BECKETT WRESTLING ALMANAC

BECKETT - THE #1 AUTHORITY ON COLLECTIBLES

THE HOBBY'S MOST RELIABLE AND RELIED UPON SOURCE ™

Founder: Dr. James Beckett III
Edited by Matt Bible and the Price Guide Staff of Beckett Collectibles LLC

Manufactured in the United States of America I Published by Beckett Collectibles LLC

BECKETT

Beckett Collectibles LLC
2700 Summit Ave, Ste 100, Plano, TX 75074
(866) 287-9383 • beckett.com

First Printing
ISBN: 978-1-953801-91-3

BECKETT WRESTLING ALMANAC

NUMBER 5

BECKETT - THE #1 AUTHORITY ON COLLECTIBLES

COVER BACKGROUND: GETTY IMAGES, COVER FIGURES: PHOTOGRAPHED BY DANIEL MOSCOSO

CONTENTS

BECKETT WRESTLING ALMANAC - NUMBER 5

IN MEMORIAM

ABOUT THE AUTHOR

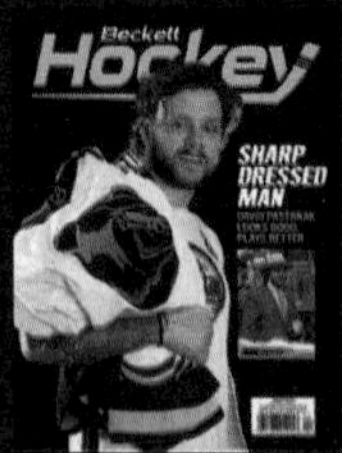

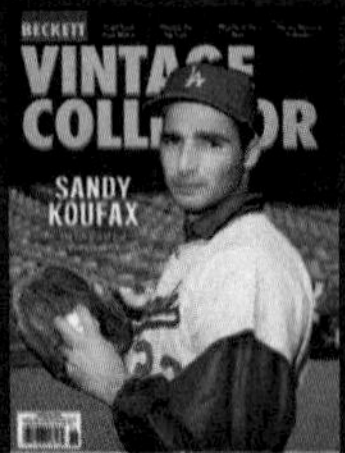

Based in Dallas, Beckett Collectibles LLC is the leading publisher of sports and specialty market collectible products in the U.S. Beckett operates Beckett.com and is the premier publisher of monthly sports and entertainment collectibles magazines.

The growth of Beckett Collectibles sports magazines, ***Beckett Baseball, Beckett Basketball, Beckett Football, Beckett Hockey*** and ***Beckett Vintage Collector,*** is another indication of the unprecedented popularity of sports cards. Founded in 1984 by Dr. James Beckett, Beckett sports magazines contain the most extensive and accepted Price Guide, collectible superstar covers, colorful feature articles, the Hot List, tips for beginners, information on errors and varieties, autograph collecting tips and profiles of the sport's hottest stars. Published 12 times a year, ***Beckett Baseball*** is the hobby's largest baseball periodical.

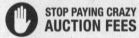

2022 TOP 5 PRODUCTS

1. PANINI PRIZM WWE

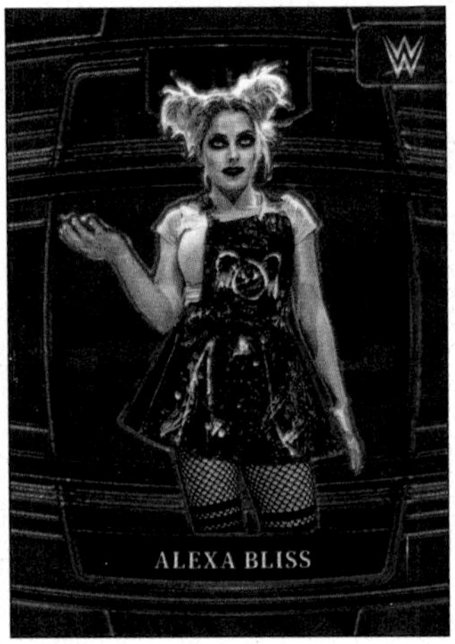

2. SELECT WWE

3. PANINI CHRONICLES WWE

4. PANINI WWE NXT

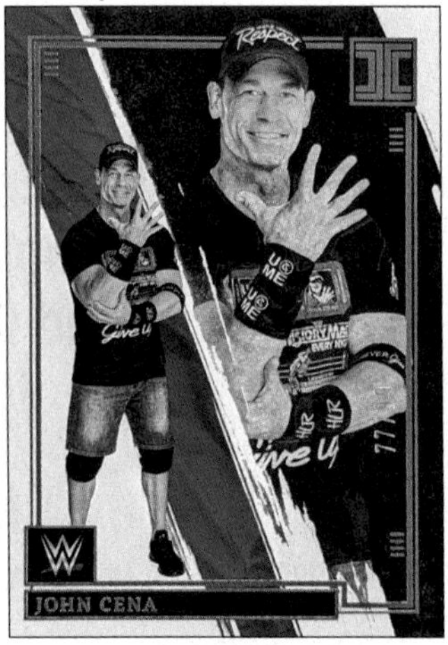

5. PANINI IMPECCABLE WWE

2022 TOP 5 INSERT SETS

1. PANINI PRIZM WWE COLOR BLAST

2. PANINI IMPECCABLE WWE SILVER WWE LOGOS/LEGENDS LOGOS

3. UPPER DECK AEW CANVAS

4. PANINI IMPECCABLE WWE STAINLESS STARS

5. PANINI CHRONICLES WWE IT'S ALL ABOUT THE GAME

2022 TOP 5 AUTOGRAPHED CARDS

1. PANINI IMPECCABLE WWE IMPECCABLE HALL OF FAME AUTOGRAPHS #HFUKT UNDERTAKER/22

2. PANINI IMPECCABLE WWE IMPECCABLE CHAMPIONSHIP DEBUTS AUTOGRAPHS #CDHHG HULK HOGAN/84

3. UPPER DECK AEW AUTOGRAPHS #3 MJF C

4. REVOLUTION WWE AUTOGRAPHS #AGSCA STONE COLD STEVE AUSTIN

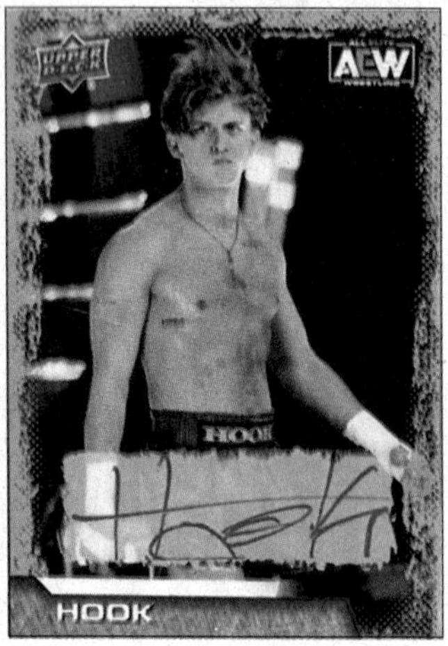

5. UPPER DECK AEW AUTOGRAPHS #80 HOOK

2022 TOP 5 ACTION FIGURES/ FIGURINES

1. JAZWARES AEW UNMATCHED SERIES 4 CM PUNK/5,000* CH

2. MATTEL WWE ELITE COLLECTION EXCLUSIVES WOLFPAC HULK HOGAN RSC

3. JAZWARES AEW UNMATCHED SERIES 4 CODY RHODES/3,000* R

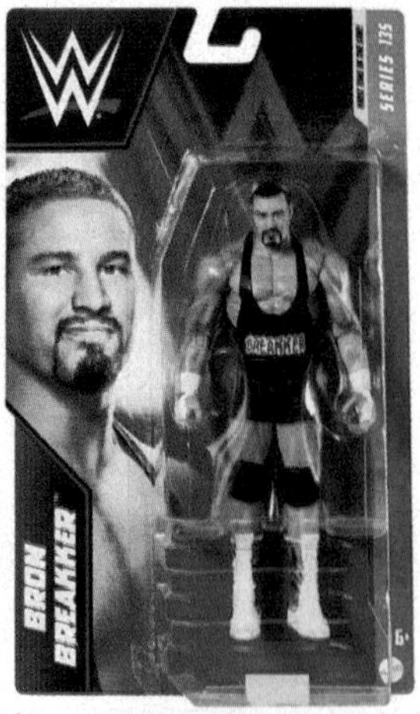

4. MATTEL WWE SERIES 135 BRON BREAKKER

5. JAZWARES AEW UNMATCHED SERIES 5 DARBY ALLIN LJN

BASEBALL CARD
Exchange

ALL-TIME TOP 10

WRESTLING ROOKIE CARDS (MEN)

1. 1985 TOPPS WWF #1 HULK HOGAN

2. 2002 FLEER WWE ROYAL RUMBLE #7 JOHN CENA

3. 1988 WONDERAMA NWA #1 RIC FLAIR

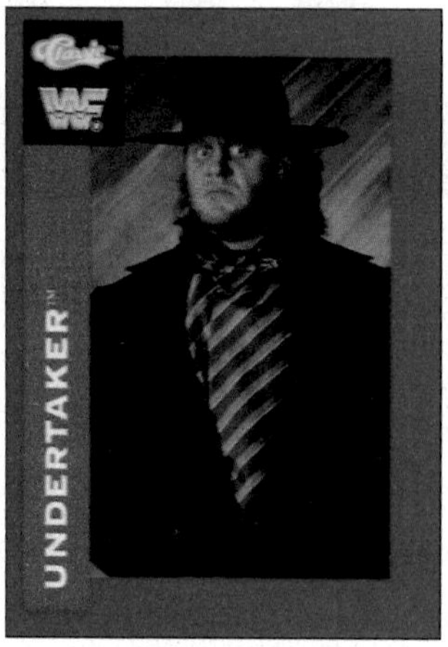

4. 1991 CLASSIC WWF SUPERSTARS #64 UNDERTAKER

5. 1998 DUOCARDS WWF #15 THE ROCK

6. 1995 CARDZ WCW MAIN EVENT #29 STEVE AUSTIN

7. 2002 FLEER WWE ROYAL RUMBLE #4 BROCK LESNAR

8. 2004 PACIFIC TNA #34 CM PUNK

9. 1985 TOPPS WWF #7 ROWDY RODDY PIPER

10. 1985-86 O-PEE-CHEE WWF SERIES 2 #63 RANDY SAVAGE (& ELIZABETH)

ALL-TIME TOP 10

WRESTLING ROOKIE CARDS (WOMEN)

1. 2001 FLEER WWF RAW IS WAR #17 TRISH STRATUS

2. 2001 FLEER WWF RAW IS WAR #6 LITA

3. 2015 TOPPS HERITAGE WWE #104 CHARLOTTE FLAIR

4. 2015 TOPPS HERITAGE WWE #109 SASHA BANKS

5. 2015 TOPPS CHROME WWE #92 ALEXA BLISS NXT

6. 2016 TOPPS WWE DIVAS REVOLUTION #16 BECKY LYNCH

7. 2016 TOPPS WWE NXT #5 ASUKA

8. 1998 DUOCARDS WWF #63 CHYNA BBB

9. 1995 ACTION PACKED WWF #8 ALUNDRA BLAYZE (MADUSA)

10. 1985 TOPPS WWF #13 FABULOUS MOOLAH

2023 Beckett® Wrestling Almanac Collectibles Price Guide

The World's Most-Trusted Source in Collecting

Welcome to the Beckett® Wrestling Almanac. This 5th edition is an enhanced and expanded volume with the addition of new releases, updated prices, and changes to older listings. The Beckett® Wrestling Almanac will do what no other publication has done -- give you the most complete and comprehensive collectible listings possible. The prices were added to the checklists just prior to printing and reflect not the author's opinions or desires, but the going retail prices for each collectible, based on the marketplace such as conventions and shows, hobby shops, online trading, auction results and other first-hand reports of realized sales.

What is the best price guide available on the market today? Of course sellers will prefer the price guide with the highest prices, while buyers will naturally prefer the one with the lower prices. Accuracy, however, is the true test. Compared to other price guides, The Beckett® Wrestling Almanac may not always have the highest or lowest values, but the accuracy of both our checklists and pricing – produced with the utmost integrity – will make it the most widely used reference book in the hobby.

LISTINGS AND SECTIONS

Each collection is personal and reflects the individuality of its owner. There are no set rules on how to collect. Since collecting is a hobby or leisure pastime, what you collect, how much you collect, and how much time and money you spend collecting are entirely up to you. The funds you have available for collecting and your own personal taste should determine how you collect.

It is not possible to collect every card and action figure ever produced. Therefore, beginners, as well as intermediate and advanced collectors, usually specialize in some way. One of the reasons this hobby is popular is that individual collectors can define and tailor their collecting methods to match their own tastes.

Many collectors select complete sets from particular years or acquire only certain wrestlers/athletes, while some collectors are only interested in collecting certain figures or autographs.

WHAT'S LISTED

Products listed in the Price Guide typically:

- Are produced by licensed manufacturers
- Are widely available
- Have market activity on single items
- International releases

HOW IT'S LISTED

Unlike regular Beckett® Almanacs, the sort order of this publication is somewhat unique. Like the others, all listings are organized 1) alphabetically then 2) chronologically.

WHAT THE COLUMNS MEAN

The LO and HI columns reflect current retail selling ranges. The HI column on the right generally represents the full retail selling price. The LO column on the left generally represents the lowest price one would expect to find with extensive shopping.

GRADING

All cards in the price guide are based on NrMint to Mint condition. Damaged cards are generally sold for 25 to 75 percent of Mint value. Toy prices are based on Mint condition. Toys that are loose (out-of-package) are generally sold for 50 percent of the listed price, but may list for less/more depending on market sales.

CURRENCY

This price guide is intended to reflect the entire North American market. While not all of the cards are produced in the United States, they will reflect the market value in U.S. dollars.

GLOSSARY/LEGEND

Our glossary defines terms most frequently used in the collecting hobby. Some of these terms are common to other types of collecting while others may have several meanings depending on the use and context.

7-11	7-11 Exclusive
AMZ	Amazon Exclusive
ARGO	Argo's Exclusive
BJ	BJ's Exclusive
BL	Big Lots Exclusive
CAN	Issued in Canada
CH	Chase Figure
FB	Flashback
FCE	Fall Convention Exclusive
FHQ	Funko Headquarters Exclusive
FL	Foot Locker Exclusive
FP	First Piece in an Action Figure Line
FYE	fYe Exclusive
GITD	Glow-in-the-Dark
GS	GameStop Exclusive
HILLS	Hills Exclusive
HT	Hot Topic Exclusive
KB	Kay-Bee Toys Exclusive
KM	K-Mart Exclusive
LE	Limited Edition
MA	Mail-Away
MANIA TIX	WrestleMania Ticket Mail-In Exclusive
MEI	Meijer Exclusive
NYC TF	New York City Toy Fair Exclusive
NYCC	New York Comic Con
OL	Internet/Online Exclusive
PROFIG	Profigures.com Exclusive
RTWM21 TOUR	- Road to WrestleMania 21 Tour Giveaway Exclusive
RSC	Ringside Collectibles Exclusive
RSF	Ringside Fest Exclusive
SC	Sam's Club Exclusive
SCE	Summer Convention Exclusive
SDCC	San Diego Comic Con Exclusive
SE	Special Edition
TAR	Target Exclusive
TFM	Toyfare Magazine Exclusive
TRU	Toys R Us Exclusive
UK	Issued in United Kingdom
US	Issued in the United States
V	Vaulted (applies only to Funko products)
WG	Walgreens Exclusive
WM	Walmart Exclusive
WRMS	WrestleMania Shop Exclusive
WWE SZ	WWE Shopzone Exclusive

As with any new publication, we appreciate reader feedback. If you have any questions, concerns, corrections or suggestions, please contact us at: **nonsports@beckett.com**

Trading Cards

1994 Action Packed WWF

COMPLETE SET (42)	20.00	50.00
COMPLETE FACTORY SET (42)	25.00	60.00
UNOPENED BOX (24 PACKS)		
UNOPENED PACK (6 CARDS)		
COLOSSAL CRUSHERS (30-36)		
1 Bam Bam Bigelow	1.25	3.00
2 I.R.S.	.75	2.00
3 Doink the Clown	.40	1.00
4 Diesel RC	3.00	8.00
5 Razor Ramon	.25	.60
6 Ludvig Borga RC	.20	.50
7 Shawn Michaels	.40	1.00
8 Yokozuna	1.25	3.00
9 Head Shrinkers	.20	.50
10 Bushwhackers	.20	.50
11 Bob Backlund	.20	.50
12 Undertaker	5.00	12.00
13 Macho Man Randy Savage	.50	1.25
14 Adam Bomb RC	.20	.50
15 Bret Hit Man Hart	.60	1.50
16 Luna RC	.25	.60
17 1-2-3 Kid RC	1.50	4.00
18 Owen Hart	3.00	8.00
19 Lex Luger	.60	1.50
20 Bastion Booger RC	.20	.50
21 Quebecers	.20	.50
22 Marty Jannetty	.20	.50
23 Freddie Blassie	.25	.60
24 Stenier Brothers	.25	.60
25 Smoking Gunns	.20	.50
26 Andre the Giant	2.00	5.00
27 Paul Bearer	.30	.75
28 M.O.M.	.20	.50
29 Tatanka	.20	.50
30 Yokozuna CC	2.00	5.00
31 Diesel CC	2.00	5.00
32 Adam Bomb CC	.20	.50
33 Bastion Booger CC	.20	.50
34 Earthquake CC	.20	.50
35 Mabel CC RC	.20	.50
36 Ludvig Borga CC	.20	.50
37 Razor Ramon	2.50	6.00
38 Shawn Michaels	2.00	5.00
39 Macho Man Randy Savage	2.00	5.00
40 Bret Hit Man Hart	2.00	5.00
41 Steiner Brothers	.25	.60
42 Undertaker/Paul Bearer CC	4.00	10.00

1994 Action Packed WWF 24 Kt Gold Leaf

COMPLETE SET (6)	25.00	60.00
STATED ODDS 1:24		
1G Razor Ramon	15.00	40.00
2G Shawn Michaels	8.00	20.00
3G Macho Man Randy Savage	6.00	15.00
4G Bret Hit Man Hart	6.00	15.00
5G Steiner Brothers	5.00	12.00
6G Undertaker/Paul Bearer	10.00	25.00

1994 Action Packed WWF Autographed Prototypes

1 Macho Man Randy Savage	500.00	1000.00
2 Undertaker	300.00	600.00

1994 Action Packed WWF Prototypes

COMPLETE SET (2)	3.00	8.00
1 Macho Man Randy Savage	2.00	5.00
2 Undertaker	2.50	6.00

1995 Action Packed WWF

COMPLETE SET (42)	15.00	40.00
COMPLETE FACTORY SET (42)	15.00	40.00
UNOPENED BOX (24 PACKS)		
UNOPENED PACK (6 CARDS)		
1 Bret Hit Man Hart	.30	.75
2 Undertaker	.75	2.00
3 Razor Ramon	.40	1.00
4 Diesel	.20	.50
5 Heavenly Bodies	.20	.50
6 Doink the Clown	.20	.50
7 Lex Luger	.25	.60
8 Alundra Blayze RC	.50	1.25
9 Yokozuna	.20	.50
10 Bam Bam Bigelow	.25	.60
11 British Bulldog	.25	.60
12 Crush	.20	.50
13 King Kong Bundy	.25	.60
14 Nikolai Volkoff	.20	.50
15 Tatanka	.20	.50
16 Paul Bearer	.30	.75
17 Head Shrinkers	.20	.50
18 Duke the Dumpster RC	.20	.50
19 Dink RC	.20	.50
20 Bushwhackers	.20	.50
21 Diesel	.20	.50
22 Mabel	.20	.50
23 Smoking Gunns	.20	.50
24 Undertaker	1.25	3.00
25 Shawn Michaels DD	.75	2.00
26 Owen Hart DD	.50	1.25
27 Jim The Anvil Neidhart DD	.25	.60
28 Mr. Fuji DD	.20	.50
29 IRS DD	.60	1.50
30 Luna DD	.40	1.00
31 Well Dunn DD	.20	.50
32 Jerry The King Lawler DD RC	.40	1.00
33 Double J Jeff Jarrett DD RC	.25	.60
34 Mr. Bob Backlund DD	.20	.50
35 Bull Nakano DD RC	.20	.50
36 Million Dollar Man Ted DiBiase DD	.30	.75
37 1-2-3 Kid HFR	.20	.50
38 Shawn Michaels HFR	.40	1.00
39 Adam Bomb HFR	.20	.50
40 Bob Spark Plugg Holly HFR RC	.25	.60
41 Bret "Hit Man" Hart HFR	.40	1.00
42 Bam Bam Bigelow HFR	.25	.60

1995 Action Packed WWF 24 Kt Gold Leaf

COMPLETE SET (12)	30.00	75.00
STATED ODDS 1:96		
G1 Shawn Michaels	6.00	15.00
G2 Owen Hart	6.00	15.00
G3 Jim The Anvil Neidhart	4.00	10.00
G4 Mr. Fuji	4.00	10.00
G5 IRS	4.00	10.00
G6 Luna	5.00	12.00
G7 Well Dunn	3.00	8.00
G8 Jerry The King Lawler	5.00	12.00
G9 Double J Jeff Jarrett	4.00	10.00
G10 Mr. Bob Backlund	4.00	10.00
G11 Bull Nakano	3.00	8.00
G12 Ted Dibiase	5.00	12.00

1995 Action Packed WWF Promos

LT1 Lawrence Taylor WMXI	15.00	40.00
MM1 Diesel	6.00	15.00
MM2 Undertaker	10.00	25.00

2018 All In Series 1

COMPLETE SET (36)	50.00	100.00
1 All In	.60	1.50
2 Cody	4.00	10.00
3 Brandi	2.50	6.00
4 Kenny Omega	5.00	12.00
5 Matt Jackson	2.50	6.00
6 Nick Jackson	2.50	6.00
7 Nick Aldis	1.25	3.00
8 Stephen Amell	2.00	5.00
9 Joey Janela	2.00	5.00
10 Penelope Ford	3.00	8.00
11 Tessa Blanchard	2.50	6.00
12 Kazuchika Okada	2.00	5.00
13 Kota Ibushi	2.00	5.00
14 Penta El Zero M	2.50	6.00
15 Rey Fenix	3.00	8.00
16 El Bandido	.60	1.50
17 Flip Gordon	.60	1.50
18 MJF	25.00	60.00
19 Adam Page	4.00	10.00
20 Joey Ryan	3.00	8.00
21 Rey Mysterio	1.50	4.00
22 Jerry Lynn	.60	1.50
23 Jay Lethal	2.00	5.00
24 Burnard	.60	1.50
25 Briscoe Brothers	.75	2.00
26 Best Friends	2.00	5.00
27 Chelsea Green	5.00	12.00
28 Britt Baker	15.00	40.00
29 Madison Rayne	2.50	6.00
30 Marty Scurll	.60	1.50
31 SoCal Uncensored	2.00	5.00
32 BTE	.60	1.50
33 Masa	.60	1.50
34 Bury	.60	1.50
35 Cracker Barrel	.60	1.50
36 Checklist	.75	2.00

1999 Artbox WWF MotionCardz

COMPLETE SET (40)	10.00	25.00
UNOPENED BOX (24 PACKS)		
UNOPENED PACK (8 CARDS)		
1 The Undertaker SM	.40	1.00
2 Stone Cold Steve Austin SM	.50	1.25
3 Kane SM	.40	1.00
4 Kane SM	.40	1.00
5 Road Dogg SM	.40	1.00
6 The Rock SM	.60	1.50
7 Stone Cold Steve Austin SM	.50	1.25
8 The Undertaker SM	.75	2.00
9 The Undertaker/Kane	.40	1.00
10 The Undertaker/Kane	.40	1.00
11 The Undertaker/Kane	.40	1.00
12 The Undertaker/Kane	.40	1.00
13 The Undertaker/Kane	.40	1.00
14 The Undertaker/Kane	.40	1.00
15 The Undertaker/Kane	.40	1.00
16 The Undertaker/Kane	.40	1.00
17 D-Generation X	.40	1.00
18 D-Generation X	.40	1.00
19 D-Generation X	.40	1.00
20 D-Generation X	.40	1.00
21 D-Generation X	.40	1.00
22 D-Generation X	.40	1.00
23 D-Generation X	.40	1.00
24 D-Generation X	.40	1.00
25 The Rock	.60	1.50
26 The Rock	.60	1.50
27 The Rock	.75	2.00
28 The Rock	.75	2.00
29 The Rock	.75	2.00
30 The Rock	.60	1.50
31 The Rock	.60	1.50
32 The Rock	2.00	5.00
33 Stone Cold Steve Austin	.50	1.25
34 Stone Cold Steve Austin	.50	1.25
35 Stone Cold Steve Austin	.50	1.25
36 Stone Cold Steve Austin	.50	1.25
37 Stone Cold Steve Austin	.50	1.25
38 Stone Cold Steve Austin	.50	1.25
39 Stone Cold Steve Austin	.50	1.25
40 Stone Cold Steve Austin	.50	1.25
R1 Sable Revealed	5.00	12.00

1999 Artbox WWF MotionCardz Attitudes

COMPLETE SET (4)	8.00	20.00
STATED ODDS 1:12		
AT1 Undertaker	6.00	15.00
AT2 No Holds Barred	1.50	4.00

AT3 Kane	1.25	3.00
AT4 D-Generation X	2.00	5.00

1999 Artbox WWF MotionCardz Temporary Tattooz

COMPLETE SET (8)	6.00	15.00
STATED ODDS 1:1		
WWF11 Stone Cold 3:16 Logo	1.25	3.00
WWF12 Kane	1.00	2.50
WWF13 Undertaker	1.25	3.00
WWF14 Stone Cold Skull Logo	1.25	3.00
WWF15 Stone Cold Skull Logo	1.25	3.00
WWF16 Stone Cold Skull Logo	1.25	3.00
WWF17 Raw Is War Logo	.75	2.00
WWF18 War Zone Logo	.75	2.00

1999 Artbox WWF MotionCardz Promos

P1 Val Venis/Taka Michinoku	4.00	10.00
P2 Undertaker/Road Dogg	5.00	12.00

2001 Artbox WWF Slams! MotionCardz

COMPLETE SET (45)	12.00	30.00
COMPLETE SET W/O SP (40)		
UNOPENED BOX (24 PACKS)		
UNOPENED PACK (4 CARDS)		
SP 41-44 STATED ODDS 1:12		
SP 45 STATED ODDS 1:240		
1 Test	.25	.60
2 Rikishi vs. Val Venis	.25	.60
3 The Undertaker vs. HHH FM	1.00	2.50
4 Bradshaw vs. Edge FM	.60	1.50
5 Trish Stratus FM	6.00	15.00
6 HHH vs. Chris Jericho	1.00	2.50
7 The Rock vs. Chris Benoit	1.00	2.50
8 Scotty 2 Hotty/Grandmaster Sexay FM	.25	.60
9 Road Dogg vs. Chris Jericho FM	.40	1.00
10 Bradshaw vs. Edge	.60	1.50
11 The Rock FM	2.50	6.00
12 D-Von & Buh-Buh Ray vs. Edge	.60	1.50
13 Buh-Buh Ray Dudley vs. Christian	.40	1.00
14 Trish vs. Lita FM	1.50	4.00
15 Rikishi vs. Val Venis	.25	.60
16 Steve Blackman	.15	.40
17 Steve Blackman vs. Crash Holly	.15	.40
18 Kurt Angle vs. The Undertaker	.75	2.00
19 The Undertaker vs. HHH	1.00	2.50
20 Lita vs. Test	1.00	2.50
21 Edge and Christian vs. Kane	.60	1.50
22 Bob Hardcore Holly vs. Kurt Angle	.60	1.50
23 Buh-Buh Ray vs. Road Dogg	.25	.60
24 X-Pac vs. Buh-Buh Ray Dudley	.25	.60
25 Commissioner Foley FM	.60	1.50
26 Faarooq vs. X-Pac	.25	.60
27 X-Pac vs. Faarooq	.25	.60
28 Chyna vs. Edge	.60	1.50
29 Buh-Buh Ray Dudley vs. Edge	.60	1.50
30 Hardyz vs. Dudley Boyz	.40	1.00
31 Steve Austin vs. Mr. Ass #1	1.00	2.50
32 The Rock	1.00	2.50
33 Stephanie vs. Buh-Buh Ray Dudley	.75	2.00
34 The Rock vs. Shane McMahon	2.50	6.00
35 Mankind vs. Prince Albert FM	.60	1.50
36 Grandmaster Sexay vs. Test FM	.25	.60
37 Rock & Mick Foley vs. Chris Benoit	1.00	2.50
38 Chris Benoit vs. Eddie Guerrero	.60	1.50
39 Edge vs. Buh-Buh Ray Dudley	.60	1.50
40 Val Venis vs. Rikishi	.25	.60
41 Kurt Angle/Hardcore Holly SP	1.00	2.50
42 Kane vs. Kurt Angle SP	1.00	2.50
43 Steve Blackman/Shano Mac SP	1.00	2.50
44 Matt Hardy SP	1.00	2.50
45 The Godfather SP		

1997 Cardinal WWF Trivia Game Cards Series 1

COMPLETE SET (30)	200.00	400.00
1 Stone Cold Steve Austin	60.00	120.00
2 Justin Bradshaw	2.50	6.00
3 Brakus	2.00	5.00
4 British Bulldog	3.00	8.00
5 Crush	1.50	4.00
6 Diesel	2.00	5.00
7 Faarooq	1.50	4.00
8 Flash Funk	1.25	3.00
9 Doug Furnas	1.25	3.00
10 Henry Godwinn	1.25	3.00
11 Phineas Godwinn	1.25	3.00
12 The Goon	1.25	3.00
13 Bret Hit Man Hart	5.00	12.00
14 Owen Hart	3.00	8.00
15 Hunter Hearst-Helmsley	15.00	40.00
16 Bob Holly	2.00	5.00
17 Goldust	2.50	6.00
18 Ahmed Johnson	1.50	4.00
19 Philip LaFon	1.25	3.00
20 Jerry Lawler	2.00	5.00
21 Rocky Maivia	150.00	300.00
22 Mankind	4.00	10.00
23 Marc Mero	1.25	3.00
24 Shawn Michaels	3.00	8.00
25 Aldo Montoya	1.25	3.00
26 Papa Shango	1.25	3.00
27 Sycho Sid	2.00	5.00
28 The Sultan	1.25	3.00
29 Undertaker	10.00	25.00
30 Vader	2.00	5.00

2001 Cardinal WWF Trivia Game Cards Series 3

NNO Al Snow	1.50	4.00
NNO APA	1.50	4.00
NNO The Big Show	2.00	5.00
NNO Chris Benoit		
NNO Chris Jericho		
NNO Chyna	15.00	40.00
NNO Debra		
NNO Dudley Boyz	1.50	4.00
NNO Edge & Christian	1.50	4.00
NNO Hardy Boyz	3.00	8.00
NNO Kane		
NNO K-Kwik		
NNO Kurt Angle	10.00	25.00
NNO Lita	15.00	40.00
NNO Perry Saturn w/Terri		
NNO Rhyno		
NNO Rikishi		
NNO The Rock	20.00	50.00
NNO RTC		
NNO Steve Blackman	1.50	4.00
NNO Stone Cold Steve Austin	10.00	25.00
NNO Tazz		
NNO Test		
NNO Too Cool		
NNO Triple H w/Stephanie McMahon-Helmsley		
NNO Trish Stratus	25.00	60.00
NNO Undertaker	8.00	20.00
NNO Vince McMahon	4.00	10.00
NNO William Regal	1.50	4.00
NNO X-Pac	1.50	4.00

1995 CARDZ WCW Main Event

COMPLETE SET (100)	30.00	75.00
UNOPENED BOX (36 PACKS)	300.00	500.00
UNOPENED PACK (8 CARDS)	8.00	15.00
1 Wild Cat Willie	.20	.50
2 Hulk Hogan	2.00	5.00
3 Ric Flair	.30	.75
4 Sting	.25	.60
5 Macho Man Randy Savage	.20	.50
6 Frank Andersson RC	.10	.25
7 Marcus Bagwell RC	1.00	2.50
8 The Patriot RC	.10	.25
9 Paul Roma	.10	.25
10 Paul Orndorff	.12	.30
11 Blacktop Bully	.10	.25
12 Bobby Eaton	.10	.25
13 Diamond Dallas Page	.25	.60
14 Meng	.10	.25
15 Bunkhouse Buck RC	.10	.25
16 Booker T RC	8.00	20.00
17 Stevie Ray RC	.10	.25
18 Brad Armstrong	.10	.25
19 Arn Anderson	.12	.30
20 Lord Steven Regal RC	.75	2.00
21 Johnny B. Badd	.10	.25
22 Flyin Brian	.30	.75
23 Big Bubba	.10	.25
24 Dustin Rhodes	.12	.30
25 Jerry Sags	.10	.25
26 Brian Knobs	.10	.25
27 Kevin Sullivan	.10	.25
28 Vader	.12	.30
29 Stunning Steve Austin RC	15.00	40.00
30 Alex Wright RC	.10	.25
31 Avalanche	.10	.25
32 Butcher	.10	.25
33 Hacksaw Jim Duggan	.20	.50
34 Dave Sullivan RC	.10	.25
35 Nasty Boys	.10	.25
36 Harlem Heat	1.25	3.00
37 Pretty Wonderful	.10	.25
38 Stars & Stripes	.10	.25
39 Monster Maniacs	.40	1.00
40 Jimmy Hart	.20	.50
41 Sister Sherri	.12	.30
42 Harley Race	.10	.25
43 Colonel Parker RC	.10	.25
44 Gary Cappetta RC	.10	.25
45 Mean Gene Okerlund	.60	1.50
46 Bobby Heenan	.20	.50
47 Tony Schiavone	.10	.25
48 Eric Bischoff RC	.40	1.00
49 Gordon Solie RC	.10	.25
50 Larry Zbyszko	.12	.30
51 Nick Bockwinkel RC	.10	.25
52 Diamond Doll RC	2.00	5.00
53 Das Wunderkind Alex Wright RC	.10	.25
54 Harlem Heat	1.25	3.00
55 Dave Sullivan RC	.10	.25
56 Atomic Leg Drop	.40	1.00
57 Scorpion Death Lock	.25	.60
58 Power Bomb	.12	.30
59 Bulldog	.12	.30
60 Sleeper	.10	.25
61 Sunset Flip	.10	.25
62 Hollywood & Vine	5.00	12.00
63 Vadersault	.12	.30
64 Pit Stop	.10	.25
65 Flying Elbow	.20	.50
66 Figure Four Leglock	.30	.75
67 Headlock	.40	1.00
68 Hulk Hogan/Ric Flair	2.50	6.00
69 Hulk Hogan/Ric Flair	2.50	6.00
70 Hogan/Vader	.20	.50
71 Rhodes/Anderson	.20	.50
72 Macho Man Randy Savage	.40	1.00
73 Macho Man Randy Savage	.40	1.00
74 Macho Man Randy Savage	.40	1.00
75 Macho Man Randy Savage	.40	1.00
76 Ric Flair	.30	.75
77 Ric Flair	.30	.75
78 Ric Flair	.30	.75
79 Ric Flair	.30	.75
80 Sting	.30	.75
81 Sting	.30	.75
82 Sting	.30	.75
83 Hulk Hogan	2.00	5.00
84 Hulk Hogan	2.00	5.00
85 Hulk Hogan	2.00	5.00
86 Hulk Hogan	2.00	5.00
87 Hulk Hogan	2.00	5.00
88 Hulk Hogan	2.00	5.00
89A Uncensored	.10	.25
89B Spring Stampede	.10	.25
90 Starrcade 1994	.10	.25
91 Halloween Havoc 1994	.10	.25
92 Fall Brawl	.10	.25
93 Bash at the Beach	.10	.25
94 Slamboree 1994	.10	.25
95A Superbrawl IV	.10	.25
95B Superbrawl V	.10	.25
96 Arn Anderson	.12	.30
97 Harlem Heat	1.25	3.00
98 Vader	.12	.30
99 Hulk Hogan	2.00	5.00
100 Checklist	.10	.25

1995 CARDZ WCW Main Event Promos

P1 Hulk Hogan	1.50	4.00
P2 Sting	1.25	3.00
NNO Hogan vs. Flair TEK	2.00	5.00
NNO Clash of the Champions KKLZ		

1986 Carnation Major League Wrestling

COMPLETE SET (6)	150.00	300.00
NNO Kamala	15.00	40.00
NNO The Koloffs	20.00	50.00
NNO Ric Flair	75.00	150.00
NNO Rick Martel	15.00	40.00
NNO The Road Warriors	30.00	75.00
NNO Sergeant Slaughter	25.00	60.00

1993 Catcher Quartett WWF Series 5

A1 Bret Hit Man Hart

A2 Undertaker	6.00	15.00
A3 Hulk Hogan	6.00	15.00
A4 Crush	1.25	3.00
B1 Mr. Perfect	3.00	8.00
B2 Bam Bam Bigelow		
B3 Kamala	1.50	4.00
B4 Money Inc.		
C1 Doink	1.00	2.50
C2 Macho Man Randy Savage		
C3 Big Boss Man	1.00	2.50
C4 Tatanka	1.00	2.50
D1 Virgil	1.00	2.50
D2 Papa Shango	2.00	5.00
D3 Shawn Michaels	3.00	8.00
D4 Repo Man	1.00	2.50
E1 Hacksaw Jim Duggan	1.25	3.00
E2 Razor Ramon		
E3 Bushwhackers		
E4 Nasty Boys	1.00	2.50
F1 Giant Gonzalez	1.00	2.50
F2 Head Shrinkers	1.00	2.50
F3 Beverly Brothers	1.25	3.00
F4 Damian Demento		
G1 Bob Backlund	1.00	2.50
G2 Brutus The Barber Beefcake	1.50	4.00
G3 Lex Luger	2.00	5.00
G4 Steiner Brothers	2.50	6.00
H1 Yokozuna	6.00	15.00
H2 El Matador	1.00	2.50
H3 Paul Bearer		
H4 Billy of the Smoking Gunns	1.00	2.50

1993 Catcher Quartett WWF Series 7

A1 Bret Hit Man Hart		
A2 Undertaker	5.00	12.00
A3 Hulk Hogan		
A4 Crush		
B1 Mr. Perfect		
B2 Bam Bam Bigelow	1.50	4.00
B3 Kamala		
B4 Money Inc.	1.00	2.50
C1 Doink		
C2 Macho Man Randy Savage		
C3 Big Boss Man		
C4 Tatanka	1.00	2.50
D1 Virgil	1.00	2.50
D2 Papa Shango		
D3 Shawn Michaels		
D4 Repo Man		
E1 Hacksaw Jim Duggan		
E2 Razor Ramon	4.00	10.00
E3 Bushwhackers	1.00	2.50
E4 Knobbs of the Nasty Boys		
F1 Giant Gonzalez	1.00	2.50
F2 Head Shrinkers	1.00	2.50
F3 Beverly Brothers		
F4 Damian Demento		
G1 Bob Backlund	1.00	2.50
G2 Brutus The Barber Beefcake		
G3 Lex Luger	2.50	6.00
G4 Steiner Brothers	1.50	4.00
H1 Yokozuna		
H2 El Matador		
H3 Paul Bearer	1.00	2.50
H4 The Smoking Gunns	1.00	2.50

1993 Catcher Quartett WWF Series 8

A1 Bret Hit Man Hart		
A2 Undertaker		
A3 Hulk Hogan		
A4 Crush	1.00	2.50
B1 Mr. Perfect	2.50	6.00
B2 Bam Bam Bigelow	1.25	3.00
B3 Kamala		
B4 Money Inc.	1.00	2.50
C1 Doink	1.00	2.50
C2 Macho Man Randy Savage		8.00
C3 Big Boss Man		
C4 Tatanka		
D1 Virgil		
D2 Papa Shango	2.00	5.00
D3 Shawn Michaels	2.50	6.00
D4 Repo Man		
E1 Hacksaw Jim Duggan	1.25	3.00
E2 Razor Ramon	2.50	6.00
E3 Luke of the Bushwhackers	1.00	2.50
E4 Nasty Boys		
F1 Giant Gonzalez		
F2 Head Shrinkers		
F3 Beverly Brothers	1.25	3.00
F4 Damian Demento		
G1 Bob Backlund		
G2 Brutus The Barber Beefcake		
G3 Lex Luger		
G4 Steiner Brothers	3.00	8.00
H1 Yokozuna	8.00	20.00
H2 El Matador		
H3 Paul Bearer	1.00	2.50
H4 Billy of the Smoking Gunns		

1991 Championship Marketing WCW

COMPLETE SET (110)	12.00	30.00
UNOPENED BOX (36 PACKS)		
UNOPENED PACK (16 CARDS)		
1 Sting	.30	.75
2 Arn Anderson	.15	.40
3 Michael Hayes	.12	.30
4 Rick Steiner	.15	.40
5 The Fabulous Freebirds	.15	.40
6 The Steiner Brothers	.15	.40
7 Lex Luger	.15	.40
8 Ric Flair	.50	1.25
9 Tom Zenk RC	.12	.30
10 Sid Vicious RC	.12	.30
11 Brian Pillman	.12	.30
12 Ric Flair	.50	1.25
13 Sid Vicious RC	.12	.30
14 The Four Horsemen	.50	1.25
15 Jim Ross RC	.12	.30
16 Ron Simmons	.15	.40
17 Barry Windham	.12	.30
18 Sid Vicious RC	.12	.30
19 Sid Vicious RC	.12	.30
20 Sting and Ric	.50	1.25
21 Beautiful Bobby Punishes Opponent	.12	.30
22 New Champion/Sting	.30	.75
23 Paul E. with Mouth Open	.12	.30
24 Michael Hayes	.12	.30
25 Scott Steiner RC	.15	.40
26 Rick Steiner	.15	.40
27 World TV Champion/Arn Anderson	.15	.40
28 Barry Windham with Arms Raised	.12	.30
29 Tommy Rich RC	.12	.30
30 Ricky Morton	.12	.30
31 Horsemen Press Conference	.50	1.25
32 The Freebirds	.15	.40
33 Terry Taylor	.12	.30
34 Dirty Dutch Mantell RC	.15	.40
35 Nature Boy Ric Flair	.50	1.25
36 Lex Presses Ric	.50	1.25
37 Lex and Sting	.15	.40
38 Flyin' Brian RC	.12	.30
39 Ric Flair	.50	1.25
40 Sting and Lex	.30	.75
41 Missy Hyatt	.15	.40
42 Three Out of Four/Horsemen	.12	.30
43 Sid Vicious in Action	.12	.30
44 Terry Taylor vs. Z-Man	.12	.30
45 Southern Boys	.12	.30
46 Sting	.30	.75
47 What Did You Say?/Ric Flair	.50	1.25
48 Arn, Paul E. and Ric Flair	.50	1.25
49 Sting	.30	.75
50 Say Uncle/Sid Vicious	.12	.30
51 Paul E. Dangerously RC	.12	.30
52 Sting and Ric	.50	1.25
53 Sting, Jim and Lex	.30	.75
54 What a Belt!/Sting	.30	.75
55 Sting	.30	.75
56 Ric All In White	.50	1.25
57 Lex Presses Ric II	.50	1.25
58 El Gigante	.15	.40
59 Arn Says My Turn	.15	.40
60 Sid Vicious RC	.12	.30
61 Brian and Ric	.50	1.25
62 Flyin Brian	.12	.30
63 The Fabulous Freebirds	.15	.40
64 No Sid This High	.12	.30
65 El Gigante RC	.12	.30
66 Ric, Jim and Sting	.50	1.25
67 No It's Mine/Flair, JR & Sting	.50	1.25
68 Golden Nature Boy	.50	1.25
69 Missy and Scott	.15	.40
70 Ron Simmons	.15	.40
71 Telephone/Paul E. Dangerously	.12	.30
72 Jimmy Jam Garvin	.15	.40
73 Ric Flair in Pink Robe	.50	1.25
74 Beautiful Bobby	.12	.30
75 Lex Luger	.15	.40
76 Z-Man RC	.12	.30
77 Where's The Door?/Ric Flair	.50	1.25
78 El Gigante RC	.12	.30
79 What Do You Think?/Ric Flair	.50	1.25
80 6 Time World Champion/Ric Flair	.50	1.25
81 Missy Hyatt	.15	.40
82 The New Champion/Sting	.30	.75
83 Celebration/Sting	.30	.75
84 USA Sting	.30	.75
85 Sting Is Injured	.30	.75
86 Let's Get Busy/Sting	.30	.75
87 Courage of a Champion/Sting	.30	.75
88 No Hold the Anchovies Paul E. Dangerously	.12	.30
89 Lex Presses Ric III	.50	1.25
90 Barry Windham	.12	.30
91 Heads or Tails/Ric Flair & Lex Luger	.50	1.25
92 U.S. Heavyweight Champion/Lex Luger	.15	.40
93 Getting Ready For Battle/Lex Luger	.15	.40
94 Lex Wins the Title	.15	.40
95 Ric Goes Too Far	.50	1.25
96 El Gigante and the Champ/Sting	.30	.75
97 Z-Man RC	.12	.30
98 World Tag-Team Champions Doom with Teddy Long	.12	.30
99 Missy in Evening Gown	.15	.40
100 Missy Hyatt	.15	.40
101 Tony (Schiavone) in Front of Chicago Building	.12	.30
102 Ricky Morton	.12	.30
103 Flyin Brian	.12	.30
104 The Steiners Want Sting Revenge	.15	.40
105 Z-Man Tom Zenk RC	.12	.30
106 Southern Boys	.12	.30
107 Teddy R. Long	.12	.30
108 Arn Anderson in Action	.15	.40
109 Sting in Action	.30	.75
110 Doom	.12	.30

1991 Championship Marketing WCW Puzzle

COMPLETE SET (110)	6.00	15.00
STATED ODDS 1:1		
1 Puzzle Card	.12	.30
2 Puzzle Card	.12	.30
3 Puzzle Card	.12	.30
4 Puzzle Card	.12	.30
5 Puzzle Card	.12	.30
6 Puzzle Card	.12	.30
7 Puzzle Card	.12	.30
8 Puzzle Card	.12	.30
9 Puzzle Card	.12	.30
10 Puzzle Card	.12	.30
11 Puzzle Card	.12	.30
12 Puzzle Card	.12	.30
13 Puzzle Card	.12	.30
14 Puzzle Card	.12	.30
15 Puzzle Card	.12	.30
16 Puzzle Card	.12	.30
17 Puzzle Card	.12	.30
18 Puzzle Card	.12	.30
19 Puzzle Card	.12	.30
20 Puzzle Card	.12	.30
21 Puzzle Card	.12	.30
22 Puzzle Card	.12	.30
23 Puzzle Card	.12	.30
24 Puzzle Card	.12	.30
25 Puzzle Card	.12	.30
26 Puzzle Card	.12	.30
27 Puzzle Card	.12	.30
28 Puzzle Card	.12	.30
29 Puzzle Card	.12	.30
30 Puzzle Card	.12	.30
31 Puzzle Card	.12	.30
32 Puzzle Card	.12	.30
33 Puzzle Card	.12	.30
34 Puzzle Card	.12	.30
35 Puzzle Card	.12	.30
36 Puzzle Card	.12	.30
37 Puzzle Card	.12	.30
38 Puzzle Card	.12	.30
39 Puzzle Card	.12	.30
40 Puzzle Card	.12	.30
41 Puzzle Card	.12	.30
42 Puzzle Card	.12	.30
43 Puzzle Card	.12	.30
44 Puzzle Card	.12	.30
45 Puzzle Card	.12	.30
46 Puzzle Card	.12	.30

47 Puzzle Card	.12	.30
48 Puzzle Card	.12	.30
49 Puzzle Card	.12	.30
50 Puzzle Card	.12	.30
51 Puzzle Card	.12	.30
52 Puzzle Card	.12	.30
53 Puzzle Card	.12	.30
54 Puzzle Card	.12	.30
55 Puzzle Card	.12	.30
56 Puzzle Card	.12	.30
57 Puzzle Card	.12	.30
58 Puzzle Card	.12	.30
59 Puzzle Card	.12	.30
60 Puzzle Card	.12	.30
61 Puzzle Card	.12	.30
62 Puzzle Card	.12	.30
63 Puzzle Card	.12	.30
64 Puzzle Card	.12	.30
65 Puzzle Card	.12	.30
66 Puzzle Card	.12	.30
67 Puzzle Card	.12	.30
68 Puzzle Card	.12	.30
69 Puzzle Card	.12	.30
70 Puzzle Card	.12	.30
71 Puzzle Card	.12	.30
72 Puzzle Card	.12	.30
73 Puzzle Card	.12	.30
74 Puzzle Card	.12	.30
75 Puzzle Card	.12	.30
76 Puzzle Card	.12	.30
77 Puzzle Card	.12	.30
78 Puzzle Card	.12	.30
79 Puzzle Card	.12	.30
80 Puzzle Card	.12	.30
81 Puzzle Card	.12	.30
82 Puzzle Card	.12	.30
83 Puzzle Card	.12	.30
84 Puzzle Card	.12	.30
85 Puzzle Card	.12	.30
86 Puzzle Card	.12	.30
87 Puzzle Card	.12	.30
88 Puzzle Card	.12	.30
89 Puzzle Card	.12	.30
90 Puzzle Card	.12	.30
91 Puzzle Card	.12	.30
92 Puzzle Card	.12	.30
93 Puzzle Card	.12	.30
94 Puzzle Card	.12	.30
95 Puzzle Card	.12	.30
96 Puzzle Card	.12	.30
97 Puzzle Card	.12	.30
98 Puzzle Card	.12	.30
99 Puzzle Card	.12	.30
100 Puzzle Card	.12	.30
101 Puzzle Card	.12	.30
102 Puzzle Card	.12	.30
103 Puzzle Card	.12	.30
104 Puzzle Card	.12	.30
105 Puzzle Card	.12	.30
106 Puzzle Card	.12	.30
107 Puzzle Card	.12	.30
108 Puzzle Card	.12	.30
109 Puzzle Card	.12	.30
110 Puzzle Card	.12	.30

1987 Circle K Coca-Cola WWF Supermatch

COMPLETE SET (20)	30.00	75.00
1 Hulk Hogan	10.00	25.00
2 Hercules and Bobby Heenan	2.00	5.00
3 The Hart Foundation	2.50	6.00
4 Randy Macho Man Savage	3.00	8.00
5 Koko B. Ware	1.25	3.00
6 George The Animal Steele	1.25	3.00
7 Ricky The Dragon Steamboat	1.50	4.00
8 The Honky Tonk Man	2.00	5.00
9 Hacksaw Jim Duggan	1.25	3.00
10 Kamala and Kimchee	2.50	6.00
11 Billy Jack Haynes	1.25	3.00
12 Junk Yard Dog	1.50	4.00
13 Jake The Snake Roberts	4.00	10.00
14 The Killer Bees	1.25	3.00
15 Tito Santana	1.25	3.00
16 The Can-Am Connection	1.25	3.00
17 Andre the Giant	6.00	15.00
18 Elizabeth	3.00	8.00
19 The British Bulldogs	2.00	5.00
20 The Iron Sheik	1.25	3.00

1990 Classic WWF

COMPLETE FACTORY SET (145)	10.00	25.00
UNOPENED BOX (36 PACKS)		
UNOPENED PACK (15 CARDS)		
1 Hulk Hogan	.60	1.50
2 Big Boss Man	.10	.25
3 Ravishing Rick Rude	.15	.40
4 Macho Man Randy Savage	.40	1.00
5 The Ultimate Warrior	.25	.60
6 Demolition	.10	.25
7 Jake The Snake Roberts	.25	.60
8 Million Dollar Man Ted DiBiase	.15	.40
9 Hacksaw Jim Duggan	.15	.40
10 Andre the Giant	.40	1.00
11 Miss Elizabeth	.15	.40
12 Brutus The Barber Beefcake	.15	.40
13 Rowdy Roddy Piper	.75	2.00
14 Jimmy Superfly Snuka	.25	.60
15 Bushwhackers	.10	.25
16 Dusty Rhodes	.10	.25
17 Hercules	.10	.25
18 Sensational Queen Sherri	.15	.40
19 Mr. Perfect	.15	.40
20 Rick Martel	.60	1.50
21 Tito Santana	.10	.25
22 Mr. Fuji	.10	.25
23 Jimmy Hart	.15	.40
24 Brother Love	.10	.25
25 Akeem	.10	.25
26 Bad News Brown	.10	.25
27 Honky Tonk Man	.15	.40
28 The Rockers	.15	.40
29 Koko B. Ware	.15	.40
30 Bobby The Brain Heenan	.15	.40
31 Dino Bravo	.10	.25
32 The Genius	.10	.25
33 Greg The Hammer Valentine	.15	.40
34 Virgil	.10	.25
35 Haku	.10	.25
36 Rugged Ronnie Garvin	.10	.25
37 Bret Hit Man Hart	.15	.40
38 Hart Foundation	.15	.40
39 Red Rooster	.10	.25
40 Hillbilly Jim	.10	.25
41 Slick		
42 The Widow Maker	.10	.25
43 The Ultimate Warrior	.25	.60
44 Honky Tonk Man	.15	.40
45 Bret Hit Man Hart	.15	.40
46 Jim Neidhart	.15	.40
47 Bushwhackers	.10	.25
48 Paul Roma	.10	.25
49 Barry Horowitz	.10	.25
50 Brooklyn Brawler	.10	.25
51 Mean Gene Okerlund	.10	.25
52 Gorilla Monsoon	.10	.25
53 Jesse The Body Ventura	.40	1.00
54 Sean Mooney	.10	.25
55 Danny Davis	.10	.25
56 Jack Tunney	.10	.25
57 Hulk Hogan	.60	1.50
58 Big Boss Man	.10	.25
59 Ravishing Rick Rude	.15	.40
60 Macho Man Randy Savage	.40	1.00
61 The Ultimate Warrior	.25	.60
62 Demolition	.10	.25
63 Jake The Snake Roberts	.25	.60
64 Million Dollar Man Ted DiBiase	.15	.40
65 Hacksaw Jim Duggan	.15	.40
66 Andre the Giant	.40	1.00
67 Miss Elizabeth	.15	.40
68 Brutus The Barber Beefcake	.15	.40
69 Jimmy Superfly Snuka	.25	.60
70 Bushwhackers	.10	.25
71 Dusty Rhodes	.10	.25
72 Hercules	.10	.25
73 Sensational Queen Sherri	.15	.40
74 Mr. Perfect	1.00	2.50
75 Jimmy Hart	.15	.40
76 Andre the Giant	.40	1.00
77 Brother Love	.10	.25
78 Akeem	.10	.25
79 Bad News Brown	.10	.25
80 Honky Tonk Man	.15	.40
81 The Rockers	.15	.40
82 Koko B. Ware	.15	.40
83 Bobby The Brain Heenan	.15	.40
84 Dino Bravo	.10	.25
85 The Genius	.10	.25
86 Greg The Hammer Valentine	.15	.40
87 Virgil	.10	.25
88 Haku	.10	.25
89 Rugged Ronnie Garvin	.10	.25
90 Hulk Hogan	.60	1.50
91 Red Rooster	.10	.25
92 Hillbilly Jim	.10	.25
93 The Widow Maker	.10	.25
94 Freddie Blassie	.10	.25
95 Bret Hit Man Hart	.15	.40
96 Jim Neidhart	.15	.40
97 Demolition	.10	.25
98 Paul Roma	.10	.25
99 Barry Horowitz	.10	.25
100 Brooklyn Brawler	.10	.25
101 Danny Davis	.10	.25
102 Hulk Hogan	.60	1.50
103 Big Boss Man	.10	.25
104 Ravishing Rick Rude	.15	.40
105 Macho Man Randy Savage	.40	1.00
106 The Ultimate Warrior	.25	.60
107 Demolition	.10	.25
108 Jake The Snake Roberts	1.25	3.00
109 Million Dollar Man Ted DiBiase	.15	.40
110 Hacksaw Jim Duggan	.15	.40
111 Andre the Giant	.40	1.00
112 Miss Elizabeth	.15	.40
113 Brutus The Barber Beefcake	.15	.40
114 Jimmy Superfly Snuka	.25	.60
115 Tito Santana	.10	.25
116 Bushwhackers	.10	.25
117 Honky Tonk Man	.15	.40
118 The Rockers	.15	.40
119 Koko B. Ware	.15	.40
120 Haku	.10	.25
121 The Rockers	.15	.40
122 Red Rooster	.10	.25
123 Bret Hit Man Hart	2.50	6.00
124 Jim Neidhart	.75	2.00
125 Hulk Hogan	.60	1.50
126 Macho Man Randy Savage	1.50	4.00
127 The Ultimate Warrior	1.50	4.00
128 Demolition	1.25	3.00
129 Hulk Hogan	3.00	8.00
130 Andre the Giant	2.00	5.00
131 Jimmy Superfly Snuka	.25	.60
132 Bushwhackers	.10	.25
133 Honky Tonk Man	.15	.40
134 The Rockers	1.25	3.00
135 Haku	.10	.25
136 Miss Elizabeth	1.00	2.50
137 Macho Madness	.40	1.00
138 Honky Tonk Man	.15	.40
139 The Ultimate Warrior	1.50	4.00
140 Million Dollar Man Ted DiBiase	.15	.40
141 Simply Ravishing	.15	.40
142 Big Boss Man	.10	.25
143 Brutus The Barber Beefcake	.15	.40
144 Koko B. Ware	.15	.40
145 Hulk Hogan Rules	.60	1.50

1990 Classic WWF History of WrestleMania

COMPLETE SET (150)	10.00	25.00
COMPLETE FACTORY SET (150)		
UNOPENED BOX (36 PACKS)		
UNOPENED PACK (15 CARDS)		
*TRADEMARK: .6X TO 1.5X BASIC CARDS		
1 Greg The Hammer Valentine Junk Yard Dog	.12	.30
2 Tito Santana Masked Executioner	.10	.25
3 Hulk Hogan	.50	1.25
4 Dream Team British Bulldogs	.10	.25
5 Battle Royal	.10	.25
6 Battle Royal	.10	.25
7 Battle Royal	.10	.25
8 Brutus The Barber Beefcake British Bulldogs	.12	.30
9 Tito Santana Junk Yard Dog Funk Brothers	.12	.30
10 Greg The Hammer Valentine	.12	.30
11 Hulk Hogan King Kong Bundy	.50	1.25
12 Macho Man Randy Savage George The Animal Steele	.20	.50
13 Macho Man Randy Savage George The Animal Steele	.20	.50
14 Hulk Hogan King Kong Bundy	.50	1.25

15 Hulk Hogan	.50	1.25
King Kong Bundy		
16 Andre the Giant	.40	1.00
17 Slick	.10	.25
Tito Santana		
18 Rowdy Roddy Piper	.20	.50
Adrian Adonis		
19 Andre the Giant	.50	1.25
Hulk Hogan		
20 Jim Neidhart	.10	.25
Dynamite Kid		
21 Davey Boy Smith	.12	.30
Danny Davis		
22 Slick	.10	.25
Tito Santana		
23 Stadium Scene	.10	.25
24 Honky Tonk Man	.15	.40
Jake The Snake Roberts		
25 Brutus The Barber Beefcake	.12	.30
Adrian Adonis		
26 Hulk Hogan	.50	1.25
Andre the Giant		
27 Hulk Hogan	.50	1.25
Andre the Giant		
28 Hulk Hogan	.50	1.25
Andre the Giant		
29 Million Dollar Man	.20	.50
Macho Man Randy Savage		
30 Million Dollar Man	.20	.50
Macho Man Randy Savage		
31 Million Dollar Man	.20	.50
Macho Man Randy Savage		
32 Hulk Hogan	.50	1.25
Macho Man Randy Savage		
33 Hulk Hogan	.50	1.25
Macho Man Randy Savage		
34 Hulk Hogan	.50	1.25
Andre the Giant		
35 Hulk Hogan	.50	1.25
Andre the Giant		
36 Hulk Hogan	.50	1.25
Andre the Giant		
37 Hulk Hogan	.50	1.25
Andre the Giant		
38 Hulk Hogan	.50	1.25
Andre the Giant		
39 Hulk Hogan	.50	1.25
Andre the Giant		
40 Hulk Hogan	.50	1.25
41 Hulk Hogan	.50	1.25
42 Brutus The Barber Beefcake	.12	.30
43 Brutus The Barber Beefcake	.12	.30
Honky Tonk Man		
44 Honky Tonk Man	.12	.30
Brutus The Barber Beefcake		
45 Rick Martel	.10	.25
Demolition		
46 Demolition	.10	.25
Strike Force		
47 Ravishing Rick Rude	.15	.40
Jake The Snake Roberts		
48 Hercules	.12	.30
Ultimate Warrior		
49 The Hammer	.20	.50
Macho Man Randy Savage		
50 The Hammer	.20	.50
Macho Man Randy Savage		
51 Hulk Hogan	.50	1.25
52 Million Dollar Man	.40	1.00
Virgil		
Andre the Giant		
53 Hulk Hogan	.50	1.25
Macho Man Randy Savage		
54 Macho Man Randy Savage	.20	.50
Akeem		
55 Ring Scene	.10	.25
56 Bobby The Brain Heenan	.10	.25
Koko B. Ware		
57 Battle Royal	.10	.25
58 Million Dollar Man	.12	.30
Hacksaw Jim Duggan		
59 Dino Bravo	.10	.25
Don Muraco		
60 Jake The Snake Roberts	.15	.40
Rick Rude		
61 Hercules	.12	.30
Ultimate Warrior		
62 Jake The Snake Roberts	.15	.40
Rick Rude		
63 Hercules	.12	.30
Ultimate Warrior		
64 Hercules	.12	.30
Ultimate Warrior		
65 Hercules	.12	.30
Ultimate Warrior		
66 Mr. Fuji	.10	.25
Ax		
67 Demolition	.10	.25
Tito Santana		
68 Rick Martel	.10	.25
Smash		
69 Honky Tonk Man	.12	.30
Brutus The Barber Beefcake		
70 Bret Hit Man Hart	.12	.30
Bad News Brown		
71 Bret Hit Man Hart	.12	.30
Bad News Brown		
72 Bret Hit Man Hart	.12	.30
Bad News Brown		
73 Bad News Brown	.10	.25
74 Power of Pain	.10	.25
Demolition		
75 Million Dollar Man	.12	.30
Virgil		
76 Mr. Fuji	.10	.25
Ax		
77 Demolition	.10	.25
78 Andre the Giant	.40	1.00
Jake The Snake Roberts		
79 Bret Hit Man Hart	.12	.30
Honky Tonk Man		
80 Brooklyn Brawler	.10	.25
81 King Haku	.10	.25
Hercules		
82 King Haku	.10	.25
Hercules		
83 Million Dollar Man	.12	.30
Brutus The Barber Beefcake		
84 Dino Bravo	.10	.25
Ronnie Garvin		
85 Bad News Brown	.12	.30
Hacksaw Jim Duggan		
86 Bad News Brown	.12	.30
Hacksaw Jim Duggan		
87 Bret Hit Man Hart	.12	.30
Greg The Hammer Valentine		
88 Bret Hit Man Hart	.12	.30
Honky Tonk Man		
89 Mr. Perfect	.12	.30
Blue Blazer		
90 Bobby The Brain Heenan	.12	.30
91 Bushwhackers	.10	.25
Rougeau Brothers		
92 Bushwhackers	.10	.25
Rougeau Brothers		
93 Dino Bravo	.10	.25
Ronnie Garvin		
94 Hulk Hogan	.50	1.25
Macho Man Randy Savage		
95 Hulk Hogan	.50	1.25
Macho Man Randy Savage		
96 Hulk Hogan	.50	1.25
Macho Man Randy Savage		
97 Akeem	.15	.40
Shawn Michaels		
98 The Rockers	.12	.30
Akeem		
99 Hulk Hogan	.50	1.25
Macho Man Randy Savage		
100 Hulk Hogan	.50	1.25
Macho Man Randy Savage		
101 Hulk Hogan	.50	1.25
Macho Man Randy Savage		
102 Hulk Hogan	.50	1.25
Macho Man Randy Savage		
103 Hulk Hogan	.50	1.25
Macho Man Randy Savage		
104 Ravishing Rick Rude	.12	.30
Ultimate Warrior		
105 Ravishing Rick Rude	.12	.30
Ultimate Warrior		
106 The Ultimate Warrior	.12	.30
107 Hulk Hogan	.50	1.25
Macho Man Randy Savage		
108 Marty Jannetty	.10	.25
Akeem		
109 Brutus The Barber Beefcake	.12	.30
Virgil		
110 Ravishing Rick Rude	.12	.30
Ultimate Warrior		
111 Ravishing Rick Rude	.12	.30
Ultimate Warrior		
112 Ravishing Rick Rude	.12	.30
Ultimate Warrior		
113 Haku	.40	1.00
Andre the Giant		
114 Million Dollar Man	.15	.40
Jake The Snake Roberts		
115 Barbarian	.10	.25
Tito Santana		
116 Rick Martel	.10	.25
Koko B. Ware		
117 Million Dollar Man Ted DiBiase	.12	.30
118 Hacksaw Jim Duggan	.12	.30
Bravo		
119 Hacksaw Jim Duggan	.12	.30
Bravo		
120 Hacksaw Jim Duggan	.12	.30
Bravo		
121 Macho King	.10	.25
Dusty Rhodes		
122 American Dream	.15	.40
Sapphire		
Miss Elizabeth		
123 Macho Man Randy Savage	.20	.50
124 Hart Foundation	.12	.30
125 Dusty Rhodes	.20	.50
Macho Man Randy Savage		
126 American Dream	.12	.30
Sapphire		
Queen Sherri		
127 Bad News	.20	.50
Rowdy Roddy Piper		
128 Brutus The Barber Beefcake	.12	.30
Genius		
129 Sato	.10	.25
Tanaka		
Marty Jannetty		
130 Big Boss Man	.10	.25
Akeem		
131 Sato	.15	.40
Shawn Michaels		
132 Hulk Hogan	.50	1.25
Ultimate Warrior		
133 Hulk Hogan	.50	1.25
Ultimate Warrior		
134 Hulk Hogan	.50	1.25
Ultimate Warrior		
135 Hulk Hogan	.50	1.25
Immortal One		
136 The Ultimate Warrior	.12	.30
137 Rhythm and Blues	.10	.25
138 Ravishing Rick Rude	.15	.40
Superfly Jimmy Snuka		
139 Rhythm and Blues	.12	.30
Jimmy Hart		
140 Demolition	.10	.25
141 Andre the Giant	.40	1.00
Bobby Heenan		
142 Haku	.10	.25
Smash		
143 Smash	.10	.25
Haku		
Ax		
144 Brutus The Barber Beefcake	.12	.30
Mr.Perfect		
145 Hulk Hogan	.50	1.25
Ultimate Warrior		
146 Brutus The Barber Beefcake	.12	.30
147 The Ultimate Warrior	.12	.30
148 Bushwhackers	.10	.25
149 The Rockers	.12	.30
150 Dusty Rhodes	.10	.25

1991 Classic WWF Superstars

COMPLETE SET (150)	50.00	100.00
COMPLETE FACTORY SET (150)	100.00	200.00
UNOPENED BOX (36 PACKS)		
UNOPENED PACK (12 CARDS)		
*EUROPEAN: SAME VALUE		
1 Hulk Hogan	.50	1.25
2 Ultimate Warrior	.30	.75
3 Texas Tornado RC	.12	.30
4 Jake The Snake Roberts	.20	.50
5 Big Boss Man	.10	.25
6 Hacksaw Jim Duggan	.12	.30
7 Davey Boy Smith	.12	.30
8 The Model Rick Martel	.10	.25
9 Million Dollar Man Ted DiBiase	.12	.30
10 Bobby Heenan	.75	2.00
11 Rockers	.15	.40

12 Legion of Doom	.12	.30
13 Tugboat RC	.10	.25
14 Power & Glory	.10	.25
15 Bushwackers	.10	.25
16 Macho King Randy Savage	.30	.75
17 Koko B. Ware	.10	.25
18 Superfly Jimmy Snuka	.15	.40
19 Davey Boy Smith	.12	.30
20 Sensational Queen Sherri	.12	.30
21 Barbarian	.10	.25
22 Virgil	.10	.25
23 Nasty Boys	1.00	2.50
24 Million Dollar Man Ted DiBiase	.12	.30
25 Big Boss Man	.10	.25
26 Sgt. Slaughter RC	.15	.40
27 Barbarian	.10	.25
28 Nasty Boys	.10	.25
29 Mr. Perfect	.15	.40
30 Undertaker RC	6.00	15.00
31 Rowdy Roddy Piper	.40	1.00
32 The Mountie RC	.10	.25
33 Davey Boy Smith	.12	.30
34 General Adnan RC	.10	.25
35 Hulk Hogan	.50	1.25
36 Ultimate Warrior	.30	.75
37 Texas Tornado RC	.12	.30
38 Hacksaw Jim Duggan	.12	.30
39 Jake The Snake Roberts	.20	.50
40 Hulk Hogan	.50	1.25
41 The Model Rick Martel	.10	.25
42 Earthquake RC	.10	.25
43 Jimmy Hart	.15	.40
44 Rockers	.15	.40
45 Slick	.10	.25
46 Legion of Doom	.12	.30
47 Mr. Fuji	.10	.25
48 Tugboat RC	.10	.25
49 Power & Glory	.10	.25
50 Bushwackers	.10	.25
51 Macho King Randy Savage	.30	.75
52 Hulk Hogan	.50	1.25
53 Koko B. Ware	.10	.25
54 Superfly Jimmy Snuka	.15	.40
55 Haku	.10	.25
56 Sensational Queen Sherri	.12	.30
57 Nasty Boys	.10	.25
58 Virgil	.10	.25
59 Million Dollar Man Ted DiBiase	.12	.30
60 Big Boss Man	.10	.25
61 Sgt. Slaughter RC	.15	.40
62 Barbarian	.10	.25
63 Mr. Perfect	.15	.40
64 Undertaker RC	20.00	50.00
65 Rowdy Roddy Piper	.40	1.00
66 The Mountie RC	.10	.25
67 General Adnan RC	.10	.25
68 The Dragon Ricky Steamboat	.12	.30
69 Hulk Hogan	.50	1.25
70 Ultimate Warrior	.30	.75
71 Texas Tornado RC	.12	.30
72 Hacksaw Jim Duggan	.12	.30
73 Jake The Snake Roberts	.20	.50
74 The Model Rick Martel	.10	.25
75 Earthquake RC	.10	.25
76 Mr. Fuji	.10	.25
77 Jimmy Hart	.15	.40
78 Rockers	.15	.40
79 Legion of Doom	.12	.30
80 Tugboat RC	.10	.25
81 Paul Roma	.10	.25
82 Power & Glory	.10	.25
83 Bushwackers	.10	.25
84 Macho King Randy Savage	.30	.75
85 General Adnan RC	.10	.25
86 The Mountie RC	.10	.25
87 Rowdy Roddy Piper	.40	1.00
88 Undertaker RC	5.00	12.00
89 Mr. Perfect	.15	.40
90 Sgt. Slaughter RC	.15	.40
91 Hulk Hogan	.50	1.25
92 Earthquake RC	.10	.25
93 Paul Bearer RC	1.50	4.00
94 Koko B. Ware	.10	.25
95 Superfly Jimmy Snuka	.15	.40
96 Sensational Queen Sherri	.12	.30
97 Sgt. Slaughter RC	.15	.40
98 Rowdy Roddy Piper	.40	1.00
99 Hulk Hogan	.50	1.25
100 Ultimate Warrior	.30	.75
101 Texas Tornado RC	.12	.30
102 The Model Rick Martel	.10	.25
103 Earthquake RC	.10	.25
104 Legion of Doom	.12	.30
105 Bret Hart	.75	2.00
106 Undertaker RC	15.00	40.00
107 Mr. Perfect	.15	.40
108 Sgt. Slaughter w/General Adnan	.15	.40
109 Big Boss Man	.10	.25
110 Million Dollar Man Ted DiBiase	.12	.30
111 Hulk Hogan	.50	1.25
112 Legion Of Doom	.12	.30
113 Mr. Perfect	.15	.40
114 Ultimate Warrior	.30	.75
115 Big Boss Man	.10	.25
116 Hacksaw Jim Duggan	.12	.30
117 Power & Glory w/Slick	.10	.25
118 Macho King Randy Savage	.30	.75
119 Bushwackers	.10	.25
120 Tugboat RC	.10	.25
121 Mr. Perfect	.15	.40
122 Barbarian	.10	.25
123 Hulk Hogan	.50	1.25
124 Ultimate Warrior	3.00	8.00
125 Big Boss Man	1.00	2.50
126 Hacksaw Jim Duggan	1.50	4.00
127 Jake The Snake Roberts	2.50	6.00
128 The Model Rick Martel	.10	.25
129 The Dragon Ricky Steamboat	.12	.30
130 Mr. Perfect	1.50	4.00
131 Haku	.10	.25
132 Million Dollar Man Ted DiBiase	.12	.30
133 Texas Tornado RC	.12	.30
134 Macho King Randy Savage	.30	.75
135 Macho King Randy Savage	.30	.75
136 Legion of Doom	.12	.30
137 Rockers	.15	.40
138 Earthquake RC	.10	.25
139 Superfly Jimmy Snuka	.15	.40
140 Hulk Hogan	3.00	8.00
141 The Dragon Ricky Steamboat	1.50	4.00
142 Sgt. Slaughter RC	2.00	5.00
143 Texas Tornado RC	.12	.30
144 Million Dollar Man Ted DiBiase	.12	.30
145 Earthquake RC	.10	.25
146 Legion of Doom	.12	.30
147 Rockers	.15	.40
148 Macho King Randy Savage	2.00	5.00
149 Earthquake RC	.10	.25
150 The Model Rick Martel	.10	.25

1994 Coliseum Video WWF Akklaim Strategy Tips

COMPLETE SET (4)	5.00	12.00
NNO Doink	2.00	5.00
NNO Luna Vachon	2.00	5.00
NNO Shawn Michaels	2.50	6.00
NNO Yokozuna	2.00	5.00

1994 Coliseum Video WWF Bret Hart

COMPLETE SET (5)	2.50	6.00
1 Bret Hitman Hart	.75	2.00
2 Bret Hitman Hart	.75	2.00
3 Bret Hitman Hart	.75	2.00
4 Bret Hitman Hart	.75	2.00
5 Bret Hitman Hart	.75	2.00

1993 Coliseum Video WWF Collectors Cards

COMPLETE SET (9)	10.00	25.00
COLISEUM VIDEO RENTAL EXCLUSIVE		
1 Hulk Hogan/Mr. T	2.50	6.00
2 King Kong Bundy/Hulk Hogan	2.50	6.00
3 Andre The Giant/Hulk Hogan	2.00	5.00
4 Macho Man Randy Savage/Miss Elizabeth	2.00	5.00
5 Macho Man Randy Savage/Hulk Hogan	4.00	10.00
6 Ultimate Warrior	1.50	4.00
7 Sgt. Slaughter/Hulk Hogan	2.00	5.00
8 Macho Man Randy Savage	1.50	4.00
9 Wrestlemania IX	1.25	3.00

1993 Coliseum Video WWF Lenticular

COMPLETE SET (5)	10.00	25.00
NNO Bret Hit Man Hart	4.00	10.00
NNO Hulk Hogan	3.00	8.00
NNO Mr. Perfect	2.50	6.00
NNO Tatanka	1.50	4.00
NNO The Undertaker	5.00	12.00

2000 Comic Images WWF Axxess Fan Fest

COMPLETE SET (3)		
1 Big Show	4.00	10.00
2 Triple H	6.00	15.00
3 The Rock	10.00	25.00

2000 Comic Images WWF The Divas Promos

COMPLETE SET (8)	12.00	30.00
P1 Chyna	3.00	8.00
P2 Debra	2.50	6.00
P3 Ivory	2.00	5.00
P4 Jacqueline	2.00	5.00
P5 The Kat	2.00	5.00
P6 Terri	3.00	8.00
P7 Tori	2.00	5.00
P8 Trish	4.00	10.00

2000 Comic Images WWF No Mercy

COMPLETE SET (81)	8.00	20.00
UNOPENED BOX (36 PACKS)		
UNOPENED PACK (7 CARDS)		
1 Mankind	.50	1.25
2 Cactus Jack	.50	1.25
3 Stone Cold Steve Austin	.75	2.00
4 Hardcore Holly	.20	.50
5 Al Snow	.20	.50
6 Road Dogg	.12	.30
7 Big Boss Man	.20	.50
8 The Undertaker	.60	1.50
9 Kane	.50	1.25
10 The Rock	.75	2.00
11 Vince McMahon	.50	1.25
12 Shane McMahon	.30	.75
13 Edge/Christian	.50	1.25
14 The Hardy Boyz	.30	.75
15 The Dudley Boyz	.20	.50
16 The Acolytes	.30	.75
17 Faarooq	.12	.30
18 Bradshaw	.30	.75
19 X-Pac	.20	.50
20 The Big Show	.30	.75
21 Viscera	.12	.30
22 Prince Albert	.12	.30
23 Test	.20	.50
24 Mr. Ass	.12	.30
25 Triple H	.75	2.00
26 Chyna	.50	1.25
27 Ken Shamrock	.20	.50
28 Godfather	.12	.30
29 Chris Jericho	.30	.75
30 Tazz RC	.20	.50
31 Hardcore Belt	.12	.30
32 D-Generation X	.30	.75
33 Gangrel	.12	.30
34 The Headbangers	.12	.30
35 British Bulldog	.20	.50
36 D'Lo Brown	.12	.30
37 Mark Henry	.12	.30
38 Kurt Angle RC	12.00	30.00
39 Mean Street Posse	.12	.30
40 Rikishi Phatu	.20	.50
41 Too Cool	.12	.30
42 Mick Foley	.50	1.25
43 Shawn Michaels	.50	1.25
44 The Undertaker	.60	1.50
45 Stone Cold Steve Austin	.75	2.00
46 Legion Of Doom	.40	1.00
47 Wild Samoans	.20	.50
48 Sgt. Slaughter	.30	.75
49 Mankind/The Rock	.75	2.00
50 Mankind/The Rock	.75	2.00
51 Mankind/The Undertaker	.60	1.50
52 Mankind/Triple H	.75	2.00
53 Mankind/Ken Shamrock	.50	1.25
54 The Rock/Triple H	.75	2.00
55 The Undertaker/Shawn Michaels	.60	1.50
56 The Hardy Boyz/Edge/Christian	.50	1.25
57 The Undertaker/Kane	.60	1.50
58 Undertaker/Kane/Austin	.75	2.00
59 Kane/Vince McMahon/Undertaker	.60	1.50
60 Steve Austin/Kane	.75	2.00
61 Steve Austin/Dude Love	.75	2.00
62 Steve Austin/Undertaker	.75	2.00
63 Steve Austin/Undertaker	.75	2.00
64 Steve Austin/Vince McMahon	.75	2.00
65 Steve Austin/Shane & Vince McMahon	.75	2.00
66 Shane McMahon/Test	.30	.75
67 Al Snow/Big Boss Man	.20	.50
68 Al Snow/Hardcore Holly	.20	.50
69 Al Snow/Minis	.20	.50

70 Ivory/Luna	.50	1.25
71 Ken Shamrock/Steve Blackman	.20	.50
72 Mr. Ass/Hardcore Holly	.20	.50
73 The Acolytes	.30	.75
74 New Age Outlaws/Mankind/Kane	.50	1.25
75 Vince McMahon/Mankind	.50	1.25
76 Sgt. Slaughter/Triple H	.75	2.00
77 Shawn Michaels/The Undertaker	.60	1.50
78 The Rock/Mankind	.75	2.00
79 Triple H/Cactus Jack	.75	2.00
80 The Hardy Boyz/The Dudley Boyz	.30	.75
81 Checklist	.12	.30

2000 Comic Images WWF No Mercy Hardcore Champions Holofoil

COMPLETE SET (8)	3.00	8.00
RANDOMLY INSERTED INTO PACKS		
C1 Mankind	1.25	3.00
C2 Big Bossman	.50	1.25
C3 Road Dogg	.50	1.25
C4 Hardcore Holly	.50	1.25
C5 Al Snow	.50	1.25
C6 Mr. Ass	.50	1.25
C7 British Bulldog	.50	1.25
C8 Test	.50	1.25

2000 Comic Images WWF No Mercy Piece of the Ring Relics

COMPLETE SET (4)	12.00	30.00
RANDOMLY INSERTED INTO PACKS		
P1 Ring Mat	6.00	15.00
P2 Road Dogg Hat	4.00	10.00
P3 Chris Jericho Shirt	8.00	20.00
P4 D-Generation X Shirt	5.00	12.00

2000 Comic Images WWF No Mercy Promos

COMPLETE SET (3)	1.50	4.00
RANDOMLY INSERTED INTO PACKS		
P1 Mankind/The Rock	.75	2.00
P2 The Undertaker/Kane	.75	2.00
P3 Vince McMahon	.75	2.00

2000 Comic Images WWF Rock Solid

COMPLETE SET (72)	10.00	25.00
UNOPENED BOX (36 PACKS)	100.00	150.00
UNOPENED PACK (7 CARDS)	3.00	4.00
1 Title Card	.30	.75
2 Reeling 'Em In	.30	.75
3 Catching Up	.30	.75
4 The People's Threads	.30	.75
5 Sweet Ride	.30	.75
6 The Rock's Roots	.30	.75
7 Shirt Off His Back	.30	.75
8 Electrifying Threads	.30	.75
9 In For A Trim	.30	.75
10 Laying It Down In Miami	.30	.75
11 Electrifying Author	.30	.75
12 The Little People's Champ	.30	.75
13 A Class Act	.30	.75
14 The Fans Bring It	.30	.75
15 They Smell It	.30	.75
16 Another Happy Customer	.30	.75
17 Author, Author	.30	.75
18 Who's The Champ	.15	.75
19 Rocky Rocky Rocky	.30	.75
20 Action, Rock	.30	.75
21 The People's Host	.30	.75
22 Hot, Hot, Hot	.30	.75
23 Getting Cheffy With It	.30	.75
24 The Best-Selling Author	.30	.75
25 The People's Show	.30	.75
26 Check Right In	.30	.75
27 Stretch 'Em Out, Rock	.30	.75
28 Electrifying	.30	.75
29 Rough Landing	.30	.75
30 Goin' Down	.30	.75
31 Off With The Pad	.30	.75
32 Table For One	.30	.75
33 Rock Bottom	.30	.75
34 Over The Top	.30	.75
35 His Own Medicine	.30	.75
36 Not A Friendly Hug	.30	.75
37 Who's The Game	.30	.75
38 The End In Near	.30	.75
39 Say Cheese	.30	.75
40 Respect	.30	.75
41 Taker Takes One	.30	.75
42 Some Pain For Kane	.30	.75
43 Big Blow To The Big Show	.30	.75
44 One Giant Hit For Mankind	.30	.75
45 Crippling The Crippler	.30	.75
46 Take That, Boss	.30	.75
47 Shane Can Smell It	.30	.75
48 Double Trouble	.30	.75
49 Olympic Zero	.30	.75
50 Turn That Camera Sideways And	.30	.75
51 Raw Is Who	.30	.75
52 Rock vs. Brooklyn Brawler	.30	.75
53 Rock vs. Faarooq	.30	.75
54 Rock vs. Triple H	.30	.75
55 Rock vs. Ken Shamrock & Mankind	.30	.75
56 Rock vs. Mr. Ass	.30	.75
57 Rock vs. Steve Austin	.30	.75
58 Rock vs. Mankind	.30	.75
59 Rock vs. Mankind	.30	.75
60 Rock vs. Chris Benoit	.30	.75
61 Rock vs. Triple H	.30	.75
62 Rock vs. Vince McMahon	.30	.75
63 Rock vs. Triple H	.30	.75
64 Rock vs. Mankind	.30	.75
65 Rock 'N' Sock Wins First Title	.30	.75
66 Rock 'N' Sock Wins Third Title	.30	.75
67 CL Rock on runway	.30	.75
68 CL Rock in crowd	.30	.75
69 CL Rock w/Mick Foley	.30	.75
70 CL Rock w/Kane	.30	.75
71 CL Rock w/Steve Austin	.30	.75
72 CL Rock w/Stevie Richards	.30	.75

2000 Comic Images WWF Rock Solid Holofoil

COMPLETE SET (6)	8.00	20.00
STATED ODDS 1:18		
C1 Rock Bottom	2.50	6.00
C2 Lethal Style	2.50	6.00
C3 The People's Champ	2.50	6.00
C4 The People's Elbow	2.50	6.00
C5 Kickin' Back	2.50	6.00
C6 Lights, Camera, Rock	2.50	6.00

2000 Comic Images WWF Rock Solid Promos

P1 Rock w/Sunglasses	1.50	4.00
P2 Rock on Ropes	1.50	4.00
P3 Rock Lounging	1.50	4.00

1999 Comic Images WWF SmackDown

COMPLETE SET (72)	6.00	15.00
UNOPENED BOX (36 PACKS)		
UNOPENED PACK (7 CARDS)		
*CHROMIUM: .5X TO 1.2X BASIC CARDS		
1 Title Card	.10	.25
2 Stone Cold Steve Austin	.60	1.50
3 The Rock	.60	1.50
4 The Big Show	.15	.40
5 Mankind	.30	.75
6 The Undertaker	.40	.75
7 X-Pac	.15	.40
8 Triple H	.50	1.25
9 The Road Dogg	.15	.40
10 Mr. Ass	.15	.40
11 Al Snow	.15	.40
12 Big Boss Man	.15	.40
13 Kane	.20	.50
14 D'Lo Brown	.10	.25
15 Droz	.10	.25
16 Edge	.50	1.25
17 Gangrel RC	.10	.25
18 Christian RC	.15	.40
19 Godfather	.15	.40
20 Prince Albert RC	.10	.25
21 Mark Henry	.10	.40
22 Jeff Jarrett	.15	.40
23 Chyna	.50	1.25
24 Mideon RC	.10	.25
25 Hardcore Holly	.15	.40
26 Test RC	.10	.25
27 Val Venis	.10	.25
28 Viscera	.10	.25
29 Too Cool	.10	.25
30 The Hardy Boyz	.20	.50
31 Debra RC	.20	.50
32 Tori RC	.20	.50
33 P.M.S.	.20	.50
34 Ken Shamrock	.20	.50
35 Jerry The King Lawler	.15	.40
36 Meat RC	.10	.25
37 Steve Blackman	.10	.25
38 Paul Bearer	.15	.40
39 Ivory RC	.20	.50
40 Shane McMahon RC	.15	.40
41 Vince McMahon	.30	.75
42 Stone Cold Steve Austin	.60	1.50
43 The Undertaker	.40	1.00
44 The Big Show	.15	.40
45 The Rock	.60	1.50
46 Mankind	.30	.75
47 Triple H/Chyna	.50	1.25
48 X-Pac	.15	.40
49 Kane	.20	.50
50 Ken Shamrock	.20	.50
51 Mean Street Posse	.10	.25
52 Test RC	.10	.25
53 Steve Austin/Undertaker	.40	1.00
54 The Rock/Triple H	.40	1.00
55 S.McMahon/The Rock/V.McMahon	.40	1.00
56 The Undertaker/Kane	.30	.75
57 Vince McMahon	.20	.60
58 The Rock/Mick Foley	.40	1.00
59 The Big Show	.15	.40
60 Stone Cold Steve Austin/The Rock	.40	1.00
61 Vince McMahon	.20	.50
62 Mankind/Vince McMahon	.30	.75
63 The Big Show	.20	.50
64 X-Pac/Shane McMahon	.10	.25
65 Mr. Ass	.10	.25
66 Vince McMahon/Shane McMahon	.20	.50
67 Stone Cold Steve Austin	.30	.75
68 The Rock	.40	1.00
69 The Brood	.30	.75
70 X-Pac/Road Dogg	.15	.40
71 Jeff Jarrett/Debra	.15	.40
72 Checklist	.10	.25

1999 Comic Images WWF SmackDown Chromium

COMPLETE SET (90)	6.00	15.00
1 Title Card	.12	.30
2 Stone Cold Steve Austin	.75	2.00
3 The Rock	.75	2.00
4 The Big Show	.20	.50
5 Mankind	.30	.75
6 The Undertaker	.40	1.00
7 X-Pac	.20	.50
8 Triple H	.60	1.50
9 The Road Dogg	.20	.50
10 Mr. Ass	.12	.30
11 Al Snow	.20	.50
12 Big Boss Man	.20	.50
13 Kane	.25	.60
14 D'Lo Brown	.12	.30
15 Droz	.12	.30
16 Edge	.60	1.50
17 Gangrel RC	.12	.30
18 Christian RC	.20	.50
19 Godfather	.20	.50
20 Prince Albert RC	.12	.30
21 Mark Henry	.12	.30
22 Jeff Jarrett	.20	.50
23 Chyna	.25	.60
24 Mideon RC	.12	.30
25 Hardcore Holly	.20	.50
26 Test RC	.12	.30
27 Val Venis	.12	.30
28 Viscera	.12	.30
29 Shawn Michaels	.40	1.00
30 The Hardy Boyz	.30	.75
31 Debra RC	.30	.75
32 Tori RC	.30	.75
33 P.M.S.	.30	.75
34 Ken Shamrock	.12	.30
35 Jerry The King Lawler	.20	.50
36 Meat RC	.12	.30
37 Steve Blackman	.12	.30
38 Paul Bearer	.20	.50
39 Ivory RC	.30	.75
40 Shane McMahon RC	.20	.50
41 Vince McMahon	.40	1.00
42 Stone Cold Steve Austin	.75	2.00
43 The Undertaker	.40	1.00
44 The Big Show	.20	.50
45 The Rock	.75	2.00
46 Mankind	.30	.75

47 Triple H/Chyna	.60	1.50
48 X-Pac	.20	.50
49 Kane	.25	.60
50 Ken Shamrock	.12	.30
51 Mean Street Posse	.12	.30
52 Test RC	.12	.30
53 Steve Austin/Undertaker	.50	1.25
54 The Rock/Triple H	.50	1.25
55 S.McMahon/The Rock/V.McMahon	.50	1.25
56 The Undertaker/Kane	.40	1.00
57 Vince McMahon	.30	.75
58 The Rock/Mick Foley	.30	.75
59 The Big Show	.25	.60
60 Stone Cold Steve Austin/The Rock	.50	1.25
61 Vince McMahon	.30	.75
62 Mankind/Vince McMahon	.30	.75
63 The Big Show	.25	.60
64 X-Pac/Shane McMahon	.20	.50
65 Mr. Ass	.12	.30
66 Vince McMahon/Shane McMahon	.25	.60
67 Stone Cold Steve Austin	.50	1.25
68 The Rock	.50	1.25
69 The Brood	.30	.75
70 X-Pac/Road Dogg	.20	.50
71 Jeff Jarrett/Debra	.20	.50
72 The Undertaker/Big Boss Man	.25	.60
73 Four-Way Match	.20	.50
74 Triple Threat Match	.20	.50
75 Shane McMahon/X-Pac	.20	.50
76 Triple H/Kane	.50	1.25
77 Stone Cold Steve Austin	.75	2.00
78 Mr. Ass	.20	.50
79 Road Dogg/Chyna	.20	.50
80 Road Dogg/X-Pac	.20	.50
81 Shane/Vince McMahon	.30	.75
82 Kane/The Big Show	.30	.75
83 X-Pac/Hardcore Holly	.20	.50
84 Triple H/The Rock	.60	1.50
85 Undertaker/Steve Austin	.60	1.50
86 Jeff Jarrett/Edge	.50	1.25
87 D'Lo Brown/Mideon	.12	.30
88 Big Boss Man/Al Snow	.20	.50
89 Acolytes/Hardy Boyz	.30	.75
90 Checklist	.12	.30

1999 Comic Images WWF SmackDown 22KT Gold Signatures

COMPLETE SET (6)	50.00	100.00
STATED ODDS 1:80		
1 Stone Cold Steve Austin	12.00	30.00
2 The Undertaker	10.00	25.00
3 The Rock	20.00	50.00
4 Triple H	12.00	30.00
5 The Big Show	12.00	30.00
6 Mankind	8.00	20.00
SE Stone Cold Steve Austin Special Edition		

1999 Comic Images WWF SmackDown Autographs

COMPLETE SET (8)		
STATED ODDS 1:80		
NNO Al Snow	6.00	15.00
NNO Big Boss Man	15.00	40.00
NNO D'Lo Brown	6.00	15.00
NNO Godfather	6.00	15.00
NNO The Hardy Boyz	15.00	40.00
NNO Hardcore Holly	6.00	15.00
NNO Ivory	12.00	30.00
NNO Tori	6.00	15.00

1999 Comic Images WWF SmackDown Chrome Inserts

COMPLETE SET (6)	5.00	12.00
STATED ODDS 1:18		
C1 Stone Cold Steve Austin	1.50	4.00
C2 The Corporate Ministry	1.00	2.50
C3 X-Pac/Kane	.60	1.50
C4 The Brood	1.00	2.50
C5 Mankind	1.00	2.50
C6 The Rock	1.50	4.00

1999 Comic Images WWF SmackDown Promos

P1 Stone Cold Steve Austin	1.50	4.00
(Non-Sport Update Exclusive)		
P2 The Rock	2.00	5.00
P3 Mankind	1.00	2.50

1999-05 Danbury Mint WWF/WWE 22kt Gold

COMPLETE SET (124)	250.00	500.00
1 Andre The Giant	3.00	8.00
2 Ken Shamrock	2.00	5.00
3 Stone Cold Steve Austin	4.00	10.00
3 Bob Backlund	2.00	5.00
4 The Rock	4.00	10.00
5 B.A. Billy Gunn	1.50	4.00
6 Road Dogg	1.50	4.00
7 Gorilla Monsoon	1.50	4.00
8 Val Venis	1.00	2.50
9 Al Snow	1.25	3.00
10 Kane	2.00	5.00
11 Jesse The Body Ventura	2.50	6.00
12 Undertaker	5.00	12.00
13 Shawn Michaels	6.00	15.00
14 Jerry The King Lawler	4.00	10.00
15 Lita	3.00	8.00
16 Fabulous Moolah	2.50	6.00
17 Rikishi Fatu	1.25	3.00
18 Big Boss Man	1.00	2.50
19 Jim Ross	4.00	10.00
20 The Iron Sheik	1.25	3.00
21 Hardy Boyz	3.00	8.00
22 Trish Stratus	6.00	15.00
23 Chris Jericho	4.00	10.00
24 Sgt. Slaughter	1.50	4.00
25 Triple H	2.50	6.00
26 Stephanie McMahon-Helmsley	2.00	5.00
27 Chris Benoit	8.00	20.00
28 Captain Lou Albano	2.50	6.00
29 George The Animal Steele	2.00	5.00
30 X-Pac	1.25	3.00
31 Vince McMahon	2.00	5.00
32 Shane O Mac	2.50	6.00
33 Stone Cold Steve Austin	3.00	8.00
33 Bob Backlund	2.00	5.00
34 Chyna	3.00	8.00
35 Dudley Boyz	2.50	6.00
36 British Bulldog	2.50	6.00
37 Jimmy Superfly Snuka	1.50	4.00
38 Mankind	4.00	10.00
39 Tazz	2.00	5.00
40 Big Show	1.50	4.00
41 Kurt Angle	2.50	6.00
42 Eddie Guerrero	4.00	10.00
43 Debra	2.00	5.00
44 Mr. Fuji	1.25	3.00
45 The Godfather	2.50	6.00
46 Edge/Christian	2.50	6.00
47 Too Cool	1.25	3.00
48 Test	1.25	3.00
49 The Acolytes	1.50	4.00
50 Steve Blackman	2.50	6.00
51 William Regal	2.00	5.00
52 Ric Flair	5.00	12.00
53 Tajiri	2.00	5.00
54 Rhyno	1.25	3.00
55 Stacy Keibler	6.00	15.00
56 K-Kwik	1.25	3.00
57 Crash Holly	1.25	3.00
58 Molly Holly	1.50	4.00
59 Albert	1.50	4.00
60 Perry Saturn	2.00	5.00
61 Booker T	2.50	6.00
62 Kaientai	1.25	3.00
63 Jacqueline	1.25	3.00
64 Steven Richards	1.25	3.00
65 Raven	1.50	4.00
66 Rob Van Dam	2.00	5.00
67 Earl Hebner	2.50	6.00
68 Spike Dudley	1.25	3.00
69 Hardcore Holly	3.00	8.00
70 Linda McMahon	1.50	4.00
71 Hollywood Hulk Hogan	12.00	30.00
72 Nidia	2.50	6.00
73 Garrison Cade	4.00	10.00
74 Luther Reigns	4.00	10.00
75 Eric Bischoff	3.00	8.00
76 Gail Kim	8.00	20.00
77 Matt Hardy	2.50	6.00
78 Scott Steiner	8.00	20.00
79 Tyson Tomko	6.00	15.00
80 Miss Jackie	3.00	8.00
81 Ivory	4.00	10.00
82 Billy/Chuck	2.00	5.00
83 Chavo Guerrero	3.00	8.00
84 Jamie Noble	2.00	5.00
85 Mark Henry	3.00	8.00
86 Tommy Dreamer	2.50	6.00
87 Diamond Dallas Page	2.00	5.00
88 Mark Jindrak	2.50	6.00
89 Victoria	2.50	6.00
90 Kevin Nash	3.00	8.00
91 Eugene	3.00	8.00
92 John Cena	6.00	15.00
93 Rey Mysterio	4.00	10.00
94 Muhammad Hassan	5.00	12.00
95 The Hurricane	2.00	5.00
96 Matt Morgan	2.50	6.00
97 Sable	5.00	12.00
98 Rene/Kenzo	2.50	6.00
99 Billy Kidman	2.00	5.00
100 Goldust	2.00	5.00
101 Theodore Long	2.50	6.00
102 JBL	6.00	15.00
103 Lance Storm	2.00	5.00
104 Zach Gowen	3.00	8.00
105 FBI	1.25	3.00
106 Edge	6.00	15.00
107 Randy Orton	2.50	6.00
108 Maven	1.50	4.00
109 La Resistance	2.00	5.00
110 Chavo Guerrero	3.00	8.00
111 Basham Brothers	2.50	6.00
112 Bubba Ray Dudley	2.50	6.00
113 The Coach	4.00	10.00
114 Heidenreich	5.00	12.00
115 Benjamin/Haas	2.50	6.00
116 Jazz	2.50	6.00
117 Batista	2.50	6.00
118 Goldberg	6.00	15.00
119 Torrie Wilson	4.00	10.00
120 Brock Lesnar	3.00	8.00
B1 Mankind Bonus	15.00	40.00
B2 Cactus Jack Bonus	15.00	40.00

2002 Doritos WWF Super Stars

COMPLETE SET (12)	5.00	12.00
1 The Rock	.75	2.00
2 Stone Cold Steve Austin	.75	2.00
3 Kurt Angle	.50	1.25
4 Booker T	.25	.60
5 Triple H	.75	2.00
6 Edge	.50	1.25
7 Rob Van Dam	.25	.60
8 Chris Jericho	.40	1.00
9 Undertaker	.50	1.25
10 Jeff Hardy	.40	1.00
11 Lita	.75	2.00
12 Trish Stratus	1.25	3.00

1998 DuoCards WWF

COMPLETE SET (72)	50.00	100.00
UNOPENED BOX (30 PACKS)		
UNOPENED PACK (7 CARDS)		
1 WWF Attitude	.10	.25
2 Mr. Vince McMahon RC	4.00	10.00
3 Commissioner Slaughter	.20	.50
4 Mr. Pat Patterson RC	.10	.25
5 Mr. Gerald Brisco RC	.15	.40
6 WWF Champion	.60	1.50
7 WWF Tag Team Champions	.20	.50
8 WWF IC Champ/The Rock	15.00	40.00
9 WWF European Champion	.10	.25
10 WWF Light Heavyweight Champion	.10	.25
11 Stone Cold Steve Austin	3.00	8.00
12 Undertaker	3.00	8.00
13 Shawn Michaels	2.50	6.00
14 Ken Shamrock	2.00	5.00
15 The Rock RC	12.00	30.00
16 Triple H RC	6.00	10.00
17 Kane RC	5.00	12.00
18 Owen Hart	.30	1.00
19 Mankind RC	.30	.75
20 Dude Love RC	.30	.75
21 Cactus Jack RC	1.50	4.00
22 Sable RC	.30	.75
23 X-Pac	.20	.50
24 D'Lo Brown RC	.10	.25
25 Mark Henry RC	.10	.25
26 Bradshaw RC	.50	1.25
27 The Godfather	.10	.25
28 Double J	.10	.25
29 Dustin Runnels	.10	.25
30 Marvelous Marc Mero	.10	.25
31 Steve Blackman RC	.40	1.00
32 Al Snow and Head RC	.15	.40
33 Taka Michinoku RC	.10	.25
34 Badd Ass Billy Gunn RC	.20	.50

35 Savio Vega	.10	.25
36 Dr. Death Steve Williams	.10	.25
37 Steven Regal	.15	.40
38 Faarooq	.15	.40
39 Scorpio RC	.10	.25
40 Kurrgan RC	.10	.25
41 Luna	.10	.25
42 Dan The Beast Severn	.15	.40
43 Golga	.10	.25
44 Giant Silva RC	.10	.25
45 Road Dog Jesse James RC	.20	.50
46 Edge RWT RC	4.00	10.00
47 Darren Droz Drozdov RWT RC	.10	.25
48 Val Venis RWT RC	.15	.40
49 Papi Chulo RWT RC	.10	.25
50 Tiger Ali Singh RWT RC	.15	.40
51 D-Generation X FW	.20	.50
52 The Nation FW	.20	.60
53 Kaientai FW	.10	.25
54 Kane w/Mankind DD	1.50	4.00
55 New Age Outlaws DD	.20	.50
56 Headbangers DD	.10	.25
57 D.O.A. DD	.10	.25
58 L.O.D. 2000 DD	.15	.40
59 Southern Justice DD	.10	.25
60 Too Much DD	.10	.25
61 Los Boricuas DD	.10	.25
62 Paul Bearer BBB	.10	.25
63 Chyna BBB RC	2.50	6.00
64 Jackyl BBB RC	.10	.25
65 Jim Cornette BBB	.15	.40
66 Yamaguchi-San BBB RC	.10	.25
67 Jacqueline BBB RC	.15	.40
68 Paul Ellering BBB	.10	.25
69 Jim Ross MTR	.15	.40
70 Jerry The King Lawler MTR	1.50	4.00
71 Raw is War	.10	.25
72 Checklist	.10	.25

1998 DuoCards WWF Autographs

STATED ODDS 1:100

NNO Billy Gunn	10.00	25.00
NNO Chyna	60.00	120.00
NNO Hawk	150.00	300.00
NNO Jacqueline	5.00	12.00
NNO Mankind	25.00	60.00
NNO Owen Hart	400.00	800.00
NNO Paul Bearer	50.00	100.00
NNO Road Dog Jesse James	12.00	30.00
NNO Sable	15.00	40.00
NNO Sable - Unsigned	6.00	15.00
NNO Steve Blackman	10.00	25.00
NNO The Rock	1500.00	3000.00
NNO Redemption Card	2.00	5.00

1998 DuoCards WWF Stone Cold's Greatest Hitz

COMPLETE SET (8)	15.00	30.00
STATED ODDS 1:20		
OMNI1 1996 King of the Ring	2.00	5.00
OMNI2 WM 13 Submission Match	2.00	5.00
OMNI3 1998 Royal Rumble	2.00	5.00
OMNI4 Wrestlemania XIV	2.00	5.00
OMNI5 King of the Ring	2.00	5.00
OMNI6 Raw is War	2.00	5.00
BONUS1 D-X In Your House	2.00	5.00
BONUS2 Arrest That Hyperlink	2.00	5.00

1998 DuoCards WWF Promos

1 Stone Cold Steve Austin	3.00	8.00
2 Sable	1.25	3.00
3 D-Generation X	2.00	5.00
4 Dude Love/Steve Austin	2.00	5.00

1999 Eastman Kodak WWF Collectible Motion

COMPLETE SET (6)	15.00	40.00
NNO Mankind	3.00	8.00
NNO The Rock	6.00	15.00
NNO Stone Cold Hell Yeah	6.00	15.00
NNO Stone Cold Stuns McMahon	6.00	15.00
NNO The Undertaker	5.00	12.00

2004 Edibas WWE Lamincards

COMPLETE SET (120)	15.00	40.00
UNOPENED BOX (24 PACKS)		
UNOPENED PACK (4 CARDS)		
1 Chris Benoit	.75	2.00
2 Randy Orton	.75	2.00
3 Kane	1.25	3.00
4 Chris Jericho	.75	2.00
5 Ric Flair	1.50	4.00
6 Rob Conway RC	.30	.75
7 Val Venis	.50	1.25
8 Chuck Palumbo	.50	1.25
9 Rosey	.30	.75
10 Tyson Tomko RC	.50	1.25
11 Shawn Michaels	2.00	5.00
12 The Rock	2.00	5.00
13 Shelton Benjamin RC	.30	.75
14 Christian	1.00	2.50
15 Mark Henry	.50	1.25
16 Test	.50	1.25
17 A-Train	.30	.75
18 Eric Bischoff	.50	1.25
19 Jonathan Coachman RC	.30	.75
20 Jerry The King Lawler	.75	2.00
21 Jim Ross	.50	1.25
22 Gail Kim RC	1.25	3.00
23 Ivory	1.25	3.00
24 Jazz	.75	2.00
25 Lita	2.00	5.00
26 Molly	1.50	4.00
27 Nidia	.75	2.00
28 Stacy Keibler	3.00	8.00
29 Trish Stratus	3.00	8.00
30 Victoria	1.50	4.00
31 Undertaker	1.50	4.00
32 JBL	.75	2.00
33 Eddie Guerrero	1.50	4.00
34 Booker T	1.25	3.00
35 Kurt Angle	1.25	3.00
36 John Cena	2.00	5.00
37 Rob Van Dam	1.25	3.00
38 Rene Dupree RC	.50	1.25
39 Rey Mysterio	.75	2.00
40 Paul Heyman	.30	.75
41 Hardcore Holly	.50	1.25
42 Paul London RC	.30	.75
43 Charlie Haas	.30	.75
44 Bubba Ray	.50	1.25
45 Billy Kidman	.30	.75
46 D-Von Dudley	.50	1.25
47 Chavo Guerrero	.50	1.25
48 Nunzio	.30	.75
49 Scotty 2 Hotty	.50	1.25
50 Johnny Stamboli	.30	.75
51 Danny Basham RC	.30	.75
52 Luther Reigns RC	.30	.75
53 Orlando Jordan RC	.30	.75
54 Akio RC	.30	.75
55 Big Show	1.25	3.00
56 Rico	.30	.75
57 Tazz	.50	1.25
58 Kenzo Suzuki RC	.30	.75
59 Theodore Long	.30	.75
60 Jon Heidenreich RC	.30	.75
61 Funaki	.50	1.25
62 Spike Dudley	.50	1.25
63 Hiroko RC	.30	.75
64 Dawn Marie	.75	2.00
65 Miss Jackie	1.25	3.00
66 Torrie Wilson	3.00	8.00
67 Chris Benoit LOGO	.75	2.00
68 Randy Orton LOGO	.75	2.00
69 Triple H LOGO	2.00	5.00
70 Batista LOGO	1.25	3.00
71 Kane LOGO	1.25	3.00
72 Chris Jericho LOGO	.75	2.00
73 Ric Flair LOGO	1.50	4.00
74 Shawn Michaels LOGO	2.00	5.00
75 Rob Conway LOGO	.30	.75
76 Stacy Keibler LOGO	3.00	8.00
77 Ivory LOGO	1.25	3.00
78 Molly Holly LOGO	1.50	4.00
79 Eddie Guerrero LOGO	1.50	4.00
80 Undertaker LOGO	1.50	4.00
81 Booker T LOGO	1.25	3.00
82 Kurt Angle LOGO	1.25	3.00
83 Rob Van Dam LOGO	1.25	3.00
84 Rey Mysterio LOGO	.75	2.00
85 Hardcore Holly LOGO	.50	1.25
86 Paul London LOGO	.30	.75
87 Billy Kidman LOGO	.30	.75
88 Dawn Marie LOGO	.75	2.00
89 Miss Jackie LOGO	1.25	3.00
90 Torrie Wilson LOGO	3.00	8.00
91 Chavo Guerrero LOGO	.50	1.25
92 Chuck Palumbo LOGO	.50	1.25
93 Mark Henry LOGO	.50	1.25
94 Orlando Jordan LOGO	.30	.75
95 Rico LOGO	.30	.75
96 The Rock LOGO	2.00	5.00
97 Scotty 2 Hotty LOGO	.50	1.25
98 Lita LOGO	2.00	5.00
99 Victoria LOGO	1.50	4.00
100 Gail Kim LOGO	1.25	3.00
101 Benoit vs. Flair IA	1.50	4.00
102 Jericho vs. Michaels IA	2.00	5.00
103 Hurricane vs. The Rock IA	2.00	5.00
104 Orton vs. Benoit IA	.75	2.00
105 Kane vs. Jericho IA	1.25	3.00
106 Test vs. Richards IA	.50	1.25
107 HHH vs. Benoit IA	2.00	5.00
108 Benjamin vs. Orton IA	.75	2.00
109 Conway vs. Hurricane IA	.30	.75
110 Jericho vs. Edge IA	1.25	3.00
111 Guerrero vs. Angle IA	1.50	4.00
112 Orton vs. The Rock IA	2.00	5.00
113 Akio vs. Moore IA	.30	.75
114 Big Show vs. RVD IA	1.25	3.00
115 Dudleys vs. La Resistance IA	.40	1.00
116 Cena vs. Big Show IA	2.00	5.00
117 JBL vs. Mysterio IA	.75	2.00
118 Nunzio vs. Chavo IA	.50	1.25
119 Booker T vs. Guerrero IA	1.50	4.00
120 Undertaker vs. Cena IA	2.00	5.00

2005 Edibas WWE Lamincards

COMPLETE SET (150)	15.00	40.00
UNOPENED BOX (24 PACKS)		
UNOPENED PACK (4 CARDS)		
1 Al Snow	.30	.75
2 Batista	.75	2.00
3 Booker T	.50	1.25
4 Candice RC	2.00	5.00
5 Chris Benoit	1.25	3.00
6 Christian	1.00	2.50
7 Doug Basham	.30	.75
8 Eddie Guerrero	1.50	4.00
9 Funaki	.30	.75
10 Hardcore Holly	.50	1.25
11 Heidenreich	.30	.75
12 John Bradshaw Layfield	.50	1.25
13 Joey Mercury RC	.30	.75
14 Johnny Nitro RC	.30	.75
15 Melina RC	1.50	4.00
16 Michelle McCool RC	1.50	4.00
17 Nunzio	.30	.75
18 Orlando Jordan	.30	.75
19 Paul London	.30	.75
20 Randy Orton	.30	.75
21 Rey Mysterio	1.00	2.50
22 Scotty 2 Hotty	.50	1.25
23 Sylvain Grenier RC	.30	.75
24 Torrie Wilson	3.00	8.00
25 Undertaker	1.50	4.00
26 William Regal	.50	1.25
27 Antonio RC	.30	.75
28 Big Show	1.25	3.00
29 Carlito RC	.30	.75
30 Chris Jericho	1.00	2.50
31 Christy Hemme RC	3.00	8.00
32 Danny Basham	.30	.75
33 Edge	1.00	2.50
34 Eugene	.75	2.00
35 Gene Snitzky RC	.30	.75
36 Jerry The King Lawler	.75	2.00
37 John Cena	2.00	5.00
38 Kane	1.00	2.50
39 Kerwin White RC	.30	.75
40 Kurt Angle	1.25	3.00
41 Lita	2.00	5.00
42 Rene Dupree	.30	.75
43 Ric Flair	1.50	4.00
44 Rob Van Dam	1.00	2.50
45 Romeo RC	.30	.75
46 Rosey	.30	.75
47 Shawn Michaels	1.50	4.00
48 Shelton Benjamin	.30	.75
49 Stacy Keibler	3.00	8.00
50 Tajiri	.30	.75
51 The Hurricane	.30	.75
52 The Rock	2.00	5.00
53 Triple H	1.50	4.00
54 Trish Stratus	3.00	8.00
55 Tyson Tomko	.30	.75
56 Val Venis	.50	1.25
57 Victoria	2.00	5.00
58 Viscera	.30	.75

59 Sicilian Slide	.30	.75
60 The Worm	.50	1.25
61 Clothesline from Hell	.50	1.25
62 Tombstone Piledriver	1.50	4.00
63 Frog Splash	1.50	4.00
64 Crippler Crossface	1.25	3.00
65 ChokeSlam	1.50	4.00
66 Scissors Kick	.50	1.25
67 619	1.50	4.00
68 Flying Headbutt	1.25	3.00
69 Book-End	.50	1.25
70 The Walls of Jericho	1.00	2.50
71 Moonsault	2.00	5.00
72 Gory Bomb	.40	1.00
73 FU	2.00	5.00
74 Rock Bottom	2.00	5.00
75 Super Splash	.30	.75
76 Sweet Chin Music	1.50	4.00
77 Show Stopper	1.25	3.00
78 Ankle Lock	1.25	3.00
79 Twist of Fate	3.00	8.00
80 Chick Kick	3.00	8.00
81 Five Star Frog Splash	1.00	2.50
82 Bear Hug	.30	.75
83 Clothesline	.20	.50
84 Head Lock	.30	.75
85 Boston Crab	1.50	4.00
86 Chinlock	.20	.50
87 Jumping Foot Stomp	.20	.50
88 Shoulder Block	.30	.75
89 Right Hand	.20	.50
90 Hip Toss	2.00	5.00
91 Sleeper Hold	.30	.75
92 Hard Kick	.20	.50
93 Leap Frog	.20	.50
94 Head Lock	1.00	2.50
95 Pescado	1.00	2.50
96 Chinlock	.30	.75
97 Spinebuster	2.00	5.00
98 Chinlock	.20	.50
99 Vertical Suplex	.20	.50
100 Moonsault	1.00	2.50
101 One Leg Boston Crab	1.25	3.00
102 One Leg Boston Crab	.30	.75
103 Rope Walk	1.50	4.00
104 Bulldog	.20	.50
105 Drop Kick	1.00	2.50
106 Clothesline	.30	.75
107 Back Kick	1.00	2.50
108 Clothesline	.30	.75
109 Forearm	1.25	3.00
110 Face Slam	.20	.50
111 Head Lock	.20	.50
112 Belly to Back Suplex	1.50	4.00
113 Shoulder Tackle	2.00	5.00
114 Armbar	1.50	4.00
115 Big Boot	1.50	4.00
116 Armbar	1.50	4.00
117 Sharpshooter	2.00	5.00
118 Gorilla Press Slam	1.25	3.00
119 Double Flying Clothesline	.20	.50
120 Batista	.75	2.00
121 Booker T	.50	1.25
122 Chris Benoit	1.25	3.00
123 Christian	1.00	2.50
124 Eddie Guerrero	1.50	4.00
125 John Bradshaw Layfield	.50	1.25
126 Randy Orton	.30	.75
127 Rey Mysterio	1.00	2.50
128 Undertaker	1.50	4.00
129 Big Show	1.25	3.00
130 Carlito RC	.30	.75
131 John Cena	2.00	5.00
132 Kane	1.00	2.50
133 Kurt Angle	1.25	3.00
134 Shawn Michaels	1.50	4.00
135 The Hurricane	.30	.75
136 Triple H	1.50	4.00
137 Val Venis	.50	1.25
138 The Rock	2.00	5.00
139 Hulk Hogan	2.00	5.00
140 Sgt. Slaughter	.75	2.00
141 The Iron Sheik	.75	2.00
142 WWE Champion	.20	.50
143 WWE Intercontinental Champion	.20	.50
144 WWE Tag Team Champion	.20	.50
145 WWE Champion	.20	.50
146 WWE Tag Team Champion	.20	.50
147 WWE U.S. Champion	.20	.50
148 WWE Heavyweight Champion	.20	.50
149 WWE Cruiserweight Champion	.20	.50
150 WWE Women's Champion	.20	.50

2007 eTopps WWE

COMPLETE SET W/O AU (6)	50.00	100.00
STATED PRINT RUN 999 SERIAL #'d SETS		
WILSON AU STATED PRINT RUN TO 867*		
1 Batista	2.00	5.00
2 John Cena	3.00	8.00
3 Shawn Michaels	8.00	20.00
4 The Rock	125.00	250.00
5 Undertaker	10.00	25.00
6 Rowdy Roddy Piper	2.50	6.00
7 Torrie Wilson AU/867	50.00	100.00

1964 Exhibit

COMPLETE SET (16)	50.00	100.00
NNO Andre Drapp	5.00	12.00
NNO Antonio Rocca	3.00	8.00
NNO Bruno Sammartino	15.00	40.00
NNO Buddy Rogers	8.00	20.00
NNO Count Billy Vargo	3.00	8.00
NNO Cowboy Bob Ellis	3.00	8.00
NNO Don Leo Jonathan	3.00	8.00
NNO Enrique Torres	3.00	8.00
NNO Hard Boiled Haggerty	3.00	8.00
NNO Haystacks Calhoun	6.00	15.00
NNO Jerry Graham	3.00	8.00
NNO Lou Thesz	8.00	20.00
NNO Pat O'Connor	3.00	8.00
NNO Pepper Gomez	3.00	8.00
NNO Roy Heffernan	3.00	8.00
NNO Sailor Art Thomas	3.00	8.00

2010 FCW Summer Slamarama

NNO Bo Rotunda	12.00	30.00
NNO Darren Young	10.00	25.00
NNO Duke Rotunda		
NNO Heath Slater	8.00	20.00
NNO Joe Hennig	12.00	30.00
NNO Justin Angel	8.00	20.00
NNO Kaval	10.00	25.00
NNO Naomi Knight	30.00	75.00
NNO Savannah	10.00	25.00
NNO Skip Sheffield (Ryback)	8.00	20.00
NNO Tyler Reks	8.00	20.00
NNO Wade Barrett	10.00	25.00

2011 FCW Summer Slamarama

NNO AJ	100.00	200.00
NNO Aksana	6.00	15.00
NNO Bo Rotundo	6.00	15.00
NNO Brad Maddox	4.00	10.00
NNO Briley Pierce	3.00	8.00
NNO Brodus Clay	5.00	12.00
NNO Calvin Raines	2.50	6.00
NNO Conor O'Brian	2.50	6.00
NNO Damien Sandow	8.00	20.00
NNO Dean Ambrose	20.00	50.00
NNO Hunico	3.00	8.00
NNO Husky Harris	75.00	150.00
NNO Jinder Mahal	8.00	20.00
NNO Kenneth Cameron	2.50	6.00
NNO Leo Kruger	4.00	10.00
NNO Mason Ryan	3.00	8.00
NNO Peter Orlov	2.50	6.00
NNO Raquel Diaz	3.00	8.00
NNO Richie Steamboat	6.00	15.00
NNO Roman Leakee	100.00	200.00
NNO Seth Rollins	75.00	150.00
NNO Titus O'Neill	5.00	12.00
NNO Xavier Woods	6.00	15.00

2012 FCW Summer Slamarama

NNO Bo Dallas	3.00	8.00
NNO Brad Maddox	2.00	5.00
NNO Briley Pierce	2.00	5.00
NNO Caylee Turner	1.50	4.00
NNO CJ Parker	1.50	4.00
NNO Jake Carter	1.50	4.00
NNO Mike Dalton	6.00	15.00
NNO Paige	125.00	250.00
NNO Raquel Diaz	3.00	8.00
NNO Richie Steamboat	2.00	5.00
NNO Rick Victor	1.50	4.00
NNO Sofia Cortez	2.50	6.00
NNO Summer Rae	30.00	75.00

2020 Finest WWE

COMPLETE SET W/SP (125)		
COMPLETE SET W/O SP (100)	25.00	60.00
COMMON SP (101-125)		
*REFRACTOR: .5X TO 1.2X BASIC CARDS		
*X-FRACTOR: .6X TO 1.5X BASIC CARDS		
*BLUE/150: .75X TO 2X BASIC CARDS		
*GREEN/99: 1X TO 2.5X BASIC CARDS		
*ORANGE/50: 1.2X TO 3X BASIC CARDS		
*BLACK/25: 4X TO 10X BASIC CARDS		
*GOLD/10: UNPRICED DUE TO SCARCITY		
*RED/5: UNPRICED DUE TO SCARCITY		
*SUPERFR/1: UNPRICED DUE TO SCARCITY		
SP STATED ODDS (101-125) 1:80		
1 Angel Garza RC	.60	1.50
2 Akam	.60	1.50
3 Aleister Black	1.00	2.50
4 Andrade	.75	2.00
5 Angelo Dawkins	.50	1.25
6 Asuka	2.00	5.00
7 Austin Theory RC	.75	2.00
8 Becky Lynch	2.00	5.00
9 Bianca Belair	1.25	3.00
10 Bobby Lashley	1.00	2.50
11 Murphy	.60	1.50
12 Charlotte Flair	2.00	5.00
13 Drew McIntyre	1.00	2.50
14 Edge	1.00	2.50
15 Erik	.50	1.25
16 Humberto Carrillo	.75	2.00
17 Ivar	.50	1.25
18 Kairi Sane	1.00	2.50
19 Kevin Owens	.60	1.50
20 Lana	1.25	3.00
21 Liv Morgan	1.25	3.00
22 Montez Ford	.50	1.25
23 Nia Jax	.75	2.00
24 R-Truth	.50	1.25
25 Randy Orton	1.25	3.00
26 Rezar	.50	1.25
27 Ricochet	.75	2.00
28 Riddick Moss	.50	1.25
29 Ruby Riott	.75	2.00
30 Samoa Joe	.75	2.00
31 Seth Rollins	1.00	2.50
32 Shayna Baszler	1.50	4.00
33 Zelina Vega	1.00	2.50
34 AJ Styles	1.50	4.00
35 Alexa Bliss	3.00	8.00
36 Bayley	1.00	2.50
37 Big E	.50	1.25
38 Braun Strowman	1.25	3.00
39 The Fiend Bray Wyatt	1.50	4.00
40 Carmella	1.25	3.00
41 Cesaro	.50	1.25
42 Daniel Bryan	1.50	4.00
43 Dolph Ziggler	.50	1.25
44 Elias	1.00	2.50
45 Jeff Hardy	1.25	3.00
46 Jey Uso	.50	1.25
47 Jimmy Uso	.50	1.25
48 John Morrison	.50	1.25
49 King Corbin	.60	1.50
50 Kofi Kingston	.75	2.00
51 Lacey Evans	1.25	3.00
52 Mandy Rose	2.50	6.00
53 Matt Riddle	1.00	2.50
54 Mojo Rawley	.50	1.25
55 Mustafa Ali	.75	2.00
56 Naomi	1.00	2.50
57 Nikki Cross	1.00	2.50
58 Otis	.75	2.00
59 Robert Roode	.50	1.25
60 Roman Reigns	1.25	3.00
61 Sami Zayn	.60	1.50
62 Sasha Banks	2.50	6.00
63 Sheamus	.60	1.50
64 Shinsuke Nakamura	1.00	2.50
65 Shorty G	.50	1.25
66 Sonya Deville	1.25	3.00
67 Tamina	.60	1.50
68 The Miz	.75	2.00
69 Tucker	.50	1.25
70 Xavier Woods	.50	1.25
71 Adam Cole	1.25	3.00
72 Bobby Fish	.50	1.25
73 Cameron Grimes RC	.50	1.25
74 Candice LeRae	1.50	4.00
75 Chelsea Green	2.50	6.00
76 Dakota Kai	1.00	2.50
77 Damian Priest RC	.50	1.25
78 Dominik Dijakovic	.50	1.25

79 Finn Balor 1.25 3.00
80 Io Shirai .75 2.00
81 Isaiah Swerve Scott RC .60 1.50
82 Johnny Gargano 1.00 2.50
83 Kacy Catanzaro 1.00 2.50
84 Karrion Kross RC 1.00 2.50
85 Keith Lee .50 1.25
86 Kushida RC .60 1.50
87 Kyle OíReilly .60 1.50
88 Mia Yim 1.00 2.50
89 Pete Dunne .50 1.25
90 Rhea Ripley 2.00 5.00
91 Roderick Strong 1.00 2.50
92 Scarlett RC 2.00 5.00
93 Shotzi Blackheart RC 1.50 4.00
94 Tegan Nox RC 1.25 3.00
95 Tommaso Ciampa 1.00 2.50
96 Tyler Breeze .60 1.50
97 Velveteen Dream .60 1.50
98 Kay Lee Ray RC .75 2.00
99 Toni Storm 1.25 3.00
100 Walter RC 1.00 2.50
101 Big Show SP
102 Jinder Mahal SP
103 Natalya SP
104 Ember Moon SP
105 Dana Brooke SP
106 Jaxson Ryker SP RC
107 Kalisto SP
108 Kane SP
109 Aliyah SP
110 Bronson Reed SP RC
111 Robert Stone SP
112 Santos Escobar SP RC
113 Jordan Devlin SP RC
114 Mercedes Martinez SP RC
115 John Cena SP
116 Rob Gronkowski SP
117 Ronda Rousey SP
118 The Rock SP
119 Triple H SP
120 Undertaker SP
121 Batista SP
122 Bret Hit Man Hart SP
123 Goldberg SP
124 Shawn Michaels SP
125 Stone Cold Steve Austin SP

2020 Finest WWE Autographs

*GREEN/99: .6X TO 1.2X BASIC AUTOS
*ORANGE/50 .6X TO 1.5X BASIC AUTOS
*BLACK/25: UNPRICED DUE TO SCARCITY
*GOLD/10: UNPRICED DUE TO SCARCITY
*RED/5: UNPRICED DUE TO SCARCITY
*SUPERFR/1: UNPRICED DUE TO SCARCITY
STATED ODDS 1:17

AAB Aleister Black 8.00 20.00
AAC Adam Cole 10.00 25.00
AAD Angelo Dawkins 5.00 12.00
AAG Angel Garza 12.00 30.00
AAJ AJ Styles 15.00 40.00
AAN Andrade 5.00 12.00
AAS Asuka 30.00 75.00
ABA Bayley 25.00 60.00
ABB Bianca Belair 15.00 40.00
ABD Roman Reigns 15.00 40.00
ABE Big E 6.00 15.00
ABM Murphy 5.00 12.00
ABO Bobby Lashley 8.00 20.00
ABW The Fiend Bray Wyatt 30.00 75.00
ACG Cameron Grimes 10.00 25.00
ACS Cesaro 6.00 15.00
ADD Dominik Dijakovic 5.00 12.00
ADK Dakota Kai 20.00 50.00
ADM Drew McIntyre 15.00 40.00
ADZ Dolph Ziggler 6.00 15.00
AEK Erik 5.00 12.00
AFB Finn Balor 10.00 25.00
AIO Io Shirai 30.00 75.00
AIS Isaiah Swerve Scott 8.00 20.00
AJE Jey Uso 6.00 15.00
AJG Johnny Gargano 5.00 12.00
AJH Jeff Hardy 12.00 30.00
AKC King Corbin 6.00 15.00
AKL Keith Lee 10.00 25.00
AKU Kushida 5.00 12.00
ALM Liv Morgan 20.00 50.00
AMA Mandy Rose 25.00 60.00
AMF Montez Ford 6.00 15.00
AMY Mia Yim 10.00 25.00
ANC Nikki Cross 10.00 25.00
AOT Otis 8.00 20.00
AQS Shayna Baszler 10.00 25.00
ARC Ricochet 10.00 25.00
ARH Rhea Ripley 50.00 100.00
ARR Ruby Riott 15.00 40.00
ART R-Truth 8.00 20.00
ASB Sasha Banks 50.00 100.00
ASG Shorty G 5.00 12.00
ASH Sheamus 6.00 15.00
ASJ Samoa Joe 5.00 12.00
ASN Shinsuke Nakamura 8.00 20.00
ASR Seth Rollins 10.00 25.00
ATB Tyler Breeze 5.00 12.00
ATC Tucker 6.00 15.00
ATN Tegan Nox 30.00 75.00
ATO Tommaso Ciampa 10.00 25.00
AVD Velveteen Dream 5.00 12.00
AZV Zelina Vega 15.00 40.00

2020 Finest WWE Decade's Finest Debuts

COMPLETE SET (9) 6.00 15.00
*GOLD/50: .6X TO 1.5X BASIC CARDS
*RED/5: UNPRICED DUE TO SCARCITY
*SUPERFR/1: UNPRICED DUE TO SCARCITY
STATED ODDS 1:11

D1 Daniel Bryan 2.00 5.00
D2 Roman Reigns 1.50 4.00
D3 Seth Rollins 1.25 3.00
D4 Kevin Owens .75 2.00
D5 Samoa Joe 1.00 2.50
D6 Braun Strowman 1.50 4.00
D7 AJ Styles 2.00 5.00
D8 Shinsuke Nakamura 1.25 3.00
D9 Adam Cole 1.50 4.00
D10 Ronda Rousey 3.00 8.00

2020 Finest WWE Decade's Finest Debuts Autographs

*GOLD/50: .5X TO 1.2X BASIC AUTOS
*RED/5: UNPRICED DUE TO SCARCITY
*SUPERFR/1: UNPRICED DUE TO SCARCITY
STATED ODDS 1:124

DAC Adam Cole 12.00 30.00
DAJ AJ Styles 12.00 30.00
DKO Kevin Owens 6.00 15.00
DSJ Samoa Joe 6.00 15.00
DSN Shinsuke Nakamura 8.00 20.00

2020 Finest WWE Decade's Finest Returns

COMPLETE SET (17) 12.00 30.00
*GOLD/50: .6X TO 1.5X BASIC CARDS
*RED/5: UNPRICED DUE TO SCARCITY
*SUPERFR/1: UNPRICED DUE TO SCARCITY
STATED ODDS 1:7

R1 Bret Hit Man Hart 1.50 4.00
R2 Booker T 1.25 3.00
R3 Diesel 1.00 2.50
R4 The Rock 3.00 8.00
R5 Kane .75 2.00
R6 Undertaker 2.50 6.00
R7 Ultimate Warrior 1.50 4.00
R9 Shane McMahon 1.00 2.50
R10 Seth Rollins 1.25 3.00
R11 Goldberg 2.50 6.00
R12 Paige 1.50 4.00
R13 Daniel Bryan 2.00 5.00
R14 Bobby Lashley 1.25 3.00
R15 Roman Reigns 1.50 4.00
R16 Trish Stratus 3.00 8.00
R17 Batista 1.00 2.50
R18 Sasha Banks 3.00 8.00

2020 Finest WWE Decade's Finest Returns Autographs

*GOLD/50: .5X TO 1.2X BASIC AUTOS
*RED/5: UNPRICED DUE TO SCARCITY
*SUPERFR/1: UNPRICED DUE TO SCARCITY
STATED ODDS 1:106

RBL Bobby Lashley 8.00 20.00
RRR Roman Reigns 20.00 50.00
RSB Sasha Banks 50.00 100.00
RSR Seth Rollins 8.00 20.00

2020 Finest WWE Decade's Finest Superstars

COMPLETE SET (10) 10.00 25.00
*GOLD/50: .6X TO 1.5X BASIC CARDS
*RED/5: UNPRICED DUE TO SCARCITY
*SUPERFR/1: UNPRICED DUE TO SCARCITY
STATED ODDS 1:11

S1 Becky Lynch 2.50 6.00
S2 Charlotte Flair 2.50 6.00
S3 Daniel Bryan 2.00 5.00
S4 John Cena 2.50 6.00
S5 Kofi Kingston 1.00 2.50
S6 Randy Orton 1.50 4.00
S7 Roman Reigns 1.50 4.00
S8 Seth Rollins 1.25 3.00
S9 Sheamus .75 2.00
S10 The Miz 1.00 2.50

2020 Finest WWE Decade's Finest Superstars Autographs

*GOLD/50: .5X TO 1.2X BASIC AUTOS
*RED/5: UNPRICED DUE TO SCARCITY
*SUPERFR/1: UNPRICED DUE TO SCARCITY
STATED ODDS 1:123

SKK Kofi Kingston 6.00 15.00
SRR Roman Reigns 15.00 40.00
SSR Seth Rollins 12.00 30.00

2020 Finest WWE Finest Careers Die-Cuts

COMPLETE SET (10) 30.00 75.00
*GOLD/50: .6X TO 1.5X BASIC CARDS
*RED/5: UNPRICED DUE TO SCARCITY
*SUPERFR/1: UNPRICED DUE TO SCARCITY
STATED ODDS 1:48

C1 Austin 3:16 Is Born 6.00 15.00
C2 Stunner Heard Around World 6.00 15.00
C3 First WWE Championship 6.00 15.00
C4 Zamboni Mayhem 6.00 15.00
C5 Cementing the Boss' Car 6.00 15.00
C6 Raining on Corporation's Parade 6.00 15.00
C7 Stone Cold's Final Match 6.00 15.00
C8 Chasing Down Mr. McMahon 6.00 15.00
C9 Mr. McMahon Inducts Austin 6.00 15.00
C10 Celebrating Raw's 25th Anniversary6.00 15.00

2020 Finest WWE Finest Tag Teams

COMPLETE SET (17) 12.00 30.00
*GOLD/50: .6X TO 1.5X BASIC CARDS
*RED/5: UNPRICED DUE TO SCARCITY
*SUPERFR/1: UNPRICED DUE TO SCARCITY
STATED ODDS 1:7

TT1 Akam/Rezar 1.00 2.50
TT2 Montez Ford/Angelo Dawkins .75 2.00
TT3 Kairi Sane/Asuka 3.00 8.00
TT4 Billie Kay/Peyton Royce 1.50 4.00
TT5 Ivar/Erik .75 2.00
TT6 Alexa Bliss/Nikki Cross 5.00 12.00
TT7 Sasha Banks/Bayley 4.00 10.00
TT8 Big E/Kofi Kingston 1.25 3.00
TT9 John Morrison/The Miz 1.25 3.00
TT10 Jimmy Uso/Jey Uso .75 2.00
TT11 Tucker/Otis 1.25 3.00
TT12 Bobby Fish/Kyle OíReilly 1.00 2.50
TT13 Pete Dunne/Matt Riddle 1.50 4.00
TT14 Wesley Blake/Steve Cutler 1.00 2.50
TT15 Wolfgang/Mark Coffey 1.00 2.50
TT16 James Drake/Zack Gibson 1.00 2.50
TT17 Marcel Barthel/Fabian Aichner .75 2.00

2020 Finest WWE Finest Tag Teams Autographs

*GOLD REF/25: UNPRICED DUE TO SCARCITY
*RED REF/5: UNPRICED DUE TO SCARCITY
*SUPERFR/1: UNPRICED DUE TO SCARCITY
STATED ODDS 1:74

TTBC Alexa Bliss/Nikki Cross 75.00 150.00
TTBH Sasha Banks/Bayley 100.00 200.00
TTHM Tucker/Otis 20.00 50.00
TTII Billie Kay/Peyton Royce 60.00 120.00
TTIM Marcel Barthel/Fabian Aichner 10.00 25.00
TTMM John Morrison/The Miz 30.00 75.00
TTSP Angelo Dawkins/Montez Ford 15.00 40.00
TTUE Bobby Fish/Kyle O'Reilly 15.00 40.00
TTVR Ivar/Erik 10.00 25.00

2021 Finest WWE

*REF: .5X TO 1.2X BASIC CARDS
*XFRAC: .6X TO 1.5X BASIC CARDS
*BLUE/150: .75X TO 2X BASIC CARDS
*GREEN/99: 1X TO 2.5X BASIC CARDS

*ROSE G/75: 1.2X TO 3X BASIC CARDS
*GOLD/50: 1.5X TO 4X BASIC CARDS
*ORANGE/25: 2X TO 5X BASIC CARDS
*ORANGE SP/25: UNPRICED DUE TO SCARCITY
*BLACK/10: UNPRICED DUE TO SCARCITY
*RED/5: UNPRICED DUE TO SCARCITY
*SUPER/1: UNPRICED DUE TO SCARCITY

1 AJ Styles	1.50	4.00
2 Akira Tozawa	.60	1.50
3 Alexa Bliss	3.00	8.00
4 Asuka	2.00	5.00
5 Becky Lynch	2.00	5.00
6 Bobby Lashley	1.25	3.00
7 Charlotte Flair	2.50	6.00
8 Cedric Alexander	.50	1.25
9 Damian Priest	.75	2.00
10 Dana Brooke	.50	1.25
11 Drew McIntyre	1.25	3.00
12 Elias	.50	1.25
13 Humberto Carrillo	.50	1.25
14 Jaxson Ryker	.50	1.25
15 Jeff Hardy	1.25	3.00
16 Jinder Mahal	.60	1.50
17 John Morrison	1.00	2.50
18 Keith Lee	1.00	2.50
19 Kofi Kingston	1.25	3.00
20 Lacey Evans	1.25	3.00
21 MACE	.50	1.25
22 Mandy Rose	2.50	6.00
23 Mustafa Ali	.60	1.50
24 MVP	.50	1.25
25 Naomi	.60	1.50
26 Nia Jax	1.00	2.50
27 Nikki A.S.H.	1.00	2.50
28 Omos RC	1.00	2.50
29 R-Truth	.60	1.50
30 Randy Orton	1.50	4.00
31 Reggie RC	.60	1.50
32 Rhea Ripley	1.50	4.00
33 Ricochet	1.00	2.50
34 Riddle	1.25	3.00
35 Shayna Baszler	1.00	2.50
36 Sheamus	.75	2.00
37 Shelton Benjamin	.75	2.00
38 T-BAR	.60	1.50
39 Titus O'Neil	.50	1.25
40 The Miz	.75	2.00
41 Xavier Woods	.50	1.25
42 Angelo Dawkins	.60	1.50
43 Apollo Crews	.60	1.50
44 Bayley	1.25	3.00
45 Bianca Belair	1.25	3.00
46 Big E	1.00	2.50
47 Carmella	1.25	3.00
48 Cesaro	.50	1.25
49 Chad Gable	.50	1.25
50 Commander Azeez RC	.60	1.50
51 Dolph Ziggler	1.00	2.50
52 Dominik Mysterio RC	.60	1.50
53 Edge	2.00	5.00
54 Finn Balor	1.25	3.00
55 Jey Uso	.50	1.25
56 Kevin Owens	1.00	2.50
57 Baron Corbin	.50	1.25
58 Liv Morgan	2.00	5.00
59 Montez Ford	.50	1.25
60 Tegan Nox	1.25	3.00
61 Otis	.60	1.50
62 Paul Heyman	.60	1.50
63 Rey Mysterio	1.25	3.00
64 Rick Boogs RC	.50	1.25
65 Robert Roode	.60	1.50
66 Roman Reigns	2.50	6.00
67 Sasha Banks	2.50	6.00
68 Sami Zayn	.75	2.00
69 Seth Rollins	1.25	3.00
70 Shinsuke Nakamura	1.25	3.00
71 Shotzi	2.00	5.00
72 Sonya Deville	1.25	3.00
73 Toni Storm	1.50	4.00
74 Zelina Vega	1.00	2.50
75 Aliyah	1.00	2.50
76 Adam Cole	1.50	4.00
77 Austin Theory	1.00	2.50
78 Candice LeRae	2.00	5.00
79 Cameron Grimes	1.00	2.50
80 Dakota Kai	1.00	2.50
81 Danny Burch	.60	1.50
82 Drake Maverick	.50	1.25
83 Ember Moon	.60	1.50
84 Indi Hartwell RC	1.50	4.00
85 Io Shirai	1.00	2.50
86 Isaiah Swerve Scott	.75	2.00
87 James Drake	.50	1.25
88 Johnny Gargano	1.00	2.50
89 Karrion Kross	2.00	5.00
90 Kyle O'Reilly	.75	2.00
91 Oney Lorcan	.50	1.25
92 Pete Dunne	1.00	2.50
93 Raquel Gonzalez	1.25	3.00
94 Roderick Strong	.75	2.00
95 Santos Escobar	.75	2.00
96 Scarlett	2.50	6.00
97 Timothy Thatcher RC	.50	1.25
98 Tommaso Ciampa	1.25	3.00
99 Zack Gibson	.50	1.25
100 John Cena	2.50	6.00
101 Angel Garza SP	10.00	25.00
102 Eva Marie SP	15.00	40.00
103 Mansoor SP RC	15.00	40.00
104 Jimmy Uso SP	10.00	25.00
105 Tamina SP	12.00	30.00
106 Cameron Grimes SP	12.00	30.00
107 Dexter Lumis SP	10.00	25.00
108 Isaiah Swerve Scott SP	8.00	20.00
109 Kushida SP	15.00	40.00
110 Zoey Stark SP RC	8.00	20.00
111 Fabian Aichner SP	8.00	20.00
112 Kay Lee Ray SP	12.00	30.00
113 Marcel Barthel SP	8.00	20.00
114 Trent Seven SP	15.00	40.00
115 Tyler Bate SP	8.00	20.00
116 Walter SP	20.00	50.00
117 John Cena SP	30.00	75.00
118 Kane SP	10.00	25.00
119 Goldberg SP	25.00	60.00
120 Booker T SP	12.00	30.00
121 Rob Van Dam SP	20.00	50.00
122 Stacy Keibler SP	50.00	100.00

2021 Finest WWE Autographs

*GREEN/99: .6X TO 1.5X BASIC AUTOS
*GOLD/50: .75X TO 2X BASIC AUTOS
*ORANGE/25: UNPRICED DUE TO SCARCITY
*BLACK/10: UNPRICED DUE TO SCARCITY
*RED/5: UNPRICED DUE TO SCARCITY
*SUPER/1: UNPRICED DUE TO SCARCITY
RANDOMLY INSERTED INTO PACKS

RAAC Apollo Crews	5.00	12.00
RAAD Angelo Dawkins	5.00	12.00
RAAT Austin Theory	12.00	30.00
RABI Big E	8.00	20.00
RACE Cesaro	6.00	15.00
RACG Chad Gable	5.00	12.00
RACL Candice LeRae	8.00	20.00
RACR Carmella	10.00	25.00
RADK Dakota Kai	12.00	30.00
RADO Dominik Mysterio	10.00	25.00
RADP Damian Priest	6.00	15.00
RAEM Ember Moon	8.00	20.00
RAHC Humberto Carrillo	5.00	12.00
RAIH Indi Hartwell	12.00	30.00
RAIS Io Shirai	10.00	25.00
RAJG Johnny Gargano	5.00	12.00
RAJM John Morrison	6.00	15.00
RAJR Jaxson Ryker	6.00	15.00
RAKC King Corbin	5.00	12.00
RAKK Karrion Kross	10.00	25.00
RAKO Kyle O'Reilly	5.00	12.00
RAKT Commander Azeez	8.00	20.00
RALM Liv Morgan	25.00	60.00
RAMR Mandy Rose	25.00	60.00
RAMV MVP	5.00	12.00
RANJ Nia Jax	5.00	12.00
RAOM Omos	25.00	60.00
RAOT Otis	6.00	15.00
RARB Robert Roode	5.00	12.00
RARC Ricochet	10.00	25.00
RARE Mia Yim	10.00	25.00
RARG Raquel Gonzalez	12.00	30.00
RARH R-Truth	5.00	12.00
RARI Riddle	12.00	30.00
RARR Rhea Ripley	10.00	25.00
RASB Shayna Baszler	6.00	15.00
RASC Scarlett	20.00	50.00
RASE Santos Escobar	6.00	15.00
RASO Shotzi Blackheart	25.00	60.00
RASZ Sami Zayn	6.00	15.00
RATO Titus O'Neil	5.00	12.00
RAXW Xavier Woods	6.00	15.00

2021 Finest WWE Autographs Gold Refractors

RAA Asuka	25.00	60.00
RAE Edge	30.00	75.00
RAAB Alexa Bliss	125.00	250.00
RAAS AJ Styles	25.00	60.00
RABE Becky Lynch	100.00	200.00
RABL Bobby Lashley	15.00	40.00
RADM Drew McIntyre	15.00	40.00
RADZ Dolph Ziggler	12.00	30.00
RAJH Jeff Hardy	30.00	75.00
RAKF Kofi Kingston	12.00	30.00
RARM Rey Mysterio	30.00	75.00
RASA Sasha Banks	100.00	200.00
RASM Sheamus	8.00	20.00
RASR Seth Rollins	50.00	100.00
RATM The Miz	15.00	40.00

2021 Finest WWE Autographs Green Refractors

RASN Shinsuke Nakamura	8.00	20.00

2021 Finest WWE Deadman's Tombstone Career Tribute Die-Cuts

COMPLETE SET (13)	25.00	60.00

*ORANGE/25: 4X TO 10X BASIC CARDS
*RED/5: UNPRICED DUE TO SCARCITY
*SUPER/1: UNPRICED DUE TO SCARCITY
RANDOMLY INSERTED INTO PACKS

UT1 Debut of the Deadman	3.00	8.00
UT2 Defeating the Doppelganger	3.00	8.00
UT3 Deadman's Hand	3.00	8.00
UT4 Burning Brothers	3.00	8.00
UT5 Fall of Mankind	3.00	8.00
UT6 Stephanie's Teddy Bear	3.00	8.00
UT7 The Deadman Returns	3.00	8.00
UT8 Lightning Fright	3.00	8.00
UT9 Royal Rumble Match Winner	3.00	8.00
UT10 Rated-R Chokeslam	3.00	8.00
UT11 Career vs. Streak	3.00	8.00
UT12 End of an Era	3.00	8.00
UT13 A Phenomenal Ending	3.00	8.00

2021 Finest WWE Legacies

*ORANGE/25: UNPRICED DUE TO SCARCITY
*RED/5: UNPRICED DUE TO SCARCITY
*SUPER/1: UNPRICED DUE TO SCARCITY
RANDOMLY INSERTED INTO PACKS

L1 AJ Styles Shawn Michaels	2.50	6.00
L2 Bayley Macho Man Randy Savage	2.00	5.00
L3 Bianca Belair Mr. Perfect	2.00	5.00
L4 Carmella Miss Elizabeth	2.00	5.00
L5 Cesaro Bruno Sammartino	.75	2.00
L6 Jeff Hardy Undertaker	2.00	5.00
L7 Mandy Rose Trish Stratus	4.00	10.00
L8 Montez Ford Booker T	.75	2.00
L9 Rhea Ripley Beth Phoenix	2.50	6.00
L10 Roman Reigns The Rock	8.00	20.00
L11 R-Truth John Cena	1.00	2.50
L12 Sasha Banks Eddie Guerrero	4.00	10.00
L13 The Miz Ultimate Warrior	3.00	8.00
L14 Bobby Lashley Ron Simmons	2.00	5.00
L15 Randy Orton Jake The Snake Roberts	2.50	6.00
L16 Dave Mastiff Vader	.75	2.00
L17 Paul Heyman Bobby The Brain Heenan	1.00	2.50

2021 Finest WWE Legacies Autographs

*ORANGE/25: UNPRICED DUE TO SCARCITY
*RED/5: UNPRICED DUE TO SCARCITY
*SUPER/1: UNPRICED DUE TO SCARCITY

RANDOMLY INSERTED INTO PACKS

LC	Carmella	15.00	40.00
LAC	Cesaro	10.00	25.00
LAS	AJ Styles	12.00	30.00
LBB	Bianca Belair	20.00	50.00
LJH	Jeff Hardy	25.00	60.00
LMR	Mandy Rose	30.00	75.00
LRR	Rhea Ripley	25.00	60.00
LRT	R-Truth	10.00	25.00
LTM	The Miz	10.00	25.00

2021 Finest WWE Rumble Pops

*ORANGE/25: UNPRICED DUE TO SCARCITY
*RED/5: UNPRICED DUE TO SCARCITY
*SUPER/1: UNPRICED DUE TO SCARCITY
RANDOMLY INSERTED INTO PACKS

RP1	Mick Foley	2.00	5.00
RP2	John Cena	5.00	12.00
RP3	Diesel	1.50	4.00
RP4	Triple H	4.00	10.00
RP5	AJ Styles	3.00	8.00
RP6	Goldberg	4.00	10.00
RP7	Trish Stratus	5.00	12.00
RP8	Rey Mysterio	2.50	6.00
RP9	Becky Lynch	4.00	10.00
RP10	Edge	4.00	10.00

2021 Finest WWE Rumble Pops Autographs

*ORANGE/25: UNPRICED DUE TO SCARCITY
*RED/5: UNPRICED DUE TO SCARCITY
*SUPER/1: UNPRICED DUE TO SCARCITY
RANDOMLY INSERTED INTO PACKS

RG	Goldberg	50.00	100.00
RAJ	AJ Styles	10.00	25.00
RBL	Becky Lynch	60.00	120.00
RMF	Mick Foley	25.00	60.00
RRM	Rey Mysterio	20.00	50.00

2021 Finest WWE Sole Survivors

*ORANGE/25: UNPRICED DUE TO SCARCITY
*RED/5: UNPRICED DUE TO SCARCITY
*SUPER/1: UNPRICED DUE TO SCARCITY
RANDOMLY INSERTED INTO PACKS

SS1	Hulk Hogan	4.00	10.00
SS2	Lex Luger	1.00	2.50
SS3	Razor Ramon	1.25	3.00
SS4	Randy Orton	2.50	6.00
SS5	Kofi Kingston	2.00	5.00
SS6	Dolph Ziggler	1.50	4.00
SS7	Roman Reigns	4.00	10.00
SS8	Asuka	3.00	8.00
SS9	Nia Jax	1.50	4.00
SS10	The British Bulldog	1.25	3.00

2021 Finest WWE Sole Survivors Autographs

*ORANGE/25: UNPRICED DUE TO SCARCITY
*RED/5: UNPRICED DUE TO SCARCITY
*SUPER/1: UNPRICED DUE TO SCARCITY
RANDOMLY INSERTED INTO PACKS

SA	Asuka	20.00	50.00
SDZ	Dolph Ziggler	6.00	15.00
SKK	Kofi Kingston	8.00	20.00
SLL	Lex Luger	15.00	40.00
SRR	Roman Reigns	75.00	150.00

2021 Finest WWE Triple Autographs

COMMON AUTO 30.00 75.00
*ORANGE/25: UNPRICED DUE TO SCARCITY
*RED/5: UNPRICED DUE TO SCARCITY
RANDOMLY INSERTED INTO PACKS

TAAN	The Usos/Reigns	250.00	500.00
TALA	Barrett/McIntyre/Sheamus	30.00	75.00
TALF	Mendoza/Wilde/Escobar	30.00	75.00
TAND	Big E/Woods/Kingston	75.00	150.00

2021 Finest WWE Uncrowned Greatness

COMPLETE SET (20) 10.00 25.00
*ORANGE/25: UNPRICED DUE TO SCARCITY
*RED/5: UNPRICED DUE TO SCARCITY
*SUPER/1: UNPRICED DUE TO SCARCITY
RANDOMLY INSERTED INTO PACKS

UG1	Bam Bam Bigelow	1.25	3.00
UG2	Brutus The Barber Beefcake	.75	2.00
UG3	DDP	1.00	2.50
UG4	Dusty Rhodes	2.00	5.00
UG5	Harley Race	.60	1.50
UG6	Jake The Snake Roberts	1.00	2.50
UG7	Jerry The King Lawler	1.00	2.50
UG8	Junkyard Dog	.60	1.50
UG9	Lex Luger	.75	2.00
UG10	Ted DiBiase	1.25	3.00
UG11	Mr. Perfect	2.00	5.00
UG12	Ravishing Rick Rude	.75	2.00
UG13	Ricky The Dragon Steamboat	1.00	2.50
UG14	Rikishi	.75	2.00
UG15	Ron Simmons	1.00	2.50
UG16	Rowdy Roddy Piper	1.50	4.00
UG17	Scott Hall	1.00	2.50
UG18	The British Bulldog	1.00	2.50
UG19	Wade Barrett	.60	1.50
UG20	William Regal	1.00	2.50

2021 Finest WWE Uncrowned Greatness Autographs

*ORANGE/25: UNPRICED DUE TO SCARCITY
*RED/5: UNPRICED DUE TO SCARCITY
*SUPER/1: UNPRICED DUE TO SCARCITY
RANDOMLY INSERTED INTO PACKS

UR	Rikishi	10.00	25.00
UBB	Brutus The Barber Beefcake	12.00	30.00
UFR	Ron Simmons	12.00	30.00
UJL	Jerry The King Lawler	20.00	50.00
UJR	Jake The Snake Roberts	25.00	60.00
ULL	Lex Luger	15.00	40.00
URS	Ricky The Dragon Steamboat	15.00	40.00
UTD	Ted DiBiase	15.00	40.00
UWB	Wade Barrett	10.00	25.00
UWR	William Regal	10.00	25.00
UDDP	DDP	20.00	50.00

2002 Fleer WWE Absolute Divas

COMPLETE SET (100) 15.00 40.00
UNOPENED BOX (24 PACKS)
UNOPENED PACK (8 CARDS)
*DIVA GEM: .75X TO 2X BASIC CARDS

1	Trish Stratus	1.25	3.00
2	Terri	.60	1.50
3	Ivory	.50	1.25
4	Lita	.75	2.00
5	Jackie RC	.50	1.25
6	Stacy Keibler RC	1.25	3.00
7	Torrie Wilson RC	1.25	3.00
8	Jacqueline	.30	.75
9	Molly	.30	.75
10	Jazz RC	.30	.75
11	Stephanie McMahon	.60	1.50
12	Nidia RC	.30	.75
13	Dawn Marie RC	.30	.75
14	Victoria RC	.60	1.50
15	Linda RC	.30	.75
16	Trish Stratus	1.25	3.00
17	Terri	1.25	3.00
18	Ivory	.50	1.25
19	Lita	.75	2.00
20	Jazz RC	.30	.75
21	Stacy Keibler RC	1.25	3.00
22	Torrie Wilson RC	1.25	3.00
23	Jacqueline	.30	.75
24	Molly	.30	.75
25	Stephanie McMahon	.60	1.50
26	Trish Stratus	1.25	3.00
27	Terri	.60	1.50
28	Ivory	.50	1.25
29	Lita	.75	2.00
30	Jackie RC	.50	1.25
31	Stacy Keibler RC	1.25	3.00
32	Torrie Wilson RC	1.25	3.00
33	Jacqueline	.30	.75
34	Molly	.30	.75
35	Jazz RC	.30	.75
36	Trish Stratus	1.25	3.00
37	Terri	.60	1.50
38	Ivory	.50	1.25
39	Lita	.75	2.00
40	Stacy Keibler RC	1.25	3.00
41	Torrie Wilson RC	1.25	3.00
42	Jacqueline	.30	.75
43	Molly	.30	.75
44	Jazz RC	.30	.75
45	Lita PS	.75	2.00
46	Bubba Ray PS	.20	.50
47	Jamie Noble PS RC	.20	.50
48	Matt Hardy PS	.30	.75
49	Brock Lesnar with Paul Heyman PS	1.25	3.00
50	William Regal PS	.20	.50
51	Triple H PS	.75	2.00
52	Vince McMahon PS	.50	1.25
53	Booker T PS	.50	1.25
54	Tajiri PS	.20	.50
55	Steven Richards PS	.20	.50
56	Chris Jericho PS	.30	.75
57	D-Von Dudley PS	.20	.50
58	Rob Van Dam PS RC	.50	1.25
59	The Rock PS	.75	2.00
60	Ric Flair PS	.60	1.50
61	Bradshaw PS	.30	.75
62	Hollywood Hulk Hogan PS	1.25	3.00
63	Hurricane PS RC	.20	.50
64	Jeff Hardy PS	.30	.75
65	Kurt Angle PS	.50	1.25
66	Jazz DM	.30	.75
67	Trish Stratus DM	1.25	3.00
68	Molly DM	.30	.75
69	Lita DM	.75	2.00
70	Stacy Keibler DM	1.25	3.00
71	Torrie Wilson DM	1.25	3.00
72	Trish Stratus DM	1.25	3.00
73	Jacqueline DM	.30	.75
74	Ivory DM	.50	1.25
75	Trish Stratus DM	1.25	3.00
76	Lita DM	.75	2.00
77	Terri DM	.60	1.50
78	Jacqueline DM	.30	.75
79	Molly DM	.30	.75
80	Dawn Marie DM	.30	.75
81	Lita GOF	.75	2.00
82	Jacqueline GOF	.30	.75
83	Molly GOF	.30	.75
84	Stacy Keibler GOF	1.25	3.00
85	Ivory GOF	.50	1.25
86	Trish Stratus GOF	1.25	3.00
87	Torrie Wilson GOF	1.25	3.00
88	Terri GOF	.60	1.50
89	Victoria GOF	.60	1.50
90	Jazz GOF	.30	.75
91	Trish Stratus GOF	1.25	3.00
92	Torrie Wilson GOF	1.25	3.00
93	Ivory GOF	.50	1.25
94	Lita GOF	.75	2.00
95	Dawn Marie GOF	.30	.75
96	Terri GOF	.60	1.50
97	Linda GOF	.30	.75
98	Stacy Keibler GOF	1.25	3.00
99	Molly GOF	.30	.75
100	Jackie GOF	.50	1.25

2002 Fleer WWE Absolute Divas Cover Shots

COMPLETE SET (10) 12.00 30.00
STATED ODDS 1:12 HOBBY

1	Ivory	1.25	3.00
2	Jacqueline	.75	2.00
3	Lita	2.50	6.00
4	Dawn Marie	.75	2.00
5	Stacy Keibler (w/Dudley Boyz)	5.00	12.00
6	Terri	1.50	4.00
7	Torrie Wilson	3.00	8.00
8	Trish Stratus	5.00	12.00
9	Stephanie McMahon	6.00	15.00
10	Stacy & Torrie	4.00	10.00

2002 Fleer WWE Absolute Divas Diva Ink

STATED ODDS 1:198 HOBBY
CARDS AVAILABLE BY EXCH ONLY

NNO	Dawn Marie	20.00	50.00
NNO	Jackie	15.00	40.00
NNO	Linda	10.00	25.00
NNO	Stacy Keibler	125.00	250.00
NNO	Torrie Wilson	100.00	200.00

2002 Fleer WWE Absolute Divas Inter-Actions

COMPLETE SET (20) 10.00 25.00
STATED ODDS 1:6 HOBBY

1	Swimsuit Competition	1.50	4.00
2	Terri Wins The Hardcore Championship	.75	2.00
3	Six-Person Intergender Match	1.50	4.00
4	Bra And Panties Paddle On A Pole Match	.75	2.00
5	Mixed Tag Team Match	1.50	4.00
6	Tag Team	1.50	4.00
7	Bikini Match	1.50	4.00
8	Table Match	.40	1.00
9	Mixed Tag Team Match	1.50	4.00
10	Tag Team Hardcore Women's Title Match	1.50	4.00

11 Tag Team	1.50	4.00
12 Judgment Day Match	1.50	4.00
13 Gravy Bowl Match	1.50	4.00
14 Tag Team Match	1.50	4.00
15 Wrestlemania X-8 Triple Threat	1.00	2.50
16 Tag Team	.40	1.00
17 Swimsuit Competition	.40	1.00
18 Women's Title Match-KOTR	1.50	4.00
19 Bra And Panties Match (Women's Title)	1.50	4.00
20 Lingerie Match	1.50	4.00

2002 Fleer WWE Absolute Divas Lip Service

STATED PRINT RUN 50 SER. #'d SETS
CARDS AVAILABLE BY EXCH ONLY

NNO Dawn Marie	50.00	100.00
NNO Jackie	20.00	50.00
NNO Linda	6.00	15.00
NNO Stacy Keibler	200.00	400.00
NNO Torrie Wilson	150.00	300.00

2002 Fleer WWE Absolute Divas Material Girls

STATED ODDS 1:36 HOBBY

NNO Dawn Marie	4.00	10.00
Skirt		
NNO Ivory	2.00	5.00
Mat		
NNO Jazz	2.00	5.00
Mat		
NNO Lita	3.00	8.00
Mat		
NNO Lita	6.00	15.00
Top		
NNO Molly	4.00	10.00
Top		
NNO Nidia	4.00	10.00
Shorts		
NNO Stacy Keibler	30.00	75.00
Top		
NNO Stacy Keibler	15.00	40.00
T-Shirt		
NNO Terri	6.00	15.00
Outfit		
NNO Torrie Wilson	8.00	20.00
Bikini		
NNO Trish Stratus	10.00	25.00
Mat		
NNO Trish Stratus	20.00	50.00
Top		
NNO Victoria	6.00	15.00
Shorts		

2002 Fleer WWE Absolute Divas Mini-Posters

COMPLETE SET (30)	8.00	20.00
STATED ODDS 1:1 HOBBY		
NNO Booker T	.40	1.00
NNO Brock Lesnar/Paul Heyman	1.00	2.50
NNO Chris Jericho	.25	.60
NNO Dawn Marie	.25	.60
NNO Hollywood Hulk Hogan	1.00	2.50
NNO Ivory	.40	1.00
NNO Jackie (orange border)	.40	1.00
NNO Jackie (yellow border)	.40	1.00
NNO Jacqueline	.25	.60
NNO Jazz	.25	.60
NNO Jeff Hardy	.25	.60
NNO Kurt Angle	.40	1.00
NNO Lita (blue border)	.60	1.50
NNO Lita (purple border)	.60	1.50
NNO Matt Hardy	.25	.60
NNO Molly	.25	.60
NNO Nidia	.25	.60
NNO Rob Van Dam	.40	1.00
NNO The Rock	.60	1.50
NNO Stacy Keibler (purple border)	1.00	2.50
NNO Stacy Keibler (red border)	1.00	2.50
NNO Stephanie McMahon	.50	1.25
NNO Terri (orange border)	.50	1.25
NNO Terri (purple border)	.50	1.25
NNO Torrie Wilson (black outfit)	1.00	2.50
NNO Torrie Wilson (blue outfit)	1.00	2.50
NNO Triple H	.60	1.50
NNO Trish Stratus (red border)	1.00	2.50
NNO Trish Stratus (yellow border)	1.00	2.50
NNO Victoria	.50	1.25

2002 Fleer WWE Absolute Divas Signed with a Kiss

STATED PRINT RUN 50 SER. #'d SETS
AVAILABLE BY EXCH ONLY

NNO Dawn Marie	60.00	120.00
NNO Ivory	20.00	50.00
NNO Jackie	25.00	60.00
NNO Linda	15.00	40.00
NNO Lita	50.00	100.00
NNO Stacy Keibler	500.00	1000.00
NNO Torrie Wilson	200.00	400.00

2002 Fleer WWE Absolute Divas Tropical Pleasures

COMPLETE SET (10)	12.00	30.00
STATED ODDS 1:12 HOBBY		
1 Ivory	1.25	3.00
2 Trish Stratus	3.00	8.00
3 Lita	2.00	5.00
4 Lita and Trish Stratus	3.00	8.00
5 Stacy Keibler	3.00	8.00
6 Terri	1.50	4.00
7 Torrie Wilson	3.00	8.00
8 Jacqueline	.75	2.00
9 Molly Holly	.75	2.00
10 Victoria	1.50	4.00

2002 Fleer WWE Absolute Divas Wardrobe Closet

STATED ODDS 1:23 HOBBY

NNO Lita	6.00	15.00
Jacket		
NNO Molly	4.00	10.00
Top		
NNO Nidia	3.00	8.00
Shorts		
NNO Stacy Keibler	15.00	40.00
T-Shirt		
NNO Torrie Wilson	12.00	30.00
Pants		
NNO Torrie Wilson	12.00	30.00
Top		
NNO Trish Stratus	20.00	50.00
Top		
NNO Victoria	5.00	12.00
Top		

2003 Fleer WWE Aggression

COMPLETE SET (89)	10.00	25.00
UNOPENED BOX (24 PACKS)		
UNOPENED PACK (5 CARDS)		
1 Goldberg	.75	2.00
2 Batista	.50	1.25
3 Booker T	.50	1.25
4 Bradshaw	.30	.75
5 Bubba Ray Dudley	.20	.50
6 Chief Morley	.20	.50
7 Chris Jericho	.30	.75
8 Chris Nowinski	.12	.30
9 Christian	.30	.75
10 D-Von Dudley	.20	.50
11 Eric Bischoff	.20	.50
12 Goldust	.12	.30
13 Ivory	.50	1.25
14 Jacqueline	.30	.75
15 Jazz	.20	.50
16 Jamal RC	.20	.50
17 Charlie Haas RC	.12	.30
18 Kane	.50	1.25
19 Kevin Nash	.60	1.50
20 Lance Storm	.12	.30
21 Al Snow	.12	.30
22 Lita	.75	2.00
23 Maven	.12	.30
24 Molly	.60	1.50
25 Randy Orton	.30	.75
26 Ric Flair	.60	1.50
27 Rico	.12	.30
28 Rob Van Dam	.50	1.25
29 Rosey RC	.12	.30
30 Scott Steiner	.60	1.50
31 Shawn Michaels	.75	2.00
32 Spike Dudley	.20	.50
33 Stacy Keibler	1.25	3.00
34 Steven Richards	.20	.50
35 Stone Cold Steve Austin	.75	2.00
36 Terri	.60	1.50
37 Test	.20	.50
38 The Hurricane	.12	.30
39 Tommy Dreamer	.12	.30
40 Trish Stratus	1.25	3.00
41 Triple H	.75	2.00
42 Victoria	.60	1.50
43 William Regal	.30	.75
44 Big Show	.50	1.25
45 Bill DeMott	.12	.30
46 Billy Kidman	.12	.30
47 Brock Lesnar	1.25	3.00
48 Chavo Guerrero	.20	.50
49 Chuck Palumbo	.20	.50
50 Chris Benoit	.30	.75
51 Crash	.12	.30
52 Dawn Marie	.60	1.50
53 Edge	.50	1.25
54 Eddie Guerrero	.60	1.50
55 Funaki	.20	.50
56 Sable	.75	2.00
57 Hulk Hogan	.75	2.00
58 Jamie Noble	.12	.30
59 John Cena	.75	2.00
60 Johnny Stamboli RC	.12	.30
61 Kurt Angle	.50	1.25
62 Mark Henry	.20	.50
63 Matt Hardy	.30	.75
64 Nathan Jones RC	.12	.30
65 Nidia	.30	.75
66 Nunzio RC	.12	.30
67 Rey Mysterio	.30	.75
68 Rhyno	.50	1.25
69 Rikishi	.30	.75
70 Shannon Moore RC	.12	.30
71 The Rock	.75	2.00
72 Tajiri	.12	.30
73 Torrie Wilson	1.25	3.00
74 Tazz	.20	.50
75 Undertaker	.60	1.50
76 A-Train	.12	.30
77 Paul Heyman	.12	.30
78 Brian Kendrick RC	.20	.50
79 Torrie Wilson DL	1.25	3.00
80 Sable DL	.75	2.00
81 Lita DL	.75	2.00
82 Ivory DL	.50	1.25
83 Jacqueline DL	.30	.75
84 Jazz DL	.20	.50
85 Molly DL	.60	1.50
86 Stacy Keibler DL	1.25	3.00
87 Terri DL	.60	1.50
88 Trish Stratus DL	1.25	3.00
89 Nidia DL	.30	.75

2003 Fleer WWE Aggression Matitude

COMPLETE SET (10)	10.00	25.00
STATED ODDS 1:12 HOBBY		
1 Triple H	2.00	5.00
2 The Rock	2.00	5.00
3 Brock Lesnar	3.00	8.00
4 Stone Cold Steve Austin	2.00	5.00
5 Kurt Angle	1.25	3.00
6 Chris Jericho	.75	2.00
7 Hulk Hogan	2.00	5.00
8 Scott Steiner	1.50	4.00
9 Rob Van Dam	1.25	3.00
10 Undertaker	1.50	4.00

2003 Fleer WWE Aggression Matitude Event Used

MR The Rock	4.00	10.00
MU Undertaker	3.00	8.00
MBL Brock Lesnar	3.00	8.00
MCJ Chris Jericho	2.50	6.00
MHH Hollywood Hulk Hogan	6.00	15.00
MKA Kurt Angle	4.00	10.00
MSA Stone Cold Steve Austin	3.00	8.00
MSS Scott Steiner	2.00	5.00
MTR Triple H	3.00	8.00
MRVD Rob Van Dam	2.00	5.00

2003 Fleer WWE Aggression Matitude Event Used Jumbo Images

STATED PRINT RUN 50 SER.#'d SETS

MR The Rock	15.00	40.00
MU Undertaker	15.00	40.00
MBL Brock Lesnar	20.00	50.00
MCJ Chris Jericho	10.00	25.00
MHH Hollywood Hulk Hogan	25.00	60.00
MKA Kurt Angle	12.00	30.00
MSA Stone Cold Steve Austin	15.00	40.00
MSS Scott Steiner	12.00	30.00
MTH Triple H	15.00	40.00
MRVD Rob Van Dam	10.00	25.00

2003 Fleer WWE Aggression Queens of the Ring

COMPLETE SET (10) 25.00 60.00
STATED ODDS 1:8 HOBBY

1	Lita	3.00	8.00
2	Ivory	2.00	5.00
3	Jacqueline	1.25	3.00
4	Jazz	.75	2.00
5	Molly	2.50	6.00
6	Stacy Keibler	5.00	12.00
7	Terri	2.50	6.00
8	Trish Stratus	5.00	12.00
9	Nidia	1.25	3.00
10	Torrie Wilson	5.00	12.00

2003 Fleer WWE Aggression Queens of the Ring Autographs

STATED PRINT RUN 50 SER.#'d SETS
SK AVAILABLE AT NATIONAL ONLY
SK STATED PRINT RUN 1500 CARDS

NNO	Ivory/50	30.00	75.00
NNO	Molly Holly/50	50.00	75.00
NNO	Stacy Keibler/50	125.00	250.00
NNO	Stacy Keibler NSCC	30.00	75.00
NNO	Terri/50	60.00	125.00
NNO	Trish Stratus/50	125.00	250.00

2003 Fleer WWE Aggression Queens of the Ring Event Used

STATED ODDS 1:115 HOBBY

QRI	Ivory	10.00	25.00
QRJ	Jacqueline	8.00	20.00
QRL	Lita	12.00	30.00
QRN	Nidia	8.00	20.00
QRT	Terri	12.00	30.00
QRJA	Jazz	8.00	20.00
QRMH	Molly Holly	8.00	20.00
QRSK	Stacy Keibler	20.00	50.00
QRTS	Trish Stratus	15.00	40.00
QRTW	Torrie Wilson	20.00	50.00

2003 Fleer WWE Aggression Ring Leaders

COMPLETE SET (15) 8.00 20.00
STATED ODDS 1:4 HOBBY

1	Triple H	1.25	3.00
2	The Rock	1.25	3.00
3	Brock Lesnar	2.00	5.00
4	Stone Cold Steve Austin	1.25	3.00
5	The Hurricane	.20	.50
6	Undertaker	1.00	2.50
7	Kane	.75	2.00
8	Chris Jericho	.50	1.25
9	Hulk Hogan	1.25	3.00
10	Scott Steiner	1.00	2.50
11	Rob Van Dam	.75	2.00
12	Shawn Michaels	1.25	3.00
13	Chris Benoit	.50	1.25
14	Edge	.75	2.00
15	Booker T	.75	2.00

2003 Fleer WWE Aggression Ring Leaders Event Used

STATED ODDS 1:29 HOBBY

RLE	Edge	6.00	15.00
RLH	The Hurricane	3.00	8.00
RLK	Kane	4.00	10.00
RLR	The Rock	8.00	20.00
RLU	Undertaker	6.00	15.00
RLBL	Brock Lesnar	8.00	20.00
RLBT	Booker T	3.00	8.00
RLCB	Chris Benoit	4.00	10.00
RLCJ	Chris Jericho	4.00	10.00
RLHH	Hollywood Hulk Hogan	8.00	20.00
RLSA	Stone Cold Steve Austin	8.00	20.00
RLSM	Shawn Michaels	4.00	10.00
RLSS	Scott Steiner	4.00	10.00
RLTH	Triple H	6.00	15.00
RLRVD	Rob Van Dam	4.00	10.00

2004 Fleer WWE Chaos

COMPLETE SET (95) 10.00 25.00
UNOPENED BOX (24 PACKS)
UNOPENED PACK (5 CARDS)
*GOLD: 1X TO 2.5X BASIC CARDS

1	Stone Cold Steve Austin	1.25	3.00
2	Test	.30	.75
3	Jazz	.50	1.25
4	Kurt Angle	.75	2.00
5	Batista	.75	2.00
6	The Hurricane		
7	Rey Mysterio	.50	1.25
8	Steven Richards	.30	.75
9	Goldberg	1.50	4.00
10	Chris Benoit	.50	1.25
11	Doug Basham	.20	.50
12	Torrie Wilson	2.00	5.00
13	Booker T	.75	2.00
14	Lance Storm	.20	.50
15	Rhyno	.75	2.00
16	Matt Hardy	.50	1.25
17	Maven	.20	.50
18	Rico	.20	.50
19	Rodney Mack RC	.20	.50
20	Jacqueline	.60	1.50
21	Rosey	.20	.50
22	Rikishi	.50	1.25
23	Scotty 2 Hotty	.30	.75
24	Mark Jindrak RC	.20	.50
25	Spike Dudley	.30	.75
26	Shawn Michaels	1.25	3.00
27	Paul Heyman	.20	.50
28	Val Venis	.30	.75
29	Shannon Moore	.20	.50
30	Triple H	1.25	3.00
31	Rob Conway RC	.20	.50
32	Edge	.75	2.00
33	A-Train	.20	.50
34	Big Show	.75	2.00
35	Theodore Long	.20	.50
36	Shelton Benjamin RC	.20	.50
37	Billy Gunn	.25	.60
38	Billy Kidman	.20	.50
39	Bradshaw	.50	1.25
40	Kane	.75	2.00
41	Charlie Haas	.20	.50
42	Chavo Guerrero	.30	.75
43	The Rock	1.25	3.00
44	Danny Basham RC	.20	.50
45	Chuck Palumbo	.30	.75
46	D-Von Dudley	.30	.75
47	Eddie Guerrero	1.00	2.50
48	Rene Dupree RC	.30	.75
49	Tajiri	.20	.50
50	Undertaker	1.00	2.50
51	Rob Van Dam	.75	2.00
52	Ric Flair	1.00	2.50
53	Matt Morgan RC	.25	.60
54	Eric Bischoff	.30	.75
55	Garrison Cade RC	.20	.50
56	Funaki	.30	.75
57	Brock Lesnar	2.00	5.00
58	Chris Jericho	.50	1.25
59	Hardcore Holly	.30	.75
60	Ultimo Dragon	.20	.50
61	Jamie Noble	.20	.50
62	Scott Steiner	1.00	2.50
63	John Cena	1.25	3.00
64	Randy Orton	.50	1.25
65	Johnny Stamboli	.20	.50
66	Nunzio	.20	.50
67	Bubba Ray Dudley	.30	.75
68	Mark Henry	.30	.75
69	Christian	.60	1.50
70	Jazz SI	.50	1.25
71	Torrie Wilson SI	2.00	5.00
72	Trish Stratus SI	2.00	5.00
73	Dawn Marie SI	.50	1.25
74	Stacy Keibler SI	2.00	5.00
75	Nidia SI	.50	1.25
76	Shaniqua SI RC	.50	1.25
77	Lita SI	1.25	3.00
78	Jacqueline SI	.60	1.50
79	Victoria SI	1.00	2.50
80	Terri SI	1.00	2.50
81	Ivory SI	.75	2.00
82	Gail Kim SI RC	.75	2.00
83	Miss Jackie SI	.75	2.00
84	Molly SI	1.00	2.50
85	Sable SI	1.25	3.00
86	Brock Lesnar PI	2.00	5.00
87	Triple H PI	1.25	3.00
88	Kurt Angle PI	.75	2.00
89	Batista PI	.75	2.00
90	Test PI	.30	.75
91	Randy Orton PI	.50	1.25
92	Scott Steiner PI	1.00	2.50
93	Booker T PI	.75	2.00
94	The Rock PI	1.25	3.00
95	Goldberg PI	1.50	4.00

2004 Fleer WWE Chaos Controlled Chaos

COMPLETE SET (15) 8.00 20.00
STATED ODDS 1:6 HOBBY AND RETAIL

1	Brock Lesnar	2.00	5.00
2	Chris Benoit	.50	1.25
3	Triple H	1.25	3.00
4	Kurt Angle	.75	2.00
5	Kane	.75	2.00
6	Shawn Michaels	1.25	3.00
7	Edge	.75	2.00
8	Chris Jericho	.50	1.25
9	Stone Cold	1.25	3.00
10	Big Poppa Pump	1.00	2.50
11	Undertaker	1.00	2.50
12	Rob Van Dam	.75	2.00
13	Ric Flair	1.00	2.50
14	The Rock	1.25	3.00
15	Goldberg	1.50	4.00

2004 Fleer WWE Chaos Showing Off

COMPLETE SET (16) 12.50 30.00
STATED ODDS 1:4 HOBBY AND RETAIL

1	Lita	1.50	4.00
2	Jacqueline	.75	2.00
3	Ivory	1.00	2.50
4	Dawn Marie	.60	1.50
5	Stacy Keibler	2.50	6.00
6	Nidia	.60	1.50
7	Molly Holly	1.25	3.00
8	Jazz	.60	1.50
9	Torrie Wilson	2.50	6.00
10	Victoria	1.25	3.00
11	Terri	1.25	3.00
12	Trish Stratus	2.50	6.00
13	Sable	1.50	4.00
14	Miss Jackie	1.00	2.50
15	Shaniqua	.60	1.50
16	Gail Kim	1.00	2.50

2004 Fleer WWE Chaos Showing Off Autographs

STATED PRINT RUN 25 SER.#'d SETS

NNO	Dawn Marie	50.00	100.00
NNO	Gail Kim	60.00	125.00
NNO	Ivory	60.00	125.00
NNO	Jacqueline	30.00	75.00
NNO	Jazz	50.00	100.00
NNO	Lita	75.00	150.00
NNO	Molly	50.00	100.00
NNO	Miss Jackie	60.00	125.00
NNO	Nidia	30.00	75.00
NNO	Sable	75.00	150.00
NNO	Shaniqua	30.00	75.00
NNO	Stacy Keibler	100.00	200.00
NNO	Terri	100.00	200.00
NNO	Torrie Wilson	60.00	120.00
NNO	Trish Stratus	125.00	250.00
NNO	Victoria	30.00	75.00

2004 Fleer WWE Chaos Showing Off Memorabilia

STATED ODDS 1:36 HOBBY; 1:72 RETAIL

SOI	Ivory	5.00	12.00
SOJ	Jacqueline	4.00	10.00
SOJ	Jazz	4.00	10.00
SOL	Lita	6.00	15.00
SOM	Molly	5.00	12.00
SON	Nidia	4.00	10.00
SOS	Sable	6.00	15.00
SOS	Shaniqua	4.00	10.00
SOT	Terri	6.00	15.00
SOV	Victoria	5.00	12.00
SODM	Dawn Marie	5.00	12.00
SOGK	Gail Kim	6.00	15.00
SOMJ	Miss Jackie	6.00	15.00
SOSK	Stacy Keibler	10.00	25.00
SOTS	Trish Stratus	10.00	25.00
SOTW	Torrie Wilson	10.00	25.00

2004 Fleer WWE Chaos Tuff Guys

COMPLETE SET (12) 12.00 30.00
STATED ODDS 1:12 HOBBY AND RETAIL

1	The Rock	2.50	6.00
2	Eddie Guerrero	2.00	5.00
3	Triple H	2.50	6.00

4	Kurt Angle	1.50	4.00
5	Undertaker	2.00	5.00
6	Shawn Michaels	2.50	6.00
7	Rob Van Dam	1.50	4.00
8	Stone Cold Steve Austin	2.50	6.00
9	Chris Benoit	1.00	2.50
10	Brock Lesnar	4.00	10.00
11	Chris Jericho	1.00	2.50
12	Kane	1.50	4.00

2004 Fleer WWE Chaos Tuff Guys Event Used Mat

STATED ODDS 1:8 RETAIL

TGK	Kane	2.00	5.00
TGU	Undertaker	2.50	6.00
TGBL	Brock Lesnar	6.00	15.00
TGCB	Chris Benoit	1.50	4.00
TGCJ	Chris Jericho	1.50	4.00
TGEG	Eddie Guerrero	1.50	4.00
TGKA	Kurt Angle	2.00	5.00
TGRV	Rob Van Dam	1.50	4.00
TGSA	Stone Cold Steve Austin	3.00	8.00
TGSM	Shawn Michaels	2.50	6.00
TGTH	Triple H	2.50	6.00
TGTR	The Rock	3.00	8.00

2004 Fleer WWE Chaos Tuff Guys Event Worn Memorabilia

STATED ODDS 1:12 HOBBY EXCLUSIVE

TGK	Kane	3.00	8.00
TGU	Undertaker	4.00	10.00
TGBL	Brock Lesnar	5.00	12.00
TGCB	Chris Benoit	5.00	15.00
TGCJ	Chris Jericho	2.50	6.00
TGEG	Eddie Guerrero	3.00	10.00
TGKA	Kurt Angle	4.00	10.00
TGRV	Rob Van Dam	2.50	6.00
TGSA	Stone Cold Steve Austin	5.00	12.00
TGSM	Shawn Michaels	3.00	8.00
TGTH	Triple H	4.00	10.00
TGTR	The Rock	5.00	12.00

2003 Fleer WWE Divine Divas

COMPLETE SET (90) 10.00 25.00
UNOPENED BOX (24 PACKS)
UNOPENED PACK (5 CARDS)

1	Lita	.60	1.50
2	Jacqueline	.25	.60
3	Ivory	.40	1.00
4	Dawn Marie	.50	1.25
5	Stacy Keibler	1.00	2.50
6	Nidia	.25	.60
7	Molly	.50	1.25
8	Jazz	.15	.40
9	Torrie Wilson	1.00	2.50
10	Victoria	.50	1.25
11	Terri	.50	1.25
12	Trish Stratus	1.00	2.50
13	Sable	.60	1.50
14	Lita	.60	1.50
15	Jacqueline	.25	.60
16	Ivory	.40	1.00
17	Dawn Marie	.50	1.25
18	Stacy Keibler	1.00	2.50
19	Nidia	.25	.60
20	Molly	.50	1.25
21	Jazz	.15	.40
22	Torrie Wilson	1.00	2.50
23	Victoria	.50	1.25
24	Terri	.50	1.25
25	Trish Stratus	1.00	2.50
26	Sable	.60	1.50
27	Lita	.60	1.50
28	Jacqueline	.25	.60
29	Ivory	.40	1.00
30	Dawn Marie	.50	1.25
31	Stacy Keibler	1.00	2.50
32	Nidia	.25	.60
33	Molly	.50	1.25
34	Jazz	.15	.40
35	Torrie Wilson	1.00	2.50
36	Victoria	.50	1.25
37	Terri	.50	1.25
38	Trish Stratus	1.00	2.50
39	Sable	.60	1.50
40	Lita	.60	1.50
41	Jacqueline	.25	.60
42	Ivory	.40	1.00
43	Dawn Marie	.50	1.25
44	Stacy Keibler	1.00	2.50
45	Nidia	.25	.60
46	Molly	.50	1.25
47	Jazz	.15	.40
48	Torrie Wilson	1.00	2.50
49	Victoria	.50	1.25
50	Terri	.50	1.25
51	Trish Stratus	1.00	2.50
52	Sable	.60	1.50
53	Lita	.60	1.50
54	Jacqueline	.25	.60
55	Ivory	.40	1.00
56	Dawn Marie	.50	1.25
57	Stacy Keibler	1.00	2.50
58	Nidia	.25	.60
59	Molly	.50	1.25
60	Jazz	.15	.40
61	Torrie Wilson	1.00	2.50
62	Victoria	.50	1.25
63	Terri	.50	1.25
64	Trish Stratus	1.00	2.50
65	Sable	.60	1.50
66	Lita	.60	1.50
67	Jacqueline	.25	.60
68	Ivory	.40	1.00
69	Dawn Marie	.50	1.25
70	Stacy Keibler	1.00	2.50
71	Nidia	.25	.60
72	Molly	.50	1.25
73	Jazz	.15	.40
74	Torrie Wilson	1.00	2.50
75	Victoria	.50	1.25
76	Terri	.50	1.25
77	Trish Stratus	1.00	2.50
78	Sable	.60	1.50
79	Triple H/Victoria DT	.60	1.50
80	Trish Stratus/The Rock DT	1.00	2.50
81	Sable/Brock Lesnar DT	1.00	2.50
82	Lita/Edge DT	.60	1.50
83	Stacy Keibler/Scott Steiner DT	1.00	2.50
84	Terri/Stone Cold Steve Austin DT	.60	1.50
85	Chris Jericho/Ivory DT	.25	.60
86	Kurt Angle/Torrie Wilson DT	1.00	2.50
87	Booker T/Jazz DT	.40	1.00
88	Gail Kim/Kane DT	.40	1.00
89	Nidia/Jamie Noble DT	.25	.60
90	Zach Gowen/Stephanie DT	.50	1.25

2003 Fleer WWE Divine Divas Dress Code Memorabilia

STATED ODDS 1:288 HOBBY

NNO	Dawn Marie	10.00	25.00
NNO	Ivory	30.00	75.00
NNO	Molly	12.00	30.00
NNO	Nidia	12.00	30.00
NNO	Sable	20.00	50.00
NNO	Stacy Keibler	50.00	100.00
NNO	Trish Stratus	25.00	60.00
NNO	Victoria	10.00	25.00

2003 Fleer WWE Divine Divas Hugs and Kisses

COMPLETE SET (14) 15.00 40.00
STATED ODDS 1:8

NNO	Dawn Marie	1.50	4.00
NNO	Gail Kim	1.25	3.00
NNO	Ivory	1.25	3.00
NNO	Lita	2.00	5.00
NNO	Miss Jackie	1.25	3.00
NNO	Molly	1.50	4.00
NNO	Nidia	.75	2.00
NNO	Sable	2.00	5.00
NNO	Shaniqua	.75	2.00
NNO	Stacy Keibler	3.00	8.00
NNO	Terri	1.50	4.00
NNO	Torrie Wilson	3.00	8.00
NNO	Trish Stratus	3.00	8.00
NNO	Victoria	1.50	4.00

2003 Fleer WWE Divine Divas Hugs and Kisses Autographs

STATED PRINT RUN 25 SER.#'d SETS

NNO	Dawn Marie	50.00	100.00
NNO	Gail Kim	60.00	125.00
NNO	Ivory	30.00	75.00
NNO	Jazz	30.00	75.00
NNO	Miss Jackie	60.00	125.00
NNO	Lita	75.00	150.00
NNO	Molly	50.00	100.00
NNO	Nidia	30.00	75.00
NNO	Sable	125.00	250.00
NNO	Shaniqua	30.00	75.00
NNO	Stacy Keibler	200.00	350.00
NNO	Terri	100.00	200.00
NNO	Trish Stratus	125.00	250.00
NNO	Victoria	60.00	125.00
NNO	Torrie Wilson	125.00	250.00

2003 Fleer WWE Divine Divas On Location

COMPLETE SET (16) 20.00 50.00
STATED ODDS 1:12 HOBBY AND RETAIL

1	Jacqueline	1.00	2.50
2	Jazz	.60	1.50
3	Nidia	1.00	2.50
4	Dawn Marie	2.00	5.00
5	Torrie Wilson	4.00	10.00
6	Lita	2.50	6.00
7	Sable	2.50	6.00
8	Ivory	1.50	4.00
9	Stacy Keibler	4.00	10.00
10	Trish Stratus	4.00	10.00
11	Terri	2.00	5.00
12	Victoria	2.00	5.00
13	Molly	2.00	5.00
14	Miss Jackie	1.50	4.00
15	Shaniqua	1.00	2.50
16	Gail Kim	1.50	4.00

2003 Fleer WWE Divine Divas On Location Memorabilia

STATED ODDS 1:24 HOBBY; 1:96 RETAIL

NNO	Dawn Marie	5.00	12.00
NNO	Ivory	6.00	15.00
NNO	Miss Jackie	6.00	15.00
NNO	Molly	5.00	12.00
NNO	Nidia	4.00	10.00
NNO	Sable	8.00	20.00
NNO	Shaniqua	4.00	10.00
NNO	Victoria	6.00	15.00

2003 Fleer WWE Divine Divas With Love

1	Lita	1.25	3.00
2	Jacqueline	.50	1.25
3	Ivory	.75	2.00
4	Dawn Marie	1.00	2.50
5	Stacy Keibler	2.00	5.00
6	Nidia	.50	1.25
7	Molly	1.00	2.50
8	Jazz	.30	.75
9	Torrie Wilson	2.00	5.00
10	Victoria	1.00	2.50
11	Terri	1.00	2.50
12	Trish Stratus	2.00	5.00
13	Sable	1.25	3.00
14	Shaniqua	.50	1.25
15	Gail Kim	.75	2.00
16	Miss Jackie	.75	2.00

2003 Fleer WWE Divine Divas With Love Autographs

STATED PRINT RUN 100 SER.#'d SETS

NNO	Dawn Marie	12.00	30.00
NNO	Gail Kim	15.00	40.00
NNO	Ivory	20.00	50.00
NNO	Jacqueline	12.00	30.00
NNO	Jazz	12.00	30.00
NNO	Miss Jackie	15.00	40.00
NNO	Molly	15.00	40.00
NNO	Nidia	12.00	30.00
NNO	Sable	100.00	200.00
NNO	Shaniqua	12.00	30.00
NNO	Stacy Keibler	75.00	150.00
NNO	Trish Stratus	50.00	100.00
NNO	Victoria	15.00	40.00

2003 Fleer WWE Divine Divas With Love Memorabilia

NNO	Dawn Marie	4.00	10.00
NNO	Gail Kim	6.00	15.00
NNO	Ivory	6.00	15.00
NNO	Jacqueline	3.00	8.00
NNO	Miss Jackie	5.00	12.00
NNO	Molly	4.00	10.00
NNO	Nidia	3.00	8.00
NNO	Sable	15.00	40.00
NNO	Shaniqua	3.00	8.00
NNO	Stacy Keibler	20.00	50.00
NNO	Trish Stratus	8.00	20.00
NNO	Victoria	4.00	10.00

2003 Fleer WWE Divine Divas Promo

5 Stacy Keibler	1.50	4.00

2004 Fleer WWE Divine Divas 2005

COMPLETE SET (80)	10.00	25.00
UNOPENED BOX		
UNOPENED PACK		
1 Lita	.50	1.25
2 Ivory	.30	.75
3 Dawn Marie	.20	.50
4 Stacy Keibler	.75	2.00
5 Nidia	.20	.50
6 Molly Holly	.40	1.00
7 Jazz	.20	.50
8 Torrie Wilson	.75	2.00
9 Victoria	.40	1.00
10 Trish Stratus	.75	2.00
11 Sable	.50	1.25
12 Miss Jackie	.30	.75
13 Gail Kim RC	.30	.75
14 Lita	.50	1.25
15 Ivory	.30	.75
16 Dawn Marie	.20	.50
17 Stacy Keibler	.75	2.00
18 Nidia	.20	.50
19 Molly Holly	.40	1.00
20 Jazz	.20	.50
21 Torrie Wilson	.75	2.00
22 Victoria	.40	1.00
23 Trish Stratus	.75	2.00
24 Sable	.50	1.25
25 Miss Jackie	.30	.75
26 Gail Kim RC	.30	.75
27 Lita	.50	1.25
28 Ivory	.30	.75
29 Dawn Marie	.20	.50
30 Stacy Keibler	.75	2.00
31 Torrie Wilson	.20	.50
32 Molly Holly	.40	1.00
33 Jazz	.20	.50
34 Torrie Wilson	.75	2.00
35 Victoria	.40	1.00
36 Trish Stratus	.75	2.00
37 Sable	.50	1.25
38 Miss Jackie	.30	.75
39 Gail Kim RC	.30	.75
40 Lita	.50	1.25
41 Ivory	.30	.75
42 Dawn Marie	.20	.50
43 Stacy Keibler	.75	2.00
44 Stacy Keibler	.75	2.00
45 Molly Holly	.40	1.00
46 Jazz	.20	.50
47 Torrie Wilson	.75	2.00
48 Victoria	.40	1.00
49 Trish Stratus	.75	2.00
50 Sable	.50	1.25
51 Miss Jackie	.30	.75
52 Gail Kim RC	.30	.75
53 Trish/Victoria CF	.75	2.00
54 Jazz & Gail Kim CF	.30	.75
55 Victoria & Molly Holly CF	.40	1.00
56 Sable/Torri/Stacy/Jackie CF	.75	2.00
57 Gail Kim & Lita CF	.50	1.25
58 Molly Holly & Gail Kim CF	.40	1.00
59 Jazz & Trish Stratus CF	.75	2.00
60 Lita & Trish Stratus CF	.75	2.00
61 Stacy Keibler & Miss Jackie CF	.75	2.00
62 Victoria & Gail Kim CF	.40	1.00
63 Molly Holly & Trish Stratus CF	.75	2.00
64 Sable & Torrie Wilson CF	.75	2.00
65 Victoria & Jazz CF	.40	1.00
66 Triple H OS	.50	1.25
67 Chris Jericho OS	.20	.50
68 Kurt Angle OS	.30	.75
69 Christian OS	.25	.60
70 Eric Bischoff OS	.12	.30
71 Shawn Michaels OS	.50	1.25
72 Eddie Guerrero OS	.40	1.00
73 Undertaker OS	.40	1.00
74 Booker T OS	.30	.75
75 Tyson Tomko OS RC	.12	.30
76 Chris Benoit OS	.20	.50
77 Eugene OS RC	.12	.30
78 Randy Orton OS	.20	.50
79 Edge OS	.30	.75
80 Babe of the Year Trish Stratus	.75	2.00

2004 Fleer WWE Divine Divas 2005 Body and Soul

COMPLETE SET (10)	8.00	20.00
STATED ODDS 1:8 HOBBY		
1 Dawn Marie	.60	1.50
2 Stacy Keibler	2.50	6.00
3 Torrie Wilson	2.50	6.00
4 Trish Stratus	2.50	6.00
5 Victoria	1.25	3.00
6 Miss Jackie	1.00	2.50
7 Lita	1.50	4.00
8 Ivory	1.00	2.50
9 Nidia	.60	1.50
10 Sable	1.50	4.00

2004 Fleer WWE Divine Divas 2005 Body and Soul Memorabilia

STATED ODDS 1:288 HOBBY		
BSDM Dawn Marie	4.00	10.00
BSIV Ivory	6.00	15.00
BSLI Lita	8.00	20.00
BSMJ Miss Jackie	5.00	12.00
BSNI Nidia	4.00	10.00
BSSA Sable	8.00	20.00
BSSK Stacy Keibler	10.00	25.00
BSTS Trish Stratus	10.00	25.00
BSTW Torrie Wilson	8.00	20.00
BSVI Victoria	6.00	15.00

2004 Fleer WWE Divine Divas 2005 Divas Uncensored

COMPLETE SET (13)	15.00	40.00
STATED ODDS 1:12 HOBBY		
1 Dawn Marie	1.25	3.00
2 Jazz	1.25	3.00
3 Sable	3.00	8.00
4 Nidia	1.25	3.00
5 Victoria	2.50	6.00
6 Gail Kim	2.00	5.00
7 Ivory	2.00	5.00
8 Molly Holly	2.50	6.00
9 Trish Stratus	5.00	12.00
10 Lita	3.00	8.00
11 Stacy Keibler	5.00	12.00
12 Torrie Wilson	5.00	12.00
13 Miss Jackie	2.00	5.00

2004 Fleer WWE Divine Divas 2005 Divas Uncensored Memorabilia

STATED ODDS 1:24 HOBBY		
DUL Lita	6.00	15.00
DUDM Dawn Marie	4.00	10.00
DUGK Gail Kim	4.00	10.00
DUIV Ivory	5.00	12.00
DUJA Jazz	3.00	8.00
DUMH Molly Holly	4.00	10.00
DUMJ Miss Jackie	5.00	12.00
DUNI Nidia	3.00	8.00
DUSA Sable	6.00	15.00
DUSK Stacy Keibler	12.00	30.00
DUTS Trish Stratus	8.00	20.00
DUTW Torrie Wilson	12.00	30.00
DUVI Victoria	4.00	10.00

2004 Fleer WWE Divine Divas 2005 Femme Physique

COMPLETE SET (13)	8.00	20.00
STATED ODDS 1:4 HOBBY		
1 Lita	1.25	3.00
2 Ivory	.75	2.00
3 Dawn Marie	.50	1.25
4 Stacy Keibler	2.00	5.00
5 Nidia	.50	1.25
6 Molly Holly	1.00	2.50
7 Jazz	.50	1.25
8 Torrie Wilson	2.00	5.00
9 Victoria	1.00	2.50
10 Trish Stratus	2.00	5.00
11 Sable	1.25	3.00
12 Miss Jackie	.75	2.00
13 Gail Kim	.75	2.00

2004 Fleer WWE Divine Divas 2005 Femme Physique Memorabilia

STATED ODDS 1:28 HOBBY		
FPL Lita	6.00	15.00
FPDM Dawn Marie	3.00	8.00
FPGK Gail Kim	3.00	8.00
FPIV Ivory	4.00	10.00
FPJA Jazz	3.00	8.00
FPMH Molly Holly	4.00	10.00
FPMJ Miss Jackie	5.00	12.00
FPNI Nidia	3.00	8.00
FPSA Sable	6.00	15.00
FPSK Stacy Keibler	8.00	20.00
FPTS Trish Stratus	8.00	20.00
FPTW Torrie Wilson	8.00	20.00
FPVI Victoria	4.00	10.00

2004 Fleer WWE Divine Divas 2005 Hugs and Kisses Autographs

STATED PRINT RUN 15 SER.#'d SETS		
HKDM Dawn Marie	50.00	100.00
HKIV Ivory	60.00	125.00
HKLI Lita	150.00	300.00
HKMJ Miss Jackie	60.00	125.00
HKNI Nidia	50.00	100.00
HKSA Sable	250.00	500.00
HKSK Stacy Keibler	250.00	500.00
HKTM Torrie Wilson	125.00	250.00
HKTS Trish Stratus	200.00	400.00
HKVI Victoria	60.00	125.00

2002 Fleer WWE KB Toys SmackDown! Shut Your Mouth

1 Kurt Angle	2.00	5.00
2 The Rock	5.00	12.00
3 Undertaker	2.50	6.00
4 Trish Stratus	4.00	10.00
5 Stacy Keibler	4.00	10.00
6 Triple H	2.50	6.00
7 Chris Jericho	2.00	5.00
8 Booker T	1.25	3.00
9 Rob Van Dam	1.25	3.00
10 Hollywood Hulk Hogan	4.00	10.00

2002 Fleer WWE Raw vs. SmackDown

COMPLETE SET (90)	12.00	30.00
UNOPENED BOX (24 PACKS)		
UNOPENED PACK (8 CARDS)		
1 The Rock	.75	2.00
2 Undertaker	.60	1.50
3 Kurt Angle	.50	1.25
4 Kevin Nash	.60	1.50
5 Jim Ross	.20	.50
6 X-Pac	.20	.50
7 Chris Benoit	.30	.75
8 Kane	.50	1.25
9 Hollywood Hulk Hogan	1.25	3.00
10 Rob Van Dam RC	.50	1.25
11 Billy Gunn	.20	.50
12 Chuck Palumbo RC	.20	.50
13 Booker T	.50	1.25
14 Edge	.50	1.25
15 Big Show	.50	1.25
16 Rikishi	.30	.75
17 Bubba Ray Dudley	.20	.50
18 D-Von Dudley	.20	.50
19 Brock Lesnar	6.00	15.00
20 Mark Henry	.20	.50
21 William Regal	.20	.50
22 Maven RC	.12	.30
23 Lita	.75	2.00
24 Billy Kidman	.12	.30
25 Bradshaw	.30	.75
26 Tajiri	.20	.50
27 Steven Richards	.20	.50
28 Chris Jericho	.30	.75
29 Matt Hardy	.30	.75
30 Ivory	.50	1.25
31 Raven	.20	.50
32 Albert	.12	.30
33 Jeff Hardy	.30	.75
34 The Hurricane RC	.20	.50
35 Jerry Lawler	.30	.75
36 Al Snow	.20	.50
37 D'Lo Brown	.12	.30
38 Diamond Dallas Page	.20	.50
39 Shawn Stasiak	.12	.30
40 Torrie Wilson RC	1.25	3.00
41 Terri	.60	1.50
42 Scotty 2 Hotty	.20	.50
43 Jacqueline	.30	.75
44 Stacy Keibler RC	1.25	3.00
45 Goldust	.12	.30
46 Christian	.30	.75
47 Trish Stratus	1.25	3.00
48 Test	.20	.50
49 Justin Credible	.12	.30

50 Faarooq	.12	.30
51 Boss Man	.12	.30
52 Tazz	.20	.50
53 Tommy Dreamer RC	.12	.30
54 Hardcore Holly	.20	.50
55 Crash	.12	.30
56 The Big Valbowski	.20	.50
57 Molly Holly	.30	.75
58 Perry Saturn	.12	.30
59 Spike Dudley	.20	.50
60 Lance Storm RC	.12	.30
61 Triple H	.75	2.00
62 Vince McMahon	.50	1.25
63 Ric Flair	.60	1.50
64 nWo	.20	.50
65 Rico RC	.12	.30
66 Debra QR	.30	.75
67 Jazz QR RC	.30	.75
68 Lita QR	.75	2.00
69 Ivory QR	.50	1.25
70 Terri QR	.60	1.50
71 Torrie Wilson QR	1.25	3.00
72 Jacqueline QR	.30	.75
73 Stacy Keibler QR	1.25	3.00
74 Trish Stratus QR	1.25	3.00
75 Molly Holly QR	.30	.75
76 Rob Van Dam/Kurt Angle RVS	.50	1.25
77 Big Show/Rikishi RVS	.50	1.25
78 Undertaker/DDP RVS	.60	1.50
79 Stone Cold/The Rock RVS	2.00	5.00
80 William Regal/Chris Jericho RVS	.20	.50
81 Bubba Ray Dudley/D-Von Dudley RVS	.20	.50
82 Trish Stratus/Torrie Wilson RVS	1.25	3.00
83 Lita/Stacy Keibler RVS	1.25	3.00
84 Jacqueline/Ivory RVS	.50	1.25
85 Raven/Tajiri RVS	.20	.50
86 Brock Lesnar/The Rock RVS	5.00	12.00
87 Booker T/Edge RVS	.50	1.25
88 Goldust/The Hurricane RVS	.20	.50
89 Bradshaw/Faarooq RVS	.30	.75
90 Kane/Hulk Hogan RVS	1.25	3.00

2002 Fleer WWE Raw vs. SmackDown Catch Phrases

COMPLETE SET (15)	6.00	15.00
STATED ODDS 1:4 HOBBY		
CP1 The Rock	1.25	3.00
CP2 Ric Flair	1.00	2.50
CP3 Kurt Angle	.75	2.00
CP4 Stone Cold Steve Austin	1.25	3.00
CP5 Tazz	.30	.75
CP6 Raven	.30	.75
CP7 Trish Stratus	2.00	5.00
CP8 Triple H	1.25	3.00
CP9 The Big Valbowski	.30	.75
CP10 Booker T	.75	2.00
CP11 Chris Jericho	.50	1.25
CP12 Hollywood Hulk Hogan	2.00	5.00
CP13 nWo	.30	.75
CP14 Jim Ross	.30	.75
CP15 Chris Benoit	.50	1.25

2002 Fleer WWE Raw vs. SmackDown Exposure

COMPLETE SET (10)	8.00	20.00
STATED ODDS 1:8 HOBBY		
XP1 Debra	.60	1.50
XP2 Ivory	1.00	2.50
XP3 Jacqueline	.60	1.50
XP4 Jazz	.60	1.50
XP5 Lita	1.50	4.00
XP6 Molly Holly	.60	1.50
XP7 Stacy Keibler	2.50	6.00
XP8 Terri	1.25	3.00
XP9 Torrie Wilson	2.50	6.00
XP10 Trish Stratus	2.50	6.00

2002 Fleer WWE Raw vs. SmackDown Pay-Per-View Relics

COMPLETE SET (5)	30.00	75.00
STATED ODDS 1:33 HOBBY		
NNO Kurt Angle/Kane	6.00	15.00
NNO Ric Flair/Undertaker	10.00	25.00
NNO The Rock/Hulk Hogan	20.00	50.00
NNO Scott Hall/Steve Austin	10.00	25.00
NNO William Regal/Rob Van Dam	6.00	15.00

2002 Fleer WWE Raw vs. SmackDown Pop-Ups

COMPLETE SET (10)	20.00	50.00
STATED ODDS 1:HOBBY BOX		
NNO Chris Jericho	1.25	3.00
NNO Hollywood Hulk Hogan	5.00	12.00
NNO Kurt Angle	2.00	5.00
NNO Lita	3.00	8.00
NNO The Rock	3.00	8.00
NNO Stacy Keibler	5.00	12.00
NNO Stone Cold Steve Austin	3.00	8.00
NNO Triple H	3.00	8.00
NNO Trish Stratus	5.00	12.00
NNO Undertaker	2.50	6.00

2002 Fleer WWE Raw vs. SmackDown Raw Certified

STATED ODDS 1:72		
NNO Kevin Nash	10.00	25.00
NNO Rob Van Dam	8.00	20.00
NNO Spike Dudley	8.00	20.00
NNO William Regal	8.00	20.00
NNO X-Pac	8.00	20.00

2002 Fleer WWE Raw vs. SmackDown SmackDown Authentics

STATED ODDS 1:36 HOBBY		
NNO Billy Gunn Headband	4.00	10.00
NNO Chuck Palumbo Headband	4.00	10.00
NNO DDP Pants	5.00	12.00
NNO Edge Shirt	6.00	15.00
NNO Hollywood Hulk Hogan Shirt	8.00	20.00
NNO Triple H Shirt	6.00	15.00
NNO Undertaker Shirt	6.00	15.00

2002 Fleer WWE Raw vs. SmackDown Triple Exposure

NNO Lita/Debra/Molly	25.00	60.00
NNO Molly/Stacy Keibler/Debra	30.00	75.00
NNO Terri/Torrie/Stacy	75.00	150.00

2002 Fleer WWE Raw vs. SmackDown Ultimate Exposure

STATED ODDS 1:96 HOBBY		
NNO Debra Jacket	8.00	20.00
NNO Lita Top	10.00	25.00
NNO Molly Holly Swimsuit	6.00	15.00
NNO Molly Holly Top	6.00	15.00
NNO Stacy Keibler Shirt	12.00	30.00
NNO Terri Dress	10.00	25.00
NNO Torrie Wilson Stocking	12.00	30.00

2002 Fleer WWE Royal Rumble

COMPLETE SET W/CENA (90)	125.00	250.00
COMPLETE SET W/O CENA (89)	50.00	100.00
UNOPENED PACK (8 CARDS)		
UNOPENED BOX (24 PACKS)		
1 Big Show	.50	1.25
2 Booker T	.50	1.25
3 Bradshaw	.30	.75
4 Brock Lesnar	30.00	75.00
5 Bubba Ray Dudley	.20	.50
6 Chris Nowinski RC	.12	.30
7 John Cena RC	75.00	200.00
8 D'Lo Brown	.12	.30
9 Eddie Guerrero	.60	1.50
10 Goldust	.12	.30
11 Jacqueline	.30	.75
12 Jazz RC	.30	.75
13 Jeff Hardy	.30	.75
14 Randy Orton RC	12.00	30.00
15 Kane	.50	1.25
16 Kevin Nash	.60	1.50
17 Lita	.75	2.00
18 Mark Henry	.20	.50
19 Matt Hardy	.30	.75
20 Molly	.30	.75
21 Rob Van Dam RC	.50	1.25
22 Raven	.20	.50
23 Shawn Michaels	.75	2.00
24 Shawn Stasiak	.12	.30
25 Spike Dudley	.20	.50
26 Steven Richards	.20	.50
27 Terri	.60	1.50
28 Ric Flair	.60	1.50
29 William Regal	.20	.50
30 X-Pac	.20	.50
31 Al Snow	.20	.50
32 Billy	.20	.50
33 Billy Kidman	.12	.30
34 Chris Benoit	.30	.75
35 Christian	.30	.75
36 Chuck RC	.20	.50
37 D-Von	.20	.50
38 Paul Heyman	.12	.30
39 Edge	.50	1.25
40 Faarooq	.12	.30
41 Funaki	.20	.50
42 Chris Jericho	.30	.75
43 Hollywood Hulk Hogan	1.25	3.00
44 The Hurricane RC	.20	.50
45 Ivory	.50	1.25
46 Kurt Angle	.50	1.25
47 Maven RC	.12	.30
48 Nidia RC	.30	.75
49 Rico RC	.12	.30
50 The Rock	.75	2.00
51 Tajiri	.20	.50
52 Torrie Wilson RC	1.25	3.00
53 Triple H	.75	2.00
54 Scotty 2 Hotty	.20	.50
55 Stacy Keibler RC	1.25	3.00
56 Lance Storm RC	.12	.30
57 Tazz	.20	.50
58 Test	.20	.50
59 Eric Bischoff	.12	.30
60 Jackie RC	.50	1.25
61 Victoria RC	.60	1.50
62 Stephanie	.60	1.50
63 Vince McMahon	.50	1.25
64 Rikishi	.30	.75
65 Jerry Lawler	.30	.75
66 Jim Ross	.20	.50
67 Deacon Batista RC	12.00	30.00
68 Shane McMahon	.30	.75
69 Albert	.12	.30
70 Trish Stratus	1.25	3.00
71 Undertaker	.60	1.50
72 Dawn Marie RC	.30	.75
73 Chavo Guerrero	.20	.50
74 Rey Mysterio	.30	.75
75 Tommy Dreamer RC	.12	.30
76 Eddie Guerrero AKA	.60	1.50
77 Brock Lesnar AKA	6.00	15.00
78 Chris Benoit AKA	.30	.75
79 Triple H AKA	.75	2.00
80 Undertaker AKA	.60	1.50
81 The Rock AKA	.75	2.00
82 Jim Ross AKA	.20	.50
83 Jerry Lawler AKA	.30	.75
84 Ric Flair AKA	.60	1.50
85 Shawn Stasiak AKA	.12	.30
86 Kurt Angle AKA	.50	1.25
87 Shawn Michaels AKA	.75	2.00
88 Hulk Hogan AKA	1.25	3.00
89 Rob Van Dam AKA	.50	1.25
90 J.Hardy/M.Hardy/Lita AKA	.75	2.00

2002 Fleer WWE Royal Rumble AKA Memorabilia

STATED ODDS 1:24 HOBBY		
NNO Triple H Ring Mat	4.00	10.00
NNO Undertaker Ring Mat	4.00	10.00

2002 Fleer WWE Royal Rumble Divastating

COMPLETE SET (15)	10.00	25.00
STATED ODDS 1:8 HOBBY		
D1 Ivory	1.00	2.50
D2 Torrie Wilson	2.50	6.00
D3 Terri	1.25	3.00
D4 Stacy Keibler	2.50	6.00
D5 Trish Stratus	2.50	6.00
D6 Molly	.60	1.50
D7 Stephanie McMahon	4.00	10.00
D8 Jazz	.60	1.50

D9 Jacqueline	.60	1.50
D10 Lita	1.50	4.00
D11 Dawn Marie	.60	1.50
D12 Nidia	.60	1.50
D13 Linda	.60	1.50
D14 Jackie	1.00	2.50
D15 Victoria	1.25	3.00

2002 Fleer WWE Royal Rumble Divastating Autographs

PRINT RUN 100 SER. #'d SETS		
NNO Lita	50.00	100.00
NNO Stacy Keibler	75.00	150.00
NNO Terri	25.00	60.00
NNO Torrie Wilson	60.00	120.00

2002 Fleer WWE Royal Rumble Divastating Memorabilia

STATED ODDS 1:48 HOBBY		
NNO Dawn Marie	8.00	20.00
Dress		
NNO Ivory	6.00	15.00
Undergarment		
NNO Jazz	4.00	10.00
Ring Mat		
NNO Stacy Keibler	10.00	25.00
Shirt		
NNO Torrie Wilson	10.00	25.00
Skirt		
NNO Trish Stratus	15.00	40.00
Pants		

2002 Fleer WWE Royal Rumble Factions

COMPLETE SET (5)	20.00	50.00
STATED ODDS 1:120		
F1 The Nation of Domination	6.00	15.00
F2 The Corporation	6.00	15.00
F3 The Radicalz	6.00	15.00
F4 D-Generation X	6.00	15.00
F5 New World Order	6.00	15.00

2002 Fleer WWE Royal Rumble Factions Memorabilia

STATED ODDS 1:48 HOBBY		
NNO The Rock	8.00	20.00
Shirt		
NNO Shawn Michaels	6.00	15.00
D-X Shirt		
NNO Shawn Michaels	6.00	15.00
nWo Shirt		
NNO X-Pac	4.00	10.00
Shirt		

2002 Fleer WWE Royal Rumble Gimmick Matches

COMPLETE SET (10)	6.00	15.00
STATED ODDS 1:4 HOBBY		
GM1 Triple H/Chris Jericho	1.25	3.00
GM2 Undertaker/Jeff Hardy	1.00	2.50
GM3 Rob Van Dam/Eddie Guerrero	1.00	2.50
GM4 Kurt Angle/Edge	.75	2.00
GM5 Rob Van Dam/Jeff Hardy	.75	2.00
GM6 Stacy Keibler/Trish Stratus	2.00	5.00
GM7 The Rock/Trish Stratus	2.00	5.00
GM8 Kurt Angle/Shane McMahon	.75	2.00
GM9 Chris Jericho/Kane	.75	2.00
GM10 Kurt Angle/Edge	.75	2.00

2002 Fleer WWE Royal Rumble Gimmick Matches Dual Memorabilia

STATED PRINT RUN 25 SER. #'d SETS		
NNO The Rock/Trish Stratus	15.00	40.00
NNO Stacy Keibler/Trish Stratus	20.00	50.00
NNO Triple H/Chris Jericho	20.00	50.00
NNO Undertaker/Jeff Hardy	50.00	100.00

2002 Fleer WWE Royal Rumble Gimmick Matches Memorabilia

STATED ODDS 1:24 HOBBY		
NNO Chris Jericho	6.00	15.00
Shirt (Hell in a Cell)		
NNO Chris Jericho	6.00	15.00
Shirt (Last Man Standing)		
NNO Edge	8.00	20.00
Shirt (Cage Match)		
NNO Edge	8.00	20.00
Shirt (Hair vs Hair)		
NNO Jeff Hardy	8.00	20.00
Shirt (Ladder Match)		
NNO Jeff Hardy	8.00	20.00
Tank Top (Hardcore Match)		
NNO Stacy Keibler	10.00	25.00
Shirt (Gravy Bowl Match)		
NNO Triple H	8.00	20.00
Shirt (Hell in a Cell)		
NNO Trish Stratus	10.00	25.00
Pants (Gender Match)		
NNO Trish Stratus	10.00	25.00
Shirt (Gender Match)		
NNO Trish Stratus	10.00	25.00
Shirt (Gravy Bowl Match)		
NNO Undertaker	8.00	20.00
Shirt (Ladder Match)		

2002 Fleer WWE Royal Rumble Memorabilia

STATED ODDS 1:24 HOBBY		
NNO Brock Lesnar	30.00	75.00
Shirt		
NNO Chris Benoit	6.00	15.00
Ring Skirt		
NNO Edge	6.00	15.00
Ring Mat		
NNO Funaki	3.00	8.00
Shirt		
NNO Hollywood Hulk Hogan	15.00	40.00
T-Shirt		
NNO The Hurricane	3.00	8.00
Ring Mat		
NNO Kane	5.00	12.00
Ring Mat		
NNO Kurt Angle	5.00	12.00
Ring Mat		
NNO Maven	3.00	8.00
T-Shirt		
NNO Rey Mysterio	10.00	25.00
Shirt		
NNO Rob Van Dam	4.00	10.00
Ring Mat		
NNO The Rock	10.00	25.00
Ring Mat		
NNO Scotty 2 Hotty	4.00	10.00
Jeans		
NNO Shawn Michaels	5.00	12.00
Shirt		
NNO Tazz	3.00	8.00
Sweat Pants		

2002 Fleer WWE Royal Rumble Recap

COMPLETE SET (10)	15.00	40.00
STATED ODDS 1:24 HOBBY		
RR1 Kane	1.50	4.00
RR2 Kane vs The Undertaker	2.00	5.00
RR3 Triple H vs Cactus Jack	2.50	6.00
RR4 Vince McMahon	1.50	4.00
RR5 Stone Cold	2.50	6.00
RR6 Hollywood Hulk Hogan	4.00	10.00
RR7 Ric Flair	2.00	5.00
RR8 The Rock vs Mankind	2.50	6.00
RR9 Shawn Michaels	2.50	6.00
RR10 Mae Young	1.00	2.50

2003 Fleer WWE WrestleMania XIX

COMPLETE SET (90)	12.50	30.00
UNOPENED BOX (24 PACKS)		
UNOPENED PACK (5 CARDS)		
1 Scott Steiner	.60	1.50
2 Scotty 2 Hotty	.20	.50
3 Albert	.12	.30
4 Kurt Angle	.50	1.25
5 Batista	.50	1.25
6 Chris Benoit	.30	.75
7 Big Show	.50	1.25
8 Billy	.20	.50
9 Eric Bischoff	.20	.50
10 Bradshaw	.30	.75
11 D'Lo Brown	.20	.50
12 John Cena	.75	2.00
13 Christian	.30	.75
14 Chuck	.20	.50
15 Tommy Dreamer	.12	.30
16 Bubba Ray Dudley	.20	.50
17 Spike Dudley	.20	.50
18 D-Von	.20	.50
19 Edge	.50	1.25
20 Ron Simmons	.20	.50
21 Ric Flair	.60	1.50
22 Funaki	.20	.50
23 Goldust	.12	.30
24 Crash	.12	.30
25 Eddie Guerrero	.60	1.50
26 Triple H	.75	2.00
27 Jeff Hardy	.30	.75
28 Matt Hardy	.30	.75
29 Hollywood Hulk Hogan	.75	2.00
30 The Hurricane	.12	.30
31 Chris Jericho	.30	.75
32 Kane	.50	1.25
33 Billy Kidman	.12	.30
34 Jerry Lawler	.30	.75
35 Brock Lesnar	1.25	3.00
36 Mark Henry	.20	.50
37 Maven	.12	.30
38 Godfather	.12	.30
39 Johnny Stamboli RC	.12	.30
40 Shawn Michaels	.75	2.00
41 Rey Mysterio	.30	.75
42 Kevin Nash	.60	1.50
43 Chris Nowinski	.12	.30
44 Randy Orton	.30	.75
45 Raven	.30	.75
46 William Regal	.30	.75
47 Steven Richards	.20	.50
48 Rico	.12	.30
49 Rikishi	.30	.75
50 The Rock	.75	2.00
51 Jim Ross	.20	.50
52 Al Snow	.12	.30
53 Jamie Noble	.12	.30
54 Lance Storm	.12	.30
55 Booker T	.50	1.25
56 Tajiri	.12	.30
57 Tazz	.20	.50
58 Test	.20	.50
59 Undertaker	.60	1.50
60 Rob Van Dam	.50	1.25
61 Lilian Garcia RC	1.50	4.00
62 Dawn Marie	.60	1.50
63 Trish Stratus	1.25	3.00
64 Jackie	.50	1.25
65 Victoria	.60	1.50
66 Stephanie	.60	1.50
67 Torrie Wilson	1.25	3.00
68 Stacy Keibler	1.25	3.00
69 Nidia	.30	.75
70 Ivory	.50	1.25
71 Terri	.60	1.50
72 Jacqueline	.30	.75
73 Jazz	.20	.50
74 Lita	.75	2.00
75 Molly	.60	1.50
76 Undertaker MM	.60	1.50
77 Kane MM	.50	1.25
78 Hollywood Hulk Hogan MM	.75	2.00
79 The Rock MM	.75	2.00
80 Triple H MM	.75	2.00
81 Kurt Angle MM	.50	1.25
82 Chris Jericho MM	.30	.75
83 Trish Stratus MM	1.25	3.00
84 Shawn Michaels MM	.75	2.00
85 Ivory MM	.50	1.25
86 Lita MM	.75	2.00
87 Jeff Hardy MM	.30	.75
88 Ric Flair MM	.60	1.50
89 Rikishi MM	.30	.75
90 Stone Cold Steve Austin MM	.75	2.00

2003 Fleer WWE WrestleMania XIX Diva Las Vegas

COMPLETE SET (2)		
NNO Dawn Marie/1350	8.00	20.00
NNO Torrie Wilson/150	20.00	50.00

2003 Fleer WWE WrestleMania XIX Flashbacks

COMPLETE SET (6)	30.00	60.00
STATED ODDS 1:48 HOBBY		
NNO Chris Jericho	4.00	10.00
NNO Hollywood Hulk Hogan	12.00	30.00
NNO Kurt Angle	6.00	15.00
NNO Stone Cold Steve Austin	6.00	15.00
NNO Triple H	10.00	25.00
NNO Undertaker	10.00	25.00

2003 Fleer WWE WrestleMania XIX Mat Finish

COMPLETE SET (10)	40.00	80.00
STATED ODDS 1:24 HOBBY		
NNO Brock Lesnar	6.00	15.00
NNO Edge	5.00	12.00
NNO The Hurricane	4.00	10.00
NNO Kurt Angle	5.00	12.00
NNO Rob Van Dam	4.00	10.00
NNO The Rock	6.00	15.00
NNO Stone Cold Steve Austin	6.00	15.00
NNO Triple H	5.00	12.00
NNO Trish Stratus	6.00	15.00
NNO Undertaker	5.00	12.00

2003 Fleer WWE WrestleMania XIX Title Shots

COMPLETE SET (7)	50.00	100.00
STATED ODDS 1:48 HOBBY		
NNO Brock Lesnar	10.00	25.00
NNO Kane	6.00	15.00
NNO Kurt Angle	8.00	20.00
NNO Rob Van Dam	6.00	15.00
NNO The Rock	12.00	30.00
NNO Triple H	8.00	20.00
NNO Undertaker	8.00	20.00

2004 Fleer WWE WrestleMania XX

COMPLETE SET (84)	10.00	25.00
UNOPENED BOX (24 PACKS)		
UNOPENED PACK (5 CARDS)		
*GOLD: .75X TO 2X BASIC CARDS		
1 Batista	.50	1.25
2 A-Train	.12	.30
3 Chris Jericho	.30	.75
4 Bill DeMott	.12	.30
5 Goldberg	1.00	2.50
6 Undertaker	.60	1.50
7 Kevin Nash	.60	1.50
8 Eddie Guerrero	.60	1.50
9 Mark Henry	.20	.50
10 John Cena	.75	2.00
11 Ric Flair	.60	1.50
12 Shannon Moore	.12	.30
13 Scott Steiner	.60	1.50
14 Brock Lesnar	1.25	3.00
15 Shawn Michaels	.75	2.00
16 Basham Brothers	.12	.30
17 Mark Jindrak & Garrison Cade	.12	.30
18 Chavo Guerrero	.20	.50
19 Eric Bischoff	.20	.50
20 Ultimo Dragon	.12	.30
21 Triple H	.75	2.00
22 The World's Greatest Tag Team	.12	.30
23 La Resistance	.12	.30
24 Rhyno	.50	1.25
25 Rico	.12	.30
26 Edge	.50	1.25
27 Steven Richards	.20	.50
28 Jerry The King Lawler	.30	.75
29 Vince McMahon	.50	1.25
30 Linda McMahon	.20	.50
31 Stephanie McMahon	.60	1.50
32 Shane McMahon	.30	.75
33 Jim Ross	.20	.50
34 Chris Nowinski	.12	.30
35 Tazz	.20	.50
36 Maven	.12	.30
37 Sean O'Haire RC	.12	.30
38 Dudley Boyz	.20	.50
39 The Hurricane		
40 Rey Mysterio	.30	.75
41 Test	.20	.50
42 Tajiri	.12	.30
43 Stone Cold Steve Austin	.75	2.00
44 Chris Benoit	.30	.75
45 The Rock	.75	2.00
46 APA	.30	.75
47 Rosey	.12	.30
48 Rodney Mack RC	.12	.30
49 Matt Hardy	.30	.75
50 Randy Orton	.30	.75
51 Kurt Angle	.50	1.25
52 Lance Storm	.12	.30
53 FBI		
54 Kane	.50	1.25
55 Billy Kidman	.12	.30
56 Christian	.40	1.00
57 Big Show	.50	1.25
58 Booker T	.50	1.25
59 Sable RD	.75	2.00
60 Lita RD	.75	2.00
61 Ivory RD	.50	1.25
62 Stacy Keibler RD	1.25	3.00
63 Molly RD	.60	1.50
64 Torrie Wilson RD	1.25	3.00
65 Terri RD	.60	1.50
66 Shaniqua RD RC	.30	.75
67 Gail Kim RC	.50	1.25
68 Miss Jackie RD	.50	1.25
69 Victoria RD	.60	1.50
70 Jazz RD	.30	.75
71 Nidia RD	.30	.75
72 Dawn Marie RD	.30	.75
73 Jacqueline RD	.40	1.00
74 Trish Stratus RD	1.25	3.00
75 Ric Flair MM	.60	1.50
76 Shawn Michaels MM	.75	2.00
77 Shawn Michaels MM	.75	2.00
78 Undertaker MM	.60	1.50
79 Stone Cold Steve Austin MM	.75	2.00
80 The Rock MM	.75	2.00
81 Triple H MM	.75	2.00
82 Steve Austin & The Rock MM	.75	2.00
83 Triple H MM	.75	2.00
84 Brock Lesnar MM	1.25	3.00

2004 Fleer WWE WrestleMania XX Champions and Contenders

COMPLETE SET (17)	8.00	20.00
STATED ODDS 1:4 HOBBY AND RETAIL		
1 Kurt Angle	1.50	4.00
Brock Lesnar		
2 Steve Austin	2.00	5.00
The Rock		
3 Trish Stratus	1.50	4.00
Jazz		
4 Triple H	1.00	2.50
Booker T		
5 Kane	.60	1.50
Big Show		
6 Eddie Guerrero	.75	2.00
Test		
7 Undertaker	.75	2.00
Ric Flair		
8 Edge & Christian	.60	1.50
Dudley Boyz		
9 Jazz	1.00	2.50
Lita		
10 Triple H	1.00	2.50
The Rock		
11 Shane McMahon	.60	1.50
Vince McMahon		
12 Chris Benoit	.40	1.00
Chris Jericho		
13 Rob Van Dam	.60	1.50
William Regal		
14 Trish Stratus	1.50	4.00
Victoria		
15 Matt Hardy	.40	1.00
Rey Mysterio		
16 Steve Austin	1.00	2.50
Shawn Michaels		
17 Triple H	1.00	2.50
Chris Jericho		

2004 Fleer WWE WrestleMania XX Champions and Contenders Dual Memorabilia

STATED ODDS 1:144 HOBBY		
CCDJ/L Jazz	6.00	12.00
Lita		
CCDK/BS Kane	6.00	12.00
Big Show		
CCDSA/R Steve Austin	10.00	20.00
The Rock		
CCDTS/J Trish Stratus	10.00	20.00
Jazz		
CCDCB/CJ Chris Benoit	5.00	10.00
Chris Jericho		
CCDKA/BL Kurt Angle	7.50	15.00
Brock Lesnar		
CCDMH/RM Matt Hardy	6.00	12.00
Rey Mysterio		
CCDSA/SM Steve Austin	7.50	15.00
Shawn Michaels		
CCDTH/BT Triple H	6.00	12.00
Booker T		
CCDTH/CJ Triple H	6.00	12.00
Chris Jericho		

2004 Fleer WWE WrestleMania XX Champions and Contenders Memorabilia

STATED ODDS 1:18 HOBBY		
CCSJ Jazz	3.00	8.00
CCSK Kane	4.00	10.00
CCSL Lita	5.00	12.00
CCSR The Rock	6.00	15.00
CCST Test	3.00	8.00
CCSU Undertaker	5.00	12.00
CCSBL Brock Lesnar	6.00	15.00
CCSBT Booker T	3.00	8.00
CCSCB Chris Benoit	3.00	8.00
CCSCJ Chris Jericho	3.00	8.00
CCSKA Kurt Angle	4.00	10.00
CCSMH Matt Hardy	5.00	12.00
CCSSA Stone Cold Steve Austin	6.00	15.00
CCSSM Shawn Michaels	5.00	12.00
CCSTH Triple H	5.00	12.00
CCSTS Trish Stratus	6.00	15.00
CCSRVD Rob Van Dam	3.00	8.00

2004 Fleer WWE WrestleMania XX Road to WrestleMania

COMPLETE SET (10)	20.00	50.00
STATED ODDS 1:24 HOBBY AND RETAIL		
1 Shawn Michaels	3.00	8.00
2 Trish Stratus	5.00	12.00
3 Brock Lesnar	5.00	12.00
4 Stone Cold Steve Austin	3.00	8.00
5 Undertaker	2.50	6.00
6 Scott Steiner	2.50	6.00
7 Lita	3.00	8.00
8 Triple H	3.00	8.00
9 The Rock	3.00	8.00
10 Kurt Angle	2.00	5.00

2004 Fleer WWE WrestleMania XX To the Mat Memorabilia

STATED ODDS 1:48 HOBBY		
1 Lita	6.00	15.00
2 Stacy Keibler	8.00	20.00
3 Molly	4.00	10.00
4 Torrie Wilson	8.00	20.00
5 Gail Kim	4.00	10.00
6 Victoria	5.00	12.00
7 Miss Jackie	5.00	12.00
8 Trish Stratus	8.00	20.00
9 Sable	6.00	15.00
10 Ivory	5.00	12.00

2004 Fleer WWE WrestleMania XX To the Mat Memorabilia Autographs

STATED PRINT RUN 50 SER.#'d SETS		
TTML Lita	50.00	100.00
TTMS Sable	30.00	75.00
TTMSK Stacy Keibler	60.00	120.00
TTMTS Trish Stratus	75.00	150.00
TTMTW Torrie Wilson	30.00	75.00

2002 Fleer WWF All Access

COMPLETE SET (100)	8.00	20.00
UNOPENED BOX (24 PACKS)		
UNOPENED PACK (8 CARDS)		
16 The Rock	2.00	5.00
1 Justin Credible	.12	.30
2 Shane McMahon	.30	.75
3 Tajiri	.20	.50
4 Jerry Lynn	.12	.30
5 Christian	.30	.75
6 Haku	.12	.30
7 Kurt Angle	.50	1.25
8 Albert	.12	.30
9 Chris Jericho	.30	.75
10 Jeff Hardy	.30	.75
11 Triple H	.75	2.00
12 The One Billy Gunn	.20	.50
13 Booker T	.50	1.25
14 Funaki	.20	.50
15 Chris Benoit	.30	.75
17 Bradshaw	.30	.75
18 Stephanie McMahon-Helmsley	2.00	5.00
19 Crash Holly	.12	.30
20 Rhyno	.30	.75
21 Faarooq	.12	.30

22 Al Snow	.20	.50
23 Hardcore Holly	.20	.50
24 Rikishi	.30	.75
25 Rob Van Dam RC	.50	1.25
26 X-Pac	.20	.50
27 D-Von Dudley	.20	.50
28 Kane	.50	1.25
29 Spike Dudley	.20	.50
30 William Regal	.20	.50
31 Taka Michinoku	.12	.30
32 Mick Foley	.50	1.25
33 Undertaker	.60	1.50
34 Edge	.50	1.25
35 Stone Cold Steve Austin	.75	2.00
36 Jim Ross	.20	.50
37 Bubba Ray Dudley	.20	.50
38 Steve Blackman	.12	.30
39 Test	.20	.50
40 Molly Holly	.30	.75
41 Vince Mcmahon	.50	1.25
42 Stacy Keibler RC	1.25	3.00
43 Torrie Wilson RC	1.25	3.00
44 Perry Saturn	.12	.30
45 Raven	.20	.50
46 Scotty 2 Hotty	.20	.50
47 Big Show	.50	1.25
48 Matt Hardy	.30	.75
49 Tazz	.20	.50
50 The Hurricane RC	.20	.50
51 Kane OTM	.50	1.25
52 Mick Foley OTM	.50	1.25
53 Lita OTM	.75	2.00
54 Justin Credible OTM	.12	.30
55 Big Show OTM	.50	1.25
56 Chris Benoit OTM	.30	.75
57 Stone Cold OTM	.75	2.00
58 Edge OTM	.50	1.25
59 Trish Stratus OTM	2.50	6.00
60 Faarooq OTM	.12	.30
61 Linda McMahon OTM	.20	.50
62 Matt Hardy OTM	.30	.75
63 Diamond Dallas Page OTM	.20	.50
64 The Hurricane OTM	.20	.50
65 Kurt Angle OTM	.50	1.25
66 Ric Flair OTM	.60	1.50
67 Undertaker OTM	.60	1.50
68 Tajiri OTM	.20	.50
69 Vince McMahon OTM	.50	1.25
70 Chris Jericho OTM	.30	.75
71 Triple H OTM	.75	2.00
72 Tazz OTM	.20	.50
73 Rob Van Dam OTM	.50	1.25
74 Sgt. Slaughter OTM	.30	.75
75 The Rock OTM	.75	2.00
76 Jim Ross OTM	.20	.50
77 Bradshaw OTM	.30	.75
78 Matt Hardy OTM	.30	.75
79 Perry Saturn OTM	.12	.30
80 X-Pac OTM	.20	.50
81 Maven RR RC	.12	.30
82 Molly Holly RR	.30	.75
83 Big Show RR	.50	1.25
84 Edge RR	.50	1.25
85 Stone Cold Steve Austin RR	.75	2.00
86 Vince McMahon RR	.50	1.25
87 Jeff Hardy RR	.30	.75
88 Kane RR	.50	1.25
89 Lita RR	.75	2.00
90 Ivory RR	.50	1.25
91 Kurt Angle RR	.50	1.25
92 Triple H RR	.75	2.00
93 Rob Van Dam RR	.50	1.25
94 Trish Stratus RR	1.25	3.00
95 Nidia RR RC	.30	.75
96 Matt Hardy RR	.30	.75
97 Christian RR	.30	.75
98 Mick Foley RR	.50	1.25
99 The Rock RR	.75	2.00
100 Undertaker RR	.60	1.50

2002 Fleer WWF All Access All Access Memorabilia

STATED ODDS 1:15

AAMF Funaki	3.00	8.00
AAMH The Hurricane SP		
AAMK Kane	12.00	30.00
AAMU Undertaker	20.00	50.00
AAMA Stone Cold Steve Austin	12.00	30.00
AAMJH Jeff Hardy	5.00	12.00
AAMKA Kurt Angle		
AAMMH Molly Holly	5.00	12.00
AAMSH Scotty 2 Hotty	4.00	10.00
AAMSK Stacy Keibler	15.00	40.00
AAMT1 Tajiri	3.00	8.00
AAMT2 Tazz	3.00	8.00
AAMTH Triple H	6.00	15.00
AAMTW Torrie Wilson	8.00	20.00
AAMDVD D-Von Dudley	5.00	12.00
AAMRVD Rob Van Dam	4.00	10.00

2002 Fleer WWF All Access Famous Rides

COMPLETE SET (12)	5.00	12.00
STATED ODDS 1:6		
FR1 Diamond Dallas Page's Pink Cadillac	.30	.75
FR2 Stone Cold's Truck	1.25	3.00
FR3 The Rock's Limo	1.25	3.00
FR4 D-Generation X's Tank Jeep	.30	.75
FR5 Stone Cold Destroys Vince's Vette	1.25	3.00
FR6 Vince McMahon's Jet	.75	2.00
FR7 Big Show's Purple Car	.75	2.00
FR8 Kurt Angle's Scooter	.75	2.00
FR9 Jeff Hardy's Motorcycle	.50	1.25
FR10 Stone Cold's 18-Wheeler	1.25	3.00
FR11 D-Generation X's Bus	.30	.75
FR12 Al Snow's Lil' Racecar	.30	.75

2002 Fleer WWF All Access Match Makers

COMPLETE SET (15)	6.00	15.00
STATED ODDS 1:6		
MM1 Triple H & Stephanie	1.00	2.50
MM2 Kane & Undertaker	.75	2.00
MM3 Debra & Stone Cold	1.00	2.50
MM4 Dudley Boyz	.25	.60
MM5 The Rock & Mick Foley	1.00	2.50
MM6 Edge & Christian	.60	1.50
MM7 Stephanie & Chris Jericho	.75	2.00
MM8 Kurt Angle & Triple H	1.00	2.50
MM9 The Rock & Stone Cold	1.00	2.50
MM10 Kaientai	.25	.60
MM11 Benoit & Jericho	.40	1.00
MM12 Stone Cold & Undertaker	1.00	2.50
MM13 Kurt Angle & The Rock	1.00	2.50
MM14 Matt Hardy, Lita & Jeff Hardy	1.00	2.50
MM15 Mr. McMahon & Stone Cold	1.00	2.50

2002 Fleer WWF All Access Match Makers Memorabilia

STATED ODDS 1:95

MMDB Dudley Boyz	15.00	40.00
MMEC Edge & Christian	12.00	30.00
MMKU Kane & Undertaker	10.00	25.00
MMRKA Kurt Angle & The Rock	12.00	30.00
MMRMF The Rock & Mick Foley	12.00	30.00
MMRSA The Rock & Stone Cold	15.00	40.00
MMSAU Stone Cold & Undertaker	12.00	30.00

2002 Fleer WWF All Access Off the Mat Autographs

RANDOMLY INSERTED INTO PACKS

NNO The Hurricane	12.00	30.00
NNO Jim Ross	30.00	75.00
NNO Lita	50.00	100.00
NNO Rob Van Dam	25.00	60.00
NNO Stacy Keibler	100.00	200.00
NNO Torrie Wilson	30.00	80.00
NNO Triple H	250.00	500.00
NNO Trish Stratus	60.00	120.00

2002 Fleer WWF All Access Pay-Per-View Posters

COMPLETE SET (8)	15.00	40.00
STATED ODDS 1:33		
PPV1 Backlash	3.00	8.00
PPV2 Invasion	2.00	5.00
PPV3 Judgment Day	3.00	8.00
PPV4 No Mercy	2.00	5.00
PPV5 No Way Out	2.00	5.00
PPV6 SummerSlam	3.00	8.00
PPV7 Unforgiven	3.00	8.00
PPV8 Vengeance	3.00	8.00
PPV9 WrestleMania X-7	3.00	8.00
PPV10 Survivor Series	5.00	12.00

2001 Fleer WWF Championship Clash

COMPLETE SET (80)	8.00	20.00
UNOPENED BOX (24 PACKS)		
UNOPENED PACK (5 CARDS)		
1 The Rock	4.00	10.00
2 K-Kwik RC	.12	.30
3 Steve Blackman	.12	.30
4 Eddie Guerrero	.50	1.25
5 Jerry Lynn RC	.12	.30
6 Christian	.30	.75
7 Kane	.50	1.25
8 Tazz	.20	.50
9 Stone Cold Steve Austin	.75	2.00
10 Crash Holly RC	.12	.30
11 Matt Hardy RC	.30	.75
12 Undertaker	.60	1.50
13 Al Snow	.20	.50
14 Tajiri RC	.12	.30
15 Scotty 2 Hotty RC	.20	.50
16 Dean Malenko	.20	.50
17 Raven	.12	.30
18 Big Show	.50	1.25
19 Jeff Hardy RC	.30	.75
20 Spike Dudley RC	.20	.50
21 Chris Jericho	.30	.75
22 Kurt Angle	.50	1.25
23 Test	.20	.50
24 Chris Benoit	.30	.75
25 William Regal	.20	.50
26 Rikishi	.20	.50
27 D-Von Dudley RC	.20	.50
28 Mick Foley	.50	1.25
29 Triple H	.75	2.00
30 Albert	.12	.30
31 Haku	.12	.30
32 Perry Saturn	.12	.30
33 The One Billy Gunn	.12	.30
34 Hardcore Holly	.20	.50
35 Shane McMahon	.30	.75
36 Edge	.50	1.25
37 Rhyno RC	.20	.50
38 Bubba Ray Dudley RC	.20	.50
39 Justin Credible RC	.12	.30
40 X-Pac	.20	.50
41 The Rock PC	2.50	6.00
42 K-Kwik PC	.12	.30
43 Steve Blackman PC	.12	.30
44 Eddie Guerrero PC	.50	1.25
45 Jerry Lynn PC	.12	.30
46 Christian PC	.30	.75
47 Kane PC	.50	1.25
48 Tazz PC	.20	.50
49 Stone Cold Steve Austin PC	.75	2.00
50 Crash Holly PC	.12	.30
51 Matt Hardy PC	.30	.75
52 Undertaker PC	.60	1.50
53 Al Snow PC	.20	.50
54 Tajiri PC	.12	.30
55 Scotty 2 Hotty PC	.20	.50
56 Dean Malenko PC	.20	.50
57 Raven PC	.12	.30
58 Big Show PC	.50	1.25
59 Jeff Hardy PC	.30	.75
60 Spike Dudley PC	.20	.50
61 Chris Jericho PC	.30	.75
62 Kurt Angle PC	.50	1.25
63 Test PC	.20	.50
64 Chris Benoit PC	.30	.75
65 William Regal PC	.20	.50
66 Rikishi PC	.20	.50
67 D-Von Dudley PC	.20	.50
68 Mick Foley PC	.50	1.25
69 Triple H PC	.75	2.00
70 Albert PC	.12	.30
71 Haku PC	.12	.30
72 Perry Saturn PC	.12	.30
73 The One Billy Gunn PC	.12	.30
74 Hardcore Holly PC	.20	.50
75 Shane McMahon PC	.30	.75
76 Edge PC	.50	1.25
77 Rhyno PC	.20	.50
78 Bubba Ray Dudley PC	.20	.50
79 Justin Credible PC	.12	.30
80 X-Pac PC	.20	.50

2001 Fleer WWF Championship Clash Divas Private Collection

STATED ODDS 1:30 HOBBY; 1:576 RETAIL

DPDE Debra	10.00	25.00
Skirt		
DPTO Tori	6.00	15.00

Skirt/Tights		
DPCIV Ivory	8.00	20.00
Scarf		
DPCMH Molly Holly	4.00	10.00
Halter Top		
DPCTE Terri	7.50	15.00
Dress		
DPCLBT Lita	25.00	50.00
Bikini Top		
DPCLTS Lita	10.00	25.00
T-Shirt		

2001 Fleer WWF Championship Clash Divas Private Signing

COMPLETE SET (8)	175.00	350.00
STATED ODDS 1:120		
CARDS 1-4 AVAIL.IN CHAMP.CLASH		
CARDS 5-8 AVAIL.IN ULT DIVA COL.		
HOBBY EXCLUSIVE		
DPSD Debra	100.00	200.00
DPSI Ivory	30.00	75.00
DPSJ Jacqueline	20.00	40.00
DPSL Lita	25.00	50.00
DPSMH Molly Holly	75.00	150.00
DPSSM Stephanie McMahon-Helmsley	200.00	400.00
DPSTE Terri	25.00	50.00
DPSTS Trish Stratus	150.00	300.00

2001 Fleer WWF Championship Clash Females

COMPLETE SET (9)	12.00	30.00
STATED ODDS 1:4 HOBBY; 1:7 RETAIL		
WF1 Ivory	.75	2.00
WF2 Trish Stratus	6.00	15.00
WF3 Lita	1.25	3.00
WF4 Molly Holly	4.00	10.00
WF5 Debra	3.00	8.00
WF6 Stephanie McMahon	5.00	12.00
WF7 Terri	1.00	2.50
WF8 Jacqueline	.75	2.00
WF9 Tori	1.00	2.50

2001 Fleer WWF Championship Clash Main Event Memorabilia

COMPLETE SET (9)	25.00	60.00
STATED ODDS 1:24 HOBBY; 1:144 RETAIL		
SA Steve Austin	5.00	12.00
Ring Skirt		
BKR Big Show vs. Kane vs. Raven	3.00	8.00
Ring Mat		
EGT Test vs. Eddie Guerrero	2.50	6.00
Ring Mat		
CBCJ Chris Benoit vs. Chris Jericho	12.00	30.00
Ring Skirt		
CJWR William Regal vs. Chris Jericho	3.00	8.00
Ring Mat		
KATH Triple H vs. Kurt Angle	6.00	15.00
Ring Skirt		
SATR Steve Austin vs. The Rock	5.00	12.00
Ring Mat		
SMKA Shane McMahon vs. Kurt Angle	3.00	8.00
Garbage Can SP		
SAKACJ Kurt Angle vs. Chris Jericho vs. Steve Austin	4.00	10.00
Steel Chair SP		

2001 Fleer WWF Championship Clash Piece of the Champion

STATED ODDS 1:24 HOBBY; 1:576 RETAIL		
PCB Bradshaw	10.00	20.00
T-Shirt		
PCCJ Chris Jericho	12.00	30.00
T-Shirt		
PCER Essa Rios	6.00	12.00
Pants		
PCFA Faarooq (spelled Faaroog)		
Knee Brace UER SP		
PCFN Funaki	6.00	12.00
T-Shirt		
PCJH Jeff Hardy	15.00	40.00
T-Shirt		
PCKA K. Angle	125.00	250.00
Gold Medal Strap SP		
PCKA2 Kurt Angle	15.00	30.00
T-Shirt		
PCMH Matt Hardy	15.00	30.00
T-Shirt		
PCSA Steve Austin	15.00	30.00
T-Shirt		
PCSH Scotty 2 Hotty	10.00	25.00
Pants		
PCTM Taka Michinoku	6.00	12.00
T-Shirt		
PCXP X- Pac	10.00	20.00
Bandana		

2002 Fleer WWF Divas Magazine Series 1

1 Lita	.40	1.00
2 Lita	.40	1.00
3 Lita	.40	1.00
4 Jacqueline	.20	.50
5 Jacqueline	.20	.50
6 Jacqueline	.20	.50
7 Torrie	.60	1.50
8 Torrie	.60	1.50
9 Torrie	.60	1.50

2002 Fleer WWF Divas Magazine Series 2

1 Trish	.60	1.50
2 Trish	.60	1.50
3 Trish	.60	1.50
4 Ivory	.20	.50
5 Ivory	.20	.50
6 Ivory	.20	.50
7 Terri	.30	.75
8 Terri	.30	.75
9 Terri	.30	.75

2002 Fleer WWF Divas Magazine Series 3

1 Stacy	.60	1.50
2 Stacy	.60	1.50
3 Stacy	.60	1.50
4 Sharmell	.20	.50
5 Sharmell	.20	.50
6 Sharmell	.20	.50
7 Molly	.20	.50
8 Molly	.20	.50
9 Molly	.20	.50

2001 Fleer WWF KB Toys Get Real

COMPLETE SET (18)	12.00	30.00
UNOPENED PACK (3 CARDS)	1.50	2.00
1 The Rock	2.50	6.00
2 Undertaker	2.50	6.00
3 Kane	1.25	3.00
4 Stone Cold Steve Austin	2.00	5.00
5 Kurt Angle	.75	2.00
6 Triple H	.75	2.00
7 Albert	.50	1.25
8 The Dudley Boyz	1.25	3.00
9 The Hardy Boyz	1.50	4.00
10 Lita	3.00	8.00
11 Edge	1.50	4.00
12 Christian	.60	1.50
13 Tazz	.50	1.25
14 Raven	.75	2.00
15 Chris Jericho	2.00	5.00
16 Jacqueline	.75	2.00
17 Ivory	.75	2.00
18 Trish Stratus	2.50	6.00

2001 Fleer WWF Raw Is War

COMPLETE SET (100)	8.00	20.00
UNOPENED BOX (24 PACKS)		
UNOPENED PACK (8 CARDS)		
1 Stone Cold Steve Austin	.75	2.00
2 Triple H	.75	2.00
3 Mick Foley	.50	1.25
4 Dean Malenko	.20	.50
5 Chris Jericho	.30	.75
6 Lita RC	6.00	15.00
7 Bubba Ray Dudley RC	.20	.50
8 JR	.20	.50
9 Bull Buchanan RC	.12	.30
10 Kane	.50	1.25
11 Gerald Brisco	.20	.50
12 The Goodfather	.20	.50
13 Matt Hardy RC	.30	.75
14 Rikishi	.20	.50
15 Vince McMahon	.50	1.25
16 Ivory	.50	1.25
17 Trish Stratus RC	3.00	8.00
18 Test	.20	.50
19 Raven	.12	.30
20 Albert	.12	.30
21 Val Venis	.20	.50
22 Tazz	.20	.50
23 Chyna	.50	1.25
24 Molly Holly RC	.50	1.25
25 Christian	.30	.75
26 Edge	.50	1.25
27 William Regal	.20	.50
28 Crash Holly RC	.12	.30
29 Jeff Hardy RC	.30	.75
30 Kurt Angle	.50	1.25
31 K-Kwik RC	.12	.30
32 Bradshaw	.30	.75
33 Terri RC	.60	1.50
34 Bob Hardcore Holly	.20	.50
35 Grandmaster Sexay RC		
36 Perry Saturn	.12	.30
37 D-Von Dudley RC	.20	.50
38 The One Billy Gunn	.12	.30
39 The Rock	2.50	6.00
40 Eddie Guererro	.50	1.25
41 Steven Richards RC	.20	.50
42 Pat Patterson	.20	.50
43 Chris Benoit	.30	.75
44 Big Show	.50	1.25
45 Faarooq	.12	.30
46 Steve Blackman	.12	.30
47 Undertaker	.60	1.50
48 Jacqueline	.50	1.25
49 Scotty Too Hotty RC	.20	.50
50 Chris Jericho WZ	.30	.75
51 APA WZ	.30	.75
52 Billy Gunn vs. Val Venis WZ	.20	.50
53 Taka Michinoku WZ	.12	.30
54 Triple H vs.The Rock WZ	.75	2.00
55 Edge & Christian WZ	.50	1.25
56 Big Show WZ	.50	1.25
57 Hardy Boyz vs. Edge & Christian WZ	.50	1.25
58 Debra WZ	.60	1.50
59 Kurt Angle WZ	.50	1.25
60 Kaientai WZ	.12	.30
61 Rock & Undertaker vs. Edge & Christian WZ	.75	2.00
62 Right to Censor WZ	.50	1.25
63 Undertaker WZ	.60	1.50
64 Billy Gunn with Chyna WZ	.50	1.25
65 Dudleyz vs. Edge & Christian WZ	.50	1.25
66 Lita vs. Trish Stratus WZ	1.25	3.00
67 The Rock WZ	2.50	6.00
68 Stephanie McMahon-Helmsley WZ RC	3.00	8.00
69 Dudley Boyz WZ	.20	.50
70 Triple H WZ	.75	2.00
71 Steve Austin vs. Vince McMahon WZ	2.50	6.00
72 Shane McMahon WZ	.30	.75
73 Perry Saturn with Terri WZ	.60	1.50
74 Too Cool WZ	.20	.50
75 Triple H WZ	.50	1.25
76 Hardy Boyz WZ	2.00	5.00
77 Stone Cold Steve Austin WZ	2.50	6.00
78 Undertaker vs. Kane WZ	.60	1.50
79 Hardcore/Molly/Crash Holly WZ	.50	1.25
80 William Regal WZ	.20	.50
81 Steve Austin vs. Kurt Angle WZ	.75	2.00
82 Vince McMahon WZ	.50	1.25
83 Right to Censor vs. Hardy Boyz WZ	.30	.75
84 Kane WZ	.50	1.25
85 The Rock vs. Undertaker SE	.60	1.50
86 Steve Austin vs. William Regal SE	.60	1.50
87 Steve Austin vs. Chris Benoit SE	.60	1.50
88 Steve Austin vs. Rikishi vs. Angle SE	.60	1.50
89 Chris Jericho vs. The Rock SE	.60	1.50
90 Steve Austin vs. Kurt Angle SE	.60	1.50
91 Steve Austin vs. Edge & Christian & Angle SE	.60	1.50
92 Triple H vs. Kurt Angle SE	.60	1.50
93 Undertaker vs. The Rock SE	.60	1.50
94 Chris Jericho vs. Benoit SE	.30	.75
95 Rock vs. HHH vs. Kurt Angle SE	.60	1.50
96 Shane McMahon vs. The Rock SE	.60	1.50
97 Triple H vs. The Rock SE	.60	1.50
98 The Rock vs. Kane SE	.60	1.50
99 Lita vs. Stephanie SE	.60	1.50
100 The Rock vs. Benoit SE	.60	1.50

2001 Fleer WWF Raw Is War Booty

STATED ODDS 1:26 HOBBY; 1:134 RETAIL		
NNO Chris Benoit	10.00	25.00
Ring Skirt		
NNO Chris Jericho	10.00	25.00

Ring Skirt
NNO Dudley Boyz 8.00 20.00
Ring Skirt
NNO Edge & Christian 10.00 25.00
Ring Skirt
NNO Hardy Boyz 10.00 25.00
Ring Mat
NNO Kane 6.00 15.00
Ring Skirt
NNO Kurt Angle 12.00 30.00
T-Shirt
NNO Mick Foley 10.00 25.00
Ring Mat
NNO The One Billy Gunn 12.00 30.00
Ring Trunks
NNO The Rock 20.00 50.00
Ring Mat
NNO Stone Cold Steve Austin 20.00 50.00
Ring Mat
NNO Triple H 10.00 25.00
Ring Mat
NNO Undertaker 10.00 25.00
Ring Mat
NNO Vince McMahon 8.00 20.00
Ring Mat
NNO William Regal 6.00 15.00
Ring Skirt

2001 Fleer WWF Raw Is War Booty Autographs

STATED ODDS 1:354
EXCH.EXPIRATION: 07/01/2002

NNO Christian 20.00 50.00
NNO Edge 30.00 75.00
NNO Triple H
NNO Undertaker 400.00 800.00

2001 Fleer WWF Raw Is War Famous Nicknames

COMPLETE SET (14) 25.00 60.00
STATED ODDS 1:15 HOBBY; 1:20 RETAIL

FN1 Chyna 3.00 8.00
FN2 Steve Austin 4.00 10.00
FN3 Kurt Angle 3.00 8.00
FN4 Billy Gunn 1.50 4.00
FN5 Triple H 3.00 8.00
FN6 Lita 5.00 12.00
FN7 Steve Blackman 1.50 4.00
FN8 The Rock 4.00 10.00
FN9 Shawn Michaels 3.00 8.00
FN10 Chris Jericho 3.00 8.00
FN11 Chris Benoit 2.50 6.00
FN12 Undertaker 3.00 8.00
FN13 Jim Ross 1.25 3.00
FN14 Eddie Guerrero 1.50 4.00

2001 Fleer WWF Raw Is War Femme Fatale

COMPLETE SET (20) 10.00 25.00
STATED ODDS 1:2 HOBBY AND RETAIL

FF1 Trish Stratus 2.50 6.00
FF2 Molly Holly .25 .60
FF3 Terri .40 1.00
FF4 Lita 2.00 5.00
FF5 Tori .30 .75
FF6 Trish Stratus 2.50 6.00
FF7 Molly Holly .25 .60
FF8 Terri .40 1.00
FF9 Lita 2.00 5.00
FF10 Tori .30 .75
FF11 Trish Stratus 2.50 6.00
FF12 Molly Holly .25 .60
FF13 Terri .40 1.00
FF14 Lita 2.00 5.00
FF15 Tori .30 .75
FF16 Trish Stratus 2.50 6.00
FF17 Molly Holly .25 .60
FF18 Terri .40 1.00
FF19 Lita 2.00 5.00
FF20 Tori .30 .75

2001 Fleer WWF Raw Is War Raw Is Jericho

COMPLETE SET (15) 4.00 10.00
STATED ODDS 1:2 HOBBY AND RETAIL

RJ1 The Rock .40 1.00
RJ2 Stone Cold Steve Austin .40 1.00
RJ3 Chris Benoit .40 1.00
RJ4 Kurt Angle .40 1.00
RJ5 Edge and Christian .40 1.00
RJ6 Kane .40 1.00
RJ7 Undertaker .40 1.00
RJ8 Chyna .40 1.00
RJ9 Triple H .40 1.00
RJ10 McMahon Family .40 1.00
RJ11 Dudley Boyz .40 1.00
RJ12 Hardy Boyz .40 1.00
RJ13 Divas .40 1.00
RJ14 Mick Foley .40 1.00
RJ15 Chris Jericho .40 1.00

2001 Fleer WWF Raw Is War TLC

COMPLETE SET (15) 10.00 25.00
STATED ODDS 1:5 HOBBY; 1:10 RETAIL

TLC1 Hardy Boyz vs. Dudley Boyz vs. Edge & Christian .60 1.50
TLC2 Hardy Boyz 1.25 3.00
TLC3 Dudley Boyz 1.25 3.00
TLC4 Edge & Christian 1.25 3.00
TLC5 Rock/Dudleyz vs. Angle/Edge/Christian .60 1.50
TLC6 Jericho/Dudleyz vs. Angle/Edge/Christian .60 1.50
TLC7 Bob Holly vs. Steve Blackman .60 1.50
TLC8 Triple H 1.25 3.00
TLC9 Stone Cold Steve Austin 1.50 4.00
TLC10 Kane 1.00 2.50
TLC11 Chris Jericho 1.25 3.00
TLC12 Kurt Angle 1.25 3.00
TLC13 Big Show 1.00 2.50
TLC14 Undertaker 1.25 3.00
TLC15 The Rock 1.50 4.00

2001 Fleer WWF The Ultimate Diva Collection

COMPLETE SET (100) 20.00 50.00
COMPLETE SET W/O SP (85) 10.00 25.00
UNOPENED BOX (24 PACKS)
UNOPENED PACK (8 CARDS)
*GOLD (1-85): 1X TO 2.5X BASIC CARDS
*GOLD SP (86-100): 2X TO 5X BASIC CARDS
HEDONISM STATED ODDS 1:4

1 Trish Stratus RC .60 1.50
2 Debra .30 .75
3 Ivory .25 .60
4 Jacqueline .25 .60
5 Lita RC .40 1.00
6 Molly Holly RC .25 .60
7 Terri RC .30 .75
8 Trish Stratus RC .60 1.50
9 Debra .30 .75
10 Ivory .25 .60
11 Jacqueline .25 .60
12 Lita RC .40 1.00
13 Molly Holly RC .25 .60
14 Debra .30 .75
15 Trish Stratus RC .60 1.50
16 Debra .30 .75
17 Ivory .25 .60
18 Jacqueline .25 .60
19 Lita RC .40 1.00
20 Molly Holly RC .25 .60
21 Terri RC .30 .75
22 Trish Stratus RC .60 1.50
23 Debra .30 .75
24 Ivory .25 .60
25 Jacqueline .25 .60
26 Lita RC .40 1.00
27 Molly Holly RC .25 .60
28 Terri RC .30 .75
29 Trish Stratus RC .60 1.50
30 Debra .30 .75
31 Ivory .25 .60
32 Jacqueline .25 .60
33 Lita RC .40 1.00
34 Molly Holly RC .25 .60
35 Terri RC .30 .75
36 Trish Stratus RC .60 1.50
37 Debra .30 .75
38 Ivory .25 .60
39 Jacqueline .25 .60
40 Lita RC .40 1.00
41 Molly Holly RC .25 .60
42 Terri RC .30 .75
43 Trish Stratus RC .60 1.50
44 Debra .30 .75
45 Ivory .25 .60
46 Jacqueline .25 .60
47 Lita RC .40 1.00
48 Molly Holly RC .25 .60
49 Terri RC .30 .75
50 Trish Stratus RC .60 1.50
51 Debra .30 .75
52 Ivory .25 .60
53 Jacqueline .25 .60
54 Lita RC .40 1.00
55 Molly Holly RC .25 .60
56 The Rock RP .60 1.50
57 Stone Cold Steve Austin RP .60 1.50
58 Triple H RP .60 1.50
59 Undertaker RP .50 1.25
60 APA RP .25 .60
61 The Hardy Boyz RP .25 .60
62 Dudley Boyz RP .15 .40
63 Chris Jericho RP .25 .60
64 Kurt Angle RP .40 1.00
65 Kane RP .40 1.00
66 Debra ITR .30 .75
67 Jacqueline ITR .25 .60
68 Lita ITR .40 1.00
69 Trish Stratus ITR .60 1.50
70 Lita ITR .40 1.00
71 Molly Holly ITR .25 .60
72 Jacqueline ITR .25 .60
73 Terri ITR .30 .75
74 Ivory ITR .25 .60
75 Debra ITR .30 .75
76 Molly Holly ITR .25 .60
77 Lita ITR .40 1.00
78 Ivory ITR .25 .60
79 Terri ITR .30 .75
80 Trish Stratus ITR .60 1.50
81 M.Holly/T.Stratus ITR .60 1.50
82 M.Holly/Jacqueline ITR .25 .60
83 Lita/T.Stratus ITR .60 1.50
84 M.Holly/Lita ITR .40 1.00
85 Terri/T.Stratus ITR .60 1.50
86 Debra HED SP .75 2.00
87 Terri HED SP .75 2.00
88 Lita HED SP 1.00 2.50
89 Trish Stratus HED SP 1.50 4.00
90 Jacqueline HED SP .60 1.50
91 Debra HED SP .75 2.00
92 Terri HED SP .75 2.00
93 Lita HED SP 1.00 2.50
94 Trish Stratus HED SP 1.50 4.00
95 Jacqueline HED SP .60 1.50
96 Debra HED SP .75 2.00
97 Terri HED SP .75 2.00
98 Lita HED SP 1.00 2.50
99 Trish Stratus HED SP 1.50 4.00
100 Jacqueline HED SP .60 1.50

2001 Fleer WWF The Ultimate Diva Collection The Bad and The Beautiful

COMPLETE SET (15) 10.00 20.00
STATED ODDS 1:4 HOBBY; 1:8 RETAIL

1 Trish Stratus 1.25 3.00
2 Jacqueline .50 1.25
3 Ivory .50 1.25
4 Molly Holly .50 1.25
5 Lita .75 2.00
6 Terri .60 1.50
7 Trish Stratus 1.25 3.00
8 Jacqueline .50 1.25
9 Debra .60 1.50
10 Ivory .50 1.25
11 Molly Holly .50 1.25
12 Debra .60 1.50
13 Terri .60 1.50
14 Lita .75 2.00
15 Trish Stratus 1.25 3.00

2001 Fleer WWF The Ultimate Diva Collection Diva Ink

COMPLETE SET (2) 150.00 300.00
STATED ODDS 1:104 HOBBY; 1:1,787 RETAIL
EXCH.EXPIRATION: 1/1/2003

NNO Debra 20.00 40.00
NNO Ivory 30.00 60.00
NNO Jacqueline 20.00 40.00
NNO Lita 30.00 60.00
NNO Molly Holly 20.00 40.00
NNO Terri 30.00 60.00
NNO Trish Stratus 40.00 80.00

2001 Fleer WWF The Ultimate Diva Collection Kiss and Tell

COMPLETE SET (12) 15.00 30.00

STATED ODDS 1:12 HOBBY; 1:20 RETAIL

1 Vince McMahon Trish Stratus	3.00	8.00
2 Kurt Angle Stephanie McMahon-Helmsley	1.50	4.00
3 Chris Jericho Terri	1.50	4.00
4 Stone Cold Steve Austin Debra	2.00	5.00
5 Triple H Stephanie McMahon-Helmsley	2.00	5.00
6 APA Jacqueline	1.25	3.00
7 Perry Saturn Terri	1.50	4.00
8 Undertaker Ivory	1.50	4.00
9 The Hardy Boyz Lita	2.00	5.00
10 The Rock Trish Stratus	3.00	8.00
11 Dudley Boyz Molly Holly	1.25	3.00
12 Kane Ivory	1.25	3.00

2001 Fleer WWF The Ultimate Diva Collection Matching Set

COMPLETE SET (8)	25.00	60.00
COMMON CARD (1-8)	4.00	10.00
SEMISTARS	5.00	12.00
UNLISTED STARS	6.00	15.00
NNO Debra/Stone Cold	8.00	20.00
NNO Jacqueline/APA	4.00	10.00
NNO Jacqueline/Bradshaw	5.00	12.00
NNO Lita/Jeff Hardy	6.00	15.00
NNO Lita/Matt Hardy	8.00	20.00
NNO Molly Holly/Spike Dudley	5.00	12.00
NNO Terri/Perry Saturn	6.00	15.00
NNO Trish Stratus/Big Show	6.00	15.00

2001 Fleer WWF The Ultimate Diva Collection National Assets

COMPLETE SET (15)	15.00	30.00

STATED ODDS 1:12 HOBBY; 1:20 RETAIL

1 Lita	1.50	4.00
2 Debra	1.25	3.00
3 Ivory	1.00	2.50
4 Terri	1.25	3.00
5 Trish Stratus	2.50	6.00
6 Terri	1.25	3.00
7 Molly Holly	1.00	2.50
8 Jacqueline	1.00	2.50
9 Debra	1.25	3.00
10 Molly Holly	1.00	2.50
11 Trish Stratus	2.50	6.00
12 Terri	1.25	3.00
13 Ivory	1.00	2.50
14 Jacqueline	1.00	2.50
15 Lita	1.50	4.00

2001 Fleer WWF The Ultimate Diva Collection Ring Accessories

COMPLETE SET (7)	20.00	50.00
COMMON CARD (1-7)	4.00	8.00
SEMISTARS	4.00	10.00
UNLISTED STARS	5.00	12.00
NNO Debra	4.00	8.00
NNO Ivory	5.00	12.00
NNO Jacqueline	4.00	10.00
NNO Lita	7.50	15.00
NNO Molly Holly	5.00	10.00
NNO Terri	5.00	12.00
NNO Trish Stratus	15.00	40.00

2001 Fleer WWF The Ultimate Diva Collection Signed with a Kiss

RANDOMLY INSERTED INTO PACKS
STATED PRINT RUN 50 SERIAL #'d SETS
EXCH.EXPIRATION: 1/1/2003

NNO Debra	30.00	75.00
NNO Ivory	20.00	50.00
NNO Jacqueline	15.00	40.00
NNO Lita	75.00	150.00
NNO Molly Holly	75.00	150.00
NNO Terri Runnels	15.00	40.00
NNO Trish Stratus	600.00	1200.00

2001 Fleer WWF WrestleMania

COMPLETE SET (100)	8.00	20.00

UNOPENED BOX (28 PACKS)
UNOPENED PACK (7 CARDS)
*CH GOLD: 1.2X TO 3X BASIC CARDS

1 The Rock	2.00	5.00
2 D-Von Dudley RC	.20	.50
3 Matt Hardy RC	.30	.75
4 Test	.20	.50
5 Raven	.12	.30
6 Chris Benoit	.30	.75
7 Jeff Hardy RC	.30	.75
8 Shane McMahon	.30	.75
9 Brooklyn Brawler	.12	.30
10 Gerald Brisco	.20	.50
11 Linda McMahon RC	.20	.50
12 Albert	.12	.30
13 Eddie Guerrero	.50	1.25
14 Mick Foley	.50	1.25
15 The Goodfather	.20	.50
16 Buh-Buh Ray Dudley RC	.20	.50
17 Grandmaster Sexay RC	.20	.50
18 Scotty 2 Hotty RC	.20	.50
19 William Regal	.20	.50
20 Big Boss Man	.20	.50
21 Edge	.50	1.25
22 Mideon	.12	.30
23 Al Snow	.20	.50
24 Stephanie McMahon-Helmsley RC	8.00	20.00
25 Dean Malenko	.20	.50
26 Tazz	.20	.50
27 Bull Buchanan RC	.12	.30
28 Hardcore Holly	.20	.50
29 Sgt. Slaughter	.30	.75
30 X-Pac	.20	.50
31 Christian	.30	.75
32 Jim JR Ross	.20	.50
33 Steve Blackman	.12	.30
34 Fabulous Moolah	.20	.50
35 Gangrel	.12	.30
36 Rikishi	.20	.50
37 Vince McMahon	.50	1.25
38 Essa Rios	.12	.30
39 Pat Patterson	.20	.50
40 Triple H	.75	2.00
41 K-Kwik RC	.12	.30
42 Crash Holly RC	.12	.30
43 Kane	.50	1.25
44 Steven Richards RC	.20	.50
45 Joey Abs RC	.12	.30
46 The One Billy Gunn	.12	.30
47 Faarooq	.12	.30
48 Undertaker	.60	1.50
49 Tiger Ali Singh	.12	.30
50 D'Lo Brown	.12	.30
51 Kurt Angle	.50	1.25
52 Stone Cold Steve Austin	.75	2.00
53 Chaz RC	.12	.30
54 Chris Jericho	.30	.75
55 Jerry The King Lawler	.20	.50
56 Mae Young RC	.20	.50
57 Bradshaw	.30	.75
58 Funaki RC	.12	.30
59 Perry Saturn	.12	.30
60 Val Venis	.20	.50
61 Tori DIVAS	.60	1.50
62 Debra DIVAS	.60	1.50
63 Chyna DIVAS	.50	1.25
64 Ivory DIVAS	.50	1.25
65 Jacqueline DIVAS	.50	1.25
66 The Kat DIVAS RC	.15	.40
67 Lita DIVAS RC	2.50	6.00
68 Trish Stratus DIVAS RC	3.00	8.00
69 Molly Holly DIVAS RC	.50	1.25
70 Terri DIVAS RC	.60	1.50
71 Edge & Christian TT	.50	1.25
72 Hardy Boyz TT	.30	.75
73 Dudley Boyz TT	.20	.50
74 T & A TT	.20	.50
75 Right to Censor TT	.20	.50
76 The Radicalz TT	.50	1.25
77 The Hollys TT	.20	.50
78 K-Kwik & Road Dogg TT	.12	.30
79 Lo Down TT	.12	.30
80 Too Cool TT	.20	.50
81 I Pity the Fool WR	.20	.50
82 Hulkamania Runs Wild WR	.60	1.50
83 Rage in the Cage WR	.60	1.50
84 A New Attendance Record WR	.12	.30
85 The Proud Chairman WR	.50	1.25
86 Brain Awakens Sleeping Giant WR	.40	1.00
87 Stars and Stripes Challenge WR	.12	.30
88 Don't Do It, Roddy WR	.30	.75
89 When in Rome WR	.20	.50
90 Megabucks vs. Megamaniacs WR	1.50	4.00
91 Good Friends, Better Enemies WR	.15	.40
92 Enter the Rattlesnake WR	.75	2.00
93 Dark Days Cometh WR	.60	1.50
94 Rock/Rikishi Early Years WR	.75	2.00
95 Hardcore Highlight WR	.12	.30
96 Rough Night for Charlie Hustle WR	.12	.30
97 The Stone Cold Age Begins WR	.75	2.00
98 Strike Two for the Hit King WR	.20	.50
99 The Rattlesnake Reigns Supreme WR	.75	2.00
100 Tag Team Daredevils WR	.12	.30

2001 Fleer WWF WrestleMania Foreign Objects

COMPLETE SET (9)	150.00	300.00
UNLISTED STARS	20.00	50.00

STATED ODDS 1:63 HOBBY EXCLUSIVE

NNO Chris Jericho Jersey	10.00	25.00
NNO Dudley Boyz Table SP	75.00	150.00
NNO The Rock T-Shirt	15.00	40.00
NNO Stone Cold Steve Austin T-Shirt	12.00	30.00
NNO Triple H Jeans	10.00	25.00
NNO Triple H T-Shirt	10.00	25.00
NNO Trish Stratus Shirt	20.00	50.00
NNO Trish Stratus Skirt	30.00	75.00
NNO Undertaker T-Shirt	10.00	25.00

2001 Fleer WWF WrestleMania Lip Service

STATED PRINT RUN 50 SERIAL #'d SETS
EXCH.EXPIRATION: 04/01/2002
HOBBY EXCLUSIVE

NNO Chyna	200.00	400.00
NNO Ivory	50.00	100.00
NNO Jacqueline	25.00	60.00
NNO Lita	175.00	350.00
NNO Molly Holly	75.00	150.00
NNO Terri	50.00	100.00
NNO Tori	30.00	75.00
NNO Trish Stratus	250.00	500.00

2001 Fleer WWF WrestleMania The People's Champion

COMPLETE SET (15)	2.00	5.00

STATED ODDS 1:2

PC1 The People's Elbow	.20	.50
PC2 The Rock on the Mic	.20	.50
PC3 The People's Eyebrow	.20	.50
PC4 Blood From a Rock	.20	.50
PC5 Football Career	.20	.50
PC6 The Rock, The Author	.20	.50
PC7 The Great One	.20	.50
PC8 The Brahma Bull	.20	.50
PC9 Layeth the Smackdown	.20	.50
PC10 The Rock Bottom	.20	.50
PC11 Can You Smell?	.20	.50
PC12 Just Bring It Jabroni	.20	.50
PC13 Five-Time WWF Champion	.20	.50
PC14 The Millions And Millions	.20	.50
PC15 Not Just a WWF Superstar	.20	.50

2001 Fleer WWF WrestleMania Signature Moves

COMPLETE SET (15)	40.00	80.00

STATED ODDS 1:24 HOBBY EXCLUSIVE

SM1 The Rock	6.00	12.00
SM2 Stone Cold Steve Austin	6.00	12.00
SM3 Kurt Angle	5.00	10.00
SM4 Triple H	5.00	10.00
SM5 Chris Jericho	5.00	10.00
SM6 Chris Benoit	4.00	8.00
SM7 Undertaker	5.00	10.00
SM8 Kane	4.00	8.00
SM9 Too Cool	4.00	8.00
SM10 Hardy Boyz	5.00	10.00
SM11 Dudley Boyz	5.00	10.00
SM12 Tazz	5.00	10.00

SM13 Eddie Guerrero	2.00	5.00
SM14 The One Billy Gunn	2.00	5.00
SM15 Lita	7.50	15.00

2001 Fleer WWF WrestleMania Signature Moves Autographs

COMPLETE SET (4)		
RANDOM INSERTS IN PACKS		
STATED PRINT RUN 500 SERIAL #'d SETS		
STRATUS PROMO ONLY AVAILABLE AT '01 NSCC		
NNO Bubba Ray Dudley	20.00	50.00
NNO D-Von Dudley	15.00	40.00
NNO Kurt Angle	50.00	100.00
NNO Stone Cold Steve Austin	400.00	750.00
NNO Trish Stratus	75.00	150.00
(NSCC Exclusive)		

2001 Fleer WWF WrestleMania Stone Cold Said So

COMPLETE SET (15)	5.00	12.00
STATED ODDS 1:2		
SC1 The Rock	2.50	6.00
SC2 Kurt Angle	.50	1.25
SC3 Rikishi	.30	.75
SC4 Chris Benoit	.40	1.00
SC5 Chris Jericho	.50	1.25
SC6 Triple H	.50	1.25
SC7 Vince McMahon	.40	1.00
SC8 Undertaker	.50	4.00
SC9 Kane	.40	1.00
SC10 Stephanie McMahon-Helmsley	1.50	4.00
SC11 X-Pac	.30	.75
SC12 Mick Foley	.50	1.25
SC13 Tazz	.50	1.25
SC14 Shane McMahon	.40	1.00
SC15 The One Billy Gunn	.30	.75

2015 Frame By Frame WWE Flip Madness Collection

COMPLETE SET W/SP (36)		
COMPLETE SET W/O SP (20)		
UNOPENED BOX (24 PACKS)		
UNOPENED PACK (1 FLIPBOOK)		
COMMON GOLD SP (21-30)	1.25	3.00
COMMON TITANIUM SP (31-36)	2.00	5.00
1 Batista	1.50	4.00
2 Big Show	1.50	4.00
3 Brock Lesnar	2.50	6.00
4 Cesaro	.60	1.50
5 Roman Reigns	1.50	4.00
6 Daniel Bryan	2.50	6.00
7 Dean Ambrose	1.50	4.00
8 Dolph Ziggler	1.00	2.50
9 Goldust	.60	1.50
10 John Cena	3.00	8.00
11 Kofi Kingston	.60	1.50
12 Mark Henry	1.00	2.50
13 Randy Orton	2.50	6.00
14 Ryback	.60	1.50
15 Seth Rollins	1.00	2.50
16 Sheamus	1.50	4.00
17 The Miz	1.00	2.50
18 King Barrett	.60	1.50
19 Triple H	2.50	6.00
20 Undertaker	2.50	6.00
21 Big Show SP	3.00	8.00
22 Brock Lesnar SP	5.00	12.00
23 Cesaro SP	1.25	3.00
24 Dolph Ziggler SP	2.00	5.00
25 Goldust SP	1.25	3.00
26 Roman Reigns SP	3.00	8.00
27 Ryback SP	1.25	3.00
28 Sheamus SP	3.00	8.00
29 Triple H SP	5.00	12.00
30 Undertaker SP	5.00	12.00
31 Daniel Bryan SP	8.00	20.00
32 Dean Ambrose SP	5.00	12.00
33 John Cena SP	10.00	25.00
34 Randy Orton SP	8.00	20.00
35 Seth Rollins SP	3.00	8.00
36 King Barrett SP	2.00	5.00

1988 Gold Bond WWF

COMPLETE SET (12)	15.00	40.00
NNO Andre the Giant	5.00	12.00
NNO Bobby The Brain Heenan	4.00	10.00
NNO Elizabeth	3.00	8.00
NNO George The Animal Steele	2.50	6.00
NNO Hillbilly Jim	2.00	5.00
NNO Honky Tonk Man	2.00	5.00
NNO Hulk Hogan	5.00	12.00
NNO Koko B. Ware	1.50	4.00
NNO The Million Dollar Man Ted DiBiase	3.00	8.00
NNO Randy Macho Man Savage	3.00	8.00
NNO Ricky The Dragon Steamboat	1.50	4.00
NNO Strike Force	1.50	4.00

1989 Gold Bond WWF

COMPLETE SET (12)		
NNO Andre the Giant	3.00	8.00
NNO Bobby The Brain Heenan		
NNO Brutus The Barber Beefcake	1.50	4.00
NNO Demolition (Ax & Smash)		
NNO Hacksaw Jim Duggan	2.50	6.00
NNO Hercules		
NNO Hulk Hogan	6.00	15.00
NNO Jake The Snake Roberts	3.00	8.00
NNO Macho Man Randy Savage	4.00	10.00
NNO Million Dollar Man Ted DiBiase	1.50	4.00
NNO Miss Elizabeth	3.00	8.00
NNO Ultimate Warrior		

1990 Gold Bond WWF

COMPLETE SET (12)	12.00	30.00
NNO Andre the Giant	2.50	6.00
NNO Bobby The Brain Heenan	2.00	5.00
NNO Brutus The Barber Beefcake	1.50	4.00
NNO Demolition	1.50	4.00
NNO Hulk Hogan	3.00	8.00
NNO Hulk Hogan	4.00	10.00
No Holds Barred		
NNO Macho Man Randy Savage	3.00	8.00
NNO Million Dollar Man Ted Dibiase	1.50	4.00
NNO Ravishing Rick Rude	1.50	4.00
NNO Rowdy Roddy Piper	3.00	8.00
NNO Ultimate Warrior	3.00	8.00
NNO Wrestlemania III	1.00	2.50

1991 Gold Bond WWF

COMPLETE SET (12)		
NNO Big Boss Man		
NNO Honky Tonk Man		
NNO Hulk Hogan	3.00	8.00
NNO Jake The Snake Roberts	2.00	5.00
NNO Macho King Randy Savage	3.00	8.00
NNO Million Dollar Man Ted Dibiase	5.00	12.00
NNO Mr. Perfect	4.00	10.00
NNO Rowdy Roddy Piper	3.00	8.00
NNO Sensational Queen Sherri	10.00	25.00
NNO Sgt. Slaughter	2.50	6.00
NNO Superfly Jimmy Snuka		
NNO Ultimate Warrior		

1985 Golden Hulk Hogan's Rock 'n' Wrestling Card Game

NNO Andre the Giant		
NNO Big John Studd		
NNO Fabulous Moolah		
NNO Hillbilly Jim		
NNO Hulk Hogan		
NNO Hulk Hogan/Iron Sheik Flip Card		
NNO Iron Sheik		
NNO Jimmy "Superfly" Snuka		
NNO Junkyard Dog		
NNO Mr. Fuji		
NNO Nikolai Volkoff		
NNO Rowdy Roddy Piper		
NNO Tito Santana		
NNO Wendi Richter		

1992 Good Humor WWF

COMPLETE SET (12)		
NNO Big Boss Man		
NNO Bret Hit Man Hart	6.00	15.00
NNO Elizabeth	3.00	8.00
NNO Hulk Hogan	12.00	30.00
NNO Legion of Doom		
NNO Macho Man Randy Savage	5.00	12.00
NNO Million Dollar Man Ted Dibiase	3.00	8.00
NNO Mr. Perfect		
NNO Rowdy Roddy Piper	5.00	12.00
NNO Sid Justice		
NNO The Nasty Boys		
NNO The Undertaker	6.00	15.00

2002 Good Humor WWF

COMPLETE SET (10)	15.00	40.00
NNO Chris Jericho	1.50	4.00
NNO Dudley Boyz	1.50	4.00
NNO Edge & Christian	2.50	6.00
NNO Hardy Boyz	1.50	4.00
NNO Kane	2.50	6.00
NNO Kurt Angle	2.50	6.00
NNO The Rock	4.00	10.00
NNO Stone Cold Steve Austin	4.00	10.00
NNO Triple H	4.00	10.00
NNO The Undertaker	3.00	8.00

1990 Hasbro WWF Flips Trading Cards

NNO Big Boss Man	1.25	3.00
NNO Brutus The Barber Beefcake	1.50	4.00
NNO The Bushwhackers		
NNO Hacksaw Jim Duggan	4.00	10.00
NNO Hulk Hogan	6.00	15.00
NNO Jake The Snake Roberts		
NNO Macho King Randy Savage	5.00	12.00
NNO Million Dollar Man Ted Dibiase		
NNO The Rockers		
NNO Ultimate Warrior		

1988 Hostess WWF WrestleMania IV Stickers

1 Jake The Snake Roberts		
2 Billy Jack Haynes		
3 Brutus The Barber Beefcake	.40	1.00
4 Randy Macho Man Savage and Elizabeth		
5 Koko B. Ware	.40	1.00
6 George The Animal Steele		
7 Hulk Hogan	4.00	10.00
8 Junkyard Dog		
9 Magnificent Muraco	.40	1.00
10 Bam Bam Bigelow	.75	2.00
11 Elizabeth		
12 The Honky Tonk Man	.75	2.00
13 Ted DiBiase	.40	1.00
14 The Natural Butch Reed	.40	1.00
15 Ravishing Rick Rude		
16 Killer Khan		
17 Bobby The Brain Heenan		
18 Jimmy Hart		
19 Slick The Doctor of Style		
20 Hulk Hogan	8.00	20.00
21 Mr. Fuji		
22 Oliver Humperdink		
23 Strike Force		
24 The British Bulldogs		
25 The Killer Bees		
26 Demolition Ax and Smash		
27 The Islanders		
28 Ken Patera		
29 The Rougeau Brothers		
30 The Hart Foundation		
31 Strike Force		
32 Jesse The Body Ventura		
33 Hillbilly Jim		
34 Randy Macho Man Savage		

1987 Hostess Munchies WWF Stickers

COMPLETE SET (20)	10.00	20.00
NNO British Bulldogs	.20	.50
NNO Don Muraco	.15	.40
NNO George The Animal Steele	.40	1.00
NNO Hillbilly Jim	.20	.50
NNO Honky Tonk Man	.20	.50
NNO Hulk Hogan	3.00	8.00
NNO Hulk Hogan	3.00	8.00
NNO Iron Sheik and Nikoli Volkoff	.25	.60
NNO Jake The Snake Roberts	.50	1.25
NNO Junkyard Dog	.20	.50
NNO Kamala	.15	.40
NNO King Kong Bundy	.20	.50
NNO Koko B. Ware	.15	.40
NNO Outback Jack	.15	.40
NNO Paul Mr. Wonderful Orndorff	.20	.50
NNO Randy Savage and Elizabeth	1.50	4.00
NNO Ricky The Dragon Steamboat	.20	.50
NNO Rowdy Roddy Piper	1.25	3.00
NNO Sika	.40	1.00
NNO Tito Santana	.15	.40

1999 Hot Shots WWF Stickers

COMPLETE SET (212)	12.00	30.00
1 Stone Cold Steve Austin	.75	2.00
2 Stone Cold Steve Austin	.75	2.00
3 Stone Cold Steve Austin	.75	2.00
4 Stone Cold Steve Austin	.75	2.00

5 Stone Cold Steve Austin	.75	2.00
6 Stone Cold Steve Austin	.75	2.00
7 Stone Cold Steve Austin	.75	2.00
8 Stone Cold Steve Austin	.75	2.00
9 Stone Cold Steve Austin	.75	2.00
10 Stone Cold Steve Austin	.75	2.00
11 Stone Cold Steve Austin	.75	2.00
12 Stone Cold Steve Austin	.75	2.00
13 Stone Cold Steve Austin	.75	2.00
14 Stone Cold Steve Austin	.75	2.00
15 Stone Cold Steve Austin	.75	2.00
16 Stone Cold Steve Austin	.75	2.00
17 Stone Cold Steve Austin	.75	2.00
18 Stone Cold Steve Austin	.75	2.00
19 The Rock	.75	2.00
20 The Rock	.75	2.00
21 The Rock	.75	2.00
22 The Rock	.75	2.00
23 The Rock	.75	2.00
24 The Rock	.75	2.00
25 The Rock	.75	2.00
26 The Rock	.75	2.00
27 The Rock	.75	2.00
28 The Rock	.75	2.00
29 The Rock	.75	2.00
30 The Rock	.75	2.00
31 The Rock	.75	2.00
32 The Rock	.75	2.00
33 The Rock	.75	2.00
34 The Rock	.75	2.00
35 The Rock	.75	2.00
36 The Rock	.75	2.00
37 Big Show	.25	.60
38 Big Show	.25	.60
39 Big Show	.25	.60
40 Big Show	.25	.60
41 Big Show	.25	.60
42 Big Show	.25	.60
43 Undertaker	.60	1.50
44 Undertaker	.60	1.50
45 Undertaker	.60	1.50
46 Undertaker	.60	1.50
47 Undertaker	.60	1.50
48 Undertaker	.60	1.50
49 Undertaker	.60	1.50
50 Undertaker	.60	1.50
51 Undertaker	.60	1.50
52 Undertaker	.60	1.50
53 Undertaker	.60	1.50
54 Undertaker	.60	1.50
55 Undertaker	.60	1.50
56 Undertaker	.60	1.50
57 Undertaker	.60	1.50
58 Undertaker	.60	1.50
59 Undertaker	.60	1.50
60 Undertaker	.60	1.50
61 Acolytes	.12	.30
62 Corporate Ministry	.12	.30
63 Viscera	.12	.30
64 Chyna	.20	.50
65 Chyna	.20	.50
66 Big Boss Man	.12	.30
67 Big Boss Man	.12	.30
68 Viscera	.12	.30
69 Corporate Ministry	.12	.30
70 Big Boss Man	.12	.30
71 Acolytes	.12	.30
72 Paul Bearer	.15	.40

73 Ken Shamrock	.15	.40
74 Ken Shamrock	.15	.40
75 Ken Shamrock	.15	.40
76 Ken Shamrock	.15	.40
77 Ken Shamrock	.15	.40
78 Ken Shamrock	.15	.40
79 Mankind	.30	.75
80 Mankind	.30	.75
81 Mankind	.30	.75
82 Mankind	.30	.75
83 Mankind	.30	.75
84 Mankind	.30	.75
85 Mankind	.30	.75
86 Mankind	.30	.75
87 Mankind	.30	.75
88 Mankind	.30	.75
89 Mankind	.30	.75
90 Mankind	.30	.75
91 Vince McMahon	.20	.50
92 Vince McMahon	.20	.50
93 Vince McMahon	.20	.50
94 Vince McMahon	.20	.50
95 Vince McMahon	.20	.50
96 Vince McMahon	.20	.50
97 Shane McMahon	.20	.50
98 Shane McMahon	.20	.50
99 Shane McMahon	.20	.50
100 Shane McMahon	.20	.50
101 Shane McMahon	.20	.50
102 Shane McMahon	.20	.50
103 Triple H	.30	.75
104 Triple H	.30	.75
105 Triple H	.30	.75
106 Triple H	.30	.75
107 Triple H	.30	.75
108 Triple H	.30	.75
109 Jeff Jarrett	.25	.60
110 Jeff Jarrett	.25	.60
111 Jeff Jarrett	.25	.60
112 Jeff Jarrett	.25	.60
113 Jeff Jarrett	.25	.60
114 Jeff Jarrett	.25	.60
115 Debra	.30	.75
116 Debra	.30	.75
117 Debra	.30	.75
118 Debra	.30	.75
119 Debra	.30	.75
120 Debra	.30	.75
121 Kane	.25	.60
122 Kane	.25	.60
123 Kane	.25	.60
124 Kane	.25	.60
125 Kane	.25	.60
126 Kane	.25	.60
127 Kane	.25	.60
128 Kane	.25	.60
129 Kane	.25	.60
130 Kane	.25	.60
131 Kane	.25	.60
132 Kane	.25	.60
133 X-Pac	.25	.60
134 X-Pac	.25	.60
135 X-Pac	.25	.60
136 X-Pac	.25	.60
137 X-Pac	.25	.60
138 X-Pac	.25	.60
139 Road Dogg	.25	.60
140 Road Dogg	.25	.60

141 Road Dogg	.25	.60
142 Road Dogg	.25	.60
143 Road Dogg	.25	.60
144 Road Dogg	.25	.60
145 Billy Gunn	.25	.60
146 Billy Gunn	.25	.60
147 Billy Gunn	.25	.60
148 Billy Gunn	.25	.60
149 Billy Gunn	.25	.60
150 Billy Gunn	.25	.60
151 Al Snow	.15	.40
152 Al Snow	.15	.40
153 Al Snow	.15	.40
154 Al Snow	.15	.40
155 Al Snow	.15	.40
156 Al Snow	.15	.40
157 Val Venis	.15	.40
158 Val Venis	.15	.40
159 Val Venis	.15	.40
160 Val Venis	.15	.40
161 Val Venis	.15	.40
162 Val Venis	.15	.40
163 The Brood	.30	.75
164 Edge	.30	.75
165 The Brood	.30	.75
166 Christian	.25	.60
167 Edge	.30	.75
168 Christian	.25	.60
169 Gangrel	.12	.30
170 Gangrel	.12	.30
171 Gangrel	.12	.30
172 Gangrel	.12	.30
173 Gangrel	.12	.30
174 Gangrel	.12	.30
175 D-Lo Brown	.12	.30
176 D-Lo Brown	.12	.30
177 D-Lo Brown	.12	.30
178 D-Lo Brown	.12	.30
179 Mark Henry	.15	.40
180 Mark Henry	.15	.40
181 Goldust	.25	.60
182 Goldust	.25	.60
183 Goldust	.25	.60
184 Goldust	.25	.60
185 Goldust	.25	.60
186 Goldust	.25	.60
187 Godfather	.20	.50
188 Godfather	.20	.50
189 Godfather	.20	.50
190 Godfather	.20	.50
191 Godfather	.20	.50
192 Godfather	.20	.50
193 PMS	.15	.40
194 PMS	.15	.40
195 PMS	.15	.40
196 PMS	.15	.40
197 PMS	.15	.40
198 PMS	.15	.40
199 Nicole Bass	.12	.30
200 Droz	.12	.30
201 Shawn Michaels	.40	1.00
202 Ivory	.20	.50
203 Droz	.12	.30
204 Hardcore Holly	.12	.30
205 Test	.12	.30
206 Tiger Ali Singh	.12	.30
207 Tiger Ali Singh	.12	.30
208 Kurrgan	.12	.30

209 Test	.12	.30
210 Shawn Michaels	.40	1.00
211 Test	.12	.30
212 Raw Is War	.12	.30

1991 Imagine Wrestling Legends

COMPLETE SET (60)	25.00	60.00
1 Bruno Sammartino	1.25	3.00
2 Buddy Rogers	.75	2.00
3 Ivan Koloff	.75	2.00
4 Lou Albano	.40	1.00
5 Billy Graham	1.00	2.50
6 Killer Kowalski	1.00	2.50
7 Lou Thesz	1.25	3.00
8 Domenic DeNucci	.40	1.00
9 Bruno Sammartino	1.25	3.00
10 Buddy Rogers	.75	2.00
11 Ivan Koloff	.75	2.00
12 Lou Albano	.40	1.00
13 Billy Graham	1.00	2.50
14 Killer Kowalski	1.00	2.50
15 Lou Thesz	1.25	3.00
16 Bill Miller	.40	1.00
17 Domenic DeNucci	.40	1.00
18 Bruno Sammartino	1.25	3.00
19 Antonio Rocca	.40	1.00
20 Buddy Rogers	.75	2.00
21 Ivan Koloff	.75	2.00
22 Primo Carnerra	.75	2.00
23 Lou Albano	.40	1.00
24 Bruno Sammartino	1.25	3.00
25 Crusher Lisowski	.75	2.00
26 Billy Graham	1.00	2.50
27 Killer Kowalski	1.00	2.50
28 Domenic DeNucci	.40	1.00
29 Rocca & Perez	.75	2.00
30 Bill Watts	.40	1.00
31 BoBo Brazil	.75	2.00
32 Lou Thesz	1.25	3.00
33 Pedro Morales	1.00	2.50
34 Johnny Valentine	.75	2.00
35 Argentine Apollo	.40	1.00
36 Billy Graham	1.00	2.50
37 Haystacks Calhoun	.40	1.00
38 Bruno Sammartino	1.25	3.00
39 The Destroyer	.75	2.00
40 Buddy Rogers	.75	2.00
41 Ray Stevens	.75	2.00
42 Lou Albano	.40	1.00
43 Edouard Carpentier	.40	1.00
44 Killer Kowalski	1.00	2.50
45 Bob Backlund	1.00	2.50
46 Killer Kowalski	1.00	2.50
47 Mil Mascaras	1.00	2.50
48 Domenic DeNucci	.40	1.00
49 Smasher Sloan	.40	1.00
50 Ivan Koloff	.75	2.00
51 Lou Albano	.40	1.00
52 Lou Thesz	1.25	3.00
53 Harly Race UER	1.25	3.00
54 Billy Graham	1.00	2.50
55 Domenic DeNucci	.40	1.00
56 Hawk & Hansen	.75	2.00
57 Lou Thesz	1.25	3.00
58 Ivan Koloff	.75	2.00
59 Buddy Rogers	.75	2.00
60 Bruno Sammartino	1.25	3.00

61	Bruno Sammartino AU	50.00	100.00
62	Buddy Rogers AU	25.00	60.00
63	Lou Thesz AU	25.00	60.00
64	Billy Graham AU	15.00	40.00
65	Ivan Koloff AU	15.00	40.00
66	Killer Kowalski AU	30.00	75.00
67	Lou Albano AU	20.00	50.00
68	Domenic DeNucci AU	12.00	30.00

2022 Immaculate Collection WWE

STATED PRINT RUN 65 SER.#'d SETS
*MARKET INFO UNAVAILABLE AT PRESS TIME

1 Shawn Michaels
2 Dakota Kai
3 Triple H
4 Finn Balor
5 Junkyard Dog
6 Macho Man Randy Savage
7 Matt Riddle
8 Asuka
9 Razor Ramon
10 Booker T
11 Shayna Baszler
12 Damian Priest
13 Trish Stratus
14 Gigi Dolin
15 Kane
16 Ted DiBiase
17 Natalya
18 Bam Bam Bigelow
19 Rey Mysterio
20 Bret "Hit Man" Hart
21 Shinsuke Nakamura
22 Diesel
23 Tyler Bate
24 Goldberg
25 Karrion Kross
26 Mr. Perfect
27 Nikki Bella
28 Batista
29 Rhea Ripley
30 British Bulldog
31 Shotzi
32 Dolph Ziggler
33 Ultimate Warrior
34 Gunther
35 Katana Chance
36 Rowdy Roddy Piper
37 Nikkita Lyons
38 Bayley
39 Ricochet
40 Brock Lesnar
41 Solo Sikoa
42 Dominik Mysterio
43 Umaga
44 Hollywood Hogan
45 Kevin Owens
46 Stone Cold Steve Austin
47 Braun Strowman
48 Becky Lynch
49 The Rock
50 Bruno Sammartino
51 Sonya Deville
52 Drew McIntyre
53 Vader
54 Ilja Dragunov
55 Kofi Kingston
56 Bobby Lashley
57 Omos
58 Bianca Belair
59 Roman Reigns
60 Butch
61 Stacy Keibler
62 Dusty Rhodes
63 Xavier Woods
64 IYO SKY
65 Lacey Evans
66 Cody Rhodes
67 Paul Bearer
68 Big Boss Man
69 Ronda Rousey
70 Carmella
71 Terry Funk
72 Eddie Guerrero
73 X-Pac
74 Jey Uso
75 Liv Morgan
76 Alba Fyre
77 Paul Heyman
78 Big E
79 Roxanne Perez
80 Charlotte Flair
81 The Miz
82 Edge
83 Yokozuna
84 Jimmy Uso
85 Mandy Rose
86 Alexa Bliss
87 Randy Orton
88 Big John Studd
89 Scarlett
90 Chyna
91 Austin Theory
92 Elektra Lopez
93 Johnny Gargano
94 John Cena
95 Mankind
96 Andre the Giant
97 Raquel Rodriguez
98 Bobby Heenan
99 Seth Rollins
100 Tommaso Ciampa

2022 Immaculate Collection WWE All-Time Greats Signatures

*GOLD/10: UNPRICED DUE TO SCARCITY
*PLATINUM/1: UNPRICED DUE TO SCARCITY
RANDOMLY INSERTED INTO PACKS

1 Jeff Jarrett/49
2 Jerry Lawler/75
3 Lita/99
4 Ted DiBiase/99
5 Shawn Michaels/75
6 Batista/99
7 Superstar Billy Graham/99
8 Cactus Jack/75
9 Trish Stratus/99
10 Goldberg/75
11 X-Pac/75
12 John Cena/99
13 Road Dogg/75
14 Stone Cold Steve Austin/49
15 Nikki Bella/75
16 Cowboy Bob Orton/60
17 Triple H/99
18 Gerald Brisco/99
19 Undertaker/49
20 Hulk Hogan/35

2022 Immaculate Collection WWE The Bloodline Autograph

STATED PRINT RUN 25 SER.#'d SETS

1 Sikoa/Reigns/Usos/Afa/Sika/Rikishi

2022 Immaculate Collection WWE Dual Autographed Memorabilia

*PLATINUM/1: UNPRICED DUE TO SCARCITY
STATED PRINT RUN 10 SER.#'d SETS

1 R.Orton/M.Riddle
2 B.Lynch/B.Belair
3 Shanky/J.Mahal
4 AJ Styles/Edge
5 Edge/D.Priest
6 S.Rollins/B.Lesnar
7 Brutus & Julius Creed
8 K.Carter/K.Chance
9 A.Dawkins/M.Ford
11 Jimmy & Jey Uso
12 D.McIntyre/H.Corbin
13 LA Knight/Gunther
14 R.Reigns/B.Lesnar
15 J.Reid/R.Fowler
16 Ciampa/B.Breakker
17 J.Jayne/G.Dolin
20 Azeez/A.Crews
21 Ivar/Erik
22 B.Lashley/Omos
23 Natalya/S.Baszler
24 B.Lesnar/D.McIntyre
25 M.Rose/C.Jade
26 D.Ziggler/B.Breakker
27 MVP/Omos
28 K.Wilson/E.Prince
29 Dominik & Rey Mysterio
30 R.Ripley/D.Priest

2022 Immaculate Collection WWE Dual Autographs

*PLATINUM/1: UNPRICED DUE TO SCARCITY
STATED PRINT RUN 25 SER.#'d SETS

1 D.Priest/R.Ripley
2 B.Lynch/B.Belair
3 K.Angle/G.Steveson
4 B.Lesnar/R.Reigns
5 I.Dragunov/J.Devlin
6 Julius & Brutus Creed
7 R.Orton/C.Rhodes
8 K.Chance/K.Carter
9 Rey & Dominik Mysterio
10 M.Riddle/RVD
11 Jey & Jimmy Uso
12 H.Corbin/D.McIntyre
13 T.Stratus/Lita
14 Undertaker/Kane
15 J.Reid/R.Fowler
16 J.Jayne/G.Dolin
17 Kama/Faarooq
18 S.Baszler/R.Rousey
19 R.Orton/M.Riddle
20 K.Owens/S.Austin
21 Erik/Ivar
22 B.Lashley/Omos
23 S.Baszler/Natalya
24 The Bushwhackers
25 B.Lesnar/G.Steveson
26 Afa/Sika
27 A.Dawkins/M.Ford
29 D.Priest/Edge
30 R.Rousey/C.Flair
31 J.Mahal/Shanky
32 Edge/AJ Styles
33 I.Sheik/H.Hogan
34 Faarooq/Bradshaw
35 The Bella Twins
36 HHH/S.McMahon
38 K.Wilson/E.Prince
39 Azeez/A.Crews
40 C.Rhodes/S.Rollins

2022 Immaculate Collection WWE Heralded Signatures

*GOLD/10: UNPRICED DUE TO SCARCITY
*PLATINUM/1: UNPRICED DUE TO SCARCITY
STATED PRINT RUN 95-99 SETS

1 Stan Hansen/99
2 Jerry Lawler/99
3 Road Dogg/99
4 Beth Phoenix/95
5 Papa Shango/99
6 Ted DiBiase/99
7 Michelle McCool/99
8 Bushwhacker Luke/99
9 Cowboy Bob Orton/99
10 Greg Valentine/99
11 Terri Runnels/99
12 Jimmy Hart/99
13 Rob Van Dam/99
14 Booker T/99
16 Rikishi/99
17 Tyson Kidd/99
18 Diamond Dallas Page/99
19 Gerald Brisco/99
20 Hacksaw Jim Duggan/99
21 The Boogeyman/99
22 Kurt Angle/99
23 Superstar Billy Graham/99
24 Iron Sheik/99
25 1-2-3 Kid/99
26 Alundra Blayze/99
27 Al Snow/99
28 Don Muraco/99
29 Jerry Sags/99
30 Paul Heyman/99
31 The Sandman/99
32 Michael Hayes/99
33 Teddy Long/99
35 Kelly Kelly/99
36 Brutus Beefcake/99
37 Brian Knobs/99
38 Ron Simmons/99
39 Johnny Rodz/99
40 Ivory/99

2022 Immaculate Collection WWE Immaculate Celebrations Autographs

RANDOMLY INSERTED INTO PACKS

1 Shawn Michaels/60
2 Booker T/49

3 Diamond Dallas Page/75
4 Hulk Hogan/49
5 John Cena/99
6 Big E/49
7 Bobby Lashley/49
8 Randy Orton/49
9 Undertaker/49
10 Goldberg/75

2022 Immaculate Collection WWE Immaculate Inductions Autographs

RANDOMLY INSERTED INTO PACKS

1 Jerry Lawler/75
2 Undertaker/49
3 Kevin Nash/75
4 Michael Hayes/99
5 Bushwhacker Butch/75
6 Stan Hansen/49
7 Don Muraco/75
8 Superstar Billy Graham/99
10 Teddy Long/49
11 Hacksaw Jim Duggan/99
12 Johnny Rodz/99
13 Torrie Wilson/10
14 Ricky The Dragon Steamboat/49
15 Bushwhacker Luke/75
16 Stone Cold Steve Austin
17 Goldberg/75
18 Ted DiBiase/99
19 Jeff Jarrett/49
20 The Honky Tonk Man/49

2022 Immaculate Collection WWE Immaculate Ink

*GOLD/10: UNPRICED DUE TO SCARCITY
*PLATINUM/1: UNPRICED DUE TO SCARCITY
STATED PRINT RUN 99 SER.#'d SETS

1 Kevin Owens
3 Leilani Kai
4 Angelo Dawkins
5 MVP
6 Ricochet
7 Ivar
8 Jason Jordan
10 The Blue Meanie
11 Austin Theory
12 Montez Ford
13 Simon Dean
14 Apollo Crews
15 Butch
16 Jey Uso
18 Mosh
19 Dory Funk Jr.
20 Thrasher
21 Haku
22 Damian Priest
26 Erik
28 Stevie Richards
29 The Miz
30 Tom Prichard

2022 Immaculate Collection WWE Immaculate Milestones Autographs

RANDOMLY INSERTED INTO PACKS

1 John Cena/99
2 Kane/75
3 Hulk Hogan/49
4 Undertaker/49
5 Natalya/49
6 Roman Reigns/49
7 Booker T/49
8 Drew McIntyre/49
9 Randy Orton/49
10 Rey Mysterio/49

2022 Immaculate Collection WWE Immaculate Moments Autographs

RANDOMLY INSERTED INTO PACKS

1 Kofi Kingston/49
2 Triple H/99
3 Mankind/75
4 Goldberg/75
5 Cody Rhodes/99
6 Roman Reigns/49
7 Hulk Hogan/49
8 Shawn Michaels/60
9 Kane/75
10 Stone Cold Steve Austin/49

2022 Immaculate Collection WWE Immaculate Nicknames Autographs

STATED PRINT RUN 25 SER.#'d SETS

1 Triple H
2 Shawn Michaels
3 Randy Orton
4 AJ Styles
5 Undertaker
6 Dolph Ziggler
7 Beth Phoenix
8 Batista
9 Jimmy Hart
10 Seth Rollins
11 Hulk Hogan
12 Mick Foley
13 Alexa Bliss
14 Cowboy Bob Orton
15 Bret "Hit Man" Hart
16 Charlotte Flair
17 Don Muraco
18 Greg Valentine
19 Jerry Lawler
20 Ted DiBiase
21 Kane
22 Diesel
23 Kevin Owens
24 Lex Luger
25 The Miz
26 Natalya
27 Ricochet
28 Rob Van Dam
29 Ronda Rousey
30 Shayna Baszler

2022 Immaculate Collection WWE The Immaculate Standard Memorabilia

STATED PRINT RUN 99 SER.#'d SETS

1 Bayley
2 Sheamus
3 Austin Theory
4 Kevin Owens
5 Gable Steveson
6 IYO SKY
7 Alexa Bliss
8 Queen Zelina
9 Gigi Dolin
10 Ivy Nile
11 Mandy Rose
12 The Miz
13 Carmelo Hayes
14 Shotzi
15 Roman Reigns
16 Jacy Jayne
17 Charlotte Flair
18 Rhea Ripley
19 Liv Morgan
20 Jey Uso
21 AJ Styles
22 Brutus Creed
23 Drew McIntyre
24 Finn Balor
25 Bron Breakker
26 Lacey Evans
27 Becky Lynch
28 Matt Riddle
29 Randy Orton
30 Jimmy Uso
31 Sonya Deville
32 Julius Creed
33 Edge
34 Bobby Lashley
35 Xavier Woods
36 Nikki A.S.H.
37 Bianca Belair
38 Carmella
39 Rey Mysterio
40 Alba Fyre
41 Asuka
42 Natalya
43 Katana Chance
44 Grayson Waller
45 Brock Lesnar
46 Omos
47 Cora Jade
48 Dominik Mysterio
49 Seth Rollins
50 Kofi Kingston

2022 Immaculate Collection WWE Jumbo Memorabilia Hoodie

RANDOMLY INSERTED INTO PACKS

1 Brutus Creed/4
3 Erik/10
4 Edge/14
11 Butch/27
20 Seth Rollins/26
26 Grayson Waller/18
29 Alexa Bliss/50
31 Carmelo Hayes/50
45 Julius Creed/4
50 Sheamus/22
53 IYO SKY/4
63 Ivar/12
68 Ridge Holland/29
78 Roderick Strong/1
83 Jey Uso/24
86 Drew McIntyre/26
93 Jimmy Uso/24

2022 Immaculate Collection WWE Jumbo Memorabilia Shirt

RANDOMLY INSERTED INTO PACKS

1 Brutus Creed/50
2 Tyler Bate/50
3 Erik/38
5 Jinder Mahal/50
6 Noam Dar/27
7 Lash Legend/32
8 Rampage Brown/27
9 AJ Styles/50
10 Santos Escobar/50
11 Butch/50
12 Veer Mahaan/34
13 Ezekiel/37
14 Carmella/50
15 Joaquin Wilde/50
17 Liv Morgan/50
18 Raquel Rodriguez/50
19 Alba Fyre/35
20 Seth Rollins/29
21 Cameron Grimes/50
22 Wes Lee/50
23 Gigi Dolin/50
24 Axiom/13
25 Joe Gacy/40
26 Grayson Waller/7
27 Mandy Rose/50
28 Reggie/50
29 Alexa Bliss/50
30 Shanky/50
31 Carmelo Hayes/40
32 Xavier Woods/50
33 Happy Corbin/50
34 Mark Coffey/27
35 JD McDonagh/27
36 Rey Mysterio/50
37 man.soor/50
38 Rhea Ripley/50
39 Angelo Dawkins/50
40 Shayna Baszler/40
41 Tommaso Ciampa/29
42 Xia Li/50
43 Indi Hartwell/50
44 Dolph Ziggler/28
45 Julius Creed/50
46 Dominik Mysterio/50
47 Meiko Satomura/50
48 Ricochet/50
49 Apollo Crews/50
50 Sheamus/24
51 Commander Azeez/38
52 Xyon Quinn/34
53 IYO SKY/36
54 Jinny/22
55 Kayden Carter/50
57 Montez Ford/50
58 Matt Riddle/42
59 Asuka/50
60 Shinsuke Nakamura/50
61 Damian Priest/50
62 Zoey Stark/30
63 Ivar/50
64 Blair Davenport/22
65 Kevin Owens/50
67 MVP/47
68 Ridge Holland/50

69 Becky Lynch/19
70 Shotzi/50
71 Dana Brooke/26
72 Ilja Dragunov/50
73 Jacy Jayne/50
74 Aoife Valkyrie/27
75 Kofi Kingston/50
77 Nikki A.S.H./50
78 Roderick Strong/50
79 Bianca Belair/50
80 Bobby Lashley/50
81 Doudrop/50
82 Joe Coffey/27
83 Jey Uso/44
84 Natalya/20
85 Max Dupri/41
86 Drew McIntyre/24
87 Odyssey Jones/31
88 Roman Reigns/50
89 Boa/30
90 The Miz/50
91 Drew Gulak/50
92 Wolfgang/18
93 Jimmy Uso/50
94 Sonya Deville/50
95 Lacey Evans/50
96 Cora Jade/20
97 Otis/50
98 Sami Zayn/50
99 Bron Breakker/50
100 Von Wagner/24

2022 Immaculate Collection WWE Jumbo Memorabilia Specialty

RANDOMLY INSERTED INTO PACKS

16 Finn Balor/9
38 Rhea Ripley/41
39 Angelo Dawkins/50
57 Montez Ford/50
58 Matt Riddle/8
69 Becky Lynch/35

2022 Immaculate Collection WWE Jumbo Ring Canvas

STATED PRINT RUN 99 SER.#'d SETS

1 Roman Reigns
2 Cameron Grimes
3 Cody Rhodes
4 Mandy Rose
5 Stone Cold Steve Austin
6 Bron Breakker
7 Edge
8 Brock Lesnar
9 Jimmy Uso
10 Rey Mysterio
11 The Miz
12 Carmelo Hayes
13 Seth Rollins
14 Cora Jade
15 Randy Orton
16 AJ Styles
17 Gable Steveson
18 Jey Uso
19 Kevin Owens
20 Bianca Belair
21 Tony D'Angelo
22 Charlotte Flair
23 Gunther
24 Matt Riddle
25 Theory
26 Pat McAfee
27 Dominik Mysterio
28 Drew McIntyre
29 Raquel Gonzalez
30 Becky Lynch
31 Tommaso Ciampa
32 Ronda Rousey
33 Dolph Ziggler
34 Bobby Lashley
35 Bianca Belair
36 Becky Lynch
37 Damian Priest
38 The Miz
39 Bobby Lashley
40 Theory
41 Rey Mysterio
42 Dominik Mysterio
43 Pat McAfee
44 Jimmy Uso
45 Jey Uso
46 Liv Morgan
47 Ronda Rousey
48 Roman Reigns
49 Brock Lesnar
50 Finn Balor

2022 Immaculate Collection WWE Marks of Greatness Autographs

*GOLD/10: UNPRICED DUE TO SCARCITY
*PLATINUM/1: UNPRICED DUE TO SCARCITY
RANDOMLY INSERTED INTO PACKS

2 Brother Love/99
4 Liv Morgan/49
5 Jey Uso/49
6 Ronda Rousey/99
7 Carmelo Hayes/49
8 Rey Mysterio/49
9 Io Shirai/49
10 Bayley/49
11 Solo Sikoa/99
12 Carmella/49
13 Meiko Satomura/60
14 Shinsuke Nakamura/49
15 Alba Fyre/49
16 Goldberg/75
17 Ciampa/49
18 Seth Rollins/49
19 Ludwig Kaiser/99
20 Bianca Belair/49
21 Santos Escobar/49
22 Otis/99
24 Montez Ford/49
25 Bron Breakker/49
26 Finn Balor/49
27 Cora Jade/49
28 Alexa Bliss/49
29 Mandy Rose/49
30 Big E/49
31 Gunther/49
32 man.soor/99
34 Jimmy Uso/49
35 Cameron Grimes/49
37 Giovanni Vinci/99
38 Asuka/49
39 Raquel Rodriguez/49
40 Ezekiel/99

2022 Immaculate Collection WWE Memorabilia Autographs

*RED/25: UNPRICED DUE TO SCARCITY
*GOLD/10: UNPRICED DUE TO SCARCITY
*ACETATE/8: UNPRICED DUE TO SCARCITY
*ACE.FOTL/3-6: UNPRICED DUE TO SCARCITY
*GREEN/5: UNPRICED DUE TO SCARCITY
*PLATINUM/1: UNPRICED DUE TO SCARCITY
STATED PRINT RUN 99 SER.#'d SETS

1 Drew McIntyre
2 Liv Morgan
3 Io Shirai
4 Natalya
5 AJ Styles
6 Jimmy Uso
7 Becky Lynch
8 Ciampa
9 Nikki A.S.H.
10 Gigi Dolin
11 Edge
12 Omos
13 Kevin Owens
14 Randy Orton
15 Alexa Bliss
16 Seth Rollins
17 Bianca Belair
18 Apollo Crews
19 Carmella
20 Raquel Rodriguez
21 Finn Balor
22 Jey Uso
23 Kofi Kingston
24 Rey Mysterio
25 Asuka
26 Shinsuke Nakamura
28 Damian Priest
29 Charlotte Flair
30 Rhea Ripley
31 Gunther
32 Ricochet
33 Mandy Rose
34 Xia Li
36 The Miz
37 Bobby Lashley
38 Dominik Mysterio
39 Dolph Ziggler
40 Xavier Woods

2022 Immaculate Collection WWE Modern Marks Autographs

*GOLD/10: UNPRICED DUE TO SCARCITY
*PLATINUM/1: UNPRICED DUE TO SCARCITY
STATED PRINT RUN 99 SER.#'d SETS

2 Shotzi/99
3 Omos/99
4 Kit Wilson/99
5 Otis/99
6 Stevie Turner/99
7 Xyon Quinn/99
8 Dana Brooke/99
9 Liv Morgan/99
10 man.soor/99
12 Reggie/99
13 Elton Prince/99
14 Queen Zelina/99
15 Sonya Deville/99
17 Rip Fowler/99
19 Kofi Kingston/99
20 Nikki A.S.H./99
21 Boa/99
22 Jagger Reid/99
23 Jinny/99
24 Damian Priest/49
26 Matt Riddle/99
27 Robert Roode/99
28 Carmella/99
29 Sheamus/99
30 Ridge Holland/99

2022 Immaculate Collection WWE Premium Memorabilia Autographs

*RED/25: UNPRICED DUE TO SCARCITY
*GOLD/10: UNPRICED DUE TO SCARCITY
*ACETATE/8: UNPRICED DUE TO SCARCITY
*ACE.FOTL/3-6: UNPRICED DUE TO SCARCITY
*GREEN/5: UNPRICED DUE TO SCARCITY
*PLATINUM/1: UNPRICED DUE TO SCARCITY
STATED PRINT RUN 49-99 SETS

2 Dana Brooke/99
3 Brock Lesnar/49
4 Rick Boogs/99
5 Edge/99
6 Kofi Kingston/99
7 Jey Uso/99
8 Roman Reigns/49
9 Shayna Baszler/99
10 Ciampa/49
11 Becky Lynch/99
12 Katana Chance/99
13 Carmella/99
14 Santos Escobar/49
15 Finn Balor/75
16 Mandy Rose/99
17 Jimmy Uso/99
18 Montez Ford/99
19 Sheamus/99
20 Theory/99
21 Bianca Belair/99
22 Alba Fyre/49
23 Charlotte Flair/99
25 Gunther/99
26 Natalya/99
27 Omos/99
28 Seth Rollins/49
29 AJ Styles/99
30 Cameron Grimes/99
32 Queen Zelina/99
33 Dolph Ziggler/99
34 Shotzi/99
35 Io Shirai/49
36 Randy Orton/49
37 Matt Riddle/99
38 Shinsuke Nakamura/99
39 Alexa Bliss/99
40 Drew Gulak/99
41 Bobby Lashley/99
42 Reggie/99
43 Drew McIntyre/49
44 Sonya Deville/99
45 Kevin Owens/99
46 Rey Mysterio/99

47 Sami Zayn/99
48 The Miz/99
49 Asuka/99
50 Doudrop/99

2022 Immaculate Collection WWE Quad Autographs

*PLATINUM/1: UNPRICED DUE TO SCARCITY
STATED PRINT RUN SER.#'d SETS
UNPRICED DUE TO SCARCITY

1 HBK/HHH/X-Pac/Road Dogg
2 HBK/Edge/Orton/Cena
3 Usos/Sika/Afa
4 Miz/Ziggler/RVD/Edge
5 Usos/Dawkins/Ford
6 Bliss/Asuka/Carmella/Bayley
7 Rousey/Lesnar/Baszler/Riddle
8 Undertaker/Austin/Mankind./HHH
9 Faarooq/Kane/X-Pac/Bradshaw
10 Goldberg/Lashley

2022 Immaculate Collection WWE Rookie Memorabilia Autographs

*RED/25: UNPRICED DUE TO SCARCITY
*GOLD/10: UNPRICED DUE TO SCARCITY
*ACETATE/8: UNPRICED DUE TO SCARCITY
*ACE.FOTL/6: UNPRICED DUE TO SCARCITY
*GREEN/5: UNPRICED DUE TO SCARCITY
*PLATINUM/1: UNPRICED DUE TO SCARCITY
STATED PRINT RUN 99 SER.#'d SETS

101 Von Wagner
102 Grayson Waller
103 Jacy Jayne
104 Bron Breakker
105 Joe Gacy
106 Carmelo Hayes
107 Ivy Nile
108 Cora Jade
109 Veer Mahaan
110 Gable Steveson

2022 Immaculate Collection WWE Shadowbox Signatures

*GOLD/10: UNPRICED DUE TO SCARCITY
*PLATINUM/1: UNPRICED DUE TO SCARCITY
STATED PRINT RUN 49-99 SETS

1 Blair Davenport/99
2 Lash Legend/99
6 Cody Rhodes/99
7 Ivy Nile/49
8 Joe Gacy/49
9 Axiom/99
11 Brutus Creed/49
12 Noam Dar/99
14 Solo Sikoa/99
15 Gigi Dolin/49
16 Von Wagner/49
17 Jacy Jayne/49
18 Julius Creed/49
20 Kit Wilson/49
21 Butch/49
22 Odyssey Jones/99
23 Drew Gulak/49
24 Stevie Turner/99
25 Grayson Waller/49
26 Wes Lee/99
27 Jinny/99
28 Katana Chance/49
29 Angelo Dawkins/49
30 Max Dupri/49
31 Damian Priest/49
33 Elton Prince/49
35 Indi Hartwell/99
36 Xyon Quinn/99
38 Kayden Carter/49
39 Aoife Valkyrie/99
40 Lacey Evans/99

2022 Immaculate Collection WWE Standout Memorabilia

*RED/25: UNPRICED DUE TO SCARCITY
*GOLD/10: UNPRICED DUE TO SCARCITY
*PLATINUM/1: UNPRICED DUE TO SCARCITY
STATED PRINT RUN 99 SER.#'d SETS

1 Indi Hartwell
2 Xavier Woods
3 Joaquin Wilde
4 Lacey Evans
5 AJ Styles
6 Rampage Brown
7 Bron Breakker
8 Roman Reigns
9 Dana Brooke
10 Shinsuke Nakamura
11 Ivar
12 Xyon Quinn
13 JD McDonagh
14 man.soor
15 Alexa Bliss
16 Reggie
17 Butch
18 Santos Escobar
19 Doudrop
20 Bobby Lashley
21 Jey Uso
22 Wolfgang
23 Kayden Carter
24 Montez Ford
25 Apollo Crews
26 Ricochet
27 Carmelo Hayes
28 Seth Rollins
29 Erik
30 Carmella
31 Jinder Mahal
32 Liv Morgan
33 Kofi Kingston
34 Odyssey Jones
35 Bianca Belair
36 Ridge Holland
37 Commander Azeez
38 Shayna Baszler
39 Gigi Dolin
40 Veer Mahaan

2022 Immaculate Collection WWE Superstar Swatches

*RED/25: UNPRICED DUE TO SCARCITY
*GOLD/10: UNPRICED DUE TO SCARCITY
*PLATINUM/1: UNPRICED DUE TO SCARCITY
STATED PRINT RUN 99 SER.#'d SETS

1 Alba Fyre
2 Nikki A.S.H.
3 Brutus Creed
4 Matt Riddle
5 Carmella
6 Sheamus
7 IYO SKY
8 Wes Lee
9 Joe Gacy
10 Lash Legend
11 Angelo Dawkins
12 Otis
13 Cameron Grimes
14 Roderick Strong
15 Drew Gulak
16 Shotzi
17 Jacy Jayne
18 Xia Li
19 Julius Creed
20 Mandy Rose
21 Asuka
22 Raquel Rodriguez
23 Tommaso Ciampa
24 Sami Zayn
25 Ezekiel
26 The Miz
27 Jimmy Uso
28 Zoey Stark
29 Kevin Owens
30 Meiko Satomura
31 Boa
32 Rhea Ripley
33 Damian Priest
34 Shanky
35. Happy Corbin
36 Tyler Bate
37 Jinny
38 Blair Davenport
39 Max Dupri
40 MVP

2022 Immaculate Collection WWE Triple Autographs

*PLATINUM/1: UNPRICED DUE TO SCARCITY
STATED PRINT RUN 5-10 SETS

1 Undertaker/HBK/HHH/10
2 Waller/Breakker/Hayes/10
3 Ziggler/Breakker/Ciampa/10
4 Woods/Big E/Kingston/10
5 Kelly/McCool/Phoenix/10
6 Rollins/McMahon/HHH/10
7 Faarooq/Undertaker/Bradshaw/10
8 The Usos/Reigns/10
9 D-Von/Spike/Bubba Ray/10
11 Nash/Hart/Jarrett/5
12 DiBiase/Knight/Grimes/10
13 Flair/Lynch/Bayley/10
14 Orton/HHH/Batista/10
15 Wilson/McCool/Kelly/10
16 Mark & Joe Coffey/Wolfgang/10
17 Hart/Honky Tonk Man/Valentine/10
18 Rose/Dolin/Jayne/10
20 Butch/Holland/Sheamus/10

2021 Impact Wrestling Complete Series

COMPLETE SET (40)	60.00	120.00
COMPLETE S1 SET (10)		
COMPLETE S2 SET (10)		
COMPLETE S3 SET (10)		
COMPLETE S4 SET (10)		
1 Mike Tenay	1.50	3.00
2 Abyss	1.25	3.00
3 Bobby Roode	1.50	4.00
4 Christian Cage	2.50	6.00
5 Gail Kim	4.00	10.00
6 Madison Rayne	5.00	12.00
7 Scott D'Amore	1.25	3.00
8 Chris Sabin	1.25	3.00
9 Matt Cardona	6.00	15.00
10 Matthew Rehwoldt		
11 Brian Myers	6.00	15.00
12 Deonna Purrazzo	10.00	25.00
13 Moose	8.00	20.00
14 Big LG	2.50	6.00
15 Karl Anderson	3.00	8.00
16 Eric Young	2.50	6.00
17 Rich Swann	2.00	5.00
18 Sami Callihan		
19 Suicide	5.00	12.00
20 Rosemary		
21 Tasha Steelz		
22 Ace Austin	6.00	15.00
23 Chris Bey	1.50	4.00
24 Eddie Edwards	3.00	8.00
25 Heath	3.00	8.00
26 Havok	1.25	3.00
27 Jordynne Grace	6.00	15.00
28 Josh Alexander		
29 Willie Mack	2.00	5.00
30 Crazzy Steve	1.25	3.00
31 VBD		
32 Hernandez	1.25	3.00
33 Jake Something	1.25	3.00
34 Johnny Swinger	3.00	8.00
35 Tenille Dashwood	4.00	10.00
36 Taylor Wilde	3.00	8.00
37 Trey Miguel	2.00	5.00
38 Rohit Raju		
39 Petey Williams	1.25	3.00
40 Steve Maclin	1.25	3.00

2021 Impact Wrestling Complete Series Autographs

STATED ODDS 1:SET

M3 Moose	20.00	50.00
AA2 Ace Austin	15.00	40.00
BM1 Brian Myers		
CS1 Chris Sabin	15.00	40.00
DP2 Deonna Purrazzo	50.00	100.00
JG3 Jordynne Grace	25.00	60.00
JS1 Johnny Swinger	10.00	25.00
LG1 Big LG	12.00	30.00
MC2 Matt Cardona	30.00	75.00
TD2 Tenille Dashwood	20.00	50.00
TM3 Trey Miguel	15.00	40.00
TS3 Tasha Steelz	30.00	75.00

1991 Impel WCW

COMPLETE SET (162)	6.00	15.00
UNOPENED BOX (36 PACKS)		
UNOPENED PACK (12 CARDS)		
1 Sting	.20	.50
2 Sting	.20	.50
3 Sting	.20	.50
4 Sting	.20	.50
5 Sting	.20	.50

6 Sting	.20	.50
7 Sting	.20	.50
8 Sting	.20	.50
9 Sting	.20	.50
10 Sting	.20	.50
11 Sting	.20	.50
12 Sting	.20	.50
13 Sting	2.00	5.00
14 Lex Luger	.10	.25
15 Lex Luger	.10	.25
16 Lex Luger	.10	.25
17 Lex Luger	.10	.25
18 Lex Luger	.10	.25
19 Lex Luger	.10	.25
20 Lex Luger	.10	.25
21 Lex Luger	.10	.25
22 Lex Luger	.10	.25
23 Lex Luger	.10	.25
24 Sid Vicious RC	.07	.20
25 Sid Vicious RC	.07	.20
26 Sid Vicious RC	.07	.20
27 Sid Vicious RC	.07	.20
28 Sid Vicious RC	.07	.20
29 Sid Vicious RC	.07	.20
30 Sid Vicious RC	.07	.20
31 Sid Vicious RC	.07	.20
32 Sid Vicious RC	.07	.20
33 Sid Vicious RC	.07	.20
34 Sid Vicious RC	.07	.20
35 Sid Vicious RC	.07	.20
36 Ric Flair	.30	.75
37 Ric Flair	.30	.75
38 Ric Flair	.30	.75
39 Ric Flair	.30	.75
40 Ric Flair	.30	.75
41 Ric Flair	.30	.75
42 Ric Flair	.30	.75
43 Ric Flair	.30	.75
44 Ric Flair	.30	.75
45 Ric Flair	.30	.75
46 Ric Flair	.30	.75
47 Ric Flair	2.00	5.00
48 Arn Anderson	.10	.25
49 Arn Anderson	.10	.25
50 Arn Anderson	.10	.25
51 Arn Anderson	.10	.25
52 Arn Anderson	.10	.25
53 Arn Anderson	.10	.25
54 Arn Anderson	.10	.25
55 Flyin Brian	.07	.20
56 Flyin Brian	.07	.20
57 Flyin Brian	.07	.20
58 Flyin Brian	.07	.20
59 Flyin Brian	.07	.20
60 Flyin Brian	.07	.20
61 Flyin Brian	.07	.20
62 Flyin Brian	.07	.20
63 Flyin Brian	.07	.20
64 Flyin Brian	.07	.20
65 Z-Man RC	.07	.20
66 Z-Man RC	.07	.20
67 Z-Man RC	.07	.20
68 Terry Taylor	.07	.20
69 Terry Taylor	.07	.20
70 Terry Taylor	.07	.20
71 Terry Taylor	.07	.20
72 Terry Taylor	.07	.20
73 Terry Taylor	.07	.20
74 Terry Taylor	.07	.20
75 Terry Taylor	.07	.20
76 Dutch Mantell RC	.10	.25
77 Dutch Mantell RC	.10	.25
78 Dutch Mantell RC	.10	.25
79 Dutch Mantell RC	.10	.25
80 Dutch Mantell RC	.10	.25
81 Dutch Mantell RC	.10	.25
82 Mr. Wall Street	.07	.20
83 Mr. Wall Street	.07	.20
84 Mr. Wall Street	.07	.20
85 El Gigante RC	.07	.20
86 El Gigante RC	.07	.20
87 El Gigante RC	.07	.20
88 El Gigante RC	.07	.20
89 El Gigante RC	.07	.20
90 El Gigante RC	.07	.20
91 El Gigante RC	.07	.20
92 El Gigante RC	.07	.20
93 Tommy Rich RC	.07	.20
94 Tommy Rich RC	.07	.20
95 Tommy Rich RC	.07	.20
96 Tommy Rich RC	.07	.20
97 Ricky Morton	.07	.20
98 Ricky Morton	.07	.20
99 Ricky Morton	.07	.20
100 Ricky Morton	.07	.20
101 Ricky Morton	.07	.20
102 Ricky Morton	.07	.20
103 Steiner Brothers	.10	.25
104 Steiner Brothers	.10	.25
105 Steiner Brothers	.10	.25
106 Steiner Brothers	.10	.25
107 Steiner Brothers	.10	.25
108 Steiner Brothers	.10	.25
109 Steiner Brothers	.10	.25
110 Steiner Brothers	.10	.25
111 Steiner Brothers	.10	.25
112 Steiner Brothers	.10	.25
113 Steiner Brothers	.10	.25
114 Steiner Brothers	.10	.25
115 Steiner Brothers	.10	.25
116 Steiner Brothers	.10	.25
117 Fabulous Freebirds	.10	.25
118 Fabulous Freebirds	.10	.25
119 Fabulous Freebirds	.10	.25
120 Fabulous Freebirds	.10	.25
121 Fabulous Freebirds	.10	.25
122 Fabulous Freebirds	.10	.25
123 Fabulous Freebirds	.10	.25
124 Fabulous Freebirds	.10	.25
125 Fabulous Freebirds	.10	.25
126 Fabulous Freebirds	.10	.25
127 Fabulous Freebirds	.10	.25
128 Fabulous Freebirds	.10	.25
129 Southern Boys	.07	.20
130 Southern Boys	.07	.20
131 Southern Boys	.07	.20
132 Southern Boys	.07	.20
133 Southern Boys	.07	.20
134 Southern Boys	.07	.20
135 Southern Boys	.07	.20
136 Southern Boys	.07	.20
137 Southern Boys	.07	.20
138 Southern Boys	.07	.20
139 Doom	.10	.25
140 Doom	.10	.25
141 Doom	.10	.25
142 Doom	.10	.25
143 Doom	.10	.25
144 Doom	.10	.25
145 Doom	.10	.25
146 Doom	.10	.25
147 Doom	.10	.25
148 Doom	.10	.25
149 Doom	.10	.25
150 Doom	.10	.25
151 Teddy Long	.07	.20
152 Teddy Long	.07	.20
153 Teddy Long	.07	.20
154 Jim Ross RC	.07	.20
155 Jim Ross RC	.07	.20
156 Jim Ross RC	.07	.20
157 Missy Hyatt	.10	.25
158 Missy Hyatt	.10	.25
159 Missy Hyatt	.10	.25
160 Missy Hyatt	.10	.25
161 Checklist	.07	.20
162 Checklist	.07	.20
NNO Sting HOLO	8.00	20.00

2018 Leaf Legends of Wrestling Autographs

UNOPENED BOX (8 CARDS)
*GREEN/15: UNPRICED DUE TO SCARCITY
*GOLD/10: UNPRICED DUE TO SCARCITY
*PURPLE/5: UNPRICED DUE TO SCARCITY
*RED/1: UNPRICED DUE TO SCARCITY

LWC1 Christian	5.00	12.00
LWE1 Edge	8.00	20.00
LWK1 Konnan	4.00	10.00
LWR1 Ricochet	15.00	40.00
LWS1 Slick	5.00	12.00
LW2CS 2 Cold Scorpio	4.00	10.00
LWAS1 Alexis Smirnoff	12.00	30.00
LWBF1 Bad Luck Fale	6.00	15.00
LWBH1 Bret Hart	8.00	20.00
LWBL1 Bobby Lashley	6.00	15.00
LWBVR Baron Von Raschke	10.00	25.00
LWBW1 Barry Windham	5.00	12.00
LWCJ1 Chris Jericho	8.00	20.00
LWCK1 Corporal Kirchner	5.00	12.00
LWCR1 Cody Rhodes	15.00	40.00
LWDK1 Dynamite Kid	12.00	30.00
LWGS1 The Great Sasuke	6.00	15.00
LWGV1 Greg Valentine	5.00	12.00
LWHT1 Hiroshi Tanahashi	6.00	15.00
LWJB1 Jim Brunzell	4.00	10.00
LWJH1 Jimmy Hart	5.00	12.00
LWJR1 Jacques Rougeau	4.00	10.00
LWJR2 Jake Roberts	6.00	15.00
LWJR3 Jim Ross	6.00	15.00
LWJV1 Jesse Ventura	20.00	50.00
LWJV2 Jesse Ventura	20.00	50.00
LWKF1 Kazuyuki Fujita	8.00	20.00
LWKI1 Kota Ibushi	10.00	25.00
LWKK1 Kendo Kashin	4.00	10.00
LWKN1 Kevin Nash	6.00	15.00
LWKO1 Kazuchika Okada	12.00	30.00
LWKO2 Kenny Omega	25.00	60.00
LWKS1 Katsuyori Shibata	8.00	20.00
LWLH1 Larry Hennig	12.00	30.00
LWMS1 Minoru Suzuki	8.00	20.00
LWMW1 Mikey Whipwreck	4.00	10.00
LWPE1 Penta El Zero M	10.00	25.00
LWPO1 Pierre Ouellet	6.00	15.00
LWRF1 Ric Flair	15.00	40.00
LWRR1 Rocky Romero	4.00	10.00
LWSD1 Shane Douglas	4.00	10.00
LWSH1 Sam Houston	5.00	12.00
LWTI1 Tomohiro Ishii	12.00	30.00
LWTL1 Tanga Loa	12.00	30.00
LWTN1 Tetsuya Naito	12.00	30.00
LWTT1 Tama Tonga	10.00	25.00
LWWO1 Will Ospreay	12.00	30.00

2018 Leaf Legends of Wrestling Dual Autographs

LWD1 Edge /Christian	12.00	30.00
LWD2 C.Jericho/Christian	10.00	25.00
LWD3 K.Ibushi/B.L.Fale	8.00	20.00
LWD4 B.Hart/K.Nash		
LWD5 K.Nash/Konnan	10.00	25.00
LWD6 Konnan/S.Douglas		
LWD7 S.Douglas/2 Cold Scorpio	8.00	20.00
LWD8 J.Rougeau/P.Ouellet		
LWD9 2 Cold Scorpio/M.Whipwreck		
LWD10 B.L.Fale/T.Loa	12.00	30.00
LWD11 B.Windham/2 Cold Scorpio	8.00	20.00
LWD12 C.Rhodes/Christian		
LWD13 G.Valentine/J.Roberts	8.00	20.00
LWD14 L.Hennig/B.Von Raschke		
LWD15 Minoru Suzuki Tomohiro Ishii	15.00	40.00

2018 Leaf Legends of Wrestling Originals Update Autographs

E1 Edge (2014)	6.00	15.00
S3 Sunny (2014)	8.00	20.00
BW1 The Bushwackers (2014)	15.00	40.00
DB1 Dick Beyer (2017)	8.00	20.00
FE1 Fedor Emelianenko (2016)	12.00	30.00
JB1 Jim Brunzell (2017)	6.00	15.00
KS1 Kazuski Sakuraba (2016)	8.00	20.00
MTA Magnum T.A. (2017)	6.00	15.00
PP1 Pat Patterson (2014)	6.00	15.00
PVZ Paige VanZant (2016)	10.00	25.00
RG1 Royce Gracie (2016)	12.00	30.00
RMJ Rey Mysterio Jr. (2017)	10.00	25.00
RS1 Ricky Steamboat (2017)	8.00	20.00
RS2 Ryan Shamrock (2017)	5.00	12.00
SL1 Stan Lane (2014)	5.00	12.00
SR2 Stevie Richards (2014)	5.00	12.00

2012 Leaf Originals Wrestling

*YELLOW/99: .5X TO 1.2X BASIC AUTOS
*BLUE/25: .6X TO 1.5X BASIC AUTOS
*RED/10: UNPRICED DUE TO SCARCITY
*BLACK/1: UNPRICED DUE TO SCARCITY
*P.P.BLACK/1: UNPRICED DUE TO SCARCITY
*P.P.CYAN/1: UNPRICED DUE TO SCARCITY
*P.P.MAGENTA/1: UNPRICED DUE TO SCARCITY
*P.P.YELLOW/1: UNPRICED DUE TO SCARCITY
*A.A.: SAME VALUE AS BASIC AUTOS
*A.A.YELLOW/25: .6X TO 1.5X BASIC AUTOS
*A.A.BLUE/10: UNPRICED DUE TO SCARCITY
*A.A.RED/5: UNPRICED DUE TO SCARCITY
*A.A.BLACK/1: UNPRICED DUE TO SCARCITY
*A.A.P.P.BLACK/1: UNPRICED DUE TO SCARCITY
*A.A.P.P.CYAN/1: UNPRICED DUE TO SCARCITY
*A.A.P.P.MAGENTA/1: UNPRICED DUE TO SCARCITY
*A.A.P.P.YELLOW/1: UNPRICED DUE TO SCARCITY

ATB Abdullah the Butcher 10.00 25.00
BB1 Bob Backlund 10.00 25.00
BB2 Brutus Beefcake 8.00 20.00
BB3 Buff Bagwell 8.00 20.00
BH1 Bobby Heenan 12.00 30.00
BH2 Bret Hart 40.00 80.00
BO1 Cowboy Bob Orton Jr. 8.00 20.00
BS1 Bruno Sammartino 15.00 40.00
DDP Diamond Dallas Page 8.00 20.00
DS1 Dan Severn 6.00 15.00
GJG Jimmy Garvin 6.00 15.00
GS1 George Steele 10.00 25.00
GV1 Greg Valentine 8.00 20.00
HH1 Hulk Hogan 60.00 120.00
HJ1 Hillbilly Jim 10.00 25.00
HTM The Honky Tonk Man 10.00 25.00
IK1 Ivan Koloff 8.00 20.00
IP1 The Polish Hammer Ivan Putski 8.00 20.00
JD1 Hacksaw Jim Duggan 12.00 30.00
JH1 Jimmy Hart 10.00 25.00
JN1 Jim Neidhart 8.00 20.00
JR1 Jake Roberts 12.00 30.00
KA1 Kamala 8.00 20.00
KBW Koko B. Ware 8.00 20.00
KN1 Kevin Nash 15.00 40.00
KS1 Ken Shamrock 8.00 20.00
LL1 Lex Luger 10.00 25.00
LP1 Lanny Poffo 6.00 15.00
LZ1 Larry Zbyszko 6.00 15.00
MH1 Missy Hyatt 6.00 15.00
MJ1 Marty Jannetty 6.00 15.00
NK1 Nikita Koloff 8.00 20.00
NV1 Nikolai Volkoff 8.00 20.00
OMG One Man Gang 8.00 20.00
PO1 Paul Orndorff 25.00 60.00
PR1 Pete Rose 12.00 30.00
RM1 Rick Martel 6.00 15.00
RRP Rowdy Roddy Piper 75.00 150.00
RS1 Rick Steiner 6.00 15.00
SBG Billy Graham 25.00 50.00
SH1 Scott Hall 12.00 30.00
SID Sid 8.00 20.00
SS1 Scott Steiner 8.00 20.00
TA1 Tony Atlas 6.00 15.00
TAT Tatanka 8.00 20.00
TDB Ted DiBiase 10.00 25.00
TIS The Iron Sheik 15.00 40.00
TNB Ric Flair 30.00 75.00
TS1 Tito Santana 8.00 20.00
VAD Vader 25.00 60.00
WR1 Wendi Richter 8.00 20.00
PARWA Road Warrior Animal LOS 30.00 75.00

2014 Leaf Originals Wrestling

UNOPENED BOX (5 CARDS)
*YELLOW/99: SAME VALUE AS BASIC AUTOS
*BLUE/25: .5X TO 1.2X BASIC AUTOS
*RED/10: UNPRICED DUE TO SCARCITY
*BLACK/1: UNPRICED DUE TO SCARCITY
*P.P.BLACK/1: UNPRICED DUE TO SCARCITY
*P.P.CYAN/1: UNPRICED DUE TO SCARCITY
*P.P.MAGENTA/1: UNPRICED DUE TO SCARCITY
*P.P.YELLOW/1: UNPRICED DUE TO SCARCITY
*ALT.ART./ .5X TO 1.2X BASIC AUTOS
*A.A.YELLOW/25: .6X TO 1.5X BASIC AUTOS
*A.A.BLUE/10: UNPRICED DUE TO SCARCITY
*A.A.RED/5: UNPRICED DUE TO SCARCITY
*A.A.BLACK/1: UNPRICED DUE TO SCARCITY
*A.A.P.P.BLACK/1: UNPRICED DUE TO SCARCITY
*A.A.P.P.CYAN/1: UNPRICED DUE TO SCARCITY
*A.A.P.P.MAGENTA/1: UNPRICED DUE TO SCARCITY
*A.A.P.P.YELLOW/1: UNPRICED DUE TO SCARCITY

AF1 Francine 5.00 12.00
AG1 Gangrel SP 6.00 15.00
AG2 Godfather 5.00 12.00
AG3 Goldberg 50.00 100.00
AM1 Maryse 6.00 15.00
AR1 Raven 5.00 12.00
AS1 Sabu 12.00 30.00
AS2 Samu 6.00 15.00
AS2 Sting 25.00 60.00
AS3 Sandman 5.00 12.00
AW1 Warlord 5.00 12.00
AZ1 Zeus 5.00 12.00
A2CS 2 Cold Scorpio SP 5.00 12.00
AAB1 Adam Bomb 5.00 12.00
AAS1 Al Snow 5.00 12.00
ABH1 Bob Holly 5.00 12.00
ABH1 Bobby Heenan SP 12.00 30.00
ABM1 Balls Mahoney 5.00 12.00
ABM1 Blue Meanie 5.00 12.00
ACM1 Candice Michelle SP 10.00 25.00
ADA1 Demolition Ax 5.00 12.00
ADK1 Dynamite Kid SP 12.00 30.00
ADM1 Don Muraco 5.00 12.00
ADR1 Dennis Rodman SP 15.00 40.00
ADS1 Demolition Smash 5.00 12.00
AGB1 Gerald Brisco 5.00 12.00
AHH1 Hulk Hogan SP 75.00 150.00
AIS1 Iron Sheik 6.00 15.00
AJD1 J.J. Dillon 5.00 12.00
AJH1 Jeff Hardy SP 10.00 25.00
AJR2 Jake Roberts SP 10.00 25.00
AKK1 Kelly Kelly 6.00 15.00
AKKB King Kong Bundy 15.00 40.00
AKN1 Kevin Nash 8.00 20.00
AKP1 Ken Patera 5.00 12.00
AKVE Kevin Von Erich 6.00 15.00
ALS1 Lance Storm 5.00 12.00
AMK1 Maria Kanellis 6.00 15.00
AMT1 Mike Tyson SP 80.00 150.00
AOA1 Ole Anderson 25.00 60.00
ARF1 Ric Flair SP 75.00 150.00
ARF2 Rikishi Fatu 10.00 25.00
ARG1 Robert Gibson 5.00 12.00
ARM1 Ricky Morton 5.00 12.00
ARP1 Roddy Piper SP 50.00 100.00
ARS1 Ron Simmons 6.00 15.00
ASH1 Scott Hall 15.00 40.00
ASR1 Stevie Ray SP 6.00 15.00
ATB1 The Barbarian 5.00 12.00
ATD1 Tommy Dreamer 5.00 12.00
ATF1 Terry Funk 25.00 60.00
ATNB The Nasty Boys 8.00 20.00
ATS1 Trish Stratus 20.00 50.00
AVV1 Val Venis 5.00 12.00

2014 Leaf Originals Wrestling Flair's Epic Battles

*YELLOW/25: X TO X BASIC AUTO
*BLUE/10: UNPRICED DUE TO SCARCITY
*RED/5: UNPRICED DUE TO SCARCITY
*BLACK/1: UNPRICED DUE TO SCARCITY
*P.P.BLACK/1: UNPRICED DUE TO SCARCITY
*P.P.CYAN/1: UNPRICED DUE TO SCARCITY
*P.P.MAGENTA/1: UNPRICED DUE TO SCARCITY
*P.P.YELLOW/1: UNPRICED DUE TO SCARCITY

RFBH1 Ric Flair 80.00 150.00
Bret Hart
RFHH1 Ric Flair/Hulk Hogan 120.00 250.00
RFRM1 Ric Flair/Ricky Morton 20.00 50.00
RFRP1 Ric Flair/Roddy Piper 80.00 150.00

2017 Leaf Originals Wrestling Autographs

*YELLOW/99: .6X TO 1.5X BASIC AUTOS
*BLUE/25: .75X TO 2X BASIC AUTOS
*RED/10: 1X TO 2.5X BASIC CARDS
*BLACK/1: UNPRICED DUE TO SCARCITY
*ALT.ART: SAME VALUE AS BASIC AUTOS
*ALT.YELLOW/25: .75X TO 2X BASIC AUTOS
*ALT.BLUE/10: 1X TO 2.5X BASIC AUTOS
*ALT.RED/5: UNPRICED DUE TO SCARCITY
*ALT.BLACK/1: UNPRICED DUE TO SCARCITY

K1 Konnan 8.00 20.00
V2 Victoria 5.00 12.00
BB1 B. Brian Blair 5.00 12.00
BL1 Bobby Lashley 5.00 12.00
BW1 Barry Windham 6.00 15.00
DFJ Dory Funk Jr. 6.00 15.00
DLB D'Lo Brown 5.00 12.00
DM2 Dutch Mantel 5.00 12.00
JR1 Jacques Rougeau 5.00 12.00
JR2 Jim Ross 8.00 20.00
LK1 Leilani Kai 5.00 12.00
MF1 Manny Fernandez 5.00 12.00
MM1 Marc Mero 5.00 12.00
MVP MVP 6.00 15.00
SB1 Shelton Benjamin 6.00 15.00
SD1 Shane Douglas 5.00 12.00
TW1 Torrie Wilson 8.00 20.00

2017 Leaf Originals Wrestling '14 Design Autographs

*YELLOW/50-99: .6X TO 1.5X BASIC AUTOS
*BLUE/25: .75X TO 2X BASIC AUTOS
*RED/10: 1X TO 2.5X BASIC AUTOS
*BLACK/1: UNPRICED DUE TO SCARCITY
*P.P.BLACK/1: UNPRICED DUE TO SCARCITY
*P.P.CYAN/1: UNPRICED DUE TO SCARCITY
*P.P.MAGENTA/1: UNPRICED DUE TO SCARCITY
*P.P.YELLOW/1: UNPRICED DUE TO SCARCITY
*ALT.ART: SAME VALUE AS BASIC AUTOS
*ALT.YELLOW/25: .75X TO 2X BASIC AUTOS
*ALT.BLUE/10: 1X TO 2.5X BASIC AUTOS
*ALT.RED/5: UNPRICED DUE TO SCARCITY
*ALT.BLACK/1: UNPRICED DUE TO SCARCITY
*ALT.P.P.BLACK/1: UNPRICED DUE TO SCARCITY
*ALT.P.P.CYAN/1: UNPRICED DUE TO SCARCITY
*ALT.P.P.MAGENTA/1: UNPRICED DUE TO SCARCITY
*ALT.P.P.YELLOW/1: UNPRICED DUE TO SCARCITY

C1 Chyna 20.00 50.00
H1 Haku 6.00 15.00
S1 Slick 5.00 12.00
BE1 Bobby Eaton 5.00 12.00
BG1 Billy Gunn 5.00 12.00
BH2 Bret Hart 15.00 40.00
BR1 Butch Reed 5.00 12.00
BT1 Booker T 8.00 20.00
CH1 Christy Hemme 6.00 15.00
CJ1 Chris Jericho 8.00 20.00
DC1 Dennis Condrey 5.00 12.00
DH1 Danny Hodge 6.00 15.00
EB1 Eric Bischoff 5.00 12.00
JC1 Jim Cornette 6.00 15.00
JJ1 Jeff Jarrett 6.00 15.00
JL1 Jushin Liger 8.00 20.00
KS1 Kevin Sullivan 5.00 12.00
MF1 Mick Foley 8.00 20.00
MH1 Matt Hardy 5.00 12.00
RVD Rob Van Dam 5.00 12.00
TB1 Tully Blanchard 5.00 12.00
TR1 Terri Runnels 6.00 15.00
WS1 Wild Samoans 8.00 20.00
XP1 X-Pac 6.00 15.00

2017 Leaf Originals Wrestling '16 Design Autographs

*YELLOW/50: .6X TO 1.5X BASIC AUTOS
*BLUE/25: .75X TO 2X BASIC AUTOS
*RED/10: 1X TO 2.5X BASIC AUTOS
*BLACK/1: UNPRICED DUE TO SCARCITY
*ALT.ART: SAME VALUE AS BASIC AUTOS
*ALT.YELLOW/25: .75X TO 2X BASIC AUTOS
*ALT.BLUE/10: 1X TO 2.5X BASIC AUTOS
*ALT.RED/5: UNPRICED DUE TO SCARCITY
*ALT.BLACK/1: UNPRICED DUE TO SCARCITY

HH1 Hulk Hogan 20.00 50.00
KS1 Kazushi Sakuraba 12.00 30.00

2016 Leaf Signature Series Wrestling

UNOPENED BOX (8 CARDS)
*BLUE/7-50: UNPRICED DUE TO SCARCITY
*GREEN/5-25: UNPRICED DUE TO SCARCITY
*RED/3-10: UNPRICED DUE TO SCARCITY
*BLACK/2-5: UNPRICED DUE TO SCARCITY
*PURPLE/1: UNPRICED DUE TO SCARCITY
*P.P.BLACK/1: UNPRICED DUE TO SCARCITY
*P.P.CYAN/1: UNPRICED DUE TO SCARCITY
*P.P.MAGENTA/1: UNPRICED DUE TO SCARCITY
*P.P.BLACK/1: UNPRICED DUE TO SCARCITY

1 6-Pac 8.00 20.00
2 Adam Bomb 8.00 20.00
3 Adam Pearce 8.00 20.00
4 Al Snow 6.00 15.00
5 Balls Mahoney 10.00 25.00
6 The Barbarian 8.00 20.00
7 Barry Windham 10.00 25.00
8 Goldberg 25.00 60.00
9 Blue Meanie 8.00 20.00
10 Bob Holly 6.00 15.00
11 Bobby Heenan 30.00 75.00
12 Bolo Mongol/Ax 10.00 25.00
13 Brutus Beefcake 8.00 20.00
14 Bushwacker Luke 8.00 20.00
15 Carlito 6.00 15.00
16 Carlos Colon 10.00 25.00
17 Chris Masters 6.00 15.00
18 Christopher Daniels 6.00 15.00
19 Christy Hemme 12.00 30.00
20 Debra McMichael 10.00 25.00
21 Dennis Condrey 6.00 15.00
22 Dennis Rodman 15.00 40.00
23 Dynamite Kid 10.00 25.00
24 Ezekiel Jackson 6.00 15.00
25 Fifi/Wendy Barlow 10.00 25.00
26 Francine 10.00 25.00

27 Frankie Kazarian	6.00	15.00
28 Gangrel	6.00	15.00
29 Greg Valentine	10.00	25.00
30 Harley Race	12.00	30.00
31 Headshrinker Fatu	8.00	20.00
32 Hulk Hogan	30.00	80.00
33 Jeff Jarrett	10.00	25.00
34 Gerald Brisco	6.00	15.00
35 Jesus	6.00	15.00
36 Jimmy Garvin	6.00	15.00
37 Jimmy Hart	8.00	20.00
38 J.J. Dillon	8.00	20.00
39 Jushin Liger	15.00	40.00
40 Kama	6.00	15.00
Kama Mustafa		
41 Kamala	8.00	20.00
42 Kelly Kelly	15.00	40.00
43 Ken Patera	8.00	20.00
44 Kevin Nash	10.00	25.00
45 Kevin Sullivan	10.00	25.00
46 King Kong Bundy	10.00	25.00
47 King Mo	6.00	15.00
48 Lanny Poffo	6.00	15.00
49 Larry Zbyszko	8.00	20.00
50 Lita	15.00	40.00
51 Maria Kanellis	10.00	25.00
52 Marlena	12.00	30.00
53 Masato Tanaka	8.00	20.00
54 Matt Hardy	8.00	20.00
55 Matt Striker	6.00	15.00
56 Mike Tyson	50.00	100.00
57 Mil Mascaras	30.00	80.00
58 Nick Bockwinkel	30.00	75.00
59 Nikita Koloff	8.00	20.00
60 Nikolai Volkoff	8.00	20.00
61 Ole Anderson	10.00	25.00
62 Papa Shango	8.00	20.00
63 Pat Tanaka	6.00	15.00
64 Pete Rose	15.00	40.00
65 Reby Sky	8.00	20.00
66 Repo Man	12.00	30.00
67 Ric Flair	20.00	50.00
68 Rick Steiner	10.00	25.00
69 Ricky Morton	8.00	20.00
70 Robert Gibson	8.00	20.00
71 Ron Simmons	8.00	20.00
72 Sabu	8.00	20.00
73 Samu	6.00	15.00
74 Scott Hall	15.00	40.00
75 Scott Norton	6.00	15.00
76 Sid Vicious	10.00	25.00
77 Steve Corino	6.00	15.00
78 Stevie Ray	8.00	20.00
79 Sunny	12.00	30.00
80 Terri Runnels	10.00	25.00
81 The Godfather	6.00	15.00
82 Iron Sheik	12.00	30.00
83 Tito Santana	10.00	25.00
84 Tommy Dreamer	8.00	20.00
85 Tully Blanchard	10.00	25.00
86 Val Venis	6.00	15.00
87 Warlord	6.00	15.00
88 Wendi Richter	15.00	40.00
89 Wrath	8.00	20.00
90 X-Pac	8.00	20.00
91 Zeus	12.00	30.00
92 Zodiac	8.00	20.00

2016 Leaf Signature Series Wrestling Adversaries

*BLUE/15-25: UNPRICED DUE TO SCARCITY
*GREEN/10: UNPRICED DUE TO SCARCITY
*RED/5: UNPRICED DUE TO SCARCITY
*BLACK/3: UNPRICED DUE TO SCARCITY
*PURPLE/1: UNPRICED DUE TO SCARCITY
*P.P.BLACK/1: UNPRICED DUE TO SCARCITY
*P.P.CYAN/1: UNPRICED DUE TO SCARCITY
*P.P.MAGENTA/1: UNPRICED DUE TO SCARCITY
*P.P.YELLOW/1: UNPRICED DUE TO SCARCITY
RANDOMLY INSERTED INTO PACKS

ADV01 S.Corino/T.Funk	15.00	40.00
ADV02 R.Flair/J.Garvin	20.00	50.00
ADV03 123 Kid/S.Hall	12.00	30.00
ADV05 B.Windham/B.Beefcake	12.00	30.00
ADV06 B.Eaton/R.Morton	12.00	30.00
ADV07 Carlito/Sabu	10.00	25.00
ADV09 S.Douglas/C.Daniels	10.00	25.00
ADV10 C.Hemme/V.Sky	20.00	50.00
ADV11 T.Dreamer/Francine	15.00	40.00
ADV12 Raven /F.Kazarian	10.00	25.00
ADV13 Animal/K.Sullivan	12.00	30.00
ADV14 Sandman/M.Striker	10.00	25.00
ADV15 Bushwacker Luke/P.Tanaka	12.00	30.00
ADV16 T.Dreamer/Sabu	15.00	40.00
ADV17 Zeus/H.Hogan	60.00	120.00

2016 Leaf Signature Series Wrestling Hall of Fame

*BLUE/15-50: UNPRICED DUE TO SCARCITY
*GREEN/10-25: UNPRICED DUE TO SCARCITY
*RED/5-10: UNPRICED DUE TO SCARCITY
*BLACK/3-5: UNPRICED DUE TO SCARCITY
*PURPLE/1: UNPRICED DUE TO SCARCITY
*P.P.BLACK/1: UNPRICED DUE TO SCARCITY
*P.P.CYAN/1: UNPRICED DUE TO SCARCITY
*P.P.MAGENTA/1: UNPRICED DUE TO SCARCITY
*P.P.YELLOW/1: UNPRICED DUE TO SCARCITY
RANDOMLY INSERTED INTO PACKS

HOF01 Bobby Heenan	20.00	50.00
HOF02 Carlos Colon	10.00	25.00
HOF03 Iron Sheik	10.00	25.00
HOF04 Wendi Richter	10.00	25.00
HOF05 Ron Simmons	10.00	25.00
HOF06 Nick Bockwinkel	50.00	100.00
HOF07 Ric Flair	25.00	60.00
HOF08 Mil Mascaras	30.00	80.00
HOF09 Harley Race	12.00	30.00
HOF10 Pete Rose	15.00	40.00
HOF11 Mike Tyson	50.00	100.00

2016 Leaf Signature Series Wrestling Ring Showdowns

*BLUE/7-50: UNPRICED DUE TO SCARCITY
*GREEN/5-10: UNPRICED DUE TO SCARCITY
*RED/3-5: UNPRICED DUE TO SCARCITY
*BLACK/2-3: UNPRICED DUE TO SCARCITY
*PURPLE/1: UNPRICED DUE TO SCARCITY
*P.P.BLACK/1: UNPRICED DUE TO SCARCITY
*P.P.CYAN/1: UNPRICED DUE TO SCARCITY
*P.P.MAGENTA/1: UNPRICED DUE TO SCARCITY
*P.P.YELLOW/1: UNPRICED DUE TO SCARCITY
RANDOMLY INSERTED INTO PACKS

RS201 Steve Corino/Greg Valentine	12.00	30.00
RS202 B.Bagwell/S.Norton	10.00	25.00
RS203 X-Pac /V.Venis	10.00	25.00
RS204 123 Kid/P.Tanaka	10.00	25.00
RS206 A.Bomb/Virgil	8.00	20.00
RS207 A.Snow/Raven	10.00	25.00
RS208 B.Mahoney/Sabu	15.00	40.00
RS209 Gangrel/Blue Meanie	10.00	25.00
RS210 H.Hogan/B.Beefcake	25.00	60.00
RS211 B.Beefcake/Masked Superstar	20.00	50.00
RS213 X-Pac /Gangrel	8.00	20.00
RS214 Gangrel /Godfather	8.00	20.00
RS215 K.Patera/T.Atlas	12.00	30.00
RS216 M.Bennett/S.Richards	8.00	20.00
RS217 M.Hardy/M.Bennett	12.00	30.00
RS218 R.Steiner/Vincent	8.00	20.00
RS219 K.Nash/R.Steiner	15.00	40.00
RS220 K.Nash/S.Vicious	15.00	40.00
RS222 T.Runnels/S.Richards	10.00	25.00
RS224 H.Hogan/D.Rodman	50.00	100.00

2016 Leaf Signature Series Wrestling Team Effort

*BLUE/7-50: UNPRICED DUE TO SCARCITY
*GREEN/5-25: UNPRICED DUE TO SCARCITY
*RED/3-10: UNPRICED DUE TO SCARCITY
*BLACK/2-5: UNPRICED DUE TO SCARCITY
*PURPLE/1: UNPRICED DUE TO SCARCITY
*P.P.BLACK/1: UNPRICED DUE TO SCARCITY
*P.P.CYAN/1: UNPRICED DUE TO SCARCITY
*P.P.MAGENTA/1: UNPRICED DUE TO SCARCITY
*P.P.YELLOW/1: UNPRICED DUE TO SCARCITY
RANDOMLY INSERTED INTO PACKS

TE01 S.Corino/A.Pearce	12.00	30.00
TE02 K.Patera/S.Norton	10.00	25.00
TE03 Konnan/S.Norton	20.00	50.00
TE05 J.Garvin/Precious	15.00	40.00
TE06 Ax/Smash	20.00	50.00
TE08 B.Eaton/D.Condrey	12.00	30.00
TE09 S.Lane/B.Eaton	12.00	30.00
TE10 S.Too Hotty/B.Christopher	15.00	40.00
TE11 B.Knobbs/J.Sags	12.00	30.00
TE13 J.Cornette/D.Condrey	10.00	25.00
TE14 Kama/Tatanka	10.00	25.00
TE15 C.Michelle/K.Kelly	12.00	30.00
TE16 N.Koloff/K.Kruschev	15.00	40.00
TE18 T.Runnels/V.Venis	15.00	40.00
TE19 N.Jackson/M.Jackson	8.00	20.00
TE20 M.Kanellis/M.Bennett	15.00	40.00
TE21 R.Steiner/S.Steiner	20.00	50.00
TE22 R.Morton/R.Gibson	12.00	30.00
TE23 Rikishi Fatu	8.00	20.00
Samu		
TE24 Tori/X-Pac	12.00	30.00

2020 Leaf Ultimate Wrestling Ultimate Stars Autographs

*PURPLE/45>: X TO X BASIC AUTOS
*PLATINUM/25>: UNPRICED DUE TO SCARCITY
*RED/10>: UNPRICED DUE TO SCARCITY
*EMERALD/5>: UNPRICED DUE TO SCARCITY
*SILVER/3>: UNPRICED DUE TO SCARCITY
*GOLD/1: UNPRICED DUE TO SCARCITY
*P.P.BLACK/1: UNPRICED DUE TO SCARCITY
*P.P.CYAN/1: UNPRICED DUE TO SCARCITY
*P.P.MAGENTA/1: UNPRICED DUE TO SCARCITY
*P.P.YELLOW/1: UNPRICED DUE TO SCARCITY

USE1 Edge	12.00	30.00
USG1 Goldberg	25.00	60.00
USK1 Kamala	10.00	25.00
UST1 Tugboat/Typhoon/Shockmaster	20.00	50.00
USW1 Warlord	8.00	20.00
USAA1 Arn Anderson	12.00	30.00
USAP1 Adam Page	15.00	40.00
USBB1 Britt Baker	12.00	30.00
USBB1 Brutus Beefcake	6.00	15.00
USBH1 Bret Hart	15.00	40.00
USBL1 Brother Love	8.00	20.00
USBOJ Bob Orton Jr.	6.00	15.00
USBP1 Brian Pillman Jr.	6.00	15.00
USBV1 Baron Von Raschke	10.00	25.00
USBW1 Barry Windham	10.00	25.00
USCC1 Colt Cabana	6.00	15.00
USCM1 Cima	5.00	12.00
USCR1 Cody Rhodes	15.00	40.00
USDA1 Demolition Ax	8.00	20.00
USDF1 Don Frye	6.00	15.00
USDS1 Demolition Smash	12.00	30.00
USEB1 Eric Bischoff	10.00	25.00
USED1 El Hijo del Fantasma	6.00	15.00
USFG1 Flip Gordon	5.00	12.00
USFL1 Flamita	5.00	12.00
USFU1 Funaki	6.00	15.00
USGM1 The Great Muta	15.00	40.00
USHH1 Hulk Hogan	60.00	120.00
USHT1 Hiroshi Tanahashi	8.00	20.00
USHTM The Honky Tonk Man	10.00	25.00
USJB1 Josh Barnett	10.00	25.00
USJH1 Jimmy Hart	8.00	20.00
USJL1 Jushin Liger	15.00	40.00
USKBW Koko B. Ware	10.00	25.00
USKI1 Kota Ibushi	15.00	40.00
USKO1 Kenny Omega	15.00	40.00
USKS1 Ken Shamrock	15.00	40.00
USLH1 Larry Hennig	10.00	25.00
USMF1 Manny Fernandez	6.00	15.00
USMF1 Mick Foley	15.00	40.00
USMS1 Minoru Suzuki	10.00	25.00
USPE1 Penta El Zero M	10.00	25.00
USPF1 Penelope Ford	10.00	25.00
USPS1 Perry Saturn	5.00	12.00
USRF1 Ric Flair	25.00	60.00
USRS1 Ricky Steamboat	10.00	25.00
USSS1 Sumie Sakai	5.00	12.00
USSV1 Sid Vicious	6.00	15.00
USTA1 Tony Atlas	6.00	15.00
USTB1 The Barbarian	6.00	15.00
USTB1 Tully Blanchard	10.00	25.00
USTD1 Ted DiBiase	10.00	25.00
USTF1 Terry Funk	15.00	40.00
USTS1 Tito Santana	8.00	20.00
USTZ1 Tazz	8.00	20.00
USVP1 Vampiro	8.00	20.00
USYH1 Yoshi-Hashi	6.00	15.00

2020 Leaf Ultimate Wrestling Clearly Dominant Autographs

*PINK/10-15: UNPRICED DUE TO SCARCITY
*PLATINUM/10: UNPRICED DUE TO SCARCITY
*GREEN/4-6: UNPRICED DUE TO SCARCITY
*RED/3-5: UNPRICED DUE TO SCARCITY
*SILVER/2-3: UNPRICED DUE TO SCARCITY
*GOLD/1: UNPRICED DUE TO SCARCITY
STATED PRINT RUN 25 SER.#'d SETS

CDG1 Goldberg	20.00	50.00
CDAA1 Arn Anderson	15.00	40.00

CDBH1	Bret Hart	20.00	50.00
CDCJ1	Chris Jericho	15.00	40.00
CDGM1	The Great Muta	30.00	75.00
CDHH1	Hulk Hogan	75.00	150.00
CDHT1	Hiroshi Tanahashi	12.00	30.00
CDJL1	Jushin Liger	20.00	50.00
CDJV1	Jesse Ventura		
CDKK1	Kenta Kobashi	25.00	60.00
CDKN1	Kevin Nash	12.00	30.00
CDKO1	Kenny Omega	25.00	60.00
CDMF1	Mick Foley	15.00	40.00
CDRF1	Ric Flair	50.00	100.00

2020 Leaf Ultimate Wrestling Enshrined Autographs

*PURPLE/35>: UNPRICED DUE TO SCARCITY
*PLATINUM/10-15: UNPRICED DUE TO SCARCITY
*RED/7-10: UNPRICED DUE TO SCARCITY
*EMERALD/5: UNPRICED DUE TO SCARCITY
*SILVER/3: UNPRICED DUE TO SCARCITY
*GOLD/1: UNPRICED DUE TO SCARCITY
*P.P.BLACK/1: UNPRICED DUE TO SCARCITY
*P.P.CYAN/1: UNPRICED DUE TO SCARCITY
*P.P.MAGENTA/1: UNPRICED DUE TO SCARCITY
*P.P.YELLOW/1: UNPRICED DUE TO SCARCITY
RANDOMLY INSERTED INTO PACKS

EBB1	Brutus Beefcake	6.00	15.00
EBH1	Bret Hart	15.00	40.00
EBOJ	Bob Orton Jr.	8.00	20.00
EHH1	Hulk Hogan	50.00	100.00
EJH1	Jimmy Hart	6.00	15.00
EKBW	Koko B. Ware	6.00	15.00
EKN1	Kevin Nash	10.00	25.00
ERS1	Ricky Steamboat	12.00	30.00
ETA1	Tony Atlas	6.00	15.00

2020 Leaf Ultimate Wrestling Ultimate Ring Queens Autographs

*PURPLE/6-25: UNPRICED DUE TO SCARCITY
*PLATINUM/5-10: UNPRICED DUE TO SCARCITY
*RED/4-7: UNPRICED DUE TO SCARCITY
*EMERALD/3-5: UNPRICED DUE TO SCARCITY
*SILVER/2-3: UNPRICED DUE TO SCARCITY
*GOLD/1: UNPRICED DUE TO SCARCITY
*P.P.BLACK/1: UNPRICED DUE TO SCARCITY
*P.P.CYAN/1: UNPRICED DUE TO SCARCITY
*P.P.MAGENTA/1: UNPRICED DUE TO SCARCITY
*P.P.YELLOW/1: UNPRICED DUE TO SCARCITY
RANDOMLY INSERTED INTO PACKS

RQBB1	Britt Baker	25.00	60.00
RQBR1	Brandi Rhodes	15.00	40.00
RQIV1	Ivelisse	8.00	20.00
RQJH1	Jackie Haas	8.00	20.00
RQPF1	Penelope Ford	12.00	30.00
RQRS1	Ryan Shamrock		
RQSB1	Scarlett Bordeaux	25.00	60.00
RQTB1	Tessa Blanchard	15.00	40.00
RQVI1	Victoria	6.00	15.00

2020 Leaf Ultimate Wrestling Ultimate Signatures 2

*PLATINUM/25>: UNPRICED DUE TO SCARCITY
*RED/15>: UNPRICED DUE TO SCARCITY
*EMERALD/5>: UNPRICED DUE TO SCARCITY
*SILVER/2-3: UNPRICED DUE TO SCARCITY
*GOLD/1: UNPRICED DUE TO SCARCITY
*P.P.BLACK/1: UNPRICED DUE TO SCARCITY
*P.P.CYAN/1: UNPRICED DUE TO SCARCITY
*P.P.MAGENTA/1: UNPRICED DUE TO SCARCITY
*P.P.YELLOW/1: UNPRICED DUE TO SCARCITY
RANDOMLY INSERTED INTO PACKS

US201	Ax/Smash	20.00	50.00
US202	Barbarian/Warlord	15.00	40.00
US203	B.Baker/P.Ford	25.00	60.00
US204	B.Beefcake/H.Hogan	60.00	120.00
US205	C.Cabana/T.Yano	15.00	40.00
US206	K.Omega/Cima	20.00	50.00
US207	E.Bischoff/T.Funk	20.00	50.00
US208	Honky Tonk Man/J.B. Badd	10.00	25.00
US209	T.DiBiase/J.Hart	12.00	30.00
US210	K.B. Ware/Bushwacker Luke	12.00	30.00
US211	S.Vicious/Vampiro	12.00	30.00
US212	Tazz/Funaki	12.00	30.00
US213	Tully & Tessa Blanchard	25.00	60.00
US214	T.Santana/T.DiBiase	15.00	40.00
US215	K.B. Ware/Warlord	10.00	25.00
US216	M.Foley/Edge	20.00	50.00
US217	Kat/Victoria	10.00	25.00
US218	Victoria/B.Reed	10.00	25.00
US219	T.Tonga/T.Loa	12.00	30.00
US220	A.Page/Y.Takahashi	15.00	40.00
US221	H.Hogan/D.Rodman	100.00	200.00

2020 Leaf Ultimate Wrestling Ultimate Signatures 4

*PURPLE/10-25: UNPRICED DUE TO SCARCITY
*PLATINUM/7-10: UNPRICED DUE TO SCARCITY
*RED/6-7: UNPRICED DUE TO SCARCITY
*EMERALD/4-5: UNPRICED DUE TO SCARCITY
*SILVER/3: UNPRICED DUE TO SCARCITY
*GOLD/1: UNPRICED DUE TO SCARCITY
*P.P.BLACK/1: UNPRICED DUE TO SCARCITY
*P.P.CYAN/1: UNPRICED DUE TO SCARCITY
*P.P.MAGENTA/1: UNPRICED DUE TO SCARCITY
*P.P.YELLOW/1: UNPRICED DUE TO SCARCITY
RANDOMLY INSERTED INTO PACKS

US401	Anderson/Blanchard/Flair/Windham		
US402	Barbarian/Warlord/Ax/Smash	60.00	120.00

1999 Little Caesar's WCW/nWo Lenticular

COMPLETE SET (4)	3.00	8.00
NNO Diamond Dallas Page	1.25	3.00
NNO Goldberg	2.50	6.00
NNO Hollywood Hogan	2.00	5.00
NNO Sting	2.50	6.00

1991 Mello Smello WWF Stickers

COMPLETE SET (6)	15.00	40.00
1 Hulk Hogan	10.00	25.00
2 The Bushwhackers	3.00	8.00
3 Big Boss Man	3.00	8.00
4 The Ultimate Warrior	6.00	15.00
5 The Legion of Doom	6.00	15.00
6 Jake The Snake Roberts	4.00	10.00

2008 Merlin WWE Heroes Stickers

COMPLETE SET (230)	50.00	100.00
1 RAW Logo	.15	.40
2 SmackDown Logo	.15	.40
3 ECW Logo	.15	.40
4 Randy Orton	.40	1.00
5 Randy Orton	.40	1.00
6 Randy Orton	.40	1.00
7 Randy Orton	.40	1.00
8 Randy Orton	.40	1.00
9 Randy Orton	.40	1.00
10 Randy Orton	.40	1.00
11 Randy Orton	.40	1.00
12 Randy Orton	.40	1.00
13 Randy Orton	.40	1.00
14 Randy Orton	.40	1.00
15 Undertaker	.75	2.00
16 Undertaker	.75	2.00
17 Undertaker	.75	2.00
18 Undertaker	.75	2.00
19 Undertaker	.75	2.00
20 Undertaker	.75	2.00
21 Undertaker	.75	2.00
22 Undertaker	.75	2.00
23 Undertaker	.75	2.00
24 Undertaker	.75	2.00
25 Undertaker	.75	2.00
26 Shawn Michaels	1.00	2.50
27 Shawn Michaels	1.00	2.50
28 Shawn Michaels	1.00	2.50
29 Shawn Michaels	1.00	2.50
30 Shawn Michaels	1.00	2.50
31 Shawn Michaels	1.00	2.50
32 Shawn Michaels	1.00	2.50
33 Shawn Michaels	1.00	2.50
34 Shawn Michaels	1.00	2.50
35 Shawn Michaels	1.00	2.50
36 Shawn Michaels	1.00	2.50
37 MVP	.25	.60
38 MVP	.25	.60
39 MVP	.25	.60
40 MVP	.25	.60
41 MVP	.25	.60
42 MVP	.25	.60
43 Michelle McCool	.75	2.00
44 Michelle McCool	.75	2.00
45 Michelle McCool	.75	2.00
46 Michelle McCool	.75	2.00
47 Michelle McCool	.75	2.00
48 Triple H	1.00	2.50
49 Triple H	1.00	2.50
50 Triple H	1.00	2.50
51 Triple H	1.00	2.50
52 Triple H	1.00	2.50
53 Triple H	1.00	2.50
54 Triple H	1.00	2.50
55 Triple H	1.00	2.50
56 Triple H	1.00	2.50
57 Triple H	1.00	2.50
58 Triple H	1.00	2.50
59 Batista	.60	1.50
60 Batista	.60	1.50
61 Batista	.60	1.50
62 Batista	.60	1.50
63 Batista	.60	1.50
64 Batista	.60	1.50
65 Batista	.60	1.50
66 Batista	.60	1.50
67 Batista	.60	1.50
68 Batista	.60	1.50
69 Batista	.60	1.50
70 Umaga	.25	.60
71 Umaga	.25	.60
72 Umaga	.25	.60
73 Umaga	.25	.60
74 Umaga	.25	.60
75 Umaga	.25	.60
76 Hornswoggle	.25	.60
77 Hornswoggle	.25	.60
78 Hornswoggle	.25	.60
79 Hornswoggle	.25	.60
80 Hornswoggle	.25	.60
81 Matt Hardy	.60	1.50
82 Matt Hardy	.60	1.50
83 Matt Hardy	.60	1.50
84 Matt Hardy	.60	1.50
85 Matt Hardy	.60	1.50
86 Matt Hardy	.60	1.50
87 Matt Hardy	.60	1.50
88 Matt Hardy	.60	1.50
89 Matt Hardy	.60	1.50
90 Matt Hardy	.60	1.50
91 Matt Hardy	.60	1.50
92 CM Punk	.15	.40
93 CM Punk	.15	.40
94 CM Punk	.15	.40
95 CM Punk	.15	.40
96 CM Punk	.15	.40
97 CM Punk	.15	.40
98 The Miz	.25	.60
99 The Miz	.25	.60
100 The Miz	.25	.60
101 The Miz	.25	.60
102 The Miz	.25	.60
103 Ken Kennedy	.40	1.00
104 Ken Kennedy	.40	1.00
105 Ken Kennedy	.40	1.00
106 Ken Kennedy	.40	1.00
107 Ken Kennedy	.40	1.00
108 Ken Kennedy	.40	1.00
109 Melina	.60	1.50
110 Melina	.60	1.50
111 Melina	.60	1.50
112 Melina	.60	1.50
113 Melina	.60	1.50
114 John Morrison	.15	.40
115 John Morrison	.15	.40
116 John Morrison	.15	.40
117 John Morrison	.15	.40
118 John Morrison	.15	.40
119 Elijah Burke	.15	.40
120 Elijah Burke	.15	.40
121 Elijah Burke	.15	.40
122 Elijah Burke	.15	.40
123 Elijah Burke	.15	.40
124 Elijah Burke	.15	.40
125 Kane	.60	1.50
126 Kane	.60	1.50
127 Kane	.60	1.50
128 Kane	.60	1.50
129 Kane	.60	1.50
130 Kane	.60	1.50
131 Kane	.60	1.50
132 Kane	.60	1.50
133 Kane	.60	1.50
134 Kane	.60	1.50
135 Kane	.60	1.50
136 John Cena	1.00	2.50
137 John Cena	1.00	2.50
138 John Cena	1.00	2.50
139 John Cena	1.00	2.50
140 John Cena	1.00	2.50
141 John Cena	1.00	2.50

142	John Cena	1.00	2.50
143	John Cena	1.00	2.50
144	John Cena	1.00	2.50
145	John Cena	1.00	2.50
146	John Cena	1.00	2.50
147	Rey Mysterio	.40	1.00
148	Rey Mysterio	.40	1.00
149	Rey Mysterio	.40	1.00
150	Rey Mysterio	.40	1.00
151	Rey Mysterio	.40	1.00
152	Rey Mysterio	.40	1.00
153	Rey Mysterio	.40	1.00
154	Rey Mysterio	.40	1.00
155	Rey Mysterio	.40	1.00
156	Rey Mysterio	.40	1.00
157	Rey Mysterio	.40	1.00
158	Chris Jericho	.40	1.00
159	Chris Jericho	.40	1.00
160	Chris Jericho	.40	1.00
161	Chris Jericho	.40	1.00
162	Chris Jericho	.40	1.00
163	Chris Jericho	.40	1.00
164	Beth Phoenix	.75	2.00
165	Beth Phoenix	.75	2.00
166	Beth Phoenix	.75	2.00
167	Beth Phoenix	.75	2.00
168	Beth Phoenix	.75	2.00
169	Chavo Guerrero	.25	.60
170	Chavo Guerrero	.25	.60
171	Chavo Guerrero	.25	.60
172	Chavo Guerrero	.25	.60
173	Chavo Guerrero	.25	.60
174	The Great Khali	.15	.40
175	The Great Khali	.15	.40
176	The Great Khali	.15	.40
177	The Great Khali	.15	.40
178	The Great Khali	.15	.40
179	The Great Khali	.15	.40
180	Shelton Benjamin	.15	.40
181	Shelton Benjamin	.15	.40
182	Shelton Benjamin	.15	.40
183	Shelton Benjamin	.15	.40
184	Shelton Benjamin	.15	.40
185	Boogeyman	.25	.60
186	Boogeyman	.25	.60
187	Boogeyman	.25	.60
188	Boogeyman	.25	.60
189	Boogeyman	.25	.60
190	Boogeyman	.25	.60
191	Edge	.60	1.50
192	Edge	.60	1.50
193	Edge	.60	1.50
194	Edge	.60	1.50
195	Edge	.60	1.50
196	Edge	.60	1.50
197	Edge	.60	1.50
198	Edge	.60	1.50
199	Edge	.60	1.50
200	Edge	.60	1.50
201	Edge	.60	1.50
202	Jeff Hardy	.60	1.50
203	Jeff Hardy	.60	1.50
204	Jeff Hardy	.60	1.50
205	Jeff Hardy	.60	1.50
206	Jeff Hardy	.60	1.50
207	Jeff Hardy	.60	1.50
208	Jeff Hardy	.60	1.50
209	Jeff Hardy	.60	1.50
210	Jeff Hardy	.60	1.50
211	Jeff Hardy	.60	1.50
212	Jeff Hardy	.60	1.50
213	Undertaker/Mark Henry	.75	2.00
214	CM Punk/Miz	.25	.60
215	Carlito/Mr. Anderson	.40	1.00
P1	Undertaker	.75	2.00
P2	World Title	.15	.40
P3	Randy Orton	.40	1.00
P4	Batista	.60	1.50
P5	Rey Mysterio	.40	1.00
P6	Triple H	1.00	2.50
P7	WWE Title	.15	.40
P8	John Cena	1.00	2.50
P9	Randy Orton	.40	1.00
P10	Edge	.60	1.50
P11	JBL	.15	.40
P12	Beth Phoenix	.75	2.00
P13	WWE Women's Title	.15	.40
P14	Melina	.60	1.50
P15	Mickie James	1.00	2.50

1986 Monty Gum Wrestling

	COMPLETE SET (100)	75.00	150.00
	UNOPENED BOX (50 PACKS)		
	UNOPENED PACK		
1	Rip Rogers	.40	1.00
2	Chris Adams	.25	.75
3	Black Bart	.20	.50
4	Steve Regal	.60	1.50
5	Gino Hernandez	.40	1.00
6	Ricky Steamboat	.75	2.00
7	The Road Warriors	1.00	2.50
8	Joe LeDuc	.60	1.50
9	Fritz Von Erich	.60	1.50
10	Kevin Von Erich	.60	1.50
11	Kerry Von Erich	.60	1.50
12	Baron Von Raschke UER	.20	.50
13	Sgt. Slaughter	.75	2.00
14	Magnificent Don Muraco	.40	1.00
15	Bobby Jaggers	.20	.50
16	Wahoo McDaniel	2.00	5.00
17	The Great Kabuki & Sunshine	1.00	2.50
18	The Iron Sheik	.30	.75
19	Greg Valentine	.50	1.25
20	Rick Martel	.40	1.00
21	The Road Warriors	1.00	2.50
22	Hulk Hogan	4.00	10.00
23	Kerry Von Erich	1.00	2.50
24	David Schultz	1.25	3.00
25	The Road Warriors	1.25	3.00
26	Nikita Koloff	.25	.60
27	Baron Von Raschke	.20	.50
28	Hercules Hernandez	.50	1.25
29	The RPM's	.30	.75
30	Buzz Sawyer	1.00	2.50
31	Junkyard Dog UER	.40	1.00
32	Nikita Koloff	.40	1.00
33	Krusher Khruschev & Ivan Koloff	.20	.50
34	Kevin Von Erich (Ric Flair) UER	.75	2.00
35	Kerry Von Erich	.75	2.00
36	Bobby Fulton & Tommy Rogers	.75	2.00
37	Magnificent Don Muraco	.20	.50
38	Rick Martel	.40	1.00
39	Rick Martel	.20	.50
40	Rick Martel	.75	2.00
41	Gino Hernandez	.20	.50
42	Terry Taylor	.50	1.25
43	Rock 'N Roll Express	.75	2.00
44	Billy Jack Haynes & Rick Rude	.50	1.25
45	Billy Jack Haynes & Rick Rude	.50	1.25
46	Arn Anderson & Brett Sawyer	.40	1.00
47	Kerry Von Erich	.75	2.00
48	Rick Martel & Nick Bockwinkel	.20	.50
49	Hulk Hogan (w/Joan Rivers)	8.00	20.00
50	Hulk Hogan & Cyndi Lauper	4.00	10.00
51	Hulk Hogan & Muhammed Ali	8.00	20.00
52	Hulk Hogan & M.Ali (Stallone) UER	4.00	10.00
53	Tully Blanchard	1.25	3.00
54	Bruno Sammartino/Nikolai Volkoff	.75	2.00
55	Bruno Sammartino	1.25	3.00
56	B.Sammartino & Killer Kowalski	.50	1.25
57	B.Sammartino & Johnny Valentine	.75	2.00
58	Ric Flair & Kerry Von Erich	1.00	2.50
59	Ric Flair	5.00	12.00
60	Ric Flair & Dusty Rhodes	4.00	10.00
61	Hulk Hogan & Nick Bockwinkel	5.00	12.00
62	Hulk Hogan	8.00	20.00
63	Hulk Hogan & Ken Patera	3.00	8.00
64	Dusty Rhodes & Manny Fernandez	.30	.75
65	Dusty Rhodes	3.00	8.00
66	Dusty Rhodes & King Curtis	.75	2.00
67	The Missing Link	.75	2.00
68	The Road Warriors	1.00	2.50
69	Precious Paul Ellering	.20	.50
70	Fabulous Free-Birds: Terry Gordy	.75	2.00
71	Fabulous Freebirds: Michael Hayes	1.25	3.00
72	Jim Cornette UER	.75	2.00
73	Jesse Barr	.25	.60
74	Rip Rogers & Bugsy McGraw	.30	.75
75	Konga, the Barbarian	.40	1.00
76	Eric Embry	.20	.50
77	Magnum T.A. Terry Allen	1.50	4.00
78	Magnum T.A. Terry Allen	1.25	3.00
79	Greg Allen (Valentine) UER	.30	.75
80	Tully Blanchard	.40	1.00
81	The Sheepherders	.75	2.00
82	Tito Santana	.40	1.00
83	The One Man Gang	.75	2.00
84	Gary Hart	.20	.50
85	Brett Sawyer	.20	.50
86	Ron Bass	.20	.50
87	Hulk Hogan	6.00	15.00
88	Rick Flair UER	2.00	5.00
89	Rick Flair & Sgt. Slaughter UER	1.50	4.00
90	Rick Flair UER	6.00	15.00
91	Sgt. Slaughter	.75	2.00
92	Rick Steamboat	1.25	3.00
93	King Kong Brody	.50	1.25
94	Randy Savage	12.00	30.00
95	Dusty Rhodes	1.00	2.50
96	King Kong Bundy	.50	1.25
97	Nikita Koloff	.75	2.00
98	Nikita Koloff & Dusty Rhodes	.50	1.25
99	Butch Reed	.40	1.00
100	Konga, the Barbarian	.75	2.00

2005 NBC Universal WWE RAW Ringside Sweepstakes

	COMPLETE SET (4)	4.00	10.00
NNO	Carlito	1.25	3.00
NNO	John Cena	2.00	5.00
NNO	Torrie Wilson	1.50	4.00
NNO	Triple H	1.25	3.00

1985 O'Quinn Wrestling All-Stars

	COMPLETE SET (54)	150.00	300.00
	ONLY AVAILABLE IN WRESTLING ALL STARS MAGAZINE		
1	Hulk Hogan	30.00	75.00
2	Ric Flair	20.00	50.00
3	Rick Martel	2.50	6.00
4	Sergeant Slaughter	3.00	8.00
5	The Iron Sheik	6.00	15.00
6	Kamala	3.00	8.00
7	Dusty Rhodes	3.00	8.00
8	Paul Orndorff	2.50	6.00
9	The Fabulous Freebirds	3.00	8.00
10	Big John Studd	2.50	6.00
11	Kerry Von Erich	2.50	6.00
12	Jimmy Valiant	2.50	6.00
13	Baron Von Raschke	6.00	15.00
14	Missing Link	2.50	6.00
15	Roddy Piper	12.00	30.00
16	Terry Taylor	2.50	6.00
17	Superstar Billy Graham	3.00	8.00
18	Carlos Colon	2.50	6.00
19	Kevin Sullivan	3.00	8.00
20	Tommy Rich	2.50	6.00
21	(Jesse) The Body Ventura	8.00	20.00
22	Kevin Von Erich	2.50	6.00
23	King Kong Bundy	4.00	10.00
24	Wahoo McDaniel	3.00	8.00
25	Greg Valentine	3.00	8.00
26	Ken Patera	2.50	6.00
27	Terry Allen	2.50	6.00
28	Rock n Roll Express	4.00	10.00
29	Jerry Lawler	6.00	15.00
30	Junkyard Dog	3.00	8.00
31	Barry Windham	3.00	8.00
32	The Youngbloods	2.50	6.00
33	Ricky Steamboat	4.00	10.00
34	Superfly Snuka	3.00	8.00
35	The Road Warriors	12.00	30.00
36	Bob Orton	5.00	12.00
37	Mil Mascaras	3.00	8.00
38	Ivan Putski	2.50	6.00
39	Jimmy Garvin	2.50	6.00
40	Mike Von Erich	2.50	6.00
41	Chris Adams	2.50	6.00
42	Brad Armstrong	2.50	6.00
43	Gino Hernandez	4.00	10.00
44	Tully Blanchard	4.00	10.00
45	The Sheepherders	2.50	6.00
46	Andre The Giant	25.00	60.00
47	The Fabulous Ones	2.50	6.00
48	The Tonga Kid	2.50	6.00
49	Masked Superstar	3.00	8.00
50	Billy Haynes	3.00	8.00
51	Adrian Street	2.50	6.00
52	Pedro Morales	3.00	8.00
53	David Sammartino	3.00	8.00
54	Bruno Sammartino	5.00	12.00

1985 O-Pee-Chee WWF

	COMPLETE SET W/HOGAN (66)	200.00	400.00
	COMPLETE SET W/O HOGAN (60)	30.00	75.00
	UNOPENED BOX (36 PACKS)		
	UNOPENED PACK (9 CARDS+1 STICKER)		
	RINGSIDE ACTION (22-56)		
	SUPERSTARS SPEAK (57-66)		
1	Hulk Hogan RC	75.00	150.00

2 The Iron Sheik RC	1.00	2.50
3 Captain Lou Albano RC	.75	2.00
4 Junk Yard Dog RC	1.00	2.50
5 Paul Mr. Wonderful Orndorff RC	.60	1.50
6 Jimmy Superfly Snuka RC	.60	1.50
7 Rowdy Roddy Piper RC	6.00	15.00
8 Wendi Richter RC	.75	2.00
9 Greg The Hammer Valentine RC	1.00	2.50
10 Brutus Beefcake RC	1.00	2.50
11 Jesse The Body Ventura RC	3.00	8.00
12 Big John Studd RC	.60	1.50
13 Fabulous Moolah RC	1.25	3.00
14 Tito Santana RC	1.25	3.00
15 Hillbilly Jim RC	1.00	2.50
16 Hulk Hogan RC	100.00	200.00
17 Mr. Fuji RC	.75	2.00
18 Rotundo & Windham	.75	2.00
19 Moondog Spot RC	.50	1.25
20 Chief Jay Strongbow RC	.50	1.25
21 George The Animal Steele RC	1.25	3.00
22 Let Go of My Toe! RA	.50	1.25
23 Lock 'Em Up! RA	.50	1.25
24 Scalp 'Em! RA	.50	1.25
25 Going for the Midsection! RA	.75	2.00
26 Up in the Air! RA	.60	1.50
27 All Tied Up! RA	1.50	4.00
28 Here She Comes! RA	.50	1.25
29 Stretched to the Limit! RA	3.00	8.00
30 Over He Goes! RA	1.00	2.50
31 An Appetite for Mayhem! RA	.60	1.50
32 Putting on Pressure! RA	.50	1.25
33 Smashed on a Knee! RA	.75	2.00
34 A Fist Comes Flying! RA	.50	1.25
35 Lemme' Out of This! RA	.50	1.25
36 No Fair Chokin'! RA	.50	1.25
37 Attacked by an Animal! RA	.50	1.25
38 One Angry Man! RA	1.25	3.00
39 Someone's Going Down! RA	1.25	3.00
40 Strangle Hold! RA	2.00	5.00
41 Bending an Arm! RA	.50	1.25
42 Ready for a Pile Driver! RA	.75	2.00
43 Face to the Canvas! RA	.50	1.25
44 Paul Wants It All! RA	.75	2.00
45 Kick to the Face! RA	3.00	8.00
46 Ready for Action! RA	.50	1.25
47 Putting on the Squeeze! RA	.60	1.50
48 Giants in Action! RA	1.50	4.00
49 Camel Clutch! RA	.60	1.50
50 Pile Up! RA	2.00	5.00
51 Can't Get Away! RA	.60	1.50
52 Going for the Pin! RA	.50	1.25
53 Ready to Fly! RA	2.00	5.00
54 Crusher in a Crusher! RA	.50	1.25
55 Fury of the Animal! RA	.75	2.00
56 Wrong Kind of Music! RA	6.00	15.00
57 Who's your next challenger? SS	2.50	6.00
58 This dog has got a mean bite! SS	.75	2.00
59 I don't think I'll ask that... SS	1.25	3.00
60 You Hulkster fans lift... SS	8.00	20.00
61 This ain't my idea... SS	1.00	2.50
62 You mean Freddie Blassie is... SS	1.25	3.00
63 Mppgh Ecch Oong. SS	1.00	2.50
64 It's the rock n' wrestling... SS	.75	2.00
65 Arrrggghhhh! SS	.60	1.50
66 They took my reindeer! SS	.60	1.50

1985 O-Pee-Chee WWF Stickers

COMPLETE SET W/HOGAN (22)	50.00	100.00
COMPLETE SET W/O HOGAN (17)	12.00	30.00
STATED ODDS 1:1		
1 Hulk Hogan	15.00	40.00
2 Captain Lou Albano	.75	2.00
3 Brutus Beefcake	1.25	3.00
4 Jesse Ventura	2.00	5.00
5 The Iron Sheik	1.50	4.00
6 Wendi Richter	1.25	3.00
7 Jimmy Snuka	.75	2.00
8 Ivan Putski	1.00	2.50
9 Hulk Hogan	4.00	10.00
10 Junk Yard Dog	1.25	3.00
11 Hulk Hogan	6.00	15.00
12 Captain Lou Albano	.75	2.00
13 Captain Lou Albano	.75	2.00
14 Freddy Blassie & Iron Sheik	.75	2.00
15 Jimmy Snuka	.75	2.00
16 Hulk Hogan	10.00	25.00
17 Iron Sheik	1.50	4.00
18 Rene Goulet & S.D. Jones	1.25	3.00
19 Junk Yard Dog	.75	2.00
20 Wendi Richter	1.25	3.00
21 Le gÈant FerrÈ	3.00	8.00
22 Hulk Hogan	8.00	20.00

1985-86 O-Pee-Chee WWF Series 2

COMPLETE SET (75)	60.00	120.00
UNOPENED BOX (36 PACKS)		
UNOPENED PACK (10 CARDS)		
1 Nikolai Volkoff RC	4.00	10.00
2 The Magnificent Muraco RC	1.25	3.00
3 Tony Atlas RC	2.00	5.00
4 Jim The Anvil Neidhart RC	.40	1.00
5 Ricky Steamboat RC	.75	2.00
6 The British Bulldogs	1.50	4.00
7 King Kong Bundy RC	3.00	8.00
8 Bobby The Brain Heenan RC	1.25	3.00
9 Lei Lani Kai RC	.40	1.00
10 Snaky Squeeze!	.75	2.00
11 Savage Attack!	15.00	40.00
12 Cowboy Bob Orton RC	.50	1.25
13 Showing the Flag	1.25	3.00
14 Showboating!	1.50	4.00
15 Terry Funk RC	1.25	3.00
16 Martial Artist!	1.25	3.00
17 Don't Call Me Beach Bum	.75	2.00
18 Up and Over!	.30	1.00
19 Brewing Up Trouble!	.40	1.00
20 A Leg Up!	.75	2.00
21 About To Explode	.40	1.00
22 Twister!	.50	1.25
23 Headed For the Turnbuckle	5.00	12.00
24 Hercules Hernandez RC	2.50	6.00
25 Leggo' My Head!	.40	1.00
26 The Dragon Has Struck!	.40	1.00
27 Top Dog	1.00	2.50
28 Watch Out For Me	1.25	3.00
29 It's Time For A Little Road Work!	.60	1.50
30 Karate Chop!	.60	1.50
31 Crafty Fuji	.75	2.00
32 Bulldog Grip!	.60	1.50
33 Jake The Snake RC	4.00	10.00
34 Siva Afi RC	.60	1.50
35 This Is Gonna' Hurt!	1.25	3.00
36 Military Press!	.60	1.50
37 Tower Of Strength!	.40	1.00
38 Bulldog Grip!	.40	1.00
39 Piggyback!	2.00	5.00
40 Shove Off!	.40	1.00
41 Jimmy Mouth of the South Hart RC	1.25	3.00
42 Fliperoo!	.50	1.25
43 Ring Toss!	.50	1.25
44 Uncle Elmer RC	.50	1.25
45 Iran and Russia - Number One?	1.25	3.00
46 The Killer Bees	.50	1.25
47 Secret Plans	.50	1.25
48 Davey Boy Smith RC	1.50	4.00
49 Aerial Escape!	.40	1.00
50 Caught by Kong!	.60	1.50
51 Banging Away!	1.50	4.00
52 All American Boy!	.40	1.00
53 Fiji Fury!	.40	1.00
54 What d'ya mean...	1.00	2.50
55 Do you know any way...	.40	1.00
56 Those are the biggest feet...	.40	1.00
57 I make sukiyaki...	1.25	3.00
58 This guy really looks sick.	.40	1.00
59 Nikolai, he sings...	.40	1.00
60 The Animal In Love!	.40	1.00
61 Hoss Funk RC	.75	2.00
62 Can I autograph your cast?	.60	1.50
63 Randy Savage RC & Elizabeth RC	12.00	30.00
64 I don't know...	.40	1.00
65 If anybody calls you...	.40	1.00
66 It's rock and wrestling - forever!	2.00	5.00
67 Wrestlers vs. Football Greats	1.25	3.00
68 Big Men Battle	.50	1.25
69 Help Coming	.40	1.00
70 The Body Struts His Stuff	.40	1.00
71 In the Corner	1.25	3.00
72 Plenty of Beef	.75	2.00
73 Battle Royal Winner	.50	1.25
74 Working for a Position	.40	1.00
75 Ready for a War!	1.50	4.00

1987 O-Pee-Chee WWF

COMPLETE SET (75)	60.00	120.00
UNOPENED BOX (36 PACKS)		
UNOPENED PACK (10 CARDS)		
1 Bret "Hit Man" Hart RC	25.00	60.00
2 Andre the Giant RC	6.00	15.00
3 Hulk Hogan	5.00	12.00
4 Frankie	.75	2.00
5 Koko B. Ware RC	.75	2.00
6 Tito Santana	.60	1.50
7 Randy Savage & Elizabeth	10.00	25.00
8 Billy Jack Haynes RC	.40	1.00
9 Hercules & Bobby Heenan	.40	1.00
10 King Harley Race RC	.60	1.50
11 Kimchee & Kamala	.40	1.00
12 Bravo/Johnny V/Valentine	.50	1.25
13 Honky Tonk Man RC	1.00	2.50
14 Outback Jack RC	.40	1.00
15 King Kong Bundy	1.25	3.00
16 The Magnificent Muraco	.40	1.00
17 Mr. Fuji and Killer Khan	.75	2.00
18 The Natural Butch Reed RC	.60	1.50
19 Davey Boy Smith	.75	2.00
20 The Dynamite Kid RC	.40	1.00
21 Ricky The Dragon Steamboat	1.50	4.00
22 Two-Man Clothesline RA	.40	1.00
23 Ref Turned Wrestler RA	.75	2.00
24 Ready to Strike RA	.60	1.50
25 In the Outback RA	.40	1.00
26 The Hulkster Explodes RA	2.00	5.00
27 Double Whammy RA	.40	1.00
28 Spoiling for a Fight RA	.40	1.00
29 Flip Flop RA	.40	1.00
30 Islanders Attack RA	.40	1.00
31 King Harley Parades RA	.40	1.00
32 Backbreaker RA	.40	1.00
33 Double Dropkick RA	.40	1.00
34 The Loser Must Bow RA	.40	1.00
35 American-Made RA	2.50	6.00
36 A Challenge Answered RA	2.00	5.00
37 Champ in the Ring RA	4.00	10.00
38 Listening to Hulkamania RA	2.00	5.00
39 Heading for the Ring RA	.40	1.00
40 Out to Destroy RA	.40	1.00
41 Tama Takes a Beating RA	.40	1.00
42 Bundy in Mid-Air RA	.40	1.00
43 Karate Stance RA	.40	1.00
44 Her Eyes on Randy RA	2.50	6.00
45 The Olympian Returns RA	.40	1.00
46 Reed Is Riled RA	.40	1.00
47 Flying Bodypress RA	.40	1.00
48 Hooking the Leg RA	.40	1.00
49 A Belly Buster WMIII	.40	1.00
50 Revenge on Randy WMIII	.75	2.00
51 Fighting the Full Nelson WMIII	.40	1.00
52 Honky Tonk Goes Down WMIII	.40	1.00
53 Over the Top WMIII	.40	1.00
54 The Giant Is Slammed WMIII	1.25	3.00
55 Out of the Ring WMIII	.75	2.00
56 And Still Champion WMIII	1.50	4.00
57 Harts Hit Concrete WMIII	.40	1.00
58 The Challenge RA	1.25	3.00
59 Bearhug RA	.40	1.00
60 Fantastic Bodypress RA	.40	1.00
61 Aerial Maneuvers RA	.40	1.00
62 Ready to Sting! RA	.40	1.00
63 Showing Off RA	.40	1.00
64 Scare Tactics RA	.40	1.00
65 Taking a Bow RA	.60	1.50
66 Out to Eat a Turnbuckle RA	.40	1.00
67 Nice guys finish last! SS	.40	1.00
68 Here's how we keep... SS	.40	1.00
69 Urrggh. Nice! SS	.40	1.00
70 No Kamala...him not dinner! SS	.40	1.00
71 We are the original destroyers. SS	.40	1.00
72 I think the fans are mad at me. SS	.40	1.00
73 You ain't nothin'... SS	.40	1.00
74 I'm gonna take a big bit... SS	.40	1.00
75 Good! SS	.40	1.00

2004 Pacific TNA

COMPLETE SET (75)	10.00	25.00
UNOPENED BOX (24 PACKS)	85.00	100.00
UNOPENED PACK (5 CARDS)	4.00	5.00
*RED: .6X TO 1.5X BASIC CARDS		
1 April RC	.20	.50
2 Chelsea RC	.12	.30
3 Goldylocks RC	.75	2.00
4 Lollipop RC	.30	.75
5 Athena RC	.20	.50
6 Abyss RC	.30	.75
7 Jeremy Borash RC	.12	.30
8 Traci RC	.50	1.25
9 D'Lo Brown	.20	.50

10 Christopher Daniels RC	.12	.30
11 Delirious RC	.12	.30
12 Simon Diamond RC	.12	.30
13 Julio Dinero RC	.12	.30
14 Shane Douglas	.12	.30
15 Sonjay Dutt RC	.12	.30
16 Ekmo Fatu	.20	.50
17 Glenn Gilberti	.12	.30
18 Juventud Guerrera	.12	.30
19 Chris Harris RC	.12	.30
20 Don Harris RC	.12	.30
21 Ron Harris RC	.12	.30
22 Chris Hero RC	.12	.30
23 BG James	.20	.50
24 Jeff Jarrett	.60	1.50
25 Kid Kash RC	.12	.30
26 Frankie Kazarian RC	.12	.30
27 Ron Killings	.20	.50
28 Konnan	.12	.30
29 Lazz RC	.12	.30
30 Jerry Lynn	.12	.30
31 Father James Mitchell RC	.12	.30
32 Kevin Northcutt RC	.12	.30
33 Nosawa RC	.12	.30
34 CM Punk RC	20.00	50.00
35 Raven	.50	1.25
36 Dusty Rhodes	.30	.75
37 Vince Russo RC	.12	.30
38 Chris Sabin RC	.12	.30
39 Sandman	.20	.50
40 Rick Santel RC	.12	.30
41 Michael Shane RC	.12	.30
42 Shark Boy RC	.12	.30
43 Sonny Siaki	.12	.30
44 Sinn RC	.12	.30
45 Slash RC	.12	.30
46 James Storm RC	.20	.50
47 AJ Styles RC	12.00	30.00
48 Johnny Swinger RC	.12	.30
49 Terry Taylor	.12	.30
50 Trinity RC	.20	.50
51 Chris Vaughn RC	.12	.30
52 Ryan Wilson RC	.12	.30
53 David Young RC	.12	.30
54 Scott Hudson RC	.12	.30
55 Mike Tenay RC	.12	.30
56 Don West RC	.12	.30
57 Don Callis	.12	.30
58 Erik Watts RC	.12	.30
59 Rudy Charles RC	.12	.30
60 Mike Posey RC	.12	.30
61 Andrew Thomas RC	.12	.30
62 3Live Kru	.20	.50
63 America's Most Wanted	.20	.50
64 D'Lo Brown	.20	.50
65 Simon Diamond	.12	.30
66 Jeff Jarrett	.60	1.50
67 Raven	.50	1.25
68 Dusty Rhodes	.30	.75
69 Chris Sabin	.12	.30
70 Sonny Siaki RC	.12	.30
71 AJ Styles RC	6.00	15.00
72 Chris Vaughn RC	.12	.30
73 Trinity RC	.20	.50
74 Goldylocks RC	.75	2.00
75 Lollipop RC	.30	.75

2004 Pacific TNA Event-Used

STATED PRINT RUN 1,525 SER.#'d SETS

1 America's Most Wanted	4.00	8.00
2 AJ Styles	5.00	10.00
3 D'Lo Brown	4.00	8.00
4 Raven	4.00	8.00
5 BG James	4.00	8.00

2004 Pacific TNA Event-Used Limited Edition

NOT AVAILABLE IN PACKS

1 TNA Babes	15.00	40.00
2 America's Most Wanted	15.00	40.00

2004 Pacific TNA Legends and Superstars Autographs

COMPLETE SET (6)
STATED ODDS 1:24 HOBBY

1 Rowdy Roddy Piper	75.00	150.00
3 Jeff Jarrett	10.00	25.00
4 Terry Taylor	5.00	12.00
5 Dusty Rhodes	100.00	200.00
6 Harley Race	30.00	75.00
7 Raven	5.00	12.00

2004 Pacific TNA Main Event Autographs

STATED ODDS 1:24 HOBBY

NNO AJ Styles Red Border SP	15.00	40.00
NNO AJ Styles Gold Border SP	15.00	40.00
NNO AMW DUAL AU	6.00	15.00
NNO April	4.00	10.00
NNO Goldylocks	4.00	10.00
NNO Lollipop	5.00	12.00
NNO Chris Vaughn	4.00	10.00
NNO Trinity	4.00	10.00

2004 Pacific TNA Tag Teams

COMPLETE SET (8)	2.00	5.00
STATED ODDS 1:5 HOBBY		
1 Diamond/Swinger	.30	.75
2 The Naturals	.30	.75
3 3Live Kru	.50	1.25
4 The Gathering	2.00	5.00
5 Red Shirt Security	.30	.75
6 Black Shirt Security	.30	.75
7 Gilberti/Young	.30	.75
8 America's Most Wanted	.50	1.25

2004 Pacific TNA Tattoos

COMPLETE SET (28)	3.00	8.00
STATED ODDS 1:1 HOBBY		
1 TNA Logo 1	.12	.30
2 TNA Logo 2	.12	.30
3 TNA Logo 3	.12	.30
4 Total Non-Stop Action	.12	.30
5 PTC Logo 1	.12	.30
6 PTC Logo 2	.12	.30
7 PTC Logo 3	.12	.30
8 Raven	.50	1.25
9 AJ Styles	.30	.75
10 Jeff Jarrett	.60	1.50
11 D'Lo Brown	.20	.50
12 Chris Harris	.12	.30
13 James Storm	.20	.50
14 Shark Boy	.12	.30
15 Ron Killings	.20	.50
16 Konnan	.12	.30
17 BG James	.20	.50
18 Chris Sabin	.12	.30
19 Michael Shane	.12	.30
20 Sonny Siaki	.12	.30
21 Chris Vaughn	.12	.30
22 Trinity	.20	.50
23 America's Most Wanted	.20	.50
24 3Live Kru	.20	.50
25 Red Shirt Security	.12	.30
26 Black Shirt Security	.12	.30
27 Lollipop	.30	.75
28 Goldylocks	.75	2.00

2022 Panini Chronicles WWE

*BRONZE: .6X TO 1.5X BASIC CARDS
*SILVER: .75X TO 2X BASIC CARDS
*RED/199: 1.2X TO 3X BASIC CARDS
*BLUE/99: 2X TO 5X BASIC CARDS
*GREEN/99: 2X TO 5X BASIC CARDS
*PURPLE/49: 4X TO 10X BASIC CARDS
*GREEN SP/25: UNPRICED DUE TO SCARCITY
*GOLD/10: UNPRICED DUE TO SCARCITY
*BLACK/1: UNPRICED DUE TO SCARCITY
*GOLD VINYL/1: UNPRICED DUE TO SCARCITY
*NEBULA/1: UNPRICED DUE TO SCARCITY
*PLATINUM/1: UNPRICED DUE TO SCARCITY

1 Alexa Bliss	1.50	4.00
2 Happy Corbin	.30	.75
3 Liv Morgan	1.25	3.00
4 Josh Briggs RC	.25	.60
5 Bam Bam Bigelow	.40	1.00
6 Molly Holly	.30	.75
7 Robert Roode	.30	.75
8 Akira Tozawa	.30	.75
9 Bron Breakker RC	1.00	2.50
10 Commander Azeez	.30	.75
11 Asuka	1.00	2.50
12 The Honky Tonk Man	.30	.75
13 Mandy Rose	1.25	3.00
14 Junkyard Dog	.30	.75
15 D-Lo Brown	.25	.60
16 Montez Ford	.25	.60
17 R-Truth	.30	.75
18 Angel	.25	.60
19 Cora Jade RC	.75	2.00
20 Cowboy Bob Orton	.25	.60
21 Becky Lynch	1.00	2.50
22 Humberto	.25	.60
23 Rhea Ripley	.75	2.00
24 Ken Shamrock	.30	.75
25 Rick Steiner	.40	1.00
26 Mr. T	.50	1.25
27 Shelton Benjamin	.40	1.00
28 Angelo Dawkins	.30	.75
29 Gable Steveson RC	1.25	3.00
30 Dana Brooke	.25	.60
31 Brock Lesnar	1.25	3.00
32 Ilja Dragunov	.25	.60
33 Roman Reigns	1.50	4.00
34 Lex Luger	.30	.75
35 Karrion Kross	.50	1.25
36 Mustafa Ali	.30	.75
37 Sid Vicious	.30	.75
38 Big Boss Man	.40	1.00
39 Bayley	.60	1.50
40 Dominik Mysterio	.30	.75
41 Charlotte Flair	1.00	2.50
42 Ivar	.25	.60
43 Ronda Rousey	1.50	4.00
44 Ludwig Kaiser	.30	.75
45 Hulk Hogan	1.25	3.00
46 MVP	.25	.60
47 Tamina	.30	.75
48 Big John Studd	.25	.60
49 Nikkita Lyons RC	.60	1.50
50 Don Muraco	.25	.60
51 The American Nightmare Cody Rhodes	.60	1.50
52 Jagger Reid	.25	.60
53 Elektra Lopez RC	.60	1.50
54 Mace	.25	.60
55 Macho Man Randy Savage	1.00	2.50
56 Otis	.30	.75
57 T-Bar	.25	.60
58 British Bulldog	.40	1.00
59 Roxanne Perez RC	.75	2.00
60 Erik	.25	.60
61 Edge	1.00	2.50
62 Jey Uso	.30	.75
63 Bret "Hit Man" Hart	.60	1.50
64 Madcap Moss	.25	.60
65 Stone Cold Steve Austin	1.25	3.00
66 Ravishing Rick Rude	.50	1.25
67 Umaga	.25	.60
68 Captain Lou Albano	.30	.75
69 Solo Sikoa RC	.60	1.50
70 Ezekiel	.25	.60
71 Finn Balor	.60	1.50
72 Jim "The Anvil" Neidhart	.30	.75
73 Goldberg	1.00	2.50
74 man.soor	.25	.60
75 Triple H	1.00	2.50
76 Reggie	.30	.75
77 Vader	.30	.75
78 Cedric Alexander	.25	.60
79 Tony D'Angelo RC	.75	2.00
80 Freddie Blassie	.30	.75
81 Gigi Dolin	1.00	2.50
82 Jimmy Uso	.30	.75
83 The Rock	2.50	6.00
84 Meiko Satomura RC	.75	2.00
85 Ultimate Warrior	1.00	2.50
86 Ridge Holland	.25	.60
87 Xavier Woods	.30	.75
88 Chad Gable	.25	.60
89 Veer Mahaan	.60	1.50
90 The Godfather	.25	.60
91 John Cena	.75	2.00
92 Jinder Mahal	.30	.75
93 Shawn Michaels	1.00	2.50
94 Michael Hayes	.25	.60
95 Undertaker	1.25	3.00
96 Road Dogg	.30	.75
97 X-Pac	.30	.75
98 Chief Jay Strongbow	.40	1.00
99 AJ Styles	.75	2.00
100 Greg Valentine	.25	.60
101 Asuka	1.00	2.50
Contenders		
102 Finn Balor	.60	1.50
Contenders		
103 Becky Lynch	1.00	2.50
Contenders		
104 John Cena	.75	2.00

Contenders
105 Brock Lesnar 1.25 3.00
Contenders
106 Charlotte Flair 1.00 2.50
Contenders
107 AJ Styles .75 2.00
Contenders
108 The American Nightmare Cody Rhodes .60 1.50
Contenders
109 Alexa Bliss 1.50 4.00
Contenders
110 Edge 1.00 2.50
Contenders
111 Carmelo Hayes .30 .75
Donruss Rated Rookies
112 Nikkita Lyons .60 1.50
Donruss Rated Rookies
113 Joe Gacy .60 1.50
Donruss Rated Rookies
114 Roxanne Perez .75 2.00
Donruss Rated Rookies
115 Solo Sikoa .60 1.50
Donruss Rated Rookies
116 Bron Breakker 1.00 2.50
Donruss Rated Rookies
117 Tony D'Angelo .75 2.00
Donruss Rated Rookies
118 Cora Jade .75 2.00
Donruss Rated Rookies
119 Veer Mahaan .60 1.50
Donruss Rated Rookies
120 Gable Steveson 1.25 3.00
Donruss Rated Rookies
121 Liv Morgan 1.25 3.00
Absolute
122 Bret "Hit Man" Hart .60 1.50
Absolute
123 Mandy Rose 1.25 3.00
Absolute
124 The Rock 2.50 6.00
Absolute
125 Rhea Ripley .75 2.00
Absolute
126 Goldberg 1.00 2.50
Absolute
127 Roman Reigns 1.50 4.00
Absolute
128 Ronda Rousey 1.50 4.00
Absolute
129 Gigi Dolin 1.00 2.50
Absolute
130 Solo Sikoa .60 1.50
Absolute
131 Damian Priest .50 1.25
Origins
132 Randy Orton .60 1.50
Origins
133 Eddie Guerrero .75 2.00
Origins
134 Gunther .60 1.50
Origins
135 Axiom .30 .75
Origins
136 Jake Roberts .40 1.00
Origins
137 Batista .50 1.25
Origins
138 Kit Wilson .25 .60
Origins
139 Brie Bella .50 1.25
Origins
140 Nathan Frazer .25 .60
Origins
141 Shawn Michaels 1.00 2.50
Legacy
142 Andre The Giant 1.00 2.50
Legacy
143 Chyna .50 1.25
Legacy
144 Hulk Hogan 1.25 3.00
Legacy
145 Macho Man Randy Savage 1.00 2.50
Legacy
146 Stone Cold Steve Austin 1.25 3.00
Legacy
147 Triple H 1.00 2.50
Legacy
148 Ultimate Warrior 1.00 2.50
Legacy
149 Undertaker 1.25 3.00
Legacy
150 Batista .50 1.25
Legacy
151 Edris Enofe .25 .60
Luminance
152 Rowdy Roddy Piper .60 1.50
Luminance
153 Big E .50 1.25
Luminance
154 Shinsuke Nakamura .60 1.50
Luminance
155 Brooks Jensen .25 .60
Luminance
156 Carmella .60 1.50
Luminance
157 Bayley .60 1.50
Luminance
158 Valentina Feroz .40 1.00
Luminance
159 Alba Fyre .60 1.50
Luminance
160 Guru Raaj .25 .60
Luminance
161 Aleah James .30 .75
Playoff
162 Raquel Rodriguez .60 1.50
Playoff
163 Beth Phoenix .50 1.25
Playoff
164 Roderick Strong .40 1.00
Playoff
165 Shotzi 1.00 2.50
Playoff
166 John "Bradshaw" Layfield .25 .60
Playoff
167 Terry Funk .40 1.00
Playoff
168 Kofi Kingston .60 1.50
Playoff
169 Von Wagner .25 .60
Playoff
170 Nikki A.S.H. .40 1.00
Playoff
171 Dante Chen .25 .60
Prestige
172 Nikki Bella .60 1.50
Prestige
173 Elektra Lopez .60 1.50
Prestige
174 Ru Feng .25 .60
Prestige
175 Ikemen Jiro .25 .60
Prestige
176 Sonya Deville .60 1.50
Prestige
177 Jerry Lawler .50 1.25
Prestige
178 Kevin Owens .50 1.25
Prestige
179 Bruno Sammartino .60 1.50
Prestige
180 Razor Ramon .50 1.25
Prestige
181 Tiffany Stratton .40 1.00
Rookies & Stars
182 Grayson Waller .60 1.50
Rookies & Stars
183 Blair Davenport .25 .60
Rookies & Stars
184 Ivy Nile .25 .60
Rookies & Stars
185 Shanky .25 .60
Rookies & Stars
186 Jacy Jayne .60 1.50
Rookies & Stars
187 Brutus Creed .30 .75
Rookies & Stars
188 Julius Creed .60 1.50
Rookies & Stars
189 Elton Prince .30 .75
Rookies & Stars
190 Wendy Choo .50 1.25
Rookies & Stars
191 Drew McIntyre .50 1.25
Score
192 Trish Stratus 1.25 3.00
Score
193 IYO SKY .50 1.25
Score
194 Kayden Carter .50 1.25
Score
195 Alundra Blayze .30 .75
Score
196 Odyssey Jones .25 .60
Score
197 Bianca Belair .75 2.00
Score
198 Queen Zelina .40 1.00
Score
199 Cameron Grimes .50 1.25
Score
200 Superstar Billy Graham .25 .60
Score
201 Carmelo Hayes .30 .75
Black
202 Kevin Owens .50 1.25
Black
203 Nikki Bella .60 1.50
Black
204 Brutus Creed .30 .75
Black
205 Aliyah .50 1.25
Black
206 Gorilla Monsoon .40 1.00
Black
207 Kofi Kingston .60 1.50
Black
208 AJ Styles .75 2.00
Black
209 Ricky "The Dragon" Steamboat .50 1.25
Black
210 Asuka 1.00 2.50
Black
211 Xia Li .50 1.25
Black
212 Bayley .60 1.50
Black
213 Andre Chase .25 .60
Black
214 Doudrop .40 1.00
Black
215 Amari Miller .25 .60
Black
216 Jacy Jayne .60 1.50
Black
217 Odyssey Jones .25 .60
Black
218 Alexa Bliss 1.50 4.00
Black
219 Shanky .25 .60
Black
220 Bron Breakker 1.00 2.50
Black
221 Charlotte Flair 1.00 2.50
Certified
222 Terry Funk .40 1.00
Certified
223 Tiffany Stratton .40 1.00
Certified
224 Rowdy Roddy Piper .60 1.50
Certified
225 Butch .50 1.25
Certified
226 Aoife Valkyrie .50 1.25
Certified
227 Grayson Waller .60 1.50
Certified
228 The Miz .40 1.00
Certified
229 Becky Lynch 1.00 2.50
Certified
230 Ricochet .50 1.25
Certified
231 Cora Jade .75 2.00
Certified
232 Yokozuna .30 .75
Certified
233 Beth Phoenix .50 1.25
Certified
234 Bodhi Hayward .30 .75
Certified
235 Drew McIntyre .50 1.25
Certified
236 Big E .50 1.25
Certified
237 Jake Roberts .40 1.00
Certified
238 Oliver Carter .25 .60
Certified
239 Brock Lesnar 1.25 3.00
Certified

240 Shayna Baszler Certified	.50	1.25
241 Finn Balor Elite	.60	1.50
242 Alba Fyre Elite	.60	1.50
243 Axiom Elite	.30	.75
244 Shinsuke Nakamura Elite	.60	1.50
245 Cactus Jack Elite	.50	1.25
246 Bobby "The Brain" Heenan Elite	.40	1.00
247 John "Bradshaw" Layfield Elite	.25	.60
248 Omos Elite	.50	1.25
249 The American Nightmare Cody Rhodes Elite	.60	1.50
250 Sheamus Elite	.40	1.00
251 Gable Steveson Elite	1.25	3.00
252 Yulisa Leon Elite	.25	.60
253 Bianca Belair Elite	.75	2.00
254 Stacy Keibler Elite	.75	2.00
255 The Great Khali Elite	.30	.75
256 The All Mighty Bobby Lashley Elite	.50	1.25
257 Lacey Evans Elite	.60	1.50
258 Matt Riddle Elite	.60	1.50
259 Edge Elite	1.00	2.50
260 The Miz Elite	.40	1.00
261 Liv Morgan Illusions	1.25	3.00
262 Shinsuke Nakamura Illusions	.60	1.50
263 Bret "Hit Man" Hart Illusions	.60	1.50
264 Trick Williams Illusions	.25	.60
265 Big E Illusions	.50	1.25
266 Butch Illusions	.50	1.25
267 Duke Hudson Illusions	.25	.60
268 Jerry Lawler Illusions	.50	1.25
269 Gigi Dolin Illusions	1.00	2.50
270 Paul Bearer Illusions	.30	.75
271 Mandy Rose Illusions	1.25	3.00
272 Theory Illusions	.60	1.50
273 Dude Love Illusions	.50	1.25
274 Booker T Illusions	.50	1.25
275 Cameron Grimes Illusions	.50	1.25
276 Carmella Illusions	.60	1.50
277 Gunther Illusions	.60	1.50
278 Lash Legend Illusions	.25	.60
279 John Cena Illusions	.75	2.00
280 Rikishi Illusions	.30	.75
281 Blair Davenport XR	.25	.60
282 Diamond Dallas Page XR	.30	.75
283 Dusty Rhodes XR	.60	1.50
284 Jinny XR	.25	.60
285 Rhea Ripley XR	.75	2.00
286 Paul Heyman XR	.40	1.00
287 Ronda Rousey XR	1.50	4.00
288 Shotzi XR	1.00	2.50
289 Goldberg XR	1.00	2.50
290 Cactus Jack XR	.50	1.25
291 Carmella XR	.60	1.50
292 Cruz Del Toro XR	.40	1.00
293 Guru Raaj XR	.25	.60
294 Malik Blade XR	.25	.60
295 Roman Reigns XR	1.50	4.00
296 Rob Van Dam XR	.50	1.25
297 Solo Sikoa XR	.60	1.50
298 The All Mighty Bobby Lashley XR	.50	1.25
299 Aleah James XR	.30	.75
300 Ciampa XR	.60	1.50
301 Ciampa Phoenix	.60	1.50
302 Mr. Perfect Curt Hennig Phoenix	.50	1.25
303 Joaquin Wilde Phoenix	.40	1.00
304 Rowdy Roddy Piper Phoenix	.60	1.50
305 Roxanne Perez Phoenix	.75	2.00
306 Alundra Blayze Phoenix	.30	.75
307 Rhea Ripley Phoenix	.75	2.00
308 Cruz Del Toro Phoenix	.40	1.00
309 Aliyah Phoenix	.50	1.25
310 Indi Hartwell Phoenix	.75	2.00
311 Eddie Guerrero Phoenix	.75	2.00
312 Queen Zelina Phoenix	.40	1.00
313 Mankind Phoenix	.50	1.25
314 Sonya Deville Phoenix	.60	1.50
315 Ronda Rousey Phoenix	1.50	4.00
316 The All Mighty Bobby Lashley Phoenix	.50	1.25
317 The Rock Phoenix	2.50	6.00
318 Edris Enofe Phoenix	.25	.60
319 Bobby "The Brain" Heenan Phoenix	.40	1.00
320 Julius Creed Phoenix	.60	1.50
321 Ikemen Jiro Phoenix	.25	.60
322 Roderick Strong Phoenix	.40	1.00
323 Trish Stratus Phoenix	1.25	3.00
324 Torrie Wilson Phoenix	.60	1.50
325 Roman Reigns Phoenix	1.50	4.00
326 Mandy Rose Flux	1.25	3.00
327 Torrie Wilson Flux	.60	1.50
328 Gigi Dolin Flux	1.00	2.50
329 Doudrop Flux	.40	1.00
330 Elektra Lopez Flux	.60	1.50
331 Dusty Rhodes Flux	.60	1.50
332 Solo Sikoa Flux	.60	1.50
333 Faarooq Flux	.30	.75
334 Ru Feng Flux	.25	.60
335 Trish Stratus Flux	1.25	3.00
336 Liv Morgan Flux	1.25	3.00
337 Andre Chase Flux	.25	.60
338 Shawn Michaels Flux	1.00	2.50
339 Dude Love Flux	.50	1.25
340 IYO SKY Flux	.50	1.25
341 Scott Steiner Flux	.40	1.00
342 Randy Orton Flux	.60	1.50
343 Gene Okerlund Flux	.40	1.00
344 Stevie Turner Flux	.25	.60
345 Trick Williams Flux	.25	.60
346 John Cena Flux	.75	2.00
347 Kevin Nash Flux	.40	1.00
348 Damian Priest Flux	.50	1.25
349 Duke Hudson Flux	.25	.60
350 Katana Chance Flux	.50	1.25
351 The American Nightmare Cody Rhodes Donruss Optic	.60	1.50
352 Lacey Evans Donruss Optic	.60	1.50
353 Andre The Giant Donruss Optic	1.00	2.50
354 Paul Heyman Donruss Optic	.40	1.00
355 Nikki Bella Donruss Optic	.60	1.50
356 Sami Zayn Donruss Optic	.40	1.00
357 Million Dollar Man Ted DiBiase Donruss Optic	.40	1.00
358 Bruno Sammartino Donruss Optic	.60	1.50
359 Finn Balor Donruss Optic	.60	1.50
360 Superstar Billy Graham Donruss Optic	.25	.60
361 Charlotte Flair Donruss Optic	1.00	2.50
362 Rikishi Donruss Optic	.30	.75
363 Diesel Donruss Optic	.40	1.00
364 Rey Mysterio Donruss Optic	.60	1.50
365 Rick Boogs Donruss Optic	.30	.75
366 Seth ìFreakinî Rollins Donruss Optic	.60	1.50
367 Brie Bella Donruss Optic	.50	1.25
368 Stacy Keibler Donruss Optic	.75	2.00
369 Edge Donruss Optic	1.00	2.50
370 Kevin Owens Donruss Optic	.50	1.25
371 Brock Lesnar Donruss Optic	1.25	3.00
372 Omos Donruss Optic	.50	1.25
373 Gene Okerlund Donruss Optic	.40	1.00
374 Undertaker Donruss Optic	1.25	3.00
375 Terry Gordy Donruss Optic	.25	.60

376 The Miz .40 1.00
Spectra
377 Iron Sheik .30 .75
Spectra
378 Raquel Rodriguez .60 1.50
Spectra
379 AJ Styles .75 2.00
Spectra
380 Bodhi Hayward .30 .75
Spectra
381 Becky Lynch 1.00 2.50
Spectra
382 Ricochet .50 1.25
Spectra
383 Amari Miller .25 .60
Spectra
384 Shayna Baszler .50 1.25
Spectra
385 Kurt Angle .60 1.50
Spectra
386 Theory .60 1.50
Spectra
387 Kayden Carter .50 1.25
Spectra
388 Sami Zayn .40 1.00
Spectra
389 Alexa Bliss 1.50 4.00
Spectra
390 Billy Gunn .30 .75
Spectra
391 Chyna .50 1.25
Spectra
392 Matt Riddle .60 1.50
Spectra
393 Booker T .50 1.25
Spectra
394 Sheamus .40 1.00
Spectra
395 Randy Orton .60 1.50
Spectra
396 Xia Li .50 1.25
Spectra
397 Natalya .40 1.00
Spectra
398 Johnny Rodz .25 .60
Spectra
399 Asuka 1.00 2.50
Spectra
400 Trick Williams .25 .60
Spectra
401 Stone Cold Steve Austin 1.25 3.00
Noir
402 Rikishi .30 .75
Noir
403 Elton Prince .30 .75
Noir
404 Nathan Frazer .25 .60
Noir
405 AJ Styles .75 2.00
Noir
406 Valentina Feroz .40 1.00
Noir
407 Gigi Dolin 1.00 2.50
Noir
408 IRS .30 .75
Noir
409 Bron Breakker 1.00 2.50
Noir
410 Ken Shamrock .30 .75
Noir
411 Undertaker 1.25 3.00
Noir
412 Drew McIntyre .50 1.25
Noir
413 Isla Dawn .30 .75
Noir
414 Razor Ramon .50 1.25
Noir
415 Becky Lynch 1.00 2.50
Noir
416 1-2-3 Kid .30 .75
Noir
417 Mandy Rose 1.25 3.00
Noir
418 Joaquin Wilde .40 1.00
Noir
419 Bret "Hit Man" Hart .60 1.50
Noir
420 Nikolai Volkoff .25 .60
Noir
421 Dante Chen .25 .60
Noir
422 Stevie Turner .25 .60
Noir
423 Bianca Belair .75 2.00
Noir
424 Santos Escobar .40 1.00
Noir
425 The American Nightmare Cody Rhodes.60 1.50
Noir
426 The Great Khali .30 .75
Noir
427 Ronda Rousey 1.50 4.00
Noir
428 Malik Blade .25 .60
Noir
429 Shawn Michaels 1.00 2.50
Noir
430 Paul Bearer .30 .75
Noir
431 John Cena .75 2.00
National Treasures
432 Mr. Perfect Curt Hennig .50 1.25
National Treasures
433 Cora Jade .75 2.00
National Treasures
434 Papa Shango .25 .60
National Treasures
435 Triple H 1.00 2.50
National Treasures
436 The Hurricane .25 .60
National Treasures
437 Brooks Jensen .25 .60
National Treasures
438 Ivy Nile .25 .60
National Treasures
439 Alexa Bliss 1.50 4.00
National Treasures
440 Rey Mysterio .60 1.50
National Treasures
441 Roxanne Perez .75 2.00
National Treasures
442 Randy Orton .60 1.50
National Treasures
443 Goldberg 1.00 2.50
National Treasures
444 Santos Escobar .40 1.00
National Treasures
445 Andre The Giant 1.00 2.50
National Treasures
446 Von Wagner .25 .60
National Treasures
447 Diamond Dallas Page .30 .75
National Treasures
448 Kevin Owens .50 1.25
National Treasures
449 Brock Lesnar 1.25 3.00
National Treasures
450 Karrion Kross .50 1.25
National Treasures
451 Rhea Ripley .75 2.00
National Treasures
452 Ricky "The Dragon" Steamboat .50 1.25
National Treasures
453 Hulk Hogan 1.25 3.00
National Treasures
454 Stephanie McMahon .40 1.00
National Treasures
455 Aoife Valkyrie .50 1.25
National Treasures
456 Yulisa Leon .25 .60
National Treasures
457 Faarooq .30 .75
National Treasures
458 Nikki A.S.H. .40 1.00
National Treasures
459 Edge 1.00 2.50
National Treasures
460 Lash Legend .25 .60
National Treasures
461 Liv Morgan 1.25 3.00
One
462 The Rock 2.50 6.00
One
463 Stacy Keibler .75 2.00
One
464 Chyna .50 1.25
One
465 Gorilla Monsoon .40 1.00
One
466 Rey Mysterio .60 1.50
One
467 Isla Dawn .30 .75
One
468 Yokozuna .30 .75
One
469 Asuka 1.00 2.50
One
470 Kit Wilson .25 .60
One
471 Roman Reigns 1.50 4.00
One
472 Batista .50 1.25
One
473 Macho Man Randy Savage 1.00 2.50
One
474 Million Dollar Man Ted DiBiase .40 1.00
One
475 Tiffany Stratton .40 1.00
One
476 Torrie Wilson .60 1.50
One
477 Indi Hartwell .75 2.00
One
478 Jinny .25 .60
One
479 Charlotte Flair 1.00 2.50
One
480 Mankind .50 1.25
One
481 Gable Steveson 1.25 3.00
One
482 Rob Van Dam .50 1.25
One
483 Ultimate Warrior 1.00 2.50
One
484 The Boogeyman .25 .60
One
485 Captain Lou Albano .30 .75
One
486 Wendy Choo .50 1.25
One
487 Iron Sheik .30 .75
One
488 Katana Chance .50 1.25
One
489 Finn Balor .60 1.50
One
490 Oliver Carter/8
One
491 Roxanne Perez/8
Gala
492 Gable Steveson/8
Gala
493 Solo Sikoa/8
Gala
494 Bron Breakker/8
Gala
495 Carmelo Hayes/8
Gala
496 Tony D'Angelo/8
Gala
497 Nikkita Lyons/8
Gala
498 Cora Jade/8
Gala
499 Joe Gacy/8
Gala
500 Veer Mahaan/8
Gala

2022 Panini Chronicles WWE Absolute Tools of the Trade Signatures

*PRIME/10: UNPRICED DUE TO SCARCITY
*SUPER PRIME/1: UNPRICED DUE TO SCARCITY
STATED PRINT RUN 75-99

TTADK Angelo Dawkins/99 5.00 12.00
TTASK Asuka/99 20.00 50.00
TTATH Theory/99 20.00 50.00
TTBTC Butch/99 10.00 25.00
TTCGR Cameron Grimes/99 12.00 30.00
TTCHY Carmelo Hayes/49 20.00 50.00
TTDBK Dana Brooke/99 8.00 20.00
TTDDP Doudrop/99 10.00 25.00
TTDPR Damian Priest/99 6.00 15.00
TTDZG Dolph Ziggler/99 8.00 20.00
TTGGD Gigi Dolin/75 60.00 150.00
TTGTH Gunther/99 12.00 30.00
TTIDG Ilja Dragunov/99 5.00 12.00
TTISH IYO SKY/99 25.00 60.00

TTJGC Joe Gacy/99	6.00	15.00
TTJJN Jacy Jayne/99	25.00	60.00
TTJUS Jey Uso/99	12.00	30.00
TTJUS Jimmy Uso/99	15.00	40.00
TTKCC Katana Chance/99	15.00	40.00
TTKCO Kayden Carter/99	10.00	25.00
TTKWD Xavier Woods/99	8.00	20.00
TTLEV Lacey Evans/99	25.00	60.00
TTLVM Liv Morgan/99	60.00	150.00
TTMIZ The Miz/99	10.00	25.00
TTMSM Meiko Satomura/75		
TTMVP MVP/99	6.00	15.00
TTMZF Montez Ford/99	8.00	20.00
TTNTL Natalya/99	10.00	25.00
TTODY Odyssey Jones/99	5.00	12.00
TTOTS Otis/99	8.00	20.00
TTQZL Queen Zelina/99	15.00	40.00
TTRCH Ricochet/99	12.00	30.00
TTRGE Reggie/99	5.00	12.00
TTRHL Ridge Holland/99	6.00	15.00
TTRRP Rhea Ripley/99	30.00	75.00
TTRST Roderick Strong/99	5.00	12.00
TTSBZ Shayna Baszler/99	15.00	40.00
TTSES Santos Escobar/75	5.00	12.00
TTSZI Shotzi/99	30.00	75.00
TTVMH Veer Mahaan/99	8.00	20.00

2022 Panini Chronicles WWE Contenders Rookie Ticket Autographs

*RED: .6X TO 1.5X BASIC AUTOS
*CRACKED ICE/10: UNPRICED DUE TO SCARCITY
*CHAMPIONSHIP/1: UNPRICED DUE TO SCARCITY
RANDOMLY INSERTED INTO PACKS

RSAVK Aoife Valkyrie	12.00	30.00
RSAXM Axiom	6.00	15.00
RSBBK Bron Breakker	25.00	60.00
RSBCR Brutus Creed	6.00	15.00
RSGSV Gable Steveson EXCH	30.00	75.00
RSJNY Jinny	8.00	20.00
RSLLG Lash Legend	6.00	15.00
RSSSK Solo Sikoa	40.00	100.00
RSSTN Stevie Turner	12.00	30.00
RSVMH Veer Mahaan	6.00	15.00

2022 Panini Chronicles WWE Crown Royale Silhouettes Autographs

*PRIME/10: UNPRICED DUE TO SCARCITY
*SUPER PRIME/1: UNPRICED DUE TO SCARCITY
STATED PRINT RUN 99 SER.#'d SETS

SLACR Apollo Crews/99	5.00	12.00
SLADK Angelo Dawkins/99	5.00	12.00
SLASH Nikki A.S.H./99	15.00	40.00
SLBCD Brutus Creed/99	6.00	15.00
SLCJD Cora Jade/99	75.00	200.00
SLDMY Dominik Mysterio/99	10.00	25.00
SLDPR Damian Priest/99	10.00	25.00
SLERK Erik/99	6.00	15.00
SLGVC Giovanni Vinci/99	6.00	15.00
SLGWL Grayson Waller/99	12.00	30.00
SLHPC Happy Corbin/99	6.00	15.00
SLIHW Indi Hartwell/99	15.00	40.00
SLIVR Ivar/99	8.00	20.00
SLJCD Julius Creed/99	6.00	15.00
SLJMH Jinder Mahal/99	6.00	15.00
SLJQW Joaquin Wilde/99	6.00	15.00
SLJRD Jagger Reid/99	6.00	15.00
SLJUS Jey Uso/99	12.00	30.00
SLKKG Kofi Kingston/99	10.00	25.00
SLKLR Alba Fyre/49	20.00	50.00
SLKOW Kevin Owens/99	20.00	50.00
SLLLG Lash Legend/99	12.00	30.00
SLMBT Ludwig Kaiser/99	8.00	20.00
SLMFD Montez Ford/99	8.00	20.00
SLMXD Max Dupri/99	12.00	30.00
SLOMS Omos/99	6.00	15.00
SLRBG Rick Boogs/99	10.00	25.00
SLRDL Matt Riddle/99	15.00	40.00
SLRMY Rey Mysterio/99	30.00	75.00
SLRQG Raquel Rodriguez/99	25.00	60.00
SLRST Roderick Strong/99	5.00	12.00
SLSDV Sonya Deville/99	20.00	50.00
SLSHM Sheamus/99	10.00	25.00
SLSZN Sami Zayn/99	15.00	40.00
SLTBT Tyler Bate/99	5.00	12.00
SLTCP Ciampa/49	6.00	15.00
SLVWG Von Wagner/99	8.00	20.00
SLZST Zoey Stark/99	12.00	30.00

2022 Panini Chronicles WWE Donruss Optic Rated Rookie Signatures

*RED: .6X TO 1.5X BASIC AUTOS
*GOLD/10: UNPRICED DUE TO SCARCITY
*GOLD VINYL/1: UNPRICED DUE TO SCARCITY
RANDOMLY INSERTED INTO PACKS

RRGSV Gable Steveson EXCH	20.00	50.00
RRAOF Aoife Valkyrie	12.00	30.00
RRAXM Axiom	8.00	20.00
RRBBK Bron Breakker	30.00	75.00
RRCJD Cora Jade	75.00	150.00
RRINY Ivy Nile	15.00	40.00
RRJCD Julius Creed	6.00	15.00
RROJN Odyssey Jones	6.00	15.00
RRSHY Shanky	6.00	15.00
RRSSK Solo Sikoa	60.00	150.00

2022 Panini Chronicles WWE Flux Autographs

*RED: .6X TO 1.5X BASIC AUTOS
*GOLD/10: UNPRICED DUE TO SCARCITY
*BLACK/1: UNPRICED DUE TO SCARCITY
RANDOMLY INSERTED INTO PACKS

FXABS Alexa Bliss	100.00	250.00
FXACR Apollo Crews	5.00	12.00
FXADK Angelo Dawkins	4.00	10.00
FXAJS AJ Styles	15.00	40.00
FXBTH Butch	6.00	15.00
FXCAZ Commander Azeez	4.00	10.00
FXCOR The American Nightmare Cody Rhodes EXCH	75.00	200.00
FXDGL Drew Gulak	5.00	12.00
FXDMY Dominik Mysterio	10.00	25.00
FXDPS Damian Priest	8.00	20.00
FXDZG Dolph Ziggler	6.00	15.00
FXEZK Ezekiel	6.00	15.00
FXHPC Happy Corbin	6.00	15.00
FXJMH Jinder Mahal	6.00	15.00
FXJMU Jimmy Uso	10.00	25.00
FXJUS Jey Uso	12.00	30.00
FXJWD Joaquin Wilde	4.00	10.00
FXKOW Kevin Owens	15.00	40.00
FXMFD Montez Ford	10.00	25.00
FXMIZ The Miz	12.00	30.00
FXMVP MVP	6.00	15.00
FXRDL Matt Riddle	12.00	30.00
FXRHL Ridge Holland	10.00	25.00
FXRRP Rhea Ripley	25.00	60.00
FXRRS Roman Reigns	50.00	125.00
FXSDV Sonya Deville	12.00	30.00
FXSZI Shotzi	30.00	75.00
FXTON Titus O'Neil	4.00	10.00
FXXLI Xia Li	15.00	40.00
FXZST Zoey Stark	10.00	25.00

2022 Panini Chronicles WWE Hall of Fame Autographs

*RED: .6X TO 1.5X BASIC AUTOS
*GOLD/10: UNPRICED DUE TO SCARCITY
*PLATINUM/1: UNPRICED DUE TO SCARCITY
RANDOMLY INSERTED INTO PACKS

HFDDP Diamond Dallas Page	12.00	30.00
HFDSL Diesel	25.00	60.00
HFHHG Hulk Hogan	125.00	300.00
HFISH Iron Sheik	20.00	50.00
HFKAG Kurt Angle	15.00	40.00
HFMDM Million Dollar Man Ted DiBiase	15.00	40.00
HFRVD Rob Van Dam	12.00	30.00
HFSCA Stone Cold Steve Austin	125.00	300.00
HFTSH Trish Stratus	40.00	100.00

2022 Panini Chronicles WWE It's All About the Game

COMPLETE SET (50)	500.00	1200.00

RANDOMLY INSERTED INTO PACKS

1 Hunter Hearst Helmsley	15.00	40.00
2 Hunter Hearst Helmsley	15.00	40.00
3 Hunter Hearst Helmsley	15.00	40.00
4 Hunter Hearst Helmsley	15.00	40.00
5 Hunter Hearst Helmsley	15.00	40.00
6 Hunter Hearst Helmsley	15.00	40.00
7 Triple H	15.00	40.00
8 Triple H	15.00	40.00
9 Triple H	15.00	40.00
10 Triple H	15.00	40.00
11 Triple H	15.00	40.00
12 Triple H	15.00	40.00
13 Triple H	15.00	40.00
14 Triple H	15.00	40.00
15 Triple H	15.00	40.00
16 Triple H	15.00	40.00
17 Triple H	15.00	40.00
18 Triple H	15.00	40.00
19 Triple H	15.00	40.00
20 Triple H	15.00	40.00
21 Triple H	15.00	40.00
22 Triple H	15.00	40.00
23 Triple H	15.00	40.00
24 Triple H	15.00	40.00
25 Triple H	15.00	40.00
26 Triple H	15.00	40.00
27 Triple H	15.00	40.00
28 Triple H	15.00	40.00
29 Triple H	15.00	40.00
30 Triple H	15.00	40.00
31 Triple H	15.00	40.00
32 Triple H	15.00	40.00
33 Triple H	15.00	40.00
34 Triple H	15.00	40.00
35 Triple H	15.00	40.00
36 Triple H	15.00	40.00
37 Triple H	15.00	40.00
38 Triple H	15.00	40.00
39 Triple H	15.00	40.00
40 Triple H	15.00	40.00
41 Triple H	15.00	40.00
42 Triple H	15.00	40.00
43 Triple H	15.00	40.00
44 Triple H	15.00	40.00
45 Triple H	15.00	40.00
46 Triple H	15.00	40.00
47 Triple H	15.00	40.00
48 Triple H	15.00	40.00
49 Triple H	15.00	40.00
50 Triple H	15.00	40.00

2022 Panini Chronicles WWE National Pride Signatures

*RED: .6X TO 1.5X BASIC AUTOS
*GOLD/10: UNPRICED DUE TO SCARCITY
*BLACK/1: UNPRICED DUE TO SCARCITY
RANDOMLY INSERTED INTO PACKS

NPASK Asuka	20.00	50.00
NPEGE Edge	15.00	40.00
NPFBL Finn Balor	12.00	30.00
NPGSV Gable Steveson EXCH	20.00	50.00
NPGTH Gunther	10.00	25.00
NPHHG Hulk Hogan	125.00	300.00
NPISH Iron Sheik	15.00	40.00
NPJDG Hacksaw Jim Duggan	12.00	30.00
NPKAG Kurt Angle	20.00	50.00
NPMCF Mark Coffey	6.00	15.00
NPMSR man.soor	6.00	15.00
NPNTL Natalya	8.00	20.00
NPSHK Shinsuke Nakamura	10.00	25.00
NPSHY Shanky	6.00	15.00
NPTSH Trish Stratus	30.00	75.00
NPWBT Wade Barrett	10.00	25.00
NPWGN Wolfgang	6.00	15.00
NPWRG William Regal	12.00	30.00

2022 Panini Chronicles WWE National Treasures Memorabilia Autographs

*GOLD/10: UNPRICED DUE TO SCARCITY
*PLATINUM/1: UNPRICED DUE TO SCARCITY
STATED PRINT RUN 49 SER.#'d SETS

NTMRS Mandy Rose	75.00	200.00
NTBBL Bianca Belair	50.00	125.00
NTRRN Roman Reigns	100.00	250.00
NTBLS Brock Lesnar	100.00	250.00
NTSFR Seth ìFreakinî Rollins	50.00	125.00
NTCML Carmella	50.00	125.00
NTDMC Drew McIntyre	25.00	60.00
NTAJS AJ Styles	25.00	60.00
NTFBL Finn Balor	25.00	60.00
NTKOW Kevin Owens	30.00	75.00
NTASK Asuka	60.00	125.00
NTRMY Rey Mysterio	40.00	100.00
NTBBK Bron Breakker	50.00	125.00
NTSKN Shinsuke Nakamura	25.00	60.00
NTCFL Charlotte Flair EXCH	60.00	150.00
NTEGE Edge	30.00	75.00
NTABS Alexa Bliss	150.00	400.00
NTGSV Gable Steveson	40.00	100.00
NTBLY Becky Lynch EXCH	150.00	400.00

2022 Panini Chronicles WWE Origins Autographs

*RED: .6X TO 1.5X BASIC AUTOS
*GOLD/10: UNPRICED DUE TO SCARCITY
*PLATINUM/1: UNPRICED DUE TO SCARCITY
RANDOMLY INSERTED INTO PACKS

OAAFA Afa	8.00	20.00
OABBF Brutus Beefcake	15.00	40.00
OABGM The Boogeyman	8.00	20.00
OABHH Bret "Hit Man" Hart	50.00	125.00
OABKT Booker T	12.00	30.00
OABLV Brother Love		
OABPH Beth Phoenix	15.00	40.00
OABWB Bushwhacker Butch	12.00	30.00
OABWL Bushwhacker Luke	12.00	30.00
OADDP Diamond Dallas Page	10.00	25.00
OADMR Don Muraco	12.00	30.00
OAFRQ Faarooq	10.00	25.00
OAGFT The Godfather	10.00	25.00
OAGVL Greg Valentine	12.00	30.00
OAHHH Triple H EXCH	75.00	200.00
OAISH Iron Sheik	25.00	60.00
OAIVY Ivory	8.00	20.00
OAJBL John "Bradshaw" Layfield	10.00	25.00
OAJDG Hacksaw Jim Duggan	15.00	40.00
OAJHT Jimmy Hart	12.00	30.00
OAJLW Jerry Lawler	15.00	40.00
OAKAG Kurt Angle	15.00	40.00
OAKKL Kelly Kelly	12.00	30.00
OAKNE Kane	15.00	40.00
OAKNS Kevin Nash	20.00	50.00
OALLC Lex Luger	12.00	30.00
OAMDM Million Dollar Man Ted DiBiase	15.00	40.00
OAMHY Molly Holly	10.00	25.00
OAMMC Michelle McCool	12.00	30.00
OARDG Road Dogg	10.00	25.00
OARKI Rikishi	10.00	25.00
OARRS Ronda Rousey	75.00	200.00
OARVD Rob Van Dam	15.00	40.00
OASBG Superstar Billy Graham	12.00	30.00
OASHM Shane Helms	8.00	20.00
OASKA Sika	8.00	20.00
OATON Titus O'Neil	8.00	20.00
OAWBT Wade Barrett	8.00	20.00
OAWRG William Regal	12.00	30.00
OAXPC X-Pac	15.00	40.00

2022 Panini Chronicles WWE Phoenix Autographs

*RED: .6X TO 1.5X BASIC AUTOS
*GOLD/10: UNPRICED DUE TO SCARCITY
*GOLD VINYL/1: UNPRICED DUE TO SCARCITY
RANDOMLY INSERTED INTO PACKS

PAACR Apollo Crews	5.00	12.00
PAADK Angelo Dawkins	5.00	12.00
PAASH Nikki A.S.H.	8.00	20.00
PAATH Theory	15.00	40.00
PABBL Bianca Belair	20.00	50.00
PABCH Butch	6.00	15.00
PABDV Blair Davenport	10.00	25.00
PABGE Big E	6.00	15.00
PABLY Bayley	15.00	40.00
PACAZ Commander Azeez	5.00	12.00
PACFL Charlotte Flair EXCH	30.00	75.00
PACOR The American Nightmare Cody Rhodes EXCH	75.00	200.00
PADDP Doudrop	10.00	25.00
PADGL Drew Gulak	5.00	12.00
PADPS Damian Priest	8.00	20.00
PADZG Dolph Ziggler	8.00	20.00
PAERK Erik	5.00	12.00
PAEZK Ezekiel	6.00	15.00
PAHCB Happy Corbin	6.00	15.00
PAIVR Ivar	5.00	12.00
PAJMH Jinder Mahal		
PAJMU Jimmy Uso	15.00	40.00
PAJQW Joaquin Wilde	5.00	12.00
PAJRD Jagger Reid	5.00	12.00
PAJUS Jey Uso	12.00	30.00
PALEV Lacey Evans	12.00	30.00
PAMFD Montez Ford	6.00	15.00
PAMVP MVP	6.00	15.00
PAOMS Omos	5.00	12.00
PAOTS Otis	6.00	15.00
PAQZL Queen Zelina	12.00	30.00
PARGE Reggie	5.00	12.00
PARHL Ridge Holland	6.00	15.00
PARMY Rey Mysterio	20.00	50.00
PARPF Rip Fowler	5.00	12.00
PASDV Sonya Deville	12.00	30.00
PASHM Sheamus	8.00	20.00
PATON Titus O'Neil	5.00	12.00
PAXLI Xia Li	12.00	30.00
PAXWD Xavier Woods	6.00	15.00

2022 Panini Chronicles WWE Signatures

*RED: .6X TO 1.5X BASIC AUTOS
*GOLD/10: UNPRICED DUE TO SCARCITY
*PLATINUM/1: UNPRICED DUE TO SCARCITY
RANDOMLY INSERTED INTO PACKS

CSBBL Brie Bella	15.00	40.00
CSBHH Bret "Hit Man" Hart	40.00	100.00
CSBOA Boa	6.00	15.00
CSBTS Batista	50.00	125.00
CSDDP Diamond Dallas Page	12.00	30.00
CSEPC Elton Prince	6.00	15.00
CSGBG Goldberg	40.00	100.00
CSGVC Giovanni Vinci	6.00	15.00
CSJCF Joe Coffey	6.00	15.00
CSJCN John Cena	75.00	200.00
CSJDM JD McDonagh	6.00	15.00
CSJLW Jerry Lawler	20.00	50.00
CSJQW Joaquin Wilde	8.00	20.00
CSJRD Jagger Reid	6.00	15.00
CSJRZ Johnny Rodz	8.00	20.00
CSKAG Kurt Angle	15.00	40.00
CSKCT Kayden Carter	10.00	25.00
CSKNE Kane	30.00	75.00
CSKNH Kevin Nash	15.00	40.00
CSKWL Kit Wilson	6.00	15.00
CSLTA Lita	20.00	50.00
CSMBT Ludwig Kaiser	6.00	15.00
CSMCF Mark Coffey	6.00	15.00
CSMDM Million Dollar Man Ted DiBiase	12.00	30.00
CSMKN Mankind	30.00	75.00
CSNBL Nikki Bella	20.00	50.00
CSRDG Road Dogg	10.00	25.00
CSRKI Rikishi	10.00	25.00
CSRPF Rip Fowler	6.00	15.00
CSRSM Ron Simmons	12.00	30.00
CSSHM Shawn Michaels	75.00	200.00
CSTBT Tyler Bate	6.00	15.00
CSTSH Trish Stratus	30.00	75.00
CSUTK Undertaker	125.00	300.00
CSWGG Wolfgang	6.00	15.00
CSWLE Wes Lee	6.00	15.00
CSXNQ Xyon Quinn	6.00	15.00

2022 Panini Impeccable WWE

UNOPENED BOX (1 PACK)
UNOPENED PACK (9 CARDS)
*SILVER/49: .6X TO 1.5X BASIC CARDS
*GOLD/35: .75X TO 2X BASIC CARDS
*HOLO SILVER/25: UNPRICED DUE TO SCARCITY
*HOLO GOLD/10: UNPRICED DUE TO SCARCITY
*PLATINUM/1: UNPRICED DUE TO SCARCITY
STATED PRINT RUN 99 SER.#'d SETS

1 The Rock	12.00	30.00
2 Rhea Ripley	5.00	12.00
3 Ivar	2.00	5.00
4 AJ Styles	4.00	10.00
5 Ricochet	3.00	8.00
6 Damian Priest	4.00	10.00
7 Ronda Rousey	15.00	40.00
8 Otis	2.50	6.00
9 Cameron Grimes	2.50	6.00
10 Alexa Bliss	30.00	75.00
11 Stone Cold Steve Austin	20.00	50.00
12 Tamina	2.00	5.00
13 Jey Uso	2.50	6.00
14 Akira Tozawa	3.00	8.00
15 Ridge Holland	2.00	5.00
16 Dolph Ziggler	2.50	6.00
17 Chyna	10.00	25.00
18 Randy Orton	4.00	10.00
19 Eddie Guerrero	10.00	25.00
20 Becky Lynch	20.00	50.00
21 Undertaker	15.00	40.00
22 Angel	2.00	5.00
23 Jimmy Uso	2.50	6.00
24 Angelo Dawkins	2.00	5.00
25 Roman Reigns	8.00	20.00
26 Dominik Mysterio	2.50	6.00
27 Shayna Baszler	3.00	8.00
28 Reggie	2.00	5.00
29 Dusty Rhodes	4.00	10.00
30 Bianca Belair	6.00	15.00
31 Triple H	5.00	12.00
32 Big E	2.50	6.00
33 Jinder Mahal	2.00	5.00
34 Apollo Crews	2.00	5.00
35 Sami Zayn	3.00	8.00
36 Edge	5.00	12.00
37 Shotzi	12.00	30.00
38 Rey Mysterio	4.00	10.00
39 Solo Sikoa	10.00	25.00
40 Carmella	10.00	25.00
41 Cactus Jack	8.00	20.00
42 The American Nightmare Cody Rhodes	25.00	60.00
43 Xavier Woods	2.50	6.00
44 Theory	4.00	10.00
45 Sheamus	3.00	8.00
46 Finn Balor	6.00	15.00
47 Xia Li	5.00	12.00
48 Riddle	5.00	12.00
49 Ciampa	3.00	8.00
50 Dana Brooke	2.00	5.00
51 Bruno Sammartino	2.50	6.00
52 Drew Gulak	2.50	6.00
53 Kofi Kingston	3.00	8.00
54 The All Mighty Bobby Lashley	3.00	8.00
55 Shinsuke Nakamura	4.00	10.00
56 Kevin Owens	5.00	12.00
57 Asuka	12.00	30.00
58 Robert Roode	2.00	5.00
59 Santos Escobar	2.00	5.00
60 Doudrop	2.00	5.00
61 Ultimate Warrior	8.00	20.00
62 Drew McIntyre	5.00	12.00
63 Mace	2.00	5.00
64 Brock Lesnar	8.00	20.00
65 Aliyah	2.00	5.00
66 The Miz	2.50	6.00
67 Bayley	6.00	15.00
68 R-Truth	2.00	5.00
69 Goldberg	4.00	10.00
70 Liv Morgan	30.00	75.00
71 Andre the Giant	10.00	25.00
72 Erik	2.00	5.00
73 Madcap Moss	2.00	5.00
74 Cedric Alexander	2.00	5.00
75 Charlotte Flair	8.00	20.00
76 Montez Ford	2.00	5.00
77 John Cena	6.00	15.00
78 Seth Freakin Rollins	6.00	15.00
79 Raquel Rodriguez	15.00	40.00
80 Maryse	12.00	30.00
81 Meiko Satomura	2.00	5.00
82 Happy Corbin	2.00	5.00
83 Mansoor	2.00	5.00
84 Chad Gable	2.00	5.00
85 Hulk Hogan	25.00	60.00
86 MVP	2.00	5.00
87 Lacey Evans	8.00	20.00
88 Shelton Benjamin	2.00	5.00
89 Alba Fyre	5.00	12.00
90 Nikki A.S.H.	3.00	8.00
91 Ilja Dragunov	2.00	5.00
92 Humberto	2.00	5.00
93 Rick Boogs	2.00	5.00
94 Commander Azeez	2.00	5.00
95 Natalya	3.00	8.00
96 Omos	2.00	5.00
97 Shanky	2.00	5.00
98 T-Bar	2.00	5.00
99 Mandy Rose	20.00	50.00
100 Queen Zelina	6.00	15.00

2022 Panini Impeccable WWE Elegance Memorabilia Autographs

*HOLO SILVER/25: .6X TO 1.5X BASIC AUTOS
*HOLO GOLD/10: UNPRICED DUE TO SCARCITY
*PLATINUM/1: UNPRICED DUE TO SCARCITY
RANDOMLY INSERTED INTO PACKS

EMABS Alexa Bliss	100.00	250.00
EMACR Apollo Crews	8.00	20.00
EMADK Angelo Dawkins	10.00	25.00
EMAJS AJ Styles	20.00	50.00
EMASK Asuka	30.00	75.00
EMBBL Bianca Belair	30.00	75.00
EMBLS The All Mighty Bobby Lashley	12.00	30.00
EMBLS Brock Lesnar	75.00	200.00
EMBLY Becky Lynch	40.00	100.00
EMCFL Charlotte Flair EXCH	60.00	150.00
EMCGR Cameron Grimes	8.00	20.00
EMCML Carmella	20.00	50.00
EMDDR Doudrop	8.00	20.00

EMDMC Drew McIntyre	25.00	60.00
EMDMY Dominik Mysterio	8.00	20.00
EMDPS Damian Priest	10.00	25.00
EMDZG Dolph Ziggler	10.00	25.00
EMEGD Edge	30.00	75.00
EMFBL Finn Balor	15.00	40.00
EMGGD Gigi Dolin	60.00	150.00
EMGTH Gunther	10.00	25.00
EMIDG Ilja Dragunov	12.00	30.00
EMISH Io Shirai	25.00	60.00
EMJMH Jinder Mahal	8.00	20.00
EMJMU Jimmy Uso	15.00	40.00
EMJUS Jey Uso	15.00	40.00
EMKKG Kofi Kingston	8.00	20.00
EMKOW Kevin Owens	15.00	40.00
EMLAK LA Knight	15.00	40.00
EMLVM Liv Morgan	100.00	250.00
EMMFD Montez Ford	12.00	30.00
EMMIZ The Miz	15.00	40.00
EMNTA Natalya	10.00	25.00
EMOMS Omos	12.00	30.00
EMOTS Otis	8.00	20.00
EMRDL Riddle	20.00	50.00
EMRMY Rey Mysterio	25.00	60.00
EMROR Randy Orton EXCH	40.00	100.00
EMRQG Raquel Rodriguez		
EMRRN Roman Reigns EXCH	60.00	150.00
EMRRP Rhea Ripley	40.00	100.00
EMSDV Sonya Deville	15.00	40.00
EMSHM Sheamus	10.00	25.00
EMSHN Shinsuke Nakamura	15.00	40.00
EMSHZ Shotzi	30.00	75.00
EMSRL Seth Freakin Rollins	30.00	75.00
EMSZN Sami Zayn	15.00	40.00
EMTCP Ciampa	10.00	25.00

2022 Panini Impeccable WWE Elegance Rookie Memorabilia Autographs

*HOLO SILVER/25: .6X TO 1.5X BASIC AUTOS
*HOLO GOLD/10: UNPRICED DUE TO SCARCITY
*PLATINUM/1: UNPRICED DUE TO SCARCITY
STATED PRINT RUN 99 SER.#'d SETS

101 Bron Breakker	60.00	150.00
102 Carmelo Hayes	20.00	50.00
103 Gable Steveson EXCH	25.00	60.00
104 Grayson Waller	12.00	30.00
105 Ivy Nile	20.00	50.00
106 Joe Gacy	12.00	30.00
107 Von Wagner	12.00	30.00
108 Cora Jade	75.00	200.00
109 Jacy Jayne	40.00	100.00
110 Veer Mahaan	12.00	30.00

2022 Panini Impeccable WWE Illustrious Ink

*HOLO SILVER/25: .6X TO 1.5X BASIC AUTOS
*HOLO GOLD/10: UNPRICED DUE TO SCARCITY
*PLATINUM/1: UNPRICED DUE TO SCARCITY
STATED PRINT RUN 99 SER.#'d SETS

ILAFA Afa	15.00	40.00
ILAML Amale	12.00	30.00
ILBOA Boa	6.00	15.00
ILCJD Cora Jade	75.00	200.00
ILCJK Cactus Jack	60.00	150.00
ILCML Carmella	30.00	75.00
ILDBK Dana Brooke	8.00	20.00
ILDDP Diamond Dallas Page	30.00	75.00
ILDGL Drew Gulak	12.00	30.00
ILDMR Don Muraco	15.00	40.00
ILDMS Dave Mastiff	6.00	15.00
ILDMY Dominik Mysterio	12.00	30.00
ILFRQ Faarooq	12.00	30.00
ILIVR Ivar EXCH	6.00	15.00
ILJCR Julius Creed	8.00	20.00
ILJDG Hacksaw Jim Duggan	25.00	60.00
ILJLW Jerry Lawler	25.00	60.00
ILJNY Jinny	10.00	25.00
ILJWL Joaquin Wilde	6.00	15.00
ILKWD Xavier Woods	12.00	30.00
ILKWL Kenny Williams	6.00	15.00
ILMCF Mark Coffey	6.00	15.00
ILMRS Mandy Rose	50.00	125.00
ILODY Odyssey Jones	6.00	15.00
ILOTS Otis	10.00	25.00
ILRHL Ridge Holland	6.00	15.00
ILSDV Sonya Deville	12.00	30.00
ILSKA Sika	10.00	25.00
ILTMN Teoman	6.00	15.00
ILZST Zoey Stark	15.00	40.00

2022 Panini Impeccable WWE Immortal Ink

*HOLO SILVER/25: .6X TO 1.5X BASIC AUTOS
*HOLO GOLD/10: UNPRICED DUE TO SCARCITY
*PLATINUM/1: UNPRICED DUE TO SCARCITY
STATED PRINT RUN 99 SER.#'d SETS

IMABZ Alundra Blayze	15.00	40.00
IMBBK Brutus Beefcake	20.00	50.00
IMBBL Brie Bella	25.00	60.00
IMBHT Bret "Hit Man" Hart	100.00	250.00
IMBKT Booker T	25.00	60.00
IMBLV Brother Love	12.00	30.00
IMBOR Cowboy Bob Orton	12.00	30.00
IMBPX Beth Phoenix	12.00	30.00
IMBWB Bushwhacker Butch	15.00	40.00
IMBWL Bushwhacker Luke	15.00	40.00
IMGFT The Godfather	12.00	30.00
IMGVL Greg Valentine	12.00	30.00
IMISH Iron Sheik	25.00	60.00
IMIVY Ivory	20.00	50.00
IMJBL John "Bradshaw" Layfield	12.00	30.00
IMJHT Jimmy Hart	12.00	30.00
IMJLW Jerry Lawler	25.00	60.00
IMKLY Kelly Kelly	25.00	60.00
IMLTA Lita	40.00	100.00
IMMDM Million Dollar Man Ted DiBiase	20.00	50.00
IMMHL Molly Holly	15.00	40.00
IMMHY Michael Hayes	12.00	30.00
IMNBL Nikki Bella	40.00	100.00
IMPGE Paige	50.00	125.00
IMRKI Rikishi	15.00	40.00
IMRVD Rob Van Dam	25.00	60.00
IMSBG Superstar Billy Graham	12.00	30.00
IMSML Shawn Michaels	100.00	250.00
IMUTK Undertaker	250.00	500.00
IMXPC X-Pac	20.00	50.00

2022 Panini Impeccable WWE Impeccable Championship Debuts Autographs

STATED PRINT RUN 1-99

CDABS Alexa Bliss/16		
CDAJS AJ Styles/16		
CDASK Asuka/18		
CDBBL Bianca Belair/21	250.00	600.00
CDBLS Brock Lesnar/2		
CDBLS The All Mighty Bobby Lashley/21	150.00	400.00
CDBLY Becky Lynch/16		
CDBPX Beth Phoenix/11		
CDBTS Batista/5		
CDCFL Charlotte Flair/15		
CDDMI Drew McIntyre/20	100.00	250.00
CDDZG Dolph Ziggler/11		
CDEGE Edge/6		
CDFBL Finn Balor/16		
CDGLB Goldberg/98	100.00	250.00
CDHHG Hulk Hogan/84	500.00	1200.00
CDISH Iron Sheik/83	75.00	200.00
CDJBL John "Bradshaw" Layfield/4		
CDJCN John Cena/5		
CDKKG Kofi Kingston/19		
CDKLY Kelly Kelly/9		
CDLTA Lita/1		
CDMFL Mankind/99	150.00	400.00
CDMMC Michelle McCool/8 EXCH		
CDPGE Paige/14		
CDROR Randy Orton/4		
CDRYM Rey Mysterio/6		
CDSCA Stone Cold Steve Austin/98	400.00	1000.00
CDSHM Sheamus/9		
CDSRL Seth Freakin Rollins/15		

2022 Panini Impeccable WWE Impeccable Championships Signatures

STATED PRINT RUN 2-16
UNPRICED DUE TO SCARCITY

ICABS Alexa Bliss/5 EXCH
ICABZ Alundra Blayze/3
ICAJS AJ Styles/2
ICBHT Bret "Hit Man" Hart/7
ICBLS Brock Lesnar/10
ICBLY Becky Lynch/6
ICBTS Batista/6
ICCFL Charlotte Flair/13
ICEGE Edge/11
ICGLB Goldberg/4
ICHHG Hulk Hogan/12
ICJCN John Cena/16
ICMKN Mankind/3
ICROR Randy Orton/14
ICRRN Roman Reigns/5
ICSCA Stone Cold Steve Austin/6
ICSRL Seth Freakin Rollins/4
ICTPH Triple H/14
ICTSH Trish Stratus/7
ICUKT Undertaker/7

2022 Panini Impeccable WWE Impeccable Hall of Fame Signatures

STATED PRINT RUN 4-96

HFABZ Alundra Blayze/15		
HFBBF Brutus Beefcake/19		
HFBHT Bret "Hit Man" Hart/6		
HFBKT Booker T/13		
HFBOR Cowboy Bob Orton/5		
HFBPX Beth Phoenix/17		
HFDDP Diamond Dallas Page/17		
HFEGE Edge/12		
HFFRQ Ron Simmons/12		
HFGFT The Godfather/17		
HFGLB Goldberg/18		
HFGVL Greg Valentine/4		
HFHHG Hulk Hogan/5		
HFIPT Ivan Putski/95 EXCH	40.00	100.00
HFISH Iron Sheik/5		
HFIVY Ivory/18		
HFJBL JBL/20	100.00	250.00
HFJHT Jimmy Hart/5		
HFJKL Jerry Lawler/7		
HFJRZ Johnny Rodz/96	40.00	100.00
HFKNE Kane/21	200.00	500.00
HFLTA Lita/14		
HFMDM Million Dollar Man Ted DiBiase/10		
HFMHL Molly Holly/21	75.00	200.00
HFRKI Rikishi/15		
HFRVD Rob Van Dam/21	100.00	250.00
HFSML Shawn Michaels/11		
HFTSH Trish Stratus/13		
HFTWL Torrie Wilson/19		
HFUKT Undertaker/22	1500.00	4000.00

2022 Panini Impeccable WWE Impeccable Jumbo Materials

STATED PRINT RUN 35 SER.#'d SETS

JMABS Alexa Bliss	30.00	75.00
JMAJS AJ Styles	8.00	20.00
JMASK Asuka	15.00	40.00
JMBBL Bianca Belair	10.00	25.00
JMBLS Brock Lesnar	25.00	60.00
JMBLS The All Mighty Bobby Lashley	6.00	15.00
JMBLY Becky Lynch	40.00	100.00
JMBRK Bron Breakker	12.00	30.00
JMCFL Charlotte Flair	25.00	60.00
JMCML Carmella	40.00	100.00
JMCRD The American Nightmare Cody Rhodes	20.00	50.00
JMDMI Drew McIntyre	6.00	15.00
JMEGE Edge	12.00	30.00
JMFBL Finn Balor	12.00	30.00
JMLVM Liv Morgan	75.00	200.00
JMROR Randy Orton	12.00	30.00
JMRRN Roman Reigns	12.00	30.00
JMRYM Rey Mysterio	10.00	25.00
JMSCA Stone Cold Steve Austin	20.00	50.00
JMSRL Seth Freakin Rollins	15.00	40.00

2022 Panini Impeccable WWE Impeccable WrestleMania Signatures

STATED PRINT RUN 7-27

IWAJS AJ Styles/7
IWBLS Brock Lesnar/11
IWBTS Batista/7
IWEGE Edge/13
IWHHG Hulk Hogan/12
IWJBL JBL/10
IWJCA John Cena/15
IWKAN Kurt Angle/9
IWKKG Kofi Kingston/11
IWKNE Kane/17
IWMIZ The Miz/10
IWROR Randy Orton/18
IWRRN Roman Reigns/9 EXCH
IWRYM Rey Mysterio/13
IWSCA Stone Cold Steve Austin/8

IWSHM Sheamus/10		
IWSML Shawn Michaels/17		
IWSRL Seth Freakin Rollins/11		
IWTPH Triple H/23 EXCH	500.00	1200.00
IWUTK Undertaker/27	800.00	1500.00

2022 Panini Impeccable WWE Indelible Ink

*HOLO SILVER/25: UNPRICED DUE TO SCARCITY
*HOLO GOLD/10: UNPRICED DUE TO SCARCITY
*PLATINUM/1: UNPRICED DUE TO SCARCITY
STATED PRINT RUN 99 SER.#'d SETS

INASH Nikki A.S.H.	10.00	25.00
INBGM The Boogeyman	15.00	40.00
INBTS Batista EXCH	30.00	75.00
INCAZ Commander Azeez	6.00	15.00
INDDR Doudrop	8.00	20.00
INDLN Dani Luna EXCH	8.00	20.00
INEPC Elton Prince	8.00	20.00
INERK Erik	5.00	12.00
INFAB Fabian Aichner	5.00	12.00
INFMW Flash Morgan Webster	5.00	12.00
INGBS Gerald Brisco	12.00	30.00
INGSV Gable Steveson EXCH	25.00	60.00
INHCN The Hurricane	12.00	30.00
ININY Ivy Nile	12.00	30.00
INJDV Jordan Devlin	6.00	15.00
INKAN Kurt Angle EXCH	30.00	75.00
INKCY Katana Chance	20.00	50.00
INKNS Diesel EXCH	25.00	60.00
INKWS Kit Wilson	6.00	15.00
INLEV Lacey Evans	15.00	40.00
INLLG Lex Luger	20.00	50.00
INMAD Mark Andrews EXCH	6.00	15.00
INMMC Michelle McCool EXCH	20.00	50.00
INMRS Mandy Rose	50.00	125.00
INMSR Mansoor	5.00	12.00
INMVP MVP	6.00	15.00
INOMS Omos		
INRBG Rick Boogs	10.00	25.00
INRCO Ricochet	12.00	30.00
INRRD Robert Roode	6.00	15.00
INRRP Rhea Ripley	30.00	75.00
INSHY Shanky	6.00	15.00
INSHZ Shotzi	40.00	100.00
INSTN Stevie Turner	12.00	30.00
INTBT Tyler Bate	5.00	12.00
INWRG William Regal	12.00	30.00
INXLI Xia Li	30.00	75.00
INXQN Xyon Quinn	8.00	20.00
INZGB Zack Gibson	5.00	12.00

2022 Panini Impeccable WWE Silver WWE Legends Logos

*GOLD/1: UNPRICED DUE TO SCARCITY
STATED PRINT RUN 35 SER.#'d SETS

1 Junkyard Dog	75.00	200.00
2 Paul Bearer	60.00	150.00
3 Alundra Blayze	40.00	100.00
4 Rowdy Roddy Piper	100.00	250.00
5 Bret "Hit Man" Hart	125.00	300.00
6 Stone Cold Steve Austin	125.00	300.00
7 Diesel	75.00	200.00
8 Triple H	100.00	250.00
9 Hulk Hogan	200.00	500.00
10 Undertaker	200.00	500.00
11 Macho Man Randy Savage	150.00	400.00
12 Razor Ramon	100.00	250.00
13 Andre the Giant	125.00	300.00
14 Terry Gordy	30.00	100.00
15 Brie Bella	60.00	150.00
16 Million Dollar Man Ted DiBiase	75.00	200.00
17 Dusty Rhodes	75.00	200.00
18 Trish Stratus	125.00	300.00
19 Iron Sheik	40.00	100.00
20 Vader	50.00	125.00
21 Mankind	100.00	250.00
22 Rob Van Dam	60.00	150.00
23 Batista	60.00	150.00
24 Shawn Michaels	125.00	300.00
25 Bruno Sammartino	60.00	150.00
26 Superstar Billy Graham	75.00	200.00
27 Eddie Guerrero	100.00	250.00
28 Ultimate Warrior	200.00	500.00
29 JBL	40.00	100.00
30 X-Pac	60.00	150.00
31 Nikki Bella	75.00	200.00
32 The Rock	250.00	600.00
33 Booker T	50.00	125.00
34 Stacy Keibler	125.00	300.00
35 Chyna	100.00	250.00
36 Terry Funk	60.00	150.00
37 Goldberg	100.00	250.00
38 Umaga	40.00	100.00
39 Jerry Lawler	60.00	150.00
40 Yokozuna	60.00	150.00

2022 Panini Impeccable WWE Silver WWE Logos

*GOLD/1: UNPRICED DUE TO SCARCITY
STATED PRINT RUN 35 SER.#'d SETS

1 Jimmy Uso	60.00	150.00
2 Seth Freakin Rollins	60.00	150.00
3 Big E	50.00	125.00
4 Cora Jade	150.00	400.00
5 Solo Sikoa	75.00	200.00
6 Kofi Kingston	50.00	125.00
7 AJ Styles	100.00	250.00
8 Asuka	125.00	300.00
9 Jey Uso	60.00	150.00
10 Bayley	50.00	125.00
11 Roman Reigns	100.00	250.00
12 Raquel Rodriguez	40.00	100.00
13 Sami Zayn	60.00	150.00
14 Bron Breakker	75.00	200.00
15 Carmella	100.00	250.00
16 The All Mighty Bobby Lashley	60.00	150.00
17 Damian Priest	40.00	100.00
18 Drew McIntyre	60.00	150.00
19 The American Nightmare Cody Rhodes	125.00	300.00
20 Liv Morgan	200.00	500.00
21 Dominik Mysterio	40.00	100.00
22 Ilja Dragunov	50.00	125.00
23 Edge	50.00	125.00
24 Grayson Waller	50.00	125.00
25 Riddle	50.00	125.00
26 Shinsuke Nakamura	75.00	200.00
27 Ronda Rousey	200.00	500.00
28 Brock Lesnar	125.00	300.00
29 Randy Orton	75.00	200.00
30 Charlotte Flair	125.00	300.00
31 Bianca Belair	60.00	150.00
32 Mandy Rose	200.00	500.00
33 Rey Mysterio	60.00	150.00
34 Finn Balor	100.00	250.00
35 Ciampa	40.00	100.00
36 Kevin Owens	75.00	200.00
37 Alexa Bliss	250.00	600.00
38 The Miz	50.00	125.00
39 Becky Lynch	100.00	250.00
40 John Cena	125.00	300.00

2022 Panini Impeccable WWE Stainless Stars

*ORANGE/25: UNPRICED DUE TO SCARCITY
*RED FOTL/15: UNPRICED DUE TO SCARCITY
*GOLD/10: UNPRICED DUE TO SCARCITY
*PLATINUM/1: UNPRICED DUE TO SCARCITY
STATED PRINT RUN 99 SER.#'d SETS

1 Undertaker	20.00	50.00
2 Mandy Rose	20.00	50.00
3 Triple H	12.00	30.00
4 Solo Sikoa	10.00	25.00
5 The Rock	30.00	75.00
6 Drew McIntyre	6.00	15.00
7 Stone Cold Steve Austin	20.00	50.00
8 Charlotte Flair	15.00	40.00
9 Randy Orton	8.00	20.00
10 Seth Freakin Rollins	10.00	25.00
11 Roman Reigns	15.00	40.00
12 Bron Breakker	15.00	40.00
13 Edge	10.00	25.00
14 Ciampa	6.00	15.00
15 Ronda Rousey	25.00	60.00
16 Brock Lesnar	12.00	30.00
17 The American Nightmare Cody Rhodes	40.00	100.00
18 John Cena	15.00	40.00
19 Becky Lynch	15.00	40.00
20 Raquel Rodriguez	8.00	20.00
21 Bianca Belair	10.00	25.00
22 Cora Jade	30.00	75.00
23 Rey Mysterio	8.00	20.00
24 The All Mighty Bobby Lashley	6.00	15.00
25 Alexa Bliss	40.00	100.00

2022 Panini Impeccable WWE Stainless Stars Autographs

*BLUE/75: .5X TO 1.2X BASIC AUTOS
*PURPLE/49: .6X TO 1.5X BASIC AUTOS
*ORANGE/25: .75X TO 2X BASIC AUTOS
*GOLD/10: UNPRICED DUE TO SCARCITY
*PLATINUM/1: UNPRICED DUE TO SCARCITY
STATED PRINT RUN 99 SER.#'d SETS

SSAKD A-Kid	5.00	12.00
SSAOV Aoife Valkyrie	12.00	30.00
SSBBK Bron Breakker	40.00	100.00
SSBLS Brock Lesnar	60.00	150.00
SSBLY Becky Lynch	30.00	75.00
SSDBC Drew McIntyre	12.00	30.00
SSFBL Finn Balor	12.00	30.00
SSGBG Goldberg	40.00	100.00
SSIHW Indi Hartwell	20.00	50.00
SSIOS Io Shirai	15.00	40.00
SSKCZ Katana Chance	12.00	30.00
SSMSM Meiko Satomura	10.00	25.00
SSNDR Noam Dar	5.00	12.00
SSRMY Rey Mysterio	15.00	40.00
SSROR Randy Orton EXCH		
SSRQG Raquel Rodriguez	20.00	50.00
SSRRN Roman Reigns EXCH		
SSSES Santos Escobar	12.00	30.00
SSSRL Seth Freakin Rollins	20.00	50.00
SSSRY Sarray EXCH	8.00	20.00
SSTON Titus O'Neil	8.00	20.00
SSTSH Trish Stratus	40.00	100.00
SSTWL Torrie Wilson	30.00	75.00
SSWLE Wes Lee	8.00	20.00
SSZGB Zack Gibson	5.00	12.00

2022 Panini Impeccable WWE Superstar Autographs

*HOLO SILVER/25: .6X TO 1.5X BASIC AUTOS
*HOLO GOLD/10: UNPRICED DUE TO SCARCITY
*PLATINUM/1: UNPRICED DUE TO SCARCITY
STATED PRINT RUN 99 SER.#'d SETS

SAABS Alexa Bliss	125.00	300.00
SAADK Angelo Dawkins	6.00	15.00
SAAJS AJ Styles	20.00	50.00
SAASK Asuka	25.00	60.00
SAATH Theory	15.00	40.00
SABBL Bianca Belair	25.00	60.00
SABCR Brutus Creed	6.00	15.00
SABGE Big E	8.00	20.00
SABLS The All Mighty Bobby Lashley	15.00	40.00
SABLY Bayley	30.00	75.00
SABNB Bad News Barrett	8.00	20.00
SABTS Batista EXCH	50.00	125.00
SACFL Charlotte Flair EXCH	40.00	100.00
SAELS Ezekiel	10.00	25.00
SAEMK Emilia McKenzie	12.00	30.00
SAGBG Goldberg	60.00	150.00
SAHCB Happy Corbin	6.00	15.00
SAHHG Hulk Hogan	250.00	500.00
SAJCF Joe Coffey	5.00	12.00
SAJCN John Cena EXCH	60.00	150.00
SAJDK James Drake	5.00	12.00
SAJJN Jacy Jayne	50.00	125.00
SAKCT Kayden Carter	12.00	30.00
SAKLR Alba Fyre	15.00	40.00
SALLG Lash Legend	10.00	25.00
SALVM Liv Morgan	75.00	200.00
SAMBT Ludwig Kaiser	6.00	15.00
SAMFD Montez Ford	8.00	20.00
SANTL Natalya	10.00	25.00
SAQZL Queen Zelina	20.00	50.00
SARBR Rampage Brown	5.00	12.00
SARDG Road Dogg	15.00	40.00
SARDL Riddle	15.00	40.00
SARGE Reggie	5.00	12.00
SARST Roderick Strong	8.00	20.00
SASBG Superstar Billy Graham	20.00	50.00
SASBZ Shayna Baszler	8.00	20.00
SASCA Stone Cold Steve Austin	250.00	500.00
SATPH Triple H EXCH	75.00	200.00
SAWFG Wolfgang	5.00	12.00

2022 Panini Instant WWE

*VERSICOLOR/5: UNPRICED DUE TO SCARCITY
*BLACK/1: UNPRICED DUE TO SCARCITY

1 Undertaker/472*	6.00	15.00
2 Raquel Gonzalez/Dakota Kai/130*	6.00	15.00
3 Cameron Grimes/121*	2.50	6.00
4 Tommaso Ciampa/122*	2.50	6.00
5 MSK/126*	2.50	6.00
6 Mandy Rose/210*	8.00	20.00
7 Dolph Ziggler/120*		
8 The Usos/167*	3.00	8.00

9 Bianca Belair/167*	5.00	12.00
10 Cody Rhodes/316*	8.00	20.00
11 Charlotte Flair/283*	6.00	15.00
12 Stone Cold Steve Austin/384*	5.00	12.00
13 Triple H/268*		
14 RK-Bro/176*		
15 Gable Steveson/908*	6.00	15.00
16 Sasha Banks & Naomi/272*	4.00	10.00
17 Edge & Damian Priest/166*		
18 Roman Reigns/412*	3.00	8.00
19 Bron Breakker/588*		
20 Toxic Attraction/180*	6.00	15.00
21 Nikkita Lyons/629*	10.00	25.00
22 Cody Rhodes/130*	5.00	12.00
23 Omos/76*	3.00	8.00
24 Edge/105*		
25 Rhea Ripley/133*	4.00	10.00
26 Ronda Rousey/176*	6.00	15.00
27 Roman Reigns/Usos/117*	8.00	20.00
28 The Usos/97*	5.00	12.00
29 Bianca Belair/144*	4.00	10.00
30 Theory/123*	3.00	8.00
31 Cody Rhodes/242*	6.00	15.00
32 Finn Balor/114*	6.00	15.00
33 Gunther/120*	5.00	12.00
34 Brock Lesnar/95*		
35 John Cena/254*	5.00	12.00
36 John Cena/254*	5.00	12.00
37 John Cena/254*	5.00	12.00
38 John Cena/254*	5.00	12.00
39 John Cena/254*	5.00	12.00
40 John Cena/254*	5.00	12.00
41 John Cena/254*	5.00	12.00
42 John Cena/254*	5.00	12.00
43 John Cena/254*	5.00	12.00
44 John Cena/254*	5.00	12.00
45 John Cena/254*	5.00	12.00
46 John Cena/254*	5.00	12.00
47 John Cena/254*	5.00	12.00
48 John Cena/254*	5.00	12.00
49 John Cena/254*	5.00	12.00
50 John Cena/254*	5.00	12.00
51 John Cena/254*	5.00	12.00
52 The Almighty Bobby Lashley/69*	6.00	15.00
53 The Usos/69*	5.00	12.00
54 Liv Morgan/287*	8.00	20.00
55 Riddle/79*	6.00	15.00
56 Theory/78*	4.00	10.00
57 Cora Jade/Roxanne Perez/233*	10.00	25.00
58 Bianca Belair/95*	4.00	10.00
59 Edge/68*		
60 Pat McAfee/684*	5.00	12.00
61 Roman Reigns/145*	5.00	12.00
62 Raquel Rodriguez & Aliyah/91*		
63 Damage CTRL/67*	4.00	10.00
64 Gunther/		
65 Dominik Mysterio/		
66 Seth "Freakin" Rollins/		
67 Roman Reigns/83*	5.00	12.00
68 Pretty Deadly/84*	5.00	12.00
69 Mandy Rose/113*	6.00	15.00
70 Bron Breakker/		
71 Braun Strowman/		
72 Damage CTRL/		
73 Solo Sikoa/		
74 Ronda Rousey/69*		
75 Karrion Kross/84*		
76 Matt Riddle/83*		
77 Bray Wyatt/149*		
78 Wes Lee/84*		
79 Roxanne Perez/96*		
80 Mandy Rose/105*		
81 Bron Breakker/90*		
82 Ava Rayne/633*		
83 Becky Lynch/82*		
84 AJ Styles/87*		
85 Austin Theory/62*		
86 Sami Zayn/64*	8.00	20.00
87 Roxanne Perez/291*		
88 The American Nightmare Cody Rhodes/		
89 Rhea Ripley/		
90 Sami Zayn/	6.00	15.00

2022 Panini Prizm WWE

*GREEN: .5X TO 1.2X BASIC CARDS
*HYPER: .6X TO 1.5X BASIC CARDS
*ICE: .6X TO 1.5X BASIC CARDS
*RW&B: .75X TO 2X BASIC CARDS
*RUBY WAVE: .75X TO 2X BASIC CARDS
*SILVER: 1X TO 2.5X BASIC CARDS
*RED/299: 1.2X TO 3X BASIC CARDS
*BLUE/199: 1.5X TO 4X BASIC CARDS
*PREMIUM BOX/199: 1.5X TO 4X BASIC CARDS
*PURPLE/149: 2X TO 5X BASIC CARDS
*ORANGE/99: 2.5X TO 6X BASIC CARDS
*TEAL/49: 3X TO 8X BASIC CARDS
*GREEN PULSAR/25: UNPRICED DUE TO SCARCITY
*MOJO/25: UNPRICED DUE TO SCARCITY
*WHITE SPARKLE/20: UNPRICED DUE TO SCARCITY
*BLUE SHIM./10: UNPRICED DUE TO SCARCITY
*GOLD/10: UNPRICED DUE TO SCARCITY
*LUCKY ENV./8: UNPRICED DUE TO SCARCITY
*GOLD SHIM./3: UNPRICED DUE TO SCARCITY
*BLACK/1: UNPRICED DUE TO SCARCITY

1 Dana Brooke	.40	1.00
2 Shelton Benjamin	.60	1.50
3 Fabian Aichner	.50	1.25
4 Von Wagner RC	.40	1.00
5 Rikishi	.50	1.25
6 Kenny Williams RC	.40	1.00
7 AJ Styles	3.00	8.00
8 Mustafa Ali	.50	1.25
9 Bianca Belair	1.25	3.00
10 Rick Boogs	1.00	2.50
11 Lita	1.50	4.00
12 Shotzi	1.50	4.00
13 Flash Morgan Webster	.50	1.25
14 Wes Lee	.40	1.00
15 Jimmy Uso	.50	1.25
16 Kofi Kingston	1.00	2.50
17 A-Kid RC	.50	1.25
18 Naomi	.60	1.50
19 Blair Davenport RC	.40	1.00
20 Riddle	1.00	2.50
21 Dave Mastiff	.40	1.00
22 Stevie Turner RC	.40	1.00
23 Gable Steveson RC	15.00	40.00
24 King Woods	.50	1.25
25 Jinny RC	.40	1.00
26 Harland RC	.40	1.00
27 Akira Tozawa	.50	1.25
28 Natalya	.60	1.50
29 Bobby Lashley	1.00	2.50
30 Robert Roode	.50	1.25
31 Dolph Ziggler	.75	2.00
32 T-Bar		1.00
33 Goldberg	1.50	4.00
34 Xyon Quinn RC	.40	1.00
35 Joe Coffey	.40	1.00
36 Lewis Howley RC	.40	1.00
37 Alexa Bliss	6.00	15.00
38 Nikki A.S.H.	.60	1.50
39 Bron Breakker RC	12.00	30.00
40 Roman Reigns	2.00	5.00
41 Doudrop	.60	1.50
42 Teoman RC	.40	1.00
43 Grayson Waller RC	.40	1.00
44 Queen Zelina	.60	1.50
45 John Cena	3.00	8.00
46 Liv Morgan	2.00	5.00
47 Aliyah	.75	2.00
48 Odyssey Jones RC	1.00	2.50
49 Cameron Grimes	.75	2.00
50 Sam Stoker RC	.40	1.00
51 Drew Gulak	.50	1.25
52 Shane McMahon	1.25	3.00
53 Ilja Dragunov	.40	1.00
54 Amale RC	.40	1.00
55 Paul Heyman	.75	2.00
56 Madcap Moss	.40	1.00
57 Angel	.40	1.00
58 Guru Raaj RC	.40	1.00
59 Carmella	1.00	2.50
60 Beth Phoenix	.75	2.00
61 Duke Hudson RC	.40	1.00
62 Tommaso Ciampa	1.00	2.50
63 Io Shirai	.75	2.00
64 Angelo Dawkins	.50	1.25
65 Joseph Conners RC	.40	1.00
66 Mansoor	.40	1.00
67 Aoife Valkyrie RC	.50	1.25
68 Pete Dunne	.75	2.00
69 Cedric Alexander	.40	1.00
70 Sarray	.50	1.25
71 Elektra Lopez RC	.50	1.25
72 Tony D'Angelo RC	1.25	3.00
73 Ivar	.40	1.00
74 Apollo Crews	.50	1.25
75 Julius Creed RC	.40	1.00
76 Mark Andrews	.40	1.00
77 Eddie Guerrero	2.00	5.00
78 Randy Orton	1.25	3.00
79 Chad Gable	.40	1.00
80 The Great Khali	.50	1.25
81 Ikemen Jiro RC	.40	1.00
82 Trent Seven	.50	1.25
83 Jacy Jayne RC	.40	1.00
84 Asuka	1.50	4.00
85 Malcolm Bivens RC	.40	1.00
86 Wendy Choo RC	.75	2.00
87 Austin Theory	1.50	4.00
88 Raul Mendoza	.60	1.50
89 Commander Azeez	.50	1.25
90 Jerry Lawler	.75	2.00
91 Erik	.40	1.00
92 Valentina Feroz RC	.60	1.50
93 Ultimate Warrior	2.50	6.00
94 Malik Blade RC	.40	1.00
95 Kayden Carter	.75	2.00
96 Robert Stone RC	.40	1.00
97 Becky Lynch	2.00	5.00
98 Rey Mysterio	1.00	2.50
99 Dakota Kai	.75	2.00
100 Shayna Baszler	.75	2.00
101 Damian Priest	1.25	3.00
102 Sasha Banks	2.50	6.00
103 Saurav	.40	1.00
104 Tiffany Stratton RC	.60	1.50
105 James Drake	.40	1.00
106 Kay Lee Ray	1.00	2.50
107 Mark Coffey	.40	1.00
108 Bayley	1.00	2.50
109 Rampage Brown RC	.40	1.00
110 Dani Luna RC	.40	1.00
111 Seth Rollins	1.25	3.00
112 The Demon Finn Balor	2.50	6.00
113 Kevin Nash	.75	2.00
114 Solo Sikoa RC	1.50	4.00
115 Jack Starz RC	.40	1.00
116 Meiko Satomura RC	.50	1.25
117 Big E	.75	2.00
118 Raquel Gonzalez	1.00	2.50
119 Dante Chen RC	.40	1.00
120 Shanky RC	.40	1.00
121 Primate RC	.40	1.00
122 Tyler Bate	.50	1.25
123 Jey Uso	.50	1.25
124 Kevin Owens	1.25	3.00
125 Montez Ford	.40	1.00
126 Boa	.40	1.00
127 Reggie	.50	1.25
128 Dexter Lumis	.40	1.00
129 Sheamus	.60	1.50
130 Gigi Dolin	3.00	8.00
131 Veer Mahaan	1.00	2.50
132 Jinder Mahal	.50	1.25
133 Kushida	.60	1.50
134 MVP	.40	1.00
135 Brock Lesnar	3.00	8.00
136 Rhea Ripley	1.50	4.00
137 Dominik Mysterio	.50	1.25
138 Shinsuke Nakamura	1.00	2.50
139 Wild Boar RC	.40	1.00
140 Walter	1.00	2.50
141 Joaquin Wilde	.60	1.50
142 LA Knight	.60	1.50
143 Nash Carter	.40	1.00
144 Brutus Creed RC	.50	1.25
145 Ricochet	.75	2.00
146 Booker T	.75	2.00
147 Sonya Deville	1.00	2.50
148 Happy Corbin	.50	1.25
149 Wolfgang	.40	1.00
150 Joe Gacy RC	.40	1.00
151 Lash Legend RC	.40	1.00
152 Stacy Keibler	2.00	5.00
153 Candice LeRae	1.25	3.00
154 Ridge Holland	.40	1.00
155 Drew McIntyre	1.00	2.50
156 Tamina	.50	1.25
157 Humberto	.40	1.00
158 Xia Li	.75	2.00
159 Bruno Sammartino	1.00	2.50
160 Santos Escobar	.60	1.50
161 Noam Dar	.50	1.25
162 Carmelo Hayes RC	.50	1.25
163 Roderick Strong	.60	1.50
164 Edge	2.50	6.00
165 Chyna	2.00	5.00
166 Indi Hartwell	1.25	3.00
167 Zack Gibson	.40	1.00

168 Jordan Devlin	.40	1.00
169 Mace	.40	1.00
170 Omos	.75	2.00
171 Cesaro	.40	1.00
172 R-Truth	.50	1.25
173 Elias	.40	1.00
174 The Miz	1.50	4.00
175 Dusty Rhodes	1.00	2.50
176 Zoey Stark	.50	1.25
177 Josh Briggs RC	.40	1.00
178 Mandy Rose	2.00	5.00
179 Otis	.50	1.25
180 Charlotte Flair	2.00	5.00
181 Sami Zayn	.60	1.50
182 Emilia McKenzie RC	.60	1.50
183 Titus O'Neil	.40	1.00
184 Ivy Nile RC	.40	1.00
185 Kacy Catanzaro	.75	2.00
186 Marcel Barthel	.50	1.25
187 Persia Pirotta RC	1.50	4.00
188 Cora Jade RC	6.00	15.00
189 Lacey Evans	1.00	2.50
190 Mick Foley	1.25	3.00
191 The Rock	6.00	15.00
192 Stone Cold Steve Austin	5.00	12.00
193 Undertaker	5.00	12.00
194 Triple H	3.00	8.00
195 Hulk Hogan	2.50	6.00
196 Batista	1.25	3.00
197 Trish Stratus	3.00	8.00
198 Bret "Hit Man" Hart	1.50	4.00
199 Shawn Michaels	1.50	4.00
200 Andre the Giant	2.50	6.00

2022 Panini Prizm WWE Champion Signatures

*GREEN: .5X TO 1.2X BASIC AUTOS
*SILVER: .6X TO 1.5X BASIC AUTOS
*RED/99: .75X TO 2X BASIC AUTOS
*BLUE/49: 1X TO 2.5X BASIC AUTOS
*MOJO/25: UNPRICED DUE TO SCARCITY
*GREEN PULS./25: UNPRICED DUE TO SCARCITY
*PREMIUM BOX/20: UNPRICED DUE TO SCARCITY
*GOLD/10: UNPRICED DUE TO SCARCITY
*BLACK/1: UNPRICED DUE TO SCARCITY
*WHITE SPARKLE/1: UNPRICED DUE TO SCARCITY
RANDOMLY INSERTED INTO PACKS

CSBGE Big E	20.00	50.00
CSBLY Becky Lynch	75.00	200.00
CSCFL Charlotte Flair	60.00	150.00
CSDPS Damian Priest	15.00	40.00
CSHHO Hulk Hogan	300.00	800.00
CSRRS Roman Reigns	200.00	500.00
CSSCA Stone Cold Steve Austin	400.00	800.00
CSSKN Shinsuke Nakamura	15.00	40.00
CSTPH Triple H	250.00	600.00
CSUND Undertaker	500.00	1200.00

2022 Panini Prizm WWE Color Blast

RANDOMLY INSERTED INTO PACKS

1 Brock Lesnar	1000.00	2500.00
2 Charlotte Flair	1000.00	2500.00
3 Roman Reigns	1500.00	4000.00
4 Alexa Bliss	1500.00	4000.00
5 Goldberg	600.00	1500.00
6 Becky Lynch	1000.00	2500.00
7 John Cena	1200.00	3000.00
8 Sasha Banks	750.00	2000.00
9 Big E	750.00	2000.00
10 Bianca Belair	750.00	2000.00

2022 Panini Prizm WWE Fearless

*GREEN: .5X TO 1.2X BASIC CARDS
*SILVER: .6X TO 1.5X BASIC CARDS
*GREEN PULS./25: UNPRICED DUE TO SCARCITY
*MOJO/25: UNPRICED DUE TO SCARCITY
*GOLD/10: UNPRICED DUE TO SCARCITY
*BLACK/1: UNPRICED DUE TO SCARCITY
RANDOMLY INSERTED INTO PACKS

1 Big E	1.25	3.00
2 Asuka	2.50	6.00
3 Shinsuke Nakamura	2.50	6.00
4 Riddle	2.00	5.00
5 Alexa Bliss	10.00	25.00
6 Rhea Ripley	3.00	8.00
7 Edge	2.00	5.00
8 Sasha Banks	5.00	12.00
9 Bayley	2.50	6.00
10 The Miz	1.50	4.00
11 Roman Reigns	5.00	12.00
12 Randy Orton	3.00	8.00
13 The Demon Finn Balor	2.00	5.00
14 Brock Lesnar	3.00	8.00
15 Kofi Kingston	1.25	3.00
16 Bobby Lashley	3.00	8.00
17 AJ Styles	3.00	8.00
18 Drew McIntyre	2.50	6.00
19 Rey Mysterio	1.50	4.00
20 Goldberg	2.50	6.00
21 Charlotte Flair	4.00	10.00
22 Bianca Belair	2.50	6.00
23 John Cena	3.00	8.00
24 Seth Rollins	3.00	8.00
25 Becky Lynch	4.00	10.00

2022 Panini Prizm WWE Iconic Rivals Dual Autographs

*GOLD/10: UNPRICED DUE TO SCARCITY
*BLACK/1: UNPRICED DUE TO SCARCITY
STATED PRINT RUN 25 SER.#'d SETS

IRAC Asuka/Charlotte Flair	625.00	1250.00
IRBA Stone Cold Steve Austin Bret "Hit Man" Hart	2000.00	4000.00
IRBB Becky Lynch/Bianca Belair	200.00	400.00
IRBC Becky Lynch/Charlotte Flair	250.00	500.00
IRBD Bobby Lashley Drew McIntyre EXCH	100.00	200.00
IRBG Bobby Lashley/Goldberg EXCH	200.00	400.00
IRCL Cameron Grimes/LA Knight	60.00	120.00
IRDR Dakota Kai/Raquel Gonzalez	75.00	150.00
IRER Edge/Randy Orton	250.00	500.00
IRGH Goldberg/Hulk Hogan	750.00	1500.00
IRIW Ilja Dragunov/Walter	100.00	200.00
IRJR John Cena/Roman Reigns	1250.00	2500.00
IRKB Brock Lesnar/Kurt Angle	300.00	600.00
IRKS Kevin Owens/Sami Zayn	125.00	250.00
IRMT Mick Foley/Triple H	400.00	700.00
IRRJ John Cena/Randy Orton	1500.00	3000.00
IRRU Roman Reigns/Undertaker	750.00	1500.00
IRSA Stone Cold Steve Austin Shawn Michaels	750.00	1500.00
IRSB Brock Lesnar/Seth Rollins	400.00	700.00
IRST Shawn Michaels/Triple H	500.00	1000.00

2022 Panini Prizm WWE Legendary Signatures

*GREEN: .5X TO 1.2X BASIC AUTOS
*SILVER: .6X TO 1.5X BASIC AUTOS
*RED/99: .75X TO 2X BASIC AUTOS
*BLUE/49: 1X TO 2.5X BASIC AUTOS
*MOJO/25: UNPRICED DUE TO SCARCITY
*GREEN PULS./25: UNPRICED DUE TO SCARCITY
*GOLD/10: UNPRICED DUE TO SCARCITY
*BLACK/1: UNPRICED DUE TO SCARCITY
*WHITE SPARKLE/1: UNPRICED DUE TO SCARCITY
RANDOMLY INSERTED INTO PACKS

LSBAT Batista EXCH	300.00	600.00
LSBBL Brie Bella	15.00	40.00
LSBHT Bret "Hit Man" Hart	60.00	150.00
LSBKT Booker T	15.00	40.00
LSISH Iron Sheik	30.00	75.00
LSJLW Jerry Lawler	25.00	60.00
LSKAN Kurt Angle	25.00	60.00
LSKNE Kane	50.00	100.00
LSKNS Kevin Nash	50.00	100.00
LSLTA Lita	30.00	75.00
LSMFL Mick Foley	30.00	75.00
LSNBL Nikki Bella EXCH	60.00	120.00
LSRDG Road Dogg	15.00	40.00
LSRKS Rikishi	15.00	40.00
LSSLT Sgt. Slaughter	30.00	75.00
LSSMC Shawn Michaels	125.00	250.00
LSTST Trish Stratus	50.00	125.00

2022 Panini Prizm WWE Next Level

*GREEN: .5X TO 1.2X BASIC CARDS
*SILVER: .6X TO 1.5X BASIC CARDS
*GREEN PULS./25: UNPRICED DUE TO SCARCITY
*MOJO/25: UNPRICED DUE TO SCARCITY
*GOLD/10: UNPRICED DUE TO SCARCITY
*BLACK/1: UNPRICED DUE TO SCARCITY
RANDOMLY INSERTED INTO PACKS

1 The Demon Finn Balor	2.00	5.00
2 Big E	1.25	3.00
3 Bobby Lashley	2.50	6.00
4 Riddle	3.00	8.00
5 Rey Mysterio		6.00
6 Edge	4.00	10.00
7 Bianca Belair	3.00	8.00
8 Bayley	2.00	5.00
9 Seth Rollins	3.00	8.00
10 Roman Reigns	4.00	10.00
11 Brock Lesnar	4.00	10.00
12 Asuka	3.00	8.00
13 AJ Styles	2.50	6.00
14 Alexa Bliss	6.00	15.00
15 Goldberg	2.50	6.00
16 Sasha Banks	3.00	8.00
17 John Cena	4.00	10.00
18 The Miz	1.25	3.00
19 Becky Lynch	3.00	8.00
20 Randy Orton	2.00	5.00
21 Kofi Kingston	1.25	3.00
22 Shinsuke Nakamura	1.50	4.00
23 Drew McIntyre	2.50	6.00
24 Rhea Ripley	2.50	6.00
25 Charlotte Flair	3.00	8.00

2022 Panini Prizm WWE Prizmatic Entrances

*GREEN: .5X TO 1.2X BASIC CARDS
*SILVER: .6X TO 1.5X BASIC CARDS
*GREEN PULS./25: UNPRICED DUE TO SCARCITY
*MOJO/25: UNPRICED DUE TO SCARCITY
*GOLD/10: UNPRICED DUE TO SCARCITY
*BLACK/1: UNPRICED DUE TO SCARCITY
RANDOMLY INSERTED INTO PACKS

1 Carmella	1.50	4.00
2 Sheamus	1.25	3.00
3 Edge	3.00	8.00
4 Stone Cold Steve Austin	5.00	12.00
5 AJ Styles	1.50	4.00
6 Kane	1.50	4.00
7 Bayley	1.50	4.00
8 Rey Mysterio	2.00	5.00
9 Big E	1.25	3.00
10 Roman Reigns	4.00	10.00
11 Charlotte Flair	3.00	8.00
12 Shinsuke Nakamura	1.50	4.00
13 The Demon Finn Balor	2.50	6.00
14 John Cena	3.00	8.00
15 Alexa Bliss	6.00	15.00
16 Kofi Kingston	1.50	4.00
17 Becky Lynch	3.00	8.00
18 Rhea Ripley	2.00	5.00
19 Bobby Lashley	1.50	4.00
20 Sasha Banks	3.00	8.00
21 Drew McIntyre	2.00	5.00
22 The Miz	1.25	3.00
23 Goldberg	2.50	6.00
24 Undertaker	6.00	15.00
25 Asuka	2.50	6.00
26 Randy Orton	2.00	5.00
27 Bianca Belair	3.00	8.00
28 Riddle	2.50	6.00
29 Brock Lesnar	4.00	10.00
30 Seth Rollins	2.50	6.00

2022 Panini Prizm WWE Sensational Signatures

*GREEN: .6X TO 1.5X BASIC AUTOS
*GREEN PULS./25: UNPRICED DUE TO SCARCITY
*GOLD/10: UNPRICED DUE TO SCARCITY
*BLACK/1: UNPRICED DUE TO SCARCITY
*WHITE SPARKLE/1: UNPRICED DUE TO SCARCITY
RANDOMLY INSERTED INTO PACKS

SSACR Apollo Crews	5.00	12.00
SSADK Angelo Dawkins	5.00	12.00
SSAKD A-Kid	8.00	20.00
SSAML Amale	10.00	25.00
SSATH Austin Theory	30.00	75.00
SSBCR Brutus Creed	10.00	25.00
SSBDV Blair Davenport	10.00	25.00
SSCAZ Commander Azeez	5.00	12.00
SSCGR Cameron Grimes	8.00	20.00
SSCLR Candice LeRae	12.00	30.00
SSCMH Carmelo Hayes	25.00	60.00
SSCSR Cesaro	6.00	15.00
SSDBK Dana Brooke	10.00	25.00
SSDDP Diamond Dallas Page	15.00	40.00
SSDDR Doudrop	12.00	30.00
SSDGL Drew Gulak	5.00	12.00
SSDKI Dakota Kai	15.00	40.00
SSDLM Dexter Lumis	8.00	20.00
SSDMY Dominik Mysterio	10.00	25.00
SSDZG Dolph Ziggler	8.00	20.00
SSELS Elias	8.00	20.00
SSERK Erik	5.00	12.00

SSFAC Fabian Aichner	5.00	12.00
SSGWL Grayson Waller	20.00	50.00
SSHCB Happy Corbin	10.00	25.00
SSIHW Indi Hartwell	15.00	40.00
SSILD Ilja Dragunov	10.00	25.00
SSINL Ivy Nile	25.00	60.00
SSIVR Ivar	5.00	12.00
SSJCR Julius Creed	20.00	50.00
SSJDV Jordan Devlin	12.00	30.00
SSJJN Jacy Jayne	25.00	60.00
SSJMH Jinder Mahal	8.00	20.00
SSJMU Jimmy Uso	10.00	25.00
SSJUS Jey Uso	10.00	25.00
SSKLR Kay Lee Ray	12.00	30.00
SSKOW Kevin Owens	15.00	40.00
SSKSH Kushida	5.00	12.00
SSLAK LA Knight	15.00	40.00
SSLEV Lacey Evans	20.00	50.00
SSLVE Brother Love	15.00	40.00
SSMBT Marcel Barthel	6.00	15.00
SSMSR Mansoor	8.00	20.00
SSMST Meiko Satomura	15.00	40.00
SSMTF Montez Ford	12.00	30.00
SSMVP MVP	6.00	15.00
SSNDR Noam Dar	6.00	15.00
SSNKA Nikki A.S.H.	25.00	60.00
SSNOM Naomi	12.00	30.00
SSNSH Nash Carter	6.00	15.00
SSNTL Natalya	12.00	30.00
SSOJN Odyssey Jones	8.00	20.00
SSOTS Otis	8.00	20.00
SSPDN Pete Dunne	10.00	25.00
SSPGE Paige	100.00	200.00
SSPHE Paul Heyman EXCH	60.00	150.00
SSPPT Persia Pirotta	15.00	40.00
SSRCC Ricochet	12.00	30.00
SSRHL Ridge Holland	8.00	20.00
SSRRD Robert Roode	6.00	15.00
SSRST Roderick Strong	8.00	20.00
SSRVD Rob Van Dam EXCH	50.00	100.00
SSSBG Superstar Billy Graham	30.00	75.00
SSSBZ Shayna Baszler	10.00	25.00
SSSES Santos Escobar	10.00	25.00
SSSHK Shanky	6.00	15.00
SSSRY Sarray	12.00	30.00
SSSZY Sami Zayn	12.00	30.00
SSTBT Tyler Bate	6.00	15.00
SSTCP Tommaso Ciampa	10.00	25.00
SSTDB Million Dollar Man Ted DiBiase	50.00	100.00
SSTGK The Great Khali EXCH	15.00	40.00
SSTSV Trent Seven	6.00	15.00
SSVMH Veer Mahaan	25.00	60.00
SSVWG Von Wagner	6.00	15.00
SSWLE Wes Lee	6.00	15.00
SSXWD King Woods	12.00	30.00
SSZST Zoey Stark	10.00	25.00
SSZVG Queen Zelina	20.00	50.00

2022 Panini Prizm WWE Superstar Autographs

*GREEN: .5X TO 1.2X BASIC AUTOS
*SILVER: .6X TO 1.5X BASIC AUTOS
*RED/99: .75X TO 2X BASIC AUTOS
*BLUE/49: 1X TO 2.5X BASIC AUTOS
*GREEN PULS./25: UNPRICED DUE TO SCARCITY
*MOJO/25: UNPRICED DUE TO SCARCITY
*GOLD/10: UNPRICED DUE TO SCARCITY
*BLACK/1: UNPRICED DUE TO SCARCITY
*WHITE SPARKLE/1: UNPRICED DUE TO SCARCITY
RANDOMLY INSERTED INTO PACKS

SAABL Alexa Bliss EXCH	125.00	250.00
SAAJS AJ Styles	20.00	50.00
SAASK Asuka	30.00	75.00
SABBK Bron Breakker	250.00	500.00
SABBL Bianca Belair	25.00	60.00
SABLA Bobby Lashley EXCH	25.00	60.00
SABLS Brock Lesnar	125.00	300.00
SABLY Bayley	25.00	60.00
SACJD Cora Jade	75.00	150.00
SACML Carmella	15.00	40.00
SADMT Drew McIntyre	30.00	75.00
SAEDG Edge	30.00	75.00
SAFBL The Demon Finn Balor	30.00	75.00
SAGBG Goldberg	60.00	150.00
SAGGD Gigi Dolin	60.00	120.00
SAGST Gable Steveson	300.00	600.00
SAIDR Ilja Dragunov	10.00	25.00
SAISH Io Shirai	25.00	60.00
SAJCN John Cena	150.00	300.00
SAJGC Joe Gacy	25.00	60.00
SAKCZ Kacy Catanzaro	15.00	40.00
SAKKS Kofi Kingston	25.00	60.00
SALMG Liv Morgan	125.00	250.00
SAMRS Mandy Rose	60.00	120.00
SAOMS Omos	20.00	50.00
SARDL Riddle	30.00	75.00
SARGE Reggie	8.00	20.00
SARKB Rick Boogs	15.00	40.00
SARMS Rey Mysterio	50.00	125.00
SAROR Randy Orton	75.00	150.00
SARQG Raquel Gonzalez	25.00	60.00
SARRP Rhea Ripley	100.00	200.00
SASBK Sasha Banks	125.00	250.00
SASDV Sonya Deville	25.00	60.00
SASHM Sheamus	15.00	40.00
SASHZ Shotzi	25.00	60.00
SASRL Seth Rollins	50.00	100.00
SATMZ The Miz	25.00	60.00
SAWTR Walter	15.00	40.00
SAXLI Xia Li	15.00	40.00

2022 Panini Prizm WWE WWE Gold

COMPLETE SET (20)
*GREEN: .6X TO 1.5X BASIC CARDS
*SILVER: .75X TO 2X BASIC CARDS
*GREEN PULS./25: UNPRICED DUE TO SCARCITY
*MOJO/25: UNPRICED DUE TO SCARCITY
*GOLD/10: UNPRICED DUE TO SCARCITY
*BLACK/1: UNPRICED DUE TO SCARCITY
RANDOMLY INSERTED INTO PACKS

1 Randy Orton	2.50	6.00
2 Drew McIntyre	2.00	5.00
3 Seth Rollins	2.00	5.00
4 Tommaso Ciampa	1.50	4.00
5 The Miz	1.25	3.00
6 Alexa Bliss	15.00	40.00
7 Rey Mysterio	1.50	4.00
8 Sasha Banks	6.00	15.00
9 Triple H	3.00	8.00
10 Big E	1.25	3.00
11 Edge	3.00	8.00
12 Kofi Kingston	2.00	5.00
13 Roman Reigns	5.00	12.00
14 Bayley	2.00	5.00
15 Dolph Ziggler	2.00	5.00
16 Asuka	3.00	8.00
17 Ilja Dragunov	1.25	3.00
18 Charlotte Flair	5.00	12.00
19 Shawn Michaels	3.00	8.00
20 AJ Styles	2.50	6.00

1998 Panini WCW/nWo Photocards

COMPLETE SET (108)	15.00	40.00
UNOPENED BOX (24 PACKS)		
UNOPENED PACK (6 CARDS)		
1 Goldberg	.50	1.25
2 Goldberg	.50	1.25
3 Goldberg	.50	1.25
4 Goldberg	.50	1.25
5 Goldberg	.50	1.25
6 Goldberg	.50	1.25
7 Goldberg	.50	1.25
8 Goldberg	.50	1.25
9 Goldberg	.50	1.25
10 Goldberg	.50	1.25
11 Goldberg Logo	.50	1.25
12 Goldberg	.50	1.25
13 Goldberg	.50	1.25
14 Goldberg	.50	1.25
15 Goldberg vs. Konnan	.50	1.25
16 Disco Inferno	.12	.30
17 Sting	.50	1.25
18 Sting	.50	1.25
19 Sting	.50	1.25
20 Sting	.50	1.25
21 Sting	.50	1.25
22 Sting Logo	.75	2.00
23 Sting	.50	1.25
24 Sting	.50	1.25
25 Hollywood Hogan	.60	1.50
26 Hollywood Hogan	.60	1.50
27 Hollywood Hogan	.60	1.50
28 Hollywood Hogan Logo	.60	1.50
29 Hollywood Hogan	.60	1.50
30 Hogan vs. Luger	.60	1.50
31 Hollywood Hogan	.60	1.50
32 Ric Flair	.40	1.00
33 Diamond Dallas Page	.30	.75
34 Diamond Dallas Page	.30	.75
35 Dallas Page Logo	.30	.75
36 Diamond Dallas Page	.30	.75
37 Scott Hall	.30	.75
38 Hall vs. Piper	.30	.75
39 Scott Hall	.30	.75
40 Scott Hall	.30	.75
41 Kevin Nash	.25	.60
42 Kevin Nash	.25	.60
43 Kevin Nash Logo	.25	.60
44 Kevin Nash	.25	.60
45 Macho Man	.40	1.00
46 Macho Man Logo	.40	1.00
47 Macho Man	.40	1.00
48 Macho Man vs. Hart	.40	1.00
49 Public Enemy	.12	.30
50 Public Enemy	.12	.30
51 Lex Luger	.20	.50
52 Lex Luger	.20	.50
53 Luger vs. Hogan	.30	.75
54 Lex Luger	.20	.50
55 Lex Luger Logo	.20	.50
56 Lex Luger	.20	.50
57 Buff Bagwell	.12	.30
58 Bagwell vs. Booker T	.15	.40
59 Buff Bagwell	.12	.30
60 Anvil	.15	.40
61 Rick Steiner	.15	.40
62 Rick Steiner	.15	.40
63 Scott Steiner	.15	.40
64 Scott Steiner	.15	.40
65 Raven	.15	.40
66 Raven Logo	.15	.40
67 Raven	.15	.40
68 Glacier	.12	.30
69 Roddy Piper	.40	1.00
70 Piper vs. Hogan	.50	1.25
71 Roddy Piper	.40	1.00
72 Scott Norton	.12	.30
73 Rey Mysterio	.30	.75
74 Rey Mysterio Logo	.30	.75
75 Chris Benoit	.25	.60
76 Benoit vs. Malenko	.25	.60
77 Alex Wright	.12	.30
78 Alex Wright	.12	.30
79 Brian Adams	.12	.30
80 Brian Adams	.12	.30
81 Guerrero vs Konnan	.12	.30
82 Eddie Guerrero	.40	1.00
83 Guerrero vs Malenko	.40	1.00
84 Wrath	.15	.40
85 Chris Jericho	.40	1.00
86 Chris Jericho	.40	1.00
87 Jericho vs. Wright	.40	1.00
88 Chris Jericho	.40	1.00
89 Dean Malenko	.15	.40
90 Malenko vs. Benoit	.15	.40
91 Dean Malenko Logo	.15	.40
92 Dean Malenko	.15	.40
93 Dragon vs Wright	.15	.40
94 Dragon vs Mysterio	.25	.60
95 Konnan	.20	.50
96 Konnan	.20	.50
97 Bret Hart	.40	1.00
98 Bret Hart	.40	1.00
99 Bret Hart	.40	1.00
100 British Bulldog	.30	.75
101 Juventud vs Kidman	.15	.40
102 Juventud vs Kidman	.15	.40
103 Juventud vs Kidman	.15	.40
104 Curt Hennig	.25	.60
105 Saturn	.12	.30
106 Saturn	.12	.30
107 Saturn	.12	.30
108 Nitro Girls	.75	2.00

1999 Panini WCW/nWo Stickers

COMPLETE SET (120)	20.00	50.00
UNOPENED BOX (100 PACKS)		
UNOPENED PACK		
1 Bill Goldberg	.60	1.50
2 Kevin Nash	.30	.75
3 Diamond Dallas Page	.30	.75
4 Hollywood Hogan	.60	1.50
5 Ric Flair	.50	1.25
6 Nash & Luger Rule!	.30	.75
7 Kevin Nash	.30	.75
8 Kevin Nash	.30	.75
9 Goldberg-Nash Bash!!!	.75	2.00
10 Kevin Nash	.30	.75

11 Kevin Nash	.25	.60
12 Kevin Nash	.30	.75
13 Kevin Nash	.30	.75
14 Kevin Nash	.30	.75
15 Red & Black Attack	.25	.60
16 Who's Next?	.40	1.00
17 Bill Goldberg	.60	1.50
18 Bill Goldberg	.60	1.50
19 Bill Goldberg	.60	1.50
20 Raven's Wings Are Clipped!	.40	1.00
21 A Crushing Headlock On Konnan	.40	1.00
22 Goldberg Tattoo	.75	2.00
23 Bill Goldberg	.60	1.50
24 Bill Goldberg	.60	1.50
25 Bill Goldberg	.60	1.50
26 Hogan Hands Out A Beating!	.60	1.50
27 Hollywood Hogan	.60	1.50
28 Hollywood Hogan	.60	1.50
29 Hollywood Hogan	.60	1.50
30 Hollywood Hogan	.60	1.50
31 Hogan And His Buddy Bischoff!	.60	1.50
32 No Mercy!	.25	.60
33 Hollywood Hogan	.60	1.50
34 Hollywood Hogan	.60	1.50
35 Hollywood Hogan	.60	1.50
36 Ric Flair Struts His Stuff!	.50	1.25
37 Horsemen/Arn Anderson	.40	1.00
38 Chris Benoit	.25	.60
39 Dean Makenko	.15	.40
40 Steve McMichael	.12	.30
41 Malenko Mauls Benoit!	.20	.50
42 Ric Flair Tells It Like It Is...	.60	1.50
43 WOOOOOOOOO!!!	.50	1.25
44 Ric Flair In Action...	.40	1.00
45 Four Horsemen	.25	.60
46 Eddie Guerrero	.40	1.00
47 Juventud Guerrera	.15	.40
48 Rey Mysterio	.40	1.00
49 Juventud Jumps Kidman!	.15	.40
50 Guerrero Airborne!	.40	1.00
51 Eddie Guerrero	.40	1.00
52 Hector Garza	.12	.30
53 La Parka	.12	.30
54 Damian	.12	.30
55 Psychosis	.12	.30
56 Che, Fyre, and Spice	.40	1.00
57 Tigress	.40	1.00
58 The Happy Loving Couple...	.60	1.50
59 AC Jazz	.40	1.00
60 Whisper	.40	1.00
61 Alex Wright...	.12	.30
62 Kidman Gets Drop...	.15	.40
63 Kidman	.15	.40
64 Wrath's Guillotine Drop!	.12	.30
65 Kidman Hangs Tough!	.15	.40
66 Konnan Krushes Eddie Guerrero!	.30	.75
67 Konnan	.20	.50
68 Whisper	.40	1.00
69 British Bulldog	.30	.75
70 Disco Inferno	.12	.30
71 Van Hammer Slams Alex Wright!	.12	.30
72 Booker T.	.25	.60
73 Saturn	.12	.30
74 Ernest Miller Wrestling...	.15	.40
75 Chavo and Pepe	.15	.40
76 Diamond Dallas Page	.30	.75
77 Diamond Dallas Page	.30	.75
78 DDP Has Hart!	.40	1.00
79 DDP Gets The Drop On Sting!	.40	1.00
80 Diamond Dallas Page	.30	.75
81 Bret Hart	.40	1.00
82 Hart Gets A Leg up!	.40	1.00
83 Hart Puts The Hurt On DDP!	.40	1.00
84 DDP Gets Hit By The Hitman!	.40	1.00
85 Your Seat Is Ready!	.40	1.00
86 Scott Hall	.30	.75
87 The Pac In The House!	.30	.75
88 Scott Hall	.30	.75
89 Scott Hall	.30	.75
90 Scott Hall	.30	.75
91 Luger Lights It Up!	.20	.50
92 Luger's Got A Flair For Winning!	.20	.50
93 Lex Luger	.20	.50
94 Lex Luger	.20	.50
95 Lex Luger	.20	.50
96 Big Poppa Pump Pumps It Up!	.15	.40
97 Big Poppa Pump Pummels XXX!	.15	.40
98 NWO Bad Boy Buff Bagwell!	.12	.30
99 Big Poppa Pump Makes His Point!	.15	.40
100 Steiner's Super Bod!	.15	.40
101 Hollywood Hogan Gets Stung!	.40	1.00
102 Sting	.50	1.25
103 Scorpion	.50	1.25
104 Sting	.50	1.25
105 Sting	.50	1.25
106 Alex Wright	.12	.30
107 Chris Jericho	.40	1.00
108 Eric Bischoff	.25	.60
109 Scott Norton	.12	.30
110 Glacier	.12	.30
111 Rick Steiner	.15	.40
112 Public Enemy	.12	.30
113 Brian Adams	.12	.30
114 Bagwell Bags Rick Steiner!	.15	.40
115 The Announcers	.12	.30
116 Kendall Windham Slam...	.12	.30
117 Where The Big Boys Play!	.25	.60
118 Raven At Rest!	.15	.40
119 Wright Or Wrong?	.12	.30
120 Anvil!!! (Bam Bam Bigelow)	.20	.50

2022 Panini WWE Debut Edition

*RED: .75X TO 2X BASIC CARDS
*GREEN: 1.2X TO 3X BASIC CARDS
*GOLD: 2X TO 5X BASIC CARDS

1 Ivar	.30	.75
2 AJ Styles	1.00	2.50
3 Rick Boogs	.40	1.00
4 Damian Priest	.60	1.50
5 Naomi	.50	1.25
6 Otis	.40	1.00
7 Lacey Evans	.75	2.00
8 Veer Mahaan	.75	2.00
9 Santos Escobar	.50	1.25
10 Rhea Ripley	1.00	2.50
11 Jey Uso	.40	1.00
12 Akira Tozawa	.40	1.00
13 Ricochet	.60	1.50
14 Dolph Ziggler	.60	1.50
15 Natalya	.50	1.25
16 Randy Orton	.75	2.00
17 Carmelo Hayes RC	.40	1.00
18 Alexa Bliss	2.00	5.00
19 Cora Jade RC	2.50	6.00
20 Tamina	.40	1.00
21 Jimmy Uso	.40	1.00
22 Angelo Dawkins	.40	1.00
23 Ridge Holland	.30	.75
24 Dominik Mysterio	.40	1.00
25 Sasha Banks	2.00	5.00
26 Reggie	.40	1.00
27 Fabian Aichner	.40	1.00
28 Becky Lynch	1.25	3.00
29 Gigi Dolin	1.25	3.00
30 Angel	.30	.75
31 Jinder Mahal	.40	1.00
32 Apollo Crews	.40	1.00
33 Roman Reigns	2.00	5.00
34 Edge	1.25	3.00
35 Shayna Baszler	.60	1.50
36 Rey Mysterio	.75	2.00
37 Marcel Barthel	.40	1.00
38 Bianca Belair	1.00	2.50
39 Mandy Rose	1.50	4.00
40 Brock Lesnar	1.50	4.00
41 King Woods	.40	1.00
42 Austin Theory	.75	2.00
43 Sami Zayn	.50	1.25
44 Finn Balor	.75	2.00
45 Shotzi	1.25	3.00
46 Robert Roode	.40	1.00
47 Roderick Strong	.50	1.25
48 Carmella	.75	2.00
49 Raquel Gonzalez	.75	2.00
50 Solo Sikoa RC	2.00	5.00
51 Kofi Kingston	.75	2.00
52 Big E	.60	1.50
53 Shanky RC	.30	.75
54 Kevin Owens	.60	1.50
55 Tiffany Stratton RC	.50	1.25
56 Riddle	.75	2.00
57 Tommaso Ciampa	.75	2.00
58 Dana Brooke	.30	.75
59 Ikja Dragunov	.30	.75
60 Drew Gulak	.40	1.00
61 Mace	.30	.75
62 Bobby Lashley	.60	1.50
63 Sheamus	.50	1.25
64 The Miz	.50	1.25
65 Xia Li	.60	1.50
66 R-Truth	.40	1.00
67 Maryse	.50	1.25
68 Doudrop	.50	1.25
69 Meiko Satomura RC	1.00	2.50
70 Drew McIntyre	.60	1.50
71 Madcap Moss	.30	.75
72 Cedric Alexander	.30	.75
73 Shinsuke Nakamura	.75	2.00
74 Montez Ford	.30	.75
75 Asuka	1.25	3.00
76 Seth Rollins	.75	2.00
77 Bron Breakker RC	2.50	6.00
78 Liv Morgan	1.50	4.00
79 Trent Seven	.40	1.00
80 Erik	.30	.75
81 Mansoor	.30	.75
82 Chad Gable	.30	.75
83 Aliyah	.60	1.50
84 MVP	.30	.75
85 Bayley	.75	2.00
86 Shelton Benjamin	.50	1.25
87 Dexter Lumis	.30	.75
88 Nikki A.S.H.	.50	1.25
89 Tyler Bate	.40	1.00
90 Happy Corbin	.40	1.00
91 Jacy Jayne RC	1.50	4.00
92 Commander Azeez	.40	1.00
93 Charlotte Flair	1.25	3.00
94 Omos	.60	1.50
95 John Cena	1.00	2.50
96 T-Bar	.30	.75
97 Joe Gacy RC	.75	2.00
98 Queen Zelina	.50	1.25
99 Noam Dar	.40	1.00
100 Humberto	.30	.75
101 Humberto L	.30	.75
102 Dusty Rhodes L	.75	2.00
103 Terry Funk L	.50	1.25
104 The Great Khali L	.40	1.00
105 Undertaker L	1.50	4.00
106 Jerry Lawler L	.60	1.50
107 Mick Foley L	.60	1.50
108 Batista L	.60	1.50
109 Rob Van Dam L	.60	1.50
110 Bret Hit Man Hart L	.75	2.00
111 Shawn Michaels L	1.25	3.00
112 Eddie Guerrero L	1.00	2.50
113 Triple H L	1.25	3.00
114 Hulk Hogan L	1.50	4.00
115 Vader L	.40	1.00
116 Diesel L	.50	1.25
117 Nikki Bella L	.75	2.00
118 Beth Phoenix L	.60	1.50
119 The Rock L	3.00	8.00
120 Brie Bella L	.60	1.50
121 Stacy Keibler L	1.00	2.50
122 The Godfather L	.30	.75
123 Ultimate Warrior L	1.25	3.00
124 Iron Sheik L	.40	1.00
125 X-Pac L	.40	1.00
126 Lex Luger L	.40	1.00
127 Rikishi L	.40	1.00
128 Big John Studd L	.30	.75
129 Ron Simmons L	.40	1.00
130 Bruno Sammartino L	.75	2.00
131 Stone Cold Steve Austin L	1.50	4.00
132 Goldberg L	1.25	3.00
133 Trish Stratus L	1.50	4.00
134 John Bradshaw Layfield L	.30	.75
135 Yokozuna L	.40	1.00
136 Macho Man Randy Savage L	1.25	3.00
137 Road Dogg L	.40	1.00
138 Booker T L	.60	1.50
139 Rowdy Roddy Piper L	.75	2.00
140 Chyna L	.60	1.50
141 Million Dollar Man Ted DiBiase CH	.50	1.25
142 Brock Lesnar CH	1.50	4.00
143 Big E CH	.60	1.50
144 John Cena CH	1.00	2.50
145 Damian Priest CH	.60	1.50
146 Edge CH	1.25	3.00
147 Charlotte Flair CH	1.25	3.00
148 Stone Cold Steve Austin L	1.50	4.00
149 Tommaso Ciampa CH	.75	2.00
150 Hulk Hogan CH	1.50	4.00
151 Ilja Dragunov CH	.30	.75
152 Triple H CH	1.25	3.00
153 Becky Lynch CH	1.25	3.00
154 Randy Orton CH	.75	2.00
155 Roman Reigns CH	2.00	5.00
156 The Rock CH	3.00	8.00

157 Shinsuke Nakamura CH	.75	2.00
158 Undertaker CH	1.50	4.00
159 Mandy Rose CH	1.50	4.00
160 Bret Hit Man Hart CH	.75	2.00

2022 Panini WWE NXT

UNOPENED BOX (24 PACKS)
UNOPENED PACK (8 CARDS)
*GREEN: .5X TO 1.2X BASIC CARDS
*SILVER: .5X TO 1.2X BASIC CARDS
*RED/199: .6X TO 1.5X BASIC CARDS
*BLUE/149: .75X TO 2X BASIC CARDS
*PURPLE/99: 1.2X TO 3X BASIC CARDS
*BLACK&GOLD/75: 1.2X TO 3X BASIC CARDS
*TEAL/49: 1.5X TO 4X BASIC CARDS
*2.0/25: UNPRICED DUE TO SCARCITY
*GOLD/10: UNPRICED DUE TO SCARCITY
*BLACK/1: UNPRICED DUE TO SCARCITY

1 Sanga	.30	.75
2 Tyler Bate	.40	1.00
3 Fallon Henley RC	.30	.75
4 Alba Fyre	.75	2.00
5 Andre Chase RC	.30	.75
6 Zoey Stark	.40	1.00
7 Giovanni Vinci	.40	1.00
8 Xia Brookside RC	2.00	5.00
9 Jack Starz RC	.30	.75
10 Mark Andrews	.30	.75
11 Solo Sikoa RC	1.50	4.00
12 Wolfgang	.30	.75
13 Cora Jade RC	3.00	8.00
14 Kayden Carter	.60	1.50
15 Boa	.30	.75
16 Tiger Turan RC	.30	.75
17 Grayson Waller RC	.75	2.00
18 A-Kid RC	1.25	3.00
19 Oliver Carter RC	.30	.75
20 Mark Coffey	.30	.75
21 Nathan Frazer RC	.30	.75
22 Dani Luna RC	1.25	3.00
23 Damon Kemp RC	.30	.75
24 Lash Legend RC	1.00	2.50
25 Bron Breakker RC	1.50	4.00
26 Santos Escobar	.50	1.25
27 Ashton Smith RC	.40	1.00
28 Dave Mastiff	.30	.75
29 Malik Blade RC	.30	.75
30 Noam Dar	.40	1.00
31 Tony D'Angelo RC	1.00	2.50
32 Emilia McKenzie RC	1.00	2.50
33 Elektra Lopez RC	1.25	3.00
34 Mandy Rose	2.00	5.00
35 Brooks Jensen RC	1.25	3.00
36 Amale RC	.30	.75
37 Charlie Dempsey RC	.30	.75
38 Eddie Dennis RC	.30	.75
39 Sam Gradwell RC	.30	.75
40 Rampage Brown RC	.30	.75
41 Trick Williams RC	.30	.75
42 Stevie Turner RC	.75	2.00
43 Gigi Dolin	2.00	5.00
44 Aleah James RC	.75	2.00
45 Brutus Creed RC	1.25	3.00
46 Aoife Valkyrie RC	.60	1.50
47 Ikemen Jiro RC	.30	.75
48 Flash Morgan Webster	.40	1.00
49 Roxanne Perez RC	2.50	6.00
50 Kit Wilson RC	.30	.75
51 Von Wagner RC	.30	.75
52 Wild Boar RC	.30	.75
53 Indi Hartwell	1.00	2.50
54 Bodhi Hayward RC	.40	1.00
55 Carmelo Hayes RC	.40	1.00
56 Blair Davenport RC	1.25	3.00
57 James Drake	.30	.75
58 Ilja Dragunov	.30	.75
59 Odyssey Jones RC	.30	.75
60 Saxon Huxley RC	.30	.75
61 Wes Lee	.30	.75
62 Primate RC	.30	.75
63 Io Shirai	.60	1.50
64 Sarray	.40	1.00
65 Cameron Grimes	.60	1.50
66 Isla Dawn RC	.40	1.00
67 Joaquin Wilde	.50	1.25
68 Joe Coffey	.30	.75
69 Nikkita Lyons RC	2.50	6.00
70 Sha Samuels RC	.30	.75
71 Xyon Quinn RC	1.50	4.00
72 Roderick Strong	.50	1.25
73 Ivy Nile RC	.30	.75
74 Tiffany Stratton RC	1.50	4.00
75 Dante Chen RC	.30	.75
76 Jinny RC	.30	.75
77 Joe Gacy RC	.75	2.00
78 Jordan Devlin	.30	.75
79 Cruz Del Toro	.50	1.25
80 Teoman RC	.30	.75
81 Zack Gibson	.30	.75
82 Edris Enofe RC	.30	.75
83 Jacy Jayne RC	1.50	4.00
84 Valentina Feroz RC	.50	1.25
85 T-Bone RC	.30	.75
86 Meiko Satomura RC	1.00	2.50
87 Josh Briggs RC	.30	.75
88 Kenny Williams RC	.30	.75
89 Robert Stone RC	.30	.75
90 Trent Seven	.40	1.00
91 Amari Miller RC	.30	.75
92 Yulisa Leon RC	.30	.75
93 Katana Chance	.60	1.50
94 Wendy Choo RC	.60	1.50
95 Duke Hudson RC	.30	.75
96 Nina Samuels	.40	1.00
97 Julius Creed RC	.75	2.00
98 Elton Prince RC	.40	1.00
99 Johnny Saint RC	.30	.75
100 Triple H	1.25	3.00
101 Kevin Owens	.60	1.50
102 Bianca Belair	1.00	2.50
103 Drew McIntyre	.60	1.50
104 Montez Ford	.30	.75
105 Bayley	.75	2.00
106 Apollo Crews	.40	1.00
107 Seth Freakin Rollins	.75	2.00
108 Charlotte Flair	1.25	3.00
109 Big E	.60	1.50
110 Shayna Baszler	.60	1.50
111 Finn Balor	.75	2.00
112 Damian Priest	.60	1.50
113 Alexa Bliss	2.00	5.00
114 Angelo Dawkins	.40	1.00
115 Becky Lynch	1.25	3.00
116 Asuka	1.25	3.00
117 Tyler Breeze	.30	.75
118 Otis	.40	1.00
119 Sami Zayn	.50	1.25
120 Ricochet	.60	1.50
121 Shinsuke Nakamura	.75	2.00
122 Chad Gable	.30	.75
123 Rhea Ripley	1.00	2.50
124 Roman Reigns	2.00	5.00
125 Corey Graves	.30	.75

2022 Panini WWE NXT All-Time Highlights

*GREEN: .5X TO 1.2X BASIC CARDS
*SILVER: .5X TO 1.2X BASIC CARDS
*BLACK&GOLD/75: .75X TO 2X BASIC CARDS
*2.0/25: UNPRICED DUE TO SCARCITY
*GOLD/10: UNPRICED DUE TO SCARCITY
*BLACK/1: UNPRICED DUE TO SCARCITY
RANDOMLY INSERTED INTO PACKS

1 Seth Freakin Rollins	1.25	3.00
2 Big E	1.00	2.50
3 Tyler Breeze	.50	1.25
4 Shayna Baszler	1.00	2.50
5 Charlotte Flair	2.00	5.00
6 Charlotte Flair	2.00	5.00
7 Sami Zayn	.75	2.00
8 The Demon Finn Balor	1.25	3.00
9 Tyler Bate	.60	1.50
10 Kevin Owens	1.00	2.50
11 Pete Dunne	1.00	2.50
12 WALTER	1.25	3.00
13 The Demon Finn Balor	1.25	3.00
14 Bayley	1.25	3.00
15 The Demon Finn Balor	1.25	3.00
16 Asuka	2.00	5.00
17 Bayley	1.25	3.00
18 Bayley	1.25	3.00
19 The Demon Finn Balor	1.25	3.00
20 Shinsuke Nakamura	1.25	3.00
21 Asuka	2.00	5.00
22 Asuka	2.00	5.00
23 Shinsuke Nakamura	1.25	3.00
24 Asuka	2.00	5.00
25 Shinsuke Nakamura	1.25	3.00

2022 Panini WWE NXT Alumni Signatures

*GREEN: .5X TO 1.2X BASIC AUTOS
*RED/49: .6X TO 1.5X BASIC AUTOS
*2.0/25: UNPRICED DUE TO SCARCITY
*BLACK&GOLD/25: UNPRICED DUE TO SCARCITY
*GOLD/10: UNPRICED DUE TO SCARCITY
*BLACK/1: UNPRICED DUE TO SCARCITY
RANDOMLY INSERTED INTO PACKS

ASABS Alexa Bliss	75.00	200.00
ASACR Apollo Crews	6.00	15.00
ASASK Asuka	15.00	40.00
ASBBL Bianca Belair	15.00	40.00
ASBGE Big E	8.00	20.00
ASBLN Becky Lynch	50.00	125.00
ASBLY Bayley	15.00	40.00
ASCFL Charlotte Flair EXCH	25.00	60.00
ASCML Carmella	15.00	40.00
ASDMI Drew McIntyre	12.00	30.00
ASFBL Finn Balor	12.00	30.00
ASKOW Kevin Owens	15.00	40.00
ASLVM Liv Morgan	50.00	125.00
ASPGE Paige EXCH	60.00	150.00
ASRRN Roman Reigns	50.00	125.00
ASSBZ Shayna Baszler	10.00	25.00
ASSNK Shinsuke Nakamura	10.00	25.00
ASSRL Seth Freakin Rollins	20.00	50.00
ASSZY Sami Zayn	8.00	20.00

2022 Panini WWE NXT Dual Autographs

*GOLD/10: UNPRICED DUE TO SCARCITY
*BLACK/1: UNPRICED DUE TO SCARCITY
STATED PRINT RUN 25 SER.#'d SETS

DAAJG AJ Styles/Grayson Waller		
DABSE Bron Breakker/Santos Escobar	60.00	150.00
DABTC Bron Breakker/Tommaso Ciampa	50.00	125.00
DACGL Cameron Grimes/LA Knight	20.00	50.00
DACRD Brutus Creed/Julius Creed	60.00	150.00
DAGLS Mark Coffey/Wolfgang		
DAGYV James Drake/Zack Gibson	15.00	40.00
DAIMP Fabian Aichner/Marcel Barthel		
DAIZS Io Shirai/Zoey Stark	40.00	100.00
DAKCK Kacy Catanzaro/Kayden Carter	30.00	75.00
DAKWE Kit Wilson/Elton Prince	30.00	75.00
DAMBD Meiko Satomura/Blair Davenport	50.00	125.00
DAMRG Mandy Rose/Raquel Gonzalez		
DATSB Trent Seven/Tyler Bate	25.00	60.00
DATXC Gigi Dolin/Jacy Jayne	125.00	300.00

2022 Panini WWE NXT Gold Inserts

*GREEN: .5X TO 1.2X BASIC CARDS
*SILVER: .5X TO 1.2X BASIC CARDS
*BLACK&GOLD/75: .75X TO 2X BASIC CARDS
*2.0/25: UNPRICED DUE TO SCARCITY
*GOLD/10: UNPRICED DUE TO SCARCITY
*BLACK/1: UNPRICED DUE TO SCARCITY
RANDOMLY INSERTED INTO PACKS

1 Drew McIntyre	1.25	3.00
2 Raquel Rodriguez	1.50	4.00
3 Trent Seven	.75	2.00
4 Gigi Dolin	2.50	6.00
5 Roderick Strong	1.00	2.50
6 Charlotte Flair	2.50	6.00
7 Seth Freakin Rollins	1.50	4.00
8 Bayley	1.50	4.00
9 Finn Balor	1.50	4.00
10 Shayna Baszler	1.25	3.00
11 Bron Breakker	2.50	6.00
12 Tyler Bate	.75	2.00
13 Fabian Aichner	.75	2.00
14 Jacy Jayne	1.50	4.00
15 Ilja Dragunov	.60	1.50
16 Io Shirai	1.25	3.00
17 Kevin Owens	1.25	3.00
18 Asuka	2.50	6.00
19 Shinsuke Nakamura	1.50	4.00
20 Mandy Rose	3.00	8.00
21 Carmelo Hayes	.75	2.00
22 Ciampa	1.50	4.00
23 Ludwig Kaiser	.75	2.00
24 Corey Graves	.60	1.50
25 Dolph Ziggler	1.25	3.00

2022 Panini WWE NXT Highlights

*GREEN: .5X TO 1.2X BASIC CARDS
*SILVER: .5X TO 1.2X BASIC CARDS
*BLACK&GOLD/75: .75X TO 2X BASIC CARDS
*2.0/25: UNPRICED DUE TO SCARCITY
*GOLD/10: UNPRICED DUE TO SCARCITY

*BLACK/1: UNPRICED DUE TO SCARCITY
RANDOMLY INSERTED INTO PACKS

1 Santos Escobar	.60	1.50
2 Raquel Rodriguez	1.00	2.50
3 Finn Balor	1.00	2.50
4 Santos Escobar	.60	1.50
5 Io Shirai	.75	2.00
6 Finn Balor	1.00	2.50
7 Io Shirai	.75	2.00
8 LA Knight	.60	1.50
9 Pete Dunne	.75	2.00
10 WALTER	1.00	2.50
11 Raquel Rodriguez	1.00	2.50
12 Santos Escobar	.60	1.50
13 Kushida	.60	1.50
14 Sarray	.50	1.25
15 Indi Hartwell/Candice LeRae	1.25	3.00
16 Raquel Rodriguez	1.00	2.50
17 Kushida	.60	1.50
18 Kushida	.60	1.50
19 LA Knight	.60	1.50
20 Raquel Rodriguez	1.00	2.50
21 Kushida	.60	1.50
22 Io Shirai/Zoey Stark	.75	2.00
23 Raquel Rodriguez	1.00	2.50
24 Cameron Grimes	.75	2.00
25 Raquel Rodriguez	1.00	2.50
26 Bron Breakker	1.50	4.00
27 Ciampa	1.00	2.50
28 Roderick Strong	.60	1.50
29 Raquel Rodriguez	1.00	2.50
30 Carmelo Hayes	.50	1.25
31 Jacy Jayne/Gigi Dolin	1.50	4.00
32 Mandy Rose	2.00	5.00
33 Fabian Aichner/Ludwig Kaiser	.50	1.25
34 Ciampa	1.00	2.50
35 Solo Sikoa	1.00	2.50
36 Carmelo Hayes	.50	1.25
37 Cora Jade	1.25	3.00
38 Fabian Aichner/Ludwig Kaiser	.50	1.25
39 Cameron Grimes	.75	2.00
40 Bron Breakker	1.50	4.00
41 Cameron Grimes	.75	2.00
42 Meiko Satomura	1.25	3.00
43 Raquel Rodriguez	1.00	2.50
44 WALTER	1.00	2.50
45 Tyler Bate	.50	1.25
46 Meiko Satomura	1.25	3.00
47 A-Kid	.50	1.25
48 Ilja Dragunov	.40	1.00
49 Noam Dar	.50	1.25
50 Tyler Bate/Trent Seven	.50	1.25

2022 Panini WWE NXT Memorabilia

*GREEN: .5X TO 1.2X BASIC MEM
*RED/99: .6X TO 1.5X BASIC MEM
*BLUE/49: .75X TO 2X BASIC MEM
*2.0/25: UNPRICED DUE TO SCARCITY
*BLACK&GOLD/25: UNPRICED DUE TO SCARCITY
*GOLD/10: UNPRICED DUE TO SCARCITY
*BLACK/1: UNPRICED DUE TO SCARCITY
RANDOMLY INSERTED INTO PACKS

NXMAKD A-Kid	2.00	5.00
NXMAML Amale	2.50	6.00
NXMAOV Aoife Valkyrie	2.00	5.00
NXMBBK Bron Breakker	8.00	20.00
NXMBCD Brutus Creed	2.50	6.00
NXMBDV Blair Davenport	6.00	15.00
NXMBOA Boa	2.50	6.00
NXMCGR Cameron Grimes	2.00	5.00
NXMCHY Carmelo Hayes	2.50	6.00
NXMCJD Cora Jade	12.00	30.00
NXMDLN Dani Luna	2.50	6.00
NXMDMS Dave Mastiff	2.00	5.00
NXMELP Elton Prince	2.50	6.00
NXMEMK Emilia McKenzie	2.50	6.00
NXMFAH Giovanni Vinci	5.00	12.00
NXMFMW Flash Morgan Webster	2.00	5.00
NXMGGD Gigi Dolin	10.00	25.00
NXMGTH Gunther	2.50	6.00
NXMGWL Grayson Waller	2.50	6.00
NXMIHW Indi Hartwell	8.00	20.00
NXMIOS Io Shirai	12.00	30.00
NXMIVN Ivy Nile	2.50	6.00
NXMJCD Julius Creed	2.50	6.00
NXMJCF Joe Coffey	4.00	10.00
NXMJDR James Drake	2.50	6.00
NXMJGC Joe Gacy	5.00	12.00
NXMJJN Jacy Jayne	12.00	30.00
NXMJNY Jinny	2.50	6.00
NXMJWD Joaquin Wilde	6.00	15.00
NXMKCC Katana Chance	5.00	12.00
NXMKDC Kayden Carter	6.00	15.00
NXMKLR Alba Fyre	4.00	10.00
NXMKWL Kenny Williams	2.50	6.00
NXMKWS Kit Wilson	6.00	15.00
NXMLLG Lash Legend	2.50	6.00
NXMMAW Mark Andrews	2.50	6.00
NXMMBT Ludwig Kaiser	10.00	25.00
NXMMCF Mark Coffey	3.00	8.00
NXMMDP Max Dupri	2.00	5.00
NXMMRS Mandy Rose	12.00	30.00
NXMMSM Meiko Satomura	2.00	5.00
NXMNMD Noam Dar	2.00	5.00
NXMODJ Odyssey Jones	2.50	6.00
NXMRQG Raquel Rodriguez	5.00	12.00
NXMRST Roderick Strong	3.00	8.00
NXMSES Santos Escobar	4.00	10.00
NXMSRY Sarray	5.00	12.00
NXMSTN Stevie Turner	8.00	20.00
NXMTBT Tyler Bate	2.50	6.00
NXMTCP Ciampa	2.50	6.00
NXMTEO Teoman	2.50	6.00
NXMVWG Von Wagner	3.00	8.00
NXMWFG Wolfgang	4.00	10.00
NXMWLE Wes Lee	2.50	6.00
NXMXYQ Xyon Quinn	8.00	20.00
NXMYSV Trent Seven	3.00	8.00
NXMZGB Zack Gibson	2.50	6.00
NXMZST Zoey Stark	3.00	8.00

2022 Panini WWE NXT Memorabilia Signatures

*2.0/25: UNPRICED DUE TO SCARCITY
*GOLD/10: UNPRICED DUE TO SCARCITY
*BLACK/1: UNPRICED DUE TO SCARCITY
STATED PRINT RUN 24-99

MSBCD Brutus Creed/99	8.00	20.00
MSBOA Boa/99	6.00	15.00
MSCGR Cameron Grimes/99	10.00	25.00
MSCHY Carmelo Hayes/49	15.00	40.00
MSCJD Cora Jade/99	60.00	150.00
MSFAH Giovanni Vinci/99	6.00	15.00
MSGGD Gigi Dolin/49	40.00	100.00
MSGTH Gunther/99	12.00	30.00
MSGWL Grayson Waller/99	10.00	25.00
MSIHW Indi Hartwell/99	12.00	30.00
MSIOS Io Shirai/49	30.00	75.00
MSIVN Ivy Nile/49	15.00	40.00
MSJCD Julius Creed/99	12.00	30.00
MSJDR James Drake/99		
MSJGC Joe Gacy/99	15.00	40.00
MSJJN Jacy Jayne/99	40.00	100.00
MSJWD Joaquin Wilde/99	6.00	15.00
MSKCC Katana Chance/99	15.00	40.00
MSKDC Kayden Carter/99	10.00	25.00
MSKLR Alba Fyre/99	20.00	50.00
MSLLG Lash Legend/99	8.00	20.00
MSMBT Ludwig Kaiser/49	8.00	20.00
MSMDP Max Dupri/49	15.00	40.00
MSMRS Mandy Rose/99	40.00	100.00
MSMSM Meiko Satomura/24	12.00	30.00
MSODJ Odyssey Jones/99	10.00	25.00
MSRQG Raquel Rodriguez/49	15.00	40.00
MSRST Roderick Strong/99	8.00	20.00
MSSES Santos Escobar/99	6.00	15.00
MSSRY Sarray/99		
MSTBT Tyler Bate/99	8.00	20.00
MSTCP Ciampa/49		
MSVWG Von Wagner/99	6.00	15.00
MSWLE Wes Lee/99		
MSXYQ Xyon Quinn/99		
MSYSV Trent Seven/99	6.00	15.00
MSZGB Zack Gibson/99		
MSZST Zoey Stark/99	6.00	15.00
NXMBBK Bron Breakker/99	40.00	100.00

2022 Panini WWE NXT Signatures

*GREEN: .5X TO 1.2X BASIC AUTOS
*RED/49: .6X TO 1.5X BASIC AUTOS
*2.0/25: UNPRICED DUE TO SCARCITY
*BLACK & GOLD/25: UNPRICED DUE TO SCARCITY
*GOLD/10: UNPRICED DUE TO SCARCITY
*BLACK/1: UNPRICED DUE TO SCARCITY
RANDOMLY INSERTED INTO PACKS

NSAKD A-Kid	8.00	20.00
NSAML Amale	10.00	25.00
NSAOV Aoife Valkyrie	10.00	25.00
NSBBK Bron Breakker	30.00	75.00
NSBCD Brutus Creed	10.00	25.00
NSBDV Blair Davenport	10.00	25.00
NSBOA Boa	5.00	12.00
NSCGR Cameron Grimes	8.00	20.00
NSCHY Carmelo Hayes	12.00	30.00
NSCJD Cora Jade	40.00	100.00
NSDLN Dani Luna	8.00	20.00
NSDMS Dave Mastiff	5.00	12.00
NSELP Elton Prince	8.00	20.00
NSEMK Emilia McKenzie	8.00	20.00
NSFAH Fabian Aichner	5.00	12.00
NSFMW Flash Morgan Webster	5.00	12.00
NSGGD Gigi Dolin	40.00	100.00
NSGTH Gunther	12.00	30.00
NSGWL Grayson Waller	10.00	25.00
NSIHW Indi Hartwell	15.00	40.00
NSILD Ilja Dragunov	10.00	25.00
NSIOS Io Shirai	10.00	25.00
NSIVN Ivy Nile	10.00	25.00
NSJCD Julius Creed	12.00	30.00
NSJCF Joe Coffey	5.00	12.00
NSJGC Joe Gacy	10.00	25.00
NSJJN Jacy Jayne	25.00	60.00
NSJNY Jinny	6.00	15.00
NSKCC Kacy Catanzaro	15.00	40.00
NSKDC Kayden Carter	10.00	25.00
NSKLR Kay Lee Ray	25.00	60.00
NSKWL Kenny Williams	5.00	12.00
NSKWS Kit Wilson	6.00	15.00
NSLAK LA Knight	8.00	20.00
NSLLG Lash Legend	6.00	15.00
NSMBT Marcel Barthel	6.00	15.00
NSMRS Mandy Rose	30.00	75.00
NSMSM Meiko Satomura	10.00	25.00
NSNMD Noam Dar	6.00	15.00
NSODJ Odyssey Jones	8.00	20.00
NSRPB Rampage Brown	6.00	15.00
NSRQG Raquel Gonzalez	12.00	30.00
NSRST Roderick Strong	5.00	12.00
NSSES Santos Escobar	12.00	30.00
NSSRY Sarray	12.00	30.00
NSSTN Stevie Turner	10.00	25.00
NSTBT Tyler Bate	6.00	15.00
NSTCP Tommaso Ciampa	6.00	15.00
NSTEO Teoman	5.00	12.00
NSVWG Von Wagner	6.00	15.00
NSWFG Wolfgang	6.00	15.00
NSWLE Wes Lee	6.00	15.00
NSXYQ Xyon Quinn	6.00	15.00
NSYSV Trent Seven	6.00	15.00

2022 Panini WWE Sticker Collection

1 WWE LOGO FOIL		
2 Panini LOGO FOIL		
3 RAW Puzzle 1		
4 RAW Puzzle 2		
5 WWE World Heavyweight Championship Belt		
6 WWE RAW Women's Championship Belt		
7 NXT 2.0 Puzzle 1		
8 NXT 2.0 Puzzle 2		
9 NXT Championship Belt		
10 SmackDown Puzzle 1		
11 SmackDown Puzzle 2		
12 WWE Universal Championship Belt		
13 WWE SmackDown Women's Championship Belt		
14 NXT Women's Championship Belt		
15 WWE 24/7 Championship Belt		
16 RAW LOGO FOIL		
17 Akira Tozawa	.30	.75
18 Angelo Dawkins	.30	.75
19 Becky Lynch	1.00	2.50
20 Becky Lynch LOGO	1.00	2.50
21 Becky Lynch FOIL	1.00	2.50
22 Bobby Lashley	.50	1.25
23 Bobby Lashley LOGO	.50	1.25
24 Bobby Lashley FOIL	.50	1.25
25 Apollo Crews	.30	.75
26 Commander Azeez	.30	.75
27 Carmella	.60	1.50
28 Omos	.50	1.25
29 Tommaso Ciampa	.60	1.50
30 Damian Priest LOGO	.50	1.25
31 Damian Priest FOIL	.50	1.25
32 Damian Priest	.50	1.25
33 AJ Styles	.75	2.00
34 AJ Styles LOGO	.75	2.00
35 AJ Styles FOIL	.75	2.00
36 Cedric Alexander	.25	.60
37 Chad Gable	.25	.60

38 Bianca Belair LOGO	.75	2.00
39 Bianca Belair FOIL	.75	2.00
40 Bianca Belair		
41 Rey Mysterio	.60	1.50
42 Rey Mysterio LOGO	.60	1.50
43 Rey Mysterio FOIL	.60	1.50
44 Riddle	.60	1.50
45 Riddle FOIL	.60	1.50
46 Riddle LOGO	.60	1.50
47 Corey Graves	.25	.60
48 Dolph Ziggler	.50	1.25
49 Alexa Bliss LOGO	1.50	4.00
50 Alexa Bliss FOIL	1.50	4.00
51 Alexa Bliss	1.50	4.00
52 Edge LOGO	1.00	2.50
53 Edge FOIL	1.00	2.50
54 Edge	1.00	2.50
55 Seth Freakin Rollins	.60	1.50
56 Seth Freakin Rollins FOIL	.60	1.50
57 Seth Freakin Rollins LOGO	.60	1.50
58 Doudrop	.40	1.00
59 Dominik Mysterio	.30	.75
60 Randy Orton LOGO	.60	1.50
61 Randy Orton FOIL	.60	1.50
62 Randy Orton	.60	1.50
63 Liv Morgan	1.25	3.00
64 Liv Morgan LOGO	1.25	3.00
65 Liv Morgan FOIL	1.25	3.00
66 Finn Balor LOGO	.60	1.50
67 Finn Balor FOIL	.60	1.50
68 Finn Balor	.60	1.50
69 Kevin Owens	.50	1.25
70 Montez Ford	.25	.60
71 MVP	.25	.60
72 Nikki A.S.H.	.40	1.00
73 Rhea Ripley LOGO	.75	2.00
74 Rhea Ripley FOIL	.75	2.00
75 Rhea Ripley	.75	2.00
76 Theory	.60	1.50
77 Otis	.30	.75
78 Queen Zelina	.40	1.00
79 Dana Brooke	.25	.60
80 Reggie	.30	.75
81 Robert Roode	.30	.75
82 R-Truth	.30	.75
83 Shelton Benjamin	.40	1.00
84 Sonya Deville	.60	1.50
85 American Nightmare Cody Rhodes LOGO	.60	1.50
86 American Nightmare Cody Rhodes FOIL	.60	1.50
87 American Nightmare Cody Rhodes	.60	1.50
88 Veer	.60	1.50
89 Tamina	.30	.75
90 Ezekiel	.25	.60
91 T-Bar	.25	.60
92 The Miz	.40	1.00
93 Stephanie McMahon	.40	1.00
94 SmackDown FOIL		
95 Aliyah	.50	1.25
96 Cesaro	.25	.60
97 Roman Reigns FOIL	1.50	4.00
98 Roman Reigns	1.50	4.00
99 Roman Reigns LOGO	1.50	4.00
100 The Bloodline	1.50	4.00
101 The Bloodline LOGO		
102 The Usos	.30	.75
103 Paul Heyman	.40	1.00
104 Ivar	.25	.60
105 Erik	.25	.60
106 Brock Lesnar LOGO	1.25	3.00
107 Brock Lesnar FOIL	1.25	3.00
108 Brock Lesnar	1.25	3.00
109 Charlotte Flair LOGO	1.00	2.50
110 Charlotte Flair FOIL	1.00	2.50
111 Charlotte Flair	1.00	2.50
112 Sami Zayn	.40	1.00
113 Sami Zayn LOGO	.40	1.00
114 Sami Zayn FOIL	.40	1.00
115 Mustafa Ali	.30	.75
116 Drew Gulak	.30	.75
117 Jinder Mahal	.30	.75
118 Xavier Woods	.30	.75
119 Kofi Kingston	.60	1.50
120 Humberto	.25	.60
121 Drew McIntyre LOGO	.50	1.25
122 Drew McIntyre FOIL	.50	1.25
123 Drew McIntyre	.50	1.25
124 Naomi	.40	1.00
125 Naomi LOGO	.40	1.00
126 Naomi FOIL	.40	1.00
127 Mace	.25	.60
128 Madcap Moss	.25	.60
129 Mansoor	.25	.60
130 Jimmy Uso	.30	.75
131 Jey Uso	.30	.75
132 Sasha Banks LOGO	1.50	4.00
133 Sasha Banks	1.50	4.00
134 Sasha Banks FOIL	1.50	4.00
135 Ricochet	.50	1.25
136 Ricochet LOGO	.50	1.25
137 Ricochet FOIL	.50	1.25
138 Natalya	.40	1.00
139 Ludwig Kaiser	.30	.75
140 Gunther	.60	1.50
141 Rick Boogs	.30	.75
142 Ridge Holland	.25	.60
143 Shanky	.25	.60
144 Happy Corbin LOGO	.30	.75
145 Happy Corbin FOIL	.30	.75
146 Happy Corbin	.30	.75
147 Big E	.50	1.25
148 Big E LOGO	.50	1.25
149 Big E FOIL	.50	1.25
150 Shayna Baszler	.50	1.25
151 Sheamus	.40	1.00
152 Butch	.50	1.25
153 Sonya Deville	.60	1.50
154 Angelo Dawkins	.30	.75
155 The New Day LOGO	.60	1.50
156 The New Day FOIL	.60	1.50
157 The New Day	.60	1.50
158 Shinsuke Nakamura	.60	1.50
159 Shinsuke Nakamura LOGO	.60	1.50
160 Shinsuke Nakamura FOIL	.60	1.50
161 Xia Li	.50	1.25
162 Shotzi	1.00	2.50
163 NXT 2.0 LOGO		
164 Amari Miller	.25	.60
165 Bron Breakker LOGO	1.00	2.50
166 Bron Breakker FOIL	1.00	2.50
167 Bron Breakker	1.00	2.50
168 Andre Chase	.25	.60
169 Boa	.25	.60
170 Bodhi Hayward	.30	.75
171 Brooks Jensen	.25	.60
172 Brutus Creed	.30	.75
173 Cameron Grimes	.50	1.25
174 Cora Jade	.75	2.00
175 Dakota Kai	.50	1.25
176 Dante Chen	.25	.60
177 Dexter Lumis	.25	.60
178 Draco Anthony		
179 Mandy Rose LOGO	1.25	3.00
180 Mandy Rose FOIL	1.25	3.00
181 Mandy Rose	1.25	3.00
182 Duke Hudson	.25	.60
183 Edris Enofe	.25	.60
184 Elektra Lopez	.60	1.50
185 Fabian Aichner	.30	.75
186 Gigi Dolin	1.00	2.50
187 Grayson Waller	.60	1.50
188 Guru Raaj	.25	.60
189 Harland	.25	.60
190 Ilja Dragunov LOGO	.25	.60
191 Ilja Dragunov FOIL	.25	.60
192 Ilja Dragunov	.25	.60
193 Ikemen Jiro	.25	.60
194 Indi Hartwell	.75	2.00
195 Io Shirai	.50	1.25
196 Ivy Nile	.25	.60
197 Jacy Jayne	.60	1.50
198 James Drake	.25	.60
199 Joaquin Wilde	.40	1.00
200 Joe Gacy	.60	1.50
201 Meiko Satomura LOGO	.75	2.00
202 Meiko Satomura FOIL	.75	2.00
203 Meiko Satomura	.75	2.00
204 Josh Briggs	.25	.60
205 Julius Creed	.60	1.50
206 Kacy Catanzaro	.50	1.25
207 Alba Fyre	.60	1.50
208 Kayden Carter	.50	1.25
209 Kushida	.40	1.00
210 LA Knight	.40	1.00
211 Lash Legend	.25	.60
212 Noam Dar LOGO	.30	.75
213 Noam Dar FOIL	.30	.75
214 Noam Dar	.30	.75
215 Nathan Frazer	.25	.60
216 Malik Blade	.25	.60
217 Roxanne Perez	.75	2.00
218 Nikkita Lyons	.60	1.50
219 Carmelo Hayes LOGO	.30	.75
220 Carmelo Hayes FOIL	.30	.75
221 Carmelo Hayes	.30	.75
222 Odyssey Jones	.25	.60
223 Persia Pirotta	.25	.60
224 Raul Mendoza	.40	1.00
225 Raquel Rodriguez	.60	1.50
226 Robert Stone	.25	.60
227 Roderick Strong	.40	1.00
228 Ru Feng	.25	.60
229 Sanga	.25	.60
230 Santos Escobar	.40	1.00
231 Sarray	.30	.75
232 Solo Sikoa	.60	1.50
233 Tiffany Stratton	.40	1.00
234 Tony D'Angelo	.75	2.00
235 Trick Williams	.25	.60
236 Valentina Feroz	.40	1.00
237 Von Wagner	.25	.60
238 Wendy Choo	.50	1.25
239 Wes Lee	.25	.60
240 Xyon Quinn	.25	.60
241 Yulisa Leon	.25	.60
242 Zack Gibson	.25	.60
243 Zoey Stark	.30	.75
244 Alpha Academy Puzzle 1	.25	.60
245 Alpha Academy Puzzle 2	.30	.75
246 Otis/Chad Gable FOIL	.30	.75
247 Carmella/Queen Zelina FOIL	.60	1.50
248 Carmella Puzzle 1	.60	1.50
249 Queen Zelina Puzzle 2	.40	1.00
250 RK-Bro Puzzle 1	.60	1.50
251 RK-Bro Puzzle 2	.60	1.50
252 Randy Orton/Riddle FOIL	.60	1.50
253 Montez Ford/Angelo Dawkins FOIL	.30	.75
254 Street Profits Puzzle 1	.30	.75
255 Street Profits Puzzle 2	.25	.60
256 The Usos Puzzle 1		
257 The Usos Puzzle 2		
258 Jey Uso/Jimmy Uso FOIL	.30	.75
259 Gigi Dolin/Jacy Jayne FOIL	1.00	2.50
260 Toxic Attraction Puzzle 1	1.00	2.50
261 Toxic Attraction Puzzle 2	.60	1.50
262 Moustache Mountain Puzzle 1	.30	.75
263 Moustache Mountain Puzzle 2	.30	.75
264 Tyler Bate/Trent Seven FOIL	.30	.75
265 Kit Wilson/Elton Prince FOIL	.30	.75
266 Pretty Deadly Puzzle 1	.25	.60
267 Pretty Deadly Puzzle 2	.30	.75
268 Sasha Banks	1.50	4.00
269 Becky Lynch	1.00	2.50
270 Randy Orton	.60	1.50
271 Goldberg	1.00	2.50
272 The Rock Puzzle 1	2.50	6.00
273 The Rock Puzzle 2	2.50	6.00
274 Brock Lesnar	1.25	3.00
275 Bret Hart	.60	1.50
276 Finn Balor	.60	1.50
277 Stone Cold Steve Austin Puzzle 1	1.25	3.00
278 Stone Cold Steve Austin Puzzle 2	1.25	3.00
279 Roman Reigns Puzzle 1	1.50	4.00
280 Roman Reigns Puzzle 2	1.50	4.00
281 Triple H	1.00	2.50
282 Shawn Michaels Puzzle 1	1.00	2.50
283 Shawn Michaels Puzzle 2	1.00	2.50
284 Razor Ramon	.50	1.25
285 Ted DiBiase	.40	1.00
286 Randy Savage	1.00	2.50
287 Diesel	.40	1.00
288 AJ Styles	.75	2.00
289 Sheamus	.40	1.00
290 Undertaker Puzzle 1	1.25	3.00
291 Undertaker Puzzle 2	1.25	3.00
292 Batista	.50	1.25
293 Eddie Guerrero	.75	2.00
294 John Cena Puzzle 1	.75	2.00
295 John Cena Puzzle 2	.75	2.00
296 WrestleMania III Poster Ricky Steamboat/Randy Savage	1.00	2.50
297 WrestleMania IV Poster Warrior/Hulk Hogan	1.25	3.00
298 WrestleMania XII Poster Bret Hart/Shawn Michaels	1.00	2.50
299 WrestleMania X-Seven Poster Rock/Steve Austin	2.50	6.00
300 WrestleMania 25th Anniversary Poster Undertaker/Shawn Michaels	1.25	3.00
301 WrestleMania LOGO		
302 WrestleMania 35 Poster Rousey/Lynch/Flair	1.50	4.00

303 WrestleMania 28 Poster John Cena/Rock	2.50	6.00
304 WrestleMania 38 Poster Brock Lesnar/Roman Reigns	1.50	4.00
305 Super Showdown LOGO		
306 Extreme Rules LOGO		
307 Money in the Bank LOGO		
308 Elimination Chamber LOGO		
309 WrestleMania BackLash LOGO		
310 SummerSlam '92 Poster Bret Hart/British Bulldog	.60	1.50
311 Royal Rumble LOGO		
312 Royal Rumble 2000 Poster Cactus Jack/Triple H	1.00	2.50
313 SummerSlam LOGO		
314 SummerSlam '16 Poster John Cena/AJ Styles	.75	2.00
315 Clash of Champions LOGO		
316 SummerSlam '95 Poster Shawn Michaels/Razor Ramon	1.00	2.50
317 Hell in a Cell LOGO		
318 Survivor Series LOGO		
319 NXT TakeOver Brooklyn Poster Sasha Banks/Bayley	1.50	4.00
320 No Way Out 2004 Poster Eddie Guerrero/Brock Lesnar	1.25	3.00
321 TLC LOGO		
322 King of the Ring/Queens Crown Tournament LOGO		
323 Rob Van Dam L	.50	1.25
324 Batista L	.50	1.25
325 Hulk Hogan L FOIL	1.25	3.00
326 Hulkamania L LOGO	1.25	3.00
327 Hulk Hogan L	1.25	3.00
328 Goldberg L	1.00	2.50
329 Eddie Guerrero L	.75	2.00
330 Sgt. Slaughter L		
331 John Cena L FOIL	.75	2.00
332 John Cena L LOGO	.75	2.00
333 John Cena L	.75	2.00
334 Trish Stratus L	1.25	3.00
335 Triple H L	1.00	2.50
336 Alundra Blayze L	.30	.75
337 Jerry Lawler L	.50	1.25
338 The Rock L FOIL	2.50	6.00
339 The Rock L LOGO	2.50	6.00
340 The Rock L	2.50	6.00
341 Mean Gene Okerlund L	.40	1.00
342 Jake The Snake Roberts L	.40	1.00
343 Razor Ramon L	.50	1.25
344 Undertaker L FOIL	1.25	3.00
345 Undertaker L LOGO	1.25	3.00
346 Undertaker L	1.25	3.00
347 Iron Sheik L	.30	.75
348 Big John Studd L	.25	.60
349 X-Pac (1-2-3 Kid) L	.30	.75
350 Dusty Rhodes L	.60	1.50
351 Stone Cold Steve Austin L FOIL	1.25	3.00
352 Stone Cold Steve Austin L LOGO	1.25	3.00
353 Stone Cold Steve Austin L	1.25	3.00
354 Ravishing Rick Rude L	.50	1.25
355 Molly Holly L	.30	.75
356 Bobby The Brain Heenan L	.40	1.00
357 Ultimate Warrior L FOIL	1.00	2.50
358 Ultimate Warrior L LOGO	1.00	2.50
359 Ultimate Warrior L	1.00	2.50
360 British Bulldog L	.40	1.00
361 Ricky The Dragon Steamboat L	.50	1.25
362 Greg The Hammer Valentine L	.25	.60
363 Yokozuna L	.30	.75
364 Andre the Giant L FOIL	1.00	2.50
365 Andre the Giant L LOGO	1.00	2.50
366 Andre the Giant L	1.00	2.50
367 Big Boss Man L	.40	1.00
368 Beth Phoenix L	.50	1.25
369 Booker T L	.50	1.25
370 Macho Man Randy Savage L FOIL	1.00	2.50
371 Macho Man Randy Savage L LOGO	1.00	2.50
372 Macho Man Randy Savage L	1.00	2.50
373 Diesel L	.40	1.00
374 Chyna L	.50	1.25
375 Don Muraco L	.25	.60
376 Honky Tonk Man L	.30	.75
377 Shawn Michaels L FOIL	1.00	2.50
378 Shawn Michaels L LOGO	1.00	2.50
379 Shawn Michaels L	1.00	2.50
380 The Great Khali L	.30	.75
381 Rikishi L	.30	.75
382 Nikki Bella L	.60	1.50
383 Rowdy Roddy Piper L FOIL	.60	1.50
384 Rowdy Roddy Piper L LOGO	.60	1.50
385 Rowdy Roddy Piper L	.60	1.50
386 Harley Race L		
387 George "The Animal" Steele L		
388 Million Dollar Man Ted DiBiase L FOIL	.40	1.00
389 Million Dollar Man Ted DiBiase L LOGO	.40	1.00
390 Million Dollar Man Ted DiBiase L	.40	1.00
391 Lex Luger L	.30	.75
392 Stacy Keibler L	.75	2.00
393 Mick Foley L FOIL	.50	1.25
394 Mick Foley L LOGO	.50	1.25
395 Mick Foley L	.50	1.25
396 Vader L	.30	.75
397 Bret Hitman Hart L FOIL	.60	1.50
398 Bret Hitman Hart L LOGO	.60	1.50
399 Bret Hitman Hart L	.60	1.50
400 Nikolai Volkoff L	.25	.60
401 Curt Hennig L	.50	1.25
402 JBL HOF 2020	.25	.60
403 British Bulldog HOF 2020	.40	1.00
404 Titus O'Neil HOF 2020	.25	.60
405 The Bella Twins HOF 2020	.60	1.50
406 The nWo HOF 2020	1.25	3.00
407 Molly Holly HOF 2021	.30	.75
408 Kane HOF 2021		
409 The Great Khali HOF 2021	.30	.75
410 Rob Van Dam HOF 2021	.50	1.25
411 Hall of Fame 2022 LOGO Puzzle 1		
412 Hall of Fame 2022 LOGO Puzzle 2		
413 Undertaker HOF 2022	1.25	3.00
414 Vader HOF 2022	.30	.75

1954-55 Parkhurst Wrestling

COMPLETE SET (75)	350.00	600.00
*PREMIUM BACKS: SAME VALUE		
1 Lou Thesz RC	10.00	25.00
2 Sky Hi Lee RC	4.00	10.00
3 Whipper Billy Watson RC	4.00	10.00
4 Johnny Barend RC	4.00	10.00
5 Antonio Argentina Rocca RC	6.00	15.00
6 Dirty Dick Raines RC	4.00	10.00
7 Frank Valois RC	4.00	10.00
8 Hombre Montana RC	4.00	10.00
9 Lou Plummer RC	4.00	10.00
10 Chief Big Heart RC	4.00	10.00
11 Man Mountain Dean Jr. RC	4.00	10.00
12 Primo Carnera	10.00	25.00
13 Paul Baillargeon RC	4.00	10.00
14 Nick Roberts RC	4.00	10.00
15 Tim Geohagen RC	4.00	10.00
16 The Togo Brothers	4.00	10.00
17 Verne Gagne RC	12.00	30.00
18 Maurice Tillet RC	4.00	10.00
19 Yukon Eric RC	4.00	10.00
20 Toar Morgan RC	4.00	10.00
21 Mighty Schultz RC	4.00	10.00
22 Bill Stack RC	4.00	10.00
23 Argentina Rocca RC	6.00	15.00
24 Big Ben Morgan RC	4.00	10.00
25 Lou Pitoscia RC	4.00	10.00
26 Earl McCready & Billy Watson	4.00	10.00
27 Hans Schmidt RC	4.00	10.00
28 Lu Kim RC	4.00	10.00
29 Roy McLarity RC	4.00	10.00
30 Lord Jan Blears	4.00	10.00
31 Lee Henning & Fred Atkins	4.00	10.00
32 Jim Goon Henry RC	4.00	10.00
33 Wee Willie Davis RC	4.00	10.00
34 Yvon Robert RC	4.00	10.00
35 Joe Killer Christie RC	4.00	10.00
36 Bo Bo Brazil RC	8.00	20.00
37 The Sharpe Brothers	4.00	10.00
38 Larry Moquin RC	4.00	10.00
39 Nanjo Singh RC	4.00	10.00
40 Wladek Kowalski RC	10.00	25.00
41 Frank Sexton RC	4.00	10.00
42 George Bollas RC	4.00	10.00
43 Ray Villmer RC	4.00	10.00
44 Steve Stanlee RC	4.00	10.00
45 Tuffy McCrae & Little Beaver	4.00	10.00
46 Johnny Rougeau RC	4.00	10.00
47 Harry Lewis RC	4.00	10.00
48 Pat Flanagan RC	4.00	10.00
49 Ovila Asselin RC	4.00	10.00
50 Sammy Berg RC	4.00	10.00
51 The Mighty Ursus	4.00	10.00
52 Lou Newman RC	4.00	10.00
53 George Scott RC	4.00	10.00
54 Hans Hermann RC	4.00	10.00
55 Bob Wagner RC	4.00	10.00
56 Little Beaver/Salassi	4.00	10.00
57 Sandor Kovacs RC	4.00	10.00
58 The Mills Brothers	4.00	10.00
59 Roberto Pico RC	4.00	10.00
60 Fred Atkins RC	4.00	10.00
61 Wild Bill Longson RC	4.00	10.00
62 Bobby Managoff RC	4.00	10.00
63 Athol Layton RC	4.00	10.00
64 Warren Bockwinkle RC	4.00	10.00
65 The Mighty Atlas RC	4.00	10.00
66 Mike Sharpe RC	4.00	10.00
67 Ernie Dusek	4.00	10.00
68 Danno O'Shocker RC	4.00	10.00
69 Gorgeous George RC	20.00	50.00
70 The Great Togo RC	4.00	10.00
71 Bob Langevin RC	4.00	10.00
72 Emil Dusek RC	4.00	10.00
73 Chief Sunni War Cloud RC	4.00	10.00
74 Pat O'Connor RC	4.00	10.00
75 Baron Leone RC	5.00	12.00

1955-56 Parkhurst Wrestling

COMPLETE SET (121)	450.00	800.00
1 Frank Valois	6.00	15.00
2 Johnny Barend	4.00	10.00
3 Sky Hi Lee	4.00	10.00
4 Hans Schmidt	4.00	10.00
5 Hans Hermann	4.00	10.00
6 Bo Bo Brazil	8.00	20.00
7 Chief Sunni War Cloud	4.00	10.00
8 The Mills Brothers	4.00	10.00
9 Roy McLarity	4.00	10.00
10 Danno O'Shocker	4.00	10.00
11 Chief Big Heart	4.00	10.00
12 Bob Wagner	4.00	10.00
13 Lou Pitoscia	4.00	10.00
14 Ernie Dusek	4.00	10.00
15 Whipper Watson	4.00	10.00
16 Johnny Rougeau	4.00	10.00
17 Ovila Asselin	4.00	10.00
18 Bill Stack	4.00	10.00
19 Ken Kenneth RC	4.00	10.00
20 Lou Newman	4.00	10.00
21 Warren Bockwinkle	4.00	10.00
22 The Sharpe Brothers	4.00	10.00
23 Bobby Managoff	4.00	10.00
24 Nick Roberts	4.00	10.00
25 Lee Henning RC	4.00	10.00
26 Joe Christie	4.00	10.00
27 Larry Moquin	4.00	10.00
28 Jim Goon Henry	4.00	10.00
29 Bob Langevin	4.00	10.00
30 Roberto Pico	4.00	10.00
31 Sammy Berg	4.00	10.00
32 Mighty Atlas	4.00	10.00
33 Baron Leone	4.00	10.00
34 Hassen Bay RC	4.00	10.00
35 Allen Garfield RC	4.00	10.00
36 Don Evans RC	4.00	10.00
37 Dory Funk RC	8.00	20.00
38 Art Neilson RC	4.00	10.00
39 Don Lee Jonathan RC	4.00	10.00
40 Argentina Rocca	6.00	15.00
41 Tex McKenzie RC	4.00	10.00
42 Pat Flanagan	4.00	10.00
43 Verne Gagne	8.00	20.00
44 Selassi & Little Beaver	4.00	10.00
45 Steve Stanlee	4.00	10.00
46 Frank Sexton	4.00	10.00
47 Pat O'Connor	4.00	10.00
48 Nanjo Singh	4.00	10.00
49 Toar Morgan	4.00	10.00
50 Harry Lewis	4.00	10.00
51 Doug Hepburn RC	4.00	10.00
52 Reggie Lisowski RC	4.00	10.00
53 Kenny Ackles RC	4.00	10.00
54 Argentina Rocca	6.00	15.00
55 Herb Parks RC	4.00	10.00
56 Bearcat Wright RC	4.00	10.00
57 Yvon Robert	4.00	10.00
58 Waldo Von Sieber RC	4.00	10.00
59 Harold Nelson RC	4.00	10.00
60 Sumo Wrestlers	4.00	10.00
61 Golden Hawk RC	4.00	10.00
62 Wee Willie Davis	4.00	10.00
63 Mike Sharpe	4.00	10.00
64 Sandor Kovacs	4.00	10.00
65 Lord Blears	4.00	10.00

66 Tim Goehagen	4.00	10.00
67 Jack Laskin RC	4.00	10.00
68 Emil Dusek	4.00	10.00
69 Ben Morgan	4.00	10.00
70 Lu Kim	4.00	10.00
71 Frank Marconi RC	4.00	10.00
72 Prince Maiava RC	4.00	10.00
73 Larry Kasaboski RC	4.00	10.00
74 Frank Thompson RC	4.00	10.00
75 Yukon Eric	4.00	10.00
76 Lou Thesz	6.00	15.00
77 Bill Longson	4.00	10.00
78 Fred Atkins	4.00	10.00
79 Lord Layton	4.00	10.00
80 Dusek Brothers	4.00	10.00
81 Zorra RC	4.00	10.00
82 Lou Thesz	10.00	25.00
83 Luther Lindsey RC	4.00	10.00
84 Jack Bence RC	4.00	10.00
85 Primo Carnera	8.00	20.00
86 Kalmikoff Brothers	4.00	10.00
87 The Great Togo	4.00	10.00
88 Lou Plummer	4.00	10.00
89 Bates Ford RC	4.00	10.00
90 Ursus and Montana	4.00	10.00
91 Paul Baillargeon	4.00	10.00
92 Bill McDaniels RC	4.00	10.00
93 Ray Villmer	4.00	10.00
94 Yvon Robert	4.00	10.00
95 Gorgeous George	15.00	40.00
96 Scott Brothers	4.00	10.00
97 Bronko Nagurski	50.00	100.00
98 Pete Managoff RC	4.00	10.00
99 The Togo Brothers	4.00	10.00
100 Don Lee RC	4.00	10.00
101 Steve Patrick RC	4.00	10.00
102 George Gordienko RC	4.00	10.00
103 Vic Holbrook RC	4.00	10.00
104 Gil Mains	4.00	10.00
105 Firpo Zbyszko RC	4.00	10.00
106 Mike Paidousis RC	4.00	10.00
107 Al Oeming RC	4.00	10.00
108 Matt Murphy RC	4.00	10.00
109 Martin Hutzler RC	4.00	10.00
110 Tommy O'Toole RC	4.00	10.00
111 Steve Gob RC	4.00	10.00
112 Riot Call Wright RC	4.00	10.00
113 Leo Newman RC	4.00	10.00
114 Frank Hurley RC	4.00	10.00
115 Jack Claybourne RC	4.00	10.00
116 Ken Colley RC	4.00	10.00
117 Whipper Watson	4.00	10.00
118 Steve McGill RC	4.00	10.00
119 Buddy Rogers RC	4.00	10.00
120 Gino Garibaldi RC	4.00	10.00
121 Ed Gardenia RC	5.00	12.00

2006 Popeye's WWE Mania Moments

COMPLETE SET (21)	15.00	40.00
1 Andre the Giant	1.50	4.00
2 Rowdy Roddy Piper	1.50	4.00
3 Hulk Hogan	2.00	5.00
4 Ted Dibiase	1.25	3.00
5 Jake The Snake Roberts	1.50	4.00
6 Skydome	.60	1.50
7 Sgt. Slaughter	2.00	5.00
8 Ric Flair	1.50	4.00
9 Bobby Heenan	.75	2.00
10 Mr. Perfect	1.00	2.50
11 Bam Bam Bigelow	1.00	2.50
12 Shawn Michaels	2.00	5.00
13 Undertaker	1.50	4.00
14 Stone Cold Steve Austin	2.00	5.00
15 The Rock	2.00	5.00
16 Mick Foley	1.00	2.50
17 Kurt Angle	1.25	3.00
18 Triple H	2.00	5.00
19 Rey Mysterio	1.25	3.00
20 Chris Benoit	1.25	3.00
21 Batista / John Cena	2.00	5.00

1982 PWE Wrestling All-Stars Series A

COMPLETE SET (36)	1000.00	2000.00
CARDS PRICED IN NR-MT CONDITION		
1 Andre the Giant	150.00	300.00
2 Hulk Hogan	300.00	600.00
3 Mil Mascaras	25.00	60.00
4 Ted DiBiase	50.00	100.00
5 The Junkyard Dog	30.00	75.00
6 Dusty Rhodes	50.00	100.00
7 Jack Brisco	10.00	25.00
8 Harley Race	25.00	60.00
9 Dory Funk Jr.	10.00	25.00
10 Terry Funk	50.00	100.00
11 Nick Bockwinkel	12.00	30.00
12 Bob Backlund	20.00	50.00
13 Bruno Sammartino	20.00	50.00
14 Pedro Morales	10.00	25.00
15 Don Muraco	20.00	50.00
16 Bill Dundee	15.00	40.00
17 Steve Olsonoski	6.00	15.00
18 Tommy Rich	15.00	40.00
19 Angelo Mosca	12.00	30.00
20 Bruiser Brody	75.00	150.00
21 The Fabulous Moolah	20.00	50.00
22 Wahoo McDaniel	12.00	30.00
23 Billy Robinson	6.00	15.00
24 Ivan Koloff	15.00	40.00
25 Tony Atlas	20.00	50.00
26 Pat Patterson	20.00	50.00
27 Ric Flair	400.00	800.00
28 Ivan Putski	12.00	30.00
29 Dick Murdoch	8.00	20.00
30 The Crusher	8.00	20.00
31 Ken Patera	15.00	40.00
32 Ernie Ladd	12.00	30.00
33 Dick the Bruiser	10.00	25.00
34 Jerry Lawler	75.00	150.00
35 Cowboy Bill Watts	12.00	30.00
36 The Destroyer	10.00	25.00

1983 PWE Wrestling All-Stars Series A

COMPLETE SET (36)	250.00	500.00
CARDS PRICED IN NR-MT CONDITION		
1 Superstar (Billy) Graham	15.00	40.00
2 Tiger Mask	8.00	20.00
3 Sheik El Kaissey	6.00	15.00
4 Sgt. Jacque Goulet	5.00	12.00
5 Curt Hennig	30.00	75.00
6 Tully Blanchard	12.00	30.00
7 Jimmy Superfly Snuka	15.00	40.00
8 Gino Hernandez	8.00	20.00
9 Lou Thesz	6.00	15.00
10 Hacksaw (Jim) Duggan	25.00	60.00
11 Mr. Olympia	6.00	15.00
12 Iron Mike Sharpe	12.00	30.00
13 Jimmy Hart	20.00	50.00
14 Spike Huber	6.00	15.00
15 Steve Regal	6.00	15.00
16 Buddy Rogers	8.00	20.00
17 Jules Strongbow	10.00	25.00
18 Salvatore Bellomo	8.00	20.00
19 Bob Sweetan	6.00	15.00
20 Scott Casey	3.00	8.00
21 The Grappler	5.00	12.00
22 Big John Studd	10.00	25.00
23 Buddy Rose	5.00	12.00
24 Rocky Johnson	25.00	60.00
25 Jake Roberts	50.00	100.00
26 The Super Destroyer	3.00	8.00
27 Antonio Inoki	12.00	30.00
28 Dick Slater	6.00	15.00
29 Ken Lucas	2.00	8.00
30 Ricky Morton	15.00	40.00
31 Fred Blassie	12.00	30.00
32 Lou Albano	12.00	30.00
33 The Grand Wizard	4.00	10.00
34 Candi Divine	5.00	12.00
35 Austin Idol	4.00	10.00
36 Matt Borne	3.00	8.00

1982 PWE Wrestling All-Stars Series B

COMPLETE SET (36)	400.00	800.00
CARDS PRICED IN NR-MT CONDITION		
1 Rick Martel	10.00	25.00
2 Tony Garea	8.00	20.00
3 Bob Roop	8.00	20.00
4 Greg Gagne	12.00	30.00
5 Jim Brunzell	6.00	15.00
6 Jay Strongbow	10.00	25.00
7 Kerry Von Erich	60.00	120.00
8 S.D. Jones	6.00	15.00
9 Brad Rheingans	6.00	15.00
10 Killer Khan	15.00	40.00
11 Ricky Steamboat	50.00	100.00
12 Paul Orndorff	15.00	40.00
13 Tito Santana	25.00	60.00
14 Sergeant Slaughter	50.00	100.00
15 Verne Gagne	10.00	25.00
16 Bobby Heenan	15.00	40.00
17 Jerry Blackwell	8.00	20.00
18 Les Thornton	4.00	10.00
19 Adrian Adonis	10.00	25.00
20 Jesse Ventura	30.00	75.00
21 Buck Zum Hofe	4.00	10.00
22 Jimmy Valiant	8.00	20.00
23 Steve Keirn	5.00	12.00
24 Ray Stevens	6.00	15.00
25 The Iron Sheik	50.00	100.00
26 Mr. Wrestling II	12.00	30.00
27 Col. Buck Robley	4.00	10.00
28 Bobby Duncum	5.00	12.00
29 Mike George	4.00	10.00
30 Dino Bravo	6.00	15.00
31 Baron Von Raschke	12.00	30.00
32 Bobo Brazil	6.00	15.00
33 Greg Valentine	15.00	40.00
34 Joyce Grable	6.00	15.00
35 Sweet Brown Sugar	4.00	10.00
36 Dutch Mantell	10.00	25.00

2022 Revolution WWE

COMPLETE SET (150)	75.00	200.00
*ASTRO: .5X TO 1.2X BASIC CARDS		
*FRACTAL: .6X TO 1.5X BASIC CARDS		
*GALACTIC: .75X TO 2X BASIC CARDS		
*GROOVE: 1X TO 2.5X BASIC CARDS		
*ANGULAR/199: 1.2X TO 3X BASIC CARDS		
*COSMIC/149: 1.5X TO 4X BASIC CARDS		
*SUNBURST/99: 2X TO 5X BASIC CARDS		
*CUBIC/49: 2.5X TO 6X BASIC CARDS		
*LAVA/10: UNPRICED DUE TO SCARCITY		
1 Tony D'Angelo RC	1.25	3.00
2 Brock Lesnar	2.00	5.00
3 Meiko Satomura RC	1.25	3.00
4 Rick Boogs	.50	1.25
5 Natalya	.60	1.50
6 AJ Styles	1.25	3.00
7 Sonya Deville	1.00	2.50
8 Kevin Owens	.75	2.00
9 Nash Carter	.40	1.00
10 Alexa Bliss	2.50	6.00
11 Von Wagner RC	.40	1.00
12 Chad Gable	.40	1.00
13 Gigi Dolin	1.50	4.00
14 Ricochet	.75	2.00
15 Sasha Banks	2.50	6.00
16 Apollo Crews	.50	1.25
17 Bron Breakker RC	3.00	8.00
18 The Miz	.60	1.50
19 Wes Lee	.40	1.00
20 Becky Lynch	1.50	4.00
21 Xyon Quinn RC	.40	1.00
22 Drew McIntyre	.75	2.00
23 Jacy Jayne RC	1.50	4.00
24 Roman Reigns	2.50	6.00
25 Shayna Baszler	.75	2.00
26 Big E	.75	2.00
27 Cameron Grimes	.75	2.00
28 Montez Ford	.40	1.00
29 Odyssey Jones RC	.40	1.00
30 Bianca Belair	1.25	3.00
31 Zack Gibson	.40	1.00
32 Happy Corbin	.50	1.25
33 Mandy Rose	2.00	5.00
34 Sami Zayn	.60	1.50
35 Shotzi	1.50	4.00
36 The All Mighty Bobby Lashley	.75	2.00
37 Carmelo Hayes RC	.50	1.25
38 Angelo Dawkins	.50	1.25
39 Pete Dunne	.75	2.00
40 Carmella	1.00	2.50
41 James Drake	.40	1.00
42 Jey Uso	.50	1.25
43 Indi Hartwell	1.25	3.00
44 Sheamus	.60	1.50
45 Theory	1.00	2.50
46 Damian Priest	.75	2.00
47 Dexter Lumis	.40	1.00
48 Omos	.75	2.00
49 Rey Mysterio	1.00	2.50
50 Ronda Rousey	2.50	6.00
51 Candice LeRae	1.25	3.00
52 Jimmy Uso	.50	1.25
53 Io Shirai	.75	2.00

54 Shanky RC	.40	1.00
55 Xia Li	.75	2.00
56 Dolph Ziggler	.75	2.00
57 Fabian Aichner	.50	1.25
58 Randy Orton	1.00	2.50
59 Roderick Strong	.60	1.50
60 Doudrop	.60	1.50
61 Cora Jade RC	2.50	6.00
62 Jinder Mahal	.50	1.25
63 Katana Chance	.75	2.00
64 Shinsuke Nakamura	1.00	2.50
65 Asuka	1.50	4.00
66 Dominik Mysterio	.50	1.25
67 Grayson Waller RC	1.00	2.50
68 Riddle	1.00	2.50
69 Santos Escobar	.60	1.50
70 Liv Morgan	2.00	5.00
71 Dakota Kai	.75	2.00
72 King Woods	.50	1.25
73 Alba Fyre	1.00	2.50
74 Aliyah	.75	2.00
75 Bayley	1.00	2.50
76 Edge	1.50	4.00
77 Kushida	.60	1.50
78 Reggie	.50	1.25
79 Solo Sikoa RC	2.00	5.00
80 Nikki A.S.H.	.60	1.50
81 Gunther	1.00	2.50
82 Kofi Kingston	1.00	2.50
83 Raquel Rodriguez	1.00	2.50
84 Charlotte Flair	1.50	4.00
85 John Cena	1.25	3.00
86 Finn Balor	1.00	2.50
87 LA Knight	.60	1.50
88 Seth ìFreakinî Rollins	1.00	2.50
89 Elektra Lopez RC	1.00	2.50
90 Queen Zelina	.60	1.50
91 Ilja Dragunov	.40	1.00
92 Mansoor	.40	1.00
93 Sarray	.50	1.25
94 Naomi	.60	1.50
95 Lacey Evans	1.00	2.50
96 Gable Steveson RC	4.00	10.00
97 Ludwig Kaiser	.50	1.25
98 Veer Mahaan	1.00	2.50
99 Ciampa	1.00	2.50
100 Rhea Ripley	1.25	3.00
101 Andre The Giant	1.50	4.00
102 Bret "Hit Man" Hart	1.00	2.50
103 Faarooq	.50	1.25
104 Cactus Jack	.75	2.00
105 Ultimate Warrior	1.50	4.00
106 Dusty Rhodes	1.00	2.50
107 Hulk Hogan	2.00	5.00
108 Eddie Guerrero	1.25	3.00
109 Jerry Lawler	.75	2.00
110 Shawn Michaels	1.50	4.00
111 Rikishi	.50	1.25
112 Nikki Bella	1.00	2.50
113 Stone Cold Steve Austin	2.00	5.00
114 Chyna	.75	2.00
115 Undertaker	2.00	5.00
116 The Godfather	.40	1.00
117 Iron Sheik	.50	1.25
118 Triple H	1.50	4.00
119 Lex Luger	.50	1.25
120 Batista	.75	2.00
121 Rob Van Dam	.75	2.00
122 Bruno Sammartino	1.00	2.50
123 Million Dollar Man Ted DiBiase	.60	1.50
124 Diesel	.60	1.50
125 X-Pac	.50	1.25
126 The Great Khali	.50	1.25
127 JBL	.40	1.00
128 The Rock	4.00	10.00
129 Macho Man Randy Savage	1.50	4.00
130 Booker T	.75	2.00
131 Macho Man Randy Savage/Hulk Hogan	2.00	5.00
132 Fabian Aichner/Ludwig Kaiser	.50	1.25
133 Kane/Undertaker	2.00	5.00
134 Shawn Michaels/Triple H	1.50	4.00
135 Bret "Hit Man" Hart/Jim Neidhart	1.00	2.50
136 Erik/Ivar	.40	1.00
137 Mankind/The Rock	4.00	10.00
138 King Woods/Kofi Kingston	1.00	2.50
139 Bradshaw/Faarooq	.50	1.25
140 Randy Orton/Riddle	1.00	2.50
141 Booker T/Stevie Ray	.75	2.00
142 Gigi Dolin/Jacy Jayne	1.50	4.00
143 Edge/Randy Orton	1.50	4.00
144 Roman Reigns/Seth ìFreakinî Rollins	2.50	6.00
145 Brie Bella/Nikki Bella	1.00	2.50
146 Angelo Dawkins/Montez Ford	.50	1.25
147 Diesel/Shawn Michaels	1.50	4.00
148 Chad Gable/Otis	.50	1.25
149 Gerald Brisco/Pat Patterson	.40	1.00
150 Jey Uso/Jimmy Uso	.50	1.25

2022 Revolution WWE Autographs

*SUNBURST/99: SAME PRICE AS BASIC
*CUBIC/49: .5X TO 1.2X BASIC AUTOS
*LAVA/10: UNPRICED DUE TO SCARCITY
*KALEIDO/1: UNPRICED DUE TO SCARCITY
RANDOMLY INSERTED INTO PACKS

AGABS Alexa Bliss	100.00	250.00
AGAJS AJ Styles	20.00	50.00
AGASK Asuka	30.00	75.00
AGBBL Bianca Belair	25.00	60.00
AGBGE Big E	8.00	20.00
AGBHT Bret "Hit Man" Hart	60.00	150.00
AGBLH The All Mighty Bobby Lashley	10.00	25.00
AGBLN Becky Lynch	50.00	125.00
AGBLS Brock Lesnar	100.00	250.00
AGBLY Bayley	25.00	60.00
AGBTS Batista		
AGCLF Charlotte Flair	50.00	125.00
AGCML Carmella	15.00	40.00
AGDGZ Dolph Ziggler	8.00	20.00
AGDMC Drew McIntyre	12.00	30.00
AGDMY Dominik Mysterio	10.00	25.00
AGEGE Edge	30.00	75.00
AGFBL Finn Balor	12.00	30.00
AGGBG Goldberg	50.00	150.00
AGGSV Gable Steveson	60.00	150.00
AGGTH Gunther	12.00	30.00
AGHHG Hulk Hogan	200.00	500.00
AGHHH Triple H	100.00	250.00
AGIOS Io Shirai	20.00	50.00
AGJCN John Cena EXCH	75.00	200.00
AGKCZ Katana Chance	10.00	25.00
AGKKG Kofi Kingston	10.00	25.00
AGLIV Liv Morgan	40.00	100.00
AGMIZ The Miz	20.00	50.00
AGMRS Mandy Rose	75.00	200.00
AGOMS Omos	6.00	15.00
AGRDL Riddle	20.00	50.00
AGRMY Rey Mysterio	20.00	50.00
AGROR Randy Orton	50.00	125.00
AGRQG Raquel Rodriguez	12.00	30.00
AGRRN Roman Reigns EXCH	75.00	200.00
AGRRP Rhea Ripley	30.00	75.00
AGSBK Sasha Banks	60.00	150.00
AGSCA Stone Cold Steve Austin	300.00	750.00
AGSDV Sonya Deville	15.00	40.00
AGSHL Shawn Michaels	60.00	150.00
AGSHM Sheamus	10.00	25.00
AGSHZ Shotzi	40.00	100.00
AGSKN Shinsuke Nakamura	10.00	25.00
AGSMM Stephanie McMahon	100.00	250.00
AGSRL Seth Freakin Rollins	25.00	60.00
AGTSH Trish Stratus EXCH	40.00	100.00
AGUND Undertaker	200.00	500.00
AGXLI Xia Li	15.00	40.00

2022 Revolution WWE Liftoff

COMPLETE SET (10) 15.00 40.00
*GALACTIC: .6X TO 1.5X BASIC CARDS
*SUNBURST/99: .75X TO 2X BASIC CARDS
*CUBIC/49: 1.2X TO 3X BASIC CARDS
*LAVA/10: UNPRICED DUE TO SCARCITY
RANDOMLY INSERTED INTO PACKS

1 Bobby Lashley	1.25	3.00
2 Kofi Kingston	1.50	4.00
3 Charlotte Flair	2.50	6.00
4 Finn Balor	1.50	4.00
5 Alexa Bliss	10.00	25.00
6 Seth Rollins	1.50	4.00
7 Edge	2.50	6.00
8 Drew McIntyre	1.25	3.00
9 Rey Mysterio	1.50	4.00
10 AJ Styles	2.00	5.00

2022 Revolution WWE Shock Wave

COMPLETE SET (30) 30.00 75.00
*GALACTIC: .6X TO 1.5X BASIC CARDS
*SUNBURST/99: .75X TO 2X BASIC CARDS
*CUBIC/49: 1.2X TO 3X BASIC CARDS
*LAVA/10: UNPRICED DUE TO SCARCITY
RANDOMLY INSERTED INTO PACKS

1 Becky Lynch	2.50	6.00
2 Shinsuke Nakamura	1.50	4.00
3 Carmella	1.50	4.00
4 Xia Li	1.25	3.00
5 Doudrop	1.00	2.50
6 Roman Reigns	4.00	10.00
7 Jimmy Uso	.75	2.00
8 Montez Ford	.60	1.50
9 AJ Styles	2.00	5.00
10 Riddle	1.50	4.00
11 Big E	1.25	3.00
12 The Miz	1.00	2.50
13 Charlotte Flair	2.50	6.00
14 Bobby Lashley	1.25	3.00
15 Edge	2.50	6.00
16 Randy Orton	1.50	4.00
17 Kofi Kingston	1.50	4.00
18 Raquel Gonzalez	1.50	4.00
19 Apollo Crews	.75	2.00
20 Sami Zayn	1.00	2.50
21 Brock Lesnar	3.00	8.00
22 Gunther	1.50	4.00
23 Dolph Ziggler	1.25	3.00
24 John Cena	2.00	5.00
25 Io Shirai	1.25	3.00
26 Sasha Banks	4.00	10.00
27 Mandy Rose	3.00	8.00
28 Rhea Ripley	2.00	5.00
29 Ronda Rousey	4.00	10.00
30 Seth "Freakin" Rollins	1.50	4.00

2022 Revolution WWE Supernova

COMPLETE SET (30) 60.00 150.00
*GALACTIC: .6X TO 1.5X BASIC CARDS
*SUNBURST/99: .75X TO 2X BASIC CARDS
*CUBIC/49: 1.2X TO 3X BASIC CARDS
*LAVA/10: UNPRICED DUE TO SCARCITY
RANDOMLY INSERTED INTO PACKS

1 Drew McIntyre	2.00	5.00
2 Shotzi	4.00	10.00
3 Jey Uso	1.25	3.00
4 Gunther	2.50	6.00
5 Kevin Owens	2.00	5.00
6 Mandy Rose	5.00	12.00
7 Alexa Bliss	12.00	30.00
8 Rey Mysterio	2.50	6.00
9 Bobby Lashley	2.00	5.00
10 Sasha Banks	6.00	15.00
11 Edge	4.00	10.00
12 The Miz	1.50	4.00
13 Jimmy Uso	1.25	3.00
14 Xia Li	2.00	5.00
15 Liv Morgan	5.00	12.00
16 Randy Orton	2.50	6.00
17 Becky Lynch	4.00	10.00
18 Rhea Ripley	3.00	8.00
19 Brock Lesnar	5.00	12.00
20 Seth "Freakin" Rollins	2.50	6.00
21 Finn Balor	2.50	6.00
22 Bayley	2.50	6.00
23 John Cena	3.00	8.00
24 Queen Zelina	1.50	4.00
25 AJ Styles	3.00	8.00
26 Raquel Gonzalez	2.50	6.00
27 Big E	2.00	5.00
28 Roman Reigns	6.00	15.00
29 Charlotte Flair	4.00	10.00
30 Shinsuke Nakamura	2.50	6.00

2022 Revolution WWE Supernova Cubic

7 Alexa Bliss	40.00	100.00

2022 Revolution WWE Supernova Sunburst

7 Alexa Bliss	30.00	75.00

2022 Revolution WWE Vortex

COMPLETE SET (30) 60.00 150.00
*GALACTIC: .6X TO 1.5X BASIC CARDS
*SUNBURST/99: .75X TO 2X BASIC CARDS
*CUBIC/49: 1.2X TO 3X BASIC CARDS
*LAVA/10: UNPRICED DUE TO SCARCITY
RANDOMLY INSERTED INTO PACKS

1 Rey Mysterio	2.50	6.00
2 Bayley	2.50	6.00
3 Sasha Banks	6.00	15.00
4 Bobby Lashley	2.00	5.00
5 Brock Lesnar	5.00	12.00
6 Damian Priest	2.00	5.00

7 Finn Balor	2.50	6.00
8 John Cena	3.00	8.00
9 Liv Morgan	5.00	12.00
10 Apollo Crews	1.25	3.00
11 Ricochet	2.00	5.00
12 Becky Lynch	4.00	10.00
13 Sheamus	1.50	4.00
14 Bron Breakker	4.00	10.00
15 King Woods	1.25	3.00
16 Dominik Mysterio	1.25	3.00
17 Jey Uso	1.25	3.00
18 AJ Styles	3.00	8.00
19 Ronda Rousey	6.00	15.00
20 Asuka	4.00	10.00
21 Roman Reigns	6.00	15.00
22 Bianca Belair	3.00	8.00
23 Shotzi	4.00	10.00
24 Cora Jade	3.00	8.00
25 Queen Zelina	1.50	4.00
26 Drew McIntyre	2.00	5.00
27 Kevin Owens	2.00	5.00
28 Alexa Bliss	6.00	15.00
29 Randy Orton	2.50	6.00
30 Austin Theory	2.50	6.00

2022 Revolution WWE Vortex Cubic

28 Alexa Bliss	40.00	100.00

2022 Revolution WWE Vortex Sunburst

28 Alexa Bliss	30.00	75.00

1986 Scanlens WWF Australian

COMPLETE SET (66)	20.00	50.00
UNOPENED BOX		
UNOPENED PACK		
RINGSIDE ACTION (22-56)		
SUPERSTARS SPEAK (57-66)		
1 Hulk Hogan	100.00	200.00
2 The Iron Sheik	.20	.50
3 Captain Lou Albano	.20	.50
4 Junk Yard Dog	.20	.50
5 Paul Mr. Wonderful Orndorff	.15	.40
6 Jimmy Superfly Snuka	.15	.40
7 Rowdy Roddy Piper	2.00	5.00
8 Wendi Richter	.20	.50
9 Greg The Hammer Valentine	.15	.40
10 Brutus Beefcake	.12	.30
11 Jesse The Body Ventura	1.50	4.00
12 Big John Studd	.15	.40
13 Fabulous Moolah	.15	.40
14 Tito Santana	.12	.30
15 Hillbilly Jim	.15	.40
16 Hulk Hogan	125.00	250.00
17 Mr. Fuji	.12	.30
18 Rotundo & Windham	.12	.30
19 Moondog Spot	.12	.30
20 Chief Jay Strongbow	.12	.30
21 George "The Animal" Steele	.15	.40
22 Let Go of My Toe! RA	.15	.40
23 Lock 'Em Up! RA	.15	.40
24 Scalp 'Em! RA	.20	.50
25 Going for the Midsection! RA	.20	.50
26 Up in the Air! RA	.12	.30
27 All Tied Up! RA	.40	1.00
28 Here She Comes! RA	.12	.30
29 Stretched to the Limit! RA	2.00	5.00
30 Over He Goes! RA	.15	.40
31 An Appetite for Mayhem! RA	.15	.40
32 Putting on Pressure! RA	.20	.50
33 Smashed on a Knee! RA	.15	.40
34 A Fist Comes Flying! RA	.12	.30
35 Lemme' Out of This! RA	.12	.30
36 No Fair Chokin'! RA	.15	.40
37 Attacked by an Animal! RA	.15	.40
38 One Angry Man! RA	.40	1.00
39 Someone's Going Down! RA	.40	1.00
40 Strangle Hold! RA	.40	1.00
41 Bending an Arm! RA	.12	.30
42 Ready for a Pile Driver! RA	.15	.40
43 Face to the Canvas! RA	.12	.30
44 Paul Wants It All! RA	.15	.40
45 Kick to the Face! RA	.75	2.00
46 Ready for Action! RA	.12	.30
47 Putting on the Squeeze! RA	.20	.50
48 Giants in Action! RA	.40	1.00
49 Camel Clutch! RA	.20	.50
50 Pile Up! RA	.75	2.00
51 Can't Get Away! RA	.20	.50
52 Going for the Pin! RA	.12	.30
53 Ready to Fly! RA	.40	1.00
54 Crusher in a Crusher! RA	.20	.50
55 Fury of the Animal! RA	.15	.40
56 Wrong Kind of Music! RA	2.00	5.00
57 Who's your next challenger? SS	2.00	5.00
58 This dog has got a mean bite! SS	.20	.50
59 I don't think I'll ask... SS	.40	1.00
60 You Hulkster fans... SS	2.00	5.00
61 This ain't my idea... SS	.40	1.00
62 You mean Freddie Blassie... SS	.40	1.00
63 Mppgh Ecch Oong. SS	.20	.50
64 Rock n' wrestling... SS	.20	.50
65 Arrrggghhhh! SS	.15	.40
66 They took my reindeer! SS	.20	.50

2010 SCWA JT Smooth Series One

COMPLETE SET (9)
NNO JT Smooth Cell 3E Edition
NNO JT Smooth Evolution Fire Edition
NNO JT Smooth Special Hardcore Edition Picture
NNO Smooth Gel Bubbles Edition
NNO Smooth Gel Ultimate Fire Edition
NNO Smooth Metallic Gel Edition
NNO The Under Armour Warrior
NNO Ultimate 3E Transformation Edition
NNO Ultimate Destruction Chaos Edition

2022 Select WWE

*ELEPHANT: UNPRICED DUE TO SCARCITY
*ORANGE FLASH: X TO X BASIC CARDS
*PURPLE&ORANGE: X TO X BASIC CARDS
*RED&BLUE: X TO X BASIC CARDS
*RED WAVE: X TO X BASIC CARDS
*SCOPE: X TO X BASIC CARDS
*SILVER: X TO X BASIC CARDS
*TIGER: UNPRICED DUE TO SCARCITY
*TRI-COLOR: X TO X BASIC CARDS
*ZEBRA: UNPRICED DUE TO SCARCITY
*LT.BLUE/299: .75X TO 2X BASIC CARDS
*RED/249: X TO X BASIC CARDS
*BLUE/199: 1X TO 2.5X BASIC CARDS
*MAROON/149: 1X TO 2.5X BASIC CARDS
*WHITE/99: X TO X BASIC CARDS
*PURPLE/75: X TO X BASIC CARDS
*NEON GREEN/49: X TO X BASIC CARDS
*PINK/49: X TO X BASIC CARDS
*ORANGE/35: X TO X BASIC CARDS
*TIE-DYE/25: UNPRICED DUE TO SCARCITY
*GOLD/10: UNPRICED DUE TO SCARCITY
*GOLD FLASH/10: UNPRICED DUE TO SCARCITY
*GOLD WAVE/10: UNPRICED DUE TO SCARCITY
*LUCKY ENV/8: UNPRICED DUE TO SCARCITY
*GREEN/5: UNPRICED DUE TO SCARCITY
*BLACK/1: UNPRICED DUE TO SCARCITY
*BLACK&GOLD/1: UNPRICED DUE TO SCARCITY

1 LA Knight	.50	1.25
2 Alba Fyre	.75	2.00
3 Alexa Bliss	2.00	5.00
4 Mansoor	.30	.75
5 Brock Lesnar	1.50	4.00
6 Raquel Rodriguez	.75	2.00
7 Eddie Guerrero	1.00	2.50
8 Seth Freakin Rollins	.75	2.00
9 The Godfather	.30	.75
10 The Miz	.50	1.25
11 Jey Uso	.40	1.00
12 Meiko Satomura RC	1.00	2.50
13 AJ Styles	1.00	2.50
14 Maryse	.50	1.25
15 Bron Breakker RC	3.00	8.00
16 Rhea Ripley	1.00	2.50
17 Dominik Mysterio	.40	1.00
18 Gunther	.75	2.00
19 Goldberg	1.25	3.00
20 The Rock	3.00	8.00
21 Jerry Lawler	.60	1.50
22 Montez Ford	.30	.75
23 Angel	.30	.75
24 Mick Foley	.60	1.50
25 Cedric Alexander	.30	.75
26 Ricochet	.60	1.50
27 Doudrop	.50	1.25
28 Shawn Michaels	1.25	3.00
29 The Great Khali	.40	1.00
30 Undertaker	1.50	4.00
31 Jimmy Uso	.40	1.00
32 Kevin Owens	.60	1.50
33 Angelo Dawkins	.40	1.00
34 Shotzi	1.25	3.00
35 Diamond Dallas Page	.40	1.00
36 Riddle	.75	2.00
37 Drew McIntyre	.60	1.50
38 Shelton Benjamin	.50	1.25
39 Harland RC	.30	.75
40 Triple H	1.25	3.00
41 Jinder Mahal	.40	1.00
42 Xavier Woods	.40	1.00
43 Apollo Crews	.40	1.00
44 Liv Morgan	1.50	4.00
45 Charlotte Flair	1.25	3.00
46 Rikishi	.40	1.00
47 Dusty Rhodes	.75	2.00
48 Shinsuke Nakamura	.75	2.00
49 Indi Hartwell	1.00	2.50
50 Sheamus	.50	1.25
51 Happy Corbin	.40	1.00
52 Kofi Kingston	.75	2.00
53 Becky Lynch	1.25	3.00
54 Nikki A.S.H.	.50	1.25
55 Stone Cold Steve Austin	1.50	4.00
56 Roman Reigns	2.00	5.00
57 Edge	1.25	3.00
58 Solo Sikoa RC	2.50	6.00
59 Julius Creed RC	.75	2.00
60 Veer Mahaan	.75	2.00
61 Joe Gacy RC	.75	2.00
62 Kushida	.50	1.25
63 Big E	.60	1.50
64 Odyssey Jones RC	.30	.75
65 Cora Jade RC	2.50	6.00
66 Ciampa	.75	2.00
67 Dolph Ziggler	.60	1.50
68 Sonya Deville	.75	2.00
69 Hulk Hogan	1.50	4.00
70 Wes Lee	.30	.75
71 John Cena	1.00	2.50
72 Macho Man Randy Savage	1.25	3.00
73 Blair Davenport RC	1.50	4.00
74 Omos	.60	1.50
75 Damian Priest	.60	1.50
76 Santos Escobar	.50	1.25
77 Faarooq	.40	1.00
78 Grayson Waller RC	1.25	3.00
79 Humberto	.30	.75
80 Bayley	.75	2.00
81 Jordan Devlin	.30	.75
82 Rick Boogs	.40	1.00
83 The All Mighty Bobby Lashley	.60	1.50
84 Butch	.60	1.50
85 Bret Hit Man Hart	.75	2.00
86 Sasha Banks	2.00	5.00
87 Gigi Dolin	2.00	5.00
88 Million Dollar Man Ted DiBiase	.50	1.25
89 Ilja Dragunov	.30	.75
90 Ronda Rousey	2.00	5.00
91 Katana Chance	.60	1.50
92 Rob Van Dam	.60	1.50
93 Booker T	.60	1.50
94 Randy Orton	.75	2.00
95 Bruno Sammartino	.75	2.00
96 Von Wagner RC	.30	.75
97 Jacy Jayne RC	2.50	6.00
98 Tony D'Angelo RC	1.00	2.50
99 Io Shirai	.60	1.50
100 Michael Cole	.30	.75
101 Charlotte Flair	1.50	4.00
102 Shane McMahon	.75	2.00
103 Edge	1.50	4.00
104 Typhoon	.40	1.00
105 Jey Uso	.50	1.25
106 Kevin Owens	.75	2.00
107 AJ Styles	1.25	3.00
108 MVP	.40	1.00
109 Big E	.75	2.00
110 Ricochet	.75	2.00
111 Chyna	.75	2.00
112 Shayna Baszler	.75	2.00
113 Elektra Lopez RC	1.00	2.50
114 Ultimate Warrior	1.50	4.00
115 Jimmy Hart	.50	1.25
116 Xavier Woods	.50	1.25
117 Finn Balor	1.00	2.50
118 Natalya	.60	1.50
119 Boa	.40	1.00
120 Riddle	1.00	2.50
121 Cora Jade	3.00	8.00
122 Sheamus	.60	1.50
123 Gene Okerlund	.60	1.50
124 Von Wagner	.40	1.00

125	Jinny RC	.40	1.00
126	LA Knight	.60	1.50
127	Aliyah	.75	2.00
128	Nina Samuels	.50	1.25
129	Bret Hit Man Hart	1.00	2.50
130	Ridge Holland	.40	1.00
131	Damian Priest	.75	2.00
132	Shinsuke Nakamura	1.00	2.50
133	Gigi Dolin	2.00	5.00
134	Bad News Barrett	.40	1.00
135	Joaquin Wilde	.60	1.50
136	Elton Prince RC	.50	1.25
137	Alundra Blayze	.50	1.25
138	Oliver Carter RC	.40	1.00
139	Brock Lesnar	2.00	5.00
140	Rob Van Dam	.75	2.00
141	Dana Brooke	.40	1.00
142	Shotzi	1.50	4.00
143	Grayson Waller	1.00	2.50
144	Wolfgang	.40	1.00
145	John Cena	1.25	3.00
146	Madcap Moss	.40	1.00
147	Aoife Valkyrie RC	.75	2.00
148	Otis	.50	1.25
149	Bruno Sammartino	1.00	2.50
150	Roderick Strong	.60	1.50
151	Dave Mastiff	.40	1.00
152	The Miz	.60	1.50
153	Happy Corbin	.50	1.25
154	Xia Li	.75	2.00
155	Jordan Devlin	.40	1.00
156	Mandy Rose	2.00	5.00
157	Apollo Crews	.50	1.25
158	Queen Zelina	.60	1.50
159	Bron Breakker	3.00	8.00
160	Roman Reigns	2.50	6.00
161	Dolph Ziggler	.75	2.00
162	The Rock	4.00	10.00
163	Harland	.40	1.00
164	Zack Gibson	.40	1.00
165	Julius Creed	1.00	2.50
166	Mark Coffey	.40	1.00
167	Asuka	1.50	4.00
168	Randy Orton	1.00	2.50
169	Cactus Jack	.75	2.00
170	Kit Wilson RC	.40	1.00
171	Drew Gulak	.50	1.25
172	Ciampa	1.00	2.50
173	Indi Hartwell	2.50	6.00
174	Vader	.50	1.25
175	Kama	.40	1.00
176	Meiko Satomura	1.25	3.00
177	Becky Lynch	1.50	4.00
178	Cruz Del Toro	.60	1.50
179	Cameron Grimes	.75	2.00
180	Stone Cold Steve Austin	2.00	5.00
181	Drew McIntyre	.75	2.00
182	Tony D'Angelo	1.25	3.00
183	Jacy Jayne	2.50	6.00
184	Umaga	.40	1.00
185	Kayden Carter	.75	2.00
186	Montez Ford	.40	1.00
187	Beth Phoenix	.75	2.00
188	Reggie	.50	1.25
189	Carmella	1.00	2.50
190	Saxon Huxley RC	.40	1.00
191	Eddie Guerrero	1.25	3.00
192	Trent Seven	.50	1.25
193	Jerry Lawler	.75	2.00
194	Nikkita Lyons RC	6.00	15.00
195	Kevin Nash	.60	1.50
196	Mr. T	.75	2.00
197	Big Boss Man	.60	1.50
198	Rick Boogs	.50	1.25
199	Chad Gable	.40	1.00
200	Seth Freakin Rollins	1.00	2.50
201	Liv Morgan	3.00	8.00
202	AJ Styles	1.50	4.00
203	Nikki Bella	1.25	3.00
204	Big E	1.00	2.50
205	Ricky The Dragon Steamboat	1.00	2.50
206	Carmelo Hayes RC	1.50	4.00
207	Shawn Michaels	2.00	5.00
208	Gable Steveson RC	3.00	8.00
209	Trick Williams RC	.50	1.25
210	Io Shirai	1.00	2.50
211	Macho Man Randy Savage	2.00	5.00
212	Alexa Bliss	3.00	8.00
213	Otis	.60	1.50
214	The All Mighty Bobby Lashley	1.00	2.50
215	Riddle	1.25	3.00
216	Charlotte Flair	2.00	5.00
217	Sheamus	.75	2.00
218	Finn Balor	1.25	3.00
219	Triple H	2.00	5.00
220	Joe Gacy	1.25	3.00
221	Madcap Moss	.50	1.25
222	Amale RC	.50	1.25
223	Paul Heyman	.75	2.00
224	Bret Hit Man Hart	1.25	3.00
225	Rikishi	.60	1.50
226	Dakota Kai	1.00	2.50
227	Shinsuke Nakamura	1.25	3.00
228	Gigi Dolin	4.00	10.00
229	Ultimate Warrior	2.00	5.00
230	John Cena	1.50	4.00
231	Mandy Rose	3.00	8.00
232	Aliyah	1.00	2.50
233	Nikkita Lyons	10.00	25.00
234	Brie Bella	1.00	2.50
235	Rob Van Dam	1.00	2.50
236	Damian Priest	1.00	2.50
237	Stone Cold Steve Austin	3.00	8.00
238	Goldberg	2.50	6.00
239	Undertaker	5.00	12.00
240	Jordan Devlin	.50	1.25
241	Mankind	1.00	2.50
242	Apollo Crews	.60	1.50
243	High Chief Peter Maivia	.50	1.25
244	The British Bulldog	.75	2.00
245	Roderick Strong	.75	2.00
246	Dexter Lumis	.50	1.25
247	Solo Sikoa	2.50	6.00
248	Grayson Waller	1.25	3.00
249	Xia Brookside RC	4.00	10.00
250	Kevin Owens	1.00	2.50
251	Ludwig Kaiser	.60	1.50
252	Asuka	2.00	5.00
253	Randy Orton	1.25	3.00
254	Brock Lesnar	4.00	10.00
255	Roman Reigns	4.00	10.00
256	Diesel	.75	2.00
257	Stacy Keibler	4.00	10.00
258	Gunther	1.25	3.00
259	X-Pac	.60	1.50
260	Xavier Woods	.60	1.50
261	Maryse	.75	2.00
262	Theory	1.25	3.00
263	Raquel Rodriguez	1.25	3.00
264	Bron Breakker	5.00	12.00
265	Sami Zayn	.75	2.00
266	Doudrop	.75	2.00
267	Stephanie McMahon	.75	2.00
268	Happy Corbin	.60	1.50
269	Zoey Stark	.60	1.50
270	Kofi Kingston	1.25	3.00
271	Ashton Smith RC	.60	1.50
272	Bayley	1.25	3.00
273	Rey Mysterio	1.25	3.00
274	Cameron Grimes	1.00	2.50
275	Santos Escobar	.75	2.00
276	Drew McIntyre	1.00	2.50
277	The Miz	.75	2.00
278	Hulk Hogan	6.00	15.00
279	Ronda Rousey	5.00	12.00
280	Kushida	.75	2.00
281	Meiko Satomura	1.50	4.00
282	Becky Lynch	2.00	5.00
283	Rhea Ripley	4.00	10.00
284	Candice LeRae	1.50	4.00
285	Sasha Banks	10.00	25.00
286	Edge	2.00	5.00
287	The Rock	10.00	25.00
288	Ilja Dragunov	.50	1.25
289	Nathan Frazer RC	.50	1.25
290	LA Knight	.75	2.00
291	Montez Ford	.50	1.25
292	Bianca Belair	1.50	4.00
293	Rick Boogs	.60	1.50
294	Carmella	1.25	3.00
295	Seth Freakin Rollins	1.25	3.00
296	Fabian Aichner	.60	1.50
297	Ciampa	1.25	3.00
298	Indi Hartwell	1.50	4.00
299	The American Nightmare Cody Rhodes	12.00	30.00
300	Lex Luger	.60	1.50
301	The Rock	6.00	15.00
302	Jimmy Uso	.75	2.00
303	Mandy Rose	10.00	25.00
304	A-Kid RC	.75	2.00
305	Nikki Bella	1.50	4.00
306	The All Mighty Bobby Lashley	1.25	3.00
307	Rey Mysterio	1.50	4.00
308	Damian Priest	1.25	3.00
309	Santos Escobar	1.00	2.50
310	Erik	.60	1.50
311	Trent Seven	.75	2.00
312	Jinny	.60	1.50
313	Ludwig Kaiser	.75	2.00
314	Akira Tozawa	.75	2.00
315	Nikolai Volkoff	.60	1.50
316	Brie Bella	1.25	3.00
317	Ravishing Rick Rude	1.25	3.00
318	Dana Brooke	.60	1.50
319	Sarray	.75	2.00
320	Ikemen Jiro RC	.60	1.50
321	Tyler Bate	.75	2.00
322	John Cena	2.00	5.00
323	Booker T	1.25	3.00
324	Amari Miller RC	5.00	12.00
325	Noam Dar	.75	2.00
326	Brock Lesnar	3.00	8.00
327	Riddle	1.50	4.00
328	Dominik Mysterio	.75	2.00
329	Sasha Banks	10.00	25.00
330	Iron Sheik	.75	2.00
331	Undertaker	8.00	20.00
332	Don Muraco	.60	1.50
333	Molly Holly	.75	2.00
334	Andre Chase RC	.60	1.50
335	Omos	1.25	3.00
336	Brutus Creed RC	.75	2.00
337	Robert Roode	.75	2.00
338	Drew McIntyre	1.25	3.00
339	Michelle McCool	1.00	2.50
340	Ivar	.60	1.50
341	Xia Li	1.25	3.00
342	Stone Cold Steve Austin	3.00	8.00
343	Roxanne Perez RC	12.00	30.00
344	Theory	1.50	4.00
345	Paige	8.00	20.00
346	Carmelo Hayes	.75	2.00
347	Robert Stone RC	.60	1.50
348	Dude Love	1.25	3.00
349	Seth Freakin Rollins	1.50	4.00
350	Ivy Nile RC	.60	1.50
351	Xyon Quinn RC	.60	1.50
352	Josh Briggs RC	.60	1.50
353	Mr. Perfect Curt Hennig	1.25	3.00
354	Batista	1.25	3.00
355	Papa Shango	.60	1.50
356	Paul Heyman	1.00	2.50
357	Rocky Johnson	.75	2.00
358	Duke Hudson RC	.60	1.50
359	Shinsuke Nakamura	1.50	4.00
360	Jacy Jayne	8.00	20.00
361	Yulisa Leon RC	3.00	8.00
362	Kenny Williams RC	.60	1.50
363	Trish Stratus	8.00	20.00
364	Bayley	1.50	4.00
365	Primate RC	.60	1.50
366	Charlotte Flair	2.50	6.00
367	Rohan Raja RC	.60	1.50
368	Eddie Dennis RC	.60	1.50
369	Tamina	.75	2.00
370	James Drake	.60	1.50
371	Bron Breakker	8.00	20.00
372	Lacey Evans	1.50	4.00
373	Naomi	1.00	2.50
374	Becky Lynch	12.00	30.00
375	Queen Zelina	1.00	2.50
376	Superstar Billy Graham	.60	1.50
377	Roman Reigns	4.00	10.00
378	Edge	2.50	6.00
379	T-Bar	.60	1.50
380	JBL	.60	1.50
381	Ronda Rousey	8.00	20.00
382	Lash Legend RC	.60	1.50
383	Elton Prince	.75	2.00
384	Bianca Belair	2.00	5.00
385	Rampage Brown RC	.60	1.50
386	Commander Azeez	.75	2.00
387	R-Truth	.75	2.00
388	Ezekiel	.60	1.50
389	Terry Funk	1.00	2.50
390	Jey Uso	.75	2.00
391	Ken Shamrock	.75	2.00
392	Mace	.60	1.50
393	Natalya	1.00	2.50
394	Big E	1.25	3.00
395	Randy Orton	1.50	4.00
396	Corey Graves	.60	1.50

397 Sami Zayn	1.00	2.50
398 Kit Wilson	.60	1.50
399 The Miz	1.00	2.50
400 Jim The Anvil Neidhart	.75	2.00

2022 Select WWE Autographed Memorabilia

*TIE-DYE/25: UNPRICED DUE TO SCARCITY
*GOLD/10: UNPRICED DUE TO SCARCITY
*BLACK/1: UNPRICED DUE TO SCARCITY
STATED PRINT RUN 199 SER.#'d SETS
B.LESNAR SER.#'d TO 49 CARDS

AMABL Alexa Bliss/199	50.00	125.00
AMACR Apollo Crews/199	8.00	20.00
AMADK Angelo Dawkins/199	6.00	15.00
AMAJS AJ Styles/199	12.00	30.00
AMASK Asuka/199	30.00	75.00
AMBBL Bianca Belair/199	15.00	40.00
AMBGE Big E EXCH/199		
AMBLS Brock Lesnar/49	50.00	125.00
AMBLS The All Mighty Bobby Lashley/199	12.00	30.00
AMBLY Becky Lynch/199	30.00	75.00
AMBLY Bayley EXCH/199	25.00	60.00
AMCFL Charlotte Flair/199	25.00	60.00
AMCML Carmella/199	20.00	50.00
AMDBK Dana Brooke/199	10.00	25.00
AMDMI Drew McIntyre/199	10.00	25.00
AMDMY Dominik Mysterio/199	6.00	15.00
AMDPS Damian Priest/199	6.00	15.00
AMEDG Edge/199	30.00	75.00
AMFBL Finn Balor/199	15.00	40.00
AMJMU Jimmy Uso/199	10.00	25.00
AMJUS Jey Uso/199	10.00	25.00
AMKKG Kofi Kingston/199	6.00	15.00
AMKOW Kevin Owens/199	15.00	40.00
AMLVM Liv Morgan/199	60.00	150.00
AMMIZ The Miz/199	15.00	40.00
AMRDL Riddle/199	15.00	40.00
AMRHR Rhea Ripley/199	25.00	60.00
AMRMY Rey Mysterio/199	15.00	40.00
AMROR Randy Orton EXCH/199	30.00	75.00
AMRRN Roman Reigns/199	40.00	100.00
AMSBK Sasha Banks/199	60.00	150.00
AMSHM Sheamus/199	8.00	20.00
AMSHZ Shotzi/199	30.00	75.00
AMSKN Shinsuke Nakamura/199	10.00	25.00
AMSRL Seth Freakin Rollins/199	15.00	40.00

2022 Select WWE Championship

*FLASH: .5X TO 1.2X BASIC CARDS
*SILVER: .6X TO 1.5X BASIC CARDS
*GOLD/10: UNPRICED DUE TO SCARCITY
*BLACK/1: UNPRICED DUE TO SCARCITY
RANDOMLY INSERTED INTO PACKS

1 The All Mighty Bobby Lashley	1.25	3.00
2 Undertaker	3.00	8.00
3 Randy Orton	1.50	4.00
4 Becky Lynch	2.50	6.00
5 Stone Cold Steve Austin	3.00	8.00
6 John Cena	2.00	5.00
7 The Rock	6.00	15.00
8 Brock Lesnar	3.00	8.00
9 Roman Reigns	4.00	10.00
10 Charlotte Flair	2.50	6.00

2022 Select WWE Global Icons

*FLASH: .5X TO 1.2X BASIC CARDS
*SILVER: .6X TO 1.5X BASIC CARDS
*GOLD/10: UNPRICED DUE TO SCARCITY
*BLACK/1: UNPRICED DUE TO SCARCITY
RANDOMLY INSERTED INTO PACKS

1 Finn Balor	2.00	5.00
2 Hacksaw Jim Duggan	1.00	2.50
3 Bret "Hit Man" Hart	2.00	5.00
4 The Great Khali	1.00	2.50
5 Sheamus	1.25	3.00
6 Gunther	2.00	5.00
7 Trish Stratus	4.00	10.00
8 Drew McIntyre	1.50	4.00
9 Pat Patterson	.75	2.00
10 Iron Sheik	1.00	2.50
11 Meiko Satomura	2.50	6.00
12 The British Bulldog	1.25	3.00
13 Becky Lynch	3.00	8.00
14 Asuka	3.00	8.00
15 Yokozuna	1.00	2.50
16 Rey Mysterio	2.00	5.00
17 Shinsuke Nakamura	2.00	5.00
18 Andre The Giant	3.00	8.00
19 Kevin Owens	1.50	4.00
20 Hulk Hogan	4.00	10.00

2022 Select WWE Hall of Fame Selections

*FLASH: .5X TO 1.2X BASIC CARDS
*SILVER: .6X TO 1.5X BASIC CARDS
*GOLD/10: UNPRICED DUE TO SCARCITY
*BLACK/1: UNPRICED DUE TO SCARCITY
RANDOMLY INSERTED INTO PACKS

1 Stone Cold Steve Austin	3.00	8.00
2 Booker T	1.25	3.00
3 Shawn Michaels	2.50	6.00
4 Ultimate Warrior	2.50	6.00
5 Trish Stratus	3.00	8.00
6 Macho Man Randy Savage	2.50	6.00
7 Kevin Nash	1.00	2.50
8 Edge	2.50	6.00
9 Ricky "The Dragon" Steamboat	1.25	3.00
10 Dusty Rhodes	1.50	4.00
11 Eddie Guerrero	2.00	5.00
12 Mick Foley	1.25	3.00
13 The British Bulldog	1.00	2.50
14 Rikishi	.75	2.00
15 Superstar Billy Graham	.60	1.50
16 Jerry Lawler	1.25	3.00
17 Hulk Hogan	3.00	8.00
18 Bret "Hit Man" Hart	1.50	4.00
19 Mr. Perfect Curt Hennig	1.25	3.00
20 Million Dollar Man Ted DiBiase	1.00	2.50

2022 Select WWE Legendary Signatures

*RED WAVE: SAME VALUE AS BASIC
*RED/99: .5X TO 1.2X BASIC AUTOS
*BLUE/49: .6X TO 1.5X BASIC AUTOS
*TIE-DYE/25: UNPRICED DUE TO SCARCITY
*GOLD/10: UNPRICED DUE TO SCARCITY
*GOLD WAVE/5: UNPRICED DUE TO SCARCITY
*BLACK/1: UNPRICED DUE TO SCARCITY
RANDOMLY INSERTED INTO PACKS

LSBKT Booker T	12.00	30.00
LSBPH Beth Phoenix	8.00	20.00
LSHHH Triple H	100.00	250.00
LSJCN John Cena EXCH	50.00	125.00
LSKNE Kane	10.00	25.00
LSLTA Lita	12.00	30.00
LSNBL Nikki Bella	12.00	30.00
LSRKI Rikishi	8.00	20.00
LSSCA Stone Cold Steve Austin	100.00	250.00
LSUND Undertaker	100.00	250.00

2022 Select WWE NXT 2.0

*FLASH: .5X TO 1.2X BASIC CARDS
*SILVER: .6X TO 1.5X BASIC CARDS
*GOLD/10: UNPRICED DUE TO SCARCITY
*BLACK/1: UNPRICED DUE TO SCARCITY
RANDOMLY INSERTED INTO PACKS

1 Gigi Dolin	2.50	6.00
2 LA Knight	1.00	2.50
3 Carmelo Hayes	.75	2.00
4 Raquel Rodriguez	1.50	4.00
5 Ilja Dragunov	.60	1.50
6 Ludwig Kaiser	.75	2.00
7 Dakota Kai	1.25	3.00
8 Nikkita Lyons	1.50	4.00
9 Gunther	1.50	4.00
10 Jordan Devlin	.60	1.50
11 Bron Breakker	2.50	6.00
12 Cameron Grimes	1.25	3.00
13 Ciampa	1.50	4.00
14 Jacy Jayne	1.50	4.00
15 Meiko Satomura	2.00	5.00
16 Fabian Aichner	.75	2.00
17 Grayson Waller	1.50	4.00
18 Santos Escobar	1.00	2.50
19 Mandy Rose	3.00	8.00
20 Io Shirai	1.25	3.00

2022 Select WWE Phenomenon

*FLASH: .5X TO 1.2X BASIC CARDS
*SILVER: .6X TO 1.5X BASIC CARDS
*GOLD/10: UNPRICED DUE TO SCARCITY
*BLACK/1: UNPRICED DUE TO SCARCITY
RANDOMLY INSERTED INTO PACKS

1 Finn Balor	1.50	4.00
2 Bianca Belair	2.00	5.00
3 Omos	1.25	3.00
4 AJ Styles	2.00	5.00
5 Rey Mysterio	1.50	4.00
6 Seth Freakin Rollins	1.50	4.00
7 Shawn Michaels	2.50	6.00
8 Big E	1.25	3.00
9 Mankind	1.25	3.00
10 Stone Cold Steve Austin	3.00	8.00
11 Rob Van Dam	1.25	3.00
12 Becky Lynch	2.50	6.00
13 Kofi Kingston	1.50	4.00
14 Randy Orton	1.50	4.00
15 Roman Reigns	4.00	10.00
16 Kevin Owens	1.25	3.00
17 Shinsuke Nakamura	1.50	4.00
18 Undertaker	3.00	8.00
19 Drew McIntyre	1.25	3.00
20 The Miz	1.00	2.50
21 Edge	2.50	6.00
22 Rhea Ripley	2.00	5.00
23 Xavier Woods	.75	2.00
24 Riddle	1.50	4.00
25 Sheamus	1.00	2.50
26 Brock Lesnar	3.00	8.00
27 Sasha Banks	4.00	10.00
28 The Rock	6.00	15.00
29 Bron Breakker	2.50	6.00
30 Charlotte Flair	2.50	6.00

2022 Select WWE Ringside Action Signatures

*RED WAVE: .5X TO 1.2X BASIC AUTOS
*RED/99: .6X TO 1.5X BASIC AUTOS
*BLUE/49: .75X TO 2X BASIC AUTOS
*TIE-DYE/25: UNPRICED DUE TO SCARCITY
*GOLD/10: UNPRICED DUE TO SCARCITY
*GOLD WAVE/5: UNPRICED DUE TO SCARCITY
*BLACK/1: UNPRICED DUE TO SCARCITY
RANDOMLY INSERTED INTO PACKS

RAABL Alexa Bliss	50.00	125.00
RAACR Apollo Crews	6.00	15.00
RABBK Bron Breakker	30.00	75.00
RABDV Blair Davenport	10.00	25.00
RABGE Big E	8.00	20.00
RABLY Bayley	15.00	40.00
RACAZ Commander Azeez	5.00	12.00
RACFL Charlotte Flair	25.00	60.00
RACGR Cameron Grimes	8.00	20.00
RACHY Carmelo Hayes	10.00	25.00
RACJD Cora Jade	40.00	100.00
RADDR Doudrop	8.00	20.00
RADGL Drew Gulak	5.00	12.00
RADKI Dakota Kai	15.00	40.00
RADMI Drew McIntyre	12.00	30.00
RADZG Dolph Ziggler	8.00	20.00
RAFBL Finn Balor	12.00	30.00
RAGTH Gunther	12.00	30.00
RAGWL Grayson Waller	10.00	25.00
RAIVR Ivar	5.00	12.00
RAJDV Jordan Devlin	6.00	15.00
RAJMH Jinder Mahal	8.00	20.00
RAJUS Jey Uso	10.00	25.00
RAKCT Katana Chance	10.00	25.00
RAKWD Xavier Woods	5.00	12.00
RALAK LA Knight	8.00	20.00
RALEV Lacey Evans	10.00	25.00
RAMIZ The Miz	8.00	20.00
RAMZF Montez Ford	8.00	20.00
RANKA Nikki A.S.H.	6.00	15.00
RANOM Naomi	6.00	15.00
RAOMS Omos	6.00	15.00
RARCC Ricochet	8.00	20.00
RARGE Reggie	5.00	12.00
RARHD Ridge Holland	5.00	12.00
RARMY Rey Mysterio	15.00	40.00
RARQG Raquel Rodriguez	12.00	30.00
RARRD Robert Roode	6.00	15.00
RARRN Roman Reigns	40.00	100.00
RASBZ Shayna Baszler	10.00	25.00
RASKN Shinsuke Nakamura	8.00	20.00
RASRL Seth Freakin Rollins	12.00	30.00
RAVWG Von Wagner	6.00	15.00
RAXLI Xia Li	12.00	30.00

2022 Select WWE Selective Swatches

*TIE-DYE/25: UNPRICED DUE TO SCARCITY
*GOLD/10: UNPRICED DUE TO SCARCITY
*BLACK/1: UNPRICED DUE TO SCARCITY
RANDOMLY INSERTED INTO PACKS

SWABL Alexa Bliss	12.00	30.00
SWACR Apollo Crews	3.00	8.00

SWADK Angelo Dawkins	2.50	6.00
SWAJS AJ Styles	5.00	12.00
SWASK Asuka	5.00	12.00
SWBBL Bianca Belair	4.00	10.00
SWBLS The All Mighty Bobby Lashley	3.00	8.00
SWBLS Brock Lesnar	5.00	12.00
SWBLY Becky Lynch	10.00	25.00
SWCFL Charlotte Flair	6.00	15.00
SWCML Carmella	5.00	12.00
SWDBK Dana Brooke	2.50	6.00
SWDMI Drew McIntyre	3.00	8.00
SWDMY Dominik Mysterio	2.50	6.00
SWDPS Damian Priest	2.50	6.00
SWEDG Edge	4.00	10.00
SWFBL Finn Balor	5.00	12.00
SWJMU Jimmy Uso	4.00	10.00
SWJUS Jey Uso	4.00	10.00
SWKKG Kofi Kingston	3.00	8.00
SWKOW Kevin Owens	4.00	10.00
SWLVM Liv Morgan	12.00	30.00
SWMIZ The Miz	2.50	6.00
SWRDL Riddle	3.00	8.00
SWRHR Rhea Ripley	5.00	12.00
SWRKO Randy Orton	3.00	8.00
SWRMY Rey Mysterio	3.00	8.00
SWRRN Roman Reigns	6.00	15.00
SWSBK Sasha Banks	8.00	20.00
SWSHM Sheamus	4.00	10.00
SWSHZ Shotzi	6.00	15.00
SWSKN Shinsuke Nakamura	3.00	8.00
SWSRL Seth Freakin Rollins	3.00	8.00

2022 Select WWE Signature Selections

*FLASH: X TO X BASIC AUTOS
*TIE-DYE/25: UNPRICED DUE TO SCARCITY
*GOLD/10: UNPRICED DUE TO SCARCITY
*GOLD FLASH/10: UNPRICED DUE TO SCARCITY
*BLACK/1: UNPRICED DUE TO SCARCITY
*BLACK FLASH/1: UNPRICED DUE TO SCARCITY
RANDOMLY INSERTED INTO PACKS
BLASTER EXCLUSIVE

SNAKD A-Kid	8.00	20.00
SNALB Alundra Blayze		
SNAML Amale	10.00	25.00
SNAOF Aoife Valkyrie	10.00	25.00
SNBBF Brutus Beefcake	10.00	25.00
SNBBK Bron Breakker	30.00	75.00
SNBBL Brie Bella	15.00	40.00
SNBCD Brutus Creed	10.00	25.00
SNBDV Blair Davenport	10.00	25.00
SNBLS Brock Lesnar	100.00	250.00
SNBLY Becky Lynch	60.00	150.00
SNBOA Boa	5.00	12.00
SNBTA Batista		
SNBWB Bushwhacker Butch	6.00	15.00
SNBWL Bushwhacker Luke	6.00	15.00
SNCBO Cowboy Bob Orton	6.00	15.00
SNCGR Cameron Grimes	8.00	20.00
SNCHY Carmelo Hayes	10.00	25.00
SNCJD Cora Jade	40.00	100.00
SNCLR Candice LeRae	12.00	30.00
SNDLM Dexter Lumis	8.00	20.00
SNDLN Dani Luna	8.00	20.00
SNDMI Drew McIntyre	12.00	30.00
SNDMS Dave Mastiff	5.00	12.00
SNEDG Edge	30.00	75.00
SNEMK Emilia McKenzie	8.00	20.00
SNEPC Elton Prince	8.00	20.00
SNFAI Fabian Aichner	5.00	12.00
SNFBL Finn Balor	12.00	30.00
SNFMW Flash Morgan Webster	5.00	12.00
SNGBS Gerald Brisco	8.00	20.00
SNGHV Greg Valentine	10.00	25.00
SNGSV Gable Steveson	40.00	100.00
SNGTH Gunther	12.00	30.00
SNGWL Grayson Waller	10.00	25.00
SNHCN The Hurricane	8.00	20.00
SNHHG Hulk Hogan	150.00	400.00
SNIHW Indi Hartwell	15.00	40.00
SNILU Brother Love	15.00	40.00
SNINY Ivy Nile		
SNIOS Io Shirai	12.00	30.00
SNISH Iron Sheik		
SNJBL JBL	8.00	20.00
SNJCD Julius Creed	12.00	30.00
SNJCF Joe Coffey	5.00	12.00
SNJDK James Drake	8.00	20.00
SNJDV Jordan Devlin	6.00	15.00
SNJHT Jimmy Hart	12.00	30.00
SNJJN Jacy Jayne	25.00	60.00
SNJKL Jerry Lawler	25.00	60.00
SNJNY Jinny EXCH	6.00	15.00
SNJWD Joaquin Wilde	6.00	15.00
SNKCY Katana Chance	10.00	25.00
SNKDC Kayden Carter	10.00	25.00
SNKLR Alba Fyre		
SNKLY Kelly Kelly	10.00	25.00
SNKNY Kenny Williams	5.00	12.00
SNKSH Kushida	5.00	12.00
SNKWS Kit Wilson	6.00	15.00
SNLSH Lash Legend	6.00	15.00
SNLXL Lex Luger		
SNMAD Mark Andrews	5.00	12.00
SNMBL Ludwig Kaiser	6.00	15.00
SNMCF Mark Coffey	5.00	12.00
SNMHL Molly Holly	10.00	25.00
SNMHY Michael Hayes	8.00	20.00
SNMKS Meiko Satomura	10.00	25.00
SNMRS Mandy Rose	40.00	100.00
SNNMD Noam Dar	6.00	15.00
SNNOM Naomi	6.00	15.00
SNODY Odyssey Jones	8.00	20.00
SNPDN Pete Dunne	10.00	25.00
SNPGE Paige	60.00	150.00
SNPSA Persia Pirotta	10.00	25.00
SNRKO Randy Orton EXCH		
SNRMY Rey Mysterio	15.00	40.00
SNRPB Rampage Brown	6.00	15.00
SNRQG Raquel Rodriguez	12.00	30.00
SNRRD Robert Roode	6.00	15.00
SNRRN Roman Reigns	40.00	100.00
SNRST Roderick Strong	8.00	20.00
SNRVD Rob Van Dam		
SNSGS Sgt. Slaughter	12.00	30.00
SNSHB Sasha Banks	40.00	100.00
SNSHM Shawn Michaels	60.00	150.00
SNSHY Shanky	6.00	15.00
SNSRL Seth Freakin Rollins	20.00	50.00
SNSRY Sarray	12.00	30.00
SNSTN Stevie Turner	10.00	25.00
SNTBT Tyler Bate EXCH	6.00	15.00
SNTEO Teoman	5.00	12.00
SNTSV Trent Seven	6.00	15.00
SNVWG Von Wagner	6.00	15.00
SNWFG Wolfgang	6.00	15.00
SNWSL Wes Lee	6.00	15.00
SNXLI Xia Li	12.00	30.00
SNXQN Xyon Quinn	6.00	15.00
SNZGB Zack Gibson		
SNZST Zoey Stark	10.00	25.00

2022 Select WWE Signatures

*RED WAVE: X TO X BASIC AUTOS
*RED/99: X TO X BASIC AUTOS
*BLUE/49: X TO X BASIC AUTOS
*TIE-DYE/25: UNPRICED DUE TO SCARCITY
*GOLD/10: UNPRICED DUE TO SCARCITY
*GOLD WAVE/5: UNPRICED DUE TO SCARCITY
*BLACK/1: UNPRICED DUE TO SCARCITY
RANDOMLY INSERTED INTO PACKS

SGADW Angelo Dawkins	5.00	12.00
SGAJS AJ Styles	20.00	50.00
SGASK Asuka	30.00	75.00
SGATH Theory	8.00	20.00
SGBBL Bianca Belair	20.00	50.00
SGBLS Brock Lesnar	100.00	250.00
SGBLS The All Mighty Bobby Lashley	10.00	25.00
SGBLY Becky Lynch	60.00	150.00
SGCML Carmella	15.00	40.00
SGDBK Dana Brooke	10.00	25.00
SGDMY Dominik Mysterio	10.00	25.00
SGDPS Damian Priest	10.00	25.00
SGEDG Edge	30.00	75.00
SGELS Ezekiel	8.00	20.00
SGERK Erik	5.00	12.00
SGGGD Gigi Dolin	50.00	100.00
SGHCB Happy Corbin	10.00	25.00
SGIOS Io Shirai	12.00	30.00
SGJGC Joe Gacy		
SGJMU Jimmy Uso	10.00	25.00
SGKKG Kofi Kingston	10.00	25.00
SGKLR Alba Fyre		
SGKOW Kevin Owens	15.00	40.00
SGKSH Kushida	5.00	12.00
SGLVM Liv Morgan	40.00	100.00
SGMKS Meiko Satomura	10.00	25.00
SGMRS Mandy Rose	40.00	100.00
SGMSR Mansoor	6.00	15.00
SGMVP MVP	6.00	15.00
SGNTY Natalya	12.00	30.00
SGOTS Otis	8.00	20.00
SGPDN Pete Dunne	10.00	25.00
SGQZL Queen Zelina	15.00	40.00
SGRBG Rick Boogs	8.00	20.00
SGRDL Riddle	15.00	40.00
SGRHR Rhea Ripley	30.00	75.00
SGRKO Randy Orton		
SGSBK Sasha Banks	4.00	10.00
SGSDV Sonya Deville	15.00	40.00
SGSES Santos Escobar	10.00	25.00
SGSHM Sheamus	10.00	25.00
SGSHZ Shotzi	25.00	60.00
SGSZN Sami Zayn	12.00	30.00
SGTMC Ciampa		
SGVMH Veer Mahaan	12.00	30.00

2022 Select WWE Sparks

*TIE-DYE/25: UNPRICED DUE TO SCARCITY
*GOLD/10: UNPRICED DUE TO SCARCITY
*BLACK/1: UNPRICED DUE TO SCARCITY
RANDOMLY INSERTED INTO PACKS

1 Becky Lynch	10.00	25.00
2 Roman Reigns	8.00	20.00
3 Kofi Kingston	3.00	8.00
4 Rey Mysterio	5.00	12.00
5 Shinsuke Nakamura	5.00	12.00
6 Damian Priest	3.00	8.00
7 Shotzi	6.00	15.00
8 Bianca Belair	6.00	15.00
9 Brock Lesnar	4.00	10.00
10 Liv Morgan	12.00	30.00
12 Edge	5.00	12.00
13 The All Mighty Bobby Lashley	3.00	8.00
14 Sasha Banks	10.00	25.00
15 The Miz	3.00	8.00
16 Seth Freakin Rollins	3.00	8.00
17 AJ Styles	4.00	10.00
18 Asuka	4.00	10.00
19 Jimmy Uso	2.50	6.00
20 Rhea Ripley	8.00	20.00
21 Charlotte Flair	5.00	12.00
22 Drew McIntyre	3.00	8.00
23 Jey Uso	2.50	6.00
24 Apollo Crews	2.50	6.00
25 Randy Orton	3.00	8.00
26 Carmella	4.00	10.00
27 Alexa Bliss	12.00	30.00
28 Finn Balor	4.00	10.00
29 Kevin Owens	3.00	8.00

2006 7-11 WWE Slam Philippines

COMPLETE SET (36)	20.00	50.00
1 Finlay	.75	2.00
2 William Regal	.75	2.00
3 Batista	1.25	3.00
4 Matt Hardy	.75	2.00
5 Lashley	.75	2.00
6 Rey Mysterio	1.25	3.00
7 Brian Kendrick	.30	.75
8 Paul London	.30	.75
9 Vito	.30	.75
10 Michelle McCool	1.50	4.00
11 Mr. Kennedy	.75	2.00
12 Booker T	.75	2.00
13 Undertaker	1.50	4.00
14 Ashley	1.25	3.00
15 Big Show	1.25	3.00
16 Rob Van Dam	.75	2.00
17 Nitro	.50	1.25
18 Hulk Hogan	2.00	5.00
19 Edge	1.25	3.00
20 Ric Flair	1.50	4.00
21 Carlito	1.25	3.00
22 Umaga	.50	1.25
23 Torrie Wilson	3.00	8.00
24 John Cena	2.00	5.00
25 Randy Orton	.75	2.00
26 Kane	1.25	3.00
27 Candice Michelle	2.00	5.00
28 Mickie James	2.00	5.00
29 Triple H	2.00	5.00
30 Shawn Michaels	2.00	5.00
31 Undertaker	1.50	4.00
32 Rey Mysterio	1.25	3.00
33 Batista	1.25	3.00
34 Triple H	2.00	5.00
35 John Cena	2.00	5.00
36 Shawn Michaels	2.00	5.00

1997 Stridex WWF

COMPLETE SET (7)	8.00	20.00
NNO Header Card	.75	2.00
NNO Ahmed Johnson	.75	2.00
NNO Bret Hit Man Hart	2.00	5.00
NNO Shawn Michaels	2.00	5.00
NNO Stone Cold Steve Austin	3.00	8.00
NNO Sycho Sid	1.25	3.00
NNO Undertaker	3.00	8.00

1987 Stuart WWF Canadian

COMPLETE SET (16)	15.00	40.00
*CUT: X TO X BASIC CARDS		
1 Brutus The Barber Beefcake	1.25	3.00
2 Les Freres Rougeau Brothers	1.00	2.50
3 Strike Force	1.25	3.00
4 The Honky Tonk Man	1.25	3.00
5 Randy Savage with Elizabeth	4.00	10.00
6 Hulk Hogan	6.00	15.00
7 Demolition	1.25	3.00
8 Koko B. Ware	1.00	2.50
9 Ted DiBiase UER	1.50	4.00
10 Slick The Doctor of Style	1.25	3.00
11 British Bulldogs	1.25	3.00
12 Bobby The Brain Heenan	1.50	4.00
13 Jimmy Hart	1.25	3.00
14 George The Animal Steele	1.50	4.00
15 Jake The Snake Roberts	2.00	5.00
16 The Junk Yard Dog	1.25	3.00

1991 Swanson WWF Wrestling Canadian

COMPLETE SET (12)	30.00	75.00
NNO Big Boss Man	3.00	8.00
NNO Bret Hitman Hart	5.00	12.00
NNO The Bushwhackers	4.00	10.00
NNO Hulk Hogan	8.00	20.00
NNO Jake The Snake Roberts	2.50	6.00
NNO Legion of Doom	5.00	12.00
NNO Macho Man Randy Savage	6.00	15.00
NNO Million Dollar Man Ted DiBiase	3.00	8.00
NNO The Mountie	2.50	6.00
NNO Rockers Marty and Shawn	5.00	12.00
NNO Texas Tornado	2.50	6.00
NNO Ultimate Warrior	6.00	15.00

1994 Titan Sports WWF Vending Hologram Stickers

COMPLETE SET (10)	8.00	20.00
NNO Adam Bomb	1.00	2.50
NNO Bret Hitman Hart	2.00	5.00
NNO Doink	1.00	2.50
NNO Lex Luger	1.50	4.00
NNO Ludvig Borga	1.00	2.50
NNO Macho Man Randy Savage	2.00	5.00
NNO Razor Ramon	1.25	3.00
NNO Tatanka	1.00	2.50
NNO Undertaker	3.00	8.00
NNO Yokozuna	1.25	3.00

2013 Topps Best of WWE

COMPLETE SET (110)	8.00	20.00
UNOPENED BOX (24 PACKS)		
UNOPENED PACK (7 CARDS)		
*BLUE: .6X TO 1.5X BASIC CARDS		
*BRONZE: .6X TO 1.5X BASIC CARDS		
*SILVER: 2.5X TO 6X BASIC CARDS		
*GOLD/10: 5X TO 12X BASIC CARDS		
*P.P.BLACK/1: UNPRICED DUE TO SCARCITY		
*P.P.CYAN/1: UNPRICED DUE TO SCARCITY		
*P.P.MAGENTA/1: UNPRICED DUE TO SCARCITY		
*P.P.YELLOW/1: UNPRICED DUE TO SCARCITY		
1 The Rock	.75	2.00
2 Brock Lesnar/John Cena	.75	2.00
3 Daniel Bryan/AJ Lee	.75	2.00
4 Dusty Rhodes/Cody Rhodes	.25	.60
5 AJ Lee/Kaitlyn	.75	2.00
6 Layla/Nikki Bella	.30	.75
7 Cody Rhodes	.15	.40
8 CM Punk/Chris Jericho	.60	1.50
9 John Cena/Brock Lesnar	.75	2.00
10 Brock Lesnar/Triple H	.60	1.50
11 Kofi Kingston/R-Truth	.15	.40
12 Damien Sandow	.15	.40
13 John Laurinaitis/Big Show	.30	.75
14 Christian/Cody Rhodes	.15	.40
15 John Laurinaitis/John Cena	.75	2.00
16 AJ Lee/Kane	.75	2.00
17 Big Show/Mr. McMahon	.30	.75
18 CM Punk/Kane	.60	1.50
19 John Cena/John Laurinaitis	.75	2.00
20 Dolph Ziggler/Jack Swagger	.25	.60
21 AJ Lee	.75	2.00
22 Zack Ryder	.15	.40
23 AJ Lee/CM Punk	.75	2.00
24 Dolph Ziggler	.25	.60
25 John Cena	.75	2.00
26 AJ Lee/Daniel Bryan	.75	2.00
27 D-Generation X	.60	1.50
28 Dude Love/Brodus Clay	.60	1.50
29 Trish Stratus/Triple H	.75	2.00
30 AJ Lee/Daniel Bryan	.75	2.00
31 The Miz/Christian	.25	.60
32 APA/Heath Slater	.15	.40
33 Undertaker/Kane	.60	1.50
34 John Cena/Big Show	.75	2.00
35 CM Punk/The Rock	.75	2.00
36 Daniel Bryan	.40	1.00
37 Mr.McMahon/Booker T	.25	.60
38 Daniel Bryan	.40	1.00
39 Brock Lesnar/Shawn Michaels	.60	1.50
40 Antonio Cesaro/Santino Marella	.15	.40
41 Daniel Bryan/Kane	.40	1.00
42 Brock Lesnar/Triple H	.60	1.50
43 Dolph Ziggler/Chris Jericho	.60	1.50
44 Daniel Bryan/Kane	.40	1.00
45 CM Punk/Jerry Lawler	.60	1.50
46 Kane/Daniel Bryan	.40	1.00
47 CM Punk/Paul Heyman	.60	1.50
48 Kaitlyn	.30	.75
49 Kane/Bryan/Truth	.40	1.00
50 Eve	.60	1.50
51 CM Punk/John Cena	.75	2.00
52 CM Punk/Mr. McMahon	.60	1.50
53 Kofi Kingston/The Miz	.25	.60
54 AJ Lee/Vickie Guerrero	.75	2.00
55 Big Show/Sheamus	.30	.75
56 Brad Maddox/Ryback	.15	.40
57 Vickie Guerrero/John Cena	.75	2.00
58 Big Show/Sheamus	.30	.75
59 Randy Orton/Alberto Del Rio	.50	1.25
60 CM Punk/Jerry Lawler	.60	1.50
61 Ryback/Brad Maddox	.15	.40
62 Team Ziggler/Team Foley	.25	.60
63 Shield/Cena/Ryback	.75	2.00
64 John Cena/AJ Lee	.75	2.00
65 John Cena/Dolph Ziggler	.75	2.00
66 Vicki/AJ Lee/Maddox	.75	2.00
67 Cody Rhodes	.15	.40
68 Reigns/Bryan/Ambrose	.40	1.00
69 AJ Lee/Cena/Ziggler	.75	2.00
70 Big E Langston/John Cena	.75	2.00
71 8 Divas	.60	1.50
72 John Cena/Alberto Del Rio	.75	2.00
73 Great Khali	.15	.40
74 Wade Barrett/Kofi Kingston	.15	.40
75 Dolph Ziggler/AJ Lee	.75	2.00
76 Antonio Cesaro/Great Khali	.15	.40
77 CM Punk/Ryback	.60	1.50
78 The Rock/CM Punk	.75	2.00
79 Alberto Del Rio/Big Show	.30	.75
80 Kaitlyn/Eve	.60	1.50
81 Kane/Daniel Bryan	.40	1.00
82 Chris Jericho	.60	1.50
83 Bo Dallas	.15	.40
84 John Cena	.75	2.00
85 The Rock/CM Punk	.75	2.00
86 Brock Lesnar/Mr. McMahon	.60	1.50
87 Jack Swagger	.25	.60
88 Roman Reigns/Ryback	.25	.60
89 The Rock/CM Punk	.75	2.00
90 Vickie Guerrero/Brad Maddox	.25	.60
91 The Rock	.75	2.00
92 Heyman/McMahon/Brock/HHH	.60	1.50
93 John Cena/CM Punk	.75	2.00
94 The Deadman	.60	1.50
95 Ted Dibiase	.25	.60
96 Outlaws/Primo/Epico	.15	.40
97 CM Punk/Randy Orton	.60	1.50
98 Undertaker	.60	1.50
99 Brie Bella/Nikki Bella	.60	1.50
100 CM Punk/Undertaker	.60	1.50
101 Mick Foley/Chris Jericho	.60	1.50
102 Trish Stratus	.75	2.00
103 Booker T	.25	.60
104 Bob Backlund	.40	1.00
105 Bruno Sammartino	.40	1.00
106 The Miz/Wade Barrett	.25	.60
107 Fandango/Chris Jericho	.60	1.50
108 Undertaker/CM Punk	.60	1.50
109 Triple H/Brock Lesnar	.60	1.50
110 John Cena/The Rock	.75	2.00

2013 Topps Best of WWE Autographs

STATED ODDS 1:48 HOBBY AND RETAIL		
NNO American Dream Dusty Rhodes	200.00	400.00
NNO Big E Langston	30.00	75.00
NNO Bob Backlund	15.00	40.00
NNO Brie Bella	15.00	40.00
NNO Bruno Sammartino	75.00	150.00
NNO Cactus Jack	15.00	40.00
NNO Damien Sandow	10.00	25.00
NNO Dean Ambrose	30.00	75.00
NNO Dude Love	150.00	300.00
NNO JBL	10.00	25.00
NNO Lilian Garcia	20.00	50.00
NNO Mankind	50.00	100.00
NNO Mick Foley	20.00	50.00
NNO Nikki Bella	15.00	40.00
NNO Paul Heyman	30.00	75.00
NNO Roman Reigns	150.00	300.00
NNO Seth Rollins	100.00	200.00
NNO Trish Stratus	30.00	75.00
NNO Vickie Guerrero	10.00	25.00

2013 Topps Best of WWE Dual Autographs

STATED PRINT RUN 10 SER. #'d SETS		
NNO Brie Bella/Nikki Bella	75.00	150.00
NNO B.Sammartino/B.Backlund		
NNO D.Sandow/Big E	25.00	60.00
NNO D.Ambrose/P.Heyman	60.00	120.00
NNO J.Swagger/V.Guerrero	25.00	60.00
NNO JBL/L.Garcia	50.00	100.00
NNO M.Foley/T.Stratus	50.00	100.00
NNO R.Dogg/B.Gunn	75.00	150.00
NNO S.Rollins/R.Reigns	200.00	400.00
NNO S.Michaels/X-Pac	100.00	200.00

2013 Topps Best of WWE Jerry Lawler Portraits

COMPLETE SET (10)	30.00	80.00
*P.P.BLACK/1: UNPRICED DUE TO SCARCITY		
*P.P.CYAN/1: UNPRICED DUE TO SCARCITY		
*P.P.MAGENTA/1: UNPRICED DUE TO SCARCITY		
*P.P.YELLOW/1: UNPRICED DUE TO SCARCITY		
RANDOMLY INSERTED INTO RETAIL PACKS		
1 CM Punk	6.00	15.00
2 R-Truth	1.50	4.00
3 Undertaker	6.00	15.00
4 Kane	3.00	8.00
5 Paul Bearer	2.50	6.00
6 Vickie Guerrero	2.50	6.00
7 Stone Cold Steve Austin	6.00	15.00
8 Sgt. Slaughter	2.50	6.00
9 Vader	1.50	4.00
10 Doink the Clown	1.50	4.00

2013 Topps Best of WWE Swatch Relics

STATED ODDS 1:24 HOBBY EXCLUSIVE		
NNO AJ Lee/Shirt	20.00	50.00
NNO AJ Lee/Teddy Bear	60.00	120.00
NNO Brodus Clay/Shirt	4.00	10.00
NNO CM Punk/Shirt	6.00	15.00
NNO Damien Sandow Shirt	4.00	10.00
NNO Daniel Bryan/Shirt	5.00	12.00
NNO Dean Ambrose/Shirt	5.00	12.00
NNO Dolph Ziggler/Shirt	5.00	12.00
NNO Great Khali/Referee Shirt	4.00	10.00
NNO John Cena/Hat	40.00	80.00
NNO John Cena/Headband		
NNO John Cena/Shirt	6.00	15.00
NNO John Cena/Wristband	40.00	80.00
NNO Miz/Shirt	4.00	10.00
NNO Randy Orton/Shirt	5.00	12.00
NNO Roman Reigns/Shirt	5.00	12.00
NNO Ryback/Shirt	4.00	10.00
NNO Seth Rollins/Shirt	6.00	15.00
NNO Sheamus/Shirt	4.00	10.00
NNO Wade Barrett/Shirt	4.00	10.00

2013 Topps Best of WWE Top 10 Catchphrases

COMPLETE SET (10)	4.00	10.00
*P.P.BLACK/1: UNPRICED DUE TO SCARCITY		

*P.P.CYAN/1: UNPRICED DUE TO SCARCITY
*P.P.MAGENTA/1: UNPRICED DUE TO SCARCITY
*P.P.YELLOW/1: UNPRICED DUE TO SCARCITY
STATED ODDS OVERALL 3:1 HOBBY AND RETAIL

1 The Rock/If Ya Smell	3.00	8.00
2 Undertaker/Rest in Peace	1.50	4.00
3 John Cena/You Can't See Me!	1.25	3.00
4 Booker T/Can You Dig It, Sucka?	.30	.75
5 The Miz/Because I'm the Miz...	.30	.75
6 Daniel Bryan/Yes!	.50	1.25
7 CM Punk/Best in the World	.75	2.00
8 Zack Ryder/Woo Woo Woo	.20	.50
9 Damien Sandow/You're Welcome!	.20	.50
10 Vickie Guerrero/Excuse Me!	.30	.75

2013 Topps Best of WWE Top 10 Finishers

COMPLETE SET (10) 5.00 12.00
*P.P.BLACK/1: UNPRICED DUE TO SCARCITY
*P.P.CYAN/1: UNPRICED DUE TO SCARCITY
*P.P.MAGENTA/1: UNPRICED DUE TO SCARCITY
*P.P.YELLOW/1: UNPRICED DUE TO SCARCITY
STATED ODDS OVERALL 3:1 HOBBY AND RETAIL

1 Undertaker/Tombstone	2.50	6.00
2 Stone Cold Steve Austin/Stunner	1.50	4.00
3 Randy Orton/RKO	.75	2.00
4 Shawn Michaels/Sweet Chin Music	.75	2.00
5 Triple H/Pedigree	.75	2.00
6 The Rock/Rock Bottom	1.00	2.50
7 John Cena/Attitude Adjustment	1.00	2.50
8 CM Punk/GTS	.75	2.00
9 Rey Mysterio/619	.50	1.25
10 Eddie Guerrero/Frog Splash	.20	.50

2013 Topps Best of WWE Top 10 Greatest WWE Moments

COMPLETE SET (10) 5.00 12.00
*P.P.BLACK/1: UNPRICED DUE TO SCARCITY
*P.P.CYAN/1: UNPRICED DUE TO SCARCITY
*P.P.MAGENTA/1: UNPRICED DUE TO SCARCITY
*P.P.YELLOW/1: UNPRICED DUE TO SCARCITY
STATED ODDS OVERALL 3:1 HOBBY AND RETAIL

1 Undertaker/Shawn Michaels	2.50	6.00
2 Triple H	1.50	4.00
3 John Cena	1.25	3.00
4 The Rock/John Cena	1.00	2.50
5 Eddie Guerrero/Brock Lesnar	.75	2.00
6 The Rock/Hollywood Hogan	1.00	2.50
7 John Cena/JBL	1.00	2.50
8 CM Punk	.75	2.00
9 CM Punk/John Cena	1.00	2.50
10 Mr. McMahon	.20	.50

2013 Topps Best of WWE Top 10 Intercontinental Champions

COMPLETE SET (10) 3.00 8.00
*P.P.BLACK/1: UNPRICED DUE TO SCARCITY
*P.P.CYAN/1: UNPRICED DUE TO SCARCITY
*P.P.MAGENTA/1: UNPRICED DUE TO SCARCITY
*P.P.YELLOW/1: UNPRICED DUE TO SCARCITY
STATED ODDS OVERALL 3:1 HOBBY AND RETAIL

1 Randy Orton	2.00	5.00
2 Rey Mysterio	1.00	2.50
3 Christian	.25	.60
4 Kofi Kingston	.20	.50
5 Cody Rhodes	.20	.50
6 Wade Barrett	.20	.50
7 Dolph Ziggler	.30	.75
8 William Regal	.25	.60
9 Santino Marella	.20	.50
10 Ezekiel Jackson	.20	.50

2013 Topps Best of WWE Top 10 Rivalries

COMPLETE SET (10) 5.00 12.00
*P.P.BLACK/1: UNPRICED DUE TO SCARCITY
*P.P.CYAN/1: UNPRICED DUE TO SCARCITY
*P.P.MAGENTA/1: UNPRICED DUE TO SCARCITY
*P.P.YELLOW/1: UNPRICED DUE TO SCARCITY
STATED ODDS OVERALL 3:1 HOBBY AND RETAIL

1 Shawn Michaels/Undertaker	2.50	6.00
2 Undertaker/Triple H	1.50	4.00
3 John Cena/The Rock	1.25	3.00
4 Undertaker/Kane	.75	2.00
5 CM Punk/John Cena	1.00	2.50
6 Triple H/Shawn Michaels	.75	2.00
7 Triple H/Randy Orton	.75	2.00
8 John Cena/Brock Lesnar	1.00	2.50
9 Triple H/Batista	.75	2.00
10 Rey Mysterio/Eddie Guerrero	.50	1.25

2013 Topps Best of WWE Top 10 Trash Talkers

COMPLETE SET (10) 5.00 12.00
*P.P.BLACK/1: UNPRICED DUE TO SCARCITY
*P.P.CYAN/1: UNPRICED DUE TO SCARCITY
*P.P.MAGENTA/1: UNPRICED DUE TO SCARCITY
*P.P.YELLOW/1: UNPRICED DUE TO SCARCITY
STATED ODDS OVERALL 3:1 HOBBY AND RETAIL

1 Stone Cold Steve Austin	2.50	6.00
2 The Rock	2.00	5.00
3 CM Punk	1.00	2.50
4 Triple H	.75	2.00
5 Rowdy Roddy Piper	.50	1.25
6 John Cena	1.00	2.50
7 The Miz	.30	.75
8 Shawn Michaels	.75	2.00
9 Paul Heyman	.20	.50
10 AJ Lee	1.00	2.50

2013 Topps Best of WWE Top 10 2K14

COMPLETE SET (10) 60.00 120.00
RANDOMLY INSERTED INTO PACKS

1 John Cena	15.00	40.00
2 Triple H	8.00	20.00
3 The Rock	20.00	50.00
4 Undertaker	10.00	25.00
5 CM Punk		
6 Sheamus		
7 Brock Lesnar	8.00	20.00
8 Eddie Guerrero	8.00	20.00
9 The Miz	6.00	15.00
10 JBL	6.00	15.00

2013 Topps Best of WWE Top 10 Undertaker Matches

COMPLETE SET (10) 5.00 12.00
*P.P.BLACK/1: UNPRICED DUE TO SCARCITY
*P.P.CYAN/1: UNPRICED DUE TO SCARCITY
*P.P.MAGENTA/1: UNPRICED DUE TO SCARCITY
*P.P.YELLOW/1: UNPRICED DUE TO SCARCITY
STATED ODDS OVERALL 3:1 HOBBY AND RETAIL

1 Vs. Triple H	2.50	6.00
2 Vs. Shawn Michaels	1.50	4.00
3 Vs. Shawn Michaels	1.00	2.50
4 Vs. Triple H	.75	2.00
5 Vs. Stone Cold Steve Austin	.75	2.00
6 Wins Royal Rumble	.75	2.00
7 Vs. Batista	.75	2.00
8 Vs. Kane	.75	2.00
9 Vs. Randy Orton	.75	2.00
10 Vs. CM Punk	.75	2.00

2013 Topps Best of WWE Top 10 World Heavyweight Champions

COMPLETE SET (10) 4.00 10.00
*P.P.BLACK/1: UNPRICED DUE TO SCARCITY
*P.P.CYAN/1: UNPRICED DUE TO SCARCITY
*P.P.MAGENTA/1: UNPRICED DUE TO SCARCITY
*P.P.YELLOW/1: UNPRICED DUE TO SCARCITY
STATED ODDS OVERALL 3:1 HOBBY AND RETAIL

1 Undertaker	2.50	6.00
2 Triple H	1.50	4.00
3 Randy Orton	.75	2.00
4 Batista	.50	1.25
5 Sheamus	.40	1.00
6 Rey Mysterio	.50	1.25
7 Kane	.40	1.00
8 CM Punk	.75	2.00
9 Booker T	.30	.75
10 Daniel Bryan	.50	1.25

2013 Topps Best of WWE Top 10 WWE Champions

COMPLETE SET (10) 5.00 12.00
*P.P.BLACK/1: UNPRICED DUE TO SCARCITY
*P.P.CYAN/1: UNPRICED DUE TO SCARCITY
*P.P.MAGENTA/1: UNPRICED DUE TO SCARCITY
*P.P.YELLOW/1: UNPRICED DUE TO SCARCITY
STATED ODDS OVERALL 3:1 HOBBY AND RETAIL

1 John Cena	3.00	8.00
2 Triple H	1.50	4.00
3 The Rock	1.25	3.00
4 Undertaker	.75	2.00
5 CM Punk	.75	2.00
6 Sheamus	.40	1.00
7 Brock Lesnar	.75	2.00
8 Eddie Guerrero	.20	.50
9 The Miz	.30	.75
10 JBL	.30	.75

2013 Topps Best of WWE Top 10 WWE Tag Team Champions

COMPLETE SET (10) 3.00 8.00
*P.P.BLACK/1: UNPRICED DUE TO SCARCITY
*P.P.CYAN/1: UNPRICED DUE TO SCARCITY
*P.P.MAGENTA/1: UNPRICED DUE TO SCARCITY
*P.P.YELLOW/1: UNPRICED DUE TO SCARCITY
STATED ODDS OVERALL 3:1 HOBBY AND RETAIL

1 D-Generation X	2.50	6.00
2 Team Hell No	1.00	2.50
3 Rey Mysterio/Eddie Guerrero	.60	1.50
4 Big Show/Kane	.40	1.00
5 Kofi Kingston/R-Truth	.20	.50
6 Air Boom	.20	.50
7 ShoMiz	.40	1.00
8 Ted DiBiase/Cody Rhodes	.25	.60
9 Curt Hawkins/Zack Ryder	.20	.50
10 Primo & Epico	.20	.50

2013 Topps Best of WWE WrestleMania 29 Mat Relics

STATED ODDS 1:48 HOBBY AND RETAIL

NNO Alberto Del Rio	4.00	10.00
NNO Big E Langston	4.00	10.00
NNO Big Show	4.00	10.00
NNO Brock Lesnar	5.00	12.00
NNO Chris Jericho	5.00	12.00
NNO CM Punk	12.00	30.00
NNO Daniel Bryan	5.00	12.00
NNO Dolph Ziggler	4.00	10.00
NNO Fandango	6.00	15.00
NNO Jack Swagger	4.00	10.00
NNO John Cena	6.00	20.00
NNO Kane	5.00	12.00
NNO Mark Henry	4.00	10.00
NNO Randy Orton	6.00	15.00
NNO Ryback	5.00	12.00
NNO Sheamus	4.00	10.00
NNO The Shield	6.00	15.00
NNO Triple H	5.00	12.00
NNO Undertaker	8.00	20.00
NNO The Rock	15.00	40.00

2014 Topps Chrome WWE

COMPLETE SET (110) 8.00 20.00
UNOPENED BOX (24 PACKS)
UNOPENED PACK (4 CARDS)
*REF.: .4X TO 1.2X BASIC CARDS
*ATOMIC REF.: .6X TO 1.5X BASIC CARDS
*XFRACTOR: .6X TO 1.5X BASIC CARDS
*GOLD REF./50: 2X TO 5X BASIC CARDS
*SUPERFR./1: UNPRICED DUE TO SCARCITY
*P.P.BLACK/1: UNPRICED DUE TO SCARCITY
*P.P.CYAN/1: UNPRICED DUE TO SCARCITY
*P.P.MAGENTA/1: UNPRICED DUE TO SCARCITY
*P.P.YELLOW/1: UNPRICED DUE TO SCARCITY

1 AJ Lee	1.50	4.00
2 Alex Riley	.30	.75
3 Big E Langston	.30	.75
4 Bo Dallas RC	.30	.75
5 Brad Maddox RC	.30	.75
6 Bray Wyatt	.75	2.00
7 Brie Bella	1.00	2.50
8 Brock Lesnar	1.25	3.00
9 Brodus Clay	.30	.75
10 Cameron	.50	1.25
11 Chris Jericho	.75	2.00
12 CM Punk	1.25	3.00
13 Curtis Axel	.30	.75
14 Daniel Bryan	.50	1.25
15 David Otunga	.30	.75
16 Dean Ambrose	.75	2.00
17 Diego	.30	.75
18 Dolph Ziggler	.50	1.25
19 Erick Rowan RC	.50	1.25
20 Eva Marie RC	1.25	3.00
21 Fandango	.50	1.25
22 Fernando	.30	.75
23 Jack Swagger	.50	1.25
24 Jerry The King Lawler	.75	2.00
25 John Cena	1.50	4.00
26 JoJo RC	.50	1.25
27 Justin Roberts	.30	.75

28 Kane	.75	2.00
29 Kofi Kingston	.30	.75
30 Luke Harper RC	.50	1.25
31 El Torito RC	.30	.75
32 Michael Cole	.30	.75
33 The Miz	.50	1.25
34 Naomi	.50	1.25
35 Nikki Bella	1.00	2.50
36 Paul Heyman	.30	.75
37 R-Truth	.30	.75
38 Randy Orton	1.25	3.00
39 Rey Mysterio	.75	2.00
40 The Rock	1.50	4.00
41 Rob Van Dam	.75	2.00
42 Roman Reigns	.75	2.00
43 Ryback	.30	.75
44 Santino Marella	.50	1.25
45 Scott Stanford	.30	.75
46 Seth Rollins	.30	.75
47 Stephanie McMahon	.50	1.25
48 Summer Rae RC	1.25	3.00
49 Tamina Snuka	.50	1.25
50 Tensai	.30	.75
51 Triple H	1.25	3.00
52 Zack Ryder	.30	.75
53 Zeb Colter	.50	1.25
54 Aksana	.75	2.00
55 Alberto Del Rio	.75	2.00
56 Alicia Fox	.50	1.25
57 Antonio Cesaro	.30	.75
58 Big Show	.75	2.00
59 Booker T	.50	1.25
60 Camacho	.30	.75
61 Christian	.30	.75
62 Cody Rhodes	.30	.75
63 Curt Hawkins	.30	.75
64 Damien Sandow	.30	.75
65 Darren Young	.30	.75
66 Drew McIntyre	.30	.75
67 Ezekiel Jackson	.50	1.25
68 The Great Khali	.30	.75
69 Heath Slater	.30	.75
70 Hornswoggle	.50	1.25
71 Hunico	.30	.75
72 JBL	.50	1.25
73 Jey Uso	.30	.75
74 Jimmy Uso	.30	.75
75 Jinder Mahal	.30	.75
76 Josh Mathews	.30	.75
77 Justin Gabriel	.30	.75
78 Goldust	.30	.75
79 Layla	.75	2.00
80 Lilian Garcia	.75	2.00
81 Mark Henry	.50	1.25
82 Natalya	1.00	2.50
83 Renee Young RC	1.25	3.00
84 Ricardo Rodriguez	.30	.75
85 Rosa Mendes	.50	1.25
86 Sheamus	.75	2.00
87 Sin Cara	.75	2.00
88 Theodore Long	.30	.75
89 Titus O'Neil	.30	.75
90 Tony Chimel	.30	.75
91 Tyson Kidd	.30	.75
92 Undertaker	1.25	3.00
93 Vickie Guerrero	.50	1.25
94 Bad News Barrett	.30	.75
95 William Regal	.50	1.25
96 Andre the Giant L	1.25	3.00
97 Billy Gunn L	.50	1.25
98 Bob Backlund L	.50	1.25
99 Diamond Dallas Page L	.50	1.25
100 Eddie Guerrero L	.50	1.25
101 Honky Tonk Man L	.50	1.25
102 Jim Ross L	.50	1.25
103 Junkyard Dog L	.50	1.25
104 Kevin Nash L	.75	2.00
105 Larry Zbyszko L	.50	1.25
106 Mick Foley L	.75	2.00
107 Paul Bearer L	.50	1.25
108 Road Dogg L	.50	1.25
109 Shawn Michaels L	1.25	3.00
110 X-Pac L	.30	.75

2014 Topps Chrome WWE Autographs

*REFRACTOR/50: .5X TO 1.2X BASIC AUTOS
*RED REF./25: .75X TO 2X BASIC AUTOS
*GOLD REF./10: UNPRICED DUE TO SCARCITY
*SUPERFR./1: UNPRICED DUE TO SCARCITY

NNO Aksana	15.00	40.00
NNO Alicia Fox	5.00	12.00
NNO Diamond Dallas Page	12.00	30.00
NNO Dolph Ziggler	10.00	25.00
NNO Fandango	6.00	15.00
NNO Honky Tonk Man	8.00	20.00
NNO Kane	20.00	50.00
NNO Natalya	12.00	30.00
NNO Roman Reigns	100.00	200.00
NNO Sin Cara	5.00	12.00

2014 Topps Chrome WWE Championship Plates

*SUPERFR./1: UNPRICED DUE TO SCARCITY
SP CARDS ARE SER.#'d TO 25

NNO AJ Lee SP	75.00	150.00
NNO Alicia Fox	12.00	30.00
NNO Batista	15.00	40.00
NNO Brie Bella	15.00	40.00
NNO Chris Jericho SP	20.00	50.00
NNO Cody Rhodes	8.00	20.00
NNO Cody Rhodes and Goldust	8.00	20.00
NNO Daniel Bryan World Title	12.00	30.00
NNO Daniel Bryan WWE Title	12.00	30.00
NNO Dolph Ziggler	12.00	30.00
NNO Edge and Christian	15.00	40.00
NNO Greg The Hammer Valentine	8.00	20.00
NNO Honky Tonk Man	12.00	30.00
NNO John Cena SP	20.00	50.00
NNO Natalya	15.00	40.00
NNO Nikki Bella	15.00	40.00
NNO Randy Orton	20.00	50.00
NNO Ravishing Rick Rude	8.00	20.00
NNO Rey Mysterio	12.00	30.00
NNO Ricky The Dragon Steamboat	8.00	20.00
NNO RVD and Rey Mysterio	12.00	30.00
NNO Sgt. Slaughter	25.00	60.00
NNO Shawn Michaels World Title	20.00	50.00
NNO Shawn Michaels WWE Title	20.00	50.00
NNO Sheamus	12.00	30.00
NNO The Shield SP	120.00	200.00
NNO ShoMiz	12.00	30.00
NNO Stone Cold Steve Austin SP	25.00	60.00
NNO Triple H	20.00	50.00
NNO Undertaker SP	25.00	60.00

2014 Topps Chrome WWE Champions Tribute Batista

COMPLETE SET (5) 5.00 12.00
*P.P.BLACK/1: UNPRICED DUE TO SCARCITY
*P.P.CYAN/1: UNPRICED DUE TO SCARCITY
*P.P.MAGENTA/1: UNPRICED DUE TO SCARCITY
*P.P.YELLOW/1: UNPRICED DUE TO SCARCITY
STATED OVERALL ODDS 1:6

1 Batista	1.50	4.00
2 Batista	1.50	4.00
3 Batista	1.50	4.00
4 Batista	1.50	4.00
5 Batista	1.50	4.00

2014 Topps Chrome WWE Champions Tribute Eddie Guerrero

COMPLETE SET (5) 2.50 6.00
*P.P.BLACK/1: UNPRICED DUE TO SCARCITY
*P.P.CYAN/1: UNPRICED DUE TO SCARCITY
*P.P.MAGENTA/1: UNPRICED DUE TO SCARCITY
*P.P.YELLOW/1: UNPRICED DUE TO SCARCITY
STATED OVERALL ODDS 1:6

1 Eddie Guerrero	.75	2.00
2 Eddie Guerrero	.75	2.00
3 Eddie Guerrero	.75	2.00
4 Eddie Guerrero	.75	2.00
5 Eddie Guerrero	.75	2.00

2014 Topps Chrome WWE Champions Tribute Edge

COMPLETE SET (5) 4.00 10.00
*P.P.BLACK/1: UNPRICED DUE TO SCARCITY
*P.P.CYAN/1: UNPRICED DUE TO SCARCITY
*P.P.MAGENTA/1: UNPRICED DUE TO SCARCITY
*P.P.YELLOW/1: UNPRICED DUE TO SCARCITY
STATED OVERALL ODDS 1:6

1 Edge	1.25	3.00
2 Edge	1.25	3.00
3 Edge	1.25	3.00
4 Edge	1.25	3.00
5 Edge	1.25	3.00

2014 Topps Chrome WWE Champions Tribute Iron Sheik

*P.P.BLACK/1: UNPRICED DUE TO SCARCITY
*P.P.CYAN/1: UNPRICED DUE TO SCARCITY
*P.P.MAGENTA/1: UNPRICED DUE TO SCARCITY
*P.P.YELLOW/1: UNPRICED DUE TO SCARCITY
STATED OVERALL ODDS 1:6

1 Iron Sheik	.75	2.00
2 Iron Sheik	.75	2.00
3 Iron Sheik	.75	2.00
4 Iron Sheik	.75	2.00
5 Iron Sheik	.75	2.00

2014 Topps Chrome WWE Champions Tribute JBL

COMPLETE SET (5) 2.50 6.00
*P.P.BLACK/1: UNPRICED DUE TO SCARCITY
*P.P.CYAN/1: UNPRICED DUE TO SCARCITY
*P.P.MAGENTA/1: UNPRICED DUE TO SCARCITY
*P.P.YELLOW/1: UNPRICED DUE TO SCARCITY
STATED OVERALL ODDS 1:6

1 JBL	.75	2.00
2 JBL	.75	2.00
3 JBL	.75	2.00
4 JBL	.75	2.00
5 JBL	.75	2.00

2014 Topps Chrome WWE Champions Tribute Kevin Nash

COMPLETE SET (5) 4.00 10.00
*P.P.BLACK/1: UNPRICED DUE TO SCARCITY
*P.P.CYAN/1: UNPRICED DUE TO SCARCITY
*P.P.MAGENTA/1: UNPRICED DUE TO SCARCITY
*P.P.YELLOW/1: UNPRICED DUE TO SCARCITY
STATED OVERALL ODDS 1:6

1 Kevin Nash	1.25	3.00
2 Kevin Nash	1.25	3.00
3 Kevin Nash	1.25	3.00
4 Kevin Nash	1.25	3.00
5 Kevin Nash	1.25	3.00

2014 Topps Chrome WWE Champions Tribute Mick Foley

COMPLETE SET (5) 4.00 10.00
*P.P.BLACK/1: UNPRICED DUE TO SCARCITY
*P.P.CYAN/1: UNPRICED DUE TO SCARCITY
*P.P.MAGENTA/1: UNPRICED DUE TO SCARCITY
*P.P.YELLOW/1: UNPRICED DUE TO SCARCITY
STATED OVERALL ODDS 1:6

1 Mick Foley	1.25	3.00
2 Mick Foley	1.25	3.00
3 Mick Foley	1.25	3.00
4 Mick Foley	1.25	3.00
5 Mick Foley	1.25	3.00

2014 Topps Chrome WWE Champions Tribute Sgt. Slaughter

COMPLETE SET (5) 4.00 10.00
*P.P.BLACK/1: UNPRICED DUE TO SCARCITY
*P.P.CYAN/1: UNPRICED DUE TO SCARCITY
*P.P.MAGENTA/1: UNPRICED DUE TO SCARCITY
*P.P.YELLOW/1: UNPRICED DUE TO SCARCITY
STATED OVERALL ODDS 1:6

1 Sgt. Slaughter	1.25	3.00
2 Sgt. Slaughter	1.25	3.00
3 Sgt. Slaughter	1.25	3.00
4 Sgt. Slaughter	1.25	3.00
5 Sgt. Slaughter	1.25	3.00

2014 Topps Chrome WWE Champions Tribute Shawn Michaels

COMPLETE SET (5) 6.00 15.00
*P.P.BLACK/1: UNPRICED DUE TO SCARCITY
*P.P.CYAN/1: UNPRICED DUE TO SCARCITY
*P.P.MAGENTA/1: UNPRICED DUE TO SCARCITY
*P.P.YELLOW/1: UNPRICED DUE TO SCARCITY
STATED OVERALL ODDS 1:6

1 Shawn Michaels	2.00	5.00
2 Shawn Michaels	2.00	5.00
3 Shawn Michaels	2.00	5.00
4 Shawn Michaels	2.00	5.00
5 Shawn Michaels	2.00	5.00

2014 Topps Chrome WWE Champions Tribute Yokozuna

COMPLETE SET (5)	2.50	6.00

*P.P.BLACK/1: UNPRICED DUE TO SCARCITY
*P.P.CYAN/1: UNPRICED DUE TO SCARCITY
*P.P.MAGENTA/1: UNPRICED DUE TO SCARCITY
*P.P.YELLOW/1: UNPRICED DUE TO SCARCITY
STATED OVERALL ODDS 1:6

1 Yokozuna	.75	2.00
2 Yokozuna	.75	2.00
3 Yokozuna	.75	2.00
4 Yokozuna	.75	2.00
5 Yokozuna	.75	2.00

2014 Topps Chrome WWE Dual Autographs

STATED PRINT RUN 5 SER.#'d SETS

NNO D.Bryan/B.Wyatt	150.00	300.00
NNO D.Rhodes/J.Swagger	100.00	200.00
NNO J.Cena/R.Orton	150.00	300.00
NNO L.Harper/E.Rowan	100.00	200.00

2014 Topps Chrome WWE Jerry Lawler's Tributes

COMPLETE SET (10)	10.00	25.00

*P.P.BLACK/1: UNPRICED DUE TO SCARCITY
*P.P.CYAN/1: UNPRICED DUE TO SCARCITY
*P.P.MAGENTA/1: UNPRICED DUE TO SCARCITY
*P.P.YELLOW/1: UNPRICED DUE TO SCARCITY
STATED ODDS 1:12 HOBBY AND RETAIL

1 The Iron Sheik	1.00	2.50
2 Sgt. Slaughter	1.50	4.00
3 Yokozuna	1.00	2.50
4 Kevin Nash	1.50	4.00
5 Shawn Michaels	2.50	6.00
6 Mick Foley	1.50	4.00
7 Eddie Guerrero	1.00	2.50
8 JBL	1.00	2.50
9 Batista	2.00	5.00
10 Edge	1.50	4.00

2014 Topps Chrome WWE Kiss

NNO AJ Lee	50.00	100.00
NNO Aksana	20.00	50.00
NNO Alicia Fox	20.00	50.00
NNO Cameron	30.00	60.00
NNO Eva Marie	30.00	80.00
NNO Naomi	30.00	60.00
NNO Tamina Snuka	12.00	30.00
NNO Vickie Guerrero	12.00	30.00

2014 Topps Chrome WWE Kiss Autographs

NNO AJ Lee	250.00	400.00
NNO Aksana	30.00	75.00
NNO Cameron	30.00	75.00
NNO Tamina Snuka	30.00	75.00
NNO Vickie Guerrero	75.00	150.00

2014 Topps Chrome WWE NXT Prospects

COMPLETE SET (20)	30.00	75.00

*P.P.BLACK/1: UNPRICED DUE TO SCARCITY
*P.P.CYAN/1: UNPRICED DUE TO SCARCITY
*P.P.MAGENTA/1: UNPRICED DUE TO SCARCITY
*P.P.YELLOW/1: UNPRICED DUE TO SCARCITY
STATED ODDS 1:3 HOBBY AND RETAIL

1 Adrian Neville	1.25	3.00
2 Alexander Rusev	1.50	4.00
3 Baron Corbin	.60	1.50
4 Bayley	5.00	12.00
5 Charlotte	12.00	30.00
6 CJ Parker	.60	1.50
7 Konnor O'Brian	.60	1.50
8 Corey Graves	.60	1.50
9 Emma	2.00	5.00
10 Enzo Amore	1.25	3.00
11 Jason Jordan	.60	1.50
12 Leo Kruger	.60	1.50
13 Mojo Rawley	.60	1.50
14 Paige	8.00	20.00
15 Rick Viktor	.60	1.50
16 Sami Zayn	1.25	3.00
17 Sasha Banks	10.00	25.00
18 Sylvester Lefort	.60	1.50
19 Tyler Breeze	.60	1.50
20 Xavier Woods	.60	1.50

2014 Topps Chrome WWE Royal Rumble Mat Relics

*SUPERFR/1: UNPRICED DUE TO SCARCITY
STATED ODDS

NNO Alberto Del Rio	4.00	10.00
NNO Alexander Rusev	6.00	15.00
NNO Batista	10.00	25.00
NNO Big E	3.00	8.00
NNO Billy Gunn	5.00	12.00
NNO Bray Wyatt	8.00	20.00
NNO Brock Lesnar	8.00	20.00
NNO Cody Rhodes	3.00	8.00
NNO Daniel Bryan	8.00	20.00
NNO El Torito	3.00	8.00
NNO Goldust	3.00	8.00
NNO JBL	5.00	12.00
NNO John Cena	10.00	25.00
NNO Kane	6.00	15.00
NNO Kevin Nash	8.00	20.00
NNO Randy Orton	8.00	20.00
NNO Rey Mysterio	8.00	20.00
NNO Road Dogg	5.00	12.00
NNO Roman Reigns	10.00	25.00
NNO Sheamus	6.00	15.00

2014 Topps Chrome WWE Swatch Relics

NNO Alberto Del Rio	6.00	15.00
NNO Bray Wyatt	12.00	30.00
NNO Curtis Axel	3.00	8.00
NNO Damien Sandow	3.00	8.00
NNO Daniel Bryan	8.00	20.00
NNO Diego	3.00	8.00
NNO Dolph Ziggler	5.00	12.00
NNO Fernando	3.00	8.00
NNO Goldust	3.00	8.00
NNO Jack Swagger	6.00	15.00
NNO John Cena	12.00	30.00
NNO Kofi Kingston	3.00	8.00
NNO Mark Henry	5.00	12.00
NNO The Miz	5.00	12.00
NNO Rey Mysterio	8.00	20.00
NNO Undertaker	15.00	40.00

2014 Topps Chrome WWE WrestleMania DVD Promo

P1 John Cena

2015 Topps Chrome WWE

COMPLETE SET (100)	8.00	20.00
UNOPENED BOX (24 PACKS)	60.00	80.00
UNOPENED PACK (4 CARDS)	3.50	4.00

*REF.: .4X TO 1.2X BASIC CARDS
*ATOMIC: .6X TO 1.5X BASIC CARDS
*XFRACTOR: .6X TO 1.5X BASIC CARDS
*PULSAR/75: 1.5X TO 4X BASIC CARDS
*GOLD/50: 2X TO 5X BASIC CARDS
*SILVER WAVE/20: 3X TO 8X BASIC CARDS
*SHIMMER/10: 5X TO 12X BASIC CARDS
*RED/5: UNPRICED DUE TO SCARCITY
*SUPERFR./1: UNPRICED DUE TO SCARCITY
*P.P.BLACK/1: UNPRICED DUE TO SCARCITY
*P.P.CYAN/1: UNPRICED DUE TO SCARCITY
*P.P.MAGENTA/1: UNPRICED DUE TO SCARCITY
*P.P.YELLOW/1: UNPRICED DUE TO SCARCITY

1 Adam Rose RC	.30	.75
2 AJ Lee	1.25	3.00
3 Alicia Fox	.50	1.25
4 Bad News Barrett	.25	.60
5 Batista	.60	1.50
6 Big E	.40	1.00
7 Big Show	.60	1.50
8 Bo Dallas	.25	.60
9 Booker T	.40	1.00
10 Bray Wyatt	1.00	2.50
11 Brie Bella	.75	2.00
12 Brock Lesnar	1.00	2.50
13 Cameron	.40	1.00
14 Cesaro	.25	.60
15 Chris Jericho	.60	1.50
16 Christian	.25	.60
17 Curtis Axel	.25	.60
18 Damien Mizdow	.40	1.00
19 Daniel Bryan	1.00	2.50
20 Darren Young	.25	.60
21 David Otunga	.25	.60
22 Dean Ambrose	.60	1.50
23 Diego	.25	.60
24 Dolph Ziggler	.40	1.00
25 Eden	.40	1.00
26 Emma RC	.40	1.00
27 Erick Rowan	.40	1.00
28 Eva Marie	1.00	2.50
29 Fandango	.25	.60
30 Fernando	.25	.60
31 Goldust	.25	.60
32 Heath Slater	.25	.60
33 Hornswoggle	.40	1.00
34 Jack Swagger	.40	1.00
35 Jerry The King Lawler	.40	1.00
36 Jey Uso	.25	.60
37 Jimmy Uso	.25	.60
38 John Cena	1.25	3.00
39 Justin Gabriel	.25	.60
40 Kane	.60	1.50
41 Kofi Kingston	.25	.60
42 Lana RC	1.00	2.50
43 Layla	.60	1.50
44 Lilian Garcia	.60	1.50
45 Luke Harper	.40	1.00
46 Mark Henry	.40	1.00
47 The Miz	.40	1.00
48 Naomi	.40	1.00
49 Natalya	.75	2.00
50 Nikki Bella	.75	2.00
51 Paige RC	1.25	3.00
52 Paul Heyman	.25	.60
53 R-Truth	.25	.60
54 Randy Orton	2.00	5.00
55 Renee Young	1.00	2.50
56 Rey Mysterio	.60	1.50
57 The Rock	1.25	3.00
58 Rob Van Dam	.60	1.50
59 Roman Reigns	.60	1.50
60 Rosa Mendes	.40	1.00
61 Rusev RC	.60	1.50
62 Ryback	.25	.60
63 Seth Rollins	.40	1.00
64 Sheamus	.60	1.50
65 Sin Cara	.40	1.00
66 Stardust	.25	.60
67 Stephanie McMahon	.40	1.00
68 Summer Rae	1.00	2.50
69 Tamina Snuka	.40	1.00
70 Titus O'Neil	.25	.60
71 El Torito	.25	.60
72 Triple H	1.00	2.50
73 Tyson Kidd	.25	.60
74 Undertaker	1.00	2.50
75 William Regal	.40	1.00
76 Xavier Woods	.40	1.00
77 Zack Ryder	.25	.60
78 Zeb Colter	.40	1.00
79 Bret Hit Man Hart	.75	2.00
80 Bruno Sammartino	.60	1.50
81 George The Animal Steele	.30	.75
82 Gerald Brisco	.40	1.00
83 Hulk Hogan	1.25	3.00
84 Larry Zbyszko	.40	1.00
85 Mouth of the South Jimmy Hart	.30	.75
86 Pat Patterson	.25	.60
87 Ric Flair	1.25	3.00
88 Rowdy Roddy Piper	.75	2.00
89 Sting	.60	1.50
90 Ultimate Warrior	.75	2.00
91 Aiden English NXT RC	.30	.75
92 Alexa Bliss NXT RC	12.00	30.00
93 Angelo Dawkins NXT RC	.30	.75
94 Bull Dempsey NXT RC	.40	1.00
95 Colin Cassady NXT RC	.40	1.00
96 Hideo Itami NXT RC	.25	.60
97 Kalisto NXT RC	.40	1.00
98 Marcus Louis NXT RC	.40	1.00
99 Sawyer Fulton NXT RC	.40	1.00
100 Tye Dillinger NXT RC	.40	1.00

2015 Topps Chrome WWE Autographs

*PULSAR/75: .5X TO 1.2X BASIC AUTOS
*GOLD/10: .75X TO 2X BASIC AUTOS
*RED/5: UNPRICED DUE TO SCARCITY

NNO Adam Rose	6.00	15.00
NNO Brie Bella	12.00	30.00
NNO Bruno Sammartino	15.00	40.00
NNO Eva Marie	20.00	50.00
NNO Hulk Hogan	200.00	400.00
NNO Lana	25.00	60.00
NNO Lita	20.00	50.00

NNO Nikki Bella	25.00	60.00
NNO Renee Young	12.00	30.00
NNO Roman Reigns	100.00	200.00

2015 Topps Chrome WWE Commemorative Championship Plates

*PULSAR/75: .6X TO 1.5X BASIC PLATES
*RED/5: UNPRICED DUE TO SCARCITY

NNO Adrian Neville NXT Champion	6.00	15.00
NNO Adrian Neville NXT Tag Champion	6.00	15.00
NNO Big E	5.00	12.00
NNO Bo Dallas	3.00	8.00
NNO Charlotte	10.00	25.00
NNO Corey Graves	6.00	15.00
NNO Erick Rowan	5.00	12.00
NNO Kalisto	5.00	12.00
NNO Konnor	8.00	20.00
NNO Luke Harper	5.00	12.00
NNO Paige	15.00	40.00
NNO Seth Rollins	6.00	15.00
NNO Sin Cara	5.00	12.00
NNO Viktor	8.00	20.00

2015 Topps Chrome WWE Diva Kiss

RANDOMLY INSERTED INTO PACKS

NNO Brie Bella	20.00	50.00
NNO Cameron	10.00	25.00
NNO Eden	10.00	25.00
NNO Emma	30.00	60.00
NNO Naomi	20.00	40.00
NNO Natalya	20.00	50.00
NNO Nikki Bella	40.00	80.00
NNO Renee Young	25.00	60.00
NNO Summer Rae	25.00	60.00
NNO Tamina Snuka	10.00	25.00

2015 Topps Chrome WWE Diva Kiss Autographs

*RED REF./5: UNPRICED DUE TO SCARCITY
*SUPERFR./1: UNPRICED DUE TO SCARCITY
STATED PRINT RUN 25 SER.#'d SETS

NNO Brie Bella	50.00	100.00
NNO Cameron	12.00	30.00
NNO Eden	15.00	40.00
NNO Emma	25.00	60.00
NNO Naomi	15.00	50.00
NNO Natalya	20.00	50.00
NNO Nikki Bella	50.00	100.00
NNO Renee Young	75.00	150.00
NNO Summer Rae	30.00	75.00
NNO Tamina Snuka	15.00	40.00

2015 Topps Chrome WWE Dual Autographs

STATED PRINT RUN 5 SER. #'d SETS
UNPRICED DUE TO SCARCITY

1 AJ Lee/Paige
2 D.Ambrose/S.Rollins
3 Emma/Eden
4 J.Cena/B.Wyatt

2015 Topps Chrome WWE King of the Ring Sign Relics

*RED/5: UNPRICED DUE TO SCARCITY
*SUPERFR./1: UNPRICED DUE TO SCARCITY
STATED ODDS 1:1,156 HOBBY

NNO Billy Gunn	5.00	12.00
NNO Bret Hit Man Hart	12.00	30.00
NNO Brock Lesnar	15.00	40.00
NNO Don Muraco	5.00	12.00
NNO Edge	8.00	20.00
NNO Harley Race	5.00	12.00
NNO King Booker	5.00	12.00
NNO Million Dollar Man Ted DiBiase	5.00	12.00
NNO Sheamus	8.00	20.00
NNO Stone Cold Steve Austin	10.00	25.00
NNO Tito Santana	5.00	12.00
NNO Triple H	8.00	20.00
NNO William Regal	5.00	12.00

2015 Topps Chrome WWE Night of Champions Mat Relics

RANDOMLY INSERTED INTO PACKS
*PULSAR/75: .6X TO 1.5X BASIC RELICS

1 AJ Lee	12.00	30.00
2 Brock Lesnar	10.00	25.00
3 Cesaro	2.50	6.00
4 Chris Jericho	6.00	15.00
5 Dean Ambrose	6.00	15.00
6 Dolph Ziggler	4.00	10.00
7 John Cena	12.00	30.00
8 Mark Henry	4.00	10.00
9 The Miz	4.00	10.00
10 Nikki Bella	8.00	20.00
11 Paige	12.00	30.00
12 Randy Orton	10.00	25.00
13 Rusev	6.00	15.00
14 Seth Rollins	4.00	10.00
15 Sheamus	6.00	15.00

2015 Topps Chrome WWE Night of Champions Turnbuckle Relics

*SUPERFR./1: UNPRICED DUE TO SCARCITY
STATED PRINT RUN 33 SER.#'d SETS

NNO AJ Lee	80.00	150.00
NNO Brock Lesnar	15.00	40.00
NNO Chris Jericho	12.00	30.00
NNO Dean Ambrose	25.00	50.00
NNO John Cena	25.00	60.00
NNO Nikki Bella	15.00	40.00
NNO Paige	25.00	60.00
NNO Randy Orton	15.00	40.00
NNO Seth Rollins	8.00	20.00

2015 Topps Chrome WWE NXT Autographs

*GOLD/10: .75X TO 2X BASIC AUTOS
*ATOMIC/5: UNPRICED DUE TO SCARCITY
*RED/5: UNPRICED DUE TO SCARCITY
*SUPERFR./1: UNPRICED DUE TO SCARCITY
RANDOMLY INSERTED INTO PACKS

NNO Aiden English	6.00	15.00
NNO Alexa Bliss	200.00	350.00
NNO Charlotte	30.00	80.00
NNO Colin Cassady	12.00	30.00
NNO Sawyer Fulton	5.00	12.00

2015 Topps Chrome WWE Swatch Relics

RANDOMLY INSERTED INTO PACKS
*PULSAR/75: .1X TO 2.5X BASIC RELICS

NNO Cesaro	1.50	4.00
NNO Curtis Axel	1.50	4.00
NNO Damien Mizdow	2.50	6.00
NNO Daniel Bryan	6.00	15.00
NNO Darren Young	1.50	4.00
NNO Diego	1.50	4.00
NNO Jack Swagger	2.50	6.00
NNO Jerry The King Lawler	2.50	6.00
NNO Jimmy Uso	1.50	4.00
NNO John Cena	8.00	20.00
NNO Kofi Kingston	1.50	4.00
NNO Mark Henry	2.50	6.00
NNO Paige	8.00	20.00
NNO Randy Orton	6.00	15.00
NNO Sheamus	4.00	10.00
NNO Titus O'Neil	1.50	4.00
NNO Tyson Kidd	1.50	4.00
NNO Zack Ryder	1.50	4.00

2015 Topps Chrome WWE Ultimate Warrior Commemorative Face Paint Plate

*PULSAR REF/75: 1.2X TO 3X BASIC MEM
RANDOMLY INSERTED INTO PACKS

NNO Ultimate Warrior	5.00	12.00

2020 Topps Chrome WWE

COMPLETE SET (100)	15.00	40.00

*REF: .5X TO 1.2X BASIC CARDS
*XFRAC: .6X TO 1.5X BASIC CARDS
*GREEN/99: 1.2X TO 3X BASIC CARDS
*GOLD/50: 2X TO 5X BASIC CARDS
*ORANGE/25: UNPRICED DUE TO SCARCITY
*BLACK/10: UNPRICED DUE TO SCARCITY
*RED/5: UNPRICED DUE TO SCARCITY
*SUPER/1: UNPRICED DUE TO SCARCITY

1 AJ Styles	1.25	3.00
2 Aleister Black	.75	2.00
3 Alexa Bliss	2.50	6.00
4 Mustafa Ali	.60	1.50
5 Andrade	.60	1.50
6 Asuka	1.50	4.00
7 King Corbin	.50	1.25
8 Bayley	.75	2.00
9 Becky Lynch	1.50	4.00
10 Big E	.40	1.00
11 Big Show	.50	1.25
12 Billie Kay	.75	2.00
13 Bobby Lashley	.75	2.00
14 Braun Strowman	1.00	2.50
15 The Fiend Bray Wyatt	1.25	3.00
16 Brock Lesnar	1.50	4.00
17 Murphy	.50	1.25
18 Carmella	1.00	2.50
19 Cesaro	.40	1.00
20 Charlotte Flair	1.50	4.00
21 Daniel Bryan	1.25	3.00
22 Drake Maverick	.40	1.00
23 Drew McIntyre	.75	2.00
24 Elias	.40	1.00
25 Erik	.40	1.00
26 Ember Moon	.75	2.00
27 Finn Balor	1.00	2.50
28 Humberto Carrillo	.60	1.50
29 Ivar	.40	1.00
30 Jeff Hardy	1.00	2.50
31 Jey Uso	.40	1.00
32 Jimmy Uso	.40	1.00
33 John Cena	1.50	4.00
34 Kairi Sane	.75	2.00
35 Kane	.50	1.25
36 Karl Anderson	.40	1.00
37 Kevin Owens	.50	1.25
38 Kofi Kingston	.60	1.50
39 Lana	1.00	2.50
40 Lacey Evans	1.00	2.50
41 Luke Gallows	.40	1.00
42 Mandy Rose	2.00	5.00
43 Naomi	.75	2.00
44 Natalya	.60	1.50
45 Nia Jax	.60	1.50
46 Nikki Cross	.75	2.00
47 Peyton Royce	.75	2.00
48 Randy Orton	1.00	2.50
49 Ricochet	.60	1.50
50 Roman Reigns	1.00	2.50
51 Ronda Rousey	2.00	5.00
52 R-Truth	.40	1.00
53 Ruby Riott	.60	1.50
54 Rusev	.50	1.25
55 Sami Zayn	.50	1.25
56 Samoa Joe	.60	1.50
57 Sasha Banks	2.00	5.00
58 Seth Rollins	.75	2.00
59 Sheamus	.50	1.25
60 Shinsuke Nakamura	.75	2.00
61 Shorty G	.40	1.00
62 Sonya Deville	1.00	2.50
63 The Miz	.60	1.50
64 The Rock	2.00	5.00
65 Triple H	1.00	2.50
66 Undertaker	1.50	4.00
67 Xavier Woods	.40	1.00
68 Zelina Vega	.75	2.00
69 Adam Cole	1.00	2.50
70 Angel Garza RC	.50	1.25
71 Angelo Dawkins	.40	1.00
72 Bianca Belair	1.00	2.50
73 Boa RC	.40	1.00
74 Bobby Fish	.40	1.00
75 Bronson Reed RC	.40	1.00
76 Cameron Grimes RC	.40	1.00
77 Candice LeRae	1.25	3.00
78 Damian Priest RC	.40	1.00
79 Dexter Lumis RC	.40	1.00
80 Io Shirai	.60	1.50
81 Isaiah Swerve Scott RC	.50	1.25
82 Joaquin Wilde RC	.40	1.00
83 Johnny Gargano	.75	2.00
84 Kushida RC	.50	1.25
85 Kyle O'Reilly	.50	1.25
86 Lio Rush	.40	1.00
87 Matt Riddle	.75	2.00
88 Mia Yim	.75	2.00
89 Montez Ford	.40	1.00
90 Roderick Strong	.75	2.00
91 Shayna Baszler	1.25	3.00
92 Velveteen Dream	.50	1.25
93 Alexander Wolfe	.40	1.00
94 Fabian Aichner	.40	1.00

95 Marcel Barthel RC	.40	1.00
96 Pete Dunne	.40	1.00
97 Rhea Ripley	1.50	4.00
98 Toni Storm	1.00	2.50
99 Travis Banks RC	.40	1.00
100 Walter RC	.75	2.00

2020 Topps Chrome WWE Autographs

*GREEN/99: .5X TO 1.2X BASIC AUTOS
*GOLD/50: .6X TO 1.5X BASIC AUTOS
*ORANGE/25: UNPRICED DUE TO SCARCITY
*BLACK/10: UNPRICED DUE TO SCARCITY
*RED/5: UNPRICED DUE TO SCARCITY
*SUPER/1: UNPRICED DUE TO SCARCITY
RANDOMLY INSERTED INTO PACKS

AAB Aleister Black	8.00	20.00
AAC Adam Cole	10.00	25.00
AAL Alexa Bliss	60.00	120.00
AAN Andrade	8.00	20.00
AAS AJ Styles	12.00	30.00
ABY Bayley	20.00	50.00
ACF Charlotte Flair	20.00	50.00
ADB Daniel Bryan	8.00	20.00
ADM Drew McIntyre	12.00	30.00
AFB Finn Balor	12.00	30.00
AHC Humberto Carrillo	6.00	15.00
AIS Io Shirai	30.00	75.00
AKC King Corbin	6.00	15.00
AKK Kofi Kingston	6.00	15.00
AKU Kushida	8.00	20.00
ALE Lacey Evans	15.00	40.00
AMA Mustafa Ali	8.00	20.00
ARH Rhea Ripley	30.00	75.00
ASB Shayna Baszler	10.00	25.00
ASD Johnny Gargano	6.00	15.00
ASJ Samoa Joe	6.00	15.00
ASN Shinsuke Nakamura	12.00	30.00
ASR Seth Rollins	8.00	20.00
ATM The Miz	8.00	20.00

2020 Topps Chrome WWE Big Legends

COMPLETE SET (25)	12.00	30.00

*GREEN/99: .75X TO 2X BASIC CARDS
*GOLD/50: 1.2X TO 3X BASIC CARDS
*ORANGE/25: UNPRICED DUE TO SCARCITY
*BLACK/10: UNPRICED DUE TO SCARCITY
*RED/5: UNPRICED DUE TO SCARCITY
*SUPER/1: UNPRICED DUE TO SCARCITY
RANDOMLY INSERTED INTO PACKS

BL1 Alundra Blayze	1.00	2.50
BL2 Boogeyman	.60	1.50
BL3 Booker T	1.25	3.00
BL4 Brutus The Barber Beefcake	.60	1.50
BL5 Christian	.75	2.00
BL6 Eve	1.25	3.00
BL7 Gerald Brisco	.60	1.50
BL8 The Godfather	.60	1.50
BL9 The Hurricane	.60	1.50
BL10 Jerry The King Lawler	1.50	4.00
BL11 Kerry Von Erich	1.00	2.50
BL12 Kevin Nash	1.00	2.50
BL13 Kurt Angle	1.50	4.00
BL14 Mick Foley	1.25	3.00
BL15 Molly Holly	.75	2.00
BL16 Pat Patterson	.60	1.50
BL17 Razor Ramon	1.00	2.50
BL18 Ric Flair	2.50	6.00
BL19 Rikishi	.60	1.50
BL20 Road Dogg Jesse James	.75	2.00
BL21 Ron Simmons	1.00	2.50
BL22 Sgt. Slaughter	1.25	3.00
BL23 The Million Dollar Man Ted DiBiase	1.25	3.00
BL24 Wendi Richter	.75	2.00
BL25 X-Pac	.60	1.50

2020 Topps Chrome WWE Big Legends Autographs

*GREEN/99: .5X TO 1.2X BASIC CARDS
*GOLD/50: .6X TO 1.5X BASIC CARDS
*ORANGE/25: UNPRICED DUE TO SCARCITY
*BLACK/10: UNPRICED DUE TO SCARCITY
*RED/5: UNPRICED DUE TO SCARCITY
*SUPER/1: UNPRICED DUE TO SCARCITY
RANDOMLY INSERTED INTO PACKS

BLJJ Road Dogg Jesse James	10.00	25.00
BLJL Jerry The King Lawler	12.00	30.00
BLHBK Shawn Michaels		

2020 Topps Chrome WWE Fantasy Matches

COMPLETE SET (22)	15.00	40.00

*GREEN/99: .6X TO 1.5X BASIC CARDS
*GOLD/50: .75X TO 2X BASIC CARDS
*ORANGE/25: UNPRICED DUE TO SCARCITY
*BLACK/10: UNPRICED DUE TO SCARCITY
*RED/5: UNPRICED DUE TO SCARCITY
*SUPER/1: UNPRICED DUE TO SCARCITY
RANDOMLY INSERTED INTO PACKS

FM1 Samoa Joe/John Cena	2.50	6.00
FM2 Beth Phoenix/Chyna	1.50	4.00
FM3 Batista/Ultimate Warrior	1.50	4.00
FM4 AJ Styles/Mr. Perfect	2.00	5.00
FM5 Drew McIntyre/Booker T	1.25	3.00
FM6 The Miz/Rowdy Roddy Piper	1.50	4.00
FM7 Roman Reigns/The Rock	3.00	8.00
FM8 Randy Orton/DDP	1.50	4.00
FM9 Bret Hit Man Hart/Daniel Bryan	2.00	5.00
FM10 Alexa Bliss/Trish Stratus	4.00	10.00
FM11 Charlotte Flair/Lita	2.50	6.00
FM12 The Fiend/Jake The Snake Roberts	2.00	5.00
FM13 Seth Rollins/Shawn Michaels	1.50	4.00
FM14 Kurt Angle/Ken Shamrock	1.50	4.00
FM15 Mankind/Jeff Hardy	1.50	4.00
FM16 Braun Strowman/Goldberg	2.50	6.00
FM17 Finn Balor/Undertaker	2.50	6.00
FM18 Rick Rude/Robert Roode	.75	2.00
FM19 KO/Stone Cold Steve Austin	3.00	8.00
FM20 Big Show/Vader	1.00	2.50
FM21 Randy Savage/Kofi Kingston	2.00	5.00
FM22 Andrade/Eddie Guerrero	1.50	4.00

2020 Topps Chrome WWE Fantasy Matches Autographs

*BLACK/10: UNPRICED DUE TO SCARCITY
*RED/5: UNPRICED DUE TO SCARCITY
*SUPER/1: UNPRICED DUE TO SCARCITY
STATED PRINT RUN 25 SER.#'d SETS

FMKK Jeff Hardy/Mankind	75.00	150.00
FMLC Charlotte Flair/Lita	125.00	250.00
FMSA Seth Rollins/Shawn Michaels	75.00	150.00
FMTA Alexa Bliss/Trish Stratus	250.00	500.00

2020 Topps Chrome WWE Image Variations

COMPLETE SET (25)
*GREEN/99: .5X TO 1.2X BASIC CARDS
*GOLD/50: .6X TO 1.5X BASIC CARDS
*ORANGE/25: UNPRICED DUE TO SCARCITY
*BLACK/10: UNPRICED DUE TO SCARCITY
*RED/5: UNPRICED DUE TO SCARCITY
*SUPER/1: UNPRICED DUE TO SCARCITY
RANDOMLY INSERTED INTO PACKS

IV1 AJ Styles	2.00	5.00
IV2 Alexa Bliss	5.00	12.00
IV3 Mustafa Ali	1.50	4.00
IV4 Asuka	3.00	8.00
IV5 Bayley	1.50	4.00
IV6 Becky Lynch	6.00	15.00
IV7 Bianca Belair	2.50	6.00
IV8 The Fiend Bray Wyatt	4.00	10.00
IV9 Carmella	4.00	10.00
IV10 Charlotte Flair	5.00	12.00
IV11 Ember Moon	1.50	4.00
IV12 Finn Balor	2.00	5.00
IV13 Jeff Hardy	2.50	6.00
IV14 Kairi Sane	3.00	8.00
IV15 Kofi Kingston	1.50	4.00
IV16 Lacey Evans	3.00	8.00
IV17 Matt Riddle	2.50	6.00
IV18 Naomi	2.50	6.00
IV19 Nikki Cross	3.00	8.00
IV20 Ricochet	2.00	5.00
IV21 Samoa Joe	2.00	5.00
IV22 Seth Rollins	2.00	5.00
IV23 Sonya Deville	2.50	6.00
IV24 Velveteen Dream	2.00	5.00
IV25 King Corbin	1.50	4.00

2020 Topps Chrome WWE Shocking Wins

COMPLETE SET (25)	12.00	30.00

*GREEN/99: .5X TO 1.2X BASIC CARDS
*GOLD/50: .6X TO 1.5X BASIC CARDS
*ORANGE/25: UNPRICED DUE TO SCARCITY
*BLACK/10: UNPRICED DUE TO SCARCITY
*RED/5: UNPRICED DUE TO SCARCITY
*SUPER/1: UNPRICED DUE TO SCARCITY
RANDOMLY INSERTED INTO PACKS

SW1 Ron Simmons	1.00	2.50
SW2 The 1-2-3 Kid	.60	1.50
SW3 Yokozuna	1.00	2.50
SW4 Shawn Michaels	1.50	4.00
SW5 Kevin Nash	1.00	2.50
SW6 Mankind	1.25	3.00
SW7 Jeff Hardy	1.50	4.00
SW8 Brock Lesnar	2.50	6.00
SW9 The Hurricane	.60	1.50
SW10 Eddie Guerrero	1.50	4.00
SW11 Shelton Benjamin	.75	2.00
SW12 Bobby Lashley	1.25	3.00
SW13 Sheamus	.75	2.00
SW14 The Miz	1.00	2.50
SW15 Sheamus	.75	2.00
SW16 Lord Tensai	.60	1.50
SW17 Bo Dallas	.60	1.50
SW18 Fandango	.60	1.50
SW19 Brock Lesnar	2.50	6.00
SW20 Paige	1.50	4.00
SW21 Charlotte Flair	2.50	6.00
SW22 Heath Slater	.60	1.50
SW23 Kevin Owens	.75	2.00
SW24 Finn Balor	1.50	4.00
SW25 Jinder Mahal	.60	1.50

2020 Topps Chrome WWE Shocking Wins Autographs

*GREEN/99: .5X TO 1.2X BASIC AUTOS
*GOLD/50: .6X TO 1.5X BASIC AUTOS
*ORANGE/25: UNPRICED DUE TO SCARCITY
*BLACK/10: UNPRICED DUE TO SCARCITY
*RED/5: UNPRICED DUE TO SCARCITY
*SUPER/1: UNPRICED DUE TO SCARCITY
RANDOMLY INSERTED INTO PACKS

SWABD Bo Dallas	5.00	12.00
SWACF Charlotte Flair	15.00	40.00
SWAFB Finn Balor	12.00	30.00
SWAJH Jeff Hardy	10.00	25.00
SWAJL Jerry The King Lawler		
SWAJM Jinder Mahal		
SWAKO Kevin Owens	6.00	15.00
SWALA Bobby Lashley	5.00	12.00
SWALT Lord Tensai	5.00	12.00
SWAMA Mustafa Ali	5.00	12.00
SWAMK Mankind		
SWASB Shelton Benjamin	6.00	15.00
SWASH Sheamus		
SWASM Sheamus	8.00	20.00
SWATM The Miz	8.00	20.00
SWAZR Zack Ryder		

2021 Topps Chrome WWE

COMPLETE SET (100)
*REFRACTOR: .5X TO 1.2X BASIC CARDS
*AQUA/150: .75X TO 2X BASIC CARDS
*GREEN/99: 1X TO 2.5X BASIC CARDS
*GOLD/50: 1.5X TO 4X BASIC CARDS
*ORANGE/25: UNPRICED DUE TO SCARCITY
*BLACK/10: UNPRICED DUE TO SCARCITY
*RED/5: UNPRICED DUE TO SCARCITY
*SUPERFR/1: UNPRICED DUE TO SCARCITY

1 AJ Styles	1.25	3.00
2 Akira Tozawa	.50	1.25
3 Alexa Bliss	2.50	6.00
4 Andrade	.60	1.50
5 Angel Garza	.50	1.25
6 Arturo Ruas RC	.40	1.00
7 Asuka	1.50	4.00
8 Becky Lynch	1.50	4.00
9 Bobby Lashley	1.00	2.50
10 Braun Strowman	1.00	2.50
11 The Fiend Bray Wyatt	1.50	4.00
12 Charlotte Flair	2.00	5.00
13 Charly Caruso	1.00	2.50
14 Dabba-Kato RC	.40	1.00
15 Drew Gulak	.50	1.25
16 Drew McIntyre	1.00	2.50
17 Gran Metalik	.40	1.00
18 John Morrison	.75	2.00
19 Edge	1.50	4.00
20 Erik	.40	1.00
21 Ivar	.40	1.00
22 Jeff Hardy	1.00	2.50
23 Keith Lee	.75	2.00
24 King Corbin	.40	1.00
25 Kofi Kingston	1.00	2.50
26 Lacey Evans	1.00	2.50

27 Lince Dorado	.40	1.00
28 Mandy Rose	2.00	5.00
29 Riddle	1.00	2.50
30 Naomi	.50	1.25
31 Nikki Cross	.75	2.00
32 Mustafa Ali	.50	1.25
33 MVP	.40	1.00
34 Nia Jax	.75	2.00
35 Peyton Royce	.75	2.00
36 R-Truth	.50	1.25
37 Randy Orton	1.25	3.00
38 Riddick Moss	.50	1.25
39 Samoa Joe	.75	2.00
40 Shayna Baszler	.75	2.00
41 Sheamus	.60	1.50
42 Shelton Benjamin	.60	1.50
43 Dominik Dijakovic	.50	1.25
44 The Miz	.60	1.50
45 Xavier Woods	.40	1.00
46 Aleister Black	1.00	2.50
47 Angelo Dawkins	.50	1.25
48 Apollo Crews	.50	1.25
49 Bayley	1.00	2.50
50 Bianca Belair	1.00	2.50
51 Big E	.75	2.00
52 Billie Kay	.75	2.00
53 Cesaro	.40	1.00
54 Daniel Bryan	1.50	4.00
55 Dolph Ziggler	.75	2.00
56 Kalisto	.50	1.25
57 Kayla Braxton	.75	2.00
58 Kevin Owens	.75	2.00
59 Liv Morgan	1.50	4.00
60 Montez Ford	.40	1.00
61 Murphy	.50	1.25
62 Natalya	.60	1.50
63 Otis	.50	1.25
64 Roman Reigns	2.00	5.00
65 Ruby Riott	.75	2.00
66 Sasha Banks	2.00	5.00
67 Sami Zayn	.60	1.50
68 Seth Rollins	1.00	2.50
69 Shinsuke Nakamura	1.00	2.50
70 Chad Gable	.40	1.00
71 Sonya Deville	1.00	2.50
72 Adam Cole	1.25	3.00
73 Aliyah	.75	2.00
74 Austin Theory	.75	2.00
75 Bobby Fish	.50	1.25
76 Bronson Reed	.50	1.25
77 Cameron Grimes	.75	2.00
78 Candice LeRae	1.50	4.00
79 Dakota Kai	.75	2.00
80 Damian Priest	.60	1.50
81 Dexter Lumis	.40	1.00
82 Finn Balor	1.00	2.50
83 Io Shirai	.75	2.00
84 Isaiah Swerve Scott	.60	1.50
85 Johnny Gargano	.75	2.00
86 Karrion Kross	1.50	4.00
87 Kyle O'Reilly	.60	1.50
88 Kushida	.60	1.50
89 Raquel Gonzalez	1.00	2.50
90 Rhea Ripley	1.25	3.00
91 Ridge Holland RC	.40	1.00
92 Robert Stone	.40	1.00
93 Roderick Strong	.60	1.50
94 Santos Escobar	.60	1.50
95 Scarlett	2.00	5.00
96 Shotzi Blackheart	1.50	4.00
97 Tegan Nox	1.00	2.50
98 Timothy Thatcher RC	.40	1.00
99 Tommaso Ciampa	1.00	2.50
100 Velveteen Dream	.50	1.25

2021 Topps Chrome WWE 5 Timers Club

COMPLETE SET (20) 20.00 50.00
*GREEN/99: .5X TO 1.2X BASIC CARDS
*GOLD/50: .6X TO 1.5X BASIC CARDS
*ORANGE/25: UNPRICED DUE TO SCARCITY
*BLACK/10: UNPRICED DUE TO SCARCITY
*RED/5: UNPRICED DUE TO SCARCITY
*SUPERFR/1: UNPRICED DUE TO SCARCITY
RANDOMLY INSERTED INTO PACKS

5T1 Booker T	1.25	3.00
5T2 Bret Hit Man Hart	1.50	4.00
5T3 Charlotte Flair	3.00	8.00
5T4 Dolph Ziggler	1.25	3.00
5T5 Edge	2.50	6.00
5T6 John Cena	3.00	8.00
5T7 Kevin Nash	1.00	2.50
5T8 Kofi Kingston	1.50	4.00
5T9 Lex Luger	.75	2.00
5T10 Randy Orton	2.00	5.00
5T11 Rey Mysterio	1.50	4.00
5T12 Ric Flair	2.50	6.00
5T13 R-Truth	.75	2.00
5T14 Sasha Banks	3.00	8.00
5T15 Stone Cold Steve Austin	3.00	8.00
5T16 The Miz	1.00	2.50
5T17 The Rock	6.00	15.00
5T18 Triple H	2.50	6.00
5T19 Trish Stratus	3.00	8.00
5T20 William Regal	1.00	2.50

2021 Topps Chrome WWE 5 Timers Club Autographs

*GOLD/50: .5X TO 1.2X BASIC AUTOS
*ORANGE/25: .6X TO 1.5X BASIC AUTOS
*BLACK/10: UNPRICED DUE TO SCARCITY
*RED/5: UNPRICED DUE TO SCARCITY
*SUPERFR/1: UNPRICED DUE TO SCARCITY
*P.P.BLACK/1: UNPRICED DUE TO SCARCITY
*P.P.CYAN/1: UNPRICED DUE TO SCARCITY
*P.P.MAGENTA/1: UNPRICED DUE TO SCARCITY
*P.P.YELLOW/1: UNPRICED DUE TO SCARCITY
STATED PRINT RUN 99 SER.#'d SETS

5TABT Booker T	15.00	40.00
5TACF Charlotte Flair	75.00	150.00
5TAKK Kofi Kingston	12.00	30.00
5TARM Rey Mysterio	50.00	100.00
5TASB Sasha Banks	75.00	150.00
5TATM The Miz	12.00	30.00
5TATS Trish Stratus	75.00	150.00
5TAWR William Regal	15.00	40.00

2021 Topps Chrome WWE Autographs

*GREEN/99: .5X TO 1.2X BASIC AUTOS
*GOLD/50: .6X TO 1.5X BASIC AUTOS
*ORANGE/25: UNPRICED DUE TO SCARCITY
*BLACK/10: UNPRICED DUE TO SCARCITY
*RED/5: UNPRICED DUE TO SCARCITY
*SUPERFR/1: UNPRICED DUE TO SCARCITY
*P.P.BLACK/1: UNPRICED DUE TO SCARCITY
*P.P.CYAN/1: UNPRICED DUE TO SCARCITY
*P.P.MAGENTA/1: UNPRICED DUE TO SCARCITY
*P.P.YELLOW/1: UNPRICED DUE TO SCARCITY
RANDOMLY INSERTED INTO PACKS

AAA Aliyah	12.00	30.00
AAB Alexa Bliss	75.00	150.00
AAC Apollo Crews	5.00	12.00
AAD Angelo Dawkins	6.00	15.00
AAJ AJ Styles	12.00	30.00
AAS Asuka	15.00	40.00
ABA Bayley	20.00	50.00
ABB Bianca Belair	15.00	40.00
ABE Big E	6.00	15.00
ABH Shotzi Blackheart	25.00	60.00
ABK Billie Kay	15.00	40.00
ABL Bobby Lashley	10.00	25.00
ABR Bronson Reed	5.00	12.00
ACL Candice LeRae	12.00	30.00
ACS Cesaro	6.00	15.00
ADL Dexter Lumis	6.00	15.00
ADP Damian Priest	8.00	20.00
AFB Finn Balor	12.00	30.00
AGM Gran Metalik	6.00	15.00
AIS Io Shirai	15.00	40.00
AJG Johnny Gargano	5.00	12.00
AJM John Morrison	8.00	20.00
AKC King Corbin	6.00	15.00
AKO Kevin Owens	12.00	30.00
AKR Karrion Kross	15.00	40.00
AKY Kyle O'Reilly	6.00	15.00
ALM Liv Morgan	30.00	75.00
AMA Mustafa Ali	5.00	12.00
AMF Montez Ford	6.00	15.00
AMR Mandy Rose	20.00	50.00
ANC Nikki Cross	10.00	25.00
ANJ Nia Jax	8.00	20.00
AOT Otis	5.00	12.00
APR Peyton Royce	15.00	40.00
ARB Ruby Riott	15.00	40.00
ARG Raquel Gonzalez	20.00	50.00
ARP Rhea Ripley	20.00	50.00
ARS Robert Stone	5.00	12.00
ASB Shayna Baszler	10.00	25.00
ASC Scarlett	50.00	100.00
ASD Sonya Deville	15.00	40.00
ASG Chad Gable	5.00	12.00
ASM Sheamus	6.00	15.00
ASN Shinsuke Nakamura	10.00	25.00
ASR Seth Rollins	10.00	25.00
ASS Isaiah Swerve Scott	6.00	15.00
AST Roderick Strong	6.00	15.00
ATC Tommaso Ciampa	8.00	20.00
ATK Dakota Kai	12.00	30.00
ATT Timothy Thatcher	6.00	15.00
AXW Xavier Woods	6.00	15.00
ABAY Adam Cole	25.00	60.00
ABRO Riddle	15.00	40.00
ADMC Drew McIntyre		
ALEE Keith Lee	8.00	20.00
AMVP MVP	6.00	15.00

2021 Topps Chrome WWE Best of In Your House

COMPLETE SET (25) 25.00 60.00
*GREEN/99: .5X TO 1.2X BASIC CARDS
*GOLD/50: .6X TO 1.5X BASIC CARDS
*ORANGE/25: UNPRICED DUE TO SCARCITY
*BLACK/10: UNPRICED DUE TO SCARCITY
*RED/5: UNPRICED DUE TO SCARCITY
*SUPERFR/1: UNPRICED DUE TO SCARCITY
RANDOMLY INSERTED INTO PACKS

IYH1 Shawn Michaels	2.50	6.00
IYH2 Razor Ramon	1.00	2.50
IYH3 Hunter Hearst Helmsley	2.50	6.00
IYH4 Undertaker	3.00	8.00
IYH5 Razor Ramon	1.00	2.50
IYH6 Shawn Michaels	2.50	6.00
IYH7 Mark Henry	.60	1.50
IYH8 HBK	2.50	6.00
IYH9 Stone Cold Steve Austin	3.00	8.00
IYH10 Undertaker	3.00	8.00
IYH11 Ken Shamrock	.75	2.00
IYH12 Shawn Michaels/Undertaker	3.00	8.00
IYH13 Shawn Michaels	2.50	6.00
IYH14 Kane	1.00	2.50
IYH15 Triple H	2.50	6.00
IYH16 Shawn Michaels	2.50	6.00
IYH17 Undertaker	3.00	8.00
IYH18 Stone Cold Steve Austin	3.00	8.00
IYH19 Steve Austin/Undertaker	3.00	8.00
IYH20 Christian	1.00	2.50
IYH21 Ken Shamrock	.75	2.00
IYH22 Stone Cold Steve Austin	3.00	8.00
IYH23 Finn Balor	1.50	4.00
IYH24 Keith Lee	1.25	3.00
IYH25 Io Shirai	1.25	3.00

2021 Topps Chrome WWE Cruiserweight Greats

COMPLETE SET (10) 4.00 10.00
*GREEN/99: .5X TO 1.2X BASIC CARDS
*GOLD/50: .6X TO 1.5X BASIC CARDS
*ORANGE/25: UNPRICED DUE TO SCARCITY
*BLACK/10: UNPRICED DUE TO SCARCITY
*RED/5: UNPRICED DUE TO SCARCITY
*SUPERFR/1: UNPRICED DUE TO SCARCITY
FAT PACK EXCLUSIVES

CG1 Akira Tozawa	.60	1.50
CG2 Angel Garza	.60	1.50
CG3 Cedric Alexander	.50	1.25
CG4 Drew Gulak	.60	1.50
CG5 Jordan Devlin	.50	1.25
CG6 Kalisto	.60	1.50
CG7 Murphy	.60	1.50
CG8 Santos Escobar	.75	2.00
CG9 The Brian Kendrick	.50	1.25
CG10 Tony Nese	.50	1.25

2021 Topps Chrome WWE Cruiserweight Greats Autographs

*ORANGE/25: .5X TO 1.2X BASIC AUTOS
*BLACK/10: UNPRICED DUE TO SCARCITY
*RED/5: UNPRICED DUE TO SCARCITY
*SUPERFR/1: UNPRICED DUE TO SCARCITY
FAT PACK EXCLUSIVES
STATED PRINT RUN 50 SER.#'d SETS

CGAAG Angel Garza	5.00	15.00
CGAAT Akira Tozawa	6.00	15.00
CGACA Cedric Alexander	8.00	20.00
CGAKL Kalisto	6.00	15.00
CGAMP Murphy	6.00	15.00
CGASE Santos Escobar	10.00	25.00
CGATN Tony Nese	8.00	20.00

2021 Topps Chrome WWE Great Feats of Strength

COMPLETE SET (10) 6.00 15.00
*GREEN/99: .5X TO 1.2X BASIC CARDS
*GOLD/50: .6X TO 1.5X BASIC CARDS
*ORANGE/25: UNPRICED DUE TO SCARCITY
*BLACK/10: UNPRICED DUE TO SCARCITY
*RED/5: UNPRICED DUE TO SCARCITY
*SUPERFR/1: UNPRICED DUE TO SCARCITY
BLASTER BOX EXCLUSIVES

GF1 Beth Phoenix	1.00	2.50
GF2 Mark Henry	.50	1.25
GF3 Mark Henry	.50	1.25
GF4 Titus O'Neil	.50	1.25
GF5 Braun Strowman	1.25	3.00
GF6 Ronda Rousey	2.50	6.00
GF7 Bobby Lashley	1.25	3.00
GF8 Cesaro	.50	1.25
GF9 Tyler Bate	.60	1.50
GF10 Bianca Belair	1.25	3.00

2021 Topps Chrome WWE Great Feats of Strength Autographs

BLASTER BOX EXCLUSIVES

GFABB Bianca Belair
GFABE Big E
GFABP Beth Phoenix
GFACS Cesaro
GFARR Ronda Rousey
GFATO Titus O'Neil
GFATY Tyler Bate
GFAWS Mark Henry

2021 Topps Chrome WWE Image Variations

*GREEN/99: 1X TO 2.5X BASIC CARDS
*GOLD/50: 1.5X TO 4X BASIC CARDS
*ORANGE/25: UNPRICED DUE TO SCARCITY
*BLACK/10: UNPRICED DUE TO SCARCITY
*RED/5: UNPRICED DUE TO SCARCITY
*SUPERFR/1: UNPRICED DUE TO SCARCITY
RANDOMLY INSERTED INTO PACKS

IV1 AJ Styles	3.00	8.00
IV2 Angel Garza	1.25	3.00
IV3 Asuka	6.00	15.00
IV4 Bray Wyatt	3.00	8.00
IV5 Erik	1.25	3.00
IV6 Gran Metalik	1.25	3.00
IV7 Keith Lee	2.00	5.00
IV8 King Corbin	2.00	5.00
IV9 Lince Dorado	1.50	4.00
IV10 Mandy Rose	8.00	20.00
IV11 Riddle	2.00	5.00
IV12 MVP	1.25	3.00
IV13 Naomi	1.25	3.00
IV14 Samoa Joe	1.25	3.00
IV15 Shayna Baszler	1.50	4.00
IV16 Sheamus	1.25	3.00
IV17 The Miz	1.25	3.00
IV18 Bianca Belair	2.50	6.00
IV19 Seth Rollins	1.50	4.00
IV20 Bayley	2.00	5.00
IV21 Big E	1.50	4.00
IV22 Cesaro	1.25	3.00
IV23 Dolph Ziggler	1.25	3.00
IV24 Kalisto	1.25	3.00
IV25 Kayla Braxton	2.50	6.00
IV26 Sasha Banks	6.00	15.00
IV27 Shinsuke Nakamura	2.00	5.00
IV28 Santos Escobar	1.25	3.00
IV29 Shotzi Blackheart	5.00	12.00
IV30 Velveteen Dream	1.25	3.00

2021 Topps Chrome WWE Slam Attax

COMPLETE SET (200) 125.00 250.00
*REF.: .5X TO 1.2X BASIC CARDS
*SPECKLE: .6X TO 1.5X BASIC CARDS
*YELLOW/99: .75X TO 2X BASIC CARDS
*GREEN/50: 1.2X TO 3X BASIC CARDS
*ORANGE/25: UNPRICED DUE TO SCARCITY
*BLACK/10: UNPRICED DUE TO SCARCITY
*RED WAVE/5: UNPRICED DUE TO SCARCITY
*SUPERFR/1: UNPRICED DUE TO SCARCITY

1 Adam Cole	1.00	2.50
2 AJ Styles	1.00	2.50
3 Akira Tozawa	.40	1.00
4 Danny Burch	.40	1.00
5 Alexa Bliss	2.00	5.00
6 Angel Garza	.40	1.00
7 Angelo Dawkins	.40	1.00
8 Apollo Crews	.40	1.00
9 Asuka	1.25	3.00
10 Austin Theory	.60	1.50
11 Bayley	.75	2.00
12 Becky Lynch	1.25	3.00
13 Bianca Belair	.75	2.00
14 Big E	.60	1.50
15 Doudrop	.50	1.25
16 Bobby Lashley	.75	2.00
17 Fabian Aichner	.40	1.00
18 Jimmy Uso	.30	.75
19 Cameron Grimes	.60	1.50
20 Candice LeRae	1.25	3.00
21 Carmella	.75	2.00
22 Cedric Alexander	.30	.75
23 Cesaro	.30	.75
24 Chad Gable	.30	.75
25 Charlotte Flair	1.50	4.00
26 Dakota Kai	.60	1.50
27 Damian Priest	.50	1.25
28 Dana Brooke	.30	.75
29 Flash Morgan Webster	.40	1.00
30 Dexter Lumis	.30	.75
31 Dolph Ziggler	.60	1.50
32 Dominik Mysterio RC	.40	1.00
33 Drew McIntyre	.75	2.00
34 Edge	1.25	3.00
35 Elias	.30	.75
36 Ember Moon	.40	1.00
37 Dominik Mysterio RC	.40	1.00
38 Finn Balor	.75	2.00
39 Indi Hartwell RC	1.00	2.50
40 Io Shirai	.60	1.50
41 Isaiah "Swerve" Scott	.50	1.25
42 Ivar	.30	.75
43 James Drake	.30	.75
44 Jeff Hardy	.75	2.00
45 Jey Uso	.30	.75
46 John Morrison	.60	1.50
47 Johnny Gargano	.60	1.50
48 Jordan Devlin	.30	.75
49 Kacy Catanzaro	.60	1.50
50 Karrion Kross	1.25	3.00
51 Kay Lee Ray	.75	2.00
52 Keith Lee	.60	1.50
53 Kevin Owens	.60	1.50
54 Lince Dorado	.30	.75
55 Baron Corbin	.30	.75
56 Kofi Kingston	.75	2.00
57 Jinder Mahal	.40	1.00
58 Kushida	.50	1.25
59 Kyle OíReilly	.50	1.25
60 Lacey Evans	.75	2.00
61 Gran Metalik	.30	.75
62 Reggie RC	.40	1.00
63 Liv Morgan	1.25	3.00
64 Mace	.30	.75
65 Mandy Rose	1.50	4.00
66 Marcel Barthel	.40	1.00
67 Mark Andrews	.30	.75
68 Zelina Vega	.60	1.50
69 Montez Ford	.30	.75
70 Humberto Carrillo	.30	.75
71 Mustafa Ali	.40	1.00
72 Naomi	.40	1.00
73 Nash Carter RC	.30	.75
74 Natalya	.50	1.25
75 Nia Jax	.60	1.50
76 Nikki A.S.H.	.60	1.50
77 Oney Lorcan	.30	.75
78 Otis	.40	1.00
79 Pete Dunne	.60	1.50
80 R-Truth	.40	1.00
81 Randy Orton	1.00	2.50
82 Raquel Gonzalez	.75	2.00
83 Rey Mysterio	.75	2.00
84 Rhea Ripley	1.00	2.50
85 Ricochet	.60	1.50
86 Riddle	.75	2.00
87 Robert Roode	.40	1.00
88 Roderick Strong	.50	1.25
89 Roman Reigns	1.50	4.00
90 MVP	.30	.75
91 Sami Zayn	.50	1.25
92 Santos Escobar	.50	1.25
93 Sasha Banks	1.50	4.00
94 Scarlett	1.50	4.00
95 Seth Rollins	.75	2.00
96 Shayna Baszler	.60	1.50
97 Sheamus	.50	1.25
98 Shelton Benjamin	.50	1.25
99 Shinsuke Nakamura	.75	2.00
100 Shotzi	1.25	3.00
101 T-Bar	.40	1.00
102 Tamina	.40	1.00
103 Tegan Nox	.75	2.00
104 Omos RC	.60	1.50
105 The Miz	.50	1.25
106 Timothy Thatcher RC	.30	.75
107 Tommaso Ciampa	.75	2.00
108 Toni Storm	1.00	2.50
109 Trent Seven	.40	1.00
110 Tyler Bate	.40	1.00
111 Ilja Dragunov	.30	.75
112 Walter	.75	2.00
113 Wes Lee RC	.30	.75
114 Xavier Woods	.30	.75
115 Zack Gibson	.30	.75
116 Mankind 25th ANN	.60	1.50
117 ìStone Coldî Steve Austin 25th ANN	1.50	4.00
118 Hulk Hogan 25th ANN	1.50	4.00
119 The Rock 25th ANN	3.00	8.00
120 The Undertaker TYT	1.50	4.00
121 The Undertaker TYT	1.50	4.00
122 The Undertaker TYT	1.50	4.00
123 The Undertaker TYT	1.50	4.00
124 The Undertaker TYT	1.50	4.00
125 Apollo Crews BS	.40	1.00
126 Bianca Belair BS	.75	2.00
127 Big E BS	.60	1.50
128 Cesaro BS	.30	.75
129 Damian Priest BS	.50	1.25
130 Jey Uso BS	.30	.75
131 Liv Morgan BS	1.25	3.00
132 Rhea Ripley BS	1.00	2.50
133 Riddle BS	.75	2.00
134 Andre the Giant L	1.25	3.00
135 Batista L	.60	1.50
136 Bret ìHit Manî Hart L	.75	2.00
137 Hulk Hogan L	1.50	4.00
138 ìMacho Manî Randy Savage L	2.00	5.00
139 Mankind L	.60	1.50
140 Shawn Michaels L	1.25	3.00
141 ìStone Coldî Steve Austin L	1.50	4.00
142 Trish Stratus L	1.50	4.00
143 Ultimate Warrior L	1.25	3.00
144 Apollo Crews BL	.40	1.00
145 Bayley BL	.75	2.00
146 Sasha Banks BL	1.50	4.00
147 Sheamus BL	.50	1.25
148 Asuka ER	1.25	3.00
149 Cesaro ER	.30	.75
150 Kevin Owens ER	.60	1.50
151 Seth Rollins ER	.75	2.00
152 Drew McIntyre SS	.75	2.00
153 Mandy Rose SS	1.50	4.00
154 Montez Ford SS	.30	.75
155 Roman Reigns SS	1.50	4.00
156 Dominik Mysterio PB	.40	1.00
157 Keith Lee PB	.60	1.50
158 Riddle PB	.75	2.00
159 Shayna Baszler PB	.60	1.50
160 Angelo Dawkins COC	.40	1.00
161 Bobby Lashley COC	.75	2.00
162 Sami Zayn COC	.50	1.25
163 Shinsuke Nakamura COC	.75	2.00
164 AJ Styles SRS	1.00	2.50
165 Lacey Evans SRS	.75	2.00
166 Nia Jax SRS	.60	1.50
167 The Miz SRS	.50	1.25
168 Big E TLC	.60	1.50
169 Cedric Alexander TLC	.30	.75
170 Otis TLC	.40	1.00
171 Randy Orton TLC	1.00	2.50
172 Bianca Belair RR	.75	2.00
173 Edge RR	1.25	3.00
174 Rhea Ripley RR	1.00	2.50
175 Asuka ICONS	1.25	3.00
176 Bayley ICONS	.75	2.00
177 Becky Lynch ICONS	1.25	3.00
178 Charlotte Flair ICONS	1.50	4.00
179 John Cena ICONS	1.50	4.00
180 Kofi Kingston ICONS	.75	2.00
181 Randy Orton ICONS	1.00	2.50
182 Seth Rollins ICONS	.75	2.00
183 Alexa Bliss 100	2.00	5.00
184 Bianca Belair 100	.75	2.00
185 Drew McIntyre 100	.75	2.00
186 Bobby Lashley 100	.75	2.00

187	Sasha Banks 100	1.50	4.00
188	Big E 100	.60	1.50
189	Edge 100	1.25	3.00
190	Hollywood Hulk Hogan nWo SR	1.50	4.00
191	Roman Reigns 100	1.50	4.00
192	AJ Styles F	1.00	2.50
193	Bobby Lashley F	.75	2.00
194	Drew McIntyre F	.75	2.00
195	Io Shirai F	.60	1.50
196	Jey Uso F	.30	.75
197	Randy Orton F	1.00	2.50
198	Rhea Ripley F	1.00	2.50
199	Roman Reigns F	1.50	4.00
200	John Cena nWo UR	6.00	15.00

2021 Topps Chrome WWE Slam Attax Autographs

STATED ODDS 1:54

AB Big E
AR Reckoning
AAB Alexa Bliss
AAC Adam Cole
AAJ AJ Styles
ABB Bianca Belair
ABH Bret ìHit Manî Hart
ABL Becky Lynch
ACF Charlotte Flair
ACL Candice LeRae
ADM Drew McIntyre
AED Edge
AFA Fabian Aichner
AFB Finn Balor
AGM Gran Metalik
AHH Hulk Hogan
AIS Io Shirai
AJC John Cena
AJR Jaxson Ryker
AKR Kay Lee Ray
AKU Kushida
AKY Kyle OíReilly
AMA Ali
AMF Mick Foley
AMY Mia Yim
ANC Nikki A.S.H.
ANM Naomi
ANT Natalya
ARC Ricochet
ARR Rhea Ripley
ARR Roman Reigns
ARS Roderick Strong
ASB Sasha Banks
ASH Shelton Benjamin
ASN Shinsuke Nakamura
AT7 Trent Seven
ATC Tommaso Ciampa
ATM The Miz
ATS Toni Storm
ATY Tyler Bate
AWT Walter
AXW Xavier Woods
AZV Zelina Vega
AHHH Triple H

2006 Topps Heritage Chrome WWE

COMPLETE SET (90) 10.00 25.00
UNOPENED BOX (24 PACKS)
UNOPENED PACK (5 CARDS)
*REFRACTORS: .75X TO 2X BASIC CARDS
*X-FRACTORS: 1.5X TO 4X BASIC CARDS
*SUPERFR./25: 10X TO 25X BASIC CARDS

1	John Cena	4.00	10.00
2	Batista	.75	2.00
3	Carlito	.75	2.00
4	Orlando Jordan	.20	.50
5	Paul London	.20	.50
6	Johnny Nitro	.30	.75
7	Joey Mercury	.20	.50
8	The Hurricane	.20	.50
9	Rosey	.20	.50
10	The Rock	10.00	25.00
11	Stone Cold Steve Austin	1.25	3.00
12	Hulk Hogan	1.25	3.00
13	Big Show	.75	2.00
14	The Boogeyman RC	.30	.75
15	Danny Basham	.20	.50
16	Edge	.75	2.00
17	Finlay	.50	1.25
18	Eugene	.20	.50
19	Joey Styles RC	.20	.50
20	Jonathan Coachman	.20	.50
21	Kane	.75	2.00
22	Kid Kash	.20	.50
23	Kurt Angle	.75	2.00
24	Rene Dupree	.30	.75
25	Ric Flair	1.00	2.50
26	Rob Van Dam	.50	1.25
27	Shawn Michaels	1.25	3.00
28	Triple H	1.25	3.00
29	Chavo Guerrero	.30	.75
30	Val Venis	.30	.75
31	Viscera	.30	.75
32	Steven Richards	.30	.75
33	Booker T	.50	1.25
34	Chris Benoit	.75	2.00
35	Ken Kennedy RC	.50	1.25
36	Doug Basham	.30	.75
37	Lashley RC	.50	1.25
38	Funaki	.30	.75
39	Hardcore Holly	.30	.75
40	JBL	.50	1.25
41	Paul Burchill RC	.20	.50
42	Psicosis	.20	.50
43	Super Crazy	.30	.75
44	Shelton Benjamin	.20	.50
45	Chris Masters	.30	.75
46	Nunzio	.20	.50
47	Randy Orton	.50	1.25
48	Rey Mysterio	.75	2.00
49	Scotty 2 Hotty	.30	.75
50	Tazz	.30	.75
51	Theodore Long	.20	.50
52	Undertaker	1.00	2.50
53	William Regal	.50	1.25
54	Antonio	.20	.50
55	Romeo	.20	.50
56	Snitsky	.30	.75
57	Robert Conway	.30	.75
58	Mickie James DV RC	1.25	3.00
59	Sharmell DV	.75	2.00
60	Trish Stratus DV	2.00	5.00
61	Torrie Wilson DV	2.00	5.00
62	Ashley DV RC	.75	2.00
63	Lita DV	1.25	3.00
64	Lilian Garcia DV	1.00	2.50
65	Maria DV	.75	2.00
66	Stacy Keibler DV	2.00	5.00
67	Victoria DV	1.25	3.00
68	Candice Michelle DV	1.25	3.00
69	Michelle McCool DV	1.00	2.50
70	Melina DV	.75	2.00
71	The British Bulldog L	.75	2.00
72	Chief Jay Strongbow L	.30	.75
73	Classy Freddie Blassie L	.30	.75
74	Cowboy Bob Orton L	.50	1.25
75	Bobby The Brain Heenan L	.50	1.25
76	Gorilla Monsoon L	.30	.75
77	Hillbilly Jim L	.30	.75
78	Iron Sheik L	.75	2.00
79	Jake The Snake Roberts L	.60	1.50
80	Jerry The King Lawler L	.60	1.50
81	Junkyard Dog L	.60	1.50
82	Mouth of the South Jimmy Hart L	.75	2.00
83	Mr. Wonderful Paul Orndorff L	.75	2.00
84	Nikolai Volkoff L	.50	1.25
85	Rowdy Roddy Piper L	1.00	2.50
86	Sgt. Slaughter L	.75	2.00
87	Superstar Billy Graham L RC	.30	.75
88	Million-Dollar Man Ted DiBiase L	.75	2.00
89	Godfather L	.30	.75
90	Checklist	.20	.50

2006 Topps Heritage Chrome WWE Autographs

GROUP A ODDS: 1:404 HOBBY
GROUP B ODDS: 1:719 HOBBY
GROUP C ODDS: 1:167 HOBBY
GROUP D ODDS: 1:31 HOBBY

NNO	Ashley D	12.00	30.00
NNO	Big Show D	12.00	30.00
NNO	Bobby The Brain Heenan D	125.00	250.00
NNO	Boogeyman D	10.00	25.00
NNO	Booker T A	8.00	20.00
NNO	Carlito C	6.00	15.00
NNO	Chavo Guerrero D	6.00	15.00
NNO	Chief Jay Strongbow D	12.00	30.00
NNO	Chris Benoit D	300.00	600.00
NNO	Hillbilly Jim D	30.00	75.00
NNO	JBL A	25.00	60.00
NNO	Jerry The King Lawler D	15.00	40.00
NNO	John Cena D	75.00	150.00
NNO	Kane B	12.00	30.00
NNO	Ken Kennedy D	6.00	15.00
NNO	Kurt Angle C	10.00	25.00
NNO	Lashley D	15.00	40.00
NNO	Lilian Garcia D	12.00	30.00
NNO	Lita D	15.00	40.00
NNO	Mickie James D	15.00	40.00
NNO	Rey Mysterio D	20.00	50.00
NNO	Sgt. Slaughter D	20.00	50.00
NNO	Shawn Michaels D	75.00	150.00
NNO	Tazz C	15.00	40.00
NNO	Torrie Wilson D	15.00	40.00
NNO	Trish Stratus C	25.00	60.00
NNO	Victoria D	12.00	30.00

2006 Topps Heritage Chrome WWE Ringside Relics

COMPLETE SET (2) 10.00 25.00
RETAIL EXCLUSIVE

NNO	JBL/Batista	6.00	15.00
NNO	Melina/T.Wilson	8.00	20.00

2007 Topps Heritage II Chrome WWE

COMPLETE SET (100) 10.00 25.00
UNOPENED BOX (24 PACKS)
UNOPENED PACK (5 CARDS)
*REFRACTORS: .8X TO 2X BASIC CARDS
*X-FRACTORS: 1.5X TO 4X BASIC CARDS
*SUPERFR/25: 10X TO 25X BASIC CARDS

1	John Cena	1.25	3.00
2	Batista	.75	2.00
3	Carlito	.75	2.00
4	Tatanka	.20	.50
5	Highlanders	.30	.75
6	Johnny Nitro	.30	.75
7	The Great Khali	.30	.75
8	Gregory Helms	.20	.50
9	Jeff Hardy	.50	1.25
10	The Rock	1.50	4.00
11	Stone Cold Steve Austin	1.25	3.00
12	Matt Striker	.20	.50
13	Montel Vontavious Porter RC	.30	.75
14	The Boogeyman	.30	.75
15	Mark Henry	.30	.75
16	Edge	.75	2.00
17	Finlay	.50	1.25
18	Eugene	.20	.50
19	Sandman	.30	.75
20	Sabu RC	.20	.50
21	Kane	.75	2.00
22	Brian Kendrick/Paul London	.50	1.25
23	Rene Dupree	.30	.75
24	Ric Flair	.75	2.00
25	Rob Van Dam	.75	2.00
26	Shawn Michaels	1.25	3.00
27	Triple H	1.25	3.00
28	Chavo Guerrero	.30	.75
29	Vito	.20	.50
30	Viscera	.50	1.25
31	King Booker	.75	2.00
32	Chris Benoit	.50	1.25
33	Ken Kennedy	.50	1.25
34	Bobby Lashley	.75	2.00
35	Funaki	.30	.75
36	Matt Hardy	.50	1.25
37	JBL	.50	1.25
38	Paul Burchill	.20	.50
39	CM Punk	.30	.75
40	Super Crazy	.30	.75
41	Shelton Benjamin	.20	.50
42	Chris Masters	.75	2.00
43	Little Guido Maritato	.20	.50
44	Randy Orton	.75	2.00
45	Rey Mysterio	.50	1.25
46	Scotty 2 Hotty	.30	.75
47	Kenny Dykstra RC	.30	.75
48	Undertaker	1.00	2.50
49	William Regal	.50	1.25
50	Charlie Haas	.20	.50
51	Umaga	.30	.75
52	Snitsky	.30	.75
53	Rob Conway	.20	.50
54	Mr. McMahon	.75	2.00
55	Shane McMahon	.50	1.25
56	Stephanie McMahon	1.00	2.50
57	Linda McMahon	.30	.75
58	Mickie James DV	1.00	2.50
59	Sharmell DV	.50	1.25
60	Torrie Wilson DV	1.50	4.00

61 Ashley DV	.75	2.00
62 Michelle McCool DV	1.00	2.50
63 Layla DV RC	.75	2.00
64 Maria DV	.75	2.00
65 Kristal DV	.75	2.00
66 Victoria DV	1.00	2.50
67 Candice Michelle DV	1.00	2.50
68 Jillian Hall DV	1.00	2.50
69 Melina DV	.75	2.00
70 Mean Gene Okerlund L	.50	1.25
71 Don Muraco L	.30	.75
72 Paul Bearer L	.30	.75
73 One Man Gang L	.30	.75
74 Dusty Rhodes L	.50	1.25
75 Bushwhackers L	.20	.50
76 The Wild Samoans L	.30	.75
77 Bam Bam Bigelow L	.50	1.25
78 Mr. Perfect Curt Hennig L	.50	1.25
79 The British Bulldog L	.75	2.00
80 Earthquake L	.30	.75
81 Rocky Johnson L RC	.30	.75
82 Papa Shango L	.25	.60
83 Jerry The King Lawler	.50	1.25
84 High Chief Peter Maivia L	.20	.50
85 Arn Anderson L	.20	.50
86 Mick Foley L	.75	2.00
87 Ravishing Rick Rude L	.50	1.25
88 Doink L	.20	.50
89 Andre The Giant L	.75	2.00
90 Batista TR	.75	2.00
91 Triple H TR	1.25	3.00
92 Carlito TR	.75	2.00
93 John Cena TR	1.25	3.00
94 Rey Mysterio TR	.50	1.25
95 Andre The Giant TR	.75	2.00
96 Iron Sheik TR	.75	2.00
97 Jerry The King Lawler TR	.50	1.25
98 Rowdy Roddy Piper TR	.75	2.00
99 Superstar Billy Graham TR	.30	.75
100 Cena/Booker/Ashley/Mysterio CL	1.25	3.00

2007 Topps Heritage II Chrome WWE Autographs

STATED ODDS 1:24 HOBBY EXCLUSIVE

NNO Ashley	12.00	30.00
NNO Jeff Hardy	15.00	40.00
NNO John Cena	25.00	60.00
NNO Ken Kennedy	8.00	20.00
NNO Layla	10.00	25.00
NNO Melina	10.00	25.00
NNO Michelle McCool	10.00	25.00
NNO Mickie James	15.00	40.00
NNO Sabu	10.00	25.00
NNO Sandman	15.00	40.00
NNO Sharmell	6.00	15.00
NNO Torrie Wilson	15.00	40.00
NNO William Regal	10.00	25.00

2007 Topps Heritage II Chrome WWE Mini

COMPLETE SET (5)

1 John Cena
2 Rey Mysterio
3 Andre The Giant
4 Hulk Hogan
5 Batista

2007 Topps Heritage II Chrome WWE Ringside Relics

STATED ODDS 1:24 RETAIL EXCLUSIVE

NNO Jeff Hardy/Carlito	4.00	10.00
NNO Kane/Umaga	4.00	10.00
NNO Lita/Mickie James	6.00	15.00

2008 Topps Heritage III Chrome WWE

COMPLETE SET (90)	8.00	20.00
UNOPENED BOX (24 PACKS)		
UNOPEND PACK (5 CARDS)		
*REFRACTORS: .8X TO 2X BASIC CARDS		
*X-FRACTORS: 1.5X TO 4X BASIC CARDS		
*SUPERFR./25: 10X TO 25X BASIC CARDS		
1 John Cena	1.25	3.00
2 Batista	.75	2.00
3 Rey Mysterio	.50	1.25
4 Stone Cold	1.25	3.00
5 The Great Khali	.20	.50
6 Chris Jericho	.50	1.25
7 Edge	.75	2.00
8 Hard Core Holly	.30	.75
9 Umaga	.30	.75
10 Montel Vontavious Porter	.30	.75
11 Stevie Richards	.30	.75
12 Deuce	.20	.50
13 Lance Cade	.20	.50
14 Super Crazy	.30	.75
15 Chuck Palumbo	.30	.75
16 Domino	.20	.50
17 Trevor Murdoch	.20	.50
18 Zack Ryder	.20	.50
19 Festus RC	.20	.50
20 Mark Henry	.30	.75
21 Boogeyman	.30	.75
22 Brian Kendrick	.30	.75
23 Tommy Dreamer	.20	.50
24 Charlie Haas	.20	.50
25 JBL	.20	.50
26 Armando Estrada	.20	.50
27 CM Punk	.20	.50
28 Triple H	1.25	3.00
29 Shannon Moore	.20	.50
30 Hacksaw Jim Duggan	.50	1.25
31 Jeff Hardy	.75	2.00
32 Kane	.75	2.00
33 Ron Simmons	.20	.50
34 Finlay	.30	.75
35 The Miz	.30	.75
36 Kenny Dykstra	.30	.75
37 Snitsky	.30	.75
38 Jesse RC	.20	.50
39 Santino Marella	.20	.50
40 Cody Rhodes	.20	.50
41 Shelton Benjamin	.20	.50
42 Hornswoggle	.30	.75
43 Big Daddy V	.30	.75
44 Matt Striker	.20	.50
45 Curt Hawkins	.20	.50
46 William Regal	.50	1.25
47 Jimmy Wang Yang	.20	.50
48 Elijah Burke	.20	.50
49 Chavo Guerrero	.30	.75
50 Paul London	.20	.50
51 Mr. Kennedy	.50	1.25
52 John Morrison	.20	.50
53 Matt Hardy	.75	2.00
54 Shawn Michaels	1.25	3.00
55 Randy Orton	.50	1.25
56 Ric Flair	.75	2.00
57 Undertaker	1.00	2.50
58 Torrie Wilson DV	1.50	4.00
59 Candice DV	1.00	2.50
60 Michelle McCool DV	1.00	2.50
61 Melina DV	.75	2.00
62 Cherry DV	.75	2.00
63 Jillian DV	.75	2.00
64 Ashley DV	.75	2.00
65 Maria DV	.75	2.00
66 Kelly Kelly DV	.75	2.00
67 Mickie James DV	1.25	3.00
68 Maryse DV	.75	2.00
69 Victoria DV	1.00	2.50
70 Anderson/Blanchard L	.30	.75
71 Brian Pillman L	.30	.75
72 Dean Malenko L	.50	1.25
73 Funk Brothers L	.30	.75
74 Dusty Rhodes L	.50	1.25
75 The Freebirds L	.30	.75
76 Jimmy Superfly Snuka L	.50	1.25
77 Jimmy Garvin L	.30	.75
78 Papa Shango L	.20	.50
79 Pat Patterson L	.20	.50
80 Bam Bam Bigelow L	.50	1.25
81 Gorilla Monsoon L	.50	1.25
82 Ted Dibiase L	.50	1.25
83 Rocky Johnson L	.30	.75
84 Bruiser Brody L RC	.30	.75
85 Kamala L	.30	.75
86 Earthquake L	.30	.75
87 Vader L	.30	.75
88 Jack and Gerry Brisco L	.30	.75
89 Cowboy Bob Orton L	.50	1.25
100 Checklist	.20	.50

2008 Topps Heritage III Chrome WWE Allen and Ginter Superstars

COMPLETE SET (10)	6.00	15.00
*REFRACTORS: .8X TO 2X BASIC CARDS		
*X-FRACTORS: 1.5X TO 4X BASIC CARDS		
*SUPERFR/25: 10X TO 25X BASIC CARDS		
1 John Cena	1.25	3.00
2 Batista	.75	2.00
3 Rey Mysterio	.50	1.25
4 Triple H	1.25	3.00
5 Shawn Michaels	1.25	3.00
6 Undertaker	1.00	2.50
7 Rowdy Roddy Piper	.75	2.00
8 Chief Jay Strongbow	.50	1.25
9 Sgt. Slaughter	.50	1.25
10 Iron Sheik	.75	2.00

2008 Topps Heritage III Chrome WWE Autographs

STATED ODDS 1:24 HOBBY EXCLUSIVE

NNO Ashley	25.00	60.00
NNO Carlito	6.00	15.00
NNO Cherry	8.00	20.00
NNO Chuck Palumbo	6.00	15.00
NNO Festus	6.00	15.00
NNO Jeff Hardy	15.00	40.00
NNO Jesse	8.00	20.00
NNO Kane	25.00	60.00
NNO Layla	8.00	20.00
NNO Montel Vontavious Porter	6.00	15.00
NNO Tommy Dreamer	6.00	15.00
NNO Trevor Murdoch	6.00	15.00

2008 Topps Heritage III Chrome WWE Mini-Cards

COMPLETE SET (5)

1 Stone Cold Steve Austin
2 John Cena
3 Edge
4 Umaga
5 The Great Khali

2008 Topps Heritage III Chrome WWE Ringside Relics

STATED ODDS 1:24 RETAIL EXCLUSIVE

NNO Hardcore Holly vs. Carlito	4.00	10.00
NNO Mickie James vs. Beth Phoenix	4.00	10.00
NNO Mr. Kennedy vs. Shawn Michaels	5.00	12.00

2006 Topps Heritage II WWE

COMPLETE SET (90)	8.00	20.00
UNOPENED BOX (24 PACKS)		
UNOPENED PACK (5 CARDS)		
1 John Cena	.75	2.00
2 Batista	.40	1.00
3 Carlito	.30	.75
4 Tatanka	.12	.30
5 Paul London/Brian Kendrick	.30	.75
6 Johnny Nitro	.12	.30
7 The Great Khali RC	.40	1.00
8 Gregory Helms	.12	.30
9 Gunnar Scott RC	.30	.75
10 The Rock	.75	2.00
11 Stone Cold Steve Austin	.75	2.00
12 Hulk Hogan	.75	2.00
13 Big Show	.40	1.00
14 The Boogeyman RC	.20	.50
15 Mark Henry	.30	.75
16 Edge	.40	1.00
17 Finlay	.30	.75
18 Eugene	.12	.30
19 Matt Striker RC	.12	.30
20 Jake and Jesse Gymini	.20	.50
21 Kane	.50	1.25
22 Kid Kash	.20	.50
23 Kurt Angle	.75	2.00
24 Rene Dupree	.12	.30
25 Ric Flair	.60	1.50
26 Rob Van Dam	.50	1.25
27 Shawn Michaels	.60	1.50
28 Triple H	.75	2.00
29 Chavo Guerrero	.30	.75
30 Vito RC	.12	.30
31 Viscera	.20	.50
32 Steven Richards	.20	.50
33 Booker T	.30	.75
34 Chris Benoit	.30	.75
35 Ken Kennedy RC	.30	.75
36 Goldust	.30	.75
37 Bobby Lashley RC	.30	.75
38 Funaki	.20	.50
39 Matt Hardy	.20	.50
40 JBL	.40	1.00
41 Paul Burchill RC	.12	.30
42 Psicosis	.12	.30
43 Super Crazy	.20	.50

44 Shelton Benjamin	.12	.30
45 Chris Masters	.40	1.00
46 Little Guido Maritato RC	.12	.30
47 Randy Orton	.40	1.00
48 Rey Mysterio	.30	.75
49 Scotty 2 Hotty	.20	.50
50 Tazz	.20	.50
51 Spirit Squad	.20	.50
52 Undertaker	.60	1.50
53 William Regal	.30	.75
54 Charlie Haas	.12	.30
55 Umaga	.20	.50
56 Snitsky	.20	.50
57 Rob Conway	.12	.30
58 Mickie James DV RC	.75	2.00
59 Sharmell DV	.40	1.00
60 Torrie Wilson DV	.75	2.00
61 Ashley DV RC	.40	1.00
62 Lita DV	.60	1.50
63 Beth Phoenix DV RC	1.50	4.00
64 Maria DV	.50	1.25
65 Kristal DV RC	.40	1.00
66 Victoria DV	.60	1.50
67 Candice Michelle DV	.60	1.50
68 Jillian Hall DV RC	.50	1.25
69 Melina DV	.50	1.25
70 Mean Gene Okerlund L	.30	.75
71 Don Muraco L	.20	.50
72 Paul Bearer L	.20	.50
73 One Man Gang L	.20	.50
74 Dusty Rhodes L	.30	.75
75 Bushwhackers L	.20	.50
76 The Wild Samoans L	.30	.75
77 Bam Bam Bigelow L	.20	.50
78 Mr. Perfect Curt Hennig L	.30	.75
79 The British Bulldog L	.50	1.25
80 Earthquake L	.20	.50
81 Kamala L	.30	.75
82 Koko B Ware L	.20	.50
83 Jerry The King Lawler L	.30	.75
84 High Chief Peter Maivia L RC	.12	.30
85 Arn Anderson L	.12	.30
86 Mick Foley L	.50	1.25
87 Ravishing Rick Rude L	.30	.75
88 Vader L	.30	.75
89 Andre The Giant L	.50	1.25
90 Checklist	.12	.30

2006 Topps Heritage II WWE Autographs

SEMISTARS	8.00	20.00
UNLISTED STARS	10.00	25.00
STATED ODDS 1:24 HOBBY EXCLUSIVE		
NNO Ashley	10.00	25.00
NNO Bobby Lashley	8.00	20.00
NNO Booker T	15.00	40.00
NNO Brian Kendrick	8.00	20.00
NNO Carlito	8.00	20.00
NNO Charlie Haas	6.00	15.00
NNO Chavo Guerrero	6.00	15.00
NNO Edge	20.00	50.00
NNO Gene Snitsky	6.00	15.00
NNO Jamie Noble	6.00	15.00
NNO Jillian Hall	10.00	25.00
NNO John Cena	60.00	120.00
NNO Johnny Nitro	8.00	20.00
NNO Kane	12.00	30.00
NNO Ken Kennedy	8.00	20.00
NNO Kurt Angle	12.00	30.00
NNO Melina	10.00	25.00
NNO Michelle McCool	15.00	40.00
NNO Mickie James	15.00	40.00
NNO The Miz	8.00	20.00
NNO Paul London	6.00	15.00
NNO Randy Orton	30.00	75.00
NNO Sharmell	8.00	20.00
NNO Shawn Michaels	75.00	150.00
NNO Umaga	15.00	40.00
NNO Vito	6.00	15.00

2006 Topps Heritage II WWE Magazine Promos

COMPLETE SET (9)	4.00	10.00
WWE MAGAZINE EXCLUSIVE		
W1 John Cena	1.00	2.50
W2 Triple H	1.00	2.50
W3 Edge	.75	2.00
W4 Batista	.60	1.50
W5 Undertaker	.60	1.50
W6 Rey Mysterio	.60	1.50
W7 Hulk Hogan	1.00	2.50
W8 Rowdy Roddy Piper	.75	2.00
W9 Sgt. Slaughter	.75	2.00

2006 Topps Heritage II WWE Magnets

COMPLETE SET (9)	6.00	15.00
STATED ODDS 1:4 RETAIL EXCLUSIVE		
1 John Cena	1.50	4.00
2 Batista	1.00	2.50
3 Carlito	.60	1.50
4 Shawn Michaels	1.50	4.00
5 Triple H	1.50	4.00
6 Rey Mysterio	.60	1.50
7 Edge	1.00	2.50
8 Hulk Hogan	1.50	4.00
9 Torrie Wilson	2.00	5.00

2006 Topps Heritage II WWE Raw vs. Smackdown

COMPLETE SET (2)	.75	2.00
V1 John Cena	.60	1.50
V2 Rey Mysterio	.40	1.00

2006 Topps Heritage II WWE Ringside Relics

COMPLETE SET (8)		
STATED ODDS 1:24 HOBBY		
NNO Big Show	8.00	20.00
NNO Carlito	5.00	12.00
NNO Hulk Hogan	10.00	25.00
NNO John Cena Hat	30.00	75.00
NNO John Cena Shirt	10.00	25.00
NNO Psicosis	5.00	12.00
NNO Shawn Michaels	12.00	30.00
NNO Triple H	8.00	20.00

2006 Topps Heritage II WWE Ringside Relics Doubles

NNO Gregory Helms Super Crazy	5.00	12.00
NNO Ken Kennedy Gunner Scott	5.00	12.00
NNO Bobby Lashley King Booker	5.00	12.00

2006 Topps Heritage II WWE Tin Inserts

COMPLETE SET (6)	6.00	15.00
STATED ODDS 1:RETAIL TIN		
TLB1 John Cena	2.50	6.00
TLB2 Hulk Hogan	2.00	5.00
TLB3 Edge	1.50	4.00
TLB4 Triple H	2.00	5.00
TLB5 Rey Mysterio	1.00	2.50
TLB6 Andre The Giant	1.50	4.00

2006 Topps Heritage II WWE Toppers

COMPLETE SET (12)	4.00	10.00
B1-B3 STATED ODDS 1:HOBBY BOX		
B4-B9 STATED ODDS 1:RETAIL TIN		
B10-B12 STATED ODDS 1:2 RETAIL BLISTER		
B1 D-Generation X	1.00	2.50
B2 Edge & Lita	.75	2.00
B3 Armando Alejandro Estrada/Umaga	.30	.75
B4 Booker T & Sharmell	.60	1.50
B5 Johnny Nitro & Melina	.60	1.50
B6 Spirit Squad	.30	.75
B7 D-Generation X	1.00	2.50
B8 Edge & Lita	.75	2.00
B9 Armando Alejandro Estrada/Umaga	.30	.75
B10 The Great Khali/Daivari	.30	.75
B11 Highlanders	.30	.75
B12 Brian Kendrick/Paul London	.60	1.50

2006 Topps Heritage II WWE Turkey Red Legends

COMPLETE SET (12)	6.00	15.00
STATED ODDS 1:6 HOBBY EXCLUSIVE		
1 Rowdy Roddy Piper	1.00	2.50
2 Jake The Snake Roberts	.60	1.50
3 Sgt. Slaughter	.75	2.00
4 Chief Jay Strongbow	.30	.75
5 Jerry The King Lawler	.60	1.50
6 Gorilla Monsoon	.30	.75
7 Iron Sheik	.75	2.00
8 Junkyard Dog	.75	2.00
9 Superstar Billy Graham	.30	.75
10 Classy Freddie Blassie	.30	.75
11 Bobby The Brain Heenan	.50	1.25
12 Andre The Giant	1.00	2.50

2006 Topps Heritage II WWE Turkey Red Superstars

COMPLETE SET (12)	10.00	20.00
STATED ODDS 1:6 RETAIL EXCLUSIVE		
1 John Cena	1.50	4.00
2 Batista	1.00	2.50
3 Carlito	.60	1.50
4 Big Show	1.00	2.50
5 Shawn Michaels	1.50	4.00
6 Rey Mysterio	.60	1.50
7 Kurt Angle	1.00	2.50
8 Edge	1.00	2.50
9 Rob Van Dam	.60	1.50
10 Triple H	1.50	4.00
11 Hulk Hogan	1.50	4.00
12 Ric Flair	1.25	3.00

2007 Topps Heritage III WWE

COMPLETE SET (90)	8.00	20.00
UNOPENED BOX (24 PACKS)		
UNOPENED PACK (5 CARDS)		
1 John Cena	1.00	2.50
2 Batista	.60	1.50
3 Rey Mysterio	.40	1.00
4 Stone Cold Steve Austin	1.00	2.50
5 The Great Khali	.25	.60
6 Carlito	.60	1.50
7 Edge	.60	1.50
8 Hardcore Holly	.40	1.00
9 Umaga	.25	.60
10 Montel Vontavious Porter RC	.25	.60
11 Stevie Richards	.25	.60
12 Deuce RC	.15	.40
13 Lance Cade	.15	.40
14 Super Crazy	.25	.60
15 Chuck Palumbo	.15	.40
16 Domino RC	.15	.40
17 Trevor Murdoch	.15	.40
18 Val Venis	.40	1.00
19 Bobby Lashley	.60	1.50
20 Mark Henry	.25	.60
21 Boogeyman	.25	.60
22 Brian Kendrick	.25	.60
23 Tommy Dreamer	.20	.50
24 Charlie Haas	.15	.40
25 JBL	.40	1.00
26 Armando Estrada RC	.15	.40
27 CM Punk	.25	.60
28 Triple H	1.00	2.50
29 Shannon Moore	.15	.40
30 Hacksaw Jim Duggan	.25	.60
31 Jeff Hardy	.40	1.00
32 Kane	.60	1.50
33 Ron Simmons	.25	.60
34 Finlay	.40	1.00
35 The Miz RC	.30	.75
36 Kenny Dykstra RC	.25	.60
37 Snitsky	.25	.60
38 Chris Masters	.60	1.50
39 Santino Marella RC	.20	.50
40 Cody Rhodes RC	8.00	20.00
41 Shelton Benjamin	.15	.40
42 Hornswoggle RC	.20	.50
43 Big Daddy V	.40	1.00
44 Matt Striker	.15	.40
45 Jamie Noble	.15	.40
46 William Regal	.40	1.00
47 Jimmy Wang Yang	.15	.40
48 Elijah Burke RC	.15	.40
49 Chavo Guerrero	.25	.60
50 Paul London	.40	1.00
51 Mr. Kennedy	.40	1.00
52 John Morrison	.25	.60
53 Matt Hardy	.40	1.00
54 Shawn Michaels	1.00	2.50
55 Randy Orton	.60	1.50
56 Ric Flair	.60	1.50
57 Undertaker	.75	2.00
58 Torrie Wilson DV	1.25	3.00
59 Candice DV	.75	2.00
60 Michelle McCool DV	.75	2.00

61 Melina DV	.60	1.50
62 Cherry DV RC	.15	.40
63 Jillian DV	.75	2.00
64 Ashley DV	.60	1.50
65 Maria DV	.60	1.50
66 Kelly Kelly DV RC	.40	1.00
67 Mickie James DV	.75	2.00
68 Maryse DV RC	.30	.75
69 Victoria DV	.75	2.00
70 Anderson/Blanchard L	.15	.40
71 Brian Pillman L	.15	.40
72 Dean Malenko L	.15	.40
73 Funk Brothers Dory & Terry L	.15	.40
74 Dusty Rhodes L	.40	1.00
75 The Freebirds L	.15	.40
76 Jimmy Superfly Snuka L	.25	.60
77 Jimmy Garvin L	.15	.40
78 Papa Shango L	.20	.50
79 Pat Patterson L	.15	.40
80 Bam Bam Bigelow L	.40	1.00
81 Gorilla Monsoon L	.30	.75
82 Ted DiBiase L	.30	.75
83 Rocky Johson L RC	.25	.60
84 Bruiser Brody L RC	.15	.40
85 Kamala L	.20	.50
86 Earthquake L	.25	.60
87 Vader L	.25	.60
88 Jack and Gerry Brisco L	.15	.40
89 Cowboy Bob Orton L	.20	.50
90 John Cena CL	1.00	2.50

2007 Topps Heritage III WWE Allen and Ginter Legends

COMPLETE SET (12)	6.00	15.00
STATED ODDS 1:6 HOBBY EXCLUSIVE		
1 Rowdy Roddy Piper	1.00	2.50
2 Chief Jay Strongbow	.30	.75
3 Sgt. Slaughter	.60	1.50
4 Iron Sheik	.60	1.50
5 Don Muraco	.20	.50
6 Ravishing Rick Rude	.60	1.50
7 Classy Freddie Blassie	.30	.75
8 Bobby The Brain Heenan	.60	1.50
9 The British Bulldog	.60	1.50
10 Jake The Snake Roberts	.60	1.50
11 Nikolai Volkoff	.60	1.50
12 Junkyard Dog	1.00	2.50

2007 Topps Heritage III WWE Allen and Ginter Superstars

COMPLETE SET (12)	10.00	25.00
STATED ODDS 1:6 RETAIL EXCLUSIVE		
1 John Cena	1.50	4.00
2 Batista	.75	2.00
3 Rey Mysterio	.60	1.50
4 Carlito	.60	1.50
5 Edge	.75	2.00
6 Bobby Lashley	.60	1.50
7 Mr. Kennedy	.75	2.00
8 Triple H	1.50	4.00
9 Shawn Michaels	1.25	3.00
10 Undertaker	1.25	3.00
11 Ric Flair	1.25	3.00
12 Booker T	.75	2.00

2007 Topps Heritage III WWE Allen and Ginter Tin Inserts

COMPLETE SET (6)
STATED ODDS 1:1 TIN EXCLUSIVES
1 John Cena
2 Batista
3 Ric Flair
4 Undertaker
5 Edge
6 Shawn Michaels

2007 Topps Heritage III WWE Autographs

STATED ODDS 1:24 HOBBY EXCLUSIVE		
NNO Candice	8.00	20.00
NNO Carlito	6.00	15.00
NNO Cherry	6.00	15.00
NNO Chuck Palumbo	6.00	15.00
NNO CM Punk	75.00	150.00
NNO Deuce	6.00	15.00
NNO Domino	6.00	15.00
NNO Hacksaw Jim Duggan	15.00	40.00
NNO Jeff Hardy	20.00	50.00
NNO John Cena	75.00	150.00
NNO Kane	12.00	30.00
NNO Kelly Kelly	20.00	50.00
NNO Lance Cade	6.00	15.00
NNO Maria	12.00	30.00
NNO Miz	12.00	30.00
NNO Montel Vontavious Porter	8.00	20.00
NNO Randy Orton	25.00	60.00
NNO Stevie Richards	6.00	15.00
NNO Super Crazy	6.00	15.00
NNO Torrie Wilson	10.00	25.00
NNO Trevor Murdoch	6.00	15.00
NNO Victoria	12.00	30.00

2007 Topps Heritage III WWE Event-Used Mat Ringside Relics

STATED ODDS 1:24 RETAIL EXCLUSIVE		
NNO John Cena/Randy Orton	4.00	10.00
NNO Rey Mysterio/Chavo Guerrero	3.00	8.00
NNO Triple H/King Booker	4.00	10.00

2007 Topps Heritage III WWE Ringside Relics

STATED ODDS 1:24 HOBBY EXCLUSIVE		
NNO Bobby Lashley	5.00	10.00
NNO Carlito	5.00	10.00
NNO John Cena	6.00	12.00
NNO Matt Hardy	5.00	10.00
NNO Mr. Kennedy	5.00	10.00

2007 Topps Heritage III WWE Magnets

COMPLETE SET (9)	6.00	15.00
STATED ODDS 1:4 RETAIL		
1 John Cena	1.50	4.00
2 Batista	1.00	2.50
3 Rey Mysterio	.60	1.50
4 Carlito	1.00	2.50
5 Edge	1.00	2.50
6 Bobby Lashley	1.00	2.50
7 Mr. Kennedy	.60	1.50
8 Triple H	1.50	4.00
9 Ric Flair	1.00	2.50

2007 Topps Heritage III WWE Ringside Bonus

COMPLETE SET (16)	25.00	60.00
STATED ODDS 4:1 WAL-MART BLASTER		
R1 John Cena	5.00	12.00
R2 Carlito	2.50	6.00
R3 CM Punk	2.50	6.00
R4 Randy Orton	4.00	10.00
R5 Hornswoggle	1.50	4.00
R6 Jamie Noble	1.50	4.00
R7 Super Crazy	1.50	4.00
R8 Great Khali	2.50	6.00
R9 Jeff Hardy	3.00	8.00
R10 Matt Hardy	3.00	8.00
R11 Chavo Guerrero	1.50	4.00
R12 Finlay	1.50	4.00
R13 Kane	3.00	8.00
R14 Hardcore Holly	2.50	6.00
R15 Rey Mysterio	3.00	8.00
R16 Jimmy Wang Yang	1.50	4.00

2007 Topps Heritage III WWE Ringside Rookie Bonus

COMPLETE SET (4)	10.00	25.00
STATED ODDS 1:1 WAL-MART BLASTER		
RK1 Cody Rhodes	4.00	10.00
RK2 Santino Marella	4.00	10.00
RK3 Deuce	3.00	8.00
RK4 Domino	3.00	8.00

2007 Topps Heritage III WWE Superstar Team

1 Brian Kendrick/Paul London	.20	.50
2 C.Haas/S.Benjamin	.12	.30
3 Lance Cade/Trevor Murdoch	.12	.30

2007 Topps Heritage III WWE Superstar Team Oversized

COMPLETE SET (3)
STATED ODDS 1:1 HOBBY EXCLUSIVES
1 Brian Kendrick/Paul London
2 Charlie Haas/Shelton Benjamin
3 Lance Cade/Trevor Murdoch

2007 Topps Heritage III WWE Tin Inserts

COMPLETE SET (6)
STATED ODDS 1:1 TIN EXCLUSIVES
B1 John Cena
B2 Batista
B3 Ric Flair
B4 Undertaker
B5 Edge
B6 Shawn Michaels

2008 Topps Heritage IV WWE

COMPLETE SET (90)	8.00	20.00
UNOPENED BOX (24 PACKS)		
UNOPENED PACK (5 CARDS)		
1 Armando Estrada	.12	.30
2 Ricky Ortiz RC	.12	.30
3 Bam Neely RC	.12	.30
4 Batista	.50	1.25
5 Big Show	.30	.75
6 Brian Kendrick	.20	.50
7 Carlito	.30	.75
8 Chavo Guerrero	.20	.50
9 Chris Jericho	.30	.75
10 CM Punk	.12	.30
11 Cody Rhodes	.12	.30
12 Undertaker	.60	1.50
13 Curt Hawkins	.12	.30
14 D-Lo Brown	.20	.50
15 Edge	.50	1.25
16 Evan Bourne RC	.12	.30
17 Ezekiel RC	.20	.50
18 Festus RC	.12	.30
19 Finlay	.20	.50
20 The Great Khali	.12	.30
21 Hardcore Holly	.20	.50
22 Hornswoggle	.20	.50
23 Jamie Noble	.12	.30
24 John Bradshaw Layfield	.12	.30
25 Jeff Hardy	.50	1.25
26 Jesse RC	.12	.30
27 John Cena	.75	2.00
28 John Morrison	.12	.30
29 JTG	.12	.30
30 Kane	.50	1.25
31 Kofi Kingston RC	.20	.50
32 Lance Cade	.12	.30
33 Mark Henry	.20	.50
34 Matt Hardy	.50	1.25
35 Primo Colon RC	.12	.30
36 Mike Knox	.12	.30
37 The Miz	.20	.50
38 Mr. Kennedy	.30	.75
39 MVP	.20	.50
40 Paul Burchill	.12	.30
41 Randy Orton	.30	.75
42 Rey Mysterio	.30	.75
43 Santino Marella	.12	.30
44 Shad	.12	.30
45 Shawn Michaels	.75	2.00
46 Shelton Benjamin	.12	.30
47 Snitsky	.20	.50
48 Super Crazy	.20	.50
49 Ted DiBiase Jr. RC	.30	.75
50 Tommy Dreamer	.12	.30
51 Tony Atlas	.12	.30
52 Triple H	.75	2.00
53 Umaga	.20	.50
54 Vladimir Kozlov RC	.20	.50
55 Zack Ryder	.12	.30
56 Tiffany DV RC	.60	1.50
57 Beth Phoenix DV	.60	1.50
58 Candice DV	.60	1.50
59 Eve DV RC	.50	1.25
60 Jillian DV	.50	1.25
61 Katie Lea Burchill DV RC	.50	1.25
62 Kelly Kelly DV	.50	1.25
63 Layla DV	.50	1.25
64 Lilian Garcia DV	.50	1.25
65 Maria DV	.50	1.25
66 Maryse DV	.50	1.25
67 Melina DV	.50	1.25
68 Michelle McCool DV	.60	1.50
69 Mickie James DV	.75	2.00
70 Natalya DV RC	.50	1.25
71 Victoria DV	.60	1.50
72 Tazz/Jim Ross A	.12	.30
73 Jerry Lawler/Michael Cole A	.12	.30
74 Matt Striker/Todd Grisham A	.12	.30
75 Bobby The Brain Heenan	.50	1.25

76 Brian Pillman L	.20	.50
77 Gerald Brisco L	.20	.50
78 Jack Brisco L RC	.20	.50
79 Mr. Perfect Curt Hennig	.30	.75
80 Mr. Wonderful Paul Orndorff	.30	.75
81 Rowdy Roddy Piper	.50	1.25
82 Superfly Jimmy Snuka	.30	.75
83 British Bulldog L	.30	.75
84 Hillbilly Jim L	.30	.75
85 Junkyard Dog L	.30	.75
86 Mean Gene Okerlund	.30	.75
87 Million-Dollar Man Ted DiBiase	.30	.75
88 Tully Blanchard L	.20	.50
89 Dusty Rhodes L	.30	.75
90 Checklist	.12	.30

2008 Topps Heritage IV WWE Allen and Ginter Legends

COMPLETE SET (12)	6.00	15.00
STATED ODDS 1:6 HOBBY		
1 Bobby The Brain Heenan	.60	1.50
2 Junkyard Dog	1.00	2.50
3 Hillbilly Jim	.60	1.50
4 British Bulldog	.60	1.50
5 Mean Gene Okerlund	.60	1.50
6 Mr. Perfect Curt Hennig	.40	1.00
7 Rowdy Roddy Piper	1.00	2.50
8 Jimmy Superfly Snuka	.60	1.50
9 Mr. Wonderful Paul Orndorff	.40	1.00
10 Million-Dollar Man Ted DiBiase	.60	1.50
11 Tully Blanchard	.40	1.00
12 Brian Pillman	.40	1.00

2008 Topps Heritage IV WWE Allen and Ginter Superstars

COMPLETE SET (12)	10.00	25.00
STATED ODDS 1:6 RETAIL EXCLUSIVE		
1 Batista	2.00	5.00
2 John Cena	3.00	8.00
3 Chavo Guerrero	1.25	3.00
4 Chris Jericho	1.25	3.00
5 Edge	2.00	5.00
6 Triple H	3.00	8.00
7 Jeff Hardy	2.00	5.00
8 Matt Hardy	2.00	5.00
9 Mr. Kennedy	1.25	3.00
10 CM Punk	1.25	3.00
11 Rey Mysterio	1.25	3.00
12 Undertaker	2.50	6.00

2008 Topps Heritage IV WWE Autographs

RANDOM INSERTS IN PACKS		
STATED ODDS 1:24 HOBBY/TARGET/WALMART		
NNO Beth Phoenix	12.00	30.00
NNO Carlito	25.00	60.00
NNO Chavo Guerrero	8.00	20.00
NNO Cody Rhodes	15.00	40.00
NNO Deuce	6.00	15.00
NNO John Cena	75.00	150.00
NNO Kofi Kingston	12.00	30.00
NNO Layla	15.00	40.00
NNO Matt Hardy	12.00	30.00
NNO Mickie James	75.00	150.00
NNO Natalya	12.00	30.00
NNO Tazz	6.00	15.00
NNO Ted DiBiase Jr.	12.00	30.00

2008 Topps Heritage IV WWE Blister Bonus

COMPLETE SET (3)
RANDOMLY INSERTED INTO PACKS
RETAIL EXCLUSIVE

1 Edge
2 John Cena
3 Matt Hardy

2008 Topps Heritage IV WWE Magnets

COMPLETE SET (9)	12.00	30.00
STATED ODDS 1:4 RETAIL EXCLUSIVE		
1 John Cena	3.00	8.00
2 Mr. Kennedy	1.25	3.00
3 CM Punk	2.50	6.00
4 Chris Jericho	1.25	3.00
5 Batista	2.00	5.00
6 Triple H	3.00	8.00
7 Edge	2.00	5.00
8 Mickie James	3.00	8.00
9 Melina	2.00	5.00

2008 Topps Heritage IV WWE Mat Relics

STATED ODDS 1:24 RETAIL EXCLUSIVES		
NNO Batista vs. Paul Burchill	3.00	8.00
NNO John Cena vs. Cody Rhodes	5.00	12.00
NNO John Cena vs. Ted DiBiase	5.00	12.00

2008 Topps Heritage IV WWE Ringside Rookies

COMPLETE SET (4)	15.00	40.00
STATED ODDS 1:WALMART BLASTER		
RK1 Ted DiBiase Jr.	8.00	20.00
RK2 Vladimir Kozlov	4.00	10.00
RK3 Evan Bourne	5.00	12.00
RK4 Natalya	8.00	20.00

2008 Topps Heritage IV WWE Ringside Superstars

COMPLETE SET (16)	30.00	80.00
STATED ODDS 4:1 WALMART BLASTER		
R1 John Cena	6.00	15.00
R2 Batista	4.00	10.00
R3 CM Punk	2.00	5.00
R4 Rey Mysterio	2.50	6.00
R5 Triple H	6.00	15.00
R6 Undertaker	5.00	12.00
R7 MVP	2.00	5.00
R8 Jeff Hardy	4.00	10.00
R9 Matt Hardy	4.00	10.00
R10 Tommy Dreamer	2.00	5.00
R11 Mark Henry	2.00	5.00
R12 John Morrison	2.00	5.00
R13 Mickie James	6.00	15.00
R14 Beth Phoenix	5.00	12.00
R15 Candice	5.00	12.00
R16 Michelle McCool	5.00	12.00

2008 Topps Heritage IV WWE Shirt Relics

STATED ODDS		
NNO Jeff Hardy	7.50	15.00
NNO MVP	6.00	12.00
NNO Rey Mysterio	6.00	12.00

2008 Topps Heritage IV WWE Tin Inserts

COMPLETE SET (6)	12.00	30.00
STATED ODDS 1:TIN RETAIL EXCLUSIVE		
1 John Cena	4.00	10.00
2 Rey Mysterio	2.50	6.00
3 Shawn Michaels	4.00	10.00
4 Edge	2.50	6.00
5 Randy Orton	2.50	6.00
6 Triple H	4.00	10.00

2005 Topps Heritage WWE

COMPLETE SET (90)	8.00	20.00
UNOPENED BOX (24 PACKS)		
UNOPENED PACK (5 CARDS)		
1 John Cena	1.25	3.00
2 Batista	.50	1.25
3 Carlito RC	.20	.50
4 Orlando Jordan	.20	.50
5 Paul London	.20	.50
6 Johnny Nitro RC	.20	.50
7 Joey Mercury RC	.20	.50
8 Hurricane	.20	.50
9 Rosey	.20	.50
10 The Rock	1.25	3.00
11 Stone Cold Steve Austin	1.25	3.00
12 Hulk Hogan	1.25	3.00
13 Big Show	.75	2.00
14 Chris Jericho	.60	1.50
15 Danny Basham	.20	.50
16 Edge	.60	1.50
17 Eric Bischoff	.30	.75
18 Eugene	.50	1.25
19 Jim Ross	.30	.75
20 Jonathan Coachman	.20	.50
21 Kane	.60	1.50
22 Heidenreich	.20	.50
23 Kurt Angle	.75	2.00
24 Rene Dupree	.20	.50
25 Ric Flair	1.00	2.50
26 Rob Van Dam	.60	1.50
27 Shawn Michaels	1.00	2.50
28 Tajiri	.20	.50
29 Triple H	1.00	2.50
30 Kerwin White RC	.20	.50
31 Val Venis	.30	.75
32 Viscera	.20	.50
33 Steven Richards	.20	.50
34 Booker T	.30	.75
35 Chris Benoit	.75	2.00
36 Christian	.60	1.50
37 Doug Basham	.20	.50
38 Eddie Guerrero	1.00	2.50
39 Funaki	.20	.50
40 Hardcore Holly	.30	.75
41 JBL	.30	.75
42 Juventud	.20	.50
43 Psicosis	.20	.50
44 Super Crazy RC	.20	.50
45 Shelton Benjamin	.20	.50
46 Chris Masters RC	.20	.50
47 Nunzio	.20	.50
48 Randy Orton	.20	.50
49 Rey Mysterio	.60	1.50
50 Scotty 2 Hotty	.30	.75
51 Tazz	.20	.50
52 Theodore Long	.20	.50
53 Undertaker	1.00	2.50
54 William Regal	.30	.75
55 Antonio	.20	.50
56 Romeo RC	.20	.50
57 Snitsky RC	.20	.50
58 Robert Conway	.20	.50
59 Sharmell DV	1.00	2.50
60 Trish Stratus DV	2.00	5.00
61 Torrie Wilson DV	2.00	5.00
62 Christy Hemme DV RC	2.00	5.00
63 Lita DV	1.25	3.00
64 Lilian Garcia DV	1.00	2.50
65 Maria DV RC	1.25	3.00
66 Stacy Keibler DV	2.00	5.00
67 Victoria DV	1.25	3.00
68 Candice Michelle DV RC	1.25	3.00
69 Michelle McCool DV RC	1.00	2.50
70 Melina DV RC	1.00	2.50
71 The British Bulldog L	.30	.75
72 Chief Jay Strongbow L	.20	.50
73 Classy Freddie Blassie L	.20	.50
74 Cowboy Bob Orton L	.30	.75
75 Bobby The Brain Heenan L	.30	.75
76 Gorilla Monsoon L	.20	.50
77 Hillbilly Jim L	.30	.75
78 Iron Sheik L	.50	1.25
79 Jake The Snake Roberts L	.50	1.25
80 Jerry The King Lawler L	.50	1.25
81 Junkyard Dog L	.50	1.25
82 Mouth of the South Jimmy Hart L	.60	1.50
83 Mr. Wonderful Paul Orndorff L	.60	1.50
84 Nikolái Volkoff L	.30	.75
85 Rowdy Roddy Piper L	1.00	2.50
86 Sgt. Slaughter L	.50	1.25
87 Superstar Billy Graham L	.30	.75
88 The Million Dollar Man Ted DiBiase L	.60	1.50
89 Godfather L	.20	.50
90 Hogan/Cena/Batista CL	1.25	3.00

2005 Topps Heritage WWE Autographs

OVERALL STATED ODDS 1:36
HEMME ODDS 1:1574 H
ANGLE, HOGAN, SHIEK ODDS 1:530 H
MICHAELS, SLAUGHTER, WILSON ODDS 1:520 H
CENA, KANE, KIEBLER, LAWLER, PIPER, STRATUS, STRONGBOW ODDS 1:510
HILLBILLY, HEENAN ODDS 1:473 RETAIL

NNO Bobby The Brain Heenan RET	75.00	150.00
NNO Chief Jay Strongbow	20.00	50.00
NNO Christy Hemme	50.00	100.00
NNO Hillbilly Jim RET	25.00	60.00
NNO Hulk Hogan	300.00	600.00
NNO Iron Sheik	15.00	40.00
NNO Jerry The King Lawler	15.00	40.00
NNO John Cena	200.00	400.00
NNO Kane	25.00	60.00
NNO Kurt Angle	25.00	60.00
NNO Lita	30.00	75.00
NNO Rowdy Roddy Piper	200.00	400.00
NNO Sgt. Slaughter	15.00	40.00
NNO Shawn Michaels	125.00	250.00
NNO Stacy Keibler	75.00	150.00
NNO Torrie Wilson	30.00	75.00
NNO Trish Stratus	50.00	100.00

2005 Topps Heritage WWE Event-Used Mat Ringside Relics

STATED ODDS 1:12 RETAIL EXCLUSIVES

NNO Booker T/Christian
NNO Rey Mysterio/Eddie Guerrero
NNO JBL/Batista

2005 Topps Heritage WWE Event-Worn Ringside Relics

OVERALL STATED ODDS 1:17
EUGENE ODDS 1:214
MICHAELS ODDS 1:196
ANGLE ODDS 1:185
JERICHO ODDS 1:158
TRIPLE H ODDS 1:104
CENA ODDS 1:89
HOGAN ODDS 1:70

NNO Chris Jericho	6.00	15.00
NNO Eugene	8.00	20.00
NNO Hulk Hogan	10.00	25.00
NNO John Cena	10.00	30.00
NNO Kurt Angle	8.00	20.00
NNO Shawn Michaels	10.00	25.00
NNO Triple H	10.00	25.00

2005 Topps Heritage WWE Stickers

COMPLETE SET (10)	12.50	30.00
STATED ODDS 1:4 HOBBY		
1 Hulk Hogan	2.00	5.00
2 The Rock	2.00	5.00
3 Batista	.75	2.00
4 Shawn Michaels	1.50	4.00
5 Carlito	.30	.75
6 Kurt Angle	1.25	3.00
7 Triple H	1.50	4.00
8 John Cena	2.00	5.00
9 Torrie Wilson	3.00	8.00
10 Christy Hemme	3.00	8.00

2005 Topps Heritage WWE World's Greatest Wrestling Managers DVD Promos

COMPLETE SET (4)	3.00	8.00
STATED ODDS 1:SET PER DVD		
V1 Bobby The Brain Heenan	1.25	3.00
V2 Classy Freddie Blassie	.60	1.50
V3 Mouth of the South Jimmy Hart	.75	2.00
V4 Paul Bearer	1.25	3.00

2005 Topps Heritage WWE Promo

NNO John Cena	1.50	4.00

2012 Topps Heritage WWE

COMPLETE SET (110)	10.00	25.00
UNOPENED BOX (24 PACKS)		
UNOPENED PACK (9 CARDS)		
*RED: X TO X BASIC CARDS		
*SILVER: .75X TO 2X BASIC CARDS		
*BLACK: 5X TO 12X BASIC CARDS		
*GOLD/10: UNPRICED DUE TO SCARCITY		
1 AJ Lee	.75	2.00
2 Aksana RC	.40	1.00
3 Alberto Del Rio	.40	1.00
4 Alicia Fox	.25	.60
5 Beth Phoenix	.40	1.00
6 Big Show	.40	1.00
7 Brock Lesnar	.60	1.50
8 Brodus Clay	.15	.40
9 Cameron RC	.25	.60
10 Chris Jericho	.60	1.50
11 Christian	.15	.40
12 CM Punk	.60	1.50
13 Cody Rhodes	.15	.40
14 Damien Sandow RC	.15	.40
15 Daniel Bryan	.15	.40
16 Dolph Ziggler	.25	.60
17 Eve	.60	1.50
18 Jack Swagger	.25	.60
19 John Cena	.75	2.00
20 Kaitlyn	.40	1.00
21 Kane	.40	1.00
22 Ryback	.15	.40
23 Kofi Kingston	.15	.40
24 Layla	.40	1.00
25 Lilian Garcia	.40	1.00
26 Mark Henry	.25	.60
27 The Miz	.25	.60
28 Naomi RC	.25	.60
29 Natalya	.60	1.50
30 R-Truth	.15	.40
31 Randy Orton	.60	1.50
32 Rey Mysterio	.40	1.00
33 The Rock	.75	2.00
34 Rosa Mendes	.25	.60
35 Santino Marella	.25	.60
36 Sheamus	.40	1.00
37 Kama Mustafa	.15	.40
38 Tamina Snuka	.25	.60
39 Tensai	.15	.40
40 Triple H	.60	1.50
41 Tyson Kidd	.15	.40
42 Undertaker	.60	1.50
43 Zack Ryder	.15	.40
44 Batista	.25	.60
45 Booker T	.25	.60
46 Cactus Jack	.60	1.50
47 Dude Love	.60	1.50
48 Jerry The King Lawler	.40	1.00
49 Jim Ross	.15	.40
50 Kevin Nash	.25	.60
51 Mankind	.60	1.50
52 Mick Foley	.60	1.50
53 Shawn Michaels	.60	1.50
54 Stone Cold Steve Austin	.75	2.00
55 Trish Stratus	.75	2.00
56 Akeem	.15	.40
57 The American Dream Dusty Rhodes	.25	.60
58 Andre The Giant	.75	2.00
59 Arn Anderson	.25	.60
60 Barry Windham	.25	.60
61 Big Boss Man	.15	.40
62 Big John Studd	.25	.60
63 Bobby The Brain Heenan	.25	.60
64 Brian Pillman	.25	.60
65 The British Bulldog	.25	.60
66 Bushwhacker Butch	.15	.40
67 Bushwhacker Luke	.15	.40
68 Chief Jay Strongbow	.25	.60
69 Classy Freddie Blassie	.25	.60
70 Cowboy Bob Orton	.25	.60
71 Dean Malenko	.25	.60
72 Doink The Clown	.25	.60
73 Don Muraco	.25	.60
74 The Godfather	.15	.40
75 Gorilla Monsoon	.25	.60
76 Greg The Hammer Valentine	.25	.60
77 Hacksaw Jim Duggan	.25	.60
78 Harley Race	.25	.60
79 Hillbilly Jim	.25	.60
80 Howard Finkel RC	.25	.60
81 The Iron Sheik	.25	.60
82 Irwin R. Schyster	.15	.40
83 Jake The Snake Roberts	.25	.60
84 Jimmy Superfly Snuka	.25	.60
85 Junkyard Dog	.25	.60
86 Sin Cara	.40	1.00
87 Kamala	.25	.60
88 Koko B. Ware	.25	.60
89 Mean Gene Okerlund	.25	.60
90 Michael PS Hayes	.15	.40
91 Million Dollar Man Ted DiBiase	.25	.60
92 Mr. Perfect	.25	.60
93 Mr. Wonderful Paul Orndorff	.25	.60
94 Nikolai Volkoff	.25	.60
95 One Man Gang	.15	.40
96 Papa Shango	.15	.40
97 Paul Bearer	.15	.40
98 Ravishing Rick Rude	.25	.60
99 Ricky The Dragon Steamboat	.25	.60
100 Road Warrior Animal	.25	.60
101 Road Warrior Hawk	.25	.60
102 Rocky Johnson	.25	.60
103 Rowdy Roddy Piper	.40	1.00
104 Sgt. Slaughter	.25	.60
105 Terry Funk	.25	.60
106 Tito Santana	.25	.60
107 Tom Prichard RC	.15	.40
108 Tully Blanchard	.25	.60
109 Vader	.25	.60
110 Yokozuna	.25	.60

2012 Topps Heritage WWE Allen and Ginter

COMPLETE SET (30)	30.00	75.00
STATED ODDS 1:6 HOBBY AND RETAIL		
1 Brock Lesnar	3.00	8.00
2 Christian	.75	2.00
3 CM Punk	3.00	8.00
4 Daniel Bryan	.75	2.00
5 John Cena	4.00	10.00
6 Kelly Kelly	3.00	8.00
7 Kofi Kingston	.75	2.00
8 Layla	2.00	5.00
9 Randy Orton	3.00	8.00
10 Sheamus	2.00	5.00
11 Booker T	1.25	3.00
12 Diesel	1.25	3.00
13 Mankind	3.00	8.00
14 Stone Cold Steve Austin	4.00	10.00
15 Trish Stratus	4.00	10.00
16 The American Dream Dusty Rhodes	1.25	3.00
17 Andre The Giant	4.00	10.00
18 Big Boss Man	.75	2.00
19 Big John Studd	1.25	3.00
20 Cowboy Bob Orton	1.25	3.00
21 Doink The Clown	1.25	3.00
22 Hacksaw Jim Duggan	1.25	3.00
23 Kamala	1.25	3.00
24 Koko B. Ware	1.25	3.00
25 Papa Shango	.75	2.00
26 Paul Bearer	.75	2.00
27 Ricky The Dragon Steamboat	1.25	3.00
28 Terry Funk	1.25	3.00
29 Vader	1.25	3.00
30 Yokozuna	1.25	3.00

2012 Topps Heritage WWE Andre the Giant Tribute

COMPLETE SET (10)	8.00	20.00
*SILVER/85: 1X TO 2.5X BASIC CARDS		
*GOLD/10: UNPRICED DUE TO SCARCITY		
STATED ODDS 1:8 HOBBY AND RETAIL		
1 Andre the Giant	1.25	3.00
2 Andre the Giant	1.25	3.00
3 Andre the Giant	1.25	3.00
4 Andre the Giant	1.25	3.00
5 Andre the Giant	1.25	3.00
6 Andre the Giant	1.25	3.00
7 Andre the Giant	1.25	3.00
8 Andre the Giant	1.25	3.00
9 Andre the Giant	1.25	3.00
10 Andre the Giant	1.25	3.00

2012 Topps Heritage WWE Autographs

STATED ODDS HOBBY EXCLUSIVE 1:44		
STATED ODDS RETAIL EXCLUSIVE 1:120		
NNO Akeem	25.00	60.00
NNO Cameron	15.00	40.00
NNO CM Punk	50.00	100.00
NNO Doink The Clown	100.00	200.00
NNO The Godfather	25.00	60.00
NNO Howard Finkel	20.00	50.00
NNO Irwin R. Schyster	25.00	60.00
NNO Jake The Snake Roberts	20.00	50.00
NNO John Cena	75.00	150.00
NNO Kama Mustafa	10.00	25.00
NNO Kamala	15.00	40.00
NNO Layla	10.00	25.00
NNO Mean Gene Okerlund	15.00	40.00
NNO Michael PS Hayes	10.00	25.00
NNO Naomi	15.00	40.00
NNO Natalya	12.00	30.00
NNO One Man Gang	25.00	60.00
NNO Papa Shango	20.00	50.00
NNO Paul Bearer	75.00	150.00
NNO Vader	30.00	75.00

2012 Topps Heritage WWE Fabled Tag Teams

COMPLETE SET (10)	6.00	15.00
STATED ODDS 1:12 HOBBY AND RETAIL		
1 Nikolai Volkoff/Iron Sheik	.75	2.00
2 The Brain Busters	.75	2.00
3 Big Boss Man/Akeem	.50	1.25
4 The Road Warriors	.75	2.00
5 The Bushwhackers	.50	1.25
6 Money Inc	.75	2.00
7 The Rock N Sock Connection	2.50	6.00
8 The Brothers of Destruction	2.00	5.00
9 The Two-Man Power Trip	2.50	6.00
10 D-Generation X	2.00	5.00

2012 Topps Heritage WWE Family History

COMPLETE SET (10)	6.00	15.00
STATED ODDS 1:8 HOBBY AND RETAIL		

1 B.Orton/R.Orton	2.00	5.00
2 T.DiBiase Sr./T.DiBiase Jr.	.75	2.00
3 J.Snuka/T.Snuka	.75	2.00
4 R.Johnson/The Rock	2.50	6.00
5 Yokozuna	.75	2.00
The Usos		
6 B.Bulldog/Natalya	2.00	5.00
7 D.Rhodes/C.Rhodes	.75	2.00
8 Animal/J.Laurinaitis	.50	1.25
9 Mr. Perfect/M.McGillicutty	.75	2.00
10 P.Bearer/Kane	1.25	3.00

2012 Topps Heritage WWE Jerry the King Lawler Portraits

COMPLETE SET (10)	12.00	30.00
STATED ODDS 1:24 HOBBY AND RETAIL		
1 Big Show	2.50	6.00
2 Brodus Clay	1.00	2.50
3 CM Punk	4.00	10.00
4 Hornswoggle	1.50	4.00
5 Kelly Kelly	4.00	10.00
6 Rey Mysterio	2.50	6.00
7 Santino Marella	1.50	4.00
8 Sheamus	2.50	6.00
9 The Miz	1.50	4.00
10 Undertaker	4.00	10.00

2012 Topps Heritage WWE Ringside Action

COMPLETE SET (55)	10.00	25.00
STATED ODDS 1:1 HOBBY AND RETAIL		
1 Superfly Splash	.60	1.50
Jimmy Superfly Snuka		
2 Double A Spinebuster	.60	1.50
3 Stone Cold Stunner	2.00	5.00
4 Perfect-Plex	.60	1.50
5 Cobra Clutch	.60	1.50
6 DDT	.60	1.50
7 Flying Fist Drop	1.00	2.50
8 Figure Four Leglock	.60	1.50
9 Mandible Claw	1.50	4.00
10 Jackknife Powerbomb	.60	1.50
11 Superplex	.60	1.50
12 Running Powerslam	.60	1.50
13 Doomsday Device	.60	1.50
14 Bionic Elbow	.60	1.50
15 Camel Clutch	.60	1.50
16 Flying Cross-body Press	.60	1.50
17 Three Point Stance Clothesline	.60	1.50
18 Scissor Kick	.60	1.50
19 Rude Awakening	.60	1.50
20 Chokeslam	1.00	2.50
21 Lariat	.60	1.50
22 Texas Cloverleaf	.60	1.50
23 Flying Splash	.60	1.50
24 Million Dollar Dream	.60	1.50
25 Rock Bottom	2.00	5.00
26 F-5	1.50	4.00
27 Battering Ram	.40	1.00
28 The Write-Off	.40	1.00
29 Killswitch	.40	1.00
30 Sidewalk Slam	.40	1.00
31 Flying Forearm	.60	1.50
32 Pimp Drop	.40	1.00
The Godfather		
33 The Whoopie Cushion		
34 Diving Headbutt	.60	1.50
35 STF	.40	1.00
36 619	1.00	2.50
38 G.T.S. (Go to Sleep)	1.50	4.00
39 World's Strongest Slam	.60	1.50
40 RKO	1.50	4.00
41 Moonsault Side Slam	1.00	2.50
42 Vader Bomb	.60	1.50
43 Air Pillman	.60	1.50
44 The Claw	.40	1.00
45 Banzai Drop	.60	1.50
46 Wasteland	.40	1.00
47 Brogue Kick	1.00	2.50
48 Attitude Adjustment	2.00	5.00
49 Reverse Piledriver	.60	1.50
50 Knockout Punch	.60	1.50
51 The Walls of Jericho	1.50	4.00
52 Sweet Chin Music	1.50	4.00
53 Batista Bomb	.60	1.50
54 Pedigree	1.50	4.00
55 Yes! Lock	.40	1.00
86 Dream Street	.60	1.50

2012 Topps Heritage WWE Shirt Relics

TWO AUTO OR MEM PER HOBBY BOX		
STATED ODDS 1:97 RETAIL		
NNO Alberto Del Rio/Scarf	6.00	15.00
NNO Batista	6.00	15.00
NNO CM Punk	6.00	15.00
NNO Cody Rhodes	5.00	12.00
NNO Daniel Bryan	5.00	12.00
NNO Dolph Ziggler	6.00	15.00
NNO John Cena	8.00	20.00
NNO Kofi Kingston	5.00	12.00
NNO Mark Henry	5.00	12.00
NNO The Miz	5.00	12.00
NNO Randy Orton	6.00	15.00
NNO Rey Mysterio	6.00	15.00
NNO R-Truth	5.00	12.00
NNO Santino Marella	5.00	12.00
NNO Sheamus	5.00	12.00
NNO Stone Cold Steve Austin	8.00	20.00
NNO Wade Barrett	5.00	12.00
NNO Zack Ryder	5.00	12.00

2012 Topps Heritage WWE Stickers

COMPLETE SET (18)	10.00	25.00
STATED ODDS 1:4 HOBBY AND RETAIL		
1 Ricky The Dragon Steamboat	.75	2.00
2 Rey Mysterio	1.25	3.00
3 Trish Stratus	2.50	6.00
4 Undertaker	2.00	5.00
5 Mankind	2.00	5.00
6 Ravishing Rick Rude	.75	2.00
7 Sin Cara	1.25	3.00
8 Vader	.75	2.00
9 Dude Love	2.00	5.00
10 Jake The Snake Roberts	.75	2.00
11 Gorilla Monsoon	.75	2.00
12 Greg The Hammer Valentine	.75	2.00
13 Rowdy Roddy Piper	1.25	3.00
14 Doink The Clown	.75	2.00
15 Booker T	.75	2.00
16 Koko B. Ware	.75	2.00
17 Kamala	.75	2.00
18 Kane	1.25	3.00

2012 Topps Heritage WWE The Superstars Speak

COMPLETE SET (20)	8.00	20.00
STATED ODDS 1:4 HOBBY AND RETAIL		
1 Stone Cold Steve Austin	2.00	5.00
2 Cactus Jack	1.50	4.00
3 Booker T	.60	1.50
4 Road Warrior Hawk	.60	1.50
5 Gorilla Monsoon	.60	1.50
6 Rowdy Roddy Piper	1.00	2.50
7 The American Dream Dusty Rhodes	.60	1.50
8 Classy Freddie Blassie	.60	1.50
9 The Iron Sheik	.60	1.50
10 Trish Stratus	2.00	5.00
11 The Rock	2.00	5.00
12 Mr. Perfect	.60	1.50
13 Kevin Nash	.60	1.50
14 Mankind	1.50	4.00
15 Hacksaw Jim Duggan	.60	1.50
16 Jim Ross	.40	1.00
17 Vader	.60	1.50
18 Million Dollar Man Ted DiBiase	.60	1.50
19 Yokozuna	.40	1.00
20 Sgt. Slaughter	.60	1.50

2012 Topps Heritage WWE Wrestlemania XXVII Mat Relics

TWO AUTO OR MEM PER HOBBY BOX		
STATED ODDS 1:97 RETAIL		
NNO Alberto Del Rio	6.00	15.00
NNO Big Show	6.00	15.00
NNO Booker T	4.00	10.00
NNO Christian	4.00	10.00
NNO CM Punk	6.00	15.00
NNO Cody Rhodes	5.00	12.00
NNO Dolph Ziggler	4.00	10.00
NNO Ezekiel Jackson	4.00	10.00
NNO Heath Slater	4.00	10.00
NNO Jerry The King Lawler	5.00	12.00
NNO John Cena	6.00	15.00
NNO Justin Gabriel	5.00	12.00
NNO Kane	5.00	12.00
NNO Kofi Kingston	5.00	12.00
NNO Layla	6.00	15.00
NNO Michael Cole	4.00	10.00
NNO The Miz	4.00	10.00
NNO Randy Orton	6.00	15.00
NNO The Rock	8.00	20.00
NNO Santino Marella	5.00	12.00
NNO Stone Cold Steve Austin	8.00	20.00
NNO Triple H	6.00	15.00
NNO Trish Stratus	8.00	20.00
NNO Undertaker	6.00	15.00
NNO Wade Barrett	5.00	12.00

2015 Topps Heritage WWE

COMPLETE SET (110)	12.00	30.00
UNOPENED BOX (24 PACKS)		
UNOPENED PACK (9 CARDS)		
*BLACK: .75X TO 2X BASIC CARDS		
*SILVER: 5X TO 12X BASIC CARDS		
*GOLD/10: 8X TO 20X BASIC CARDS		
*RED/1: UNPRICED DUE TO SCARCITY		
*P.P.BLACK/1: UNPRICED DUE TO SCARCITY		
*P.P.CYAN/1: UNPRICED DUE TO SCARCITY		
*P.P.MAGENTA/1: UNPRICED DUE TO SCARCITY		
*P.P.YELLOW/1: UNPRICED DUE TO SCARCITY		
1 The American Dream Dusty Rhodes	.25	.60
2 The Acolytes	.25	.60
3 Bob Backlund	.15	.40
4 Bam Bam Bigelow	.20	.50
5 Booker T	.25	.60
6 Bret Hit Man Hart	.50	1.25
7 The British Bulldog	.25	.60
8 Bruno Sammartino	.40	1.00
9 The Bushwhackers	.15	.40
10 Cowboy Bob Orton	.15	.40
11 D-Generation X	.60	1.50
12 Diamond Dallas Page	.30	.75
13 Doink the Clown	.15	.40
14 Earthquake	.15	.40
15 Edge	.40	1.00
16 The Foreign Legion	.25	.60
17 The Four Horsemen	.50	1.25
18 The Funks	.20	.50
19 Eddie Guerrero	.40	1.00
20 George The Animal Steele	.20	.50
21 Papa Shango	.15	.40
22 Hacksaw Jim Duggan	.25	.60
23 Hillbilly Jim	.25	.60
24 Rob Van Dam	.40	1.00
25 Jake The Snake Roberts	.25	.60
26 Jerry The King Lawler	.25	.60
27 Jim Ross	.25	.60
28 Junkyard Dog	.20	.50
29 Kamala	.20	.50
30 The King Harley Race	.25	.60
31 Koko B. Ware	.20	.50
32 Money Inc.	.25	.60
33 Mr. Perfect Curt Hennig	.25	.60
34 Mr. Wonderful Paul Orndorff	.25	.60
35 The Nasty Boys	.25	.60
36 The Outsiders	.40	1.00
37 Ravishing Rick Rude	.25	.60
38 Ricky The Dragon Steamboat	.25	.60
39 Rocky Johnson	.25	.60
40 Rowdy Roddy Piper	.50	1.25
41 Rhythm & Blues	.25	.60
42 Sgt. Slaughter	.25	.60
43 Lex Luger & Sting	.40	1.00
44 Stone Cold Steve Austin	.75	2.00
45 Tito Santana	.25	.60
46 The Twin Towers	.20	.50
47 Ultimate Warrior	.50	1.25
48 Vader	.20	.50
49 Virgil	.15	.40
50 Yokozuna	.25	.60
51 Eve	.30	.75
52 Lita	.60	1.50
53 Trish Stratus	.75	2.00
54 Alicia Fox	.30	.75
55 The Bella Twins	.50	1.25
56 Emma RC	.25	.60
57 Lana RC	.60	1.50
58 Naomi	.25	.60
59 Natalya	.50	1.25
60 Paige RC	.75	2.00
61 King Barrett	.15	.40
62 Batista	.40	1.00
63 Big Show	.40	1.00
64 Bo Dallas	.15	.40
65 Bray Wyatt	.60	1.50
66 Brock Lesnar	.60	1.50

67 Chris Jericho	.40	1.00
68 Christian	.15	.40
69 Damien Sandow	.15	.40
70 Daniel Bryan	.60	1.50
71 Dean Ambrose	.40	1.00
72 Dolph Ziggler	.25	.60
73 Goldust	.15	.40
74 J & J Security	.15	.40
75 John Cena	.75	2.00
76 Kalisto RC	.25	.60
77 Kane	.40	1.00
78 Luke Harper	.25	.60
79 Mark Henry	.25	.60
80 The Miz	.25	.60
81 Neville RC	.30	.75
82 The New Day	.25	.60
83 The Prime Time Players	.15	.40
84 R-Truth	.15	.40
85 Randy Orton	.60	1.50
86 The Rock	.75	2.00
87 Fandango	.15	.40
88 Roman Reigns	.40	1.00
89 Rusev RC	.40	1.00
90 Ryback	.15	.40
91 Santino Marella	.15	.40
92 Seth Rollins	.25	.60
93 Sheamus	.40	1.00
94 Sin Cara	.25	.60
95 Stardust	.15	.40
96 Cesaro	.15	.40
97 Undertaker	.60	1.50
98 The Usos	.15	.40
99 William Regal	.25	.60
100 Zack Ryder	.15	.40
101 Alexa Bliss RC	4.00	10.00
102 Baron Corbin RC	.25	.60
103 Bull Dempsey RC	.25	.60
104 Charlotte RC	.50	1.25
105 Finn Balor RC	.50	1.25
106 Hideo Itami RC	.15	.40
107 Kevin Owens RC	.50	1.25
108 Sami Zayn RC	.25	.60
109 Sasha Banks RC	6.00	15.00
110 Tyler Breeze RC	.15	.40
111 Steve Austin 2K16 SP		
111B Steve Austin 2K16 SP Black		
111C Steve Austin 2K16 SP Blue		
111D Steve Austin 2K16 SP Yellow		

2015 Topps Heritage WWE 2K16

COMPLETE SET (8) 10.00 25.00
*BLACK/50: 1.2X TO 3X BASIC CARDS
*P.P.BLACK/1: UNPRICED DUE TO SCARCITY
*P.P.CYAN/1: UNPRICED DUE TO SCARCITY
*P.P.MAGENTA/1: UNPRICED DUE TO SCARCITY
*P.P.YELLOW/1: UNPRICED DUE TO SCARCITY

1 Stone Cold Steve Austin	4.00	10.00
2 Daniel Bryan	3.00	8.00
3 Finn Balor	2.50	6.00
4 King Barrett	.75	2.00
5 Paige	4.00	10.00
6 Paul Heyman	.75	2.00
7 Seth Rollins	1.25	3.00
8 Stone Cold Steve Austin	4.00	10.00

2015 Topps Heritage WWE Autographs

*BLACK/50: .5X TO 1.2X BASIC AUTOS
*SILVER/25: .75X TO 2X BASIC AUTOS
*GOLD/10: UNPRICED DUE TO SCARCITY
*RED/1: UNPRICED DUE TO SCARCITY

NNO Alundra Blayze	8.00	20.00
NNO Daniel Bryan	12.00	30.00
NNO Dean Ambrose	15.00	40.00
NNO Dolph Ziggler	10.00	25.00
NNO Eva Marie	15.00	40.00
NNO Finn Balor	20.00	50.00
NNO Hideo Itami	10.00	25.00
NNO John Cena	30.00	75.00
NNO Neville	10.00	25.00
NNO Pat Patterson	10.00	25.00
NNO Roman Reigns	60.00	120.00
NNO Sasha Banks	125.00	250.00
NNO Seth Rollins	15.00	40.00

2015 Topps Heritage WWE Money in the Bank Relics

*BLACK/50: .5X TO 1.2X BASIC MEM
*SILVER/25: .75X TO 2X BASIC MEM
*GOLD/10: UNPRICED DUE TO SCARCITY
*RED/1: UNPRICED DUE TO SCARCITY

NNO Big E	3.00	8.00
NNO Big Show	5.00	12.00
NNO Darren Young	2.00	5.00
NNO Dean Ambrose	5.00	12.00
NNO Dolph Ziggler	3.00	8.00
NNO John Cena	10.00	25.00
NNO Kane	5.00	12.00
NNO Kevin Owens	6.00	15.00
NNO King Barrett	2.00	5.00
NNO Kofi Kingston	2.00	5.00
NNO Neville	4.00	10.00
NNO Nikki Bella	6.00	15.00
NNO Paige	10.00	25.00
NNO Randy Orton	8.00	20.00
NNO Roman Reigns	5.00	12.00
NNO R-Truth	2.00	5.00
NNO Ryback	2.00	5.00
NNO Seth Rollins	3.00	8.00
NNO Sheamus	5.00	12.00
NNO Titus O'Neil	2.00	5.00
NNO Xavier Woods	3.00	8.00

2015 Topps Heritage WWE nWo Autographs

RANDOMLY INSERTED INTO PACKS

NNO Big Show	20.00	50.00
NNO Booker T	12.00	30.00
NNO Bret Hit Man Hart	25.00	60.00
NNO Kevin Nash	20.00	50.00
NNO Lex Luger	12.00	30.00
NNO Shawn Michaels	60.00	120.00
NNO X-Pac	15.00	40.00

2015 Topps Heritage WWE nWo Tribute

COMPLETE SET (10) 10.00 25.00
RANDOMLY INSERTED INTO PACKS

31 Scott Hall	2.50	6.00
32 Kevin Nash	2.50	6.00
33 The Giant	2.50	6.00
34 Syxx	2.00	5.00
35 Miss Elizabeth	2.00	5.00
36 Mr. Wallstreet	1.00	2.50
37 Big Bubba Rogers	1.00	2.50
38 Curt Hennig	1.50	4.00
39 Bret Hit Man Hart	3.00	8.00
40 Stevie Ray	1.00	2.50

2015 Topps Heritage WWE NXT Called Up

COMPLETE SET (30) 8.00 20.00
*P.P.BLACK/1: UNPRICED DUE TO SCARCITY
*P.P.CYAN/1: UNPRICED DUE TO SCARCITY
*P.P.MAGENTA/1: UNPRICED DUE TO SCARCITY
*P.P.YELLOW/1: UNPRICED DUE TO SCARCITY
STATED ODDS 1:1

1 Bad News Barrett	.30	.75
2 David Otunga	.30	.75
3 Heath Slater	.30	.75
4 Darren Young	.30	.75
5 Daniel Bryan	1.25	3.00
6 Ryback	.30	.75
7 Alex Riley	.30	.75
8 Curtis Axel	.30	.75
9 Naomi	.50	1.25
10 Titus OíNeil	.30	.75
11 Dean Ambrose	.75	2.00
12 Roman Reigns	.75	2.00
13 Seth Rollins	.50	1.25
14 Big E	.50	1.25
15 Bo Dallas	.30	.75
16 Bray Wyatt	1.25	3.00
17 Luke Harper	.50	1.25
18 Erick Rowan	.50	1.25
19 Adam Rose	.40	1.00
20 Summer Rae	1.25	3.00
21 Xavier Woods	.50	1.25
22 Emma	.50	1.25
23 Byron Saxton	.30	.75
24 Rusev	.75	2.00
25 Lana	1.25	3.00
26 Paige	1.50	4.00
27 Konnor	.40	1.00
28 Viktor	.30	.75
29 Kalisto	.50	1.25
30 Neville	.60	1.50

2015 Topps Heritage WWE Rookie of the Year

COMPLETE SET (30) 10.00 25.00
*P.P.BLACK/1: UNPRICED DUE TO SCARCITY
*P.P.CYAN/1: UNPRICED DUE TO SCARCITY
*P.P.MAGENTA/1: UNPRICED DUE TO SCARCITY
*P.P.YELLOW/1: UNPRICED DUE TO SCARCITY
STATED ODDS 1:1

1 Mr. Wonderful Paul Orndorff	.50	1.25
2 Rowdy Roddy Piper	1.00	2.50
3 Davey Boy Smith	.50	1.25
4 Jake The Snake Roberts	.50	1.25
5 Ultimate Warrior	1.00	2.50
6 Shawn Michaels	1.25	3.00
7 Earthquake	.30	.75
8 Undertaker	1.25	3.00
9 I.R.S.	.30	.75
10 Razor Ramon	.75	2.00
11 Diesel	.75	2.00
12 Kama	.30	.75
13 Hunter Hearst Helmsley	1.25	3.00
14 Mark Henry	.50	1.25
15 Kane	.75	2.00
16 Edge	.75	2.00
17 Chris Jericho	.75	2.00
18 Lita	1.25	3.00
19 Brock Lesnar	1.25	3.00
20 Joey Mercury	.30	.75
21 The Miz	.50	1.25
22 Santino Marella	.30	.75
23 Dolph Ziggler	.50	1.25
24 Sheamus	.75	2.00
25 Daniel Bryan	1.25	3.00
26 Sin Cara	.50	1.25
27 Dean Ambrose	.75	2.00
28 Bray Wyatt	1.25	3.00
29 Rusev	.75	2.00
30 Neville	.60	1.50

2015 Topps Heritage WWE Swatch Relics

*BLACK/50: .5X TO 1.2 BASIC MEM
*GOLD/10: UNPRICED DUE TO SCARCITY
*RED/1: UNPRICED DUE TO SCARCITY

NNO Aiden English	3.00	8.00
NNO Baron Corbin	4.00	10.00
NNO Bayley	5.00	12.00
NNO Becky Lynch	5.00	12.00
NNO Big E	4.00	10.00
NNO Big Show	6.00	15.00
NNO Bo Dallas	2.50	6.00
NNO Bray Wyatt	10.00	25.00
NNO Cesaro	2.50	6.00
NNO Charlotte	8.00	20.00
NNO Colin Cassady	4.00	10.00
NNO Curtis Axel	2.50	6.00
NNO Damien Sandow	2.50	6.00
NNO Daniel Bryan	10.00	25.00
NNO Darren Young	2.50	6.00
NNO Dean Ambrose	6.00	15.00
NNO Dolph Ziggler	4.00	10.00
NNO Enzo Amore	2.50	6.00
NNO Finn Balor	8.00	20.00
NNO Goldust	2.50	6.00
NNO Jack Swagger	4.00	10.00
NNO Jimmy Uso	2.50	6.00
NNO John Cena	12.00	30.00
NNO Kalisto	4.00	10.00
NNO Kevin Owens	8.00	20.00
NNO King Barrett	2.50	6.00
NNO Kofi Kingston	2.50	6.00
NNO Konnor	3.00	8.00
NNO Luke Harper	4.00	10.00
NNO Luke Harper	4.00	10.00
NNO Mojo Rawley	2.50	6.00
NNO Natalya	8.00	20.00
NNO Neville	5.00	12.00
NNO Randy Orton	10.00	25.00
NNO Roman Reigns	6.00	15.00
NNO Rusev	6.00	15.00
NNO Ryback	2.50	6.00
NNO Samoa Joe	6.00	15.00
NNO Sasha Banks	5.00	12.00
NNO Seth Rollins	4.00	10.00
NNO Sheamus	6.00	15.00
NNO Simon Gotch	2.50	6.00
NNO Sin Cara	4.00	10.00

NNO	Tamina	4.00	10.00
NNO	The Miz	4.00	10.00
NNO	Titus O'Neil	2.50	6.00
NNO	Tyler Breeze	2.50	6.00
NNO	Viktor	2.50	6.00
NNO	Xavier Woods	4.00	10.00
NNO	Zack Ryder	2.50	6.00

2015 Topps Heritage WWE Then and Now

COMPLETE SET (30) 10.00 25.00
*P.P.BLACK/1: UNPRICED DUE TO SCARCITY
*P.P.CYAN/1: UNPRICED DUE TO SCARCITY
*P.P.MAGENTA/1: UNPRICED DUE TO SCARCITY
*P.P.YELLOW/1: UNPRICED DUE TO SCARCITY
STATED ODDS 1:1

1	Batista	.75	2.00
2	Big Show	.75	2.00
3	Booker T	.50	1.25
4	Brock Lesnar	1.25	3.00
5	Chris Jericho	.75	2.00
6	Christian	.30	.75
7	Daniel Bryan	1.25	3.00
8	Damien Sandow	.30	.75
9	Darren Young	.30	.75
10	Dean Ambrose	.75	2.00
11	Edge	.75	2.00
12	Goldust	.30	.75
13	Hornswoggle	.50	1.25
14	Jamie Noble	.30	.75
15	JBL	.30	.75
16	Joey Mercury	.30	.75
17	John Cena	1.50	4.00
18	Kane	.75	2.00
19	Mark Henry	.50	1.25
20	The Miz	.50	1.25
21	Randy Orton	1.25	3.00
22	Ryback	.30	.75
23	Seth Rollins	.50	1.25
24	Sting	.75	2.00
25	Stone Cold Steve Austin	1.50	4.00
26	Triple H	1.25	3.00
27	Trish Stratus	1.50	4.00
28	Undertaker	1.25	3.00
29	William Regal	.50	1.25
30	Zack Ryder	.30	.75

2016 Topps Heritage WWE

COMPLETE SET (110) 10.00 25.00
UNOPENED BOX (24 PACKS)
UNOPENED PACKS (9 CARDS)
*BRONZE/99: .75X TO 2X BASIC CARDS
*SILVER/50: 1.2X TO 3X BASIC CARDS
*BLUE/25: 2X TO 5X BASIC CARDS
*GOLD/10: 4X TO 10X BASIC CARDS
*RED/1: UNPRICED DUE TO SCARCITY
*P.P.BLACK/1: UNPRICED DUE TO SCARCITY
*P.P.CYAN/1: UNPRICED DUE TO SCARCITY
*P.P.MAGENTA/1: UNPRICED DUE TO SCARCITY
*P.P.YELLOW/1: UNPRICED DUE TO SCARCITY

1	AJ Styles	1.00	2.50
2	Alberto Del Rio	.40	1.00
3	Big E	.25	.60
4	Big Show	.50	1.25
5	Braun Strowman RC	.30	.75
6	Bray Wyatt	1.00	2.50
7	Brock Lesnar	1.25	3.00
8	Bubba Ray Dudley	.50	1.25
9	Cesaro	.50	1.25
10	Chris Jericho	.60	1.50
11	D-Von Dudley	.40	1.00
12	Dean Ambrose	.75	2.00
13	Dolph Ziggler	.30	.75
14	Erick Rowan	.25	.60
15	Goldust	.40	1.00
16	Jack Swagger	.25	.60
17	Jey Uso	.25	.60
18	Jimmy Uso	.25	.60
19	John Cena	1.25	3.00
20	Kalisto	.60	1.50
21	Kane	.40	1.00
22	Kevin Owens	.60	1.50
23	Karl Anderson RC	.25	.60
24	Kofi Kingston	.25	.60
25	Luke Harper	.25	.60
26	Neville	.60	1.50
27	Randy Orton	.60	1.50
28	The Rock	1.25	3.00
29	Roman Reigns	.75	2.00
30	Rusev	.60	1.50
31	Luke Gallows	.30	.75
32	Seth Rollins	.40	1.00
33	Sheamus	.60	1.50
34	Sin Cara	.30	.75
35	Zack Ryder	.25	.60
36	Sting	.60	1.50
37	Triple H	1.00	2.50
38	Tyson Kidd	.25	.60
39	Undertaker	1.00	2.50
40	Xavier Woods	.25	.60
41	Alicia Fox	.40	1.00
42	Becky Lynch RC	.75	2.00
43	Brie Bella	.50	1.25
44	Charlotte	.75	2.00
45	Eva Marie	.50	1.25
46	Lana	1.00	2.50
47	Mandy Rose RC	6.00	15.00
48	Naomi	.40	1.00
49	Natalya	.40	1.00
50	Nikki Bella	.75	2.00
51	Paige	.75	2.00
52	Rosa Mendes	.25	.60
53	Sasha Banks	.75	2.00
54	Summer Rae	.60	1.50
55	Tamina	.30	.75
56	Aiden English	.25	.60
57	Angelo Dawkins	.25	.60
58	Apollo Crews RC	.25	.60
59	Asuka RC	1.00	2.50
60	Bayley RC	.60	1.50
61	Baron Corbin	.30	.75
62	Carmella RC	.60	1.50
63	Colin Cassady	.50	1.25
64	Enzo Amore RC	.50	1.25
65	Finn Balor	.75	2.00
66	Hideo Itami	.30	.75
67	Nia Jax RC	.40	1.00
68	Sami Zayn	.40	1.00
69	Samoa Joe	.60	1.50
70	Simon Gotch RC	.40	1.00
71	Alundra Blayze L	.40	1.00
72	American Dream Dusty Rhodes L	.25	.60
73	Andre The Giant L	.75	2.00
74	Bam Bam Bigelow L	.30	.75
75	Bret Hit Man Hart L	.60	1.50
76	The British Bulldog L	.30	.75
77	Bruno Sammartino L	.30	.75
78	Daniel Bryan L	1.00	2.50
79	Diamond Dallas Page L	.40	1.00
80	Eddie Guerrero L	.60	1.50
81	Edge L	.60	1.50
82	Eve L	.50	1.25
83	The Honky Tonk Man L	.25	.60
84	Irwin R. Schyster L	.25	.60
85	Jake The Snake Roberts L	.50	1.25
86	Jim The Anvil Neidhart L	.25	.60
87	Kevin Nash L	.60	1.50
88	Lex Luger L	.40	1.00
89	Lita L	.75	2.00
90	Macho Man Randy Savage L	.60	1.50
91	Million Dollar Man Ted DiBiase L	.30	.75
92	Miss Elizabeth L	.25	.60
93	Mr. Perfect Curt Hennig L	.60	1.50
94	Ravishing Rick Rude L	.40	1.00
95	Ric Flair L	1.00	2.50
96	Ricky The Dragon Steamboat L	.30	.75
97	Rikishi L	.30	.75
98	Road Dogg L	.40	1.00
99	Rob Van Dam L	.50	1.25
100	Ron Simmons L	.60	1.50
101	Rowdy Roddy Piper L	.75	2.00
102	Scott Hall L	.60	1.50
103	Sensational Sherri L	.40	1.00
104	Shawn Michaels L	1.00	2.50
105	The Iron Sheik L	.25	.60
106	Stone Cold Steve Austin L	1.25	3.00
107	Tatanka L	.25	.60
108	Trish Stratus L	1.25	3.00
109	Ultimate Warrior L	.60	1.50
110	X-Pac L	.40	1.00
113	Macho Man Randy Savage SP		

2016 Topps Heritage WWE All-Star Patches

*BRONZE/99: .5X TO 1.2X BASIC MEM
*SILVER/50: .6X TO 1.5X BASIC MEM
*BLUE/25: .75X TO 2X BASIC MEM
*GOLD/10: UNPRICED DUE TO SCARCITY
*P.P.BLACK/1: UNPRICED DUE TO SCARCITY
*P.P.CYAN/1: UNPRICED DUE TO SCARCITY
*P.P.MAGENTA/1: UNPRICED DUE TO SCARCITY
*P.P.YELLOW/1: UNPRICED DUE TO SCARCITY
RANDOMLY INSERTED INTO PACKS

NNO	Andre the Giant	6.00	15.00
NNO	Bam Bam Bigelow	2.50	6.00
NNO	Bayley	5.00	12.00
NNO	Big Van Vader	4.00	10.00
NNO	Booker T	4.00	10.00
NNO	Bret Hit Man Hart	5.00	12.00
NNO	Brock Lesnar	10.00	25.00
NNO	Bubba Ray Dudley	4.00	10.00
NNO	Curt Hennig	5.00	12.00
NNO	D-Von Dudley	3.00	8.00
NNO	Finn Balor	6.00	15.00
NNO	The Giant	4.00	10.00
NNO	Hideo Itami	2.50	6.00
NNO	John Cena	10.00	25.00
NNO	Kevin Nash	5.00	12.00
NNO	Lex Luger	3.00	8.00
NNO	Macho Man Randy Savage	5.00	12.00
NNO	Ric Flair	8.00	20.00
NNO	Rob Van Dam	4.00	10.00
NNO	The Rock	10.00	25.00
NNO	Sami Zayn	3.00	8.00
NNO	Samoa Joe	5.00	12.00
NNO	Scott Hall	5.00	12.00
NNO	Sting	5.00	12.00
NNO	Stone Cold Steve Austin	10.00	25.00
NNO	Syxx	3.00	8.00
NNO	Terry Funk	2.00	5.00
NNO	Triple H	8.00	20.00
NNO	Ultimate Warrior	5.00	12.00
NNO	Undertaker	8.00	20.00

2016 Topps Heritage WWE Autographs

*SILVER/50: .5X TO 1.2X BASIC AUTOS
*BLUE/25: .6X TO 1.5X BASIC AUTOS
*GOLD/10: 1X TO 2.5X BASIC AUTOS
*P.P.BLACK/1: UNPRICED DUE TO SCARCITY
*P.P.CYAN/1: UNPRICED DUE TO SCARCITY
*P.P.MAGENTA/1: UNPRICED DUE TO SCARCITY
*P.P.YELLOW/1: UNPRICED DUE TO SCARCITY
RANDOMLY INSERTED INTO PACKS

NNO	Asuka	20.00	50.00
NNO	Bayley	15.00	40.00
NNO	Becky Lynch	30.00	75.00
NNO	Big E	6.00	15.00
NNO	Brian Knobbs	6.00	15.00
NNO	Brie Bella	10.00	25.00
NNO	Brock Lesnar	60.00	120.00
NNO	Dean Ambrose	12.00	30.00
NNO	Finn Balor	15.00	40.00
NNO	Hideo Itami	10.00	25.00
NNO	Jake The Snake Roberts	15.00	40.00
NNO	Jerry Sags	6.00	15.00
NNO	Jim The Anvil Neidhart	5.00	12.00
NNO	John Cena	20.00	50.00
NNO	Kevin Owens	10.00	25.00
NNO	Kofi Kingston	6.00	15.00
NNO	Nia Jax	8.00	20.00
NNO	Nikki Bella	10.00	25.00
NNO	Roman Reigns	30.00	75.00
NNO	Sami Zayn	10.00	25.00
NNO	Samoa Joe	12.00	30.00
NNO	Sasha Banks	25.00	60.00
NNO	Sting	25.00	60.00
NNO	Tatanka	5.00	12.00
NNO	Tyler Breeze	6.00	15.00
NNO	Typhoon	5.00	12.00
NNO	Xavier Woods	6.00	15.00

2016 Topps Heritage WWE Diva Kiss

GOLD/10: UNPRICED DUE TO SCARCITY
RANDOMLY INSERTED INTO PACKS

NNO	Asuka	125.00	250.00
NNO	Billie Kay	20.00	50.00
NNO	Charlotte	25.00	60.00
NNO	Dasha Fuentes	30.00	75.00
NNO	Mandy Rose	60.00	120.00
NNO	Naomi	12.00	30.00
NNO	Nia Jax	20.00	50.00
NNO	Peyton Royce	30.00	75.00

2016 Topps Heritage WWE Diva Kiss Autographs

*GOLD/10: UNPRICED DUE TO SCARCITY
*P.P.BLACK/1: UNPRICED DUE TO SCARCITY
*P.P.CYAN/1: UNPRICED DUE TO SCARCITY

*P.P.MAGENTA/1: UNPRICED DUE TO SCARCITY
*P.P.YELLOW/1: UNPRICED DUE TO SCARCITY
RANDOMLY INSERTED INTO PACKS

NNO Asuka 200.00 350.00
NNO Billie Kay 50.00 100.00
NNO Charlotte 100.00 200.00
NNO Dasha Fuentes 30.00 80.00
NNO Mandy Rose 50.00 100.00
NNO Naomi 20.00 50.00
NNO Nia Jax 60.00 120.00
NNO Peyton Royce 80.00 150.00

2016 Topps Heritage WWE Dual Autographs

STATED PRINT RUN 11 SER.#'d SETS

NNO Asuka/N.Jax 50.00 100.00
NNO B.Knobbs/J.Sags 25.00 60.00
NNO Charlotte/B.Lynch 125.00 250.00
NNO F.Balor/S.Joe 80.00 150.00
NNO J.Roberts/J.Neidhart 50.00 100.00
NNO J.Cena/Sting 100.00 200.00
NNO K.Owens/D.Ziggler 60.00 120.00
NNO N.Bella/B.Bella 60.00 120.00
NNO R.Reigns/D.Ambrose 50.00 100.00
NNO S.Zayn/H.Itami 25.00 60.00
NNO S.Banks/Bayley 125.00 250.00
NNO Tatanka 25.00 60.00
Typhoon

2016 Topps Heritage WWE NXT University of Central Florida Mat Relics

*BRONZE/99: .5X TO 1.2X BASIC MEM
GOLD/10: UNPRICED DUE TO SCARCITY
STATED PRINT RUN 99 SER.#'d SETS

NNO Alex Riley 2.50 6.00
NNO Asuka 10.00 25.00
NNO Bayley 6.00 15.00
NNO Carmella 6.00 15.00
NNO Colin Cassady 5.00 12.00
NNO Enzo Amore 5.00 12.00
NNO Nia Jax 4.00 10.00
NNO Sami Zayn 4.00 10.00
NNO Samoa Joe 6.00 15.00
NNO Tye Dillinger 3.00 8.00

2016 Topps Heritage WWE Record Breakers

COMPLETE SET (30) 12.00 30.00
*P.P.BLACK/1: UNPRICED DUE TO SCARCITY
*P.P.CYAN/1: UNPRICED DUE TO SCARCITY
*P.P.MAGENTA/1: UNPRICED DUE TO SCARCITY
*P.P.YELLOW/1: UNPRICED DUE TO SCARCITY

1 Bruno Sammartino .40 1.00
2 John Cena 1.50 4.00
3 Brock Lesnar 1.50 4.00
4 Andre the Giant 1.00 2.50
5 Ric Flair 1.25 3.00
6 Triple H 1.25 3.00
7 Randy Orton 1.00 2.50
8 Edge 1.00 2.50
9 Honky Tonk Man .40 1.00
10 Chris Jericho 1.00 2.50
11 Lex Luger .60 1.50
12 Ric Flair 1.50 4.00
13 Nikki Bella 1.25 3.00
14 Eve Torres .75 2.00
15 The Dudley Boyz .75 2.00
16 Edge 1.00 2.50
17 Finn Balor 1.25 3.00
18 Paige 1.25 3.00
19 The Ascension .40 1.00
20 Neville 1.00 2.50
21 The British Bulldog .50 1.25
22 Big Boss Man .60 1.50
23 Harlem Heat .75 2.00
24 Undertaker 1.50 4.00
25 Stone Cold Steve Austin 2.00 5.00
26 Roman Reigns 1.25 3.00
27 Kane .60 1.50
28 Triple H 1.50 4.00
29 Kane .60 1.50
30 Bret Hit Man Hart 1.00 2.50

2016 Topps Heritage WWE Survivor Series 2015 Mat Relics

*BRONZE/99: SAME VALUE AS BASIC MEM
*SILVER/50: .5X TO 1.2X BASIC MEM
*BLUE/25: .6X TO 1.5X BASIC MEM
*GOLD/10: UNPRICED DUE TO SCARCITY
*P.P.BLACK/1: UNPRICED DUE TO SCARCITY
*P.P.CYAN/1: UNPRICED DUE TO SCARCITY
*P.P.MAGENTA/1: UNPRICED DUE TO SCARCITY
*P.P.YELLOW/1: UNPRICED DUE TO SCARCITY
RANDOMLY INSERTED INTO PACKS

NNO Alberto Del Rio 4.00 10.00
NNO Bray Wyatt 10.00 25.00
NNO Bubba Ray Dudley 5.00 12.00
NNO Charlotte 8.00 20.00
NNO D-Von Dudley 4.00 10.00
NNO Dean Ambrose 8.00 20.00
NNO Dolph Ziggler 3.00 8.00
NNO Goldust 4.00 10.00
NNO Jey Uso 2.50 6.00
NNO Jimmy Uso 2.50 6.00
NNO Kalisto 6.00 15.00
NNO Kane 4.00 10.00
NNO Kevin Owens 6.00 15.00
NNO Luke Harper 2.50 6.00
NNO Paige 8.00 20.00
NNO Roman Reigns 8.00 20.00
NNO Sheamus 6.00 15.00
NNO Titus O'Neil 2.50 6.00
NNO Tyler Breeze 2.50 6.00
NNO Undertaker 10.00 25.00

2016 Topps Heritage WWE Swatch Relics

*BRONZE/150: SAME VALUE AS BASIC MEM
*SILVER/50: .5X TO 1.2X BASIC MEM
*BLUE/25: .6X TO 1.5X BASIC MEM
*GOLD/10: UNPRICED DUE TO SCARCITY
*P.P.BLACK/1: UNPRICED DUE TO SCARCITY
*P.P.CYAN/1: UNPRICED DUE TO SCARCITY
*P.P.MAGENTA/1: UNPRICED DUE TO SCARCITY
*P.P.YELLOW/1: UNPRICED DUE TO SCARCITY
RANDOMLY INSERTED INTO PACKS

1 Aiden English 2.50 6.00
2 Alberto Del Rio 4.00 10.00
3 Asuka 10.00 25.00
4 Bayley 6.00 15.00
5 Big E 2.50 6.00
6 Bray Wyatt 10.00 25.00
7 Brock Lesnar 12.00 30.00
8 Bubba Ray Dudley 5.00 12.00
9 Cesaro 5.00 12.00
10 Charlotte 8.00 20.00
11 D-Von Dudley 4.00 10.00
12 Dean Ambrose 8.00 20.00
13 Dolph Ziggler 3.00 8.00
14 Finn Balor 8.00 20.00
15 Jey Uso 2.50 6.00
16 Jimmy Uso 2.50 6.00
17 John Cena 12.00 30.00
18 Kevin Owens 6.00 15.00
19 Kofi Kingston 2.50 6.00
20 Paige 8.00 20.00
21 Roman Reigns 8.00 20.00
22 Samoa Joe 6.00 15.00
23 Sheamus 6.00 15.00
24 Simon Gotch 4.00 10.00
25 Xavier Woods 2.50 6.00
26 Zack Ryder 2.50 6.00

2016 Topps Heritage WWE Turn Back the Clock

COMPLETE SET (15) 10.00 25.00
*P.P.BLACK/1: UNPRICED DUE TO SCARCITY
*P.P.CYAN/1: UNPRICED DUE TO SCARCITY
*P.P.MAGENTA/1: UNPRICED DUE TO SCARCITY
*P.P.YELLOW/1: UNPRICED DUE TO SCARCITY
RANDOMLY INSERTED INTO PACKS

1 The Iron Sheik .50 1.25
2 Andre the Giant 1.50 4.00
3 Ricky The Dragon Steamboat .60 1.50
4 Jake The Snake Roberts 1.00 2.50
5 Texas Tornado .75 2.00
6 Big Boss Man .75 2.00
7 Hacksaw Jim Duggan .50 1.25
8 Rowdy Roddy Piper 1.50 4.00
9 Tatanka .50 1.25
10 Undertaker 2.00 5.00
11 Macho Man Randy Savage 1.25 3.00
12 Sgt. Slaughter .60 1.50
13 Shawn Michaels 2.00 5.00
14 Bret Hit Man Hart 1.25 3.00
15 The British Bulldog .60 1.50

2016 Topps Heritage WWE WCW/nWo All-Stars

COMPLETE SET (40) 20.00 50.00
*P.P.BLACK/1: UNPRICED DUE TO SCARCITY
*P.P.CYAN/1: UNPRICED DUE TO SCARCITY
*P.P.MAGENTA/1: UNPRICED DUE TO SCARCITY
*P.P.YELLOW/1: UNPRICED DUE TO SCARCITY

1 Scott Hall 1.50 4.00
2 Kevin Nash 1.50 4.00
3 Trillionaire Ted DiBiase .75 2.00
4 The Giant 1.25 3.00
5 Syxx 1.00 2.50
6 Vincent .60 1.50
7 Miss Elizabeth .60 1.50
8 Mr. Wallstreet .60 1.50
9 Big Bubba Rogers 1.00 2.50
10 Macho Man Randy Savage 1.50 4.00
11 Curt Hennig 1.50 4.00
12 Rick Rude 1.00 2.50
13 Dusty Rhodes .60 1.50
14 Bret Hit Man Hart 1.50 4.00
15 Stevie Ray .60 1.50
16 Lex Luger 1.00 2.50
17 Sting 1.50 4.00
18 Shawn Michaels 2.50 6.00
19 Booker T 1.25 3.00
20 Ric Flair 2.50 6.00
21 Arn Anderson .60 1.50
22 Diamond Dallas Page 1.00 2.50
23 Rowdy Roddy Piper 2.00 5.00
24 Ultimate Warrior 1.50 4.00
25 The British Bulldog .75 2.00
26 Jim The Anvil Neidhart .60 1.50
27 Hacksaw Jim Duggan .60 1.50
28 Chris Jericho 1.50 4.00
29 Eddie Guerrero 1.50 4.00
30 Dean Malenko .60 1.50
31 Mr. Wonderful Paul Orndorff .60 1.50
32 Terry Funk .60 1.50
33 Larry Zbyszko .60 1.50
34 John Tenta .60 1.50
35 Bam Bam Bigelow .75 2.00
36 Brian Pillman .75 2.00
37 Steven Regal .60 1.50
38 Brian Knobbs .60 1.50
39 Jerry Sags .75 2.00
40 Madusa .75 2.00

2017 Topps Heritage WWE

COMPLETE SET (100) 10.00 25.00
UNOPENED BOX (24 PACKS)
UNOPENED PACK (9 CARDS)
*BRONZE: .5X TO 1.2X BASIC CARDS
*BLUE/99: .75X TO 2X BASIC CARDS
*SILVER/25: 1.2X TO 3X BASIC CARDS
*GOLD/10: 2X TO 5X BASIC CARDS
*RED/1: UNPRICED DUE TO SCARCITY
*P.P.BLACK/1: UNPRICED DUE TO SCARCITY
*P.P.CYAN/1: UNPRICED DUE TO SCARCITY
*P.P.MAGENTA/1: UNPRICED DUE TO SCARCITY
*P.P.YELLOW/1: UNPRICED DUE TO SCARCITY

1 Asuka 1.25 3.00
2 Bobby Roode 1.00 2.50
3 Ember Moon RC 1.00 2.50
4 Eric Young .75 2.00
5 Hideo Itami .60 1.50
6 Johnny Gargano .40 1.00
7 Liv Morgan .60 1.50
8 Tommaso Ciampa .40 1.00
9 The Rock 2.00 5.00
10 Alicia Fox .60 1.50
11 Austin Aries .75 2.00
12 Bayley 1.25 3.00
13 Big Cass .50 1.25
14 Big E .50 1.25
15 Bob Backlund .40 1.00
16 The Brian Kendrick .40 1.00
17 Brock Lesnar 2.00 5.00
18 Cesaro .75 2.00
19 Charlotte Flair 1.50 4.00
20 Chris Jericho 1.00 2.50
21 Enzo Amore 1.25 3.00
22 Finn Balor 1.50 4.00
23 Goldberg 1.50 4.00
24 Karl Anderson .40 1.00
25 Kevin Owens 1.00 2.50
26 Kofi Kingston .50 1.25
27 Lana 1.25 3.00
28 Luke Gallows .60 1.50

29	Mick Foley	1.00	2.50
30	Roman Reigns	1.25	3.00
31	Rusev	.75	2.00
32	Sami Zayn	.50	1.25
33	Samoa Joe	1.25	3.00
34	Sasha Banks	1.25	3.00
35	Seth Rollins	1.25	3.00
36	Sheamus	.75	2.00
37	Triple H	1.00	2.50
38	Xavier Woods	.50	1.25
39	AJ Styles	2.00	5.00
40	Alexa Bliss	2.00	5.00
41	Baron Corbin	.60	1.50
42	Becky Lynch	1.25	3.00
43	Bray Wyatt	1.00	2.50
44	Carmella	1.00	2.50
45	Chad Gable	.50	1.25
46	Daniel Bryan	1.50	4.00
47	Dean Ambrose	1.25	3.00
48	Dolph Ziggler	.60	1.50
49	Heath Slater	.40	1.00
50	Jason Jordan	.50	1.25
51	Jey Uso	.50	1.25
52	Jimmy Uso	.50	1.25
53	John Cena	2.00	5.00
54	Kalisto	.60	1.50
55	Kane	.50	1.25
56	Luke Harper	.40	1.00
57	Maryse	.75	2.00
58	The Miz	.75	2.00
59	Mojo Rawley	.50	1.25
60	Naomi	.75	2.00
61	Natalya	.75	2.00
62	Nikki Bella	1.00	2.50
63	Randy Orton	1.00	2.50
64	Rhyno	.40	1.00
65	Shinsuke Nakamura	1.00	2.50
66	Undertaker	1.50	4.00
67	Zack Ryder	.40	1.00
68	Alundra Blayze L	.50	1.25
69	Andre the Giant L	.75	2.00
70	Batista L	.75	2.00
71	Bret Hit Man Hart L	.75	2.00
72	British Bulldog L	.40	1.00
73	Brutus The Barber Beefcake L	.40	1.00
74	Diamond Dallas Page L	.50	1.25
75	Dusty Rhodes L	.50	1.25
76	Edge L	1.00	2.50
77	Fit Finlay L	.40	1.00
78	Jake The Snake Roberts L	.50	1.25
79	Jim The Anvil Neidhart L	.40	1.00
80	Ken Shamrock L	.40	1.00
81	Kevin Nash L	.60	1.50
82	Lex Luger L	.50	1.25
83	Terri Runnels L	.40	1.00
84	Macho Man Randy Savage L	.75	2.00
85	Million Dollar Man Ted DiBiase L	.50	1.25
86	Mr. Perfect L	.75	2.00
87	Ravishing Rick Rude L	.60	1.50
88	Ric Flair L	1.00	2.50
89	Rob Van Dam L	.75	2.00
90	Ron Simmons L	.50	1.25
91	Rowdy Roddy Piper L	.75	2.00
92	Scott Hall L	.50	1.25
93	Sgt. Slaughter L	.50	1.25
94	Shawn Michaels L	1.00	2.50
95	Sid Vicious L	.50	1.25
96	Sting L	1.25	3.00
97	Stone Cold Steve Austin L	1.50	4.00
98	Trish Stratus L	1.50	4.00
99	Ultimate Warrior L	.75	2.00
100	Wendi Richter L	.50	1.25

2017 Topps Heritage WWE Thirty Years of SummerSlam

COMPLETE SET (50) 5.00 12.00
*P.P.BLACK/1: UNPRICED DUE TO SCARCITY
*P.P.CYAN/1: UNPRICED DUE TO SCARCITY
*P.P.MAGENTA/1: UNPRICED DUE TO SCARCITY
*P.P.YELLOW/1: UNPRICED DUE TO SCARCITY
STATED ODDS 2:1

1	Ultimate Warrior	.50	1.25
2	The Mega Powers	.50	1.25
3	Ultimate Warrior	.50	1.25
4	Texas Tornado	.25	.60
5	Hart Foundation	.50	1.25
6	Ultimate Warrior	.50	1.25
7	Bret Hit Man Hart	.50	1.25
8	Virgil	.25	.60
9	Ultimate Warrior	.50	1.25
10	British Bulldog	.25	.60
11	Lex Luger	.30	.75
12	Alundra Blayze	.30	.75
13	Razor Ramon	.30	.75
14	Shawn Michaels	.60	1.50
15	Diesel	.40	1.00
16	Mankind	.60	1.50
17	Shawn Michaels	.60	1.50
18	Mankind	.60	1.50
19	Bret Hit Man Hart	.50	1.25
20	Triple H	.60	1.50
21	Stond Cold Steve Austin	1.00	2.50
22	Unholy Alliance	1.00	2.50
23	Mankind	.60	1.50
24	X-Pac	.25	.60
25	X-Pac	.25	.60
26	The Rock	1.25	3.00
27	Shawn Michaels	.60	1.50
28	Brock Lesnar	1.25	3.00
29	Kane	.30	.75
30	Kurt Angle	.50	1.25
31	JBL	.30	.75
32	John Cena	1.25	3.00
33	Edge	.60	1.50
34	John Cena	1.25	3.00
35	Undertaker	1.00	2.50
36	Randy Orton	.60	1.50
37	Randy Orton	.60	1.50
38	Team WWE	1.00	2.50
39	Randy Orton	.60	1.50
40	Brock Lesnar	1.25	3.00
41	Daniel Bryan	1.00	2.50
42	Randy Orton	.60	1.50
43	Roman Reigns	.75	2.00
44	Brock Lesnar	1.25	3.00
45	Seth Rollins	.75	2.00
46	Undertaker	1.00	2.50
47	Charlotte	1.00	2.50
48	AJ Styles	1.25	3.00
49	Finn Balor	1.00	2.50
50	Brock Lesnar	1.25	3.00

2017 Topps Heritage WWE Autographed NXT TakeOver Toronto 2016 Mat Relics

STATED ODDS 1:9,056
STATED PRINT RUN 10 SER. #'d SETS
UNPRICED DUE TO SCARCITY

NNO Asuka
NNO Booby Roode
NNO Johnny Gargano
NNO Mickie James
NNO Samoa Joe
NNO Shinsuke Nakamura
NNO Tommaso Ciampa

2017 Topps Heritage WWE Autographed Survivor Series 2016 Mat Relics

STATED ODDS 1:3,544
STATED PRINT RUN 10 SER. #'d SETS
UNPRICED DUE TO SCARCITY

NNO AJ Styles
NNO Alexa Bliss
NNO Alicia Fox
NNO Bayley
NNO Becky Lynch
NNO Braun Strowman
NNO Bray Wyatt
NNO Brock Lesnar
NNO Carmella
NNO Charlotte Flair
NNO Chris Jericho
NNO Goldberg
NNO Kevin Owens
NNO Natalya
NNO Randy Orton
NNO Roman Reigns
NNO Sasha Banks
NNO Seth Rollins

2017 Topps Heritage WWE Autographs

*BLUE/50: .5X TO 1.2X BASIC AUTOS
*SILVER/25: .6X TO 1.5X BASIC AUTOS
*GOLD/10: UNPRICED DUE TO SCARCITY
*RED/1: UNPRICED DUE TO SCARCITY
*P.P.BLACK/1: UNPRICED DUE TO SCARCITY
*P.P.CYAN/1: UNPRICED DUE TO SCARCITY
*P.P.MAGENTA/1: UNPRICED DUE TO SCARCITY
*P.P.YELLOW/1: UNPRICED DUE TO SCARCITY
STATED ODDS 1:24

NNO	AJ Styles	15.00	40.00
NNO	Alexa Bliss	60.00	120.00
NNO	Asuka	25.00	60.00
NNO	Bayley	15.00	40.00
NNO	Becky Lynch	50.00	100.00
NNO	Bobby Roode	12.00	30.00
NNO	Bray Wyatt	12.00	30.00
NNO	Bret Hit Man Hart	20.00	50.00
NNO	Brutus The Barber Beefcake	12.00	30.00
NNO	Charlotte Flair	20.00	50.00
NNO	Chris Jericho	10.00	25.00
NNO	Dean Ambrose	8.00	20.00
NNO	Ember Moon	6.00	15.00
NNO	Eric Young	6.00	15.00
NNO	Finn Balor	15.00	40.00
NNO	Fit Finlay	10.00	25.00
NNO	Goldberg	30.00	80.00
NNO	Kevin Owens	8.00	20.00
NNO	Sasha Banks	20.00	50.00
NNO	Shinsuke Nakamura	15.00	40.00
NNO	Sting	20.00	50.00

2017 Topps Heritage WWE Autographs Blue

STATED ODDS 1:93
STATED PRINT RUN 50 SER.#'d SETS

NNO	Undertaker	120.00	250.00

2017 Topps Heritage WWE Autographs Silver

NNO	Brock Lesnar	30.00	75.00

2017 Topps Heritage WWE Bizarre SummerSlam Matches

COMPLETE SET (10) 3.00 8.00
*P.P.BLACK/1: UNPRICED DUE TO SCARCITY
*P.P.CYAN/1: UNPRICED DUE TO SCARCITY
*P.P.MAGENTA/1: UNPRICED DUE TO SCARCITY
*P.P.YELLOW/1: UNPRICED DUE TO SCARCITY
STATED ODDS 1:3

1	Big Boss Man	.40	1.00
2	Undertaker	1.25	3.00
3	Mankind	.75	2.00
4	British Bulldog	.30	.75
5	X-Pac	.30	.75
6	Ken Shamrock	.30	.75
7	Kane	.40	1.00
8	Ric Flair	.75	2.00
9	Bray Wyatt	.75	2.00
10	Rusev	.60	1.50

2017 Topps Heritage WWE Commemorative Patches

*BRONZE/99: .5X TO 1.2X BASIC MEM
*BLUE/50: .6X TO 1.5X BASIC MEM
*SILVER/25: .75X TO 2X BASIC MEM
*GOLD/10: UNPRICED DUE TO SCARCITY
*RED/1: UNPRICED DUE TO SCARCITY
*P.P.BLACK/1: UNPRICED DUE TO SCARCITY
*P.P.CYAN/1: UNPRICED DUE TO SCARCITY
*P.P.MAGENTA/1: UNPRICED DUE TO SCARCITY
*P.P.YELLOW/1: UNPRICED DUE TO SCARCITY
STATED ODDS 1:115

NNO	AJ Styles	6.00	15.00
NNO	Asuka	4.00	10.00
NNO	Bobby Roode	3.00	8.00
NNO	Charlotte Flair	5.00	12.00
NNO	Chris Jericho	3.00	8.00
NNO	Dean Ambrose	4.00	10.00
NNO	Dolph Ziggler	2.00	5.00
NNO	Ember Moon	3.00	8.00
NNO	Eric Young	2.50	6.00
NNO	Hideo Itami	2.00	5.00
NNO	John Cena	6.00	15.00
NNO	Kevin Owens	3.00	8.00
NNO	The Miz	2.50	6.00
NNO	Ric Flair	3.00	8.00
NNO	Roman Reigns	4.00	10.00
NNO	Rowdy Roddy Piper	2.50	6.00
NNO	Seth Rollins	4.00	10.00
NNO	Shawn Michaels	3.00	8.00
NNO	Sting	4.00	10.00
NNO	Trish Stratus	5.00	12.00

2017 Topps Heritage WWE Dual Autographs

STATED ODDS 1:2,264
STATED PRINT RUN 10 SER.#'d SETS

RANDOMLY INSERTED INTO PACKS

NNO Big E/K.Kingston/10	30.00	75.00
NNO B.Sammartino/L.Zbyszko/9	100.00	200.00
NNO J.Lawler/M.Cole/10	50.00	100.00
NNO Primo/Epico/10	25.00	60.00
NNO S.Rollins/R.Reigns/10	60.00	120.00

2017 Topps Heritage WWE Kiss

*GOLD/10: UNPRICED DUE TO SCARCITY
*RED/1: UNPRICED DUE TO SCARCITY
STATED ODDS 1:685

NNO Alexa Bliss	150.00	300.00
NNO Asuka	25.00	60.00
NNO Carmella	60.00	120.00
NNO Charlotte Flair	100.00	200.00
NNO Dana Brooke	30.00	75.00
NNO Ember Moon	20.00	50.00
NNO Liv Morgan	75.00	150.00

2017 Topps Heritage WWE Kiss Autographs

*GOLD/10: UNPRICED DUE TO SCARCITY
*RED/1: UNPRICED DUE TO SCARCITY
STATED ODDS 1:2,717

NNO Alexa Bliss	500.00	1000.00
NNO Asuka	75.00	150.00
NNO Carmella	60.00	120.00
NNO Charlotte Flair	60.00	120.00
NNO Dana Brooke	75.00	150.00
NNO Ember Moon	50.00	100.00
NNO Liv Morgan	50.00	100.00

2017 Topps Heritage WWE NXT TakeOver Toronto 2016 Mat Relics

*BRONZE/99: .5X TO 1.2X BASIC MEM
*BLUE/50: .6X TO 1.5X BASIC MEM
*SILVER/25: .75X TO 2X BASIC MEM
*GOLD/10: UNPRICED DUE TO SCARCITY
*RED/1: UNPRICED DUE TO SCARCITY
*P.P.BLACK/1: UNPRICED DUE TO SCARCITY
*P.P.CYAN/1: UNPRICED DUE TO SCARCITY
*P.P.MAGENTA/1: UNPRICED DUE TO SCARCITY
*P.P.YELLOW/1: UNPRICED DUE TO SCARCITY
RANDOMLY INSERTED INTO PACKS

NNO Akam	1.50	4.00
NNO Asuka	5.00	12.00
NNO Bobby Roode	4.00	10.00
NNO Johnny Gargano	1.50	4.00
NNO Mickie James	2.50	6.00
NNO Rezar	1.50	4.00
NNO Samoa Joe	5.00	12.00
NNO Shinsuke Nakamura	4.00	10.00
NNO Tommaso Ciampa	1.50	4.00
NNO Tye Dillinger	1.50	4.00

2017 Topps Heritage WWE Roster Updates

COMPLETE SET (10)	12.00	30.00

*P.P.BLACK/1: UNPRICED DUE TO SCARCITY
*P.P.CYAN/1: UNPRICED DUE TO SCARCITY
*P.P.MAGENTA/1: UNPRICED DUE TO SCARCITY
*P.P.YELLOW/1: UNPRICED DUE TO SCARCITY
RANDOMLY INSERTED INTO PACKS

R1 Alexander Wolfe	2.00	5.00
R2 Kassius Ohno	1.50	4.00
R3 Nikki Cross	3.00	8.00
R4 Roderick Strong	2.00	5.00
R5 Tye Dillinger	1.50	4.00
R6 Cedric Alexander	2.50	6.00
R7 Gentleman Jack Gallagher	3.00	8.00
R8 Neville	2.50	6.00
R9 Rich Swann	1.50	4.00
R10 TJ Perkins	1.50	4.00

2017 Topps Heritage WWE Shirt Relics

*BLUE/50: .5X TO 1.2X BASIC MEM
*SILVER/25: .6X TO 1.5X BASIC MEM
*GOLD/10: UNPRICED DUE TO SCARCITY
*RED/1: UNPRICED DUE TO SCARCITY

RC Carmella	5.00	12.00
RN Naomi	4.00	10.00
RS Sheamus	4.00	10.00
RAA Andrade Cien Almas	2.00	5.00
RAC Apollo Crews	2.50	6.00
RAE Aiden English	2.00	5.00
RAF Alicia Fox	3.00	8.00
RBK Becky Lynch	6.00	15.00
RBL Brock Lesnar	10.00	25.00
RBR Bobby Roode	5.00	12.00
RCA Curtis Axel	2.00	5.00
RCF Charlotte Flair	8.00	20.00
RDY Darren Young	2.00	5.00
RHI Hideo Itami	3.00	8.00
RJC John Cena	10.00	25.00
RJG Johnny Gargano	2.00	5.00
RJJ JoJo	3.00	8.00
RKA Karl Anderson	2.00	5.00
RLH Luke Harper	2.00	5.00
RNJ No Way Jose	2.00	5.00
RNN Natalya	4.00	10.00
RRO Randy Orton	5.00	12.00
RSB Sasha Banks	6.00	15.00
RSN Shinsuke Nakamura	5.00	12.00
RSR Seth Rollins	6.00	15.00
RSU Summer Rae	5.00	12.00
RTC Tommaso Ciampa	2.00	5.00
RZR Zack Ryder	2.00	5.00

2017 Topps Heritage WWE SummerSlam All-Stars

COMPLETE SET (30)	6.00	15.00

*P.P.BLACK/1: UNPRICED DUE TO SCARCITY
*P.P.CYAN/1: UNPRICED DUE TO SCARCITY
*P.P.MAGENTA/1: UNPRICED DUE TO SCARCITY
*P.P.YELLOW/1: UNPRICED DUE TO SCARCITY
STATED ODDS 1:1

1 Undertaker	1.50	4.00
2 Edge	1.00	2.50
3 Triple H	1.00	2.50
4 Bret Hit Man Hart	.75	2.00
5 Shawn Michaels	1.00	2.50
6 Randy Orton	1.00	2.50
7 Kane	.50	1.25
8 Ultimate Warrior	.75	2.00
9 Rob Van Dam	.75	2.00
10 Brock Lesnar	2.00	5.00
11 Big Show	.50	1.25
12 Chris Jericho	1.00	2.50
13 Kurt Angle	.75	2.00
14 John Cena	2.00	5.00
15 Tatanka	.40	1.00
16 Jerry The King Lawler	.50	1.25
17 Earthquake	.40	1.00
18 Irwin R. Schyster	.40	1.00
19 British Bulldog	.30	.75
20 Stone Cold Steve Austin	1.50	4.00
21 Daniel Bryan	1.50	4.00
22 Mick Foley	1.00	2.50
23 The Rock	1.50	4.00
24 Sheamus	.75	2.00
25 Kofi Kingston	.50	1.25
26 X-Pac	.40	1.00
27 Dolph Ziggler	.60	1.50
28 Ric Flair	1.00	2.50
29 Texas Tornado	.40	1.00
30 Typhoon	.40	1.00

2017 Topps Heritage WWE Survivor Series 2016 Mat Relics

*BRONZE/99: .5X TO 1.2X BASIC MEM
*BLUE/50: .6X TO 1.5X BASIC MEM
*SILVER/25: .75X TO 2X BASIC MEM
*GOLD/10: UNPRICED DUE TO SCARCITY
*RED/1: UNPRICED DUE TO SCARCITY
*P.P.BLACK/1: UNPRICED DUE TO SCARCITY
*P.P.CYAN/1: UNPRICED DUE TO SCARCITY
*P.P.MAGENTA/1: UNPRICED DUE TO SCARCITY
*P.P.YELLOW/1: UNPRICED DUE TO SCARCITY
STATED ODDS 1:175

NNO AJ Styles	6.00	15.00
NNO Alexa Bliss	15.00	40.00
NNO Alicia Fox	5.00	12.00
NNO Bayley	6.00	15.00
NNO Becky Lynch	6.00	15.00
NNO Braun Strowman	5.00	12.00
NNO Bray Wyatt	6.00	15.00
NNO Brock Lesnar	8.00	20.00
NNO Carmella	5.00	12.00
NNO Charlotte Flair	6.00	15.00
NNO Chris Jericho	6.00	15.00
NNO Dean Ambrose	4.00	10.00
NNO Goldberg	6.00	15.00
NNO Kevin Owens	5.00	12.00
NNO Natalya	4.00	10.00
NNO Randy Orton	5.00	12.00
NNO Roman Reigns	5.00	12.00
NNO Sasha Banks	8.00	20.00
NNO Seth Rollins	5.00	12.00
NNO Shane McMahon	6.00	15.00

2018 Topps Heritage WWE

COMPLETE SET W/SP (119)	25.00	60.00
COMPLETE SET W/O SP (110)	10.00	25.00
UNOPENED BOX (24 PACKS)		
UNOPENED PACK (6 CARDS)		

*BRONZE: .6X TO 1.5X BASIC CARDS
*BLUE/99: .75X TO 2X BASIC CARDS
*SILVER/25: 2X TO 5X BASIC CARDS
*GOLD/10: UNPRICED DUE TO SCARCITY
*RED/1: UNPRICED DUE TO SCARCITY
*P.P.BLACK/1: UNPRICED DUE TO SCARCITY
*P.P.CYAN/1: UNPRICED DUE TO SCARCITY
*P.P.MAGENTA/1: UNPRICED DUE TO SCARCITY
*P.P.YELLOW/1: UNPRICED DUE TO SCARCITY

1 AJ Styles	1.00	2.50
2 Akira Tozawa	.40	1.00
3 Alexa Bliss	1.25	3.00
4 Alicia Fox	.40	1.00
5 Apollo Crews	.25	.60
6 Ariya Daivari	.25	.60
7 Asuka	.75	2.00
8 Baron Corbin	.40	1.00
9 Bayley	.40	1.00
10 Becky Lynch	.60	1.50
11 Big Cass	.30	.75
12 Big E	.30	.75
13 Big Show	.25	.60
14 Bobby Roode	.40	1.00
15 Braun Strowman	.60	1.50
16 Bray Wyatt	.60	1.50
17 Brie Bella	.50	1.25
18 Carmella	.50	1.25
19 Cedric Alexander	.25	.60
20 Cesaro	.50	1.25
21 Chad Gable	.25	.60
22 Charlotte Flair	.75	2.00
23 Chris Jericho	.60	1.50
24 Dean Ambrose	.50	1.25
25 Drew Gulak	.25	.60
26 Elias	.60	1.50
27 Fandango	.25	.60
28 Finn Balor	.60	1.50
29 Gentleman Jack Gallagher	.30	.75
30 Goldust	.50	1.25
31 Jason Jordan	.25	.60
32 Jeff Hardy	.50	1.25
33 Jey Uso	.25	.60
34 Jimmy Uso	.25	.60
35 Jinder Mahal	.30	.75
36 John Cena	1.00	2.50
37 Kalisto	.25	.60
38 Kane	.40	1.00
39 Karl Anderson	.25	.60
40 Kevin Owens	.60	1.50
41 Kofi Kingston	.30	.75
42 Kurt Angle	.60	1.50
43 Lana	.60	1.50
44 Liv Morgan	.50	1.25
45 Luke Gallows	.30	.75
46 Mandy Rose	.60	1.50
47 Maria Kanellis	.60	1.50
48 Maryse	.50	1.25
49 Woken Matt Hardy	.60	1.50
50 Mickie James	.50	1.25
51 Mojo Rawley	.25	.60
52 Mustafa Ali	.25	.60
53 Naomi	.30	.75
54 Natalya	.30	.75
55 Nia Jax	.40	1.00
56 Nikki Bella	.50	1.25
57 Noam Dar	.25	.60
58 Paige	.60	1.50
59 Pete Dunne RC	.25	.60
60 R-Truth	.30	.75
61 Randy Orton	.60	1.50
62 Rhyno	.25	.60
63 Roman Reigns	.60	1.50
64 Ruby Riott	.40	1.00
65 Rusev	.40	1.00
66 Sami Zayn	.25	.60
67 Samoa Joe	.50	1.25
68 Sarah Logan RC	.25	.60
69 Sasha Banks	.75	2.00
70 Seth Rollins	.60	1.50
71 Shane McMahon	.50	1.25
72 Sheamus	.50	1.25
73 Shelton Benjamin	.30	.75

74	Shinsuke Nakamura	.60	1.50
75	Sin Cara	.30	.75
76	Sonya Deville	.50	1.25
77	Stephanie McMahon	.50	1.25
78	Tamina	.25	.60
79	The Brian Kendrick	.40	1.00
80	The Miz	.50	1.25
81	The Rock	1.25	3.00
82	Titus O'Neil	.25	.60
83	Tony Nese	.25	.60
84	Triple H	.60	1.50
85	Tye Dillinger	.25	.60
86	Tyler Bate	.25	.60
87	Tyler Breeze	.25	.60
88	Undertaker	1.00	2.50
89	Xavier Woods	.30	.75
90	Zack Ryder	.25	.60
91	Adam Cole RC	.30	.75
92	Aleister Black	.30	.75
93	Alexander Wolfe	.25	.60
94	Andrade Cien Almas	.40	1.00
95	Billie Kay	.50	1.25
96	Bobby Fish RC	.25	.60
97	Drew McIntyre	.40	1.00
98	Ember Moon	.50	1.25
99	Eric Young	.30	.75
100	Johnny Gargano	.25	.60
101	Kairi Sane RC	.60	1.50
102	Kassius Ohno	.25	.60
103	Killian Dain	.30	.75
104	Kyle O'Reilly RC	.30	.75
105	Nikki Cross	.40	1.00
106	Oney Lorcan	.30	.75
107	Peyton Royce	.60	1.50
108	Roderick Strong	.25	.60
109	Tommaso Ciampa	.25	.60
110	Velveteen Dream	.25	.60
111	Aiden English SP	1.25	3.00
112	Ariya Daivari SP	1.25	3.00
113	Dash Wilder SP	1.50	4.00
114	Harper SP	2.00	5.00
115	Konnor SP	1.25	3.00
116	R-Truth SP	1.50	4.00
117	Rowan SP	2.00	5.00
118	Scott Dawson SP	1.50	4.00
119	Viktor SP	1.25	3.00

2018 Topps Heritage WWE Autographed NXT TakeOver War Games 2017 Mat Relics

STATED PRINT RUN 10 SER.#'d SETS
UNPRICED DUE TO SCARCITY

NXTAAC Adam Cole
NXTABF Bobby Fish
NXTADM Drew McIntyre
NXTAEM Ember Moon
NXTAKD Killian Dain
NXTAKO Kyle O'Reilly
NXTARS Roderick Strong

2018 Topps Heritage WWE Autographed Survivor Series 2017 Mat Relics

STATED PRINT RUN 10 SER.#'d SETS
UNPRICED DUE TO SCARCITY

SSAAJ AJ Styles
SSAAS Asuka
SSABR Booby Roode
SSABS Braun Strowman
SSAKA Kurt Angle
SSANJ Nia Jax
SSARO Randy Orton
SSASB Sasha Banks
SSASJ Samoa Joe
SSASN Shinsuke Nakamura
SSATH Triple H

2018 Topps Heritage WWE Autographed TLC 2017 Mat Relics

STATED PRINT RUN 10 SER.#'d SETS
UNPRICED DUE TO SCARCITY

TLCAAJ AJ Styles
TLCABS Braun Strowman
TLCAKA Kurt Angle
TLCASH Sheamus
TLCATM The Miz

2018 Topps Heritage WWE Autographed TLC Commemorative Medallion Relics

STATED PRINT RUN 10 SER.#'d SETS
UNPRICED DUE TO SCARCITY

CTMAAJ AJ Styles
CTMABC Baron Corbin
CTMABS Braun Strowman
CTMADZ Dolph Ziggler
CTMAKA Kane
CTMAKA Kurt Angle
CTMAMZ The Miz
CTMASA Sheamus
CTMASH Sheamus
CTMATM The Miz

2018 Topps Heritage WWE Autographs

*BLUE/50: .5X TO 1.2X BASIC AUTOS
*SILVER/25: .6X TO 1.5X BASIC AUTOS
*GOLD/10: UNPRICED DUE TO SCARCITY
*RED/1: UNPRICED DUE TO SCARCITY
STATED PRINT RUN 99 SER.#'d SETS

AAB	Alexa Bliss	50.00	100.00
AAC	Adam Cole	15.00	40.00
AAS	AJ Styles	15.00	40.00
AAS	Asuka	12.00	30.00
ABA	Bayley	12.00	30.00
ABE	Big E	5.00	12.00
ABL	Becky Lynch	15.00	40.00
ABS	Braun Strowman	12.00	30.00
ACF	Charlotte Flair	15.00	40.00
AFB	Finn Balor	12.00	30.00
AJH	Jeff Hardy	12.00	30.00
AKA	Kurt Angle	10.00	25.00
AKK	Kofi Kingston	6.00	15.00
AKO	Kevin Owens	6.00	15.00
ALM	Liv Morgan	10.00	25.00
AMH	Matt Hardy	10.00	25.00
AMR	Mandy Rose	15.00	40.00
ASB	Sasha Banks	12.00	30.00
ASN	Shinsuke Nakamura	10.00	25.00
AXW	Xavier Woods	5.00	12.00
AALB	Aleister Black	6.00	15.00

2018 Topps Heritage WWE Autographs Silver

ACA	Carmella	12.00	30.00
ASM	Stephanie McMahon	75.00	150.00
ATH	Triple H	150.00	300.00
AUN	Undertaker	125.00	250.00

2018 Topps Heritage WWE Big Legends

COMPLETE SET (50) 12.00 30.00
*BRONZE/99: .75X TO 2X BASIC CARDS
*BLUE/50: 1.2X TO 3X BASIC CARDS
*SILVER/25: 1.5X TO 4X BASIC CARDS
*GOLD/10: UNPRICED DUE TO SCARCITY
*RED/1: UNPRICED DUE TO SCARCITY
*P.P.BLACK/1: UNPRICED DUE TO SCARCITY
*P.P.CYAN/1: UNPRICED DUE TO SCARCITY
*P.P.MAGENTA/1: UNPRICED DUE TO SCARCITY
*P.P.YELLOW/1: UNPRICED DUE TO SCARCITY
STATED ODDS 2:1; 4:1 FAT PACK

BL1	Alundra Blayze	.30	.75
BL2	Andre the Giant	.60	1.50
BL3	Bam Bam Bigelow	.50	1.25
BL4	Bob Backlund	.30	.75
BL5	Booker T	.50	1.25
BL6	Bret Hit Man Hart	.75	2.00
BL7	British Bulldog	.60	1.50
BL8	Bruno Sammartino	.50	1.25
BL9	Brutus The Barber Beefcake	.30	.75
BL10	Cowboy Bob Orton	.30	.75
BL11	Dean Malenko	.30	.75
BL12	Diamond Dallas Page	.50	1.25
BL13	Dusty Rhodes	.60	1.50
BL14	Eddie Guerrero	.75	2.00
BL15	Edge	.75	2.00
BL16	George The Animal Steele	.40	1.00
BL17	Greg The Hammer Valentine	.30	.75
BL18	Hacksaw Jim Duggan	.30	.75
BL19	Harley Race	.30	.75
BL20	The Honky Tonk Man	.30	.75
BL21	Iron Sheik	.30	.75
BL22	Irwin R. Schyster	.30	.75
BL23	Jake The Snake Roberts	.40	1.00
BL24	Jerry The King Lawler	.60	1.50
BL25	Jim The Anvil Neidhart	.50	1.25
BL26	Kerry Von Erich	.30	.75
BL27	Kevin Nash	.60	1.50
BL28	Kevin Von Erich	.50	1.25
BL29	Larry Zbyszko	.30	.75
BL30	Lex Luger	.40	1.00
BL31	Lita	.75	2.00
BL32	Macho Man Randy Savage	1.00	2.50
BL33	Michael P.S. Hayes	.30	.75
BL34	Mick Foley	.60	1.50
BL35	Million Dollar Man Ted DiBiase	.40	1.00
BL36	Mr. Perfect	.40	1.00
BL37	Mr. Wonderful Paul Orndorff	.30	.75
BL38	Nikolai Volkoff	.30	.75
BL39	Ravishing Rick Rude	.40	1.00
BL40	Ric Flair	1.00	2.50
BL41	Ricky The Dragon Steamboat	.50	1.25
BL42	Ron Simmons	.40	1.00
BL43	Rowdy Roddy Piper	.75	2.00
BL44	Scott Hall	.60	1.50
BL45	Sgt. Slaughter	.40	1.00
BL46	Sid Vicious	.30	.75
BL47	Sting	.75	2.00
BL48	Stone Cold Steve Austin	1.50	4.00
BL49	Trish Stratus	1.25	3.00
BL50	Ultimate Warrior	1.25	3.00

2018 Topps Heritage WWE Big Legends Autographs

*SILVER/25: UNPRICED DUE TO SCARCITY
*GOLD/10: UNPRICED DUE TO SCARCITY
*RED/1: UNPRICED DUE TO SCARCITY

BLAAB	Alundra Blayze	6.00	15.00
BLABB	Brutus The Barber Beefcake	6.00	15.00
BLABH	Bret Hit Man Hart	25.00	60.00
BLAIS	Irwin R. Schyster	10.00	25.00
BLAJD	Hacksaw Jim Duggan	8.00	20.00
BLAJR	Jake The Snake Roberts	15.00	40.00
BLAST	Sting	25.00	60.00
BLATD	Million Dollar Man Ted DiBiase	12.00	30.00
BLATS	Trish Stratus	30.00	75.00
BLADDP	Diamond Dallas Page	10.00	25.00

2018 Topps Heritage WWE Dual Autographs

STATED PRINT RUN 10 SER.#'d SETS
UNPRICED DUE TO SCARCITY

DACC Epico/Primo/9
DAKR B.Kay/P.Royce/10
DALC M.Cole/J.Lawler/10
DATM S.McMahon/Triple H/10
DAUT Triple H/Undertaker/10

2018 Topps Heritage WWE Kiss

*GOLD/10: UNPRICED DUE TO SCARCITY
*RED/1: UNPRICED DUE TO SCARCITY
STATED ODDS

KCAB	Alexa Bliss	60.00	120.00
KCAF	Alicia Fox	15.00	40.00
KCAS	Asuka	30.00	75.00
KCCC	Charly Caruso	50.00	100.00
KCDB	Dana Brooke	20.00	50.00
KCDF	Dasha Fuentes	15.00	40.00
KCMR	Mandy Rose	50.00	100.00
KCNA	Natalya	15.00	40.00
KCNA	Naomi	15.00	40.00
KCRY	Renee Young	20.00	50.00

2018 Topps Heritage WWE Kiss Autographs

*GOLD/10: UNPRICED DUE TO SCARCITY
*RED/1: UNPRICED DUE TO SCARCITY
STATED PRINT RUN 25 SER.#'d SETS

KAAB	Alexa Bliss	150.00	300.00
KAAF	Alicia Fox	50.00	100.00
KAAS	Asuka	60.00	120.00
KACC	Charly Caruso	30.00	75.00
KADB	Dana Brooke	50.00	100.00
KADF	Dasha Fuentes	30.00	75.00
KAMR	Mandy Rose	75.00	150.00
KANA	Natalya	25.00	60.00
KARY	Renee Young	30.00	75.00

2018 Topps Heritage WWE Manufactured Coins

1	John Cena	8.00	20.00
2	Brock Lesnar	6.00	15.00
3	AJ Styles	5.00	12.00
4	Roman Reigns	5.00	12.00
5	Seth Rollins	5.00	12.00
6	Dean Ambrose	4.00	10.00
7	Braun Strowman	4.00	10.00
8	Samoa Joe	4.00	10.00

9 Shinsuke Nakamura	5.00	12.00
10 Kevin Owens	4.00	10.00

2018 Topps Heritage WWE NXT TakeOver War Games 2017 Mat Relics

*BRONZE/99: .5X TO 1.2X BASIC MEM
*BLUE/50: .6X TO 1.5X BASIC MEM
*SILVER/25: .75X TO 2X BASIC MEM
*GOLD/10: UNPRICED DUE TO SCARCITY
*RED/1: UNPRICED DUE TO SCARCITY
STATED PRINT RUN 299 SER.#'d SETS

NXTAA Andrade Cien Almas	2.50	6.00
NXTAC Adam Cole	8.00	20.00
NXTAW Alexander Wolfe	2.50	6.00
NXTBF Bobby Fish	4.00	10.00
NXTDM Drew McIntyre	2.50	6.00
NXTEM Ember Moon	3.00	8.00
NXTEY Eric Young	3.00	8.00
NXTKD Killian Dain	3.00	8.00
NXTKO Kyle O'Reilly	3.00	8.00
NXTRS Roderick Strong	2.50	6.00

2018 Topps Heritage WWE Shirt Relics

*BLUE/50: .5X TO 1.2X BASIC MEM
*SILVER/25: .6X TO 1.5X BASIC MEM
*GOLD/10: UNPRICED DUE TO SCARCITY
*RED/1: UNPRICED DUE TO SCARCITY
STATED PRINT RUN 99 SER.#'d SETS

SRAB Alexa Bliss	12.00	30.00
SRAE Aiden English	4.00	10.00
SRAF Alicia Fox	3.00	8.00
SRAK Akam	3.00	8.00
SRAW Alexander Wolfe	3.00	8.00
SRBE Becky Lynch	5.00	12.00
SRBL Brock Lesnar	6.00	15.00
SRCA Carmella	5.00	12.00
SRDW Dash Wilder	3.00	8.00
SREM Ember Moon	5.00	12.00
SREY Eric Young	3.00	8.00
SRGD Goldust	3.00	8.00
SRJC John Cena	6.00	15.00
SRJJ JoJo	5.00	12.00
SRNC Nikki Cross	5.00	12.00
SRRE Rezar	3.00	8.00
SRRR Roman Reigns	8.00	20.00
SRRY Renee Young	5.00	12.00
SRSD Scott Dawson	3.00	8.00
SRSR Seth Rollins	5.00	12.00

2018 Topps Heritage WWE Survivor Series 2017 Mat Relics

*BRONZE/99: .5X TO 1.2X BASIC MEM
*BLUE/50: .6X TO 1.5X BASIC MEM
*SILVER/25: .75X TO 2X BASIC MEM
*GOLD/10: UNPRICED DUE TO SCARCITY
*RED/1: UNPRICED DUE TO SCARCITY
STATED PRINT RUN 299 SER.#'d SETS

SSAB Alexa Bliss	10.00	25.00
SSAJ AJ Styles	3.00	8.00
SSAS Asuka	5.00	12.00
SSBA Bayley	3.00	8.00
SSBL Brock Lesnar	4.00	10.00
SSBR Bobby Roode	3.00	8.00
SSBS Braun Strowman	4.00	10.00
SSCF Charlotte Flair	5.00	12.00
SSDA Dean Ambrose	2.50	6.00
SSFB Finn Balor	3.00	8.00
SSJC John Cena	4.00	10.00
SSKA Kurt Angle	2.50	6.00
SSNJ Nia Jax	2.50	6.00
SSRO Randy Orton	2.50	6.00
SSRR Roman Reigns	3.00	8.00
SSSB Sasha Banks	6.00	15.00
SSSJ Samoa Joe	4.00	10.00
SSSN Shinsuke Nakamura	3.00	8.00
SSSR Seth Rollins	3.00	8.00
SSTH Triple H	4.00	10.00

2018 Topps Heritage WWE Tag Teams and Stables

COMPLETE SET (20)	6.00	15.00

*BRONZE/99: .5X TO 1.2X BASIC CARDS
*BLUE/50: .6X TO 1.5X BASIC CARDS
*SILVER/25: 1.2X TO 3X BASIC CARDS
*GOLD/10: UNPRICED DUE TO SCARCITY
*RED/1: UNPRICED DUE TO SCARCITY
STATED ODDS 1:2; 2:1 FAT PACK

TT1 Cesaro & Sheamus	.75	2.00
TT2 The Shield	1.00	2.50
TT3 The Hardy Boyz	1.00	2.50
TT4 Heath Slater & Rhyno	.40	1.00
TT5 Luke Gallows & Karl Anderson	.50	1.25
TT6 The Miz & The Miztourage	.75	2.00
TT7 The Revival	.50	1.25
TT8 Bludgeon Brothers	.60	1.50
TT9 Breezango	.40	1.00
TT10 Shelton Benjamin & Chad Gable	.50	1.25
TT11 Kevin Owens & Sami Zayn	1.00	2.50
TT12 The Hype Bros	.40	1.00
TT13 Jinder Mahal & The Singh Brothers	.50	1.25
TT14 The New Day	.60	1.50
TT15 The Authors of Pain	.40	1.00
TT16 Heavy Machinery	.40	1.00
TT17 The Iiconics	1.00	2.50
TT18 SAnitY	.60	1.50
TT19 The Street Profits	.40	1.00
TT20 Undisputed ERA	.50	1.25

2018 Topps Heritage WWE TLC 2017 Mat Relics

*BRONZE/99: .5X TO 1.2X BASIC MEM
*BLUE/50: .6X TO 1.5X BASIC MEM
*SILVER/25: .75X TO 2X BASIC MEM
*GOLD/10: UNPRICED DUE TO SCARCITY
*RED/1: UNPRICED DUE TO SCARCITY
STATED PRINT RUN 299 SER.#'d SETS

TLCAJ AJ Styles	4.00	10.00
TLCBS Braun Strowman	2.00	5.00
TLCCE Cesaro	2.00	5.00
TLCDA Dean Ambrose	3.00	8.00
TLCFB Finn Balor	4.00	10.00
TLCKA Kurt Angle	4.00	10.00
TLCKN Kane	3.00	8.00
TLCSH Sheamus	2.00	5.00
TLCSR Seth Rollins	5.00	12.00
TLCTM The Miz	2.00	5.00

2018 Topps Heritage WWE TLC Commemorative Medallion Relics

*BRONZE/99: .5X TO 1.2X BASIC MEM
*BLUE/50: .6X TO 1.5X BASIC MEM
*SILVER/25: .75X TO 2X BASIC MEM
*GOLD/10: UNPRICED DUE TO SCARCITY
*RED/1: UNPRICED DUE TO SCARCITY
STATED PRINT RUN 199 SER.#'d SETS

CTMAB Alexa Bliss	10.00	25.00
CTMAJ AJ Styles	5.00	12.00
CTMBC Baron Corbin	4.00	10.00
CTMBL Becky Lynch	6.00	15.00
CTMBS Braun Strowman	5.00	12.00
CTMCE Cesaro	3.00	8.00
CTMDA Dean Ambrose	3.00	8.00
CTMDE Dean Ambrose	3.00	8.00
CTMDZ Dolph Ziggler	3.00	8.00
CTMJC John Cena	5.00	12.00
CTMKA Kurt Angle	3.00	8.00
CTMKA Kane	3.00	8.00
CTMKL Kalisto	3.00	8.00
CTMMZ The Miz	3.00	8.00
CTMRL Seth Rollins	4.00	10.00
CTMRR Roman Reigns	5.00	12.00
CTMSA Sheamus	3.00	8.00
CTMSH Sheamus	3.00	8.00
CTMSR Seth Rollins	3.00	8.00
CTMTM The Miz	3.00	8.00

2018 Topps Heritage WWE Top 10 Rookies

COMPLETE SET (10)	4.00	10.00

*BRONZE/99: .5X TO 1.2X BASIC CARDS
*BLUE/50: .6X TO 1.5X BASIC CARDS
*SILVER/25: .75X TO 2X BASIC CARDS
*GOLD/10: UNPRICED DUE TO SCARCITY
*RED/1: UNPRICED DUE TO SCARCITY
*P.P.BLACK/1: UNPRICED DUE TO SCARCITY
*P.P.CYAN/1: UNPRICED DUE TO SCARCITY
*P.P.MAGENTA/1: UNPRICED DUE TO SCARCITY
*P.P.YELLOW/1: UNPRICED DUE TO SCARCITY
STATED ODDS 1:3; 1:1 FAT PACK

TR1 Asuka	1.25	3.00
TR2 Shinsuke Nakamura	1.00	2.50
TR3 Bobby Roode	.60	1.50
TR4 Samoa Joe	.75	2.00
TR5 Tyler Bate	.40	1.00
TR6 Pete Dunne	.40	1.00
TR7 Dash Wilder	.50	1.25
TR8 Scott Dawson	.50	1.25
TR9 Elias	1.00	2.50
TR10 Tye Dillinger	.40	1.00

2018 Topps Heritage WWE Top 10 Rookies Autographs

*SILVER/25: .5X TO 1.2X BASIC AUTOS
*GOLD/10: UNPRICED DUE TO SCARCITY
*RED/1: UNPRICED DUE TO SCARCITY
STATED PRINT RUN 50 SER.#'d SETS

TTRAAS Asuka	15.00	40.00
TTRABR Bobby Roode	10.00	25.00
TTRADW Dash Wilder	5.00	12.00
TTRAEL Elias	25.00	60.00
TTRASD Scott Dawson	5.00	12.00
TTRASJ Samoa Joe	10.00	25.00
TTRASN Shinsuke Nakamura	12.00	30.00
TTRATD Tye Dillinger	6.00	15.00

2018 Topps Heritage WWE Triple Mat Relics

*SILVER/25: .5X TO 1.2X BASIC MEM
*GOLD/10: UNPRICED DUE TO SCARCITY
*RED/1: UNPRICED DUE TO SCARCITY
STATED PRINT RUN 50 SER.#'d SETS

TMBL Brock Lesnar	8.00	20.00
TMCF Charlotte Flair	12.00	30.00
TMDA Dean Ambrose	10.00	25.00
TMJC John Cena	10.00	25.00
TMKO Kevin Owens	8.00	20.00
TMTH Triple H	8.00	20.00
TMTM The Miz	8.00	20.00
TMUD Undertaker	15.00	40.00

2021 Topps Heritage WWE

COMPLETE SET (100)	10.00	25.00

*FOIL: .6X TO 1.5X BASIC CARDS
*GREEN/99: .75X TO 2X BASIC CARDS
*BLUE/25: 1.5X TO 4X BASIC CARDS
*RED/10: UNPRICED DUE TO SCARCITY
*FOILFRACTOR/1: UNPRICED DUE TO SCARCITY

1 AJ Styles	1.00	2.50
2 Akira Tozawa	.40	1.00
3 Alexa Bliss	2.00	5.00
4 Angel Garza	.40	1.00
5 Asuka	1.25	3.00
6 Bobby Lashley	.75	2.00
7 Cedric Alexander	.30	.75
8 Charlotte Flair	1.50	4.00
8 Charlotte Flair SP (peacock)	30.00	75.00
9 Damian Priest	.50	1.25
10 Dana Brooke	.30	.75
11 Drew McIntyre	.75	2.00
12 Doudrop	.50	1.25
13 Elias	.30	.75
14 Erik	.30	.75
15 Eva Marie	.75	2.00
16 Gran Metalik	.30	.75
17 Humberto Carrillo	.30	.75
18 Ivar	.30	.75
19 Jeff Hardy	.75	2.00
20 John Morrison	.60	1.50
21 Keith Lee	.60	1.50
22 Kofi Kingston	.75	2.00
23 Lacey Evans	.75	2.00
24 Lince Dorado	.30	.75
25 MACE	.30	.75
26 Mandy Rose	1.50	4.00
26 Mandy Rose SP (roses)	30.00	75.00
27 Mustafa Ali	.40	1.00
28 MVP	.30	.75
29 Naomi	.40	1.00
30 Nia Jax	.60	1.50
31 Nikki ASH	.60	1.50
32 Omos RC	.60	1.50
33 Randy Orton	1.00	2.50
33 Randy Orton SP (viper)	15.00	40.00
34 Rhea Ripley	1.00	2.50
35 Ricochet	.60	1.50
36 Riddick Moss	.40	1.00
37 Riddle	.75	2.00
38 R-Truth	.40	1.00
39 Shayna Baszler	.60	1.50
40 Sheamus	.50	1.25
40 Sheamus SP (great white shark)	12.00	30.00
41 Shelton Benjamin	.50	1.25

42 T-BAR	.40	1.00
43 The Fiend Bray Wyatt	1.25	3.00
44 The Miz	.50	1.25
45 Titus O'Neil	.30	.75
46 Xavier Woods	.30	.75
47 Angelo Dawkins	.40	1.00
48 Apollo Crews	.40	1.00
49 Baron Corbin	.30	.75
49 Baron Corbin SP (wolf)	8.00	20.00
50 Bayley	.75	2.00
51 Bianca Belair	.75	2.00
52 Big E	.60	1.50
53 Carmella	.75	2.00
54 Cesaro	.30	.75
55 Chad Gable	.30	.75
56 Commander Azeez RC	.40	1.00
57 Dolph Ziggler	.60	1.50
58 Dominik Mysterio RC	.40	1.00
59 Edge	1.25	3.00
60 Jey Uso	.30	.75
61 Jimmy Uso	.30	.75
62 Kevin Owens	.60	1.50
63 Liv Morgan	1.25	3.00
64 Mia Yim	.40	1.00
65 Montez Ford	.30	.75
66 Natalya	.50	1.25
67 Otis	.40	1.00
67 Otis SP (worm)	15.00	40.00
68 Rey Mysterio	.75	2.00
69 Robert Roode	.40	1.00
70 Roman Reigns	1.50	4.00
70 Roman Reigns SP (dog)	30.00	75.00
71 Sami Zayn	.50	1.25
72 Sasha Banks	1.50	4.00
72 Sasha Banks SP (stacks of cash)	25.00	60.00
73 Seth Rollins	.75	2.00
74 Shinsuke Nakamura	.75	2.00
74 Shinsuke Nakamura SP (king's crown)	10.00	25.00
75 Tamina	.40	1.00
76 Zelina Vega	.60	1.50
77 Adam Cole	1.00	2.50
78 Boa	.30	.75
79 Cameron Grimes	.60	1.50
80 Candice LeRae	1.25	3.00
81 Dakota Kai	.60	1.50
82 Ember Moon	.40	1.00
83 Finn Balor	.75	2.00
84 Io Shirai	.60	1.50
85 Indi Hartwell RC	1.00	2.50
86 Johnny Gargano	.60	1.50
87 Karrion Kross	1.25	3.00
88 Kushida	.50	1.25
89 Kyle O'Reilly	.50	1.25
90 Santos Escobar	.50	1.25
91 Samoa Joe	.60	1.50
92 Scarlett	1.50	4.00
93 Shotzi	1.25	3.00
94 Timothy Thatcher RC	.30	.75
95 Tommaso Ciampa	.75	2.00
96 Toni Storm	1.00	2.50
97 Xia Li	.60	1.50
98 Becky Lynch	1.25	3.00
99 John Cena	1.50	4.00
100 Triple H	1.25	3.00

2021 Topps Heritage WWE Allen and Ginter

COMPLETE SET (30) 12.00 30.00
RANDOMLY INSERTED INTO PACKS

AG1 AJ Styles	1.00	2.50
AG2 Alexa Bliss	2.00	5.00
AG3 Asuka	1.25	3.00
AG4 Bayley	.75	2.00
AG5 Becky Lynch	1.25	3.00
AG6 Big E	.60	1.50
AG7 Charlotte Flair	1.50	4.00
AG8 Diesel	.50	1.25
AG9 Drew McIntyre	.75	2.00
AG10 Eddie Guerrero	1.50	4.00
AG11 Kane	.50	1.25
AG12 Kevin Owens	.60	1.50
AG13 Mr. Perfect	1.00	2.50
AG14 Macho Man Randy Savage	2.00	5.00
AG15 Million Dollar Man Ted DiBiase	.60	1.50
AG16 Razor Ramon	.50	1.25
AG17 Rikishi	.40	1.00
AG18 Roman Reigns	1.50	4.00
AG19 Sasha Banks	1.50	4.00
AG20 Seth Rollins	.75	2.00
AG21 Shinsuke Nakamura	.75	2.00
AG22 Typhoon	.30	.75
AG23 Sycho Sid	.50	1.25
AG24 The 1-2-3 Kid	.40	1.00
AG25 The Fiend Bray Wyatt	1.25	3.00
AG26 The Miz	.50	1.25
AG27 The Rock	3.00	8.00
AG28 Ultimate Warrior	1.25	3.00
AG29 Vader	.50	1.25
AG30 The Godfather	.40	1.00

2021 Topps Heritage WWE Autographs

*GREEN/99: .5X TO 1.2X BASIC AUTOS
*PURPLE/50: .6X TO 1.5X BASIC AUTOS
*BLUE/25: 1.2X TO 3X BASIC AUTOS
*RED/10: UNPRICED DUE TO SCARCITY
*GOLD/1: UNPRICED DUE TO SCARCITY
STATED ODDS 1:264
STATED PRINT RUN 199 SER.#'d SETS

AS Sasha Banks	60.00	120.00
AAB Alexa Bliss	75.00	150.00
AAC Apollo Crews	6.00	15.00
AAJ AJ Styles	10.00	25.00
AAS Asuka	15.00	40.00
ABE Big E	6.00	15.00
ABL Bobby Lashley	8.00	20.00
ACI Tommaso Ciampa	6.00	15.00
ACM Carmella	8.00	20.00
ACS Cesaro	6.00	15.00
ADM Drew McIntyre	8.00	20.00
ADZ Dolph Ziggler	6.00	15.00
AEM Ember Moon	5.00	12.00
AFB Finn Balor	10.00	25.00
AIS Io Shirai	10.00	25.00
AJC John Cena		
AJM John Morrison	8.00	20.00
AKA Karrion Kross	10.00	25.00
AKO Kevin Owens	6.00	15.00
AKU Kushida	5.00	12.00
ALD Lince Dorado	6.00	15.00
ALM Liv Morgan	25.00	60.00
AMA Mustafa Ali	5.00	12.00
ANJ Nia Jax	5.00	12.00
ARH Rhea Ripley	15.00	40.00
ART R-Truth	5.00	12.00
ASB Shayna Baszler	5.00	12.00
ASE Santos Escobar	6.00	15.00
ASH Shotzi Blackheart	25.00	60.00
ASL Scarlett	20.00	50.00
ASN Shinsuke Nakamura	8.00	20.00
ASR Seth Rollins	10.00	25.00
ASZ Sami Zayn	8.00	20.00
ATT Timothy Thatcher	6.00	15.00
ABRO Riddle	12.00	30.00
AJEY Jey Uso	5.00	12.00
AKOR Kyle O'Reilly	8.00	20.00
AMVP MVP	5.00	12.00
AREY Rey Mysterio	15.00	40.00

2021 Topps Heritage WWE Dual Autographs

*BLUE/25: .5X TO 1.2X BASIC AUTOS
*RED/10: UNPRICED DUE TO SCARCITY
*GOLD/1: UNPRICED DUE TO SCARCITY
STATED ODDS 1:3,796
STATED PRINT RUN 50 SER.#'d SETS

DAJB S.Baszler/N.Jax	25.00	60.00
DAND K.Kingston/X.Woods	20.00	50.00
DART Mace/T-Bar	15.00	40.00
DASP M.Ford/A.Dawkins	20.00	50.00
DAVR Ivar/Erik	12.00	30.00
DAGYV J.Drake/Z.Gibson	12.00	30.00
DALHP G.Metalik/L.Dorado	20.00	50.00

2021 Topps Heritage WWE The Miz Superstar Tribute

COMPLETE SET (20) 6.00 15.00
STATED ODDS 1:3

TM1 The Miz	.60	1.50
TM2 The Miz	.60	1.50
TM3 The Miz	.60	1.50
TM4 The Miz	.60	1.50
TM5 The Miz	.60	1.50
TM6 The Miz	.60	1.50
TM7 The Miz	.60	1.50
TM8 The Miz	.60	1.50
TM9 The Miz	.60	1.50
TM10 The Miz	.60	1.50
TM11 The Miz	.60	1.50
TM12 The Miz	.60	1.50
TM13 The Miz	.60	1.50
TM14 The Miz	.60	1.50
TM15 The Miz	.60	1.50
TM16 The Miz	.60	1.50
TM17 The Miz	.60	1.50
TM18 The Miz	.60	1.50
TM19 The Miz	.60	1.50
TM20 The Miz	.60	1.50

2021 Topps Heritage WWE The Miz Superstar Tribute Autographs

*RED/10: UNPRICED DUE TO SCARCITY
STATED ODDS 1:4,181
STATED PRINT RUN 25 SER.#'d SETS

AMZ6 The Miz
AMZ9 The Miz
AMZ11 The Miz
AMZ15 The Miz
AMZ19 The Miz

2021 Topps Heritage WWE Sketch Card Reproduction

COMPLETE SET (10)
STATED ODDS 1:24

SCR1 Eddie Guerrero
SCR2 Edge
SCR3 John Cena
SCR4 Randy Orton
SCR5 Triple H
SCR6 Undertaker
SCR7 Jeff Hardy
SCR8 Kane
SCR9 MVP
SCR10 Rey Mysterio

2021 Topps Heritage WWE Superstar Stickers

COMPLETE SET (18) 12.00 30.00
STATED ODDS 1:4

S1 AJ Styles	1.00	2.50
S2 Alexa Bliss	2.00	5.00
S3 Bayley	.75	2.00
S4 Becky Lynch	1.25	3.00
S5 Charlotte Flair	1.50	4.00
S6 D-Generation X	1.25	3.00
S7 Finn Balor	.75	2.00
S8 Jeff Hardy	.75	2.00
S9 John Cena	1.50	4.00
S10 Randy Orton	1.00	2.50
S11 Asuka	1.25	3.00
S12 Rey Mysterio	.75	2.00
S13 Roman Reigns	1.50	4.00
S14 Sasha Banks	1.50	4.00
S15 Seth Rollins	.75	2.00
S16 Shinsuke Nakamura	.75	2.00
S17 The Miz	.50	1.25
S18 The New Day	.75	2.00
S19 Naomi	.40	1.00
S20 Undertaker	1.50	4.00

2021 Topps Heritage WWE Superstars Speak

COMPLETE SET (10) 8.00 20.00
STATED ODDS 1:12

SS1 Batista	.75	2.00
SS2 Booker T	.75	2.00
SS3 Goldberg	1.50	4.00
SS4 John Cena	2.00	5.00
SS5 Macho Man Randy Savage	2.50	6.00
SS6 Ric Flair	1.50	4.00
SS7 The Fiend Bray Wyatt	1.50	4.00
SS8 The Miz	.60	1.50
SS9 Undertaker	2.00	5.00
SS10 Ron Simmons	.60	1.50

2020 Topps Immortal Championship Wrestling Series 1

NNO Axel Lennox
NNO Bin Hamin
NNO Brut VanSlyke
NNO Christina Marie
NNO Greek God Papadon
NNO Justin Credible

NNO Mattick
NNO Mike Skyros
NNO Pat Sawyer
NNO Referee Sideburns
NNO Richard Holliday
NNO Rick Recon
NNO Sean Carr
NNO Sean Carr
NNO Slyck Wagner Brown

2011 Topps Jim Ross JR's BarBQ Sauce Autograph Exclusive

NNO Jim Ross

2017 Topps Legends of WWE

COMPLETE SET (100)	8.00	20.00
UNOPENED BOX (12 PACKS)		
UNOPENED PACK (5 CARDS)		

*BRONZE: .6X TO 1.5X BASIC CARDS
*SILVER/99: .75X TO 2X BASIC CARDS
*BLUE/50: 1.2X TO 3X BASIC CARDS
*GOLD/10: UNPRICED DUE TO SCARCITY
*RED/1: UNPRICED DUE TO SCARCITY

1 Brock Lesnar	1.25	3.00
2 Goldberg	1.00	2.50
3 The Rock	1.25	3.00
4 Hunter Hearst Helmsley	.60	1.50
5 Undertaker	1.00	2.50
6 Afa	.25	.60
7 Alundra Blayze	.30	.75
8 Andre the Giant	.50	1.25
9 Bam Bam Bigelow	.40	1.00
10 The Berzerker	.25	.60
11 Big Boss Man	.30	.75
12 Big John Studd	.30	.75
13 Bob Backlund	.25	.60
14 Bobby The Brain Heenan	.40	1.00
15 The Boogeyman	.25	.60
16 Booker T	.30	.75
17 Bret Hit Man Hart	.50	1.25
18 Brian Knobbs	.25	.60
19 British Bulldog	.25	.60
20 Bruno Sammartino	.40	1.00
21 Brutus The Barber Beefcake	.25	.60
22 Cowboy Bob Orton	.40	1.00
23 D'Lo Brown	.25	.60
24 Daniel Bryan	1.00	2.50
25 Dean Malenko	.30	.75
26 Diamond Dallas Page	.30	.75
27 Don Muraco	.25	.60
28 Dory Funk Jr.	.25	.60
29 Dusty Rhodes	.30	.75
30 Earthquake	.25	.60
31 Eddie Guerrero	.50	1.25
32 Edge	.60	1.50
33 Eve Torres	.40	1.00
34 Fit Finlay	.25	.60
35 General Adnan	.25	.60
36 George The Animal Steele	.40	1.00
37 Gerald Brisco	.25	.60
38 The Goon RC	.25	.60
39 Greg The Hammer Valentine	.30	.75
40 Hacksaw Jim Duggan	.40	1.00
41 Haku	.25	.60
42 Harley Race	.30	.75
43 The Honky Tonk Man	.30	.75
44 Iron Sheik	.30	.75
45 Irwin R. Schyster	.25	.60
46 Jake The Snake Roberts	.30	.75
47 The Godfather	.25	.60
48 Jerry The King Lawler	.30	.75
49 Jerry Sags	.25	.60
50 Jim The Anvil Neidhart	.25	.60
51 Junkyard Dog	.30	.75
52 Mike Rotunda	.25	.60
53 Ken Shamrock	.25	.60
54 Kerry Von Erich	.25	.60
55 Kevin Nash	.40	1.00
56 Kevin Von Erich	.40	1.00
57 Larry Zbyszko	.30	.75
58 Lex Luger	.30	.75
59 Macho Man Randy Savage	.50	1.25
60 Magnum T.A.	.25	.60
61 Michael P.S. Hayes	.30	.75
62 Mick Foley	.60	1.50
63 Million Dollar Man Ted DiBiase	.30	.75
64 Miss Elizabeth	.40	1.00
65 Mr. Perfect	.50	1.25
66 Mr. Wonderful Paul Orndorff	.30	.75
67 Nikolai Volkoff	.30	.75
68 Norman Smiley	.30	.75
69 Papa Shango	.25	.60
70 Pat Patterson	.25	.60
71 Ravishing Rick Rude	.40	1.00
72 Ric Flair	.60	1.50
73 Ricky The Dragon Steamboat	.50	1.25
74 Road Dogg	.40	1.00
75 Rob Van Dam	.50	1.25
76 Rocky Johnson	.25	.60
77 Ron Simmons	.30	.75
78 Rowdy Roddy Piper	.50	1.25
79 Scott Hall	.30	.75
80 Sgt. Slaughter	.30	.75
81 Sensational Sherri	.30	.75
82 Sid Vicious	.30	.75
83 Sika RC	.25	.60
84 Stevie Ray	.25	.60
85 Sting	.75	2.00
86 Stone Cold Steve Austin	1.00	2.50
87 Tatanka	.25	.60
88 Tatsumi Fujinami	.25	.60
89 Terri Runnels	.25	.60
90 Terry Taylor	.25	.60
91 Trish Stratus	1.00	2.50
92 Tully Blanchard	.30	.75
93 Typhoon	.25	.60
94 Ultimate Warrior	.50	1.25
95 Umaga	.25	.60
96 Virgil	.25	.60
97 The Warlord	.25	.60
98 Wendi Richter	.30	.75
99 X-Pac	.25	.60
100 Yokozuna	.40	1.00

2017 Topps Legends of WWE Autographed Retired Championship Belt Relics

*GOLD/10: UNPRICED DUE TO SCARCITY
*BLACK/5: UNPRICED DUE TO SCARCITY
*RED/1: UNPRICED DUE TO SCARCITY
RANDOMLY INSERTED INTO PACKS

ARCAB Alundra Blayze	8.00	20.00
ARCBH Bret Hit Man Hart	15.00	40.00
ARCBP Beth Phoenix	8.00	20.00
ARCBR Bret Hit Man Hart	15.00	40.00
ARCBS Big Show	10.00	25.00
ARCBT Booker T	15.00	40.00
ARCCF Charlotte Flair	15.00	40.00
ARCCH Chris Jericho	20.00	50.00
ARCCJ Chris Jericho	20.00	50.00
ARCDM Dean Malenko	6.00	15.00
ARCET Eve Torres	12.00	30.00
ARCGO Goldberg	30.00	75.00
ARCIV Ivory	8.00	20.00
ARCJA Jim The Anvil Neidhart	6.00	15.00
ARCJB JBL	8.00	20.00
ARCMA Maryse	12.00	30.00
ARCMD Alundra Blayze	6.00	15.00
ARCRD Road Dogg	6.00	15.00
ARCRF Ric Flair	60.00	120.00
ARCST Sting	30.00	75.00
ARCTD Ted DiBiase	10.00	25.00
ARCTS Trish Stratus	25.00	60.00
ARCWR Wendi Richter	10.00	25.00

2017 Topps Legends of WWE Autographed Shirt Relics

*SILVER/50: X TO X BASIC AUTOS
*BLUE/25: X TO X BASIC AUTOS
*GOLD/10: UNPRICED DUE TO SCARCITY
*BLACK/5: UNPRICED DUE TO SCARCITY
*RED/1: UNPRICED DUE TO SCARCITY
STATED ODDS

ARBH Bret Hit Man Hart
ARBS Big Show
ARDP Diamond Dallas Page
ARED Edge
ARIR The Iron Sheik
ARKN Kevin Nash
ARLL Lex Luger
ARMA Mankind
ARMF Mick Foley
ARRD Road Dogg
ARRS Ricky The Dragon Steamboat
ARSM Shawn Michaels
ARST Sting
ARTB Tully Blanchard
ARTD Million Dollar Man Ted DiBiase

2017 Topps Legends of WWE Autographs

*BRONZE/99: .5X TO 1.2X BASIC AUTOS
*SILVER/50: .6X TO 1.5X BASIC AUTOS
*BLUE/25: .75X TO 2X BASIC AUTOS
*GOLD/10: UNPRICED DUE TO SCARCITY
*BLACK/5: UNPRICED DUE TO SCARCITY
*RED/1: UNPRICED DUE TO SCARCITY
STATED PRINT RUN 199 SER.#'d SETS

LAAB Alundra Blayze	8.00	20.00
LAAL Albert	6.00	15.00
LABF Brutus The Barber Beefcake	12.00	30.00
LABM Bret Hit Man Hart	30.00	75.00
LABT Booker T	6.00	15.00
LADP Diamond Dallas Page	12.00	30.00
LAED Edge	12.00	30.00
LAET Eve Torres	10.00	25.00
LAFF Fit Finlay	6.00	15.00
LAGD Goldust	8.00	20.00
LAGV Greg The Hammer Valentine	6.00	15.00
LAHA Hacksaw Jim Duggan	12.00	30.00
LAIR Irwin R. Schyster	5.00	12.00
LAJA Jim The Anvil Neidhart	20.00	50.00
LAKE Kane	10.00	25.00
LAKN Kevin Nash	12.00	30.00
LAKS Ken Shamrock	10.00	25.00
LALL Lex Luger	12.00	30.00
LAMF Mick Foley	20.00	50.00
LAMP Michael P.S. Hayes	6.00	15.00
LANS Norman Smiley	5.00	12.00
LAPE Paul Ellering	10.00	25.00
LARS Ricky The Dragon Steamboat	15.00	40.00
LASM Shawn Michaels	15.00	40.00
LASS Sgt. Slaughter	10.00	25.00
LAST Sting	25.00	60.00
LASV Sid Vicious	6.00	15.00
LATA Tatanka	10.00	25.00
LATD Million Dollar Man Ted DiBiase	15.00	40.00
LATH The Boogeyman	6.00	15.00
LAWE Wendi Richter	6.00	15.00
LAWR William Regal	6.00	15.00

2017 Topps Legends of WWE Autographs Bronze

*BRONZE: .5X TO 1.2X BASIC AUTOS

LAGO Goldberg	20.00	50.00

2017 Topps Legends of WWE Autographs Silver

STATED PRINT RUN 50 SER.#'d SETS

LAUN Undertaker	150.00	300.00

2017 Topps Legends of WWE Dual Autographs

STATED PRINT RUN 10 SER.#'d SETS
RANDOMLY INSERTED INTO PACKS

DADS T.DiBiase/IRS	50.00	100.00
DAFB R.Flair/T.Blanchard	50.00	100.00
DAHN J.Neidhart/B.Hart	75.00	150.00
DARB A.Blayze/W.Richter	30.00	60.00
DASV I.Sheik/N.Volkoff	30.00	75.00
DASZ L.Zbyszko/B.Sammartino	30.00	75.00
DATM HHH/S.McMahon	500.00	1000.00
DAUK Kane/Undertaker	300.00	500.00
DAUS Sting/Undertaker	300.00	600.00
DASTL L.Luger Sting	100.00	200.00

2017 Topps Legends of WWE Legendary Bouts

COMPLETE SET (20)	6.00	15.00
RANDOMLY INSERTED INTO PACKS		
1 Undertaker/Shawn Michaels	1.25	3.00
2 Bret Hart/Steve Austin	1.25	3.00
3 Randy Savage/Ricky Steamboat	.60	1.50
4 Ultimate Warrior/Randy Savage	.60	1.50
5 Bret Hart/The British Bulldog	.30	.75
6 Bret Hart/Shawn Michaels	.75	2.00
7 The Rock/Steve Austin	1.50	4.00
8 Undertaker/Shawn Michaels	1.25	3.00
9 John Cena/Brock Lesnar	1.50	4.00
10 Mr. Perfect/Bret Hart	.60	1.50
11 Razor Ramon/Shawn Michaels	.75	2.00
12 Ric Flair/Mr. Perfect	.60	1.50
13 Randy Orton/Cactus Jack	.75	2.00
14 Ric Flair Wins 1992 Royal Rumble	.75	2.00
15 Undertaker/Triple H	1.25	3.00
16 Ric Flair/Randy Savage	.75	2.00

17 Chris Jericho/Shawn Michaels .75 2.00
18 Triple H/Cactus Jack .75 2.00
19 Sting's Squad./Dangerous Alliance 1.00 2.50
20 Edge/John Cena 1.50 4.00

2017 Topps Legends of WWE Retired Titles

COMPLETE SET (22) 5.00 12.00
RANDOMLY INSERTED INTO PACKS
1 Bret Hit Man Hart .75 2.00
2 Ric Flair 1.00 2.50
3 Terry Funk .40 1.00
4 Triple H 1.00 2.50
5 Money Inc. .50 1.25
6 The Outsiders .60 1.50
7 Terry Taylor & Greg Valentine .50 1.25
8 The Glamour Girls .40 1.00
9 Trish Stratus 1.50 4.00
10 Nikki Bella 1.00 2.50
11 Ted DiBiase .50 1.25
12 Tatsumi Fujinami .40 1.00
13 British Bulldog .40 1.00
14 Ricky Steamboat .75 2.00
15 Rob Van Dam .75 2.00
16 Chris Jericho 1.00 2.50
17 Dean Malenko .50 1.25
18 Tatsumi Fujinami .40 1.00
19 Brian Pillman .40 1.00
20 Bradshaw .50 1.25
21 Norman Smiley .50 1.25
22 Virgil .40 1.00

2017 Topps Legends of WWE Shirt Relics

STATED PRINT RUN 299 SER.#'d SETS
ARBH Bret Hit Man Hart 5.00 12.00
ARBL Brock Lesnar 4.00 10.00
ARBS Big Show 3.00 8.00
ARDP Diamond Dallas Page 3.00 8.00
ARED Edge 3.00 8.00
ARIR The Iron Sheik 2.50 6.00
ARKN Kevin Nash 2.50 6.00
ARLL Lex Luger 2.50 6.00
ARMA Mankind 2.50 6.00
ARMF Mick Foley 3.00 8.00
ARRD Road Dogg 2.50 6.00
ARRS Ricky The Dragon Steamboat 3.00 8.00
ARSM Shawn Michaels 6.00 15.00
ARST Sting 6.00 15.00
ARTB Tully Blanchard 2.50 6.00
ARTD Million Dollar Man Ted DiBiase 3.00 8.00

2017 Topps Legends of WWE Triple Autographs

TAFSG Flair/Sting/Goldberg 150.00 300.00
TAHNH Neidhart/J.Hart/B.Hart 125.00 250.00
TALJM D.Love/Cactus Jack/Mankind 100.00 250.00
TANSL Luger/Nash/Sting 100.00 200.00

2018 Topps Legends of WWE

COMPLETE SET (100) 15.00 40.00
UNOPENED BOX (12 PACKS)
UNOPENED PACK (5 CARDS)
*BRONZE: .6X TO 1.5X BASIC CARDS
*SILVER/50: 1X TO 2.5X BASIC CARDS
*BLUE/25: 1.5X TO 4X BASIC CARDS
*GOLD/10: UNPRICED DUE TO SCARCITY
*BLACK/5: UNPRICED DUE TO SCARCITY
*RED/1: UNPRICED DUE TO SCARCITY
*P.P.BLACK/1: UNPRICED DUE TO SCARCITY
*P.P.CYAN/1: UNPRICED DUE TO SCARCITY
*P.P.MAGENTA/1: UNPRICED DUE TO SCARCITY
*P.P.YELLOW/1: UNPRICED DUE TO SCARCITY
1 Andre the Giant .60 1.50
2 Bam Bam Bigelow .50 1.25
3 Batista .50 1.25
4 Big John Studd .30 .75
5 Bob Backlund .30 .75
6 Bobby The Brain Heenan .50 1.25
7 Booker T .50 1.25
8 Bret Hit Man Hart .75 2.00
9 Chief Jay Strongbow .50 1.25
10 Classy Freddie Blassie .30 .75
11 Cowboy Bob Orton .30 .75
12 D'Lo Brown .30 .75
13 Diamond Dallas Page .50 1.25
14 Don Muraco .30 .75
15 Dusty Rhodes .60 1.50
16 Eddie Guerrero .75 2.00
17 Edge .75 2.00
18 Fit Finlay .30 .75
19 George The Animal Steele .40 1.00
20 Gorilla Monsoon .60 1.50
21 Hacksaw Jim Duggan .30 .75
22 Harley Race .30 .75
23 Honky Tonk Man .30 .75
24 Jake The Snake Roberts .40 1.00
25 Jim Ross .50 1.25
26 Jerry The King Lawler .60 1.50
27 Jim The Anvil Neidhart .50 1.25
28 Junkyard Dog .30 .75
29 Ken Shamrock .40 1.00
30 Kevin Nash .60 1.50
31 Kevin Von Erich .50 1.25
32 Kurt Angle .75 2.00
33 Lex Luger .40 1.00
34 Mark Henry .40 1.00
35 Million Dollar Man Ted DiBiase .40 1.00
36 Mr. Perfect .40 1.00
37 Mr. Wonderful Paul Orndorff .30 .75
38 Papa Shango .30 .75
39 Pat Patterson .30 .75
40 Ravishing Rick Rude .40 1.00
41 Ric Flair 1.00 2.50
42 Ricky The Dragon Steamboat .50 1.25
43 Rowdy Roddy Piper .75 2.00
44 Sgt. Slaughter .40 1.00
45 Shawn Michaels 1.00 2.50
46 Sid Vicious .30 .75
47 Stevie Ray .30 .75
48 Sting .75 2.00
49 Stone Cold Steve Austin 1.50 4.00
50 Tatanka .30 .75
51 Tatsumi Fujinami .30 .75
52 Ultimate Warrior 1.25 3.00
53 Vader .40 1.00
54 William Regal .50 1.25
55 Yokozuna .40 1.00
56 Big Show .30 .75
57 Bobby Lashley .60 1.50
58 The Brian Kendrick .50 1.25
59 Daniel Bryan .75 2.00
60 Dolph Ziggler .40 1.00
61 Jeff Hardy .60 1.50
62 Goldust .60 1.50
63 John Cena 1.25 3.00
64 Kane .50 1.25
65 Woken Matt Hardy .75 2.00
66 Randy Orton .75 2.00
67 The Rock 1.50 4.00
68 Shelton Benjamin .40 1.00
69 Undertaker 1.25 3.00
70 Triple H .75 2.00
IC1 X-Pac/1-2-3 Kid .40 1.00
IC2 Albert/Tensai .30 .75
IC3 Big Bubba Rogers/Big Boss Man .30 .75
IC4 Brutus Beefcake/The Zodiac .30 .75
IC5 The Booty Man/The Disciple .30 .75
IC6 Earthquake/The Shark .30 .75
IC7 Kama Mustafa/Kama .30 .75
IC8 The Godfather/Goodfather .30 .75
IC9 Trillionaire/Million Dollar Man .40 1.00
WD1 Alundra Blayze .30 .75
WD2 Beth Phoenix .60 1.50
WD3 Eve Torres .60 1.50
WD4 Lita .75 2.00
WD5 Miss Elizabeth .75 2.00
WD6 Sherri Martel .60 1.50
WD7 Stephanie McMahon .60 1.50
WD8 Terri Runnels .40 1.00
WD9 Trish Stratus 1.25 3.00
IC10 Colonel Mustafa/Iron Sheik .30 .75
IC11 Michael Wallstreet/IRS .30 .75
IC12 Umaga/Jamal .30 .75
IC13 Road Dogg/Jesse James .30 .75
IC14 Macho Man/Macho King R.Savage 1.00 2.50
IC15 Dok Hendrix/Michael P.S. Hayes .30 .75
IC16 Scott Hall/Razor Ramon .60 1.50
IC17 Faarooq/Ron Simmons .40 1.00
IC18 Terry Taylor/Red Rooster .30 .75
IC19 Tugboat/Typhoon .30 .75
IC20 Virgil/Vincent .30 .75
WD10 Wendi Richter .30 .75

2018 Topps Legends of WWE Autographed Commemorative Hall of Fame Rings

*SILVER/50: .5X TO 1.2X BASIC AUTOS
*BLUE/25: .6X TO 1.5X BASIC AUTOS
*GOLD/10: UNPRICED DUE TO SCARCITY
*BLACK/5: UNPRICED DUE TO SCARCITY
*RED/1: UNPRICED DUE TO SCARCITY
STATED PRINT RUN 99 SER.#'d SETS
HOFAB Alundra Blayze 10.00 25.00
HOFBH Bret Hit Man Hart 15.00 40.00
HOFBP Beth Phoenix 12.00 30.00
HOFBT Booker T 15.00 40.00
HOFDP Diamond Dallas Page 10.00 25.00
HOFEG Edge 10.00 25.00
HOFHR Harley Race 15.00 40.00
HOFJD Hacksaw Jim Duggan 10.00 25.00
HOFJL Jerry The King Lawler 20.00 50.00
HOFJR Jake The Snake Roberts 12.00 30.00
HOFKA Kurt Angle 12.00 30.00
HOFKN Kevin Nash 12.00 30.00
HOFLT Lita 20.00 50.00
HOFMH Mark Henry 10.00 25.00
HOFPO Mr. Wonderful Paul Orndorff 12.00 30.00
HOFRD Ricky The Dragon Steamboat 10.00 25.00
HOFRF Ric Flair/84 30.00 75.00
HOFRR Razor Ramon 15.00 40.00
HOFSS Sgt. Slaughter 12.00 30.00
HOFST Sting 25.00 60.00
HOFWR Wendi Richter 10.00 25.00

2018 Topps Legends of WWE Autographed Dual Relics

*GOLD/10: UNPRICED DUE TO SCARCITY
*BLACK/5: UNPRICED DUE TO SCARCITY
*RED/1: UNPRICED DUE TO SCARCITY
STATED PRINT RUN 25 SER.#'d SETS
ADRGD Goldust 12.00 30.00
ADRJH Jeff Hardy 15.00 40.00
ADRMH Woken Matt Hardy 20.00 50.00

2018 Topps Legends of WWE Autographed Shirt Relics

*SILVER/50: .5X TO 1.2X BASIC AUTOS
*BLUE/25: .6X TO 1.5X BASIC AUTOS
*GOLD/10: UNPRICED DUE TO SCARCITY
*BLACK/5: UNPRICED DUE TO SCARCITY
*RED/1: UNPRICED DUE TO SCARCITY
STATED PRINT RUN 99 SER.#'d SETS
ASRDP Diamond Dallas Page 10.00 25.00
ASREG Edge 12.00 30.00
ASRIS The Iron Sheik 10.00 25.00
ASRKN Kevin Nash 15.00 40.00
ASRLL Lex Luger 10.00 25.00
ASRMH Woken Matt Hardy 8.00 20.00
ASRRD Road Dogg
ASRRS Ricky The Dragon Steamboat 8.00 20.00
ASRST Sting 15.00 40.00

2018 Topps Legends of WWE Autographs

*BRONZE/99: SAME VALUE AS BASIC AUTOS
*SILVER/50: .5X TO 1.2X BASIC AUTOS
*BLUE/25: .6X TO 1.5X BASIC AUTOS
*GOLD/10: UNPRICED DUE TO SCARCITY
*BLACK/5: UNPRICED DUE TO SCARCITY
*RED/1: UNPRICED DUE TO SCARCITY
*P.P.BLACK/1: UNPRICED DUE TO SCARCITY
*P.P.CYAN/1: UNPRICED DUE TO SCARCITY
*P.P.MAGENTA/1: UNPRICED DUE TO SCARCITY
*P.P.YELLOW/1: UNPRICED DUE TO SCARCITY
STATED ODDS
AAB Alundra Blayze 6.00 15.00
AAF Afa 5.00 12.00
ABE Brutus The Barber Beefcake 8.00 20.00
ABH Bret Hit Man Hart 12.00 30.00
ABN Brian Knobbs 6.00 15.00
ABS Big Show 8.00 20.00
ABT Booker T 8.00 20.00
ACB Cowboy Bob Orton 5.00 12.00
ACJ Chris Jericho 12.00 30.00
ADB Daniel Bryan 10.00 25.00
ADP Diamond Dallas Page 6.00 15.00
AED Edge 12.00 30.00
AFA Faarooq 5.00 12.00
AFF Fit Finlay 6.00 15.00
AGD Goldust 6.00 15.00
AGO The Goon 10.00 25.00
AHA Haku 8.00 20.00
AHR Harley Race 8.00 20.00
AHT Honky Tonk Man 6.00 15.00
AIR Irwin R. Schyster 5.00 12.00
AJD Hacksaw Jim Duggan 10.00 25.00
AJH Jimmy Hart 6.00 15.00

AJJ JJ Dillon 6.00 15.00
AJL Jerry The King Lawler 8.00 20.00
AJS Jake The Snake Roberts 10.00 25.00
AKA Kurt Angle 12.00 30.00
AKE Kane 6.00 15.00
AKN Kevin Nash 6.00 15.00
ALL Lex Luger 8.00 20.00
ALT Lita 12.00 30.00
AMA Mankind 6.00 15.00
AMC Michael Cole 5.00 12.00
AMD Million Dollar Man Ted DiBiase 8.00 20.00
ANB Jerry Sags 5.00 12.00
ANS Norman Smiley 6.00 15.00
APE Paul Ellering 8.00 20.00
APS Michael P.S. Hayes 6.00 15.00
ARH Rhyno 5.00 12.00
ARO Randy Orton 10.00 25.00
ARS Ricky The Dragon Steamboat 10.00 25.00
ASI Sika 6.00 15.00
ASR Stevie Ray 6.00 15.00
ASS Sgt. Slaughter 6.00 15.00
AST Sting 15.00 40.00
ASV Sid Vicious 6.00 15.00
ATA Magnum T.A. 6.00 15.00
ATG The Godfather 6.00 15.00
ATK Tatanka 5.00 12.00
ATS Trish Stratus 20.00 50.00
ATT Terry Taylor 5.00 12.00
ATW The Warlord 5.00 12.00
AWD Wendi Richter 6.00 15.00
AWR William Regal 8.00 20.00

2018 Topps Legends of WWE Autographs Silver

STATED PRINT RUN 50 SER.#'d SETS

ASM Stephanie McMahon 75.00 150.00
ATH Triple H 125.00 250.00
AUD Undertaker 100.00 200.00

2018 Topps Legends of WWE Dual Autographs

DABW Bushwhackers
DADX HHH/HBK
DAGG J.Martin/L.Kai
DAHF P.Orndorff/H.Race
DAHH Booker T/S.Ray

2018 Topps Legends of WWE Relics

RANDOMLY INSERTED INTO PACKS

SRBH Bret Hit Man Hart 5.00 12.00
SRDP Diamond Dallas Page 3.00 8.00
SREG Edge 3.00 8.00
SRGD Goldust 2.50 6.00
SRIS The Iron Sheik 2.50 6.00
SRJC John Cena 5.00 12.00
SRKN Kevin Nash 3.00 8.00
SRLL Lex Luger 2.50 6.00
SRMH Woken Matt Hardy 2.00 5.00
SRRD Road Dogg 2.00 5.00
SRRS Ricky The Dragon Steamboat 2.00 5.00
SRST Sting 3.00 8.00
SRTD Million Dollar Man Ted DiBiase 2.00 5.00

2018 Topps Legends of WWE Triple Autographs

STATED PRINT RUN 10 SER.#'d SETS
UNPRICED DUE TO SCARCITY

TAMHF K.Angle/HHH/S,McMahon
TAMOD Faarooq/Edge/Undertaker
TATCM HHH/Undertaker/Faarooq

2021 Topps Living WWE

1 Stone Cold Steve Austin/5,521* 8.00 20.00
2 Trish Stratus/3,546* 8.00 20.00
3 The Miz/1,582* 2.50 6.00
4 Maryse/1,592* 2.50 6.00
5 Erik/1,116* 1.50 4.00
6 Ivar/1,135* 1.50 4.00
7 Bobby Lashley/1,031* 4.00 10.00
8 MVP/1,024* 1.50 4.00
9 Jeff Hardy/1,699* 4.00 10.00
10 Undertaker/3,231* 8.00 20.00
11 Shinsuke Nakamura/962* 4.00 10.00
12 Akira Tozawa/968* 2.00 5.00
13 Jey Uso/800* 1.50 4.00
14 Jimmy Uso/785* 1.50 4.00
15 Mia Yim/792* 2.00 5.00
16 Keith Lee/786* 3.00 8.00
17 Sami Zayn/825* 2.50 6.00
18 Edge/1,022* 6.00 15.00
19 Sheamus/758* 2.50 6.00
20 Cesaro/744* 1.50 4.00
21 Titus O'Neil/696* 1.50 4.00
22 Roman Reigns/1,105* 8.00 20.00
23 Braun Strowman/839 4.00 10.00
24 Alexa Bliss/1,601* 10.00 25.00
25 Drew McIntyre/674* 4.00 10.00
26 Jinder Mahal/718* 2.00 5.00
27 Carmella/683* 4.00 10.00
28 R-Truth/619* 2.00 5.00
29 Aleister Black/606* 4.00 10.00
30 Ricochet/565* 3.00 8.00
31 Eddie Guerrero/925* 8.00 20.00
32 Sasha Banks/1,242* 8.00 20.00
33 Nikki Cross/541* 3.00 8.00
34 Finn Balor/570* 4.00 10.00
35 Angelo Dawkins/529* 2.00 5.00
36 Montez Ford/529* 1.50 4.00
37 Dolph Ziggler/551* 3.00 8.00
38 Robert Roode/512* 2.00 5.00
39 Karrion Kross/686* 6.00 15.00
40 Scarlett/936* 8.00 20.00
41 Bianca Belair/671* 4.00 10.00
42 Naomi/621* 2.00 5.00
43 Kayden Carter/483* 3.00 8.00
44 Kacy Catanzaro/554* 3.00 8.00
45 Mr. America (Hulk Hogan)/1,216* 8.00 20.00
46 Lex Luger/713* 2.00 5.00
47 Rey Mysterio/676* 4.00 10.00
48 Dominik Mysterio/563* 2.00 5.00
49 Miss Elizabeth/1,142* 3.00 8.00
50 Macho Man Randy Savage/1,866* 10.00 25.00
51 Beth Phoenix/1,142* 3.00 8.00
52 Lacey Evans/564* 4.00 10.00
53 Bobby "The Brain" Heenan/701* 2.50 6.00
54 Razor Ramon/769* 2.50 6.00
55 AJ Styles//574* 5.00 12.00
56 Omos/544* 3.00 8.00
57 Kane/658* 2.50 6.00
58 Rob Van Dam/527* 3.00 8.00
59 Seth Rollins/643* 4.00 10.00
60 Becky Lynch/932* 6.00 15.00
61 British Bulldog/646* 2.50 6.00
62 Bret Hart/1,013* 4.00 10.00
63 Cedric Alexander/430* 1.50 4.00
64 Shelton Benjamin/431* 2.50 6.00
65 Dakota Kai/490* 3.00 8.00
66 Raquel Gonzalez/572* 4.00 10.00
67 John Morrison/426* 3.00 8.00
68 Franky Monet/483* 3.00 8.00
69 Natalya/442* 2.50 6.00
70 Tamina/404* 2.00 5.00
71 Rikishi/485* 2.00 5.00
72 Yokozuna/506* 2.50 6.00
73 Asuka/767* 6.00 15.00
74 Io Shirai/663* 3.00 8.00
75 Apollo Crews/412* 2.00 5.00
76 Commander Azeez/412* 2.00 5.00
77 Papa Shango/648* 2.00 5.00
78 Ultimate Warrior/1,267* 6.00 15.00
79 Riddle/509* 4.00 10.00
80 Randy Orton/601* 5.00 12.00
81 Rocky Johnson/827* 3.00 8.00
82 The Rock/3,671* 15.00 40.00
83 Gobbledy Gooker/565* 1.50 4.00
84 Big E/485* 3.00 8.00
85 Kofi Kingston/424* 4.00 10.00
86 Xavier Woods/419* 1.50 4.00
87 Shotzi Blackheart/769* 6.00 15.00
88 Charlotte Flair/796* 8.00 20.00
89 Billy Gunn/491* 2.00 5.00
90 Road Dogg/496* 2.00 5.00
91 Chyna/596* 3.00 8.00
92 X-Pac/516* 2.00 5.00
93 John Cena/
94 Mick Foley/
95 Shawn Michaels/
96 Triple H/

2021 Topps Living WWE Rainbow Foil

STATED PRINT RUN 50 SER.#'d SETS
VIP PARTY EXCLUSIVE

1 Stone Cold Steve Austin 100.00 200.00

2016-18 Topps Now WWE

1 Brock Lesnar/132* 6.00 15.00
2 Finn Balor/221* 5.00 12.00
3 Dean Ambrose/114* 6.00 15.00
4 Charlotte/124* 6.00 15.00
5 AJ Styles/127* 8.00 20.00
6 AJ Styles/191* 6.00 15.00
7 Becky Lynch/212* 8.00 20.00
8 Heath Slater and Rhyno/104* 4.00 10.00
9 Kane/81* 12.00 30.00
10 The Miz/85* 6.00 15.00
11 Kevin Owens/68* 5.00 12.00
12 The New Day/61* 15.00 40.00
13 Charlotte/88* 5.00 12.00
14 Roman Reigns/61* 8.00 20.00
15 Chris Jericho/62* 10.00 25.00
16 AJ Styles/73* 5.00 12.00
17 Naomi/70* 8.00 20.00
18 Heath Slater & Rhyno/65* 8.00 20.00
19 Dolph Ziggler/73* 5.00 12.00
20 Bray Wyatt/86* 5.00 12.00
21 Nikki Bella/87* 5.00 12.00
22 Goldberg/249* 6.00 15.00
23 Kevin Owens/98* 8.00 20.00
24 Charlotte Flair/151* 6.00 15.00
25 Roman Reigns/69* 5.00 12.00
26 New Day/70* 5.00 12.00
27 Brian Kendrick/72* 5.00 12.00
28 The Miz/59* 5.00 12.00
29 Edge/58* 5.00 12.00
30 Undertaker/126* 8.00 20.00
31 Goldberg/125* 6.00 15.00
32 Team Smackdown Live Men/62* 5.00 12.00
33 Team Raw Women/88* 4.00 10.00
34 Team Raw Tag Team/60* 5.00 12.00
35 The Brian Kendrick/59* 5.00 12.00
36 The Miz/60* 5.00 12.00
37 AJ Styles/122* 4.00 10.00
38 Alexa Bliss/180* 15.00 40.00
39 The Miz/82* 4.00 10.00
40 Nikki Bella/93* 6.00 15.00
41 Baron Corbin/91* 4.00 10.00
42 Randy Orton & Bray Wyatt/115* 5.00 12.00
43A Kevin Owens/65* 4.00 10.00
44 Cesaro & Sheamus/65* 4.00 10.00
45 Sami Zayn/68* 4.00 10.00
46 Seth Rollins/63* 4.00 10.00
47 Rich Swann/65* 4.00 10.00
48A Charlotte Flair/108* 6.00 15.00
49 Naomi/Nikki Bella/Becky Lynch/88* 4.00 10.00
50 Luke Gallows & Karl Anderson/64* 4.00 10.00
51 Charlotte Flair/100* 4.00 10.00
52 Kevin Owens/62* 6.00 15.00
53 Neville/61* 5.00 12.00
54A John Cena/82* 6.00 15.00
55 Goldberg/Undertaker/73* 6.00 15.00
56A Randy Orton/85* 5.00 12.00
57 Nia Jax/83* 6.00 15.00
58 Bray Wyatt/102* 5.00 12.00
59 Naomi/82* 6.00 15.00
60 Randy Orton/54* 6.00 15.00
61 Nikki Bella & Natalya/74* 6.00 15.00
62 American Alpha/39* 4.00 10.00
63 Becky Lynch/73* 6.00 15.00
64 Bayley/288* 6.00 15.00
65 Goldberg/223* 8.00 20.00
66 Bayley/153* 5.00 12.00
67 Roman Reigns/64* 5.00 12.00
68 Neville/73* 5.00 12.00
69 Sasha Banks/141* 5.00 12.00
70 Luke Gallows & Karl Anderson/74* 5.00 12.00
71 Samoa Joe/81* 5.00 12.00
72 Undertaker/172* 6.00 15.00
73 Naomi/72* 5.00 12.00
74 Goldberg/64* 8.00 20.00
75 Randy Orton/69* 5.00 12.00
76 John Cena/Nikki Bella/91* 5.00 12.00
77 Hardy Boyz/114* 8.00 20.00
78 Bayley/97* 5.00 12.00
79 Kevin Owens/71* 5.00 12.00
80 Shinsuke Nakamura/78* 8.00 20.00
82 Tye Dillinger/37* 10.00 25.00
81 Finn Balor/46* 10.00 25.00
83 The Revival/46* 5.00 12.00
84 Dean Ambrose/Miz/Maryse/40* 5.00 12.00
85 Alexa Bliss/123* 10.00 25.00
86 Kevin Owens/49* 5.00 12.00
87 Charlotte Flair/57* 8.00 20.00
88 Braun Strowman/55* 5.00 12.00
89 Bray Wyatt/49* 5.00 12.00
90 Seth Rollins/50* 5.00 12.00
91 Alexa Bliss/223* 10.00 25.00
92 The Hardy Boyz/65* 5.00 12.00
93 Chris Jericho/56* 5.00 12.00

94 Shinsuka Nakamura/96*	5.00	12.00
95 The Usos/		
96 Sami Zayn/41*	5.00	12.00
97 Natalya Carmella Tamina/49*	5.00	12.00
98 Kevin Owens/44*	5.00	12.00
99 Jinder Mahal/69*	5.00	12.00
100 The Miz/60*	5.00	12.00
101 Sasha Banks/Rich Swann/78*	6.00	15.00
102 Alexa Bliss/264*	8.00	20.00
103 Cesaro & Sheamus/53*	4.00	10.00
104 Neville/53*	4.00	10.00
105 Samoa Joe/56*	4.00	10.00
106 Carmella/112*	6.00	15.00
107 The Usos/41*	5.00	12.00
108 Naomi/49*	5.00	12.00
109 Jinder Mahal/41*	4.00	10.00
110 Baron Corbin/60*	4.00	10.00
111 Brock Lesnar/61*	6.00	15.00
112 Braun Strowman/39*	4.00	10.00
113 The Miz/33*	4.00	10.00
114 Sasha Banks/103*	5.00	12.00
115 Cesaro & Sheamus/33*	4.00	10.00
116 Big Cass/32*	4.00	10.00
117 Bray Wyatt/37*	4.00	10.00
118 Neville/32*	4.00	10.00
119 Jinder Mahal/50*	4.00	10.00
120 The New Day/49*	4.00	10.00
121 John Cena/59*	4.00	10.00
122 Kevin Owens/44*	4.00	10.00
123 Natalya/44*	4.00	10.00
124 Baron Corbin/38*	4.00	10.00
125 HHH & Stephanie/Connor's Cure/216*	4.00	10.00
126 Natalya/62*	4.00	10.00
127 Sasha Banks/114*	6.00	15.00
128 Dean Ambrose & Seth Rollins/80*	5.00	12.00
129 AJ Styles/63*	5.00	12.00
130 Jinder Mahal/38*	5.00	12.00
131 Brock Lesnar/50*	5.00	12.00
132 Brock Lesnar/51*	5.00	12.00
133 Enzo Amore/48*	5.00	12.00
134 Roman Reigns/46*	5.00	12.00
135 Alexa Bliss/138*	10.00	25.00
136 Ambrose/Rollins/38*	5.00	12.00
137 Finn Balor/40*	5.00	12.00
138 Kevin Owens/39*	5.00	12.00
139 Bobby Roode/32*	5.00	12.00
140 Jinder Mahal/29*	5.00	12.00
141 Natalya/53*	5.00	12.00
142 Baron Corbin/30*	5.00	12.00
143 The Usos/32*	5.00	12.00
144 Angle/Rollins/Ambrose/75*	5.00	12.00
145 Alexa Bliss/191*	8.00	20.00
146 The Demon Finn Balor/94*	5.00	12.00
147 Asuka/146*	6.00	15.00
148 Enzo Amore/55*	4.00	10.00
149 Sasha Banks/100*	5.00	12.00
150 The Shield/50*	4.00	10.00
151 Team Raw Women/35*	4.00	10.00
152 Charlotte Flair/102*	6.00	15.00
153 Team Raw Men/	4.00	10.00
154 AJ Styles/65*	4.00	10.00
155 Kevin Owens & Sami Zayn/34*	4.00	10.00
156 Charlotte Flair/63*	6.00	15.00
157 The Usos/33*	4.00	10.00
158 Dolph Ziggler/33*	4.00	10.00
159 Scott Hall/89*	4.00	10.00
160 Undertaker/147*	6.00	15.00
161 The Miz/88*	4.00	10.00
162 John Cena/91*	6.00	15.00
163 Stone Cold Steve Austin/153*	8.00	20.00

2016-18 Topps Now WWE Relics

STATED PRINT RUN 25 SER.#'d SETS

43B Kevin Owens	20.00	50.00
48B Charlotte Flair	60.00	120.00
54B John Cena	50.00	100.00
56B Randy Orton	25.00	60.00
72A Undertaker	80.00	150.00
74A Goldberg	15.00	40.00
75A Randy Orton	20.00	50.00
76A John Cena/Nikki Bella	30.00	75.00
127A Sasha Banks	60.00	120.00
128A Dean Ambrose & Seth Rollins	30.00	75.00
131A Brock Lesnar	30.00	75.00
144A Kurt Angle	30.00	75.00
147A Asuka	50.00	100.00
163A Stone Cold Steve Austin	60.00	120.00

2018 Topps Now WWE

COMPLETE SET (72)	300.00	600.00
1 AJ Styles/99*	6.00	15.00
2 Shinsuke Nakamura/127*	5.00	12.00
3 Cesaro & Sheamus/82*	5.00	12.00
4 Lita/102*	6.00	15.00
5 Trish Stratus/186*	8.00	20.00
6 Asuka/145*	6.00	15.00
7 Alexa Bliss/171*	10.00	25.00
8 Asuka/140*	6.00	15.00
9 Woken Matt Hardy/56*	6.00	15.00
10 Roman Reigns/59*	6.00	15.00
11 AJ Styles/53*	5.00	12.00
12 Asuka/103*	6.00	15.00
13 Charlotte Flair/101*	6.00	15.00
14 Randy Orton/67*	5.00	12.00
15 Shinsuke Nakamura/50*	5.00	12.00
16 Daniel Bryan/125*	6.00	15.00
17 Woken Matt Hardy/76*	8.00	20.00
18 Cedric Alexander/74*	8.00	20.00
19 Naomi/87*	8.00	20.00
20 Seth Rollins/77*	8.00	20.00
21 Charlotte Flair/261*	8.00	20.00
22 Jinder Mahal/64*	5.00	12.00
23 The Bludgeon Brothers/67*	5.00	12.00
24 The Undertaker/145*	8.00	20.00
25 Daniel Bryan/93*	8.00	20.00
26 Nia Jax/115*	5.00	12.00
27 AJ Styles/85*	5.00	12.00
28 Braun Strowman/67*	5.00	12.00
29 Brock Lesnar/44*	5.00	12.00
30 Ronda Rousey/1342*	12.00	30.00
31 Braun Strowman/66*	5.00	12.00
32 Daniel Bryan/52*	6.00	15.00
33 Undertaker/62*	8.00	20.00
34 AJ Styles/52*	6.00	15.00
35 John Cena/66*	5.00	12.00
36 Seth Rollins/37*	6.00	15.00
37 Daniel Bryan/30*	12.00	30.00
38 Roman Reigns/33*	8.00	20.00
39 Alexa Bliss/301*	8.00	20.00
40 AJ Styles/101*	6.00	15.00
41 Alexa Bliss/304*	10.00	25.00
42 Braun Strowman/101*	5.00	12.00
43 Bobby Lashley/47*	8.00	20.00
44 Alexa Bliss/175*	10.00	25.00
45 AJ Styles/58*	8.00	20.00
46 Dolph Ziggler/48*	6.00	15.00
47 Seth Rollins/80*	6.00	15.00
48 Charlotte Flair/191*	8.00	20.00
49 Ronda Rousey/970*	8.00	20.00
50 Roman Reigns/79*	12.00	30.00
51 Becky Lynch/172*	5.00	12.00
52 Dolph Ziggler/Drew McIntyre/73*	5.00	12.00
53 AJ Styles/74*	5.00	12.00
54 Ronda Rousey/299*	6.00	15.00
55 John Cena/64*	5.00	12.00
56 IIconics/146*	5.00	12.00
57 AJ Styles/64*	4.00	10.00
58 Ronda Rousey/Bellas/166*	6.00	15.00
59 Triple H/72*	4.00	10.00
60 Buddy Murphy/64*	10.00	25.00
61 Trish Stratus & Lita/212*	6.00	15.00
62 Nia Jax/139*	12.00	30.00
63 Toni Storm/239*	8.00	20.00
64 Shayna Baszler/149*	6.00	15.00
65 Becky Lynch/325*	5.00	12.00
66 Ronda Rousey/324*	5.00	12.00
67 Seth Rollins/63*	10.00	25.00
68 Charlotte Flair/143*	8.00	20.00
69 Brock Lesnar/63*	10.00	25.00
70 Asuka/270*	4.00	10.00
71 Daniel Bryan/70*	6.00	15.00
72 Ronda Rousey/295*	5.00	12.00

2018 Topps Now WWE Relics

*GOLD/1: UNPRICED/SCARCITY

2A Shinsuke Nakamura	25.00	60.00
6A Asuka	75.00	150.00
24A The Undertaker	25.00	60.00
25A Daniel Bryan	30.00	75.00
29A Brock Lesnar	60.00	120.00
30A Ronda Rousey	150.00	300.00
48A Charlotte Flair	30.00	75.00
49A Ronda Rousey	100.00	200.00
50A Roman Reigns		
68A Charlotte Flair	50.00	100.00
69A Brock Lesnar		

2019 Topps Now WWE

1 Women's Royal Rumble/166*	8.00	20.00
2 Men's Royal Rumble/75*	5.00	12.00
3 Asuka/186*	6.00	15.00
4 Ronda Rousey/268*	6.00	15.00
5 Daniel Bryan/90*	5.00	12.00
6 Brock Lesnar/91*	6.00	15.00
7 Becky Lynch/279*	6.00	15.00
8 Seth Rollins/113*	5.00	12.00
9 WM35 Men's Preview/100*	4.00	10.00
10 WM35 Women's Preview/215*	5.00	12.00
11 Seth Rollins/157*	4.00	10.00
12 Roman Reigns/119*	4.00	10.00
13 Kurt Angle/127*	6.00	15.00
14 Kofi Kingston/217*	4.00	10.00
15 The IIconics/211*	3.00	8.00
16 Triple H/95*	3.00	8.00
17 John Cena/136*	4.00	10.00
18 Becky Lynch/710*	6.00	15.00
19 Seth Rollins/58*	6.00	15.00
20 Kofi Kingston/49*	5.00	12.00
21 Rey Mysterio/48*	8.00	20.00
22 Bayley/164*	5.00	12.00
23 Charlotte Flair/140*	6.00	15.00
24 Becky Lynch/163*	5.00	12.00
25 Bayley/138*	5.00	12.00
26 Brock Lesnar/49*	5.00	12.00
27 Mansoor/29*	12.00	30.00
28 Randy Orton/26*	6.00	15.00
29 Undertaker/31*	6.00	15.00
30 Drew Gulak/45*	5.00	12.00
31 Becky Lynch/109*	6.00	15.00
32 Ricochet/48*	5.00	12.00
33 Bayley/81*	8.00	20.00
34 Seth Rollins w/Becky Lynch/111*	6.00	15.00
35 Undertaker & Roman Reigns/58*	6.00	15.00
36 AJ Styles/57*	5.00	12.00
37 Bayley/81*	5.00	12.00
38 Seth Rollins & Becky Lynch/91*	5.00	12.00
39 Brock Lesnar/55*	5.00	12.00
40 Becky Lynch vs. Natalya/58*	6.00	15.00
41 Kofi Kingston vs. Randy Orton/29*	4.00	10.00
42 Brock Lesnar vs. Seth Rollins/29*	8.00	20.00
43 Becky Lynch/159*	8.00	20.00
44 AJ Styles/67*	4.00	10.00
45 Charlotte Flair/171*	6.00	15.00
46 The Fiend Bray Wyatt/	8.00	20.00
47 Seth Rollins//96*	4.00	10.00
48 Bayley//96*	5.00	12.00
49 Samoa Joe/26*	6.00	15.00
50 Cedric Alexander/26*	3.00	8.00
51 Elias/29*	3.00	8.00
52 Andrade/28*	5.00	12.00
53 Ricochet/31*	4.00	10.00
54 Baron Corbin/31*	4.00	10.00
55 Ali/20*		
56 Chad Gable/56*	6.00	15.00
57 Baron Corbin/21*		
58 Samoa Joe and Ricochet/21*		
59 Elias/21*		
60 Chad Gable/20*		
61 Baron Corbin/30*		
62 Chad Gable/31*	6.00	15.00
63 Bayley/101*		
64 Sasha Banks/172*	5.00	12.00
65 Kofi Kingston/55*		
66 Erick Rowan/55*		
67 Seth Rollins/66*		
68 Baron Corbin/		
69 Rock & Becky Lynch/118*	6.00	15.00
70 Becky & Charlotte/81*	6.00	15.00
71 Kevin Owens/41*	5.00	12.00
72 Roman Reigns/38*		
73 Roman Reigns & Daniel Bryan/44*		
74 Kabuki Warriors/74*	5.00	12.00
75 Charlotte Flair/75*	6.00	15.00
76 Becky Lynch/110*	4.00	10.00
77 The Fiend Bray Wyatt/182*	8.00	20.00
78 Team Hogan/36*	5.00	12.00
79 Natalya/Lacey Evans/104*		
80 AJ Styles/34*		
81 Mansoor/34*		
82 The OC/34*	5.00	12.00
83 Brock Lesnar/34*	6.00	15.00
84 Team NXT Women/79*	6.00	15.00
85 Roderick Strong/43*	6.00	15.00
86 Adam Cole/43*	6.00	15.00
87 The Fiend Bray Wyatt/80*	8.00	20.00
88 Team SmackDown Men/38*	8.00	20.00
89 Brock Lesnar/43*	5.00	12.00
90 Shayna Baszler/61*	8.00	20.00
91 The New Day/29*		
92 Aleister Black/29*		

93 King Corbin/24*
94 Bray Wyatt/50* 6.00 15.00
95 The Kabuki Warriors/70* 5.00 12.00

2020 Topps Now WWE

1 Roman Reigns/51* 6.00 15.00
2 Charlotte Flair/170* 6.00 15.00
3 Bayley/77* 3.00 8.00
4 The Fiend/85* 5.00 12.00
5 Becky Lynch/152* 6.00 15.00
6 Drew McIntyre/*76 3.00 8.00
7 Undertaker/77* 6.00 15.00
8 The Miz & John Morrison/40*
9 Roman Reigns/41* 6.00 15.00
10 Bayley/83* 3.00 8.00
11 Goldberg/67* 6.00 15.00
12 Alexa Bliss & Nikki Cross/160* 10.00 25.00
13 Becky Lynch/162* 6.00 15.00
14 Sami Zayn/66* 3.00 8.00
15 John Morrison/56* 4.00 10.00
16 Kevin Owens/61* 3.00 8.00
17 Braun Strowman/75* 6.00 15.00
18 Undertaker/141* 6.00 15.00
19 Rob Gronkowski/393* 2.50 6.00
20 Charlotte Flair/153* 6.00 15.00
21 Aleister Black/55*
22 Edge/96* 4.00 10.00
23 Street Profits/71* 4.00 10.00
24 Bayley/105* 8.00 20.00
25 The Fiend Bray Wyatt/107* 6.00 15.00
26 Drew McIntyre/105* 3.00 8.00
27 The New Day/45*
28 Bayley/75* 3.00 8.00
29 Braun Strowman/55*
30 Drew McIntyre/59*
31 Asuka/155* 6.00 15.00
32 Otis/78* 2.50 6.00
33 Bayley & Sasha Banks/148* 8.00 20.00
34 Sheamus/38*
35 Braun Strowman/40*
36 Drew McIntyre/41*
37 Randy Orton/84* 4.00 10.00
38 Cesaro & Nakamura/38*
39 Seth Rollins/31*
40 Drew McIntyre/36*
41 Bayley/73* 3.00 8.00
42 The Fiend Bray Wyatt/116* 5.00 12.00
43 Drew McIntyre/79* 3.00 8.00
44 Asuka/209* 6.00 15.00
45 Seth Rollins/57*
46 Mandy Rose/93* 8.00 20.00
47 Bayley/128* 3.00 8.00
48 Roman Reigns/86* 4.00 10.00
49 Roman Reigns/73* 4.00 10.00
50 Rey & Dominik Mysterio/97* 3.00 8.00
51 Shayna Baszler & Nia Jax/72* 5.00 12.00
52 Bobby Lashley/45*
53 Roman Reigns/62* 4.00 10.00
54 Drew McIntyre/52*
55 Asuka/102* 6.00 15.00
56 Sami Zayn/52*
57 Roman Reigns/61* 4.00 10.00
58 The Miz/39*
59 Sasha Banks/163* 8.00 20.00
60 Randy Orton/73* 4.00 10.00
61 Team RAW (men)/68* 5.00 12.00
62 Street Profits/55*
63 Bobby Lashley/65* 3.00 8.00
64 Sasha Banks/261* 8.00 20.00
65 Team RAW (women)/129* 4.00 10.00
66 Roman Reigns/65* 4.00 10.00
67 Undertaker/736* 6.00 15.00
68 Drew McIntyre
69 Sasha Banks 8.00 20.00
70 The Hurt Business
71 Asuka & Charlotte Flair 6.00 15.00
72 Roman Reigns
73 Randy Orton

2020 Topps Now WWE Autographs

*RED/10: UNPRICED DUE TO SCARCITY
*GOLD/1: UNPRICED DUE TO SCARCITY
STATED PRINT RUN 25 SER.#'d SETS
31A Asuka 75.00 150.00
32A Otis 30.00 75.00
DMA Dominik Mysterio 60.00 120.00

2020 Topps Now WWE Relics

1A Drew McIntyre 30.00 75.00
2A Charlotte Flair 50.00 100.00

2021 Topps Now WWE

1 Drew McIntyre/181* 3.00 8.00
2 Sasha Banks/426* 6.00 15.00
3 Bianca Belair/342* 3.00 8.00
4 Roman Reigns/160* 6.00 15.00
5 Edge/224* 5.00 12.00
6 Bobby Lashley/132* 3.00 8.00
7 Alexa Bliss/679* 8.00 20.00
8 The Fiend Bray Wyatt/487* 8.00 20.00
9 Bobby Lashley/118* 3.00 8.00
10 Cesaro/130* 1.25 3.00
11 AJ Styles & Omos/141* 4.00 10.00
12 Braun Strowman/153* 3.00 8.00
13 Bianca Belair/286* 3.00 8.00
14 Randy Orton/
15 Kevin Owens/116* 2.50 6.00
16 Sheamus/144* 3.00 8.00
17 Apollo Crews/118* 1.50 4.00
18 Shayna Baszler & Nia Jax/135* 2.50 6.00
19 Rhea Ripley/475* 4.00 10.00
20 Roman Reigns/193* 6.00 15.00
21 John Cena/293* 6.00 15.00
22 RK-Bro/197* 4.00 10.00
23 Becky Lynch/437* 5.00 12.00
24 Roman Reigns/189* 6.00 15.00
25 Damian Priest/201* 2.00 5.00
26 Edge/207* 5.00 12.00
27 Charlotte Flair/285* 6.00 15.00
28 Bobby Lashley/120* 3.00 8.00
29 Big E/

2021 Topps Now WWE Autographs

STATED PRINT RUN 25 SER.#'d SETS
6A Bobby Lashley
29A Big E

2021 Topps Now WWE Mat Relics

STATED PRINT RUN 25 SER.#'d SETS
13A Bianca Belair
20A Roman Reigns
23A Becky Lynch 50.00 100.00
24A Roman Reigns
27A Charlotte Flair 30.00 75.00

SS1A Goldberg
SS2A John Cena

2017 Topps Now WWE Countdown to NXT TakeOver Orlando

1 Asuka vs. Ember Moon 5.00 12.00
2 Bobby Roode vs. Nakamura 5.00 12.00
3 AOP vs. Revival vs. #DIY 5.00 12.00
4 Aleister Black vs. Andrade 5.00 12.00
5 Dillinger/Strong/Jose/Ruby vs. Sanity 5.00 12.00

2017 Topps Now WWE Countdown to WrestleMania

1 Goldberg vs. Brock Lesnar 5.00 12.00
2 Bray Wyatt vs. Randy Orton 5.00 12.00
3 Chris Jericho vs. Kevin Owens 6.00 15.00
4 Undertaker vs. Roman Reigns 8.00 20.00
5 Bayley/Charlotte/Sasha/Nia 8.00 20.00
6 SD Women's Title Match 12.00 30.00
7 Cena & Nikki vs. Miz & Maryse 5.00 12.00
8 Seth Rollins vs. HHH 5.00 12.00
9 AJ Styles vs. Shane McMahon 5.00 12.00
10 Dean Ambrose vs. Baron Corbin 5.00 12.00
11 Neville vs. Austin Aries 5.00 12.00

2017 Topps Now WWE SummerSlam

STATED PRINT RUN 36 SER.#'d SETS
UNPRICED DUE TO SCARCITY
1 Lesnar/Reigns/Samoa Joe/Strowman
2 Jinder Mahal vs. Nakamura
3 Alexa Bliss vs. Sasha Banks
4 Naomi vs. Natalya
5 AJ Styles vs. Kevin Owens
6 Akira Tozawa vs. Neville
7 Cesaro/Sheamus vs. Ambrose/Rollins
8 New Day vs. Usos
9 John Cena vs. Baron Corbin
10 Randy Orton vs. Rusev
11 The Demon Finn Balor vs. Bray Wyatt
12 Big Show vs. Big Cass

2021 Topps Now WWE Turn Back the Clock

COMPLETE SET (9)
1 Ron Simmons/149*
2 King Booker/113*
3 Alicia Fox/109*
4 Mark Henry/107*
5 Big E/104*
6 Sasha Banks/257*
7 Naomi/110*
8 Ember Moon/108*
9 Kofi Kingston/146*

2016-18 Topps Now WWE NXT

1 Samoa Joe/43*
2 Asuka/77* 20.00 50.00
3 DIY/58*
4 Authors of Pain/44*
5 Bobby Roode/40*
7 Eric Young/50* 6.00 15.00
8 Roderick Strong/71* 6.00 15.00
9 The Authors of Pain/49* 5.00 12.00
10 Asuka/87* 5.00 12.00
11 Bobby Roode/56* 6.00 15.00
12 Seth Rollins/62* 6.00 15.00
13 Bobby Roode/74* 5.00 12.00
14 Asuka/117* 5.00 12.00
15 Roderick Strong/27* 4.00 10.00
16 Asuka/74* 4.00 10.00
17 Bobby Roode/25* 4.00 10.00
18 The Authors of Pain/27* 4.00 10.00
19 Tommaso Ciampa/43* 4.00 10.00
20 Sanity/47* 5.00 12.00
21 Asuka/86* 5.00 12.00
22 Drew McIntyre/46* 5.00 12.00
23 Adam Cole/104* 5.00 12.00
24 Undisputed Era/57* 5.00 12.00
25 Andrade Cien Almas/46* 5.00 12.00
26 Ember Moon/63* 5.00 12.00

2016-18 Topps Now WWE NXT Relics

4B Asuka 30.00 75.00
5B Bobby Roode 8.00 20.00

2018 Topps Now WWE NXT

1 The Undisputed Era/38* 5.00 12.00
2 Ember Moon/56* 5.00 12.00
3 Aleister Black/54* 5.00 12.00
4 Andrade Cien Almas/31* 5.00 12.00
5 Adam Cole/80* 8.00 20.00
6 Shayna Baszler/80* 8.00 20.00
7 The Undisputed Era/50* 8.00 20.00
8 Aleister Black/56* 8.00 20.00
9 Johnny Gargano/51* 8.00 20.00
10 Kairi Sane/196*
11 Tommaso Ciampa/66*

2019 Topps Now WWE NXT

1 War Raiders/67* 6.00 15.00
2 Johnny Gargano/77* 3.00 8.00
3 Shayna Baszler/71* 6.00 15.00
4 Tommaso Ciampa/65* 4.00 10.00
5 War Raiders/91* 4.00 10.00
6 Johnny Gargano/131* 4.00 10.00
7 Shayna Baszler/104* 5.00 12.00
8 Velveteen Dream/93* 6.00 15.00
9 Matt Riddle/36* 4.00 10.00
10 Street Profits/34* 5.00 12.00
11 Velveteen Dream/36* 5.00 12.00
12 Shayna Baszler/36* 5.00 12.00
13 Adam Cole/56* 5.00 12.00
14 The Street Profits/64* 4.00 10.00
15 Io Shirai/93* 5.00 12.00
16 The Velveteen Dream/65* 4.00 10.00
17 Shayna Baszler/80* 5.00 12.00
18 Adam Cole/86* 4.00 10.00
19 Candice LeRae/110* 8.00 20.00
20 Roderick Strong/31* 6.00 15.00
21 Team Ripley/79*
22 Pete Dunne/46*
23 Finn Balor/38*
25 The Undisputed Era/22*
26 Tyler Bate/24*
27 Kay Lee Ray/45*
28 Gallus/36*

2020 Topps Now WWE NXT

1 Jordan Devlin/48* 6.00 15.00
2 #DIY/
3 Rhea Ripley/131* 5.00 12.00
4 Imperium/37* 8.00 20.00
5 Adam Cole/35* 5.00 12.00
6 The Broserweights/38* 6.00 15.00

7 Rhea Ripley/81*	5.00	12.00
8 Finn Balor/29*	8.00	20.00
9 Dakota Kai/88*	4.00	10.00
10 Keith Lee/34*	5.00	12.00
11 Finn Balor/42*		
12 Keith Lee/48*		
13 Adam Cole/64*		
14 Karrion Kross/88*		
15 Io Shirai/314*		
16 Io Shirai/94*		
17 Dexter Lumis/67*		
18 Tegan Nox/227*		
19 Candice LeRae/85*		
20 Keith Lee/125*		
21A Karrion Kross/		
21B Damian Priest/35*		
22A Io Shirai/		
22B Kushida/57*		
23A Damian Priest/		
23B Santos Escobar/47*		
24 Io Shirai/110*		
25 Finn Balor/*40		
26 Johnny Gargano/28*		
27 Dexter Lumis/36*		
28 Rhea Ripley/83*		
29 Io Shirai/96*		
30 Team Candice/95*	15.00	40.00
31 Johnny Gargano/42*		
32 The Undisputed Era/61*		
LR Leon Ruff/148*	5.00	12.00

2020 Topps Now WWE NXT Autograph

LRA Leon Ruff	30.00	75.00

2017 Topps Now WWE NXT TakeOver Brooklyn III

1 Bobby Roode vs. Drew McIntyre	6.00	15.00
2 Asuka vs. Ember Moon	8.00	20.00
3 AOP vs. SAnitY	6.00	15.00
4 Aleister Black vs. Hideo Itami	6.00	15.00
5 Andrade vs. Johnny Gargano	6.00	15.00

2021 Topps On-Demand WWE Best of British

1 British Bulldog
2 Drew McIntyre
3 Paige
4 Bret "Hit Man" Hart vs. British Bulldog
5 Macho Man Randy Savage vs. Ultimate Warrior
6 Papa Shango vs. Tito Santana
7 Grizzled Young Veterans
8 William Regal
9 Wade Barrett
10 Tyler Bate
11 Pete Dunne
12 Flash Morgan Webster
13 Piper Niven
14 Zack Gibson
15 Joe Coffey
16 Mark Coffey
17 Wolfgang
18 Danny Burch
19 Trent Seven
20 Mark Andrews
21 Gallus
22 Nikki Cross
23 Kay Lee Ray
24 James Drake
25 AJ Styles vs. Jinder Mahal
26 Becky Lynch
27 Finn Balor
28 Sheamus
29 Jordan Devlin
30 Killian Dain

2021 Topps On-Demand WWE Best of British Autographs

*GREEN/99: X TO X BASIC AUTOS
*BLUE/49: X TO X BASIC AUTOS
*PURPLE/25: X TO X BASIC AUTOS
*RED/10: UNPRICED DUE TO SCARCITY
*ORANGE/5: UNPRICED DUE TO SCARCITY
*GOLD/1: UNPRICED DUE TO SCARCITY
STATED ODDS

NNO AJ Styles
NNO Becky Lynch
NNO Bret Hart
NNO Drew McIntyre
NNO Finn Balor
NNO James Drake
NNO Kay Lee Ray
NNO Killian Dain
NNO Mark Andrews
NNO Mark Coffey
NNO Nikki Cross
NNO Pete Dunne
NNO Sheamus
NNO Trent Seven
NNO Tyler Bate
NNO Wade Barrett
NNO William Regal
NNO Wolfgang

2019 Topps On-Demand WWE Mother's Day

COMPLETE SET (9)	12.00	30.00
STATED PRINT RUN 107 ANNCD SETS		
1 Beth Phoenix	2.00	5.00
2 Eve Torres	1.50	4.00
3 Lacey Evans	2.50	6.00
4 Maryse	1.50	4.00
5 Mickie James	3.00	8.00
6 Naomi	2.00	5.00
7 Tamina	1.25	3.00
8 Trish Stratus	6.00	15.00
9 Stephanie McMahon	3.00	8.00

2021 Topps On-Demand WWE Summer of Cena

COMPLETE SET (15)	20.00	50.00
*PURPLE/25: 2X TO 5X BASIC CARDS		
*RED/10: UNPRICED DUE TO SCARCITY		
*ORANGE/5: UNPRICED DUE TO SCARCITY		
*GOLD/1: UNPRICED DUE TO SCARCITY		
STATED PRINT RUN ANNCD SETS		
NNO John Cena	2.50	6.00
NNO Shocking Return	2.50	6.00
NNO The Ultimate Face-Off	2.50	6.00
NNO Opening RAW	2.50	6.00
NNO Meeting the Bro	2.50	6.00
NNO Crushing Corbin	2.50	6.00
NNO Contract Is Signed	2.50	6.00
NNO Masters of the Mic	2.50	6.00
NNO Vegas Can See Him!	2.50	6.00
NNO Vegas Classic	2.50	6.00
NNO John Cena vs. Booker T	2.50	6.00
NNO John Cena vs. Randy Orton	2.50	6.00
NNO John Cena vs. Batista	2.50	6.00
NNO John Cena By the Numbers	2.50	6.00
NNO SummerSlam 2021 Poster Image	2.50	6.00

2020 Topps On-Demand WWE 30 Years of the Deadman

COMPLETE SET (40)	12.00	30.00
STATED PRINT RUN 278 SER.#'d SETS		

2020 Topps On-Demand WWE 30 Years of the Deadman Rest in Peace Relic

*NAVY BLUE/50: .75X TO 2X BASIC MEM		
*PURPLE/30: 1X TO 2.5X BASIC MEM		
*GRAY/15: UNPRICED DUE TO SCARCITY		
*BLACK/5: UNPRICED DUE TO SCARCITY		
*GOLD/1: UNPRICED DUE TO SCARCITY		
STATED PRINT RUN 99 SER.#'d SETS		
C1 Undertaker	12.00	30.00

2019 Topps On-Demand WWE WrestleMania 35 Roster

COMPLETE SET (10)	25.00	60.00
STATED PRINT RUN 75 SER.#'d SETS		
1 Kurt Angle	3.00	8.00
2 Kofi Kingston	2.50	6.00
3 The New Daniel Bryan	6.00	15.00
4 Becky Lynch	6.00	15.00
5 Charlotte Flair	6.00	15.00
6 Ronda Rousey	8.00	20.00
7 Seth Rollins	4.00	10.00
8 Brock Lesnar	6.00	15.00
9 Triple H	4.00	10.00
10 Dave Batista	4.00	10.00

2010 Topps Platinum WWE

COMPLETE SET (125)	12.00	30.00
UNOPENED BOX (24 PACKS)		
UNOPENED PACK (7 CARDS)		
*RAINBOW: .8X TO 2X BASIC CARDS		
*X-FRACTOR: 1X TO 2.5X BASIC CARDS		
*GREEN/499: 1.25X TO 3X BASIC CARDS		
*BLUE/199: 2X TO 5X BASIC CARDS		
*GOLD/50: 3X TO 8X BASIC CARDS		
*RED/1: UNPRICED DUE TO SCARCITY		
*P.P.BLACK/1: UNPRICED DUE TO SCARCITY		
*P.P.CYAN/1: UNPRICED DUE TO SCARCITY		
*P.P.MAGENTA/1: UNPRICED DUE TO SCARCITY		
*P.P.YELLOW/1: UNPRICED DUE TO SCARCITY		
1 John Cena	1.00	2.50
2 Finlay	.30	.75
3 Shad	.20	.50
4 Dean Malenko	.30	.75
5 Christian	.30	.75
6 Kane	.50	1.25
7 Luke Gallows	.20	.50
8 The Miz	.30	.75
9 Gail Kim	.50	1.25
10 Iron Sheik	.50	1.25
11 Eli Cottonwood RC	.20	.50
12 High Chief Peter Maivia	.20	.50
13 Earthquake	.30	.75
14 Melina	.75	2.00
15 Paul Bearer	.30	.75
16 Rosa Mendes RC	.30	.75
17 Ricky The Dragon Steamboat	.30	.75
18 Darren Young RC	.30	.75
19 Animal UER/Hawk on Front	.20	.50
20 JTG	.20	.50
21 Evan Bourne	.20	.50
22 Jake The Snake Roberts	.50	1.25
23 Edge	.75	2.00
24 Beth Phoenix	.75	2.00
25 Jey Uso RC	.20	.50
26 The Great Khali	.20	.50
27 Jimmy Superfly Snuka	.50	1.25
28 Layla	.50	1.25
29 Mark Henry	.30	.75
30 Arn Anderson	.30	.75
31 Jimmy Uso RC	.20	.50
32 Bushwhacker Luke	.20	.50
33 Jerry The King Lawler	.30	.75
34 Chris Masters	.20	.50
35 Bushwhacker Butch	.20	.50
36 Hawk UER/Animal on Front	.20	.50
37 Big Show	.50	1.25
38 Tamina RC	.20	.50
39 Hacksaw Jim Duggan	.30	.75
40 Cowboy Bob Orton	.30	.75
41 Percy Watson RC	.20	.50
42 Ted DiBiase	.30	.75
43 Curt Hawkins	.20	.50
44 Husky Harris RC	.40	1.00
45 Tyler Reks RC	.20	.50
46 Mr. Perfect Curt Hennig	.30	.75
47 Jillian	.75	2.00
48 CM Punk	.75	2.00
49 Vance Archer	.20	.50
50 Tiffany	.30	.75
51 Hillbilly Jim	.30	.75
52 David Otunga RC	.30	.75
53 Jack Swagger	.20	.50
54 Maryse	.75	2.00
55 Triple H	1.00	2.50
56 Michelle McCool	.75	2.00
57 Alex Riley RC	.20	.50
58 One Man Gang	.30	.75
59 Kofi Kingston	.30	.75
60 Zack Ryder	.20	.50
61 Doink	.20	.50
62 Sergeant Slaughter	.50	1.25
63 Dusty Rhodes	.50	1.25
64 Kelly Kelly	.75	2.00
65 Theodore Long	.20	.50
66 Chris Jericho	.50	1.25
67 Heath Slater RC	.30	.75
68 Natalya	.75	2.00
69 Rocky Johnson	.20	.50
70 Kaval RC	.20	.50
71 Eve	.75	2.00
72 Bobby The Brain Heenan	.30	.75
73 Undertaker	.75	2.00
74 Bam Bam Bigelow	.30	.75
75 Classy Freddie Blassie	.50	1.25
76 MVP	.30	.75
77 Goldust	.30	.75
78 Chavo Guerrero	.30	.75
79 Brian Pillman	.50	1.25
80 Lucky Cannon RC	.20	.50
81 Drew McIntyre RC	.30	.75
82 Ranjin Singh	.20	.50

83 Papa Shango	.20	.50
84 William Regal	.50	1.25
85 Titus O'Neil RC	.20	.50
86 Trent Barreta RC	.20	.50
87 Nikki Bella	.75	2.00
88 R-Truth	.20	.50
89 Vader	.30	.75
90 Skip Sheffield RC	.30	.75
91 Tyson Kidd	.20	.50
92 Michael Tarver RC	.30	.75
93 John Morrison	.30	.75
94 Michael McGillicutty RC	.20	.50
95 Koko B. Ware	.30	.75
96 Don Muraco	.30	.75
97 Randy Orton	.75	2.00
98 Harley Race	.30	.75
99 British Bulldog	.30	.75
100 Sheamus RC	.30	.75
101 Justin Gabriel RC	.30	.75
102 Yoshi Tatsu RC	.20	.50
103 Ezekiel Jackson	.20	.50
104 Terry Funk	.50	1.25
105 Mr. Wonderful Paul Orndorff	.50	1.25
106 David Hart Smith	.20	.50
107 Ravishing Rick Rude	.30	.75
108 Nikolai Volkoff	.30	.75
109 Cody Rhodes	.20	.50
110 Hornswoggle	.30	.75
111 Primo	.20	.50
112 Santino Marella	.20	.50
113 Rey Mysterio	.50	1.25
114 Wade Barrett RC	.30	.75
115 Dolph Ziggler	.30	.75
116 Million Dollar Man Ted DiBiase	.30	.75
117 Chief Jay Strongbow	.20	.50
118 Vladimir Kozlov	.30	.75
119 Junkyard Dog	.50	1.25
120 Vickie Guerrero	.20	.50
121 Rowdy Roddy Piper	.75	2.00
122 Kamala	.30	.75
123 Brie Bella	.75	2.00
124 Caylen Croft RC	.20	.50
125 Alicia Fox	.30	.75
CL Checklist	.20	.50

2010 Topps Platinum WWE Autographed Relics

*BLUE/99: .75X TO 1.5X BASIC AUTOS
*GOLD/25: 1X TO 2X BASIC AUTOS
STATED PRINT RUN 275 SER. #'d SETS

1 John Cena	20.00	50.00
5 Christian	10.00	25.00
8 The Miz	10.00	25.00
21 Evan Bourne	12.00	30.00
23 Edge	15.00	40.00
37 Big Show	15.00	40.00
48 CM Punk	35.00	70.00
59 Kofi Kingston	12.00	30.00
76 MVP	10.00	25.00
97 Randy Orton	15.00	40.00

2010 Topps Platinum WWE Autographs

*BLUE/99: .75X TO 1.5X BASIC AUTOS
*GOLD/25: 1X TO 2X BASIC AUTOS
*RED/1: UNPRICED DUE TO SCARCITY
*P.P.BLACK/1: UNPRICED DUE TO SCARCITY
*P.P.CYAN/1: UNPRICED DUE TO SCARCITY
*P.P.MAGENTA/1: UNPRICED DUE TO SCARCITY
*P.P.YELLOW/1: UNPRICED DUE TO SCARCITY
STATED PRINT RUN 271 SER.#'d SETS

6 Kane	15.00	40.00
42 Ted DiBiase	12.00	30.00
43 Curt Hawkins	6.00	15.00
45 Tyler Reks	6.00	15.00
52 David Otunga	8.00	20.00
54 Maryse	20.00	50.00
56 Michelle McCool	20.00	50.00
60 Zack Ryder	8.00	20.00
64 Kelly Kelly	20.00	50.00
65 Theodore Long	8.00	20.00
66 Chris Jericho	25.00	60.00
81 Drew McIntyre	12.00	30.00
86 Trent Barreta	8.00	20.00
114 Wade Barrett	12.00	30.00
115 Dolph Ziggler	12.00	30.00
124 Caylen Croft UER/Misspelled Caylan	8.00	20.00
125 Alicia Fox	12.00	30.00

2010 Topps Platinum WWE Legendary Superstars

COMPLETE SET (25)	5.00	12.00

*GREEN/499: .5X TO 1.25X BASIC CARDS
*BLUE/199: .6X TO 1.5X BASIC CARDS
*GOLD/50: 1.2X TO 3X BASIC CARDS
*RED/1: UNPRICED DUE TO SCARCITY
STATED ODDS 1:4

LS1 Evan Bourne/Jimmy Snuka	.60	1.50
LS2 Dolph Ziggler/Paul Orndorff	.60	1.50
LS3 Randy Orton/Jake Roberts	1.00	2.50
LS4 Goldust/Papa Shango	.40	1.00
LS5 R-Truth/Koko B. Ware	.40	1.00
LS6 The Miz/Michael Hayes	.40	1.00
LS7 Mark Henry/One Man Gang	.40	1.00
LS8 Big Show/Vader	.60	1.50
LS9 William Regal/Arn Anderson	.60	1.50
LS10 John Cena/Dusty Rhodes	1.25	3.00
LS11 Drew McIntyre/Rick Rude	.40	1.00
LS12 Edge/Brian Pillman	1.00	2.50
LS13 Chris Jericho/Roddy Piper	1.00	2.50
LS14 The Usos/Wild Samoans	.40	1.00
LS15 Kane/Bam Bam Bigelow	.60	1.50
LS16 Daniel Bryan/Dean Malenko	.40	1.00
LS17 Sheamus/Iron Sheik	.60	1.50
LS18 Triple H/Harley Race	1.25	3.00
LS19 Curt Hawkins/Curt Hennig	.40	1.00
LS20 Ted DiBiase/Tully Blanchard	.40	1.00
LS21 MVP/Ted DiBiase	.40	1.00
LS22 Rey Mysterio/Ricky Steamboat	.60	1.50
LS23 CM Punk/Terry Funk	1.00	2.50
LS24 Brothers of Destruction	1.00	2.50
Legion of Doom		
LS25 Wade Barrett/British Bulldog	.40	1.00

2010 Topps Platinum WWE Platinum Performance

COMPLETE SET (25)	6.00	15.00

*GREEN/499: .5X TO 1.25X BASIC CARDS
*BLUE/199: .6X TO 1.5X BASIC CARDS
*GOLD/50: 1.2X TO 3X BASIC CARDS
*RED/1: UNPRICED DUE TO SCARCITY
STATED ODDS 1:4

PP1 Pat Patterson	.40	1.00
PP2 Bobby The Brain Heenan	.40	1.00
PP3 Chris Jericho	.60	1.50
PP4 Randy Orton	1.00	2.50
PP5 Hacksaw Jim Duggan	.40	1.00
PP6 Triple H	1.25	3.00
PP7 CM Punk	1.00	2.50
PP8 The British Bulldog	.40	1.00
PP9 Beth Phoenix	1.00	2.50
PP10 John Cena	1.25	3.00
PP11 Jimmy Superfly Snuka	.60	1.50
PP12 Sheamus	.40	1.00
PP13 Chris Jericho	.60	1.50
PP14 Big Show	.60	1.50
PP15 Rey Mysterio	.60	1.50
PP16 The Hart Dynasty	.40	1.00
PP17 Undertaker	1.00	2.50
PP18 Million Dollar Man Ted DiBiase	.40	1.00
PP19 Vladimir Kozlov	.40	1.00
PP20 Edge	1.00	2.50
PP21 John Morrison	.40	1.00
PP22 Harley Race	.40	1.00
PP23 MVP	.40	1.00
PP24 Eve	1.00	2.50
PP25 Ricky The Dragon Steamboat	.40	1.00

2010 Topps Platinum WWE Relics

*GREEN/399: .5X TO 1.25X BASIC MEM
*BLUE/99: .6X TO 1.5X BASIC MEM
*GOLD/50: 1.2X TO 3X BASIC MEM
*RED/10: UNPRICED DUE TO SCARCITY
STATED ODDS ONE PER HOBBY BOX

1 John Cena	8.00	20.00
5 Christian	5.00	12.00
8 The Miz	5.00	12.00
23 Edge	6.00	15.00
37 Big Show	6.00	15.00
48 CM Punk	8.00	20.00
55 Triple H	8.00	20.00
59 Kofi Kingston	5.00	12.00
76 MVP	5.00	12.00
88 R-Truth	5.00	12.00
91 Tyson Kidd	6.00	15.00
93 John Morrison	8.00	20.00
97 Randy Orton	10.00	25.00
100 Sheamus	6.00	15.00
106 David Hart Smith	5.00	12.00

2010 Topps Platinum WWE Triple Relics

STATED PRINT RUN 99 SER.#'d SETS

PTR1 TripleH/Cena/Edge	25.00	50.00
PTR2 Morrison/Kingston/Miz	20.00	40.00
PTR3 Bourne/Truth/Christian	20.00	40.00
PTR4 Rhodes/Bourne/MVP	20.00	40.00
PTR5 Christian/Edge/Kidd	20.00	40.00
PTR6 Sheamus/Mysterio/Orton/75	25.00	50.00
PTR7 Cena/Sheamus/Morrison	25.00	50.00
PTR8 Orton/Smith/Marella	25.00	50.00
PTR9 Show/Edge/Punk	20.00	40.00
PTR10 Punk/Miz/Mysterio/75	20.00	40.00

1999 Topps WCW Embossed

COMPLETE SET (72)	10.00	25.00
UNOPENED BOX (36 PACKS)		
UNOPENED PACK (8 CARDS)		
1 Title Card	.12	.30
2 Buff Bagwell	.12	.30
3 Lash LeRoux RC	.12	.30
4 Chris Benoit	.20	.50
5 Rick Steiner	.20	.50
6 Diamond Dallas Page	.25	.60
7 Disco Inferno	.12	.30
8 Bobby Duncum, Jr. RC	.12	.30
9 Vampiro RC	.12	.30
10 Rowdy Roddy Piper	.40	1.00
11 Arn Anderson	.25	.60
12 Sid Vicious	.12	.30
13 Macho Man Randy Savage	.40	1.00
14 Ric Flair	1.00	2.50
15 Saturn	.12	.30
16 Goldberg	.30	1.00
17 Steven Regal	.12	.30
18 Juventud Guerrera	.20	.50
19 Chavo Guerrero, Jr.	.12	.30
20 Eddy Guerrero	.20	.50
21 Shane Douglas RC	.12	.30
22 Sting	.60	1.50
23 Rey Mysterio, Jr.	.30	.75
24 Booker T.	.20	.50
25 Stevie Ray	.12	.30
26 Bret Hart	.20	.50
27 Barry Windham	.12	.30
28 Scott Norton	.12	.30
29 Curt Hennig	.25	.60
30 Kaos RC	.12	.30
31 Scotty Riggs	.12	.30
32 Hugh Morrus	.12	.30
33 Ernest The Cat Miller	.12	.30
34 Kanyon	.12	.30
35 Kaz Hayashi	.12	.30
36 Billy Kidman	.12	.30
37 Konnan	.12	.30
38 Psychosis	.12	.30
39 Lenny Lane RC	.12	.30
40 Lodi	.12	.30
41 Meng	.12	.30
42 Dean Malenko	.12	.30
43 Prince Iaukea RC	.12	.30
44 Berlyn	.12	.30
45 David Flair RC	.12	.30
46 Evan Karagias RC	.12	.30
47 Jimmy Hart P	.20	.50
48 JJ Dillon P	.12	.30
49 Charles Robinson P RC	.12	.30
50 Hardcore Hak DHD RC	.12	.30
51 Brian Knobs DHD	.12	.30
52 Bam Bam Bigelow DHD	.20	.50
53 Jerry Flynn DHD RC	.12	.30
54 Fit Finlay DHD	.12	.30
55 Hulk Hogan	2.00	5.00
56 Kevin Nash	.30	.75
57 Scott Steiner	.30	.75
58 Lex Luger	.25	.60
59 Scott Hall	.12	.30
60 Horace Hogan RC	.12	.30
61 Vincent	.12	.30
62 Kimberly WOW	.20	.50
63 Chae WOW	.20	.50
64 Spice WOW	.20	.50
65 Tygress WOW	.20	.50
66 Fyre WOW	.20	.50
67 A.C. Jazz WOW	.20	.50
68 Storm WOW RC	.20	.50
69 Asya WOW RC	.20	.50
70 Madusa WOW	.20	.50
71 Gorgeous George WOW RC	.20	.50

72 Miss Elizabeth WOW	.30	.75
NNO Hulk Hogan RR	25.00	50.00

1999 Topps WCW Embossed Authentic Signatures

STATED ODDS 1:49

NNO Asya	20.00	50.00
NNO Barbarian	50.00	100.00
NNO Blitzkrieg	15.00	40.00
NNO Brad Armstrong	25.00	60.00
NNO Buff Bagwell	75.00	150.00
NNO Chastity	30.00	75.00
NNO Chris Adams	50.00	100.00
NNO Dave Taylor	20.00	50.00
NNO Doug Dillinger	15.00	40.00
NNO Eric Watts	30.00	75.00
NNO Gorgeous George	100.00	200.00
NNO Hacksaw Jim Duggan	30.00	75.00
NNO Horace Hogan	25.00	60.00
NNO Jerry Flynn	25.00	60.00
NNO Kendall Windham	75.00	150.00
NNO Lash Laroux	20.00	50.00
NNO Lex Luger	60.00	120.00
NNO Lizmark, Jr.	20.00	50.00
NNO Madusa	50.00	100.00
NNO Outrageous Evan Karagios	20.00	50.00
NNO Sarge Buddy Lee Parker	20.00	50.00
NNO Scott Hudson	30.00	75.00
NNO Scotty Putsky	25.00	60.00
NNO Steve Regal	50.00	100.00
NNO Tank Abbott	50.00	100.00
NNO Tough Tom	20.00	50.00
NNO Van Hammer	30.00	75.00

1999 Topps WCW Embossed Chrome

COMPLETE SET (5)		12.00
STATED ODDS 1:6		
1 Buff Bagwell/Lex Luger	1.50	4.00
2 Goldberg/Kevin Nash	2.50	6.00
3 Randy Savage/Gorgeous George	2.50	6.00
4 Ric Flair/David Flair	2.00	5.00
5 Scott Steiner/Rick Steiner	1.25	3.00

1999 Topps WCW Embossed Promos

P1 Buff Bagwell	1.00	2.50
P2 Gorgeous George	1.50	4.00

1998 Topps WCW/nWo

COMPLETE SET (72)	30.00	75.00
UNOPENED BOX (36 PACKS)		
UNOPENED PACK (4 CARDS)		
1 Hollywood Hogan	4.00	10.00
2 Sting	1.25	3.00
3 Kevin Nash	.40	1.00
4 Macho Man Randy Savage	1.25	3.00
5 Bret Hart	1.25	3.00
6 Lex Luger	.30	.75
7 Giant RC	3.00	8.00
8 Diamond Dallas Page	.40	1.00
9 Goldberg RC	10.00	25.00
10 Scott Hall	.75	2.00
11 Rick Steiner	.20	.50
12 Scott Steiner	.30	.75
13 Buff Bagwell	.60	1.50
14 Scott Norton RC	.12	.30
15 Booker T	.20	.50
16 Rowdy Roddy Piper	1.50	4.00
17 Chris Benoit RC	3.00	8.00
18 Raven RC	.12	.30
19 Chris Jericho RC	4.00	10.00
20 Ravishing Rick Rude	.30	.75
21 Konnan RC	.12	.30
22 Saturn RC	.12	.30
23 Sick Boy RC	.12	.30
24 British Bulldog	.20	.50
25 Juventud Guerrera RC	.12	.30
26 Dean Malenko RC	.12	.30
27 Eddy Guerrero RC	4.00	10.00
28 Chavo Guerrero Jr. RC	.12	.30
29 Ultimo Dragon RC	.12	.30
30 Disco Inferno RC	.12	.30
31 Wrath	.12	.30
32 Rey Mysterio Jr. RC	8.00	20.00
33 Psychosis RC	.12	.30
34 Stevie Ray	.12	.30
35 Jimmy Hart	.20	.50
36 Steve McMichael	.20	.50
37 Curt Hennig	.30	.75
38 Meng	.12	.30
39 Vincent	.12	.30
40 Fit Finley RC	.12	.30
41 Jay Leno	3.00	8.00
42 Alex Wright	.12	.30
43 Tenay/Schiavone/Heenan	.12	.30
44 Hugh Morrus RC	.12	.30
45 Kaz Hayashi RC	.12	.30
46 Kanyon RC	.12	.30
47 The Disciple	.20	.50
48 Jim Neidhart	.12	.30
49 Arn Anderson	.20	.50
50 Eric Bischoff	1.25	3.00
51 Ernest Miller RC	.12	.30
52 Miss Elizabeth	2.00	5.00
53 Gene Okerlund	.20	.50
54 Ric Flair	.75	2.00
55 Brian Adams	.20	.50
56 Lodi RC	.12	.30
57 Riggs RC	.12	.30
58 Fyre NG RC	1.25	3.00
59 Chae NG RC	1.25	3.00
60 Kimberly NG	1.25	3.00
61 Spice NG RC	1.25	3.00
62 A.C. Jazz NG RC	1.25	3.00
63 Tygress NG RC	1.25	3.00
64 Whisper NG RC	1.25	3.00
65 Hollywood Hogan ICON	5.00	12.00
66 Macho Man Randy Savage ICON	1.25	3.00
67 Rowdy Roddy Piper ICON	1.25	3.00
68 Goldberg CH	2.00	5.00
69 Chris Jericho CH	3.00	8.00
70 Bret Hart CH	.30	.75
71 Kidman CH RC	.12	.30
72 Checklist (Hogan/Goldberg)	.12	2.00

1998 Topps WCW/nWo Authentic Signatures

STATED ODDS 1:40 HOBBY

NNO Alex Wright	25.00	60.00
NNO Arn Anderson	75.00	150.00
NNO Bobby Heenan	125.00	250.00
NNO Chris Benoit	500.00	1000.00
NNO Chris Jericho	300.00	600.00
NNO Dean Malenko	100.00	200.00
NNO Diamond Dallas Page	125.00	250.00
NNO The Disciple	25.00	60.00
NNO Disco Inferno	25.00	60.00
NNO Eddy Guerrero	750.00	1500.00
NNO Ernest Miller	100.00	200.00
NNO Fit Finley	30.00	75.00
NNO Fyre	30.00	75.00
NNO Gene Okerlund	100.00	200.00
NNO Giant	125.00	250.00
NNO Hollywood Hogan	300.00	500.00
NNO Jimmy Hart	30.00	75.00
NNO Juventud Guerrera	30.00	75.00
NNO Kanyon	25.00	60.00
NNO Kaz Hayashi	30.00	75.00
NNO Kevin Nash	50.00	100.00
NNO Kidman	60.00	120.00
NNO Konnan	30.00	75.00
NNO Lodi	20.00	50.00
NNO Meng	30.00	75.00
NNO Mike Tenay	15.00	40.00
NNO Psychosis	75.00	150.00
NNO Raven	50.00	100.00
NNO Riggs	50.00	100.00
NNO Saturn	30.00	75.00
NNO Sick Boy	50.00	100.00
NNO Spice	30.00	75.00
NNO Tony Schiavone	60.00	120.00
NNO Tygress	25.00	60.00
NNO Vincent	15.00	40.00
NNO Whisper	25.00	60.00
NNO Wrath	30.00	75.00

1998 Topps WCW/nWo Chrome

COMPLETE SET (10)	20.00	40.00
STATED ODDS 1:12 HOBBY EXCLUSIVE		
C1 Goldberg	8.00	20.00
C2 Diamond Dallas Page	2.50	6.00
C3 Macho Man Randy Savage	6.00	15.00
C4 Sting	6.00	15.00
C5 Hollywood Hogan	12.00	30.00
C6 Kevin Nash	2.50	6.00
C7 Konnan	1.25	3.00
C8 Bret Hart	3.00	8.00
C9 Giant	2.00	5.00
C10 Lex Luger	2.00	5.00

1998 Topps WCW/nWo Retail Stickers

COMPLETE SET (10)	5.00	12.00
STATED ODDS 1:1 RETAIL EXCLUSIVE		
S1 Goldberg	2.00	5.00
S2 Diamond Dallas Page	.60	1.50
S3 Macho Man Randy Savage	1.50	4.00
S4 Sting	2.50	6.00
S5 Hollywood Hogan	2.00	5.00
S6 Kevin Nash	.50	1.25
S7 Konnan	.40	1.00
S8 Bret Hart	1.25	3.00
S9 Giant	.60	1.50
S10 Lex Luger	.40	1.00

1998 Topps WCW/nWo Promos

P1 Hollywood Hogan	1.00	2.50
P2 Sting	1.25	3.00
P3 Macho Man	.75	2.00
P4 Diamond Dallas Page	.60	1.50
P5 Goldberg	1.00	2.50

1999 Topps WCW/nWo Nitro

COMPLETE SET (72)	6.00	15.00
UNOPENED BOX (36 PACKS)		
UNOPENED PACK (8 CARDS)		
1 Checklist	.12	.30
2 Bret Hart	.25	.60
3 Diamond Dallas Page	.25	.60
4 Goldberg	.30	.75
5 Rick Steiner	.20	.50
6 Booker T	.20	.50
7 Chris Jericho	.20	.50
8 Saturn	.12	.30
9 Bam Bam Bigelow	.20	.50
10 Chavo Guerrero, Jr.	.12	.30
11 Disco Inferno	.12	.30
12 Wrath	.12	.30
13 Rey Misterio, Jr.	.25	.60
14 Meng	.12	.30
15 Super Calo RC	.12	.30
16 Glacier RC	.12	.30
17 Silver King RC	.12	.30
18 Kaos RC	.12	.30
19 Lenny Lane RC	.12	.30
20 Norman Smiley RC	.40	1.00
21 Kidman	.12	.30
22 Alex Wright	.12	.30
23 Kanyon	.12	.30
24 Raven	.12	.30
25 Lodi	.12	.30
26 Ernest Miller	.20	.50
27 The Disciple	.20	.50
28 Bobby Duncum, Jr. RC	.12	.30
29 Barry Windham	.12	.30
30 Konnan	.12	.30
31 Buff Bagwell	.12	.30
32 Eric Bischoff	.12	.30
33 Hollywood Hogan	1.50	4.00
34 Scott Hall	.12	.30
35 Horace Hogan RC	.12	.30
36 Scott Steiner	.25	.60
37 Stevie Ray	.12	.30
38 Brian Adams	.12	.30
39 Vincent	.12	.30
40 Curt Hennig	.25	.60
41 Macho Man Randy Savage	.40	1.00
42 Sting	.60	1.50
43 Kevin Nash	.30	.75
44 Lex Luger	.25	.60
45 Ric Flair	1.00	2.50
46 Arn Anderson	.20	.50
47 Dean Malenko	.12	.30
48 Chris Benoit	.25	.60
49 Steve McMichael	.20	.50
50 Juventud Guerrera	.12	.30
51 Eddie Guerrero	.20	.50
52 Psychosis	.12	.30
53 La Parka RC	.12	.30
54 Damian RC	.12	.30
55 Hector Garza RC	.12	.30
56 Miss Elizabeth	.30	.75
57 Kimberly	.20	.50
58 Spice	.20	.50
59 A.C. Jazz	.20	.50
60 Tygress	.20	.50
61 Whisper	.20	.50
62 Chae	.20	.50
63 Fyre	.20	.50

64 Storm RC	.20	.50
65 Goldberg Triumphant	.30	.75
66 The Venomous Bite of Sting	.40	1.00
67 Hogan for President	.60	1.50
68 Kevin Nash Is God	.30	.75
69 DDP Is Back Again	.25	.60
70 Larry Zbyszko/Bobby Heenan	.20	.50
71 Doug Dellinger	.12	.30
72 Sonny Onoo RC	.12	.30

1999 Topps WCW/nWo Nitro Authentic Signatures

STATED ODDS 1:40 HOBBY

NNO A.C. Jazz	25.00	60.00
NNO Bam Bam Bigelow	150.00	300.00
NNO Billy Silverman	30.00	75.00
NNO Bret Hart	100.00	200.00
NNO Brian Adams	100.00	200.00
NNO Chae	20.00	50.00
NNO Charles Robinson	25.00	60.00
NNO Chavo Guerrero, Jr.	15.00	40.00
NNO Curt Hennig	250.00	400.00
NNO Cyclope	12.00	30.00
NNO Damian	50.00	100.00
NNO David Penzer	15.00	40.00
NNO El Dandy	10.00	25.00
NNO Glacier	75.00	150.00
NNO Goldberg	200.00	400.00
NNO Hector Garza	12.00	30.00
NNO Hugh Morrus	25.00	60.00
NNO Jim Neidhart	50.00	100.00
NNO Kenny Kaos	15.00	40.00
NNO Kimberly	125.00	250.00
NNO La Parka	50.00	100.00
NNO Larry Zbyszko	25.00	60.00
NNO Lenny Lane	25.00	60.00
NNO Macho Man Randy Savage	500.00	1000.00
NNO Ms. Elizabeth	400.00	800.00
NNO Nick Patrick	10.00	25.00
NNO Norman Smiley	12.00	30.00
NNO Prince Iaukea	10.00	25.00
NNO Rick Steiner	100.00	200.00
NNO Scott Hall	125.00	250.00
NNO Scott Norton	20.00	50.00
NNO Silver King	10.00	25.00
NNO Sonny Onoo	30.00	75.00
NNO Sting	150.00	300.00
NNO Storm	50.00	100.00
NNO Super Calo	10.00	25.00
NNO Ultimo Dragon	30.00	75.00

1999 Topps WCW/nWo Nitro Chrome

COMPLETE SET (12) 30.00 60.00
STATED ODDS 1:12 HOBBY

C1 Sting/Luger v. Hogan/Nash	3.00	8.00
C2 Hogan v. Sting	4.00	10.00
C3 Hogan v. Savage	3.00	8.00
C4 Savage v. Sting	2.50	6.00
C5 Nash v. Giant	3.00	8.00
C6 Hogan/Hart v. Savage/Piper	4.00	10.00
C7 DDP v. Hogan	3.00	8.00
C8 DDP v. Hogan	3.00	8.00
C9 WCW v. The Pac v. Hollywood	3.00	8.00
C10 Goldberg v. DDP	2.50	6.00
C11 60 Man 3 Ring Battle Royal	1.50	4.00
C12 Nash v. Goldberg	3.00	8.00

1999 Topps WCW/nWo Nitro Stickers

COMPLETE SET (12) 3.00 6.00
STATED ODDS 1:1 RETAIL

S1 Sting/Luger v. Hogan/Nash	.40	1.00
S2 Hogan v. Sting	.40	1.00
S3 Hogan v. Savage	.30	.75
S4 Savage v. Sting	.20	.50
S5 Nash v. Giant	.20	.50
S6 Hogan/Hart v. Savage/Piper	.40	1.00
S7 DDP v. Hogan	.40	1.00
S8 DDP v. Hogan	.40	1.00
S9 WCW v. The Pac v. Hollywood	.40	1.00
S10 Goldberg v. DDP	.30	.75
S11 60 Man 3 Ring Battle Royal	.20	.50
S12 Nash v. Goldberg	.30	.75

1999 Topps WCW/nWo Nitro Promos

D1 IS DEALER EXCLUSIVE

B1 Nash and Nitro Girls DE	3.00	8.00
H1 Goldberg	2.00	5.00
H2 Kevin Nash	.75	2.00
H3 Goldberg	1.25	3.00
R1 Goldberg		

2009 Topps WWE

COMPLETE SET (90) 15.00 30.00
UNOPENED BOX (24 PACKS)
UNOPENED PACK (7 CARDS)
*GOLD/500: 1.2X TO 3X BASIC CARDS
*BLACK/40: 5X TO 12X BASIC CARDS
*PLATINUM/1: UNPRICED DUE TO SCARCITY

1 Hurricane Helms	.15	.40
2 Carlito	.40	1.00
3 CM Punk	.25	.60
4 Maria	.60	1.50
5 Kofi Kingston	.15	.40
6 Primo	.15	.40
7 Rey Mysterio	.40	1.00
8 Natalya	.60	1.50
9 Tommy Dreamer	.15	.40
10 Michelle McCool	.60	1.50
11 Undertaker	.75	2.00
12 Big Show	.40	1.00
13 Charlie Haas	.15	.40
14 Chris Jericho	.40	1.00
15 Evan Bourne	.15	.40
16 Layla	.40	1.00
17 Christian	.40	1.00
18 Cody Rhodes	.15	.40
19 Dolph Ziggler RC	.25	.60
20 Randy Orton	.40	1.00
21 Edge	.60	1.50
22 Mickie James	.75	2.00
23 Festus	.15	.40
24 Finlay	.25	.60
25 Ted DiBiase	.25	.60
26 Goldust	.25	.60
27 Melina	.60	1.50
28 Hornswoggle	.25	.60
29 Jack Swagger RC	.15	.40
30 Jim Ross	.15	.40
31 Mark Henry	.25	.60
32 Katie Lea Burchill	.40	1.00
33 Mike Knox	.15	.40
34 Kelly Kelly	.60	1.50
35 Matt Hardy	.60	1.50
36 Montel Vontavious Porter	.25	.60
37 R-Truth	.15	.40
38 John Cena	1.00	2.50
39 William Regal	.40	1.00
40 Santino Marella	.15	.40
41 Tyson Kidd RC	.15	.40
42 Maryse	.40	1.00
43 Shelton Benjamin	.15	.40
44 The Brian Kendrick	.25	.60
45 The Great Khali	.15	.40
46 Eve	.60	1.50
47 The Miz	.25	.60
48 Triple H	1.00	2.50
49 Vladimir Kozlov	.25	.60
50 Alicia Fox RC	.25	.60
51 Beth Phoenix	.75	2.00
52 Gail Kim	.40	1.00
53 Jerry The King Lawler	.25	.60
54 Theodore Long	.15	.40
55 Batista	.60	1.50
56 Tiffany	.25	.60
57 Ranjin Singh RC	.15	.40
58 Tony Atlas	.15	.40
59 Kane	.60	1.50
60 Shawn Michaels	1.00	2.50
61 Chavo Guerrero	.25	.60
62 John Morrison	.25	.60
63 Jamie Noble	.15	.40
64 Jimmy Wang Yang	.15	.40
65 Kung Fu Naki	.15	.40
66 Paul Burchill	.15	.40
67 Jillian Hall	.60	1.50
68 David Hart Smith	.15	.40
69 Curt Hawkins	.15	.40
70 DJ Gabriel RC	.15	.40
71 Ezekiel Jackson	.15	.40
72 Jesse	.15	.40
73 Zack Ryder	.15	.40
74 JTG	.15	.40
75 Shad Gaspard	.15	.40
76 Ricky Ortiz	.15	.40
77 Brie Bella RC	5.00	12.00
78 Nikki Bella RC	6.00	15.00
79 CM Punk	.25	.60
80 Santina Marella	.15	.40
81 Chris Jericho	.40	1.00
82 Matt Hardy	.60	1.50
83 Rey Mysterio	.40	1.00
84 Undertaker/Shawn Michaels	1.00	2.50
85 Edge	.60	1.50
86 John Cena	1.00	2.50
87 Randy Orton	.40	1.00
88 Triple H	1.00	2.50
89 Stone Cold Steve Austin	1.00	2.50
90 John Cena CL	1.00	2.50

2009 Topps WWE Autographs

STATED ODDS 1:54 HOBBY; 1:172 RETAIL

NNO Arn Anderson	20.00	50.00
NNO Beth Phoenix	12.00	30.00
NNO Evan Bourne	6.00	15.00
NNO Gail Kim	12.00	30.00
NNO Jim Ross	10.00	25.00
NNO John Cena	30.00	75.00
NNO John Morrison	15.00	40.00
NNO Maryse	30.00	75.00
NNO Michelle McCool	12.00	30.00
NNO Mickie James	15.00	40.00
NNO Ricky Steamboat	12.00	30.00
NNO Santino Marella	6.00	15.00
NNO Tiffany	12.00	30.00

2009 Topps WWE Dual Autographs

STATED ODDS 1:55 HOBBY EXCLUSIVE

NNO Bob & Randy Orton	60.00	120.00
NNO Carlito/Primo	12.00	30.00
NNO Dusty & Cody Rhodes	150.00	300.00
NNO Ted DiBiase Sr. & Jr.	12.00	30.00

2009 Topps WWE Event-Worn Ringside Relics

STATED ODDS 1:24 HOBBY; 1:84 RETAIL

NNO Christian	6.00	15.00
NNO Cody Rhodes	6.00	15.00
NNO Miz (looking left)	5.00	12.00
NNO Miz (looking right)	5.00	12.00
NNO Santino Marella (hands apart)	6.00	15.00
NNO Santino Marella (hands clasped)	6.00	15.00
NNO Shawn Michaels (no hat)	8.00	20.00
NNO Shawn Michaels (w/hat)	8.00	20.00
NNO Ted DiBiase	6.00	15.00
NNO Triple H	8.00	20.00

2009 Topps WWE Historical Commemorative Patches

COMPLETE SET (4) 12.00 30.00
STATED ODDS 1:RETAIL BLASTER BOX

P1 John Cena WrestleMania	6.00	15.00
P2 John Cena The Bash	6.00	15.00
P3 John Cena SummerSlam	6.00	15.00
P4 John Cena Royal Rumble	6.00	15.00

2009 Topps WWE Judgment Day Mat Relic Autographs

STATED ODDS 1:215 HOBBY EXCLUSIVE

NNO Christian	25.00	60.00
NNO Edge	30.00	75.00
NNO Randy Orton	30.00	75.00
NNO Rey Mysterio	20.00	50.00

2009 Topps WWE Legends of the Ring

COMPLETE SET (20) 8.00 20.00
*GOLD/2250: .75X TO 2X BASIC CARDS
*PLATINUM/1: UNPRICE DUE TO SCARCITY
STATED ODDS 1:1 HOBBY AND RETAIL

1 Bam Bam Bigelow	1.00	2.50
2 British Bulldog	1.00	2.50
3 Chief Jay Strongbow	.60	1.50
4 Dean Malenko	1.00	2.50
5 Don Muraco	.40	1.00
6 Dusty Rhodes	1.00	2.50
7 Iron Sheik	1.00	2.50
8 Jake The Snake Roberts	1.00	2.50
9 Jimmy Superfly Snuka	1.00	2.50
10 Junkyard Dog	1.00	2.50
11 Mr. Perfect	1.00	2.50
12 Nikolai Volkoff	.60	1.50
13 Ravishing Rick Rude	1.00	2.50
14 Sgt. Slaughter	1.00	2.50

15 Superstar Billy Graham	1.00	2.50
16 Terry Funk	.60	1.50
17 Vader	.60	1.50
18 The Wild Samoans	.60	1.50
19 Gorilla Monsoon	1.00	2.50
20 Mr. Wonderful Paul Orndorff	.60	1.50

2009 Topps WWE Reign of Honor

COMPLETE SET (10) 6.00 15.00
STATED ODDS 1:6 HOBBY AND RETAIL

1 John Cena	1.50	4.00
2 Triple H	1.50	4.00
3 Jack Swagger	.25	.60
4 Rey Mysterio	.60	1.50
5 MVP	.40	1.00
6 Melina	1.00	2.50
7 Maryse	.60	1.50
8 Primo & Carlito	.60	1.50
9 Shawn Michaels	1.50	4.00
10 Undertaker	1.25	3.00

2009 Topps WWE Sketches

STATED ODDS 1:2,857 HOBBY EXCLUSIVE
UNPRICED DUE TO SCARCITY

NNO Eve
Beauty Is in the Eye of the Owner
NNO Eve/Musical Notes
NNO Eve/Passion
NNO Eve/Speak What You Feel
NNO J.Lawler/Batista
NNO J.Lawler/Big Show
NNO J.Lawler/Edge
NNO J.Lawler/Jack Swagger
NNO J.Lawler/Rey Mysterio
NNO J.Lawler/Triple H
NNO J.Lawler/Undertaker
NNO Natalya/Balance
NNO Natalya/Calm
NNO Natalya/Energy
NNO Natalya
Glory
NNO Natalya/Happy
NNO Natalya/Honour
NNO Natalya/Peace
NNO Natalya/Pride
NNO Natalya/Sparkle
NNO Natalya/Spirit
NNO Santino/Island
NNO Santino/Landscape
NNO Santino/Map of Italy
NNO Santino/Muscle
NNO Santino/Santina
NNO Santino/Santino
NNO Santino/Self Portrait 1
NNO Santino/Self Portrait 2
NNO Santino/Self Portrait 3
NNO Santino/Self Portrait w/belt

2009 Topps WWE Tin Inserts

1 Jack Swagger
2 Triple H
3 Chris Jericho
4 Rey Mysterio

2009 Topps WWE Topps Town

COMPLETE SET (30) 6.00 15.00
STATED ODDS 1:1 HOBBY AND RETAIL

1 Batista	.50	1.25
2 Beth Phoenix	.60	1.50
3 Chris Jericho	.30	.75
4 Christian	.30	.75
5 CM Punk	.20	.50
6 Cody Rhodes	.12	.30
7 Dolph Ziggler	.20	.50
8 Edge	.50	1.25
9 Evan Bourne	.12	.30
10 Gail Kim	.30	.75
11 Jack Swagger	.12	.30
12 John Cena	.75	2.00
13 John Morrison	.20	.50
14 Kofi Kingston	.12	.30
15 Maria	.50	1.25
16 Maryse	.30	.75
17 Matt Hardy	.50	1.25
18 Melina	.50	1.25
19 Michelle McCool	.50	1.25
20 Mickie James	.60	1.50
21 Montel Vontavious Porter	.20	.50
22 Randy Orton	.30	.75
23 Rey Mysterio	.30	.75
24 R-Truth	.12	.30
25 Santino Marella	.12	.30
26 Shawn Michaels	.75	2.00
27 Ted DiBiase	.20	.50
28 The Miz	.20	.50
29 Triple H	.75	2.00
30 Undertaker	.60	1.50

2010 Topps WWE

COMPLETE SET (110) 10.00 25.00
UNOPENED BOX (24 PACKS)
UNOPENED PACK (7 CARDS)
*BLUE/2010: 1X TO 2.5X BASIC CARDS
*SILVER/999: 1.2X TO 3X BASIC CARDS
*GOLD/50: 4X TO 10X BASIC CARDS
*RED/1: UNPRICED DUE TO SCARCITY
*P.P.BLACK/1: UNPRICED DUE TO SCARCITY
*P.P.CYAN/1: UNPRICED DUE TO SCARCITY
*P.P.MAGENTA/1: UNPRICED DUE TO SCARCITY
*P.P.YELLOW/1: UNPRICED DUE TO SCARCITY

1 John Cena	.75	2.00
2 Layla	.40	1.00
3 William Regal	.40	1.00
4 John Morrison	.25	.60
5 Matt Hardy	.40	1.00
6 Alicia Fox	.25	.60
7 Yoshi Tatsu RC	.15	.40
8 Nikki Bella	.60	1.50
9 Randy Orton	.60	1.50
10 Luke Gallows	.15	.40
11 MVP	.25	.60
12 Michelle McCool	.60	1.50
13 JTG	.15	.40
14 Rosa Mendes RC	.25	.60
15 Beth Phoenix	.60	1.50
16 Chris Jericho	.40	1.00
17 Kane	.40	1.00
18 Mark Henry	.25	.60
19 Tyson Kidd	.15	.40
20 Santino Marella	.15	.40
21 Theodore Long	.15	.40
22 Big Show	.40	1.00
23 Kofi Kingston	.25	.60
24 Vladimir Kozlov	.25	.60
25 Vance Archer	.15	.40
26 Brie Bella	.60	1.50
27 Ezekiel Jackson	.15	.40
28 David Hart Smith	.15	.40
29 Trent Baretta RC	.15	.40
30 Kelly Kelly	.60	1.50
31 Goldust	.25	.60
32 Maryse	.60	1.50
33 Tyler Reks RC	.15	.40
34 Serena RC	.25	.60
35 Melina	.60	1.50
36 CM Punk	.60	1.50
37 Drew McIntyre RC	.25	.60
38 Jillian	.60	1.50
39 Cody Rhodes	.15	.40
40 Ted DiBiase	.25	.60
41 Finlay	.25	.60
42 Dolph Ziggler	.25	.60
43 Triple H	.75	2.00
44 Hornswoggle	.25	.60
45 R-Truth	.15	.40
46 The Miz	.25	.60
47 Primo	.15	.40
48 Jack Swagger	.15	.40
49 Caylen Croft RC	.15	.40
50 Rey Mysterio	.40	1.00
51 Chris Masters	.15	.40
52 Chavo Guerrero	.25	.60
53 Shad	.15	.40
54 Ranjin Singh	.15	.40
55 Sheamus RC	.25	.60
56 Vickie Guerrero	.15	.40
57 Evan Bourne	.15	.40
58 Edge	.60	1.50
59 The Undertaker	.60	1.50
60 Zack Ryder	.15	.40
61 Natalya	.60	1.50
62 The Great Khali	.15	.40
63 Eve	.60	1.50
64 Christian	.25	.60
65 Michael Tarver RC	.25	.60
66 Skip Sheffield RC	.25	.60
67 Wade Barrett RC	.25	.60
68 Daniel Bryan RC	8.00	20.00
69 Darren Young RC	.25	.60
70 David Otunga RC	.25	.60
71 Heath Slater RC	.25	.60
72 Justin Gabriel RC	.25	.60
73 Undertaker 18-0	.60	1.50
74 ShowMiz	.40	1.00
75 The Dude Busters	.15	.40
76 The Straight Edge Society	.60	1.50
77 Hart Dynasty	.60	1.50
78 Mr. Perfect Curt Hennig	.25	.60
79 Dean Malenko	.25	.60
80 Don Muraco	.25	.60
81 Akeem	.25	.60
82 Doink the Clown	.15	.40
83 Earthquake	.25	.60
84 Hillbilly Jim	.25	.60
85 Mr. Wonderful Paul Orndorff	.40	1.00
86 Nikolai Volkoff	.25	.60
87 Papa Shango	.15	.40
88 Vader	.25	.60
89 Sgt. Slaughter	.40	1.00
90 Junkyard Dog	.40	1.00
91 Bobby The Brain Heenan	.25	.60
92 Harley Race	.25	.60
93 The American Dream Dusty Rhodes	.40	1.00
94 Jake The Snake Roberts	.40	1.00
95 The Iron Sheik	.40	1.00
96 Koko B. Ware	.25	.60
97 Brian Pillman	.40	1.00
98 Jimmy Superfly Snuka	.40	1.00
99 Mean Gene Okerland UER	.25	.60
100 Million Dollar Man Ted DiBiase	.25	.60
101 The Bushwackers	.15	.40
102 Paul Bearer	.25	.60
103 Rowdy Roddy Piper	.60	1.50
104 Terry Funk	.40	1.00
105 Kamala	.25	.60
106 Cowboy Bob Orton	.25	.60
107 The Road Warriors	.40	1.00
108 Ravishing Rick Rude	.25	.60
109 Bam Bam Bigelow	.25	.60
110 Classy Freddie Blassie	.40	1.00
CH1 Checklist 1/2	.15	.40
CH3 Checklist 3/4	.15	.40

2010 Topps WWE Autographs

*GOLD/25: .6X TO 1.5X BASIC AUTOS
*RED/1: UNPRICED DUE TO SCARCITY
*P.P.BLACK/1: UNPRICED DUE TO SCARCITY
*P.P.CYAN/1: UNPRICED DUE TO SCARCITY
*P.P.MAGENTA/1: UNPRICED DUE TO SCARCITY
*P.P.YELLOW/1: UNPRICED DUE TO SCARCITY
OVERALL AUTO ODDS 1:BOX

ABP Beth Phoenix		
ABS Big Show	12.00	30.00
ACC Caylen Croft	6.00	15.00
ACH Christian		
ACM CM Punk	20.00	50.00
ACR Cody Rhodes	8.00	20.00
ADM Drew McIntyre	10.00	25.00
ADS David Hart Smith	8.00	20.00
AEB Evan Bourne	6.00	15.00
AED Edge	12.00	30.00
AEJ Ezekiel Jackson	6.00	15.00
AGK Gail Kim	12.00	30.00
AJC John Cena	30.00	75.00
AJM John Morrison	10.00	25.00
AJT JTG	6.00	15.00
AKK Kofi Kingston	8.00	20.00
ALG Luke Gallows	6.00	15.00
AMM Michelle McCool	12.00	30.00
ARM Rosa Mendes	10.00	25.00
ARO Randy Orton	20.00	50.00
ART R-Truth	8.00	20.00
ASE Serena	10.00	25.00
ASH Shad	6.00	15.00
ATB Trent Baretta	6.00	15.00
ATD Ted DiBiase	10.00	25.00
ATH Triple H		
ATK Tyson Kidd	8.00	20.00
ATM Miz	12.00	30.00
AVA Vance Archer	6.00	15.00
AZR Zack Ryder	8.00	20.00
ASAN Santino Marella	10.00	25.00
ASHE Sheamus	12.00	30.00
JCA1 John Cena	50.00	100.00

2010 Topps WWE Championship Material

COMPLETE SET (50) 20.00 50.00
*PUZZLE BACK: .5X TO 1.2X BASIC CARDS

*IC PUZZLE: .5X TO 1.2X BASIC CARDS
STATED ODDS 1:6 HOBBY AND RETAIL

C1 Christian	.50	1.25
C2 John Morrison	.50	1.25
C3 John Morrison	.50	1.25
C4 The Miz & John Morrison	.50	1.25
C5 CM Punk	1.25	3.00
C6 CM Punk	1.25	3.00
C7 Kofi Kingston & CM Punk	1.25	3.00
C8 The Miz	.50	1.25
C9 The Hart Dynasty	1.25	3.00
C10 Goldust	.50	1.25
C11 Triple H	1.50	4.00
C12 Edge & Chris Jericho	1.25	3.00
C13 Christian	.50	1.25
C14 Chris Jericho & Big Show	.75	2.00
C15 Chris Jericho	.75	2.00
C16 Randy Orton	1.25	3.00
C17 Big Show & The Miz	.75	2.00
C18 Edge & Christian	1.25	3.00
C19 Edge	1.25	3.00
C20 Mark Henry	.50	1.25
C21 Chavo Guerrero	.50	1.25
C22 Matt Hardy	.75	2.00
C23 Undertaker & Kane	1.25	3.00
C24 Kane	.75	2.00
C25 Kane	.75	2.00
C26 R-Truth	.30	.75
C27 John Cena	1.50	4.00
C28 Big Show	.75	2.00
C29 Ted DiBiase & Cody Rhodes	.50	1.25
C30 Drew McIntyre	.50	1.25
C31 Rey Mysterio	.75	2.00
C32 Jack Swagger	.30	.75
C33 William Regal	.75	2.00
C34 Kofi Kingston	.50	1.25
C35 Santino Marella	.30	.75
C36 Ted DiBiase	.75	2.00
C37 Michelle McCool	1.25	3.00
C38 Maryse	1.25	3.00
C39 Edge & Randy Orton	1.25	3.00
C40 Jillian	1.25	3.00
C41 Melina	1.25	3.00
C42 MVP	.50	1.25
C43 Kofi Kingston	.50	1.25
C44 Matt Hardy	.75	2.00
C45 Finlay	.50	1.25
C46 Mr. Perfect	.50	1.25
C47 Don Muraco	.50	1.25
C48 Ravishing Rick Rude	.50	1.25
C49 Rowdy Roddy Piper	1.25	3.00
C50 British Bulldog	.50	1.25

2010 Topps WWE Dual Autographs

*GOLD/25: .5X TO 1.2X BASIC AUTOS
*RED/1: UNPRICED DUE TO SCARCITY
*P.P.BLACK/1: UNPRICED DUE TO SCARCITY
*P.P.CYAN/1: UNPRICED DUE TO SCARCITY
*P.P.MAGENTA/1: UNPRICED DUE TO SCARCITY
*P.P.YELLOW/1: UNPRICED DUE TO SCARCITY
STATED PRINT RUN 99 SER.#'d SETS

DABM E.Bourne/D.McIntyre	10.00	25.00
DACB C.Croft/T.Baretta	8.00	20.00
DACO J.Cena/R.Orton	50.00	100.00
DADR T.DiBiase/C.Rhodes	12.00	30.00
DAES Edge Big Show	15.00	40.00
DAJC E.Jackson/Christian		
DAJS JTG Shad	8.00	20.00
DAJT E.Jackson/R-Truth	8.00	20.00
DAKM K.Kingston/Miz	12.00	30.00
DAMP J.Morrison/CM Punk	20.00	50.00
DAPG CM Punk/L.Gallows	20.00	50.00
DAPS CM Punk Serena	15.00	40.00
DARM Z.Ryder/R.Mendes	12.00	30.00
DASK D.Smith/T.Kidd	8.00	20.00
DASP S.Marella/B.Phoenix		
DASS S.Marella/Sheamus	12.00	30.00
DAKMC G.Kim/M.McCool	15.00	40.00

2010 Topps WWE Elimination Chamber Canvas

COMPLETE SET (19) 60.00 120.00
*GOLD/50: .75X TO 2X BASIC CARDS
*RED/1: UNPRICED DUE TO SCARCITY
OVERALL RELIC ODDS 1:2 RETAIL EXCLUSIVE

EC1 John Cena	8.00	20.00
EC2 Sheamus	2.50	6.00
EC3 Triple H	8.00	20.00
EC4 Randy Orton	6.00	15.00
EC5 Ted DiBiase Jr.	2.50	6.00
EC6 Kofi Kingston	2.50	6.00
EC7 Drew McIntyre	2.50	6.00
EC8 Kane	4.00	10.00
EC9 Michelle McCool	6.00	15.00
EC10 Layla	4.00	10.00
EC11 Maryse	6.00	15.00
EC12 The Miz	2.50	6.00
EC13 MVP	2.50	6.00
EC14 Chris Jericho	4.00	10.00
EC15 The Undertaker	6.00	15.00
EC16 John Morrison	2.50	6.00
EC17 CM Punk	6.00	15.00
EC18 Rey Mysterio	4.00	10.00
EC19 R-Truth	2.50	6.00

2010 Topps WWE Favorite Finishers

COMPLETE SET (25) 8.00 20.00
STATED ODDS 1:4 HOBBY AND RETAIL

FF1 Dolph Ziggler	.40	1.00
FF2 Jack Swagger	.25	.60
FF3 Edge	1.00	2.50
FF4 CM Punk	1.00	2.50
FF5 Sheamus	.40	1.00
FF6 Evan Bourne	.25	.60
FF7 Undertaker	1.00	2.50
FF8 John Cena	1.25	3.00
FF9 The Hart Dynasty	1.00	2.50
FF10 Yoshi Tatsu	.25	.60
FF11 Drew McIntyre	.40	1.00
FF12 MVP	.40	1.00
FF13 John Morrison	.40	1.00
FF14 Randy Orton	1.00	2.50
FF15 Big Show	.60	1.50
FF16 Kofi Kingston	.40	1.00
FF17 Matt Hardy	.60	1.50
FF18 Kane	.60	1.50
FF19 Christian	.40	1.00
FF20 Mark Henry	.40	1.00
FF21 Triple H	1.25	3.00
FF22 Beth Phoenix	1.00	2.50
FF23 Rey Mysterio	.60	1.50
FF24 Chris Jericho	.60	1.50
FF25 The Miz	.40	1.00

2010 Topps WWE History Of

COMPLETE SET (25) 10.00 25.00
STATED ODDS 1:8 HOBBY AND RETAIL

HO1 Chris Jericho	.75	2.00
HO2 Triple H	1.50	4.00
HO3 Edge	1.25	3.00
HO4 Jack Swagger	.30	.75
HO5 John Morrison	.50	1.25
HO6 The Undertaker	1.25	3.00
HO7 Kane	.75	2.00
HO8 The Miz	.50	1.25
HO9 Finlay	.50	1.25
HO10 Michelle McCool	1.25	3.00
HO11 Rey Mysterio	.75	2.00
HO12 Natalya	1.25	3.00
HO13 John Cena	1.50	4.00
HO14 Kelly Kelly	1.25	3.00
HO15 Ted DiBiase	.50	1.25
HO16 Randy Orton	1.25	3.00
HO17 Kofi Kingston	.50	1.25
HO18 Big Show	.75	2.00
HO19 Santino Marella	.30	.75
HO20 Goldust	.50	1.25
HO21 Christian	.50	1.25
HO22 William Regal	.75	2.00
HO23 British Bulldog	.50	1.25
HO24 Junkyard Dog	.75	2.00
HO25 Mr. Perfect	.50	1.25

2010 Topps WWE National Heroes

COMPLETE SET (25) 10.00 25.00
STATED ODDS 1:8 HOBBY AND RETAIL

NH1 John Cena	1.50	4.00
NH2 Maryse	1.25	3.00
NH3 Jack Swagger	.30	.75
NH4 Edge	1.25	3.00
NH5 Chris Jericho	.75	2.00
NH6 William Regal	.75	2.00
NH7 Finlay	.50	1.25
NH8 Yoshi Tatsu	.30	.75
NH9 Sheamus	.50	1.25
NH10 Sgt. Slaughter	.75	2.00
NH11 Vladimir Kozlov	.50	1.25
NH12 The Great Khali	.30	.75
NH13 Kamala	.50	1.25
NH14 Nikolai Volkoff	.50	1.25
NH15 Iron Shiek	.75	2.00
NH16 Wild Samoans	.30	.75
NH17 Kofi Kingston	.50	1.25
NH18 Drew McIntyre	.50	1.25
NH19 Santino Marella	.30	.75
NH20 Rey Mysterio	.75	2.00
NH21 Mark Henry	.50	1.25
NH22 Christian	.50	1.25
NH23 Tyson Kidd	.30	.75
NH24 Chavo Guerrero	.50	1.25
NH25 The British Bulldog	.50	1.25

2010 Topps WWE Signature Swatches

STATED PRINT RUN 25 SER. #'d SETS

SSSBS Big Show	60.00	120.00
SSSCG Chavo Guerrero	25.00	60.00
SSSCH Christian	30.00	80.00
SSSCJ Chris Jericho	50.00	100.00
SSSCM CM Punk	60.00	120.00
SSSCR Cody Rhodes	25.00	60.00
SSSDS David Hart Smith	25.00	60.00
SSSEB Evan Bourne	25.00	60.00
SSSED Edge	50.00	100.00
SSSJC John Cena	100.00	200.00
SSSJM John Morrison	50.00	100.00
SSSKK Kofi Kingston	30.00	80.00
SSSMH Matt Hardy	30.00	80.00
SSSRM Rey Mysterio	50.00	100.00
SSSRO Randy Orton	100.00	200.00
SSSSA Santino Marella EXCH	50.00	100.00
SSSSH Shad	25.00	60.00
SSSTD Ted DiBiase Jr.	25.00	60.00
SSSTK Tyson Kidd	30.00	80.00
SSSTM The Miz	30.00	80.00
SSSJTG JTG	25.00	60.00
SSSMVP MVP	30.00	80.00

2010 Topps WWE Superstar Jumbo Swatches

STATED PRINT RUN 30 SER.#'d SETS

SSSBS Big Show	50.00	100.00
SSSCG Chavo Guerrero		
SSSCH Christian	40.00	80.00
SSSCJ Chris Jericho		
SSSCM CM Punk	50.00	100.00
SSSCR Cody Rhodes	20.00	50.00
SSSDS David Hart Smith	25.00	60.00
SSSEB Evan Bourne	25.00	60.00
SSSED Edge	50.00	100.00
SSSJC John Cena	60.00	120.00
SSSJM John Morrison	40.00	80.00
SSSKK Kofi Kingston	40.00	80.00
SSSMH Matt Hardy EXCH	50.00	100.00
SSSRM Rey Mysterio	40.00	80.00
SSSRO Randy Orton	40.00	80.00
SSSSA Santino Marella EXCH	25.00	60.00
SSSSH Shad		
SSSTD Ted DiBiase Jr.		
SSSTH Triple H		
SSSTK Tyson Kidd	25.00	60.00
SSSTM The Miz	40.00	80.00
SSSTU The Undertaker		
SSSJTG JTG		
SSSMVP MVP	25.00	60.00

2010 Topps WWE Superstar Swatches

*GOLD/99: .5X TO 1.2X BASIC CARDS
*RED/1: UNPRICED DUE TO SCARCITY
OVERALL RELIC ODDS 1:BOX

JCR1 John Cena	15.00	30.00
SBS Big Show	5.00	12.00
SCG Chavo Guerrero		
SCH Christian	5.00	12.00
SCJ Chris Jericho		
SCM CM Punk	5.00	12.00
SCR Cody Rhodes	4.00	10.00
SDS David Hart Smith	4.00	10.00
SEB Evan Bourne	5.00	12.00
SED Edge	6.00	15.00
SJC John Cena	10.00	25.00
SJM John Morrison	6.00	15.00
SKK Kofi Kingston	5.00	12.00
SMH Matt Hardy EXCH	8.00	20.00

SRM Rey Mysterio	8.00	20.00
SRO Randy Orton	10.00	25.00
SSA Santino Marella EXCH	5.00	12.00
SSH Shad		
STD Ted DiBiase EXCH	6.00	15.00
STH Triple H EXCH	20.00	50.00
STK Tyson Kidd	4.00	10.00
STM The Miz	4.00	10.00
STU The Undertaker		
SJTG JTG		
SMVP MVP	4.00	10.00

2010 Topps WWE Topps Town

COMPLETE SET (25) 10.00 25.00
STATED ODDS 1:6 HOBBY AND RETAIL

TT1 John Cena	1.25	3.00
TT2 Jack Swagger	.25	.60
TT3 Rey Mysterio	.60	1.50
TT4 The Miz	.40	1.00
TT5 Kane	.60	1.50
TT6 Triple H	1.25	3.00
TT7 MVP	.40	1.00
TT8 The Undertaker	1.00	2.50
TT9 John Morisson	.40	1.00
TT10 Randy Orton	1.00	2.50
TT11 Kofi Kingston	.40	1.00
TT12 Michelle McCool	1.00	2.50
TT13 Cody Rhodes	.25	.60
TT14 Edge	1.00	2.50
TT15 Kelly Kelly	1.00	2.50
TT16 Ted DiBiase	.40	1.00
TT17 Chris Jericho	.60	1.50
TT18 CM Punk	1.00	2.50
TT19 Big Show	.60	1.50
TT20 Beth Phoenix	1.00	2.50
TT21 Sheamus	.40	1.00
TT22 Christian	.40	1.00
TT23 R-Truth	.25	.60
TT24 Ezekiel Jackson	.25	.60
TT25 Maryse	1.00	2.50

2010 Topps WWE When They Were Young

RANDOMLY INSERTED INTO PACKS

WTWY1 John Cena
WTWY2 William Regal
WTWY3 Jack Swagger
WTWY4 Chris Jericho
WTWY5 Big Show
WTWY6 Natalya
WTWY7 The Miz
WTWY8 Sheamus
WTWY9 Chavo Guerrero
WTWY10 Shad
WTWY11 Hornswoggle
WTWY12 Jerry Lawler
WTWY13 Santino Marella
WTWY14 Melina
WTWY15 Ted DiBiase Jr.
WTWY16 Cody Rhodes
WTWY17 Christian
WTWY18 Kelly Kelly
WTWY19 Rosa Mendes
WTWY20 CM Punk
WTWY21 Shelton Benjamin
WTWY22 Evan Bourne
WTWY23 R-Truth
WTWY24 Zack Ryder
WTWY25 Triple H

2010 Topps WWE World Championship Material

COMPLETE SET (25) 12.00 30.00
*PUZZLE: .5X TO 1.2X BASIC CARDS
STATED ODDS 1:6 HOBBY AND RETAIL

W1 John Cena	1.50	4.00
W2 John Cena	1.50	4.00
W3 Triple H	1.50	4.00
W4 Triple H	1.50	4.00
W5 Chris Jericho	.75	2.00
W6 Superstar Billy Graham	.75	2.00
W7 Chris Jericho	.75	2.00
W8 Sheamus	.50	1.25
W9 Randy Orton	1.25	3.00
W10 Randy Orton	1.25	3.00
W11 Kane	.75	2.00
W12 Undertaker	1.25	3.00
W13 Undertaker	1.25	3.00
W14 Rey Mysterio	.75	2.00
W15 Jack Swagger	.30	.75
W16 Melina	1.25	3.00
W17 Edge	1.25	3.00
W18 Beth Phoenix	1.25	3.00
W19 Edge	1.25	3.00
W20 Michelle McCool	1.25	3.00
W21 Big Show	.75	2.00
W22 CM Punk	1.25	3.00
W23 Sgt. Slaughter	.75	2.00
W24 The Iron Sheik	.75	2.00
W25 John Cena	1.50	4.00

2011 Topps WWE

COMPLETE SET (113) 10.00 25.00
UNOPENED BOX (24 PACKS)
UNOPENED PACK (7 CARDS)
*BLUE/2011: .8X TO 2X BASIC CARDS
*BLACK/999: 1.5X TO 4X BASIC CARDS
*GOLD/50: 4X TO 10X BASIC CARDS
*RED/1: UNPRICED DUE TO SCARCITY
*P.P.BLACK/1: UNPRICED DUE TO SCARCITY
*P.P.CYAN/1: UNPRICED DUE TO SCARCITY
*P.P.MAGENTA/1: UNPRICED DUE TO SCARCITY
*P.P.YELLOW/1: UNPRICED DUE TO SCARCITY

1 John Cena	.75	2.00
2 Randy Orton	.60	1.50
3 Rey Mysterio	.40	1.00
4 Wade Barrett	.15	.40
5 John Morrison	.25	.60
6 Natalya	.60	1.50
7 Primo	.15	.40
8 Justin Gabriel	.15	.40
9 Johnny Curtis RC	.15	.40
10 Josh Mathews	.15	.40
11 Michael McGillicutty	.15	.40
12 Jey Uso	.15	.40
13 Dolph Ziggler	.25	.60
14 Alex Riley	.15	.40
15 Kharma	.25	.60
16 Ranjin Singh	.15	.40
17 Chris Masters	.15	.40
18 Ted DiBiase	.25	.60
19 Percy Watson	.15	.40
20 Hornswoggle	.25	.60
21 David Otunga	.15	.40
22 Booker T	.25	.60
23 Mason Ryan RC	.15	.40
24 Tamina	.15	.40
25 CM Punk	.40	1.00
26 Jack Korpela RC	.15	.40
27 Kelly Kelly	.60	1.50
28 William Regal	.25	.60
29 Beth Phoenix	.40	1.00
30 The Great Khali	.15	.40
31 Michael Cole	.15	.40
32 Brodus Clay RC	.15	.40
33 Goldust	.15	.40
34 Jimmy Uso	.15	.40
35 Kofi Kingston	.15	.40
36 Matt Striker	.15	.40
37 Nikki Bella	.60	1.50
38 Yoshi Tatsu	.15	.40
39 Ricardo Rodriguez RC	.15	.40
40 Cody Rhodes	.15	.40
41 Brie Bella	.60	1.50
42 Ezekiel Jackson	.25	.60
43 Vladimir Kozlov	.25	.60
44 Sheamus	.25	.60
45 Vickie Guerrero	.25	.60
46 Alicia Fox	.25	.60
47 Drew McIntyre	.15	.40
48 Todd Grisham	.15	.40
49 Jack Swagger	.25	.60
50 Tyson Kidd	.15	.40
51 Alberto Del Rio RC	.40	1.00
52 Heath Slater	.15	.40
53 Evan Bourne	.15	.40
54 JTG	.15	.40
55 Kaitlyn RC	.40	1.00
56 Big Show	.40	1.00
57 Tyler Reks	.15	.40
58 Layla	.40	1.00
59 Justin Roberts	.15	.40
60 R-Truth	.15	.40
61 Daniel Bryan	.15	.40
62 Gail Kim	.40	1.00
63 The Miz	.25	.60
64 Chavo Guerrero	.15	.40
65 Curt Hawkins	.15	.40
66 Maryse	.60	1.50
67 Kane	.40	1.00
68 Santino Marella	.25	.60
69 Mark Henry	.25	.60
70 David Hart Smith	.15	.40
71 Rosa Mendes	.25	.60
72 Jerry The King Lawler	.40	1.00
73 Undertaker	.60	1.50
74 Melina	.60	1.50
75 Sin Cara RC	.40	1.00
76 Eve	.60	1.50
77 Theodore Long	.15	.40
78 Zack Ryder	.15	.40
79 Christian	.15	.40
80 Triple H	.75	2.00
81 Edge	.60	1.50
82 The Rock	.75	2.00
83 Darren Young	.15	.40
84 Lucky Cannon	.15	.40
85 Titus O'Neil	.15	.40
86 Byron Saxton RC	.15	.40
87 Conor O'Brian RC	.15	.40
88 Jacob Novak RC	.15	.40
89 The American Dream Dusty Rhodes	.25	.60
90 The British Bulldog	.25	.60
91 Million Dollar Man Ted DiBiase	.25	.60
92 Rowdy Roddy Piper	.60	1.50
93 Mr. Perfect	.40	1.00
94 The Iron Sheik	.40	1.00
95 Cowboy Bob Orton	.25	.60
96 Jake The Snake Roberts	.40	1.00
97 Ravishing Rick Rude	.25	.60
98 Doink the Clown	.25	.60
99 Big Boss Man	.25	.60
100 Bushwhacker Luke	.25	.60
101 Bushwhacker Butch	.25	.60
102 Yokozuna	.25	.60
103 Sgt. Slaughter	.40	1.00
104 Papa Shango	.15	.40
105 Hawk	.40	1.00
106 Animal	.40	1.00
107 Kamala	.25	.60
108 Terry Funk	.25	.60
109 Junkyard Dog	.40	1.00
110 Hacksaw Jim Duggan	.40	1.00
CL1 Checklist 1	.15	.40
CL2 Checklist 2	.15	.40
CL3 Checklist 3	.15	.40

2011 Topps WWE Autographs

NNO Alberto Del Rio	15.00	40.00
NNO Alex Riley	10.00	25.00
NNO Big Show	12.00	30.00
NNO Brie Bella	20.00	50.00
NNO Christian	10.00	25.00
NNO David Otunga	6.00	15.00
NNO Drew McIntyre	8.00	20.00
NNO Evan Bourne	6.00	15.00
NNO Eve	12.00	30.00
NNO Ezekiel Jackson	10.00	25.00
NNO John Cena	25.00	60.00
NNO Kane	12.00	30.00
NNO Kofi Kingston	10.00	25.00
NNO Mark Henry	10.00	25.00
NNO Michael McGillicutty	6.00	15.00
NNO Nikki Bella	20.00	50.00
NNO Randy Orton	20.00	50.00
NNO R-Truth	8.00	20.00
NNO Sin Cara	10.00	25.00
NNO The Miz	10.00	25.00

2011 Topps WWE Catchy Phrases

COMPLETE SET (10) 5.00 10.00
*P.P.BLACK/1: UNPRICED DUE TO SCARCITY
*P.P.CYAN/1: UNPRICED DUE TO SCARCITY
*P.P.MAGENTA/1: UNPRICED DUE TO SCARCITY
*P.P.YELLOW/1: UNPRICED DUE TO SCARCITY
STATED ODDS 1:8 HOBBY AND RETAIL

CP1 John Cena	1.50	4.00
CP2 The Miz	.50	1.25
CP3 The Rock	1.50	4.00
CP4 Undertaker	1.25	3.00
CP5 Triple H	1.50	4.00
CP6 Rey Mysterio	.75	2.00
CP7 Christian	.30	.75
CP8 Zack Ryder	.30	.75
CP9 Goldust	.30	.75
CP10 Vickie Guerrero	.50	1.25

2011 Topps WWE Dual Autographs

STATED PRINT RUN 70 SER.#'d SETS

NNO	A.Del Rio/Christian	25.00	60.00
NNO	Big Show/M.Henry	20.00	50.00
NNO	Brie Bella & Nikki Bella	60.00	120.00
NNO	D.Otunga/M.McGillicutty	12.00	30.00
NNO	Eve/K.Kingston	25.00	60.00
NNO	J.Cena/R-Truth	30.00	75.00
NNO	Kane/E.Jackson	15.00	40.00
NNO	R.Orton/E.Bourne	25.00	60.00
NNO	S.Cara/D.McIntyre	15.00	40.00
NNO	Miz/A.Riley	20.00	50.00

2011 Topps WWE Electrifying Entrances

COMPLETE SET (25) 10.00 25.00
*P.P.BLACK/1: UNPRICED DUE TO SCARCITY
*P.P.CYAN/1: UNPRICED DUE TO SCARCITY
*P.P.MAGENTA/1: UNPRICED DUE TO SCARCITY
*P.P.YELLOW/1: UNPRICED DUE TO SCARCITY
STATED ODDS 1:8 HOBBY AND RETAIL

EE1	Undertaker	1.25	3.00
EE2	John Cena	1.50	4.00
EE3	Triple H	1.50	4.00
EE4	Rey Mysterio	.75	2.00
EE5	R-Truth	.30	.75
EE6	Randy Orton	1.25	3.00
EE7	The Miz	.50	1.25
EE8	Big Show	.75	2.00
EE9	Kofi Kingston	.30	.75
EE10	Sheamus	.50	1.25
EE11	Alberto Del Rio	.75	2.00
EE12	Kane	.75	2.00
EE13	Christian	.30	.75
EE14	Jack Swagger	.50	1.25
EE15	Sin Cara	.75	2.00
EE16	Wade Barrett	.30	.75
EE17	John Morrison	.50	1.25
EE18	Drew McIntyre	.30	.75
EE19	Daniel Bryan	.30	.75
EE20	Cody Rhodes	.30	.75
EE21	Ted DiBiase	.50	1.25
EE22	Dolph Ziggler	.50	1.25
EE23	Santino Marella	.50	1.25
EE24	The Great Khali	.30	.75
EE25	Kharma	.50	1.25

2011 Topps WWE Heritage

COMPLETE SET (50) 12.00 30.00
P.P.BLACK/1: UNPRICED DUE TO SCARCITY
P.P.CYAN/1: UNPRICED DUE TO SCARCITY
P.P.MAGENTA/1: UNPRICED DUE TO SCARCITY
P.P.YELLOW/1: UNPRICED DUE TO SCARCITY
STATED ODDS 1:4 HOBBY AND RETAIL

H1	Stone Cold Steve Austin	1.00	2.50
H2	Shawn Michaels	1.00	2.50
H3	Trish Stratus	1.25	3.00
H4	Booker T	.40	1.00
H5	Jerry The King Lawler	.60	1.50
H6	Michael PS Hayes	.25	.60
H7	The American Dream Dusty Rhodes	.40	1.00
H8	The British Bulldog	.40	1.00
H9	Million Dollar Man Ted DiBiase	.40	1.00
H10	Rowdy Roddy Piper	1.00	2.50
H11	Mr. Perfect	.60	1.50
H12	Mean Gene Okerlund	.40	1.00
H13	Jimmy Superfly Snuka	.60	1.50
H14	Paul Bearer	.40	1.00
H15	Irwin R. Schyster	.25	.60
H16	Vader	.40	1.00
H17	Akeem	.25	.60
H18	Bobby The Brain Heenan	.40	1.00
H19	Kama Mustafa	.25	.60
H20	Howard Finkel	.25	.60
H21	Don Muraco	.40	1.00
H22	Harley Race	.40	1.00
H23	Brian Pillman	.40	1.00
H24	The Iron Sheik	.60	1.50
H25	Koko B. Ware	.40	1.00
H26	Gorilla Monsoon	.40	1.00
H27	Jake The Snake Roberts	.60	1.50
H28	Ravishing Rick Rude	.40	1.00
H29	Doink the Clown	.25	.60
H30	Big Boss Man	.40	1.00
H31	Jim Ross	.25	.60
H32	Rocky Johnson	.40	1.00
H33	Terry Funk	.40	1.00
H34	Big John Studd	.25	.60
H35	The Godfather	.25	.60
H36	Hillbilly Jim	.40	1.00
H37	Barry Windham	.25	.60
H38	Tito Santana	.25	.60
H39	Nikolai Volkoff	.40	1.00
H40	Arn Anderson	.40	1.00
H41	Tully Blanchard	.40	1.00
H42	One Man Gang	.25	.60
H43	Dean Malenko	.25	.60
H44	Classy Freddie Blassie	.40	1.00
H45	Tom Prichard	.25	.60
H46	Yokozuna	.40	1.00
H47	Mr. Wonderful Paul Orndorff	.40	1.00
H48	Sgt. Slaughter	.60	1.50
H49	Diesel	.40	1.00
H50	Batista	.40	1.00

2011 Topps WWE Masters of the Mat Relics

*GOLD/50: 1X TO 2.5X BASIC MEM
*RED/1: UNPRICED DUE TO SCARCITY
STATED ODDS 1:69

NNO	Alberto Del Rio	2.50	6.00
NNO	Big Show	2.50	6.00
NNO	Christian	2.50	6.00
NNO	Cody Rhodes	2.50	6.00
NNO	Daniel Bryan	2.50	6.00
NNO	Dolph Ziggler	2.50	6.00
NNO	Drew McIntyre	2.50	6.00
NNO	Jack Swagger	2.50	6.00
NNO	John Cena	5.00	12.00
NNO	John Morrison	2.50	6.00
NNO	Kane	2.50	6.00
NNO	Kofi Kingston	2.50	6.00
NNO	Mark Henry	2.50	6.00
NNO	Randy Orton	4.00	10.00
NNO	Rey Mysterio	3.00	8.00
NNO	R-Truth	2.50	6.00
NNO	Santino Marella	2.50	6.00
NNO	Sheamus	2.50	6.00
NNO	Sin Cara	2.50	6.00
NNO	Ted DiBiase	2.50	6.00
NNO	The Great Khali	2.50	6.00
NNO	The Miz	2.50	6.00
NNO	Triple H	4.00	10.00
NNO	Undertaker	4.00	10.00
NNO	Wade Barrett	2.50	6.00

2011 Topps WWE Prestigious Pairings

COMPLETE SET (15) 6.00 15.00
*P.P.BLACK/1: UNPRICED DUE TO SCARCITY
*P.P.CYAN/1: UNPRICED DUE TO SCARCITY
*P.P.MAGENTA/1: UNPRICED DUE TO SCARCITY
*P.P.YELLOW/1: UNPRICED DUE TO SCARCITY
STATED ODDS 1:8 HOBBY AND RETAIL

PP1	Big Show/Kane	.75	2.00
PP2	Marella/Kozlov	.50	1.25
PP3	Phoenix/Kelly	1.25	3.00
PP4	Lawler/Ross	.75	2.00
PP5	Swagger/Cole	.50	1.25
PP6	Orton/Mysterio	1.25	3.00
PP7	Cena/Cara	1.50	4.00
PP8	Jimmy Uso/Jay Uso	.30	.75
PP9	Ziggler/Guerrero	.50	1.25
PP10	Edge/Christian	1.25	3.00
PP11	Del Rio/Clay	.75	2.00
PP12	Ziggler/Sheamus	.50	1.25
PP13	Morrison/Bryan	.50	1.25
PP14	Torres/Kim	1.25	3.00
PP15	R-Truth/Morrison	.50	1.25

2011 Topps WWE Ringside Relics Ring Skirts

*GOLD/50: .6X TO 1.5X BASIC MEM
*RED/1: UNPRICED DUE TO SCARCITY
STATED ODDS 1:180

NNO	Alberto Del Rio	3.00	8.00
NNO	Big Show	3.00	8.00
NNO	Christian	3.00	8.00
NNO	Daniel Bryan	3.00	8.00
NNO	Dolph Ziggler	3.00	8.00
NNO	Jack Swagger	3.00	8.00
NNO	John Cena	6.00	15.00
NNO	John Morrison	3.00	8.00
NNO	Kane	3.00	8.00
NNO	Kofi Kingston	3.00	8.00
NNO	Randy Orton	5.00	12.00
NNO	Rey Mysterio	4.00	10.00
NNO	R-Truth	3.00	8.00
NNO	Santino Marella	3.00	8.00
NNO	Sheamus	3.00	8.00
NNO	Sin Cara	3.00	8.00
NNO	The Miz	3.00	8.00
NNO	Triple H	5.00	12.00
NNO	Undertaker	6.00	15.00
NNO	Wade Barrett	3.00	8.00

2011 Topps WWE Superstar Swatches

*GOLD/50: .6X TO 1.5X BASIC CARDS
*RED/1: UNPRICED DUE TO SCARCITY
STATED ODDS 1:126

NNO	Christian	4.00	10.00
NNO	Cody Rhodes	4.00	10.00
NNO	Daniel Bryan	5.00	12.00
NNO	Drew McIntyre	4.00	10.00
NNO	Heath Slater	4.00	10.00
NNO	Jack Swagger	4.00	10.00
NNO	Kofi Kingston	4.00	10.00
NNO	Randy Orton	5.00	12.00
NNO	R-Truth	4.00	10.00
NNO	Santino Marella	4.00	10.00
NNO	Sheamus	4.00	10.00
NNO	Stone Cold Steve Austin	6.00	15.00
NNO	Ted DiBiase	4.00	10.00
NNO	The Miz	4.00	10.00
NNO	Wade Barrett	4.00	10.00

2012 Topps WWE

COMPLETE SET (93) 15.00 40.00
COMPLETE SET W/O SP (90) 10.00 25.00
UNOPENED BOX (24 PACKS)
UNOPENED PACK (7 CARDS)
*BLUE: 1X TO 2.5X BASIC CARDS
*GOLD: 2.5X TO 6X BASIC CARDS
*PURPLE: 2.5X TO 6X BASIC CARDS
*RED: 2.5X TO 6X BASIC CARDS
*SILVER: 2.5X TO 6X BASIC CARDS
*BLACK: 8X TO 20X BASIC CARDS
*PLATINUM/1: UNPRICED DUE TO SCARCITY
*P.P.BLACK/1: UNPRICED DUE TO SCARCITY
*P.P.CYAN/1: UNPRICED DUE TO SCARCITY
*P.P.MAGENTA/1: UNPRICED DUE TO SCARCITY
*P.P.YELLOW/1: UNPRICED DUE TO SCARCITY

1	John Cena	.75	2.00
2	Randy Orton	.60	1.50
3	Beth Phoenix	.40	1.00
4	Sheamus	.40	1.00
5	Brock Lesnar	.60	1.50
6	Daniel Bryan	.15	.40
7A	Mick Foley	.60	1.50
7B	Cactus Jack SP	4.00	10.00
7C	Dude Love SP	4.00	10.00
7D	Mankind SP	4.00	10.00
8	Cody Rhodes	.15	.40
9	Cameron RC	.25	.60
10	Christian	.15	.40
11	Kelly Kelly	.60	1.50
12	Hornswoggle	.25	.60
13	Brodus Clay	.15	.40
14	Aksana RC	.40	1.00
15	Epico RC	.15	.40
16	Mark Henry	.25	.60
17	Maxine RC	.40	1.00
18	Jey Uso	.15	.40
19	Zack Ryder	.15	.40
20	Ricardo Rodriguez	.15	.40
21	JTG	.15	.40
22	Hunico RC	.15	.40
23	Kofi Kingston	.15	.40
24	Matt Striker	.15	.40
25	Kane	.40	1.00
26	Jimmy Uso	.15	.40
27	Naomi RC	.25	.60
28	The Great Khali	.15	.40
29	Tyler Reks	.15	.40
30	Josh Matthews	.15	.40
31	Derrick Bateman RC	.15	.40
32	Camacho RC	.15	.40
33	Kharma	.25	.60
34	Heath Slater	.15	.40
35	Evan Bourne	.15	.40
36	Yoshi Tatsu	.15	.40
37	Big Show	.40	1.00
38	Ryback	.15	.40
39	Percy Watson	.15	.40
40	Kaitlyn	.40	1.00
41	The Miz	.25	.60
42	William Regal	.25	.60
43	Michael Cole	.15	.40

44 Wade Barrett .15 .40
45 Rey Mysterio .40 1.00
46 Alicia Fox .25 .60
47 Triple H .60 1.50
48 Layla .40 1.00
49 Chris Jericho .60 1.50
50 Jinder Mahal .15 .40
51 Eve .60 1.50
52 Johnny Curtis .15 .40
53 Tensai .15 .40
54 Titus O'Neil .15 .40
55 Vickie Guerrero .25 .60
56 Justin Gabriel .15 .40
57 Primo .15 .40
58 Booker T .25 .60
59 Goldust .15 .40
60 Natalya .60 1.50
61 Jack Swagger .25 .60
62 Ezekiel Jackson .25 .60
63 John Laurinaitis .15 .40
64 Ted DiBiase .25 .60
65 R-Truth .15 .40
66 Trent Barreta .15 .40
67 Jerry The King Lawler .40 1.00
68 Tyson Kidd .15 .40
69 David Otunga .15 .40
70 Rosa Mendes .25 .60
71 Michael McGillicutty .15 .40
72 Drew McIntyre .15 .40
73 Alex Riley .15 .40
74 Theodore Long .15 .40
75 Dolph Ziggler .25 .60
76 Sin Cara .40 1.00
77 Justin Roberts .15 .40
78 Alberto Del Rio .40 1.00
79 Curt Hawkins .15 .40
80 Tamina Snuka .25 .60
81 Mason Ryan .15 .40
82 Darren Young .15 .40
83 Scott Stanford RC .15 .40
84 Lilian Garcia .40 1.00
85 Santino Marella .25 .60
86 Antonio Cesaro RC .15 .40
87 The Rock .75 2.00
88 AJ .75 2.00
89 CM Punk .60 1.50
90 Undertaker .60 1.50

2012 Topps WWE Autographs

STATED ODDS 1:470 HOBBY AND RETAIL

NNO Booker T 15.00 40.00
NNO Cactus Jack 50.00 100.00
NNO Chris Jericho 30.00 75.00
NNO Dude Love 50.00 100.00
NNO Epico 8.00 20.00
NNO Hunico 8.00 20.00
NNO John Laurinaitis 12.00 30.00
NNO Mankind 50.00 100.00
NNO Mick Foley 30.00 75.00
NNO Primo 8.00 20.00
NNO Triple H

2012 Topps WWE Classic Hall of Famers

COMPLETE SET (35) 10.00 25.00
*P.P.BLACK/1: UNPRICED DUE TO SCARCITY
*P.P.CYAN/1: UNPRICED DUE TO SCARCITY
*P.P.MAGENTA/1: UNPRICED DUE TO SCARCITY
*P.P.YELLOW/1: UNPRICED DUE TO SCARCITY
STATED ODDS 1:4 HOBBY AND RETAIL

1 Chief Jay Strongbow .40 1.00
2 Classy Freddie Blassie .40 1.00
3 Gorilla Monsoon .40 1.00
4 Jimmy Superfly Snuka .40 1.00
5 Big John Studd .40 1.00
6 Bobby The Brain Heenan .40 1.00
7 Don Muraco .40 1.00
8 Greg The Hammer Valentine .40 1.00
9 Harley Race .40 1.00
10 Junkyard Dog .40 1.00
11 Sgt. Slaughter .40 1.00
12 Tito Santana .40 1.00
13 Cowboy Bob Orton .40 1.00
14 The Iron Sheik .40 1.00
15 Mr. Wonderful Paul Orndorff .40 1.00
16 Nikolai Volkoff .40 1.00
17 Rowdy Roddy Piper .60 1.50
18 Mean Gene Okerlund .40 1.00
19 The American Dream Dusty Rhodes .40 1.00
20 Mr. Perfect Curt Hennig .40 1.00
21 Rocky Johnson .40 1.00
22 Terry Funk .40 1.00
23 Howard Finkel .40 1.00
24 Koko B. Ware .40 1.00
25 Ricky The Dragon Steamboat .40 1.00
26 Stone Cold Steve Austin 1.25 3.00
27 Million Dollar Man Ted DiBiase .40 1.00
28 Hacksaw Jim Duggan .40 1.00
29 Road Warrior Hawk .40 1.00
30 Road Warrior Animal .40 1.00
31 Shawn Michaels 1.00 2.50
32 Edge .60 1.50
33 Arn Anderson .40 1.00
34 Barry Windham .40 1.00
35 Tully Blanchard .40 1.00

2012 Topps WWE Classic Hall of Famers Autographs

STATED ODDS 1:269 HOBBY AND RETAIL

NNO Animal 25.00 60.00
NNO Barry Windham 12.00 30.00
NNO Don Muraco 20.00 50.00
NNO Greg The Hammer Valentine 25.00 60.00
NNO Harley Race 50.00 100.00
NNO Jimmy Superfly Snuka 100.00 200.00
NNO Koko B. Ware 15.00 40.00
NNO Mr. Wonderful Paul Orndorff 100.00 200.00
NNO Nikolai Volkoff 15.00 30.00
NNO Terry Funk 75.00 150.00
NNO Tito Santana 20.00 50.00
NNO Tully Blanchard 15.00 40.00

2012 Topps WWE Diva Kiss

STATED ODDS 1:1,125

NNO AJ 100.00 175.00
NNO Aksana 30.00 80.00
NNO Alicia Fox 30.00 80.00
NNO Beth Phoenix 30.00 80.00
NNO Kaitlyn 20.00 50.00
NNO Kelly Kelly 25.00 60.00
NNO Layla 50.00 100.00
NNO Maxine 20.00 50.00
NNO Natalya 30.00 80.00
NNO Rosa Mendes 30.00 80.00
NNO Cameron 20.00 50.00
NNO Naomi 30.00 80.00
NNO Tamina Snuka 30.00 80.00

2012 Topps WWE Divas Class of 2012

COMPLETE SET (15) 8.00 20.00
*P.P.BLACK/1: UNPRICED DUE TO SCARCITY
*P.P.CYAN/1: UNPRICED DUE TO SCARCITY
*P.P.MAGENTA/1: UNPRICED DUE TO SCARCITY
*P.P.YELLOW/1: UNPRICED DUE TO SCARCITY
STATED ODDS 1:4 HOBBY AND RETAIL

1 AJ 2.50 6.00
2 Aksana 1.25 3.00
3 Alicia Fox .75 2.00
4 Beth Phoenix 1.25 3.00
5 Cameron .75 2.00
6 Eve 2.00 5.00
7 Kaitlyn 1.25 3.00
8 Kelly Kelly 2.00 5.00
9 Layla 1.25 3.00
10 Lilian Garcia 1.25 3.00
11 Maxine 1.25 3.00
12 Naomi .75 2.00
13 Natalya 2.00 5.00
14 Rosa Mendes .75 2.00
15 Tamina Snuka .75 2.00

2012 Topps WWE Divas Class of 2012 Autographs

STATED ODDS 1:364

NNO Aksana 20.00 50.00
NNO Alicia Fox 15.00 40.00
NNO Beth Phoenix 15.00 40.00
NNO Kaitlyn 30.00 75.00
NNO Kelly Kelly 30.00 75.00
NNO Lilian Garcia 20.00 50.00
NNO Maxine 15.00 40.00
NNO Rosa Mendes 15.00 40.00
NNO Tamina Snuka 20.00 50.00

2012 Topps WWE Dual Autographs

STATED ODDS 1:2,245 HOBBY EXCLUSIVE

NNO Jimmy & Tamina Snuka 100.00 200.00
NNO Maxine/Kaitlyn 30.00 75.00
NNO Primo/Epico 20.00 50.00
NNO T.Blanchard/B.Windham 25.00 60.00

2012 Topps WWE First Class Champions

COMPLETE SET (20) 10.00 25.00
*P.P.BLACK/1: UNPRICED DUE TO SCARCITY
*P.P.CYAN/1: UNPRICED DUE TO SCARCITY
*P.P.MAGENTA/1: UNPRICED DUE TO SCARCITY
*P.P.YELLOW/1: UNPRICED DUE TO SCARCITY
STATED ODDS 1:6 HOBBY AND RETAIL

1 The Iron Shiek .50 1.25
2 Sgt. Slaughter .50 1.25
3 Undertaker 1.25 3.00
4 Yokozuna .50 1.25
5 Diesel .50 1.25
6 Shawn Michaels 1.25 3.00
7 Stone Cold Steve Austin 1.50 4.00
8 The Rock 1.50 4.00
9 Mankind 1.25 3.00
10 Triple H 1.25 3.00
11 Big Show .75 2.00
12 Chris Jericho 1.25 3.00
13 Brock Lesnar 1.25 3.00
14 John Cena 1.50 4.00
15 Edge .75 2.00
16 Randy Orton 1.25 3.00
17 Batista .50 1.25
18 Sheamus .75 2.00
19 The Miz .50 1.25
20 CM Punk 1.25 3.00

2012 Topps WWE Shirt Relics

*BLACK/50: .8X TO 2X BASIC MEM
*PLATINUM/1: UNPRICED DUE TO SCARCITY
STATED ODDS 1:112

NNO Alberto Del Rio 5.00 12.00
NNO Big Show 6.00 15.00
NNO Brodus Clay 5.00 12.00
NNO Camacho 5.00 12.00
NNO CM Punk 6.00 15.00
NNO Cody Rhodes 5.00 12.00
NNO Daniel Bryan 5.00 12.00
NNO Dolph Ziggler 6.00 15.00
NNO Hornswoggle 5.00 12.00
NNO Hunico 4.00 10.00
NNO Jerry Lawler 6.00 15.00
NNO John Cena 10.00 25.00
NNO Kofi Kingston 5.00 12.00
NNO Mark Henry 4.00 10.00
NNO Randy Orton 6.00 15.00
NNO R-Truth 4.00 10.00
NNO Santino Marella 4.00 10.00
NNO Sheamus 5.00 12.00
NNO The Miz 5.00 12.00
NNO Zack Ryder 5.00 12.00
NNO Natalya 5.00 12.00
NNO Christian 5.00 12.00
NNO Chris Jericho 6.00 15.00
NNO Evan Bourne 3.00 8.00
NNO Heath Slater 4.00 10.00
NNO Jack Swagger 4.00 10.00
NNO Justin Gabriel 3.00 8.00
NNO Michael McGillicutty 3.00 8.00
NNO Ted DiBiase 3.00 8.00
NNO Wade Barrett 4.00 10.00

2012 Topps WWE Top Class Matches Punk's Picks

COMPLETE SET (10) 5.00 12.00
*P.P.BLACK/1: UNPRICED DUE TO SCARCITY
*P.P.CYAN/1: UNPRICED DUE TO SCARCITY
*P.P.MAGENTA/1: UNPRICED DUE TO SCARCITY
*P.P.YELLOW/1: UNPRICED DUE TO SCARCITY
STATED ODDS 1:6

1 Wins ECW Championship 1.00 2.50
2 Wins Money in the Bank 1.00 2.50
3 Wins Intercontinental Title 1.00 2.50
4 Wins World Heavyweight Championship1.00 2.50
5 Loses His Hair 1.00 2.50
6 Wins the WWE Championship 1.00 2.50
7 Unifies the WWE Championship 1.00 2.50
8 Reclaims the WWE Championship 1.00 2.50
9 Victorious at WrestleMania XXVIII 1.00 2.50
10 Turns Back Jericho Again 1.00 2.50

2012 Topps WWE World Class Events

COMPLETE SET (10) 5.00 12.00

*P.P.BLACK/1: UNPRICED DUE TO SCARCITY
*P.P.CYAN/1: UNPRICED DUE TO SCARCITY
*P.P.MAGENTA/1: UNPRICED DUE TO SCARCITY
*P.P.YELLOW/1: UNPRICED DUE TO SCARCITY
STATED ODDS 1:6

1 WrestleMania XXVII	1.00	2.50
2 Money in the Bank 2011	1.00	2.50
3 SummerSlam 2011	1.00	2.50
4 Hell in a Cell 2011	1.00	2.50
5 Vengeance 2011	1.00	2.50
6 Survivor Series 2011	1.00	2.50
7 Tables, Ladders and Chairs 2011	1.00	2.50
8 Royal Rumble 2012	1.00	2.50
9 Elimination Chamber 2012	1.00	2.50
10 WrestleMania XXVIII	1.00	2.50

2012 Topps WWE WrestleMania XXVIII Mat Relics

*BLACK/50: .8X TO 2X BASIC MEM
*PLATINUM/1: UNPRICED DUE TO SCARCITY
STATED ODDS 1:109

NNO Beth Phoenix	6.00	15.00
NNO Big Show	6.00	15.00
NNO Booker T	5.00	12.00
NNO Chris Jericho	6.00	15.00
NNO CM Punk	10.00	25.00
NNO Cody Rhodes	5.00	12.00
NNO Daniel Bryan	5.00	12.00
NNO David Otunga	5.00	12.00
NNO Dolph Ziggler	5.00	12.00
NNO Eve	6.00	15.00
NNO Jack Swagger	6.00	15.00
NNO John Cena	10.00	25.00
NNO Kane	6.00	15.00
NNO Kelly Kelly	8.00	20.00
NNO Kofi Kingston	5.00	12.00
NNO Mark Henry	5.00	12.00
NNO Randy Orton	6.00	15.00
NNO R-Truth	5.00	12.00
NNO Santino Marella	5.00	12.00
NNO Sheamus	6.00	15.00
NNO The Miz	5.00	12.00
NNO The Rock	10.00	25.00
NNO Triple H	8.00	20.00
NNO Undertaker	10.00	25.00
NNO Zack Ryder	6.00	15.00

2013 Topps WWE

COMPLETE SET (110) 8.00 20.00
UNOPENED BOX (24 PACKS)
UNOPENED PACK (7 CARDS)
*BLACK: 2.5X TO 6X BASIC CARDS
*SILVER: 4X TO 10X BASIC CARDS
*GOLD/10: 15X TO 40X BASIC CARDS
*P.P.BLACK/1: UNPRICED DUE TO SCARCITY
*P.P.CYAN/1: UNPRICED DUE TO SCARCITY
*P.P.MAGENTA/1: UNPRICED DUE TO SCARCITY
*P.P.YELLOW/1: UNPRICED DUE TO SCARCITY

1 AJ Lee	.75	2.00
2 Alex Riley	.15	.40
3 Big E Langston RC	.15	.40
4 Big Show	.30	.75
5 Brock Lesnar	.60	1.50
6 Brodus Clay	.15	.40
7 Cameron	.25	.60
8 CM Punk	.60	1.50
9 Daniel Bryan	.40	1.00
10 David Otunga	.15	.40
11 Dean Ambrose RC	.25	.60
12 Dolph Ziggler	.25	.60
13 Epico	.15	.40
14 Evan Bourne	.15	.40
15 Eve	.60	1.50
16 Jack Swagger	.25	.60
17 Jerry The King Lawler	.30	.75
18 John Cena	.75	2.00
19 JTG	.15	.40
20 Justin Roberts	.15	.40
21 Kane	.30	.75
22 Kofi Kingston	.15	.40
23 Mason Ryan	.15	.40
24 Michael Cole	.15	.40
25 Michael McGillicutty	.15	.40
26 The Miz	.25	.60
27 Naomi	.40	1.00
28 Paul Heyman	.15	.40
29 Primo	.15	.40
30 R-Truth	.15	.40
31 Rey Mysterio	.40	1.00
32 The Rock	.75	2.00
33 Roman Reigns RC	30.00	75.00
34 Rosa Mendes	.25	.60
35 Ryback	.15	.40
36 Santino Marella	.15	.40
37 Scott Stanford	.15	.40
38 Seth Rollins RC	10.00	25.00
39 Tamina Snuka	.20	.50
40 Tensai	.15	.40
41 Triple H	.60	1.50
42 Vickie Guerrero	.25	.60
43 Zack Ryder	.15	.40
44 Aksana	.25	.60
45 Alberto Del Rio	.30	.75
46 Alicia Fox	.25	.60
47 Antonio Cesaro	.15	.40
48 Booker T	.25	.60
49 Camacho	.15	.40
50 Christian	.15	.40
51 Cody Rhodes	.15	.40
52 Damien Sandow	.15	.40
53 Darren Young	.15	.40
54 Drew McIntyre	.15	.40
55 Ezekiel Jackson	.15	.40
56 The Great Khali	.15	.40
57 Heath Slater	.15	.40
58 Hornswoggle	.15	.40
59 Hunico	.15	.40
60 Jey Uso	.15	.40
61 Jimmy Uso	.15	.40
62 Jinder Mahal	.15	.40
63 Fandango	.15	.40
64 Josh Mathews	.15	.40
65 Justin Gabriel	.15	.40
66 Kaitlyn	.30	.75
67 Layla	.30	.75
68 Lilian Garcia	.40	1.00
69 Mark Henry	.20	.50
70 Matt Striker	.15	.40
71 Natalya	.30	.75
72 Percy Watson	.15	.40
73 Randy Orton	.50	1.25
74 Ricardo Rodriguez	.15	.40
75 Sheamus	.30	.75
76 Sin Cara	.25	.60
77 Ted DiBiase	.20	.50
78 Theodore Long	.15	.40
79 Titus O'Neil	.15	.40
80 Tyson Kidd	.15	.40
81 Undertaker	.60	1.50
82 Wade Barrett	.15	.40
83 William Regal	.20	.50
84 Yoshi Tatsu	.15	.40
85 The American Dream Dusty Rhodes	.25	.60
86 Big John Studd	.25	.60
87 The British Bulldog	.25	.60
88 The Bushwhackers	.15	.40
89 Cowboy Bob Orton	.25	.60
90 Dean Malenko	.15	.40
91 Hacksaw Jim Duggan	.25	.60
92 Greg The Hammer Valentine	.15	.40
93 Harley Race	.25	.60
94 The Iron Sheik	.25	.60
95 Jake The Snake Roberts	.25	.60
96 Jimmy Superfly Snuka	.25	.60
97 Junkyard Dog	.25	.60
98 Million Dollar Man Ted DiBiase	.25	.60
99 Mr. Perfect	.25	.60
100 Mr. Wonderful Paul Orndorff	.25	.60
101 Nikolai Volkoff	.25	.60
102 Ravishing Rick Rude	.25	.60
103 Ricky The Dragon Steamboat	.25	.60
104 Rowdy Roddy Piper	.40	1.00
105 Sgt. Slaughter	.25	.60
106 Terry Funk	.25	.60
107 Tito Santana	.25	.60
108 Tom Prichard	.15	.40
109 Vader	.15	.40
110 Yokozuna	.15	.40

2013 Topps WWE Autographed Relics

STATED ODDS 1:9,550
UNPRICED DUE TO SCARCITY

NNO Alicia Fox
NNO Daniel Bryan
NNO Dolph Ziggler
NNO Kofi Kingston
NNO Ryback
NNO Sin Cara

2013 Topps WWE Autographs

STATED ODDS 1:79 HOBBY AND RETAIL

NNO AJ Lee	75.00	150.00
NNO Alicia Fox	8.00	20.00
NNO Antonio Cesaro	10.00	25.00
NNO Bushwhacker Butch	12.00	30.00
NNO Bushwhacker Luke	8.00	20.00
NNO Cowboy Bob Orton	10.00	25.00
NNO Daniel Bryan	15.00	40.00
NNO Dean Malenko	12.00	30.00
NNO Dolph Ziggler	12.00	30.00
NNO Eve	12.00	30.00
NNO Jack Swagger	10.00	25.00
NNO Kaitlyn	15.00	40.00
NNO Kofi Kingston	8.00	20.00
NNO Michael Cole	8.00	20.00
NNO Million Dollar Man Ted DiBiase	15.00	40.00
NNO Randy Orton	20.00	50.00
NNO Rosa Mendes	10.00	25.00
NNO Ryback	10.00	25.00
NNO Sin Cara	10.00	25.00
NNO Tom Prichard	8.00	20.00

2013 Topps WWE Diva Kiss

STATED ODDS 1:568 HOBBY AND RETAIL

NNO AJ Lee	100.00	175.00
NNO Aksana	25.00	50.00
NNO Alicia Fox	15.00	40.00
NNO Cameron	25.00	50.00
NNO Eve	40.00	80.00
NNO Kaitlyn	40.00	80.00
NNO Layla	30.00	60.00
NNO Naomi	15.00	40.00
NNO Natalya	30.00	60.00
NNO Rosa Mendes	25.00	50.00

2013 Topps WWE Diva Snapshots

COMPLETE SET (10) 20.00 40.00
STATED ODDS 1:24 HOBBY AND RETAIL

NNO AJ Lee	6.00	15.00
NNO Aksana	2.00	5.00
NNO Alicia Fox	2.00	5.00
NNO Cameron	2.00	5.00
NNO Eve	5.00	12.00
NNO Kaitlyn	2.50	6.00
NNO Layla	2.50	6.00
NNO Naomi	3.00	8.00
NNO Natalya	2.50	6.00
NNO Rosa Mendes	2.00	5.00

2013 Topps WWE Shirt Relics

STATED ODDS 1:24 HOBBY; 1:96 RETAIL

NNO Alicia Fox Skirt	6.00	15.00
NNO Big Show/Hat	6.00	15.00
NNO Brodus Clay/Pants	4.00	10.00
NNO CM Punk/Shirt	9.00	20.00
NNO Damien Sandow/Shirt	5.00	12.00
NNO Daniel Bryan/Shirt	5.00	12.00
NNO Dolph Ziggler/Shirt	5.00	12.00
NNO Kofi Kingston/Shirt	5.00	12.00
NNO Paul Heyman/Suit	6.00	15.00
NNO R-Truth/Shirt	5.00	12.00
NNO Rey Mysterio/Shirt	6.00	15.00
NNO Ryback/Shirt	8.00	20.00
NNO Santino Marella/Puppet	6.00	15.00
NNO Sheamus/Shirt	6.00	15.00
NNO Sin Cara Shirt	5.00	12.00
NNO The Miz/Shirt	4.00	10.00
NNO Titus O'Neil/Shirt	4.00	10.00
NNO Wade Barrett/Shirt	5.00	12.00
NNO CM Punk/Sock SP	30.00	60.00

2013 Topps WWE SummerSlam Mat Relics

STATED ODDS 1:102

NNO AJ Lee	8.00	20.00
NNO Aksana	4.00	10.00
NNO Alberto Del Rio	5.00	12.00
NNO Antonio Cesaro	4.00	10.00
NNO Big Show	4.00	10.00
NNO Brock Lesnar	6.00	15.00
NNO CM Punk	6.00	15.00
NNO Daniel Bryan	4.00	10.00
NNO Darren Young	4.00	10.00
NNO Dolph Ziggler	5.00	12.00
NNO Jerry The King Lawler	5.00	12.00
NNO John Cena	8.00	20.00

NNO	Kane	5.00	12.00
NNO	Kofi Kingston	4.00	10.00
NNO	Paul Heyman	5.00	12.00
NNO	R-Truth	4.00	10.00
NNO	Santino Marella	4.00	10.00
NNO	Sheamus	4.00	10.00
NNO	The Miz	4.00	10.00
NNO	Titus O'Neil	4.00	10.00
NNO	Triple H	6.00	15.00
NNO	Vickie Guerrero	4.00	10.00

2013 Topps WWE Triple Autographs

STATED ODDS 1:12,637 HOBBY AND RETAIL
UNPRICED DUE TO SCARCITY

NNO Luke/Butch/DiBiase
NNO Bryan/Cesaro/Kaitlyn
NNO Eve/Fox/Mendes
NNO Swagger/SinCara/Ryback
NNO R.Orton/B.Orton/Cole

2013 Topps WWE Triple Threat Tier Three

COMPLETE SET (30) 5.00 12.00
*TIER TWO: .5X TO 1.2X TIER THREE
*TIER ONE: .8X TO 2X TIER THREE
*T3 P.P.BLACK/1: UNPRICED DUE TO SCARCITY
*T3 P.P.CYAN/1: UNPRICED DUE TO SCARCITY
*T3 P.P.MAGENTA/1: UNPRICED DUE TO SCARCITY
*T3 P.P.YELLOW/1: UNPRICED DUE TO SCARCITY
*T2 P.P.BLACK/1: UNPRICED DUE TO SCARCITY
*T2 P.P.CYAN/1: UNPRICED DUE TO SCARCITY
*T2 P.P.MAGENTA/1: UNPRICED DUE TO SCARCITY
*T2 P.P.YELLOW/1: UNPRICED DUE TO SCARCITY
*T1 P.P.BLACK/1: UNPRICED DUE TO SCARCITY
*T1 P.P.CYAN/1: UNPRICED DUE TO SCARCITY
*T1 P.P.MAGENTA/1: UNPRICED DUE TO SCARCITY
*T1 P.P.YELLOW/1: UNPRICED DUE TO SCARCITY
STATED ODDS 1:2 HOBBY AND RETAIL

TT1	Dolph Ziggler	.30	.75
TT2	John Cena	1.00	2.50
TT3	Jack Swagger	.30	.75
TT4	The Miz	.30	.75
TT5	Prime Time Players	.20	.50
TT6	Wade Barrett	.20	.50
TT7	Santino Marella	.20	.50
TT8	Brock Lesnar	.75	2.00
TT9	Sin Cara	.30	.75
TT10	Rey Mysterio	.50	1.25
TT11	Damien Sandow	.20	.50
TT12	Randy Orton	.60	1.50
TT13	Cody Rhodes	.20	.50
TT14	Eve	.75	2.00
TT15	Kane	.40	1.00
TT16	Big Show	.40	1.00
TT17	AJ Lee	1.00	2.50
TT18	Mark Henry	.25	.60
TT19	Triple H	.75	2.00
TT20	Ryback	.20	.50
TT21	Zack Ryder	.20	.50
TT22	Daniel Bryan	.50	1.25
TT23	Alberto Del Rio	.40	1.00
TT24	Christian	.20	.50
TT25	Tyson Kidd	.20	.50
TT26	CM Punk	.75	2.00
TT27	The Rock	1.00	2.50
TT28	Undertaker	.75	2.00
TT29	Kofi Kingston	.20	.50
TT30	Sheamus	.40	1.00

2013 Topps WWE 2K14 Phenom Edition Promo

NNO Undertaker

2014 Topps WWE

COMPLETE SET (110) 10.00 25.00
UNOPENED BOX (24 PACKS)
UNOPENED PACK (7 CARDS)
*BLACK: .75X TO 2X BASIC CARDS
*SILVER: 1.5X TO 4X BASIC CARDS
*GOLD/10: 6X TO 15X BASIC CARDS
*RED/1: UNPRICED DUE TO SCARCITY
*P.P.BLACK/1: UNPRICED DUE TO SCARCITY
*P.P.CYAN/1: UNPRICED DUE TO SCARCITY
*P.P.MAGENTA/1: UNPRICED DUE TO SCARCITY
*P.P.YELLOW/1: UNPRICED DUE TO SCARCITY

1	AJ Lee	.75	2.00
2	Alex Riley	.15	.40
3	Big E Langston	.15	.40
4	Bo Dallas RC	.15	.40
5	Brad Maddox RC	.15	.40
6	Bray Wyatt	.40	1.00
7	Brie Bella	.50	1.25
8	Brock Lesnar	.60	1.50
9	Brodus Clay	.15	.40
10	Cameron	.25	.60
11	Chris Jericho	.40	1.00
12	CM Punk	.60	1.50
13	Curtis Axel	.15	.40
14	Daniel Bryan	.25	.60
15	David Otunga	.15	.40
16	Dean Ambrose	.40	1.00
17	Diego	.15	.40
18	Dolph Ziggler	.25	.60
19	Erick Rowan RC	.25	.60
20	Eva Marie RC	.60	1.50
21	Fandango	.25	.60
22	Fernando	.15	.40
23	Jack Swagger	.25	.60
24	Jerry The King Lawler	.40	1.00
25	John Cena	.75	2.00
26	Jojo RC	.25	.60
27	Justin Roberts	.15	.40
28	Kane	.40	1.00
29	Kofi Kingston	.15	.40
30	Luke Harper RC	.25	.60
31	El Torito RC	.15	.40
32	Michael Cole	.15	.40
33	The Miz	.25	.60
34	Naomi	.25	.60
35	Nikki Bella	.50	1.25
36	Paul Heyman	.15	.40
37	R-Truth	.15	.40
38	Randy Orton	.60	1.50
39	Rey Mysterio	.40	1.00
40	The Rock	.75	2.00
41	Rob Van Dam	.40	1.00
42	Roman Reigns	.40	1.00
43	Ryback	.15	.40
44	Santino Marella	.25	.60
45	Scott Stanford	.15	.40
46	Seth Rollins	.15	.40
47	Stephanie McMahon	.25	.60
48	Summer Rae RC	.60	1.50
49	Tamina Snuka	.25	.60
50	Tensai	.15	.40
51	Triple H	.60	1.50
52	Zack Ryder	.15	.40
53	Zeb Colter	.25	.60
54	Aksana	.40	1.00
55	Alberto Del Rio	.40	1.00
56	Alicia Fox	.25	.60
57	Antonio Cesaro	.15	.40
58	Big Show	.40	1.00
59	Booker T	.25	.60
60	Camacho	.15	.40
61	Christian	.15	.40
62	Cody Rhodes	.15	.40
63	Curt Hawkins	.15	.40
64	Damien Sandow	.15	.40
65	Darren Young	.15	.40
66	Drew McIntyre	.15	.40
67	Ezekiel Jackson	.25	.60
68	The Great Khali	.15	.40
69	Heath Slater	.15	.40
70	Hornswoggle	.25	.60
71	Hunico	.15	.40
72	JBL	.25	.60
73	Jey Uso	.15	.40
74	Jimmy Uso	.15	.40
75	Jinder Mahal	.15	.40
76	Josh Mathews	.15	.40
77	Justin Gabriel	.15	.40
78	Kaitlyn	.40	1.00
79	Layla	.40	1.00
80	Lilian Garcia	.40	1.00
81	Mark Henry	.25	.60
82	Natalya	.50	1.25
83	Renee Young RC	.60	1.50
84	Ricardo Rodriguez	.15	.40
85	Rosa Mendes	.25	.60
86	Sheamus	.40	1.00
87	Sin Cara	.40	1.00
88	Theodore Long	.15	.40
89	Titus O'Neil	.15	.40
90	Tony Chimel	.15	.40
91	Tyson Kidd	.15	.40
92	Undertaker	.60	1.50
93	Vickie Guerrero	.25	.60
94	Wade Barrett	.15	.40
95	William Regal	.25	.60
96	Andre The Giant L	.60	1.50
97	Billy Gunn L	.25	.60
98	Bob Backlund L	.25	.60
99	Diamond Dallas Page L	.25	.60
100	Eddie Guerrero L	.25	.60
101	Honky Tonk Man L	.25	.60
102	Jim Ross L	.25	.60
103	Junkyard Dog L	.25	.60
104	Kevin Nash L	.40	1.00
105	Larry Zbyszko L	.25	.60
106	Mick Foley L	.40	1.00
107	Paul Bearer L	.25	.60
108	Road Dogg L	.25	.60
109	Shawn Michaels L	.60	1.50
110	X-Pac L	.15	.40

2014 Topps WWE Autographs

*BLACK/50: .5X TO 1.2X BASIC AUTOS
*SILVER/25: .6X TO 1.5X BASIC AUTOS
*GOLD/10: UNPRICED DUE TO SCARCITY
*RED/1: UNPRICED DUE TO SCARCITY
*P.P.BLACK/1: UNPRICED DUE TO SCARCITY
*P.P.CYAN/1: UNPRICED DUE TO SCARCITY
*P.P.MAGENTA/1: UNPRICED DUE TO SCARCITY
*P.P.YELLOW/1: UNPRICED DUE TO SCARCITY

NNO	AJ Lee	60.00	120.00
NNO	Billy Gunn	8.00	20.00
NNO	Bray Wyatt	30.00	75.00
NNO	Daniel Bryan	15.00	40.00
NNO	Erick Rowan	6.00	15.00
NNO	Eva Marie	12.00	30.00
NNO	Jack Swagger	8.00	20.00
NNO	John Cena	75.00	150.00
NNO	JoJo	6.00	15.00
NNO	Luke Harper	8.00	20.00
NNO	Randy Orton	30.00	75.00
NNO	Renee Young	15.00	40.00
NNO	Road Dogg	12.00	30.00
NNO	Shawn Michaels	30.00	75.00
NNO	Summer Rae	15.00	40.00
NNO	X-Pac	8.00	20.00

2014 Topps WWE Champions

COMPLETE SET (30) 10.00 25.00
*P.P.BLACK/1: UNPRICED DUE TO SCARCITY
*P.P.CYAN/1: UNPRICED DUE TO SCARCITY
*P.P.MAGENTA/1: UNPRICED DUE TO SCARCITY
*P.P.YELLOW/1: UNPRICED DUE TO SCARCITY
STATED ODDS 1:4 HOBBY AND RETAIL

1	Bruno Sammartino	.40	1.00
2	Bob Backlund	.40	1.00
3	The Iron Sheik	.40	1.00
4	Andre The Giant	1.00	2.50
5	Sgt. Slaughter	.60	1.50
6	Undertaker	1.00	2.50
7	Yokozuna	.40	1.00
8	Diesel	.60	1.50
9	Shawn Michaels	1.00	2.50
10	Stone Cold Steve Austin	1.25	3.00
11	Kane	.60	1.50
12	The Rock	1.25	3.00
13	Mankind	.60	1.50
14	Triple H	1.00	2.50
15	Big Show	.60	1.50
16	Chris Jericho	.60	1.50
17	Brock Lesnar	1.00	2.50
18	Eddie Guerrero	.40	1.00
19	JBL	.40	1.00
20	John Cena	1.25	3.00
21	Edge	.60	1.50
22	Rob Van Dam	.60	1.50
23	Randy Orton	1.00	2.50
24	Batista	.75	2.00
25	Sheamus	.60	1.50
26	The Miz	.40	1.00
27	CM Punk	1.00	2.50
28	Rey Mysterio	.60	1.50
29	Alberto Del Rio	.60	1.50
30	Daniel Bryan	.40	1.00

2014 Topps WWE Championship Belts

STATED PRINT RUN 400 SETS

NNO	AJ Lee	10.00	25.00
NNO	Andre The Giant	8.00	20.00
NNO	Brie Bella	6.00	15.00
NNO	British Bulldog	4.00	10.00

NNO Chris Jericho 5.00 12.00
NNO Christian 2.00 5.00
NNO CM Punk 12.00 30.00
NNO Daniel Bryan 3.00 8.00
NNO D-Generation X 8.00 20.00
NNO Edge 5.00 12.00
NNO Jeri-Show 5.00 12.00
NNO Jimmy Superfly Snuka 3.00 8.00
NNO John Cena 10.00 25.00
NNO Kaitlyn 5.00 12.00
NNO Kofi Kingston 2.00 5.00
NNO Kofi Kingston/R-Truth 2.00 5.00
NNO Layla 5.00 12.00
NNO The Miz 3.00 8.00
NNO Mr. Perfect Curt Hennig 2.50 6.00
NNO Nikki Bella 6.00 15.00
NNO Randy Orton 8.00 20.00
NNO Ravishing Rick Rude 2.00 5.00
NNO Rey Mysterio/Eddie Guerrero 5.00 12.00
NNO Ricky The Dragon Steamboat 2.00 5.00
NNO The Rock 10.00 25.00
NNO Rowdy Roddy Piper 5.00 12.00
NNO Stone Cold Steve Austin 10.00 25.00
NNO Team Hell No 5.00 12.00
NNO Triple H 8.00 20.00
NNO Undertaker 8.00 20.00

2014 Topps WWE Diva Kiss

STATED PRINT RUN 100 SETS

NNO AJ Lee 150.00 225.00
NNO Brie Bella 50.00 100.00
NNO Eva Marie 30.00 75.00
NNO JoJo 25.00 60.00
NNO Kaitlyn 25.00 60.00
NNO Lilian Garcia 25.00 60.00
NNO Natalya 25.00 60.00
NNO Nikki Bella 50.00 100.00
NNO Renee Young 35.00 75.00
NNO Summer Rae 60.00 120.00

2014 Topps WWE Diva Kiss Autographs

COMMON AUTO 60.00 120.00
STATED PRINT RUN 20 SETS

NNO AJ Lee 200.00 400.00
NNO Eva Marie 125.00 250.00
NNO JoJo 60.00 120.00
NNO Renee Young 75.00 150.00
NNO Summer Rae 125.00 250.00

2014 Topps WWE Greatest Championship Contenders

COMPLETE SET (10) 5.00 12.00
*P.P.BLACK/1: UNPRICED DUE TO SCARCITY
*P.P.CYAN/1: UNPRICED DUE TO SCARCITY
*P.P.MAGENTA/1: UNPRICED DUE TO SCARCITY
*P.P.YELLOW/1: UNPRICED DUE TO SCARCITY
STATED ODDS 1:12

1 Ricky The Dragon Steamboat .50 1.25
2 Mr. Perfect .60 1.50
3 Ravishing Rick Rude .50 1.25
4 Million Dollar Man Ted DiBiase .60 1.50
5 Rowdy Roddy Piper 1.25 3.00
6 Mr. Wonderful Paul Orndorff .50 1.25
7 Jake The Snake Roberts .75 2.00
8 Jimmy Superfly Snuka .75 2.00
9 The British Bulldog 1.00 2.50
10 The American Dream Dusty Rhodes 1.00 2.50

2014 Topps WWE Greatest Championship Matches

COMPLETE SET (20) 8.00 20.00
*P.P.BLACK/1: UNPRICED DUE TO SCARCITY
*P.P.CYAN/1: UNPRICED DUE TO SCARCITY
*P.P.MAGENTA/1: UNPRICED DUE TO SCARCITY
*P.P.YELLOW/1: UNPRICED DUE TO SCARCITY
STATED ODDS 1:8 HOBBY AND RETAIL

1 The Rock/Steve Austin .75 2.00
2 John Cena/CM Punk .75 2.00
3 John Cena/HBK .75 2.00
4 The Rock/Mankind .75 2.00
5 Triple H/Cactus Jack .60 1.50
6 HBK/Mankind .60 1.50
7 John Cena/RVD .75 2.00
8 Brock Lesnar/Undertaker .60 1.50
9 Rey Mysterio/John Cena .75 2.00
10 HHH/Chris Jericho .60 1.50
11 Steve Austin/The Rock .75 2.00
12 Randy Orton/John Cena .75 2.00
13 CM Punk/John Cena .75 2.00
14 The Rock/HHH .75 2.00
15 Brock Lesnar/Eddie Guerrero .60 1.50
16 John Cena/JBL .75 2.00
17 The Rock/Brock Lesnar .75 2.00
18 Steve Austin/Chris Jericho .75 2.00
19 CM Punk/Chris Jericho .60 1.50
20 Mankind/The Rock .75 2.00

2014 Topps WWE NXT Prospects

COMPLETE SET (20) 15.00 40.00
*P.P.BLACK/1: UNPRICED DUE TO SCARCITY
*P.P.CYAN/1: UNPRICED DUE TO SCARCITY
*P.P.MAGENTA/1: UNPRICED DUE TO SCARCITY
*P.P.YELLOW/1: UNPRICED DUE TO SCARCITY
STATED ODDS 1:2 HOBBY AND RETAIL

1 Adrian Neville .60 1.50
2 Alexander Rusev .75 2.00
3 Baron Corbin .30 .75
4 Bayley 3.00 8.00
5 Charlotte 6.00 15.00
6 CJ Parker .30 .75
7 Konnor O'Brian .30 .75
8 Corey Graves .30 .75
9 Emma 1.50 4.00
10 Enzo Amore .60 1.50
11 Jason Jordan .30 .75
12 Leo Kruger .30 .75
13 Mojo Rawley .30 .75
14 Paige 5.00 12.00
15 Rick Viktor .30 .75
16 Sami Zayn .60 1.50
17 Sasha Banks 6.00 15.00
18 Sylvester Lefort .30 .75
19 Tyler Breeze .30 .75
20 Xavier Woods .30 .75

2014 Topps WWE Quad Autograph

NNO Shawn Michaels/X-Pac
Road Dogg/Billy Gunn

2014 Topps WWE Stone Cold Steve Austin Tribute

COMPLETE SET (10) 5.00 12.00
*P.P.BLACK/1: UNPRICED DUE TO SCARCITY
*P.P.CYAN/1: UNPRICED DUE TO SCARCITY
*P.P.MAGENTA/1: UNPRICED DUE TO SCARCITY
*P.P.YELLOW/1: UNPRICED DUE TO SCARCITY
STATED ODDS 1:12 HOBBY AND RETAIL

1 Stone Cold Steve Austin 1.00 2.50
2 Stone Cold Steve Austin 1.00 2.50
3 Stone Cold Steve Austin 1.00 2.50
4 Stone Cold Steve Austin 1.00 2.50
5 Stone Cold Steve Austin 1.00 2.50
6 Stone Cold Steve Austin 1.00 2.50
7 Stone Cold Steve Austin 1.00 2.50
8 Stone Cold Steve Austin 1.00 2.50
9 Stone Cold Steve Austin 1.00 2.50
10 Stone Cold Steve Austin 1.00 2.50

2014 Topps WWE SummerSlam Mat Relics

NNO AJ Lee 12.00 30.00
NNO Alberto Del Rio 6.00 15.00
NNO Big E Langston 2.50 6.00
NNO Bray Wyatt 6.00 15.00
NNO Brie Bella 8.00 20.00
NNO Brock Lesnar 10.00 25.00
NNO Christian 2.50 6.00
NNO CM Punk 10.00 25.00
NNO Cody Rhodes 2.50 6.00
NNO Damien Sandow 2.50 6.00
NNO Daniel Bryan 4.00 10.00
NNO Dean Ambrose 10.00 25.00
NNO Dolph Ziggler 4.00 10.00
NNO John Cena 12.00 30.00
NNO Kaitlyn 6.00 15.00
NNO Kane 6.00 15.00
NNO Natalya 8.00 20.00
NNO Randy Orton 10.00 25.00
NNO Rob Van Dam 6.00 15.00
NNO Triple H 10.00 25.00

2014 Topps WWE Swatch Relics

NNO Brodus Clay/Shirt 3.00 8.00
NNO Christian/Shirt 3.00 8.00
NNO CM Punk/Shirt 6.00 15.00
NNO Damien Sandow/Shirt 3.00 8.00
NNO Daniel Bryan/Shirt 4.00 10.00
NNO Darren Young/Shirt 3.00 8.00
NNO Dean Ambrose/Shirt 8.00 20.00
NNO Dolph Ziggler/Shirt 5.00 12.00
NNO Hornswoggle/Shirt 3.00 8.00
NNO John Cena/Shirt 8.00 20.00
NNO Mark Henry/Shirt 4.00 10.00
NNO The Miz/Shirt 3.00 8.00
NNO Randy Orton/Shirt 6.00 15.00
NNO Roman Reigns/Shirt 12.00 30.00
NNO Ryback/Shirt 3.00 8.00
NNO Seth Rollins 6.00 15.00
Shirt
NNO Undertaker/Pants 12.00 30.00
NNO Wade Barrett/Shirt 3.00 8.00

2014 Topps WWE Triple Autographs

OVERALL TRIPLE AUTO PRINT RUN 25
UNPRICED DUE TO SCARCITY

NNO AJ Lee
Summer Rae
Renee Young
NNO Bray Wyatt
Luke Harper
Erick Rowan
NNO Eva Marie
JoJo
Jack Swagger
NNO John Cena
Daniel Bryan
Randy Orton

2014 Topps WWE Promo

P1 Shawn Michaels
(WWE 50 Book Exclusive)

2015 Topps WWE

COMPLETE SET (100) 8.00 20.00
UNOPENED BOX (24 PACKS)
UNOPENED PACK (7 CARDS)
*BLACK: 2X TO 5X BASIC CARDS
*SILVER: 3X TO 8X BASIC CARDS
*GOLD/10: 6X TO 15X BASIC CARDS
*RED/1: UNPRICED DUE TO SCARCITY
*P.P.BLACK/1: UNPRICED DUE TO SCARCITY
*P.P.CYAN/1: UNPRICED DUE TO SCARCITY
*P.P.MAGENTA/1: UNPRICED DUE TO SCARCITY
*P.P.YELLOW/1: UNPRICED DUE TO SCARCITY

1 Adam Rose RC .20 .50
2 AJ Lee .75 2.00
3 Alex Riley .15 .40
4 Alicia Fox .30 .75
5 Bad News Barrett .15 .40
6 Batista .40 1.00
7 Big E .25 .60
8 Big Show .40 1.00
9 Bo Dallas .15 .40
10 Booker T .25 .60
11 Bray Wyatt .60 1.50
12 Brie Bella .50 1.25
13 Brock Lesnar .60 1.50
14 Byron Saxton .15 .40
15 Cameron .25 .60
16 Cesaro .15 .40
17 Chris Jericho .40 1.00
18 Christian .15 .40
19 Curtis Axel .15 .40
20 Damien Mizdow .15 .40
21 Daniel Bryan .60 1.50
22 Darren Young .15 .40
23 David Otunga .15 .40
24 Dean Ambrose .40 1.00
25 Diego .15 .40
26 Dolph Ziggler .25 .60
27 Eden .25 .60
28 Emma RC .25 .60
29 Erick Rowan .25 .60
30 Eva Marie .60 1.50
31 Fandango .15 .40
32 Fernando .15 .40
33 Goldust .15 .40
34 Heath Slater .15 .40
35 Hornswoggle .25 .60
36 Jack Swagger .25 .60
37 Jason Albert .15 .40
38 JBL .15 .40
39 Jerry The King Lawler .25 .60
40 Jey Uso .15 .40
41 Jimmy Uso .15 .40
42 John Cena .75 2.00

43 Justin Gabriel	.15	.40
44 Kane	.40	1.00
45 Kofi Kingston	.15	.40
46 Lana RC	.60	1.50
47 Layla	.40	1.00
48 Lilian Garcia	.40	1.00
49 Luke Harper	.25	.60
50 Mark Henry	.25	.60
51 Michael Cole	.15	.40
52 The Miz	.25	.60
53 Naomi	.25	.60
54 Natalya	.50	1.25
55 Nikki Bella	.50	1.25
56 Paige RC	.75	2.00
57 Paul Heyman	.15	.40
58 R-Truth	.15	.40
59 Randy Orton	.60	1.50
60 Renee Young	.60	1.50
61 Rey Mysterio	.40	1.00
62 The Rock	.75	2.00
63 Rob Van Dam	.40	1.00
64 Roman Reigns	.40	1.00
65 Rosa Mendes	.25	.60
66 Rusev RC	.40	1.00
67 Ryback	.15	.40
68 Santino Marella	.15	.40
69 Scott Stanford	.15	.40
70 Seth Rollins	.25	.60
71 Sheamus	.40	1.00
72 Sin Cara	.25	.60
73 Stardust	.15	.40
74 Stephanie McMahon	.25	.60
75 Summer Rae	.60	1.50
76 Tamina Snuka	.25	.60
77 Titus O'Neil	.15	.40
78 Tom Phillips RC	.15	.40
79 Tony Chimel	.15	.40
80 El Torito	.15	.40
81 Triple H	.60	1.50
82 Tyson Kidd	.15	.40
83 Undertaker	.60	1.50
84 William Regal	.25	.60
85 Xavier Woods	.25	.60
86 Zack Ryder	.15	.40
87 Zeb Colter	.25	.60
88 Bret The Hit Man Hart	.50	1.25
89 Bruno Sammartino	.40	1.00
90 George The Animal Steele	.20	.50
91 Gerald Brisco	.25	.60
92 Hulk Hogan	.75	2.00
93 Larry Zbyszko	.25	.60
94 Mouth of the South Jimmy Hart	.20	.50
95 Pat Patterson	.15	.40
96 Ric Flair	.75	2.00
97 Rowdy Roddy Piper	.50	1.25
98 Sting	.40	1.00
99 Ultimate Warrior	.50	1.25
100 Virgil	.15	.40

2015 Topps WWE Athletic Tape Relics

*RED/1: UNPRICED DUE TO SCARCITY
STATED PRINT RUN 20 SER.#'d SETS

NNO Cesaro	30.00	80.00
NNO Curtis Axel	25.00	60.00
NNO Daniel Bryan	120.00	200.00
NNO Darren Young	15.00	40.00
NNO Jack Swagger	15.00	40.00
NNO Rey Mysterio	30.00	80.00
NNO Ryback	25.00	60.00
NNO Zack Ryder	50.00	100.00

2015 Topps WWE Autographs

*BLACK/50: .6X TO 1.5X BASIC AUTOS
*SILVER/25: .75X to 2X BASIC AUTOS
*GOLD/10: 1X TO 2.5X BASIC AUTOS
*RED/1: UNPRICED DUE TO SCARCITY
*P.P.BLACK/1: UNPRICED DUE TO SCARCITY
*P.P.CYAN/1: UNPRICED DUE TO SCARCITY
*P.P.MAGENTA/1: UNPRICED DUE TO SCARCITY
*P.P.YELLOW/1: UNPRICED DUE TO SCARCITY
RANDOMLY INSERTED INTO PACKS

NNO AJ Lee	75.00	150.00
NNO Bray Wyatt	15.00	40.00
NNO Bret Hit Man Hart	25.00	60.00
NNO Eden	20.00	50.00
NNO Emma	15.00	40.00
NNO George The Animal Steele	15.00	40.00
NNO Hulk Hogan	125.00	250.00
NNO Jack Swagger	6.00	15.00
NNO John Cena	25.00	60.00
NNO Larry Zbyszko	6.00	15.00
NNO Mouth of the South Jimmy Hart	6.00	15.00
NNO Paige	75.00	150.00
NNO Ric Flair	15.00	40.00
NNO Rowdy Roddy Piper	25.00	60.00
NNO Rusev	20.00	50.00
NNO Seth Rollins	15.00	40.00

2015 Topps WWE Championship Plates

*GOLD/10: UNPRICED DUE TO SCARCITY
*RED/1: UNPRICED DUE TO SCARCITY
RANDOMLY INSERTED INTO PACKS

NNO AJ Lee	15.00	40.00
NNO Batista and Rey Mysterio	6.00	15.00
NNO Big Show	6.00	15.00
NNO Booker T	6.00	15.00
NNO Brie Bella	8.00	20.00
NNO Brock Lesnar	8.00	20.00
NNO Bruno Sammartino	6.00	15.00
NNO Cesaro	6.00	15.00
NNO Dean Ambrose	8.00	20.00
NNO Dolph Ziggler	8.00	20.00
NNO Edge and Chris Jericho	6.00	15.00
NNO Eve	10.00	25.00
NNO Hulk Hogan	12.00	30.00
NNO John Cena	10.00	25.00
NNO Kane	6.00	15.00
NNO Kane and Big Show	6.00	15.00
NNO Lex Luger	6.00	15.00
NNO New Age Outlaws	8.00	20.00
NNO Nikki Bella	12.00	30.00
NNO Paige	15.00	40.00
NNO Randy Orton	6.00	15.00
NNO Razor Ramon	8.00	20.00
NNO Rey Mysterio	6.00	15.00
NNO Ric Flair/US Title	10.00	25.00
NNO Ric Flair/WWE Title	12.00	30.00
NNO Rock	8.00	20.00
NNO Triple H	6.00	15.00
NNO Ultimate Warrior/IC Title	6.00	15.00
NNO Ultimate Warrior/WWE Title	10.00	25.00
NNO Usos	8.00	20.00

2015 Topps WWE Crowd Chants Oh No

COMPLETE SET (10) 4.00 10.00
*P.P.BLACK/1: UNPRICED DUE TO SCARCITY
*P.P.CYAN/1: UNPRICED DUE TO SCARCITY
*P.P.MAGENTA/1: UNPRICED DUE TO SCARCITY
*P.P.YELLOW/1: UNPRICED DUE TO SCARCITY
RANDOMLY INSERTED INTO PACKS

1 The Montreal Incident	.40	1.00
2 Mr. McMahon/The Rock	.40	1.00
3 Eve/Zack Ryder	1.00	2.50
4 Brad Maddox/Ryback	.40	1.00
5 Damien Sandow/Cody Rhodes	.40	1.00
6 Big Show/John Cena	.40	1.00
7 Randy Orton/Daniel Bryan	1.25	3.00
8 Triple H/Daniel Bryan	.75	2.00
9 Wyatt Family/John Cena	.50	1.25
10 Streak Ends	1.00	2.50

2015 Topps WWE Crowd Chants One More Match

COMPLETE SET (10) 4.00 10.00
*P.P.BLACK/1: UNPRICED DUE TO SCARCITY
*P.P.CYAN/1: UNPRICED DUE TO SCARCITY
*P.P.MAGENTA/1: UNPRICED DUE TO SCARCITY
*P.P.YELLOW/1: UNPRICED DUE TO SCARCITY
RANDOMLY INSERTED INTO PACKS

1 Cowboy Bob Orton	.40	1.00
2 Edge	.50	1.25
3 Shawn Michaels	.50	1.25
4 Million Dollar Man Ted DiBiase	.40	1.00
5 Bruno Sammartino	.40	1.00
6 Ric Flair	.75	2.00
7 Rowdy Roddy Piper	.50	1.25
8 Hulk Hogan	1.25	3.00
9 Jake The Snake Roberts	.40	1.00
10 Stone Cold Steve Austin	1.25	3.00

2015 Topps WWE Crowd Chants This Is Awesome

COMPLETE SET (10) 4.00 10.00
*P.P.BLACK/1: UNPRICED DUE TO SCARCITY
*P.P.CYAN/1: UNPRICED DUE TO SCARCITY
*P.P.MAGENTA/1: UNPRICED DUE TO SCARCITY
*P.P.YELLOW/1: UNPRICED DUE TO SCARCITY
RANDOMLY INSERTED INTO PACKS

1 Rock beats Cena	.75	2.00
2 DX Reunites	.75	2.00
3 Bob Backlund HOF	.40	1.00
4 Dolph Ziggler/Alberto Del Rio	.40	1.00
5 Big Show/Triple H	.40	1.00
6 Kofi Kingston	.40	1.00
7 Wyatt Family/The Shield	.40	1.00
8 Hogan/Austin/Rock	1.25	3.00
9 Daniel Bryan	.40	1.00
10 Paige/AJ Lee	2.50	6.00

2015 Topps WWE Crowd Chants USA

COMPLETE SET (10) 5.00 12.00
*P.P.BLACK/1: UNPRICED DUE TO SCARCITY
*P.P.CYAN/1: UNPRICED DUE TO SCARCITY
*P.P.MAGENTA/1: UNPRICED DUE TO SCARCITY
*P.P.YELLOW/1: UNPRICED DUE TO SCARCITY
RANDOMLY INSERTED INTO PACKS

1 Hulk Hogan	1.50	4.00
2 Sgt. Slaughter	.75	2.00
3 Hacksaw Jim Duggan	.40	1.00
4 Lex Luger	.40	1.00
5 The US Express	.40	1.00
6 Jack Swagger	.40	1.00
7 The American Dream Dusty Rhodes	.40	1.00
8 John Cena	1.25	3.00
9 The Rock	1.50	4.00
10 Undertaker	1.25	3.00

2015 Topps WWE Crowd Chants WOOOOOO

COMPLETE SET (10) 4.00 10.00
*P.P.BLACK/1: UNPRICED DUE TO SCARCITY
*P.P.CYAN/1: UNPRICED DUE TO SCARCITY
*P.P.MAGENTA/1: UNPRICED DUE TO SCARCITY
*P.P.YELLOW/1: UNPRICED DUE TO SCARCITY
RANDOMLY INSERTED INTO PACKS

1 Ric Flair/Royal Rumble	.75	2.00
2 Ric Flair/Randy Savage	.60	1.50
3 Ric Flair/Eric Bischoff	.60	1.50
4 Ric Flair/Jeff Jarrett	.60	1.50
5 Evolution	.60	1.50
6 Ric Flair/Carlito	.60	1.50
7 Ric Flair/Roddy Piper	.60	1.50
8 Ric Flair HOF	1.25	3.00
9 Shawn Michaels/Ric Flair	.60	1.50
10 Four Horsemen HOF	1.25	3.00

2015 Topps WWE Crowd Chants YES! YES! YES!

COMPLETE SET (10) 5.00 12.00
*P.P.BLACK/1: UNPRICED DUE TO SCARCITY
*P.P.CYAN/1: UNPRICED DUE TO SCARCITY
*P.P.MAGENTA/1: UNPRICED DUE TO SCARCITY
*P.P.YELLOW/1: UNPRICED DUE TO SCARCITY
RANDOMLY INSERTED INTO PACKS

1 Daniel Bryan/Kane	.75	2.00
2 Team Hell No/Tag Champs	1.25	3.00
3 Team Hell No/Ziggler & Big E	.75	2.00
4 Daniel Bryan/WWE Title	.75	2.00
5 Locker Room/Daniel Bryan	.75	2.00
6 Daniel Bryan/Second Title	.75	2.00
7 Daniel Bryan/Wyatt Family	.75	2.00
8 Yes Movement	.75	2.00
9 Daniel Bryan/Triple H	.75	2.00
10 Daniel Bryan WWE World TItle	1.25	3.00

2015 Topps WWE Crowd Chants You Still Got It

COMPLETE SET (10) 2.50 6.00
*P.P.BLACK/1: UNPRICED DUE TO SCARCITY
*P.P.CYAN/1: UNPRICED DUE TO SCARCITY
*P.P.MAGENTA/1: UNPRICED DUE TO SCARCITY
*P.P.YELLOW/1: UNPRICED DUE TO SCARCITY
RANDOMLY INSERTED INTO PACKS

1 Ricky The Dragon Steamboat	.40	1.00
2 Booker T	.40	1.00
3 Chris Jericho	.40	1.00
4 Vader	.40	1.00
5 Road Warrior Animal	.40	1.00
6 Jerry The King Lawler	.40	1.00
7 Rob Van Dam	.40	1.00
8 Goldust	.40	1.00
9 Billy Gunn	.40	1.00
10 Road Dogg	.40	1.00

2015 Topps WWE Diva Kiss

*GOLD/10: .5X TO 1.2X BASIC KISS
*RED/1: UNPRICED DUE TO SCARCITY
RANDOMLY INSERTED INTO PACKS

NNO Alicia Fox	20.00	50.00
NNO Eva Marie	25.00	60.00
NNO Eve Torres	25.00	60.00
NNO Lana	30.00	80.00
NNO Layla	15.00	40.00
NNO Lilian Garcia	15.00	40.00
NNO Paige	150.00	300.00
NNO Rosa Mendes	15.00	40.00
NNO Trish Stratus	30.00	80.00
NNO Lita	25.00	60.00

2015 Topps WWE Diva Kiss Autographs

*GOLD/10: UNPRICED DUE TO SCARCITY
*RED/1: UNPRICED DUE TO SCARCITY
STATED PRINT RUN 15 SER.#'d SETS

NNO Alicia Fox	40.00	100.00
NNO Eva Marie	80.00	200.00
NNO Eve Torres	40.00	100.00
NNO Lana	80.00	200.00
NNO Layla	50.00	125.00
NNO Lilian Garcia	50.00	125.00
NNO Paige	100.00	250.00
NNO Rosa Mendes	30.00	80.00
NNO Trish Stratus	100.00	250.00
NNO Lita	80.00	200.00

2015 Topps WWE King of the Ring Relics

*RED/1: UNPRICED DUE TO SCARCITY
RANDOMLY INSERTED INTO PACKS

NNO Billy Gunn	12.00	30.00
NNO Bret Hit Man Hart	25.00	60.00
NNO Brock Lesnar	15.00	40.00
NNO Don Muraco	12.00	30.00
NNO Edge	20.00	50.00
NNO Harley Race	20.00	50.00
NNO King Booker	15.00	40.00
NNO Million Dollar Man Ted DiBiase	20.00	50.00
NNO Sheamus	15.00	40.00
NNO Stone Cold Steve Austin	25.00	60.00
NNO Tito Santana	15.00	40.00
NNO Triple H	25.00	60.00
NNO William Regal	12.00	30.00

2015 Topps WWE NXT Prospects

COMPLETE SET (10)	6.00	15.00
STATED ODDS 1:3		
1 Aiden English	1.00	2.50
2 Alexa Bliss	12.00	30.00
3 Angelo Dawkins	1.00	2.50
4 Bull Dempsey	1.50	4.00
5 Colin Cassady	1.25	3.00
6 Hideo Itami	2.00	5.00
7 Kalisto	1.25	3.00
8 Marcus Louis	1.00	2.50
9 Sawyer Fulton	1.00	2.50
10 Tye Dillinger	1.00	2.50

2015 Topps WWE SummerSlam Mat Relics

*GOLD/10: UNPRICED DUE TO SCARCITY
*RED/1: UNPRICED DUE TO SCARCITY
RANDOMLY INSERTED INTO PACKS

NNO AJ Lee	12.00	30.00
NNO Bray Wyatt	6.00	15.00
NNO Brie Bella	6.00	15.00
NNO Brock Lesnar	8.00	20.00
NNO Cesaro	5.00	12.00
NNO Chris Jericho	8.00	20.00
NNO Dean Ambrose	6.00	15.00
NNO Dolph Ziggler	8.00	20.00
NNO Jack Swagger	5.00	12.00
NNO John Cena	6.00	15.00
NNO Miz	5.00	12.00
NNO Nikki Bella	6.00	15.00
NNO Paige	15.00	40.00
NNO Randy Orton	5.00	12.00
NNO Rob Van Dam	5.00	12.00
NNO Roman Reigns	8.00	20.00
NNO Rusev	6.00	15.00
NNO Seth Rollins	5.00	12.00
NNO Stephanie McMahon	8.00	20.00
NNO Triple H	8.00	20.00

2015 Topps WWE Swatch Relics

*GOLD/10: UNPRICED DUE TO SCARCITY
*RED/1: UNPRICED DUE TO SCARCITY
RANDOMLY INSERTED INTO PACKS

NNO AJ Lee	15.00	40.00
NNO Big E	5.00	12.00
NNO Big Show	5.00	12.00
NNO Bo Dallas	6.00	15.00
NNO Bray Wyatt	10.00	25.00
NNO Brie Bella	6.00	15.00
NNO Dolph Ziggler	6.00	15.00
NNO Fandango	5.00	12.00
NNO Goldust	5.00	12.00
NNO Jey Uso	5.00	12.00
NNO John Cena	6.00	15.00
NNO The Miz	5.00	12.00
NNO Natalya	6.00	15.00
NNO Nikki Bella	6.00	15.00
NNO Paige	15.00	40.00
NNO Randy Orton	6.00	15.00
NNO Seth Rollins	6.00	15.00
NNO Stardust	5.00	12.00

2015 Topps WWE Triple Autographs

STATED PRINT RUN 5 SER.#'d SETS
UNPRICED DUE TO SCARCITY

NNO AJ/Paige/Emma
NNO Wyatt/Rusev/Hart
NNO Hogan/Flair/Piper
NNO Cena/Ambrose/Rollins
NNO Paige/Emma/Eden

2016 Topps WWE

COMPLETE SET (100)	10.00	25.00
UNOPENED BOX (24 PACKS)		
UNOPENED PACK (8 CARDS)		
*BRONZE: 1.2X TO 3X BASIC CARDS		
*SILVER: 2X TO 5X BASIC CARDS		
*GOLD/10: UNPRICED DUE TO SCARCITY		
*RED/1: UNPRICED DUE TO SCARCITY		
*P.P.BLACK/1: UNPRICED DUE TO SCARCITY		
*P.P.CYAN/1: UNPRICED DUE TO SCARCITY		
*P.P.MAGENTA/1: UNPRICED DUE TO SCARCITY		
*P.P.YELLOW/1: UNPRICED DUE TO SCARCITY		
1 Adam Rose	.20	.50
2 Alberto Del Rio	.30	.75
3 Alicia Fox	.30	.75
4 The Ascension	.20	.50
5 Becky Lynch RC	.60	1.50
6 Big Show	.40	1.00
7 Bo Dallas	.20	.50
8 Booker T	.40	1.00
9 Brie Bella	.40	1.00
10 Bubba Ray Dudley	.40	1.00
11 The Bunny	.20	.50
12 Byron Saxton	.20	.50
13 Cesaro	.40	1.00
14 Charlotte	.60	1.50
15 Corey Graves RC	.12	.30
16 Curtis Axel	.20	.50
17 D-Von Dudley	.30	.75
18 Damien Sandow	.20	.50
19 Dolph Ziggler	.25	.60
20 Fandango	.20	.50
21 Goldust	.30	.75
22 Jason Albert	.20	.50
23 JBL	.25	.60
24 Jerry The King Lawler	.40	1.00
25 Kalisto	.50	1.25
26 Kevin Owens	.50	1.25
27 Lana	.75	2.00
28 Mandy Rose RC	2.00	5.00
29 Mark Henry	.25	.60
30 The Miz	.30	.75
31 Naomi	.30	.75
32 Natalya	.30	.75
33 Neville	.50	1.25
34 Nikki Bella	.60	1.50
35 Paige	.60	1.50
36 Titus O'Neil	.20	.50
37 R-Truth	.20	.50
38 Rusev	.50	1.25
39 Ryback	.25	.60
40 Sasha Banks	.60	1.50
41 Sin Cara	.25	.60
42 Stardust	.20	.50
43 Summer Rae	.50	1.25
44 Tamina	.25	.60
45 Tyler Breeze	.20	.50
46 Tyson Kidd	.20	.50
47 The Usos	.20	.50
48 William Regal	.20	.50
49 Zeb Colter	.20	.50
50 Alundra Blayze L	.25	.60
51 American Dream Dusty Rhodes L	.20	.50
52 Andre the Giant L	.60	1.50
53 Bam Bam Bigelow L	.25	.60
54 Barry Windham L	.20	.50
55 Batista L	.40	1.00
56 The Brain Busters L	.20	.50
57 The British Bulldog L	.25	.60
58 The Bushwhackers L	.20	.50
59 Christian L	.30	.75
60 Dangerous Danny Davis L	.20	.50
61 Doink the Clown L	.20	.50
62 Edge L	.50	1.25
63 Eve Torres L	.40	1.00
64 George The Animal Steele L	.25	.60
65 The Godfather L	.25	.60
66 Irwin R. Schyster L	.20	.50
67 Jake The Snake Roberts L	.40	1.00
68 Jim Ross L	.30	.75
69 J.J. Dillon L	.20	.50
70 Kamala L	.20	.50
71 Kerry Von Erich L	.30	.75
72 Kevin Nash L	.50	1.25
73 Kevin Von Erich L RC	.30	.75
74 Lita L	.60	1.50
75 Macho King Randy Savage L	.50	1.25
76 Mike Rotunda L	.20	.50
77 Million Dollar Man Ted DiBiase L	.25	.60
78 Miss Elizabeth L	.20	.50
79 Mr. X L	.20	.50
80 The Nasty Boys L	.20	.50
81 The Natural Disasters L	.20	.50
82 Bret Hit Man Hart L	.50	1.25
83 Papa Shango L	.25	.60
84 Ric Flair L	.75	2.00
85 Rikishi L	.25	.60
86 Road Dogg L	.30	.75
87 Rob Van Dam L	.40	1.00
88 Faarooq L	.50	1.25
89 Rowdy Roddy Piper L	.60	1.50
90 Santino Marella L	.25	.60
91 Scott Hall L	.50	1.25
92 Sensational Sherri L	.30	.75
93 Shawn Michaels L	.75	2.00
94 Stevie Ray L	.20	.50
95 Superstar Billy Graham L	.20	.50
96 Tatsumi Fujinami L RC	.20	.50
97 Trish Stratus L	1.00	2.50
98 Ultimate Warrior L	.50	1.25
99 Virgil L	.20	.50
100 X-Pac L	.30	.75

2016 Topps WWE 2K17 NXT TakeOver London Mat Relics

*PURPLE/299: SAME VALUE AS BASIC
*GREEN/199: .5X TO 1.2X BASIC MEM
*BRONZE/99: .6X TO 1.5X BASIC MEM
*SILVER/50: .75X TO 2X BASIC MEM
*BLUE/25: UNPRICED DUE TO SCARCITY
*GOLD/10: UNPRICED DUE TO SCARCITY
RANDOMLY INSERTED INTO PACKS

NNO Asuka	5.00	12.00
NNO Emma	6.00	15.00
NNO Dana Brooke	3.00	8.00
NNO Dash Wilder	2.50	6.00
NNO Scott Dawson	2.50	6.00
NNO Enzo Amore	3.00	8.00
NNO Colin Cassady	3.00	8.00
NNO Carmella	6.00	15.00
NNO Baron Corbin	4.00	10.00
NNO Apollo Crews	3.00	8.00
NNO Bayley	5.00	12.00
NNO Nia Jax	3.00	8.00
NNO Finn Balor	5.00	12.00
NNO Samoa Joe	3.00	8.00

2016 Topps WWE Authority Perspectives

COMPLETE SET (18)	12.00	30.00
*P.P.BLACK/1: UNPRICED DUE TO SCARCITY		
*P.P.CYAN/1: UNPRICED DUE TO SCARCITY		
*P.P.MAGENTA/1: UNPRICED DUE TO SCARCITY		
*P.P.YELLOW/1: UNPRICED DUE TO SCARCITY		
RANDOMLY INSERTED INTO PACKS		
*ANTI-AUTHORITY: SAME VALUE		
1A Triple H	2.50	6.00

2A Stephanie McMahon	1.00	2.50
3A Seth Rollins	1.00	2.50
4A Kane	1.00	2.50
5A J&J Security	.60	1.50
6A The New Day	1.50	4.00
7A The Wyatt Family	1.25	3.00
8A King Barrett	.60	1.50
9A Sheamus	1.50	4.00
10A John Cena	3.00	8.00
11A Sting	1.50	4.00
12A The Rock	3.00	8.00
13A Reigns/Ambrose	2.00	5.00
14A Randy Orton	1.50	4.00
15A Brock Lesnar	3.00	8.00
16A Undertaker	2.50	6.00
17A Chris Jericho	1.50	4.00
18A Daniel Bryan	2.50	6.00

2016 Topps WWE Autographs

*BRONZE/50: .5X TO 1.2X BASIC AUTOS
*SILVER/25: .75X TO 2X BASIC AUTOS
*GOLD/10: UNPRICED DUE TO SCARCITY
*RED/1: UNPRICED DUE TO SCARCITY
*P.P.BLACK/1: UNPRICED DUE TO SCARCITY
*P.P.CYAN/1: UNPRICED DUE TO SCARCITY
*P.P.MAGENTA/1: UNPRICED DUE TO SCARCITY
*P.P.YELLOW/1: UNPRICED DUE TO SCARCITY
RANDOMLY INSERTED INTO PACKS

NNO Apollo Crews	10.00	25.00
NNO Alberto Del Rio	10.00	25.00
NNO Asuka	30.00	80.00
NNO Bayley	25.00	60.00
NNO Becky Lynch	15.00	40.00
NNO Braun Strowman	10.00	25.00
NNO Bray Wyatt	10.00	25.00
NNO Bubba Ray Dudley	8.00	20.00
NNO Charlotte	12.00	30.00
NNO D-Von Dudley	6.00	15.00
NNO Dean Ambrose	10.00	25.00
NNO Finn Balor	15.00	40.00
NNO JJ Dillion	6.00	15.00
NNO John Cena	15.00	40.00
NNO Luke Harper	25.00	60.00
NNO Natalya	8.00	20.00
NNO Nia Jax	12.00	30.00
NNO Ric Flair	30.00	75.00
NNO Rikishi	6.00	15.00
NNO Roman Reigns	10.00	25.00
NNO Samoa Joe	8.00	20.00
NNO Seth Rollins	8.00	20.00
NNO Sting	25.00	60.00
NNO Superstar Billy Graham	15.00	40.00

2016 Topps WWE Diva Kiss

*GOLD/10: UNPRICED DUE TO SCARCITY
*RED/1: UNPRICED DUE TO SCARCITY
STATED PRINT RUN 99 SER.#'d SETS

NNO Alicia Fox	30.00	75.00
NNO Alundra Blayze	60.00	120.00
NNO Bayley	75.00	150.00
NNO Becky Lynch	150.00	300.00
NNO Brie Bella	30.00	75.00
NNO Charlotte	125.00	250.00
NNO Lana	50.00	100.00
NNO Lita	25.00	60.00
NNO Nikki Bella	60.00	120.00
NNO Sasha Banks	150.00	300.00
NNO Trish Stratus	200.00	400.00

2016 Topps WWE Diva Kiss Autographs

*GOLD/10: UNPRICED DUE TO SCARCITY
*RED/1: UNPRICED DUE TO SCARCITY
*P.P.BLACK/1: UNPRICED DUE TO SCARCITY
*P.P.CYAN/1: UNPRICED DUE TO SCARCITY
*P.P.MAGENTA/1: UNPRICED DUE TO SCARCITY
*P.P.YELLOW/1: UNPRICED DUE TO SCARCITY
STATED PRINT RUN 25 SER.#'d SETS

NNO Alicia Fox	30.00	80.00
NNO Alundra Blayze	30.00	80.00
NNO Bayley	100.00	200.00
NNO Becky Lynch	400.00	800.00
NNO Brie Bella	150.00	300.00
NNO Charlotte	150.00	300.00
NNO Lana	60.00	120.00
NNO Lita	50.00	100.00
NNO Nikki Bella	50.00	100.00
NNO Sasha Banks	250.00	500.00
NNO Trish Stratus	250.00	500.00

2016 Topps WWE Medallions

*BRONZE/50: .5X TO 1.2X BASIC MEM
*SILVER/25: .6X TO 1.5X BASIC MEM
*GOLD/10: UNPRICED DUE TO SCARCITY
*RED/1: UNPRICED DUE TO SCARCITY
STATED PRINT RUN 299 SER.#'d SETS

NNO Big E	2.00	5.00
NNO Braun Strowman	2.50	6.00
NNO Bray Wyatt	8.00	20.00
NNO Brock Lesnar	10.00	25.00
NNO Chris Jericho	5.00	12.00
NNO Daniel Bryan	8.00	20.00
NNO Dean Ambrose	6.00	15.00
NNO Jamie Noble	2.00	5.00
NNO Joey Mercury	2.00	5.00
NNO John Cena	10.00	25.00
NNO Kane	3.00	8.00
NNO King Barrett	2.00	5.00
NNO Kofi Kingston	2.00	5.00
NNO Luke Harper	2.00	5.00
NNO Randy Orton	5.00	12.00
NNO The Rock	10.00	25.00
NNO Roman Reigns	6.00	15.00
NNO Seth Rollins	3.00	8.00
NNO Sheamus	5.00	12.00
NNO Stephanie McMahon	3.00	8.00
NNO Sting	5.00	12.00
NNO Triple H	8.00	20.00
NNO Undertaker	8.00	20.00
NNO Xavier Woods	2.00	5.00

2016 Topps WWE NXT Inserts

COMPLETE SET (28)	8.00	20.00

*P.P.BLACK/1: UNPRICED DUE TO SCARCITY
*P.P.CYAN/1: UNPRICED DUE TO SCARCITY
*P.P.MAGENTA/1: UNPRICED DUE TO SCARCITY
*P.P.YELLOW/1: UNPRICED DUE TO SCARCITY
STATED ODDS 1:1

1 Aiden English	.30	.75
2 Alexa Bliss	4.00	10.00
3 Angelo Dawkins	.30	.75
4 Apollo Crews	.30	.75
5 Asuka	4.00	10.00
6 Baron Corbin	.40	1.00
7 Bayley	.75	2.00
8 Billie Kay	.75	2.00
9 Blake	.30	.75
10 Carmella	.75	2.00
11 Chad Gable	.40	1.00
12 Colin Cassady	.60	1.50
13 Dana Brooke	.75	2.00
14 Dash Wilder	.40	1.00
15 Scott Dawson	.30	.75
16 Enzo Amore	.60	1.50
17 Finn Balor	2.00	5.00
18 Hideo Itami	.40	1.00
19 Jason Jordan	.40	1.00
20 Mojo Rawley	.30	.75
21 Murphy	.30	.75
22 Nia Jax	.50	1.25
23 Peyton Royce	.75	2.00
24 Sami Zayn	.50	1.25
25 Samoa Joe	.75	2.00
26 Sawyer Fulton	.40	1.00
27 Simon Gotch	.50	1.25
28 Tye Dillinger	.40	1.00

2016 Topps WWE NXT TakeOver Brooklyn Mat Relics

*BRONZE/50: .5X TO 1.2X BASIC MEM
*SILVER/25: .6X TO 1.5X BASIC MEM
*GOLD/10: UNPRICED DUE TO SCARCITY
*RED/1: UNPRICED DUE TO SCARCITY
*P.P.BLACK/1: UNPRICED DUE TO SCARCITY
*P.P.CYAN/1: UNPRICED DUE TO SCARCITY
*P.P.MAGENTA/1: UNPRICED DUE TO SCARCITY
*P.P.YELLOW/1: UNPRICED DUE TO SCARCITY
STATED PRINT RUN 199 SER.#'d SETS

NNO Aiden English	2.50	6.00
NNO Alexa Bliss	12.00	30.00
NNO Apollo Crews	2.50	6.00
NNO Baron Corbin	3.00	8.00
NNO Bayley	6.00	15.00
NNO Blake	2.50	6.00
NNO Finn Balor	8.00	20.00
NNO Kevin Owens	6.00	15.00
NNO Murphy	2.50	6.00
NNO Samoa Joe	6.00	15.00
NNO Sasha Banks	8.00	20.00
NNO Simon Gotch	4.00	10.00
NNO Tye Dillinger	3.00	8.00
NNO Tyler Breeze	2.50	6.00

2016 Topps WWE Shirt Relics

*BRONZE/50: .5X TO 1.2X BASIC MEM
*SILVER/25: .6X TO 1.5X BASIC MEM
*GOLD/10: UNPRICED DUE TO SCARCITY
*RED/1: UNPRICED DUE TO SCARCITY
*P.P.BLACK/1: UNPRICED DUE TO SCARCITY
*P.P.CYAN/1: UNPRICED DUE TO SCARCITY
*P.P.MAGENTA/1: UNPRICED DUE TO SCARCITY
*P.P.YELLOW/1: UNPRICED DUE TO SCARCITY
RANDOMLY INSERTED INTO PACKS

NNO Aiden English	3.00	8.00
NNO Alberto Del Rio	5.00	12.00
NNO Alicia Fox	5.00	12.00
NNO Apollo Crews	3.00	8.00
NNO Bayley	8.00	20.00
NNO Becky Lynch	10.00	25.00
NNO Braun Strowman	4.00	10.00
NNO Bray Wyatt	12.00	30.00
NNO Brie Bella	6.00	15.00
NNO Bubba Ray Dudley	6.00	15.00
NNO Cesaro	6.00	15.00
NNO Charlotte	10.00	25.00
NNO Dean Ambrose	10.00	25.00
NNO D-Von Dudley	5.00	12.00
NNO Finn Balor	10.00	25.00
NNO John Cena	15.00	40.00
NNO Kevin Owens	8.00	20.00
NNO Luke Harper	3.00	8.00
NNO Naomi	5.00	12.00
NNO Natalya	5.00	12.00
NNO Neville	8.00	20.00
NNO Paige	10.00	25.00
NNO Roman Reigns	10.00	25.00
NNO Samoa Joe	8.00	20.00
NNO Sasha Banks	10.00	25.00
NNO Seth Rollins	5.00	12.00
NNO Simon Gotch	5.00	12.00
NNO Tamina	4.00	10.00
NNO Tyler Breeze	3.00	8.00
NNO Zack Ryder	3.00	8.00

2016 Topps WWE SummerSlam Mat Relics

*BRONZE/50: .5X TO 1.2X BASIC MEM
*SILVER/25: .6X TO 1.5X BASIC MEM
*GOLD/10: UNPRICED DUE TO SCARCITY
*RED/1: UNPRICED DUE TO SCARCITY
*P.P.BLACK/1: UNPRICED DUE TO SCARCITY
*P.P.CYAN/1: UNPRICED DUE TO SCARCITY
*P.P.MAGENTA/1: UNPRICED DUE TO SCARCITY
*P.P.YELLOW/1: UNPRICED DUE TO SCARCITY
STATED PRINT RUN 199 SER.#'d SETS

NNO Big Show	4.00	10.00
NNO Bray Wyatt	8.00	20.00
NNO Brock Lesnar	10.00	25.00
NNO Cesaro	4.00	10.00
NNO Dean Ambrose	6.00	15.00
NNO Dolph Ziggler	2.50	6.00
NNO John Cena	10.00	25.00
NNO Kevin Owens	5.00	12.00
NNO King Barrett	2.00	5.00
NNO Luke Harper	2.00	5.00
NNO The Miz	3.00	8.00
NNO Neville	5.00	12.00
NNO Randy Orton	5.00	12.00
NNO Roman Reigns	6.00	15.00
NNO Rusev	5.00	12.00
NNO Ryback	2.50	6.00
NNO Seth Rollins	3.00	8.00
NNO Sheamus	5.00	12.00
NNO Stardust	2.00	5.00
NNO Undertaker	8.00	20.00

2016 Topps WWE Superstars of Canada Autographs

STATED PRINT RUN 25 SER.#'d SETS

NNO Chris Jericho	15.00	40.00
NNO Christian	12.00	30.00
NNO Edge	25.00	60.00
NNO Kevin Owens	12.00	30.00
NNO Natalya	12.00	30.00
NNO Renee Young	15.00	40.00
NNO Sami Zayn	10.00	25.00
NNO Trish Stratus	50.00	100.00

NNO Tyson Kidd 6.00 15.00
NNO Viktor 6.00 15.00

2016 Topps WWE Triple Autographs

STATED PRINT RUN 11 SER.#'d SETS

NNO Alberto Del Rio 50.00 100.00
Superstar Billy Graham
Rikishi
NNO Bayley/Asuka/Nia Jax 75.00 150.00
NNO Wyatt/Harper/Strowman 100.00 200.00
NNO Charlotte 100.00 200.00
Becky Lynch
Natalya
NNO Balor/Samoa Joe/Crews 100.00 200.00
NNO Cena/Dudley Boyz 75.00 150.00
NNO Rollins/Ambrose/Reigns 125.00 250.00
NNO Sting/Flair/Dillon 150.00 300.00

2017 Topps WWE

COMPLETE SET W/O SP (100) 8.00 20.00
COMPLETE SET W/SP (120)
UNOPENED BOX (24 PACKS)
UNOPENED PACK (7 CARDS)
*BRONZE: .5X TO 1.2X BASIC CARDS
*BLUE/99: 1X TO 2.5X BASIC CARDS
*SILVER/25: 2X TO 5X BASIC CARDS
*GOLD/10: 4X TO 10X BASIC CARDS
*RED/1: UNPRICED DUE TO SCARCITY
*P.P.BLACK/1: UNPRICED DUE TO SCARCITY
*P.P.CYAN/1: UNPRICED DUE TO SCARCITY
*P.P.MAGENTA/1: UNPRICED DUE TO SCARCITY
*P.P.YELLOW/1: UNPRICED DUE TO SCARCITY

1A The Rock 1.25 3.00
1B The Rock SP Just Bring It 10.00 25.00
2 Tyson Kidd .25 .60
3 Booker T .30 .75
4 Byron Saxton .25 .60
5A Bayley .75 2.00
5B Bayley SP Leaping 5.00 12.00
6 Big Cass .30 .75
7A Big E .30 .75
7B Big E SP Big Splash 3.00 8.00
8 Bob Backlund .25 .60
9A Brian Kendrick .25 .60
9B Brian Kendrick SP Jacket 3.00 8.00
10A Brock Lesnar 1.25 3.00
10B Brock Lesnar SP Outside Ring 8.00 20.00
11 Chad Patton RC .25 .60
12 Charly Caruso RC .25 .60
13A Chris Jericho .60 1.50
13B Chris Jericho SP Walls of Jericho 6.00 15.00
14 Corey Graves .25 .60
15 Darrick Moore RC .25 .60
16 Enzo Amore .75 2.00
17A Finn Balor 1.00 2.50
17B Finn Balor SP Entrance/No Logo 10.00 25.00
18A Goldberg 1.00 2.50
18B Goldberg SP Jacket 12.00 30.00
19 JoJo .40 1.00
20 John Cone RC .25 .60
21 Karl Anderson .25 .60
22A Kofi Kingston .30 .75
22B Kofi Kingston SP Leaping 6.00 15.00
23 Luke Gallows .40 1.00
24 Michael Cole .25 .60
25 Mick Foley .60 1.50
26A Nia Jax .40 1.00
26B Nia Jax SP Pink Gear 5.00 12.00
27 Paige .60 1.50
28 Paul Heyman .25 .60
29 Rod Zapata RC .25 .60
30 Shawn Bennett RC .25 .60
31 TJ Perkins RC .25 .60
32 Titus O'Neil .25 .60
33A Triple H .60 1.50
33B Triple H SP No Mic 10.00 25.00
34A Xavier Woods .30 .75
34B Xavier Woods 2.50 6.00
35A AJ Styles 1.25 3.00
35B AJ Styles 12.00 30.00
36A Alexa Bliss 1.25 3.00
36B Alexa Bliss SP Flip 15.00 40.00
37 Andrea D'Marco RC .25 .60
38A Carmella .60 1.50
38B Carmella SP Microphone 6.00 15.00
39 Chad Gable .30 .75
40 Charles Robinson .25 .60
41 Dan Engler RC .25 .60
42 David Otunga .25 .60
43 Greg Hamilton .25 .60
44 Jason Ayers RC .25 .60
45 Jason Jordan .30 .75
46 JBL .30 .75
47A John Cena 1.25 3.00
47B John Cena SP
48A Kane .30 .75
48B Kane SP Facing Forward 8.00 20.00
49 Luke Harper .25 .60
50 Maryse .50 1.25
51 Mauro Ranallo .25 .60
52 Mike Chioda RC .25 .60
53A The Miz .50 1.25
53B Miz SP In the Ring 8.00 20.00
54 Mojo Rawley .30 .75
55A Randy Orton .60 1.50
55B Randy Orton SP RKO 6.00 15.00
56 Renee Young .40 1.00
57 Ryan Tran RC .25 .60
58A Undertaker 1.00 2.50
58B Undertaker SP Silhouette 20.00 50.00
59 Zack Ryder .25 .60
60 Alexander Wolfe RC .30 .75
61 Aliyah .30 .75
62A Asuka .75 2.00
62B Asuka SP/(mask) 8.00 20.00
63A Austin Aries .50 1.25
63B Austin Aries SP Cape 6.00 15.00
64 Billie Kay .30 .75
65A Bobby Roode .60 1.50
65B Bobby Roode SP 8.00 20.00
66 Cathy Kelley .25 .60
67 Dash Wilder .25 .60
68 Dasha Fuentes .30 .75
69 Danilo Anfibio RC .25 .60
70 Drake Wuertz RC .25 .60
71 Eddie Orengo RC .25 .60
72 Ember Moon RC .60 1.50
73 Eric Young .50 1.25
74 Hideo Itami .40 1.00
75 Johnny Gargano .25 .60
76 Liv Morgan .40 1.00
77 Nick Miller RC .25 .60
78 Nikki Cross RC .50 1.25
79 Oney Lorcan .25 .60
80 Paul Ellering .25 .60
81 Peyton Royce .40 1.00
82 Roderick Strong RC .30 .75
83A Samoa Joe .75 2.00
83B Samoa Joe SP
84 Scott Dawson .25 .60
85 Shane Thorne RC .25 .60
86A Shinsuke Nakamura .60 1.50
86B Shinsuke Nakamura SP Jacket 6.00 15.00
87 Tommaso Ciampa .25 .60
88 Tye Dillinger .25 .60
89 William Regal .30 .75
90 Norman Smiley .30 .75
91 Ric Flair .60 1.50
92 Terri Runnels .25 .60
93 Beth Phoenix .25 .60
94 Eric Bischoff .25 .60
95 Ivory .25 .60
96 Judy Martin RC .25 .60
97 Kelly Kelly .50 1.25
98 Leilani Kai .25 .60
99 Princess Victoria RC .25 .60
100 Torrie Wilson .60 1.50

2017 Topps WWE Autographed Shirt Relics

STATED ODDS 1:3,524

NNO Bayley 30.00 75.00
NNO Big E 15.00 40.00
NNO Bray Wyatt 30.00 75.00
NNO Carmella 25.00 60.00
NNO Cesaro 15.00 40.00
NNO Dolph Ziggler 15.00 40.00
NNO John Cena 50.00 100.00
NNO Karl Anderson 15.00 40.00
NNO Kevin Owens 15.00 40.00
NNO Kofi Kingston 15.00 40.00
NNO The Miz 30.00 75.00
NNO Randy Orton 30.00 80.00
NNO Roman Reigns
NNO Seth Rollins 25.00 60.00
NNO Shinsuke Nakamura
NNO Xavier Woods

2017 Topps WWE Autographs

*BLUE/50: .6X TO 1.5X BASIC AUTOS
*SILVER/25: .75X TO 2X BASIC AUTOS
*GOLD/10: UNPRICED DUE TO SCARCITY
*RED/1: UNPRICED DUE TO SCARCITY
STATED ODDS 1:50

5 Bayley 15.00 40.00
6 Big Cass 8.00 20.00
7 Big E 6.00 15.00
10 Brock Lesnar 50.00 100.00
13 Chris Jericho 12.00 30.00
16 Enzo Amore 10.00 25.00
18 Goldberg 50.00 100.00
21 Karl Anderson 6.00 15.00
22 Kofi Kingston 6.00 15.00
23 Luke Gallows 5.00 12.00
34 Xavier Woods 6.00 15.00
38 Carmella 10.00 25.00
53 The Miz 5.00 12.00
62 Asuka 15.00 40.00
64 Billie Kay 8.00 20.00
81 Peyton Royce 10.00 25.00
83 Samoa Joe 6.00 15.00
91 Ric Flair 15.00 40.00
92 Terri Runnels 10.00 25.00
93 Beth Phoenix 6.00 15.00
94 Eric Bischoff 8.00 20.00
96 Judy Martin 6.00 15.00
97 Kelly Kelly 15.00 40.00
98 Leilani Kai 6.00 15.00
100 Torrie Wilson 10.00 25.00

2017 Topps WWE Autographs Blue

STATED ODDS 1:99
STATED PRINT RUN 50 SER.#'d SETS

58 Undertaker 150.00 300.00

2017 Topps WWE Autographs Silver

STATED ODDS 1:116
STATED PRINT RUN 25 SER.#'d SETS

25 Mick Foley 15.00 40.00

2017 Topps WWE Breaking Ground

COMPLETE SET (10) 5.00 12.00
STATED ODDS 1:2

1 Baron Corbin 1.00 2.50
2 Dana Brooke 1.25 3.00
3 Tyler Breeze .60 1.50
4 Jason Jordan .75 2.00
5 Tyler Breeze .60 1.50
6 The Superstars 1.00 2.50
7 Bayley 2.00 5.00
8 Scott Hall .75 2.00
9 Sami Zayn .75 2.00
10 Tyler Breeze .60 1.50

2017 Topps WWE Championship Relics

*BLUE/50: .5X TO 1.2X BASIC MEM
*SILVER/25: .6X TO 1.5X BASIC MEM
*GOLD/10: 1X TO 2.5X BASIC MEM
*RED/1: UNPRICED DUE TO SCARCITY
STATED ODDS 1:277

NNO AJ Styles 10.00 25.00
NNO Becky Lynch 6.00 15.00
NNO Charlotte Flair 8.00 20.00
NNO Dean Ambrose 6.00 15.00
NNO Dean Ambrose 6.00 15.00
NNO Dolph Ziggler 3.00 8.00
NNO Finn Balor 8.00 20.00
NNO Kalisto 3.00 8.00
NNO Kevin Owens/NXT Title 5.00 12.00
NNO Kevin Owens/Universal Title 5.00 12.00
NNO The Miz 4.00 10.00
NNO The New Day 4.00 10.00
NNO Rhyno & Heath Slater 2.00 5.00
NNO Roman Reigns/US Title 6.00 15.00
NNO Roman Reigns/WWE Title 6.00 15.00
NNO Rusev 4.00 10.00
NNO Sasha Banks 6.00 15.00
NNO Seth Rollins 6.00 15.00
NNO Triple H 5.00 12.00
NNO Zack Ryder 2.00 5.00

2017 Topps WWE Kiss

*GOLD/10: .6X TO 1.5X BASIC KISS
*RED/1: UNPRICED DUE TO SCARCITY
STATED ODDS 1:125

NNO Asuka 25.00 60.00
NNO Becky Lynch 15.00 40.00

NNO Charlotte Flair	25.00	60.00
NNO Maryse	20.00	50.00
NNO Naomi	15.00	40.00
NNO Summer Rae	12.00	30.00

2017 Topps WWE NXT Autographed TakeOver Brooklyn II Mat Relics

STATED PRINT RUN 10 SER.#'d SETS

NNO Asuka
NNO Austin Aries
NNO Bayley
NNO Samoa Joe
NNO Shinsuke Nakamura

2017 Topps WWE NXT TakeOver Brooklyn II Mat Relics

*BRONZE/199: SAME VALUE AS BASIC MEM
*BLUE/50: .5X TO 1.2X BASIC MEM
*SILVER/25: .6X TO 1.5X BASIC MEM
*GOLD/10: 1X TO 2.5X BASIC MEM
*RED/1: UNPRICED DUE TO SCARCITY
STATED ODDS 1:369

NNO Andrade Cien Almas	2.00	5.00
NNO Asuka	6.00	15.00
NNO Austin Aries	4.00	10.00
NNO Bayley	6.00	15.00
NNO Bobby Roode	5.00	12.00
NNO Johnny Gargano	2.00	5.00
NNO No Way Jose	2.00	5.00
NNO Samoa Joe	6.00	15.00
NNO Shinsuke Nakamura	5.00	12.00
NNO Tommaso Ciampa	2.00	5.00

2017 Topps WWE Roster Updates

COMPLETE SET (20)	8.00	20.00
RANDOMLY INSERTED INTO PACKS		
R1 Tamina	1.25	3.00
R2 Cedric Alexander	1.50	4.00
R3 Gran Metalik	2.00	5.00
R4 Jack Gallagher	2.00	5.00
R5 Lince Dorado	1.25	3.00
R6 Noam Dar	1.00	2.50
R7 Rich Swann	1.00	2.50
R8 Stephanie McMahon	1.25	3.00
R9 Shane McMahon	1.50	4.00
R10 Tom Phillips	1.00	2.50
R11 Andrade Cien Almas	1.00	2.50
R12 Mandy Rose	1.25	3.00
R13 Mike Rome	1.00	2.50
R14 No Way Jose	1.00	2.50
R15 Otis Dozovic	1.25	3.00
R16 Riddick Moss	1.25	3.00
R17 Tian Bing	1.00	2.50
R18 Tino Sabbatelli	1.25	3.00
R19 Tye Dillinger	1.00	2.50
R20 Tucker Knight	2.50	6.00

2017 Topps WWE Shirt Relics

*BLUE/50: .5X TO 1.2X BASIC MEM
*SILVER/25: .6X TO 1.5X BASIC MEM
*GOLD/10: 1X TO 2.5X BASIC MEM
*RED/1: UNPRICED DUE TO SCARCITY
STATED ODDS 1:185
STATED PRINT RUN 199 SER.#'d SETS

NNO Andrade Cien Almas	2.00	5.00
NNO Baron Corbin	3.00	8.00
NNO Bayley	6.00	15.00
NNO Big E	2.50	6.00
NNO Bobby Roode	5.00	12.00
NNO Bray Wyatt	5.00	12.00
NNO Carmella	5.00	12.00
NNO Cesaro	4.00	10.00
NNO Chad Gable	2.50	6.00
NNO Dolph Ziggler	3.00	8.00
NNO Heath Slater	2.00	5.00
NNO Jason Jordan	2.50	6.00
NNO John Cena	10.00	25.00
NNO Johnny Gargano	2.00	5.00
NNO Karl Anderson	2.00	5.00
NNO Kevin Owens	5.00	12.00
NNO Kofi Kingston	2.50	6.00
NNO The Miz	4.00	10.00
NNO No Way Jose	2.00	5.00
NNO Randy Orton	5.00	12.00
NNO Roman Reigns	6.00	15.00
NNO Seth Rollins	6.00	15.00
NNO Shinsuke Nakamura	5.00	12.00
NNO Tommaso Ciampa	2.00	5.00
NNO Xavier Woods	2.50	6.00

2017 Topps WWE Stone Cold Podcast

COMPLETE SET (8)	8.00	20.00
STATED ODDS 1:4		
1 Triple H	2.00	5.00
2 Paul Heyman	.75	2.00
3 Edge & Christian	2.00	5.00
4 Brock Lesnar	4.00	10.00
5 Big Show	1.00	2.50
6 Mick Foley	2.00	5.00
7 AJ Styles	4.00	10.00
8 Dean Ambrose	2.50	6.00

2017 Topps WWE Autographed SummerSlam 2016 Mat Relics

STATED PRINT RUN 10 SER.#'d SETS
UNPRICED DUE TO SCARCITY

NNO AJ Styles
NNO Big Cass
NNO Brock Lesnar
NNO Charlotte Flair
NNO Chris Jericho
NNO Dean Ambrose
NNO Dolph Ziggler
NNO Enzo Amore
NNO Finn Balor
NNO John Cena
NNO Karl Anderson
NNO Kevin Owens
NNO Kofi Kingston
NNO Luke Gallows
NNO Randy Orton
NNO Roman Reigns
NNO Rusev
NNO Sasha Banks
NNO Seth Rollins
NNO Xavier Woods

2017 Topps WWE SummerSlam 2016 Mat Relics

*BRONZE/199: SAME VALUE AS BASIC MEM
*BLUE/50: .5X TO 1.2X BASIC MEM
*SILVER/25: .6X TO 1.5X BASIC MEM
*GOLD/10: 1X TO 2.5X BASIC MEM
*RED/1: UNPRICED DUE TO SCARCITY
STATED ODDS 1:184
STATED PRINT RUN 299 SER.#'d SETS

NNO AJ Styles	10.00	25.00
NNO Big Cass	2.50	6.00
NNO Brock Lesnar	10.00	25.00
NNO Charlotte Flair	8.00	20.00
NNO Chris Jericho	5.00	12.00
NNO Dean Ambrose	6.00	15.00
NNO Dolph Ziggler	3.00	8.00
NNO Enzo Amore	6.00	15.00
NNO Finn Balor	8.00	20.00
NNO John Cena	10.00	25.00
NNO Karl Anderson	2.00	5.00
NNO Kevin Owens	5.00	12.00
NNO Kofi Kingston	2.50	6.00
NNO Luke Gallows	3.00	8.00
NNO Randy Orton	5.00	12.00
NNO Roman Reigns	6.00	15.00
NNO Rusev	4.00	10.00
NNO Sasha Banks	6.00	15.00
NNO Seth Rollins	6.00	15.00
NNO Xavier Woods	2.50	6.00

2017 Topps WWE Total Divas

COMPLETE SET (20)	12.00	30.00
STATED ODDS 1:2		
1 Nikki Bella	1.25	3.00
2 Brie Bella	1.25	3.00
3 Natalya	1.00	2.50
4 The Bellas	1.25	3.00
5 Mandy Rose	.60	1.50
6 Natalya	1.00	2.50
7 Nikki Bella	1.25	3.00
8 Nikki Bella	1.25	3.00
9 Alicia Fox	.75	2.00
10 Natalya	1.00	2.50
11 Brie Bella	1.25	3.00
12 Brie Bella	1.25	3.00
13 John Cena	2.50	6.00
14 Daniel Bryan	2.00	5.00
15 Natalya	1.00	2.50
16 The Bella Twins	1.25	3.00
17 Nikki Bella	1.25	3.00
18 Mandy Rose	.60	1.50
19 Alicia Fox	.75	2.00
20 Nikki Bella	1.25	3.00

2017 Topps WWE Triple Autographs

STATED ODDS 1:1,762		
NNO Bayley/Jax/Morgan		
NNO Big E/Kingston/Woods	60.00	120.00
NNO Kay/Royce/Aliyah		
NNO Lesnar/Goldberg/Bischoff	250.00	400.00
NNO C.Kelly/Fuentes/Young	75.00	150.00
NNO Martin/Kai/Victoria		
NNO K.Kelly/Wilson/Phoenix	75.00	150.00

2017 Topps WWE Undertaker Tribute

COMPLETE SET (40)	15.00	40.00
1 Undertaker	2.00	5.00
2 Undertaker	2.00	5.00
3 Undertaker	2.00	3.00
4 Undertaker	2.00	5.00
5 Undertaker	2.00	5.00
6 Undertaker	2.00	5.00
7 Undertaker	2.00	5.00
8 Undertaker	2.00	5.00
9 Undertaker	2.00	5.00
10 Undertaker	2.00	5.00
11 Undertaker	2.00	5.00
12 Undertaker	2.00	5.00
13 Undertaker	2.00	5.00
14 Undertaker	2.00	5.00
15 Undertaker	2.00	5.00
16 Undertaker	2.00	5.00
17 Undertaker	2.00	5.00
18 Undertaker	2.00	5.00
19 Undertaker	2.00	5.00
20 Undertaker	2.00	5.00
21 Undertaker	2.00	5.00
22 Undertaker	2.00	5.00
23 Undertaker	2.00	5.00
24 Undertaker	2.00	5.00
25 Undertaker	2.00	5.00
26 Undertaker	2.00	5.00
27 Undertaker	2.00	5.00
28 Undertaker	2.00	5.00
29 Undertaker	2.00	5.00
30 Undertaker	2.00	5.00
31 Undertaker	2.00	5.00
32 Undertaker	2.00	5.00
33 Undertaker	2.00	5.00
34 Undertaker	2.00	5.00
35 Undertaker	2.00	5.00
36 Undertaker	2.00	5.00
37 Undertaker	2.00	5.00
38 Undertaker	2.00	5.00
39 Undertaker	2.00	5.00
40 Undertaker	2.00	5.00

2018 Topps WWE

COMPLETE SET W/O SP (100)	8.00	20.00
UNOPENED BOX (24 PACKS)		
UNOPENED PACK (7 CARDS)		

*BRONZE: .5X TO 1.2X BASIC CARDS
*BLUE/99: .75X TO 2X BASIC CARDS
*SILVER/25: 2X TO 5X BASIC CARDS
*GOLD/10: UNPRICED DUE TO SCARCITY
*RED/1: UNPRICED DUE TO SCARCITY
*P.P.BLACK/1: UNPRICED DUE TO SCARCITY
*P.P.CYAN/1: UNPRICED DUE TO SCARCITY
*P.P.MAGENTA/1: UNPRICED DUE TO SCARCITY
*P.P.YELLOW/1: UNPRICED DUE TO SCARCITY

1A Adam Cole RC	.30	.75
1B Adam Cole SP Shirtless	12.00	30.00
2A AJ Styles	1.00	2.50
2B AJ Styles SP Shirtless	20.00	50.00
3 Akam	.25	.60
4 Akira Tozawa	.40	1.00
5A Aleister Black	.30	.75
5B Aleister Black SP Mid-Air	6.00	15.00
6 Alicia Fox	.40	1.00
7 Andrade Cien Almas	.40	1.00
8 Apollo Crews	.25	.60
9 Ariya Daivari	.25	.60
10 Asuka	.75	2.00
11A Big E	.30	.75
11B Big E SP Microphone	2.50	6.00
12 Billie Kay	.50	1.25
13 Bo Dallas	.25	.60
14A Bobby Roode	.40	1.00
14B Bobby Roode SP In Action	10.00	25.00
15 Bobby Fish RC	.25	.60

16 Booker T .40 1.00
17 The Brian Kendrick .40 1.00
18 Brie Bella .50 1.25
19 Byron Saxton .25 .60
20A Carmella .50 1.25
20B Carmella SP In Ring 12.00 30.00
21 Cathy Kelley .50 1.25
22 Cedric Alexander .25 .60
23 Chad Gable .25 .60
24A Charlotte Flair .75 2.00
24B Charlotte Flair SP Close-Up 12.00 30.00
25 Christy St. Cloud RC .30 .75
26 Curt Hawkins .25 .60
27 Curtis Axel .25 .60
28 Daniel Bryan .60 1.50
29 Drew Gulak .25 .60
30A Drew McIntyre .40 1.00
30B Drew McIntyre SP Close-Up 2.50 6.00
31 Elias .60 1.50
32A Ember Moon .50 1.25
32B Ember Moon SP In Between Ropes 6.00 15.00
33 Gentleman Jack Gallagher .30 .75
34 Gran Metalik .25 .60
35 Greg Hamilton .40 1.00
36 Heath Slater .25 .60
37 Hideo Itami .25 .60
38 Jerry The King Lawler .50 1.25
39 Jey Uso .25 .60
40 Jim Ross .40 1.00
41 Jimmy Uso .25 .60
42A Jinder Mahal .30 .75
42B Jinder Mahal SP Shirtless
43 John Cena 1.00 2.50
44 Johnny Gargano .25 .60
45A Kairi Sane RC .60 1.50
45B Kairi Sane SP Mid-Air
46 Kayla Braxton RC .25 .60
47A Kevin Owens .60 1.50
47B Kevin Owens SP Red Background 8.00 20.00
48A Kofi Kingston .30 .75
48B Kofi Kingston SP Cross Body 2.50 6.00
49 Kurt Angle .60 1.50
50A Kyle O'Reilly RC .30 .75
50B Kyle O'Reilly SP Straightfaced 2.50 6.00
51 Lana .60 1.50
52 Lita .60 1.50
53 Maria Kanellis .60 1.50
54 Maryse .50 1.25
55 Mauro Ranallo .25 .60
56 Mean Gene Okerlund .30 .75
57 Michael Cole .25 .60
58 Mickie James .50 1.25
59 Mike Kanellis .60 1.50
60 Mike Rome .25 .60
61 The Miz .50 1.25
62 Montez Ford .25 .60
63 Mr. McMahon .50 1.25
64 Mustafa Ali .25 .60
65 Naomi .30 .75
66A Natalya .30 .75
66B Natalya SP Pointing Up 12.00 30.00
67 Neville .40 1.00
68 Nia Jax .40 1.00
69 Nigel McGuinness RC .25 .60
70 Noam Dar .25 .60
71 Paige .60 1.50
72 Paul Ellering .30 .75
73 Percy Watson .25 .60
74 Pete Dunne RC .25 .60
75 Peyton Royce .60 1.50
76 Rezar .25 .60
77 Rhyno .25 .60
78 Big Cass .30 .75
79 The Rock 1.25 3.00
80 Roderick Strong .25 .60
81 Samir Singh RC .25 .60
82 Shane McMahon .50 1.25
83 Shelton Benjamin .30 .75
84 Sin Cara .30 .75
85 Sonya Deville .50 1.25
86 Stephanie McMahon .50 1.25
87 Sunil Singh RC .25 .60
88 Tamina .25 .60
89 Titus O'Neil .25 .60
90 TJP .30 .75
91 Tommaso Ciampa .25 .60
92 Tony Nese .25 .60
93 Tony Chimel .25 .60
94 Triple H .60 1.50
95 Tyler Bate .25 .60
96A Undertaker 1.00 2.50
96B Undertaker SP Kneeling 10.00 25.00
97 William Regal .40 1.00
98A Xavier Woods .30 .75
98B Xavier Woods SP Cross Body 5.00 12.00
99 Zack Ryder .25 .60
100 Zelina Vega RC .25 .60

2018 Topps WWE Autographed Commemorative Championship Medallions

STATED PRINT RUN 10 SER.#'d SETS
UNPRICED DUE TO SCARCITY
CCAJ AJ Styles
CCAT Akira Tozawa
CCBW Bray Wyatt
CCCJ Chris Jericho
CCJM Jinder Mahal
CCKO Kevin Owens
CCNA Natalya
CCNO Naomi
CCRO Randy Orton
CCTM The Miz

2018 Topps WWE Autographed Dual Mat Relics

STATED PRINT RUN 10 SER.#'d SETS
UNPRICED DUE TO SCARCITY
DMRDB Daniel Bryan
DMRSM Stephanie McMahon
DMRTH Triple H
DMRUT Undertaker
DNRDA Dean Ambrose

2018 Topps WWE Autographed NXT TakeOver Brooklyn III Mat Relics

STATED PRINT RUN 10 SER.#'d SETS
UNPRICED DUE TO SCARCITY
TBRAB Aleister Black
TBRAC Adam Cole
TBRAS Asuka
TBRBR Bobby Roode
TBRDM Drew McIntyre
TBREM Ember Moon
TBREY Eric Young
TBRHI Hideo Itami
TBRJG Johnny Gargano

2018 Topps WWE Autographed Shirt Relics

STATED PRINT RUN 10 SER.#'d SETS
UNPRICED DUE TO SCARCITY
SRAE Aiden English
SRAF Alicia Fox
SREY Eric Young
SRGD Goldust
SRJJ JoJo
SRNA Natalya
SRRY Renee Young
SRSJ Samoa Joe

2018 Topps WWE Autographed SummerSlam 2017 Mat Relics

STATED PRINT RUN 10 SER.#'d SETS
UNPRICED DUE TO SCARCITY
SMRAJ AJ Styles
SMRBC Baron Corbin
SMRBS Braun Strowman
SMRBW Bray Wyatt
SMRCO Cesaro
SMRDA Dean Ambrose
SMRJM Jinder Mahal
SMRKO Kevin Owens
SMRNA Natalya
SMRNO Naomi
SMRSB Sasha Banks
SMRSH Sheamus
SMRSJ Samoa Joe
SMRSN Shinsuke Nakamura

2018 Topps WWE Autographs

*BLUE/50: .5X TO 1.2X BASIC AUTOS
*SILVER/25: .6X TO 1.5X BASIC AUTOS
*GOLD/10: UNPRICED DUE TO SCARCITY
*RED/1: UNPRICED DUE TO SCARCITY
1 Adam Cole 20.00 50.00
2 AJ Styles 15.00 40.00
4 Akira Tozawa 5.00 12.00
5 Aleister Black 10.00 25.00
8 Apollo Crews 4.00 10.00
10 Asuka 15.00 40.00
11 Big E 8.00 20.00
14 Bobby Roode 6.00 15.00
15 Bobby Fish 12.00 30.00
18 Brie Bella 10.00 25.00
20 Carmella 12.00 30.00
24 Charlotte Flair 15.00 40.00
30 Drew McIntyre 8.00 20.00
32 Ember Moon 10.00 25.00
42 Jinder Mahal 5.00 12.00
45 Kairi Sane 30.00 75.00
47 Kevin Owens 6.00 15.00
48 Kofi Kingston 6.00 15.00
49 Kurt Angle 12.00 30.00
50 Kyle O'Reilly 12.00 30.00
61 The Miz 5.00 12.00
65 Naomi 4.00 10.00
66 Natalya 6.00 15.00
68 Nia Jax 10.00 25.00
80 Roderick Strong 5.00 12.00
83 Shelton Benjamin 5.00 12.00
88 Tamina 4.00 10.00
89 Titus O'Neil 5.00 12.00
98 Xavier Woods 6.00 15.00

2018 Topps WWE Commemorative Championship Medallions

*BRONZE/99: .5X TO 1.2X BASIC MEM
*BLUE/50: .6X TO 1.5X BASIC MEM
*SILVER/25: .75X TO 2X BASIC MEM
*GOLD/10: UNPRICED DUE TO SCARCITY
*RED/1: UNPRICED DUE TO SCARCITY
CCAA American Alpha 3.00 8.00
CCAB Alexa Bliss 10.00 25.00
CCAJ AJ Styles 6.00 15.00
CCAS Dean Ambrose & Seth Rollins 8.00 20.00
CCAT Akira Tozawa 3.00 8.00
CCAX Alexa Bliss 8.00 20.00
CCBA Bayley 8.00 20.00
CCBL Brock Lesnar 10.00 25.00
CCBW Bray Wyatt 3.00 8.00
CCCJ Chris Jericho 4.00 10.00
CCCS Cesaro & Sheamus 2.50 6.00
CCGA Luke Gallows & Karl Anderson 2.50 6.00
CCHB The Hardy Boyz 6.00 15.00
CCJC John Cena 5.00 12.00
CCJM Jinder Mahal 2.50 6.00
CCKA Kalisto 2.50 6.00
CCKO Kevin Owens 4.00 10.00
CCNA Natalya 2.50 6.00
CCND The New Day 2.50 6.00
CCNO Naomi 2.50 6.00
CCRO Randy Orton 4.00 10.00
CCTM The Miz 2.50 6.00
CCTU The Usos 3.00 8.00
CCWF The Wyatt Family 5.00 12.00

2018 Topps WWE Dual Mat Relics

*SILVER/25: .6X TO 1.5X BASIC MEM
*GOLD/10: UNPRICED DUE TO SCARCITY
*RED/1: UNPRICED DUE TO SCARCITY
DMRBL Brock Lesnar 10.00 25.00
DMRBY Bayley 10.00 25.00
DMRDA Dean Ambrose 6.00 15.00
DMRDB Daniel Bryan 8.00 20.00
DMRRR Roman Reigns 6.00 15.00
DMRSM Stephanie McMahon 15.00 40.00
DMRSR Seth Rollins 5.00 12.00
DMRTH Triple H 6.00 15.00
DMRTR The Rock 8.00 20.00
DMRUT Undertaker 12.00 30.00

2018 Topps WWE Evolution

COMPLETE SET (50) 15.00 40.00
E1 The Giant .40 1.00
E2 Big Show .40 1.00
E3 Big Show .40 1.00
E4 Booker T .60 1.50
E5 G.I. Bro .60 1.50
E6 King Booker .60 1.50
E7 Booker T .60 1.50
E8 Brock Lesnar 1.50 4.00
E9 Brock Lesnar 1.50 4.00
E10 Chris Jericho 1.00 2.50
E11 Chris Jericho 1.00 2.50
E12 Daniel Bryan 1.00 2.50
E13 Daniel Bryan 1.00 2.50
E14 Daniel Bryan 1.00 2.50
E15 The Rock 2.00 5.00

E16 The Rock	2.00	5.00
E17 Goldust	.75	2.00
E18 Seven	.75	2.00
E19 American Nightmare Dustin Rhodes	.75	2.00
E20 Goldust	.75	2.00
E21 Jerry The King Lawler	.75	2.00
E22 Jerry The King Lawler	.75	2.00
E23 John Cena	1.50	4.00
E24 Doctor of Thuganomics John Cena	1.50	4.00
E25 John Cena	1.50	4.00
E26 Kane	.60	1.50
E27 Kane	.60	1.50
E28 Corporate Kane	.60	1.50
E29 Kane	.60	1.50
E30 Kurt Angle	1.00	2.50
E31 Kurt Angle	1.00	2.50
E32 Mark Henry	.50	1.25
E33 Mark Henry	.50	1.25
E34 Mark Henry	.50	1.25
E35 Cactus Jack	.75	2.00
E36 Mankind	.75	2.00
E37 Dude Love	.75	2.00
E38 Mick Foley	.75	2.00
E39 Randy Orton	1.00	2.50
E40 Randy Orton	1.00	2.50
E41 Hunter Hearst Helmsley	1.00	2.50
E42 Triple H	1.00	2.50
E43 The Game Triple H	1.00	2.50
E44 COO Triple H	1.00	2.50
E45 Undertaker	1.50	4.00
E46 Undertaker	1.50	4.00
E47 Undertaker	1.50	4.00
E48 The American Bad-Ass Undertaker	1.50	4.00
E49 Big Evil Undertaker	1.50	4.00
E50 Undertaker	1.50	4.00

2018 Topps WWE Kiss

*GOLD/10: UNPRICED DUE TO SCARCITY
*RED/1: UNPRICED DUE TO SCARCITY

KBX Billie Kay	20.00	50.00
KDB Dana Brooke	15.00	40.00
KEM Ember Moon	20.00	50.00
KKS Kairi Saine	30.00	75.00
KLM Liv Morgan	25.00	60.00
KMA Maryse	15.00	40.00
KNA Natalya	15.00	40.00
KPR Peyton Royce	25.00	60.00
KSD Sonya Deville	50.00	100.00

2018 Topps WWE Kiss Autographs

*GOLD/10: UNPRICED DUE TO SCARCITY
*RED/1: UNPRICED DUE TO SCARCITY
STATED PRINT RUN 25 SER.#'d SETS

NNO Billie Kay	30.00	75.00
NNO Dana Brooke	30.00	75.00
NNO Ember Moon	60.00	120.00
NNO Kairi Saine	50.00	100.00
NNO Liv Morgan	50.00	100.00
NNO Maryse	50.00	100.00
NNO Mickie James	75.00	150.00
NNO Natalya	30.00	75.00
NNO Peyton Royce	30.00	75.00
NNO Sonya Deville	60.00	120.00

2018 Topps WWE NXT TakeOver Brooklyn III Mat Relics

*BRONZE/199: .5X TO 1.2X BASIC MEM
*BLUE/50: .6X TO 1.5X BASIC MEM
*SILVER/25: .75X TO 2X BASIC MEM
*GOLD/10: UNPRICED DUE TO SCARCITY
*RED/1: UNPRICED DUE TO SCARCITY

TBRAA Andrade Cien Almas	3.00	8.00
TBRAB Aleister Black	3.00	8.00
TBRAC Adam Cole	6.00	15.00
TBRAS Asuka	6.00	15.00
TBRBR Bobby Roode	3.00	8.00
TBRDM Drew McIntyre	3.00	8.00
TBREM Ember Moon	4.00	10.00
TBREY Eric Young	3.00	8.00
TBRHI Hideo Itami	3.00	8.00
TBRJG Johnny Gargano	3.00	8.00

2018 Topps WWE Roster Updates

COMPLETE SET (20)	15.00	40.00
R1 Aiden English	1.00	2.50
R2 Aliyah	1.50	4.00
R3 Angelo Dawkins	1.00	2.50
R4 Buddy Murphy	1.25	3.00
R5 Charly Caruso	1.50	4.00
R6 Corey Graves	1.25	3.00
R7 Dana Brooke	2.00	5.00
R8 Dasha Fuentes	1.50	4.00
R9 Epico Colon	1.00	2.50
R10 JoJo	1.00	2.50
R11 Konnor	1.00	2.50
R12 Lars Sullivan	1.00	2.50
R13 Lio Rush	1.00	2.50
R14 Primo Colon	1.00	2.50
R15 R-Truth	1.25	3.00
R16 Renee Young	1.50	4.00
R17 Sarah Logan	1.00	2.50
R18 Tom Phillips	1.00	2.50
R19 Viktor	1.00	2.50
R20 Wesley Blake	1.25	3.00

2018 Topps WWE Shirt Relics

*BLUE/50: .6X TO 1.5X BASIC MEM
*SILVER/25: .75X TO 2X BASIC MEM
*GOLD/10: UNPRICED DUE TO SCARCITY
*RED/1: UNPRICED DUE TO SCARCITY

SRAE Aiden English	3.00	8.00
SRAF Alicia Fox	3.00	8.00
SRAW Alexander Wolfe	2.50	6.00
SRBL Brock Lesnar	6.00	15.00
SRDW Dash Wilder	2.50	6.00
SREY Eric Young	3.00	8.00
SRGD Goldust	3.00	8.00
SRJC John Cena	8.00	20.00
SRJJ JoJo	5.00	12.00
SRNA Natalya	3.00	8.00
SRNC Nikki Cross	6.00	15.00
SRRR Roman Reigns	4.00	10.00
SRRY Renee Young	6.00	15.00
SRSD Scott Dawson	3.00	8.00
SRSJ Samoa Joe	4.00	10.00

2018 Topps WWE SummerSlam 2017 Mat Relics

*BRONZE/199: .5X TO 1.2X BASIC MEM
*BLUE/50: .6X TO 1.5X BASIC MEM
*SILVER/25: .75X TO 2X BASIC MEM
*GOLD/10: UNPRICED DUE TO SCARCITY
*RED/1: UNPRICED DUE TO SCARCITY

SMRAB Alexa Bliss	8.00	20.00
SMRAJ AJ Styles	5.00	12.00
SMRBC Baron Corbin	2.50	6.00
SMRBL Brock Lesnar	4.00	10.00
SMRBS Braun Strowman	5.00	12.00
SMRBW Bray Wyatt	2.50	6.00
SMRCO Cesaro	2.50	6.00
SMRDA Dean Ambrose	2.50	6.00
SMRFB Finn Balor	4.00	10.00
SMRJC John Cena	5.00	12.00
SMRJM Jinder Mahal	2.50	6.00
SMRKO Kevin Owens	2.50	6.00
SMRNA Natalya	3.00	8.00
SMRNO Naomi	2.50	6.00
SMRRR Roman Reigns	3.00	8.00
SMRSB Sasha Banks	8.00	20.00
SMRSH Sheamus	2.50	6.00
SMRSJ Samoa Joe	2.50	6.00
SMRSN Shinsuke Nakamura	4.00	10.00
SMRSR Seth Rollins	2.50	6.00

2018 Topps WWE Triple Autographs

STATED PRINT RUN 10 SER.#'d SETS
UNPRICED DUE TO SCARCITY

TADAY Big E
Kofi Kingston
Xavier Woods
TAERA Cole/Fish/O'Reilly
TAHOJ Ambrose/Rollins/Reigns
TAMIZ Miz/Axel/Dallas
TARAW HHH/S.McMahon/Angle
TATWF Bray Wyatt
Luke Harper
Erick Rowan

2021 Topps WWE

COMPLETE SET (200)	15.00	40.00

*FOILBOARD: .6X TO 1.5X BASIC CARDS
*AQUA/299: .75X TO 2X BASIC CARDS
*LT GREEN/199: 1.2X TO 3X BASIC CARDS
*DK GREEN/99: 1.5X TO 4X BASIC CARDS
*CITRINE/75: 2X TO 5X BASIC CARDS
*ORANGE/50: 2.5X TO 6X BASIC CARDS
*PURPLE/25: UNPRICED DUE TO SCARCITY
*BLUE/10: UNPRICED DUE TO SCARCITY
*BLACK/5: UNPRICED DUE TO SCARCITY
*RED/1: UNPRICED DUE TO SCARCITY
*P.P.BLACK/1: UNPRICED DUE TO SCARCITY
*P.P.CYAN/1: UNPRICED DUE TO SCARCITY
*P.P.MAGENTA/1: UNPRICED DUE TO SCARCITY
*P.P.YELLOW/1: UNPRICED DUE TO SCARCITY

1 Kofi Kingston	.60	1.50
2 Otis	.30	.75
3 Usos	.50	1.25
4 Miz	.40	1.00
5 King Corbin's Court	.50	1.25
6 Drew McIntyre	.60	1.50
7 John Morrison	.50	1.25
8 John Morrison	.50	1.25
9 Roman Reigns	1.25	3.00
10 Edge	1.00	2.50
11 Drew McIntyre	.60	1.50
12 Miz & John Morrison	.50	1.25
13 King Corbin	.25	.60
14 Randy Orton	.75	2.00
15 Angel Garza	.30	.75
16 Drew McIntyre	.60	1.50
17 Angel Garza	.30	.75
18 King Corbin	.25	.60
19 Drew McIntyre	.60	1.50
20 Street Profits	.50	1.25
21 Usos	.60	1.50
22 Seth Rollins	.60	1.50
23 Randy Orton	.75	2.00
24 Roman Reigns	1.25	3.00
25 Undertaker	1.25	3.00
26 Miz & John Morrison	.50	1.25
27 Angel Garza	.30	.75
28 Goldberg	1.00	2.50
29 Usos	.40	1.00
30 Angel Garza	.30	.75
31 Randy Orton	.75	2.00
32 Dolph Ziggler	.50	1.25
33 Miz & John Morrison	.50	1.25
34 Sami Zayn	.60	1.50
35 AJ Styles	.75	2.00
36 Edge	1.00	2.50
37 Elias	.25	.60
38 Edge	1.00	2.50
39 Elias	.25	.60
40 Dolph Ziggler	.50	1.25
41 Street Profits	.30	.75
42 Miz & John Morrison	.50	1.25
43 King Corbin	.25	.60
44 Kevin Owens & Street Profits	.25	.60
45 Cesaro	.25	.60
46 John Morrison	.50	1.25
47 Kevin Owens	.50	1.25
48 Undertaker	1.25	3.00
49 Elias	.25	.60
50 Otis	.30	.75
51 Edge	1.00	2.50
52 Street Profits	.50	1.25
53 Drew McIntyre	.60	1.50
54 Drew McIntyre	.60	1.50
55 Sheamus	.40	1.00
56 Seth Rollins	.60	1.50
57 Big E	.50	1.25
58 Apollo Crews	.30	.75
59 Rey Mysterio	.60	1.50
60 Drew McIntyre	.60	1.50
61 King Corbin	.25	.60
62 Lucha House Party	.40	1.00
63 Drew McIntyre	.60	1.50
64 Otis	.30	.75
65 AJ Styles	.75	2.00
66 Viking Raiders	.25	.60
67 New Day	.50	1.25
68 Drew McIntyre	.60	1.50
69 Otis	.30	.75
70 Bobby Lashley	.60	1.50
71 Rey Mysterio	.60	1.50
72 Randy Orton	1.00	2.50
73 Elias	.25	.60
74 Bobby Lashley	.25	.60
75 Drew McIntyre	.60	1.50
76 AJ Styles	.75	2.00
77 Jeff Hardy	.60	1.50
78 Apollo Crews	.30	.75
79 Drew McIntyre	.60	1.50
80 Drew McIntyre	.60	1.50
81 Sheamus	.40	1.00
82 Jeff Hardy	.60	1.50
83 Bobby Lashley	.60	1.50
84 Bobby Lashley & MVP	.60	1.50
85 AJ Styles	.75	2.00

86 Cesaro & Nakamura .60 1.50
87 Sheamus .40 1.00
88 Drew McIntyre .60 1.50
89 Randy Orton .75 2.00
90 Cesaro & Nakamura .60 1.50
91 Seth Rollins .60 1.50
92 Drew McIntyre .60 1.50
93 Street Profits .30 .75
94 Seth Rollins .60 1.50
95 Drew McIntyre .60 1.50
96 AJ Styles .75 2.00
97 Alexa Bliss 1.50 4.00
98 Aliyah .50 1.25
99 Asuka 1.00 2.50
100 Becky Lynch 1.00 2.50
101 Bobby Lashley .60 1.50
102 Cedric Alexander .25 .60
103 Charlotte Flair 1.25 3.00
104 Damian Priest .40 1.00
105 Dana Brooke .25 .60
106 Drew Gulak .30 .75
107 Drew McIntyre .60 1.50
108 Doudrop .40 1.00
109 Elias .25 .60
110 Eva Marie .60 1.50
111 Jeff Hardy .60 1.50
112 Jaxson Ryker .25 .60
113 John Morrison .50 1.25
114 Keith Lee .50 1.25
115 Kofi Kingston .60 1.50
116 Lacey Evans .60 1.50
117 Mace .25 .60
118 Mansoor RC .25 .60
119 MVP .25 .60
120 Mustafa Ali .30 .75
121 Naomi .30 .75
122 Nia Jax .50 1.25
123 Nikki A.S.H. .50 1.25
124 Omos RC .50 1.25
125 Randy Orton .75 2.00
126 Reggie RC .30 .75
127 Rhea Ripley .75 2.00
128 Ricochet .50 1.25
129 Riddle .60 1.50
130 Shayna Baszler .50 1.25
131 Sheamus .40 1.00
132 Shelton Benjamin .40 1.00
133 T-Bar .30 .75
134 The Miz .40 1.00
135 Xavier Woods .25 .60
136 Angelo Dawkins .30 .75
137 Apollo Crews .30 .75
138 Baron Corbin .25 .60
139 Bayley .60 1.50
140 Bianca Belair .60 1.50
141 Big E .50 1.25
142 Carmella .60 1.50
143 Cesaro .25 .60
144 Chad Gable .25 .60
145 Commander Azeez RC .30 .75
146 Dolph Ziggler .50 1.25
147 Dominik Mysterio RC .30 .75
148 Finn Balor .60 1.50
149 Jey Uso .25 .60
150 Jimmy Uso .25 .60
151 Kevin Owens .50 1.25
152 King Nakamura .60 1.50
153 Liv Morgan 1.00 2.50
154 Montez Ford .25 .60
155 Natalya .40 1.00
156 Nox .60 1.50
157 Otis .30 .75
158 Rey Mysterio .60 1.50
159 Rick Boogs RC .25 .60
160 Robert Roode .30 .75
161 Roman Reigns 1.25 3.00
162 Sami Zayn .40 1.00
163 Sasha Banks 1.25 3.00
164 Seth Rollins .60 1.50
165 Shotzi 1.00 2.50
166 Sonya Deville .60 1.50
167 Tamina .30 .75
168 Toni Storm .75 2.00
169 Zelina Vega .50 1.25
170 Austin Theory .50 1.25
171 Candice LeRae 1.00 2.50
172 Dakota Kai .50 1.25
173 Dexter Lumis .25 .60
174 Ember Moon .30 .75
175 Io Shirai .50 1.25
176 Indi Hartwell RC .75 2.00
177 Isaiah "Swerve" Scott .40 1.00
178 Johnny Gargano .50 1.25
179 Karrion Kross 1.00 2.50
180 Kyle O'Reilly .40 1.00
181 Mandy Rose 1.25 3.00
182 Pete Dunne .50 1.25
183 Raquel Gonzalez .60 1.50
184 Roderick Strong .40 1.00
185 Samoa Joe .50 1.25
186 Santos Escobar .40 1.00
187 Sarray RC .30 .75
188 Scarlett 1.25 3.00
189 Timothy Thatcher RC .25 .60
190 Tommaso Ciampa .60 1.50
191 Walter .60 1.50
192 Batista .50 1.25
193 British Bulldog .40 1.00
194 Edge 1.00 2.50
195 Goldberg 1.00 2.50
196 JBL .25 .60
197 Kane .40 1.00
198 Molly Holly .30 .75
199 Rob Van Dam .50 1.25
200 John Cena 1.25 3.00

2021 Topps WWE Autographed Mat Relics

*RED/1: UNPRICED DUE TO SCARCITY
STATED ODDS 1:4,986
STATED PRINT RUN 10 SER.#'d SETS

MRAB Big E
MRAR Riddle
MRMY Mia Yim
MRAAG Angel Garza
MRAFA Fabian Aichner
MRAFB Finn Balor
MRAJD Jordan Devlin
MRAJG Johnny Gargano
MRAKL Keith Lee
MRAMB Marcel Barthel
MRARM Rey Mysterio
MRARR Rhea Ripley
MRARS Roderick Strong
MRATC Tommaso Ciampa
MRAWT WALTER
MRABOB Bobby Lashley
MRADOM Dominik Mysterio
MRANIA Nia Jax
MRAROM Roman Reigns
MRASHA Shayna Baszler

2021 Topps WWE Autographs

*GREEN/99: .6X TO 1.5X BASIC AUTOS
*ORANGE/50: .75X TO 2X BASIC AUTOS
*PURPLE/25: UNPRICED DUE TO SCARCITY
*BLUE/10: UNPRICED DUE TO SCARCITY
*BLACK/5: UNPRICED DUE TO SCARCITY
*RED/1: UNPRICED DUE TO SCARCITY
*P.P.BLACK/1: UNPRICED DUE TO SCARCITY
*P.P.CYAN/1: UNPRICED DUE TO SCARCITY
*P.P.MAGENTA/1: UNPRICED DUE TO SCARCITY
*P.P.YELLOW/1: UNPRICED DUE TO SCARCITY
STATED PRINT RUN 150 SER.#'d SETS

AC Carmella 12.00 30.00
AE Big E 6.00 15.00
AAS AJ Styles 10.00 25.00
AAT Austin Theory
ABB Bianca Belair 12.00 30.00
ABE Becky Lynch 50.00 100.00
ABL Bobby Lashley 10.00 25.00
ACF Charlotte Flair 30.00 75.00
ADM Drew McIntyre 15.00 40.00
ADP Damian Priest 6.00 15.00
AED Edge 25.00 60.00
AFB Finn Balor 10.00 25.00
AJH Jeff Hardy 15.00 40.00
AJU Jey Uso 6.00 15.00
AKC King Corbin 5.00 12.00
AKF Kofi Kingston 6.00 15.00
AKK Karrion Kross
AKL Keith Lee
AKN Asuka 25.00 60.00
AKO Kevin Owens 8.00 20.00
ALM Liv Morgan 30.00 75.00
AMR Riddle 10.00 25.00
AOT Otis 6.00 15.00
AQS Shayna Baszler 6.00 15.00
ARH Rhea Ripley 12.00 30.00
ARM Rey Mysterio 15.00 40.00
ARR Roman Reigns 30.00 75.00
ARU Robert Roode 5.00 12.00
ASB Sasha Banks 50.00 100.00
ASD Sonya Deville 8.00 20.00
ASN Shinsuke Nakamura 10.00 25.00
ASR Seth Rollins 10.00 25.00
ASZ Sami Zayn 6.00 15.00
AUN Apollo Crews 5.00 12.00
AXW Xavier Woods 5.00 12.00
AMVP MVP 5.00 12.00

2021 Topps WWE Coolest Mixed Tag Teams

COMPLETE SET (11) 6.00 15.00
STATED ODDS 1:10

MT1 Charlotte Flair & AJ Styles 1.50 4.00
MT2 Finn Balor & Bayley .75 2.00
MT3 John Cena & Trish Stratus 1.50 4.00
MT4 Sasha Banks & Roman Reigns 1.50 4.00
MT5 R-Truth & Carmella .75 2.00
MT6 The Miz & Asuka 1.25 3.00
MT7 Stephanie McMahon & Triple H 1.25 3.00
MT8 Jimmy Uso & Naomi .40 1.00
MT9 Seth Rollins & Becky Lynch 1.25 3.00
MT10 Johnny Gargano & Candice LeRae 1.25 3.00
MT11 Natalya & Shinsuke Nakamura .75 2.00

2021 Topps WWE Hall of Fame Tribute

COMPLETE SET (18) 8.00 20.00
STATED ODDS 1:12

HOF1 Razor .50 1.25
HOF2 Diesel .50 1.25
HOF3 ...The New World Order .50 1.25
HOF4 Hollywood Hulk Hogan 1.50 4.00
HOF5 The Outsiders .50 1.25
HOF6 The nWo PPV 1.50 4.00
HOF7 Syxx .40 1.00
HOF8 Kevin Nash .50 1.25
HOF9 Fingerpoke of Doom .50 1.25
HOF10 Scott Hall .75 2.00
HOF11 Hollywood Hulk Hogan 1.50 4.00
HOF12 Kevin Nash .50 1.25
HOF13 Scott Hall .50 1.25
HOF14 Scott Hall .50 1.25
HOF15 The nWo 1.50 4.00
HOF16 The nWo .50 1.25
HOF17 Scott Hall .50 1.25
HOF18 Icon vs. Icon 3.00 8.00

2021 Topps WWE Hall of Fame Tribute Autographs

STATED PRINT RUN 25 SER.#'d SETS

NWOKN Kevin Nash 15.00 40.00
NWOSW Syxx 12.00 30.00

2021 Topps WWE Locker Room Veterans Booklet Autograph

ABC The Miz/R-Truth/Rey Mysterio/Randy Orton/Jeff Hardy/Shelton Benjamin
Sheamus/Natalya/Edge/Bobby Lashley/MVP/Kofi Kingston

2021 Topps WWE Manufactured Match Film Strip Relics

*AQUA/299: X TO 1.2X BASIC MEM
*LT GREEN/199: X TO 1.5X BASIC MEM
*DK GREEN/99: X TO 2X BASIC MEM
*CITRINE/75: X TO 2.5X BASIC MEM
*ORANGE/50: X TO 3X BASIC MEM
*PURPLE/25: UNPRICED DUE TO SCARCITY
*BLUE/10: UNPRICED DUE TO SCARCITY
*BLACK/5: UNPRICED DUE TO SCARCITY
*RED/1: UNPRICED DUE TO SCARCITY
STATED ODDS 1:74

FSAJ AJ Styles vs. John Cena 6.00 15.00
FSBB Bret Hart vs. British Bulldog 5.00 12.00
FSBC Becky Lynch vs. Charlotte Flair 8.00 20.00
FSBP Bret Hart vs. Mr. Perfect 5.00 12.00
FSHA Bret Hart vs. "Stone Cold" Steve Austin 6.00 15.00
FSHG Hulk Hogan vs. Andre the Giant 10.00 25.00
FSHM Bret Hart vs. Shawn Michaels 5.00 12.00
FSHU Hulk Hogan vs. Ultimate Warrior 15.00 40.00
FSJE John Cena vs. Edge
FSKU Undertaker vs. Kane 5.00 12.00
FSLU Bobby Lashley vs. Umaga 5.00 12.00
FSMF Shawn Michaels vs. Ric Flair 5.00 12.00
FSMR Randy Savage vs. Ric Flair 6.00 15.00

FSNC Natalya vs. Charlotte Flair		
FSPR Mr. Perfect vs. Ric Flair	4.00	12.00
FSRC The Rock vs. John Cena	6.00	15.00
FSRH The Rock vs. Hulk Hogan	10.00	25.00
FSRS Razor Ramon vs. Shawn Michaels	10.00	25.00
FSSB Sasha Banks vs. Bayley	6.00	15.00
FSSC Sami Zayn vs. Cesaro	4.00	12.00
FSSM Shawn Michaels vs. Mankind	5.00	12.00
FSSS Randy Savage vs. Ricky Steamboat	12.00	30.00
FSST Shawn Michaels vs. Triple H	5.00	12.00
FSSW Randy Savage vs. Ultimate Warrior	8.00	20.00
FSTJ The Miz vs. John Cena		
FSBCA Becky Lynch vs. Charlotte Flair vs. Asuka	6.00	15.00
FSFBL Charlotte Flair vs. Sasha Banks vs. Becky Lynch	5.00	12.00
FSRA2 The Rock vs. Steve Austin	8.00	20.00
FSRA3 The Rock vs. Steve Austin	8.00	20.00
FSRC2 The Rock vs. John Cena	6.00	15.00
FSUH2 Undertaker vs. Triple H	6.00	15.00
FSUH3 Undertaker vs. Triple H	6.00	15.00
FSUM1 Undertaker vs. Shawn Michaels	6.00	15.00
FSUM2 Undertaker vs. Shawn Michaels	6.00	15.00
FSUM3 Undertaker vs. Shawn Michaels	6.00	15.00
FSUMK Undertaker vs. Mankind	5.00	12.00
FSACJG Adam Cole vs. Johnny Gargano	5.00	12.00
FSKOSZ Kevin Owens vs. Sami Zayn	5.00	12.00
FSTCJG Tommaso Ciampa vs. Johnny Gargano	5.00	12.00

2021 Topps WWE Mat Relics

*AQUA/299: .5X TO 1.2X BASIC MEM
*LT GREEN/199: .6X TO 1.5X BASIC MEM
*DK GREEN/99: .75X TO 2X BASIC MEM
*CITRINE/75: 1X TO 2.5X BASIC MEM
*ORANGE/50: 1.2X TO 3X BASIC MEM
*PURPLE/25: UNPRICED DUE TO SCARCITY
*BLUE/10: UNPRICED DUE TO SCARCITY
*BLACK/5: UNPRICED DUE TO SCARCITY
*RED/1: UNPRICED DUE TO SCARCITY
STATED ODDS 1:49

MRB Big E	1.25	3.00
MRR Riddle	1.50	4.00
MRAC Adam Cole	2.00	5.00
MRAG Angel Garza	.75	2.00
MRAS Asuka	2.50	6.00
MRBA Bayley	1.50	4.00
MRBB Bianca Belair	1.50	4.00
MRBF Bobby Fish	.75	2.00
MRBL Becky Lynch	8.00	20.00
MRBR Robert Roode	2.50	6.00
MRCS Cesaro	2.00	5.00
MRDA Dana Brooke	2.00	5.00
MRDK Dakota Kai	4.00	10.00
MRDM Finn Balor	5.00	12.00
MRFA Fabian Aichner	2.50	6.00
MRFB Finn Balor	5.00	12.00
MRGM Gran Metalik	2.00	5.00
MRID Ilja Dragunov	2.00	5.00
MRIS Isaiah "Swerve" Scott	3.00	8.00
MRJD Jordan Devlin	2.00	5.00
MRJG Johnny Gargano	4.00	10.00
MRJH Jeff Hardy	5.00	12.00
MRJM Jinder Mahal	2.50	6.00
MRKL Keith Lee	4.00	10.00
MRKO Kevin Owens	4.00	10.00
MRKR Kyle O'Reilly	3.00	8.00
MRLA Bobby Lashley	5.00	12.00
MRLM Liv Morgan	8.00	20.00
MRMA Mustafa Ali	2.50	6.00
MRMB Marcel Barthel	2.50	6.00
MRMY Mia Yim	2.50	6.00
MRNJ Nia Jax	4.00	10.00
MROT Otis	2.50	6.00
MRRM Rey Mysterio	5.00	12.00
MRRR Rhea Ripley	6.00	15.00
MRRS Roderick Strong	3.00	8.00
MRSB Sasha Banks	10.00	25.00
MRSD Sonya Deville	5.00	12.00
MRSG Chad Gable	2.00	5.00
MRSN Shinsuke Nakamura	5.00	12.00
MRSR Seth Rollins	5.00	12.00
MRT7 Trent Seven	2.50	6.00
MRTC Tommaso Ciampa	5.00	12.00
MRTO Titus O'Neil	2.00	5.00
MRTS Toni Storm	6.00	15.00
MRTY Tyler Bate	2.50	6.00
MRWT WALTER	5.00	12.00
MRBOB Bobby Lashley	5.00	12.00
MRDOM Dominik Mysterio	2.50	6.00
MRKLR Kay Lee Ray	5.00	12.00
MRMIZ The Miz	3.00	8.00
MRNIA Nia Jax	4.00	10.00
MRROM Roman Reigns	10.00	25.00
MRSHA Shayna Baszler	4.00	10.00

2021 Topps WWE Memorable Entrances

COMPLETE SET (9)	6.00	15.00
STATED ODDS 1:10		
ME1 Rhythm & Blues	.40	1.00
ME2 Bobby "The Brain" Heenan	.50	1.25
ME3 Macho King Randy Savage	2.00	5.00
ME4 Shawn Michaels	1.25	3.00
ME5 John Cena	1.50	4.00
ME6 Undertaker	1.50	4.00
ME7 Triple H	1.25	3.00
ME8 Sasha Banks	1.50	4.00
ME9 Roman Reigns	1.50	4.00

2021 Topps WWE RKO Outta Nowhere

COMPLETE SET (10)	6.00	15.00
STATED ODDS 1:10		
RKO1 Undertaker	1.50	4.00
RKO2 Hulk Hogan	1.50	4.00
RKO3 Jeff Hardy	.75	2.00
RKO4 Triple H	1.25	3.00
RKO5 Dolph Ziggler	.60	1.50
RKO6 Seth Rollins	.75	2.00
RKO7 Rey Mysterio	.75	2.00
RKO8 Ricochet	.60	1.50
RKO9 AJ Styles	1.00	2.50
RKO10 Alexa Bliss	2.00	5.00

2021 Topps WWE Tag Team Autographs

*BLUE/10: UNPRICED DUE TO SCARCITY
*RED/1: UNPRICED DUE TO SCARCITY
RANDOMLY INSERTED INTO PACKS
STATED PRINT RUN 25 SER.#'d SETS

DADD Robert Roode/Dolph Ziggler	15.00	40.00
DASN Shayna Baszler/Nia Jax	15.00	40.00
DALHP Lince Dorado/Gran Metalik	12.00	30.00

2007 Topps WWE Action

COMPLETE SET (90)	8.00	20.00
UNOPENED BOX (24 PACKS)		
UNOPENED PACK (7 CARDS)		
1 John Cena	.60	1.50
2 Carlito	.40	1.00
3 Charlie Haas	.10	.25
4 Chris Masters	.40	1.00
5 Edge	.40	1.00
6 Eugene	.10	.25
7 Jim Duggan	.40	1.00
8 John Morrison	.10	.25
9 JTG RC	.10	.25
10 Kenny Dykstra RC	.15	.40
11 Lance Cade	.15	.40
12 Randy Orton	.40	1.00
13 Robbie McAllister RC	.10	.25
14 Rory McAllister RC	.10	.25
15 Shad RC	.10	.25
16 Shawn Michaels	.60	1.50
17 Shelton Benjamin	.10	.25
18 Super Crazy	.15	.40
19 Trevor Murdoch	.10	.25
20 Triple H	.60	1.50
21 Umaga	.15	.40
22 Val Venis	.25	.60
23 Viscera	.25	.60
24 Ric Flair	.40	1.00
25 The Great Khali	.15	.40
26 Jeff Hardy	.25	.60
27 Matt Hardy	.25	.60
28 Batista	.40	1.00
29 Boogeyman	.15	.40
30 Brian Kendrick	.15	.40
31 Chavo Guerrero	.15	.40
32 Santino Marella RC	.25	.60
33 Dave Taylor RC	.10	.25
34 Deuce RC	.10	.25
35 Domino RC	.10	.25
36 Finlay	.25	.60
37 Funaki	.15	.40
38 Gregory Helms	.10	.25
39 Hornswoggle RC	.15	.40
40 Jamie Noble	.10	.25
41 Jimmy Wang Yang	.10	.25
42 Kane	.40	1.00
43 King Booker	.40	1.00
44 Mark Henry	.15	.40
45 Montel Vontavious Porter RC	.15	.40
46 Mr. Kennedy	.25	.60
47 Paul London	.25	.60
48 Rey Mysterio	.25	.60
49 Scotty 2 Hotty	.15	.40
50 The Miz RC	.40	1.00
51 Balls Mahoney RC	.10	.25
52 Bobby Lashley	.40	1.00
53 CM Punk	.15	.40
54 Elijah Burke RC	.10	.25
55 Hardcore Holly	.25	.60
56 Kevin Thorn RC	.10	.25
57 Nunzio	.15	.40
58 Marcus CorVan RC	.10	.25
59 Matt Striker	.10	.25
60 Tazz	.15	.40
61 Joey Styles	.10	.25
62 Sabu RC	.10	.25
63 Sandman	.15	.40
64 Snitsky	.15	.40
65 Steve Richards	.15	.40
66 Tommy Dreamer	.15	.40
67 Undertaker/Batista	.50	1.25
68 Undertaker/Batista	.50	1.25
69 Undertaker/Batista	.50	1.25
70 J. Cena/S. Michaels	.60	1.50
71 J. Cena/S. Michaels	.60	1.50
72 J. Cena/S. Michaels	.60	1.50
73 Bobby Lashley/Umaga	.40	1.00
74 Bobby Lashley/Umaga	.40	1.00
75 Bobby Lashley/Umaga	.40	1.00
76 Mr. Kennedy	.25	.60
77 Mr. Kennedy	.25	.60
78 Mr. Kennedy	.25	.60
79 ECW Originals/New Breed	.10	.25
80 ECW Originals/New Breed	.10	.25
81 ECW Originals/New Breed	.10	.25
82 The Great Khali/Kane	.40	1.00
83 The Great Khali/Kane	.40	1.00
84 The Great Khali/Kane	.40	1.00
85 The Great Khali/Kane	.40	1.00
86 Mr. McMahon	.40	1.00
87 Mr. McMahon	.40	1.00
88 Mr. McMahon	.40	1.00
89 Mr. McMahon	.40	1.00
90 Checklist Card	.10	.25

2007 Topps WWE Action Autographs

STATED ODDS 1:48 HOBBY EXCLUSIVE
WILLIAM PERRY ODDS 1:1,392

NNO Bobby Lashley	10.00	25.00
NNO Carlito	5.00	12.00
NNO CM Punk	30.00	60.00
NNO Edge	10.00	25.00
NNO Jeff Hardy	20.00	40.00
NNO John Cena	25.00	50.00
NNO Matt Hardy	10.00	25.00
NNO Mr. Kennedy	10.00	25.00
NNO William Refrigerator Perry	40.00	80.00

2007 Topps WWE Action Lenticular Motion

COMPLETE SET (10)	5.00	12.00
STATED ODDS 1:8 RETAIL EXCLUSIVE		
1 John Cena	1.25	3.00
2 Carlito	.60	1.50
3 Shawn Michaels	1.00	2.50
4 Batista	1.00	2.50
5 Mr. Kennedy	.40	1.00
6 Bobby Lashley	.40	1.00
7 Ric Flair	1.50	4.00
8 Edge	.75	2.00
9 Rey Mysterio	.75	2.00
10 Rob Van Dam	.40	1.00

2007 Topps WWE Action Ringside Relics

COMPLETE SET (4)	10.00	25.00
STATED ODDS 1:48 HOBBY EXCLUSIVE		
NNO Carlito	3.00	8.00
NNO Edge	4.00	10.00
NNO Mr. Kennedy	3.00	8.00
NNO Shawn Michaels	5.00	12.00

2007 Topps WWE Action Tattoos

COMPLETE SET (10)	4.00	10.00

STATED ODDS 1:4 RETAIL EXCLUSIVE

1 Batista	.50	1.25
2 Booker T	.50	1.25
3 John Cena	.75	2.00
4 Edge	.50	1.25
5 Triple H	.75	2.00
6 Undertaker	.60	1.50
7 Carlito	.50	1.25
8 Ric Flair	.50	1.25
9 Rob Van Dam	.50	1.25
10 Rey Mysterio	.30	.75

2015-16 Topps WWE Bret Hart Tribute

COMPLETE SET (20)	15.00	40.00
CANADIAN EXCLUSIVES		
1 Bret Hit Man Hart	2.50	6.00
2 Bret Hit Man Hart	2.50	6.00
3 Bret Hit Man Hart	2.50	6.00
4 Bret Hit Man Hart	2.50	6.00
5 Bret Hit Man Hart	2.50	6.00
6 Bret Hit Man Hart	2.50	6.00
7 Bret Hit Man Hart	2.50	6.00
8 Bret Hit Man Hart	2.50	6.00
9 Bret Hit Man Hart	2.50	6.00
10 Bret Hit Man Hart	2.50	6.00
11 Bret Hit Man Hart	2.50	6.00
12 Bret Hit Man Hart	2.50	6.00
13 Bret Hit Man Hart	2.50	6.00
14 Bret Hit Man Hart	2.50	6.00
15 Bret Hit Man Hart	2.50	6.00
16 Bret Hit Man Hart	2.50	6.00
17 Bret Hit Man Hart	2.50	6.00
18 Bret Hit Man Hart	2.50	6.00
19 Bret Hit Man Hart	2.50	6.00
20 Bret Hit Man Hart	2.50	6.00

2015-16 Topps WWE Bret Hart Tribute Autographs and Relics

NNO Bret Hart AU/100	50.00	100.00
NNO Bret Hart MEM/100	30.00	80.00
NNO Bret Hart AU MEM/10	150.00	300.00

2016 Topps WWE Brock Lesnar Tribute

COMPLETE SET (10)	15.00	40.00
WALMART EXCLUSIVE		
1 Brock Lesnar	1.00	2.50
2 Brock Lesnar	1.00	2.50
3 Brock Lesnar	1.00	2.50
4 Brock Lesnar	1.00	2.50
5 Brock Lesnar	1.00	2.50
6 Brock Lesnar	1.00	2.50
7 Brock Lesnar	1.00	2.50
8 Brock Lesnar	1.00	2.50
9 Brock Lesnar	1.00	2.50
10 Brock Lesnar	1.00	2.50
11 Brock Lesnar	1.00	2.50
12 Brock Lesnar	1.00	2.50
13 Brock Lesnar	1.00	2.50
14 Brock Lesnar	1.00	2.50
15 Brock Lesnar	1.00	2.50
16 Brock Lesnar	1.00	2.50
17 Brock Lesnar	1.00	2.50
18 Brock Lesnar	1.00	2.50
19 Brock Lesnar	1.00	2.50
20 Brock Lesnar	1.00	2.50
21 Brock Lesnar	1.00	2.50
22 Brock Lesnar	1.00	2.50
23 Brock Lesnar	1.00	2.50
24 Brock Lesnar	1.00	2.50
25 Brock Lesnar	1.00	2.50
26 Brock Lesnar	1.00	2.50
27 Brock Lesnar	1.00	2.50
28 Brock Lesnar	1.00	2.50
29 Brock Lesnar	1.00	2.50
30 Brock Lesnar	1.00	2.50
31 Brock Lesnar	1.00	2.50
32 Brock Lesnar	1.00	2.50
33 Brock Lesnar	1.00	2.50
34 Brock Lesnar	1.00	2.50
35 Brock Lesnar	1.00	2.50
36 Brock Lesnar	1.00	2.50
37 Brock Lesnar	1.00	2.50
38 Brock Lesnar	1.00	2.50
39 Brock Lesnar	1.00	2.50
40 Brock Lesnar	1.00	2.50

2016 Topps WWE Brock Lesnar Tribute Autographs and Relics

NNO Brock Lesnar AUTO
NNO Brock Lesnar RELIC
NNO Brock Lesnar RELIC AUTO

2011 Topps WWE Champions

COMPLETE SET (90)	10.00	25.00
UNOPENED BOX (24 PACKS)		
UNOPENED PACK (7 CARDS)		
1 Undertaker/Shawn Michaels	.60	1.50
2 ShowMiz/Morrison & R-Truth	.40	1.00
3 Randy Orton/Rhodes & DiBiase	.60	1.50
4 Jack Swagger MITB	.25	.60
5 Triple H/Sheamus	.75	2.00
6 Rey Mysterio/CM Punk	.40	1.00
7 10-Diva Tag Match	.60	1.50
8 John Cena/Batista	.75	2.00
9 Sheamus	.25	.60
10 Randy Orton	.60	1.50
11 The Miz	.60	1.50
12 Rey Mysterio	.40	1.00
13 Kane	.40	1.00
14 Edge	.60	1.50
15 Dolph Ziggler	.25	.60
16 Edge	.60	1.50
17 Kofi Kingston	.15	.40
18 Dolph Ziggler	.25	.60
19 Kofi Kingston	.15	.40
20 Wade Barrett	.15	.40
21 R-Truth	.15	.40
22 The Miz	.25	.60
23 Daniel Bryan	.15	.40
24 Sheamus	.25	.60
25 David Hart Smith/Tyson Kidd	.15	.40
26 Cody Rhodes/Drew McIntyre	.15	.40
27 David Otunga/John Cena	.75	2.00
28 Heath Slater/Justin Gabriel	.15	.40
29 Santino Marella/Vladimir Kozlov	.25	.60
30 Heath Slater/Justin Gabriel	.15	.40
31 John Cena/The Miz	.75	2.00
32 Heath Slater/Justin Gabriel	.15	.40
33 Eve	.60	1.50
34 Alicia Fox	.25	.60
35 Melina	.60	1.50
36 Michelle McCool	.60	1.50
37 Natalya	.60	1.50
38 Eve	.60	1.50
39 Beth Phoenix	.40	1.00
40 Layla	.40	1.00
41 Nexus	.15	.40
42 Alberto Del Rio	.40	1.00
43 Alex Riley	.15	.40
44 Mason Ryan	.15	.40
45 Sin Cara	.40	1.00
46 Ted DiBiase	.25	.60
47 Big Show/Miz	.40	1.00
48 Randy Orton/Evan Bourne	.60	1.50
49 Big Show/CM Punk	.40	1.00
50 Kane MITB	.40	1.00
51 The Miz MITB	.25	.60
52 Kane/Undertaker	.60	1.50
53 Team SmackDown	.60	1.50
54 Sheamus KOTR	.25	.60
55 Team Mysterio	.40	1.00
56 CM Punk	.40	1.00
57 Wade Barrett	.15	.40
58 John Morrison	.25	.60
59 Booker T	.25	.60
60 Diesel	.25	.60
61 Alberto Del Rio	.40	1.00
62 Edge	.60	1.50
63 John Cena	.75	2.00
64 The Rock Returns	.75	2.00
65 Stone Cold Steve Austin	.60	1.50
66 Trish Stratus/Vickie Guerrero	.75	2.00
67 Mean Gene Okerlund	.25	.60
68 Cowboy Bob Orton	.25	.60
69 Nikolai Volkoff	.25	.60
70 Jimmy Superfly Snuka	.40	1.00
71 Tito Santana	.15	.40
72 Sgt. Slaughter	.40	1.00
73 Jim Ross	.15	.40
74 Rowdy Roddy Piper	.60	1.50
75 Daniel Bryan	.15	.40
76 The Miz	.25	.60
77 CM Punk/John Cena	.75	2.00
78 Wade Barrett	.15	.40
79 John Morrison	.25	.60
80 Drew McIntyre	.15	.40
81 Daniel Bryan	.15	.40
82 Cody Rhodes	.15	.40
83 Edge/Alberto Del Rio	.60	1.50
84 Big Show/Kane/Santino/Kofi	.40	1.00
85 Randy Orton/CM Punk	.60	1.50
86 Michael Cole/Jerry Lawler	.40	1.00
87 Undertaker/Triple H	.75	2.00
88 Trish & Morrison/LayCool & Ziggler	.75	2.00
89 The Miz/John Cena	.75	2.00
90 Checklist	.15	.40

2011 Topps WWE Champions Autographs

STATED ODDS 1:150		
NNO Dolph Ziggler	8.00	20.00
NNO Edge	15.00	40.00
NNO John Cena	25.00	60.00
NNO Kofi Kingston	12.00	30.00
NNO Layla	10.00	25.00
NNO Michelle McCool	12.00	30.00
NNO The Miz	12.00	30.00
NNO Natalya	12.00	30.00
NNO Randy Orton	20.00	50.00
NNO Santino Marella	8.00	20.00
NNO Sheamus	12.00	30.00
NNO Vladimir Kozlov	8.00	20.00

2011 Topps WWE Champions Foil

COMPLETE SET (10)	4.00	10.00
STATED ODDS 1:3		
F1 Stone Cold Steve Austin	1.00	2.50
F2 Triple H	1.25	3.00
F3 Ravishing Rick Rude	.40	1.00
F4 John Morrison	.40	1.00
F5 Edge & Christian	1.00	2.50
F6 Michelle McCool	1.00	2.50
F7 Melina	1.00	2.50
F8 The British Bulldog	.40	1.00
F9 Terry Funk	.40	1.00
F10 Booker T	.40	1.00

2009 Topps WWE Chipz

COMPLETE SET (63)	15.00	30.00
UNOPENED BOX (24 PACKS)		
UNOPENED PACK (3 CHIPS)		
1 John Cena	1.00	2.50
2 Randy Orton	.40	1.00
3 Charlie Haas	.15	.40
4 JTG	.15	.40
5 Snitsky	.25	.60
6 Shad	.15	.40
7 Shawn Michaels	1.00	2.50
8 Santino Marella	.15	.40
9 D-Lo Brown	.25	.60
10 William Regal	.40	1.00
11 Jerry Lawler	.25	.60
12 Chris Jericho	.40	1.00
13 Ted DiBiase	.40	1.00
14 Cody Rhodes	.15	.40
15 Hardcore Holly	.25	.60
16 JBL	.25	.60
17 Michael Cole	.15	.40
18 Rey Mysterio	.40	1.00
19 Batista	.60	1.50
20 Chuck Palumbo	.25	.60
21 Jamie Noble	.15	.40
22 CM Punk	.25	.60
23 Kofi Kingston	.15	.40
24 Kane	.60	1.50
25 Triple H	1.00	2.50
26 Brian Kendrick	.25	.60
27 Undertaker	.75	2.00
28 Jeff Hardy	.60	1.50
29 Umaga	.25	.60
30 Jim Ross	.15	.40
31 Edge	.60	1.50
32 Big Show	.40	1.00
33 Kenny Dykstra	.25	.60
34 Jimmy Wang Yang	.15	.40
35 Zack Ryder	.15	.40
36 Curt Hawkins	.15	.40
37 Deuce	.15	.40
38 Kung Fu Naki	.15	.40
39 R-Truth	.15	.40
40 MVP	.25	.60
41 Vladimir Kozlov	.25	.60
42 Primo	.15	.40
43 Jesse	.15	.40
44 Festus	.15	.40
45 Tazz	.15	.40

46 Shelton Benjamin	.15	.40
47 Elijah Burke	.15	.40
48 Hornswoggle	.25	.60
49 Tommy Dreamer	.15	.40
50 Mike Knox	.15	.40
51 Evan Bourne	.15	.40
52 Matt Striker	.15	.40
53 Matt Hardy	.60	1.50
54 John Morrison	.25	.60
55 Chavo Guerrero	.25	.60
56 Candice	.75	2.00
57 Jillian	.60	1.50
58 Maria	.60	1.50
59 Melina	.60	1.50
60 Michelle McCool	.60	1.50
61 Eve	.60	1.50
62 Kelly Kelly	.60	1.50
63 Victoria	.60	1.50

2009 Topps WWE Chipz Foil

COMPLETE SET (17)	10.00	20.00
STATED ODDS 1:2		
1 Randy Orton	.50	1.25
2 Shawn Michaels	1.25	3.00
3 Mr. Kennedy	.50	1.25
4 Carlito	.50	1.25
5 Shad	.20	.50
6 Chris Jericho	.50	1.25
7 The Great Khali	.20	.50
8 Matt Hardy	.75	2.00
9 MVP	.30	.75
10 Hurricane Helms	.20	.50
11 Mark Henry	.30	.75
12 Finlay	.30	.75
13 John Morrison	.30	.75
14 Boogeyman	.30	.75
15 The Miz	.30	.75
16 Beth Phoenix	1.00	2.50
17 Mickie James	1.00	2.50

2009 Topps WWE Chipz Silver

SILVER STATED ODDS 1:24		
GOLD STATED ODDS 1:72		
1 Shawn Michaels	12.00	30.00
2 Rey Mysterio	10.00	25.00
3 CM Punk	8.00	20.00
4 Kane	10.00	25.00
5 Triple H	10.00	25.00
6 Batista	10.00	25.00
7 Jeff Hardy	10.00	25.00
8 Edge	8.00	20.00
9 Randy Orton	10.00	25.00
10 John Cena GOLD	10.00	25.00

2011 Topps WWE Classic

COMPLETE SET (90)	8.00	20.00
UNOPENED BOX (24 PACKS)		
UNOPENED PACK (8 CARDS)		
*GOLD: 4X TO 10X BASIC CARDS		
1 AJ RC	8.00	20.00
2 Alberto Del Rio	.40	1.00
3 Alex Riley	.15	.40
4 Alicia Fox	.25	.60
5 Batista	.25	.60
6 Beth Phoenix	.40	1.00
7 Big Show	.40	1.00
8 Booker T	.25	.60
9 Brie Bella	.60	1.50
10 Brodus Clay	.15	.40
11 Christian	.15	.40
12 CM Punk	.40	1.00
13 Cody Rhodes	.15	.40
14 Curt Hawkins	.15	.40
15 Daniel Bryan	.15	.40
16 David Otunga	.15	.40
17 Dolph Ziggler	.25	.60
18 Drew McIntyre	.15	.40
19 Eden Stiles RC	.60	1.50
20 Edge	.60	1.50
21 Evan Bourne	.15	.40
22 Eve	.60	1.50
23 Ezekiel Jackson	.25	.60
24 Goldust	.15	.40
25 Heath Slater	.15	.40
26 Hornswoggle	.25	.60
27 Jack Swagger	.25	.60
28 Jerry The King Lawler	.40	1.00
29 Jey Uso	.15	.40
30 Jim Ross	.15	.40
31 Jimmy Uso	.15	.40
32 Jinder Mahal RC	.25	.60
33 John Cena	.75	2.00
34 John Morrison	.25	.60
35 Johnny Curtis	.15	.40
36 JTG	.15	.40
37 Justin Gabriel	.15	.40
38 Kaitlyn	.40	1.00
39 Kane	.40	1.00
40 Kelly Kelly	.60	1.50
41 Kofi Kingston	.15	.40
42 Layla	.40	1.00
43 Mark Henry	.25	.60
44 Mason Ryan	.15	.40
45 Matt Striker	.15	.40
46 Michael Cole	.15	.40
47 Michael McGillicutty	.15	.40
48 The Miz	.25	.60
49 Natalya	.60	1.50
50 Nikki Bella	.60	1.50
51 Percy Watson	.15	.40
52 Primo	.15	.40
53 R-Truth	.15	.40
54 Randy Orton	.60	1.50
55 Rey Mysterio	.40	1.00
56 Ricardo Rodriguez	.15	.40
57 The Rock	.75	2.00
58 Rosa Mendes	.25	.60
59 Santino Marella	.25	.60
60 Shawn Michaels	.60	1.50
61 Sheamus	.25	.60
62 Sin Cara RC	.40	1.00
63 Stone Cold Steve Austin	.60	1.50
64 Tamina	.15	.40
65 Ted DiBiase	.25	.60
66 Theodore Long	.15	.40
67 Trent Barreta	.15	.40
68 Triple H	.75	2.00
69 Trish Stratus	.75	2.00
70 Tyler Reks	.15	.40
71 Tyson Kidd	.15	.40
72 Undertaker	.60	1.50
73 Vickie Guerrero	.25	.60
74 Wade Barrett	.15	.40
75 William Regal	.25	.60
76 Yoshi Tatsu	.15	.40
77 Zack Ryder	.15	.40
78 The American Dream Dusty Rhodes	.25	.60
79 Arn Anderson	.25	.60
80 Big Boss Man	.25	.60
81 Bobby The Brain Heenan	.25	.60
82 Diesel	.25	.60
83 Jimmy Superfly Snuka	.40	1.00
84 Junkyard Dog	.40	1.00
85 Michael PS Hayes	.15	.40
86 Ricky The Dragon Steamboat	.40	1.00
87 The Road Warriors	.40	1.00
88 Rowdy Roddy Piper	.60	1.50
89 Sgt. Slaughter	.40	1.00
90 Yokozuna	.25	.60

2011 Topps WWE Classic Autographs

STATED ODDS 1:24 HOBBY; 1:153 RETAIL		
NNO AJ	75.00	150.00
NNO CM Punk	15.00	40.00
NNO Daniel Bryan	15.00	40.00
NNO Dolph Ziggler	8.00	20.00
NNO Hornswoggle	8.00	20.00
NNO Jack Swagger	8.00	20.00
NNO Jinder Mahal	15.00	40.00
NNO Johnny Curtis	8.00	20.00
NNO Justin Gabriel	8.00	20.00
NNO Mason Ryan	8.00	20.00
NNO Rey Mysterio	20.00	50.00
NNO R-Truth	10.00	25.00
NNO Santino Marella	8.00	20.00
NNO Sheamus	12.00	30.00
NNO Wade Barrett	8.00	20.00
NNO Zack Ryder	8.00	20.00

2011 Topps WWE Classic Relics

STATED ODDS 1:24 HOBBY; 1:48 RETAIL		
NNO Alberto Del Rio	5.00	12.00
NNO Christian	5.00	12.00
NNO CM Punk	8.00	20.00
NNO Daniel Bryan	5.00	12.00
NNO Dolph Ziggler	6.00	15.00
NNO Drew McIntyre	5.00	12.00
NNO Hornswoggle	5.00	12.00
NNO Jack Swagger	5.00	12.00
NNO Kofi Kingston	5.00	12.00
NNO The Miz	5.00	12.00
NNO Santino Marella	8.00	20.00
NNO Sheamus	5.00	12.00
NNO Zack Ryder	6.00	15.00

2011 Topps WWE Classic Promo

P1 The Rock vs. John Cena
(WWE '12 People's Edition Exclusive)

2020 Topps WWE Countdown to WrestleMania

COMPLETE SET (20)		
1 Hulk Hogan/Andre the Giant/207*	6.00	15.00
2 Hulk Hogan/Randy Savage/207*	5.00	12.00
3 Ultimate Warrior/Hulk Hogan/208*	6.00	15.00
4 Razor Ramon/170*	4.00	10.00
5 Shawn Michaels/Bret Hart/147*	5.00	12.00
6 Bret Hart/Steve Austin/149*	5.00	12.00
7 Stone Cold Steve Austin/164*	5.00	12.00
8 The Rock/172*	4.00	10.00
9 Brock Lesnar/132*		
10 Eddie Guerrero/134*		
11 Undertaker/123*	5.00	12.00
12 Undertaker/129*	4.00	10.00
13 John Cena/113*	4.00	10.00
14 Daniel Bryan/116*	4.00	10.00
15 Brock Lesnar/106*	8.00	20.00
16 Seth Rollins/116*	4.00	10.00
17 Charlotte Flair/183*	5.00	12.00
18 Kurt Angle & Ronda Rousey/194*	10.00	25.00
19 Becky Lynch/206*	8.00	20.00
20 Kofi Kingston/113*	4.00	10.00

2017 Topps WWE Daniel Bryan Tribute

COMPLETE SET (20)	8.00	20.00
1 Daniel Bryan	1.25	3.00
2 Daniel Bryan	1.25	3.00
3 Daniel Bryan	1.25	3.00
4 Daniel Bryan	1.25	3.00
5 Daniel Bryan	1.25	3.00
6 Daniel Bryan	1.25	3.00
7 Daniel Bryan	1.25	3.00
8 Daniel Bryan	1.25	3.00
9 Daniel Bryan	1.25	3.00
10 Daniel Bryan	1.25	3.00
11 Daniel Bryan	1.25	3.00
12 Daniel Bryan	1.25	3.00
13 Daniel Bryan	1.25	3.00
14 Daniel Bryan	1.25	3.00
15 Daniel Bryan	1.25	3.00
16 Daniel Bryan	1.25	3.00
17 Daniel Bryan	1.25	3.00
18 Daniel Bryan	1.25	3.00
19 Daniel Bryan	1.25	3.00
20 Daniel Bryan	1.25	3.00
21 Daniel Bryan	1.25	3.00
22 Daniel Bryan	1.25	3.00
23 Daniel Bryan	1.25	3.00
24 Daniel Bryan	1.25	3.00
25 Daniel Bryan	1.25	3.00
26 Daniel Bryan	1.25	3.00
27 Daniel Bryan	1.25	3.00
28 Daniel Bryan	1.25	3.00
29 Daniel Bryan	1.25	3.00
30 Daniel Bryan	1.25	3.00
31 Daniel Bryan	1.25	3.00
32 Daniel Bryan	1.25	3.00
33 Daniel Bryan	1.25	3.00
34 Daniel Bryan	1.25	3.00
35 Daniel Bryan	1.25	3.00
36 Daniel Bryan	1.25	3.00
37 Daniel Bryan	1.25	3.00
38 Daniel Bryan	1.25	3.00
39 Daniel Bryan	1.25	3.00
40 Daniel Bryan	1.25	3.00

2017 Topps WWE Daniel Bryan Tribute Autographs and Relics

NNO Daniel Bryan AU
NNO Daniel Bryan MEM
NNO Daniel Bryan AU MEM

2017 Topps WWE Daniel Bryan Tribute Topps Heritage WWE Autographs and Relics

RANDOMLY INSERTED INTO PACKS

1 Daniel Bryan AUTO

2 Daniel Bryan RELIC		
3 Daniel Bryan AUTO RELIC		

2017 Topps WWE Daniel Bryan Tribute Topps WWE Road to WrestleMania Autographs and Relics

NNO Daniel Bryan AU
NNO Daniel Bryan MEM
NNO Daniel Bryan AU MEM

2017 Topps WWE Daniel Bryan Tribute Topps WWE Then Now Forever Autographs and Relics

STATED ODDS

NNO Daniel Bryan AUTO	12.00	30.00
NNO Daniel Bryan RELIC	8.00	20.00
NNO Daniel Bryan AUTO RELIC		

2008 Topps WWE Decade of Decadence Ultimate Fan Edition DVD Memorabilia Promo

NNO Edge
Shirt

2016 Topps WWE Divas Revolution

COMPLETE SET (43)	15.00	40.00

*SILVER/50: 1X TO 2.5X BASIC CARDS
*PINK/25: 2.5X TO 6X BASIC CARDS
*GOLD/10: 4X TO 10X BASIC CARDS
*RED/1: UNPRICED DUE TO SCARCITY

1 Wendi Richter	.25	.60
2 Miss Elizabeth	.25	.60
3 Sensational Sherri	.40	1.00
4 Alundra Blayze	.30	.75
5 Ivory	.25	.60
6 Lita	.75	2.00
7 Trish Stratus	1.25	3.00
8 Torrie Wilson	.60	1.50
9 Leilani Kai	.25	.60
10 Kelly Kelly	.40	1.00
11 Beth Phoenix	.40	1.00
12 Eve Torres	.50	1.25
13 Alexa Bliss	6.00	15.00
14 Alicia Fox	.40	1.00
15 Cathy Kelley RC	.25	.60
16 Becky Lynch RC	4.00	10.00
17 Brie Bella	.50	1.25
18 Carmella RC	.60	1.50
19 Charlotte	3.00	8.00
20 Dana Brooke RC	.60	1.50
21 Dasha Fuentes RC	.25	.60
22 Emma	.50	1.25
23 Eva Marie	.50	1.25
24 JoJo	.25	.60
25 Lana	1.00	2.50
26 Maryse	.50	1.25
27 Naomi	.40	1.00
28 Natalya	.40	1.00
29 Nia Jax RC	.40	1.00
30 Nikki Bella	.75	2.00
31 Renee Young	.60	1.50
32 Rosa Mendes	.25	.60
33 Sasha Banks	3.00	8.00
34 Stephanie McMahon	.40	1.00
35 Summer Rae	.60	1.50
36 Tamina	.30	.75
37 Aliyah RC	.30	.75
38 Asuka RC	2.50	6.00
39 Bayley RC	.60	1.50
40 Billie Kay RC	.60	1.50
41 Liv Morgan RC	6.00	15.00
42 Peyton Royce RC	.60	1.50
43 Mandy Rose RC	3.00	8.00

2016 Topps WWE Divas Revolution Autographs

*SILVER/50: .6X TO 1.5X BASIC AUTOS
*PINK/25: .75X TO 2X BASIC AUTOS
*GOLD/10: 1.2X TO 3X BASIC AUTOS
*RED/1: UNPRICED DUE TO SCARCITY
STATED ODDS 1:9

1 Wendi Richter	12.00	30.00
4 Alundra Blayze	10.00	25.00
6 Lita	15.00	40.00
7 Trish Stratus	20.00	50.00
8 Torrie Wilson	20.00	50.00
9 Leilani Kai	6.00	15.00
10 Kelly Kelly	15.00	40.00
11 Beth Phoenix	10.00	25.00
12 Eve Torres	20.00	50.00
13 Alexa Bliss	60.00	120.00
14 Alicia Fox	12.00	30.00
16 Becky Lynch	25.00	60.00
17 Brie Bella	12.00	30.00
18 Carmella	15.00	40.00
19 Charlotte	20.00	50.00
22 Emma	15.00	40.00
26 Maryse	12.00	30.00
27 Naomi	10.00	25.00
28 Natalya	12.00	30.00
30 Nikki Bella	15.00	40.00
32 Rosa Mendes	6.00	15.00
33 Sasha Banks	20.00	50.00
35 Summer Rae	10.00	25.00
36 Tamina	10.00	25.00
38 Asuka	15.00	40.00
43 Mandy Rose	50.00	100.00

2016 Topps WWE Divas Revolution Best Matches

COMPLETE SET (9)	6.00	15.00

*SILVER/50: .5X TO 1.5X BASIC CARDS
*PINK/25: X TO 2X BASIC CARDS
*GOLD/10: 1.2X TO 3X BASIC CARDS
*RED/1: UNPRICED DUE TO SCARCITY

1 Alundra Blayze/Bull Nakano	.60	1.50
2 Trish Stratus/Lita	2.50	6.00
3 Charlotte/Natalya	1.50	4.00
4 Stephanie McMahon/Brie Bella	.75	2.00
5 Charlotte/Sasha Banks	1.50	4.00
6 Sasha Banks/Becky Lynch	1.50	4.00
7 Bayley	1.25	3.00
8 Bayley/Sasha Banks	1.25	3.00
9 Asuka/Bayley	2.00	5.00

2016 Topps WWE Divas Revolution Diva Kiss

*GOLD/10: .75X TO 2X BASIC KISS
*RED/1: UNPRICED DUE TO SCARCITY
STATED ODDS 1:15

NNO Alexa Bliss	60.00	120.00
NNO Alicia Fox	12.00	30.00
NNO Asuka	25.00	60.00
NNO Becky Lynch	20.00	50.00
NNO Billie Kay	25.00	60.00
NNO Carmella	25.00	60.00
NNO Charlotte	20.00	50.00
NNO Dana Brooke	25.00	60.00
NNO Emma	25.00	60.00
NNO Mandy Rose	20.00	40.00
NNO Maryse	20.00	50.00
NNO Natalya	20.00	50.00
NNO Nia Jax	12.00	30.00
NNO Peyton Royce	12.00	30.00
NNO Renee Young	20.00	50.00

2016 Topps WWE Divas Revolution Diva Kiss Autographs

*GOLD/10: .75X TO 2X BASIC AUTOS
*RED/1: UNPRICED DUE TO SCARCITY
STATED ODDS 1:56

NNO Alexa Bliss	120.00	200.00
NNO Alicia Fox	15.00	40.00
NNO Asuka	40.00	100.00
NNO Becky Lynch	60.00	120.00
NNO Billie Kay	25.00	60.00
NNO Carmella	60.00	120.00
NNO Charlotte	60.00	120.00
NNO Dana Brooke	25.00	60.00
NNO Emma	25.00	60.00
NNO Mandy Rose	25.00	60.00
NNO Maryse	25.00	60.00
NNO Natalya	15.00	40.00
NNO Nia Jax	15.00	40.00
NNO Peyton Royce	15.00	40.00
NNO Renee Young	20.00	50.00

2016 Topps WWE Divas Revolution Historic Women's Champions

COMPLETE SET (10)	6.00	15.00

*SILVER/50: .75X TO 2X BASIC CARDS
*PINK/25: 2X TO 5X BASIC CARDS
*GOLD/10: 3X TO 8X BASIC CARDS
*RED/1: UNPRICED DUE TO SCARCITY

1 Alundra Blayze	.50	1.25
2 Lita	1.25	3.00
3 Trish Stratus	2.00	5.00
4 Maryse	.75	2.00
5 Eve Torres	.75	2.00
6 Nikki Bella	1.25	3.00
7 Charlotte	1.25	3.00
8 Charlotte	1.25	3.00
9 Bayley	1.00	2.50
10 Charlotte	1.25	3.00

2016 Topps WWE Divas Revolution Mat Relics

*SILVER/50: .5X TO 1.2X BASIC MEM
*PINK/25: .6X TO 1.5X BASIC MEM
*GOLD/10: .75X TO 2X BASIC MEM
*RED/1: UNPRICED DUE TO SCARCITY
STATED ODDS 1:8

NNO Alexa Bliss Belfast	10.00	25.00
NNO Alexa Bliss DMF	10.00	25.00
NNO Alicia Fox Summerslam	3.00	8.00
NNO Alicia Fox WrestleMania	3.00	8.00
NNO Asuka Belfast	8.00	20.00
NNO Asuka DMF	8.00	20.00
NNO Bayley Takeover	5.00	12.00
NNO Bayley DMF	5.00	12.00
NNO Bayley Belfast	5.00	12.00
NNO Becky Lynch SummerSlam	6.00	15.00
NNO Becky Lynch NXT	6.00	15.00
NNO Brie Bella SummerSlam	4.00	10.00
NNO Brie Bella WrestleMania	4.00	10.00
NNO Carmella Belfast	5.00	12.00
NNO Carmella DMF	5.00	12.00
NNO Charlotte SummerSlam	6.00	15.00
NNO Charlotte NXT	6.00	15.00
NNO Dana Brooke NXT	5.00	12.00
NNO Emma WrestleMania	4.00	10.00
NNO Emma NXT	4.00	10.00
NNO Eve Torres WrestleMania	4.00	10.00
NNO Naomi SummerSlam	3.00	8.00
NNO Naomi WrestleMania	3.00	8.00
NNO Naomi WrestleMania	3.00	8.00
NNO Nia Jax Belfast	3.00	8.00
NNO Nia Jax DMF	3.00	8.00
NNO Nikki Bella MITB	6.00	15.00
NNO Nikki Bella SummerSlam	6.00	15.00
NNO Nikki Bella WrestleMania	6.00	15.00
NNO Peyton Royce Belfast	5.00	12.00
NNO Peyton Royce DMF	5.00	12.00
NNO Rosa Mendes WrestleMania	2.00	5.00
NNO Sasha Banks Takeover	6.00	15.00
NNO Sasha Banks SummerSlam	6.00	15.00
NNO Tamina SummerSlam	2.50	6.00

2016 Topps WWE Divas Revolution Power Couples

COMPLETE SET (10)	6.00	15.00

*RED/50: .75X TO 2X BASIC CARDS
*PINK/25: 1.2X TO 3X BASIC CARDS
*GOLD/10: 2X TO 5X BASIC CARDS
RANDOMLY INSERTED INTO PACKS

1 Miss Elizabeth/Randy Savage	1.00	2.50
2 Stephanie McMahon/HHH	1.50	4.00
3 Lita/Edge	1.25	3.00
4 Sensational Sherri/HBK	1.50	4.00
5 Trish Stratus/Christian	2.00	5.00
6 Brie Bella/Daniel Bryan	1.50	4.00
7 Queen Sherri/Randy Savage	1.00	2.50
8 Naomi/Jimmy Uso	.60	1.50
9 Rusev/Lana	1.50	4.00
10 Lita/Kane	1.25	3.00

2016 Topps WWE Divas Revolution The Revolution

COMPLETE SET (4)	4.00	10.00

*SILVER/50: .75X TO 2X BASIC CARDS
*PINK/25: 1.2X TO 3X BASIC CARDS
*GOLD/10: 1.5X TO 4X BASIC CARDS
*RED/1: UNPRICED DUE TO SCARCITY

1 Charlotte	1.50	4.00
2 Team PCB	1.25	3.00
3 Charlotte	1.50	4.00
4 Charlotte	1.50	4.00

2016 Topps WWE Divas Revolution Rivalries

COMPLETE SET (8)	5.00	12.00

*SILVER/50: 1X TO 2.5X BASIC CARDS
*PINK/25: 1.2X TO 3X BASIC CARDS
*GOLD/10: 1.5X TO 4X BASIC CARDS
*RED//1: UNPRICED DUE TO SCARCITY
RANDOMLY INSERTED INTO PACKS

1 Trish Stratus/Lita	2.00	5.00
2 Trish Stratus/Stephanie McMahon	2.00	5.00

3 Bayley/Sasha Banks	1.25	3.00
4 Charlotte/Sasha Banks	1.25	3.00
5 Charlotte/Nikki Bella	1.25	3.00
6 Becky Lynch/Charlotte	1.25	3.00
7 Brie Bella/Nikki Bella	1.25	3.00
8 Miss Elizabeth	.60	1.50
Sensational Sherri		

2016 Topps WWE Divas Revolution Shirt Relics

*SILVER/50: .5X TO 1.2X BASIC MEM
*PINK/25: .6X TO 1.5X BASIC MEM
*GOLD/10: UNPRICED DUE TO SCARCITY
*RED/1: UNPRICED DUE TO SCARCITY

NNO Alexa Bliss	12.00	30.00
NNO Alicia Fox	4.00	10.00
NNO Asuka	10.00	25.00
NNO Becky Lynch	8.00	20.00
NNO Brie Bella	5.00	12.00
NNO Carmella	6.00	15.00
NNO Charlotte	8.00	20.00
NNO JoJo	2.50	6.00
NNO Lana	10.00	25.00
NNO Naomi	4.00	10.00
NNO Natalya	4.00	10.00
NNO Renee Young	6.00	15.00
NNO Sasha Banks	8.00	20.00
NNO Summer Rae	6.00	15.00
NNO Tamina	3.00	8.00

2007 Topps WWE Dog Tags

COMPLETE SET (24)	40.00	80.00
UNOPENED BOX (24 PACKS)		
UNOPENED PACK (1 TAG+1 CARD)		
*GOLD: 1X TO 2.5X BASIC TAGS		
1 John Cena	4.00	10.00
2 Batista	2.50	6.00
3 Johnny Nitro	1.00	2.50
4 Carlito	2.50	6.00
5 Ric Flair	2.50	6.00
6 Undertaker	3.00	8.00
7 Chris Benoit	1.50	4.00
8 CM Punk	1.00	2.50
9 Booker T	2.50	6.00
10 Rob Van Dam	2.50	6.00
11 Ken Kennedy	1.50	4.00
12 Shawn Michaels	4.00	10.00
13 The Rock	5.00	12.00
14 Jeff Hardy	1.50	4.00
15 Stone Cold Steve Austin	4.00	10.00
16 Edge	2.50	6.00
17 Rey Mysterio	1.50	4.00
18 Kane	2.50	6.00
19 Randy Orton	2.50	6.00
20 Triple H	4.00	10.00
21 Sabu	.60	1.50
22 Umaga	1.00	2.50
23 Sandman	1.00	2.50
24 Bobby Lashley	2.50	6.00

2007 Topps WWE Dog Tags Trading Cards

COMPLETE SET (25)	15.00	40.00
1 John Cena	2.00	5.00
2 Batista	1.25	3.00
3 Johnny Nitro	.50	1.25
4 Carlito	1.25	3.00
5 Ric Flair	1.25	3.00
6 Undertaker	1.50	4.00
7 Chris Benoit	.75	2.00
8 CM Punk	.50	1.25
9 Booker T	1.25	3.00
10 Rob Van Dam	1.25	3.00
11 Ken Kennedy	.75	2.00
12 Shawn Michaels	2.00	5.00
13 The Rock	2.50	6.00
14 Jeff Hardy	.75	2.00
15 Stone Cold Steve Austin	2.00	5.00
16 Edge	1.25	3.00
17 Rey Mysterio	.75	2.00
18 Kane	1.25	3.00
19 Randy Orton	1.25	3.00
20 Triple H	2.00	5.00
21 Sabu	.30	.75
22 Umaga	.50	1.25
23 Sandman	.50	1.25
24 Bobby Lashley	1.25	3.00
NNO Checklist	.30	.75

2015 Topps WWE Dog Tags

COMPLETE SET (30)	15.00	40.00
*GOLD: X TO X BASIC TAGS		
1 AJ Lee	1.50	4.00
2 Bad News Barrett	.30	.75
3 Batista	.75	2.00
4 Big Show	.75	2.00
5 Bray Wyatt	1.25	3.00
6 Brock Lesnar	1.25	3.00
7 Cesaro	.30	.75
8 Chris Jericho	.75	2.00
9 Daniel Bryan	1.25	3.00
10 Dean Ambrose	.75	2.00
11 Dolph Ziggler	.50	1.25
12 Edge	.75	2.00
13 Hulk Hogan	1.50	4.00
14 Jake The Snake Roberts	.50	1.25
15 John Cena	1.50	4.00
16 Kane	.75	2.00
17 Kofi Kingston	.30	.75
18 Randy Orton	1.25	3.00
19 Rey Mysterio	.75	2.00
20 Ric Flair	1.50	4.00
21 Rob Van Dam	.75	2.00
22 The Rock	1.50	4.00
23 Roman Reigns	.75	2.00
24 Seth Rollins	.50	1.25
25 Shawn Michaels	1.25	3.00
26 Sheamus	.75	2.00
27 Stone Cold Steve Austin	1.50	4.00
28 Triple H	1.25	3.00
29 Ultimate Warrior	1.00	2.50
30 Undertaker	1.25	3.00

2015 Topps WWE Dog Tags Trading Cards

COMPLETE SET (30)	8.00	20.00
STATED ODDS 1:1		
1 AJ Lee	.75	2.00
2 Bad News Barrett	.15	.40
3 Batista	.40	1.00
4 Big Show	.40	1.00
5 Bray Wyatt	.60	1.50
6 Brock Lesnar	.60	1.50
7 Cesaro	.15	.40
8 Chris Jericho	.40	1.00
9 Daniel Bryan	.60	1.50
10 Dean Ambrose	.40	1.00
11 Dolph Ziggler	.25	.60
12 Edge	.40	1.00
13 Hulk Hogan	.75	2.00
14 Jake The Snake Roberts	.25	.60
15 John Cena	.75	2.00
16 Kane	.40	1.00
17 Kofi Kingston	.15	.40
18 Randy Orton	.60	1.50
19 Rey Mysterio	.40	1.00
20 Ric Flair	.75	2.00
21 Rob Van Dam	.40	1.00
22 The Rock	.75	2.00
23 Roman Reigns	.40	1.00
24 Seth Rollins	.25	.60
25 Shawn Michaels	.60	1.50
26 Sheamus	.40	1.00
27 Stone Cold Steve Austin	.75	2.00
28 Triple H	.60	1.50
29 Ultimate Warrior	.50	1.25
30 Undertaker	.60	1.50

2015 Topps WWE Dog Tags Relic Tags

1 Bad News Barrett
2 Big Show
3 Bray Wyatt
4 Cesaro
5 Chris Jericho
6 Daniel Bryan
7 Dolph Ziggler
8 Edge
9 Hulk Hogan
10 Kofi Kingston
11 John Cena
12 Randy Orton
13 Rey Mysterio
14 Rob Van Dam
15 Roman Reigns
16 Seth Rollins

2010 Topps WWE Dog Tags Pyrotechno Edition

COMPLETE SET (24)	12.00	30.00
UNOPENED BOX (24 PACKS)		
UNOPENED PACK (1 TAG+1 CARD)		
*GOLD: .75X TO 2X BASIC TAGS		
1 John Cena	2.50	6.00
2 Kofi Kingston	.75	2.00
3 Big Show	1.25	3.00
4 Cody Rhodes	.50	1.25
5 Ted DiBiase	.75	2.00
6 Santino Marella	.50	1.25
7 The Miz	.75	2.00
8 Triple H	2.50	6.00
9 Shawn Michaels	3.00	8.00
10 CM Punk	2.00	5.00
11 John Morrison	.75	2.00
12 Chris Jericho	1.25	3.00
13 Matt Hardy	1.25	3.00
14 Christian	.75	2.00
15 Tommy Dreamer	.50	1.25
16 Undertaker	2.00	5.00
17 Yoshi Tatsu	.50	1.25
18 Sheamus	.75	2.00
19 Finlay	.75	2.00
20 Hornswoggle	.75	2.00
21 Edge	2.00	5.00
22 Batista	2.00	5.00
23 Evan Bourne	.50	1.25
24 Randy Orton	2.00	5.00

2010 Topps WWE Dog Tags Pyrotechno Edition Trading Cards

COMPLETE SET (24)	10.00	25.00
1 John Cena	2.00	5.00
2 Kofi Kingston	.60	1.50
3 Big Show	1.00	2.50
4 Cody Rhodes	.40	1.00
5 Ted DiBiase	.60	1.50
6 Santino Marella	.40	1.00
7 The Miz	.60	1.50
8 Triple H	2.00	5.00
9 Shawn Michaels	2.50	6.00
10 CM Punk	1.50	4.00
11 John Morrison	.60	1.50
12 Chris Jericho	1.00	2.50
13 Matt Hardy	1.00	2.50
14 Christian	.60	1.50
15 Tommy Dreamer	.40	1.00
16 Undertaker	1.50	4.00
17 Yoshi Tatsu	.40	1.00
18 Sheamus	.60	1.50
19 Finlay	.60	1.50
20 Hornswoggle	.60	1.50
21 Edge	1.50	4.00
22 Batista	1.50	4.00
23 Evan Bourne	.40	1.00
24 Randy Orton	1.50	4.00

2011 Topps WWE Dog Tags Ringside Relic Edition

COMPLETE SET (24)	10.00	20.00
UNOPENED BOX (24 PACKS)		
UNOPENED PACK (1 TAG+1 CARD)		
1 CM Punk	1.00	2.50
2 Daniel Bryan	.40	1.00
3 David Otunga	.40	1.00
4 John Cena	2.00	5.00
5 John Morrison	.60	1.50
6 Justin Gabriel	.40	1.00
7 Ezekiel Jackson	.60	1.50
8 Randy Orton	1.50	4.00
9 Sheamus	.60	1.50
10 The Miz	.60	1.50
11 Wade Barrett	.40	1.00
12 Heath Slater	.40	1.00
13 Dolph Ziggler	.60	1.50
14 Edge	1.50	4.00
15 Kane	1.00	2.50
16 Undertaker	1.50	4.00
17 Alberto Del Rio	1.00	2.50
18 Jack Swagger	.60	1.50
19 Tyler Reks	.40	1.00
20 Drew McIntyre	.40	1.00
21 Rey Mysterio	1.00	2.50
22 Kaval	1.00	2.50
23 Kofi Kingston	.40	1.00
24 Big Show	1.00	2.50

2011 Topps WWE Dog Tags Ringside Relic Edition Memorabilia Tags

STATED ODDS 1:24

1 Hornswoggle	2.50	6.00
2 Sheamus	2.50	6.00
3 Kofi Kingston	2.50	6.00
4 Edge	6.00	15.00
5 Jack Swagger	2.50	6.00
6 Justin Gabriel	2.50	6.00
7 David Hart Smith	2.50	6.00
8 The Miz	2.50	6.00
9 John Cena	8.00	20.00
10 Randy Orton	6.00	15.00
11 Alex Riley	2.50	6.00
12 Heath Slater	2.50	6.00
13 Wade Barrett	2.50	6.00
14 John Morrison	2.50	6.00
15 David Otunga	2.50	6.00
16 Tyson Kidd	2.50	6.00
17 Rey Mysterio	4.00	10.00
18 Big Show	4.00	10.00

2011 Topps WWE Dog Tags Ringside Relic Edition Trading Cards

COMPLETE SET (24)	4.00	10.00
1 CM Punk	.40	1.00
2 Daniel Bryan	.15	.40
3 David Otunga	.15	.40
4 John Cena	.75	2.00
5 John Morrison	.25	.60
6 Justin Gabriel	.15	.40
7 Ezekiel Jackson	.25	.60
8 Randy Orton	.60	1.50
9 Sheamus	.25	.60
10 The Miz	.25	.60
11 Wade Barrett	.15	.40
12 Heath Slater	.15	.40
13 Dolph Ziggler	.25	.60
14 Edge	.60	1.50
15 Kane	.40	1.00
16 Undertaker	.60	1.50
17 Alberto Del Rio	.40	1.00
18 Jack Swagger	.25	.60
19 Tyler Reks	.15	.40
20 Drew McIntyre	.15	.40
21 Rey Mysterio	.40	1.00
22 Kaval	.40	1.00
23 Kofi Kingston	.15	.40
24 Big Show	.40	1.00

2011 Topps WWE Dog Tags Ringside Relic Edition Silver Insert Cards

COMPLETE SET (18)	4.00	10.00
STATED ODDS 1:24		
1 Hornswoggle	.40	1.00
2 Sheamus	.40	1.00
3 Kofi Kingston	.25	.60
4 Edge	1.00	2.50
5 Jack Swagger	.40	1.00
6 Justin Gabriel	.25	.60
7 David Hart Smith	.25	.60
8 The Miz	.40	1.00
9 John Cena	1.25	3.00
10 Randy Orton	1.00	2.50
11 Alex Riley	.25	.60
12 Heath Slater	.25	.60
13 Wade Barrett	.25	.60
14 John Morrison	.40	1.00
15 David Otunga	.25	.60
16 Tyson Kidd	.25	.60
17 Rey Mysterio	.60	1.50
18 Big Show	.60	1.50

2012 Topps WWE Dog Tags Ringside Relic Edition

COMPLETE SET (24)	15.00	40.00
UNOPENED BOX (24 PACKS)		
UNOPENED PACK (1 TAG+1 CARD)		
STATED ODDS 1:1		
1 CM Punk	2.50	6.00
2 Ted Dibiase	1.00	2.50
3 Sheamus	1.50	4.00
4 David Otunga	.60	1.50
5 The Miz	1.00	2.50
6 Jack Swagger	1.00	2.50
7 R-Truth	.60	1.50
8 Heath Slater	.60	1.50
9 Christian	.60	1.50
10 John Cena	3.00	8.00
11 Zack Ryder	.60	1.50
12 Daniel Bryan	.60	1.50
13 Hornswoggle	1.00	2.50
14 Rey Mysterio	1.50	4.00
15 Dolph Ziggler	1.00	2.50
16 Kofi Kingston	.60	1.50
17 Evan Bourne	.60	1.50
18 Santino Marella	1.00	2.50
19 Triple H	2.50	6.00
20 Sin Cara	1.50	4.00
21 The Miz	1.00	2.50
22 Stone Cold Steve Austin	3.00	8.00
23 Undertaker	2.50	6.00
24 Randy Orton	2.50	6.00

2012 Topps WWE Dog Tags Ringside Relic Edition Memorabilia Tags

STATED ODDS 1:24

1 CM Punk	6.00	15.00
2 Ted Dibiase	2.50	6.00
3 Sheamus	4.00	10.00
4 David Otunga	1.50	4.00
5 The Miz	2.50	6.00
6 Jack Swagger	2.50	6.00
7 R-Truth	1.50	4.00
8 Heath Slater	1.50	4.00
9 Christian	1.50	4.00
10 John Cena	8.00	20.00
11 Zack Ryder	1.50	4.00
12 Daniel Bryan	1.50	4.00
13 Hornswoggle	2.50	6.00
14 Rey Mysterio	4.00	10.00
15 Dolph Ziggler	2.50	6.00
16 Kofi Kingston	1.50	4.00
17 Evan Bourne	1.50	4.00

2012 Topps WWE Dog Tags Ringside Relic Edition Trading Cards

COMPLETE SET (24)	5.00	12.00
1 CM Punk	1.00	2.50
2 Ted Dibiase	.40	1.00
3 Sheamus	.60	1.50
4 David Otunga	.25	.60
5 The Miz	.40	1.00
6 Jack Swagger	.40	1.00
7 R-Truth	.25	.60
8 Heath Slater	.25	.60
9 Christian	.25	.60
10 John Cena	1.25	3.00
11 Zack Ryder	.25	.60
12 Daniel Bryan	.25	.60
13 Hornswoggle	.40	1.00
14 Rey Mysterio	.60	1.50
15 Dolph Ziggler	.40	1.00
16 Kofi Kingston	.25	.60
17 Evan Bourne	.25	.60
18 Santino Marella	.40	1.00
19 Triple H	1.00	2.50
20 Sin Cara	.60	1.50
21 The Miz	.40	1.00
22 Stone Cold Steve Austin	1.25	3.00
23 Undertaker	1.00	2.50
24 Randy Orton	1.00	2.50

2013 Topps WWE Dog Tags Signature Series

COMPLETE SET (30)		
UNOPENED BOX (24 PACKS)		
UNOPENED PACK (1 TAG+1 CARD)		
STATED ODDS 1:1		
1 John Cena	3.00	8.00
2 CM Punk	2.50	6.00
3 Ryback	.60	1.50
4 Sheamus	1.25	3.00
5 Big Show	1.25	3.00
6 Randy Orton	2.00	5.00
7 Alberto Del Rio	1.25	3.00
8 Christian	.60	1.50
9 Cody Rhodes	.60	1.50
10 Rey Mysterio	1.50	4.00
11 Sin Cara	1.00	2.50
12 Dolph Ziggler	1.00	2.50
13 Zack Ryder	.60	1.50
14 Santino	.60	1.50
15 Triple H	2.50	6.00
16 Undertaker	2.50	6.00
17 Kane	1.25	3.00
18 Daniel Bryan	1.50	4.00
19 The Miz	1.00	2.50
20 Kofi Kingston	.60	1.50
21 R-Truth	.60	1.50
22 Brodus Clay	.60	1.50
23 Wade Barrett	.60	1.50
24 The Rock	3.00	8.00
25 Cactus Jack	2.50	6.00
26 Jerry King Lawler	1.25	3.00
27 Shawn Michaels	2.50	6.00
28 Kevin Nash	.75	2.00
29 Booker T	1.00	2.50
30 Stone Cold Steve Austin	2.50	6.00

2013 Topps WWE Dog Tags Signature Series Autographed Tags

STATED ODDS 1:107

NNO AJ Lee	75.00	150.00
NNO Aksana	6.00	15.00
NNO Booker T	12.00	30.00
NNO Brodus Clay	6.00	15.00
NNO Daniel Bryan	15.00	40.00
NNO Kane	12.00	30.00
NNO Layla	6.00	15.00
NNO Natalya	10.00	25.00
NNO Tamina	6.00	15.00
NNO Zack Ryder	6.00	15.00

2013 Topps WWE Dog Tags Signature Series Divas Trading Cards

COMPLETE SET (5)
STATED ODDS 1:107

1 AJ Lee	15.00	40.00
2 Aksana	5.00	12.00
3 Layla	6.00	15.00
4 Natalya	6.00	15.00
5 Tamina	4.00	10.00

2013 Topps WWE Dog Tags Signature Series Memorabilia Tags

STATED ODDS 1:24

NNO Alberto Del Rio	3.00	8.00
NNO Brodus Clay	1.50	4.00
NNO CM Punk	6.00	15.00
NNO Cody Rhodes	1.50	4.00
NNO Daniel Bryan	4.00	10.00
NNO Dolph Ziggler	2.50	6.00
NNO John Cena	8.00	20.00
NNO Kofi Kingston	1.50	4.00
NNO The Miz	2.50	6.00
NNO Rey Mysterio	4.00	10.00
NNO R-Truth	1.50	4.00
NNO Ryback	1.50	4.00
NNO Santino	1.50	4.00
NNO Shawn Michaels	6.00	15.00
NNO Sheamus	3.00	8.00
NNO Sin Cara	2.50	6.00
NNO Wade Barrett	1.50	4.00
NNO Zack Ryder	1.50	4.00

2013 Topps WWE Dog Tags Signature Series Trading Cards

COMPLETE SET (30)	6.00	15.00
1 John Cena	1.25	3.00
2 CM Punk	1.00	2.50
3 Ryback	.25	.60
4 Sheamus	.50	1.25
5 Big Show	.50	1.25
6 Randy Orton	.75	2.00
7 Alberto Del Rio	.50	1.25
8 Christian	.25	.60
9 Cody Rhodes	.25	.60
10 Rey Mysterio	.60	1.50
11 Sin Cara	.40	1.00
12 Dolph Ziggler	.40	1.00
13 Zack Ryder	.25	.60
14 Santino	.25	.60
15 Triple H	1.00	2.50
16 Undertaker	1.00	2.50
17 Kane	.50	1.25
18 Daniel Bryan	.60	1.50
19 The Miz	.40	1.00
20 Kofi Kingston	.25	.60
21 R-Truth	.25	.60
22 Brodus Clay	.25	.60
23 Wade Barrett	.25	.60
24 The Rock	1.25	3.00
25 Cactus Jack	1.00	2.50
26 Jerry King Lawler	.50	1.25
27 Shawn Michaels	1.00	2.50
28 Kevin Nash	.30	.75

29	Booker T	.40	1.00
30	Stone Cold Steve Austin	1.00	2.50

2007 Topps WWE Dog Tags UK

COMPLETE SET (21) 25.00 60.00
UNOPENED BOX (24 PACKS)
UNOPENED PACK (1 TAG+1 CARD)
*GOLD: 1X TO 2.5X BASIC TAGS

1	John Cena	4.00	10.00
2	Batista	2.50	6.00
3	Johnny Nitro	1.00	2.50
4	Carlito	2.50	6.00
5	Ric Flair	2.50	6.00
6	Undertaker	3.00	8.00
7	CM Punk	1.00	2.50
8	Booker T	2.50	6.00
9	Ken Kennedy	1.50	4.00
10	Shawn Michaels	4.00	10.00
11	The Rock	5.00	12.00
12	Jeff Hardy	1.50	4.00
13	Stone Cold Steve Austin	4.00	10.00
14	Edge	2.50	6.00
15	Rey Mysterio	1.50	4.00
16	Kane	2.50	6.00
17	Randy Orton	2.50	6.00
18	Triple H	4.00	10.00
19	Umaga	1.00	2.50
20	Sandman	1.00	2.50
21	Bobby Lashley	2.50	6.00

2007 Topps WWE Dog Tags UK Trading Cards

COMPLETE SET (21) 12.00 30.00

1	John Cena	2.00	5.00
2	Batista	1.25	3.00
3	Johnny Nitro	.50	1.25
4	Carlito	1.25	3.00
5	Ric Flair	1.25	3.00
6	Undertaker	1.50	4.00
7	CM Punk	.50	1.25
8	Booker T	1.25	3.00
9	Ken Kennedy	.75	2.00
10	Shawn Michaels	2.00	5.00
11	The Rock	2.50	6.00
12	Jeff Hardy	.75	2.00
13	Stone Cold Steve Austin	2.00	5.00
14	Edge	1.25	3.00
15	Rey Mysterio	.75	2.00
16	Kane	1.25	3.00
17	Randy Orton	1.25	3.00
18	Triple H	2.00	5.00
19	Umaga	.50	1.25
20	Sandman	.50	1.25
21	Bobby Lashley	1.25	3.00
CL	Checklist	.30	.75

2007-08 Topps WWE DVD Collection

COMPLETE SET (17)

D1	Iron Sheik & Nikolai Volkoff
D2	Ravishing Rick Rude
D3	Mr. Perfect/Roddy Piper
D4	The Rock
D5	The Million Dollar Man Ted DiBiase
D6	The British Bulldog Davey Boy Smith
D7	Mankind
D8	Shawn Michaels
D9	Jake The Snake Roberts
D10	Sgt. Slaughter
D11	Undertaker
D12	Edge
D13	Hacksaw Jim Duggan
D14	Ric Flair
D15	Stone Cold Steve Austin
D16	Triple H
CL	Checklist

2007 Topps WWE Face-Off

COMPLETE SET (132) 20.00 50.00

1	Bobby Lashley	1.25	3.00
2	Armando Estrada RC	.30	.75
3	Brian Kendrick	.50	1.25
4	Carlito	1.25	3.00
5	Charlie Haas	.30	.75
6	Daivari RC	.30	.75
7	Jim Duggan	.50	1.25
8	Jeff Hardy	.75	2.00
9	Jerry Lawler	.75	2.00
10	Jim Ross	.40	1.00
11	John Cena	2.00	5.00
12	Jonathan Coachman	.30	.75
13	JTG RC	.30	.75
14	King Booker	1.25	3.00
15	Lance Cade	.30	.75
16	Mr. Kennedy	.75	2.00
17	Paul London	.75	2.00
18	Randy Orton	1.25	3.00
19	Robbie McAllister RC	.30	.75
20	Rory McAllister RC	.30	.75
21	Roddy Piper	1.25	3.00
22	Sandman	.50	1.25
23	Santino Marella RC	.40	1.00
24	Shad RC	.30	.75
25	Shane McMahon	.75	2.00
26	Shawn Michaels	2.00	5.00
27	Shelton Benjamin	.30	.75
28	Snitsky	.50	1.25
29	Stone Cold	2.00	5.00
30	Super Crazy	.50	1.25
31	Todd Grisham RC	.30	.75
32	Trevor Murdoch	.30	.75
33	Triple H	2.00	5.00
34	Umaga	.50	1.25
35	Val Venis	.75	2.00
36	William Regal	.75	2.00
37	Batista	1.25	3.00
38	Brett Major RC	.50	1.25
39	Brian Major RC	.30	.75
40	Chavo Guerrero	.50	1.25
41	Chris Masters	1.25	3.00
42	Dave Taylor RC	.30	.75
43	Deuce RC	.30	.75
44	Domino RC	.30	.75
45	Edge	1.25	3.00
46	Eugene	.30	.75
47	Finlay	.75	2.00
48	Funaki	.50	1.25
49	Gregory Helms	.30	.75
50	Hardcore Holly	.75	2.00
51	Hornswoggle RC	.40	1.00
52	Jamie Noble	.30	.75
53	JBL	.75	2.00
54	Jimmy Wang Yang	.30	.75
55	Kane	1.25	3.00
56	Kenny Dykstra RC	.50	1.25
57	Mark Henry	.50	1.25
58	Matt Hardy	.75	2.00
59	Michael Cole	.30	.75
60	MVP RC	.50	1.25
61	Rey Mysterio	.75	2.00
62	Ric Flair	1.25	3.00
63	Shannon Moore	.30	.75
64	The Great Khali	.50	1.25
65	Theodore Long	.40	1.00
66	Undertaker	1.50	4.00
67	Ashley	1.25	3.00
68	Candice	1.50	4.00
69	Cherry RC	.30	.75
70	Jillian	1.50	4.00
71	Kelly Kelly RC	.75	2.00
72	Maria	1.25	3.00
73	Melina	1.25	3.00
74	Michelle McCool	1.50	4.00
75	Mickie James	1.50	4.00
76	Queen Sharmell	.75	2.00
77	Torrie Wilson	2.50	6.00
78	Victoria	1.50	4.00
79	Balls Mahoney RC	.30	.75
80	Boogeyman	.50	1.25
81	CM Punk	.50	1.25
82	Elijah Burke RC	.30	.75
83	Joey Styles	.30	.75
84	John Morrison	.50	1.25
85	Kevin Thorn RC	.30	.75
86	Nunzio	.50	1.25
87	Marcus Cor Von RC	.30	.75
88	Matt Striker	.30	.75
89	Mike Knox RC	.30	.75
90	Stevie Richards	.50	1.25
91	Tazz	.50	1.25
92	The Miz RC	.60	1.50
93	Tommy Dreamer	.40	1.00
94	Big Daddy V	.30	.75
95	Kendrick / London	.75	2.00
96	Hass / Benjamin	.30	.75
97	Carlito / Masters	1.25	3.00
98	Cryme Tyme	.30	.75
99	Taylor / Regal	.75	2.00
100	Deuce / Domino	.30	.75
101	D-Generation X	1.00	2.50
102	Burke / Cor Von	.30	.75
103	Undertaker / Kane	1.50	4.00
104	Finlay / Hornswoggle	.75	2.00
105	Michaels / Cena	2.00	5.00
106	Cade / Murdoch	.30	.75
107	Kane / Boogeyman	1.25	3.00
108	Flair / Piper	1.25	3.00
109	Hardy Boys	.75	2.00
110	Highlanders	.50	1.25
111	Major Brothers	.50	1.25
112	Dusty / Cody Rhodes	.75	2.00
113	Candice / Victoria	1.50	4.00
114	Vince / Shane McMahon	1.25	3.00
115	Junkyard Dog	.60	1.50
116	British Bulldog	1.25	3.00
117	Bushwhacker Butch	.50	1.25
118	Bushwhacker Luke	.50	1.25
119	Curt Hennig	.50	1.25
120	Doink the Clown	.30	.75
121	Dusty Rhodes	.75	2.00
122	Jake Roberts	.75	2.00
123	Jimmy Snuka	.50	1.25
124	Ted Dibiase	.60	1.50
125	Nikolai Volkoff	.60	1.50
126	Paul Bearer	.50	1.25
127	Sgt. Slaughter	.75	2.00
128	Billy Graham	.50	1.25
129	Terry Funk	.30	.75
130	Bobby Heenan	.60	1.50
131	Checklist 1 CL		
132	Checklist 2 CL		.75

2007 Topps WWE Face-Off Royal Rumble Champions

COMPLETE SET (10) 12.00 30.00
RANDOMLY INSERTED INTO PACKS

R1	Batista	2.00	5.00
R2	Triple H	3.00	8.00
R3	The Rock	4.00	10.00
R4	Jim Duggan	.75	2.00
R5	Rey Mysterio	1.25	3.00
R6	Ric Flair	2.00	5.00
R7	Shawn Michaels	3.00	8.00
R8	Stone Cold Steve Austin	3.00	8.00
R9	Undertaker	2.50	6.00
R10	Mr. McMahon	2.00	5.00

2007 Topps WWE Face-Off Superstar Foil

COMPLETE SET (22) 12.00 30.00
RANDOMLY INSERTED INTO PACKS

S1	Bobby Lashley	1.50	4.00
S2	Boogeyman	.60	1.50
S3	Carlito	1.50	4.00
S4	Chavo Guerrero	.60	1.50
S5	Chris Masters	1.50	4.00
S6	CM Punk	.60	1.50
S7	Edge	1.50	4.00
S8	Fit Finlay	1.00	2.50
S9	Jeff Hardy	1.00	2.50
S10	John Cena	2.50	6.00
S11	John Morrison	.60	1.50
S12	Kane	1.50	4.00
S13	King Booker	1.50	4.00
S14	Mark Henry	.60	1.50
S15	Matt Hardy	1.00	2.50
S16	Mr. Kennedy	1.00	2.50
S17	MVP	.60	1.50
S18	Randy Orton	1.50	4.00
S19	Shelton Benjamin	.40	1.00
S20	The Great Khali	.60	1.50
S21	Tommy Dreamer	.50	1.25
S22	Umaga	.60	1.50

2020 Topps WWE Fully Loaded Autographed Gear Relics

*GREEN/50: .5X TO 1.2X BASIC AUTOS
*PURPLE/25: UNPRICED DUE TO SCARCITY
*BLUE/10: UNPRICED DUE TO SCARCITY
*RED/5: UNPRICED DUE TO SCARCITY
*GOLD/1: UNPRICED DUE TO SCARCITY
STATED ODDS 1:23
STATED PRINT RUN 199 SER.#'d SETS

SGAJ	AJ Styles	20.00	50.00
SGBL	Becky Lynch	75.00	150.00
SGFB	Finn Balor	20.00	50.00
SGSN	Shinsuke Nakamura	20.00	50.00

2020 Topps WWE Fully Loaded Autographed Chair Relics

*GREEN/50: .5X TO 1.2X BASIC AUTOS
*PURPLE/25: UNPRICED DUE TO SCARCITY
*BLUE/10: UNPRICED DUE TO SCARCITY
*RED/5: UNPRICED DUE TO SCARCITY
*GOLD/1: UNPRICED DUE TO SCARCITY
STATED ODDS 1:20
STATED PRINT RUN 99 SER.#'d SETS

CAS Asuka	50.00	100.00
CCL Candice LeRae	30.00	75.00
CDK Dakota Kai	30.00	75.00
CKC King Corbin	12.00	30.00
CRR Rhea Ripley	60.00	120.00
CSB Shayna Baszler	15.00	40.00
CTN Tegan Nox	30.00	75.00

2020 Topps WWE Fully Loaded Autographed Kiss

*PURPLE/25: .5X TO 1.2X BASIC AUTOS
*BLUE/10: UNPRICED DUE TO SCARCITY
*RED/5: UNPRICED DUE TO SCARCITY
*GOLD/1: UNPRICED DUE TO SCARCITY
STATED ODDS 1:118
STATED PRINT RUN 50 SER.#'d SETS

KBK Billie Kay		
KBL Becky Lynch		
KCC Charly Caruso		
KCF Charlotte Flair		
KCM Carmella		
KEM Ember Moon		
KLM Liv Morgan		
KMJ Mickie James	75.00	150.00
KMM Maryse		
KMR Mandy Rose		
KNC Nikki Cross	125.00	250.00
KNJ Nia Jax		
KNT Natalya	50.00	100.00
KPR Peyton Royce		
KRR Ruby Riott		
KRY Renee Young		
KSD Sonya Deville		
KVB Vanessa Borne		

2020 Topps WWE Fully Loaded Autographed Ladder Relics

*GREEN/50: .5X TO 1.2X BASIC AUTOS
*PURPLE/25: UNPRICED DUE TO SCARCITY
*BLUE/10: UNPRICED DUE TO SCARCITY
*RED/5: UNPRICED DUE TO SCARCITY
*GOLD/1: UNPRICED DUE TO SCARCITY
STATED ODDS 1:15
STATED PRINT RUN 99 SER.#'d SETS

LAJ AJ Styles	25.00	60.00
LAS Asuka	30.00	75.00
LBE Big E	15.00	40.00
LCS Cesaro	15.00	40.00
LKC King Corbin	12.00	30.00
LKK Kofi Kingston	15.00	40.00
LKO Kevin Owens	25.00	60.00
LLE Lacey Evans	30.00	75.00
LNJ Nia Jax	20.00	50.00
LOT Otis	12.00	30.00
LSZ Sami Zayn	12.00	30.00

2020 Topps WWE Fully Loaded Autographed Microphone Box Relics

*GOLD/1: UNPRICED DUE TO SCARCITY
STATED PRINT RUN 5 SER.#'d SETS
UNPRICED DUE TO SCARCITY

MCBE Big E
MCRT R-Truth
MCTM The Miz

2020 Topps WWE Fully Loaded Autographed Oversized Mat Relics

*GREEN/50: .5X TO 1.2X BASIC AUTOS
*PURPLE/25: UNPRICED DUE TO SCARCITY
*BLUE/10: UNPRICED DUE TO SCARCITY
*RED/5: UNPRICED DUE TO SCARCITY
*GOLD/1: UNPRICED DUE TO SCARCITY
STATED ODDS 1:6
STATED PRINT RUN 199 SER.#'d SETS

MAB Alexa Bliss	75.00	150.00
MAJ AJ Styles	20.00	50.00
MBA Bayley	30.00	75.00
MBL The Fiend Bray Wyatt	60.00	120.00
MBS Braun Strowman	15.00	40.00
MCF Becky Lynch	60.00	120.00
MCM Carmella	30.00	75.00
MJG Johnny Gargano	12.00	30.00
MKK Kofi Kingston	12.00	30.00
MSB Sasha Banks	75.00	150.00
MSH Sheamus	15.00	40.00
MSN Shinsuke Nakamura	15.00	40.00
MSR Seth Rollins	20.00	50.00
MTM The Miz	15.00	40.00

2020 Topps WWE Fully Loaded Autographed Table Relics

*GREEN/50: .5X TO 1.2X BASIC AUTOS
*PURPLE/25: UNPRICED DUE TO SCARCITY
*BLUE/10: UNPRICED DUE TO SCARCITY
*RED/5: UNPRICED DUE TO SCARCITY
*GOLD/1: UNPRICED DUE TO SCARCITY
STATED ODDS 1:11
STATED PRINT RUN 99 SER.#"d SETS

TAB Aleister Black	20.00	50.00
TAC Adam Cole	20.00	50.00
TAJ AJ Styles	20.00	50.00
TAS Asuka	50.00	100.00
TBF Bobby Fish	15.00	40.00
TBS Braun Strowman	15.00	40.00
TCM Carmella	30.00	75.00
TCS Cesaro	15.00	40.00
TDD Dominik Dijakovic	12.00	30.00
TKL Keith Lee	15.00	40.00
TKO Kevin Owens	15.00	40.00
TKR Kyle O'Reilly	12.00	30.00
TLA Bobby Lashley	12.00	30.00
TRS Roderick Strong	15.00	40.00
TSN Shinsuke Nakamura	15.00	40.00
TTC Tommaso Ciampa	15.00	40.00

2020 Topps WWE Fully Loaded Autographed Turnbuckle Relics

*GREEN/50: .5X TO 1.2X BASIC AUTOS
*PURPLE/25: UNPRICED DUE TO SCARCITY
*BLUE/10: UNPRICED DUE TO SCARCITY
*RED/5: UNPRICED DUE TO SCARCITY
*GOLD/1: UNPRICED DUE TO SCARCITY
STATED ODDS 1:11
STATED PRINT RUN 99 SER.#'d SETS

AAC Apollo Crews	12.00	30.00
AAG Angel Garza	12.00	30.00
AAN Andrade	15.00	40.00
AAT Austin Theory	100.00	250.00
ADM Drew McIntyre	20.00	50.00
ADZ Dolph Ziggler	12.00	30.00
AJH Jeff Hardy	25.00	60.00
ALE Lacey Evans	25.00	60.00
AMA Mustafa Ali	12.00	30.00
AMR Mandy Rose	75.00	150.00
AOT Otis	15.00	40.00
ARC Ricochet	12.00	30.00
ART R-Truth	15.00	40.00
ASB Shayna Baszler		
ASJ Samoa Joe	15.00	40.00
ATM The Miz	12.00	30.00

2020 Topps WWE Fully Loaded Autographs

STATED ODDS 1:430

AVM Mr. McMahon	300.00	600.00

2021 Topps WWE Fully Loaded Future Stars Autographs

*GOLD/99: .5X TO 1.2X BASIC AUTOS
*CITRINE/75: .6X TO 1.5X BASIC AUTOS
*ONYX/50: .75X TO 2X BASIC AUTOS
*SAPPHIRE/25: UNPRICED DUE TO SCARCITY
*RUBY/1: UNPRICED DUE TO SCARCITY
*P.P.BLACK/1: UNPRICED DUE TO SCARCITY
*P.P.CYAN/1: UNPRICED DUE TO SCARCITY
*P.P.MAGENTA/1: UNPRICED DUE TO SCARCITY
*P.P.YELLOW/1: UNPRICED DUE TO SCARCITY
STATED ODDS 1:12

SS Sarray	25.00	60.00
SW WALTER	15.00	40.00
SAT Austin Theory	12.00	30.00
SDM Dominik Mysterio		
SIH Indi Hartwell	20.00	50.00
SKK Karrion Kross		
SLK LA Knight	15.00	40.00
SNC Nash Carter	8.00	20.00
SSB Shotzi Blackheart	30.00	75.00
SSC Scarlett	50.00	100.00
STB Tyler Bate	8.00	20.00
STS Toni Storm		
STV Franky Monet	20.00	50.00
SWL Wes Lee	8.00	20.00
SZS Zoey Stark	15.00	40.00

2021 Topps WWE Fully Loaded Autographed Ladder Relics

*CITRINE/75: X TO X BASIC AUTOS
*ONYX/50: X TO X BASIC AUTOS
*SAPPHIRE/25: UNPRICED DUE TO SCARCITY
*RUBY/1: UNPRICED DUE TO SCARCITY
*DIE-CUT/1: UNPRICED DUE TO SCARCITY
STATED ODDS 1:26
STATED PRINT RUN 99 SER.#'d SETS

LCG Cameron Grimes	15.00	40.00
LCL Candice LeRae	25.00	60.00
LDP Damian Priest	12.00	30.00
LIS Io Shirai	50.00	100.00
LJG Johnny Gargano		
LJU Jimmy Uso	12.00	30.00
LSZ Sami Zayn	15.00	40.00

2021 Topps WWE Fully Loaded Autographed Metal Chair Relics

*CITRINE/75: X TO X BASIC AUTOS
*ONYX/50: X TO X BASIC AUTOS
*SAPPHIRE/25: UNPRICED DUE TO SCARCITY
*RUBY/1: UNPRICED DUE TO SCARCITY
*DIE-CUT/1: UNPRICED DUE TO SCARCITY
STATED ODDS 1:23
STATED PRINT RUN 99 SER.#'d SETS

CO Omos	25.00	60.00
CBB Bianca Belair	30.00	75.00
CDR Drew McIntyre	20.00	50.00
CIS Io Shirai	30.00	75.00
CJM John Morrison	12.00	30.00
CKO Kevin Owens	15.00	40.00
CRG Raquel Gonzalez	30.00	75.00
CSB Sasha Banks	60.00	120.00
CROM Roman Reigns	75.00	150.00

2021 Topps WWE Fully Loaded Autographed Oversized Mat Relics

*GOLD/99: X TO X BASIC AUTOS
*CITRINE/75: X TO X BASIC AUTOS
*ONYX/50: X TO X BASIC AUTOS
*SAPPHIRE/25: UNPRICED DUE TO SCARCITY
*RUBY/1: UNPRICED DUE TO SCARCITY
STATED ODDS 1:26

MA Asuka	30.00	75.00
ME Edge	25.00	60.00
MBC Baron Corbin	12.00	30.00
MCF Charlotte Flair	50.00	100.00
MFB The Demon King Finn Balor	25.00	60.00

2021 Topps WWE Fully Loaded Autographed Trash Can Relics

*GOLD/99: X TO X BASIC AUTOS
*CITRINE/75: X TO X BASIC AUTOS
*ONYX/50: X TO X BASIC AUTOS
*SAPPHIRE/25: UNPRICED DUE TO SCARCITY
*RUBY/1: UNPRICED DUE TO SCARCITY
STATED ODDS 1:34

TIS Io Shirai	50.00	100.00
TRM Raul Mendoza	10.00	25.00
TSE Santos Escobar	10.00	25.00

2021 Topps WWE Fully Loaded Autographed Superstar Gear Relics

*CITRINE/75: X TO X BASIC AUTOS
*ONYX/50: X TO X BASIC AUTOS
*SAPPHIRE/25: UNPRICED DUE TO SCARCITY
*RUBY/1: UNPRICED DUE TO SCARCITY
*DIE-CUT/1: UNPRICED DUE TO SCARCITY
STATED ODDS 1:34
STATED PRINT RUN 99 SER.#"d SETS

GC Carmella	30.00	75.00
GR Ricochet	12.00	30.00
GBE Big E	15.00	40.00
GSB Shayna Baszler	12.00	30.00
GXW Xavier Woods	12.00	30.00
GKOR Kyle O'Reilly	12.00	30.00

2021 Topps WWE Fully Loaded Autographed Table Relics

*CITRINE/75: X TO X BASIC AUTOS
*ONYX/50: X TO X BASIC AUTOS
*SAPPHIRE/25: UNPRICED DUE TO SCARCITY
*RUBY/1: UNPRICED DUE TO SCARCITY
*DIE-CUT/1: UNPRICED DUE TO SCARCITY
STATED ODDS 1:19
STATED PRINT RUN 99 SER.#'d SETS

TE Elias	10.00	25.00
TAS AJ Styles	15.00	40.00
TJH Jeff Hardy	20.00	50.00
TJU Jey Uso	10.00	25.00
TKK Kofi Kingston	15.00	40.00
TPD Pete Dunne	10.00	25.00
TRM Rey Mysterio	20.00	50.00
TRR Rhea Ripley	30.00	75.00
TSR Seth Rollins	15.00	40.00
TTM The Miz	15.00	40.00

2021 Topps WWE Fully Loaded Autographed Turnbuckle Pad Relics

*GOLD/99: X TO X BASIC AUTOS
*CITRINE/75: X TO X BASIC AUTOS
*ONYX/50: X TO X BASIC AUTOS
*SAPPHIRE/25: X TO X BASIC AUTOS
*RUBY/1: UNPRICED DUE TO SCARCITY
STATED ODDS 1:23

PN Natalya	15.00	40.00
PAD Angelo Dawkins	10.00	25.00
PKL Keith Lee	12.00	30.00
PMF Montez Ford	10.00	25.00
PSR Seth Rollins		

2021 Topps WWE Fully Loaded Legends Autographs

STATED ODDS 1:23

LG Goldberg		
LK Kane		
LU Undertaker		
LBH Bret "Hit Man" Hart		
LDL Dude Love	50.00	100.00
LPS Papa Shango	20.00	50.00
LSA Stone Cold Steve Austin		
LSK Stacy Keibler	50.00	100.00
LSM Shawn Michaels		
LTS Trish Stratus	30.00	75.00
L123 1-2-3 Kid		
LDDP Diamond Dallas Page	25.00	60.00
LHHH Triple H		
LJBL John "Bradshaw" Layfield	10.00	25.00

2019 Topps WWE Garbage Pail Kids

COMPLETE SET (13) 25.00 60.00
STATED PRINT RUN 1028 SETS PRODUCED

1 Gigantic Andre	2.50	6.00
2 Breakin' Becky	8.00	20.00
3 C-Thru Cena	4.00	10.00
4 Savage Randy	2.50	6.00
5 Mixed-Up Mick	3.00	8.00
6 Mouthy Miz & Maryse	2.50	6.00
7 Slick Ric	4.00	10.00
8 Rowdy Ronda	6.00	15.00
9 Brawlin' Rollins	3.00	8.00
10 Seething Steve	3.00	8.00
11 Chipped Rock	4.00	10.00
12 Unravelled Warrior	3.00	8.00
13 Undead Taker	5.00	10.00

2018 Topps WWE Hall of Fame Tribute

1 Andre the Giant	.60	1.50
2 Andre the Giant	.60	1.50
3 Andre the Giant	.60	1.50
4 Andre the Giant	.60	1.50
5 Andre the Giant	.60	1.50
6 Andre the Giant	.60	1.50
7 Andre the Giant	.60	1.50
8 Andre the Giant	.60	1.50
9 Andre the Giant	.60	1.50
10 Andre the Giant	.60	1.50
11 Ultimate Warrior	.60	1.50
12 Ultimate Warrior	.60	1.50
13 Ultimate Warrior	.60	1.50
14 Ultimate Warrior	.60	1.50
15 Ultimate Warrior	.60	1.50
16 Ultimate Warrior	.60	1.50
17 Ultimate Warrior	.60	1.50
18 Ultimate Warrior	.60	1.50
19 Ultimate Warrior	.60	1.50
20 Ultimate Warrior	.60	1.50
21 Ric Flair	.60	1.50
22 Ric Flair	.60	1.50
23 Ric Flair	.60	1.50
24 Ric Flair	.60	1.50
25 Ric Flair	.60	1.50
26 Ric Flair	.60	1.50
27 Ric Flair	.60	1.50
28 Ric Flair	.60	1.50
29 Ric Flair	.60	1.50
30 Ric Flair	.60	1.50
31 Rowdy Roddy Piper	.60	1.50
32 Rowdy Roddy Piper	.60	1.50
33 Rowdy Roddy Piper	.60	1.50
34 Rowdy Roddy Piper	.60	1.50
35 Rowdy Roddy Piper	.60	1.50
36 Rowdy Roddy Piper	.60	1.50
37 Rowdy Roddy Piper	.60	1.50
38 Rowdy Roddy Piper	.60	1.50
39 Rowdy Roddy Piper	.60	1.50
40 Rowdy Roddy Piper	.60	1.50

2015 Topps WWE Hulk Hogan Tribute

COMPLETE SET (30) 12.00 30.00
*GOLD/10: 4X TO 10X BASIC CARDS
*RED/1: UNPRICED DUE TO SCARCITY

1 Hulk Hogan	.75	2.00
2 Hulk Hogan	.75	2.00
3 Hulk Hogan	.75	2.00
4 Hulk Hogan	.75	2.00
5 Hulk Hogan	.75	2.00
6 Hulk Hogan	.75	2.00
7 Hulk Hogan	.75	2.00
8 Hulk Hogan	.75	2.00
9 Hulk Hogan	.75	2.00
10 Hulk Hogan	.75	2.00
11 Hulk Hogan	.75	2.00
12 Hulk Hogan	.75	2.00
13 Hulk Hogan	.75	2.00
14 Hulk Hogan	.75	2.00
15 Hulk Hogan	.75	2.00
16 Hulk Hogan	.75	2.00
17 Hulk Hogan	.75	2.00
18 Hulk Hogan	.75	2.00
19 Hulk Hogan	.75	2.00
20 Hulk Hogan	.75	2.00
21 Hulk Hogan	.75	2.00
22 Hulk Hogan	.75	2.00
23 Hulk Hogan	.75	2.00
24 Hulk Hogan	.75	2.00
25 Hulk Hogan	.75	2.00
26 Hulk Hogan	.75	2.00
27 Hulk Hogan	.75	2.00
28 Hulk Hogan	.75	2.00
29 Hulk Hogan	.75	2.00
30 Hulk Hogan	.75	2.00

2007 Topps WWE Payback

1 Shawn Michaels
2 Triple H
3 Edge
4 John Cena
5 Randy Orton
6 Val Venis
7 Kane
8 Eugene
9 Jerry Lawler
10 Lita
11 Viscera
12 Rob Conway
13 Chris Masters
14 Shelton Benjamin
15 Mickie James
16 Ric flair
17 Victoria
18 Umaga
19 Carlito
20 Johnny Nitro
21 Candice
22 torrie Wilson
23 Mick Foley
24 Hulk Hogan
25 Kenny
26 Jeff Hardy
27 Stone Cold Steve Austin
28 Charlie Haas
29 Mikey
30 Melina
31 Rory McAllister RC
32 Robbie McAllister RC
33 Rey Mysterio
34 Undertaker
35 JBL
36 Jillian Hall
37 Brian Kendrick
38 Chris Benoit
39 King Booker
40 Batista
41 Paul London
42 Chavo Guerrero Jr.
43 Gregory Helms
44 Matt Hardy
45 Tatanka
46 Paul Burchill
47 Bobby Lashley
48 Snitsky
49 Finlay
50 The Miz
51 Ashley
52 Joey Mercury
53 Psicosis
54 Super Crazy
55 The Great Khali
56 Kid Kash
57 Ken Kennedy
58 Funaki
59 Scotty 2 Hotty
60 William Regal
61 Vito
62 Michelle McCool
63 Mark Henry
64 Jamie Noble
65 Al Snow
66 Test
67 Little Guido Maritato
68 Jazz
69 Justin Credible
70 Roadkill
71 Sandman
72 Big Show
73 Tommy Dreamer
74 Tony Mamaluke
75 CM Punk
76 Hardcore Holly
77 Francine
78 Tazz
79 Rob Van Dam
80 Sabu
81 Balls Mahoney RC
82 C.W. Anderson
83 Danny Doring
84 Matt Striker
85 Mike Knox RC
86 Stevie Richards
87 Kevin Thorn RC
88 Terry Funk
89 British Bulldog
90 Sgt. Slaughter
91 Rowdy Roddy Piper
92 Million Dollar Man Ted DiBiase
93 Dusty Rhodes
94 Junkyard Dog
95 Doink The Clown
96 Jake "The Snake" Roberts

2006 Topps WWE Insider

COMPLETE SET (72) 8.00 20.00
UNOPENED BOX (24 PACKS)
UNOPENED PACK (7 CARDS)

1 Lashley RC	.30	.75
2 Big Show	.50	1.25
3 Carlito	.50	1.25
4 Chris Masters	.20	.50
5 Edge	.50	1.25
6 Gene Snitsky	.20	.50
7 Hulk Hogan	.75	2.00
8 Jerry The King Lawler	.40	1.00
9 John Cena	.75	2.00
10 Jonathan Coachman	.12	.30
11 Kane	.50	1.25
12 Chavo Guerrero	.20	.50
13 Kurt Angle	.50	1.25
14 Lance Cade	.12	.30
15 Lilian Garcia	.60	1.50
16 Lita	.75	2.00
17 Maria	.50	1.25
18 Matt Hardy	.30	.75

19 Rene Dupree	.20	.50
20 Ric Flair	.60	1.50
21 Rob Conway	.20	.50
22 Rob Van Dam	.30	.75
23 Paul Burchill RC	.12	.30
24 Kid Kash	.12	.30
25 Shawn Michaels	.75	2.00
26 Shelton Benjamin	.12	.30
27 Mickie James RC	.75	2.00
28 Stone Cold	.75	2.00
29 Gregory Helms	.12	.30
30 Trevor Murdoch RC	.12	.30
31 Triple H	.75	2.00
32 Trish Stratus	1.25	3.00
33 Mark Henry	.20	.50
34 Val Venis	.20	.50
35 Victoria	.75	2.00
36 Viscera	.20	.50
37 Batista	.50	1.25
38 Booker T	.30	.75
39 Candice Michelle	.75	2.00
40 Chris Benoit	.50	1.25
41 Boogeyman RC	.20	.50
42 Funaki	.20	.50
43 Hardcore Holly	.20	.50
44 Joey Styles RC	.12	.30
45 JBL	.30	.75
46 Joey Mercury	.12	.30
47 Johnny Nitro	.20	.50
48 Ashley RC	.50	1.25
49 Finlay	.30	.75
50 Ken Kennedy RC	.30	.75
51 Melina	.50	1.25
52 Michael Cole RC	.12	.30
53 Nunzio	.12	.30
54 Orlando Jordan	.12	.30
55 Paul London	.12	.30
56 Psicosis	.12	.30
57 Randy Orton	.30	.75
58 Rey Mysterio	.50	1.25
59 Road Warrior Animal	.25	.60
60 Kristal RC	.30	.75
61 Sharmell	.50	1.25
62 Simon Dean RC	.12	.30
63 Steven Richards	.20	.50
64 Super Crazy	.20	.50
65 Goldust	.20	.50
66 Tazz	.20	.50
67 Theodore Long	.12	.30
68 Torrie Wilson	1.25	3.00
69 Undertaker	.60	1.50
70 Vito RC	.12	.30
71 William Regal	.30	.75
72 Checklist	.10	.25

2006 Topps WWE Insider Autographs

STATED ODDS 1:24 HOBBY EXCLUSIVE

NNO Ashley	6.00	15.00
NNO Candice Michelle	12.00	30.00
NNO Carlito	30.00	80.00
NNO Chris Masters	6.00	15.00
NNO Edge	15.00	40.00
NNO Eugene	12.00	30.00
NNO Goldust	8.00	20.00
NNO Gregory Helms	8.00	20.00
NNO John Cena	75.00	150.00
NNO Kristal	8.00	20.00
NNO Lita	12.00	30.00
NNO Maria	20.00	50.00
NNO Matt Hardy	12.00	30.00
NNO Melina	8.00	20.00
NNO Mickie James	20.00	50.00
NNO Randy Orton	25.00	60.00
NNO Road Warrior (Animal)	15.00	50.00
NNO Shelton Benjamin	12.00	30.00
NNO Torrie Wilson	30.00	75.00
NNO Trish Stratus	50.00	100.00
NNO Victoria	12.00	30.00
NNO Viscera	15.00	40.00

2006 Topps WWE Insider Champions

COMPLETE SET (12) 5.00 12.00
STATED ODDS 1:6 RETAIL EXCLUSIVE

C1 John Cena	.75	2.00
C2 Ric Flair	.60	1.50
C3 Trish Stratus	1.25	3.00
C4 Rey Mysterio	.50	1.25
C5 Eddie Guerrero	.50	1.25
C6 Booker T	.30	.75
C7 Chris Benoit	.50	1.25
C8 Kurt Angle	.50	1.25
C9 Undertaker	.60	1.50
C10 Triple H	.75	2.00
C11 Stone Cold	.75	2.00
C12 Hulk Hogan	.75	2.00

2006 Topps WWE Insider Coins

COMPLETE SET (24) 12.00 30.00
STATED ODDS 1:1 RETAIL EXCLUSIVE

1 John Cena	1.50	4.00
2 Edge	1.00	2.50
3 Carlito	1.00	2.50
4 Kurt Angle	1.00	2.50
5 Randy Orton	.60	1.50
6 Shawn Michaels	1.50	4.00
7 Undertaker	1.25	3.00
8 Batista	1.00	2.50
9 Ric Flair	1.25	3.00
10 Chris Masters	.40	1.00
11 Triple H	1.50	4.00
12 Kane	1.00	2.50
13 Boogeyman	.40	1.00
14 Steve Austin	1.50	4.00
15 Trish Stratus	2.50	6.00
16 Rob Van Dam	.60	1.50
17 Chris Benoit	1.00	2.50
18 Hulk Hogan	1.50	4.00
19 JBL	.60	1.50
20 Rey Mysterio	1.00	2.50
21 Big Show	1.00	2.50
22 Booker T	.60	1.50
23 Torrie Wilson	2.50	6.00
24 Candice Michelle	1.50	4.00

2006 Topps WWE Insider Divas

COMPLETE SET (12) 10.00 25.00
STATED ODDS 1:3 RETAIL EXCLUSIVE

D1 Candice Michelle	.60	1.50
D2 Ashley	4.00	10.00
D3 Mickie James	.60	1.50
D4 Sharmell	.40	1.00
D5 Torrie Wilson	6.00	15.00
D6 Trish Stratus	5.00	12.00
D7 Jillian Hall	.40	1.00
D8 Lilian Garcia	.50	1.25
D9 Lita	.60	1.50
D10 Maria	.40	1.00
D11 Kristal	.25	.60
D12 Victoria	.60	1.50

2006 Topps WWE Insider Memorabilia

STATED ODDS 1:24 HOBBY EXCLUSIVE

NNO John Cena	6.00	15.00
NNO Kurt Angle	3.00	8.00
NNO Matt Hardy	2.00	5.00
NNO Rey Mysterio	2.00	5.00
NNO Shawn Michaels	8.00	20.00

2006 Topps WWE Insider Promos

COMPLETE SET (2)

P1 Undertaker
P2 Batista

2019 Topps WWE Intercontinental Championship 40th Anniversary

COMPLETE SET (40) 15.00 40.00
RANDOMLY INSERTED INTO PACKS

IC1 Don Muraco	.50	1.25
IC2 Macho Man Randy Savage	1.25	3.00
IC3 Ricky The Dragon Steamboat	.60	1.50
IC4 The Honky Tonk Man	.50	1.25
IC5 Ultimate Warrior	1.25	3.00
IC6 Ravishing Rick Rude	.60	1.50
IC7 Mr. Perfect	.75	2.00
IC8 Texas Tornado	.75	2.00
IC9 Bret Hit Man Hart	1.25	3.00
IC10 Rowdy Roddy Piper	1.25	3.00
IC11 Shawn Michaels	1.25	3.00
IC12 Razor Ramon	.75	2.00
IC13 Diesel	.75	2.00
IC14 Triple H	1.25	3.00
IC15 The Rock	2.50	6.00
IC16 Stone Cold Steve Austin	2.50	6.00
IC17 Ken Shamrock	.75	2.00
IC18 Road Dogg	.50	1.25
IC19 The Godfather	.50	1.25
IC20 Edge	1.25	3.00
IC21 D'Lo Brown	.50	1.25
IC22 Kurt Angle	1.00	2.50
IC23 Eddie Guerrero	1.25	3.00
IC24 Billy Gunn	.60	1.50
IC25 Jeff Hardy	1.25	3.00
IC26 Kane	.75	2.00
IC27 Albert	.50	1.25
IC28 William Regal	.75	2.00
IC29 Booker T	1.25	3.00
IC30 Randy Orton	1.25	3.00
IC31 Shelton Benjamin	.60	1.50
IC32 Ric Flair	1.50	4.00
IC33 Umaga	.50	1.25
IC34 Kofi Kingston	.75	2.00
IC35 Rey Mysterio	1.25	3.00
IC36 Drew McIntyre	.60	1.50
IC37 Dolph Ziggler	1.00	2.50
IC38 Big Show	.75	2.00
IC39 The Miz	1.00	2.50
IC40 Curtis Axel	.60	1.50

2017 Topps WWE John Cena Tribute

COMPLETE SET (40) 6.00 15.00
STATED ODDS 1:6

1 John Cena	1.00	2.50
2 John Cena	1.00	2.50
3 John Cena	1.00	2.50
4 John Cena	1.00	2.50
5 John Cena	1.00	2.50
6 John Cena	1.00	2.50
7 John Cena	1.00	2.50
8 John Cena	1.00	2.50
9 John Cena	1.00	2.50
10 John Cena	1.00	2.50
11 John Cena	1.00	2.50
12 John Cena	1.00	2.50
13 John Cena	1.00	2.50
14 John Cena	1.00	2.50
15 John Cena	1.00	2.50
16 John Cena	1.00	2.50
17 John Cena	1.00	2.50
18 John Cena	1.00	2.50
19 John Cena	1.00	2.50
20 John Cena	1.00	2.50
21 John Cena	1.00	2.50
22 John Cena	1.00	2.50
23 John Cena	1.00	2.50
24 John Cena	1.00	2.50
25 John Cena	1.00	2.50
26 John Cena	1.00	2.50
27 John Cena	1.00	2.50
28 John Cena	1.00	2.50
29 John Cena	1.00	2.50
30 John Cena	1.00	2.50
31 John Cena	1.00	2.50
32 John Cena	1.00	2.50
33 John Cena	1.00	2.50
34 John Cena	1.00	2.50
35 John Cena	1.00	2.50
36 John Cena	1.00	2.50
37 John Cena	1.00	2.50
38 John Cena	1.00	2.50
39 John Cena	1.00	2.50
40 John Cena	1.00	2.50

2018 Topps WWE Macho Man Randy Savage Tribute

1 Macho Man Randy Savage	1.25	3.00
2 Macho Man Randy Savage	1.25	3.00
3 Macho Man Randy Savage	1.25	3.00
4 Macho Man Randy Savage	1.25	3.00
5 Macho Man Randy Savage	1.25	3.00
6 Macho Man Randy Savage	1.25	3.00
7 Macho Man Randy Savage	1.25	3.00
8 Macho Man Randy Savage	1.25	3.00
9 Macho Man Randy Savage	1.25	3.00
10 Macho Man Randy Savage	1.25	3.00
11 Macho Man Randy Savage	1.25	3.00
12 Macho Man Randy Savage	1.25	3.00
13 Macho Man Randy Savage	1.25	3.00
14 Macho Man Randy Savage	1.25	3.00
15 Macho Man Randy Savage	1.25	3.00
16 Macho Man Randy Savage	1.25	3.00
17 Macho Man Randy Savage	1.25	3.00
18 Macho Man Randy Savage	1.25	3.00
19 Macho Man Randy Savage	1.25	3.00
20 Macho Man Randy Savage	1.25	3.00
21 Macho Man Randy Savage	1.25	3.00
22 Macho Man Randy Savage	1.25	3.00
23 Macho Man Randy Savage	1.25	3.00

24 Macho Man Randy Savage	1.25	3.00
25 Macho Man Randy Savage	1.25	3.00
26 Macho Man Randy Savage	1.25	3.00
27 Macho Man Randy Savage	1.25	3.00
28 Macho Man Randy Savage	1.25	3.00
29 Macho Man Randy Savage	1.25	3.00
30 Macho Man Randy Savage	1.25	3.00
31 Macho Man Randy Savage	1.25	3.00
32 Macho Man Randy Savage	1.25	3.00
33 Macho Man Randy Savage	1.25	3.00
34 Macho Man Randy Savage	1.25	3.00
35 Macho Man Randy Savage	1.25	3.00
36 Macho Man Randy Savage	1.25	3.00
37 Macho Man Randy Savage	1.25	3.00
38 Macho Man Randy Savage	1.25	3.00
39 Macho Man Randy Savage	1.25	3.00
40 Macho Man Randy Savage	1.25	3.00

2019 Topps WWE Money in the Bank

COMPLETE SET (90) 10.00 25.00
*BRONZE: .5X TO 1.2X BASIC CARDS
*GREEN/99: .75X TO 2X BASIC CARDS
*BLUE/50: 1.2X TO 3X BASIC CARDS
*PURPLE/25: 2X TO 5X BASIC CARDS
*GOLD/10: UNPRICED DUE TO SCARCITY
*BLACK/5: UNPRICED DUE TO SCARCITY
*RED/1: UNPRICED DUE TO SCARCITY

1 Aiden English	.25	.60
2 AJ Styles	1.25	3.00
3 Alexa Bliss	1.25	3.00
4 Alicia Fox	.50	1.25
5 Andrade	.30	.75
6 Ariya Daivari	.25	.60
7 Apollo Crews	.30	.75
8 Asuka	.75	2.00
9 Baron Corbin	.40	1.00
10 Bayley	.50	1.25
11 Becky Lynch	1.00	2.50
12 Beth Phoenix	.40	1.00
13 Big Show	.40	1.00
14 Big E	.25	.60
15 Bobby Lashley	.50	1.25
16 Robert Roode	.50	1.25
17 Booker T	.60	1.50
18 Braun Strowman	.60	1.50
19 Bray Wyatt	.60	1.50
20 Brock Lesnar	1.00	2.50
21 Carmella	.60	1.50
22 Cesaro	.30	.75
23 Charlotte Flair	1.00	2.50
24 Christian	.40	1.00
25 Curt Hawkins	.25	.60
26 Curtis Axel	.30	.75
27 Dana Brooke	.50	1.25
28 Daniel Bryan	1.00	2.50
29 Drew McIntyre	.30	.75
30 Elias	.50	1.25
31 Ember Moon	.60	1.50
32 Eve Torres	.30	.75
33 Fandango	.25	.60
34 Finlay	.25	.60
35 Finn Balor	.60	1.50
36 Gran Metalik	.25	.60
37 Heath Slater	.25	.60
38 Jeff Hardy	.60	1.50
39 Jey Uso	.30	.75
40 Jimmy Uso	.30	.75
41 Jinder Mahal	.50	1.25
42 John Cena	1.00	2.50
43 Kalisto	.25	.60
44 Kane	.40	1.00
45 Karl Anderson	.40	1.00
46 Kevin Owens	.60	1.50
47 Kofi Kingston	.40	1.00
48 Lacey Evans	.50	1.25
49 Lince Dorado	.25	.60
50 Luke Gallows	.40	1.00
51 Mark Henry	.30	.75
52 Maria Kanellis	.60	1.50
53 Mandy Rose	.60	1.50
54 Matt Hardy	.50	1.25
55 Mike Kanellis	.25	.60
56 Mojo Rawley	.30	.75
57 Ali	.25	.60
58 Naomi	.40	1.00
59 Natalya	.50	1.25
60 Nikki Cross	.40	1.00
61 Nia Jax	.50	1.25
62 Paige	1.00	2.50
63 Paul Heyman	.30	.75
64 Randy Orton	.60	1.50
65 Rey Mysterio	.60	1.50
66 Ric Flair	.75	2.00
67 Ricochet	.60	1.50
68 Roman Reigns	.60	1.50
69 Ronda Rousey	1.25	3.00
70 Rowan	.25	.60
71 R-Truth	.30	.75
72 Sami Zayn	.50	1.25
73 Samir Singh	.25	.60
74 Samoa Joe	.50	1.25
75 Sonya Deville	.50	1.25
76 Seth Rollins	.60	1.50
77 Sheamus	.40	1.00
78 Shelton Benjamin	.30	.75
79 Shinsuke Nakamura	.60	1.50
80 Sunil Singh	.25	.60
81 Tamina	.25	.60
82 Lord Tensai	.25	.60
83 The Miz	.50	1.25
84 Titus O'Neil	.30	.75
85 Tony Nese	.25	.60
86 Tyler Breeze	.30	.75
87 Xavier Woods	.30	.75
88 William Regal	.40	1.00
89 Zack Ryder	.30	.75
90 Zelina Vega	.40	1.00

2019 Topps WWE Money in the Bank Autographed Mat Relics

COMMON AUTO 5.00 12.00
*BLUE/50: .5X TO 1.2X BASIC AUTOS
*PURPLE/25: UNPRICED DUE TO SCARCITY
*GOLD/10: UNPRICED DUE TO SCARCITY
*BLACK/5: UNPRICED DUE TO SCARCITY
*RED/1: UNPRICED DUE TO SCARCITY
STATED ODDS 1:227
STATED PRINT RUN 99 SER.#'d SETS

MRACM Carmella	12.00	30.00
MRAFB Finn Balor	10.00	25.00
MRAKA Karl Anderson	8.00	20.00
MRAKK Kofi Kingston	6.00	15.00
MRAKO Kevin Owens	8.00	20.00
MRALG Luke Gallows	6.00	15.00
MRANT Natalya	6.00	15.00
MRART R-Truth	6.00	15.00
MRASA Samir Singh	5.00	12.00
MRASJ Samoa Joe	6.00	15.00
MRASM Sheamus	8.00	20.00
MRASN Shinsuke Nakamura	6.00	15.00
MRASR Seth Rollins	8.00	20.00
MRASU Sunil Singh	5.00	12.00
MRATO Titus O'Neil	5.00	12.00
MRATS Tamina	5.00	12.00
MRAXW Xavier Woods	5.00	12.00
MRAZR Zack Ryder	6.00	15.00

2019 Topps WWE Money in the Bank Autographed Shirt Relics

*BLUE/50: .5X TO 1.2X BASIC AUTOS
*PURPLE/25: .6X TO 1.5X BASIC AUTOS
*GOLD/10: UNPRICED DUE TO SCARCITY
*BLACK/5: UNPRICED DUE TO SCARCITY
*RED/1: UNPRICED DUE TO SCARCITY
STATED ODDS 1:453
STATED PRINT RUN 99 SER.#'d SETS

SRAAC Apollo Crews	5.00	12.00
SRAAJ AJ Styles	10.00	25.00
SRABS Braun Strowman	12.00	30.00
SRACS Cesaro	5.00	12.00
SRAHS Heath Slater	5.00	12.00
SRAKK Kofi Kingston	6.00	15.00
SRARI Ricochet	10.00	25.00
SRARR Roman Reigns		
SRASR Seth Rollins	12.00	30.00
SRASZ Sami Zayn		

2019 Topps WWE Money in the Bank Autographs

*GREEN/99: .5X TO 1.2X BASIC AUTOS
*BLUE/50: .6X TO 1.5X BASIC AUTOS
*PURPLE/25: UNPRICED DUE TO SCARCITY
*GOLD/10: UNPRICED DUE TO SCARCITY
*BLACK/5: UNPRICED DUE TO SCARCITY
*RED/1: UNPRICED DUE TO SCARCITY
STATED ODDS 1:41
STATED PRINT RUN 99 SER.#'d SETS

AAB Alexa Bliss	20.00	50.00
AAD Andrade	4.00	10.00
AAE Aiden English	4.00	10.00
AAJ AJ Styles	8.00	20.00
AAK Asuka	10.00	25.00
AAL Ali	4.00	10.00
ABC Baron Corbin	4.00	10.00
ABE Big E	4.00	10.00
ABJ Shelton Benjamin	4.00	10.00
ABK Dana Brooke	10.00	25.00
ABL Becky Lynch	12.00	30.00
ABM Matt Hardy	5.00	12.00
ABR Robert Roode	4.00	10.00
ABS Braun Strowman	5.00	12.00
ABW Bray Wyatt	6.00	15.00
ACF Charlotte Flair EXCH	12.00	30.00
ACM Carmella	6.00	15.00
ACS Cesaro	4.00	10.00
ADB Daniel Bryan	6.00	15.00
ADM Drew McIntyre	4.00	10.00
ADZ Dolph Ziggler	4.00	10.00
AEL Elias	5.00	12.00
AEM Ember Moon	6.00	15.00
AFB Finn Balor	5.00	12.00
AKK Kofi Kingston	4.00	10.00
AKL Kalisto	4.00	10.00
AKO Kevin Owens	5.00	12.00
AMA Maria Kanellis	8.00	20.00
AMG Karl Anderson	4.00	10.00
AMI Mike Kanellis	4.00	10.00
ANT Natalya	5.00	12.00
ARM Rey Mysterio	10.00	25.00
ARS Rusev	4.00	10.00
ARW Rowan	4.00	10.00
ASA Samir Singh	4.00	10.00
ASB Sasha Banks	10.00	25.00
ASJ Samoa Joe	4.00	10.00
ASM Sheamus	4.00	10.00
ASN Shinsuke Nakamura	5.00	12.00
ASR Seth Rollins	.60	15.00
ASU Sunil Singh	4.00	10.00
ASZ Sami Zayn	4.00	10.00
ATM The Miz	5.00	12.00
ATO Titus O'Neil	4.00	10.00
AXW Xavier Woods	4.00	10.00
AZR Zack Ryder	5.00	12.00
AZV Zelina Vega	8.00	20.00

2019 Topps WWE Money in the Bank Cash-In Moments

COMPLETE SET (13) 8.00 20.00
STATED ODDS 1:6

CM1 Kane	.60	1.50
CM2 The Miz	.75	2.00
CM3 Daniel Bryan	1.50	4.00
CM4 John Cena	1.50	4.00
CM5 Randy Orton	1.00	2.50
CM6 Seth Rollins	1.00	2.50
CM7 Sheamus	.60	1.50
CM8 Baron Corbin	.60	1.50
CM9 Braun Strowman	1.00	2.50
CM10 Carmella	1.00	2.50
CM11 Alexa Bliss	2.00	5.00
CM12 Bayley	.75	2.00
CM13 Brock Lesnar	1.50	4.00

2019 Topps WWE Money in the Bank Dual Autographs

*GOLD/10: UNPRICED DUE TO SCARCITY
*BLACK/5: UNPRICED DUE TO SCARCITY
*RED/1: UNPRICED DUE TO SCARCITY
STATED ODDS 1:3,663
STATED PRINT RUN 25 SER.#'d SETS

DANEW X.Woods/Big E	25.00	60.00
DABROS The Singhs	25.00	60.00
DAGOOD K.Anderson/L.Gallows	20.00	50.00
DAHRDY The Hardys	30.00	75.00

2019 Topps WWE Money in the Bank Greatest Matches and Moments

COMPLETE SET (22) 6.00 15.00
STATED ODDS 1:3

GMM1 Shelton Benjamin	.40	1.00
GMM2 Matt Hardy	.60	1.50
GMM3 Kofi Kingston	.50	1.25
GMM4 Kofi Kingston	.50	1.25
GMM5 Kofi Kingston	.50	1.25
GMM6 The Miz	.60	1.50
GMM7 Daniel Bryan	1.25	3.00
GMM8 Christian	.50	1.25
GMM9 Big Show	.50	1.25

GMM10	The Shield	.75	2.00
GMM11	John Cena	1.25	3.00
GMM12	Seth Rollins	.75	2.00
GMM13	John Cena	1.25	3.00
GMM14	Bray Wyatt	.75	2.00
GMM15	AJ Styles	1.50	4.00
GMM16	Seth Rollins	.75	2.00
GMM17	Mike & Maria Kanellis	.75	2.00
GMM18	Carmella	.75	2.00
GMM19	AJ Styles and Nakamura	1.50	4.00
GMM20	Carmella	.75	2.00
GMM21	Ember Moon	.75	2.00
GMM22	Brock Lesnar	1.25	3.00

2019 Topps WWE Money in the Bank Mat Relics

*GREEN/99: .5X TO 1.2X BASIC MEM
*BLUE/50: .6X TO 1.5X BASIC MEM
*PURPLE/25: UNPRICED DUE TO SCARCITY
*GOLD/10: UNPRICED DUE TO SCARCITY
*BLACK/5: UNPRICED DUE TO SCARCITY
*RED/1: UNPRICED DUE TO SCARCITY
STATED ODDS 1:20

MRBC	Baron Corbin	2.50	6.00
MRBE	Big E	2.50	6.00
MRBL	Bobby Lashley	2.50	6.00
MRBR	Robert Roode	2.50	6.00
MRCM	Carmella	4.00	10.00
MRFB	Finn Balor	5.00	12.00
MRJE	Jey Uso	2.50	6.00
MRJI	Jimmy Uso	2.50	6.00
MRKK	Kofi Kingston	3.00	8.00
MRKO	Kevin Owens	4.00	10.00
MRLK	Becky Lynch	5.00	12.00
MRNM	Naomi	2.50	6.00
MRNT	Natalya	2.50	6.00
MRRO	Randy Orton	3.00	8.00
MRRT	R-Truth	3.00	8.00
MRSJ	Samoa Joe	2.50	6.00
MRSM	Sheamus	2.50	6.00
MRSR	Seth Rollins	4.00	10.00
MRTO	Titus O'Neil	2.50	6.00
MRTS	Tamina	2.50	6.00
MRXW	Xavier Woods	2.50	6.00
MRZR	Zack Ryder	2.50	6.00

2019 Topps WWE Money in the Bank Money Cards

COMPLETE SET (13)		8.00	20.00
STATED ODDS 1:6			
MC1	Kane	.60	1.50
MC2	The Miz	.75	2.00
MC3	Daniel Bryan	1.50	4.00
MC4	John Cena	1.50	4.00
MC5	Randy Orton	1.00	2.50
MC6	Seth Rollins	1.00	2.50
MC7	Sheamus	.60	1.50
MC8	Baron Corbin	.60	1.50
MC9	Braun Strowman	1.00	2.50
MC10	Carmella	1.00	2.50
MC11	Alexa Bliss	2.00	5.00
MC12	Bayley	.75	2.00
MC13	Brock Lesnar	1.50	4.00

2019 Topps WWE Money in the Bank Quad Autograph

STATED ODDS 1:47,616
STATED PRINT RUN 5 SER.#'d SETS
UNPRICED DUE TO SCARCITY

QABC Owens/Styles/Nakamura/Corbin

2019 Topps WWE Money in the Bank Shirt Relics

*GREEN/99: .5X TO 1.2X BASIC MEM
*BLUE/50: .6X TO 1.5X BASIC MEM
*PURPLE/25: UNPRICED DUE TO SCARCITY
*GOLD/10: UNPRICED DUE TO SCARCITY
*BLACK/5: UNPRICED DUE TO SCARCITY
*RED/1: UNPRICED DUE TO SCARCITY
STATED ODDS 1:23
STATED PRINT RUN 199 SER.#'d SETS

SRAC	Apollo Crews	1.50	4.00
SRAJ	AJ Styles		
SRBL	Brock Lesnar	5.00	12.00
SRBS	Braun Strowman	2.50	6.00
SRCS	Cesaro	4.00	10.00
SRFB	Finn Balor		
SRHS	Heath Slater		
SRJE	Jey Uso		
SRJI	Jimmy Uso		
SRKB	Booker T	3.00	8.00
SRKK	Kofi Kingston	3.00	8.00
SRKO	Kevin Owens	3.00	8.00
SRLA	Bobby Lashley	2.50	6.00
SRMZ	The Miz	3.00	8.00
SRRI	Ricochet	5.00	12.00
SRRM	Rey Mysterio	5.00	12.00
SRRR	Roman Reigns		
SRSR	Seth Rollins	5.00	12.00
SRSZ	Sami Zayn	2.50	6.00

2019 Topps WWE Money in the Bank Triple Autographs

*GOLD/10: UNPRICED DUE TO SCARCITY
*BLACK/5: UNPRICED DUE TO SCARCITY
*RED/1: UNPRICED DUE TO SCARCITY
STATED ODDS 1:6,802
STATED PRINT RUN SER.#'d SETS

TABC	Anderson/Gallows/Styles	60.00	120.00
TANEW	Woods/Big E/Kingston	50.00	100.00

2019 Topps WWE Money in the Bank Promo

NYCC19	John Cena NYCC	5.00	12.00

2016 Topps WWE NXT

*BRONZE/50: .6X TO 1.5X BASIC CARDS
*SILVER/25: .75X TO 2X BASIC CARDS
*GOLD/10: 1.5X TO 4X BASIC CARDS
*RED/1: UNPRICED DUE TO SCARCITY

1	Aliyah RC	.75	2.00
2	Akam RC	.60	1.50
3	Andrade "Cien" Almas RC	.60	1.50
4	Angelo Dawkins	.60	1.50
5	Asuka RC	2.50	6.00
6	Austin Aries	.75	2.00
7	Billie Kay RC	1.50	4.00
8	Blake RC	.60	1.50
9	Dash Wilder RC	.75	2.00
10	Elias Samson RC	.60	1.50
11	Hideo Itami	.75	2.00
12	Johnny Gargano RC	.60	1.50
13	Liv Morgan RC	.75	2.00
14	Buddy Murphy RC	.60	1.50
15	No Way Jose RC	.60	1.50
16	Peyton Royce RC	1.50	4.00
17	Rezar RC	.60	1.50
18	Samoa Joe	1.50	4.00
19	Sawyer Fulton	.75	2.00
20	Scott Dawson RC	.60	1.50
21	Shinsuke Nakamura RC	2.50	6.00
22	Tommaso Ciampa RC	.75	2.00
23	Tye Dillinger	.75	2.00
24	Roman Reigns	2.00	5.00
25	Seth Rollins	1.00	2.50
26	Big E	.60	1.50
27	Bray Wyatt	2.50	6.00
28	Xavier Woods	.60	1.50
29	Rusev	1.50	4.00
30	Kalisto	1.50	4.00
31	Neville	1.50	4.00
32	Kevin Owens	1.50	4.00
33	Charlotte	2.00	5.00
34	Sasha Banks	2.00	5.00
35	Becky Lynch	2.00	5.00
36	Sami Zayn	1.00	2.50
37	Baron Corbin	.75	2.00
38	Big Cass	1.25	3.00
39	Enzo Amore RC	1.25	3.00
40	Aiden English	.60	1.50
41	Simon Gotch RC	1.00	2.50
42	Dana Brooke RC	1.50	4.00
43	Alexa Bliss	3.00	8.00
44	Carmella RC	1.50	4.00
45	Chad Gable RC	.75	2.00
46	Finn Balor	2.00	5.00
47	Jason Jordan RC	.75	2.00
48	Mojo Rawley RC	.60	1.50
49	Nia Jax RC	1.00	2.50
50	Bayley RC	1.50	4.00

2016 Topps WWE NXT Autographs

*BRONZE/50: .5X TO 1.2X BASIC AUTOS
*SILVER/25: .6X TO 1.5X BASIC AUTOS
*GOLD/10: UNPRICED DUE TO SCARCITY
*RED/1: UNPRICED DUE TO SCARCITY
STATED OVERALL ODDS 1:MINIBOX

NNO	Alexa Bliss	50.00	100.00
NNO	Aliyah	8.00	15.00
NNO	Andrade Cien Almas	6.00	15.00
NNO	Angelo Dawkins	6.00	15.00
NNO	Asuka	20.00	50.00
NNO	Austin Aries	10.00	25.00
NNO	Bayley	15.00	40.00
NNO	Billie Kay	20.00	50.00
NNO	Blake	6.00	15.00
NNO	Buddy Murphy	6.00	15.00
NNO	Dash Wilder	12.00	30.00
NNO	Elias Samson	15.00	40.00
NNO	Finn Balor	15.00	40.00
NNO	Hideo Itami	6.00	15.00
NNO	Johnny Gargano	6.00	15.00
NNO	Liv Morgan	40.00	100.00
NNO	Nia Jax	8.00	20.00
NNO	No Way Jose	10.00	25.00
NNO	Peyton Royce	15.00	40.00
NNO	Samoa Joe	10.00	25.00
NNO	Sawyer Fulton	10.00	25.00
NNO	Scott Dawson	6.00	15.00
NNO	Shinsuke Nakamura	10.00	25.00
NNO	Tommaso Ciampa	6.00	15.00
NNO	Tye Dillinger	10.00	25.00

2017 Topps WWE NXT

COMPLETE SET (50)
UNOPENED BOX (10 PACKS)
UNOPENED PACK (7 CARDS)
*BRONZE: .6X TO 1.5X BASIC CARDS
*BLUE/50: .75X TO 2X BASIC CARDS
*SILVER/25: 1.2X TO 3X BASIC CARDS
*GOLD/10: UNPRICED DUE TO SCARCITY
*RED/1: UNPRICED DUE TO SCARCITY
*P.P.BLACK/1: UNPRICED DUE TO SCARCITY
*P.P.CYAN/1: UNPRICED DUE TO SCARCITY
*P.P.MAGENTA/1: UNPRICED DUE TO SCARCITY
*P.P.YELLOW/1: UNPRICED DUE TO SCARCITY

1	Asuka	1.25	3.00
2	Akam	.40	1.00
3	Alexander Wolfe RC	.50	1.25
4	Aliyah	.50	1.25
5	Andrade Cien Almas	.40	1.00
6	Angelo Dawkins	.40	1.00
7	Killian Dain RC	.40	1.00
8	Billie Kay	.50	1.25
9	Bobby Roode	1.00	2.50
10	Buddy Murphy	.40	1.00
11	Elias Samson	.60	1.50
12	Ember Moon	1.00	2.50
13	Eric Young	.75	2.00
14	Hideo Itami	.60	1.50
15	Johnny Gargano	.40	1.00
16	Liv Morgan	.60	1.50
17	Mandy Rose	.50	1.25
18	Nick Miller RC	.40	1.00
19	Nikki Cross RC	.75	2.00
20	No Way Jose	.40	1.00
21	Oney Lorcan	.40	1.00
22	Otis Dozovic RC	.50	1.25
23	Peyton Royce	.60	1.50
24	Rezar	.40	1.00
25	Riddick Moss RC	.50	1.25
26	Roderick Strong	.50	1.25
27	Ruby Riot RC	.50	1.25
28	Sawyer Fulton	.40	1.00
29	Shane Thorne RC	.40	1.00
30	Tian Bing RC	.40	1.00
31	Tino Sabbatelli	.50	1.25
32	Tommaso Ciampa	.40	1.00
33	Tucker Knight RC	1.00	2.50
34	Wesley Blake	.40	1.00
35	Cathy Kelley	.40	1.00
36	Charly Caruso RC	.40	1.00
37	Mike Rome RC	.40	1.00
38	Paul Ellering	.40	1.00
39	Tom Phillips	.40	1.00
40	William Regal	.50	1.25
41	Corey Graves	.40	1.00
42	Dasha Fuentes	.50	1.25
43	Baron Corbin	.60	1.50
44	Bayley	1.25	3.00
45	Dash Wilder	.40	1.00
46	Finn Balor	1.50	4.00
47	Samoa Joe	1.25	3.00
48	Scott Dawson	.40	1.00
49	Shinsuke Nakamura	1.00	2.50
50	Tye Dillinger	.40	1.00

2017 Topps WWE NXT Autographs

*BRONZE/99: .5X TO 1.2X BASIC AUTOS
*BLUE/50: .6X TO 1.5X BASIC AUTOS
*SILVER/25: .75X TO 2X BASIC AUTOS
*GOLD/10: UNPRICED DUE TO SCARCITY
*RED/1: UNPRICED DUE TO SCARCITY
*P.P.BLACK/1: UNPRICED DUE TO SCARCITY
*P.P.CYAN/1: UNPRICED DUE TO SCARCITY
*P.P.MAGENTA/1: UNPRICED DUE TO SCARCITY
*P.P.YELLOW/1: UNPRICED DUE TO SCARCITY
RANDOMLY INSERTED INTO PACKS

RAAC Andrade Cien Almas	5.00	12.00
RAAD Angelo Dawkins	5.00	12.00
RAAK Akam	8.00	20.00
RAAL Aliyah	6.00	15.00
RAAS Asuka	20.00	50.00
RAAW Alexander Wolfe	8.00	20.00
RABD Killian Dain	5.00	12.00
RABK Billie Kay	10.00	25.00
RABM Buddy Murphy	5.00	12.00
RABR Bobby Roode	10.00	25.00
RACC Charly Caruso	8.00	20.00
RACK Cathy Kelley	8.00	20.00
RADF Dasha Fuentes	8.00	20.00
RADW Dash Wilder	5.00	12.00
RAEM Ember Moon	10.00	25.00
RAEY Eric Young	6.00	15.00
RAHI Hideo Itami	5.00	12.00
RAJG Johnny Gargano	5.00	12.00
RALM Liv Morgan	15.00	40.00
RAMR Mandy Rose	20.00	50.00
RANC Nikki Cross	10.00	25.00
RANM Nick Miller	5.00	12.00
RANW No Way Jose	5.00	12.00
RAOD Otis Dozovic	5.00	12.00
RAOL Oney Lorcan	6.00	15.00
RAPR Peyton Royce	8.00	20.00
RARE Rezar	5.00	12.00
RARM Riddick Moss	5.00	12.00
RARS Roderick Strong	5.00	12.00
RASD Scott Dawson	5.00	12.00
RASF Sawyer Fulton	5.00	12.00
RASN Shinsuke Nakamura	12.00	30.00
RAST Shane Thorne	5.00	12.00
RATB Tian Bing	5.00	12.00
RATC Tommaso Ciampa	5.00	12.00
RATK Tucker Knight	5.00	12.00
RATP Tom Phillips	5.00	12.00
RATS Tino Sabbatelli	5.00	12.00
RAWB Wesley Blake	5.00	12.00

2017 Topps WWE NXT Dual Relics

RANDOMLY INSERTED INTO PACKS
STATED PRINT RUN 25 SER.#'d SETS
UNPRICED DUE TO SCARCITY

DRAA Andrade Cien Almas
DRAS Asuka
DRBR Bobby Roode
DRBY Bayley
DREM Ember Moon
DRFB Finn Balor
DRJG Johnny Gargano
DRNJ No Way Jose
DRSD Scott Dawson
DRSJ Samoa Joe
DRSN Shinsuke Nakamura
DRTC Tommaso Ciampa

2017 Topps WWE NXT Mat Relics

*BRONZE/99: .5X TO 1.2X BASIC MEM
*BLUE/50: .6X TO 1.5X BASIC MEM
*SILVER/25: .75X TO 2X BASIC MEM
*GOLD/10: UNPRICED DUE TO SCARCITY
*RED/1: UNPRICED DUE TO SCARCITY
RANDOMLY INSERTED INTO PACKS

MRAA Andrade Cien Almas	2.00	5.00
MRAC Apollo Crews	2.50	6.00
MRAE Aiden English	2.00	5.00
MRAK Asuka	6.00	15.00
MRAS Asuka	6.00	15.00
MRAU Austin Aries	4.00	10.00
MRBC Big Cass	2.50	6.00
MRBR Bobby Roode	5.00	12.00
MRBY Bayley	6.00	15.00
MRCG Chad Gable	2.50	6.00
MRDW Dash Wilder	2.00	5.00
MREA Enzo Amore	6.00	15.00
MREM Ember Moon	5.00	12.00
MRFB Finn Balor	8.00	20.00
MRJG Johnny Gargano	2.00	5.00
MRJJ Jason Jordan	2.50	6.00
MRKO Kevin Owens	5.00	12.00
MRMR Mojo Rawley	2.50	6.00
MRSB Sasha Banks	6.00	15.00
MRSD Scott Dawson	2.00	5.00
MRSH Shinsuke Nakamura	5.00	12.00
MRSJ Samoa Joe	6.00	15.00
MRSK Asuka	6.00	15.00
MRSN Shinsuke Nakamura	5.00	12.00
MRSZ Sami Zayn	2.50	6.00
MRTB Tyler Breeze	2.00	5.00
MRTC Tommaso Ciampa	2.00	5.00
MRTD Tye Dillinger	2.00	5.00
MRZR Zack Ryder	2.00	5.00
MRBCB Baron Corbin	3.00	8.00
MRBEY Bayley	6.00	15.00
MRBLY Bayley	6.00	15.00
MRBRD Bobby Roode	5.00	12.00
MRBRH Bobby Roode	5.00	12.00
MRBYY Bayley	6.00	15.00
MRFBL Finn Balor	8.00	20.00
MRFBR Finn Balor	8.00	20.00
MRNWJ No Way Jose	2.00	5.00
MRNYJ No Way Jose	2.00	5.00
MRSJE Samoa Joe	6.00	15.00
MRSJO Samoa Joe	6.00	15.00
MRSNK Shinsuke Nakamura	5.00	12.00
MRSZN Sami Zayn	2.50	6.00
MRTDL Tye Dillinger	2.00	5.00

2017 Topps WWE NXT Matches and Moments

*BRONZE: .5X TO 1.5X BASIC CARDS
*BLUE/50: .75X TO 2X BASIC CARDS
*SILVER/25: 1.2X TO 3X BASIC CARDS
*GOLD/10: UNPRICED DUE TO SCARCITY
*RED/1: UNPRICED DUE TO SCARCITY
*P.P.BLACK/1: UNPRICED DUE TO SCARCITY
*P.P.CYAN/1: UNPRICED DUE TO SCARCITY
*P.P.MAGENTA/1: UNPRICED DUE TO SCARCITY
*P.P.YELLOW/1: UNPRICED DUE TO SCARCITY

1 Jason Jordan & Chad Gable	.50	1.25
2 Finn Balor/Samoa Joe	1.50	4.00
3 Apollo Crews	.50	1.25
4 Finn Balor/Samoa Joe	1.50	4.00
5 Finn Balor/Samoa Joe	1.50	4.00
6 Bayley	1.25	3.00
7 Apollo Crews	.50	1.25
8 Baron Corbin	.60	1.50
9 Samoa Joe	1.25	3.00
10 Samoa Joe	1.25	3.00
11 Dash/Dawson	.40	1.00
12 Dash/Dawson	.40	1.00
13 Jason Jordan/Chad Gable	.50	1.25
14 Samoa Joe/Baron Corbin	1.25	3.00
15 Dash/Dawson	.40	1.00
16 Finn Balor	1.50	4.00
17 Elias Samson	.60	1.50
18 Sami Zayn	.50	1.25
19 Finn Balor	1.50	4.00
20 Sami Zayn vs. Samoa Joe	1.25	3.00
21 Baron Corbin	.60	1.50
22 Finn Balor	1.50	4.00
23 Samoa Joe	1.25	3.00
24 The Revival	.40	1.00
25 American Alpha	.50	1.25
26 Finn Balor	1.50	4.00
27 American Alpha	.50	1.25
28 Shinsuke Nakamura	1.00	2.50
29 Asuka	1.25	3.00
30 Finn Balor	1.50	4.00
31 Apollo Crews	.50	1.25
32 Shinsuke Nakamura	1.00	2.50
33 No Way Jose	.40	1.00
34 Samoa Joe	1.25	3.00
35 Samoa Joe	1.50	4.00
36 Shinsuke Nakamura	1.00	2.50
37 Finn Balor	1.50	4.00
38 Blake/Murphy	.40	1.00
39 Johnny Gargano/Tommaso Ciampa	.40	1.00
40 Andrade Cien Almas	.40	1.00
41 The Revival	.50	1.25
42 The Authors of Pain	.40	1.00
43 Samoa Joe	1.50	4.00
44 TM-61	.40	1.00
45 Oney Lorcan	.40	1.00
46 Johnny Gargano/Tommaso Ciampa	.40	1.00
47 The Revival	.50	1.25
48 Shinsuke Nakamura	1.50	4.00
49 Shinsuke Nakamura	1.00	2.50
50 Bobby Roode	1.00	2.50

2017 Topps WWE NXT Shirt Relics

*BRONZE/99: .5X TO 1.2X BASIC MEM
*BLUE/50: .6X TO 1.5X BASIC MEM
*SILVER/25: .75X TO 2X BASIC MEM
*GOLD/10: UNPRICED DUE TO SCARCITY
*RED/1: UNPRICED DUE TO SCARCITY
RANDOMLY INSERTED INTO PACKS

SRAK Akam	2.00	5.00
SRAW Alexander Wolfe	2.50	6.00
SRBR Bobby Roode	5.00	12.00
SREM Ember Moon	5.00	12.00
SREY Eric Young	4.00	10.00
SRHI Hideo Itami	3.00	8.00
SRNC Nikki Cross	4.00	10.00
SRRZ Rezar	2.00	5.00
SRSD Scott Dawson	2.00	5.00
SRSN Shinsuke Nakamura	5.00	12.00
SRACA Andrade Cien Almas	2.00	5.00
SRAKA Asuka	6.00	15.00
SRBLY Bayley	6.00	15.00
SRNWJ No Way Jose	2.00	5.00

2018 Topps WWE NXT

UNOPENED BOX (10 PACKS)
UNOPENED PACK (7 CARDS)
*BRONZE: .6X TO 1.5X BASIC CARDS
*BLUE/50: .75X TO 2X BASIC CARDS
*SILVER/25: 1.2X TO 3X BASIC CARDS
*GOLD/10: UNPRICED DUE TO SCARCITY
*RED/1: UNPRICED DUE TO SCARCITY
*P.P.BLACK/1: UNPRICED DUE TO SCARCITY
*P.P.CYAN/1: UNPRICED DUE TO SCARCITY
*P.P.MAGENTA/1: UNPRICED DUE TO SCARCITY
*P.P.YELLOW/1: UNPRICED DUE TO SCARCITY

R1 Adam Cole RC	.50	1.25
R2 Akam	.40	1.00
R3 Aleister Black	.50	1.25
R4 Alexander Wolfe	.40	1.00
R5 Andrade Cien Almas	.60	1.50
R6 Angelo Dawkins	.40	1.00
R7 Bobby Fish RC	.40	1.00
R8 Buddy Murphy	.50	1.25
R9 Cezar Bononi RC	.40	1.00
R10 Drew McIntyre	.60	1.50
R11 Eric Young	.50	1.25
R12 Fabian Aichner RC	.40	1.00
R13 Gabriel Ealy RC	.40	1.00
R14 Kassius Ohno	.40	1.00
R15 Killian Dain	.50	1.25
R16 Kyle O'Reilly RC	.50	1.25
R17 Lars Sullivan RC	.40	1.00
R18 Lio Rush RC	.40	1.00
R19 Montez Ford	.40	1.00
R20 Nick Miller	.40	1.00
R21 No Way Jose	.50	1.25
R22 Oney Lorcan	.50	1.25
R23 Otis Dozovic	.40	1.00
R24 Paul Ellering	.50	1.25
R25 Pete Dunne RC	.40	1.00
R26 Rezar	.40	1.00
R27 Riddick Moss	.40	1.00
R28 Roderick Strong	.40	1.00
R29 Shane Thorne	.40	1.00
R30 Tino Sabbatelli	.50	1.25
R31 Tommaso Ciampa	.40	1.00
R32 Tucker Knight	.40	1.00
R33 Tyler Bate	.40	1.00
R34 Trent Seven RC	.40	1.00
R35 Velveteen Dream	.40	1.00
R36 Wesley Blake	.50	1.25
R37 Aliyah	.60	1.50
R38 Bianca Belair RC	.50	1.25
R39 Billie Kay	.75	2.00
R40 Ember Moon	.75	2.00
R41 Kairi Sane RC	1.00	2.50
R42 Lacey Evans	.50	1.25
R43 Nikki Cross	.60	1.50
R44 Peyton Royce	1.00	2.50
R45 Shayna Baszler	1.00	2.50
R46 Taynara Conti RC	.40	1.00
R47 Vanessa Borne	.40	1.00
R48 Zelina Vega	.40	1.00
R49 William Regal	.50	1.25
R50 Triple H	1.00	2.50

2018 Topps WWE NXT Autographed Shirt Relics

*BLUE/50: .5X TO 1.2X BASIC AUTOS
*SILVER/25: .6X TO 1.5X BASIC AUTOS

*GOLD/10: UNPRICED DUE TO SCARCITY
*RED/1: UNPRICED DUE TO SCARCITY
STATED PRINT RUN 99 SER.#'d SETS

ARAA Andrade Cien Almas	8.00	20.00
ARAK Akam	6.00	15.00
ARAW Alexander Wolfe	5.00	12.00
AREM Ember Moon	12.00	30.00
AREY Eric Young	8.00	20.00
ARNC Nikki Cross	10.00	25.00
ARNW No Way Jose	8.00	20.00
ARRZ Rezar	6.00	15.00

2018 Topps WWE NXT Autographs

*BRONZE/99: SAME VALUE AS BASIC
*BLUE/50: .5X TO 1.2X BASIC AUTOS
*SILVER/25: .6X TO 1.5X BASIC AUTOS
*GOLD/10: UNPRICED DUE TO SCARCITY
*RED/1: UNPRICED DUE TO SCARCITY
*P.P.BLACK/1: UNPRICED DUE TO SCARCITY
*P.P.CYAN/1: UNPRICED DUE TO SCARCITY
*P.P.MAGENTA/1: UNPRICED DUE TO SCARCITY
*P.P.YELLOW/1: UNPRICED DUE TO SCARCITY
RANDOMLY INSERTED INTO PACKS

AAA Andrade Cien Almas	4.00	10.00
AAB Aleister Black	6.00	15.00
AAC Adam Cole	8.00	20.00
AAD Angelo Dawkins	4.00	10.00
AAK Akam	4.00	10.00
AAW Alexander Wolfe	4.00	10.00
AAY Aliyah	6.00	15.00
ABB Bianca Belair	50.00	100.00
ABF Bobby Fish	10.00	25.00
ABK Billie Kay	10.00	25.00
ABM Buddy Murphy	5.00	12.00
ABY Bayley	8.00	20.00
ACB Cezar Bononi	5.00	12.00
ADA Dean Ambrose	20.00	50.00
ADM Drew McIntyre	8.00	20.00
AEM Ember Moon	8.00	20.00
AEY Eric Young	5.00	12.00
AFA Fabian Aichner	6.00	15.00
AJG Johnny Gargano	6.00	15.00
AKD Killian Dain	5.00	12.00
AKS Kairi Sane	20.00	50.00
ALE Lacey Evans	10.00	25.00
ALR Lio Rush	10.00	25.00
ALS Lars Sullivan	10.00	25.00
AMF Montez Ford	10.00	25.00
ANC Nikki Cross	6.00	15.00
ANM Nick Miller	5.00	12.00
ANW No Way Jose	4.00	10.00
AOD Otis Dozovic	5.00	12.00
AOL Oney Lorcan	5.00	12.00
AON Kassius Ohno	4.00	10.00
APD Pete Dunne	15.00	40.00
APR Peyton Royce	6.00	15.00
ARE Rezar	4.00	10.00
ARM Riddick Moss	4.00	10.00
ARS Roderick Strong	4.00	10.00
ASH Shayna Baszler	12.00	30.00
AST Shane Thorne	5.00	12.00
ATB Tyler Bate	10.00	25.00
ATC Tommaso Ciampa	5.00	12.00
ATK Tucker Knight	4.00	10.00
ATS Tino Sabbatelli	4.00	10.00
ATY Taynara Conti	20.00	50.00
AUA Kyle O'Reilly	6.00	15.00
AVB Vanessa Borne	12.00	30.00
AVD Velveteen Dream	6.00	15.00
AWB Wesley Blake	4.00	10.00
AZV Zelina Vega	20.00	50.00

2018 Topps WWE NXT Dual Autographs

*GOLD/10: UNPRICED DUE TO SCARCITY
*RED/1: UNPRICED DUE TO SCARCITY
STATED PRINT RUN 25 SER.#'d SETS

DADY Triple H/William Regal	75.00	150.00
DAID Peyton Royce/Billie Kay	75.00	150.00

2018 Topps WWE NXT Matches and Moments

*BRONZE: .6X TO 1.5X BASIC CARDS
*BLUE/50: .75X TO 2X BASIC CARDS
*SILVER/25: 1.2X TO 3X BASIC CARDS
*GOLD/10: UNPRICED DUE TO SCARCITY
*RED/1: UNPRICED DUE TO SCARCITY
*P.P.BLACK/1: UNPRICED DUE TO SCARCITY
*P.P.CYAN/1: UNPRICED DUE TO SCARCITY
*P.P.MAGENTA/1: UNPRICED DUE TO SCARCITY
*P.P.YELLOW/1: UNPRICED DUE TO SCARCITY

1 Samoa Joe	.75	2.00
2 Bobby Roode	.60	1.50
3 The Revival	.50	1.25
4 Shinsuke Nakamura	1.00	2.50
5 The Authors of Pain	.50	1.25
6 Tye Dillinger	.40	1.00
7 Bobby Roode	.60	1.50
8 Andrade "Cien" Almas	.60	1.50
9 SAnitY Debut	.60	1.50
10 #DIY Advance	.40	1.00
11 Shane Thorne	.40	1.00
12 The Authors of Pain	.50	1.25
13 Andrade "Cien" Almas	.60	1.50
14 Bobby Roode	.60	1.50
15 The Authors of Pain	.50	1.25
16 #DIY	.40	1.00
17 Samoa Joe	.75	2.00
18 SAnitY	.60	1.50
19 Samoa Joe	.75	2.00
20 Shinsuke Nakamura	1.00	2.50
21 Shinsuke Nakamura	1.00	2.50
22 Bobby Roode	.60	1.50
23 #DIY	.40	1.00
24 #DIY	.50	1.25
25 TM61	.50	1.25
26 Eric Young	.50	1.25
27 The Authors of Pain	.50	1.25
28 Seth Rollins	1.00	2.50
29 Bobby Roode	1.00	2.50
30 SAnitY	.50	1.25
31 Kassius Ohno	.40	1.00
32 The Authors of Pain	.50	1.25
33 Shinsuke Nakamura	1.00	2.50
34 Bobby Roode	.60	1.50
35 Kassius Ohno	1.00	2.50
36 SAnitY	.50	1.25
37 Aleister Black	.50	1.25
38 The Authors of Pain	.50	1.25
39 Bobby Roode	1.00	2.50
40 Oney Lorcan	.50	1.25
41 Drew McIntyre	.60	1.50
42 Tye Dillinger	.40	1.00
43 Tyler Bate	.50	1.25
44 Hideo Itami	.40	1.00
45 Hideo Itami	.40	1.00
46 Roderick Strong	.50	1.25
47 Pete Dunne	.40	1.00
48 Bobby Roode	.60	1.50
49 The Authors of Pain	.40	1.00
50 Tommaso Ciampa	.40	1.00

2018 Topps WWE NXT Triple Autographs

*GOLD/10: UNPRICED DUE TO SCARCITY
*RED/1: UNPRICED DUE TO SCARCITY
STATED ODDS

TAERA Cole/Fish/O'Reilly	50.00	100.00
TAMAG McIntyre/Almas/Gargano	30.00	75.00
TAMCA Moon/Cross/Aliyah	50.00	100.00
TASAY Young/Wolfe/Dain	25.00	60.00

2019 Topps WWE NXT

COMPLETE SET (100)	12.00	30.00

*BRONZE: .6X TO 1.5X BASIC CARDS
*BLUE/50: .75X TO 2X BASIC CARDS
*SILVER/25: 2X TO 5X BASIC CARDS
*GOLD/10: UNPRICED DUE TO SCARCITY
*RED/1: UNPRICED DUE TO SCARCITY

1 Velveteen Dream	.50	1.25
2 The Undisputed Era	.40	1.00
3 Aleister Black	.30	.75
4 Andrade	.30	.75
5 Roderick Strong	.50	1.25
6 Pete Dunne	.50	1.25
7 Johnny Gargano	.25	.60
8 Pete Dunne & Roderick Strong	.50	1.25
9 Adam Cole	.30	.75
10 Johnny Gargano	.25	.60
11 Pete Dunne & Roderick Strong	.50	1.25
12 EC3	.25	.60
13 Ricochet	.60	1.50
14 Adam Cole	.30	.75
15 Roderick Strong	.50	1.25
16 Aleister Black	.30	.75
17 Johnny Gargano	.50	1.25
18 The Viking Raiders	.30	.75
19 Ricochet	.60	1.50
20 Lars Sullivan	.25	.60
21 Kona Reeves	.30	.75
22 Pete Dunne	.50	1.25
23 The Viking Raiders	.30	.75
24 Tommaso Ciampa	.40	1.00
25 Kona Reeves	.30	.75
26 Dunne/Danny Burch/Oney Lorcan	.50	1.25
27 Lars Sullivan	.25	.60
28 EC3	.40	1.00
29 Pete Dunne	.50	1.25
30 The Undisputed Era	.50	1.25
31 Ricochet	.60	1.50
32 Aleister Black	.30	.75
33 Tommaso Ciampa	.25	.60
34 British Strong Style	.50	1.25
35 Aleister Black & Ricochet	.60	1.50
36 Moustache Mountain	.40	1.00
37 The Undisputed Era	.50	1.25
38 Johnny Gargano	.25	.60
39 The Undisputed Era	.50	1.25
40 Tommaso Ciampa	.30	.75
41 EC3	.25	.60
42 Aleister Black	.30	.75
43 Keith Lee	.25	.60
44 The Undisputed Era	.50	1.25
45 Velveteen Dream	.50	1.25
46 Ricochet	.60	1.50
47 Tommaso Ciampa	.25	.60
48 Lars Sullivan	.25	.60
49 The Undisputed Era	.50	1.25
50 The Forgotten Sons	.40	1.00
51 Jaxson Ryker	.25	.60
52 Pete Dunne	.60	1.50
53 Lars Sullivan	.25	.60
54 Keith Lee	.25	.60
55 Ricochet	.60	1.50
56 Bobby Fish	.40	1.00
57 Pete Dunne	.50	1.25
58 EC3	.25	.60
59 Johnny Gargano	.30	.75
60 Matt Riddle	.40	1.00
61 Heavy Machinery	.25	.60
62 Pete Dunne	.50	1.25
63 Aleister Black	.30	.75
64 Tommaso Ciampa	.25	.60
65 Dunne/Ricochet/Viking Raiders	.60	1.50
66 The Forgotten Sons	.40	1.00
67 EC3	.25	.60
68 Ricochet	.60	1.50
69 Dominik Dijakovic	.25	.60
70 Walter	.50	1.25
71 Tommaso Ciampa	.25	.60
72 The Viking Raiders	.30	.75
73 Johnny Gargano	.25	.60
74 Matt Riddle	.40	1.00
75 Black/Ricochet/Velveteen Dream	.25	.60
76 Rik Bugez	.40	1.00
77 Ricochet	.60	1.50
78 Velveteen Dream	.50	1.25
79 Keith Lee	.25	.60
80 DIY	.25	.60
81 Aleister Black/Ricochet	.60	1.50
82 Aleister Black/Ricochet	.60	1.50
83 Johnny Gargano	.25	.60
84 Adam Cole	.30	.75
85 Aleister Black & Ricochet	.60	1.50
86 The Viking Raiders	.30	.75
87 Velveteen Dream	.50	1.25
88 Walter	.50	1.25
89 Johnny Gargano	.50	1.25
90 Velveteen Dream	.50	1.25
91 Kushida	.25	.60
92 Matt Riddle	.40	1.00
93 The Viking Raiders	.30	.75
94 Tyler Breeze	.30	.75
95 Walter	.50	1.25
96 Imperium	.50	1.25
97 Matt Riddle	.50	1.25
98 The Street Profits	.30	.75
99 Velveteen Dream	.50	1.25
100 Adam Cole	.30	.75

2019 Topps WWE NXT Autographed Shirt Relics

*BLUE/50: .5X TO 1.2X BASIC AUTOS
*SILVER/25: UNPRICED DUE TO SCARCITY
*GOLD/10: UNPRICED DUE TO SCARCITY
*RED/1: UNPRICED DUE TO SCARCITY
STATED ODDS 1:364
STATED PRINT RUN 99 SER.#'d SETS

ASAC	Adam Cole	8.00	20.00
ASRS	Roderick Strong	6.00	15.00
ASSB	Shayna Baszler	10.00	25.00
ASVD	Velveteen Dream	6.00	15.00

2019 Topps WWE NXT Autographs

*BRONZE/99: SAME VALUE AS BASIC
*BLUE/50: .5X TO 1.2X BASIC AUTOS
*SILVER/25: UNPRICE DUE TO SCARCITY
*GOLD/10: UNPRICED DUE TO SCARCITY
*RED/1: UNPRICED DUE TO SCARCITY
*P.P.BLACK/1: UNPRICED DUE TO SCARCITY
*P.P.CYAN/1: UNPRICED DUE TO SCARCITY
*P.P.MAGENTA/1: UNPRICED DUE TO SCARCITY
*P.P.YELLOW/1: UNPRICED DUE TO SCARCITY
STATED ODDS 1:20

AE	Erik	5.00	12.00
AI	Ivar	5.00	12.00
AAC	Adam Cole	8.00	20.00
ABB	Bianca Belair	12.00	30.00
ABF	Bobby Fish	5.00	12.00
ABM	Buddy Murphy	5.00	12.00
ACG	Chelsea Green	15.00	40.00
ACL	Candice LeRae	6.00	15.00
ADD	Dominik Dijakovic	6.00	15.00
ADP	Deonna Purrazzo	6.00	15.00
AIS	Io Shirai	25.00	60.00
AJD	Jessamyn Duke	8.00	20.00
AJG	Johnny Gargano	5.00	12.00
AKL	Keith Lee	12.00	30.00
AKY	Kyle O'Reilly	5.00	12.00
ALE	Lacey Evans	15.00	40.00
AMS	Marina Shafir	5.00	12.00
AMY	Mia Yim	10.00	25.00
ANC	Nikki Cross	8.00	20.00
AOD	Otis	6.00	15.00
AOH	Kassius Ohno	5.00	12.00
APD	Pete Dunne	8.00	20.00
APM	Damian Priest	5.00	12.00
ARC	Ricochet	12.00	30.00
ARS	Roderick Strong	5.00	12.00
ASB	Shayna Baszler	6.00	15.00
ATK	Tucker	5.00	12.00
ATM	Tommaso Ciampa	8.00	20.00
ATS	Toni Storm	75.00	150.00
AVD	Velveteen Dream	5.00	12.00
AWT	Walter	15.00	40.00
ABRO	Matt Riddle	15.00	40.00

2019 Topps WWE NXT Dual Autographs

*GOLD/10: UNPRICED DUE TO SCARCITY
*RED/1: UNPRICED DUE TO SCARCITY
STATED ODDS 1:1,149
STATED PRINT RUN 25 SER.#'d SETS

DAAB	M.Barthel/F.Aichner	25.00	60.00
DAGL	C.LeRae/J.Gargano	60.00	120.00
DAMG	V.Borne/Aliyah	50.00	100.00
DASO	K.O'Reilly/R.Strong	20.00	50.00

2019 Topps WWE NXT Kiss Autographs

*GOLD/10: UNPRICED DUE TO SCARCITY
*RED/1: UNPRICED DUE TO SCARCITY
STATED ODDS 1:1,910
STATED PRINT RUN 25 SER.#'d SETS

AKAL	Aliyah	50.00	100.00
AKBB	Bianca Belair	125.00	250.00
AKCG	Chelsea Green	100.00	200.00
AKIS	Io Shirai	200.00	350.00

2019 Topps WWE NXT Roster

COMPLETE SET (50) 15.00 40.00
STATED ODDS 2:1

1	Adam Cole	.60	1.50
2	Jordan Myles	.30	.75
3	Aliyah	.50	1.25
4	Angelo Dawkins	.50	1.25
5	Bianca Belair	.30	.75
6	Bobby Fish	.75	2.00
7	Candice LeRae	1.00	2.50
8	Cathy Kelly	1.25	3.00
9	Chelsea Green	.50	1.25
10	Dakota Kai	1.00	2.50
11	Damian Priest	.50	1.25
12	Danny Burch	.50	1.25
13	Deonna Purrazzo	.50	1.25
14	Dominik Dijakovic	.50	1.25
15	Fabian Aichner	1.00	2.50
16	Humberto Carrillo	1.00	2.50
17	Io Shirai	.50	1.25
18	Jaxson Ryker	.50	1.25
19	Jessamyn Duke	.60	1.50
20	Jessi Kamea	.50	1.25
21	Johnny Gargano	.50	1.25
22	Kacy Catanzaro	1.25	3.00
23	Kassius Ohno	.75	2.00
24	Keith Lee	.50	1.25
25	Kona Reeves	.60	1.50
26	Kushida	.50	1.25
27	Kyle O'Reilly	.75	2.00
28	Marcel Barthel	1.00	2.50
29	Marina Shafir	.50	1.25
30	Matt Riddle	.75	2.00
31	Mauro Ranallo	.50	1.25
32	Mia Yim	.50	1.25
33	Montez Ford	.50	1.25
34	Oney Lorcan	.60	1.50
35	Pete Dunne	1.00	2.50
36	Raul Mendoza	.50	1.25
37	Rik Bugez	.50	1.25
38	Riddick Moss	.50	1.25
39	Roderick Strong	1.00	2.50
40	Shayna Baszler	1.00	2.50
41	Steve Cutler	.75	2.00
42	Toni Storm	2.00	5.00
43	Trent Seven	.75	2.00
44	Tyler Bate	.60	1.50
45	Vanessa Borne	.60	1.50
46	Velveteen Dream	1.00	2.50
47	Walter	1.00	2.50
48	Wesley Blake	.75	2.00
49	William Regal	.75	2.00
50	Xia Li	.50	1.25

2019 Topps WWE NXT Triple Autographs

*GOLD/10: UNPRICED DUE TO SCARCITY
*RED/1: UNPRICED DUE TO SCARCITY
STATED ODDS 1:1,442
STATED PRINT RUN 25 SER.#'d SETS

TA4H	Shafir/Baszler/Duke	60.00	120.00
TAFS	Ryker/Blake/Cutler	30.00	75.00
TAMYC	Purrazzo/Shirai/Yim	100.00	200.00

2020 Topps WWE NXT

COMPLETE SET (100) 8.00 20.00
*BRONZE: .5X TO 1.2X BASIC CARDS
*BLUE/50: .75X TO 2X BASIC CARDS
*SILVER/25: UNPRICED DUE TO SCARCITY
*GOLD/10: UNPRICED DUE TO SCARCITY
*RED/1: UNPRICED DUE TO SCARCITY

1	Imperium	.60	1.50
2	Alexander Wolfe	.60	1.50
3	Angel Garza	.40	1.00
4	Adam Cole	.75	2.00
5	Imperium	.50	1.25
6	Isaiah Swerve Scott	.40	1.00
7	Trent Seven	.30	.75
8	Killian Dain	.40	1.00
9	Johnny Gargano	.75	2.00
10	WALTER	.60	1.50
11	Pete Dunne	.30	.75
12	Tyler Bate	.50	1.25
13	Pete Dunne	.60	1.50
14	Dave Mastiff	.40	1.00
15	Street Profits	.30	.75
16	Velveteen Dream	.40	1.00
17	Adam Cole	.75	2.00
18	Flash Morgan Webster	.40	1.00
19	Mark Andrews	.30	.75
20	Moustache Mountain	.60	1.50
21	Killian Dain	.40	1.00
22	Dominik Dijakovic	.30	.75
23	Undisputed ERA	.75	2.00
24	Joe Coffey	.40	1.00
25	Mark Andrews	.40	1.00
26	WALTER	.60	1.50
27	Roderick Strong	.60	1.50
28	Mark Andrews & Flash Webster	.40	1.00
29	Roderick Strong	.60	1.50
30	Matt Riddle	.60	1.50
31	Keith Lee	.30	.75
32	Matt Riddle	.60	1.50
33	Adam Cole	.75	2.00
34	Undisputed ERA	.60	1.50
35	Finn Balor	.75	2.00
36	Tommaso Ciampa	.75	2.00
37	Gallus	.40	1.00
38	Roderick Strong	.60	1.50
39	Tommaso Ciampa	.60	1.50
40	Pete Dunne	.30	.75
41	Damian Priest	.30	.75
42	Gallus	.40	1.00
43	Angel Garza	.40	1.00
44	Roderick Strong	.60	1.50
45	Finn Balor	.75	2.00
46	Undisputed ERA	.75	2.00
47	NXT Invades SmackDown	1.00	2.50
48	Adam Cole	.75	2.00
49	Pete Dunne	.30	.75
50	Angel Garza	.40	1.00
51	Ilja Dragunov	.60	1.50
52	Imperium	.50	1.25
53	WALTER	.60	1.50
54	Finn Balor	.75	2.00
55	Keith Lee	.60	1.50
56	Damian Priest	.30	.75
57	Adam Cole	.75	2.00
58	Alexander Wolfe	.30	.75
59	NXT Invades SD DX-Style	.75	2.00
60	Pete Dunne	.30	.75
61	Finn Balor	.75	2.00
62	Team Ciampa	.60	1.50
63	Roderick Strong	.60	1.50
64	Adam Cole	.75	2.00
65	Keith Lee	.75	2.00
66	Undisputed ERA	.75	2.00
67	Finn Balor	.75	2.00
68	Gallus & Ilja Dragunov	.60	1.50
69	Tommaso Ciampa	.30	.75
70	Imperium	.60	1.50
71	Angel Garza	.40	1.00
72	Finn Balor	.75	2.00
73	Brawl Leads to Ladder Match	.30	.75
74	Johnny Gargano	.60	1.50
75	Isaiah Swerve Scott	.40	1.00
76	Austin Theory	.50	1.25
77	Ilja Dragunov	.50	1.25
78	Austin Theory	.50	1.25
79	Imperium	.30	.75
80	Undisputed ERA	.75	2.00
81	Keith Lee	.30	.75
82	Tyler Bate	.50	1.25
83	Gallus	.40	1.00
84	WALTER	.60	1.50
85	Undisputed ERA	.75	2.00
86	BroserWeights	.60	1.50
87	Johnny Gargano	.60	1.50
88	Grizzled Young Veterans	.40	1.00
89	Isaiah Swerve Scott	.40	1.00
90	Imperium	.75	2.00
91	Grizzled Young Veterans	.40	1.00
92	BroserWeights	.60	1.50
93	Keith Lee	.60	1.50
94	Jordan Devlin	.30	.75
95	Travis Banks	.30	.75
96	Finn Balor	.75	2.00
97	Jordan Devlin	.40	1.00
98	Imperium	.60	1.50
99	#DIY	.60	1.50
100	BroserWeights	.60	1.50

2020 Topps WWE NXT Autographed Mat Relics

*BLUE/50: .5X TO 1.2X BASIC AUTOS
*SILVER/25: UNPRICED DUE TO SCARCITY
*GOLD/10: UNPRICED DUE TO SCARCITY
*RED/1: UNPRICED DUE TO SCARCITY
STATED ODDS 1:12
STATED PRINT RUN 99 SER.#'d SETS

MRAAC	Adam Cole	20.00	50.00
MRABB	Bianca Belair	15.00	40.00
MRABF	Bobby Fish	12.00	30.00
MRACL	Candice LeRae	25.00	60.00
MRADK	Dakota Kai	30.00	75.00
MRAIS	Io Shirai	30.00	75.00
MRAJG	Johnny Gargano	10.00	25.00
MRAKL	Keith Lee	12.00	30.00
MRAKO	Kyle O'Reilly	10.00	25.00
MRAMR	Matt Riddle	15.00	40.00
MRARR	Rhea Ripley	50.00	100.00
MRATC	Tommaso Ciampa	12.00	30.00
MRATN	Tegan Nox	25.00	60.00
MRAVT	Velveteen Dream	12.00	30.00

2020 Topps WWE NXT Autographed Shirt Relics

*SILVER/25: UNPRICED DUE TO SCARCITY

*GOLD/10: UNPRICED DUE TO SCARCITY
*RED/1: UNPRICED DUE TO SCARCITY
STATED ODDS 1:33
STATED PRINT RUN 50 SER.#'d SETS

SRAAC	Adam Cole	20.00	50.00
SRABF	Bobby Fish	12.00	30.00
SRAFB	Finn Balor	15.00	40.00
SRAJG	Johnny Gargano	12.00	30.00
SRAKO	Kyle O'Reilly	10.00	25.00
SRAKU	Kushida	10.00	25.00
SRAMY	Mia Yim	12.00	30.00
SRAT7	Trent Seven	20.00	50.00
SRATC	Tommaso Ciampa	10.00	25.00
SRAVD	Velveteen Dream		

2020 Topps WWE NXT Called Up

COMPLETE SET (9) 6.00 15.00
RANDOMLY INSERTED INTO PACKS

CU1	Aleister Black	1.50	4.00
CU2	Angelo Dawkins	.75	2.00
CU3	Lacey Evans	2.00	5.00
CU4	Lars Sullivan	.75	2.00
CU5	Montez Ford	.75	2.00
CU6	Nikki Cross	1.50	4.00
CU7	Otis	1.25	3.00
CU8	Ricochet	1.25	3.00
CU9	Tucker	.75	2.00

2020 Topps WWE NXT Called Up Autographs

STATED PRINT RUN 25 SER.#'d SETS

CUAAB	Aleister Black		
CUAAD	Angelo Dawkins		
CUALE	Lacey Evans		
CUAMF	Montez Ford	15.00	40.00
CUANC	Nikki Cross		
CUAOT	Otis		
CUARC	Ricochet		

2020 Topps WWE NXT Dual Autographs

STATED PRINT RUN 25 SER.#'d SETS

DABB	V.Borne/Aliyah	100.00	200.00
DATK	T.Nox/D.Kai	125.00	250.00
DAUE	B.Fish/K.O'Reilly	25.00	60.00

2020 Topps WWE NXT Johnny Gargano Tribute

COMPLETE SET (20) 12.00 30.00
RANDOMLY INSERTED INTO PACKS

JG1	Johnny Gargano	1.50	4.00
JG2	Johnny Gargano	1.50	4.00
JG3	Johnny Gargano	1.50	4.00
JG4	Johnny Gargano	1.50	4.00
JG5	Johnny Gargano	1.50	4.00
JG6	Johnny Gargano	1.50	4.00
JG7	Johnny Gargano	1.50	4.00
JG8	Johnny Gargano	1.50	4.00
JG9	Johnny Gargano	1.50	4.00
JG10	Johnny Gargano	1.50	4.00
JG11	Johnny Gargano	1.50	4.00
JG12	Johnny Gargano	1.50	4.00
JG13	Johnny Gargano	1.50	4.00
JG14	Johnny Gargano	1.50	4.00
JG15	Johnny Gargano	1.50	4.00
JG16	Johnny Gargano	1.50	4.00
JG17	Johnny Gargano	1.50	4.00
JG18	Johnny Gargano	1.50	4.00
JG19	Johnny Gargano	1.50	4.00
JG20	Johnny Gargano	1.50	4.00

2020 Topps WWE NXT Johnny Gargano Tribute Autographs

*GOLD/10: UNPRICED DUE TO SCARCITY
*RED/1: UNPRICED DUE TO SCARCITY
STATED PRINT RUN 25 SER.#'d SETS

JG15	Johnny Gargano	10.00	25.00
JG16	Johnny Gargano	10.00	25.00
JG17	Johnny Gargano	10.00	25.00
JG18	Johnny Gargano	10.00	25.00
JG19	Johnny Gargano	10.00	25.00

2020 Topps WWE NXT Roster

COMPLETE SET (66) 15.00 40.00
RANDOMLY INSERTED INTO PACKS

NXT1	Adam Cole	.75	2.00
NXT2	Aliyah	.60	1.50
NXT3	Angel Garza	.40	1.00
NXT4	Austin Theory	.50	1.25
NXT5	Bianca Belair	.75	2.00
NXT6	Boa	.30	.75
NXT7	Bobby Fish	.30	.75
NXT8	Bronson Reed	.30	.75
NXT9	Cameron Grimes	.30	.75
NXT10	Candice LeRae	1.00	2.50
NXT11	Chelsea Green	1.50	4.00
NXT12	Dakota Kai	.60	1.50
NXT13	Damian Priest	.30	.75
NXT14	Danny Burch	.40	1.00
NXT15	Dexter Lumis	.30	.75
NXT16	Dominik Dijakovic	.30	.75
NXT17	Fandango	.30	.75
NXT18	Finn Balor	.75	2.00
NXT19	Io Shirai	.50	1.25
NXT20	Isaiah "Swerve" Scott	.40	1.00
NXT21	Jaxson Ryker	.40	1.00
NXT22	Jessamyn Duke	.50	1.25
NXT23	Joaquin Wilde	.30	.75
NXT24	Johnny Gargano	.60	1.50
NXT25	Keith Lee	.30	.75
NXT26	Killian Dain	.40	1.00
NXT27	Kona Reeves	.30	.75
NXT28	Kyle O'Reilly	.40	1.00
NXT29	Kushida	.40	1.00
NXT30	Mansoor	.30	.75
NXT31	Marina Shafir	.50	1.25
NXT32	Matt Riddle	.60	1.50
NXT33	Mia Yim	.60	1.50
NXT34	Oney Lorcan	.40	1.00
NXT35	Pete Dunne	.30	.75
NXT36	Raul Mendoza	.30	.75
NXT37	Rhea Ripley	1.25	3.00
NXT38	Roderick Strong	.60	1.50
NXT39	Santana Garrett	.30	.75
NXT40	Shane Thorne	.30	.75
NXT41	Shayna Baszler	1.00	2.50
NXT42	Shotzi Blackheart	1.00	2.50
NXT43	Steve Cutler	.30	.75
NXT44	Tegan Nox	.75	2.00
NXT45	Tommaso Ciampa	.60	1.50
NXT46	Tyler Breeze	.40	1.00
NXT47	Vanessa Borne	.60	1.50
NXT48	Velveteen Dream	.40	1.00
NXT49	Wesley Blake	.40	1.00
NXT50	Xia Li	.60	1.50
NXT51	Alexander Wolfe	.30	.75
NXT52	Fabian Aichner	.30	.75
NXT53	Flash Morgan Webster	.40	1.00
NXT54	Joe Coffey	.30	.75
NXT55	Jordan Devlin	.30	.75
NXT56	Kay Lee Ray	.50	1.25
NXT57	Marcel Barthel	.30	.75
NXT58	Mark Andrews	.30	.75
NXT59	Mark Coffey	.40	1.00
NXT60	Toni Storm	.75	2.00
NXT61	Trent Seven	.30	.75
NXT62	Tyler Bate	.50	1.25
NXT63	WALTER	.60	1.50
NXT64	Wolfgang	.30	.75
NXT65	James Drake	.40	1.00
NXT66	Zack Gibson	.30	.75

2020 Topps WWE NXT Roster Autographs

*BRONZE/99: .5X TO 1.2X BASIC AUTOS
*BLUE/50: .6X TO 1.5X BASIC AUTOS
*SILVER/25: UNPRICED DUE TO SCARCITY
*GOLD/10: UNPRICED DUE TO SCARCITY
*RED/1: UNPRICED DUE TO SCARCITY

AAC	Adam Cole	10.00	25.00
AAG	Angel Garza	6.00	15.00
AAL	Aliyah	10.00	25.00
AAR	Arturo Ruas	6.00	15.00
AAT	Austin Theory	12.00	30.00
ABB	Bianca Belair	20.00	50.00
ABF	Bobby Fish	5.00	12.00
ABL	Shotzi Blackheart	60.00	120.00
ABR	Bronson Reed	10.00	25.00
ACG	Cameron Grimes	6.00	15.00
ACL	Candice LeRae	20.00	50.00
ADD	Dominik Dijakovic	5.00	12.00
ADK	Dakota Kai	15.00	40.00
ADL	Dexter Lumis	20.00	50.00
ADP	Damian Priest	6.00	15.00
AFA	Fabian Aichner	5.00	12.00
AFB	Finn Balor	10.00	25.00
AIO	Io Shirai	20.00	50.00
AIS	Isaiah Swerve Scott	5.00	12.00
AJG	Johnny Gargano	8.00	20.00
AJW	Joaquin Wilde	8.00	20.00
AKC	Kayden Carter	10.00	25.00
AKL	Keith Lee	6.00	15.00
AKU	Kushida	10.00	25.00
AMB	Marcel Barthel	5.00	12.00
AMR	Matt Riddle	15.00	40.00
AMY	Mia Yim	8.00	20.00
AOL	Oney Lorcan	5.00	12.00
ARM	Raul Mendoza	6.00	15.00
ARR	Rhea Ripley	50.00	100.00
ARS	Roderick Strong	5.00	12.00
ATN	Tegan Nox	30.00	75.00
ATO	Tommaso Ciampa	6.00	15.00
AVD	Velveteen Dream	5.00	12.00

2021 Topps WWE NXT

COMPLETE SET (100) 10.00 25.00
*PURPLE: .75X TO 2X BASIC CARDS
*BLUE/50: 1.5X TO 4X BASIC CARDS
*RED/25: 2X TO 5X BASIC CARDS
*GOLD/10: UNPRICED DUE TO SCARCITY
*PLATINUM/1: UNPRICED DUE TO SCARCITY

1	Roderick Strong	.50	1.25
2	Keith Lee	.60	1.50
3	The BroserWeights	.75	2.00
4	Adam Cole	1.00	2.50
5	Johnny Gargano	.60	1.50
6	The BroserWeights	.75	2.00
7	Tommaso Ciampa	.75	2.00
8	Keith Lee	.60	1.50
9	Johnny Gargano	.60	1.50
10	Timothy Thatcher	.30	.75
11	Karrion Kross	1.50	4.00
12	Akira Tozawa	.50	1.25
13	El Hijo	.50	1.25
14	Jake Atlas	.30	.75
15	Kushida	.50	1.25
16	Isaiah "Swerve" Scott	.50	1.25
17	Imperium	.40	1.00
18	Drake Maverick	.40	1.00
19	Keith Lee	.60	1.50
20	Johnny Gargano	.60	1.50
21	Karrion Kross	1.50	4.00
22	Adam Cole	1.00	2.50
23	Akira Tozawa	.40	1.00
24	Kushida	.50	1.25
25	Jake Atlas	.30	.75
26	Imperium	.40	1.00
27	Damian Priest	.75	2.00
28	Riddle	.75	2.00
29	El Hijo	.50	1.25
30	Roderick Strong	.50	1.25
31	Drake Maverick	.50	1.25
32	Tommaso Ciampa	.75	2.00
33	Timothy Thatcher	.30	.75
34	El Hijo	.50	1.25
35	Finn B·lor	.75	2.00
36	Keith Lee	.60	1.50
37	Karrion Kross	1.25	3.00
38	El Hijo	.50	1.25
39	Adam Cole	1.00	2.50
40	Imperium	.40	1.00
41	Karrion Kross	1.25	3.00
42	Dexter Lumis	.30	.75
43	Keith Lee	.60	1.50
44	Dexter Lumis	.30	.75
45	Legado del Fantasma	.50	1.25
46	Keith Lee	.60	1.50
47	Keith Lee	.60	1.50
48	Breezango	.50	1.25
49	Bronson Reed	.40	1.00
50	Karrion Kross	1.25	3.00
51	Imperium	.40	1.00
52	Dexter Lumis	.30	.75
53	Damian Priest	.50	1.25
54	Keith Lee	.60	1.50
55	Imperium	.50	1.25
56	Karrion Kross	1.25	3.00
57	Bronson Reed	.40	1.00
58	Cameron Grimes	.60	1.50
59	Breezango	.50	1.25
60	Finn B·lor	.75	2.00
61	Damian Priest	.50	1.25
62	Karrion Kross	1.25	3.00
63	Karrion Kross	1.50	4.00
64	Breezango	.50	1.25
65	Adam Cole	1.00	2.50
66	Finn B·lor	.75	2.00

67	Breezango	.50	1.25
68	Damian Priest	.50	1.25
69	Damian Priest	.50	1.25
70	Roderick Strong & Danny Burch	.50	1.25
71	Kyle O'Reilly	.50	1.25
72	Damian Priest	.50	1.25
73	Santos Escobar	.50	1.25
74	Finn B·lor	.75	2.00
75	Cameron Grimes	.60	1.50
76	Johnny Gargano	.60	1.50
77	Undisputed ERA	.50	1.25
78	Damian Priest	.50	1.25
79	Legado del Fantasma	.50	1.25
80	Oney Lorcan & Danny Burch	.40	1.00
81	Pete Dunne	.60	1.50
82	Johnny Gargano	.60	1.50
83	Dexter Lumis	.60	1.50
84	Kushida	.50	1.25
85	Leon Ruff	.30	.75
86	Santos Escobar	.50	1.25
87	Oney Lorcan & Danny Burch	.30	.75
88	Damian Priest	.60	1.50
89	Dexter Lumis and Cameron Grimes	.60	1.50
90	Kushida	.50	1.25
91	Tommaso Ciampa	.75	2.00
92	Dexter Lumis	.60	1.50
93	Johnny Gargano	.60	1.50
94	Finn B·lor	1.50	4.00
95	Karrion Kross	1.25	3.00
96	The Way	.60	1.50
97	Kyle O'Reilly	.50	1.25
98	Leon Ruff	.30	.75
99	Damian Priest	1.25	3.00
100	Johnny Gargano	1.25	3.00

2021 Topps WWE NXT Finn Balor Tribute

COMPLETE SET (10) 5.00 12.00
RANDOMLY INSERTED INTO PACKS

FB1	Finn Balor	1.00	2.50
FB2	Finn Balor	1.00	2.50
FB3	Finn Balor	1.00	2.50
FB4	Finn Balor	1.00	2.50
FB5	Finn Balor	1.00	2.50
FB6	Finn Balor	1.00	2.50
FB7	Finn Balor	1.00	2.50
FB8	Finn Balor	1.00	2.50
FB9	Finn Balor	1.00	2.50
FB10	Finn Balor	1.00	2.50

2021 Topps WWE NXT Finn Balor Tribute Autographs

*GOLD/10: UNPRICED DUE TO SCARCITY
*PLATINUM/1: UNPRICED DUE TO SCARCITY
STATED PRINT RUN 25 SER.#'d SETS

FB14	Finn Balor	25.00	60.00
FB15	Finn Balor	25.00	60.00
FB16	Finn Balor	25.00	60.00
FB19	Finn Balor	25.00	60.00
FB20	Finn Balor	25.00	60.00

2021 Topps WWE NXT Migs Media Illustrations

COMPLETE SET (10) 6.00 15.00
RANDOMLY INSERTED INTO PACKS

MM1	Cameron Grimes	1.25	3.00
MM2	Dakota Kai	1.25	3.00
MM3	Damian Priest	1.00	2.50
MM4	Io Shirai	1.25	3.00
MM5	Kushida	1.00	2.50
MM6	Rhea Ripley	2.00	5.00
MM7	Santos Escobar	1.00	2.50
MM8	Bronson Reed	.75	2.00
MM9	Tegan Nox	1.50	4.00
MM10	Timothy Thatcher	.60	1.50

2021 Topps WWE NXT NXT Alumni

COMPLETE SET (9) 5.00 12.00
RANDOMLY INSERTED INTO PACKS

NA1	Angel Garza	.75	2.00
NA2	Bianca Belair	1.50	4.00
NA3	Jaxson Ryker	.60	1.50
NA4	Keith Lee	1.25	3.00
NA5	Riddle	1.50	4.00
NA6	Riddick Moss	.75	2.00
NA7	Shayna Baszler	1.25	3.00
NA8	Damian Priest	1.00	2.50
NA9	Rhea Ripley	2.00	5.00

2021 Topps WWE NXT NXT Alumni Autographs

*GOLD/10: UNPRICED DUE TO SCARCITY
*PLATINUM/1: UNPRICED DUE TO SCARCITY
RANDOMLY INSERTED INTO PACKS

NAAG	Angel Garza	8.00	20.00
NAJR	Jaxson Ryker	8.00	20.00
NAKL	Keith Lee	10.00	25.00
NAMR	Riddle	15.00	40.00
NARM	Riddick Moss	20.00	50.00
NASB	Shayna Baszler	15.00	40.00

2021 Topps WWE NXT Tag Team Autographs

*GOLD/10: UNPRICED DUE TO SCARCITY
*PLATINUM/1: UNPRICED DUE TO SCARCITY
STATED PRINT RUN 25 SER.#'d SETS

DABZ	Tyler Breeze/Fandango	15.00	40.00
DAER	Chase Parker/Matt Martel	50.00	100.00
DAIP	Marcel Barthel/Fabian Aichner	30.00	75.00
DAJC	Candice LeRae/Johnny Gargano	100.00	200.00
DAKS	Scarlett/Karrion Kross	250.00	500.00
DALF	Joaquin Wilde/Raul Mendoza		
DAOD	Danny Burch/Oney Lorcan	30.00	75.00
DATN	Kacy Catanzaro/Kayden Carter	100.00	200.00
DAUE	Bobby Fish/Kyle O'Reilly	20.00	50.00
DAGYV	James Drake/Zack Gibson	15.00	40.00

2021 Topps WWE NXT We Are NXT

RANDOMLY INSERTED INTO PACKS

NXT1	Adam Cole	1.25	3.00
NXT2	Aliyah	.75	2.00
NXT3	Austin Theory	.75	2.00
NXT4	Arturo Ruas	.40	1.00
NXT5	Bobby Fish	.50	1.25
NXT6	Bronson Reed	.50	1.25
NXT7	Cameron Grimes	.75	2.00
NXT8	Candice LeRae	1.50	4.00
NXT9	Chase Parker	.40	1.00
NXT10	Dakota Kai	.75	2.00
NXT11	Danny Burch	.50	1.25
NXT12	Dave Mastiff	.40	1.00
NXT13	Dexter Lumis	.40	1.00
NXT14	Drake Maverick	.40	1.00
NXT15	Fabian Aichner	.50	1.25
NXT16	Fandango	.60	1.50
NXT17	Finn Balor	1.00	2.50
NXT18	Flash Morgan Webster	.50	1.25
NXT19	Ilja Dragunov	.40	1.00
NXT20	Indi Hartwell	1.25	3.00
NXT21	Io Shirai	.75	2.00
NXT22	Isaiah Swerve Scott	.60	1.50
NXT23	Jake Atlas	.40	1.00
NXT24	James Drake	.40	1.00
NXT25	Jessi Kamea	.75	2.00
NXT26	Joaquin Wilde	.60	1.50
NXT27	Johnny Gargano	.75	2.00
NXT28	Kacy Catanzaro	.75	2.00
NXT29	Karrion Kross	1.50	4.00
NXT30	Kay Lee Ray	1.00	2.50
NXT31	Kayden Carter	.75	2.00
NXT32	Killian Dain	.40	1.00
NXT33	Kushida	.60	1.50
NXT34	Kyle O'Reilly	.60	1.50
NXT35	Malcolm Bivens	.40	1.00
NXT36	Marcel Barthel	.50	1.25
NXT37	Marina Shafir	.75	2.00
NXT38	Matt Martel	.50	1.25
NXT39	Noam Dar	.50	1.25
NXT40	Oney Lorcan	.40	1.00
NXT41	Pete Dunne	.75	2.00
NXT42	Piper Niven	.60	1.50
NXT43	Raquel Gonzalez	1.00	2.50
NXT44	Raul Mendoza	.60	1.50
NXT45	Ridge Holland	.40	1.00
NXT46	Robert Stone	.40	1.00
NXT47	Roderick Strong	.60	1.50
NXT48	Santos Escobar	.60	1.50
NXT49	Saurav	.40	1.00
NXT50	Scarlett	2.00	5.00
NXT51	Shotzi Blackheart	1.50	4.00
NXT52	Tegan Nox	1.00	2.50
NXT53	Ashante Thee Adonis	.50	1.25
NXT54	Timothy Thatcher	.40	1.00
NXT55	Tommaso Ciampa	1.00	2.50
NXT56	Toni Storm	1.25	3.00
NXT57	Trent Seven	.50	1.25
NXT58	Tyler Bate	.50	1.25
NXT59	Tyler Breeze	.50	1.25
NXT60	WALTER	1.00	2.50
NXT61	Xia Li	.75	2.00
NXT62	Zack Gibson	.40	1.00

2021 Topps WWE NXT We Are NXT Autographs

*GREEN/99: .5X TO 1.2X BASIC AUTOS
*PURPLE/75: .6X TO 1.5X BASIC AUTOS
*BLUE/50: .75X TO 2X BASIC AUTOS
*RED/25: 1.2X TO 3X BASIC AUTOS
*GOLD/10: UNPRICED DUE TO SCARCITY
*PLATINUM/1: UNPRICED DUE TO SCARCITY
*P.P.BLACK/1: UNPRICED DUE TO SCARCITY
*P.P.CYAN/1: UNPRICED DUE TO SCARCITY
*P.P.MAGENTA/1: UNPRICED DUE TO SCARCITY
*P.P.YELLOW/1: UNPRICED DUE TO SCARCITY
RANDOMLY INSERTED INTO PACKS

AAC	Adam Cole		
AAL	Aliyah		
AAT	Austin Theory	10.00	25.00
ABA	Marcel Barthel	6.00	15.00
ABF	Bobby Fish	5.00	12.00
ABR	Bronson Reed	10.00	25.00
ACG	Cameron Grimes	6.00	15.00
ACL	Candice LeRae		
ACP	Chase Parker	8.00	20.00
ADB	Danny Burch		
ADK	Dakota Kai	15.00	40.00
ADL	Dexter Lumis	10.00	25.00
ADM	Dave Mastiff	6.00	15.00
ADR	Drake Maverick	5.00	12.00
AFA	Fabian Aichner	6.00	15.00
AFD	Fandango	5.00	12.00
AFS	Kayden Carter	8.00	20.00
AID	Ilja Dragunov	15.00	40.00
AIH	Indi Hartwell	20.00	50.00
AIS	Io Shirai	15.00	40.00
AJA	Jake Atlas	5.00	12.00
AJD	James Drake	5.00	12.00
AJG	Johnny Gargano		
AJK	Jessi Kamea	10.00	25.00
AJW	Joaquin Wilde	5.00	12.00
AKC	Kacy Catanzaro	15.00	40.00
AKD	Killian Dain		
AKK	Karrion Kross	25.00	60.00
AKS	Kushida	8.00	20.00
AMM	Matt Martel	6.00	15.00
AOL	Oney Lorcan		
APD	Pete Dunne	6.00	15.00
APN	Piper Niven		
ARE	Robert Stone	4.00	12.00
ARG	Raquel Gonzalez	30.00	75.00
ARH	Ridge Holland	6.00	15.00
ARM	Raul Mendoza	5.00	12.00
ARS	Roderick Strong	8.00	20.00
ASB	Shotzi Blackheart	20.00	50.00
ASC	Scarlett		
ASE	Santos Escobar	5.00	12.00
ASW	Isaiah Swerve Scott	5.00	12.00
AT7	Trent Seven	6.00	15.00
ATB	Tyler Breeze	5.00	10.00
ATC	Tommaso Ciampa		
ATM	Ashante Thee Adonis	5.00	12.00
ATN	Tegan Nox	10.00	25.00
ATO	Toni Storm	25.00	60.00
ATT	Timothy Thatcher	6.00	15.00
ATY	Tyler Bate		
AWT	WALTER	10.00	25.00
AXL	Xia Li	10.00	25.00
AZG	Zack Gibson	6.00	15.00
AKLR	Kay Lee Ray		
AKOR	Kyle O'Reilly	6.00	15.00

2019 Topps WWE RAW

COMPLETE SET (90) 10.00 25.00
*BRONZE: .6X TO 1.5X BASIC CARDS
*BLUE/99: .75X TO 2X BASIC CARDS
*SILVER/25: 2X TO 5X BASIC CARDS
*GOLD/10: UNPRICED DUE TO SCARCITY
*BLACK/1: UNPRICED DUE TO SCARCITY
*P.P.BLACK/1: UNPRICED DUE TO SCARCITY
*P.P.CYAN/1: UNPRICED DUE TO SCARCITY
*P.P.MAGENTA/1: UNPRICED DUE TO SCARCITY
*P.P.YELLOW/1: UNPRICED DUE TO SCARCITY

1	Akam	.25	.60
2	Alexa Bliss	1.25	3.00
3	Alicia Fox	.50	1.25
4	Apollo Crews	.30	.75
5	Baron Corbin	.40	1.00

6 Batista .60 1.50
7 Bayley .50 1.25
8 Bo Dallas .30 .75
9 Bobby Lashley .50 1.25
10 Bobby Roode .50 1.25
11 Booker T .60 1.50
12 Braun Strowman .60 1.50
13 Bray Wyatt .60 1.50
14 Brie Bella .60 1.50
15 Brock Lesnar 1.00 2.50
16 Chad Gable .25 .60
17 Charly Caruso .40 1.00
18 Corey Graves .30 .75
19 Curt Hawkins .25 .60
20 Curtis Axel .30 .75
21 Dana Brooke .50 1.25
22 Dash Wilder .25 .60
23 David Otunga .25 .60
24 Dean Ambrose .60 1.50
25 Dolph Ziggler .50 1.25
26 Drake Maverick .25 .60
27 Drew McIntyre .30 .75
28 Elias .50 1.25
29 Ember Moon .60 1.50
30 Fandango .25 .60
31 Finn Balor .60 1.50
32 Gran Metalik .25 .60
33 Heath Slater .25 .60
34 Jason Jordan .30 .75
35 Jinder Mahal .50 1.25
36 Jonathan Coachman .25 .60
37 John Cena 1.00 2.50
38 JoJo .40 1.00
39 Kalisto .25 .60
40 Kane .40 1.00
41 Kayla Braxton .40 1.00
42 Kevin Owens .60 1.50
43 Konnor .25 .60
44 Kurt Angle .50 1.25
45 Lince Dorado .25 .60
46 Lio Rush .30 .75
47 Liv Morgan .75 2.00
48 Michael Cole .25 .60
49 Mickie James .60 1.50
50 Mike Rome .30 .75
51 Mojo Rawley .30 .75
52 Natalya .50 1.25
53 Nia Jax .50 1.25
54 Nikki Bella .60 1.50
55 No Way Jose .30 .75
56 Paul Heyman .30 .75
57 Renee Young .40 1.00
58 Rezar .25 .60
59 Rhyno .25 .60
60 Roman Reigns .60 1.50
61 Ronda Rousey 1.25 3.00
62 Ruby Riott .50 1.25
63 Sami Zayn .50 1.25
64 Samir Singh .25 .60
65 Sarah Logan .30 .75
66 Sasha Banks 1.00 2.50
67 Scott Dawson .25 .60
68 Seth Rollins .60 1.50
69 Stephanie McMahon .60 1.50
70 Sunil Singh .25 .60
71 Titus O'Neil .30 .75
72 Tyler Breeze .30 .75
73 Viktor .25 .60
74 Zack Ryder .30 .75
75 Akira Tozawa .25 .60
76 Ariya Daivari .25 .60
77 Buddy Murphy .30 .75
78 Cedric Alexander .25 .60
79 Drew Gulak .25 .60
80 Gentleman Jack Gallagher .30 .75
81 Hideo Itami .25 .60
82 Maria Kanellis .60 1.50
83 Mark Andrews .25 .60
84 Mike Kanellis .25 .60
85 Nigel McGuinness .25 .60
86 Noam Dar .25 .60
87 The Brian Kendrick .40 1.00
88 TJP .40 1.00
89 Tony Nese .25 .60
90 Vic Joseph RC .25 .60

2019 Topps WWE RAW Autographed Commemorative Intercontinental Championship Relics

STATED PRINT RUN 10 SER.#'d SETS
ICRAHH Triple H
ICRASM Shawn Michaels

2019 Topps WWE RAW Autographed Commemorative RAW Championship Relics

STATED PRINT RUN 10 SER.#'d SETS
UNPRICED DUE TO SCARCITY
RACAB Alexa Bliss
RACBL Bayley
RACBS Braun Strowman
RACCF Charlotte Flair
RACDA Dean Ambrose
RACFB Finn Balor
RACKO Kevin Owens
RACRRR Ronda Rousey
RACSB Sasha Banks
RACSR Seth Rollins
RACTM The Miz

2019 Topps WWE RAW Autographed Mat Relics

STATED PRINT RUN 10 SER.#'d SETS
UNPRICED DUE TO SCARCITY
DMARAB Aleister Black
DMARAJ AJ Styles
DMARAK Asuka
DMARAS Shayna Baszler
DMARBL Bobby Lashley
DMARBR Bobby Roode
DMARBS Braun Strowman
DMARCF Charlotte Flair
DMAREM Ember Moon
DMARFB Finn Balor
DMARJG Johnny Gargano
DMARJN Natalya
DMARKK Kofi Kingston
DMARKO Kevin Owens
DMARKR Kyle O'Reilly
DMARLK Becky Lynch
DMARMB Alexa Bliss
DMARNC Nikki Cross
DMARNM Naomi
DMARRC Ricochet
DMARRD Rusev
DMARRS Roderick Strong
DMARSB Sasha Banks
DMARSJ Samoa Joe
DMARSN Shinsuke Nakamura
DMARSR Seth Rollins
DMARSZ Sami Zayn
DMARTC Tomasso Ciampa
DMARTM The Miz
DMARVD Velveteen Dream
DMARRRR Ronda Rousey

2019 Topps WWE RAW Autographed Shirt Relics

STATED PRINT RUN 10 SER.#'d SETS
UNPRICED DUE TO SCARCITY
SARAB Alexa Bliss
SARDA Dean Ambrose
SARFB Finn Balor
SARKO Kevin Owens
SARRY Renee Young
SARSR Seth Rollins
SARWJ No Way Jose

2019 Topps WWE RAW Autographed Women's Revolution Relics

STATED PRINT RUN 10 SER.#'d SETS
UNPRICED DUE TO SCARCITY
DRACAB Alexa Bliss
DRACSB Sasha Banks
DRACRRR Ronda Rousey

2019 Topps WWE RAW Autographs

*BLUE/50: .5X TO 1.2X BASIC AUTOS
*SILVER/25: .6X TO 1.5X BASIC AUTOS
*GOLD/10: UNPRICED DUE TO SCARCITY
*BLACK/1: UNPRICED DUE TO SCARCITY
STATED PRINT RUN 99 SER.#'d SETS
AAB Alexa Bliss 25.00 60.00
AAC Apollo Crews
ABC Baron Corbin 5.00 12.00
ABL Bobby Lashley 5.00 12.00
ABR Bobby Roode 4.00 10.00
ABS Braun Strowman/94 5.00 12.00
ABT Booker T 5.00 12.00
ACA Cedric Alexander 4.00 10.00
ACC Charly Caruso 6.00 15.00
ACG Chad Gable 3.00 8.00
ADA Dean Ambrose 6.00 15.00
ADB Dana Brooke 6.00 15.00
ADM Drew McIntyre 5.00 12.00
AEM Ember Moon/63 8.00 20.00
AFB Finn Balor/88 12.00 30.00
AGR Corey Graves 6.00 15.00
AHO Hideo Itami 3.00 8.00
AJG Gentleman Jack Gallagher 12.00 30.00
AJJ Jason Jordan/77 5.00 12.00
AJN Natalya
AKA Kurt Angle 8.00 20.00
AKT Kalisto 4.00 10.00
ALD Lince Dorado/98 10.00 25.00
ALR Lio Rush 6.00 15.00
ARY Renee Young 6.00 12.00
ASL Sarah Logan 6.00 15.00
ASR Seth Rollins 8.00 20.00
ATB Tyler Breeze 4.00 10.00
ATN Titus O'Neil 4.00 10.00

2019 Topps WWE RAW Commemorative Intercontinental Championship Relics

RANDOMLY INSERTED INTO PACKS
ICRED Edge
ICRHH Triple H
ICRRM The Rock
ICRRR Razor Ramon
ICRSM Shawn Michaels

2019 Topps WWE RAW Commemorative RAW Championship Relics

*BRONZE/99: SAME VALUE AS BASIC
*BLUE/50: .5X TO 1.2X BASIC MEM
*SILVER/25: .6X TO 1.5X BASIC MEM
*GOLD/10: UNPRICED DUE TO SCARCITY
*BLACK/1: UNPRICED DUE TO SCARCITY
RANDOMLY INSERTED INTO PACKS
RCAB Alexa Bliss 10.00 25.00
RCBC Karl Anderson/Luke Gallows 2.00 5.00
RCBD Roman Reigns 5.00 12.00
RCBL Bayley 5.00 12.00
RCBS Braun Strowman 2.50 6.00
RCBT Curtis Axel/Bo Dallas 2.50 6.00
RCCF Charlotte Flair 4.00 10.00
RCDA Dean Ambrose 5.00 12.00
RCDZ Dolph Ziggler 2.50 6.00
RCFB Finn Balor 3.00 8.00
RCGB Goldberg 6.00 15.00
RCKO Kevin Owens 2.00 5.00
RCNJ Nia Jax 2.00 5.00
RCRR Roman Reigns 5.00 12.00
RCSB Sasha Banks 6.00 15.00
RCSD Seth Rollins/Dean Ambrose 3.00 8.00
RCSR Seth Rollins 4.00 10.00
RCTB Cesaro/Sheamus 2.00 5.00
RCTM The Miz 2.00 5.00
RCZM Drew McIntyre/Dolph Ziggler 2.50 6.00
RCRRR Ronda Rousey 12.00 30.00

2019 Topps WWE RAW Hometown Heroes

COMPLETE SET (48) 12.00 30.00
RANDOMLY INSERTED INTO PACKS
HH1 Alexa Bliss 2.00 5.00
HH2 Apollo Crews .50 1.25
HH3 Baron Corbin .60 1.50
HH4 Bayley .75 2.00
HH5 Big Show .60 1.50
HH6 Bo Dallas .50 1.25
HH7 Bobby Lashley .75 2.00
HH8 Bobby Roode .75 2.00
HH9 Booker T 1.00 2.50
HH10 Curtis Axel .50 1.25
HH11 Dana Brooke .75 2.00
HH12 Dean Ambrose 1.00 2.50
HH13 Dolph Ziggler .75 2.00
HH14 Drew McIntyre .50 1.25
HH15 Elias .75 2.00
HH16 Ember Moon 1.00 2.50
HH17 Finn Balor 1.00 2.50
HH18 Heath Slater .40 1.00
HH19 Jason Jordan .50 1.25
HH20 Jinder Mahal .75 2.00
HH21 John Cena 1.50 4.00

HH22	Kevin Owens	1.00	2.50
HH23	Liv Morgan	1.25	3.00
HH24	Mickie James	1.00	2.50
HH25	Mojo Rawley	.50	1.25
HH26	Natalya	.75	2.00
HH27	Nia Jax	.75	2.00
HH28	No Way Jose	.50	1.25
HH29	Lince Dorado	.40	1.00
HH30	Lio Rush	.50	1.25
HH31	Rhyno	.40	1.00
HH32	Roman Reigns	1.00	2.50
HH33	Ronda Rousey	2.00	5.00
HH34	Ruby Riott	.75	2.00
HH35	Sarah Logan	.50	1.25
HH36	Sasha Banks	1.50	4.00
HH37	Seth Rollins	1.00	2.50
HH38	Titus O'Neil	.50	1.25
HH39	Zack Ryder	.50	1.25
HH40	Buddy Murphy	.50	1.25
HH41	Cedric Alexander	.40	1.00
HH42	Drew Gulak	.40	1.00
HH43	Gentleman Jack Gallagher	.50	1.25
HH44	Gran Metalik	.40	1.00
HH45	Hideo Itami	.40	1.00
HH46	Kalisto	.40	1.00
HH47	Mark Andrews	.40	1.00
HH48	TJP	.60	1.50

2019 Topps WWE RAW Image Variations

RANDOMLY INSERTED INTO PACKS

IVAB	Alexa Bliss	30.00	75.00
IVAC	Apollo Crews	2.50	6.00
IVBL	Bobby Lashley	12.00	30.00
IVBR	Bobby Roode		
IVBY	Bayley	8.00	20.00
IVDG	Drew Gulak		
IVDM	Drew McIntyre	3.00	8.00
IVDZ	Dolph Ziggler		
IVEM	Ember Moon	4.00	10.00
IVFB	The Demon Finn Balor	15.00	40.00
IVJN	Natalya	5.00	12.00
IVKO	Kevin Owens	4.00	10.00
IVLL	Kalisto	2.50	6.00
IVLR	Lio Rush	3.00	8.00
IVMK	Mike Kanellis	4.00	10.00
IVMR	Mojo Rawley	4.00	10.00
IVNJ	Nia Jax	4.00	10.00
IVRR	Roman Reigns	6.00	15.00
IVRS	Drake Maverick	6.00	15.00
IVSB	Sasha Banks	12.00	30.00
IVSR	Seth Rollins	5.00	12.00
IVSZ	Sami Zayn	3.00	8.00
IVTJ	TJP	5.00	12.00
IVZR	Zack Ryder	8.00	20.00

2019 Topps WWE RAW Intercontinental Champions Autographs

*GOLD/10: UNPRICED DUE TO SCARCITY
STATED PRINT RUN 25 SER.#'d SETS

ICAHH	Triple H	100.00	200.00
ICASM	Shawn Michaels	50.00	100.00

2019 Topps WWE RAW Kiss

*SILVER/25: .6X TO 1.5X BASIC KISS
*GOLD/10: UNPRICED DUE TO SCARCITY
*BLACK/1: UNPRICED DUE TO SCARCITY
STATED PRINT RUN 50 SER.#'d SETS

KCAF	Alicia Fox	15.00	40.00
KCEM	Ember Moon	15.00	40.00
KCNJ	Nia Jax	12.00	30.00

2019 Topps WWE RAW Kiss Autographs

*GOLD/10: UNPRICED DUE TO SCARCITY
*BLACK/1: UNPRICED DUE TO SCARCITY
STATED PRINT RUN 25 SER.#'d SETS

KARAF	Alicia Fox	30.00	75.00
KARMJ	Mickie James	60.00	120.00
KARNJ	Nia Jax	20.00	50.00

2019 Topps WWE RAW Legends of RAW

COMPLETE SET (20) 6.00 15.00
RANDOMLY INSERTED INTO PACKS

LR1	Batista	.60	1.50
LR2	Bret Hitman Hart	.60	1.50
LR3	Edge	.60	1.50
LR4	Faarooq	.40	1.00
LR5	Goldberg	.75	2.00
LR6	Jerry The King Lawler	.50	1.25
LR7	Ken Shamrock	.40	1.00
LR8	Lita	.60	1.50
LR9	Mr. Perfect	.40	1.00
LR10	Mark Henry	.30	.75
LR11	Mankind	.50	1.25
LR12	Sycho Sid	.25	.60
LR13	Rikishi	.25	.60
LR14	Ric Flair	.75	2.00
LR15	Road Dogg	.25	.60
LR16	Shawn Michaels	.60	1.50
LR17	Stone Cold Steve Austin	1.25	3.00
LR18	Trish Stratus	1.25	3.00
LR19	Vader	.30	.75
LR20	X-Pac	.25	.60

2019 Topps WWE RAW Mat Relics

SEMISTARS 2.00 5.00
UNLISTED STARS 2.50 6.00
*BRONZE/99: .5X TO 1.2X BASIC MEM
*BLUE/50: .6X TO 1.5X BASIC MEM
*SILVER/25: .75X TO 2X BASIC MEM
*GOLD/10: UNPRICED DUE TO SCARCITY
*BLACK/1: UNPRICED DUE TO SCARCITY
RANDOMLY INSERTED INTO PACKS

DMRAB	Aleister Black	1.50	4.00
DMRAJ	AJ Styles	3.00	8.00
DMRAK	Asuka	6.00	15.00
DMRAS	Shayna Baszler	4.00	10.00
DMRBL	Bobby Lashley	1.50	4.00
DMRBR	Bobby Roode	2.50	6.00
DMRBS	Braun Strowman	2.00	5.00
DMRCF	Charlotte Flair	4.00	10.00
DMRCM	Carmella	5.00	12.00
DMRDB	Daniel Bryan	2.50	6.00
DMRDN	Danny Burch	2.50	6.00
DMREM	Ember Moon	3.00	8.00
DMRFB	Finn Balor	4.00	10.00
DMRJG	Johnny Gargano	2.00	5.00
DMRJN	Natalya	3.00	8.00
DMRKK	Kofi Kingston	3.00	8.00
DMRKO	Kevin Owens	2.50	6.00
DMRKR	Kyle O'Reilly	3.00	8.00
DMRLD	Lana	2.50	6.00
DMRLK	Becky Lynch	6.00	15.00
DMRLS	Lars Sullivan	1.50	4.00
DMRMB	Alexa Bliss	12.00	30.00
DMRNC	Nikki Cross	1.50	4.00
DMRNJ	Nia Jax	2.00	5.00
DMRNM	Naomi	2.50	6.00
DMROL	Oney Lorcan	2.00	5.00
DMRRC	Ricochet	3.00	8.00
DMRRD	Rusev	2.50	6.00
DMRRR	Roman Reigns	4.00	10.00
DMRRS	Roderick Strong	2.00	5.00
DMRSB	Sasha Banks	8.00	20.00
DMRSJ	Samoa Joe	2.00	5.00
DMRSN	Shinsuke Nakamura	3.00	8.00
DMRSR	Seth Rollins	4.00	10.00
DMRSZ	Sami Zayn	2.00	5.00
DMRTC	Tommaso Ciampa	2.00	5.00
DMRTM	The Miz	2.50	6.00
DMRVD	Velveteen Dream	2.00	5.00
DMRWE	Elias	2.00	5.00
DMRRRR	Ronda Rousey	10.00	25.00

2019 Topps WWE RAW Shirt Relics

*BRONZE/99: .5X TO 1.2X BASIC MEM
*BLUE/50: .6X TO 1.5X BASIC MEM
*SILVER/25: .75X TO 2X BASIC MEM
*GOLD/10: UNPRICED DUE TO SCARCITY
*BLACK/1: UNPRICED DUE TO SCARCITY
STATED PRINT RUN 199 SER.#'d SETS

SRAB	Alexa Bliss	15.00	40.00
SRDA	Dean Ambrose	6.00	15.00
SREL	Elias	4.00	10.00
SRFB	Finn Balor	8.00	20.00
SRKO	Kevin Owens	3.00	8.00
SRRR	Roman Reigns	5.00	15.00
SRSR	Seth Rollins	6.00	15.00
SRWJ	No Way Jose	3.00	6.00

2019 Topps WWE RAW Triple Autographs

*BLACK/1: UNPRICED DUE TO SCARCITY
STATED PRINT RUN 10 SER.#'d SETS
UNPRICED DUE TO SCARCITY

TAAB Bliss/Fox/James
TARS Morgan/Riott/Logan

2019 Topps WWE RAW Women's Revolution Autographs

*GOLD/10: UNPRICED DUE TO SCARCITY
*BLACK/1: UNPRICED DUE TO SCARCITY
STATED ODDS

WABL	Bayley	20.00	50.00
WARR	Ronda Rousey		
WASB	Sasha Banks	30.00	75.00

2019 Topps WWE RAW Women's Revolution Relics

DRCAB Alexa Bliss
DRCNJ Nia Jax
DRCSB Sasha Banks

2009 Topps WWE Rivals Stickers

1	Emblem WWE	.12	.30
2	WWE 1	.12	.30
3	WWE 2		.30
4	John Cena	.75	2.00
5	John Cena	.75	2.00
6	John Cena	.75	2.00
7	John Cena	.75	2.00
8	John Cena	.75	2.00
9	John Cena	.75	2.00
10	John Cena	.75	2.00
11	John Cena	.75	2.00
12	John Cena	.75	2.00
13	John Cena	.75	2.00
14	Edge	.50	1.25
15	Edge	.50	1.25
16	Edge	.50	1.25
17	Edge	.50	1.25
18	Edge	.50	1.25
19	Edge	.50	1.25
20	Edge	.50	1.25
21	Edge	.50	1.25
22	Edge	.50	1.25
23	Edge	.50	1.25
24	Kane	.50	1.25
25	Kane	.50	1.25
26	Kane	.50	1.25
27	Kane	.50	1.25
28	Kane	.50	1.25
29	The Miz	.20	.50
30	The Miz	.20	.50
31	The Miz	.20	.50
32	The Miz	.20	.50
33	The Miz	.20	.50
34	Mr. Kennedy	.30	.75
35	Mr. Kennedy	.30	.75
36	Mr. Kennedy	.30	.75
37	Mr. Kennedy	.30	.75
38	Mr. Kennedy	.30	.75
39	William Regal	.30	.75
40	William Regal	.30	.75
41	William Regal	.30	.75
42	William Regal	.30	.75
43	William Regal	.30	.75
44	Chavo Guerrero	.20	.50
45	Chavo Guerrero	.20	.50
46	Chavo Guerrero	.20	.50
47	Chavo Guerrero	.20	.50
48	Chavo Guerrero	.20	.50
49	Chavo Guerrero	.20	.50
50	Chavo Guerrero	.20	.50
51	Chavo Guerrero	.20	.50
52	Chavo Guerrero	.20	.50
53	Chavo Guerrero	.20	.50
54	CM Punk	.20	.50
55	CM Punk	.20	.50
56	CM Punk	.20	.50
57	CM Punk	.20	.50
58	CM Punk	.20	.50
59	CM Punk	.20	.50
60	CM Punk	.20	.50
61	CM Punk	.20	.50
62	CM Punk	.20	.50
63	CM Punk	.20	.50
64	The Great Khali	.12	.30
65	The Great Khali	.12	.30
66	The Great Khali	.12	.30
67	The Great Khali	.12	.30
68	The Great Khali	.12	.30
69	Finlay & Hornswoggle	.20	.50
70	Finlay & Hornswoggle	.20	.50
71	Finlay & Hornswoggle	.20	.50
72	Finlay & Hornswoggle	.20	.50

73 Finlay & Hornswoggle	.20	.50
74 Kofi Kingston	.12	.30
75 Kofi Kingston	.12	.30
76 Kofi Kingston	.12	.30
77 Kofi Kingston	.12	.30
78 Kofi Kingston	.12	.30
79 Carlito	.30	.75
80 Carlito	.30	.75
81 Carlito	.30	.75
82 Carlito	.30	.75
83 Carlito	.30	.75
84 Jeff Hardy	.50	1.25
85 Jeff Hardy	.50	1.25
86 Jeff Hardy	.50	1.25
87 Jeff Hardy	.50	1.25
88 Jeff Hardy	.50	1.25
89 Jeff Hardy	.50	1.25
90 Jeff Hardy	.50	1.25
91 Jeff Hardy	.50	1.25
92 Jeff Hardy	.50	1.25
93 Jeff Hardy	.50	1.25
94 John Morrison	.20	.50
95 John Morrison	.20	.50
96 John Morrison	.20	.50
97 John Morrison	.20	.50
98 John Morrison	.20	.50
99 John Morrison	.20	.50
100 John Morrison	.20	.50
101 John Morrison	.20	.50
102 John Morrison	.20	.50
103 John Morrison	.20	.50
104 Shawn Michaels	.75	2.00
105 Shawn Michaels	.75	2.00
106 Shawn Michaels	.75	2.00
107 Shawn Michaels	.75	2.00
108 Shawn Michaels	.75	2.00
109 Vladimir Kozlov	.20	.50
110 Vladimir Kozlov	.20	.50
111 Vladimir Kozlov	.20	.50
112 Vladimir Kozlov	.20	.50
113 Vladimir Kozlov	.20	.50
114 Big Show	.30	.75
115 Big Show	.30	.75
116 Big Show	.30	.75
117 Big Show	.30	.75
118 Big Show	.30	.75
119 JBL	.20	.50
120 JBL	.20	.50
121 JBL	.20	.50
122 JBL	.20	.50
123 JBL	.20	.50
124 Beth Phoenix	.60	1.50
125 Beth Phoenix	.60	1.50
126 Maria	.50	1.25
127 Maria	.50	1.25
128 Candice	.60	1.50
129 Melina	.50	1.25
130 Mickie James	.60	1.50
131 Candice	.60	1.50
132 Melina	.50	1.25
133 Mickie James	.60	1.50
134 Matt Hardy	.50	1.25
135 Matt Hardy	.50	1.25
136 Matt Hardy	.50	1.25
137 Matt Hardy	.50	1.25
138 Matt Hardy	.50	1.25
139 Matt Hardy	.50	1.25
140 Matt Hardy	.50	1.25
141 Matt Hardy	.50	1.25
142 Matt Hardy	.50	1.25
143 Matt Hardy	.50	1.25
144 MVP	.20	.50
145 MVP	.20	.50
146 MVP	.20	.50
147 MVP	.20	.50
148 MVP	.20	.50
149 Chris Jericho	.30	.75
150 Chris Jericho	.30	.75
151 Chris Jericho	.30	.75
152 Chris Jericho	.30	.75
153 Chris Jericho	.30	.75
154 Cody Rhodes & Ted Dibiase	.20	.50
155 Cody Rhodes & Ted Dibiase	.20	.50
156 Cody Rhodes & Ted Dibiase	.20	.50
157 Cody Rhodes & Ted Dibiase	.20	.50
158 Cody Rhodes & Ted Dibiase	.20	.50
159 Cryme Tyme	.12	.30
160 Cryme Tyme	.12	.30
161 Cryme Tyme	.12	.30
162 Cryme Tyme	.12	.30
163 Cryme Tyme	.12	.30
164 Triple H	.75	2.00
165 Triple H	.75	2.00
166 Triple H	.75	2.00
167 Triple H	.75	2.00
168 Triple H	.75	2.00
169 Triple H	.75	2.00
170 Triple H	.75	2.00
171 Triple H	.75	2.00
172 Triple H	.75	2.00
173 Triple H	.75	2.00
174 Rey Mysterio	.30	.75
175 Rey Mysterio	.30	.75
176 Rey Mysterio	.30	.75
177 Rey Mysterio	.30	.75
178 Rey Mysterio	.30	.75
179 Rey Mysterio	.30	.75
180 Rey Mysterio	.30	.75
181 Rey Mysterio	.30	.75
182 Rey Mysterio	.30	.75
183 Rey Mysterio	.30	.75
184 Shelton Benjamin	.12	.30
185 Shelton Benjamin	.12	.30
186 Shelton Benjamin	.12	.30
187 Shelton Benjamin	.12	.30
188 Shelton Benjamin	.12	.30
189 Tommy Dreamer	.12	.30
190 Tommy Dreamer	.12	.30
191 Tommy Dreamer	.12	.30
192 Tommy Dreamer	.12	.30
193 Tommy Dreamer	.12	.30
194 Santino Marella	.12	.30
195 Santino Marella	.12	.30
196 Santino Marella	.12	.30
197 Santino Marella	.12	.30
198 Santino Marella	.12	.30
199 Umaga	.20	.50
200 Umaga	.20	.50
201 Umaga	.20	.50
202 Umaga	.20	.50
203 Umaga	.20	.50
204 Randy Orton	.30	.75
205 Randy Orton	.30	.75
206 Randy Orton	.30	.75
207 Randy Orton	.30	.75
208 Randy Orton	.30	.75
209 Randy Orton	.30	.75
210 Randy Orton	.30	.75
211 Randy Orton	.30	.75
212 Randy Orton	.30	.75
213 Randy Orton	.30	.75
214 Undertaker	.60	1.50
215 Undertaker	.60	1.50
216 Undertaker	.60	1.50
217 Undertaker	.60	1.50
218 Undertaker	.60	1.50
219 Undertaker	.60	1.50
220 Undertaker	.60	1.50
221 Undertaker	.60	1.50
222 Undertaker	.60	1.50
223 Undertaker	.60	1.50
224 Mark Henry	.20	.50
225 Mark Henry	.20	.50
226 Mark Henry	.20	.50
227 Mark Henry	.20	.50
228 Mark Henry	.20	.50
229 Batista	.50	1.25
230 Batista	.50	1.25
231 Batista	.50	1.25
232 Batista	.50	1.25
233 Batista	.50	1.25
234 Jack Swagger	.12	.30
235 Jack Swagger	.12	.30
236 Jack Swagger	.12	.30
P1 RAW	.12	.30
P2 John Cena	.75	2.00
P3 Randy Orton	.30	.75
P4 JBL	.20	.50
P5 Rey Mysterio	.30	.75
P6 ECW	.12	.30
P7 John Morrison	.20	.50
P8 Mark Henry	.20	.50
P9 Chavo Guerrero	.20	.50
P10 SMACK DOWN	.12	.30
P11 Edge	.50	1.25
P12 Triple H	.75	2.00
P13 Jeff Hardy	.50	1.25
P14 Vladimir Kozlov	.20	.50

2014 Topps WWE Road to WrestleMania

COMPLETE SET (110)	12.00	30.00
UNOPENED BOX (24 PACKS)		
UNOPENED PACK (7 CARDS)		
*BRONZE: .6X TO 1.5X BASIC CARDS		
*BLUE: .75X TO 2X BASIC CARDS		
*PURPLE: .75X TO 2X BASIC CARDS		
*BLACK: 2.5X TO 6X BASIC CARDS		
*GOLD/10: UNPRICED DUE TO SCARCITY		
*P.P.BLACK/1: UNPRICED DUE TO SCARCITY		
*P.P.CYAN/1: UNPRICED DUE TO SCARCITY		
*P.P.MAGENTA/1: UNPRICED DUE TO SCARCITY		
*P.P.YELLOW/1: UNPRICED DUE TO SCARCITY		
1 Wade Barrett	.15	.40
2 Dolph Ziggler	.25	.60
3 Ryback	.15	.40
4 Kofi Kingston	.15	.40
5 Undertaker	.60	1.50
6 AJ Lee	.75	2.00
7 Brock Lesnar	.60	1.50
8 Mark Henry	.15	.40
9 Dean Ambrose	.60	1.50
10 The Shield	.75	2.00
11 Brock Lesnar	.60	1.50
12 Curtis Axel	.15	.40
13 Team Hell No	.50	1.25
14 Curtis Axel	.15	.40
15 AJ Lee	.75	2.00
16 Alberto Del Rio	.40	1.00
17 John Cena	.75	2.00
18 Mark Henry	.15	.40
19 Brad Maddox	.15	.40
20 Wyatt Family	.60	1.50
21 Damien Sandow	.25	.60
22 John Cena	.75	2.00
23 Randy Orton	.60	1.50
24 AJ Lee	.75	2.00
25 Rob Van Dam	.40	1.00
26 Vickie Guerrero	.15	.40
27 Eva Marie and JoJo	.15	.40
28 Cody Rhodes	.15	.40
29 Daniel Bryan	.75	2.00
30 Alberto Del Rio	.40	1.00
31 Bray Wyatt	.75	2.00
32 Cody Rhodes	.15	.40
33 Daniel Bryan	.75	2.00
34 Randy Orton	.60	1.50
35 Daniel Bryan	.75	2.00
36 Randy Orton	.60	1.50
37 Randy Orton	.60	1.50
38 Edge	.60	1.50
39 Randy Orton	.60	1.50
40 The Miz	.25	.60
41 Natalya & Tyson Kidd	.75	2.00
42 Daniel Bryan	.75	2.00
43 Triple H	.60	1.50
44 Daniel Bryan	.75	2.00
45 The Rhodes Brothers	.25	.60
46 Los Matadores	.15	.40
47 The Rhodes Brothers	.25	.60
48 Big Show	.40	1.00
49 The Rhodes Brothers	.25	.60
50 The Rhodes Brothers	.25	.60
51 John Cena	.75	2.00
52 Randy Orton	.60	1.50
53 John Cena	.75	2.00
54 The Authority	.25	.60
55 Big E	.15	.40
56 Xavier Woods	.15	.40
57 Rey Mysterio	.40	1.00
58 The Shield	.75	2.00
59 Team Total Divas	1.25	3.00
60 Titus O'Neil	.15	.40
61 Sin Cara	.15	.40
62 Triple H	.60	1.50
63 Daniel Bryan	.75	2.00
64 Randy Orton	.60	1.50
65 Brodus Clay	.15	.40
66 The Total Divas	1.25	3.00
67 Brock Lesnar	.60	1.50
68 Jake The Snake Roberts	.40	1.00
69 Daniel Bryan	.75	2.00
70 Batista	.60	1.50
71 New Age Outlaws	.25	.60
72 Rusev	.40	1.00
73 Kevin Nash	.40	1.00
74 Sheamus	.40	1.00
75 Batista	.40	1.00
76 Titus O'Neil	.15	.40
77 Christian	.25	.60
78 Emma	.40	1.00

79	The Wyatt Family	.60	1.50
80	Randy Orton	.60	1.50
81	Hulk Hogan	.75	2.00
82	Undertaker	.60	1.50
83	Lana	.60	1.50
84	The Usos	.25	.60
85	Big Show	.40	1.00
86	Hulk Hogan	.75	2.00
87	Daniel Bryan	.75	2.00
88	The Shield	.75	2.00
89	Kane	.40	1.00
90	The Wyatt Family	.60	1.50
91	Undertaker	.60	1.50
92	Brock Lesnar	.60	1.50
93	The Wyatt Family	.60	1.50
94	Rowdy Roddy Piper	.40	1.00
95	Jake The Snake Roberts	.40	1.00
96	Kane	.40	1.00
97	Razor Ramon	.40	1.00
98	Ultimate Warrior	.40	1.00
99	The Usos	.25	.60
100	The Real Americans	.25	.60
101	Triple H	.60	1.50
102	Daniel Bryan	.75	2.00
103	The Shield	.75	2.00
104	Kofi Kingston	.15	.40
105	Cesaro	.25	.60
106	John Cena	.75	2.00
107	Brock Lesnar	.60	1.50
108	AJ Lee	.75	2.00
109	Daniel Bryan	.75	2.00
110	Daniel Bryan	.75	2.00

2014 Topps WWE Road to WrestleMania 30 Years of WrestleMania

COMPLETE SET (60) 12.00 30.00
*P.P.BLACK/1: UNPRICED DUE TO SCARCITY
*P.P.CYAN/1: UNPRICED DUE TO SCARCITY
*P.P.MAGENTA/1: UNPRICED DUE TO SCARCITY
*P.P.YELLOW/1: UNPRICED DUE TO SCARCITY
STATED ODDS 2:1

1	The Foreign Legion	.20	.50
2	Hulk Hogan & Mr. T	1.25	3.00
3	The British Bulldogs	.20	.50
4	Hulk Hogan/King Kong Bundy	1.25	3.00
5	Ricky "The Dragon" Steamboat	.20	.50
6	Hulk Hogan vs. Andre	1.25	3.00
7	Hulk Hogan vs. Andre	1.25	3.00
8	Macho Man Randy Savage	.20	.50
9	Rick Rude	.20	.50
10	Hulk Hogan	1.25	3.00
11	Million Dollar Man Ted DiBiase	.20	.50
12	Ultimate Warrior	1.50	4.00
13	Ultimate Warrior	.60	1.50
14	Hulk Hogan	1.25	3.00
15	Macho Man Randy Savage	.75	2.00
16	Hulk Hogan	1.25	3.00
17	Yokozuna	.20	.50
18	Hulk Hogan	1.25	3.00
19	Yokozuna	.20	.50
20	Bret "Hit Man" Hart	.20	.50
21	Yokozuna & Owen Hart	.20	.50
22	Diesel	.20	.50
23	Ultimate Warrior	.60	1.50
24	Shawn Michaels	.60	1.50
25	British Bulldog & Owen Hart	.40	1.00
26	Bret "Hit Man" Hart	1.00	2.50
27	Triple H	.75	2.00
28	Stone Cold Steve Austin	1.25	3.00
29	Road Dogg	.20	.50
30	Stone Cold Steve Austin	2.00	5.00
31	Edge & Christian	.60	1.50
32	Triple H	.75	2.00
33	Edge & Christian	.60	1.50
34	Stone Cold Steve Austin	1.00	2.50
35	The Rock	2.00	5.00
36	Triple H	.75	2.00
37	Triple H	.75	2.00
38	Brock Lesnar	.75	2.00
39	Eddie Guerrero	.20	.50
40	Triple Threat Match	1.25	3.00
41	John Cena	1.00	2.50
42	Batista	.20	.50
43	Rey Mysterio	.20	.50
44	John Cena	1.25	3.00
45	Vince McMahon	.20	.50
46	John Cena	1.25	3.00
47	Shawn Michaels Retires Ric Flair	.60	1.50
48	Randy Orton	1.25	3.00
49	John Cena	1.25	3.00
50	Triple H	.75	2.00
51	Chris Jericho	.60	1.50
52	John Cena	1.25	3.00
53	Edge	.60	1.50
54	The Miz	1.25	3.00
55	CM Punk	.50	1.25
56	The Rock	1.50	4.00
57	Triple H	1.00	2.50
58	John Cena	1.50	4.00
59	Daniel Bryan	1.25	3.00
60	Daniel Bryan	1.25	3.00

2014 Topps WWE Road to WrestleMania Autographed WrestleMania 30 Mat Relics

RANDOMLY INSERTED INTO PACKS

NNO	Bray Wyatt	40.00	100.00
NNO	Cameron	12.00	30.00
NNO	Cesaro	15.00	40.00
NNO	Eve	20.00	50.00
NNO	Hulk Hogan	150.00	300.00
NNO	Jimmy Hart	20.00	30.00
NNO	Kane	25.00	60.00
NNO	Kevin Nash	30.00	80.00
NNO	Layla	12.00	30.00
NNO	Lex Luger	30.00	80.00
NNO	Naomi	20.00	50.00
NNO	Nikki Bella	30.00	80.00
NNO	Roman Reigns	40.00	100.00
NNO	Ron Simmons	30.00	80.00
NNO	Summer Rae	40.00	100.00
NNO	Trish Stratus	60.00	120.00

2014 Topps WWE Road to WrestleMania Dual Autographs

RANDOMLY INSERTED INTO PACKS

NNO	Bray Wyatt Roman Reigns	120.00	250.00
NNO	H.Hogan/J.Hart	125.00	250.00
NNO	Kane/Layla	20.00	50.00
NNO	K.Nash/R.Simmons	30.00	80.00
NNO	Lex Luger/Cesaro	50.00	100.00
NNO	Naomi/N.Bella	25.00	60.00
NNO	Trish Stratus Eve	50.00	100.00

2014 Topps WWE Road to WrestleMania Queen of WrestleMania

COMPLETE SET (8) 10.00 25.00
*P.P.BLACK/1: UNPRICED DUE TO SCARCITY
*P.P.CYAN/1: UNPRICED DUE TO SCARCITY
*P.P.MAGENTA/1: UNPRICED DUE TO SCARCITY
*P.P.YELLOW/1: UNPRICED DUE TO SCARCITY
STATED ODDS 1:12

1	Leads T&A to Victory	2.00	5.00
2	Triple Threat Match/Women's Title	2.00	5.00
3	Defeats Victoria and Jazz	2.00	5.00
4	Turns on Chris Jericho	2.00	5.00
5	Defeats Christy Hemme	2.00	5.00
6	Battles Mickie James	2.00	5.00
7	With John Morrison and Snooki	2.00	5.00
8	Hall of Fame Induction	2.00	5.00

2014 Topps WWE Road to WrestleMania The Streak

COMPLETE SET (22) 8.00 20.00
*P.P.BLACK/1: UNPRICED DUE TO SCARCITY
*P.P.CYAN/1: UNPRICED DUE TO SCARCITY
*P.P.MAGENTA/1: UNPRICED DUE TO SCARCITY
*P.P.YELLOW/1: UNPRICED DUE TO SCARCITY
STATED ODDS 1:1

1	Jimmy Superfly Snuka	.60	1.50
2	Jake The Snake Roberts	.60	1.50
3	Giant Gonzales	.60	1.50
4	King Kong Bundy	.60	1.50
5	Diesel	.60	1.50
6	Sycho Sid	.60	1.50
7	Kane	.60	1.50
8	Big Boss Man	.60	1.50
9	Triple H	.60	1.50
10	Ric Flair	.60	1.50
11	Big Show/A-Train	.60	1.50
12	Kane	.60	1.50
13	Randy Orton	.60	1.50
14	Mark Henry	.60	1.50
15	Batista	.60	1.50
16	Edge	.60	1.50
17	Shawn Michaels	.60	1.50
18	Shawn Michaels	.60	1.50
19	Triple H	.60	1.50
20	Triple H	.60	1.50
21	CM Punk	.60	1.50
22	Brock Lesnar	2.00	5.00

2014 Topps WWE Road to WrestleMania Swatch Relics

*P.P.BLACK/1: UNPRICED DUE TO SCARCITY
*P.P.CYAN/1: UNPRICED DUE TO SCARCITY
*P.P.MAGENTA/1: UNPRICED DUE TO SCARCITY
*P.P.YELLOW/1: UNPRICED DUE TO SCARCITY
RANDOMLY INSERTED INTO PACKS

NNO	Alberto Del Rio/Shirt	3.00	8.00
NNO	Big Show/Shirt	3.00	8.00
NNO	Billy Gunn/Shirt	3.00	8.00
NNO	Bray Wyatt/Shirt	4.00	10.00
NNO	Curtis Axel/Shirt	3.00	8.00
NNO	Damien Sandow/Shirt	3.00	8.00
NNO	Daniel Bryan/Shirt	10.00	25.00
NNO	Darren Young/Shirt	4.00	10.00
NNO	Dolph Ziggler/Shirt	5.00	12.00
NNO	Goldust/Shirt	3.00	8.00
NNO	Jack Swagger/Shirt	3.00	8.00
NNO	Jey Uso/Shirt	8.00	20.00
NNO	John Cena/Shirt	120.00	200.00
NNO	John Cena/Shoe	8.00	20.00
NNO	Mark Henry/Shirt	4.00	10.00
NNO	The Miz/Shirt	3.00	8.00
NNO	Natalya/Shirt	4.00	10.00
NNO	Ryback/Shirt	3.00	8.00
NNO	Tamina Snuka/Shirt	3.00	8.00
NNO	T.Stratus/Green Pants	30.00	60.00
NNO	T.Stratus/Purple Pants	30.00	60.00
NNO	Undertaker/Pants & Hat	150.00	300.00

2014 Topps WWE Road to WrestleMania Ultimate Warrior Tribute

COMPLETE SET (10) 5.00 12.00
*P.P.BLACK/1: UNPRICED DUE TO SCARCITY
*P.P.CYAN/1: UNPRICED DUE TO SCARCITY
*P.P.MAGENTA/1: UNPRICED DUE TO SCARCITY
*P.P.YELLOW/1: UNPRICED DUE TO SCARCITY
STATED ODDS 1:4

1	Defeats Honky Tonk Man	.75	2.00
2	Defeats Ravishing Rick Rude	.75	2.00
3	Defeats The Heenan Family	.75	2.00
4	Defeats Hulk Hogan for WWE Title	.75	2.00
5	Defeats Ravishing Rick Rude	.75	2.00
6	Wins Match at Survivor Series	.75	2.00
7	Defeats Macho King Randy Savage	.75	2.00
8	Returns to WWE, Defeats Triple H	.75	2.00
9	Joins WCW	.75	2.00
10	Addresses WWE Universe	.75	2.00

2014 Topps WWE Road to WrestleMania WrestleMania 30 Mat Relics

RANDOMLY INSERTED INTO PACKS

NNO	AJ Lee	12.00	30.00
NNO	Batista	4.00	10.00
NNO	Big Show	5.00	12.00
NNO	Bray Wyatt	6.00	15.00
NNO	Brock Lesnar	4.00	10.00
NNO	Cesaro	3.00	8.00
NNO	Daniel Bryan	8.00	20.00
NNO	Dean Ambrose	5.00	12.00
NNO	Hulk Hogan	10.00	25.00
NNO	Jey Uso	3.00	8.00
NNO	Jimmy Uso	3.00	8.00
NNO	John Cena	8.00	20.00
NNO	Randy Orton	6.00	15.00
NNO	The Rock	6.00	15.00
NNO	Roman Reigns	8.00	20.00
NNO	Seth Rollins	6.00	15.00
NNO	Sheamus	3.00	8.00
NNO	Stone Cold Steve Austin	6.00	15.00
NNO	Triple H	5.00	12.00
NNO	Undertaker	6.00	15.00

2014 Topps WWE Road to WrestleMania WrestleMania Autographs

*BRONZE/25: .5X TO 1.2X BASIC AUTOS
RANDOMLY INSERTED INTO PACKS

NNO Bray Wyatt	15.00	40.00
NNO Cameron	8.00	20.00
NNO Cesaro	12.00	30.00
NNO Eve	12.00	20.00
NNO Hulk Hogan	100.00	200.00
NNO Jimmy Hart	12.00	25.00
NNO Kane	15.00	40.00
NNO Kevin Nash	15.00	40.00
NNO Layla	12.00	25.00
NNO Lex Luger	12.00	30.00
NNO Naomi	12.00	30.00
NNO Nikki Bella	15.00	40.00
NNO Roman Reigns	20.00	50.00
NNO Ron Simmons	12.00	30.00
NNO Summer Rae	15.00	40.00
NNO Trish Stratus	30.00	75.00

2014 Topps WWE Road to WrestleMania WWE 2K15

STATED ODDS 1:613

1 AJ Lee	50.00	100.00
2 Bray Wyatt	15.00	40.00
3 Brock Lesnar	10.00	25.00
4 Cesaro	8.00	20.00
5 Daniel Bryan	15.00	40.00
6 Dolph Ziggler	8.00	20.00
7 Hulk Hogan	30.00	80.00
8 John Cena	30.00	80.00
9 Roman Reigns	20.00	50.00
10 Seth Rollins	20.00	50.00

2015 Topps WWE Road to WrestleMania

COMPLETE SET (110) 10.00 25.00
UNOPENED BOX (24 PACKS)
UNOPENED PACK (7 CARDS)
*BRONZE: .6X TO 1.5X BASIC CARDS
*BLUE: .75X TO 2X BASIC CARDS
*PURPLE: .75X TO 2X BASIC CARDS
*SILVER: 2.5X TO 6X BASIC CARDS
*GOLD/10: UNPRICED DUE TO SCARCITY
*RED/1: UNPRICED DUE TO SCARCITY
*P.P. BLACK/1: UNPRICED DUE TO SCARCITY
*P.P. CYAN/1: UNPRICED DUE TO SCARCITY
*P.P. MAGENTA/1: UNPRICED DUE TO SCARCITY
*P.P. YELLOW/1: UNPRICED DUE TO SCARCITY

1 Paige	.60	1.50
2 The Shield/Daniel Bryan	.30	.75
3 Daniel Bryan/Hulk Hogan	.50	1.25
4 Fandango/Summer Rae/Layla	.12	.30
5 Ultimate Warrior Tribute	.12	.30
6 Cesaro/Mark Henry	.12	.30
7 Evolution/The Shield	.50	1.25
8 Jimmy Uso/Naomi	.12	.30
9 Kane/Daniel Bryan	.30	.75
10 Bray Wyatt/John Cena	.50	1.25
11 Kane/Brie Bella	.30	.75
12 Bad News Barrett/Big E	.12	.30
13 The Shield/Evolution	.30	.75
14 Bray Wyatt/John Cena	.50	1.25
15 Daniel Bryan/Kane	.50	1.25
16 Sheamus/Dean Ambrose	.30	.75
17 Adam Rose	.15	.40
18 Bo Dallas	.12	.30
19 The Authority/Brad Maddox	.50	1.25
20 Daniel Bryan/Brie Bella	.50	1.25
21 Brie Bella	.40	1.00
22 John Cena/Bray Wyatt	.60	1.50
23 The Shield/Evolution	.30	.75
24 Batista	.30	.75
25 Seth Rollins/The Shield	.20	.50
26 The Authority/Daniel Bryan	.50	1.25
27 John Cena/Shield/Wyatts	.60	1.50
28 Stardust	.12	.30
29 John Cena/Kane	.60	1.50
30 Seth Rollins MITB	.20	.50
31 John Cena	.60	1.50
32 Bret Hit Man Hart/Damien Sandow	.40	1.00
33 Funkadactyls	.20	.50
34 Summer Rae/Layla/Fandango	.50	1.25
35 The Miz	.20	.50
36 John Cena	.60	1.50
37 Brock Lesnar/John Cena	.50	1.25
38 Stephanie McMahon/Brie Bella	.20	.50
39 Brock Lesnar/Hulk Hogan	.50	1.25
40 Dolph Ziggler/The Miz	.20	.50
41 Paige/AJ Lee	.60	1.50
42 Seth Rollins/Dean Ambrose	.20	.50
43 Roman Reigns/Randy Orton	.30	.75
44 Brock Lesnar/John Cena	.50	1.25
45 Gold & Stardust/Usos	.12	.30
46 The Miz/Dolph Ziggler	.20	.50
47 Dean Ambrose/Seth Rollins	.30	.75
48 John Cena/Brock Lesnar	.60	1.50
49 Dolph Ziggler/The Miz	.20	.50
50 The Bunny	.12	.30
51 Seth Rollins/Dean Ambrose	.20	.50
52 The Rock/Rusev	.60	1.50
53 Dean Ambrose/The Authority	.30	.75
54 Dean Ambrose/John Cena	.30	.75
55 Nikki Bella/Brie Bella	.40	1.00
56 John Cena/Randy Orton	.60	1.50
57 Bray Wyatt/Dean Ambrose	.50	1.25
58 The Authority/Randy Orton	.50	1.25
59 Rusev/Sheamus	.30	.75
60 Luke Harper/Dolph Ziggler	.20	.50
61 Miz & Mizdow/Goldust & Stardust	.20	.50
62 Divas Survivor Series Match	.12	.30
63 Nikki Bella/AJ Lee	.40	1.00
64 Sting WWE Debut	.30	.75
65 Team Cena/Team Authority	.60	1.50
66 Dolph Ziggler/Luke Harper	.20	.50
67 John Cena/Seth Rollins	.60	1.50
68 Roman Reigns	.30	.75
69 Bray Wyatt/Dean Ambrose	.50	1.25
70 Brock Lesnar/Chris Jericho	.50	1.25
71 Seth Rollins/John Cena	.20	.50
72 Dean Ambrose/Bray Wyatt	.30	.75
73 Edge & Christian	.30	.75
74 Usos/The Miz & Mizdow	.12	.30
75 The Ascension/Miz & Mizdow	.12	.30
76 Seth Rollins/John Cena	.20	.50
77 Bad New Barrett/Dolph Ziggler	.12	.30
78 Authority/Ziggler/Ryback/Rowan	.50	1.25
79 Rollins/Cena/Lesnar	.20	.50
80 Daniel Bryan	.50	1.25
81 The Ascension/nWo	.12	.30
82 Sting/Team Cena	.30	.75
83 Lesnar/Rollins/Cena	.50	1.25
84 Kane	.30	.75
85 Roman Reigns	.30	.75
86 Daniel Bryan/Kane	.50	1.25
87 Daniel Bryan/Seth Rollins	.50	1.25
88 Stardust/Goldust	.12	.30
89 Ric Flair/Triple H	.60	1.50
90 Prime Time Players	.12	.30
91 Randy Orton/The Authority	.50	1.25
92 Tyson Kidd & Cesaro/Usos	.12	.30
93 Sting/Triple H	.30	.75
94 Rusev/John Cena	.30	.75
95 Roman Reigns/Daniel Bryan	.30	.75
96 Sting/Randy Orton	.30	.75
97 Larry Zbyszko HOF	.20	.50
98 Bushwhackers HOF	.12	.30
99 Hulk Hogan/Macho Man HOF	.60	1.50
100 Kevin Nash HOF	.30	.75
101 Tyson Kidd & Cesaro	.12	.30
102 Big Show	.30	.75
103 Daniel Bryan	.50	1.25
104 Randy Orton/Seth Rollins	.50	1.25
105 Triple H/Sting	.50	1.25
106 AJ Lee & Paige/Bella Twins	.60	1.50
107 John Cena/Rusev	.60	1.50
108 The Rock/The Authority	.60	1.50
109 Undertaker/Bray Wyatt	.50	1.25
110 Rollins/Lesnar/Reigns	.20	.50

2015 Topps WWE Road to WrestleMania Autographs

*BRONZE/50: .5X TO 1.2X BASIC AUTOS
*SILVER/25: .6X TO 1.5X BASIC AUTOS
*GOLD/10: .75X TO 2X BASIC AUTOS
*RED/1: UNPRICED DUE TO SCARCITY
*P.P.BLACK/1: UNPRICED DUE TO SCARCITY
*P.P.CYAN/1: UNPRICED DUE TO SCARCITY
*P.P.MAGENTA/1: UNPRICED DUE TO SCARCITY
*P.P.YELLOW/1: UNPRICED DUE TO SCARCITY
RANDOMLY INSERTED INTO PACKS

NNO Afa	8.00	20.00
NNO Alicia Fox	6.00	15.00
NNO Bray Wyatt	12.00	30.00
NNO Brie Bella	12.00	30.00
NNO Brock Lesnar	60.00	120.00
NNO Damien Mizdow	6.00	15.00
NNO Daniel Bryan	12.00	30.00
NNO Dean Ambrose	12.00	30.00
NNO Dolph Ziggler	8.00	20.00
NNO Emma	10.00	25.00
NNO Hulk Hogan	125.00	250.00
NNO Jack Swagger	6.00	15.00
NNO Jimmy Hart	10.00	25.00
NNO Nikki Bella	15.00	40.00
NNO Razor Ramon	20.00	50.00
NNO Roman Reigns	15.00	40.00
NNO R-Truth	8.00	20.00
NNO Ryback	8.00	20.00
NNO Sika	8.00	20.00

2015 Topps WWE Road to WrestleMania Bizarre WrestleMania Matches

COMPLETE SET (10) 5.00 12.00
*P.P.BLACK/1: UNPRICED DUE TO SCARCITY
*P.P.CYAN/1: UNPRICED DUE TO SCARCITY
*P.P.MAGENTA/1: UNPRICED DUE TO SCARCITY
*P.P.YELLOW/1: UNPRICED DUE TO SCARCITY
STATED ODDS 1:4

1 Andre the Giant/Big John Studd	1.00	2.50
2 Mr.T/Rowdy Roddy Piper	1.00	2.50
3 Corporal Kirchner/Nikolai Volkoff	1.00	2.50
4 Battle Royal	1.00	2.50
5 Rowdy Roddy Piper/Adrian Adonis	1.00	2.50
6 Jake Roberts/Rick Martel	1.00	2.50
7 Rowdy Roddy Piper/Goldust	1.00	2.50
8 C.Jack & C.Charlie/New Age Outlaws	1.00	2.50
9 Gimmick Battle Royal	1.00	2.50
10 Akebono/Big Show	1.00	2.50

2015 Topps WWE Road to WrestleMania Classic WrestleMania Matches

COMPLETE SET (30) 6.00 15.00
*P.P.BLACK/1: UNPRICED DUE TO SCARCITY
*P.P.CYAN/1: UNPRICED DUE TO SCARCITY
*P.P.MAGENTA/1: UNPRICED DUE TO SCARCITY
*P.P.YELLOW/1: UNPRICED DUE TO SCARCITY
RANDOMLY INSERTED INTO PACKS

1 Harley Race/JYD	.50	1.25
2 Honky Tonk Man Jake The Snake Roberts	.50	1.25
3 Twin Towers/Rockers	.50	1.25
4 Nasty Boys/Hart Foundation	.50	1.25
5 Bret Hit Man Hart Rowdy Roddy Piper	.50	1.25
6 Money Inc/Mega-Maniacs	.50	1.25
7 Lex Luger/Mr. Perfect	.50	1.25
8 Bret Hit Man Hart	.50	1.25
9 Razor Ramon/Shawn Michaels	.50	1.25
10 Stone Cold Steve Austin Savio Vega	.50	1.25
11 Chris Jericho/Kurt Angle	.50	1.25
12 Chris Jericho/William Regal	.50	1.25
13 Eddie Guerrero/Test	.50	1.25
14 Stone Cold Steve Austin Chris Jericho	.50	1.25
15 Shawn Michaels/Chris Jericho	.50	1.25
16 John Cena/Big Show	.50	1.25
17 Christian/Chris Jericho	.50	1.25
18 Goldberg/Brock Lesnar	.50	1.25
19 Rey Mysterio/Eddie Guerrero	.50	1.25
20 Edge MITB	.50	1.25
21 Kurt Angle/Shawn Michaels	.50	1.25
22 Rob Van Dam MITB	.50	1.25
23 Edge/Mick Foley	.50	1.25
24 Shawn Michaels/Mr. McMahon	.50	1.25
25 Jack Swagger MITB	.50	1.25
26 Bret Hit Man Hart Mr. McMahon	.50	1.25
27 Randy Orton/CM Punk	.50	1.25
28 Sheamus/Daniel Bryan	.50	1.25
29 Shield/Orton Sheamus Big Show	.50	1.25
30 Team Hell No/Ziggler & Big E	.50	1.25

2015 Topps WWE Road to WrestleMania Dual Autographs

STATED PRINT RUN 10 SER.#'d SETS
UNPRICED DUE TO SCARCITY

NNO Afa/Sika
NNO Brie & Nikki Bella
NNO D.Mizdow/J.Hart
NNO D.Bryan/B.Wyatt
NNO D.Ambrose/R.Reigns
NNO D.Ziggler/Ryback
NNO Emma/A.Fox
NNO H.Hogan/R.Ramon

2015 Topps WWE Road to WrestleMania Hall of Fame

COMPLETE SET (30) 4.00 10.00

*P.P.BLACK/1: UNPRICED DUE TO SCARCITY
*P.P.CYAN/1: UNPRICED DUE TO SCARCITY
*P.P.MAGENTA/1: UNPRICED DUE TO SCARCITY
*P.P.YELLOW/1: UNPRICED DUE TO SCARCITY
STATED ODDS 1:1

1 Chief Jay Strongbow	.40	1.00
2 Classy Freddie Blassie	.25	.60
3 Gorilla Monsoon	.30	.75
4 George The Animal Steele	.30	.75
5 Jimmy Superfly Snuka	.40	1.00
6 Pat Patterson	.25	.60
7 The Magnificent Don Muraco	.40	1.00
8 Greg The Hammer Valentine	.30	.75
9 The King Harley Race	.40	1.00
10 Sgt. Slaughter	.40	1.00
11 Tito Santana	.40	1.00
12 Hulk Hogan	1.25	3.00
13 Rowdy Roddy Piper	.75	2.00
14 Cowboy Bob Orton	.25	.60
15 Mr. Wonderful Paul Orndorff	.40	1.00
16 Nikolai Volkoff	.25	.60
17 The Iron Sheik	.40	1.00
18 Bret Hit Man Hart	.75	2.00
19 The American Dream Dusty Rhodes	.40	1.00
20 Jerry The King Lawler	.40	1.00
21 Nature Boy Ric Flair	1.25	3.00
22 Rocky Johnson	.40	1.00
23 Stone Cold Steve Austin	1.25	3.00
24 Ricky The Dragon Steamboat	.40	1.00
25 Koko B. Ware	.30	.75
26 Million Dollar Man Ted DiBiase	.40	1.00
27 Heartbreak Kid Shawn Michaels	1.00	2.50
28 Hacksaw Jim Duggan	.40	1.00
29 Edge	.60	1.50
30 Ron Simmons	.40	1.00

2015 Topps WWE Road to WrestleMania HHH at WrestleMania

COMPLETE SET (10)	4.00	10.00

*P.P.BLACK/1: UNPRICED DUE TO SCARCITY
*P.P.CYAN/1: UNPRICED DUE TO SCARCITY
*P.P.MAGENTA/1: UNPRICED DUE TO SCARCITY
*P.P.YELLOW/1: UNPRICED DUE TO SCARCITY
STATED ODDS 1:2

1 Defeats Goldust	.75	2.00
2 Battles Kane	.75	2.00
3 Wins 4-Way Elimination Match	.75	2.00
4 Defeats Y2J for WWE Title	.75	2.00
5 Defeats Booker T	.75	2.00
6 Defeats Randy Orton	.75	2.00
7 Defeats Sheamus	.75	2.00
8 Faces Undertaker No Holds Barred	.75	2.00
9 Faces Undertaker Hell in a Cell	.75	2.00
10 Defeats Brock Lesnar	.75	2.00

2015 Topps WWE Road to WrestleMania Mat Relics

*SILVER/25: .6X TO 1.5X BASIC MEM
*GOLD/10: UNPRICED DUE TO SCARCITY
*RED/1: UNPRICED DUE TO SCARCITY
*P.P.BLACK/1: UNPRICED DUE TO SCARCITY
*P.P.CYAN/1: UNPRICED DUE TO SCARCITY
*P.P.MAGENTA/1: UNPRICED DUE TO SCARCITY
*P.P.YELLOW/1: UNPRICED DUE TO SCARCITY
RANDOMLY INSERTED INTO PACKS

NNO Bad News Barrett	2.00	5.00
NNO Big Show	2.50	6.00
NNO Bray Wyatt	3.00	8.00
NNO Brie Bella	4.00	10.00
NNO Brock Lesnar	3.00	8.00
NNO Damien Mizdow	2.50	6.00
NNO Daniel Bryan	5.00	12.00
NNO Dean Ambrose	3.00	8.00
NNO Dolph Ziggler	2.00	5.00
NNO John Cena	4.00	10.00
NNO Nikki Bella	4.00	10.00
NNO Paige	6.00	15.00
NNO Randy Orton	3.00	8.00
NNO Roman Reigns	4.00	10.00
NNO Rusev	2.50	6.00
NNO Ryback	2.00	5.00
NNO Seth Rollins	3.00	8.00
NNO Sting	6.00	15.00
NNO Triple H	3.00	8.00
NNO Undertaker	5.00	12.00

2015 Topps WWE Road to WrestleMania Rocking WrestleMania

COMPLETE SET (8)	5.00	12.00

*P.P.BLACK/1: UNPRICED DUE TO SCARCITY
*P.P.CYAN/1: UNPRICED DUE TO SCARCITY
*P.P.MAGENTA/1: UNPRICED DUE TO SCARCITY
*P.P.YELLOW/1: UNPRICED DUE TO SCARCITY
RANDOMLY INSERTED INTO PACKS

1 Faces Stone Cold Steve Austin	1.25	3.00
2 Takes on Stone Cold Steve Austin	1.25	3.00
3 Defeats Hollywood Hulk Hogan	1.25	3.00
4 Defeats Stone Cold Steve Austin	1.25	3.00
5 Rock 'n' Sock Reunite	1.25	3.00
6 Rock Bottoms John Cena	1.25	3.00
7 Defeats John Cena	1.25	3.00
8 Battles John Cena	1.25	3.00

2015 Topps WWE Road to WrestleMania Superstars of Canada

COMPLETE SET (10)	25.00	60.00

RANDOMLY INSERTED INTO PACKS

1 Chris Jericho	5.00	12.00
2 Christian	2.00	5.00
3 Edge	5.00	12.00
4 Kevin Owens	6.00	15.00
5 Natalya	6.00	15.00
6 Renee Young	8.00	20.00
7 Sami Zayn	3.00	8.00
8 Trish Stratus	10.00	25.00
9 Tyson Kidd	2.00	5.00
10 Viktor	2.00	5.00

2015 Topps WWE Road to WrestleMania Superstars of Canada Autographs

RANDOMLY INSERTED INTO PACKS
STATED PRINT RUN 25 SER.#'d SETS
CANADIAN EXCLUSIVES

NNO Chris Jericho	50.00	100.00
NNO Christian	25.00	60.00
NNO Edge	50.00	100.00
NNO Kevin Owens	15.00	40.00
NNO Natalya	20.00	50.00
NNO Renee Young	20.00	50.00
NNO Sami Zayn	10.00	25.00
NNO Trish Stratus	100.00	200.00
NNO Tyson Kidd	6.00	15.00
NNO Viktor	6.00	15.00

2015 Topps WWE Road to WrestleMania Swatch Relics

*P.P.BLACK/1: UNPRICED DUE TO SCARCITY
*P.P.CYAN/1: UNPRICED DUE TO SCARCITY
*P.P.MAGENTA/1: UNPRICED DUE TO SCARCITY
*P.P.YELLOW/1: UNPRICED DUE TO SCARCITY
RANDOMLY INSERTED INTO PACKS

NNO Adam Rose	4.00	10.00
NNO Brie Bella	6.00	15.00
NNO Cesaro	4.00	10.00
NNO Charlotte	10.00	25.00
NNO Dean Ambrose	8.00	20.00
NNO Damien Mizdow	4.00	10.00
NNO Dolph Ziggler	4.00	10.00
NNO Goldust	6.00	15.00
NNO Hulk Hogan	10.00	25.00
NNO John Cena	6.00	15.00
NNO Jack Swagger	5.00	12.00
NNO Nikki Bella	10.00	25.00
NNO Paige	12.00	30.00
NNO Roman Reigns	8.00	20.00
NNO Rusev	5.00	12.00
NNO Ryback	5.00	12.00
NNO Stardust	5.00	12.00
NNO Sami Zayn	6.00	15.00

2015 Topps WWE Road to WrestleMania Turnbuckle Pad Relics

RANDOMLY INSERTED INTO PACKS
STATED PRINT RUN 25 SER.#'d SETS

NNO Bad News Barrett	6.00	15.00
NNO Big Show	15.00	40.00
NNO Bray Wyatt	25.00	60.00
NNO Brie Bella	20.00	50.00
NNO Brock Lesnar	25.00	60.00
NNO Damien Mizdow	6.00	15.00
NNO Daniel Bryan	25.00	60.00
NNO Dean Ambrose	15.00	40.00
NNO Dolph Ziggler	10.00	25.00
NNO John Cena	30.00	80.00
NNO Nikki Bella	20.00	50.00
NNO Paige	30.00	80.00
NNO Randy Orton	25.00	60.00
NNO Roman Reigns	15.00	40.00
NNO Rusev	15.00	40.00
NNO Ryback	6.00	15.00
NNO Seth Rollins	10.00	25.00
NNO Sting	15.00	40.00
NNO Triple H	25.00	60.00
NNO Undertaker	25.00	60.00

2016 Topps WWE Road to WrestleMania

COMPLETE SET (110)	12.00	30.00

UNOPENED BOX (24 PACKS)
UNOPENED PACK (7 CARDS)
*BRONZE: .5X TO 1.2X BASIC CARDS
*SILVER: 2X TO 5X BASIC CARDS
*GOLD/10: UNPRICED DUE TO SCARCITY
*RED/1: UNPRICED DUE TO SCARCITY
*PP BLACK/1: UNPRICED DUE TO SCARCITY
*PP CYAN/1: UNPRICED DUE TO SCARCITY
*PP MAGENTA/1: UNPRICED DUE TO SCARCITY
*PP YELLOW/1: UNPRICED DUE TO SCARCITY
NUMBERS 111-113 ARE WWE DVD EXCLUSIVES

1 Daniel Bryan	.75	2.00
2 The Usos	.20	.50
3 Alundra Blayze	.25	.60
4 Ric Flair	.75	2.00
5 Triple H	.75	2.00
6 Hideo Itami	.25	.60
7 Damien Mizdow	.30	.75
8 Sting	.50	1.25
9 Triple H	.75	2.00
10 D-Generation X	.60	1.50
11 Rusev	.50	1.25
12 Bray Wyatt	.75	2.00
13 Roman Reigns	1.00	2.50
14 Sheamus	.50	1.25
15 Kalisto	.50	1.25
16 Brock Lesnar	1.00	2.50
17 Neville	.50	1.25
18 Big Show	.60	1.50
19 Fandango	.20	.50
20 Daniel Bryan/John Cena	1.00	2.50
21 The Miz	.30	.75
22 The New Day	.50	1.25
23 Roman Reigns	.60	1.50
24 Seth Rollins	.30	.75
25 Bad New Barrett	.20	.50
26 Sami Zayn	1.00	2.50
27 Erick Rowan	.20	.50
28 Neville	1.00	2.50
29 Daniel Bryan	.75	2.00
30 John Cena	1.00	2.50
31 Seth Rollins	.30	.75
32 Rusev	.75	2.00
33 Kevin Owens	1.00	2.50
34 Lana	.75	2.00
35 The New Day	.50	1.25
36 Kalisto	.50	1.25
37 The New Day	.50	1.25
38 Nikki Bella	.60	1.50
39 Kevin Owens	.50	1.25
40 Ryback	.25	.60
41 Dean Ambrose	.60	1.50
42 Dusty Rhodes Tribute	.20	.50
43 Bray Wyatt	.75	2.00
44 Sheamus	.50	1.25
45 Nikki Bella	.60	1.50
46 John Cena	1.00	2.50
47 The Prime Time Players	.20	.50
48 Seth Rollins	.60	1.50
49 Brock Lesnar	1.00	2.50
50 Brock Lesnar	1.00	2.50
51 Cesaro	1.00	2.50
52 Chris Jericho	.50	1.25
53 Nikki Bella	.60	1.50
54 Brock Lesnar	1.00	2.50
55 Rusev/Summer Rae	.75	2.00
56 Brock Lesnar	1.00	2.50
57 John Cena	1.00	2.50
58 Rusev	.50	1.25
59 Stardust	.20	.50
60 Brock Lesnar	1.00	2.50
61 Cesaro	.50	1.25
62 Bray Wyatt	.75	2.00
63 Charlotte	.60	1.50
64 John Cena	1.00	2.50
65 Undertaker	1.00	2.50
66 Brock Lesnar	1.00	2.50
67 John Cena/Cesaro/Randy Orton	1.00	2.50
68 Seth Rollins	.30	.75
69 John Cena	1.00	2.50

70 Dean Ambrose/Cesaro	.60	1.50
71 Rowdy Roddy Piper Tribute	.60	1.50
72 Ambrose/Reigns/Orton	.50	1.25
73 The New Day	.50	1.25
74 Undertaker	1.00	2.50
75 Ryback	.30	.75
76 Roman Reigns/Dean Ambrose	.75	2.00
77 Seth Rollins	.30	.75
78 Team PCB	.60	1.50
79 Undertaker	1.00	2.50
80 Brock Lesnar	1.00	2.50
81 The Dudley Boyz	.40	1.00
82 Braun Strowman	.25	.60
83 Sting	.50	1.25
84 Charlotte	.60	1.50
85 Sting/John Cena	1.00	2.50
86 Hideo Itami	.25	.60
87 Sami Zayn	.30	.75
88 Becky Lynch	.60	1.50
89 Kevin Owens	.50	1.25
90 Tyler Breeze/Adam Rose	.20	.50
91 Finn Balor	.60	1.50
92 Charlotte/Bayley	.60	1.50
93 Sasha Banks	.60	1.50
94 Kevin Owens	.50	1.25
95 Samoa Joe	.50	1.25
96 Kevin Owens	.50	1.25
97 Samoa Joe	.50	1.25
98 Samoa Joe	.50	1.25
99 Finn Balor/Samoa Joe	.60	1.50
100 Finn Balor	.60	1.50
101 The Vaudevillains	.20	.50
102 Sasha Banks	.60	1.50
103 Blake/Murphy	.20	.50
104 Bayley	.60	1.50
105 Bayley	.50	1.25
106 The Vaudevillains	.20	.50
107 Apollo Crews	.20	.50
108 Samoa Joe	.50	1.25
109 Bayley	.50	1.25
110 Finn Balor	.60	1.50
111 The Dudley Boyz SP		
112 Stone Cold Steve Austin SP		
113 Daniel Bryan SP		

2016 Topps WWE Road to WrestleMania Autographs

*BRONZE/50: .5X TO 1.2X BASIC AUTOS
*SILVER/25: .60X TO 1.5X BASIC AUTOS
*GOLD/10: UNPRICED DUE TO SCARCITY
*RED/1: UNPRICED DUE TO SCARCITY
*PP BLACK/1: UNPRICED DUE TO SCARCITY
*PP CYAN/1: UNPRICED DUE TO SCARCITY
*PP MAGENTA/1: UNPRICED DUE TO SCARCITY
*PP YELLOW/1: UNPRICED DUE TO SCARCITY
STATED PRINT RUN 99 SER.#'d SETS

NNO Baron Corbin	10.00	25.00
NNO Bayley	15.00	40.00
NNO Becky Lynch	25.00	60.00
NNO Brie Bella	10.00	25.00
NNO Brock Lesnar	100.00	200.00
NNO Charlotte	25.00	60.00
NNO Daniel Bryan	10.00	25.00
NNO Dean Ambrose	10.00	25.00
NNO Dory Funk Jr.	12.00	30.00
NNO Dusty Rhodes	50.00	100.00
NNO Eva Marie	15.00	40.00
NNO Gerald Brisco	6.00	15.00
NNO John Cena	20.00	50.00
NNO Kalisto	12.00	30.00
NNO Kevin Von Erich	25.00	60.00
NNO Lana	20.00	50.00
NNO Michael P.S. Hayes	10.00	25.00
NNO Neville	6.00	15.00
NNO Nikki Bella	15.00	40.00
NNO Pat Patterson	6.00	15.00
NNO Ric Flair	15.00	40.00
NNO Roman Reigns	12.00	30.00
NNO Samoa Joe	8.00	20.00
NNO Sasha Banks	25.00	60.00
NNO Seth Rollins	10.00	25.00
NNO Sting	30.00	80.00
NNO Terry Funk	50.00	100.00

2016 Topps WWE Road to WrestleMania Battleground Mat Relics

*BRONZE/50: .5X TO 1.2X BASIC MEM
*SILVER/25: .6X TO 1.5X BASIC MEM
*GOLD/10: UNPRICED DUE TO SCARCITY
*RED/1: UNPRICED DUE TO SCARCITY
*PP BLACK/1: UNPRICED DUE TO SCARCITY
*PP CYAN/1: UNPRICED DUE TO SCARCITY
*PP MAGENTA/1: UNPRICED DUE TO SCARCITY
*PP YELLOW/1: UNPRICED DUE TO SCARCITY
STATED PRINT RUN 199 SER.#'d SETS

NNO Big E	2.00	5.00
NNO Bray Wyatt	8.00	20.00
NNO Brie Bella	4.00	10.00
NNO Brock Lesnar	10.00	25.00
NNO Charlotte	6.00	15.00
NNO Darren Young	2.00	5.00
NNO John Cena	10.00	25.00
NNO Kevin Owens	5.00	12.00
NNO Kofi Kingston	2.00	5.00
NNO Luke Harper	2.00	5.00
NNO Randy Orton	5.00	12.00
NNO Roman Reigns	6.00	15.00
NNO R-Truth	2.00	5.00
NNO Sasha Banks	6.00	15.00
NNO Seth Rollins	3.00	8.00
NNO Sheamus	5.00	12.00
NNO Titus O'Neil	2.00	5.00
NNO Undertaker	8.00	20.00
NNO Wade Barrett	2.00	5.00
NNO Xavier Woods	2.00	5.00

2016 Topps WWE Road to WrestleMania Battleground Turnbuckle Pad Relics

STATED PRINT RUN 25 SER.#'d SETS

NNO Big E	5.00	12.00
NNO Bray Wyatt	20.00	50.00
NNO Brie Bella	10.00	25.00
NNO Brock Lesnar	25.00	60.00
NNO Charlotte	15.00	40.00
NNO Darren Young	5.00	12.00
NNO John Cena	25.00	60.00
NNO Kevin Owens	12.00	30.00
NNO Kofi Kingston	5.00	12.00
NNO Luke Harper	5.00	12.00
NNO Randy Orton	12.00	30.00
NNO Roman Reigns	15.00	40.00
NNO R-Truth	5.00	12.00
NNO Sasha Banks	15.00	40.00
NNO Seth Rollins	8.00	20.00
NNO Sheamus	12.00	30.00
NNO Titus O'Neil	5.00	12.00
NNO Undertaker	20.00	50.00
NNO Wade Barrett	5.00	12.00
NNO Xavier Woods	5.00	12.00

2016 Topps WWE Road to WrestleMania Dual Autographs

STATED PRINT RUN 11 SER.#'d SETS

NNO Charlotte Bayley	100.00	200.00
NNO Lana Eva Marie	100.00	200.00
NNO Neville Kalisto	30.00	75.00
NNO Pat Patterson Gerald Brisco	25.00	60.00
NNO Samoa Joe Baron Corbin	50.00	100.00
NNO Sasha Banks Becky Lynch	200.00	300.00
NNO Sting Ric Flair	225.00	350.00
NNO Terry Funk Dory Funk Jr.	50.00	100.00

2016 Topps WWE Road to WrestleMania Dusty Rhodes Tribute

COMPLETE SET (10)	3.00	8.00
STATED ODDS 1:6		
1 Dusty Rhodes	.60	1.50
2 Dusty Rhodes	.60	1.50
3 Dusty Rhodes	.60	1.50
4 Dusty Rhodes	1.00	2.50
5 Dusty Rhodes	.60	1.50
6 Dusty Rhodes	1.00	2.50
7 Dusty Rhodes	.60	1.50
8 Dusty Rhodes	.60	1.50
9 Dusty Rhodes	.60	1.50
10 Dusty Rhodes	1.50	4.00

2016 Topps WWE Road to WrestleMania Immortals

COMPLETE SET (10)	6.00	15.00
STATED ODDS 1:6		
1 Roman Reigns	1.00	2.50
2 Daniel Bryan	1.25	3.00
3 Randy Orton	.75	2.00
4 The Bellas	1.00	2.50
5 Paige	1.00	2.50
6 Triple H	1.25	3.00
7 Undertaker	1.25	3.00
8 The Rock	1.50	4.00
9 Brock Lesnar	1.50	4.00
10 John Cena	1.50	4.00

2016 Topps WWE Road to WrestleMania NXT Diva Kiss

STATED PRINT RUN 99 SER.#'d SETS

NNO Alexa Bliss	50.00	100.00
NNO Bayley	80.00	150.00
NNO Becky Lynch	50.00	100.00
NNO Carmella	25.00	60.00
NNO Charlotte	50.00	100.00
NNO Dana Brooke	20.00	50.00
NNO Eva Marie	30.00	80.00
NNO JoJo	20.00	50.00
NNO Sasha Banks	100.00	200.00

2016 Topps WWE Road to WrestleMania NXT Diva Kiss Autographs

*GOLD/10: UNPRICED DUE TO SCARCITY
*RED/1: UNPRICED DUE TO SCARCITY
*PP BLACK/1: UNPRICED DUE TO SCARCITY
*PP CYAN/1: UNPRICED DUE TO SCARCITY
*PP MAGENTA/1: UNPRICED DUE TO SCARCITY
*PP YELLOW/1: UNPRICED DUE TO SCARCITY
STATED PRINT RUN 25 SER.#'d SETS

NNO Alexa Bliss	250.00	500.00
NNO Bayley	75.00	150.00
NNO Becky Lynch	120.00	200.00
NNO Carmella	60.00	120.00
NNO Charlotte	150.00	250.00
NNO Dana Brooke	50.00	100.00
NNO Eva Marie	50.00	100.00
NNO JoJo	50.00	100.00
NNO Sasha Banks	150.00	250.00

2016 Topps WWE Road to WrestleMania Roster

COMPLETE SET (30) 10.00 25.00
*P.P.BLACK/1: UNPRICED DUE TO SCARCITY
*P.P.CYAN/1: UNPRICED DUE TO SCARCITY
*P.P.MAGENTA/1: UNPRICED DUE TO SCARCITY
*P.P.YELLOW/1: UNPRICED DUE TO SCARCITY
STATED ODDS 1:1

1 The Rock	1.50	4.00
2 Triple H	1.25	3.00
3 Undertaker	1.25	3.00
4 Sting	.75	2.00
5 Brock Lesnar	1.50	4.00
6 Seth Rollins	.50	1.25
7 Roman Reigns	1.00	2.50
8 Randy Orton	.75	2.00
9 Dean Ambrose	1.00	2.50
10 John Cena	1.50	4.00
11 Rusev	.75	2.00
12 Daniel Bryan	1.25	3.00
13 Dolph Ziggler	.40	1.00
14 King Barrett	.30	.75
15 Luke Harper	.30	.75
16 Bray Wyatt	1.25	3.00
17 The Miz	.50	1.25
18 Ryback	.40	1.00
19 Big Show	.60	1.50
20 Cesaro	.60	1.50
21 Tyson Kidd	.30	.75
22 Kofi Kingston	.30	.75
23 Big E	.30	.75
24 Xavier Woods	.30	.75
25 Brie Bella	.60	1.50
26 Nikki Bella	1.00	2.50
27 Paige	1.00	2.50
28 Naomi	.50	1.25
29 Natalya	.50	1.25
30 Lana	1.25	3.00

2016 Topps WWE Road to WrestleMania Rowdy Roddy Piper Tribute

COMPLETE SET (10) 4.00 10.00

STATED ODDS 1:6

1	Rowdy Roddy Piper	.75	2.00
2	Rowdy Roddy Piper	1.25	3.00
3	Rowdy Roddy Piper	.75	2.00
4	Rowdy Roddy Piper	.75	2.00
5	Rowdy Roddy Piper	.75	2.00
6	Rowdy Roddy Piper	.75	2.00
7	Rowdy Roddy Piper	.75	2.00
8	Rowdy Roddy Piper	.75	2.00
9	Rowdy Roddy Piper	.75	2.00
10	Rowdy Roddy Piper	.75	2.00

2016 Topps WWE Road to WrestleMania Shirt Relics

*BRONZE/50: .5X TO 1.2X BASIC MEM
*SILVER/25: .6X TO 1.5X BASIC MEM
*GOLD/10: UNPRICED DUE TO SCARCITY
*RED/1: UNPRICED DUE TO SCARCITY
*PP BLACK/1: UNPRICED DUE TO SCARCITY
*PP CYAN/1: UNPRICED DUE TO SCARCITY
*PP MAGENTA/1: UNPRICED DUE TO SCARCITY
*PP YELLOW/1: UNPRICED DUE TO SCARCITY
STATED PRINT RUN 350 SER.#'d SETS

NNO	Alicia Fox	3.00	8.00
NNO	Baron Corbin	2.50	6.00
NNO	Bayley	10.00	25.00
NNO	Becky Lynch	10.00	25.00
NNO	Big Show	4.00	10.00
NNO	Bray Wyatt	8.00	20.00
NNO	Colin Cassady	4.00	10.00
NNO	Darren Young	2.00	5.00
NNO	Dean Ambrose	6.00	15.00
NNO	John Cena	10.00	25.00
NNO	Kalisto	5.00	12.00
NNO	Kevin Owens	5.00	12.00
NNO	Kofi Kingston	2.00	5.00
NNO	Miz	3.00	8.00
NNO	Mojo Rawley	2.00	5.00
NNO	Neville	5.00	12.00
NNO	Paige	8.00	20.00
NNO	Randy Orton	5.00	12.00
NNO	Rob Van Dam	4.00	10.00
NNO	Roman Reigns	6.00	15.00
NNO	Ryback	2.50	6.00
NNO	Sami Zayn	3.00	8.00
NNO	Samoa Joe	5.00	12.00
NNO	Sasha Banks	8.00	20.00
NNO	Seth Rollins	3.00	8.00
NNO	Sheamus	5.00	12.00
NNO	Sin Cara	2.50	6.00
NNO	Summer Rae	5.00	12.00
NNO	Tyler Breeze	2.00	5.00
NNO	Xavier Woods	2.00	5.00

2016 Topps WWE Road to WrestleMania SP Inserts

STATED ODDS 1:24 HOBBY EXCLUSIVE

1	Kevin Owens	4.00	10.00
2	Charlotte	5.00	12.00
3	John Cena	8.00	20.00
4	Seth Rollins	4.00	10.00
5	Brock Lesnar	8.00	20.00
6	Tyler Breeze	1.50	4.00
7	Alberto Del Rio	8.00	20.00
8	Roman Reigns	6.00	15.00
9	Seth Rollins	2.50	6.00
10	Brock Lesnar	8.00	20.00
11	Paige	5.00	12.00
12	Goldust	2.50	6.00
13	Ryback	2.00	5.00
14	Undertaker/Kane	6.00	15.00
15	Roman Reigns	5.00	12.00
16	Sheamus	5.00	12.00
17	The New Day	1.50	4.00
18	Alberto Del Rio	2.50	6.00
19	Dean Ambrose	5.00	12.00
20	Sheamus	5.00	12.00

2016 Topps WWE Road to WrestleMania Triple Threat Autographed Dual Relics

STATED PRINT RUN 11 SER.#'d SETS

NNO	Bray Wyatt	50.00	100.00
NNO	Daniel Bryan	100.00	150.00
NNO	Dean Ambrose	25.00	60.00
NNO	John Cena	50.00	100.00
NNO	Nikki Bella	60.00	120.00
NNO	Roman Reigns	60.00	120.00
NNO	Seth Rollins	30.00	80.00

2016 Topps WWE Road to WrestleMania WWE Hall of Fame Commemorative Ring Relics

*BRONZE/50: .5X TO 1.2X BASIC MEM
*SILVER/25: .6X TO 1.5X BASIC MEM
*GOLD/10: UNPRICED DUE TO SCARCITY
RED/1: UNPRICED DUE TO SCARCITY
*P.P. BLACK/1: UNPRICED DUE TO SCARCITY
*P.P. CYAN/1: UNPRICED DUE TO SCARCITY
*P.P. MAGENTA/1: UNPRICED DUE TO SCARCITY
*P.P. YELLOW/1: UNPRICED DUE TO SCARCITY
STATED PRINT RUN 299 SER.#'d SETS

NNO	Alundra Blayze	2.00	5.00
NNO	American Dream Dusty Rhodes	1.50	4.00
NNO	Bob Backlund	1.50	4.00
NNO	Booker T	3.00	8.00
NNO	Bret Hit Man Hart	4.00	10.00
NNO	Bruno Sammartino	2.00	5.00
NNO	Don Muraco	1.50	4.00
NNO	Edge	4.00	10.00
NNO	George The Animal Steele	2.00	5.00
NNO	Hacksaw Jim Duggan	1.50	4.00
NNO	Harley Race	1.50	4.00
NNO	Iron Sheik	1.50	4.00
NNO	Jake The Snake Roberts	3.00	8.00
NNO	Jerry The King Lawler	3.00	8.00
NNO	Kevin Nash	4.00	10.00
NNO	Koko B. Ware	1.50	4.00
NNO	Larry Zbyszko	1.50	4.00
NNO	Lita	5.00	12.00
NNO	Million Dollar Man Ted DiBiase	2.00	5.00
NNO	Mr. Wonderful Paul Orndorff	1.50	4.00
NNO	Razor Ramon	4.00	10.00
NNO	Ric Flair	6.00	15.00
NNO	Ricky The Dragon Steamboat	2.00	5.00
NNO	Ron Simmons	4.00	10.00
NNO	Rowdy Roddy Piper	5.00	12.00
NNO	Sgt. Slaughter	2.00	5.00
NNO	Shawn Michaels	6.00	15.00
NNO	Stone Cold Steve Austin	8.00	20.00
NNO	Trish Stratus	8.00	20.00
NNO	Ultimate Warrior	4.00	10.00

2017 Topps WWE Road to WrestleMania

COMPLETE SET (100) 10.00 25.00
UNOPENED BOX (24 PACKS)
UNOPENED PACK (7 CARDS)
*BRONZE: .5X TO 1.2X BASIC CARDS
*BLUE/99: 1X TO 2.5X BASIC CARDS
*SILVER/25: 1.5X TO 4X BASIC CARDS
*GOLD/10: 3X TO 8X BASIC CARDS
*RED/1: UNPRICED DUE TO SCARCITY
*P.P.BLACK/1: UNPRICED DUE TO SCARCITY
*P.P.CYAN/1: UNPRICED DUE TO SCARCITY
*P.P.MAGENTA/1: UNPRICED DUE TO SCARCITY
*P.P.YELLOW/1: UNPRICED DUE TO SCARCITY

1	Roman Reigns	.60	1.50
2	Dean Ambrose	.60	1.50
3	Dean Ambrose	.60	1.50
4	John Cena	1.00	2.50
5	Charlotte	.75	2.00
6	Kalisto	.30	.75
7	Brock Lesnar	1.00	2.50
8	The Wyatt Family	.50	1.25
9	Dean Ambrose	.60	1.50
10	Kalisto	.30	.75
11	Sasha Banks	.60	1.50
12	AJ Styles	1.00	2.50
13	The Wyatt Family	.50	1.25
14	Triple H	.50	1.25
15	Triple H	.50	1.25
16	AJ Styles	1.00	2.50
17	The Rock	1.00	2.50
18	Roman Reigns/Dean Ambrose	.60	1.50
19	Brock Lesnar	1.00	2.50
20	Brock Lesnar	1.00	2.50
21	Daniel Bryan Retires	.75	2.00
22	Chris Jericho	.50	1.25
23	Kevin Owens	.50	1.25
24	Brock Lesnar	1.00	2.50
25	Kalisto	.30	.75
26	Charlotte	.75	2.00
27	AJ Styles	1.00	2.50
28	Roman Reigns/Dean Ambrose	.60	1.50
29	Brock Lesnar	1.00	2.50
30	Roman Reigns	.60	1.50
31	Shane McMahon	.30	.75
32	Dean Ambrose	.60	1.50
33	Triple H	.50	1.25
34	Undertaker	.75	2.00
35	Triple H	.50	1.25
36	Shane McMahon	.30	.75
37	Sami Zayn	.25	.60
38	The New Day	.40	1.00
39	Dean Ambrose	.60	1.50
40	Brock Lesnar	1.00	2.50
41	Triple H	.50	1.25
42	Triple H	.50	1.25
43	Roman Reigns	.60	1.50
44	Undertaker	.75	2.00
45	Brock Lesnar	1.00	2.50
46	Shane McMahon	.30	.75
47	The Godfather	.20	.50
48	Vader	.20	.50
49	The Fabulous Freebirds	.20	.50
50	John Cena	1.00	2.50
51	Sting Retires	.60	1.50
52	Kalisto	.30	.75
53	Team Total Divas	.20	.50
54	Lita	.40	1.00
55	The Usos	.25	.60
56	Zack Ryder	.20	.50
57	Chris Jericho	.50	1.25
58	Brock Lesnar	1.00	2.50
59	Charlotte	.75	2.00
60	Shane McMahon	.30	.75
61	Undertaker	.75	2.00
62	Diamond Dallas Page	.25	.60
63	Tatanka	.20	.50
64	Baron Corbin	.30	.75
65	The Rock	1.00	2.50
66	HHH/Stephanie	.50	1.25
67	Roman Reigns	.60	1.50
68	Apollo Crews	.25	.60
69	The Miz	.40	1.00
70	Maryse	.40	1.00
71	Enzo Amore/Big Cass	.60	1.50
72	Cesaro	.40	1.00
73	AJ Styles	1.00	2.50
74	Vaudevillains	.20	.50
75	Cesaro	.40	1.00
76	Gallows & Anderson	.30	.75
77	Roman Reigns	.60	1.50
	Bray Wyatt		
78	Sami Zayn	.25	.60
79	League of Nations	.20	.50
80	Dean Ambrose	.60	1.50
81	Charlotte	.75	2.00
82	Shane & Stephanie McMahon	.30	.75
83	Roman Reigns	.60	1.50
84	Dana Brooke	.40	1.00
85	Rusev	.40	1.00
86	Dean Ambrose	.60	1.50
87	Charlotte	.75	2.00
88	Roman Reigns	.60	1.50
89	Seth Rollins	.60	1.50
90	The Club	.20	.50
91	AJ Styles	1.00	2.50
92	Dean Ambrose	.60	1.50
93	Seth Rollins	.60	1.50
94	Dean Ambrose	.60	1.50
95	Team USA	.20	.50
96	Daniel Bryan	.75	2.00
	Mick Foley		
97	WWE Draft	.20	.50
98	Sasha Banks/Bayley	.60	1.50
99	John Cena/Enzo & Cass	1.00	2.50
100	Dean Ambrose	.60	1.50

2017 Topps WWE Road to WrestleMania Autographed Andre the Giant Battle Royal Trophy Relics

STATED ODDS 1:33,024
UNPRICED DUE TO SCARCITY

NNO Big Show
NNO Cesaro
NNO Curtis Axel
NNO Darren Young
NNO Goldust
NNO Heath Slater
NNO Hideo Itami
NNO Jack Swagger
NNO Kane
NNO Konnor
NNO Mark Henry

NNO	The Miz		
NNO	Viktor		

2017 Topps WWE Road to WrestleMania Andre the Giant Battle Royal Trophy Relics

*BLUE/50: .5X TO 1.2X BASIC MEM
*SILVER/25: .6X TO 1.5X BASIC MEM
*GOLD/10: .75X TO 2X BASIC MEM
*RED/1: UNPRICED DUE TO SCARCITY
*P.P.BLACK/1: UNPRICED DUE TO SCARCITY
*P.P.CYAN/1: UNPRICED DUE TO SCARCITY
*P.P.MAGENTA/1: UNPRICED DUE TO SCARCITY
*P.P.YELLOW/1: UNPRICED DUE TO SCARCITY
STATED ODDS 1:1,296

NNO	Baron Corbin	3.00	8.00
NNO	Big Show	2.50	6.00
NNO	Bo Dallas	2.00	5.00
NNO	Cesaro	4.00	10.00
NNO	Curtis Axel	2.00	5.00
NNO	Darren Young	2.00	5.00
NNO	Diamond Dallas Page	2.50	6.00
NNO	Fandango	2.00	5.00
NNO	Goldust	2.50	6.00
NNO	Heath Slater	2.00	5.00
NNO	Hideo Itami	3.00	8.00
NNO	Jack Swagger	2.00	5.00
NNO	Kane	2.50	6.00
NNO	Konnor	2.00	5.00
NNO	Mark Henry	2.00	5.00
NNO	R-Truth	2.00	5.00
NNO	Tatanka	2.00	5.00
NNO	The Miz	4.00	10.00
NNO	Tyler Breeze	2.00	5.00
NNO	Viktor	2.00	5.00

2017 Topps WWE Road to WrestleMania Autographed Shirt Relics

STATED ODDS 1:22,016
UNPRICED DUE TO SCARCITY

NNO Asuka
NNO Austin Aries
NNO Bayley
NNO Becky Lynch
NNO Big Cass
NNO Big E
NNO Bray Wyatt
NNO Cesaro
NNO Darren Young
NNO Dolph Ziggler
NNO Enzo Amore
NNO Hideo Itami
NNO John Cena
NNO Kevin Owens
NNO Kofi Kingston
NNO Natalya
NNO Randy Orton
NNO Roman Reigns
NNO Sami Zayn
NNO Sasah Banks
NNO Seth Rollins
NNO Shinsuke Nakamura
NNO Simon Gotch
NNO Xavier Woods
NNO Zack Ryder

2017 Topps WWE Road to WrestleMania Autographs

*BLUE/50: .6X TO 1.5X BASIC AUTOS
*SILVER/25: .75X TO 2X BASIC AUTOS
*GOLD/10: 1X TO 2.5X BASIC AUTOS
*RED/1: UNPRICED DUE TO SCARCITY
*P.P.BLACK/1: UNPRICED DUE TO SCARCITY
*P.P.CYAN/1: UNPRICED DUE TO SCARCITY
*P.P.MAGENTA/1: UNPRICED DUE TO SCARCITY
*P.P.YELLOW/1: UNPRICED DUE TO SCARCITY
STATED ODDS 1:36

NNO	Asuka	15.00	40.00
NNO	Austin Aries	8.00	20.00
NNO	Bayley	20.00	50.00
NNO	Becky Lynch	15.00	40.00
NNO	Big E	8.00	20.00
NNO	Bray Wyatt	12.00	30.00
NNO	Cesaro	10.00	25.00
NNO	Charlotte	12.00	30.00
NNO	Dean Ambrose	12.00	30.00
NNO	Finn Balor	12.00	30.00
NNO	Hideo Itami	6.00	15.00
NNO	John Cena		
NNO	Kevin Owens	15.00	40.00
NNO	Kofi Kingston	6.00	15.00
NNO	Lana	8.00	20.00
NNO	Lex Luger	10.00	25.00
NNO	Maryse	12.00	30.00
NNO	The Miz	6.00	15.00
NNO	Nikki Bella	15.00	40.00
NNO	Roman Reigns	30.00	75.00
NNO	Rusev	6.00	15.00
NNO	Sasha Banks	30.00	75.00
NNO	Seth Rollins	12.00	30.00
NNO	Shinsuke Nakamura	20.00	50.00
NNO	Sting	25.00	60.00

2017 Topps WWE Road to WrestleMania Kiss

*GOLD/10: .6X TO 1.5X BASIC KISS
*RED/1: UNPRICED DUE TO SCARCITY
STATED ODDS 1:91

NNO	Alexa Bliss	60.00	120.00
NNO	Becky Lynch	20.00	50.00
NNO	Carmella	20.00	50.00
NNO	Charlotte	15.00	40.00
NNO	Liv Morgan	20.00	50.00
NNO	Natalya	12.00	30.00
NNO	Nia Jax	12.00	30.00
NNO	Renee Young	12.00	30.00

2017 Topps WWE Road to WrestleMania Kiss Autographs

*GOLD/10: UNPRICED DUE TO SCARCITY
*RED/1: UNPRICED DUE TO SCARCITY
STATED ODDS 1:354

NNO	Alexa Bliss	250.00	500.00
NNO	Becky Lynch	150.00	300.00
NNO	Carmella	30.00	80.00
NNO	Charlotte	125.00	250.00
NNO	Liv Morgan	60.00	120.00
NNO	Natalya	25.00	60.00
NNO	Nia Jax	20.00	50.00
NNO	Nikki Bella	60.00	120.00
NNO	Renee Young	25.00	60.00

2017 Topps WWE Road to WrestleMania Dual Autographs

STATED ODDS 1:726
STATED PRINT RUN 10 SER.#'d SETS

NNO	Asuka/Bayley	100.00	200.00
NNO	Charlotte/R.Flair	100.00	200.00
NNO	F.Balor/H.Itami	60.00	120.00
NNO	J.Cena/N.Bella	125.00	250.00
NNO	K.Kingston/Big E	30.00	75.00
NNO	Miz/Maryse	60.00	120.00
NNO	R.Reigns/D.Ambrose		
NNO	Rusev/Lana	75.00	150.00
NNO	S.Banks/B.Lynch	100.00	200.00
NNO	S.Rollins/Cesaro	60.00	120.00
NNO	S.Nakamura/A.Aries		
NNO	Sting/L.Luger	75.00	150.00

2017 Topps WWE Road to WrestleMania Autographed NXT TakeOver Dallas Mat Relics

STATED PRINT RUN 10 SER.#'d SETS
UNPRICED DUE TO SCARCITY

NNO Asuka
NNO Austin Aries
NNO Bayley
NNO Sami Zayn
NNO Samoa Joe
NNO Shinsuke Nakamura

2017 Topps WWE Road to WrestleMania NXT TakeOver Dallas Mat Relics

*BLUE/50: .5X TO 1.2X BASIC MEM
*SILVER/25: .6X TO 1.5X BASIC MEM
*GOLD/10: .75X TO 2X BASIC MEM
*RED/1: UNPRICED DUE TO SCARCITY
*P.P.BLACK/1: UNPRICED DUE TO SCARCITY
*P.P.CYAN/1: UNPRICED DUE TO SCARCITY
*P.P.MAGENTA/1: UNPRICED DUE TO SCARCITY
*P.P.YELLOW/1: UNPRICED DUE TO SCARCITY
STATED ODDS 1:2,642

NNO	Asuka	5.00	12.00
NNO	Austin Aries	3.00	8.00
NNO	Baron Corbin	2.50	6.00
NNO	Bayley	5.00	12.00
NNO	Chad Gable	2.00	5.00
NNO	Finn Balor	6.00	15.00
NNO	Jason Jordan	2.00	5.00
NNO	Sami Zayn	2.00	5.00
NNO	Samoa Joe	5.00	12.00
NNO	Shinsuke Nakamura	4.00	10.00

2017 Topps WWE Road to WrestleMania Shirt Relics

*BLUE/50: .5X TO 1.2X BASIC MEM
*SILVER/25: .6X TO 1.5X BASIC MEM
*GOLD/10: UNPRICED DUE TO SCARCITY
*RED/1: UNPRICED DUE TO SCARCITY
*P.P.BLACK/1: UNPRICED DUE TO SCARCITY
*P.P.CYAN/1: UNPRICED DUE TO SCARCITY
*P.P.MAGENTA/1: UNPRICED DUE TO SCARCITY
*P.P.YELLOW/1: UNPRICED DUE TO SCARCITY
STATED ODDS 1:870

NNO	Asuka	4.00	10.00
NNO	Austin Aries	2.50	6.00
NNO	Becky Lynch	4.00	10.00
NNO	Big Cass	1.50	4.00
NNO	Bray Wyatt	3.00	8.00
NNO	Cesaro	2.50	6.00
NNO	Charlotte	5.00	12.00
NNO	Darren Young	1.25	3.00
NNO	Dolph Ziggler	2.00	5.00
NNO	Finn Balor	5.00	12.00
NNO	Hideo Itami	2.00	5.00
NNO	John Cena	6.00	15.00
NNO	Kofi Kingston	1.50	4.00
NNO	Natalya	2.50	6.00
NNO	No Way Jose	1.25	3.00
NNO	Randy Orton	3.00	8.00
NNO	Roman Reigns	4.00	10.00
NNO	Sasha Banks	4.00	10.00
NNO	Seth Rollins	4.00	10.00
NNO	Shinsuke Nakamura	3.00	8.00
NNO	Simon Gotch	1.25	3.00
NNO	Zack Ryder	1.25	3.00

2017 Topps WWE Road to WrestleMania Autographed Triple Threat Dual Relics

STATED ODDS 1:66,048
STATED PRINT RUN 10 SER.#'d SETS

NNO	Brock Lesnar	125.00	250.00
NNO	John Cena	125.00	200.00
NNO	Roman Reigns	60.00	120.00
NNO	Sasha Banks	120.00	200.00

2017 Topps WWE Road to WrestleMania Autographed WrestleMania 32 Mat Relics

STATED ODDS 1:33,024
UNPRICED DUE TO SCARCITY

NNO AJ Styles
NNO Becky Lynch
NNO Bray Wyatt
NNO Brie Bella
NNO Brock Lesnar
NNO Chris Jericho
NNO Dean Ambrose
NNO John Cena
NNO Kevin Owens
NNO Natalya
NNO Roman Reigns
NNO Sasha Banks
NNO Zack Ryder

2017 Topps WWE Road to WrestleMania WrestleMania 32 Mat Relics

*BLUE/50: .5X TO 1.2X BASIC MEM
*SILVER/25: .6X TO 1.5X BASIC MEM
*GOLD/10: .75X TO 2X BASIC MEM
*RED/1: UNPRICED DUE TO SCARCITY
*P.P.BLACK/1: UNPRICED DUE TO SCARCITY
*P.P.CYAN/1: UNPRICED DUE TO SCARCITY
*P.P.MAGENTA/1: UNPRICED DUE TO SCARCITY
*P.P.YELLOW/1: UNPRICED DUE TO SCARCITY
STATED ODDS 1:1,296

NNO	AJ Styles	10.00	25.00
NNO	Baron Corbin	3.00	8.00
NNO	Becky Lynch	6.00	15.00
NNO	Bray Wyatt	5.00	12.00
NNO	Brie Bella	5.00	12.00

NNO Brock Lesnar	10.00	25.00
NNO Charlotte	8.00	20.00
NNO Chris Jericho	5.00	12.00
NNO Dean Ambrose	6.00	15.00
NNO John Cena	10.00	25.00
NNO Kevin Owens	5.00	12.00
NNO Lana	6.00	15.00
NNO Natalya	4.00	10.00
NNO The Rock	10.00	25.00
NNO Roman Reigns	6.00	15.00
NNO Sasha Banks	6.00	15.00
NNO Shane McMahon	3.00	8.00
NNO Triple H	5.00	12.00
NNO Undertaker	8.00	20.00
NNO Zack Ryder	2.00	5.00

2017 Topps WWE Road to WrestleMania WrestleMania 33 Roster

COMPLETE SET (50)	10.00	25.00
STATED ODDS 2:1		
WMR1 Triple H	.75	2.00
WMR2 Stephanie McMahon	.40	1.00
WMR3 Roman Reigns	1.00	2.50
WMR4 The Rock	1.50	4.00
WMR5 John Cena	1.50	4.00
WMR6 Bray Wyatt	.75	2.00
WMR7 Erick Rowan	.30	.75
WMR8 Braun Strowman	.40	1.00
WMR9 Luke Harper	.30	.75
WMR10 Undertaker	1.25	3.00
WMR11 Shane McMahon	.50	1.25
WMR12 Brock Lesnar	1.50	4.00
WMR13 Dean Ambrose	1.00	2.50
WMR14 Charlotte	1.25	3.00
WMR15 Ric Flair	.75	2.00
WMR16 Sasha Banks	1.00	2.50
WMR17 Becky Lynch	1.00	2.50
WMR18 Chris Jericho	.75	2.00
WMR19 AJ Styles	1.50	4.00
WMR20 Baron Corbin	.50	1.25
WMR21 Kane	.40	1.00
WMR22 Big Show	.40	1.00
WMR23 Mark Henry	.30	.75
WMR24 Zack Ryder	.30	.75
WMR25 Kevin Owens	.75	2.00
WMR26 Sami Zayn	.40	1.00
WMR27 The Miz	.60	1.50
WMR28 Dolph Ziggler	.50	1.25
WMR29 Sin Cara	.40	1.00
WMR30 Kalisto	.50	1.25
WMR31 Kofi Kingston	.40	1.00
WMR32 Big E	.40	1.00
WMR33 Xavier Woods	.40	1.00
WMR34 Sheamus	.60	1.50
WMR35 Rusev	.60	1.50
WMR36 Jey Uso	.40	1.00
WMR37 Jimmy Uso	.40	1.00
WMR38 Darren Young	.30	.75
WMR39 R-Truth	.30	.75
WMR40 Goldust	.40	1.00
WMR41 Heath Slater	.30	.75
WMR42 Brie Bella	.75	2.00
WMR43 Natalya	.60	1.50
WMR44 Alicia Fox	.50	1.25
WMR45 Eva Marie	.75	2.00
WMR46 Lana	1.00	2.50
WMR47 Naomi	.60	1.50
WMR48 Tamina	.40	1.00
WMR49 Emma	.75	2.00
WMR50 Summer Rae	.75	2.00

2018 Topps WWE Road to WrestleMania

COMPLETE SET (100)	8.00	20.00
UNOPENED BOX (24 PACKS)		
UNOPENED PACK (7 CARDS)		
*BRONZE: .5X TO 1.2X BASIC CARDS		
*BLUE/99: .75X TO 2X BASIC CARDS		
*SILVER/25: 2X TO 5X BASIC CARDS		
*GOLD/10: UNPRICED DUE TO SCARCITY		
*RED/1: UNPRICED DUE TO SCARCITY		
*P.P.BLACK/1: UNPRICED DUE TO SCARCITY		
*P.P.CYAN/1: UNPRICED DUE TO SCARCITY		
*P.P.MAGENTA/1: UNPRICED DUE TO SCARCITY		
*P.P.YELLOW/1: UNPRICED DUE TO SCARCITY		
1 Roman Reigns	.60	1.50
2 Cesaro & Sheamus	.50	1.25
3 Roman Reigns	.60	1.50
4 Universal Champion Kevin Owens	.60	1.50
5 Roman Reigns	.60	1.50
6 Kevin Owens	.60	1.50
7 Team Raw defeats Team SmackDown	.50	1.25
8 Cesaro & Sheamus	.50	1.25
9 Undertaker Returns	1.00	2.50
10 Chris Jericho	.60	1.50
11 Luke Gallows & Karl Anderson	.30	.75
12 Kevin Owens	.60	1.50
13 Samoa Joe Debuts	.50	1.25
14 Kevin Owens	.60	1.50
15 Roman Reigns	.60	1.50
16 Kevin Owens	1.00	2.50
17 Roman Reigns	1.00	2.50
18 Mick Foley	.60	1.50
19 Undertaker	1.00	2.50
20 Undertaker	1.00	2.50
21 Ricky The Dragon Steamboat	.40	1.00
22 Diamond Dallas Page	.40	1.00
23 Kurt Angle Returns	.60	1.50
24 Kevin Owens	.60	1.50
25 The Hardy Boyz Return	.60	1.50
26 Seth Rollins	.60	1.50
27 Brock Lesnar	1.00	2.50
28 Roman Reigns	.60	1.50
29 Kurt Angle	.60	1.50
30 The Revival	.30	.75
31 Finn Balor	.60	1.50
32 Alexa Bliss	1.25	3.00
33 Elias	.60	1.50
34 Chris Jericho	.60	1.50
35 Bray Wyatt	.60	1.50
36 Braun Strowman	.60	1.50
37 Goldust	.50	1.25
38 The Miz	.50	1.25
39 Cesaro & Sheamus	.50	1.25
40 Samoa Joe	.50	1.25
41 Big Cass Turns	.30	.75
42 Cesaro & Sheamus	.50	1.25
43 Universal Champion Brock Lesnar	1.00	2.50
44 Kurt Angle	.60	1.50
45 Braun Strowman	.60	1.50
46 Dean Ambrose	.60	1.50
47 TJP	.30	.75
48 The Brian Kendrick	.40	1.00
49 The Brian Kendrick	.40	1.00
50 Rich Swann	.30	.75
51 Neville Returns	.40	1.00
52 Neville	.40	1.00
53 Neville	.40	1.00
54 Noam Dar	.40	1.00
55 Akira Tozawa	.40	1.00
56 WWE Champion AJ Styles	1.00	2.50
57 Dolph Ziggler	.50	1.25
58 Bray Wyatt	.60	1.50
59 Randy Orton	.60	1.50
60 The Miz	.50	1.25
61 Edge and Undertaker Return	1.00	2.50
62 Team SmackDown defeats Team Raw	1.00	2.50
63 James Ellsworth	.25	.60
64 The New Wyatt Family	.60	1.50
65 The Miz	.50	1.25
66 Baron Corbin	.40	1.00
67 AJ Styles	1.00	2.50
68 American Alpha	.25	.60
69 Dean Ambrose	.50	1.25
70 John Cena	1.00	2.50
71 Randy Orton	.60	1.50
72 Randy Orton	.60	1.50
73 Bray Wyatt	.60	1.50
74 Randy Orton	.60	1.50
75 The Usos	.40	1.00
76 Shane McMahon	1.00	2.50
77 Mojo Rawley	.25	.60
78 Dean Ambrose	.50	1.25
79 AJ Styles	1.00	2.50
80 John Cena Proposes to Nikki Bella	1.00	2.50
81 Randy Orton	.60	1.50
82 Tye Dillinger	.25	.60
83 Shinsuke Nakamura	.60	1.50
84 The Superstar Shake-Up	.75	2.00
85 Jinder Mahal	.30	.75
86 Kevin Owens	.60	1.50
87 Shinsuke Nakamura	.60	1.50
88 The Usos	.40	1.00
89 Jinder Mahal	.30	.75
90 Maria Kanellis	.60	1.50
91 WWE Champion Jinder Mahal	.30	.75
92 Baron Corbin	.40	1.00
93 AJ Styles	1.00	2.50
94 The New Day	.40	1.00
95 Kevin Owens	.60	1.50
96 John Cena	1.00	2.50
97 WWE Champion Jinder Mahal	.30	.75
98 AJ Styles	1.00	2.50
99 Shinsuke Nakamura	1.00	2.50
100 Jinder Mahal	.30	.75

2018 Topps WWE Road to WrestleMania Commemorative Andre the Giant Battle Royal Trophy Relics

*BRONZE/99: .5X TO 1.2X BASIC MEM		
*BLUE/50: .6X TO 1.5X BASIC MEM		
*SILVER/25: .75X TO 2X BASIC MEM		
*GOLD/10: UNPRICED DUE TO SCARCITY		
*RED/1: UNPRICED DUE TO SCARCITY		
STATED ODDS 1:936		
ACBR Braun Strowman	6.00	15.00
ACBS Big Show	2.50	6.00
ACCG Chad Gable	2.50	6.00
ACDZ Dolph Ziggler	2.50	6.00
ACFA Fandango	5.00	12.00
ACGO Goldust	2.50	6.00
ACHS Heath Slater	2.50	6.00
ACJI Jimmy Uso	5.00	12.00
ACJJ Jason Jordan	2.50	6.00
ACJM Jinder Mahal	2.50	6.00
ACJU Jey Uso	2.50	6.00
ACKD Killian Dain	3.00	8.00
ACLH Luke Harper	3.00	8.00
ACMH Mark Henry	2.50	6.00
ACMR Mojo Rawley	3.00	8.00
ACRH Rhyno	3.00	8.00
ACRT R-Truth	2.50	6.00
ACSZ Sami Zayn	4.00	10.00
ACTB Tian Bing	2.50	6.00
ACTBR Tyler Breeze	2.50	6.00

2018 Topps WWE Road to WrestleMania Autographed Commemorative Andre the Giant Battle Royal Trophy Re

STATED ODDS 1:24,096
STATED PRINT RUN 10 SER.#'d SETS
UNPRICED DUE TO SCARCITY

NNO Big Show
NNO Braun Strowman
NNO Dolph Ziggler
NNO Fandango
NNO Goldust
NNO Heath Slater
NNO Jey Uso
NNO Jimmy Uso
NNO Jinder Mahal
NNO Killian Dain
NNO Luke Harper
NNO Mark Henry
NNO Mojo Rawley
NNO Sami Zayn
NNO Tyler Breeze

2018 Topps WWE Road to WrestleMania Autographed Dual Relics

STATED ODDS 1:96,384
STATED PRINT RUN 10 SER.#'d SETS
UNPRICED DUE TO SCARCITY

NNO Alexa Bliss
NNO John Cena
NNO Kevin Owens
NNO Naomi
NNO Roman Reigns
NNO Shinsuke Nakamura

2018 Topps WWE Road to WrestleMania Autographed NXT TakeOver Orlando Mat Relics

STATED ODDS 1:32,128
STATED PRINT RUN 10 SER.#'d SETS
UNPRICED DUE TO SCARCITY

NNO Aleister Black
NNO Asuka
NNO Bobby Roode
NNO Eric Young
NNO Johnny Gargano
NNO Kassius Ohno
NNO Nikki Cross
NNO Roderick Strong

NNO Ruby Riot
NNO Shinsuke Nakamura
NNO Tommaso Ciampa

2018 Topps WWE Road to WrestleMania Autographed Shirt Relics

STATED ODDS 1:32,128
STATED PRINT RUN 10 SER.#'d SETS
UNPRICED DUE TO SCARCITY

NNO Becky Lynch
NNO Carmella
NNO Cesaro
NNO Goldust
NNO Karl Anderson
NNO Kevin Owens
NNO Luke Gallows
NNO Luke Harper
NNO Naomi
NNO Roman Reigns
NNO Sting
NNO Xavier Woods

2018 Topps WWE Road to WrestleMania Autographed Wrestlemania 33 Mat Relics

STATED ODDS 1:24,096
STATED PRINT RUN 10 SER.#'d SETS
UNPRICED DUE TO SCARCITY

NNO AJ Styles
NNO Charlotte Flair
NNO Chris Jericho
NNO Jeff Hardy
NNO Kevin Owens
NNO Maryse
NNO Naomi
NNO Randy Orton
NNO Roman Reigns
NNO Sasha Banks
NNO Stephanie McMahon
NNO The Miz
NNO Triple H
NNO Undertaker

2018 Topps WWE Road to WrestleMania Autographs

*BLUE/50: .5X TO 1.2X BASIC AUTOS
*SILVER/25: .6X TO 1.5X BASIC AUTOS
*GOLD/10: UNPRICED DUE TO SCARCITY
*RED/1: UNPRICED DUE TO SCARCITY
*P.P.BLACK/1: UNPRICED DUE TO SCARCITY
*P.P.CYAN/1: UNPRICED DUE TO SCARCITY
*P.P.MAGENTA/1: UNPRICED DUE TO SCARCITY
*P.P.YELLOW/1: UNPRICED DUE TO SCARCITY
STATED ODDS 1:32

AAB Aleister Black	12.00	30.00
AAL Alexa Bliss	30.00	75.00
AAS AJ Styles	15.00	40.00
ABA Bayley	12.00	30.00
ABL Becky Lynch	15.00	40.00
ABW Bray Wyatt	8.00	20.00
ACA Carmella	10.00	25.00
ACF Charlotte Flair	15.00	40.00
ADA Dean Ambrose	12.00	30.00
ADW Dash Wilder	6.00	15.00
AEM Ember Moon	12.00	30.00
AEY Eric Young	5.00	12.00
AFB Finn Balor	15.00	40.00
AJG Johnny Gargano	10.00	25.00
AJH Jeff Hardy	15.00	40.00
AJM Jinder Mahal	10.00	25.00
AKA Kassius Ohno	6.00	15.00
AKO Kevin Owens	8.00	20.00
AMH Matt Hardy	15.00	40.00
ANA Naomi	6.00	15.00
ANC Nikki Cross	10.00	25.00
ARS Roderick Strong	5.00	12.00
ASB Sasha Banks	20.00	50.00
ASD Scott Dawson	5.00	12.00
ASJ Samoa Joe	8.00	20.00
ASN Shinsuke Nakamura	12.00	30.00
ASR Seth Rollins	12.00	30.00
ATC Tommaso Ciampa	5.00	12.00
ATD Tye Dillinger	6.00	15.00
ATM The Miz	8.00	20.00
AASU Asuka	15.00	40.00
ABOR Bobby Roode	10.00	25.00
AKUA Kurt Angle	15.00	40.00
ARRI Ruby Riot	12.00	30.00

2018 Topps WWE Road to WrestleMania Autographs Silver

STATED ODDS 1:105
STATED PRINT RUN 25 SER.#'d SETS

ASM Stephanie McMahon	125.00	250.00
ATH Triple H	150.00	300.00
AUN Undertaker	150.00	300.00
ANAT Natalya	10.00	25.00

2018 Topps WWE Road to WrestleMania Dual Autographs

STATED ODDS 1:1,928
STATED PRINT RUN 10 SER.#'d SETS

DABR A.Black/B.Roode/10	60.00	120.00
DAFS F.Balor/Samoa Joe/4		
DAJT T.Ciampa/J.Gargano/10	30.00	75.00
DAMJ Matt & Jeff Hardy/10	30.00	75.00
DARK K.Ohno/R.Strong/10		
DARN N.Cross/R.Riot/10	20.00	50.00
DAUK K.Angle/Undertaker/10	250.00	400.00

2018 Topps WWE Road to WrestleMania Dual Relics

*SILVER/25: .5X TO 1.2X BASIC MEM
*GOLD/10: UNPRICED DUE TO SCARCITY
*RED/1: UNPRICED DUE TO SCARCITY
STATED PRINT RUN 50 SER.#'d SETS

DRAB Alexa Bliss	30.00	75.00
DRBL Brock Lesnar	10.00	25.00
DRJC John Cena	15.00	40.00
DRKO Kevin Owens	10.00	25.00
DRNA Naomi	12.00	30.00
DRRR Roman Reigns	10.00	25.00
DRSN Shinsuke Nakamura		
DRSR Seth Rollins	12.00	30.00

2018 Topps WWE Road to WrestleMania Kiss

*GOLD/10: UNPRICED DUE TO SCARCITY
*RED/1: UNPRICED DUE TO SCARCITY
STATED ODDS 1:112

KAB Alexa Bliss	60.00	120.00
KAS Asuka	30.00	75.00
KCA Carmella	25.00	60.00
KCF Charlotte Flair/99	25.00	60.00
KMA Maryse	20.00	50.00
KNA Naomi	12.00	30.00
KRR Ruby Riot	20.00	50.00

2018 Topps WWE Road to WrestleMania Kiss Autographs

*GOLD/10: UNPRICED DUE TO SCARCITY
*RED/1: UNPRICED DUE TO SCARCITY
STATED ODDS 1:445

NNO Alexa Bliss	120.00	250.00
NNO Asuka	50.00	100.00
NNO Becky Lynch	60.00	120.00
NNO Carmella	50.00	100.00
NNO Charlotte Flair	75.00	150.00
NNO Goldust	75.00	150.00
NNO Maryse	50.00	100.00
NNO Nikki Cross	50.00	100.00
NNO Ruby Riot	50.00	100.00

2018 Topps WWE Road to WrestleMania NXT TakeOver Orlando Mat Relics

*BRONZE/99: SAME VALUE AS BASIC MEM
*BLUE/50: .5X TO 1.2X BASIC MEM
*SILVER/25: .6X TO 1.5X BASIC MEM
*GOLD/10: UNPRICED DUE TO SCARCITY
*RED/1: UNPRICED DUE TO SCARCITY
STATED ODDS 1:1,236

MRAB Aleister Black	6.00	15.00
MRAS Asuka	6.00	15.00
MRBR Bobby Roode	6.00	15.00
MRDW Dash Wilder	2.50	6.00
MREM Ember Moon	3.00	8.00
MREY Eric Young	2.50	6.00
MRJG Johnny Gargano	3.00	8.00
MRKO Kassius Ohno	6.00	15.00
MRNC Nikki Cross	4.00	10.00
MRRR Ruby Riot	5.00	12.00
MRRS Roderick Strong	2.50	6.00
MRSD Scott Dawson	3.00	8.00
MRSN Shinsuke Nakamura	4.00	10.00
MRTC Tommaso Ciampa	3.00	8.00
MRTD Tye Dillinger	3.00	8.00

2018 Topps WWE Road to WrestleMania Road to WrestleMania 34

RTW1 The Miz & Miztourage	1.25	3.00
RTW2 Big Cass	.75	2.00
RTW3 Finn Balor	1.50	4.00
RTW4 Dean Ambrose & Seth Rollins	1.50	4.00
RTW5 Brock Lesnar	2.50	6.00
RTW6 Braun Strowman	1.50	4.00
RTW7 John Cena	2.50	6.00
RTW8 Jeff Hardy	1.25	3.00
RTW9 John Cena and Roman Reigns	2.50	6.00
RTW10 Neville	1.00	2.50
RTW11 Enzo Amore	.60	1.50
RTW12 The Brian Kendrick	1.00	2.50
RTW13 The Usos	.60	1.50
RTW14 John Cena	2.50	6.00
RTW15 Randy Orton	1.50	4.00
RTW16 AJ Styles	2.50	6.00
RTW17 Jinder Mahal	.75	2.00
RTW18 Bobby Roode	1.00	2.50
RTW19 Shelton Benjamin	.75	2.00
RTW20 Shinsuke Nakamura	1.50	4.00

2018 Topps WWE Road to WrestleMania Shirt Relics

*BLUE/50: .5X TO 1.2X BASIC MEM
*SILVER/25: .6X TO 1.5X BASIC MEM
*GOLD/10: UNPRICED DUE TO SCARCITY
*RED/1: UNPRICED DUE TO SCARCITY
STATED ODDS 1:1,890
STATED PRINT RUN 99 SER.#'d SETS

SRAB Alexa Bliss	12.00	30.00
SRBL Becky Lynch	10.00	25.00
SRBR Brock Lesnar	5.00	12.00
SRCA Carmella	6.00	15.00
SRCE Cesaro	3.00	8.00
SRCG Chad Gable	2.50	6.00
SRGO Goldust	3.00	8.00
SRJC John Cena	6.00	15.00
SRJI Jimmy Uso	2.50	6.00
SRJJ Jason Jordan	3.00	8.00
SRKA Karl Anderson	2.50	6.00
SRKO Kevin Owens	2.50	6.00
SRLG Luke Gallows	2.50	6.00
SRLH Luke Harper	3.00	8.00
SRNA Naomi	4.00	10.00
SRNW No Way Jose	2.50	6.00
SRRR Roman Reigns	4.00	10.00
SRSR Seth Rollins	4.00	10.00
SRST Sting	10.00	25.00
SRXW Xavier Woods	2.50	6.00

2018 Topps WWE Road to WrestleMania WrestleMania 33 Mat Relics

*BRONZE/99: SAME VALUE AS BASIC MEM
*BLUE/50: .5X TO 1.2X BASIC MEM
*SILVER/25: .6X TO 1.5X BASIC MEM
*GOLD/10: UNPRICED DUE TO SCARCITY
*RED/1: UNPRICED DUE TO SCARCITY
STATED ODDS 1:748
STATED PRINT RUN 199 SER.#'d SETS

WMAB Alexa Bliss	10.00	25.00
WMAS AJ Styles	8.00	20.00
WMBA Bayley	6.00	15.00
WMBR Brock Lesnar	6.00	15.00
WMBY Bray Wyatt	10.00	25.00
WMCA Carmella	5.00	12.00
WMCF Charlotte Flair	6.00	15.00
WMCJ Chris Jericho	4.00	10.00
WMDA Dean Ambrose	5.00	12.00
WMJC John Cena	6.00	15.00
WMJH Jeff Hardy	6.00	15.00
WMKO Kevin Owens	4.00	10.00
WMMA Maryse	6.00	15.00
WMMH Matt Hardy	4.00	10.00
WMNA Naomi	4.00	10.00
WMNB Nikki Bella	5.00	12.00
WMRO Randy Orton	3.00	8.00
WMRR Roman Reigns	10.00	25.00
WMSB Sasha Banks	6.00	15.00
WMSM Stephanie McMahon	6.00	15.00
WMSR Seth Rollins	5.00	12.00
WMTH Triple H	8.00	20.00
WMTM The Miz	3.00	8.00
WMUN Undertaker	15.00	40.00
WMNAT Natalya	3.00	8.00

2018 Topps WWE Road to WrestleMania WrestleMania 34 Roster

COMPLETE SET (50)	12.00	30.00
R1 Roman Reigns	.75	2.00
R2 Brock Lesnar	1.25	3.00
R3 Randy Orton	.75	2.00
R4 Bray Wyatt	.75	2.00
R5 Seth Rollins	.75	2.00
R6 Triple H	.75	2.00
R7 John Cena	1.25	3.00
R8 The Miz	.60	1.50
R9 Kevin Owens	.75	2.00
R10 Chris Jericho	.75	2.00
R11 AJ Styles	1.25	3.00
R12 Dean Ambrose	.60	1.50
R13 Baron Corbin	.50	1.25
R14 Mojo Rawley	.30	.75
R15 Jinder Mahal	.40	1.00
R16 Asuka	1.00	2.50
R17 Matt Hardy	.75	2.00
R18 Jeff Hardy	.60	1.50
R19 Luke Gallows	.40	1.00
R20 Karl Anderson	.30	.75
R21 Cesaro	.60	1.50
R22 Sheamus	.60	1.50
R23 Enzo Amore	.30	.75
R24 Big Cass	.40	1.00
R25 Bayley	.50	1.25
R26 Charlotte Flair	1.00	2.50
R27 Sasha Banks	1.00	2.50
R28 Nia Jax	.50	1.25
R29 Naomi	.40	1.00
R30 Alexa Bliss	1.50	4.00
R31 Becky Lynch	.75	2.00
R32 Mickie James	.60	1.50
R33 Natalya	.40	1.00
R34 Carmella	.60	1.50
R35 Braun Strowman	.75	2.00
R36 Big Show	.30	.75
R37 Sami Zayn	.30	.75
R38 Luke Harper	.50	1.25
R39 Dolph Ziggler	.40	1.00
R40 Fandango	.30	.75
R41 Tyler Breeze	.30	.75
R42 Jason Jordan	.30	.75
R43 Chad Gable	.30	.75
R44 Jey Uso	.30	.75
R45 Jimmy Uso	.30	.75
R46 Heath Slater	.30	.75
R47 Rhyno	.30	.75
R48 Goldust	.60	1.50
R49 R-Truth	.40	1.00
R50 Titus O'Neil	.30	.75

2019 Topps WWE Road to WrestleMania

COMPLETE SET (100)	10.00	25.00
UNOPENED BOX (24 PACKS)		
UNOPENED PACK (7 CARDS)		
*BRONZE: .5X TO 1.2X BASIC CARDS		
*BLUE/99: .75X TO 2X BASIC CARDS		
*SILVER/25: 2X TO 5X BASIC CARDS		
*GOLD/10: UNPRICED DUE TO SCARCITY		
*RED/1: UNPRICED DUE TO SCARCITY		
*P.P.BLACK/1: UNPRICED DUE TO SCARCITY		
*P.P.CYAN/1: UNPRICED DUE TO SCARCITY		
*P.P.MAGENTA/1: UNPRICED DUE TO SCARCITY		
*P.P.YELLOW/1: UNPRICED DUE TO SCARCITY		
1 Braun Strowman	.60	1.50
2 Braun Strowman	1.00	2.50
3 Roman Reigns	1.00	2.50
4 The Shield	.60	1.50
5 Kane	.40	1.00
6 Demon Finn Balor	.60	1.50
7 Kurt Angle	.50	1.25
8 SmackDown Live Siege	.50	1.25
9 Cesaro & Sheamus	.40	1.00
10 The Shield	.60	1.50
11 Triple H	.60	1.50
12 Braun Strowman	.60	1.50
13 The Shield	.60	1.50
14 Team Raw Defeat Team SmackDown	.60	1.50
15 Roman Reigns	.60	1.50
16 Matt Hardy Snaps	.50	1.25
17 Braun Strowman	.60	1.50
18 Seth Rollins & Jason Jordan	.60	1.50
19 Roman Reigns	.60	1.50
20 The Balor Club	.60	1.50
21 Stone Cold Steve Austin Returns	1.25	3.00
22 The Miz	.50	1.25
23 Cesaro & Sheamus	.40	1.00
24 John Cena	1.00	2.50
25 Elias	.50	1.25
26 Finn Balor and Seth Rollins	.60	1.50
27 Braun Strowman	.60	1.50
28 Roman Reigns	.60	1.50
29 Kurt Angle	.50	1.25
30 Braun Strowman	.60	1.50
31 John Cena	1.00	2.50
32 Braun Strowman	.60	1.50
33 John Cena	1.00	2.50
34 Woken Matt Hardy	.60	1.50
35 Seth Rollins	.60	1.50
36 Kurt Angle & Ronda Rousey	1.25	3.00
37 Undertaker	1.25	3.00
38 Braun Strowman	.60	1.50
39 Breezango	.30	.75
40 Gentleman Jack Gallagher	.40	1.00
41 Kalisto	.25	.60
42 Kalisto	.25	.60
43 Drew Gulak	.25	.60
44 Akira Tozawa	.25	.60
45 Hideo Itami	.25	.60
46 Cedric Alexander & Goldust	.25	.60
47 Drake Maverick	.25	.60
48 Mark Andrews	.25	.60
49 Buddy Murphy	.30	.75
50 Cedric Alexander	.25	.60
51 Mustafa Ali	.25	.60
52 Cedric Alexander	.25	.60
53 Buddy Murphy	.30	.75
54 Cedric Alexander	.25	.60
55 Shinsuke Nakamura	.60	1.50
56 The New Day	.40	1.00
57 Rusev	.50	1.25
58 Kevin Owens	.60	1.50
59 The Usos	.30	.75
60 Baron Corbin	.40	1.00
61 Jinder Mahal	.60	1.50
62 Kevin Owens	.60	1.50
63 Kevin Owens and Sami Zayn	.60	1.50
64 Baron Corbin	.40	1.00
65 Kevin Owens & Sami Zayn	.60	1.50
66 Shinsuka Nakamura	.60	1.50
67 AJ Styles	1.25	3.00
68 Raw Launches Counter-Siege	.60	1.50
69 Baron Corbin	.40	1.00
70 The Usos	.30	.75
71 Kevin Owens & Sami Zayn	.60	1.50
72 Mojo Rawley	.30	.75
73 Kevin Owens	.60	1.50
74 Rusev & Aiden English	.50	1.25
75 Kevin Owens & Sami Zayn	1.00	2.50
76 Kevin Owens	.60	1.50
77 Dolph Ziggler	.50	1.25
78 Kevin Owens & Sami Zayn	1.00	2.50
79 AJ Styles	1.25	3.00
80 Dolph Ziggler	.50	1.25
81 Kevin Owens	.60	1.50
82 Sami Zayn	1.25	3.00
83 Bobby Roode	.50	1.25
84 AJ Styles	1.25	3.00
85 Shinsuke Nakamura	.60	1.50
86 AJ Styles & Nakamura	1.25	3.00
87 John Cena	1.00	2.50
88 Sami Zayn	.50	1.25
89 Randy Orton	.60	1.50
90 AJ Styles	1.25	3.00
91 Daniel Bryan	1.00	2.50
92 Daniel Bryan	1.00	2.50
93 Jinder Mahal	.60	1.50
94 Bludgeon Brothers	.30	.75
95 Daniel Bryan & Shane McMahon	1.00	2.50
96 AJ Styles	1.25	3.00
97 Braun Strowman	.60	1.50
98 Shinsuka Nakamura	.60	1.50
99 The Usos	.30	.75
100 Woken Matt Hardy	.50	1.25

2019 Topps WWE Road to WrestleMania Autographed Commemorative Andre the Giant Battle Royal Trophy Relics

STATED PRINT RUN 10 SER.#'d SETS
UNPRICED DUE TO SCARCITY
BRABC Baron Corbin
BRACG Chad Gable
BRADZ Dolph Ziggler
BRAFN Fandango
BRAGD Goldust
BRAKA Karl Anderson
BRALG Luke Gallows
BRAMH Woken Matt Hardy
BRAMR Mojo Rawley
BRASB Shelton Benjamin
BRASC Sin Cara
BRATB Tyler Breeze
BRATO Titus O'Neil

2019 Topps WWE Road to WrestleMania Autographed Commemorative Intercontinental Championship Relics

STATED PRINT RUN 10 SER.#'d SETS
UNPRICED DUE TO SCARCITY
ICRBH Bret Hit Man Hart
ICRRS Ricky The Dragon Steamboat

2019 Topps WWE Road to WrestleMania Autographed Divas Revolution Relic

UNPRICED DUE TO SCARCITY
DRRABB Brie Bella

2019 Topps WWE Road to WrestleMania Autographed Mat Relics

STATED PRINT RUN 10 SER.#'d SETS
UNPRICED DUE TO SCARCITY
MRAAB Alexa Bliss
MRAAC Adam Cole
MRAAS Asuka
MRACF Charlotte Flair
MRAEM Ember Moon
MRAJG Johnny Gargano
MRAKA Kurt Angle
MRAKD Killian Dain
MRAKO Kevin Owens
MRAMH Woken Matt Hardy
MRANA Naomi
MRARC Ricochet
MRASB Shayna Baszler
MRASN Shinsuke Nakamura
MRASR Seth Rollins
MRASZ Sami Zayn
MRATC Tommaso Ciampa
MRAUN Undertaker
MRAALB Aleister Black
MRAERA Kyle O'Reilly
MRAHHH Triple H
MRARRR Ronda Rousey
MRASMC Stephanie McMahon

2019 Topps WWE Road to WrestleMania Autographed Shirt Relics

STATED PRINT RUN 10 SER.#'d SETS
UNPRICED DUE TO SCARCITY
SRAAB Alexa Bliss
SRAAF Alicia Fox
SRACM Carmella
SRAFB Finn Balor
SRAMH Woken Matt Hardy
SRARD Rusev
SRARY Renee Young
SRASR Seth Rollins

2019 Topps WWE Road to WrestleMania Autographs

*BLUE/50: .5X TO 1.2X BASIC AUTOS		
*SILVER/25: .6X TO 1.5X BASIC AUTOS		
*GOLD/10: UNPRICED DUE TO SCARCITY		
*RED/1: UNPRICED DUE TO SCARCITY		
*P.P.BLACK/1: UNPRICED DUE TO SCARCITY		
*P.P.CYAN/1: UNPRICED DUE TO SCARCITY		
*P.P.MAGENTA/1: UNPRICED DUE TO SCARCITY		
*P.P.YELLOW/1: UNPRICED DUE TO SCARCITY		
RANDOMLY INSERTED INTO PACKS		
AAB Alexa Bliss	30.00	75.00
AAE Aiden English	5.00	12.00
AAJ AJ Styles	15.00	40.00
AAS Asuka	15.00	40.00
ABE Big E	6.00	15.00
ABR Bobby Roode	6.00	15.00

ABS Braun Strowman	15.00	40.00
ACE Cesaro	5.00	12.00
ACF Charlotte Flair	20.00	50.00
ACM Carmella	12.00	30.00
ADB Daniel Bryan	10.00	25.00
AEM Ember Moon	10.00	25.00
AFB Finn Balor	15.00	40.00
AJH Jeff Hardy	15.00	40.00
AKA Kurt Angle	10.00	25.00
AKK Kofi Kingston	6.00	15.00
AKO Kevin Owens	10.00	25.00
ALM Liv Morgan EXCH	15.00	40.00
AMH Woken Matt Hardy	8.00	20.00
ANA Naomi	8.00	20.00
ANJ Nia Jax	6.00	15.00
ARD Rusev	8.00	20.00
ARW Rowan	5.00	12.00
ASB Sasha Banks	20.00	50.00
ASH Sheamus	6.00	15.00
ASJ Samoa Joe	8.00	20.00
ASN Shinsuke Nakamura	10.00	25.00
ASR Seth Rollins	10.00	25.00
ASZ Sami Zayn	5.00	12.00
ATM The Miz	6.00	15.00
AXW Xavier Woods	6.00	15.00
ARRR Ronda Rousey	125.00	250.00
ARTT Ruby Riott	12.00	30.00
AWWE Elias	12.00	30.00

2019 Topps WWE Road to WrestleMania Autographs Blue

AJM Jinder Mahal	8.00	20.00
AJEY Jey Uso	6.00	15.00
AJIM Jimmy Uso	6.00	15.00

2019 Topps WWE Road to WrestleMania Autographs Silver

AUN Undertaker	125.00	250.00
AHHH Triple H	100.00	200.00
ASMC Stephanie McMahon	75.00	150.00

2019 Topps WWE Road to WrestleMania Commemorative Andre the Giant Battle Royal Trophy Relics

*BRONZE/99: .5X TO 1.2X BASIC MEM
*BLUE/50: .6X TO 1.5X BASIC MEM
*SILVER/25: .75X TO 2X BASIC MEM
*GOLD/10: UNPRICED DUE TO SCARCITY
*RED/1: UNPRICED DUE TO SCARCITY
RANDOMLY INSERTED INTO PACKS

BRAE Aiden English	2.00	5.00
BRBC Baron Corbin	2.50	6.00
BRCG Chad Gable	3.00	8.00
BRDZ Dolph Ziggler	2.50	6.00
BRFN Fandango	2.00	5.00
BRGD Goldust	2.50	6.00
BRHS Heath Slater	2.00	5.00
BRKA Karl Anderson	2.50	6.00
BRKN Kane	3.00	8.00
BRLG Luke Gallows	2.50	6.00
BRMH Woken Matt Hardy	3.00	8.00
BRMR Mojo Rawley	2.00	5.00
BRRT R-Truth	2.00	5.00
BRRY Rhyno	2.50	6.00
BRSB Shelton Benjamin	3.00	8.00
BRSC Sin Cara	4.00	10.00
BRTB Tyler Breeze	2.50	6.00
BRTD Tye Dillinger	2.50	6.00
BRTO Titus O'Neil	2.50	6.00
BRZR Zack Ryder	3.00	8.00

2019 Topps WWE Road to WrestleMania Divas Revolution Autographs

RANDOMLY INSERTED INTO PACKS

DRABB Brie Bella
DRABL Becky Lynch
DRACF Charlotte Flair

2019 Topps WWE Road to WrestleMania Divas Revolution Relics

RANDOMLY INSERTED INTO PACKS

DRRBB Brie Bella
DRRNB Nikki Bella

2019 Topps WWE Road to WrestleMania Dual Autographs

STATED PRINT RUN 10 SER.#'d SETS
UNPRICED DUE TO SCARCITY

DAAP Akam/Rezar
DABB Rowan/Harper
DABR T.Breeze/Fandango
DABT B.Dallas/C.Axel
DADW B.Wyatt/M.Hardy
DAUSO The Usos
DAYEP S.Zayn/K.Owens

2019 Topps WWE Road to WrestleMania Intercontinental Champions Autographs

*GOLD/10: UNPRICED DUE TO SCARCITY
*RED/1: UNPRICED DUE TO SCARCITY
*P.P.BLACK/1: UNPRICED DUE TO SCARCITY
*P.P.CYAN/1: UNPRICED DUE TO SCARCITY
*P.P.MAGENTA/1: UNPRICED DUE TO SCARCITY
*P.P.YELLOW/1: UNPRICED DUE TO SCARCITY
RANDOMLY INSERTED INTO PACKS

ICABH Bret Hit Man Hart
ICARS Ricky The Dragon Steamboat

2019 Topps WWE Road to WrestleMania Kiss

*SILVER/25: .6X TO 1.2X BASIC KISS
*GOLD/10: UNPRICED DUE TO SCARCITY
*RED/1: UNPRICED DUE TO SCARCITY
STATED PRINT RUN 50 SER.#'d SETS

KCEM Ember Moon	20.00	50.00
KCKS Kairi Sane	25.00	60.00
KCLE Lacey Evans	30.00	75.00
KCNA Naomi	15.00	40.00
KCTC Taynara Conti	30.00	75.00
KCVB Vanessa Borne	15.00	40.00

2019 Topps WWE Road to WrestleMania Mat Relics

*BRONZE/99: .5X TO 1.2X BASIC MEM
*BLUE/50: .6X TO 1.5X BASIC MEM
*SILVER/25: .75X TO 2X BASIC MEM
*GOLD/10: UNPRICED DUE TO SCARCITY
*RED/1: UNPRICED DUE TO SCARCITY
RANDOMLY INSERTED INTO PACKS

MRAA Andrade Cien Almas	2.50	6.00
MRAB Alexa Bliss	10.00	25.00
MRAC Adam Cole	3.00	8.00
MRAJ AJ Styles	3.00	8.00
MRAS Asuka	5.00	12.00
MRBA Batista		
MRBS Braun Strowman	2.50	6.00
MRCA Cedric Alexander	2.00	5.00
MRCF Charlotte Flair	5.00	12.00
MRDB Daniel Bryan	3.00	8.00
MREM Ember Moon	3.00	8.00
MRFB Finn Balor	3.00	8.00
MRJC John Cena	4.00	10.00
MRJG Johnny Gargano	2.50	6.00
MRKA Kurt Angle	3.00	8.00
MRKD Killian Dain	2.00	5.00
MRKO Kevin Owens	2.00	5.00
MRLS Lars Sullivan	1.50	4.00
MRMH Woken Matt Hardy	2.50	6.00
MRNA Naomi	4.00	10.00
MRNJ Nia Jax	2.00	5.00
MRPD Pete Dunne	3.00	8.00
MRRC Ricochet	3.00	8.00
MRRR Roman Reigns	4.00	10.00
MRRS Roderick Strong		
MRSB Shayna Baszler	3.00	8.00
MRSN Shinsuke Nakamura	2.50	6.00
MRSR Seth Rollins	3.00	8.00
MRSZ Sami Zayn	1.50	4.00
MRTC Tommaso Ciampa	2.50	6.00
MRTM The Miz	2.00	5.00
MRUN Undertaker	5.00	12.00
MRVD Velveteen Dream	3.00	8.00
MRALB Aleister Black	3.00	8.00
MREC3 EC3	1.50	4.00
MRERA Kyle O'Reilly	2.50	6.00
MRHHH Triple H	3.00	8.00
MRRRR Ronda Rousey	6.00	15.00
MRSMC Stephanie McMahon	3.00	8.00
MRWWE Elias	2.00	5.00

2019 Topps WWE Road to WrestleMania Shirt Relics

*BRONZE/99: .5X TO 1.2X BASIC MEM
*BLUE/50: .6X TO 1.5X BASIC MEM
*SILVER/25: .75X TO 2X BASIC MEM
*GOLD/10: UNPRICED DUE TO SCARCITY
*RED/1: UNPRICED DUE TO SCARCITY
RANDOMLY INSERTED INTO PACKS

SRAB Alexa Bliss	15.00	30.00
SRAE Aiden English	2.50	6.00
SRAF Alicia Fox	5.00	12.00
SRBS Braun Strowman	2.50	6.00
SRCM Carmella	4.00	10.00
SRDB Daniel Bryan	3.00	8.00
SRFB Finn Balor	3.00	8.00
SRJC John Cena	4.00	10.00
SRJH Jeff Hardy	2.50	6.00
SRMH Woken Matt Hardy	4.00	10.00
SRRD Rusev		
SRRR Roman Reigns	5.00	12.00
SRRY Renee Young	2.50	6.00
SRSR Seth Rollins	4.00	10.00
SRTM The Miz	2.50	6.00
SRWWE Elias	5.00	12.00

2019 Topps WWE Road to WrestleMania Update

COMPLETE SET (20)	8.00	20.00
RANDOMLY INSERTED INTO PACKS		
U1 No Way Jose	.50	1.25
U2 Jeff Hardy	1.00	2.50
U3 Bobby Lashley	.75	2.00
U4 Samoa Joe	.75	2.00
U5 Jeff Hardy	1.00	2.50
U6 AOP	.60	1.50
U7 Kevin Owens and Sami Zayn	1.00	2.50
U8 Dolph Ziggler and Drew McIntyre	.75	2.00
U9 Kalisto	.40	1.00
U10 Drew Gulak	.40	1.00
U11 Buddy Murphy	.50	1.25
U12 Lince Dorado	.40	1.00
U13 Paige	1.50	4.00
U14 Usos	.50	1.25
U15 Randy Orton	1.00	2.50
U16 Shinsuke Nakamura	1.00	2.50
U17 Jeff Hardy	1.00	2.50
U18 Harper	.50	1.25
U19 Samoa Joe	.75	2.00
U20 AJ Styles & Daniel Bryan	2.00	5.00

2019 Topps WWE Road to WrestleMania WrestleMania 35 Roster

COMPLETE SET (50)	6.00	15.00
RANDOMLY INSERTED INTO PACKS		
WM1 Paul Heyman	.40	1.00
WM2 AJ Styles	1.50	4.00
WM3 Shinsuke Nakamura	.75	2.00
WM4 Undertaker	1.50	4.00
WM5 John Cena	1.25	3.00
WM6 Elias	.60	1.50
WM7 Kurt Angle	.60	1.50
WM8 Ronda Rousey	1.50	4.00
WM9 Triple H	.75	2.00
WM10 Stephanie McMahon	.75	2.00
WM11 Charlotte Flair	1.25	3.00
WM12 Asuka	1.00	2.50
WM13 Nia Jax	.60	1.50
WM14 Alexa Bliss	1.50	4.00
WM15 Daniel Bryan	1.25	3.00
WM16 Shane McMahon	.75	2.00
WM17 Kevin Owens	.75	2.00
WM18 Sami Zayn	.60	1.50
WM19 Seth Rollins	.75	2.00
WM20 The Miz	.60	1.50
WM21 Finn Balor	.75	2.00
WM22 Jinder Mahal	.60	1.50
WM23 Randy Orton	.75	2.00
WM24 Bobby Roode	.60	1.50
WM25 Rusev	.60	1.50
WM26 Aiden English	.30	.75
WM27 Braun Strowman	.75	2.00
WM28 Cesaro	.40	1.00
WM29 Sheamus	.50	1.25
WM30 Harper	.40	1.00
WM31 Rowan	.30	.75
WM32 Jey Uso	.40	1.00
WM33 Jimmy Uso	.40	1.00
WM34 Big E	.30	.75
WM35 Kofi Kingston	.50	1.25
WM36 Xavier Woods	.40	1.00
WM37 Cedric Alexander	.30	.75

WM38 Mustafa Ali .30 .75
WM39 Woken Matt Hardy .60 1.50
WM40 Bray Wyatt .75 2.00
WM41 Naomi .50 1.25
WM42 Bayley .60 1.50
WM43 Sasha Banks 1.25 3.00
WM44 Samoa Joe .60 1.50
WM45 Jeff Hardy .75 2.00
WM46 Bobby Lashley .60 1.50
WM47 Ember Moon .75 2.00
WM48 Carmella .75 2.00
WM49 Ruby Riott .60 1.50
WM50 Liv Morgan 1.00 2.50

2020 Topps WWE Road to WrestleMania

COMPLETE SET (100) 12.00 30.00
*FOILBOARD: .5X TO 1.2X BASIC CARDS
*BLUE/99: 1.2X TO 3X BASIC CARDS
*SILVER/25: UNPRICED DUE TO SCARCITY
*GOLD/10: UNPRICED DUE TO SCARCITY
*RED/1: UNPRICED DUE TO SCARCITY
*P.P.BLACK/1: UNPRICED DUE TO SCARCITY
*P.P.CYAN/1: UNPRICED DUE TO SCARCITY
*P.P.MAGENTA/1: UNPRICED DUE TO SCARCITY
*P.P.YELLOW/1: UNPRICED DUE TO SCARCITY

1 Lince Dorado & Gran Metalik .25 .60
2 Buddy Murphy .30 .75
3 Buddy Murphy .30 .75
4 Buddy Murphy .30 .75
5 Buddy Murphy .30 .75
6 Noam Dar .25 .60
7 Buddy Murphy .40 1.00
8 Buddy Murphy .30 .75
9 Tony Nese .25 .60
10 Buddy Murphy .30 .75
11 Tony Nese .25 .60
12 Tony Nese .25 .60
13 Tony Nese .25 .60
14 Tony Nese .25 .60
15 Roman Reigns .60 1.50
16 Seth Rollins .50 1.25
17 Dolph Ziggler & Drew McIntyre .50 1.25
18 Brock Lesnar 1.00 2.50
19 Dolph Ziggler & Drew McIntyre .50 1.25
20 Seattle Hates The Elias & KO Show .30 .75
21 Triple H 1.00 2.50
22 Roman Reigns .60 1.50
23 Dolph Ziggler .25 .60
24 Brock Lesnar 1.00 2.50
25 D-Generation X 1.00 2.50
26 Drew McIntyre .50 1.25
27 AOP .30 .75
28 Seth Rollins .50 1.25
29 Brock Lesnar 1.00 2.50
30 Team RAW Def. Team SmackDown .60 1.50
31 AOP .30 .75
32 Robert Roode & Chad Gable .25 .60
33 Finn Balor .60 1.50
34 Cena/Balor/Rollins .60 1.50
35 Bobby Lashley .50 1.25
36 Seth Rollins .50 1.25
37 Brock Lesnar 1.00 2.50
38 The Revival .25 .60
39 Baron Corbin .30 .75
40 Seth Rollins 1.00 2.50
41 The Revival .25 .60
42 Finn Balor .60 1.50
43 Baron Corbin .30 .75
44 Batista Returns .40 1.00
45 Roman Reigns Returns .60 1.50
46 Seth Rollins .50 1.25
47 Bobby Lashley .50 1.25
48 Kurt Angle .60 1.50
49 Kurt Angle .60 1.50
50 Drew McIntyre .50 1.25
51 Baron Corbin .30 .75
52 Curt Hawkins & Zack Ryder .25 .60
53 Braun Strowman .60 1.50
54 Seth Rollins .50 1.25
55 Roman Reigns .60 1.50
56 Triple H .60 1.50
57 Baron Corbin .30 .75
58 The Demon Finn Balor .60 1.50
59 The New Day .40 1.00
60 Daniel Bryan .75 2.00
61 Randy Orton .60 1.50
62 AJ Styles .75 2.00
63 Shinsuke Nakamura .50 1.25
64 The New Day .40 1.00
65 AJ Styles .75 2.00
66 Randy Orton .60 1.50
67 Big Show Helps The Bar .30 .75
68 The Miz .40 1.00
69 The Miz .50 1.25
70 Rey Mysterio .50 1.25
71 Daniel Bryan .75 2.00
72 The New Daniel Bryan .75 2.00
73 The New Daniel Bryan .75 2.00
74 The Bar .30 .75
75 AJ Styles & Mustafa Ali .75 2.00
76 Mustafa Ali .40 1.00
77 Rusev .30 .75
78 AJ Styles .75 2.00
79 Samoa Joe & Andrade .40 1.00
80 Andrade .50 1.25
81 Rey Mysterio and Andrade .50 1.25
82 Shinsuke Nakamura .50 1.25
83 The Miz & Shane McMahon .40 1.00
84 Erick Rowan .25 .60
85 R-Truth .25 .60
86 R-Truth .25 .60
87 The Usos .25 .60
88 The New Daniel Bryan .75 2.00
89 Samoa Joe .40 1.00
90 The Usos .25 .60
91 The Bar .30 .75
92 Samoa Joe .40 1.00
93 The New Daniel Bryan .75 2.00
94 Kofi Kingston .40 1.00
95 The New Day .25 .60
96 AJ Styles .75 2.00
97 The Usos .25 .60
98 Shane McMahon .40 1.00
99 Samoa Joe .40 1.00
100 Kofi Kingston .75 2.00

2020 Topps WWE Road to WrestleMania Andre the Giant Battle Royal Commemorative Trophy Relics

*BRONZE/99: .5X TO 1.2X BASIC MEM
*BLUE/50: .6X TO 1.5X BASIC MEM
*SILVER/25: UNPRICED DUE TO SCARCITY
*GOLD/10: UNPRICED DUE TO SCARCITY
*RED/1: UNPRICED DUE TO SCARCITY
STATED PRINT RUN 199 SER.#'d SETS

AGAC Apollo Crews 2.00 5.00
AGAD Andrade 2.50 6.00
AGAL Ali 2.50 6.00
AGBS Braun Strowman 4.00 10.00
AGCA Curtis Axel 2.00 5.00
AGGM Gran Metalik 4.00 10.00
AGJH Jeff Hardy 5.00 12.00
AGJM Jinder Mahal 2.00 5.00
AGKA Karl Anderson 2.50 6.00
AGKL Kalisto 2.50 6.00
AGLD Lince Dorado 2.00 5.00
AGMH Matt Hardy 4.00 10.00
AGOT Otis 6.00 15.00
AGRR Robert Roode 3.00 8.00
AGSB Shelton Benjamin 2.50 6.00
AGTB Tyler Breeze 2.50 6.00
AGTK Tucker 2.00 5.00

2020 Topps WWE Road to WrestleMania Autographed Andre the Giant Battle Royal Commemorative Trophy Re

*RED/1: UNPRICED DUE TO SCARCITY
STATED PRINT RUN 10 SER.#'d SETS
UNPRICED DUE TO SCARCITY

AGAAC Apollo Crews
AGAAD Andrade
AGAAL Ali
AGABS Braun Strowman
AGAGM Gran Metalik
AGAJH Jeff Hardy
AGAJM Jinder Mahal
AGAMH Matt Hardy
AGAOT Otis
AGATK Tucker

2020 Topps WWE Road to WrestleMania Autographed Hall of Fame Headliner Tribute Relic

HOFHTM Honky Tonk Man

2020 Topps WWE Road to WrestleMania Autographed Mat Relics

*RED/1: UNPRICED DUE TO SCARCITY
STATED PRINT RUN 10 SER.#'d SETS
UNPRICED DUE TO SCARCITY

MRAAC Adam Cole
MRAAJ AJ Styles
MRABC Becky Lynch
MRABK Billie Kay
MRABP Beth Phoenix
MRACM Carmella
MRAKA Kurt Angle
MRAKK Kofi Kingston
MRAPR Peyton Royce
MRARR Roman Reigns
MRASB Shayna Baszler
MRASJ Samoa Joe
MRAVD Velveteen Dream
MRAZR Zack Ryder

2020 Topps WWE Road to WrestleMania Autographed Shirt Relics

*RED/1: UNPRICED DUE TO SCARCITY
STATED PRINT RUN 10 SER.#'d SETS
UNPRICED DUE TO SCARCITY

SRAAB Aleister Black
SRAAD Andrade
SRAAJ AJ Styles
SRABB Bobby Lashley
SRABD Bo Dallas
SRABS Braun Strowman
SRACA Curtis Axel
SRAEL Elias
SRAFB Finn Balor
SRANJ No Way Jose
SRARC Ricochet
SRARR Ronda Rousey
SRAZR Zack Ryder

2020 Topps WWE Road to WrestleMania Autographed Women's WrestleMania Battle Royal Commemorative Trop

*RED/1: UNPRICED DUE TO SCARCITY
STATED PRINT RUN 10 SER.#'d SETS
UNPRICED DUE TO SCARCITY

WRAAS Asuka
WRACM Carmella
WRADB Dana Brooke
WRAEM Ember Moon
WRAKS Kairi Sane
WRAMJ Mickie James
WRAMK Maria Kanellis
WRAMR Mandy Rose
WRANC Nikki Cross
WRANM Naomi
WRASD Sonya Deville
WRASL Sarah Logan
WRAZV Zelina Vega

2020 Topps WWE Road to WrestleMania Autographs

*BLUE/50: .5X TO 1.2X BASIC AUTOS
*SILVER/25: UNPRICED DUE TO SCARCITY
*GOLD/10: UNPRICED DUE TO SCARCITY
*RED/1: UNPRICED DUE TO SCARCITY
*P.P.BLACK/1: UNPRICED DUE TO SCARCITY
*P.P.CYAN/1: UNPRICED DUE TO SCARCITY
*P.P.MAGENTA/1: UNPRICED DUE TO SCARCITY
*P.P.YELLOW/1: UNPRICED DUE TO SCARCITY
STATED PRINT RUN 99 SER.#'d SETS

AAB Alexa Bliss 60.00 120.00
AAJ AJ Styles 10.00 25.00
AAL Aleister Black 12.00 30.00
AAS Asuka 25.00 60.00
ABK Becky Lynch 30.00 75.00
ABS Braun Strowman 15.00 40.00
ABW Bray Wyatt 12.00 30.00
ACM Carmella 15.00 40.00
ADB Daniel Bryan 10.00 25.00
AKK Kofi Kingston 6.00 15.00
AKO Kevin Owens 8.00 20.00
AKS Kairi Sane 15.00 40.00
ALE Lacey Evans 12.00 30.00
AMA Ali 6.00 15.00
ARC Ricochet 10.00 25.00
ARR Roman Reigns 10.00 25.00
ASB Sasha Banks 25.00 60.00
ASJ Samoa Joe 6.00 15.00
ASN Shinsuke Nakamura 8.00 20.00

ASR	Seth Rollins	12.00	30.00
ATM	The Miz	6.00	15.00

2020 Topps WWE Road to WrestleMania Dual Autographs

*GOLD/10: UNPRICED DUE TO SCARCITY
*RED/1: UNPRICED DUE TO SCARCITY
STATED PRINT RUN 25 SER.#'d SETS

DAGB	K.Anderson/L.Gallows	25.00	60.00
DAHB	The Hardy Boyz	100.00	200.00
DAHM	Tucker/Otis	60.00	120.00
DAIG	Andrade/Z.Vega	30.00	75.00
DAII	B.Kay/P.Royce	100.00	200.00
DARV	S.Dawson/D.Wilder		

2020 Topps WWE Road to WrestleMania Hall of Fame Headliner Tribute

COMPLETE SET (16)		10.00	25.00
RANDOMLY INSERTED INTO PACKS			
HF1	Honky Tonk Man	1.00	2.50
HF2	Honky Tonk Man	1.00	2.50
HF3	Honky Tonk Man	1.00	2.50
HF4	Honky Tonk Man	1.50	4.00
HF5	Honky Tonk Man	1.00	2.50
HF6	Honky Tonk Man	1.00	2.50
HF7	Honky Tonk Man	1.00	2.50
HF8	Honky Tonk Man	1.00	2.50
HF9	Honky Tonk Man	1.00	2.50
HF10	Honky Tonk Man	1.00	2.50
HF11	Honky Tonk Man	1.00	2.50
HF12	Honky Tonk Man	1.00	2.50
HF13	Honky Tonk Man	1.00	2.50
HF14	Honky Tonk Man	1.00	2.50
HF15	Honky Tonk Man	1.00	2.50
HF16	Honky Tonk Man	1.00	2.50

2020 Topps WWE Road to WrestleMania Hall of Fame Headliner Tribute Autographs

STATED PRINT RUN 10 SER.#'d SETS
UNPRICED DUE TO SCARCITY

HFA1	Honky Tonk Man
HFA2	Honky Tonk Man
HFA3	Honky Tonk Man
HFA4	Honky Tonk Man
HFA5	Honky Tonk Man
HFA6	Honky Tonk Man
HFA7	Honky Tonk Man
HFA8	Honky Tonk Man
HFA9	Honky Tonk Man
HFA10	Honky Tonk Man
HFA11	Honky Tonk Man
HFA12	Honky Tonk Man
HFA13	Honky Tonk Man
HFA14	Honky Tonk Man
HFA15	Honky Tonk Man
HFA16	Honky Tonk Man

2020 Topps WWE Road to WrestleMania Mat Relics

*BRONZE/99: .5X TO 1.2X BASIC MEM
*BLUE/50: .6X TO 1.5X BASIC MEM
*SILVER/25: UNPRICED DUE TO SCARCITY
*GOLD/10: UNPRICED DUE TO SCARCITY
*RED/1: UNPRICED DUE TO SCARCITY
STATED PRINT RUN 199 SER.#'d SETS

MRAB	Aleister Black	2.00	5.00
MRAC	Adam Cole	5.00	12.00
MRAJ	AJ Styles	5.00	12.00
MRBB	Bianca Belair	4.00	10.00
MRBC	Becky Lynch	10.00	25.00
MRBK	Billie Kay	8.00	20.00
MRBM	Buddy Murphy	2.00	5.00
MRBP	Beth Phoenix	2.50	6.00
MRBS	Braun Strowman	4.00	10.00
MRBT	Batista	6.00	15.00
MRCF	Charlotte Flair	6.00	15.00
MRCH	Curt Hawkins	2.00	5.00
MRCM	Carmella	5.00	12.00
MRDB	Daniel Bryan	3.00	8.00
MRDM	Drew McIntyre	4.00	10.00
MRER	Erik	2.00	5.00
MRIS	Io Shirai	2.00	5.00
MRIV	Ivar	2.00	5.00
MRJG	Johnny Gargano	2.50	6.00
MRKA	Kurt Angle	3.00	8.00
MRKK	Kofi Kingston	4.00	10.00
MRKS	Kairi Sane	2.50	6.00
MRMR	Matt Riddle	2.00	5.00
MRNT	Natalya	3.00	8.00
MRPD	Pete Dunne	2.00	5.00
MRPR	Peyton Royce	6.00	15.00
MRRC	Ricochet	2.50	6.00
MRRM	Rey Mysterio	2.50	6.00
MRRR	Roman Reigns	4.00	10.00
MRRS	Ronda Rousey	8.00	20.00
MRSB	Shayna Baszler	5.00	12.00
MRSJ	Samoa Joe	3.00	8.00
MRTH	Triple H	3.00	8.00
MRTM	The Miz	2.50	6.00
MRTN	Tony Nese	2.00	5.00
MRVD	Velveteen Dream	2.00	5.00
MRWT	Walter	2.50	6.00
MRZR	Zack Ryder	10.00	25.00
MRJEY	Jey Uso	2.50	6.00
MRJIM	Jimmy Uso	2.50	6.00

2020 Topps WWE Road to WrestleMania Shirt Relics

*BRONZE/99: .5X TO 1.2X BASIC MEM
*BLUE/50: .6X TO 1.5X BASIC MEM
*SILVER/25: UNPRICED DUE TO SCARCITY
*GOLD/10: UNPRICED DUE TO SCARCITY
*RED/1: UNPRICED DUE TO SCARCITY
STATED PRINT RUN 199 SER.#'d SETS

SRAB	Aleister Black	4.00	10.00
SRAD	Andrade	2.50	6.00
SRAJ	AJ Styles	5.00	12.00
SRBB	Bobby Lashley	3.00	8.00
SRBD	Bo Dallas	2.00	5.00
SRBH	Bret Hit Man Hart	8.00	20.00
SRBL	Brock Lesnar	4.00	10.00
SRBS	Braun Strowman	3.00	8.00
SRBT	Booker T	3.00	8.00
SRCA	Curtis Axel	2.50	6.00
SREL	Elias	2.50	6.00
SRFB	Finn Balor	5.00	12.00
SRNJ	No Way Jose	2.00	5.00
SRRR	Ronda Rousey	20.00	50.00
SRSM	Shawn Michaels	5.00	12.00
SRSR	Stevie Ray	2.00	5.00
SRZR	Zack Ryder	2.50	6.00

2020 Topps WWE Road to WrestleMania Six-Person Autograph Booklet

STATED PRINT RUN 10 SER.#'d SETS
UNPRICED DUE TO SCARCITY
ABCMITB Rousey/Flair/Rollins/Reigns/Kingston/Lynch

2020 Topps WWE Road to WrestleMania Triple Autographs

*GOLD/10: UNPRICED DUE TO SCARCITY
*RED/1: UNPRICED DUE TO SCARCITY
STATED PRINT RUN 25 SER.#'d SETS

TALP	Dorado/Metalik/Kalisto	60.00	120.00
TAND	Woods/Big E/Kingston	75.00	150.00

2020 Topps WWE Road to WrestleMania Winningest Superstars in WrestleMania History

COMPLETE SET (10)		6.00	15.00
RANDOMLY INSERTED INTO PACKS			
WS1	Randy Orton	1.00	2.50
WS2	Shawn Michaels	1.00	2.50
WS3	Seth Rollins	.75	2.00
WS4	Macho Man Randy Savage	1.25	3.00
WS5	Rey Mysterio	.75	2.00
WS6	Kane	.50	1.25
WS7	Bret Hit Man Hart	1.00	2.50
WS8	Triple H	1.00	2.50
WS9	John Cena	1.50	4.00
WS10	Undertaker	1.50	4.00

2020 Topps WWE Road to WrestleMania Winningest Superstars in WrestleMania History Autographs

*RED/1: UNPRICED DUE TO SCARCITY
STATED PRINT RUN 10 SER.#'d SETS
UNPRICED DUE TO SCARCITY

WSA1	Randy Orton
WSA2	Shawn Michaels
WSA3	Seth Rollins
WSA4	Rey Mysterio
WSA5	Bret Hit Man Hart

2020 Topps WWE Road to WrestleMania Women's WrestleMania Battle Royal Commemorative Trophy Relics

*BRONZE/99: .5X TO 1.2X BASIC MEM
*BLUE/50: .6X TO 1.5X BASIC MEM
*SILVER/25: UNPRICED DUE TO SCARCITY
*GOLD/10: UNPRICED DUE SCARCITY
*RED/1: UNPRICED DUE TO SCARCITY
STATED PRINT RUN 199 SER.#'d SETS

WRAS	Asuka	6.00	15.00
WRCM	Carmella	5.00	12.00
WRDB	Dana Brooke	2.50	6.00
WREM	Ember Moon	3.00	8.00
WRKS	Kairi Sane	2.50	6.00
WRMJ	Mickie James	4.00	10.00
WRMK	Maria Kanellis	5.00	12.00
WRMR	Mandy Rose	8.00	20.00
WRNC	Nikki Cross	4.00	10.00
WRNM	Naomi	2.50	6.00
WRSD	Sonya Deville	3.00	8.00
WRSL	Sarah Logan	2.50	6.00
WRZV	Zelina Vega	3.00	8.00

2020 Topps WWE Road to WrestleMania WrestleMania Roster

COMPLETE SET (50)		12.00	30.00
RANDOMLY INSERTED INTO PACKS			
WM1	AJ Styles	1.00	2.50
WM2	Aleister Black	.60	1.50
WM3	Alexa Bliss	2.00	5.00
WM4	Mustafa Ali	.50	1.25
WM5	Andrade	.50	1.25
WM6	Asuka	1.25	3.00
WM7	King Corbin	.40	1.00
WM8	Bayley	.60	1.50
WM9	Becky Lynch	1.25	3.00
WM10	Big E	.30	.75
WM11	Billie Kay	.60	1.50
WM12	Bobby Lashley	.60	1.50
WM13	Braun Strowman	.75	2.00
WM14	The Fiend Bray Wyatt	1.00	2.50
WM15	Brock Lesnar	1.25	3.00
WM16	Buddy Murphy	.40	1.00
WM17	Carmella	.75	2.00
WM18	Cesaro	.30	.75
WM19	Charlotte Flair	1.25	3.00
WM20	Daniel Bryan	1.00	2.50
WM21	Drew McIntyre	.60	1.50
WM22	Elias	.30	.75
WM23	Ember Moon	.60	1.50
WM24	Erik	.30	.75
WM25	Finn Balor	.75	2.00
WM26	Ivar	.30	.75
WM27	Jeff Hardy	.75	2.00
WM28	John Cena	1.25	3.00
WM29	Kairi Sane	.60	1.50
WM30	Kevin Owens	.40	1.00
WM31	Kofi Kingston	.50	1.25
WM32	Lacey Evans	.75	2.00
WM33	Lars Sullivan	.30	.75
WM34	Mandy Rose	1.50	4.00
WM35	Matt Hardy	.60	1.50
WM36	Nikki Cross	.60	1.50
WM37	Peyton Royce	.60	1.50
WM38	Randy Orton	.75	2.00
WM39	Rey Mysterio	.60	1.50
WM40	Ricochet	.50	1.25
WM41	Roman Reigns	.75	2.00
WM42	R-Truth	.30	.75
WM43	Sami Zayn	.40	1.00
WM44	Samoa Joe	.50	1.25
WM45	Seth Rollins	.60	1.50
WM46	Shinsuke Nakamura	.60	1.50
WM47	Sonya Deville	.75	2.00
WM48	The Miz	.50	1.25
WM49	Xavier Woods	.30	.75
WM50	Zelina Vega	.60	1.50

2020 Topps WWE Road to WrestleMania Yearly Records

COMPLETE SET (10)		8.00	20.00
BLASTER EXCLUSIVE			
YR1	Asuka	2.50	6.00
YR2	Braun Strowman	1.50	4.00
YR3	Brock Lesnar	2.50	6.00
YR4	Carmella	1.50	4.00
YR5	Charlotte Flair	2.50	6.00

YR6	Daniel Bryan	2.00	5.00
YR7	Kofi Kingston	1.00	2.50
YR8	Mickie James	1.00	2.50
YR9	Pete Dunne	.60	1.50
YR10	Seth Rollins	1.25	3.00

2020 Topps WWE Road to WrestleMania Yearly Records Autographs

*RED/1: UNPRICED DUE TO SCARCITY
STATED PRINT RUN 10 SER.#'d SETS
UNPRICED DUE TO SCARCITY

YRA1 Asuka
YRA2 Braun Strowman
YRA3 Carmella
YRA4 Kofi Kingston
YRA5 Seth Rollins

2021 Topps WWE Road to WrestleMania Stickers

1	Intro	.15	.40
2	Intro	.15	.40
3	Intro	.15	.40
4	Intro	.15	.40
5	Drew McIntyre	.60	1.50
6	Drew McIntyre	.60	1.50
7	Drew McIntyre	.60	1.50
8	Drew McIntyre	.60	1.50
9	Drew McIntyre	.60	1.50
10	Drew McIntyre	.60	1.50
11	Drew McIntyre	.60	1.50
12	Drew McIntyre	.60	1.50
13	Drew McIntyre	.60	1.50
14	Drew McIntyre	.60	1.50
15	Becky Lynch	1.00	2.50
16	Becky Lynch	1.00	2.50
17	Becky Lynch	1.00	2.50
18	Becky Lynch	1.00	2.50
19	Becky Lynch	1.00	2.50
20	Becky Lynch	1.00	2.50
21	Becky Lynch	1.00	2.50
22	Becky Lynch	1.00	2.50
23	Becky Lynch	1.00	2.50
24	Becky Lynch	1.00	2.50
25	The Fiend Bray Wyatt	1.00	2.50
26	The Fiend Bray Wyatt	1.00	2.50
27	The Fiend Bray Wyatt	1.00	2.50
28	The Fiend Bray Wyatt	1.00	2.50
29	The Fiend Bray Wyatt	1.00	2.50
30	The Fiend Bray Wyatt	1.00	2.50
31	The Fiend Bray Wyatt	1.00	2.50
32	The Fiend Bray Wyatt	1.00	2.50
33	The Fiend Bray Wyatt	1.00	2.50
34	The Fiend Bray Wyatt	1.00	2.50
35	Charlotte Flair	1.25	3.00
36	Charlotte Flair	1.25	3.00
37	Charlotte Flair	1.25	3.00
38	Charlotte Flair	1.25	3.00
39	Angel Garza	.30	.75
40	Drew Gulak	.30	.75
41	Big Show	.50	1.25
42	Shayna Baszler	.50	1.25
43	Lacey Evans	.60	1.50
44	AJ Styles	.75	2.00
45	AJ Styles	.75	2.00
46	AJ Styles	.75	2.00
47	AJ Styles	.75	2.00
48	Mandy Rose	1.25	3.00
49	Dana Brooke	.25	.60
50	Elias	.25	.60
51	Nia Jax	.50	1.25
52	Braun Strowman	.60	1.50
53	Braun Strowman	.60	1.50
54	Bobby Lashley	.60	1.50
55	Bobby Lashley	.60	1.50
56	Cedric Alexander	.25	.60
57	MVP	.25	.60
58	Shelton Benjamin	.40	1.00
59	Akira Tozawa	.30	.75
60	Randy Orton	.75	2.00
61	Viking Raiders	.25	.60
62	R-Truth	.30	.75
63	Naomi	.30	.75
64	Andrade	.40	1.00
65	Nikki Cross	.50	1.25
66	The New Day	.50	1.25
67	The New Day	.50	1.25
68	The Miz	.40	1.00
69	Ricochet	.50	1.25
70	Keith Lee	.50	1.25
71	Keith Lee	.50	1.25
72	Keith Lee	.50	1.25
73	Keith Lee	.50	1.25
74	Ali	.30	.75
75	Retribution	.25	.60
76	Retribution	.25	.60
77	Lana	.30	.75
78	Sheamus	.40	1.00
79	Alexa Bliss	1.50	4.00
80	Alexa Bliss	1.50	4.00
81	Alexa Bliss	1.50	4.00
82	Gran Metalik	.25	.60
83	John Morrison	.50	1.25
84	Humberto Carrillo	.25	.60
85	Humberto Carrillo	.25	.60
86	Humberto Carrillo	.25	.60
87	Jeff Hardy	.60	1.50
88	Tucker	.25	.60
89	Asuka	1.00	2.50
90	Asuka	1.00	2.50
91	Asuka	1.00	2.50
92	Edge	1.00	2.50
93	Edge	1.00	2.50
94	Charlotte Flair	1.25	3.00
95	Number One	.15	.40
96	Surprise	.15	.40
97	Most Eliminations	.15	.40
98	Most Wins	.15	.40
99	Champion	.15	.40
100	History Maker	.15	.40
101	1988	.15	.40
102	The People's Rumble	.15	.40
103	Undertaker The Streak	1.25	3.00
104	Undertaker The Streak #1	1.25	3.00
105	Undertaker The Streak #6	1.25	3.00
106	Undertaker The Streak #7	1.25	3.00
107	Undertaker The Streak #9	1.25	3.00
108	Undertaker The Streak #12	1.25	3.00
109	Undertaker The Streak #14	1.25	3.00
110	Undertaker The Streak #17	1.25	3.00
111	Undertaker The Streak #21	1.25	3.00
112	WrestleMania	.15	.40
113	WrestleMania X	.15	.40
114	WrestleMania 13	.15	.40
115	WrestleMania XV	.15	.40
116	WrestleMania X-Seven	.15	.40
117	WrestleMania XX	.15	.40
118	WrestleMania 25	.15	.40
119	WrestleMania XXX	.15	.40
120	WrestleMania 36	.15	.40
121	Adam Cole	.75	2.00
122	Adam Cole	.75	2.00
123	Adam Cole	.75	2.00
124	The Undisputed Era	.40	1.00
125	Shotzi Blackheart	1.00	2.50
126	Dexter Lumis	.25	.60
127	Johnny Gargano	.50	1.25
128	Candice LeRae	1.00	2.50
129	Rhea Ripley	.75	2.00
130	Damian Priest	.40	1.00
131	Finn Balor	.60	1.50
132	Karrion Kross	1.00	2.50
133	Dakota Kai	.50	1.25
134	Pete Dunne	.50	1.25
135	Kushida	.40	1.00
136	Kushida	.40	1.00
137	Kushida	.40	1.00
138	Ember Moon	.30	.75
139	Tommaso Ciampa	.60	1.50
140	NXT UK	.15	.40
141	Moustache Mountain	.25	.60
142	Moustache Mountain	.25	.60
143	Trent Seven	.30	.75
144	Tyler Bate	.30	.75
145	Ilja Dragunov	.25	.60
146	Jordan Devlin	.25	.60
147	Piper Niven	.40	1.00
148	Gallus	.30	.75
149	Kay Lee Ray	.60	1.50
150	Andre the Giant	1.00	2.50
151	Macho Man Randy Savage	1.50	4.00
152	Ultimate Warrior	1.00	2.50
153	Rowdy Roddy Piper	.60	1.50
154	Bret "Hit Man" Hart	.60	1.50
155	Shawn Michaels	1.00	2.50
156	Undertaker	1.25	3.00
157	Stone Cold Steve Austin	1.25	3.00
158	The Rock	2.50	6.00
159	Triple H	1.00	2.50
160	Trish Stratus	1.25	3.00
161	Eddie Guerrero	1.25	3.00
162	Edge	1.00	2.50
163	John Cena	1.25	3.00
164	Randy Orton	.75	2.00
165	Batista	.50	1.25
166	Charlotte Flair	1.25	3.00
167	Becky Lynch	1.00	2.50
168	Roman Reigns	1.25	3.00
169	Roman Reigns	1.25	3.00
170	Roman Reigns	1.25	3.00
171	Roman Reigns	1.25	3.00
172	Roman Reigns	1.25	3.00
173	Roman Reigns	1.25	3.00
174	Roman Reigns	1.25	3.00
175	Roman Reigns	1.25	3.00
176	Roman Reigns	1.25	3.00
177	Roman Reigns	1.25	3.00
178	Roman Reigns	1.25	3.00
179	Sasha Banks	1.25	3.00
180	Sasha Banks	1.25	3.00
181	Sasha Banks	1.25	3.00
182	Sasha Banks	1.25	3.00
183	Sasha Banks	1.25	3.00
184	Sasha Banks	1.25	3.00
185	Sasha Banks	1.25	3.00
186	Sasha Banks	1.25	3.00
187	Sasha Banks	1.25	3.00
188	Sasha Banks	1.25	3.00
189	Seth Rollins	.60	1.50
190	Seth Rollins	.60	1.50
191	Seth Rollins	.60	1.50
192	Seth Rollins	.60	1.50
193	Seth Rollins	.60	1.50
194	Seth Rollins	.60	1.50
195	Seth Rollins	.60	1.50
196	Seth Rollins	.60	1.50
197	Seth Rollins	.60	1.50
198	Seth Rollins	.60	1.50
199	Bayley	.60	1.50
200	Bayley	.60	1.50
201	Bayley	.60	1.50
202	Bayley	.60	1.50
203	Rey Mysterio	.60	1.50
204	Rey Mysterio	.60	1.50
205	Rey Mysterio	.60	1.50
206	Baron Corbin	.25	.60
207	Baron Corbin	.25	.60
208	SmackDown Fact	.15	.40
209	Usos	.25	.60
210	Usos	.25	.60
211	Kevin Owens	.50	1.25
212	Bo Dallas	.25	.60
213	Big E	.50	1.25
214	Big E	.50	1.25
215	Big E	.50	1.25
216	Mojo Rawley	.25	.60
217	Tamina	.30	.75
218	Cesaro	.25	.60
219	Cesaro	.25	.60
220	Cesaro	.25	.60
221	Billie Kay	.50	1.25
222	Dolph Ziggler	.50	1.25
223	Dolph Ziggler	.50	1.25
224	Dolph Ziggler	.50	1.25
225	Street Profits	.25	.60
226	Street Profits	.25	.60
227	Street Profits	.25	.60
228	Chad Gable	.25	.60
229	Apollo Crews	.30	.75
230	Murphy	.30	.75
231	The Riott Squad	.40	1.00
232	The Riott Squad	.40	1.00
233	Aleister Black	.60	1.50
234	Bianca Belair	.60	1.50
235	Bianca Belair	.60	1.50
236	Bianca Belair	.60	1.50
237	Sami Zayn	.40	1.00
238	Kalisto	.30	.75
239	SmackDown Fact	.15	.40
240	Daniel Bryan	1.00	2.50
241	Daniel Bryan	1.00	2.50
242	Daniel Bryan	1.00	2.50
243	Natalya	.40	1.00
244	Lars Sullivan	.25	.60
245	Otis	.30	.75
246	Otis	.30	.75
247	Kane	.40	1.00
248	Shinsuke Nakamura	.60	1.50
249	Shinsuke Nakamura	.60	1.50
250	Wesley Blake	.25	.60
251	Jaxson Ryker	.25	.60

252 Steve Cutler	.25	.60
253 Carmella	.60	1.50
254 Carmella	.60	1.50
255 Carmella	.60	1.50
256 Robert Roode	.30	.75
257 Mickie James	.50	1.25
258 Main Event Shocker	.15	.40
259 Fantastic Flair	.15	.40
260 Super Cena	1.25	3.00
261 Hardcore Hell	.15	.40
262 Air Shane	.50	1.25
263 Macho Marathon	1.50	4.00
264 Asuka's Run Ended	1.00	2.50
265 Magic Mysterio	.60	1.50
266 Money, Money, Money	.15	.40
267 Mega Match	.15	.40
268 Bret Wins Big	.60	1.50
269 His Time Is Now	1.25	3.00
270 KO to Big Show	.15	.40
271 The Last Ride	.15	.40
272 I'm Sorry, I Love You	.15	.40
273 You Never Saw It Coming	.15	.40
274 Warrior to the Rescue	1.00	2.50
275 Greatest Rivals	.15	.40
276 Wyatt's World	1.00	2.50
277 Legends of the Ladder	.15	.40
278 Super Spear	.15	.40
279 The Boyz Are Back	.60	1.50
280 Dream Match	.15	.40
281 Austin Era Begins	1.25	3.00
282 Match Made in Heaven	.15	.40
283 Kofi-Mania	.60	1.50
284 The Ultimate Challenge	.15	.40
285 Best of British	.15	.40
286 The Boyhood Dream	1.00	2.50
287 Becky Two Belts	1.00	2.50
288 Stone Cold Classic	1.25	3.00
289 Icon vs. Icon	2.50	6.00
290 Drama in the Cell	.15	.40
291 Yes	.15	.40
292 End of the Streak	1.25	3.00
293 Heist of the Century	.15	.40
294 The Greatest of Them All	.15	.40
295 Sami Zayn	.40	1.00
296 Bianca Belair	.60	1.50
297 Seth Rollins	.60	1.50
298 Alexa Bliss	1.50	4.00
299 Kofi Kingston	.60	1.50
300 Big Show	.50	1.25
301 Becky Lynch	1.00	2.50
302 Charlotte Flair	1.25	3.00
303 Cesaro	.25	.60
304 Mandy Rose	1.25	3.00

2021 Topps WWE Road to WrestleMania Stickers Autographs

STATED PRINT RUN 100 ANNCD SETS

AA1 Big E	20.00	50.00
AA2 Becky Lynch	60.00	120.00
AA3 Walter	30.00	75.00
AA4 Trent Seven	30.00	75.00
AA5 Naomi	50.00	100.00

2021 Topps WWE Road to WrestleMania Stickers Firefly Funhouse Pop-Up Card

NNO Bray Wyatt

2021 Topps WWE Road to WrestleMania Stickers Gold XL

COMPLETE SET (3)

T1 Icons
T2 Superstars
T3 Future Legends

2021 Topps WWE Road to WrestleMania Stickers Limiited Edition

COMPLETE SET (4)

LE1 The Rock	2.00	5.00
LE2 The Fiend Bray Wyatt	2.50	6.00
LE3 Roman Reigns	1.50	4.00
LE4 Sasha Banks	1.50	4.00

2021 Topps WWE Road to WrestleMania Stickers Tins

NNO McIntyre/Bliss/Orton/Lashley/Strowman
NNO Rose/Banks/Bayley/Rollins/Styles
NNO Ripley/Fiend/Shirai/Reigns/Big E

2016 Topps WWE The Rock Tribute

COMPLETE SET (40)	6.00	15.00
STATED ODDS 1:6		
1 The Rock	1.00	2.50
2 The Rock	1.00	2.50
3 The Rock	1.00	2.50
4 The Rock	1.00	2.50
5 The Rock	1.00	2.50
6 The Rock	1.00	2.50
7 The Rock	1.00	2.50
8 The Rock	1.00	2.50
9 The Rock	1.00	2.50
10 The Rock	1.00	2.50
11 The Rock	1.00	2.50
12 The Rock	1.00	2.50
13 The Rock	1.00	2.50
14 The Rock	1.00	2.50
15 The Rock	1.00	2.50
16 The Rock	1.00	2.50
17 The Rock	1.00	2.50
18 The Rock	1.00	2.50
19 The Rock	1.00	2.50
20 The Rock	1.00	2.50
21 The Rock	1.00	2.50
22 The Rock	1.00	2.50
23 The Rock	1.00	2.50
24 The Rock	1.00	2.50
25 The Rock	1.00	2.50
26 The Rock	1.00	2.50
27 The Rock	1.00	2.50
28 The Rock	1.00	2.50
29 The Rock	1.00	2.50
30 The Rock	1.00	2.50
31 The Rock	1.00	2.50
32 The Rock	1.00	2.50
33 The Rock	1.00	2.50
34 The Rock	1.00	2.50
35 The Rock	1.00	2.50
36 The Rock	1.00	2.50
37 The Rock	1.00	2.50
38 The Rock	1.00	2.50
39 The Rock	1.00	2.50
40 The Rock	1.00	2.50

2019 Topps WWE Roman Reigns Leukemia and Lymphoma Society Set

COMPLETE SET (11)	8.00	20.00
STATED PRINT RUN 101 ANNCD SETS		
1 Survivor Series 2013	1.25	3.00
2 Royal Rumble 2014	1.25	3.00
3 Fastlane 2015	1.25	3.00
4 Extreme Rules 2015	1.25	3.00
5 WrestleMania 32	1.25	3.00
6 Extreme Rules 2016	1.25	3.00
7 WrestleMania 33	1.25	3.00
8 No Mercy 2017	1.25	3.00
9 SummerSlam 2018	1.25	3.00
10 RAW Return 2019	1.25	3.00
11 LLS	1.25	3.00

2019 Topps WWE Ronda Rousey Spotlight Complete Series

COMPLETE SET (40)	25.00	60.00
1 Helps The Rock Fend Off Triple H and Stephanie McMahon	1.25	3.00
2 Crashes Women's Royal Rumble	1.25	3.00
3 WWE Contract	1.25	3.00
4 Confronts HHH & Stephanie	1.25	3.00
5 Takes Down Stephanie	1.25	3.00
6 Rebuffs Absolution	1.25	3.00
7 Teams w/Kurt Angle	1.25	3.00
8 Armbars Stephanie Twice	1.25	3.00
9 Helps Natalya	1.25	3.00
10 Armbars Mickie James	1.25	3.00
11 Chases off Alexa Bliss	1.25	3.00
12 Confronts Nia Jax	1.25	3.00
13 Signs Contract for Title Match	1.25	3.00
14 Armbars Nia Jax	1.25	3.00
15 Defeats Nia Jax by DQ	1.25	3.00
16 Is Suspended	1.25	3.00
17 Violates Her Suspension	1.25	3.00
18 Wins Her RAW Debut	1.25	3.00
19 Defeats Alexa Bliss for Women's Title	1.25	3.00
20 Attacks Stephanie McMahon	1.25	3.00
21 Works with Trish Stratus	1.25	3.00
22 Stops Alexa Bliss & Alicia Fox	1.25	3.00
23 Teams with Natalya	1.25	3.00
24 Successfully Defends Title Against Bliss	1.25	3.00
25 Defeats Rudy Riott	1.25	3.00
26 Crashes Negotiations	1.25	3.00
27 Goes Toe-to-Toe with Charlotte Flair	1.25	3.00
28 Defeats Mickie James	1.25	3.00
29 Teams with Ember Moon	1.25	3.00
30 Watches Ember Moon's Back	1.25	3.00
31 Defends Women's Title Against Nia	1.25	3.00
32 Tries to Issue Open Challenge	1.25	3.00
33 Defeats Natalya to Retain Title	1.25	3.00
34 Teams with Natalya	1.25	3.00
35 Appears A Moment of Bliss	1.25	3.00
36 Tags with Sasha Banks	1.25	3.00
37 Defeats Bayley in Open Challenge	1.25	3.00
38 Defeats Liv Morgan & Sarah Logan	1.25	3.00
39 Attacks Becky Lynch	1.25	3.00
40 Defeats Dana Brooke	1.25	3.00

2010 Topps WWE Rumble Pack

COMPLETE SET (50)	5.00	12.00
UNOPENED BOX (24 PACKS)		
UNOPENED PACK (6 CARDS)		
1 Big Show	.30	.75
2 Big Show	.30	.75
3 Carlito	.30	.75
4 Chris Jericho	.30	.75
5 Christian	.20	.50
6 Christian	.20	.50
7 CM Punk	.50	1.25
8 Cody Rhodes	.12	.30
9 Cody Rhodes	.12	.30
10 Evan Bourne	.12	.30
11 Evan Bourne	.12	.30
12 Hornswoggle	.20	.50
13 Hornswoggle	.20	.50
14 Yoshi Tatsu	.12	.30
15 Yoshi Tatsu	.12	.30
16 Jack Swagger	.12	.30
17 Jack Swagger	.12	.30
18 John Cena	.60	1.50
19 John Cena	.60	1.50
20 John Morrison	.15	.40
21 John Morrison	.15	.40
22 Kane	.30	.75
23 Kane	.30	.75
24 Kofi Kingston	.20	.50
25 Kofi Kingston	.20	.50
26 Kung Fu Naki	.12	.30
27 Matt Hardy	.30	.75
28 MVP	.20	.50
29 MVP	.20	.50
30 Primo	.12	.30
31 R-Truth	.12	.30
32 R-Truth	.12	.30
33 Randy Orton	.50	1.25
34 Randy Orton	.50	1.25
35 Rey Mysterio	.30	.75
36 Rey Mysterio	.30	.75
37 Santino Marella	.12	.30
38 Shawn Michaels	.75	2.00
39 Shawn Michaels	.75	2.00
40 Sheamus	.20	.50
41 Ted DiBiase	.20	.50
42 The Miz	.20	.50
43 Undertaker	.50	1.25
44 Triple H	.60	1.50
45 Triple H	.60	1.50
46 Edge	.50	1.25
47 Edge	.50	1.25
48 Batista	.50	1.25
49 Batista	.50	1.25
50 Checklist	.12	.30

2010 Topps WWE Rumble Pack Finger Puppets

COMPLETE SET (10)	3.00	8.00
STATED ODDS 1:4		
1 Shawn Michaels	1.25	3.00
2 Rey Mysterio	.50	1.25
3 CM Punk	.75	2.00
4 Hornswoggle	.30	.75
5 Mark Henry	.30	.75
6 Hurricane Helms	.20	.50
7 Triple H	1.00	2.50
8 R-Truth	.20	.50
9 Dolph Ziggler	.30	.75
10 MVP	.30	.75

2010 Topps WWE Rumble Pack Glow-in-the-Dark

COMPLETE SET (10)	4.00	10.00
STATED ODDS 1:6		
1 John Cena	1.25	3.00
2 Undertaker	1.00	2.50
3 Rey Mysterio	.60	1.50
4 Yoshi Tatsu	.25	.60
5 The Miz	.40	1.00
6 Big Show	.60	1.50
7 Shawn Michaels	1.50	4.00
8 Triple H	1.25	3.00
9 Carlito	.60	1.50
10 Jack Swagger	.25	.60

2010 Topps WWE Rumble Pack Hidden Images

COMPLETE SET (10)	4.00	10.00
STATED ODDS 1:6		
1 John Cena	1.25	3.00
2 MVP	.40	1.00
3 Undertaker	1.00	2.50
4 Evan Bourne	.25	.60
5 CM Punk	1.00	2.50
6 Triple H	1.25	3.00
7 Christian	.40	1.00
8 Kane	.60	1.50
9 Chris Jericho	.60	1.50
10 Rey Mysterio	.60	1.50

2010 Topps WWE Rumble Pack Pop-Ups

COMPLETE SET (9)	3.00	8.00
STATED ODDS 1:4		
1 John Cena	1.00	2.50
2 Sheamus	.30	.75
3 Undertaker	.75	2.00
4 Triple H	1.00	2.50
5 Evan Bourne	.20	.50
6 Randy Orton	.75	2.00
7 John Morrison	.25	.60
8 The Miz	.30	.75
9 Edge	.75	2.00

2010 Topps WWE Rumble Pack Stickers

COMPLETE SET (30)	6.00	15.00
STATED ODDS 2:1		
1 John Cena	.75	2.00
2 John Cena	.75	2.00
3 John Cena	.75	2.00
4 Triple H	.75	2.00
5 Triple H	.75	2.00
6 Triple H	.75	2.00
7 Undertaker	.60	1.50
8 Undertaker	.60	1.50
9 Undertaker	.60	1.50
10 Rey Mysterio	.40	1.00
11 Rey Mysterio	.40	1.00
12 Rey Mysterio	.40	1.00
13 Edge	.60	1.50
14 Edge	.60	1.50
15 Edge	.60	1.50
16 Batista	.60	1.50
17 Batista	.60	1.50
18 Batista	.60	1.50
19 Shawn Michaels	1.00	2.50
20 Shawn Michaels	1.00	2.50
21 Shawn Michaels	1.00	2.50
22 CM Punk	.60	1.50
23 CM Punk	.60	1.50
24 CM Punk	.60	1.50
25 Randy Orton	.60	1.50
26 Randy Orton	.60	1.50
27 Randy Orton	.60	1.50
28 Kane	.40	1.00
29 Kofi Kingston	.25	.60
30 DX CL	1.00	2.50

2010 Topps WWE Rumble Pack Tattoos

COMPLETE SET (10)	5.00	12.00
STATED ODDS 1:6		
1 Kofi Kingston/Randy Orton	1.00	2.50
2 Christian/William Regal	.60	1.50
3 Triple H/Edge	1.25	3.00
4 Kane/Big Show	.60	1.50
5 Batista/The Undertaker	1.00	2.50
6 MVP/Jack Swagger	.40	1.00
7 Shawn Michaels/Chris Jericho	1.50	4.00
8 Rey Mysterio/CM Punk	1.00	2.50
9 John Morrison/The Miz	.40	1.00
10 John Cena/Sheamus	1.25	3.00

2018 Topps WWE Shawn Michaels Tribute

1 Shawn Michaels	1.25	3.00
2 Shawn Michaels	1.25	3.00
3 Shawn Michaels	1.25	3.00
4 Shawn Michaels	1.25	3.00
5 Shawn Michaels	1.25	3.00
6 Shawn Michaels	1.25	3.00
7 Shawn Michaels	1.25	3.00
8 Shawn Michaels	1.25	3.00
9 Shawn Michaels	1.25	3.00
10 Shawn Michaels	1.25	3.00
11 Shawn Michaels	1.25	3.00
12 Shawn Michaels	1.25	3.00
13 Shawn Michaels	1.25	3.00
14 Shawn Michaels	1.25	3.00
15 Shawn Michaels	1.25	3.00
16 Shawn Michaels	1.25	3.00
17 Shawn Michaels	1.25	3.00
18 Shawn Michaels	1.25	3.00
19 Shawn Michaels	1.25	3.00
20 Shawn Michaels	1.25	3.00
21 Shawn Michaels	1.25	3.00
22 Shawn Michaels	1.25	3.00
23 Shawn Michaels	1.25	3.00
24 Shawn Michaels	1.25	3.00
25 Shawn Michaels	1.25	3.00
26 Shawn Michaels	1.25	3.00
27 Shawn Michaels	1.25	3.00
28 Shawn Michaels	1.25	3.00
29 Shawn Michaels	1.25	3.00
30 Shawn Michaels	1.25	3.00
31 Shawn Michaels	1.25	3.00
32 Shawn Michaels	1.25	3.00
33 Shawn Michaels	1.25	3.00
34 Shawn Michaels	1.25	3.00
35 Shawn Michaels	1.25	3.00
36 Shawn Michaels	1.25	3.00
37 Shawn Michaels	1.25	3.00
38 Shawn Michaels	1.25	3.00
39 Shawn Michaels	1.25	3.00
40 Shawn Michaels	1.25	3.00

2018 Topps WWE Shawn Michaels Tribute Topps Heritage WWE Autographs and Relics

SMA1 Shawn Michaels AU	30.00	75.00
SMR1 Shawn Michaels RELIC	8.00	20.00
SMAR1 Shawn Michaels AU RELIC	60.00	120.00

2018 Topps WWE Shawn Michaels Tribute Topps WWE Road to WrestleMania Autographs and Relics

SM Shawn Michaels AU	30.00	75.00
SMR Shawn Michaels RELIC	10.00	25.00
SMAR Shawn Michaels AU RELIC	50.00	100.00

2020 Topps WWE Signature Performance Autographs

*BLUE/25: UNPRICED DUE TO SCARCITY
*RED/10: UNPRICED DUE TO SCARCITY
*ORANGE/5: UNPRICED DUE TO SCARCITY
*GOLD/1: UNPRICED DUE TO SCARCITY
STATED PRINT RUN 50 SER.#'d SETS

NNO Drew McIntyre	50.00	100.00

2008 Topps WWE Slam Attax

COMPLETE SET (172)	15.00	40.00
1 John Cena CH	1.25	3.00
2 Edge CH	.75	2.00
3 Chavo Guerrero CH	.30	.75
4 Matt Hardy CH	.75	2.00
5 Chris Jericho CH	.50	1.25
6 Triple H CH	1.25	3.00
7 Jeff Hardy CH	.75	2.00
8 Rey Mysterio CH	.50	1.25
9 Randy Orton CH	.50	1.25
10 CM Punk CH	.20	.50
11 William Regal CH	.50	1.25
12 Batista CH	.75	2.00
13 Shawn Michaels CH	1.25	3.00
14 Beth Phoenix CH	1.00	2.50
15 Kofi Kingston CH	.50	1.25
16 Undertaker CH	1.00	2.50
17 Montel Vontavious Porter FM	.30	.75
18 Kane FM	.75	2.00
19 Mr. Kennedy FM	.50	1.25
20 Big Show FM	.50	1.25
21 Carlito FM	.50	1.25
22 D-Generation X FM	.60	1.50
23 The Hardys FM	.75	2.00
24 Cryme Tyme FM	.25	.60
25 Umaga FM	.30	.75
26 JBL FM	.20	.50
27 Mark Henry FM	.30	.75
28 John Morrison FM	.20	.50
29 The Great Khali FM	.20	.50
30 Snitsky FM	.30	.75
31 Shelton Benjamin FM	.20	.50
32 Stone Cold Steve Austin FM	1.25	3.00
33 Mickie James FM	1.25	3.00
34 Finlay FM	.30	.75
35 Vladimir Kozlov FM	.20	.50
36 WWE Championship TC	.20	.50
37 Intercontinental Championship TC	.20	.50
38 Womenís Championship TC	.20	.50
39 World Tag Team Championship TC	.20	.50
40 World Heavyweight Championship TC	.20	.50
41 United States Championship TC	.20	.50
42 WWE Tag Team Championship TC	.20	.50
43 WWE Diva Championship TC	.20	.50
44 ECW Championship TC	.20	.50
45 WWE Money in the Bank Briefcase TC	.20	.50
46 Deuce	.20	.50
47 Kofi Kingston RC	.50	1.25
48 JBL	.20	.50
49 Charlie Haas	.20	.50
50 Ron Simmons	.20	.50
51 CM Punk	.20	.50
52 Chuck Palumbo	.30	.75
53 William Regal	.50	1.25
54 Paul Burchill	.20	.50
55 Rey Mysterio	.50	1.25
56 Snitsky	.30	.75
57 Paul London	.20	.50
58 Chris Jericho	.50	1.25
59 Val Venis	.25	.60
60 Jerry Lawler	.40	1.00
61 Ted DiBiase Jr. RC	.50	1.25
62 Stone Cold Steve Austin	1.25	3.00
63 Hacksaw Jim Duggan	.50	1.25
64 Todd Grisham	.20	.50
65 Jamie Noble	.20	.50
66 Batista	.75	2.00
67 D'Lo Brown	.30	.75
68 Santino Marella	.20	.50
69 Shawn Michaels	1.25	3.00
70 Michael Cole	.20	.50
71 John Cena	1.25	3.00
72 JTG	.20	.50
73 Shad	.20	.50
74 Randy Orton	.50	1.25
75 Lance Cade	.20	.50
76 Hardcore Holly	.30	.75
77 Cody Rhodes	.20	.50
78 Kane	.75	2.00
79 Mike Adamle	.20	.50
80 Ezekiel Jackson RC	.20	.50
81 Montel Vontavious Porter	.30	.75
82 Funaki	.20	.50
83 Undertaker	1.00	2.50
84 DH Smith RC	.20	.50
85 Gregory Helms	.25	.60
86 Jeff Hardy	.75	2.00
87 Vladimir Kozlov RC	.20	.50
88 The Great Khali	.20	.50
89 Jesse RC	.20	.50
90 Festus RC	.20	.50
91 Edge	.75	2.00
92 Carlito	.50	1.25
93 Vickie Guerrero	.25	.60
94 Kenny Dykstra	.30	.75
95 Mr. Kennedy	.50	1.25
96 Shelton Benjamin	.20	.50
97 Triple H	1.25	3.00
98 Justin Roberts RC	.20	.50
99 Jimmy Wang Yang	.20	.50
100 Curt Hawkins	.20	.50
101 Zack Ryder	.20	.50
102 Brian Kendrick	.30	.75
103 Big Show	.50	1.25
104 Jim Ross	.40	1.00
105 Umaga	.30	.75
106 Tazz	.30	.75

107 John Morrison	.20	.50
108 Tommy Dreamer	.20	.50
109 Mike Knox	.20	.50
110 Super Crazy	.30	.75
111 Boogeyman	.30	.75
112 Mark Henry	.30	.75
113 Chavo Guerrero	.30	.75
114 Tony Chimel RC	.20	.50
115 Finlay	.30	.75
116 Bam Neely RC	.20	.50
117 Matt Hardy	.75	2.00
118 Armando Estrada	.20	.50
119 Elijah Burke	.20	.50
120 Hornswoggle	.30	.75
121 The Miz	.30	.75
122 Ricky Ortiz RC	.20	.50
123 Evan Bourne RC	.20	.50
124 Theodore Long	.25	.60
125 Matt Striker	.20	.50
126 Natalya DV RC	.40	1.00
127 Eve DV RC	.40	1.00
128 Maria DV	.75	2.00
129 Tiffany DV RC	.30	.75
130 Katie Lea Burchill DV RC	.25	.60
131 Kelly Kelly DV	.75	2.00
132 Layla DV	.50	1.25
133 Beth Phoenix DV	1.00	2.50
134 Candice DV	1.00	2.50
135 Lilian Garcia DV	.50	1.25
136 Lena Yada DV	.25	.60
137 Victoria DV	1.00	2.50
138 Melina DV	.75	2.00
139 Maryse DV	.75	2.00
140 Michelle McCool DV	1.00	2.50
141 Jillian DV	.75	2.00
142 Mickie James DV	1.25	3.00
143 Kane & Undertaker	1.00	2.50
144 The Bushwhackers	.25	.60
145 Curt Hawkins & Zack Ryder	.20	.50
146 Finlay & Hornswoggle	.30	.75
147 Chris Jericho & Lance Cade	.50	1.25
148 Cody Rhodes & Ted Dibiase	.50	1.25
149 John Morrison & The Miz	.30	.75
150 The Hardys TT	.75	2.00
151 Jesse & Festus TT	.20	.50
152 Cryme Tyme TT	.25	.60
153 D-Generation X TT	.60	1.50
154 Chavo Guerrero / Bam Neely TT	.30	.75
155 Sgt. Slaughter HOF	.50	1.25
156 The Mouth of the South Jimmy Hart HOF	.30	.75
157 Cowboy Bob Orton HOF	.50	1.25
158 The Iron Sheik HOF	.75	2.00
159 Rowdy Roddy Piper HOF	.75	2.00
160 Pat Patterson HOF	.20	.50
161 Gerald Brisco HOF	.20	.50
162 Junkyard Dog HOF	.30	.75
163 Dusty Rhodes HOF	.50	1.25
164 Jimmy Superfly Snuka	.50	1.25
165 Tony Atlas HOF	.20	.50
166 Bobby The Brain Heenan	.50	1.25
167 Superstar Billy Graham	.25	.60
168 Gorilla Monsoon L	.50	1.25
169 Nikolai Volkoff L	.30	.75
170 Curt Hennig L	.50	1.25
171 Vader L	.30	.75
172 Stone Cold Steve Austin L	1.25	3.00

2010 Topps WWE Slam Attax

COMPLETE SET (130)	12.00	30.00
UNOPENED BOX (24 PACKS)		
UNOPENED PACK (8 CARDS)		
1 Kofi Kingston	.20	.50
2 Carlito	.30	.75
3 Primo	.12	.30
4 Jerry Lawler	.20	.50
5 Ted DiBiase	.20	.50
6 Jim Duggan	.20	.50
7 Festus	.12	.30
8 Chris Masters	.12	.30
9 Hornswoggle	.20	.50
10 Jamie Noble	.12	.30
11 Mark Henry	.20	.50
12 Justin Roberts	.12	.30
13 Santino Marella	.12	.30
14 Shawn Michaels	.75	2.00
15 Jack Swagger	.12	.30
16 Michael Cole	.12	.30
17 The Miz	.20	.50
18 Triple H	.60	1.50
19 Chavo Guerrero	.20	.50
20 Evan Bourne	.12	.30
21 Big Show	.30	.75
22 Montel Vontavious Porter	.20	.50
23 John Cena	.60	1.50
24 Randy Orton	.50	1.25
25 Cody Rhodes	.12	.30
26 Eve	.50	1.25
27 Melina	.50	1.25
28 Alicia Fox	.20	.50
29 Kelly Kelly	.50	1.25
30 Gail Kim	.30	.75
31 Jillian	.50	1.25
32 Maryse	.50	1.25
33 Sheamus RC	.20	.50
34 Brie Bella	.50	1.25
35 Nikki Bella	.50	1.25
36 Kung Fu Naki	.12	.30
37 Undertaker	.50	1.25
38 Charlie Haas	.12	.30
39 Kane	.30	.75
40 CM Punk	.50	1.25
41 Dolph Ziggler	.20	.50
42 Rey Mysterio	.30	.75
43 Chris Jericho	.30	.75
44 The Great Khali	.12	.30
45 Slam Master J	.12	.30
46 Matt Hardy	.30	.75
47 Edge	.50	1.25
48 JTG	.12	.30
49 Shad	.12	.30
50 David Hart Smith	.12	.30
51 Tyson Kidd	.12	.30
52 Mike Knox	.12	.30
53 R-Truth	.12	.30
54 John Morrison	.20	.50
55 Finlay	.20	.50
56 Beth Phoenix	.50	1.25
57 Batista	.50	1.25
58 Theodore Long	.12	.30
59 Todd Grisham	.12	.30
60 Ranjin Singh	.12	.30
61 Jimmy Wang Yang	.12	.30
62 Curt Hawkins	.12	.30
63 Jim Ross	.12	.30
64 Natalya	.50	1.25
65 Michelle McCool	.50	1.25
66 Mickie James	.60	1.50
67 Layla	.30	.75
68 Maria	.50	1.25
69 Tommy Dreamer	.12	.30
70 The Hurricane	.12	.30
71 Vladimir Kozlov	.20	.50
72 Tony Chimel	.12	.30
73 Ezekiel Jackson	.12	.30
74 Shelton Benjamin	.12	.30
75 Josh Mathews	.12	.30
76 William Regal	.30	.75
77 Paul Burchill	.12	.30
78 Gabriel	.12	.30
79 Goldust	.20	.50
80 Zack Ryder	.12	.30
81 Yoshi Tatsu	.12	.30
82 Abraham Washington RC	.12	.30
83 Tyler Reks RC	.12	.30
84 Savannah RC	.20	.50
85 Matt Striker	.12	.30
86 Christian	.20	.50
87 Rosa Mendes	.20	.50
88 Katie Lea Burchill	.30	.75
89 Tiffany	.20	.50
90 C.Rhodes/T.DiBiase	.20	.50
91 Cryme Tyme	.12	.30
92 D.Smith/T.Kidd	.12	.30
93 S.Benjamin/C.Haas	.12	.30
94 C.Jericho/Big Show	.30	.75
95 M.Henry/Hornswoggle	.20	.50
96 Iron Sheik	.30	.75
97 Ted DiBiase	.20	.50
98 Jake Roberts	.30	.75
99 Koko B. Ware	.20	.50
100 British Bulldog	.20	.50
101 Sgt. Slaughter	.30	.75
102 Rick Rude	.20	.50
103 Bam Bam Bigelow	.20	.50
104 Junkyard Dog	.30	.75
105 Roddy Piper	.50	1.25
106 Paul Orndorff	.30	.75
107 Jimmy Snuka	.30	.75
108 Nikolai Volkoff	.20	.50
109 Dusty Rhodes	.30	.75
110 Bobby Heenan	.20	.50
111 Hillbilly Jim	.20	.50
112 Curt Hennig	.20	.50
113 Bob Orton	.20	.50
114 Jerry Lawler	.20	.50
115 Earthquake	.20	.50
116 TLC Match	.12	.30
117 Steel Cage Match	.12	.30
118 Hell in a Cell Match	.12	.30
119 Stretcher Match	.12	.30
120 Casket Match	.12	.30
121 Royal Rumble	.12	.30
122 No Way Out	.12	.30
123 WrestleMania	.12	.30
124 Backlash	.12	.30
125 Judgement Day	.12	.30
126 Extreme Rules	.12	.30
127 The Bash	.12	.30
128 Night Of Champions	.12	.30
129 Summerslam	.12	.30
130 Survivor Series	.12	.30

2010 Topps WWE Slam Attax Champions

COMPLETE SET (16)	8.00	20.00
STATED ODDS 1:5		
1 John Cena	2.00	5.00
2 Edge	1.50	4.00
3 Matt Hardy	1.00	2.50
4 Chris Jericho	1.00	2.50
5 Triple H	2.00	5.00
6 Rey Mysterio	1.00	2.50
7 Randy Orton	1.50	4.00
8 CM Punk	1.50	4.00
9 Batista	1.50	4.00
10 C.Jericho/Big Show	1.00	2.50
11 Michelle McCool	1.50	4.00
12 Kofi Kingston	.60	1.50
13 Christian	.60	1.50
14 Montel Vontavious Porter	.60	1.50
15 Maryse	1.50	4.00
16 Undertaker	1.50	4.00

2010 Topps WWE Slam Attax Finishing Moves

COMPLETE SET (19)	6.00	15.00
STATED ODDS 1:6		
1 Kane	.75	2.00
2 Cody Rhodes	.30	.75
3 Ted DiBiase	.50	1.25
4 Shawn Michaels	2.00	5.00
5 John Morrison	.50	1.25
6 Carlito	.75	2.00
7 Beth Phoenix	1.25	3.00
8 Jack Swagger	.30	.75
9 Mark Henry	.50	1.25
10 Tommy Dreamer	.30	.75
11 Evan Bourne	.30	.75
12 The Great Khali	.30	.75
13 Chavo Guerrero	.50	1.25
14 Melina	1.25	3.00
15 Finlay	.50	1.25
16 Big Show	.75	2.00
17 Shelton Benjamin	.30	.75
18 R-Truth	.30	.75
19 Maria	1.25	3.00

2010 Topps WWE Slam Attax Props

COMPLETE SET (10)	5.00	12.00
STATED ODDS 1:5		
1 Steel Chair	.75	2.00
2 Sledgehammer	.75	2.00
3 Table	.75	2.00
4 Trash Can	.75	2.00
5 Ladder	.75	2.00
6 Steel Steps	.75	2.00
7 Ring Bell	.75	2.00
8 Brass Knuckles	.75	2.00
9 Shillelagh	.75	2.00
10 Kendo Stick	.75	2.00

2010 Topps WWE Slam Attax Starter Box Exclusives

COMPLETE SET (5)	6.00	15.00
STATED ODDS ONE PER STARTER BOX		
1 Chris Jericho	1.25	3.00
2 Undertaker	2.00	5.00
3 Randy Orton	2.00	5.00

4 Triple H	2.50	6.00
5 John Cena	2.50	6.00

2010 Topps WWE Slam Attax Titles

COMPLETE SET (11)	5.00	12.00
STATED ODDS 1:6		
1 WWE Championship	.75	2.00
2 Intercontinental Championship	.75	2.00
3 Women's Championship	.75	2.00
4 Word Tag Team Championship	.75	2.00
5 World Heavyweight Championship	.75	2.00
6 United States Championship	.75	2.00
7 WWE Tag Team Championship	.75	2.00
8 WWE Divas Championship	.75	2.00
9 ECW Championship	.75	2.00
10 WWE Money in the Bank Briefcase	.75	2.00
11 WWE Slammy Award	.75	2.00

2010 Topps WWE Slam Attax WrestleMania XXVI

COMPLETE SET (5)	6.00	15.00
ONE SET PER WRESTLEMANIA XXVI TIN		
1 Chris Jericho	1.00	2.50
2 John Cena	2.00	5.00
3 Randy Orton	1.50	4.00
4 Triple H	2.00	5.00
5 Undertaker	1.50	4.00

2018 Topps WWE Slam Attax Live!

COMPLETE SET (392)	25.00	60.00
1 Alexa Bliss FOIL	1.00	2.50
2 Baron Corbin FOIL	.30	.75
3 Bobby Roode FOIL	.30	.75
4 Braun Strowman FOIL	.50	1.25
5 Elias FOIL	.50	1.25
6 Finn Balor FOIL	.50	1.25
7 John Cena FOIL	.75	2.00
8 Kevin Owens FOIL	.50	1.25
9 Nia Jax FOIL	.30	.75
10 Roman Reigns FOIL	.50	1.25
11 Sami Zayn FOIL	.20	.50
12 Seth Rollins FOIL	.50	1.25
13 AJ Styles FOIL	.75	2.00
14 Rusev FOIL	.30	.75
15 Asuka FOIL	.60	1.50
16 Bludgeon Brothers FOIL	.30	.75
17 Carmella FOIL	.40	1.00
18 Charlotte Flair FOIL	.60	1.50
19 Jeff Hardy FOIL	.40	1.00
20 The Miz FOIL	.40	1.00
21 Rusev FOIL	.30	.75
22 Samoa Joe FOIL	.40	1.00
23 Shinsuke Nakamura FOIL	.50	1.25
24 The Usos FOIL	.30	.75
25 Adam Cole FOIL RC	.25	.60
26 Aleister Black FOIL	.25	.60
27 Kairi Sane FOIL RC	.50	1.25
28 Pete Dunne FOIL RC	.20	.50
29 Roderick Strong FOIL	.20	.50
30 Shayna Baszler FOIL	.50	1.25
31 Undisputed Era FOIL	.25	.60
32 Cedric Alexander FOIL	.20	.50
33 Alexa Bliss/Nia Jax FOIL	1.00	2.50
34 Bray Wyatt/Woken Matt Hardy FOIL	.50	1.25
35 Roman Reigns/Jinder Mahal FOIL	.50	1.25
36 Seth Rollins/Finn Balor FOIL	.50	1.25
37 AJ Styles/Nakamura FOIL	.75	2.00
38 Asuka/Charlotte Flair FOIL	.60	1.50
39 Bobby Roode/Randy Orton FOIL	.50	1.25
40 Daniel Bryan/The Miz FOIL	.50	1.25
41 Adam Cole/Velveteen Dream FOIL	.25	.60
42 Andrade/Aleister Black FOIL	.30	.75
43 Ember Moon/Shayna Baszler FOIL	.50	1.25
44 Bret Hart/Shawn Michaels FOIL	.60	1.50
45 Ric Flair/Chris Jericho FOIL	.60	1.50
46 Trish Stratus/Lita FOIL	.75	2.00
47 Undertaker/Kane FOIL	.75	2.00
48 X-Pac/Shane McMahon FOIL	.40	1.00
49 1-2-3 Kid	.25	.60
50 Braun Strowman	.50	1.25
51 Bret Hit Man Hart	.50	1.25
52 Chris Jericho	.50	1.25
53 Chris Jericho	.50	1.25
54 D-Generation X	.60	1.50
55 Daniel Bryan	.50	1.25
56 Daniel Bryan	.50	1.25
57 Finn Balor	.50	1.25
58 Jeff Hardy	.40	1.00
59 John Cena	.75	2.00
60 John Cena & Shawn Michaels	.75	2.00
61 Kane	.30	.75
62 Mark Henry	.25	.60
63 The Miz	.40	1.00
64 Paige	.50	1.25
65 Randy Orton	.50	1.25
66 Ric Flair	.60	1.50
67 Roman Reigns	.50	1.25
68 Sasha Banks	.60	1.50
69 Seth Rollins	.50	1.25
70 Shane McMahon	.40	1.00
71 Stephanie McMahon	.40	1.00
72 Sting	.50	1.25
73 Stone Cold Steve Austin	1.00	2.50
74 Stone Cold Steve Austin	1.00	2.50
75 Stone Cold Steve Austin	1.00	2.50
76 The Rock	1.00	2.50
77 Trish Stratus & Lita	.75	2.00
78 Ultimate Warrior	.75	2.00
79 Undertaker & Triple H	.75	2.00
80 Yokozuna	.25	.60
81 Akam	.20	.50
82 Alexa Bliss	1.00	2.50
83 Alicia Fox	.30	.75
84 Apollo Crews	.20	.50
85 Baron Corbin	.30	.75
86 Bayley	.30	.75
87 Big Show	.20	.50
88 Bo Dallas	.20	.50
89 Bobby Roode	.30	.75
90 Braun Strowman	.50	1.25
91 Bray Wyatt	.50	1.25
92 Chad Gable	.20	.50
93 Charly Caruso	.30	.75
94 Corey Graves	.25	.60
95 Curt Hawkins	.20	.50
96 Curtis Axel	.20	.50
97 Dana Brooke	.40	1.00
98 Dash Wilder	.25	.60
99 David Otunga	.25	.60
100 Dean Ambrose	.40	1.00
101 Drew McIntyre	.30	.75
102 Elias	.50	1.25
103 Ember Moon	.40	1.00
104 Fandango	.20	.50
105 Finn Balor	.50	1.25
106 Goldust	.40	1.00
107 Heath Slater	.20	.50
108 Jason Jordan	.20	.50
109 Jinder Mahal	.25	.60
110 John Cena	.75	2.00
111 JoJo	.20	.50
112 Jonathan Coachman	.20	.50
113 Kane	.30	.75
114 Kevin Owens	.50	1.25
115 Konnor	.20	.50
116 Kurt Angle	.50	1.25
117 Bobby Lashley	.40	1.00
118 Liv Morgan	.40	1.00
119 Maryse	.40	1.00
120 Woken Matt Hardy	.50	1.25
121 Michael Cole	.20	.50
122 Mickie James	.40	1.00
123 Mike Kanellis RC	.20	.50
124 Mike Rome	.20	.50
125 Mojo Rawley	.20	.50
126 Natalya	.25	.60
127 Nia Jax	.30	.75
128 No Way Jose	.25	.60
129 Renee Young	.30	.75
130 Rezar	.20	.50
131 Rhyno	.20	.50
132 Roman Reigns	.50	1.25
133 Ronda Rousey	1.00	2.50
134 Ruby Riott	.30	.75
135 Sami Zayn	.20	.50
136 Sarah Logan RC	.20	.50
137 Sasha Banks	.60	1.50
138 Scott Dawson	.25	.60
139 Seth Rollins	.50	1.25
140 Stephanie McMahon	.40	1.00
141 Titus O'Neil	.20	.50
142 Triple H	.50	1.25
143 Tyler Breeze	.20	.50
144 Viktor	.20	.50
145 Zack Ryder	.20	.50
146 Aiden English	.20	.50
147 AJ Styles	.75	2.00
148 Alexander Wolfe	.20	.50
149 Andrade Cien Almas	.30	.75
150 Asuka	.60	1.50
151 Becky Lynch	.50	1.25
152 Big Cass	.25	.60
153 Big E	.25	.60
154 Billie Kay	.40	1.00
155 Byron Saxton	.20	.50
156 Carmella	.40	1.00
157 Cesaro	.40	1.00
158 Charlotte Flair	.60	1.50
159 Chris Jericho	.50	1.25
160 Daniel Bryan	.50	1.25
161 Dasha Fuentes	.30	.75
162 Eric Young	.25	.60
163 Greg Hamilton	.30	.75
164 Harper	.30	.75
165 Jeff Hardy	.40	1.00
166 Jey Uso	.20	.50
167 Jimmy Uso	.20	.50
168 Karl Anderson	.20	.50
169 Killian Dain	.25	.60
170 Kofi Kingston	.25	.60
171 Lana	.50	1.25
172 Luke Gallows	.25	.60
173 Mandy Rose	.50	1.25
174 Maria Kanellis	.50	1.25
175 The Miz	.40	1.00
176 Naomi	.25	.60
177 Nikki Bella	.40	1.00
178 Paige	.50	1.25
179 Peyton Royce	.50	1.25
180 R-Truth	.25	.60
181 Randy Orton	.50	1.25
182 Rowan	.30	.75
183 Rusev	.30	.75
184 Samir Singh RC	.20	.50
185 Samoa Joe	.40	1.00
186 Shane McMahon	.40	1.00
187 Sheamus	.40	1.00
188 Shelton Benjamin	.25	.60
189 Shinsuke Nakamura	.50	1.25
190 Sin Cara	.25	.60
191 Sonya Deville	.40	1.00
192 Sunil Singh RC	.20	.50
193 Tamina	.20	.50
194 Tom Phillips	.20	.50
195 Tye Dillinger	.20	.50
196 Xavier Woods	.25	.60
197 Zelina Vega RC	.20	.50
198 Adam Cole RC	.25	.60
199 Aleister Black	.25	.60
200 Aliyah	.30	.75
201 Angelo Dawkins	.20	.50
202 Bianca Belair RC	.25	.60
203 Bobby Fish RC	.20	.50
204 Buddy Murphy	.25	.60
205 Cezar Bononi RC	.20	.50
206 Danny Burch RC	.20	.50
207 EC3	.20	.50
208 Fabian Aichner RC	.20	.50
209 Johnny Gargano	.20	.50
210 Kairi Sane RC	.50	1.25
211 Kassius Ohno	.20	.50
212 Kyle O'Reilly RC	.25	.60
213 Lacey Evans	.25	.60
214 Lars Sullivan RC	.20	.50
215 Lio Rush RC	.20	.50
216 Mauro Ranallo	.20	.50
217 Montez Ford	.20	.50
218 Nick Miller	.20	.50
219 Nigel McGuinness	.20	.50
220 Nikki Cross	.30	.75
221 Oney Lorcan	.25	.60
222 Otis Dozovic	.20	.50
223 Percy Watson	.20	.50
224 Pete Dunne RC	.20	.50
225 Ricochet RC	.40	1.00
226 Riddick Moss	.20	.50
227 Roderick Strong	.20	.50
228 Shane Thorne	.20	.50
229 Shayna Baszler	.50	1.25
230 Taynara Conti RC	.20	.50
231 Tino Sabatelli	.25	.60
232 Tommaso Ciampa	.20	.50
233 Trent Seven RC	.20	.50
234 Tucker Knight	.20	.50
235 Tyler Bate	.20	.50
236 Vanessa Borne	.20	.50
237 Velveteen Dream	.20	.50
238 Wesley Blake	.25	.60
239 William Regal	.30	.75
240 Akira Tozawa	.30	.75
241 Ariya Daivari RC	.20	.50

242 The Brian Kendrick	.30	.75
243 Cedric Alexander	.20	.50
244 Drake Maverick RC	.25	.60
245 Drew Gulak	.20	.50
246 Gentleman Jack Gallagher	.25	.60
247 Gran Metalik	.20	.50
248 Hideo Itami	.20	.50
249 Kalisto	.20	.50
250 Lince Dorado	.20	.50
251 Mustafa Ali	.20	.50
252 Neville	.30	.75
253 Noam Dar	.20	.50
254 TJP	.25	.60
255 Tony Nese	.20	.50
256 Alundra Blayze	.20	.50
257 Andre the Giant	.40	1.00
258 Bam Bam Bigelow	.30	.75
259 Batista	.30	.75
260 Beth Phoenix	.40	1.00
261 Big Boss Man	.20	.50
262 Billy Gunn	.25	.60
263 Bob Backlund	.20	.50
264 Bobby The Brain Heenan	.30	.75
265 Booker T	.30	.75
266 Bret Hit Man Hart	.50	1.25
267 British Bulldog	.30	.75
268 Bruno Sammartino	.30	.75
269 Chief Jay Strongbow	.30	.75
270 Classy Freddie Blassie	.20	.50
271 Cowboy Bob Orton	.20	.50
272 D'Lo Brown	.20	.50
273 Dean Malenko	.20	.50
274 Diamond Dallas Page	.30	.75
275 Dusty Rhodes	.40	1.00
276 Eddie Guerrero	.50	1.25
277 Edge	.50	1.25
278 Eve	.40	1.00
279 The Godfather	.20	.50
280 Hacksaw Jim Duggan	.20	.50
281 Harley Race	.20	.50
282 Honky Tonk Man	.20	.50
283 Howard Finkel	.20	.50
284 Iron Sheik	.20	.50
285 Irwin R. Schyster	.20	.50
286 Jake The Snake Roberts	.25	.60
287 Jerry The King Lawler	.40	1.00
288 Jim The Anvil Neidhart	.30	.75
289 Jimmy Hart	.30	.75
290 Junkyard Dog	.20	.50
291 Ken Shamrock	.25	.60
292 Kevin Nash	.40	1.00
293 Lex Luger	.25	.60
294 Lita	.50	1.25
295 Macho Man Randy Savage	.60	1.50
296 Magnificent Don Muraco	.20	.50
297 Mark Henry	.25	.60
298 Mean Gene Okerlund	.25	.60
299 Million Dollar Man Ted DiBiase	.25	.60
300 Mr. Perfect Curt Hennig	.25	.60
301 Mr. Wonderful Paul Orndorff	.20	.50
302 Norman Smiley	.20	.50
303 Papa Shango	.20	.50
304 Paul Bearer	.30	.75
305 Prince Albert	.20	.50
306 Psycho Sid	.20	.50
307 Ravishing Rick Rude	.25	.60
308 Razor Ramon	.40	1.00
309 Ric Flair	.60	1.50
310 Ricky The Dragon Steamboat	.30	.75
311 Rikishi	.20	.50
312 Road Dogg	.20	.50
313 The Rock	1.00	2.50
314 Rowdy Roddy Piper	.50	1.25
315 Sgt. Slaughter	.25	.60
316 Shawn Michaels	.60	1.50
317 Sting	.50	1.25
318 Stone Cold Steve Austin	1.00	2.50
319 Tatanka	.20	.50
320 Trish Stratus	.75	2.00
321 Ultimate Warrior	.75	2.00
322 Umaga	.20	.50
323 Undertaker	.75	2.00
324 Viscera	.20	.50
325 X-Pac	.25	.60
326 Yokozuna	.25	.60
327 The Ascension	.20	.50
328 Authors of Pain	.20	.50
329 Bray Wyatt & Woken Matt Hardy	.50	1.25
330 Breezango	.20	.50
331 Heath Slater & Rhyno	.20	.50
332 The Miztourage	.40	1.00
333 The Revival	.25	.60
334 The Riott Squad	.40	1.00
335 The Shield	.50	1.25
336 Titus Worldwide	.40	1.00
337 Absolution	.50	1.25
338 The Bar	.40	1.00
339 Bludgeon Brothers	.30	.75
340 Gallows & Anderson	.25	.60
341 The New Day	.30	.75
342 Rusev Day	.30	.75
343 The Iiconics	.50	1.25
344 SanitY	.30	.75
345 The Singh Brothers	.25	.60
346 The Usos	.30	.75
347 Danny Burch & Oney Lorcan	.25	.60
348 Heavy Machinery	.20	.50
349 Moustache Mountain	.20	.50
350 Riddick Moss & Tino Sabbatelli	.25	.60
351 The Street Profits	.20	.50
352 TM-61	.20	.50
353 Undisputed Era	.25	.60
354 Bushwhackers		.50
355 D-Generation X	.60	1.50
356 Nasty Boys	.20	.50
357 nWo	.40	1.00
358 WWE Title	.20	.50
359 Intercontinental Title	.20	.50
360 RAW Women's Title	.20	.50
361 WWE UK Title	.20	.50
362 SmackDown Women's Title	.20	.50
363 NXT Title	.20	.50
364 WWE Universal Title	.20	.50
365 NXT Women's Title	.20	.50
366 RAW Tag Team Title	.20	.50
367 SmackDown Tag Team Title	.20	.50
368 United States Title	.20	.50
369 WWE Cruiserweight Title	.20	.50
370 NXT Tag Team Title	.20	.50
371 Puzzle	.50	1.25
372 Puzzle	.75	2.00
373 Puzzle	.30	.75
374 Puzzle	.50	1.25
375 Puzzle	1.00	2.50
376 Puzzle	.50	1.25
377 Puzzle	.40	1.00
378 Puzzle	.75	2.00
379 Puzzle	.50	1.25
380 Puzzle	.50	1.25
381 Puzzle	.75	2.00
382 Puzzle	.60	1.50
383 Puzzle	1.00	2.50
384 Puzzle	1.00	2.50
385 Puzzle	.75	2.00
386 Puzzle	.20	.50
387 Puzzle	.20	.50
388 Puzzle	.20	.50
389 Steel Chair	.20	.50
390 Table	.20	.50
391 Ladder	.20	.50
392 Trash Can	.20	.50

2018 Topps WWE Slam Attax Live! Authentic Ring Mat Memorabilia

RMAA John Cena & Nikki Bella
RMAB Triple H & Stephanie McMahon
RMAC Seth Rollins
RMBA The Usos
RMBB Carmella
RMBC Baron Corbin
RMCA Sasha Banks
RMCB Braun Strowman
RMCC AJ Styles
RMDA Kurt Angle
RMDB The Miz
RMDC Dean Ambrose/Seth Rollins
RMEA Charlotte Flair
RMEB Alexa Bliss
RMEC Finn Balor
RMFA Shinsuke Nakamura
RMFB Kevin Owens
RMFC Asuka
RMGA Drew McIntyre
RMGB Braun Strowman
RMGC Andrade Cien Almas
RMHA Undisputed Era
RMHB Velveteen Dream
RMHC Kairi Sane
RMIA Aleister Black
RMIB Adam Cole
RMIC Ember Moon
RMJA Finn Balor
RMJB Elias
RMJC Jason Jordan

2018 Topps WWE Slam Attax Live! Authentic T-Shirt Memorabilia

TS1 AJ Styles
TS3 Bayley
TS5 John Cena
TS7 Karl Anderson
TS9 Roman Reigns
TS10 Sami Zayn
TS11 Tye Dillinger

2018 Topps WWE Slam Attax Live! Collector Cards

CC1 Bret Hit Man Hart
CC2 Eddie Guerrero
CC3 Shawn Michaels
CC4 Sting
CC5 Stone Cold Steve Austin
CC6 Ultimate Warrior

2018 Topps WWE Slam Attax Live! Gold Limited Edition

LEPA Roman Reigns
LEPB Daniel Bryan
LEPC Andrade Cien Almas
LEPD Sasha Banks
LEPE Asuka
LEPF Seth Rollins
LEPG John Cena
LEPH Kevin Owens

2018 Topps WWE Slam Attax Live! Silver Limited Edition

LEMB Braun Strowman
LEMC Adam Cole
LEMD Charlotte Flair
LEMF Randy Orton
LESA Ronda Rousey

2010 Topps WWE Slam Attax Mayhem

COMPLETE SET (161)	12.00	30.00
UNOPENED BOX (24 PACKS)		
UNOPENED PACK (8 CARDS)		
1 Chris Jericho	.30	.75
2 David Hart Smith	.12	.30
3 Edge	.50	1.25
4 Evan Bourne	.12	.30
5 Ezekiel Jackson	.12	.30
6 Goldust	.20	.50
7 Jerry Lawler	.20	.50
8 Jay Uso RC	.12	.30
9 Jimmy Uso RC	.12	.30
10 John Cena	.60	1.50
11 John Morrison	.20	.50
12 Justin Roberts	.12	.30
13 Mark Henry	.20	.50
14 Michael Cole	.12	.30
15 Primo	.12	.30
16 R-Truth	.12	.30
17 Randy Orton	.50	1.25
18 Ranjin Singh	.12	.30
19 Santino Marella	.12	.30
20 Sheamus RC	.20	.50
21 Ted DiBiase	.20	.50
22 The Great Khali	.12	.30
23 The Miz	.20	.50
24 Triple H	.60	1.50
25 Tyson Kidd	.12	.30
26 Vladimir Kozlov	.20	.50
27 William Regal	.30	.75
28 Yoshi Tatsu	.12	.30
29 Zack Ryder	.12	.30
30 Alicia Fox	.20	.50
31 Brie Bella	.50	1.25
32 Eve	.50	1.25
33 Gail Kim	.30	.75
34 Jillian	.50	1.25
35 Maryse	.50	1.25
36 Melina	.50	1.25
37 Natalya	.50	1.25
38 Nikki Bella	.50	1.25
39 Tamina RC	.12	.30
40 Big Show	.30	.75
41 Caylen Croft RC	.12	.30
42 Chavo Guerrero	.20	.50
43 Chris Masters	.12	.30

44 Christian	.20	.50
45 CM Punk	.50	1.25
46 Cody Rhodes	.12	.30
47 Curt Hawkins	.12	.30
48 Dolph Ziggler	.20	.50
49 Drew McIntyre RC	.20	.50
50 Finlay	.20	.50
51 Hornswoggle	.20	.50
52 Jack Swagger	.12	.30
53 JTG	.12	.30
54 Kane	.30	.75
55 Kofi Kingston	.20	.50
56 Luke Gallows	.12	.30
57 Matt Hardy	.30	.75
58 Matt Striker	.12	.30
59 Montel Vontavious Porter	.20	.50
60 Rey Mysterio	.30	.75
61 Shad	.12	.30
62 Theodore Long	.12	.30
63 Todd Grisham	.12	.30
64 Tony Chimel	.12	.30
65 Trent Barreta RC	.12	.30
66 Tyler Reks RC	.12	.30
67 Undertaker	.50	1.25
68 Vance Archer	.12	.30
69 Beth Phoenix	.50	1.25
70 Kelly Kelly	.50	1.25
71 Layla	.30	.75
72 Michelle McCool	.50	1.25
73 Rosa Mendes	.20	.50
74 Serena RC	.20	.50
75 Darren Young	.20	.50
76 David Otunga RC	.20	.50
77 Heath Slater RC	.20	.50
78 Justin Gabriel	.20	.50
79 Michael Tarver RC	.20	.50
80 Skip Sheffield RC	.20	.50
81 Wade Barrett RC	.20	.50
82 Alex Riley RC	.12	.30
83 Husky Harris	.25	.60
84 Kaval RC	.12	.30
85 Lucky Cannon	.12	.30
86 Eli Cottonwood RC	.12	.30
87 Michael McGillicutty RC	.12	.30
88 Percy Watson RC	.12	.30
89 Titus O'Neil RC	.12	.30
90 Jamie Keyes RC	.12	.30
91 David Hart Smith/Tyson Kidd	.12	.30
92 Trent Barreta/Caylen Croft	.12	.30
93 Chris Jericho/The Miz	.30	.75
94 Montel Vontavious Porter/JTG	.20	.50
95 Curt Hawkins/Vance Archer	.12	.30
96 William Regal/Vladimir Kozlov	.30	.75
97 THE USO Brothers	.12	.30
98 Iron Sheik	.30	.75
99 Jake The Snake Roberts	.30	.75
100 Koko B. Ware	.20	.50
101 British Bulldog	.20	.50
102 Sgt. Slaughter	.30	.75
103 Ravishing Rick Rude	.20	.50
104 Bam Bam Bigelow	.20	.50
105 Junkyard Dog	.30	.75
106 Ted DiBiase	.20	.50
107 Rowdy Roddy Piper	.50	1.25
108 Mr. Wonderful Paul Orndorff	.30	.75
109 Jimmy Superfly Snuka	.30	.75
110 Nikolai Volkoff	.20	.50
111 Dusty Rhodes	.30	.75
112 Bobby The Brain Heenan	.20	.50
113 Hillbilly Jim	.20	.50
114 Mr. Perfect Curt Hennig	.20	.50
115 Barry Windham	.20	.50
116 Cowboy Bob Orton	.20	.50
117 Jerry The King Lawler	.20	.50
118 Earthquake	.20	.50
119 Ricky Dragon Steamboat	.20	.50
120 Vader	.20	.50
121 Gorilla Monsoon	.12	.30
122 Terry Funk	.30	.75
123 IRS	.12	.30
124 Yokozuna	.12	.30
125 Steel Chair	.12	.30
126 Sledgehammer	.12	.30
127 Table	.12	.30
128 Trash Can	.12	.30
129 Ladder	.12	.30
130 Steel Steps	.12	.30
131 Ring Bell	.12	.30
132 Brass Knuckles	.12	.30
133 Baseball Bat	.12	.30
134 Handcuffs	.12	.30
135 Fire Extinguisher	.12	.30
136 Announcers Table	.12	.30
137 Steel Pipe	.12	.30
138 Microphone	.12	.30
139 Steel Cage Match	.12	.30
140 Hell in a Cell Match	.12	.30
141 Stretcher Match	.12	.30
142 Casket Match	.12	.30
143 Elimination Chamber Match	.12	.30
144 Ambulance Match	.12	.30
145 Backstage Brawl	.12	.30
146 Royal Rumble	.12	.30
147 Elimination Chamber	.12	.30
148 WrestleMania XXVI	.12	.30
149 Extreme Rules	.12	.30
150 WWE Over The Limit	.12	.30
151 Fatal 4 Way	.12	.30
152 Money In The Bank	.12	.30
153 SummerSlam	.12	.30
154 Night Of Champions	.12	.30
155 Hell In A Cell	.12	.30
156 WWE Bragging Rights	.12	.30
157 TLC:Tables, Ladders and Chairs	.12	.30
158 John Cena	.60	1.50
159 The Miz	.20	.50
160 Undertaker	.50	1.25
161 Rey Mysterio	.30	.75

2010 Topps WWE Slam Attax Mayhem Champions

COMPLETE SET (16)	8.00	20.00
STATED ODDS 1:6		
1 Jack Swagger	.40	1.00
2 Drew McIntyre	.60	1.50
3 John Cena	2.00	5.00
4 The Miz	.60	1.50
5 David Hart Smith/Tyson Kidd	.40	1.00
6 Eve	1.50	4.00
7 Layla	1.00	2.50
8 Triple H	2.00	5.00
9 Randy Orton	1.50	4.00
10 Chris Jericho	1.00	2.50
11 Undertaker	1.50	4.00
12 Big Show	1.00	2.50
13 Edge	1.50	4.00
14 Sheamus	.60	1.50
15 Melina	1.50	4.00
16 Kofi Kingston	.60	1.50

2010 Topps WWE Slam Attax Mayhem Finishing Moves

COMPLETE SET (26)	10.00	25.00
STATED ODDS		
1 Chavo Guerrero	.50	1.25
2 Chris Masters	.30	.75
3 Christian	.50	1.25
4 Dolph Ziggler	.50	1.25
5 Kane	.75	2.00
6 Luke Gallows	.30	.75
7 Matt Hardy	.75	2.00
8 Montel Vontavious Porter	.50	1.25
9 Undertaker	1.25	3.00
10 Evan Bourne	.30	.75
11 Mark Henry	.50	1.25
12 Rey Mysterio	.75	2.00
13 R-Truth	.30	.75
14 Ted DiBiase	.50	1.25
15 The Great Khali	.30	.75
16 The Miz	.50	1.25
17 Zack Ryder	.30	.75
18 Edge	1.25	3.00
19 Randy Orton	1.25	3.00
20 John Cena	1.50	4.00
21 John Morrison	.50	1.25
22 Jack Swagger	.30	.75
23 Beth Phoenix	1.25	3.00
24 Michelle McCool	1.25	3.00
25 Maryse	1.25	3.00
26 Gail Kim	.75	2.00

2010 Topps WWE Slam Attax Mayhem General Managers

COMPLETE SET (6)	2.50	6.00
STATED ODDS 1:6		
1 T.Long/You're Kicked Out	.75	2.00
2 T.Long/You're Kicked Out	.75	2.00
3 T.Long/You're Kicked Out	.75	2.00
4 T.Long/Return to the Ring	.75	2.00
5 T.Long/Return to the Ring	.75	2.00
6 T.Long/Return to the Ring	.75	2.00

2010 Topps WWE Slam Attax Mayhem Starter Box Exclusives

COMPLETE SET (3)	2.50	6.00
STATED ODDS ONE PER STARTER BOX		
1 Montel Vontavious Porter	.75	2.00
2 Triple H	2.50	6.00
3 Drew McIntyre	.75	2.00

2010 Topps WWE Slam Attax Mayhem Titles

COMPLETE SET (10)	5.00	12.00
STATED ODDS		
1 WWE Championship	.75	2.00
2 Intercontinental Championship	.75	2.00
3 Women's Championship	.75	2.00
4 World Tag Team Championship	.75	2.00
5 World Heavyweight Championship	.75	2.00
6 United States Championship	.75	2.00
7 WWE Tag Team Championship	.75	2.00
8 WWE Divas Championship	.75	2.00
9 WWE Money in the Bank Briefcase	.75	2.00
10 WWE Slammy Award	.75	2.00

2020 Topps WWE Slam Attax Reloaded

COMPLETE SET (352)	20.00	50.00
1 Akam	.40	1.00
2 Akira Tozawa	.30	.75
3 Aleister Black	.60	1.50
4 Andrade	.50	1.25
5 Angel Garza RC	.40	1.00
6 Angelo Dawkins	.30	.75
7 Apollo Crews	.40	1.00
8 Asuka	1.25	3.00
9 Becky Lynch	1.25	3.00
10 Bianca Belair	.75	2.00
11 Big Show	.40	1.00
12 Billie Kay	.60	1.50
13 Bobby Lashley	.60	1.50
14 Cedric Alexander	.30	.75
15 Charlotte Flair	1.25	3.00
16 Drew McIntyre	.60	1.50
17 Edge	.60	1.50
18 Erik	.30	.75
19 Humberto Carrillo	.50	1.25
20 Ivar	.30	.75
21 Jason Jordan	.30	.75
22 Jinder Mahal	.30	.75
23 Kairi Sane	.60	1.50
24 Kevin Owens	.40	1.00
25 Liv Morgan	.75	2.00
26 Montez Ford	.30	.75
27 Murphy	.40	1.00
28 Natalya	.50	1.25
29 Nia Jax	.50	1.25
30 Peyton Royce	.60	1.50
31 R-Truth	.30	.75
32 Randy Orton	.75	2.00
33 Rey Mysterio	.60	1.50
34 Rezar	.30	.75
35 Ricochet	.50	1.25
36 Shayna Baszler	1.00	2.50
37 Ruby Riott	.50	1.25
38 Samoa Joe	.50	1.25
39 Seth Rollins	.60	1.50
40 Shelton Benjamin	.40	1.00
41 Titus O'Neil	.30	.75
42 Undertaker	1.25	3.00
43 Zelina Vega	.60	1.50
44 AJ Styles	1.00	2.50
45 Alexa Bliss	2.00	5.00
46 Bayley	.60	1.50
47 Big E	.30	.75
48 Bo Dallas	.30	.75
49 Braun Strowman	.75	2.00
50 Carmella	.75	2.00
51 Cesaro	.30	.75
52 Dana Brooke	.50	1.25
53 Daniel Bryan	1.00	2.50
54 Dolph Ziggler	.30	.75
55 Elias	.30	.75
56 Ember Moon	.60	1.50
57 Goldberg	1.25	3.00
58 Gran Metalik	.30	.75
59 Jaxson Ryker RC	.40	1.00
60 Jeff Hardy	.75	2.00

61 Jey Uso	.30	.75
62 Jimmy Uso	.30	.75
63 John Morrison	.30	.75
64 Kalisto	.30	.75
65 Kane	.40	1.00
66 King Corbin	.40	1.00
67 Kofi Kingston	.50	1.25
68 Lacey Evans	.75	2.00
69 Lars Sullivan	.30	.75
70 Lince Dorado	.30	.75
71 Mandy Rose	1.50	4.00
72 Maryse	.60	1.50
73 Mickie James	.50	1.25
74 Mojo Rawley	.30	.75
75 Mustafa Ali	.50	1.25
76 Naomi	.60	1.50
77 Nikki Cross	.60	1.50
78 Otis	.50	1.25
79 Robert Roode	.30	.75
80 Roman Reigns	.75	2.00
81 Sami Zayn	.40	1.00
82 Sasha Banks	1.50	4.00
83 Sheamus	.40	1.00
84 Shinsuke Nakamura	.60	1.50
85 Shorty G	.30	.75
86 Sonya Deville	.75	2.00
87 Steve Cutler	.30	.75
88 Tamina	.40	1.00
89 The Fiend Bray Wyatt	1.00	2.50
90 The Miz	.50	1.25
91 Tucker	.30	.75
92 Wesley Blake	.40	1.00
93 Xavier Woods	.30	.75
94 Adam Cole	.75	2.00
95 Aliyah	.60	1.50
96 Arturo Ruas	.30	.75
97 Mercedes Martinez	.50	1.25
98 Boa RC	.30	.75
99 Bobby Fish	.30	.75
100 Bronson Reed RC	.30	.75
101 Cameron Grimes RC	.30	.75
102 Candice LeRae	1.00	2.50
103 Chelsea Green	1.50	4.00
104 Dakota Kai	.60	1.50
105 Damian Priest	.30	.75
106 Danny Burch	.40	1.00
107 Dexter Lumis RC	.30	.75
108 Dominik Dijakovic	.30	.75
109 Fandango	.30	.75
110 Finn Balor	.75	2.00
111 Io Shirai	.50	1.25
112 Isaiah Swerve Scott RC	.40	1.00
113 Jessamyn Duke	.50	1.25
114 Joaquin Wilde RC	.30	.75
115 Johnny Gargano	.60	1.50
116 Kacy Catanzaro	.60	1.50
117 Karrion Kross RC	.60	1.50
118 Keith Lee	.30	.75
119 Killian Dain	.40	1.00
120 Kona Reeves	.30	.75
121 Kushida	.40	1.00
122 Kyle O'Reilly	.40	1.00
123 Mansoor	.30	.75
124 Marina Shafir	.50	1.25
125 Matt Riddle	.60	1.50
126 Mia Yim	.60	1.50
127 Pete Dunne	.30	.75
128 Racquel Gonzalez RC	.50	1.25
129 Rhea Ripley	1.25	3.00
130 Roderick Strong	.60	1.50
131 Scarlett RC	1.25	3.00
132 Shane Thorne	.30	.75
133 Santana Garrett RC	.30	.75
134 Shotzi Blackheart RC	1.00	2.50
135 Tegan Nox RC	.75	2.00
136 Tommaso Ciampa	.60	1.50
137 Tyler Breeze	.40	1.00
138 Vanessa Borne	.60	1.50
139 Velveteen Dream	.40	1.00
140 Xia Li	.60	1.50
141 Alexander Wolfe	.30	.75
142 Dave Mastiff RC	.40	1.00
143 Fabian Aichner	.12	.30
144 Flash Morgan Webster RC	.40	1.00
145 Ilja Dragunov RC	.50	1.25
146 James Drake RC	.40	1.00
147 Joe Coffey RC	.30	.75
148 Jordan Devlin RC	.30	.75
149 Kay Lee Ray RC	.50	1.25
150 Ligero RC	.30	.75
151 Marcel Barthel RC	.30	.75
152 Mark Andrews	.30	.75
153 Mark Coffey RC	.40	1.00
154 Noam Dar	.30	.75
155 Piper Niven RC	.40	1.00
156 Toni Storm	.75	2.00
157 Travis Banks RC	.30	.75
158 Trent Seven	.30	.75
159 Tyler Bate	.50	1.25
160 Walter RC	.60	1.50
161 Wolfgang RC	.30	.75
162 Zack Gibson RC	.30	.75
163 Ariya Daivari	.30	.75
164 Gentleman Jack Gallagher	.40	1.00
165 Oney Lorcan	.40	1.00
166 Raul Mendoza	.30	.75
167 Samir Singh	.30	.75
168 Sunil Singh	.30	.75
169 The Brian Kendrick	.30	.75
170 Tony Nese	.30	.75
171 AOP TT	.40	1.00
172 Murphy/Austin Theory TT	.50	1.25
173 Miz/John Morrison TT	.50	1.25
174 Seth Rollins/Murphy TT	.60	1.50
175 Usos TT	.30	.75
176 Heavy Machinery TT	.50	1.25
177 Robert Roode/Dolph Ziggler TT	.30	.75
178 Street Profits TT	.30	.75
179 Viking Raiders TT	.30	.75
180 Broserweights TT	.60	1.50
181 Ever Rise TT	.30	.75
182 Danny Burch/Oney Lorcan TT	.40	1.00
183 Ricochet/Cedric Alexander TT	.50	1.25
184 Grizzled Young Veterans TT	.40	1.00
185 Alexa Bliss/Nikki Cross TT	2.00	5.00
186 Kabuki Warriors TT	1.25	3.00
187 Nakamura/Cesaro TT	.60	1.50
188 Lucha House Party TT	.30	.75
189 New Day TT	.50	1.25
190 Forgotten Sons TT	.40	1.00
191 British Strong Style TT	.50	1.25
192 Gallus TT	.40	1.00
193 The Undisputed Era TT	.75	2.00
194 Imperium TT	.60	1.50
195 Adam Cole FL	.75	2.00
196 Aleister Black FL	.60	1.50
197 Bianca Belair FL	.75	2.00
198 Dominik Dijakovic FL	.30	.75
199 Io Shirai FL	.50	1.25
200 Keith Lee FL	.30	.75
201 King Corbin FL	.40	1.00
202 Liv Morgan FL	.75	2.00
203 Matt Riddle FL	.60	1.50
204 Pete Dunne FL	.30	.75
205 Rhea Ripley FL	1.25	3.00
206 Ricochet FL	.50	1.25
207 Shayna Baszler FL	1.00	2.50
208 Tommaso Ciampa FL	.60	1.50
209 Velveteen Dream FL	.40	1.00
210 Walter FL	.60	1.50
211 Angel Garza FL	.40	1.00
212 Austin Theory FL RC	.50	1.25
213 Cameron Grimes FL	.30	.75
214 Candice LeRae FL	1.00	2.50
215 Dakota Kai FL	.60	1.50
216 Johnny Gargano FL	.60	1.50
217 Montez Ford FL	.30	.75
218 Toni Storm FL	.75	2.00
219 Lacey Evans FL	.75	2.00
220 Otis FL	.50	1.25
221 AJ Styles R	1.00	2.50
222 Asuka R	1.25	3.00
223 Rey Mysterio R	.60	1.50
224 Ruby Riott R	.50	1.25
225 Table	.20	.50
226 Ladder	.20	.50
227 Steel Chair	.20	.50
228 Trash Can	.20	.50
229 The Fiend Bray Wyatt FFH	1.00	2.50
230 Bray Wyatt FFH	1.00	2.50
231 Mercy the Buzzard FFH		1.00
232 Huskus the Pig Boy FFH	.40	
233 Ramblin' Rabbit FFH		1.00
234 Abby the Witch FFH	1.00	2.50
235 Beth Phoenix HOF	.50	1.25
236 Brutus Beefcake HOF	.30	.75
237 Dusty Rhodes HOF	.60	1.50
238 Jerry Lawler HOF	.75	2.00
239 Mark Henry HOF	.50	1.25
240 Road Dogg HOF	.40	1.00
241 Faarooq HOF	.50	1.25
242 X-Pac HOF	.30	.75
243 Big Boss Man HOF	.50	1.25
244 British Bulldog HOF	.50	1.25
245 Diamond Dallas Page HOF	.60	1.50
246 Hacksaw Jim Duggan HOF	.60	1.50
247 Kevin Nash HOF	.50	1.25
248 Mr. Perfect HOF	.50	1.25
249 Rick Rude HOF	.40	1.00
250 Razor Ramon HOF	.50	1.25
251 Ricky Steamboat HOF	.50	1.25
252 Rikishi HOF	.30	.75
253 Rowdy Roddy Piper HOF	.75	2.00
254 Sgt. Slaughter HOF	.60	1.50
255 The Honky Tonk Man HOF	.50	1.25
256 The Million Dollar Man HOF	.60	1.50
257 Andre the Giant HOF	.75	2.00
258 Batista HOF	.50	1.25
259 Booker T HOF	.60	1.50
260 Bret Hit Man Hart HOF	.75	2.00
261 Chyna HOF	.75	2.00
262 Eddie Guerrero HOF	.75	2.00
263 Lita HOF	.75	2.00
264 Randy Savage HOF	1.00	2.50
265 Mick Foley HOF	.60	1.50
266 Ric Flair HOF	1.25	3.00
267 Shawn Michaels HOF	.75	2.00
268 Diesel HOF	.50	1.25
269 Sting HOF	1.00	2.50
270 Trish Stratus HOF	1.50	4.00
271 Ultimate Warrior HOF	.75	2.00
272 Yokozuna HOF	.50	1.25
273 Andrade B	.50	1.25
274 Charlotte Flair B	1.25	3.00
275 Drew McIntyre B	.60	1.50
276 Edge B	.60	1.50
277 Sheamus B	.40	1.00
278 AJ Styles B	1.00	2.50
279 Alexa Bliss B	2.00	5.00
280 Murphy B	.40	1.00
281 The Fiend Bray Wyatt B	1.00	2.50
282 Nikki Cross B	.60	1.50
283 Adam Cole B	.75	2.00
284 Dolph Ziggler B	.30	.75
285 Rhea Ripley B	1.25	3.00
286 Io Shirai B	.50	1.25
287 Shayna Baszler B	1.00	2.50
288 Seth Rollins B	.60	1.50
289 Angel Garza B	.40	1.00
290 Goldberg B	1.25	3.00
291 Roman Reigns B	.75	2.00
292 The Miz B	.50	1.25
293 Bayley B	.60	1.50
294 Natalya B	.50	1.25
295 Randy Orton B	.75	2.00
296 Daniel Bryan B	1.00	2.50
297 Kairi Sane B	.60	1.50
298 Shorty G B	.30	.75
299 Aleister Black B	.60	1.50
300 Kevin Owens B	.40	1.00
301 Kofi Kingston B	.50	1.25
302 Shinsuke Nakamura B	.60	1.50
303 Asuka MITB	1.25	3.00
304 Otis MITB	.50	1.25
305 Universal Title	.20	.50
306 WWE Title	.20	.50
307 RAW Women's Title	.20	.50
308 SmackDown Women's Title	.20	.50
309 Intercontinental Title	.20	.50
310 United States Title	.20	.50
311 24/7 Title	.20	.50
312 RAW Tag Team Title	.20	.50
313 SmackDown Tag Team Title	.20	.50
314 WWE Women's Tag Team Title	.20	.50
315 NXT Title	.20	.50
316 NXT Women's Title	.20	.50
317 NXT North American Title	.20	.50
318 NXT Cruiserweight Title	.20	.50
319 NXT Tag Team Title	.20	.50
320 NXT UK Title	.20	.50
321 NXT UK Women's Title	.20	.50
322 NXT UK Tag Team Title	.20	.50
323 Orton/RKO	.75	2.00
324 Balor/Coup de Grace	.75	2.00
325 Goldberg/Jackhammer	1.25	3.00
326 Black/Black Mass	.60	1.50
327 Edge/Spear	.60	1.50
328 Styles/Phenomenal Forearm	1.00	2.50
329 Hardy/Swanton Bomb	.75	2.00
330 McIntyre/Claymore Kick	.60	1.50
331 Hart/Sharpshooter	.75	2.00
332 Austin/Stone Cold Stunner	1.50	4.00

333 Undertaker/Tombstone	1.25	3.00
334 Triple H/Pedigree	.75	2.00
335 Kane/Chokeslam	.40	1.00
336 Cena/Attitude Adjustment	1.25	3.00
337 Braun Strowman B	.75	2.00
338 Otis B	.50	1.25
339 Sasha Banks ICONS	1.50	4.00
340 Charlotte Flair ICONS	1.25	3.00
341 Daniel Bryan ICONS	1.00	2.50
342 Seth Rollins ICONS	.60	1.50
343 Triple H ICONS	.75	2.00
344 The Rock ICONS	1.50	4.00
345 Bret Hart ICONS	.75	2.00
346 Steve Austin ICONS	1.50	4.00
347 Roman Reigns 100 CLUB	.75	2.00
348 Asuka 100 CLUB	1.25	3.00
349 Drew McIntyre 100 CLUB	.60	1.50
350 Bray Wyatt 100 CLUB	1.00	2.50
351 Undertaker SR	1.25	3.00
352 John Cena SR	1.25	3.00

2020 Topps WWE Slam Attax Reloaded Autographs

AAB Alexa Bliss
AAC Adam Cole
AAD Angelo Dawkins
AAJ AJ Styles
AAN Andrade
AAS Asuka
ABA Bayley
ABB Bianca Belair
ABE Big E
ABL Becky Lynch
ABM Murphy
ACS Cesaro
ADB Daniel Bryan
ADM Drew McIntyre
AED Edge
AEL Elias
AEM Ember Moon
AFB Finn Balor
AJG Johnny Gargano
AKO Kevin Owens
AKS Kairi Sane
ALA Bobby Lashley
ALE Lacey Evans
AMA Mustafa Ali
AMR Mandy Rose
ANJ Nia Jax
ANM Naomi
ANT Natalya
AOO Otis
APD Pete Dunne
ARB Ruby Riott
ARC Ricochet
ARR Robert Roode
ARS Roderick Strong
ART R-Truth
ASB Shayna Baszler
ASD Sonya Deville
ASG Shorty G
ASH Shinsuke Nakamura
ATB Tyler Bate
ATC Tommaso Ciampa
ATE Aleister Black
ATM The Miz
ATS Trent Seven
AVD Velveteen Dream/50
(Topps.com Exclusive)
AXW Xavier Woods

2020 Topps WWE Slam Attax Reloaded Collector Tins

NNO Edge
NNO John Cena
NNO Sasha Banks

2020 Topps WWE Slam Attax Reloaded Exclusives

T1 Bret Hit Man Hart
T2 British Bulldog
T3 Eddie Guerrero
T4 Yokozuna
T5 Batista
T6 Diesel
T7 Lita
T8 Bayley
T9 The Fiend Bray Wyatt
T10 Kofi Kingston
T11 Velveteen Dream
T12 Kevin Owens
T13 Rhea Ripley
T14 Sasha Banks
T15 Macho Man Randy Savage
T16 Ric Flair
T17 Shawn Michaels
T18 Stone Cold Steve Austin
T19 Papa Shango
T20 Vader
T21 Booker T
T22 Daniel Bryan
T23 Drew McIntyre
T24 Randy Orton
T25 Roman Reigns
T26 King Corbin
T27 Alexa Bliss
T28 Becky Lynch
T29 Andre the Giant
T30 Bam Bam Bigelow
T31 Ultimate Warrior
T32 Rowdy Roddy Piper
T33 Razor Ramon
T34 Chyna
T35 Trish Stratus
T36 AJ Styles
T37 Braun Strowman
T38 The Miz
T39 Seth Rollins
T40 Adam Cole
T41 Charlotte Flair
T42 Asuka

2020 Topps WWE Slam Attax Reloaded Limited Edition Bronze

LEBB Becky Lynch
LECB Drew McIntyre
LERB Roman Reigns

2020 Topps WWE Slam Attax Reloaded Limited Edition Gold

LEDA The Rock
(Mega Tins Exclusive)
LEDB Undertaker
(Mega Tins Exclusive)
LEDC Stone Cold Steve Austin
(Mega Tins Exclusive)
LESA The Fiend Bray Wyatt
LETA John Cena
(Collector Tins Exclusive)
LETB Sasha Banks
(Collector Tins Exclusive)
LETC Edge
(Collector Tins Exclusive)
LEXA Daniel Bryan
(Web Wednesday Exclusive)
LEXB Charlotte Flair
(WWE Kids Magazine Exclusive)
LEXC Seth Rollins
(Web Wednesday Exclusive)
LEXD Nikki Cross
(Web Wednesday Exclusive)

2020 Topps WWE Slam Attax Reloaded Relics

M1 Drew McIntyre/T-Shirt
M2 Humberto Carrllo/T-Shirt
M3 Samoa Joe/T-Shirt
M4 Shayna Baszler/T-Shirt
M5 Sonya Deville/T-Shirt
M6 Roman Reigns vs. King Corbin/Table
M7 Triple H vs. Batista/Mat

2020 Topps WWE Slam Attax Reloaded XL

XL1 John Cena
XL2 Charlotte Flair
XL3 Braun Strowman
XL4 Bayley
XL5 Becky Lynch
XL6 Roman Reigns
XL7 Undertaker
XL8 The Fiend Bray Wyatt
XL9 Drew McIntyre
XL10 Rhea Ripley
XL11 Kofi Kingston

2016 Topps WWE Slam Attax TakeOver

COMPLETE SET (299)	25.00	60.00
1 AJ Styles	.50	1.25
2 Asuka RC	.50	1.25
3 Alberto Del Rio	.20	.50
4 Brock Lesnar	.60	1.50
5 Charlotte	.40	1.00
6 Dean Ambrose	.40	1.00
7 Finn Balor	.40	1.00
8 John Cena	.60	1.50
9 Kalisto	.30	.75
10 Kevin Owens	.30	.75
11 Roman Reigns	.40	1.00
12 Samoa Joe	.30	.75
13 Sasha Banks	.40	1.00
14 Seth Rollins	.20	.50
15 The New Day	.30	.75
16 Triple H	.50	1.25
17 AJ Styles	.50	1.25
18 Asuka RC	.50	1.25
19 Alberto Del Rio	.20	.50
20 Brock Lesnar	.60	1.50
21 Charlotte	.40	1.00
22 Dean Ambrose	.40	1.00
23 Finn Balor	.40	1.00
24 John Cena	.60	1.50
25 Kalisto	.30	.75
26 Kevin Owens	.30	.75
27 Roman Reigns	.40	1.00
28 Samoa Joe	.30	.75
29 Sasha Banks	.40	1.00
30 Seth Rollins	.20	.50
31 The New Day	.30	.75
32 Triple H	.50	1.25
33 Becky Lynch RC	.40	1.00
34 Big E	.12	.30
35 Bo Dallas	.12	.30
36 Bray Wyatt	.50	1.25
37 Charlotte	.40	1.00
38 Kalisto	.30	.75
39 Kevin Owens	.30	.75
40 Luke Harper	.12	.30
41 Neville	.25	.60
42 Paige	.40	1.00
43 Roman Reigns	.40	1.00
44 Rusev	.30	.75
45 Sasha Banks	.40	1.00
46 Seth Rollins	.20	.50
47 Tyler Breeze	.12	.30
48 Xavier Woods	.12	.30
49 MITB Briefcase	.12	.30
50 NXT Women's Title	.12	.30
51 NXT Title	.12	.30
52 NXT Tag Team Title	.12	.30
53 WWE Tag Team Title	.12	.30
54 WWE Women's Title	.12	.30
55 WWE United States Title	.12	.30
56 WWE Title	.12	.30
57 AJ Styles	.50	1.25
58 Alberto Del Rio	.20	.50
59 Apollo Crews	.12	.30
60 Asuka RC	.50	1.25
61 Baron Corbin	.15	.40
62 Bayley RC	.30	.75
63 Becky Lynch RC	.40	1.00
64 Big Cass	.25	.60
65 Braun Strowman RC	.15	.40
66 Bray Wyatt	.50	1.25
67 Brock Lesnar	.60	1.50
68 Charlotte	.40	1.00
69 Chris Jericho	.30	.75
70 Dean Ambrose	.40	1.00
71 Dolph Ziggler	.15	.40
72 Elias Samson RC	.12	.30
73 Erick Rowan	.12	.30
74 Heath Slater	.12	.30
75 Hideo Itami	.15	.40
76 Jason Jordan RC	.15	.40
77 John Cena	.60	1.50
78 Kalisto	.30	.75
79 Kevin Owens	.30	.75
80 Mojo Rawley RC	.12	.30
81 Neville	.25	.60
82 Paige	.40	1.00
83 Roman Reigns	.40	1.00
84 Rusev	.30	.75
85 Samoa Joe	.30	.75
86 Sasha Banks	.40	1.00
87 Sheamus	.30	.75
88 Triple H	.50	1.25
89 Aiden English	.12	.30
90 AJ Styles	.50	1.25

91 Alberto Del Rio	.20	.50
92 Alicia Fox	.20	.50
93 Apollo Crews	.12	.30
94 Baron Corbin	.15	.40
95 Becky Lynch RC	.40	1.00
96 Big Cass	.25	.60
97 Big E	.12	.30
98 Big Show	.25	.60
99 Bo Dallas	.12	.30
100 Booker T	.25	.60
101 Braun Strowman RC	.15	.40
102 Bray Wyatt	.50	1.25
103 Brie Bella	.25	.60
104 Brock Lesnar	.60	1.50
105 Bubba Ray Dudley	.25	.60
106 Byron Saxton	.12	.30
107 Cesaro	.25	.60
108 Charlotte	.40	1.00
109 Chris Jericho	.30	.75
110 Curtis Axel	.12	.30
111 Dana Brooke RC	.30	.75
112 Daniel Bryan	.50	1.25
113 Darren Young	.12	.30
114 David Otunga	.12	.30
115 Dean Ambrose	.40	1.00
116 Dolph Ziggler	.15	.40
117 D-Von Dudley	.20	.50
118 Emma	.25	.60
119 Enzo Amore RC	.25	.60
120 Epico	.12	.30
121 Erick Rowan	.12	.30
122 Eva Marie	.25	.60
123 Fandango	.12	.30
124 Goldust	.20	.50
125 Heath Slater	.12	.30
126 Jack Swagger	.12	.30
127 JBL	.15	.40
128 Jerry Lawler	.25	.60
129 Jey Uso	.12	.30
130 Jimmy Uso	.12	.30
131 John Cena	.60	1.50
132 JoJo	.12	.30
133 Kalisto	.30	.75
134 Kane	.20	.50
135 Karl Anderson RC	.12	.30
136 Kevin Owens	.30	.75
137 Kofi Kingston	.12	.30
138 Konnor	.12	.30
139 Lana	.50	1.25
140 Luke Gallows	.15	.40
141 Luke Harper	.12	.30
142 Mark Henry	.15	.40
143 Maryse	.25	.60
144 Mauro Ranallo RC	.12	.30
145 Michael Cole	.12	.30
146 Naomi	.20	.50
147 Natalya	.20	.50
148 Neville	.25	.60
149 Nikki Bella	.40	1.00
150 Paige	.40	1.00
151 Primo	.12	.30
152 Randy Orton	.30	.75
153 Renee Young	.30	.75
154 Roman Reigns	.40	1.00
155 Rosa Mendes	.12	.30
156 R-Truth	.12	.30
157 Rusev	.30	.75
158 Ryback	.15	.40
159 Sami Zayn	.20	.50
160 Sasha Banks	.40	1.00
161 Seth Rollins	.20	.50
162 Sheamus	.30	.75
163 Simon Gotch RC	.20	.50
164 Sin Cara	.15	.40
165 Summer Rae	.30	.75
166 Tamina	.15	.40
167 The Miz	.20	.50
168 The Rock	.60	1.50
169 Titus O'Neil	.12	.30
170 Tony Chimel	.12	.30
171 Triple H	.50	1.25
172 Tyler Breeze	.12	.30
173 Tyson Kidd	.12	.30
174 Undertaker	.50	1.25
175 Viktor	.12	.30
176 Xavier Woods	.12	.30
177 Zack Ryder	.12	.30
178 Alexa Bliss	.60	1.50
179 Angelo Dawkins	.12	.30
180 Asuka RC	.50	1.25
181 Austin Aries	.15	.40
182 Bayley RC	.30	.75
183 Billie Kay RC	.30	.75
184 Blake RC	.12	.30
185 Carmella RC	.30	.75
186 Cathy Kelley RC	.12	.30
187 Chad Gable RC	.15	.40
188 Corey Graves RC	.12	.30
189 Dash Wilder RC	.15	.40
190 Dasha Fuentes	.12	.30
191 Elias Samson RC	.12	.30
192 Finn Balor	.40	1.00
193 Greg Hamilton RC	.12	.30
194 Hideo Itami	.15	.40
195 Jason Jordan RC	.15	.40
196 Mandy Rose RC	2.00	5.00
197 Mojo Rawley RC	.12	.30
198 Murphy RC	.12	.30
199 Nia Jax RC	.20	.50
200 No Way Jose RC	.12	.30
201 Peyton Royce RC	.30	.75
202 Samoa Joe	.30	.75
203 Sawyer Fulton	.15	.40
204 Scott Dawson RC	.12	.30
205 Shinsuke Nakamura RC	.50	1.25
206 Tom Phillips	.12	.30
207 Tye Dillinger	.15	.40
208 William Regal	.12	.30
209 Adrienne Reese	.30	.75
210 Bronson Matthews RC	.12	.30
211 Oney Lorcan RC	.12	.30
212 Hugo Knox RC	.12	.30
213 King Constantine RC	.12	.30
214 Manny Andrade	.20	.50
215 Noah Kekoa RC	.12	.30
216 Tino Sabbatelli RC	.12	.30
217 Bam Bam Bigelow	.15	.40
218 Big Boss Man	.20	.50
219 Bob Backlund	.12	.30
220 Bobby Heenan	.20	.50
221 Booker T	.25	.60
222 Bret Hart	.30	.75
223 Brian Pillman	.15	.40
224 British Bulldog	.15	.40
225 Bruno Sammartino	.15	.40
226 Chief Jay Strongbow	.20	.50
227 Freddie Blassie	.15	.40
228 Bob Orton	.20	.50
229 Dean Malenko	.12	.30
230 Diamond Dallas Page	.20	.50
231 Diesel	.30	.75
232 Doink The Clown	.12	.30
233 Dusty Rhodes	.12	.30
234 Eddie Guerrero	.30	.75
235 Edge	.30	.75
236 Greg Valentine	.15	.40
237 Jim Duggan	.12	.30
238 Harley Race	.12	.30
239 Honky Tonk Man	.12	.30
240 Iron Shiek	.12	.30
241 Irwin R. Schyster	.12	.30
242 Jake Roberts	.25	.60
243 Jim Neidhart	.12	.30
244 Jimmy Hart	.15	.40
245 Junkyard Dog	.20	.50
246 Kevin Nash	.30	.75
247 Lex Luger	.20	.50
248 Lita	.40	1.00
249 Randy Savage	.30	.75
250 Don Muraco	.12	.30
251 Gene Okerlund	.15	.40
252 Ted Dibiase	.15	.40
253 Curt Hennig	.30	.75
254 Paul Orndorf	.12	.30
255 Paul Bearer	.20	.50
256 Rick Rude	.20	.50
257 Razor Ramon	.30	.75
258 Ric Flair	.50	1.25
259 Ricky Steamboat	.15	.40
260 Rikishi	.15	.40
261 Rhyno	.12	.30
262 Road Dogg	.20	.50
263 Ron Simmons	.30	.75
264 Rowdy Roddy Piper	.40	1.00
265 Sgt. Slaughter	.15	.40
266 Shawn Michaels	.50	1.25
267 Sting	.30	.75
268 Stone Cold Steve Austin	.60	1.50
269 Terry Funk	.12	.30
270 The Godfather	.15	.40
271 Trish Stratus	.60	1.50
272 Ultimate Warrior	.30	.75
273 Vader	.25	.60
274 X-Pac	.20	.50
275 Yokozuna	.25	.60
276 American Alpha	.15	.40
277 Blake/Murphy	.12	.30
278 Enzo/Cass	.25	.60
279 Gargano/Ciampa	.15	.40
280 Gallows/Anderson	.15	.40
281 The Shining Stars	.12	.30
282 Team B.A.D.	.40	1.00
283 The Ascension	.12	.30
284 The Bella Twins	.40	1.00
285 The Bushwhackers	.12	.30
286 The Dudley Boyz	.25	.60
287 The Hype Bros	.12	.30
288 The Lucha Dragons	.30	.75
289 The New Day	.30	.75
290 The Prime Time Players	.12	.30
291 The Revival	.15	.40
292 The Social Outcasts	.12	.30
293 The Usos	.12	.30
294 The Vaudevillains	.20	.50
295 The Wyatt Family	.50	1.25
296 Ladder	.12	.30
297 Steel Chair	.12	.30
298 Table	.12	.30
299 Trash Can	.12	.30

2021 Topps WWE Slam Attax

COMPLETE SET (368)	100.00	200.00
1 Adam Cole	.60	1.50
2 AJ Styles	.60	1.50
3 Akira Tozawa	.25	.60
4 Aleister Black	.50	1.25
5 Alexa Bliss	1.25	3.00
6 Alexander Wolfe	.20	.50
7 Aliyah	.40	1.00
8 August Grey RC	.20	.50
9 Angel Garza	.25	.60
10 Angelo Dawkins	.25	.60
11 Apollo Crews	.25	.60
12 Ariya Daivari	.25	.60
13 Arturo Ruas RC	.20	.50
14 Asuka	.75	2.00
15 Austin Theory	.40	1.00
16 Bayley	.50	1.25
17 Becky Lynch	.75	2.00
18 Bianca Belair	.50	1.25
19 Big E	.40	1.00
20 Billie Kay	.40	1.00
21 Bo Dallas	.20	.50
22 Boa	.20	.50
23 Bobby Fish	.25	.60
24 Bobby Lashley	.50	1.25
25 Braun Strowman	.50	1.25
26 Bronson Reed	.25	.60
27 Cameron Grimes	.40	1.00
28 Candice LeRae	.75	2.00
29 Carmella	.50	1.25
30 Cedric Alexander	.20	.50
31 Cesaro	.20	.50
32 Chad Gable	.20	.50
33 Charlotte Flair	1.00	2.50
34 Chelsea Green	.50	1.25
35 Dabba Kato RC	.25	.60
36 Dakota Kai	.40	1.00
37 Damian Priest	.30	.75
38 Dana Brooke	.20	.50
39 Daniel Bryan	.75	2.00
40 Danny Burch	.25	.60
41 Dave Mastiff	.20	.50
42 Dexter Lumis	.20	.50
43 Dolph Ziggler	.40	1.00
44 Dominik Mysterio RC	.25	.60
45 Drew Gulak	.25	.60
46 Drew McIntyre	.50	1.25
47 Edge	.75	2.00
48 Elias	.20	.50
49 Ember Moon	.25	.60
50 Erik	.20	.50
51 Fabian Aichner	.25	.60
52 Fandango	.30	.75
53 Finn Balor	.50	1.25
54 Flash Morgan	.25	.60
55 Gran Metalik	.20	.50
56 Humberto Carrillo	.20	.50
57 Ilja Dragunov	.20	.50
58 Indi Hartwell RC	.60	1.50
59 Io Shirai	.40	1.00

60 Isaiah "Swerve" Scott	.30	.75
61 Ivar	.20	.50
62 Jake Atlas RC	.20	.50
63 James Drake	.20	.50
64 Jaxson Ryker	.20	.50
65 Jeff Hardy	.50	1.25
66 Jessamyn Duke	.20	.50
67 Jey Uso	.20	.50
68 Jimmy Uso	.20	.50
69 Jinder Mahal	.25	.60
70 Joaquin Wilde	.30	.75
71 Joe Coffey	.20	.50
72 John Morrison	.40	1.00
73 Johnny Gargano	.40	1.00
74 Jordan Devlin	.20	.50
75 Kacy Catanzaro	.40	1.00
76 Kalisto	.25	.60
77 Kane	.30	.75
78 Karrion Kross	.75	2.00
79 Kay Lee Ray	.50	1.25
80 Kayden Carter	.40	1.00
81 Keith Lee	.40	1.00
82 Kevin Owens	.40	1.00
83 Killian Dain	.20	.50
84 King Corbin	.20	.50
85 Kofi Kingston	.50	1.25
86 Kona Reeves	.20	.50
87 Kushida	.30	.75
88 Kyle O'Reilly	.30	.75
89 Lacey Evans	.50	1.25
90 Lana	.25	.60
91 Leon Ruff RC	.20	.50
92 Lince Dorado	.20	.50
93 Liv Morgan	.75	2.00
94 Mace	.20	.50
95 Mandy Rose	1.00	2.50
96 Mansoor RC	.20	.50
97 Marcel Barthel	.25	.60
98 Marina Shafir	.40	1.00
99 Mark Andrews	.20	.50
100 Mark Coffey	.20	.50
101 Mercedes Martinez	.30	.75
102 Montez Ford	.20	.50
103 Murphy	.25	.60
104 Mustafa Ali	.25	.60
105 MVP	.20	.50
106 Naomi	.25	.60
107 Nash Carter RC	.20	.50
108 Natalya	.30	.75
109 Nia Jax	.40	1.00
110 Nikki Cross	.40	1.00
111 Noam Dar	.25	.60
112 Oney Lorcan	.20	.50
113 Otis	.25	.60
114 Pete Dunne	.40	1.00
115 Peyton Royce	.40	1.00
116 Piper Niven	.30	.75
117 R-Truth	.25	.60
118 Randy Orton	.60	1.50
119 Raquel Gonzalez	.50	1.25
120 Raul Mendoza	.30	.75
121 Reckoning	.25	.60
122 Rey Mysterio	.50	1.25
123 Rhea Ripley	.60	1.50
124 Ricochet	.40	1.00
125 Riddick Moss	.25	.60
126 Riddle	.50	1.25
127 Rinku (Veer Mahaan) RC	.20	.50

128 Robert Roode	.25	.60
129 Roderick Strong	.30	.75
130 Roman Reigns	1.00	2.50
131 Ruby Riott	.40	1.00
132 Sami Zayn	.30	.75
133 Samir Singh	.20	.50
134 Santos Escobar	.30	.75
135 Sasha Banks	1.00	2.50
136 Saurav RC	.20	.50
137 Scarlett	1.00	2.50
138 Seth Rollins	.50	1.25
139 Shayna Baszler	.40	1.00
140 Sheamus	.30	.75
141 Shelton Benjamin	.30	.75
142 Shinsuke Nakamura	.50	1.25
143 Shotzi Blackheart	.75	2.00
144 Slapjack	.20	.50
145 Sunil Singh	.20	.50
146 T-Bar	.25	.60
147 Tamina	.25	.60
148 Tegan Nox	.50	1.25
149 The Brian Kendrick	.20	.50
150 The Fiend Bray Wyatt	.75	2.00
151 The Miz	.30	.75
152 Timothy Thatcher RC	.20	.50
153 Tomasso Ciampa	.50	1.25
154 Toni Storm	.60	1.50
155 Tony Nese	.20	.50
156 Trent Seven	.25	.60
157 Tucker	.20	.50
158 Tyler Bate	.25	.60
159 Tyler Breeze	.25	.60
160 Tyler Rust RC	.20	.50
161 Vanessa Borne	.25	.60
162 Velveteen Dream	.25	.60
163 Walter	.50	1.25
164 Wes Lee RC	.20	.50
165 Wesley Blake	.20	.50
166 Wolfgang	.20	.50
167 Xavier Woods	.20	.50
168 Xia Lee	.40	1.00
169 Zack Gibson	.20	.50
170 Ariya Daivari & Tony Nese TT	.25	.60
171 Asuka & Charlotte TT	1.00	2.50
172 Breezango TT	.30	.75
173 Cesaro & Daniel Bryan TT	.75	2.00
174 Dakota Kai & Raquel TT	.40	1.00
175 Danny Burch & Oney Lorcan TT	.25	.60
176 Elias & Jaxson TT	.20	.50
177 Ever Rise TT	.25	.60
178 Flash Morgan Webster & Mark Andrews TT	.25	.60
179 Alpha Academy TT	.25	.60
180 Gallus TT	.25	.60
181 Grizzled Young Veterans TT	.20	.50
182 The Hurt Business TT	.30	.75
183 Imperium TT	.25	.60
184 Indus Sher TT	.20	.50
185 Kacy Catanzaro & Kayden Carter TT	.40	1.00
186 Kushida & Leon Ruff TT	.30	.75
187 Legado Del Fantasma TT	.25	.60
188 Mandy Rose & Dana Brooke TT	1.00	2.50
189 Moustache Mountain TT	.25	.60
190 MSK TT	.20	.50
191 Retribution TT	.25	.60
192 Shayna Baszler & Nia Jax TT	.40	1.00
193 Shotzi Blackheart & Ember Moon TT	.75	2.00
194 The Bollywood Boys TT	.20	.50

195 The Dirty Dawgs TT	.40	1.00
196 The Lucha House Party TT	.20	.50
197 The Miz & John Morrison TT	.40	1.00
198 The New Day TT	.40	1.00
199 The Riott Squad TT	.30	.75
200 The Robert Stone Brand TT	.20	.50
201 The Street Profits TT	.25	.60
202 The Viking Raiders TT	.20	.50
203 The Way TT	.20	.50
204 Tomasso Ciampa & Timothy Thatcher TT	.50	1.25
205 The Way FAC	.20	.50
206 The Hurt Business FAC	.30	.75
207 Imperium FAC	.25	.60
208 Retribution FAC	.25	.60
209 Styles Clash	.60	1.50
210 Twisted Bliss	1.25	3.00
211 Bayley-to-Belly	.50	1.25
212 Big Ending	.40	1.00
213 The Hurt Lock	.50	1.25
214 Powerslam	.50	1.25
215 Figure-Eight Leg-Lock	1.00	2.50
216 Claymore	.50	1.25
217 Moonsault	.40	1.00
218 Uso Splash	.20	.50
219 RKO	.60	1.50
220 Riptide	.60	1.50
221 Spear	1.00	2.50
222 Brogue Kick	.30	.75
223 Sister Abigail	.75	2.00
224 Skull-Crushing Finale	.30	.75
225 Sasha Banks	1.00	2.50
226 Sasha Banks	1.00	2.50
227 Sasha Banks	1.00	2.50
228 Riddle	.50	1.25
229 Riddle	.50	1.25
230 Riddle	.50	1.25
231 Mankind	.40	1.00
232 Stone Cold Steve Austin	1.00	2.50
233 Hulk Hogan	1.00	2.50
234 The Rock	2.00	5.00
235 Universal Championship	.15	.40
236 WWE Championship	.15	.40
237 RAW Women's Championship	.15	.40
238 SmackDown Women's Championship	.15	.40
239 Intercontinental Championship	.15	.40
240 United States Championship	.15	.40
241 24/7 Championship	.15	.40
242 RAW Tag Team Championship	.15	.40
243 SmackDown Championship	.15	.40
244 WWE Women's Tag Team Championship	.15	.40
245 NXT Championship	.15	.40
246 NXT Women's Championship	.15	.40
247 NXT North American Championship	.15	.40
248 NXT Cruiserweight Championship	.15	.40
249 NXT Tag Team Championship	.15	.40
250 NXT UK Championship	.15	.40
251 NXT UK Women's Championship	.15	.40
252 NXT UK Tag Team Championship	.15	.40
253 AJ Styles	.60	1.50
254 Alexa Bliss	1.25	3.00
255 Charlotte Flair	1.00	2.50
256 Drew McIntyre	.50	1.25
257 Randy Orton	.60	1.50
258 The Fiend Bray Wyatt	.75	2.00
259 Bayley	.50	1.25
260 Bianca Belair	.50	1.25

261 Daniel Bryan	.75	2.00
262 Kevin Owens	.40	1.00
263 Roman Reigns	1.00	2.50
264 Sasha Banks	1.00	2.50
265 Adam Cole	.60	1.50
266 Finn Balor	.50	1.25
267 Io Shirai	.40	1.00
268 Karrion Kross	.75	2.00
269 Pete Dunne	.40	1.00
270 Toni Storm	.60	1.50
271 Flash Morgan Webster	.25	.60
272 Ilja Dragunov	.20	.50
273 Kay Lee Ray	.50	1.25
274 Trent Seven	.25	.60
275 Walter	.50	1.25
276 Wolfgang	.20	.50
277 Thank You Taker	1.00	2.50
278 Thank You Taker	1.00	2.50
279 Thank You Taker	1.00	2.50
280 Thank You Taker	1.00	2.50
281 Thank You Taker	1.00	2.50
282 Daniel Bryan	.75	2.00
283 Ricochet	.40	1.00
284 Shotzi Blackheart	.75	2.00
285 WWE Logo	.15	.40
286 RAW Logo	.15	.40
287 SmackDown Logo	.15	.40
288 NXT Logo	.15	.40
289 NXT UK Logo	.15	.40
290 Andre the Giant L	.75	2.00
291 Batista L	.40	1.00
292 Bret "Hit Man" Hart L	.50	1.25
293 Hulk Hogan L	1.00	2.50
294 Macho Man Randy Savage L	1.25	3.00
295 Mankind L	.40	1.00
296 Ric Flair L	.75	2.00
297 Stone Cold Steve Austin L	1.00	2.50
298 Trish Stratus L	1.00	2.50
299 Ultimate Warrior L	.75	2.00
300 Apollo Crews	.25	.60
301 Bianca Belair	.50	1.25
302 Big E	.40	1.00
303 Billie Kay	.40	1.00
304 Cesaro	.20	.50
305 Damien Priest	.30	.75
306 Jey Uso	.20	.50
307 Liv Morgan	.75	2.00
308 Rhea Ripley	.60	1.50
309 Riddle	.50	1.25
310 Firefly Funhouse Logo	.15	.40
311 Mercy the Buzzard	.15	.40
312 Huskus the Pig Boy	.15	.40
313 Abby the Witch	.15	.40
314 Ramblin' Rabbit	.15	.40
315 The Boss	1.00	2.50
316 Friendship Frog	.15	.40
317 Apollo Crews	.25	.60
318 Bayley	.50	1.25
319 Braun Strowman	.50	1.25
320 Sheamus	.30	.75
321 Asuka	.75	2.00
322 Cesaro	.20	.50
323 Kevin Owens	.40	1.00
324 Seth Rollins	.50	1.25
325 Drew McIntyre	.50	1.25
326 Mandy Rose	1.00	2.50
327 Montez Ford	.20	.50
328 Roman Reigns	1.00	2.50

329 Dominik Mysterio RC	.25	.60
330 Keith Lee	.40	1.00
331 Riddle	.50	1.25
332 Shayna Baszler	.40	1.00
333 Angelo Dawkins	.25	.60
334 Bobby Lashley	.50	1.25
335 Sami Zayn	.30	.75
336 Shinsuke Nakamura	.50	1.25
337 AJ Styles	.60	1.50
338 Lacey Evans	.50	1.25
339 Lana	.25	.60
340 The Miz	.30	.75
341 Big E	.40	1.00
342 Cedric Alexander	.20	.50
343 Daniel Bryan	.75	2.00
344 Randy Orton	.60	1.50
345 Bianca Belair	.50	1.25
346 Billie Kay	.40	1.00
347 Edge	.75	2.00
348 Rhea Ripley	.60	1.50
349 Asuka ICON	.75	2.00
350 Bayley ICON	.50	1.25
351 Becky Lynch ICON	.75	2.00
352 Charlotte Flair ICON	1.00	2.50
353 Daniel Bryan ICON	.75	2.00
354 Kofi Kingston ICON	.50	1.25
355 Randy Orton ICON	.60	1.50
356 Seth Rollins ICON	.50	1.25
357 Hollywood Hulk Hogan SR	1.00	2.50
358 Alexa Bliss 100C	1.25	3.00
359 Bianca Belair 100C	.50	1.25
360 Drew McIntyre 100C	.50	1.25
361 Bobby Lashley 100C	.50	1.25
362 Sasha Banks 100C	1.00	2.50
363 The Fiend Bray Wyatt 100C	.75	2.00
364 Edge 100C	.75	2.00
365 Roman Reigns 100C	1.00	2.50
366 Alexa Bliss/Firefly Funhouse	1.25	3.00
367 Bray Wyatt/Firefly Funhouse	.75	2.00
368 John Cena nWo UR	1.00	2.50

2021 Topps WWE Slam Attax Autographs

RANDOMLY INSERTED INTO PACKS

AT1 Adam Cole		
AT2 Alexa Bliss		
AT3 Becky Lynch		
AT4 Bianca Belair		
AT5 Billie Kay		
AT6 The Fiend Bray Wyatt		
AT7 Candice LeRae		
AT8 Carmella	30.00	75.00
AT9 Cesaro		
AT10 Elias		
AT11 Ember Moon		
AT12 Finn Balor		
AT13 Flash Morgan Webster		
AT14 Io Shirai		
AT15 Kevin Owens		
AT17 Mark Coffey		
AT18 Mustafa Ali		
AT19 Finn Balor		
AT20 Riddle	60.00	120.00
AT21 Ruby Riott		
AT22 Pete Dunne		
AT23 Rhea Ripley		
AT24 Sasha Banks		
AT25 Shinsuke Nakamura		
AT26 Shotzi Blackheart		
AT27 The Miz	15.00	40.00
AT28 Tommaso Ciampa	25.00	60.00
AT29 Wolfgang		
AT30 Xavier Woods	15.00	40.00
AT34 Keith Lee	15.00	40.00
AT35 Lacey Evans	25.00	60.00
AT37 Asuka	50.00	100.00
AT38 Bayley		
AT39 Charlotte Flair		
AT40 Naomi	12.00	30.00
AT41 Natalya	20.00	50.00
AT42 Nikki Cross	20.00	50.00
AT43 Peyton Royce	30.00	75.00
AT44 Trish Stratus	50.00	100.00
FINDDREW Drew McIntyre/99		

2021 Topps WWE Slam Attax Boneyard Match Relics

STATED PRINT RUN 200 SER.#'d SETS

BY1 Undertaker vs. AJ Styles	50.00	100.00

2021 Topps WWE Slam Attax Champion Edition

STATED PRINT RUN 100 SER.#'d SETS

NNO Nikki A.S.H.	15.00	40.00
NNO Reggie	4.00	10.00
NNO Roman Reigns	12.00	30.00

2021 Topps WWE Slam Attax The Impossible Autographs

AT31 The Fiend/Alexa Bliss		
AT32 John Cena		
AT33 Roman Reigns		

2021 Topps WWE Slam Attax Limited Edition Bronze

RANDOMLY INSERTED INTO PACKS

LE3B The Fiend Bray Wyatt	2.00	5.00
LE4B Alexa Bliss	2.50	6.00
LE5B Roman Reigns	2.00	5.00

2021 Topps WWE Slam Attax Limited Edition Gold

COMPLETE SET (24)	75.00	150.00
RANDOMLY INSERTED INTO PACKS		
LE1G Drew McIntyre	1.50	4.00
LE2G Sasha Banks	3.00	8.00
LE3G The Fiend Bray Wyatt	4.00	10.00
LE4G Alexa Bliss	6.00	15.00
LE5G Roman Reigns	4.00	10.00
LE6G Bianca Belair	2.00	5.00
LE7G AJ Styles	2.50	6.00
LE8G Billie Kay	2.00	5.00
LE9G Big E	1.50	4.00
LE10G Daniel Bryan	2.50	6.00
LE11G Keith Lee	1.50	4.00
LE12G Liv Morgan	2.00	5.00
LE13G Riddle	3.00	8.00
LE14G Charlotte Flair	3.00	8.00
LE15G Bobby Lashley	2.00	5.00
LE16G Seth Rollins	1.50	4.00
LE17G Rhea Ripley	2.50	6.00
LE18G Becky Lynch	4.00	10.00
LE19G The Rock	6.00	15.00
LE20G John Cena	4.00	10.00
LE21G Randy Orton	3.00	8.00
LE22G Mandy Rose	4.00	10.00
LE23G Sami Zayn	1.50	4.00
LE24G Bayley	15.00	40.00

2021 Topps WWE Slam Attax Limited Edition Platinum Blue

RANDOMLY INSERTED INTO PACKS

LE3R The Fiend Bray Wyatt	10.00	25.00
LE4R Alexa Bliss	20.00	50.00
LE5R Roman Reigns	10.00	25.00

2021 Topps WWE Slam Attax Limited Edition Silver

RANDOMLY INSERTED INTO PACKS

LE3S The Fiend Bray Wyatt	3.00	8.00
LE4S Alexa Bliss	5.00	12.00
LE5S Roman Reigns	3.00	8.00

2021 Topps WWE Slam Attax Oversized

COMPLETE SET (20)	30.00	75.00
OV1 Roman Reigns	4.00	10.00
OV2 Hulk Hogan	4.00	10.00
OV3 Batista	1.50	4.00
OV4 Bret "Hit Man" Hart	2.00	5.00
OV5 Stone Cold Steve Austin	4.00	10.00
OV6 Becky Lynch	3.00	8.00
OV7 Drew McIntyre	2.00	5.00
OV8 Trish Stratus	4.00	10.00
OV9 Ultimate Warrior	3.00	8.00
OV10 Ric Flair	3.00	8.00
OV11 Karrion Kross	3.00	8.00
OV12 The Fiend Bray Wyatt	3.00	8.00
OV13 Alexa Bliss	5.00	12.00
OV14 Apollo Crews	1.00	2.50
OV15 Kevin Owens	1.50	4.00
OV16 Bianca Belair	2.00	5.00
OV17 Asuka	3.00	8.00
OV18 Cesaro	.75	2.00
OV19 Sasha Banks	4.00	10.00
OV20 Big E	1.50	4.00

2021 Topps WWE Slam Attax SP

STATED PRINT RUN 100 SER.#'d SETS

NNO The Fiend Bray Wyatt	12.00	30.00
NNO Lilly	8.00	20.00
NNO Omos	6.00	15.00

2021 Topps WWE Slam Attax Tactic Cards

COMPLETE SET (4)	3.00	8.00
RANDOMLY INSERTED INTO PACKS		
T1 Ladder	1.00	2.50
T2 Table	1.00	2.50
T3 Steel Chair	1.00	2.50
T4 Special Counsel Paul Heyman	1.00	2.50

2021 Topps WWE Slam Attax Women of WWE

COMPLETE SET (32)	10.00	25.00
RANDOMLY INSERTED INTO PACKS		
W1 Alexa Bliss	1.50	4.00
W2 Asuka	1.00	2.50
W3 Bayley	.60	1.50
W4 Becky Lynch	1.00	2.50
W5 Bianca Belair	.60	1.50
W6 Billie Kay	.50	1.25
W7 Candice LeRae	1.00	2.50
W8 Carmella	.60	1.50
W9 Charlotte Flair	1.25	3.00
W10 Dakota Kai	.50	1.25
W11 Dana Brooke	.25	.60
W12 Ember Moon	.30	.75
W13 Io Shirai	.50	1.25
W14 Kacy Catanzaro	.50	1.25
W15 Kay Lee Ray	.60	1.50
W16 Lacey Evans	.60	1.50
W17 Lana	.30	.75
W18 Liv Morgan	1.00	2.50
W19 Mandy Rose	1.25	3.00
W20 Naomi	.30	.75
W21 Natalya	.40	1.00
W22 Nia Jax	.50	1.25
W23 Nikki Cross	.50	1.25
W24 Peyton Royce	.50	1.25
W25 Piper Niven	.40	1.00
W26 Rhea Ripley	.75	2.00
W27 Ruby Riott	.50	1.25
W28 Sasha Banks	1.25	3.00
W29 Scarlett	1.25	3.00
W30 Shayna Baszler	.50	1.25
W31 Tamina	.30	.75
W32 Toni Storm	.75	2.00

2019 Topps WWE SmackDown Live

COMPLETE SET (90)	10.00	25.00

*GREEN: .5X TO 1.5X BASIC CARDS
*PURPLE/99: .75X TO 3X BASIC CARDS
*20TH ANN./20: UNPRICED DUE TO SCARCITY
*GOLD/10: UNPRICED DUE TO SCARCITY
*RED/1: UNPRICED DUE TO SCARCITY
*P.P.BLACK/1: UNPRICED DUE TO SCARCITY
*P.P.CYAN/1: UNPRICED DUE TO SCARCITY
*P.P.MAGENTA/1: UNPRICED DUE TO SCARCITY
*P.P.YELLOW/1: UNPRICED DUE TO SCARCITY

1 Aiden English	.25	.60
2 Aleister Black	.30	.75
3 Ali	.25	.60
4 Andrade	.30	.75
5 Apollo Crews	.30	.75
6 Asuka	.75	2.00
7 Bayley	.50	1.25
8 Becky Lynch	1.00	2.50
9 Big E	.25	.60
10 Billie Kay	.50	1.25
11 Bo Dallas	.30	.75
12 Buddy Murphy	.30	.75
13 Byron Saxton	.25	.60
14 Carmella	.60	1.50
15 Cesaro	.30	.75
16 Chad Gable	.25	.60
17 Charlotte Flair	1.00	2.50
18 Corey Graves	.30	.75
19 Curtis Axel	.30	.75
20 Daniel Bryan	1.00	2.50
21 Elias	.50	1.25
22 Ember Moon	.60	1.50
23 Finn Balor	.60	1.50
24 Greg Hamilton	.25	.60
25 Jeff Hardy	.60	1.50
26 Jinder Mahal	.50	1.25

27 Kairi Sane	.50	1.25
28 Kevin Owens	.60	1.50
29 Kofi Kingston	.40	1.00
30 Lana	.50	1.25
31 Lars Sullivan	.25	.60
32 Liv Morgan	.75	2.00
33 Mandy Rose	.60	1.50
34 Maryse	.30	.75
35 Matt Hardy	.50	1.25
36 Mickie James	.60	1.50
37 Otis	.25	.60
38 Paige	1.00	2.50
39 Peyton Royce	.60	1.50
40 R-Truth	.30	.75
41 Randy Orton	.60	1.50
42 Roman Reigns	.60	1.50
43 Rowan	.25	.60
44 Rusev	.50	1.25
45 Samir Singh	.25	.60
46 Sarah Schreiber RC	.25	.60
47 Sheamus	.40	1.00
48 Shelton Benjamin	.30	.75
49 Shinsuke Nakamura	.60	1.50
50 Sin Cara	.25	.60
51 Sonya Deville	.50	1.25
52 Sunil Singh	.25	.60
53 Tom Phillips	.25	.60
54 Tucker	.25	.60
55 Xavier Woods	.30	.75
56 Zelina Vega	.40	1.00
57 Big Show	.40	1.00
58 The Rock	1.25	3.00
59 Triple H	.60	1.50
60 Undertaker	1.25	3.00
61 Albert	.25	.60
62 Beth Phoenix	.40	1.00
63 Big Boss Man	.30	.75
64 The British Bulldog	.60	1.50
65 Boogeyman	.25	.60
66 King Booker	.60	1.50
67 Cactus Jack	.50	1.25
68 Christian	.40	1.00
69 Chyna	.50	1.25
70 Cowboy Bob Orton	.25	.60
71 D-Lo Brown	.25	.60
72 Diamond Dallas Page	.50	1.25
73 Eddie Guerrero	.60	1.50
74 Faarooq	.40	1.00
75 Finlay	.25	.60
76 The Godfather	.25	.60
77 Goldberg	.75	2.00
78 Jerry The King Lawler	.50	1.25
79 Kevin Nash	.40	1.00
80 Lita	.60	1.50
81 Mankind	.50	1.25
82 Paul Bearer	.30	.75
83 Rikishi	.25	.60
84 Road Dogg Jesse James	.25	.60
85 Rowdy Roddy Piper	.60	1.50
86 Scott Hall	.40	1.00
87 Stone Cold Steve Austin	1.25	3.00
88 Tatanka	.25	.60
89 Trish Stratus	1.25	3.00
90 X-Pac	.25	.60

2019 Topps WWE SmackDown Live 20 Years of SmackDown

COMPLETE SET (46)	12.00	30.00
RANDOMLY INSERTED INTO PACKS		
SD1 Undertaker & Big Show	1.50	4.00
SD2 The Rock & Mankind	1.50	4.00
SD3 Stone Cold Steve Austin	1.50	4.00
SD4 Jeff Hardy	.75	2.00
SD5 Kurt Angle	.60	1.50
SD6 Batista	.75	2.00
SD7 Rey Mysterio	.75	2.00
SD8 John Cena	1.25	3.00
SD9 Kurt Angle	.60	1.50
SD10 Kurt Angle	.60	1.50
SD11 Rey Mysterio	.75	2.00
SD12 Brock Lesnar	1.25	3.00
SD13 Brock Lesnar	1.25	3.00
SD14 Eddie Guerrero	.75	2.00
SD15 Stone Cold Steve Austin	1.50	4.00
SD16 Eddie Guerrero	.75	2.00
SD17 Undertaker	1.50	4.00
SD18 Kurt Angle	.60	1.50
SD19 Eddie Guerrero	.75	2.00
SD20 Undertaker	1.50	4.00
SD21 Kurt Angle	.60	1.50
SD22 Booker T	.75	2.00
SD23 Shawn Michaels	.75	2.00
SD24 Jeff Hardy	.75	2.00
SD25 Jeff Hardy	.75	2.00
SD26 Shawn Michaels	.75	2.00
SD27 Randy Orton	.75	2.00
SD28 Daniel Bryan	1.25	3.00
SD29 Beth Phoenix	.50	1.25
SD30 Daniel Bryan	1.25	3.00
SD31 John Cena	1.25	3.00
SD32 Cesaro	.40	1.00
SD33 Batista	.75	2.00
SD34 Wyatt Family	.40	1.00
SD35 Kevin Owens	.75	2.00
SD36 The Miz	.60	1.50
SD37 Alexa Bliss	1.50	4.00
SD38 Bray Wyatt	.75	2.00
SD39 The Usos	.40	1.00
SD40 Carmella	.75	2.00
SD41 Shinsuke Nakamura	.75	2.00
SD42 The New Day	.60	1.50
SD43 AJ Styles	1.50	4.00
SD44 John Cena	1.25	3.00
SD45 Rusev	.60	1.50
SD46 The New Day	.60	1.50

2019 Topps WWE SmackDown Live Autographed Intercontinental Championship 40th Anniversary Relics

RANDOMLY INSERTED INTO PACKS

ICRKK Kofi Kingston
ICRSB Shelton Benjamin
ICRTM The Miz

2019 Topps WWE SmackDown Live Autographed Mat Relics

STATED PRINT RUN 10 SER.#'d SETS
UNPRICED DUE TO SCARCITY

MRAAJ AJ Styles
MRABD Daniel Bryan
MRABE Big E
MRABM Buddy Murphy
MRACM Carmella
MRAJE Jey Uso
MRAJH Jeff Hardy
MRAJI Jimmy Uso
MRAKA Karl Anderson
MRAKK Kofi Kingston
MRAKS Shinsuke Nakamura
MRALG Luke Gallows
MRAMA Ali
MRAMR Mandy Rose
MRARJ Rey Mysterio
MRARM Rey Mysterio
MRART R-Truth
MRASD Sonya Deville
MRASN Shinsuke Nakamura
MRAXW Xavier Woods

2019 Topps WWE SmackDown Live Autographed Shirt Relics

STATED PRINT RUN 10 SER.#'d SETS
UNPRICED DUE TO SCARCITY

SRAC Apollo Crews
SREM Ember Moon
SRMH Matt Hardy
SRXW Xavier Woods
SRAAA Andrade
SRAAB Aleister Black
SRAEL Elias
SRAKK Kofi Kingston

2019 Topps WWE SmackDown Live Autographed SmackDown Championship Commemorative Relics

STATED PRINT RUN 10 SER.#'d SETS
UNPRICED DUE TO SCARCITY

ASCAB Alexa Bliss
ASCAJ AJ Styles
ASCBC Baron Corbin
ASCBL Becky Lynch
ASCBR Robert Roode
ASCCM Carmella
ASCKK Kofi Kingston
ASCKO Kevin Owens
ASCNM Naomi
ASCNT Natalya
ASCRO Randy Orton
ASCRT R-Truth
ASCSJ Samoa Joe
ASCSN Shinsuke Nakamura

2019 Topps WWE SmackDown Live Autographed Women's Evolution Relics

DRACCM Carmella

2019 Topps WWE SmackDown Live Autographs

*ORANGE/50: .5X TO 1.2X BASIC AUTOS
*20TH ANN./20: UNPRICED DUE TO SCARCITY
*GOLD/10: UNPRICED DUE TO SCARCITY
*RED/1: UNPRICED DUE TO SCARCITY
STATED PRINT RUN 99 SER.#'d SETS

AAA Andrade	4.00	10.00
AAL Aleister Black	12.00	30.00
ABA Bayley	10.00	25.00
ABE Becky Lynch		
ABK Billie Kay	8.00	20.00
ABL Big E	4.00	10.00
ABU Buddy Murphy	8.00	20.00
ACH Chad Gable	4.00	10.00
ACM Carmella	10.00	25.00
AEL Elias	4.00	10.00
AEM Ember Moon	8.00	20.00
AFI Finn Balor	12.00	30.00
AGH Greg Hamilton	4.00	10.00
AKE Kevin Owens	6.00	15.00
AKK Kofi Kingston	6.00	15.00
ALI Liv Morgan	15.00	40.00
AMA Ali	4.00	10.00
AMH Matt Hardy	6.00	15.00
AMR Mandy Rose	15.00	40.00
AOT Otis	10.00	25.00
APR Peyton Royce	10.00	25.00
ARR Roman Reigns	10.00	25.00
ART R-Truth	5.00	12.00
ARW Rowan	4.00	10.00
ASD Sonya Deville	6.00	15.00
ASN Shinsuke Nakamura	5.00	12.00
ATU Tucker	4.00	10.00
AXW Xavier Woods	5.00	12.00
AZV Zelina Vega	12.00	30.00

2019 Topps WWE SmackDown Live Corey Says

COMPLETE SET (19)	6.00	15.00
RANDOMLY INSERTED INTO PACKS		
CG1 AJ Styles	1.50	4.00
CG2 Asuka	1.00	2.50
CG3 Becky Lynch	1.25	3.00
CG4 Carmella	.75	2.00
CG5 Cesaro	.40	1.00
CG6 Charlotte Flair	1.25	3.00
CG7 Daniel Bryan	1.25	3.00
CG8 Jeff Hardy	.75	2.00
CG9 Randy Orton	.75	2.00
CG10 Rey Mysterio	.75	2.00
CG11 Rusev	.60	1.50
CG12 Samoa Joe	.60	1.50
CG13 Shane McMahon	.75	2.00
CG14 Sheamus	.50	1.25
CG15 Shinsuke Nakamura	.75	2.00
CG16 The Miz	.60	1.50
CG17 The New Day	.60	1.50
CG18 The Usos	.40	1.00
CG19 Undertaker	1.50	4.00

2019 Topps WWE SmackDown Live Dual Autographs

*GOLD/10: UNPRICED DUE TO SCARCITY
*RED/1: UNPRICED DUE TO SCARCITY
STATED PRINT RUN 25 SER.#'d SETS

DADB R-Truth/Carmella	20.00	50.00
DAGB K.Anderson/L.Gallows	30.00	75.00
DAII B.Kay/P.Royce	75.00	150.00
DATQ Z.Vega/Andrade	20.00	50.00
DAABS S.Deville/M.Rose	75.00	150.00

2019 Topps WWE SmackDown Live Image Variations

IV1 Aleister Black

IV2	Andrade	6.00	15.00
IV3	Big E		
IV4	Billie Kay	6.00	15.00
IV5	Charlotte Flair	15.00	40.00
IV6	Daniel Bryan	12.00	30.00
IV7	Jeff Hardy	4.00	10.00
IV8	Killian Dain		
IV9	Kofi Kingston	6.00	15.00
IV10	Mandy Rose	12.00	30.00
IV11	Peyton Royce		
IV12	R-Truth		
IV13	Shinsuke Nakamura		
IV14	Sheamus		
IV15	Shelton Benjamin	8.00	20.00
IV16	Sonya Deville	10.00	25.00
IV17	Xavier Woods	4.00	10.00
IV18	Zelina Vega		
IV19	Ali		
IV20	Matt Hardy	8.00	20.00

2019 Topps WWE SmackDown Live Intercontinental Championship 40th Anniversary Autographs

ICAKK	Kofi Kingston	8.00	20.00
ICASB	Shelton Benjamin	12.00	30.00
ICATM	The Miz	10.00	25.00

2019 Topps WWE SmackDown Live Intercontinental Championship 40th Anniversary Relics

RANDOMLY INSERTED INTO PACKS

ICRDM Drew McIntyre
ICRKK Kofi Kingston
ICRRM Rey Mysterio
ICRSB Shelton Benjamin
ICRTM The Miz

2019 Topps WWE SmackDown Live Mat Relics

*PURPLE/99: .6X TO 1.5X BASIC MEM
*ORANGE/50: .75X TO 2X BASIC MEM
*20TH ANN./20: UNPRICED DUE TO SCARCITY
*GOLD/10: UNPRICED DUE TO SCARCITY
*RED/1: UNPRICED DUE TO SCARCITY
STATED PRINT RUN 199 SER.#'d SETS

MR4H	Charlotte Flair	8.00	20.00
MRAJ	AJ Styles	4.00	10.00
MRAS	Asuka	6.00	15.00
MRAW	Alexander Wolfe	3.00	8.00
MRBD	Daniel Bryan	4.00	10.00
MRBE	Big E	2.50	6.00
MRBL	Becky Lynch	6.00	15.00
MRBM	Buddy Murphy	2.50	6.00
MRBS	Big Show	2.50	6.00
MRBT	Batista	3.00	8.00
MRCF	Charlotte Flair	6.00	15.00
MRCM	Carmella	4.00	10.00
MRCS	Cesaro	2.50	6.00
MRDB	Daniel Bryan	4.00	10.00
MREY	Eric Young	2.50	6.00
MRJE	Jey Uso	2.50	6.00
MRJH	Jeff Hardy	4.00	10.00
MRJI	Jimmy Uso	2.50	6.00
MRKA	Karl Anderson	2.50	6.00
MRKD	Killian Dain	2.50	6.00
MRKK	Kofi Kingston	3.00	8.00
MRKS	Shinsuke Nakamura	3.00	8.00
MRLG	Luke Gallows	2.50	6.00
MRLN	Lana	3.00	8.00
MRMA	Ali	2.50	6.00
MRMH	Stephanie McMahon	4.00	10.00
MRMR	Mandy Rose	6.00	15.00
MRRF	Ric Flair	5.00	12.00
MRRJ	Rey Mysterio	4.00	10.00
MRRM	Rey Mysterio	4.00	10.00
MRRO	Randy Orton	4.00	10.00
MRRS	Rusev	2.50	6.00
MRRT	R-Truth	2.50	6.00
MRSD	Sonya Deville	3.00	8.00
MRSH	Sheamus	2.50	6.00
MRSJ	Samoa Joe	2.50	6.00
MRSN	Shinsuke Nakamura	3.00	8.00
MRTH	Triple H	3.00	8.00
MRTM	The Miz	2.50	6.00
MRUT	Undertaker	6.00	15.00
MRXW	Xavier Woods	2.50	6.00

2019 Topps WWE SmackDown Live Shirt Relics

*PURPLE/99: .6X TO 1.5X BASIC MEM
*ORANGE/50: .75X TO 2X BASIC MEM
20TH ANN./20: UNPRICED DUE TO SCARCITY
*GOLD/10: UNPRICED DUE TO SCARCITY
*RED/1: UNPRICED DUE TO SCARCITY
STATED PRINT RUN 199 SER.#'d SETS

SRAA	Andrade/199	5.00	12.00
SRAB	Aleister Black/199	5.00	12.00
SRAC	Apollo Crews/199	4.00	10.00
SREL	Elias/199	5.00	12.00
SREM	Ember Moon/199	6.00	15.00
SRJH	Jeff Hardy/199	5.00	12.00
SRKA	Karl Anderson/199	4.00	10.00
SRKK	Kofi Kingston/199	4.00	10.00
SRKS	Kairi Sane/199	5.00	12.00
SRLG	Luke Gallows/199	4.00	10.00
SRLM	Liv Morgan/160	12.00	30.00
SRMH	Matt Hardy/199	4.00	10.00
SRSM	Sheamus/199	4.00	10.00
SRXW	Xavier Woods/199	6.00	15.00

2019 Topps WWE SmackDown Live SmackDown Championship Commemorative Relics

*PURPLE/99: .6X TO 1.5X BASIC MEM
*ORANGE/50: .75X TO 2X BASIC MEM
20TH ANN./20: UNPRICED DUE TO SCARCITY
*GOLD/10: UNPRICED DUE TO SCARCITY
*RED/1: UNPRICED DUE TO SCARCITY
STATED PRINT RUN 199 SER.#'d SETS

SCAB	Alexa Bliss	8.00	20.00
SCAJ	AJ Styles	5.00	12.00
SCAS	Asuka	6.00	15.00
SCBC	Baron Corbin	2.50	6.00
SCBL	Becky Lynch	10.00	25.00
SCBR	Robert Roode	2.50	6.00
SCBW	Bray Wyatt	6.00	15.00
SCCF	Charlotte Flair	4.00	10.00
SCCM	Carmella	8.00	20.00
SCDB	Daniel Bryan	5.00	12.00
SCJC	John Cena	6.00	15.00
SCJH	Jeff Hardy	5.00	12.00
SCKK	Kofi Kingston	5.00	12.00
SCKO	Kevin Owens	2.50	6.00
SCMH	Jinder Mahal	2.50	6.00
SCNM	Naomi	2.50	6.00
SCNT	Natalya	2.50	6.00
SCRO	Randy Orton	5.00	12.00
SCRT	R-Truth	3.00	8.00
SCRV	Rusev	2.50	6.00
SCSJ	Samoa Joe	2.50	6.00
SCSN	Shinsuke Nakamura	4.00	10.00
SCVP	Randy Orton	5.00	12.00

2019 Topps WWE SmackDown Live SmackDown Tag Team Championship Commemorative Relics

*PURPLE/99: .6X TO 1.5X BASIC MEM
*ORANGE/50: .75X TO 2X BASIC MEM
20TH ANN./20: UNPRICED DUE TO SCARCITY
*GOLD/10: UNPRICED DUE TO SCARCITY
*RED/1: UNPRICED DUE TO SCARCITY
STATED PRINT RUN 199 SER.#'d SETS

SCAA	Jason Jordan/Chad Gable	4.00	10.00
SCBB	Matt Hardy/Jeff Hardy	6.00	15.00
SCND	Xavier Woods/Kofi Kingston	5.00	12.00
SCPE	Rowan/Daniel Bryan	4.00	10.00
SCTB	Cesaro/Sheamus	4.00	10.00
SCUS	Jey Uso/Jimmy Uso	6.00	15.00
SCWF	Randy Orton/Bray Wyatt	5.00	12.00

2019 Topps WWE SmackDown Live Triple Autographs

*GOLD/10: UNPRICED DUE TO SCARCITY
*RED/1: UNPRICED DUE TO SCARCITY
STATED PRINT RUN 25 SER.#'d SETS

TAND	Woods/Big E/Kingston	100.00	200.00

2019 Topps WWE SmackDown Live Women's Evolution Autographs

RANDOMLY INSERTED INTO PACKS

WACM Carmella
WAMR Mandy Rose
WASD Sonya Deville

2019 Topps WWE SmackDown Live Women's Evolution Relics

RANDOMLY INSERTED INTO PACKS

DRCAK Asuka
DRCCM Carmella
DRCKS Kairi Sane

2015 Topps WWE Sting Tribute

COMPLETE SET (40)	15.00	40.00

*GOLD/10: 2X TO 5X BASIC CARDS
*RED/1: UNPRICED DUE TO SCARCITY

1	Sting	1.25	3.00
2	Sting	1.25	3.00
3	Sting	1.25	3.00
4	Sting	1.25	3.00
5	Sting	1.25	3.00
6	Sting	1.25	3.00
7	Sting	1.25	3.00
8	Sting	1.25	3.00
9	Sting	1.25	3.00
10	Sting	1.25	3.00
11	Sting	1.25	3.00
12	Sting	1.25	3.00
13	Sting	1.25	3.00
14	Sting	1.25	3.00
15	Sting	1.25	3.00
16	Sting	1.25	3.00
17	Sting	1.25	3.00
18	Sting	1.25	3.00
19	Sting	1.25	3.00
20	Sting	1.25	3.00
21	Sting	1.25	3.00
22	Sting	1.25	3.00
23	Sting	1.25	3.00
24	Sting	1.25	3.00
25	Sting	1.25	3.00
26	Sting	1.25	3.00
27	Sting	1.25	3.00
28	Sting	1.25	3.00
29	Sting	1.25	3.00
30	Sting	1.25	3.00
31	Sting	1.25	3.00
32	Sting	1.25	3.00
33	Sting	1.25	3.00
34	Sting	1.25	3.00
35	Sting	1.25	3.00
36	Sting	1.25	3.00
37	Sting	1.25	3.00
38	Sting	1.25	3.00
39	Sting	1.25	3.00
40	Sting	1.25	3.00

2015 Topps WWE Sting Tribute Autographs and Relics

*GOLD/10: UNPRICED DUE TO SCARCITY
*RED/1: UNPRICED DUE TO SCARCITY

NNO	Sting AU/Red White Blue	25.00	60.00
NNO	Sting MEM/Shirt	10.00	25.00
NNO	Sting AU MEM/Shirt	50.00	100.00

2015 Topps WWE Sting Tribute Topps Chrome WWE Autographs and Relics

*GOLD/10: UNPRICED DUE TO SCARCITY

NNO	Sting AU/WCW Belt	50.00	100.00
NNO	Sting MEM/Tights	15.00	40.00
NNO	Sting AU MEM/Tights	75.00	150.00

2015 Topps WWE Sting Tribute Topps Heritage WWE Autographs and Relics

*GOLD/10: UNPRICED DUE TO SCARCITY
*RED/1: UNPRICED DUE TO SCARCITY

NNO	Sting AU	50.00	100.00
NNO	Sting AU MEM/Glove		

2015 Topps WWE Sting Tribute Topps WWE Road to WrestleMania Autographs and Relics

*GOLD/10: UNPRICED DUE TO SCARCITY
*RED/1: UNPRICED DUE TO SCARCITY

NNO	Sting AU	50.00	100.00
NNO	Sting MEM/Boots	30.00	75.00
NNO	Sting AU MEM/Boots	75.00	150.00

2019 Topps WWE SummerSlam

COMPLETE SET (100)	10.00	25.00

*BRONZE: .6X TO 1.5X BASIC CARDS
*BLUE/99: .75X TO 2X BASIC CARDS
*SILVER/25: 2X TO 5X BASIC CARDS
*GOLD/10: UNPRICED DUE TO SCARCITY
*RED/1: UNPRICED DUE TO SCARCITY
*P.P.BLACK/1: UNPRICED DUE TO SCARCITY

*P.P.CYAN/1: UNPRICED DUE TO SCARCITY
*P.P.MAGENTA/1: UNPRICED DUE TO SCARCITY
*P.P.YELLOW/1: UNPRICED DUE TO SCARCITY

1 Akam	.25	.60
2 Baron Corbin	.40	1.00
3 Bobby Lashley	.50	1.25
4 Braun Strowman	.60	1.50
5 Bray Wyatt	.60	1.50
6 Brock Lesnar	1.00	2.50
7 Dolph Ziggler	.50	1.25
8 Drew McIntyre	.30	.75
9 Elias	.50	1.25
10 Finn Balor	.60	1.50
11 Kevin Owens	.60	1.50
12 Kurt Angle	.50	1.25
13 Rezar	.25	.60
14 Roman Reigns	.60	1.50
15 Sami Zayn	.50	1.25
16 Seth Rollins	.60	1.50
17 Titus O'Neil	.30	.75
18 Alexa Bliss	1.25	3.00
19 Bayley	.50	1.25
20 Ember Moon	.60	1.50
21 Liv Morgan	.75	2.00
22 Natalya	.50	1.25
23 Nia Jax	.50	1.25
24 Ronda Rousey	1.25	3.00
25 Ruby Riott	.50	1.25
26 Sarah Logan	.30	.75
27 Sasha Banks	1.00	2.50
28 Ali	.25	.60
29 AJ Styles	1.25	3.00
30 Andrade	.30	.75
31 Big E	.25	.60
32 Cesaro	.30	.75
33 Daniel Bryan	1.00	2.50
34 Jeff Hardy	.60	1.50
35 Kofi Kingston	.40	1.00
36 The Miz	.50	1.25
37 Randy Orton	.60	1.50
38 Rey Mysterio	.60	1.50
39 Samoa Joe	.50	1.25
40 Sheamus	.40	1.00
41 Shinsuke Nakamura	.60	1.50
42 Xavier Woods	.30	.75
43 Asuka	.75	2.00
44 Becky Lynch	1.00	2.50
45 Carmella	.60	1.50
46 Charlotte Flair	1.00	2.50
47 Mandy Rose	.60	1.50
48 Naomi	.40	1.00
49 Peyton Royce	.60	1.50
50 Zelina Vega	.40	1.00
51 Matt Hardy & Bray Wyatt	.60	1.50
52 Shelton Benjamin	.60	1.50
53 Nakamura, Rusev & English	1.25	3.00
54 The Deleters of Worlds	.60	1.50
55 Cedric Alexander	.25	.60
56 Jeff Hardy	.60	1.50
57 The Bludgeon Brothers	.30	.75
58 Seth Rollins	.60	1.50
59 AJ Styles	1.25	3.00
60 Brock Lesnar	1.00	2.50
61 Seth Rollins	.60	1.50
62 Jeff Hardy	.60	1.50
63 AJ Styles and Nakamura	.60	1.50
64 Braun Strowman	.60	1.50
65 The Deleters of Worlds	.60	1.50
66 Finn Balor	.60	1.50
67 Rusev	1.00	2.50
68 Andrade	.40	1.00
69 Cedric Alexander	.30	.75
70 The B-Team	.30	.75
71 Braun Strowman	.60	1.50
72 Shinsuke Nakamura	.60	1.50
73 Seth Rollins	.60	1.50
74 AJ Styles	1.25	3.00
75 Braun Strowman	.60	1.50
76 Dolph Ziggler	.50	1.25
77 Rusev	1.25	3.00
78 Drew McIntyre	.30	.75
79 AJ Styles & Jeff Hardy	1.25	3.00
80 The B-Team	.30	.75
81 Bobby Lashley	.50	1.25
82 AJ Styles	1.25	3.00
83 Dolph Ziggler	.60	1.50
84 Roman Reigns	.60	1.50
85 Bobby Lashley	.50	1.25
86 Randy Orton	.60	1.50
87 Drew Gulak	.25	.60
88 Baron Corbin	.60	1.50
89 Nakamura & Randy Orton	.60	1.50
90 The New Day	.40	1.00
91 Brock Lesnar	1.00	2.50
92 Cedric Alexander	.25	.60
93 Seth Rollins	.60	1.50
94 The New Day	.25	.60
95 Braun Strowman	.60	1.50
96 Samoa Joe	.50	1.25
97 The Miz	1.00	2.50
98 Finn Balor	.60	1.50
99 Shinsuke Nakamura	.60	1.50
100 Roman Reigns	.60	1.50

2019 Topps WWE SummerSlam Autographed Intercontinental Championship Manufactured Relics

UNPRICED DUE TO SCARCITY

ICRAJH Jeff Hardy
ICRAKA Kurt Angle
ICRAWR William Regal

2019 Topps WWE SummerSlam Autographed Manufactured Logo Relics

STATED PRINT RUN 10 SER.#'d SETS
UNPRICED DUE TO SCARCITY

LRABS Braun Strowman
LRAKA Kurt Angle
LRALL Lex Luger
LRAMK Mankind
LRARO Randy Orton
LRATD Ted DiBiase

2019 Topps WWE SummerSlam Autographed Mat Relics

STATED PRINT RUN 10 SER.#'d SETS
UNPRICED DUE TO SCARCITY

MRAAB Alexa Bliss
MRAAC Adam Cole
MRAAJ AJ Styles
MRABC Baron Corbin
MRABE Big E
MRABL Becky Lynch
MRABM Drew McIntyre
MRABS Braun Strowman
MRACM Carmella
MRADB Daniel Bryan
MRAEC Velveteen Dream
MRAFB Finn Balor
MRAJG Johnny Gargano
MRAJH Jeff Hardy
MRAKK Kofi Kingston
MRAKO Kevin Owens
MRAKR Kyle O'Reilly
MRAKS Kairi Sane
MRANT Natalya
MRARC Ricochet
MRARS Roderick Strong
MRARW Rowan
MRASB Shayna Baszler
MRASJ Samoa Joe
MRASN Shinsuke Nakamura
MRASR Seth Rollins
MRATB Tyler Bate
MRATM The Miz
MRATS Trent Seven
MRAVD EC3
MRAXW Xavier Woods

2019 Topps WWE SummerSlam Autographed Superstar Relics

STATED PRINT RUN 10 SER.#'d SETS
UNPRICED DUE TO SCARCITY

SRAAE Aiden English
SRAAW Alexander Wolfe
SRABS Braun Strowman
SRACS Cesaro
SRADW Dash Wilder
SRAEY Eric Young
SRAKD Killian Dain
SRASD Scott Dawson
SRASM Shawn Michaels
SRASZ Sami Zayn

2019 Topps WWE SummerSlam Autographed Women's Evolution Relics

UNPRICED DUE TO SCARCITY

ERARR Ruby Riott
ERATS Tamina

2019 Topps WWE SummerSlam Autographs

*BLUE/50: .5X TO 1.2X BASIC AUTOS
*SILVER/25: .6X TO 1.5X BASIC AUTOS
*GOLD/10: UNPRICED DUE TO SCARCITY
*RED/1: UNPRICED DUE TO SCARCITY
*P.P.BLACK/1: UNPRICED DUE TO SCARCITY
*P.P.CYAN/1: UNPRICED DUE TO SCARCITY
*P.P.MAGENTA/1: UNPRICED DUE TO SCARCITY
*P.P.YELLOW/1: UNPRICED DUE TO SCARCITY
STATED ODDS 1:24

OCAA Andrade	4.00	10.00
OCAB Alexa Bliss	30.00	75.00
OCAJ AJ Styles	12.00	30.00
OCBE Big E	4.00	10.00
OCBL Bayley	10.00	25.00
OCBR Bobby Roode	5.00	12.00
OCBS Braun Strowman	6.00	15.00
OCCF Charlotte Flair	15.00	40.00
OCCM Carmella	8.00	20.00
OCDM Drew McIntyre	6.00	15.00
OCEL Elias	8.00	20.00
OCFB Finn Balor	12.00	30.00
OCJH Jeff Hardy	12.00	30.00
OCKK Kofi Kingston	8.00	20.00
OCKO Kevin Owens	5.00	12.00
OCMM Bobby Lashley	5.00	12.00
OCMR Mandy Rose	20.00	50.00
OCRM Rey Mysterio	12.00	30.00
OCRR Ruby Riott	15.00	40.00
OCRT R-Truth	4.00	10.00
OCSD Sonya Deville	10.00	25.00
OCSJ Samoa Joe	6.00	15.00
OCSN Shinsuke Nakamura	8.00	20.00
OCTM The Miz	6.00	15.00
OCXW Xavier Woods	4.00	10.00
OCZV Zelina Vega	12.00	30.00

2019 Topps WWE SummerSlam Dual Autographs

STATED PRINT RUN 10 SER.#'d SETS
UNPRICED DUE TO SCARCITY

DAAB S.Deville/M.Rose
DABT B.Dallas/C.Axel
DAII B.Kay/P.Royce
DAMK Maria & Mike Kanellis
DAND X.Woods/K.Kingston

2019 Topps WWE SummerSlam Greatest Matches and Moments

COMPLETE SET (40) 6.00 15.00
RANDOMLY INSERTED INTO PACKS

GM1 Ultimate Warrior Def. Honky Tonk Man	.50	1.25
GM2 Warrior/Rick Rude	.60	1.50
GM3 Dusty Rhodes/Honky Tonk Man	.50	1.25
GM4 The Texas Tornado Def. Mr. Perfect	.30	.75
GM5 Macho Man Marries Elizabeth	.60	1.50
GM6 Virgil/Ted DiBiase	.25	.60
GM7 British Bulldog/Bret Hart	.50	1.25
GM8 Warrior/Randy Savage	.60	1.50
GM9 Lex Luger/Yokozuna	.30	.75
GM10 Alundra Blayze/Bull Nakano	.25	.60
GM11 Shawn Michaels/Razor Ramon	.50	1.25
GM12 Mankind/Undertaker	.40	1.00
GM13 Shawn Michaels/Vader	.60	1.50
GM14 Mankind/Triple H	.50	1.25
GM15 Steve Austin wins IC Title	1.00	2.50
GM16 Ken Shamrock/Owen Hart	.40	1.00
GM17 Steve Austin/Undertaker	1.25	3.00
GM18 Mankind/Steve Austin/HHH	.50	1.25
GM19 Rock/HHH/Kurt Angle	1.00	2.50
GM20 Kurt Angle/Steve Austin	1.25	3.00
GM21 Shawn Michaels/HHH	.60	1.50
GM22 Kurt Angle/Rey Mysterio	.40	1.00
GM23 Kurt Angle/Brock Lesnar	.50	1.25
GM24 Kurt Angle/Eddie Guerrero	.40	1.00
GM25 Rey Mysterio/Eddie Guerrero	.60	1.50
GM26 Ric Flair/Mick Foley	.75	2.00
GM27 John Cena/Randy Orton	1.00	2.50
GM28 Batista/John Cena	.50	1.25
GM29 Rey Mysterio/Dolph Ziggler	.60	1.50
GM30 Randy Orton/Sheamus	.50	1.25
GM31 Randy Orton/Christian	.60	1.50
GM32 Kane/Rey Mysterio/Undertaker	.30	.75
GM33 Miz/Rey Mysterio	.50	1.25
GM34 Daniel Bryan/John Cena	.75	2.00

GM35 Roman Reigns/Randy Orton	.60	1.50
GM36 Seth Rollins/John Cena	.50	1.25
GM37 Charlotte Flair/Sasha Banks	1.00	2.50
GM38 Finn Balor/Seth Rollins	.60	1.50
GM39 AJ Styles/John Cena	1.25	3.00
GM40 Usos/New Day	.30	.75

2019 Topps WWE SummerSlam Intercontinental Champion Autographs

STATED PRINT RUN 25 SER.#'d SETS

ICRJH Jeff Hardy	15.00	40.00
ICRWR William Regal	10.00	25.00

2019 Topps WWE SummerSlam Intercontinental Championship Manufactured Relics

RANDOMLY INSERTED INTO PACKS

ICRBT Booker T
ICRDL D'Lo Brown
ICRJH Jeff Hardy
ICRKA Kurt Angle
ICRWR William Regal

2019 Topps WWE SummerSlam Manufactured Logo Relics

*BRONZE/99: .5X TO 1.2X BASIC MEM
*BLUE/50: .6X TO 1.5X BASIC MEM
*SILVER/25: .75X TO 2X BASIC MEM
*GOLD/10: UNPRICED DUE TO SCARCITY
*RED/1: UNPRICED DUE TO SCARCITY
STATED ODDS 1:152

LRBH Bret Hit Man Hart	3.00	8.00
LRBL Brock Lesnar	6.00	15.00
LRBS Braun Strowman	3.00	8.00
LRBT Booker T	3.00	8.00
LRED Edge	3.00	8.00
LRJC John Cena	4.00	10.00
LRKA Kurt Angle	3.00	8.00
LRLL Lex Luger	2.50	6.00
LRMK Mankind	2.50	6.00
LRRO Randy Orton	4.00	10.00
LRSA Stone Cold Steve Austin	6.00	15.00
LRSM Shawn Michaels	4.00	10.00
LRTD Ted DiBiase	2.50	6.00
LRUT Undertaker	4.00	10.00
LRBDC Diesel	3.00	8.00

2019 Topps WWE SummerSlam Mat Relics

*BRONZE/99: .5X TO 1.2X BASIC MEM
*BLUE/50: .6X TO 1.5X BASIC MEM
*SILVER/25: .75X TO 2X BASIC MEM
*GOLD/10: UNPRICED DUE TO SCARCITY
*RED/1: UNPRICED DUE TO SCARCITY
RANDOMLY INSERTED INTO PACKS

MRAB Alexa Bliss	12.00	30.00
MRAC Adam Cole	3.00	8.00
MRAJ AJ Styles	3.00	8.00
MRBC Baron Corbin	1.50	4.00
MRBD Roman Reigns	3.00	8.00
MRBE Big E	1.50	4.00
MRBI Brock Lesnar	3.00	8.00
MRBL Becky Lynch	6.00	15.00
MRBM Drew McIntyre	2.50	6.00
MRBS Braun Strowman	2.50	6.00
MRCF Charlotte Flair	5.00	12.00
MRCM Carmella	4.00	10.00
MRDB Daniel Bryan		
MRDZ Dolph Ziggler	2.50	6.00
MREC Velveteen Dream	2.50	6.00
MRFB Finn Balor	4.00	10.00
MRHP Harper	2.50	6.00
MRJG Johnny Gargano	2.50	6.00
MRJH Jeff Hardy	4.00	10.00
MRKK Kofi Kingston	3.00	8.00
MRKO Kevin Owens	2.00	5.00
MRKR Kyle O'Reilly	2.00	5.00
MRKS Kairi Sane	3.00	8.00
MRNT Natalya	3.00	8.00
MRPH Paul Heyman	2.50	6.00
MRRC Ricochet	3.00	8.00
MRRR Ronda Rousey	10.00	25.00
MRRS Roderick Strong	2.50	6.00
MRRW Rowan	1.50	4.00
MRSB Shayna Baszler		
MRSJ Samoa Joe	2.00	5.00
MRSN Shinsuke Nakamura	2.00	5.00
MRSR Seth Rollins	3.00	8.00
MRTB Tyler Bate	2.50	6.00
MRTC Tommaso Ciampa	2.50	6.00
MRTM The Miz	2.00	5.00
MRTS Trent Seven	1.50	4.00
MRVD EC3	1.50	4.00
MRXW Xavier Woods	1.50	4.00

2019 Topps WWE SummerSlam Mr. SummerSlam

RANDOMLY INSERTED INTO PACKS

MSS1 Lesnar/Rock	1.25	3.00
MSS2 Lesnar/HHH	1.00	2.50
MSS3 Lesnar/Cena	1.00	2.50
MSS4 Lesnar/Orton	1.00	2.50
MSS5 Lesnar/Samoa Joe/Strowman/Reigns	1.00	2.50
MSS6 Undertaker Returns	1.25	3.00
MSS7 Undertaker/Kama	1.25	3.00
MSS8 Unholy Alliance/Kane/X-Pac	.40	1.00
MSS9 Undertaker/Edge	1.25	3.00
MSS10 Undertaker/Brock Lesnar	1.25	3.00
MSS11 Edge & Christian	.60	1.50
MSS12 Edge/Eddie Guerrero	.60	1.50
MSS13 Edge IC Title	.60	1.50
MSS14 Edge/Matt Hardy	.60	1.50
MSS15 Edge/John Cena	.60	1.50
MSS16 HHH PPV Debut	.60	1.50
MSS17 Triple H/Rock	1.25	3.00
MSS18 DX/Mr. McMahon & Shane	.60	1.50
MSS19 HHH/King Booker	.60	1.50
MSS20 HHH/A Giant	.60	1.50
MSS21 Hart Foundation	.60	1.50
MSS22 Bret Hart/Mr. Perfect	.60	1.50
MSS23 Bret Hart/Lawler	.60	1.50
MSS24 Bret Hart/Undertaker	.60	1.50
MSS25 Bret Hart Returns	.60	1.50

2019 Topps WWE SummerSlam Posters Spotlight

COMPLETE SET (4)	3.00	8.00
STATED ODDS 1:6		
SS14 '14 Cena/Lesnar	1.25	3.00
SS15 '15 Lesnar/Undertaker	1.00	2.50
SS16 '17 Collage	1.00	2.50
SS17 '18 Lesnar/Bliss/Rousey/Reigns	1.50	4.00

2019 Topps WWE SummerSlam Superstar Relics

*BRONZE/99: SAME VALUE AS BASIC
*BLUE/50: .5X TO 1.2X BASIC MEM
*SILVER/25: .6X TO 1.5X BASIC MEM
*GOLD/10: UNPRICED DUE TO SCARCITY
*RED/1: UNPRICED DUE TO SCARCITY
RANDOMLY INSERTED INTO PACKS

SRAC Apollo Crews	2.50	6.00
SRAW Alexander Wolfe	2.50	6.00
SRBS Braun Strowman	5.00	12.00
SRCS Cesaro	3.00	8.00
SRDW Dash Wilder	2.50	6.00
SRED Edge	4.00	10.00
SREY Eric Young	2.50	6.00
SRHS Heath Slater	2.50	6.00
SRJC John Cena	5.00	12.00
SRKD Killian Dain	2.50	6.00
SRRR Roman Reigns	4.00	10.00
SRSD Scott Dawson	2.50	6.00
SRSM Shawn Michaels	4.00	10.00
SRSR Seth Rollins	3.00	8.00
SRSZ Sami Zayn	2.50	6.00

2019 Topps WWE SummerSlam Women's Evolution Autographs

*GOLD/10: UNPRICED DUE TO SCARCITY
*P.P.BLACK/1: UNPRICED DUE TO SCARCITY
*P.P.CYAN/1: UNPRICED DUE TO SCARCITY
*P.P.MAGENTA/1: UNPRICED DUE TO SCARCITY
*P.P.YELLOW/1: UNPRICED DUE TO SCARCITY
STATED PRINT RUN 25 SER.#'d SETS
UNPRICED DUE TO SCARCITY

WAAF Alicia Fox
WAEM Ember Moon
WAMJ Mickie James
WANL Natalya
WARR Ruby Riott
WATS Tamina

2019 Topps WWE SummerSlam Women's Evolution Relics

STATED PRINT RUN 25 SER.#'d SETS
UNPRICED DUE TO SCARCITY

ERAF Alicia Fox
EREM Ember Moon
ERRR Ruby Riott
ERTS Tamina

2021 Topps WWE Superstars

COMPLETE SET (225)	30.00	80.00
1 Adam Cole	.60	1.50
2 AJ Styles	.60	1.50
3 Akira Tozawa	.25	.60
4 Alexa Bliss	1.25	3.00
5 Aliyah	.40	1.00
6 Angel Garza	.25	.60
7 Angelo Dawkins	.25	.60
8 Apollo Crews	.25	.60
9 Asuka	.75	2.00
10 Austin Theory	.40	1.00
11 Bayley	.40	1.00
12 Becky Lynch	.75	2.00
13 Bianca Belair	.50	1.25
14 Big E	.40	1.00
15 Bobby Lashley	.50	1.25
16 Cameron Grimes	.40	1.00
17 Candice LeRae	.75	2.00
18 Carmella	.50	1.25
19 Cedric Alexander	.20	.50
20 Cesaro	.20	.50
21 Chad Gable	.20	.50
22 Charlotte Flair	1.00	2.50
23 Commander Azeez RC	.25	.60
24 Dakota Kai	.40	1.00
25 Damian Priest	.30	.75
26 Dana Brooke	.20	.50
27 Danny Burch	.25	.60
28 Dave Mastiff	.20	.50
29 Dexter Lumis	.20	.50
30 Dolph Ziggler	.40	1.00
31 Dominik Mysterio RC	.25	.60
32 Drake Maverick	.20	.50
33 Drew Gulak	.25	.60
34 Drew McIntyre	.50	1.25
35 Edge	.75	2.00
36 Elias	.20	.50
37 Ember Moon	.25	.60
38 Erik	.20	.50
39 Eva Marie	.50	1.25
40 Fabian Aichner	.25	.60
41 Finn Balor	.50	1.25
42 Flash Morgan Webster	.25	.60
43 Franky Monet RC	.40	1.00
44 Gigi Dolin RC	.20	.50
45 Gran Metalik	.20	.50
46 Humberto Carrillo	.20	.50
47 Ilja Dragunov	.20	.50
48 Indi Hartwell RC	.60	1.50
49 Io Shirai	.40	1.00
50 Isaiah "Swerve" Scott	.30	.75
51 Ivar	.20	.50
52 James Drake	.20	.50
53 Jaxson Ryker	.20	.50
54 Jeff Hardy	.50	1.25
55 Jey Uso	.20	.50
56 Jimmy Uso	.20	.50
57 Jinder Mahal	.25	.60
58 Joaquin Wilde	.30	.75
59 Joe Coffey	.20	.50
60 John Morrison	.40	1.00
61 Johnny Gargano	.40	1.00
62 Jordan Devlin	.20	.50
63 Kacy Catanzaro	.40	1.00
64 Karrion Kross	.75	2.00
65 Kay Lee Ray	.50	1.25
66 Kayden Carter	.40	1.00
67 Keith Lee	.40	1.00
68 Kevin Owens	.40	1.00
69 Baron Corbin	.20	.50
70 Kofi Kingston	.50	1.25
71 Kushida	.30	.75
72 Kyle O'Reilly	.30	.75
73 LA Knight RC	.25	.60
74 Lacey Evans	.50	1.25
75 Liv Morgan	.75	2.00
76 Mace	.20	.50
77 Mandy Rose	1.00	2.50
78 Mansoor RC	.20	.50
79 Marcel Barthel	.25	.60
80 Mark Andrews	.20	.50
81 Mark Coffey	.20	.50
82 Montez Ford	.20	.50
83 Mustafa Ali	.25	.60

84 MVP .25 .60
85 Naomi .25 .60
86 Nash Carter RC .20 .50
87 Natalya .30 .75
88 Nia Jax .40 1.00
89 Nikki A.S.H. .40 1.00
90 Noam Dar .25 .60
91 Oney Lorcan .20 .50
92 Omos RC .40 1.00
93 Otis .25 .60
94 Pete Dunne .40 1.00
95 Doudrop .30 .75
96 R-Truth .25 .60
97 Randy Orton .60 1.50
98 Raquel Gonzalez .50 1.25
99 Mia Yim .25 .60
100 Reggie RC .25 .60
101 Rey Mysterio .50 1.25
102 Rhea Ripley .60 1.50
103 Ricochet .40 1.00
104 Riddick Moss .25 .60
105 Riddle .50 1.25
106 Robert Roode .25 .60
107 Roderick Strong .30 .75
108 Roman Reigns 1.00 2.50
109 Sami Zayn .30 .75
110 Santos Escobar .30 .75
111 Sarray RC .25 .60
112 Sasha Banks 1.00 2.50
113 Scarlett 1.00 2.50
114 Seth Rollins .50 1.25
115 Shayna Baszler .40 1.00
116 Sheamus .30 .75
117 Shelton Benjamin .30 .75
118 Shinsuke Nakamura .50 1.25
119 Shotzi .75 2.00
120 Shane Thorne .20 .50
121 T-Bar .25 .60
122 Tamina .25 .60
123 Tegan Nox .50 1.25
124 Samoa Joe .40 1.00
125 The Miz .30 .75
126 Timothy Thatcher RC .20 .50
127 Tommaso Ciampa .50 1.25
128 Toni Storm .60 1.50
129 Trent Seven .25 .60
130 Tyler Bate .25 .60
131 Walter .50 1.25
132 Wes Lee RC .20 .50
133 Wolfgang .20 .50
134 Xavier Woods .20 .50
135 Xia Li .40 1.00
136 Zack Gibson .20 .50
137 Zoey Stark RC .25 .60
138 Andre the Giant L .75 2.00
139 Bam Bam Bigelow L .40 1.00
140 Batista L .40 1.00
141 Big Boss Man L .30 .75
142 Booker T L .40 1.00
143 Bret "Hit Man" Hart L .50 1.25
144 British Bulldog L .30 .75
145 Chyna L .40 1.00
146 Doink the Clown L .20 .50
147 Eddie Guerrero L 1.00 2.50
148 Goldberg L .75 2.00
149 Honky Tonk Man L .20 .50
150 Hulk Hogan L 1.00 2.50
151 Jake "The Snake" Roberts L .30 .75
152 Kevin Nash L .30 .75
153 Lex Luger L .25 .60
154 Macho Man Randy Savage L 1.25 3.00
155 Mick Foley L .40 1.00
156 Mr. Perfect L .60 1.50
157 Papa Shango L .25 .60
158 Razor Ramon L .30 .75
159 Ricky "The Dragon" Steamboat L .30 .75
160 Rikishi L .25 .60
161 Rowdy Roddy Piper L .50 1.25
162 RVD L .40 1.00
163 Sgt. Slaughter L .30 .75
164 Shawn Michaels L .75 2.00
165 Stacy Keibler L .60 1.50
166 Stone Cold Steve Austin L 1.00 2.50
167 Trish Stratus L 1.00 2.50
168 Ultimate Warrior L .75 2.00
169 Undertaker L 1.00 2.50
170 Vader L .30 .75
171 Yokozuna L .30 .75
172 Bianca Belair UF .50 1.25
173 Bobby Lashley UF .50 1.25
174 Drew McIntyre UF .50 1.25
175 Io Shirai UF .40 1.00
176 Kevin Owens UF .40 1.00
177 Randy Orton UF .60 1.50
178 Rhea Ripley UF .60 1.50
179 Roman Reigns UF 1.00 2.50
180 John Cena UF 1.00 2.50
181 The Austin Era Begins 1.00 2.50
182 Five-Star Classic 1.00 2.50
183 Ticket to the Title 1.00 2.50
184 First WWE Championship 1.00 2.50
185 Dominating the Dude 1.00 2.50
186 The People's Stunner 1.00 2.50
187 Third Royal Rumble Win 1.00 2.50
188 Main Event Shocker 1.00 2.50
189 Last-Ever Match 1.00 2.50
190 The Winning Business WMFB .50 1.25
191 A Swiss Masterclass WMFB .20 .50
192 Omos Makes His Mark WMFB .40 1.00
193 Triumphant Turmoil WMFB .30 .75
194 Bianca Becomes the Great-est WMFB.40 1.00
195 RKO Stuns the Fiend WMFB .60 1.50
196 Owens KO's His Rival WMFB .40 1.00
197 Sheamus Solves the Riddle WMFB .30 .75
198 Crews Control WMFB .25 .60
199 Rhea Wins the Big One WMFB .60 1.50
200 Smash 'Em, Stack 'Em, Pin 'Em WMFB1.00 2.50
201 Alexa Bliss RTWM 1.25 3.00
202 Becky Lynch RTWM .75 2.00
203 Bianca Belair RTWM .50 1.25
204 Charlotte Flair RTWM 1.00 2.50
205 Drew McIntyre RTWM .50 1.25
206 Kofi Kingston RTWM .50 1.25
207 Randy Orton RTWM .60 1.50
208 Roman Reigns RTWM 1.00 2.50
209 Seth Rollins RTWM .50 1.25
210 The Rock 2.00 5.00
211 The Rock 2.00 5.00
212 The Rock 2.00 5.00
213 The Rock 2.00 5.00
214 The Rock 2.00 5.00
215 The Rock 2.00 5.00
216 The Rock 2.00 5.00
217 The Rock 2.00 5.00
218 SummerSlam 2020 SUW 1.00 2.50
219 Payback 2020 SUW 1.00 2.50
220 Clash of Champions 2020 SUW 1.00 2.50
221 Hell in a Cell 2020 SUW 1.00 2.50
222 Survivor Series 2020 SUW 1.00 2.50
223 Royal Rumble 2021 SUW 1.00 2.50
224 WrestleMania 37 SUW 1.00 2.50
225 WrestleMania Backlash SUW 1.00 2.50

2021 Topps WWE Superstars 25 Years of The Rock

COMPLETE SET (3) 8.00 20.00
*GREEN/50: .5X TO 1.2X BASIC CARDS
*PURPLE/25: .6X TO 1.5X BASIC CARDS
*TURQUOISE/10: UNPRICED DUE TO SCARCITY
*RED/5: UNPRICED DUE TO SCARCITY
*GOLD/1: UNPRICED DUE TO SCARCITY

TR1 Survivor Series Shocker 4.00 10.00
TR2 Icon vs. Icon 4.00 10.00
TR3 Magic in Miami 4.00 10.00

2021 Topps WWE Superstars Autographs Orange

*GREEN/50: X TO X BASIC AUTOS
*PURPLE/25: X TO X BASIC AUTOS
*TURQUOISE/10: UNPRICED DUE TO SCARCITY
*RED/5: UNPRICED DUE TO SCARCITY
*GOLD/1: UNPRICED DUE TO SCARCITY
STATED PRINT RUN 99 SER.#'d SETS

NNO Big E
NNO Erik
NNO King Nakamura
NNO Naomi
NNO Roderick Strong
NNO Samoa Joe
NNO Tyler Bate
NNO Zelina Vega
NNO Kofi Kingston
(2021 Black Friday Exclusive)
NNO Kofi Kingston (Kofi-Mania)
(2021 Black Friday Exclusive)

2021 Topps WWE Superstars Crystal

COMPLETE SET (6) 15.00 40.00
RANDOMLY INSERTED INTO PACKS

CR1 Alexa Bliss 6.00 15.00
CR2 Bianca Belair 3.00 8.00
CR3 Drew McIntyre 6.00 15.00
CR4 Roman Reigns 5.00 12.00
CR5 Sasha Banks 6.00 15.00
CR6 John Cena 4.00 10.00

2021 Topps WWE Superstars Iconic Matches

RANDOMLY INSERTED INTO PACKS

MA1 WrestleMania III
MA2 WrestleMania VI
MA3 SummerSlam 1992
MA4 SummerSlam 1995
MA5 WrestleMania XII
MA6 Royal Rumble 2000
MA7 WrestleMania X-Seven
MA8 WrestleMania 25
MA9 WrestleMania 28
MA10 NXT TakeOver: Brooklyn
MA11 SummerSlam 2016

2021 Topps WWE Superstars John Cena's Greatest Moments

COMPLETE SET (6) 12.00 30.00
*GREEN/50: .5X TO 1.2X BASIC CARDS
*PURPLE/25: .6X TO 1.5X BASIC CARDS
*TURQUOISE/10: UNPRICED DUE TO SCARCITY
*RED/5: UNPRICED DUE TO SCARCITY
*GOLD/1: UNPRICED DUE TO SCARCITY
RANDOMLY INSERTED INTO PACKS

JC1 First WWE Title 3.00 8.00
JC2 Legend of the Ladder 3.00 8.00
JC3 Rumble Shocker 3.00 8.00
JC4 Iconic Entrance 3.00 8.00
JC5 Revenge on the Rock 3.00 8.00
JC6 Thuganomics 4 Life 3.00 8.00

2021 Topps WWE Superstars Legends Autographs Orange

*TURQUOISE/10: UNPRICED DUE TO SCARCITY
*RED/5: UNPRICED DUE TO SCARCITY
*GOLD/1: UNPRICED DUE TO SCARCITY
STATED PRINT RUN 99 SER.#'d SETS

NNO Booker T
NNO Million Dollar Man Ted DiBiase

2021 Topps WWE Superstars Return of the Fans

COMPLETE SET (5) 6.00 15.00
*GREEN/50: .5X TO 1.2X BASIC CARDS
*PURPLE/25: .6X TO 1.5X BASIC CARDS
*TURQUOISE/10: UNPRICED DUE TO SCARCITY
*RED/5: UNPRICED DUE TO SCARCITY
*GOLD/1: UNPRICED DUE TO SCARCITY
RANDOMLY INSERTED INTO PACKS

RF1 Big E Wins the Big One 2.00 5.00
RF2 Roman Reigns Supreme 2.50 6.00
RF3 Return Heard Around the World 2.50 6.00
RF4 The Bro-Off 4.00 10.00
RF5 Superhero Cash-In 1.50 4.00

2021 Topps WWE Superstars Super Elite

COMPLETE SET (16) 15.00 40.00
*YELLOW: .5X TO 1.2X BASIC CARDS
*BLUE/299: .6X TO 1.5X BASIC CARDS
*ORANGE/99: .75X TO 2X BASIC CARDS
*GREEN/50: 1X TO 2.5X BASIC CARDS
*PURPLE/25: UNPRICED DUE TO SCARCITY
*TURQUOISE/10: UNPRICED DUE TO SCARCITY
*RED/5: UNPRICED DUE TO SCARCITY
*GOLD/1: UNPRICED DUE TO SCARCITY
RANDOMLY INSERTED INTO PACKS

SE1 AJ Styles 1.50 4.00
SE2 Alexa Bliss 3.00 8.00
SE3 Asuka 2.00 5.00
SE4 Bayley 1.00 2.50
SE5 Becky Lynch 2.00 5.00
SE6 Bianca Belair 1.25 3.00
SE7 Bobby Lashley 1.25 3.00
SE8 Charlotte Flair 2.50 6.00
SE9 Drew McIntyre 1.25 3.00
SE10 Riddle 1.25 3.00
SE11 Randy Orton 1.50 4.00
SE12 Roman Reigns 2.50 6.00
SE13 Sasha Banks 2.50 6.00
SE14 Seth Rollins 1.25 3.00

SE15 Shinsuke Nakamura	1.25	3.00
SE16 Big E	1.00	2.50

2021 Topps WWE Superstars Super Elite Icons

COMPLETE SET (9) 12.00 30.00
*YELLOW: .5X TO 1.2X BASIC CARDS
*BLUE/299: .6X TO 1.5X BASIC CARDS
*ORANGE/99: .75X TO 2X BASIC CARDS
*GREEN/50: 1X TO 2.5X BASIC CARDS
*PURPLE/25: UNPRICED DUE TO SCARCITY
*TURQUOISE/10: UNPRICED DUE TO SCARCITY
*RED/5: UNPRICED DUE TO SCARCITY
*GOLD/1: UNPRICED DUE TO SCARCITY
RANDOMLY INSERTED INTO PACKS

IC1 Andre the Giant	2.00	5.00
IC2 Bret Hit Man Hart	1.25	3.00
IC3 Hulk Hogan	2.50	6.00
IC4 John Cena	2.50	6.00
IC5 Shawn Michaels	2.00	5.00
IC6 Stone Cold Steve Austin	2.50	6.00
IC7 The Rock	5.00	12.00
IC8 Triple H	2.00	5.00
IC9 Undertaker	2.50	6.00

2016 Topps WWE Then Now Forever

COMPLETE SET (100) 10.00 25.00
UNOPENED BOX (24 PACKS)
UNOPENED PACK (7 CARDS)
*BRONZE: 1.2X TO 3X BASIC CARDS
*SILVER: 2X TO 5X BASIC CARDS
*GOLD/10: 4X TO 10X BASIC CARDS
*RED/1: UNPRICED DUE TO SCARCITY
*P.P.BLACK/1: UNPRICED DUE TO SCARCITY
*P.P.CYAN/1: UNPRICED DUE TO SCARCITY
*P.P.MAGENTA/1: UNPRICED DUE TO SCARCITY
*P.P.YELLOW/1: UNPRICED DUE TO SCARCITY

101 Aiden English	.20	.50
102 AJ Styles	.75	2.00
103 Apollo Crews RC	.20	.50
104 Baron Corbin	.25	.60
105 Big Cass	.40	1.00
106 Big E	.20	.50
107 Braun Strowman RC	.25	.60
108 Bray Wyatt	.75	2.00
109 Brock Lesnar	1.00	2.50
110 Cathy Kelley RC	.20	.50
111 Chris Jericho	.50	1.25
112 Dana Brooke RC	.50	1.25
113 Darren Young	.20	.50
114 Dasha Fuentes RC	.20	.50
115 David Otunga	.20	.50
116 Dean Ambrose	.60	1.50
117 Emma	.40	1.00
118 Enzo Amore RC	.40	1.00
119 Epico	.20	.50
120 Erick Rowan	.20	.50
121 Eva Marie	.40	1.00
122 Greg Hamilton RC	.20	.50
123 Heath Slater	.20	.50
124 Jack Swagger	.20	.50
125 John Cena	1.00	2.50
126 JoJo	.20	.50
127 Kane	.30	.75
128 Karl Anderson RC	.20	.50
129 Kofi Kingston	.20	.50
130 Luke Gallows	.25	.60
131 Luke Harper	.20	.50
132 Maryse	.40	1.00
133 Mauro Ranallo RC	.20	.50
134 Primo	.20	.50
135 Randy Orton	.50	1.25
136 Renee Young	.50	1.25
137 The Rock	1.00	2.50
138 Roman Reigns	.60	1.50
139 Rosa Mendes	.20	.50
140 Sami Zayn	.30	.75
141 Scott Stanford	.20	.50
142 Seth Rollins	.30	.75
143 Shane McMahon	.30	.75
144 Sheamus	.50	1.25
145 Simon Gotch RC	.30	.75
146 Stephanie McMahon	.30	.75
147 Tom Phillips	.20	.50
148 Tony Chimel	.20	.50
149 Triple H	.75	2.00
150 Undertaker	.75	2.00
151 Xavier Woods	.20	.50
152 Zack Ryder	.20	.50
153 Big Boss Man L	.30	.75
154 Big John Studd L	.30	.75
155 Bob Backlund L	.20	.50
156 Bobby The Brain Heenan L	.30	.75
157 Brian Pillman L	.25	.60
158 Bruno Sammartino L	.25	.60
159 Chief Jay Strongbow L	.30	.75
160 Cowboy Bob Orton L	.30	.75
161 Daniel Bryan L	.75	2.00
162 Dean Malenko L	.20	.50
163 Diamond Dallas Page L	.30	.75
164 Eddie Guerrero L	.50	1.25
165 The Funks L	.20	.50
166 Gerald Brisco L	.20	.50
167 Gorilla Monsoon L	.30	.75
168 General Adnan L	.20	.50
169 Greg The Hammer Valentine L	.25	.60
170 Hacksaw Jim Duggan L	.20	.50
171 High Chief Peter Maivia L	.20	.50
172 The Honky Tonk Man L	.20	.50
173 Howard Finkel L	.20	.50
174 Jamie Noble L	.20	.50
175 Jim The Anvil Neidhart L	.20	.50
176 Joey Mercury L	.20	.50
177 Junkyard Dog L	.30	.75
178 The King Harley Race L	.20	.50
179 Larry Zbyszko L	.20	.50
180 Lex Luger L	.30	.75
181 Mean Gene Okerlund L	.25	.60
182 Michael P.S. Hayes L	.20	.50
183 Mouth of the South Jimmy Hart L	.25	.60
184 Mr. Perfect Curt Henning L	.50	1.25
185 Mr. Wonderful Paul Orndorff L	.20	50
186 Nikolai Volkoff L	.25	.60
187 Norman Smiley L	.20	.50
188 Pat Patterson L	.20	.50
189 Paul Bearer L	.30	.75
190 Ravishing Rick Rude L	.30	.75
191 Ricky The Dragon Steamboat L	.25	.60
192 Rocky Johnson L	.25	.60
193 Sgt. Slaughter L	.25	.60
194 Sting L	.50	1.25
195 Stone Cold Steve Austin L	1.00	2.50
196 Tatanka L	.20	.50
197 Tom Prichard L	.20	.50
198 Vader L	.40	1.00
199 Viscera L	.20	.50
200 Yokozuna L	.40	1.00

2016 Topps WWE Then Now Forever Autographs

*BRONZE/50: .5X TO 1.2X BASIC AUTOS
*SILVER/25: .75X TO 2X BASIC AUTOS
*GOLD/10: 1.2X TO 3X BASIC AUTOS
*RED/1: UNPRICED DUE TO SCARCITY
*P.P.BLACK/1: UNPRICED DUE TO SCARCITY
*P.P.CYAN/1: UNPRICED DUE TO SCARCITY
*P.P.MAGENTA/1: UNPRICED DUE TO SCARCITY
*P.P.YELLOW/1: UNPRICED DUE TO SCARCITY
STATED ODDS 1:51

NNO Aiden English	6.00	15.00
NNO AJ Styles	20.00	50.00
NNO Becky Lynch	15.00	60.00
NNO Charlotte	20.00	50.00
NNO Chris Jericho	15.00	40.00
NNO Dean Ambrose	10.00	25.00
NNO Enzo Amore	12.00	30.00
NNO Hideo Itami	6.00	15.00
NNO Karl Anderson	8.00	20.00
NNO Luke Gallows	8.00	20.00
NNO Maryse	12.00	30.00
NNO Naomi	6.00	15.00
NNO Natalya	8.00	20.00
NNO Norman Smiley	6.00	15.00
NNO Ric Flair	60.00	120.00
NNO Roman Reigns	20.00	50.00
NNO R-Truth	6.00	15.00
NNO Sami Zayn	10.00	25.00
NNO Samoa Joe	6.00	15.00
NNO Sasha Banks	50.00	100.00
NNO Seth Rollins	8.00	20.00
NNO Shinsuke Nakamura	30.00	80.00
NNO Simon Gotch	6.00	15.00
NNO Sting	20.00	50.00

2016 Topps WWE Then Now Forever Diva Kiss

*GOLD/10: UNPRICED DUE TO SCARCITY
*RED/1: UNPRICED DUE TO SCARCITY
STATED ODDS 1:125
STATED PRINT RUN 99 SER.#'d SETS

NNO Alicia Fox	15.00	40.00
NNO Asuka	30.00	80.00
NNO Bayley	30.00	80.00
NNO Becky Lynch	25.00	60.00
NNO Brie Bella	20.00	50.00
NNO Carmella	25.00	60.00
NNO Charlotte	20.00	50.00
NNO Lana	20.00	50.00
NNO Nikki Bella	20.00	50.00
NNO Sasha Banks	30.00	80.00

2016 Topps WWE Then Now Forever Diva Kiss Autographs

*GOLD/10: UNPRICED DUE TO SCARCITY
*RED/1: UNPRICED DUE TO SCARCITY
STATED ODDS 1:482
STATED PRINT RUN 25 SER.#'d SETS

NNO Alicia Fox	25.00	60.00
NNO Asuka	80.00	150.00
NNO Bayley	150.00	300.00
NNO Becky Lynch	60.00	120.00
NNO Brie Bella	80.00	150.00
NNO Carmella	50.00	100.00
NNO Charlotte	60.00	120.00
NNO Lana	50.00	100.00
NNO Nikki Bella	60.00	120.00
NNO Sasha Banks	150.00	300.00

2016 Topps WWE Then Now Forever Mask and Face Paint Medallions

*BRONZE: .5X TO 1.2X BASIC MEM
*SILVER: .6X TO 1.5X BASIC MEM
*GOLD/10: UNPRICED DUE TO SCARCITY
*RED/1: UNPRICED DUE TO SCARCITY
*P.P.BLACK/1: UNPRICED DUE TO SCARCITY
*P.P.CYAN/1: UNPRICED DUE TO SCARCITY
*P.P.MAGENTA/1: UNPRICED DUE TO SCARCITY
*P.P.YELLOW/1: UNPRICED DUE TO SCARCITY
STATED ODDS 1:338

NNO Asuka	8.00	20.00
NNO Braun Strowman	5.00	12.00
NNO Goldust	10.00	25.00
NNO Kalisto	6.00	15.00
NNO Kane	5.00	12.00
NNO Papa Shango	5.00	12.00
NNO Sin Cara	5.00	12.00
NNO Sting	8.00	20.00
NNO Undertaker	10.00	25.00

2016 Topps WWE Then Now Forever NXT Prospects

COMPLETE SET (15) 12.00 30.00
STATED ODDS 1:1

1 Angelo Dawkins	1.00	2.50
2 Austin Aries	1.25	3.00
3 Asuka	4.00	10.00
4 Billie Kay	2.50	6.00
5 Blake	1.00	2.50
6 Dash Wilder	1.25	3.00
7 Elias Samson	1.00	2.50
8 Hideo Itami	1.25	3.00
9 No Way Jose	1.00	2.50
10 Peyton Royce	2.50	6.00
11 Samoa Joe	2.50	6.00
12 Sawyer Fulton	1.25	3.00
13 Scott Dawson	1.00	2.50
14 Shinsuke Nakamura	2.50	6.00
15 Tye Dillinger	1.25	3.00

2016 Topps WWE Then Now Forever NXT Rivalries

COMPLETE SET (20) 10.00 25.00
STATED ODDS 1:2

1 Shinsuke Nakamura vs. Samoa Joe	2.00	5.00
2 Finn Balor vs. Samoa Joe	1.25	3.00
3 Kevin Owens vs. Finn Balor	1.25	3.00
4 Asuka vs. Bayley	.75	2.00
5 Nia Jax vs. Asuka	1.25	3.00
6 Nia Jax vs. Bayley	1.50	4.00
7 Emma vs. Asuka	.75	2.50
8 No Way Jose vs. Austin Aries	.75	2.00
9 Baron Corbin vs. Austin Aries	.75	2.00
10 Elias Samson vs. Apollo Crews	.75	2.00
11 Baron Corbin vs. Samoa Joe	1.25	3.00
12 Emma vs. Bayley	1.25	3.00
13 Sami Zayn vs. Cesaro	.75	2.00
14 Tyler Breeze vs. Hideo Itami	.75	2.00
15 Tyler Breeze vs. Neville	.75	2.00
16 Summer Rae vs. Paige	2.00	5.00

17 Bo Dallas vs. Neville .75 2.00
18 Bray Wyatt vs. Neville .75 2.00
19 Big E vs. Bo Dallas .75 2.00
20 Big E vs. Seth Rollins .75 2.00

2016 Topps WWE Then Now Forever Royal Rumble 2016 Mat Relics

*BRONZE/50: .5X TO 1.2X BASIC MEM
*SILVER/25: .6X TO 1.5X BASIC MEM
*GOLD/10: UNPRICED DUE TO SCARCITY
*RED/1: UNPRICED DUE TO SCARCITY
*P.P.BLACK/1: UNPRICED DUE TO SCARCITY
*P.P.CYAN/1: UNPRICED DUE TO SCARCITY
*P.P.MAGENTA/1: UNPRICED DUE TO SCARCITY
*P.P.YELLOW/1: UNPRICED DUE TO SCARCITY
STATED ODDS 1:92

NNO AJ Styles 8.00 20.00
NNO Alberto Del Rio 3.00 8.00
NNO Becky Lynch 6.00 15.00
NNO Big E 2.00 5.00
NNO Big Show 4.00 10.00
NNO Braun Strowman 2.50 6.00
NNO Bray Wyatt 8.00 20.00
NNO Brock Lesnar 10.00 25.00
NNO Charlotte 6.00 15.00
NNO Chris Jericho 5.00 12.00
NNO Dean Ambrose 6.00 15.00
NNO Dolph Ziggler 2.50 6.00
NNO Erick Rowan 2.00 5.00
NNO Kalisto 5.00 12.00
NNO Kane 3.00 8.00
NNO Kevin Owens 5.00 12.00
NNO Kofi Kingston 2.00 5.00
NNO Luke Harper 2.00 5.00
NNO The Miz 3.00 8.00
NNO Ric Flair 8.00 20.00
NNO Roman Reigns 6.00 15.00
NNO Sami Zayn 3.00 8.00
NNO Sheamus 5.00 12.00
NNO Triple H 8.00 20.00
NNO Xavier Woods 2.00 5.00

2016 Topps WWE Then Now Forever Shirt Relics

*BRONZE/50: .5X TO 1.2X BASIC MEM
*SILVER/25: .6X TO 1.5X BASIC MEM
*GOLD/10: UNPRICED DUE TO SCARCITY
*RED/1: UNPRICED DUE TO SCARCITY
*P.P.BLACK/1: UNPRICED DUE TO SCARCITY
*P.P.CYAN/1: UNPRICED DUE TO SCARCITY
*P.P.MAGENTA/1: UNPRICED DUE TO SCARCITY
*P.P.YELLOW/1: UNPRICED DUE TO SCARCITY
STATED ODDS 1:102

1 Aiden English 2.00 5.00
2 Alberto Del Rio 3.00 8.00
3 Apollo Crews 2.00 5.00
4 Asuka 8.00 20.00
5 Austin Aries 2.50 6.00
6 Baron Corbin 2.50 6.00
7 Bayley 5.00 12.00
8 Big Cass 4.00 10.00
9 Big Show 4.00 10.00
10 Bo Dallas 2.00 5.00
11 Braun Strowman 2.50 6.00
12 Bray Wyatt 8.00 20.00
13 Bubba Ray Dudley 4.00 10.00
14 Cesaro 4.00 10.00
15 Curtis Axel 2.00 5.00
16 Darren Young 2.00 5.00
17 Finn Balor 6.00 15.00
18 Heath Slater 2.00 5.00
19 Jey Uso 2.00 5.00
20 Jimmy Uso 2.00 5.00
21 John Cena 10.00 25.00
22 Kalisto 5.00 12.00
23 Kevin Owens 5.00 12.00
24 Luke Harper 2.00 5.00
25 Randy Orton 5.00 12.00
26 Roman Reigns 6.00 15.00
27 Sheamus 5.00 12.00
28 Simon Gotch 3.00 8.00
29 Xavier Woods 2.00 5.00
30 Zack Ryder 2.00 5.00

2016 Topps WWE Then Now Forever Triple Autographs

STATED ODDS 1:1,362
STATED PRINT RUN 11 SER.#'d SETS

NNO English/Gotch/Amore 50.00 100.00
NNO Styles/Anderson/Gallows 125.00 250.00
NNO Cena/Jericho/R-Truth 75.00 150.00
NNO Naomi/Banks/Bayley 125.00 250.00
NNO Natalya/Charlotte/Lynch 125.00 250.00
NNO Samoa Joe/Balor/Itami 100.00 200.00
NNO Rollins/Ambrose/Reigns 120.00 250.00
NNO Nakamura/Zayn/Asuka 100.00 200.00

2016 Topps WWE Then Now Forever WWE Rivalries

COMPLETE SET (20) 10.00 25.00
STATED ODDS 1:2

1 AJ Styles vs. John Cena 1.00 2.50
2 Seth Rollins vs. Roman Reigns 1.00 2.50
3 Seth Rollins vs. Dean Ambrose 1.25 3.00
4 Dean Ambrose vs. Chris Jericho 1.25 3.00
5 Roman Reigns vs. AJ Styles 1.50 4.00
6 Chris Jericho vs. AJ Styles .75 2.00
7 Sami Zayn vs. Kevin Owens 1.25 3.00
8 Kevin Owens vs. Cesaro 1.50 4.00
9 Kevin Owens vs. Dolph Ziggler 1.25 3.00
10 Undertaker vs. Brock Lesnar 2.00 5.00
11 Roman Reigns vs. Triple H 1.25 3.00
12 Dean Ambrose vs. Triple H 1.25 3.00
13 Natalya vs. Charlotte 1.00 2.50
14 Natalya vs. Becky Lynch 1.25 3.00
15 Dolph Ziggler vs. Baron Corbin .75 2.00
16 Enzo Amore vs. Chris Jericho 1.00 2.50
17 Kalisto vs. Rusev .75 2.00
18 Rusev vs. Jack Swagger .75 2.00
19 Lana vs. Brie Bella 1.50 4.00
20 Dolph Ziggler vs. The Miz .75 2.00

2017 Topps WWE Then Now Forever

COMPLETE SET (100) 10.00 25.00
UNOPENED BOX (24 PACKS)
UNOPENED PACK (7 CARDS)
*BRONZE: .5X TO 1.2X BASIC CARDS
*BLUE/99: 1X TO 2.5X BASIC CARDS
*SILVER/25: 2X TO 5X BASIC CARDS
*GOLD/10: 4X TO 10X BASIC CARDS
*RED/1: UNPRICED DUE TO SCARCITY
*P.P.BLACK/1: UNPRICED DUE TO SCARCITY
*P.P.CYAN/1: UNPRICED DUE TO SCARCITY
*P.P.MAGENTA/1: UNPRICED DUE TO SCARCITY
*P.P.YELLOW/1: UNPRICED DUE TO SCARCITY

101 Tyler Bate RC
102 Brie Bella .60 1.50
103 Jerry The King Lawler .30 .75
104A Akira Tozawa RC .25 .60
104B Akira Tozawa SP Arms Up 8.00 20.00
105 Alicia Fox .40 1.00
106 Apollo Crews .30 .75
107 Ariya Daivari .25 .60
108 Harley Race .30 .75
109A Big Show .30 .75
109B Big Show SP Red/White/Blue 4.00 10.00
110 Bo Dallas .25 .60
111A Braun Strowman .30 .75
111B Braun Strowman SP Stomping 5.00 12.00
112A Bray Wyatt .60 1.50
112B Bray Wyatt SP White Ropes 5.00 12.00
113A Cesaro .50 1.25
113B Cesaro SP Mid-Air 5.00 12.00
114 Charly Caruso RC .25 .60
115 Curt Hawkins .25 .60
116 Curtis Axel .25 .60
117 Dana Brooke .50 1.25
118 Darren Young .25 .60
119 Dean Ambrose .75 2.00
120 Emma .60 1.50
121 Jeff Hardy .50 1.25
122 Goldust .30 .75
123 Heath Slater .25 .60
124 JoJo .40 1.00
125 Kalisto .40 1.00
126 Kurt Angle .50 1.25
127 Mark Henry .25 .60
128 Matt Hardy .60 1.50
129 Mickie James .40 1.00
130 Neville .40 1.00
131 R-Truth .25 .60
132 Rhyno .25 .60
133 Roman Reigns .75 2.00
134 Sasha Banks .75 2.00
135 Seth Rollins .75 2.00
136A Sheamus .50 1.25
136B Sheamus SP Mid-Air 4.00 10.00
137 Summer Rae .60 1.50
138 Aiden English .25 .60
139 Baron Corbin .40 1.00
140 Becky Lynch .75 2.00
141 Charlotte Flair 1.00 2.50
142A Daniel Bryan 1.00 2.50
142B Daniel Bryan SP YES! 5.00 12.00
143A Dolph Ziggler .40 1.00
143B Dolph Ziggler SP Drops Elbow 5.00 12.00
144 Epico .25 .60
145 Erick Rowan .25 .60
146 Fandango .25 .60
147 James Ellsworth RC .25 .60
148 Jey Uso .30 .75
149 Jimmy Uso .30 .75
150 Jinder Mahal .40 1.00
151A Kevin Owens .60 1.50
151B Kevin Owens SP Red/White/Blue 5.00 12.00
152 Konnor .25 .60
153 Lana .75 2.00
154 Naomi .50 1.25
155A Natalya .50 1.25
155B Natalya SP Arms Raised 6.00 15.00
156 Nikki Bella .60 1.50
157 Primo .25 .60
158A Rusev .50 1.25
158B Rusev SP Man Bun 5.00 12.00
159 Sami Zayn .30 .75
160 Shinsuke Nakamura .60 1.50
161 Sin Cara .30 .75
162 Tyler Breeze .25 .60
163 Viktor .25 .60
164 Akam .25 .60
165 Aleister Black RC .25 .60
166 Andrade Cien Almas .25 .60
167 Angelo Dawkins .25 .60
168 Buddy Murphy .25 .60
169 Drew McIntyre .25 .60
170 Elias .40 1.00
171 Kassius Ohno RC .25 .60
172 Killian Dain RC .25 .60
173 Abbey Laith RC .25 .60
174 Lacey Evans RC .40 1.00
175 Mandy Rose .30 .75
176 No Way Jose .25 .60
177 Rezar .25 .60
178 Ruby Riot RC .30 .75
179 Sawyer Fulton .25 .60
180 Wesley Blake .25 .60
181 Alundra Blayze .30 .75
182 Andre the Giant .50 1.25
183 Bret Hit Man Hart .50 1.25
184 British Bulldog .25 .60
185 Bruno Sammartino .40 1.00
186 Dusty Rhodes .30 .75
187 Edge .60 1.50
188 Jake The Snake Roberts .30 .75
189 Lex Luger .30 .75
190 Macho Man Randy Savage .50 1.25
191 Million Dollar Man Ted DiBiase .30 .75
192 Mr. Perfect .50 1.25
193 Ravishing Rick Rude .40 1.00
194 Rowdy Roddy Piper .50 1.25
195 Shawn Michaels .60 1.50
196 Sting .75 2.00
197 Stone Cold Steve Austin 1.00 2.50
198 Trish Stratus 1.00 2.50
199 Ultimate Warrior .50 1.25
200 Wendi Richter .30 .75

2017 Topps WWE Then Now Forever Autographed Dual Relics

STATED PRINT RUN 10 SER. #'d SETS
UNPRICED DUE TO SCARCITY

NNO Asuka
NNO Bayley
NNO Bobby Roode
NNO Bray Wyatt
NNO Charlotte Flair
NNO John Cena
NNO Nikki Bella
NNO Randy Orton
NNO Shinsuke Nakamura

2017 Topps WWE Then Now Forever Autographed NXT TakeOver San Antonio 2017 Mat Relics

STATED PRINT RUN 10 SER.#'d SETS
UNPRICED DUE TO SCARCITY

NNO Asuka
NNO Billie Kay

NNO Bobby Roode		
NNO Eric Young		
NNO Peyton Royce		
NNO Roderick Strong		
NNO Shinsuke Nakamura		

2017 Topps WWE Then Now Forever Autographed Royal Rumble 2017 Mat Relics

STATED PRINT RUN 10 SER. #'d SETS
UNPRICED DUE TO SCARCITY

NNO AJ Styles		
NNO Braun Strowman		
NNO Bray Wyatt		
NNO Charlotte Flair		
NNO Chris Jericho		
NNO Goldberg		
NNO Karl Anderson		
NNO Kevin Owens		
NNO Luke Gallows		
NNO Naomi		
NNO Neville		
NNO Nia Jax		
NNO Nikki Bella		
NNO Randy Orton		
NNO Roman Reigns		
NNO Undertaker		

2017 Topps WWE Then Now Forever Autographed Shirt Relics

STATED PRINT RUN 10 SER.#'d SETS
UNPRICED DUE TO SCARCITY

NNO Aiden English		
NNO Becky Lynch		
NNO Big Show		
NNO Charlotte Flair		
NNO Curtis Axel		
NNO JoJo		
NNO Kevin Owens		
NNO Naomi		
NNO Natalya		
NNO Sasha Banks		
NNO Seth Rollins		
NNO Sheamus		
NNO Sting		
NNO Summer Rae		

2017 Topps WWE Then Now Forever Autographs

*BLUE/50: .6X TO 1.5X BASIC AUTOS
*SILVER/25: .75X TO 2X BASIC AUTOS
*GOLD/10: UNPRICED DUE TO SCARCITY
*RED/1: UNPRICED DUE TO SCARCITY
STATED ODDS

102 Brie Bella	10.00	25.00
104 Akira Tozawa	8.00	20.00
105 Alicia Fox	8.00	20.00
106 Apollo Crews	6.00	15.00
111 Braun Strowman	12.00	30.00
112 Bray Wyatt	8.00	20.00
113 Cesaro	6.00	15.00
119 Dean Ambrose	10.00	25.00
121 Jeff Hardy	15.00	40.00
123 Heath Slater	5.00	12.00
126 Kurt Angle	15.00	40.00
128 Matt Hardy	15.00	40.00
134 Sasha Banks	25.00	60.00
136 Sheamus	5.00	12.00
139 Baron Corbin	5.00	12.00
140 Becky Lynch	15.00	40.00
154 Naomi	10.00	25.00
159 Sami Zayn	5.00	12.00
160 Shinsuke Nakamura	15.00	40.00
165 Aleister Black	8.00	20.00
169 Drew McIntyre	8.00	20.00
171 Kassius Ohno	6.00	15.00
172 Killian Dain	6.00	15.00
174 Lacey Evans	12.00	30.00
178 Ruby Riot	15.00	40.00
189 Lex Luger	8.00	20.00

2017 Topps WWE Then Now Forever Championship Medallion Relics

*BRONZE/99: .5X TO 1.2X BASIC MEM
*BLUE/50: .6X TO 1.5X BASIC MEM
*SILVER/25: .75X TO 2X BASIC MEM
*GOLD/10: UNPRICED DUE TO SCARCITY
*RED/1: UNPRICED DUE TO SCARCITY
RANDOMLY INSERTED INTO PACKS

NNO Aiden English	1.50	4.00
NNO American Alpha	2.00	5.00
NNO Asuka	5.00	12.00
NNO The Authors of Pain	1.50	4.00
NNO Bayley	5.00	12.00
NNO Blake & Murphy	1.50	4.00
NNO Bobby Roode	4.00	10.00
NNO The Brian Kendrick	1.50	4.00
NNO DIY	1.50	4.00
NNO Finn Balor	6.00	15.00
NNO Kevin Owens	4.00	10.00
NNO Neville	2.50	6.00
NNO The Revival	1.50	4.00
NNO Rich Swann	1.50	4.00
NNO Sami Zayn	2.00	5.00
NNO Samoa Joe	5.00	12.00
NNO Sasha Banks	5.00	12.00
NNO Shinsuke Nakamura	4.00	10.00
NNO TJ Perkins	1.50	4.00

2017 Topps WWE Then Now Forever Dual Relics

*SILVER/25: .6X TO 1.5X BASIC MEM
*GOLD/10: UNPRICED DUE TO SCARCITY
*RED/1: UNPRICED DUE TO SCARCITY
STATED PRINT RUN 50 SER.#'d SETS

NNO Asuka		
NNO Bayley		
NNO Bobby Roode	10.00	25.00
NNO Bray Wyatt		
NNO Brock Lesnar		
NNO Charlotte Flair		
NNO John Cena	12.00	30.00
NNO Nikki Bella	10.00	25.00
NNO Randy Orton		
NNO Shinsuke Nakamura	20.00	50.00

2017 Topps WWE Then Now Forever Finishers and Signature Moves

COMPLETE SET (50)	10.00	25.00
STATED ODDS 2:1		
F1 John Cena	1.50	4.00
F2 John Cena	1.50	4.00
F3 Brock Lesnar	1.50	4.00
F4 Brock Lesnar	1.50	4.00
F5 Goldberg	1.25	3.00
F6 Goldberg	1.25	3.00
F7 The Rock	1.50	4.00
F8 The Rock	1.50	4.00
F9 Triple H	.75	2.00
F10 Randy Orton	.75	2.00
F11 Undertaker	1.25	3.00
F12 Undertaker	1.25	3.00
F13 Undertaker	1.25	3.00
F14 Kane	.40	1.00
F15 Big Show	.40	1.00
F16 Big Show	.40	1.00
F17 Chris Jericho	.75	2.00
F18 Chris Jericho	.75	2.00
F19 Chris Jericho	.75	2.00
F20 Daniel Bryan	1.25	3.00
F21 Mick Foley	.75	2.00
F22 Mick Foley	.75	2.00
F23 Booker T	.40	1.00
F24 AJ Styles	1.50	4.00
F25 AJ Styles	1.50	4.00
F26 AJ Styles	1.50	4.00
F27 Finn Balor	1.25	3.00
F28 Finn Balor	1.25	3.00
F29 The Miz	.60	1.50
F30 The Miz	.60	1.50
F31 Bobby Roode	.75	2.00
F32 Shinsuke Nakamura	.75	2.00
F33 Drew McIntyre	.30	.75
F34 Aliyah	.40	1.00
F35 Andrade Cien Almas	.30	.75
F36 Dean Ambrose	1.00	2.50
F37 No Way Jose	.30	.75
F38 Ember Moon	.75	2.00
F39 Eric Young	.60	1.50
F40 Hideo Itami	.50	1.25
F41 Nikki Cross	.60	1.50
F42 Billie Kay	.40	1.00
F43 Tye Dillinger	.30	.75
F44 Buddy Murphy	.30	.75
F45 Peyton Royce	.50	1.25
F46 The Authors of Pain	.30	.75
F47 The Revival	.30	.75
F48 TM-61	.30	.75
F49 The Hype Bros.	.40	1.00
F50 #DIY	.30	.75

2017 Topps WWE Then Now Forever Kiss

*GOLD/10: UNPRICED DUE TO SCARCITY
*RED/1: UNPRICED DUE TO SCARCITY
STATED PRINT RUN 99 SER.#'d SETS

NNO Alexa Bliss	200.00	400.00
NNO Asuka	50.00	100.00
NNO Becky Lynch	125.00	250.00
NNO Billie Kay	15.00	40.00
NNO Charlotte Flair	125.00	250.00
NNO Ember Moon	30.00	75.00
NNO Liv Morgan	100.00	200.00
NNO Peyton Royce	15.00	40.00

2017 Topps WWE Then Now Forever Kiss Autographs

*GOLD/10: UNPRICED DUE TO SCARCITY
*RED/1: UNPRICED DUE TO SCARCITY
STATED PRINT RUN 25 SER.#'d SETS

NNO Alexa Bliss		
NNO Asuka	50.00	100.00
NNO Becky Lynch	50.00	100.00
NNO Billie Kay	30.00	75.00
NNO Charlotte Flair	60.00	120.00
NNO Ember Moon	25.00	60.00
NNO Liv Morgan	50.00	100.00
NNO Mickie James	60.00	120.00
NNO Nikki Bella	50.00	100.00
NNO Peyton Royce	30.00	75.00

2017 Topps WWE Then Now Forever NXT TakeOver San Antonio 2017 Mat Relics

*BRONZE/99: .5X TO 1.2X BASIC MEM
*BLUE/50: .6X TO 1.5X BASIC MEM
*SILVER/25: .75X TO 2X BASIC MEM
*GOLD/10: UNPRICED DUE TO SCARCITY
*RED/1: UNPRICED DUE TO SCARCITY
STATED PRINT RUN 350 SER.#'d SETS

NNO Akam	1.50	4.00
NNO Asuka	5.00	12.00
NNO Billie Kay	2.00	5.00
NNO Bobby Roode	4.00	10.00
NNO Eric Young	3.00	8.00
NNO Peyton Royce	2.50	6.00
NNO Rezar	1.50	4.00
NNO Roderick Strong	2.00	5.00
NNO Shinsuke Nakamura	4.00	10.00
NNO Tye Dillinger	1.50	4.00

2017 Topps WWE Then Now Forever Roster Updates

COMPLETE SET (20)	12.00	30.00
R21 Alexa Bliss	5.00	12.00
R22 Dash Wilder	1.00	2.50
R23 Jason Jordan	1.25	3.00
R24 Maryse	2.00	5.00
R25 The Miz	2.00	5.00
R26 Mustafa Ali	1.00	2.50
R27 Scott Dawson	1.00	2.50
R28 Tony Nese	1.00	2.50
R29 The New Day	2.00	5.00
R30 Samir Singh	1.00	2.50
R31 Sunil Singh	1.00	2.50
R32 Tamina	1.25	3.00
R33 Tye Dillinger	1.00	2.50
R34 Dan Matha	1.00	2.50
R35 Vanessa Borne	1.25	3.00
R36 Gabriel Ealy	1.00	2.50
R37 Kona Reeves	1.00	2.50
R38 The Velveteen Dream	1.25	3.00
R39 Steve Cutler	1.00	2.50
R40 Uriel Ealy	1.00	2.50

2017 Topps WWE Then Now Forever Royal Rumble 2017 Mat Relics

*BRONZE/99: .5X TO 1.2X BASIC MEM
*BLUE/50: .6X TO 1.5X BASIC MEM
*SILVER/25: .75X TO 2X BASIC MEM
*GOLD/10: UNPRICED DUE TO SCARCITY
*RED/1: UNPRICED DUE TO SCARCITY
RANDOMLY INSERTED INTO PACKS

NNO AJ Styles	6.00	15.00
NNO Bayley	4.00	10.00
NNO Braun Strowman	1.50	4.00
NNO Bray Wyatt	3.00	8.00
NNO Brock Lesnar	6.00	15.00

NNO Charlotte Flair	5.00	12.00
NNO Chris Jericho	3.00	8.00
NNO Goldberg	5.00	12.00
NNO John Cena	6.00	15.00
NNO Karl Anderson	1.25	3.00
NNO Kevin Owens	3.00	8.00
NNO Luke Gallows	2.00	5.00
NNO Naomi	2.50	6.00
NNO Neville	2.00	5.00
NNO Nia Jax	2.00	5.00
NNO Nikki Bella	3.00	8.00
NNO Randy Orton	3.00	8.00
NNO Rich Swann	1.25	3.00
NNO Roman Reigns	4.00	10.00
NNO Undertaker	5.00	12.00

2017 Topps WWE Then Now Forever Shirt Relics

*BLUE/50: .5X TO 1.2X BASIC MEM
*SILVER/25: .6X TO 1.5X BASIC MEM
*GOLD/10: UNPRICED DUE TO SCARCITY
*RED/1: UNPRICED DUE TO SCARCITY
RANDOMLY INSERTED INTO PACKS

NNO Aiden English	1.25	3.00
NNO Andrade Cien Almas	1.25	3.00
NNO Becky Lynch	4.00	10.00
NNO Big Show	1.50	4.00
NNO Brock Lesnar	6.00	15.00
NNO Charlotte Flair	5.00	12.00
NNO Curtis Axel	1.25	3.00
NNO Darren Young	1.25	3.00
NNO John Cena	6.00	15.00
NNO JoJo	2.00	5.00
NNO Kevin Owens	3.00	8.00
NNO Naomi	2.50	6.00
NNO Natalya	2.50	6.00
NNO No Way Jose	1.25	3.00
NNO Sasha Banks	4.00	10.00
NNO Seth Rollins	4.00	10.00
NNO Sheamus	2.50	6.00
NNO Sting	4.00	10.00
NNO Summer Rae	3.00	8.00

2017 Topps WWE Then Now Forever Triple Autographs

STATED PRINT RUN 10 SER.#'d SETS
RANDOMLY INSERTED INTO PACKS

NNO Bayley/Banks/Flair	125.00	250.00
NNO Wyatt/Orton/Harper	75.00	150.00
NNO Rollins/Reigns/Ambrose	150.00	300.00
NNO Undertaker/Lesnar/Goldberg	400.00	600.00
NNO Undertaker/Kane/Bryan	250.00	400.00

2018 Topps WWE Then Now Forever

COMPLETE SET W/SP (124)
COMPLETE SET W/O SP (100) 8.00 20.00
UNOPENED BOX (24 PACKS)
UNOPENED PACK (7 CARDS)
*BRONZE: .5X TO 1.2X BASIC CARDS
*BLUE/99: .75X TO 2X BASIC CARDS
*SILVER/25: 2X TO 5X BASIC CARDS
*GOLD/10: UNPRICED DUE TO SCARCITY
*RED/1: UNPRICED DUE TO SCARCITY
*P.P.BLACK/1: UNPRICED DUE TO SCARCITY
*P.P.CYAN/1: UNPRICED DUE TO SCARCITY
*P.P.MAGENTA/1: UNPRICED DUE TO SCARCITY
*P.P.YELLOW/1: UNPRICED DUE TO SCARCITY

101 Ronda Rousey	2.50	6.00
102 Alexa Bliss	1.25	3.00
102A Alexa Bliss SP		
103 Akam	.25	.60
104 Alexander Wolfe	.25	.60
105 Andrade	.40	1.00
105A Andrade SP		
106 Constable Baron Corbin	.40	1.00
107 Bayley	.40	1.00
107A Bayley SP		
108 Becky Lynch	.60	1.50
108A Becky Lynch SP		
109 Bianca Belair RC	.30	.75
110 Big Show	.25	.60
111 Billie Kay	.50	1.25
112 Bobby Lashley	.50	1.25
112A Bobby Lashley SP		
113 Braun Strowman	.60	1.50
113A Braun Strowman SP		
114 Bray Wyatt	.60	1.50
114A Bray Wyatt SP		
115 Candice LeRae RC	.30	.75
116 Cesaro	.50	1.25
116A Cesaro SP		
117 Cezar Bononi RC	.25	.60
118 Dakota Kai RC	.30	.75
119 Danny Burch RC	.25	.60
120 Dash Wilder	.30	.75
121 David Otunga	.30	.75
122 Dean Ambrose	.50	1.25
122A Dean Ambrose SP		
123 Dolph Ziggler	.30	.75
124 Drake Maverick RC	.30	.75
125 Drew McIntyre	.40	1.00
125A Drew McIntyre SP		
126 EC3	.30	.75
127 Ember Moon	.50	1.25
127A Ember Moon SP		
128 Eric Young	.30	.75
128A Eric Young SP		
129 Fabian Aichner RC	.25	.60
130 Fandango	.25	.60
131 Finn Balor	.60	1.50
131A Finn Balor SP		
132 Goldust	.50	1.25
133 Hanson RC	.30	.75
134 Harper	.40	1.00
135 Hideo Itami	.25	.60
136 Jason Jordan	.25	.60
137 Jeff Hardy	.50	1.25
137A Jeff Hardy SP		
138 Jonathan Coachman	.25	.60
139 Kalisto	.25	.60
140 Kane	.40	1.00
141 Karl Anderson	.25	.60
142 Kassius Ohno	.25	.60
143 Killian Dain	.30	.75
144 Kona Reeves	.25	.60
145 Lacey Evans	.30	.75
146 Lince Dorado	.25	.60
147 Liv Morgan	.50	1.25
148 Luke Gallows	.30	.75
149 Mandy Rose	.60	1.50
150 Mark Andrews RC	.25	.60
151 Woken Matt Hardy	.60	1.50
152 Mojo Rawley	.25	.60
153 Nick Miller	.25	.60
154 Nikki Bella	.50	1.25
155 Nikki Cross	.40	1.00
156 No Way Jose	.30	.75
157 Otis Dozovic	.25	.60
158 Peyton Royce	.60	1.50
159 Randy Orton	.60	1.50
159A Randy Orton SP		
160 Raul Mendoza RC	.25	.60
161 Rezar	.25	.60
162 Ricochet RC	.50	1.25
163 Riddick Moss	.25	.60
164 Roman Reigns	.60	1.50
164A Roman Reigns SP		
165 Rowan	.40	1.00
166 Rowe RC	.25	.60
167 Ruby Riott	.40	1.00
167A Ruby Riott SP		
168 Rusev	.40	1.00
168A Rusev SP		
169 Sami Zayn	.25	.60
169A Sami Zayn SP		
170 Samoa Joe	.50	1.25
170A Samoa Joe SP		
171 Sasha Banks	.75	2.00
171A Sasha Banks SP		
172 Scott Dawson	.30	.75
173 Scott Stanford	.25	.60
174 Seth Rollins	.60	1.50
174A Seth Rollins SP		
175 Shane Thorne	.25	.60
176 Shayna Baszler	.60	1.50
177 Sheamus	.50	1.25
177A Sheamus SP		
178 Shinsuke Nakamura	.60	1.50
178A Shinsuke Nakamura SP		
179 Taynara Conti RC	.25	.60
180 Tino Sabbatelli	.30	.75
181 Trent Seven RC	.25	.60
182 Tucker Knight	.25	.60
183 Tye Dillinger	.25	.60
184 Tyler Breeze	.25	.60
185 Vanessa Borne	.25	.60
186 Velveteen Dream	.25	.60
187 Zelina Vega RC	.25	.60
188 Andre the Giant	.50	1.25
189 Beth Phoenix	.50	1.25
190 Bret Hit Man Hart	.60	1.50
191 Eddie Guerrero	.60	1.50
192 Edge	.60	1.50
193 Jake The Snake Roberts	.30	.75
194 Lita	.60	1.50
195 Macho Man Randy Savage	.75	2.00
196 Million Dollar Man Ted DiBiase	.30	.75
197 Mr. Perfect	.30	.75
198 Shawn Michaels	.75	2.00
199 Sting	.60	1.50
200 Stone Cold Steve Austin	1.25	3.00

2018 Topps WWE Then Now Forever 25 Years of RAW

COMPLETE SET (50) 12.00 30.00
RANDOMLY INSERTED INTO PACKS

RAW1 Monday Night RAW Premieres	.40	1.00
RAW2 Mr. Perfect Def. Ric Flair	.40	1.00
RAW3 123 Kid vs. Bret Hart	.40	1.00
RAW4 Ringmaster Debuts	1.50	4.00
RAW5 Bret Hart Snaps	.75	2.00
RAW6 Austin injures Bret Hart	1.50	4.00
RAW7 NA Outlaws/Chainsaw Charlie	.40	1.00
RAW8 HHH Leads DX	.75	2.00
RAW9 DX Invades WCW	.75	2.00
RAW10 Stone Cold/Zamboni	1.50	4.00
RAW11 Undertaker Captures Austin	1.25	3.00
RAW12 Stone Cold/Beer Truck	1.50	4.00
RAW13 The Higher Power	.40	1.00
RAW14 Rock/This Is Your Life	.40	1.00
RAW15 HHH and Stephanie Elope	.75	2.00
RAW16 Angle/Milk Truck	.75	2.00
RAW17 HHH Returns	.75	2.00
RAW18 WWE Draft	.40	1.00
RAW19 Hardy/Undertaker	.60	1.50
RAW20 HHH Turns on HBK	.75	2.00
RAW21 HHH/Evolution	.75	2.00
RAW22 Goldberg Debuts	1.25	3.00
RAW23 HHH Def. Ric Flair	.75	2.00
RAW24 Lita Def. Trish	.75	2.00
RAW25 Batista Thumbs Down	.50	1.25
RAW26 Cena Joins RAW	1.25	3.00
RAW27 HBK/Montreal	1.00	2.50
RAW28 Mr. McMahon's Limo	.60	1.50
RAW29 Hardy Swantons Orton	.60	1.50
RAW30 Ric Flair Retires	1.00	2.50
RAW31 Bret Hart Returns	.75	2.00
RAW32 HBK Farewell	1.00	2.50
RAW33 Nexus Invades	.40	1.00
RAW34 Miz Cashes In	.60	1.50
RAW35 HHH/Taker WrestleMania	.75	2.00
RAW36 Edge Retires	.75	2.00
RAW37 Daniel Bryan Kane Hug	.75	2.00
RAW38 Dolph Ziggler Cashes In	.40	1.00
RAW39 Mark Henry Fake Retires	.40	1.00
RAW40 Yes! Movement	.75	2.00
RAW41 Seth Rollins Turns	.75	2.00
RAW42 Kevin Owens Debuts	.75	2.00
RAW43 Shane McMahon Returns	.60	1.50
RAW44 Styles Confronts Cena	1.25	3.00
RAW45 Goldberg Returns	1.25	3.00
RAW46 Angle New GM	.75	2.00
RAW47 Roman Reigns/My Yard	.75	2.00
RAW48 The Shield Reunite	.40	1.00
RAW49 Miz Wins 8th IC Title	.60	1.50
RAW50 Scott Hall Returns	.60	1.50

2018 Topps WWE Then Now Forever Autographed Royal Rumble 2018 Mat Relics

STATED PRINT RUN 10 SER.#'d SETS
UNPRICED DUE TO SCARCITY

MRARRAC Adam Cole
MRARRAJ AJ Styles
MRARRAS Asuka
MRARRBS Braun Strowman
MRARRFB Finn Balor
MRARRKK Kofi Kingston
MRARRKO Kevin Owens
MRARRMH Woken Matt Hardy
MRARRRS Rusev
MRARRSN Shinsuke Nakamura
MRARRSR Seth Rollins
MRARRSZ Sami Zayn

2018 Topps WWE Then Now Forever Autographed Shirt Relics

STATED PRINT RUN 10 SER.#'d SETS
UNPRICED DUE TO SCARCITY

SRAB Alexa Bliss		
SRAK Akam		
SRCG Chad Gable		
SRCR Carmella		
SRDZ Dolph Ziggler		
SRJC John Cena		
SRJJ Jason Jordan		
SRKA Karl Anderson		
SRLG Luke Gallows		
SRNA Naomi		
SRRZ Rezar		
SRSR Seth Rollins		

2018 Topps WWE Then Now Forever Autographs

*BLUE/99: .5X TO 1.2X BASIC AUTOS
*SILVER/25: .6X TO 1.5X BASIC AUTOS
*GOLD/10: UNPRICED DUE TO SCARCITY
*RED/1: UNPRICED DUE TO SCARCITY
RANDOMLY INSERTED INTO PACKS

102 Alexa Bliss	30.00	75.00
106 Baron Corbin	4.00	10.00
108 Becky Lynch	15.00	40.00
111 Billie Kay	10.00	25.00
113 Braun Strowman	10.00	25.00
114 Bray Wyatt	8.00	20.00
115 Candice LeRae	12.00	30.00
125 Drew McIntyre	6.00	15.00
126 EC3	10.00	25.00
127 Ember Moon	8.00	20.00
128 Eric Young	5.00	12.00
131 Finn Balor	8.00	20.00
133 Hanson	12.00	30.00
137 Jeff Hardy	8.00	20.00
142 Kassius Ohno	4.00	10.00
147 Liv Morgan	15.00	40.00
151 Woken Matt Hardy	8.00	20.00
152 Mojo Rawley	5.00	12.00
158 Peyton Royce	12.00	30.00
162 Ricochet	25.00	60.00
166 Rowe	8.00	20.00
167 Ruby Riott	12.00	30.00
168 Rusev	6.00	15.00
169 Sami Zayn	6.00	15.00
170 Samoa Joe	5.00	12.00
178 Shinsuke Nakamura	10.00	25.00
189 Beth Phoenix	10.00	25.00

2018 Topps WWE Then Now Forever Four Corner Mat Relics

*SILVER/25: .5X TO 1.2X BASIC MEM
*GOLD/10: UNPRICED DUE TO SCARCITY
STATED PRINT RUN 50 SER.#'d SETS

FCAJ AJ Styles	12.00	30.00
FCAS Asuka	10.00	25.00
FCDA Dean Ambrose	4.00	10.00
FCJC John Cena	12.00	30.00
FCRO Randy Orton	6.00	15.00
FCRR Roman Reigns	6.00	15.00
FCSN Shinsuke Nakamura	10.00	25.00
FCSR Seth Rollins	12.00	30.00
FCTH Triple H	10.00	25.00
FCUN Undertaker	15.00	40.00

2018 Topps WWE Then Now Forever Kiss

*GOLD/10: UNPRICED DUE TO SCARCITY
*RED/1: UNPRICED DUE TO SCARCITY

KCAB Alexa Bliss		
KCAS Asuka		
KCMR Mandy Rose	30.00	75.00

2018 Topps WWE Then Now Forever Kiss Autographs

*GOLD/10: UNPRICED DUE TO SCARCITY
*RED/1: UNPRICED DUE TO SCARCITY
STATED PRINT RUN 25 SER.#'d SETS

KCMJ Mickie James	60.00	120.00
KCMR Mandy Rose	50.00	100.00
KCRR Ruby Riott		

2018 Topps WWE Then Now Forever Money in the Bank 2017 Mat Relics

*BRONZE/99: .5X TO 1.2X BASIC MEM
*BLUE/50: .6X TO 1.5X BASIC MEM
*SILVER/25: .75X TO 2X BASIC MEM
*GOLD/10: UNPRICED DUE TO SCARCITY
*RED/1: UNPRICED DUE TO SCARCITY

MRMBAJ AJ Styles	8.00	20.00
MRMBBC Baron Corbin	2.50	6.00
MRMBBL Becky Lynch	6.00	15.00
MRMBCF Charlotte Flair	10.00	25.00
MRMBCR Carmella	5.00	12.00
MRMBDZ Dolph Ziggler	3.00	8.00
MRMBKO Kevin Owens	2.50	6.00
MRMBNT Natalya	3.00	8.00
MRMBSN Shinsuke Nakamura	4.00	10.00
MRMBSZ Sami Zayn	2.50	6.00
MRMBTA Tamina	2.50	6.00

2018 Topps WWE Then Now Forever NXT TakeOver Philadelphia 2018 Mat Relics

*BRONZE/99: .5X TO 1.2X BASIC MEM
*BLUE/50: .6X TO 1.5X BASIC MEM
*SILVER/25: .75X TO 2X BASIC MEM
*GOLD/10: UNPRICED DUE TO SCARCITY
*RED/1: UNPRICED DUE TO SCARCITY

MRPHAA Andrade Cien Almas	4.00	10.00
MRPHAB Aleister Black	2.50	6.00
MRPHAC Adam Cole	3.00	8.00
MRPHBF Bobby Fish	2.00	5.00
MRPHEM Ember Moon	3.00	8.00
MRPHJG Johnny Gargano	2.00	5.00
MRPHKO Kassius Ohno	3.00	8.00
MRPHOR Kyle O'Reilly	4.00	10.00
MRPHSB Shayna Baszler	3.00	8.00
MRPHVD Velveteen Dream	5.00	12.00

2018 Topps WWE Then Now Forever RAW 25 Mat Relics

*BRONZE/99: .5X TO 1.2X BASIC MEM
*BLUE/50: .6X TO 1.5X BASIC MEM
*SILVER/25: .75X TO 2X BASIC MEM
*GOLD/10: UNPRICED DUE TO SCARCITY
*RED/1: UNPRICED DUE TO SCARCITY

MR25AS Asuka	5.00	12.00
MR25EL Elias	2.50	6.00
MR25JC John Cena	6.00	15.00
MR25RR Roman Reigns	4.00	10.00
MR25SA Stone Cold Steve Austin	12.00	30.00
MR25TM The Miz	3.00	8.00

2018 Topps WWE Then Now Forever Roster Updates

COMPLETE SET (20)	15.00	40.00
RANDOMLY INSERTED INTO PACKS		
R21 Asuka	2.50	6.00
R22 Bobby Roode	1.25	3.00
R23 Chad Gable	.75	2.00
R24 Jinder Mahal	1.00	2.50
R25 Kevin Owens	2.00	5.00
R26 Konnor	.75	2.00
R27 Maria Kanellis	2.00	5.00
R28 Mike Kanellis	2.00	5.00
R29 Natalya	1.00	2.50
R30 Paige	2.00	5.00
R31 R-Truth	1.00	2.50
R32 Samir Singh	.75	2.00
R33 Sarah Logan	.75	2.00
R34 Sonya Deville	1.50	4.00
R35 Sunil Singh	.75	2.00
R36 The Miz	1.50	4.00
R37 Vic Joseph	.75	2.00
R38 Viktor	.75	2.00
R39 Zack Ryder	.75	2.00
R40 Maryse	1.50	4.00

2018 Topps WWE Then Now Forever Royal Rumble 2018 Mat Relics

*BRONZE/199: .5X TO 1.2X BASIC MEM
*BLUE/99: .6X TO 1.5X BASIC MEM
*SILVER/25: .75X TO 2X BASIC MEM
*GOLD/10: UNPRICED DUE TO SCARCITY
*RED/1: UNPRICED DUE TO SCARCITY

MRRRAA Andrade Cien Almas	2.00	5.00
MRRRAC Adam Cole	4.00	10.00
MRRRAJ AJ Styles	6.00	15.00
MRRRAS Asuka	4.00	10.00
MRRRBE Big E	2.00	5.00
MRRRBS Braun Strowman	3.00	8.00
MRRRCE Cesaro	2.50	6.00
MRRRDZ Dolph Ziggler	2.50	6.00
MRRREL Elias	3.00	8.00
MRRRFB Finn Balor	5.00	12.00
MRRRJC John Cena	6.00	15.00
MRRRJJ Jason Jordan	2.50	6.00
MRRRJM Jinder Mahal	2.00	5.00
MRRRKK Kofi Kingston	2.50	6.00
MRRRKN Kane	2.50	6.00
MRRRKO Kevin Owens	2.00	5.00
MRRRMH Woken Matt Hardy	2.50	6.00
MRRRNB Nikki Bella	5.00	12.00
MRRRRO Randy Orton	4.00	10.00
MRRRRR Roman Reigns	4.00	10.00
MRRRRS Rusev	2.50	6.00
MRRRSH Sheamus	3.00	8.00
MRRRSN Shinsuke Nakamura	3.00	8.00
MRRRSR Seth Rollins	4.00	10.00
MRRRSZ Sami Zayn	2.50	6.00
MRRRTM The Miz	2.50	6.00
MRRRXW Xavier Woods	2.50	6.00

2018 Topps WWE Then Now Forever Shirt Relics

*BLUE/99: .5X TO 1.2X BASIC MEM
*SILVER/25: .75X TO 2X BASIC MEM
*GOLD/10: UNPRICED DUE TO SCARCITY
*RED/1: UNPRICED DUE TO SCARCITY

SRAB Alexa Bliss	8.00	20.00
SRAK Akam		
SRCG Chad Gable	1.50	4.00
SRCR Carmella	3.00	8.00
SRDZ Dolph Ziggler	1.50	4.00
SRJC John Cena	4.00	10.00
SRJJ Jason Jordan	2.00	5.00
SRKA Karl Anderson		
SRLG Luke Gallows		
SRNA Naomi		
SRRZ Rezar		
SRSR Seth Rollins		

2018 Topps WWE Then Now Forever Triple Autographs

STATED PRINT RUN 10 SER.#'d SETS
UNPRICED DUE TO SCARCITY

TAABS Paige/Rose/Deville
TACLB Styles/Gallows/Anderson
TATRS Riott/Morgan/Logan
TATWW O'Neil/Crews/Brooke

2018 Topps WWE Then Now Forever Promo

NYCC2 Alexa Bliss NYCC	4.00	10.00

2016 Topps WWE Then Now Forever Stickers

1 WWE Logo FOIL	.20	.50
2 Raw Logo	.20	.50
3 Smackdown Logo	.20	.50
4 NXT Logo	.20	.50
5 WWE Legends Logo	.20	.50
6 Brock Lesnar FOIL	.60	1.50
7 Brock Lesnar	.60	1.50
8 Brock Lesnar	.60	1.50
9 Brock Lesnar	.60	1.50
10 Brock Lesnar	.60	1.50
11 Neville	.30	.75
12 Neville	.30	.75
13 Neville	.30	.75
14 Neville	.30	.75
15 Neville	.30	.75
16 The New Day FOIL	.30	.75
17 The New Day	.30	.75
18 The New Day	.30	.75
19 The New Day	.30	.75
20 The New Day	.30	.75
21 Dudley Boyz	.12	.30
22 Dudley Boyz	.12	.30
23 D-Von Dudley	.20	.50
24 Bubba Ray Dudley	.25	.60
25 Dudley Boyz	.12	.30
26 Finn Balor FOIL	.40	1.00
27 Finn Balor	.40	1.00
28 Finn Balor	.40	1.00
29 Finn Balor	.40	1.00
30 Finn Balor	.40	1.00
31 Samoa Joe	.30	.75
32 Samoa Joe	.30	.75
33 Samoa Joe	.30	.75
34 Samoa Joe	.30	.75
35 Samoa Joe	.30	.75
36 Apollo Crews	.12	.30
37 Apollo Crews	.12	.30
38 Apollo Crews	.12	.30
39 Apollo Crews	.12	.30

40	Apollo Crews	.12	.30
41	Baron Corbin	.15	.40
42	Baron Corbin	.15	.40
43	Baron Corbin	.15	.40
44	Baron Corbin	.15	.40
45	Baron Corbin	.15	.40
46	John Cena FOIL	.60	1.50
47	John Cena	.60	1.50
48	John Cena	.60	1.50
49	John Cena	.60	1.50
50	John Cena	.60	1.50
51	Seth Rollins	.20	.50
52	Seth Rollins	.20	.50
53	Seth Rollins	.20	.50
54	Seth Rollins	.20	.50
55	Seth Rollins	.20	.50
56	Roman Reigns FOIL	.40	1.00
57	Roman Reigns	.40	1.00
58	Roman Reigns	.40	1.00
59	Roman Reigns	.40	1.00
60	Roman Reigns	.40	1.00
61	Dean Ambrose FOIL	.40	1.00
62	Dean Ambrose	.40	1.00
63	Dean Ambrose	.40	1.00
64	Dean Ambrose	.40	1.00
65	Dean Ambrose	.40	1.00
66	The Wyatt Family FOIL	.50	1.25
67	Bray Wyatt	.50	1.25
68	Braun Strowman	.15	.40
69	Luke Harper	.12	.30
70	Erick Rowan	.12	.30
71	Kalisto FOIL	.30	.75
72	Kalisto	.30	.75
73	Kalisto	.30	.75
74	Kalisto	.30	.75
75	Kalisto	.30	.75
76	Bret Hart FOIL	.30	.75
77	Bret Hart	.30	.75
78	Bret Hart	.30	.75
79	Bret Hart	.30	.75
80	Bret Hart	.30	.75
81	Edge FOIL	.30	.75
82	Edge	.30	.75
83	Edge	.30	.75
84	Edge	.30	.75
85	Edge	.30	.75
86	Sting	.30	.75
87	Sting	.30	.75
88	Sting	.30	.75
89	Sting	.30	.75
90	Sting	.30	.75
91	Shawn Michaels FOIL	.50	1.25
92	Shawn Michaels	.50	1.25
93	Shawn Michaels	.50	1.25
94	Shawn Michaels	.50	1.25
95	Shawn Michaels	.50	1.25
96	Charlotte FOIL	.40	1.00
97	Alicia Fox	.20	.50
98	Becky Lynch	.40	1.00
99	Brie Bella	.25	.60
100	Lana	.50	1.25
101	Nikki Bella FOIL	.40	1.00
102	Natalya	.20	.50
103	Paige	.40	1.00
104	Sasha Banks	.40	1.00
105	Summer Rae	.30	.75
106	Naomi	.20	.50
107	Bayley FOIL	.30	.75
108	Alexa Bliss	.60	1.50
109	Asuka	.50	1.25
110	Billie Kay	.30	.75
111	Carmella	.30	.75
112	Eva Marie FOIL	.25	.60
113	Dana Brooke	.30	.75
114	Emma	.25	.60
115	Nia Jax	.20	.50
116	Peyton Royce	.30	.75
117	Dasha Fuentes	.12	.30
118	Randy Orton FOIL	.30	.75
119	Randy Orton	.30	.75
120	Randy Orton	.30	.75
121	Randy Orton	.30	.75
122	Randy Orton	.30	.75
123	Daniel Bryan FOIL	.50	1.25
124	Daniel Bryan	.50	1.25
125	Daniel Bryan	.50	1.25
126	Daniel Bryan	.50	1.25
127	Daniel Bryan	.50	1.25
128	Ryback FOIL	.15	.40
129	Ryback	.15	.40
130	Ryback	.15	.40
131	Ryback	.15	.40
132	Ryback	.15	.40
133	Dolph Ziggler FOIL	.15	.40
134	Dolph Ziggler	.15	.40
135	Dolph Ziggler	.15	.40
136	Dolph Ziggler	.15	.40
137	Dolph Ziggler	.15	.40
138	Chris Jericho	.30	.75
139	Shawn Michaels	.50	1.25
140	Steve Austin/Beer Truck	.60	1.50
141	Samoa Joe	.30	.75
142	no info		
143	Randy Orton	.30	.75
144	Bayley/Sasha Banks	.40	1.00
145	Bray Wyatt	.50	1.25
146	no info		
147	The Rock	.60	1.50
148	Ric Flair	.50	1.25
149	Daniel Bryan	.50	1.25
150	Brock Lesnar	.60	1.50
151	Kevin Owens	.30	.75
152	Finn Balor	.40	1.00
153	Bret Hart	.30	.75
154	The Rock/John Cena	.60	1.50
155	The Bellas	.40	1.00
156	Seth Rollins		
157	no info		
158	Ultimate Warrior	.30	.75
159	Roman Reigns	.40	1.00
160	League of Nations FOIL	.30	.75
161	Alberto Del Rio	.20	.50
162	Sheamus	.30	.75
163	Wade Barrett	.20	
164	Rusev	.30	.75
165	Kane FOIL	.20	.50
166	Kane	.20	.50
167	Kane	.20	.50
168	Kane	.20	.50
169	Kane	.20	.50
170	Kevin Owens FOIL	.30	.75
171	Kevin Owens	.30	.75
172	Kevin Owens	.30	.75
173	Kevin Owens	.30	.75
174	Kevin Owens	.30	.75
175	Chris Jericho FOIL	.30	.75
176	Chris Jericho	.30	.75
177	Chris Jericho	.30	.75
178	Chris Jericho	.30	.75
179	Chris Jericho	.30	.75
180	Dash/Dawson	.15	.40
181	Dash/Dawson	.15	.40
182	Dash/Dawson	.15	.40
183	Dash/Dawson	.15	.40
184	Dash/Dawson	.15	.40
185	Blake/Murphy FOIL	.12	.30
186	Murphy	.12	.30
187	Blake	.12	.30
188	Alexa Bliss/Murphy/Blake	.60	1.50
189	Blake	.12	.30
190	Enzo Amore	.25	.60
191	Enzo Amore	.25	.60
192	Enzo Amore	.25	.60
193	Enzo Amore	.25	.60
194	Enzo Amore	.25	.60
195	Colin Cassady FOIL	.25	.60
196	Colin Cassady	.25	.60
197	Colin Cassady	.25	.60
198	Colin Cassady	.25	.60
199	Colin Cassady	.25	.60
200	Eddie Guerrero FOIL	.30	.75
201	Eddie Guerrero	.30	.75
202	Eddie Guerrero	.30	.75
203	Eddie Guerrero	.30	.75
204	Eddie Guerrero	.30	.75
205	Stone Cold Steve Austin FOIL	.60	1.50
206	Stone Cold Steve Austin	.60	1.50
207	Stone Cold Steve Austin	.60	1.50
208	Stone Cold Steve Austin	.60	1.50
209	Stone Cold Steve Austin	.60	1.50
210	Razor Ramon	.30	.75
211	Razor Ramon	.30	.75
212	Razor Ramon	.30	.75
213	Razor Ramon	.30	.75
214	Razor Ramon	.30	.75
215	Ultimate Warrior FOIL	.30	.75
216	Ultimate Warrior	.30	.75
217	Ultimate Warrior	.30	.75
218	Ultimate Warrior	.30	.75
219	Ultimate Warrior	.30	.75
220	The Usos FOIL	.12	.30
221	The Usos	.12	.30
222	The Usos	.12	.30
223	The Usos	.12	.30
224	The Usos	.12	.30
225	Cesaro	.25	.60
226	Cesaro	.25	.60
227	Cesaro	.25	.60
228	Cesaro	.25	.60
229	Cesaro	.25	.60
230	The Rock FOIL	.60	1.50
231	The Rock	.60	1.50
232	The Rock	.60	1.50
233	The Rock/John Cena	.60	1.50
234	The Rock	.60	1.50
235	Undertaker FOIL	.50	1.25
236	Undertaker	.50	1.25
237	Undertaker	.50	1.25
238	Undertaker	.50	1.25
239	Undertaker	.50	1.25
240	Brock Lesnar	.60	1.50
241	Kalisto	.30	.75
242	Brock Lesnar/Undertaker	.60	1.50
243	Sting	.30	.75
244	Seth Rollins	.20	.50

2020-21 Topps WWE This Month in History

1 Jeff Hardy/95*
2 Evolution/85*
3 Boogeyman/85*
4 Trish Stratus/188*
5 Wade Barrett/78*
6 Sgt. Slaughter/89*
7 Eddie Guerrero/122*
8 Daniel Bryan/102*
9 Andre the Giant/282*
10 Mr. T/269*
11 Bret Hit Man Hart/187*
12 Road Dogg/130*
13 Mankind/147*
14 Shelton Benjamin/70*
15 Asuka/110*
16 Rob Van Dam/103*
17 Hulk Hogan/175*
18 Scott Hall/96*
19 Honky Tonk Man/
20 Yokozuna/
21 Diamond Dallas Page/
22 Sherri Martel/
23 Goldberg/
24 Undertaker/
25 Ultimate Warrior/
26 Macho Man & Elizabeth/
27 British Bulldog/
28 Stone Cold Steve Austin/
29 Shawn Michaels/
30 Trish Stratus/
31 Bayley/
32 Batista/
33 Alundra Blayze/

2020 Topps WWE 3:16 Day

COMPLETE SET (6) 15.00 40.00
STATED PRINT RUN 137 SETS

1	Stone Cold Steve Austin	4.00	10.00
2	Stone Cold Steve Austin	4.00	10.00
3	Stone Cold Steve Austin	4.00	10.00
4	Stone Cold Steve Austin	4.00	10.00
5	Stone Cold Steve Austin	4.00	10.00
6	Stone Cold Steve Austin	6.00	15.00

2019 Topps WWE Transcendent

*BLUE/15: UNPRICED DUE TO SCARCITY
*PURPLE/10: UNPRICED DUE TO SCARCITY
*BLACK/5: UNPRICED DUE TO SCARCITY
*GOLD/1: UNPRICED DUE TO SCARCITY
*RED/1: UNPRICED DUE TO SCARCITY
STATED PRINT RUN 25 SER.#'d SETS

AAB	Alexa Bliss	150.00	300.00
AAC	Adam Cole	50.00	100.00
AAJ	AJ Styles	75.00	150.00
AAL	Aleister Black	50.00	100.00
AAS	Asuka	100.00	200.00
ABB	Brie Bella	30.00	75.00
ABE	Becky Lynch	75.00	150.00
ABH	Bret Hit Man Hart	60.00	120.00
ABK	Billie Kay	30.00	75.00
ABL	Brock Lesnar	50.00	100.00
ABO	Bobby Lashley	25.00	60.00

ABR Bobby Roode	20.00	50.00
ABS Braun Strowman	30.00	75.00
ABY Bayley	50.00	100.00
ACA Carmella	30.00	75.00
ACF Charlotte Flair	100.00	200.00
ACJ Chris Jericho	60.00	120.00
ADA Dean Ambrose	30.00	75.00
ADB Daniel Bryan	50.00	100.00
AEL Elias	15.00	40.00
AFB Finn Balor	20.00	50.00
AJC John Cena	100.00	200.00
AJG Johnny Gargano	30.00	75.00
AKO Kevin Owens	15.00	40.00
ALL Lex Luger	25.00	60.00
ALV Liv Morgan	75.00	150.00
AMA Maryse	20.00	50.00
AMJ Mickie James	30.00	75.00
AMM Mr. McMahon	500.00	1000.00
AMR Mandy Rose	60.00	120.00
ANA Naomi	15.00	40.00
ANB Nikki Bella	50.00	100.00
ANT Natalya	25.00	60.00
APG Paige	100.00	200.00
APR Peyton Royce	75.00	150.00
ARD Ricky The Dragon Steamboat	20.00	50.00
ARO Randy Orton	30.00	75.00
ASA Stone Cold Steve Austin	225.00	450.00
ASB Sasha Banks	75.00	150.00
ASH Shane McMahon	200.00	400.00
ASJ Samoa Joe	15.00	40.00
ASM Stephanie McMahon	100.00	200.00
ASN Shinsuke Nakamura	25.00	60.00
ASR Seth Rollins	20.00	50.00
AST Sting	60.00	120.00
ASW Shawn Michaels	100.00	200.00
ATH Triple H	150.00	300.00
ATS Trish Stratus	75.00	150.00
AUN Undertaker	175.00	350.00
ARRR Ronda Rousey	200.00	400.00

2019 Topps WWE Transcendent Autographed Championship Titles

NNO Dean Ambrose
NNO Jeff Hardy
NNO Randy Orton
NNO Rey Mysterio
NNO Seth Rollins

2019 Topps WWE Transcendent Autographed Kiss

*BLACK/5: UNPRICED DUE TO SCARCITY
*GOLD/1: UNPRICED DUE TO SCARCITY
*RED/1: UNPRICED DUE TO SCARCITY
STATED PRINT RUN 10 SER.#'d SETS
UNPRICED DUE TO SCARCITY

KAS Asuka
KBB Brie Bella
KNB Nikki Bella
KPR Peyton Royce

2019 Topps WWE Transcendent Autographed Sketches

STATED PRINT RUN 1 SER.#'d SET
UNPRICED DUE TO SCARCITY

1 Adam Cole
2 AJ Styles
3 Aleister Black
4 Alexa Bliss
5 Asuka
6 Bayley
7 Becky Lynch
8 Billie Kay
9 Bobby Lashley
10 Bobby Roode
11 Braun Strowman
12 Bray Wyatt
13 Bret Hart
14 Brie Bella
15 Charlotte Flair
16 Daniel Bryan
17 Dean Ambrose
18 Dolph Ziggler
19 Drew McIntyre
20 Elias
21 Ember Moon
22 Finn Balor
23 Jeff Hardy
24 John Cena
25 Johnny Gargano
26 Kairi Sane
27 Kane
28 Kevin Owens
29 Kofi Kingston
30 Matt Hardy
31 Naomi
32 Nikki Bella
33 Randy Orton
34 Ric Flair
35 Ricochet
36 Roman Reigns
37 Ronda Rousey
38 Samoa Joe
39 Sasha Banks
40 Seth Rollins
41 Shawn Michaels
42 Shinsuke Nakamura
43 Sting
44 Stone Cold Steve Austin
45 The Miz
46 The Rock
47 Tommaso Ciampa
48 Triple H
49 Trish Stratus
50 Undertaker

2019 Topps WWE Transcendent Oversized Tribute Cut Signatures

STATED PRINT RUN 1 SER.#'d SET
UNPRICED DUE TO SCARCITY

CAG Andre The Giant
CBH Bobby Heenan
CBS Bruno Sammartino
CCH Mr. Perfect
CDR Dusty Rhodes
CEG Eddie Guerrero
CFB Freddie Blassie
CGM Gorilla Monsoon
CGS George Steele
CJN Jim The Anvil Neidhart
CJS Chief Jay Strongbow
CKV Kerry Von Erich
CME Miss Elizabeth
CMY Mae Young
CPB Paul Bearer
CRR Ravishing Rick Rude
CRS Macho Man Randy Savage
CSM Sherri Martel
CUG Umaga
CUM Ultimate Warrior
CYK Yokozuna
CBBB Bam Bam Bigelow
CBJS Big John Studd
CBVV Vader
CJYD Junkyard Dog
CRRR Rowdy Roddy Piper

2019 Topps WWE Transcendent Oversized Tribute Dual Cut Signatures

STATED PRINT RUN 1 SER.#'d SET
UNPRICED DUE TO SCARCITY

DCAB Andre the Giant/B.Heenan
DCBC P. Bearer/Vader
DCDS G.Steele/Junkyard Dog
DCEM Elizabeth/S.Martel
DCES G.Steele/Elizabeth
DCHH Mr. Perfect/B.Heenan
DCPE K.Von Erich/R.Piper
DCPG E.Guerrero/R.Piper
DCPW Warrior/R.Piper
DCRE D.Rhodes/Elizabeth
DCRS R.Savage/S.Martel
DCSB G.Steele/F.Blassie
DCSE R.Savage/Elizabeth
DCSH B.Heenan/J.Studd
DCSN J.Neidhart/R.Savage
DCSR B.Sammartino/R.Piper
DCSS B.Sammartino/J.Strongbow
DCSW Warrior/R.Savage
DCVB B.Bigelow/Vader
DCVM Vader/R.Savage
DCYU Umaga/Yokozuna
DCYV Vader/Yokozuna
DCNW01 C.Hennig/D.Rhodes
DCNW02 R.Savage/C.Hennig

2019 Topps WWE Transcendent VIP Party Autographs

B1 Big Show	15.00	40.00
B2 Big Show	15.00	40.00
F1 Ric Flair	75.00	150.00
F2 Ric Flair	75.00	150.00
S1 Sting	50.00	100.00
S2 Sting	50.00	100.00

2019 Topps WWE Transcendent VIP Party Dual Autograph

NNO Stephanie McMahon/Triple H	225.00	450.00

2020 Topps WWE Transcendent

COMPLETE SET (50)	500.00	750.00
STATED PRINT RUN 50 SER.#'d SETS		
1 Adam Cole	15.00	40.00
2 Andre the Giant	30.00	75.00
3 Angelo Dawkins	6.00	15.00
4 Bianca Belair	15.00	40.00
5 Big Show	8.00	20.00
6 Bruno Sammartino	15.00	40.00
7 Cain Velasquez	6.00	15.00
8 Cameron Grimes RC	6.00	15.00
9 Candice LeRae	20.00	50.00
10 Chyna	15.00	40.00
11 Damian Priest	6.00	15.00
12 Dusty Rhodes	12.00	30.00
13 Eddie Guerrero	15.00	40.00
14 Harley Race	10.00	25.00
15 Hulk Hogan	20.00	50.00
16 Io Shirai	10.00	25.00
17 Jim The Anvil Neidhart	8.00	20.00
18 John Cena	25.00	60.00
19 John Morrison	6.00	15.00
20 Johnny Gargano	12.00	30.00
21 Keith Lee	6.00	15.00
22 Kevin Nash	10.00	25.00
23 Lana	15.00	40.00
24 Lio Rush	6.00	15.00
25 Macho Man Randy Savage	20.00	50.00
26 Mandy Rose	30.00	80.00
27 Mr. Perfect Curt Hennig	10.00	25.00
28 Montez Ford	6.00	15.00
29 Mustafa Ali	10.00	25.00
30 Naomi	12.00	30.00
31 Natalya	10.00	25.00
32 Nikki Cross	12.00	30.00
33 Paul Heyman	6.00	15.00
34 Ravishing Rick Rude	8.00	20.00
35 Renee Young	8.00	20.00
36 Rhea Ripley	25.00	60.00
37 Robert Roode	6.00	15.00
38 Roderick Strong	12.00	30.00
39 Rowdy Roddy Piper	15.00	40.00
40 Rusev	8.00	20.00
41 Scott Hall	10.00	25.00
42 Shorty G	6.00	15.00
43 Sting	20.00	50.00
44 Sonya Deville	15.00	40.00
45 The British Bulldog	10.00	25.00
46 The Rock	30.00	80.00
47 Ultimate Warrior	30.00	75.00
48 Undertaker	25.00	60.00
49 Vader	10.00	25.00
50 Yokozuna	10.00	25.00

2020 Topps WWE Transcendent Autographed Replica Championship Side Plates

UNPRICED DUE TO SCARCITY

NNO AJ Styles
NNO Becky Lynch
NNO Charlotte Flair
NNO Daniel Bryan
NNO Kofi Kingston
NNO Randy Orton
NNO Roman Reigns
NNO Seth Rollins
NNO Triple H

2020 Topps WWE Transcendent Autographs

*GREEN/15: UNPRICED DUE TO SCARCITY
*PURPLE/10: UNPRICED DUE TO SCARCITY
*BLUE/5: UNPRICED DUE TO SCARCITY
*RED/1: UNPRICED DUE TO SCARCITY

AAA Andrade	25.00	60.00
AAB Aleister Black	30.00	75.00
AAJ AJ Styles	60.00	120.00
AAK Asuka	100.00	200.00
AAX Alexa Bliss	150.00	300.00

ABC King Corbin 25.00 60.00
ABD Diesel 30.00 75.00
ABH Bret Hit Man Hart 75.00 150.00
ABI Brock Lesnar 125.00 250.00
ABL Becky Lynch 75.00 150.00
ABR Braun Strowman 50.00 100.00
ABT Booker T 30.00 75.00
ABW The Fiend Bray Wyatt 100.00 200.00
ABY Bayley 50.00 100.00
ACF Charlotte Flair 100.00 200.00
ACW Sheamus 25.00 60.00
ADB Daniel Bryan 50.00 100.00
ADR Drew McIntyre 60.00 120.00
AFB Finn Balor 50.00 100.00
AGB Goldberg 75.00 150.00
AHH Hulk Hogan 250.00 500.00
AJH Jeff Hardy 60.00 120.00
AKA Kurt Angle 50.00 100.00
AKK Kofi Kingston 60.00 120.00
AKN Kane 50.00 100.00
AKO Kevin Owens 50.00 100.00
AKS Kairi Sane 75.00 150.00
ALE Lacey Evans 60.00 120.00
ALT Lita 75.00 150.00
AMF Mick Foley 30.00 75.00
AMR Matt Riddle 60.00 120.00
AQS Shayna Baszler 50.00 100.00
ARC Ricochet 25.00 60.00
ARO Randy Orton 60.00 120.00
ARR Roman Reigns 75.00 150.00
ASB Sasha Banks 125.00 250.00
ASC Stone Cold Steve Austin 350.00 700.00
ASM Shane McMahon 125.00 250.00
ASN Shinsuke Nakamura 30.00 75.00
ASR Seth Rollins 50.00 100.00
AST Stephanie McMahon 250.00 400.00
ATC Tommaso Ciampa 50.00 100.00
ATM The Miz 30.00 75.00
AUT Undertaker 300.00 500.00
AZV Zelina Vega 60.00 120.00
AHBK Shawn Michaels 125.00 250.00
AHHH Triple H 250.00 400.00
AVKM Mr. McMahon 600.00 1000.00

2020 Topps WWE Transcendent Bat Relic Autographs

RCST Sting 250.00 400.00

2020 Topps WWE Transcendent Dual Autographs

*GREEN/15: UNPRICED DUE TO SCARCITY
*PURPLE/10: UNPRICED DUE TO SCARCITY
*BLUE/5: UNPRICED DUE TO SCARCITY
*RED/1: UNPRICED DUE TO SCARCITY
STATED PRINT RUN 25 SER.#'d SETS

DAVR Erik/Ivar 75.00 150.00
DAUSO Jimmy Uso/Jey Uso 75.00 150.00

2020 Topps WWE Transcendent Image Variation Autographs

STATED PRINT RUN 1 SER.#'d SET
UNPRICED DUE TO SCARCITY

AIVAA Andrade
AIVAB Aleister Black
AIVAJ AJ Styles
AIVAK Asuka
AIVAX Alexa Bliss
AIVBC King Corbin
AIVBD Diesel
AIVBH Bret Hit Man Hart
AIVBI Brock Lesnar
AIVBL Becky Lynch
AIVBR Braun Strowman
AIVBT Booker T
AIVBW Bray Wyatt
AIVBY Bayley
AIVCF Charlotte Flair
AIVCW Sheamus
AIVDB Daniel Bryan
AIVDR Drew McIntyre
AIVFB Finn Balor
AIVGB Goldberg
AIVHH Hulk Hogan
AIVJH Jeff Hardy
AIVKA Kurt Angle
AIVKK Kofi Kingston
AIVKN Kane
AIVKO Kevin Owens
AIVKS Kairi Sane
AIVLE Lacey Evans
AIVLT Lita
AIVMF Mick Foley
AIVMR Matt Riddle
AIVQS Shayna Baszler
AIVRC Ricochet
AIVRO Randy Orton
AIVRR Roman Reigns
AIVSB Sasha Banks
AIVSC Stone Cold Steve Austin
AIVSJ Samoa Joe
AIVSM Shane McMahon
AIVSN Shinsuke Nakamura
AIVSR Seth Rollins
AIVST Stephanie McMahon
AIVTC Tommaso Ciampa
AIVTM The Miz
AIVUT Undertaker
AIVZV Zelina Vega
AIVHBK Shawn Michaels
AIVHHH Triple H
AIVVKM Mr. McMahon

2020 Topps WWE Transcendent Image Variation Dual Autographs

STATED PRINT RUN 1 SER.#'d SET
UNPRICED DUE TO SCARCITY

DAIVVR Erik/Ivar
DAIVUSO Jimmy Uso/Jey Uso

2020 Topps WWE Transcendent John Cena Superstar Tribute

COMPLETE SET (50) 250.00 500.00

JCRP1 John Cena 10.00 25.00
JCRP2 John Cena 10.00 25.00
JCRP3 John Cena 10.00 25.00
JCRP4 John Cena 10.00 25.00
JCRP5 John Cena 10.00 25.00
JCRP6 John Cena 10.00 25.00
JCRP7 John Cena 10.00 25.00
JCRP8 John Cena 10.00 25.00
JCRP9 John Cena 10.00 25.00
JCRP10 John Cena 10.00 25.00
JCRP11 John Cena 10.00 25.00
JCRP12 John Cena 10.00 25.00
JCRP13 John Cena 10.00 25.00
JCRP14 John Cena 10.00 25.00
JCRP15 John Cena 10.00 25.00
JCRP16 John Cena 10.00 25.00
JCRP17 John Cena 10.00 25.00
JCRP18 John Cena 10.00 25.00
JCRP19 John Cena 10.00 25.00
JCRP20 John Cena 10.00 25.00
JCRP21 John Cena 10.00 25.00
JCRP22 John Cena 10.00 25.00
JCRP23 John Cena 10.00 25.00
JCRP24 John Cena 10.00 25.00
JCRP25 John Cena 10.00 25.00
JCRP26 John Cena 10.00 25.00
JCRP27 John Cena 10.00 25.00
JCRP28 John Cena 10.00 25.00
JCRP29 John Cena 10.00 25.00
JCRP30 John Cena 10.00 25.00
JCRP31 John Cena 10.00 25.00
JCRP32 John Cena 10.00 25.00
JCRP33 John Cena 10.00 25.00
JCRP34 John Cena 10.00 25.00
JCRP35 John Cena 10.00 25.00
JCRP36 John Cena 10.00 25.00
JCRP37 John Cena 10.00 25.00
JCRP38 John Cena 10.00 25.00
JCRP39 John Cena 10.00 25.00
JCRP40 John Cena 10.00 25.00
JCRP41 John Cena 10.00 25.00
JCRP42 John Cena 10.00 25.00
JCRP43 John Cena 10.00 25.00
JCRP44 John Cena 10.00 25.00
JCRP45 John Cena 10.00 25.00
JCRP46 John Cena 10.00 25.00
JCRP47 John Cena 10.00 25.00
JCRP48 John Cena 10.00 25.00
JCRP49 John Cena 10.00 25.00
JCRP50 John Cena 10.00 25.00

2020 Topps WWE Transcendent John Cena Superstar Tribute Autographs

STATED PRINT RUN 1 SER.#'d SET
UNPRICED DUE TO SCARCITY

2020 Topps WWE Transcendent Sketches

STATED PRINT RUN 1 SER.#'d SET
UNPRICED DUE TO SCARCITY
ART BY DAN BERGREN

NNO AJ Styles
NNO Alexa Bliss
NNO Andrade
NNO Angel Garza
NNO Asuka
NNO Batista
NNO Bayley
NNO Becky Lynch
NNO Braun Strowman
NNO The Fiend Bray Wyatt
NNO Bret Hit Man Hart
NNO Brock Lesnar
NNO Charlotte Flair
NNO Eddie Guerrero
NNO Ember Moon
NNO Finn Balor
NNO Goldberg
NNO Hulk Hogan
NNO Jeff Hardy
NNO John Cena
NNO Kairi Sane
NNO Kane
NNO Keith Lee
NNO Kevin Owens
NNO Kofi Kingston
NNO Lacey Evans
NNO Lita
NNO Matt Riddle
NNO Mustafa Ali
NNO Pete Dunne
NNO Randy Orton
NNO Macho Man Randy Savage
NNO Ricochet
NNO Rowdy Roddy Piper
NNO Roman Reigns
NNO Ronda Rousey
NNO Sami Zayn
NNO Samoa Joe
NNO Sasha Banks
NNO Seth Rollins
NNO Shawn Michaels
NNO Shayna Baszler
NNO Shinsuke Nakamura
NNO Sting
NNO Stone Cold Steve Austin
NNO The Miz
NNO The Rock
NNO Triple H
NNO Ultimate Warrior
NNO Undertaker

2020 Topps WWE Transcendent VIP Party Black and White Pattern 1

*BLACK/WHITE 2: UNPRICED DUE TO SCARCITY
*BLACK/WHITE 3: UNPRICED DUE TO SCARCITY
*BLACK/WHITE 4: UNPRICED DUE TO SCARCITY
*BLACK/WHITE 5: UNPRICED DUE TO SCARCITY
*AQUA/PURPLE 1: UNPRICED DUE TO SCARCITY
*AQUA/PURPLE 2: UNPRICED DUE TO SCARCITY
*AQUA/PURPLE 3: UNPRICED DUE TO SCARCITY
*AQUA/PURPLE 4: UNPRICED DUE TO SCARCITY
*AQUA/PURPLE 5: UNPRICED DUE TO SCARCITY
*GREEN/YELLOW 1: UNPRICED DUE TO SCARCITY
*GREEN/YELLOW 2: UNPRICED DUE TO SCARCITY
*GREEN/YELLOW 3: UNPRICED DUE TO SCARCITY
*GREEN/YELLOW 4: UNPRICED DUE TO SCARCITY
*GREEN/YELLOW 5: UNPRICED DUE TO SCARCITY
*PURPLE/RED 1: UNPRICED DUE TO SCARCITY
*PURPLE/RED 2: UNPRICED DUE TO SCARCITY
*PURPLE/RED 3: UNPRICED DUE TO SCARCITY
*PURPLE/RED 4: UNPRICED DUE TO SCARCITY
*PURPLE/RED 5: UNPRICED DUE TO SCARCITY
*RED/YELLOW 1: UNPRICED DUE TO SCARCITY
*RED/YELLOW 2: UNPRICED DUE TO SCARCITY
*RED/YELLOW 3: UNPRICED DUE TO SCARCITY
*RED/YELLOW 4: UNPRICED DUE TO SCARCITY
*RED/YELLOW 5: UNPRICED DUE TO SCARCITY
STATED PRINT RUN 1 SER.#'d SET
UNPRICED DUE TO SCARCITY
SUMMERSLAM VIP EXCLUSIVE
ALL CARDS ARE 1/1

1 AJ Styles
2 Akira Tozawa
3 Alexa Bliss
4 Apollo Crews

5 Asuka
6 Batista
7 Bayley
8 Bianca Belair
9 Bobby Lashley
10 ìThe Fiendî Bray Wyatt
11 Carmella
12 Cesaro
13 Dakota Kai
14 Dolph Ziggler
15 Dominik Mysterio
16 Drew McIntyre
17 Edge
18 Finn Balor
19 Hulk Hogan
20 Jey Uso
21 Jinder Mahal
22 TBD
23 Kevin Owens
24 Kofi Kingston
25 Kushida
26 MVP
27 Nia Jax
28 Omos
29 Pete Dunne
30 Randy Orton
31 Raquel Gonzalez
32 Razor Ramon
33 TBD
34 Rhea Ripley
35 Ric Flair
36 Riddle
37 Roman Reigns
38 Sami Zayn
39 Santos Escobar
40 Sasha Banks
41 Scarlett
42 Seth Rollins
43 Sgt. Slaughter
44 Shayna Baszler
45 Sheamus
46 Shotzi Blackheart
47 The Miz
48 Walter
49 Xavier Woods
50 X-Pac

2020 Topps WWE Transcendent VIP Party Autographs

*AQUA/PURPLE 1: UNPRICED DUE TO SCARCITY
*AQUA/PURPLE 2: UNPRICED DUE TO SCARCITY
*BLACK/WHITE 1: UNPRICED DUE TO SCARCITY
*BLACK/WHITE 2: UNPRICED DUE TO SCARCITY
*GREEN/YELLOW 1: UNPRICED DUE TO SCARCITY
*GREEN/YELLOW 2: UNPRICED DUE TO SCARCITY
*PURPLE/RED 1: UNPRICED DUE TO SCARCITY
*PURPLE/RED 2: UNPRICED DUE TO SCARCITY
*RED/YELLOW 1: UNPRICED DUE TO SCARCITY
*RED/YELLOW 2: UNPRICED DUE TO SCARCITY
STATED PRINT RUN 1 SER.#'d SET
UNPRICED DUE TO SCARCITY
SUMMERSLAM VIP EXCLUSIVE
ALL CARDS 1/1

ABE Big E
ABP Beth Phoenix
AEM Ember Moon
AJC John Cena
AJL Jerry ìThe Kingî Lawler
AJN Jim ìThe Anvilî Neidhart
AJR Jaxson Ryker
AMK Mankind
ANN Natalya
ATA Tamina
ATR Trish Stratus
ATS Toni Storm
AJBL JBL
AKOR Kyle OìReilly

2020 Topps WWE Transcendent VIP Party On-Card Autographs

STATED PRINT RUN 25 SER.#'d SETS
SUMMERSLAM VIP EXCLUSIVE

VIPDM1 Drew McIntyre	30.00	75.00
VIPDM2 Drew McIntyre	30.00	75.00
VIPJH1 Jeff Hardy		
VIPJH2 Jeff Hardy		
VIPNC1 Nikki Ash	50.00	100.00
VIPNC2 Nikki Ash	50.00	100.00
VIPRR1 Rhea Ripley		
VIPRR2 Rhea Ripley		

2021 Topps WWE Transcendent

COMPLETE SET (50)	200.00	500.00
1 Aleister Black	8.00	20.00
2 Andre the Giant	12.00	30.00
3 Apollo Crews	4.00	10.00
4 Bam Bam Bigelow	6.00	15.00
5 Beth Phoenix	6.00	15.00
6 Big Boss Man	5.00	12.00
7 Braun Strowman	8.00	20.00
8 Candice LeRae	12.00	30.00
9 Cedric Alexander	3.00	8.00
10 Diamond Dallas Page	5.00	12.00
11 Dusty Rhodes	10.00	25.00
12 Earthquake	8.00	20.00
13 Eddie Guerrero	15.00	40.00
14 Faarooq	5.00	12.00
15 Finlay	3.00	8.00
16 Finn Balor	8.00	20.00
17 George The Animal Steele	6.00	15.00
18 Gorilla Monsoon	6.00	15.00
19 Indi Hartwell RC	10.00	25.00
20 Jerry The King Lawler	5.00	12.00
21 Jimmy Hart	4.00	10.00
22 Junkyard Dog	3.00	8.00
23 Kay Lee Ray	8.00	20.00
24 Kevin Owens	6.00	15.00
25 King Corbin	3.00	8.00
26 Lacey Evans	8.00	20.00
27 Mae Young	5.00	12.00
28 Macho King Randy Savage	20.00	50.00
29 Marlena	5.00	12.00
30 Michael Cole	3.00	8.00
31 Mr. Perfect	10.00	25.00
32 Naomi	4.00	10.00
33 Natalya	5.00	12.00
34 Nikolai Volkoff	3.00	8.00
35 Nikki Cross	6.00	15.00
36 Paul Bearer	6.00	15.00
37 Ricky The Dragon Steamboat	5.00	12.00
38 Raquel Gonzalez	8.00	20.00
39 Rob Van Dam	6.00	15.00
40 Roderick Strong	5.00	12.00
41 Rowdy Roddy Piper	8.00	20.00
42 Shayna Baszler	6.00	15.00
43 Sheamus	5.00	12.00
44 Sensational Sherri Martel	8.00	20.00
45 Shinsuke Nakamura	8.00	20.00
46 The Brian Kendrick	3.00	8.00
47 The Honky Tonk Man	3.00	8.00
48 Trent Seven	4.00	10.00
49 Tyler Bate	4.00	10.00
50 Ultimate Warrior	12.00	30.00

2021 Topps WWE Transcendent Autographed Championships

NNO AJ Styles
WWE Championship
NNO Bobby Lashley
WWE Championship
NNO Braun Strowman
SmackDown Universal Championship
NNO Drew McIntyre
WWE Championship
NNO Finn Balor
RAW Universal Championship
NNO Goldberg
RAW Universal Championship
NNO Kevin Owens
RAW Universal Championship
NNO Kofi Kingston
WWE Championship
NNO Roman Reigns
SmackDown Universal Championship
NNO Seth Rollins
RAW Universal Championship

2021 Topps WWE Transcendent Autographs

*GREEN/15: UNPRICED DUE TO SCARCITY
*PURPLE/10: UNPRICED DUE TO SCARCITY
*BLUE/5: UNPRICED DUE TO SCARCITY
*RED/1: UNPRICED DUE TO SCARCITY
*SUPERFR/1: UNPRICED DUE TO SCARCITY
STATED PRINT RUN 25 SER.#'d SETS

AAB Alexa Bliss	200.00	400.00
AAC Adam Cole	50.00	100.00
AAJ AJ Styles	25.00	60.00
AAS Asuka	100.00	200.00
ABA Bayley	30.00	75.00
ABB Bianca Belair	50.00	100.00
ABE Big E	20.00	50.00
ABH Bret "Hit Man" Hart	150.00	300.00
ABL Becky Lynch EXCH	100.00	200.00
ACF Charlotte Flair	75.00	150.00
ACS Cesaro	15.00	40.00
ADK Dakota Kai	50.00	100.00
ADP Damian Priest	15.00	40.00
ADR Drew McIntyre	25.00	60.00
AED Edge	60.00	120.00
AGB Goldberg	75.00	150.00
AIR Iron Sheik	50.00	100.00
AIS Io Shirai	75.00	150.00
AJC John Cena	150.00	300.00
AJR Jake "The Snake" Roberts	75.00	150.00
AJU Jey Uso	15.00	40.00
AKK Karrion Kross	20.00	50.00
AKL Keith Lee	15.00	40.00
AKN Kane	50.00	100.00
ALA Bobby Lashley	20.00	50.00
AMK Mankind	100.00	200.00
ANJ Nia Jax	25.00	60.00
ARM Rey Mysterio	100.00	200.00
ARO Randy Orton	50.00	100.00
ARP Rhea Ripley	60.00	120.00
ARR Roman Reigns	125.00	250.00
ASA Stone Cold Steve Austin	500.00	800.00
ASC Scarlett	60.00	120.00
ASD Sonya Deville	20.00	50.00
ASR Seth Rollins	30.00	75.00
ASS Sgt. Slaughter	50.00	100.00
AST Stephanie McMahon	150.00	300.00
ATD Million Dollar Man Ted DiBiase	30.00	75.00
ATS Toni Storm	75.00	150.00
AUT Undertaker	300.00	500.00
AVM Mr. McMahon	750.00	1500.00
AWT WALTER	15.00	40.00
AXP X-Pac	30.00	75.00
ABRO Riddle	15.00	40.00
AHBK Shawn Michaels	150.00	300.00
AHHH Triple H	200.00	400.00
AMVP MVP	15.00	40.00

2021 Topps WWE Transcendent Dual Autographs

*GREEN/15: UNPRICED DUE TO SCARCITY
*PURPLE/10: UNPRICED DUE TO SCARCITY
*BLUE/5: UNPRICED DUE TO SCARCITY
*RED/1: UNPRICED DUE TO SCARCITY
*SUPERFR/1: UNPRICED DUE TO SCARCITY
STATED PRINT RUN 25 SER.#'d SETS

TAKW The New Day	30.00	75.00
TAMM The Miz & John Morrison	25.00	60.00
TASP The Street Profits	25.00	60.00

2021 Topps WWE Transcendent Quad Autograph

*GREEN/15: UNPRICED DUE TO SCARCITY
*PURPLE/10: UNPRICED DUE TO SCARCITY
*BLUE/5: UNPRICED DUE TO SCARCITY
*RED/1: UNPRICED DUE TO SCARCITY
STATED PRINT RUN 25 SER.#'d SETS

QA4HW Becky/Sasha/Charlotte/Bayley	600.00	1000.00

2021 Topps WWE Transcendent Ric Flair Legends Tribute

COMPLETE SET (25)	125.00	300.00
STATED ODDS 1:SET PER BOX		
STATED PRINT RUN 50 SER.#'d SETS		
RF1 Ric Flair	8.00	20.00
RF2 Ric Flair	8.00	20.00
RF3 Ric Flair	8.00	20.00
RF4 Ric Flair	8.00	20.00
RF5 Ric Flair	8.00	20.00
RF6 Ric Flair	8.00	20.00
RF7 Ric Flair	8.00	20.00
RF8 Ric Flair	8.00	20.00
RF9 Ric Flair	8.00	20.00
RF10 Ric Flair	8.00	20.00
RF11 Ric Flair	8.00	20.00
RF12 Ric Flair	8.00	20.00
RF13 Ric Flair	8.00	20.00
RF14 Ric Flair	8.00	20.00
RF15 Ric Flair	8.00	20.00
RF16 Ric Flair	8.00	20.00
RF17 Ric Flair	8.00	20.00
RF18 Ric Flair	8.00	20.00
RF19 Ric Flair	8.00	20.00

RF20 Ric Flair	8.00	20.00
RF21 Ric Flair	8.00	20.00
RF22 Ric Flair	8.00	20.00
RF23 Ric Flair	8.00	20.00
RF24 Ric Flair	8.00	20.00
RF25 Ric Flair	8.00	20.00

2021 Topps WWE Transcendent The Rock Legends Tribute

COMPLETE SET (25)	200.00	500.00
STATED ODDS 1:SET PER BOX		
STATED PRINT RUN 50 SER.#'d SETS		
DJ1 The Rock	15.00	40.00
DJ2 The Rock	15.00	40.00
DJ3 The Rock	15.00	40.00
DJ4 The Rock	15.00	40.00
DJ5 The Rock	15.00	40.00
DJ6 The Rock	15.00	40.00
DJ7 The Rock	15.00	40.00
DJ8 The Rock	15.00	40.00
DJ9 The Rock	15.00	40.00
DJ10 The Rock	15.00	40.00
DJ11 The Rock	15.00	40.00
DJ12 The Rock	15.00	40.00
DJ13 The Rock	15.00	40.00
DJ14 The Rock	15.00	40.00
DJ15 The Rock	15.00	40.00
DJ16 The Rock	15.00	40.00
DJ17 The Rock	15.00	40.00
DJ18 The Rock	15.00	40.00
DJ19 The Rock	15.00	40.00
DJ20 The Rock	15.00	40.00
DJ21 The Rock	15.00	40.00
DJ22 The Rock	15.00	40.00
DJ23 The Rock	15.00	40.00
DJ24 The Rock	15.00	40.00
DJ25 The Rock	15.00	40.00

2021 Topps WWE Transcendent Sketches

UNPRICED DUE TO SCARCITY

NNO Alexa Bliss
NNO Asuka
NNO Batista
NNO Bayley
NNO Becky Lynch
NNO Booker T
NNO Braun Strowman
NNO Bray Wyatt
NNO Bret "Hit Man" Hart
NNO Charlotte Flair
NNO Daniel Bryan
NNO Drew McIntyre
NNO Eddie Guerrero
NNO Edge
NNO Finn Balor
NNO Goldberg
NNO Hulk Hogan
NNO Jeff Hardy
NNO John Cena
NNO Kane
NNO Keith Lee
NNO Kevin Owens
NNO King Corbin
NNO Macho Man Randy Savage
NNO Mick Foley
NNO Million Dollar Man Ted DiBiase
NNO Mr. Perfect
NNO Nia Jax
NNO Otis
NNO Randy Orton
NNO Razor Ramon
NNO Rey Mysterio
NNO Ric Flair
NNO Riddle
NNO Rikishi
NNO Roman Reigns
NNO Rowdy Roddy Piper
NNO Sasha Banks
NNO Sami Zayn
NNO Seth Rollins
NNO Shawn Michaels
NNO Sheamus
NNO Sgt. Slaughter
NNO Shinsuke Nakamura
NNO Stone Cold Steve Austin
NNO The New Day
NNO The Rock
NNO Ultimate Warrior
NNO Undertaker

2016 Topps WWE Triple H Tribute

COMPLETE SET (10)	12.00	30.00
TARGET EXCLUSIVES		
1 Triple H	.50	1.25
2 Triple H	.50	1.25
3 Triple H	.50	1.25
4 Triple H	.50	1.25
5 Triple H	.50	1.25
6 Triple H	1.25	3.00
7 Triple H	1.50	4.00
8 Triple H	1.25	3.00
9 Triple H	1.25	3.00
10 Triple H	1.25	3.00
11 Triple H	.50	1.25
12 Triple H	.50	1.25
13 Triple H	.50	1.25
14 Triple H	.50	1.25
15 Triple H	.50	1.25
16 Triple H	1.25	3.00
17 Triple H	1.25	3.00
18 Triple H	1.25	3.00
19 Triple H	1.25	3.00
20 Triple H	1.25	3.00
21 Triple H	.50	1.25
22 Triple H	.50	1.25
23 Triple H	.50	1.25
24 Triple H	.50	1.25
25 Triple H	.50	1.25
26 Triple H	1.25	3.00
27 Triple H	1.25	3.00
28 Triple H	1.25	3.00
29 Triple H	1.25	3.00
30 Triple H	1.25	3.00
31 Triple H	.50	1.25
32 Triple H	.50	1.25
33 Triple H	.50	1.25
34 Triple H	.50	1.25
35 Triple H	.50	1.25
36 Triple H	1.25	3.00
37 Triple H	1.25	3.00
38 Triple H	1.25	3.00
39 Triple H	1.25	3.00
40 Triple H	1.25	3.00

2020 Topps WWE Triple H 25th Anniversary

COMPLETE SET (25)	8.00	20.00
1 Triple H	.75	2.00
2 Triple H	.75	2.00
3 Triple H	.75	2.00
4 Triple H	.75	2.00
5 Triple H	.75	2.00
6 Triple H	.75	2.00
7 Triple H	.75	2.00
8 Triple H	.75	2.00
9 Triple H	.75	2.00
10 Triple H	.75	2.00
11 Triple H	.75	2.00
12 Triple H	.75	2.00
13 Triple H	.75	2.00
14 Triple H	.75	2.00
15 Triple H	.75	2.00
16 Triple H	.75	2.00
17 Triple H	.75	2.00
18 Triple H	.75	2.00
19 Triple H	.75	2.00
20 Triple H	.75	2.00
21 Triple H	.75	2.00
22 Triple H	.75	2.00
23 Triple H	.75	2.00
24 Triple H	.75	2.00
25 Triple H	.75	2.00

2020 Topps WWE Triple H 25th Anniversary Autographs

COMMON AUTO (1A-5A)	100.00	200.00
*GREEN/15: UNPRICED DUE TO SCARCITY		
*GOLD/1: UNPRICED DUE TO SCARCITY		
STATED OVERALL ODDS 1:2 W/RELICS		
STATED PRINT RUN 99 SER.#'d SETS		
1A Triple H	100.00	200.00
2A Triple H	100.00	200.00
3A Triple H	100.00	200.00
4A Triple H	100.00	200.00
5A Triple H	100.00	200.00

2020 Topps WWE Triple H 25th Anniversary Cerebral Moments

COMPLETE SET (11)	5.00	12.00
STATED PRINT RUN 260 SETS		
C1 Triple H	.75	2.00
C2 Triple H	.75	2.00
C3 Triple H	.75	2.00
C4 Triple H	.75	2.00
C5 Triple H	.75	2.00
C6 Triple H	.75	2.00
C7 Triple H	.75	2.00
C8 Triple H	.75	2.00
C9 Triple H	.75	2.00
C10 Triple H	.75	2.00
C11 Triple H	.75	2.00
C12 Triple H	.75	2.00

2020 Topps WWE Triple H 25th Anniversary Relics

COMMON MEM	30.00	75.00
STATED OVERALL ODDS 1:2 W/AUTOGRAPHS		
STATED PRINT RUN 15 SER.#'d SETS		
1R Triple H	30.00	75.00
2R Triple H	30.00	75.00
3R Triple H	30.00	75.00
4R Triple H	30.00	75.00
5R Triple H	30.00	75.00

2020 Topps WWE Triple H 25th Anniversary World Title Victories

COMPLETE SET (14)	6.00	15.00
STATED PRINT RUN 260 SETS		
T1 Triple H	.75	2.00
T2 Triple H	.75	2.00
T3 Triple H	.75	2.00
T4 Triple H	.75	2.00
T5 Triple H	.75	2.00
T6 Triple H	.75	2.00
T7 Triple H	.75	2.00
T8 Triple H	.75	2.00
T9 Triple H	.75	2.00
T10 Triple H	.75	2.00
T11 Triple H	.75	2.00
T12 Triple H	.75	2.00
T13 Triple H	.75	2.00

2008 Topps WWE Ultimate Rivals

COMPLETE SET (90)	8.00	20.00
UNOPENED BOX (24 PACKS)		
UNOPENED PACK (7 CARDS)		
1 Kane vs. Chavo Guerrero	.40	1.00
2 Batista vs. Mark Henry	.40	1.00
3 Batisita vs. The Great Khali	.40	1.00
4 Batista vs. Undertaker	.50	1.25
5 Big Daddy V vs. Boogeyman	.15	.40
6 Kendrick/London vs. Regal/Taylor	.25	.60
7 Chris Jericho vs. JBL	.25	.60
8 CM Punk vs. John Morrison	.10	.25
9 CM Punk vs. Mike Knox	.10	.25
10 CM Punk vs. Shannon Moore	.10	.25
11 C.Rhodes vs. Hardcore Holly	.15	.40
12 D-Generation X vs. Rated RKO	.25	.60
13 Elijah Burke vs. CM Punk	.10	.25
14 Finlay vs. Rey Mysterio	.25	.60
15 Finlay vs. JBL	.15	.40
16 Jamie Noble vs. The Hurricane	.12	.30
17 Jamie Noble vs. Hornswoggle	.15	.40
18 Jeff Hardy vs. John Morrison	.40	1.00
19 Jeff Hardy vs. Umaga	.40	1.00
20 John Cena vs. Carlito	.60	1.50
21 John Cena vs. Edge	.60	1.50
22 John Cena vs. Randy Orton	.60	1.50
23 Kane vs. MVP	.40	1.00
24 Kane vs. Snitsky	.40	1.00
25 Umaga vs. Kane	.40	1.00
26 Kane vs. Undertaker	.50	1.25
27 K.Dykstra vs. Chuck Palumbo	.15	.40
28 K.Dykstra vs. Shawn Michaels	.60	1.50
29 Cade/Murdoch vs. Rhodes/Holly	.15	.40
30 Deuce/Domino vs. London/Kendrick	.15	.40
31 Matt Hardy vs. Edge	.40	1.00
32 Matt Hardy vs. MVP	.40	1.00
33 T.Dreamer vs. Matt Striker	.10	.25
34 Mr. Kennedy vs. Undertaker	.50	1.25
35 Big Show vs. John Cena	.60	1.50
36 R.Mysterio vs. Chavo Guerrero	.25	.60
37 Rey Mysterio vs. MVP	.25	.60
38 Ric Flair vs. Carlito	.40	1.00
39 S.Marella vs. Steve Austin	.60	1.50
40 Shawn Michaels vs. Undertaker	.60	1.50
41 Funaki vs. Val Venis	.10	.25

42 Steve Austin vs. Mr. McMahon	.60	1.50
43 Kevin Thorn vs. Stevie Richards	.15	.40
44 Tommy Dreamer vs. Mick Foley	.50	1.25
45 Triple H vs. Batista	.60	1.50
46 Triple H vs. Mick Foley	.60	1.50
47 Randy Orton vs. Triple H	.60	1.50
48 Triple H vs. Umaga	.60	1.50
49 Shane McMahon vs. Mr. McMahon	.25	.60
50 Randy Orton vs. Jeff Hardy	.40	1.00
51 Steve Austin vs. Brian Pillman	.60	1.50
52 S.Michaels vs. British Bulldog	.60	1.50
53 Chris Jericho vs. Dean Malenko	.25	.60
54 Big Show vs. Undertaker	.50	1.25
55 Randy Orton vs. Dusty Rhodes	.25	.60
56 Shane McMahon vs. Chris Jericho	.25	.60
57 Jerry Lawler vs. Tazz	.25	.60
58 Ric Flair vs. Terry Funk	.40	1.00
59 Paul Bearer vs. Undertaker	.50	1.25
60 Rey Mysterio vs. JBL	.25	.60
61 Arn Anderson vs. Ric Flair	.40	1.00
62 Ric Flair vs. Mr.Perfect	.40	1.00
63 Ric Flair vs. Dusty Rhodes	.40	1.00
64 Kama Mustafa vs. Undertaker	.50	1.25
65 Santino Marella vs. Maria	.40	1.00
66 Mickie James vs. Melina	.60	1.50
67 Candice Michelle vs. Beth Phoenix	.50	1.25
68 Melina vs. Candice Michelle	.50	1.25
69 Kelly Kelly vs. Layla	.40	1.00
70 Victoria vs. Michelle McCool	.50	1.25
71 Mickie James vs. Beth Phoenix	.60	1.50
72 Maria vs. Melina	.40	1.00
73 Doink vs. Bam Bam Bigelow	.25	.60
74 Iron Shiek vs. Sgt. Slaughter	.40	1.00
75 Paul Orndorff vs. Bobby Heenan	.25	.60
76 J.Strongbow vs. Peter Maivia	.25	.60
77 Mick Foley vs. Terry Funk	.25	.60
78 Dusty Rhodes vs. Billy Graham	.25	.60
79 Ron Simmons vs. Vader	.15	.40
80 Jake Roberts vs. Kamala	.25	.60
81 Jake Roberts vs. Rick Rude	.25	.60
82 Jake Roberts vs. Ted DiBiase	.25	.60
83 Jake Roberts vs. Jerry Lawler	.25	.60
84 Bam Bam vs. One Man Gang	.25	.60
85 Ric Flair vs. Roddy Piper	.40	1.00
86 Rocky Johnson vs. Wild Samoans	.15	.40
87 Ted DiBiase vs. Dusty Rhodes	.25	.60
88 Sgt. Slaughter vs. Pat Patterson	.25	.60
89 Gorilla Monsoon vs. Vader	.25	.60
90 Checklist	.10	.25

2008 Topps WWE Ultimate Rivals Autographs

STATED ODDS 1:48 HOBBY EXCLUSIVE

NNO CM Punk	100.00	200.00
NNO Edge	20.00	50.00
NNO Elijah Burke	6.00	15.00
NNO John Morrison	8.00	20.00
NNO Matt Hardy	8.00	20.00
NNO Michelle McCool	12.00	30.00
NNO The Miz	8.00	20.00
NNO Stevie Richards	6.00	15.00
NNO Super Crazy	6.00	15.00
NNO Victoria	8.00	20.00

2008 Topps WWE Ultimate Rivals Motion Cards

COMPLETE SET (10)	4.00	10.00

STATED ODDS 1:8 HOBBY AND RETAIL

1 Batista vs. Edge	.60	1.50
2 Lance Cade vs. Hardcore Holly	.20	.50
3 Carlito vs. Brian Kendrick	.30	.75
4 Chavo Guerrero vs. CM Punk	.30	.75
5 Hornswoggle/Finley vs. Edge	.60	1.50
6 Lance Cade	.20	.50
7 Jeff Hardy vs. Randy Orton	.60	1.50
8 Rey Mysterio vs. Edge	.60	1.50
9 Triple H vs. Umaga	1.00	2.50
10 Undertaker vs. MVP	1.00	2.50

2008 Topps WWE Ultimate Rivals Ringside Relics

STATED ODDS 1:48 HOBBY EXCLUSIVE

NNO Carlito	3.00	8.00
NNO Charlie Haas	3.00	8.00
NNO CM Punk	3.00	8.00
NNO Edge	4.00	10.00
NNO John Cena	6.00	15.00
NNO Matt Hardy	5.00	12.00
NNO Mr. Kennedy	3.00	8.00

2008 Topps WWE Ultimate Rivals Tattoos

COMPLETE SET (10)	4.00	10.00

STATED ODDS 1:4 RETAIL EXCLUSIVE

1 John Cena	1.00	3.00
2 Batista	.60	1.50
3 Shawn Michaels	1.00	2.50
4 Edge	.60	1.50
5 Mr. Kennedy	.30	.75
6 The Undertaker	.60	1.50
7 Ric Flair	.60	1.50
8 Triple H	1.00	2.50
9 Rey Mysterio	.30	.75
10 John Morrison	.30	.75

2008 Topps WWE Ultimate Rivals Promos

P1 John Cena vs. Edge	1.00	2.50

2015 Topps WWE Undisputed

COMPLETE SET (100)	30.00	80.00

UNOPENED BOX (10 PACKS)
UNOPENED PACKS (5 CARDS)
*RED: .5X TO 1.2X BASIC CARDS
*BLACK/99: .6X TO 1.5X BASIC CARDS
*PURPLE/50: .75X TO 2X BASIC CARDS
*SILVER/25: 1.2X TO 3X BASIC CARDS
*GOLD/1: UNPRICED DUE TO SCARCITY
*PP BLACK/1: UNPRICED DUE TO SCARCITY
*PP CYAN/1: UNPRICED DUE TO SCARCITY
*PP MAGENTA/1: UNPRICED DUE TO SCARCITY
*PP YELLOW/1: UNPRICED DUE TO SCARCITY

1 Undertaker	2.50	6.00
2 Rosa Mendes	1.00	2.50
3 Lita	2.50	6.00
4 Kofi Kingston	.60	1.50
5 George The Animal Steele	.75	2.00
6 Titus O'Neil	.60	1.50
7 Stardust	.60	1.50
8 The American Dream Dusty Rhodes	1.00	2.50
9 Alicia Fox	1.25	3.00
10 Brock Lesnar	2.50	6.00
11 Zack Ryder	.60	1.50
12 Summer Rae	2.50	6.00
13 The Miz	1.00	2.50
14 Roman Reigns	1.50	4.00
15 Natalya	2.00	5.00
16 Rob Van Dam	1.50	4.00
17 Lana RC	2.50	6.00
18 Shawn Michaels	2.50	6.00
19 R-Truth	.60	1.50
20 Nature Boy Ric Flair	3.00	8.00
21 Jey Uso	.60	1.50
22 Hacksaw Jim Duggan	1.00	2.50
23 Booker T	1.00	2.50
24 Randy Orton	2.50	6.00
25 John Cena	3.00	8.00
26 Big Show	1.50	4.00
27 Cesaro	.60	1.50
28 Kevin Nash	1.50	4.00
29 Honky Tonk Man	1.00	2.50
30 Bret Hit Man Hart	2.00	5.00
31 Paige RC	3.00	8.00
32 Dolph Ziggler	1.00	2.50
33 Christian	.60	1.50
34 Ricky The Dragon Steamboat	1.00	2.50
35 Chris Jericho	1.50	4.00
36 Jerry The King Lawler	1.00	2.50
37 Kane	1.50	4.00
38 Bo Dallas	.60	1.50
39 Darren Young	.60	1.50
40 Daniel Bryan	2.50	6.00
41 Paul Heyman	.60	1.50
42 Big E	1.00	2.50
43 Sin Cara	1.00	2.50
44 Doink The Clown	.60	1.50
45 Naomi	1.00	2.50
46 Paul Bearer	1.00	2.50
47 Rusev RC	1.50	4.00
48 Mark Henry	1.00	2.50
49 Erick Rowan	1.00	2.50
50 Triple H	2.50	6.00
51 Diamond Dallas Page	1.25	3.00
52 Tyson Kidd	.60	1.50
53 The British Bulldog	1.00	2.50
54 Razor Ramon	1.50	4.00
55 Million Dollar Man Ted DiBiase	1.00	2.50
56 King Barrett	.60	1.50
57 Seth Rollins	1.00	2.50
58 Rowdy Roddy Piper	2.00	5.00
59 Ultimate Warrior	2.00	5.00
60 Trish Stratus	3.00	8.00
61 Eve Torres	1.25	3.00
62 Adam Rose RC	.75	2.00
63 Bruno Sammartino	1.50	4.00
64 JBL	.60	1.50
65 The Iron Sheik	1.00	2.50
66 Emma RC	1.00	2.50
67 Jack Swagger	1.00	2.50
68 Luke Harper	1.00	2.50
69 Konnor	.75	2.00
70 Sting	1.50	4.00
71 Bray Wyatt	2.50	6.00
72 Bob Backlund	.60	1.50
73 Eva Marie	2.50	6.00
74 Jake The Snake Roberts	1.00	2.50
75 Yokozuna	1.00	2.50
76 Nikki Bella	2.00	5.00
77 Sheamus	1.50	4.00
78 Jimmy Uso	.60	1.50
79 Fandango	.60	1.50
80 Neville RC	1.25	3.00
81 Viktor RC	.60	1.50
82 Cowboy Bob Orton	.60	1.50
83 Arn Anderson	.75	2.00
84 Damien Sandow	.60	1.50
85 Edge	1.50	4.00
86 Classy Freddie Blassie	.60	1.50
87 Dean Ambrose	1.50	4.00
88 Stephanie McMahon	1.00	2.50
89 Sgt. Slaughter	1.00	2.50
90 Mr. Perfect Curt Hennig	1.00	2.50
91 Ryback	.60	1.50
92 Big Boss Man	.60	1.50
93 Bam Bam Bigelow	.75	2.00
94 Pat Patterson	.60	1.50
95 Brie Bella	2.00	5.00
96 Cameron	1.00	2.50
97 Kalisto RC	1.00	2.50
98 The Rock	3.00	8.00
99 Goldust	.60	1.50
100 Ravishing Rick Rude	1.00	2.50

2015 Topps WWE Undisputed Autographed Relics

*BLACK/50: .6X TO 1.5X BASIC AUTOS
*PURPLE/25: 1X TO 2.5X BASIC AUTOS
*GOLD/1: UNPRICED DUE TO SCARCITY

UARAF Alicia Fox	6.00	15.00
UARAR Adam Rose	5.00	12.00
UARBB Brie Bella	12.00	30.00
UARBD Bo Dallas	5.00	12.00
UARBS Big Show	8.00	20.00
UARBW Bray Wyatt	12.00	30.00
UARCA Curtis Axel	5.00	12.00
UARCE Cesaro	10.00	25.00
UARDA Dean Ambrose	12.00	30.00
UARDB Daniel Bryan	15.00	40.00
UARDM Damien Sandow	5.00	12.00
UARDY Darren Young	5.00	12.00
UARDZ Dolph Ziggler	6.00	15.00
UARFA Fandango	5.00	12.00
UARGO Goldust	8.00	20.00
UARHS Heath Slater	5.00	12.00
UARJC John Cena	25.00	60.00
UARJS Jack Swagger	5.00	12.00
UARJU Jimmy Uso	8.00	20.00
UARKO Konnor	5.00	12.00
UARMH Mark Henry	6.00	15.00
UARNA Natalya	8.00	20.00
UARNB Nikki Bella	50.00	100.00
UARRO Randy Orton	12.00	30.00
UARRR Roman Reigns	25.00	60.00
UARSH Sheamus	10.00	25.00
UARSR Seth Rollins	15.00	40.00
UARTK Tyson Kidd	5.00	12.00
UARTM The Miz	8.00	20.00
UARTO Titus O'Neil	5.00	12.00
UARVI Viktor	5.00	12.00
UARZR Zack Ryder	5.00	12.00
UARBNB King Barrett	6.00	15.00
UARJKL Jerry The King Lawler	15.00	40.00
UARSRA Summer Rae	10.00	25.00

2015 Topps WWE Undisputed Autographs

*BLACK/50: .6X TO 1.5X BASIC AUTOS
*PURPLE/25: .75X TO 2X BASIC AUTOS

*GOLD/1: UNPRICED DUE TO SCARCITY

UAAB	Alundra Blayze	8.00	20.00
UABB	Brie Bella	12.00	30.00
UABL	Brock Lesnar	120.00	200.00
UABS	Bruno Sammartino	10.00	25.00
UABW	Bray Wyatt	8.00	20.00
UACJ	Chris Jericho	15.00	40.00
UADA	Dean Ambrose	8.00	20.00
UADB	Daniel Bryan	10.00	25.00
UADZ	Dolph Ziggler	6.00	15.00
UAED	Edge	10.00	25.00
UAEV	Eve Torres	6.00	15.00
UAIS	The Iron Sheik	20.00	50.00
UAJC	John Cena	75.00	150.00
UAJL	Jerry The King Lawler	8.00	20.00
UALI	Lita	10.00	25.00
UALT	Lawrence Taylor	75.00	150.00
UAMM	Million Dollar Man Ted DiBiase	12.00	30.00
UANA	Natalya	6.00	15.00
UANB	Nikki Bella	12.00	30.00
UANE	Neville	6.00	15.00
UAPH	Paul Heyman	8.00	20.00
UAPR	Pete Rose	20.00	50.00
UARF	Nature Boy Ric Flair	15.00	40.00
UARO	Randy Orton	25.00	60.00
UARR	Razor Ramon	60.00	120.00
UARU	Rusev	6.00	15.00
UARY	Ryback	6.00	15.00
UASM	Shawn Michaels	50.00	100.00
UASR	Seth Rollins	15.00	40.00
UATM	The Miz	8.00	20.00
UATS	Trish Stratus	50.00	100.00
UABHH	Bret Hit Man Hart	50.00	100.00
UABSH	Big Show	6.00	15.00
UARRE	Roman Reigns	50.00	100.00
UASRA	Summer Rae	12.00	30.00

2015 Topps WWE Undisputed Cage Evolution Moments

COMPLETE SET (20) 10.00 25.00
*RED: .5X TO 1.2X BASIC CARDS
*BLACK/99: .6X TO 1.5X BASIC CARDS
*PURPLE/50: .75X TO 2X BASIC CARDS
*SILVER/25: 1.2X TO 3X BASIC CARDS
*GOLD/1: UNPRICED DUE TO SCARCITY
*PP BLACK/1: UNPRICED DUE TO SCARCITY
*PP CYAN/1: UNPRICED DUE TO SCARCITY
*PP MAGENTA/1: UNPRICED DUE TO SCARCITY
*PP YELLOW/1: UNPRICED DUE TO SCARCITY

CEM1	Ultimate Warrior/Rick Rude	1.25	3.00
CEM2	Undertaker/Shawn Michaels	1.50	4.00
CEM3	Edge/Christian	1.00	2.50
CEM4	John Cena/Big Show	2.00	5.00
CEM5	Sheamus/Ryback/R-Truth Barrett/Ziggler/Henry	1.00	2.50
CEM6	Triple H/Randy Orton	1.50	4.00
CEM7	JBL/Big Show	1.00	2.50
CEM8	John Cena/Edge	2.00	5.00
CEM9	Undertaker/Edge	1.50	4.00
CEM10	Mark Henry/Big Show	1.00	2.50
CEM11	Big Show/Bryan/Henry	1.50	4.00
CEM12	Undertaker/Triple H	1.50	4.00
CEM13	Triple H/Brock Lesnar	1.50	4.00
CEM14	Cesaro/Orton/Bryan Cena/Christian/Sheamus	2.00	5.00
CEM15	John Cena/Bray Wyatt	2.00	5.00
CEM16	RVD/Jericho/HHH Booker T/Kane/HBK	1.50	4.00
CEM17	Shawn Michaels/Triple H	1.50	4.00
CEM18	Dean Ambrose/Seth Rollins	1.00	2.50
CEM19	Randy Orton/Seth Rollins	1.50	4.00
CEM20	John Cena/Seth Rollins	2.00	5.00

2015 Topps WWE Undisputed Cut Signatures

STATED PRINT RUN 1 SER.#'d SET
UNPRICED DUE TO SCARCITY

CUTBB British Bulldog
CUTJD Junkyard Dog
CUTMP Mr. Perfect Curt Hennig
CUTBBM Big Boss Man
CUTCJS Chief Jay Strongbow

2015 Topps WWE Undisputed Famous Finishers

COMPLETE SET (30) 12.00 30.00
*RED: .5X TO 1.2X BASIC CARDS
*BLACK/99: .6X TO 1.5X BASIC CARDS
*PURPLE/50: .75X TO 2X BASIC CARDS
*SILVER/25: 1.2X TO 3X BASIC CARDS
*GOLD/1: UNPRICED DUE TO SCARCITY
*PP BLACK/1: UNPRICED DUE TO SCARCITY
*PP CYAN/1: UNPRICED DUE TO SCARCITY
*PP MAGENTA/1: UNPRICED DUE TO SCARCITY
*PP YELLOW/1: UNPRICED DUE TO SCARCITY

FF1	Sweet Chin Music	2.00	5.00
FF2	Pedigree	2.00	5.00
FF3	Stratusfaction	2.50	6.00
FF4	Zig Zag	.75	2.00
FF5	Tombstone	2.00	5.00
FF6	Figure-4 Leglock	2.50	6.00
FF7	RKO	2.00	5.00
FF8	Rude Awakening	.75	2.00
FF9	Codebreaker	1.25	3.00
FF10	Brogue Kick	1.25	3.00
FF11	Sharpshooter	1.50	4.00
FF12	Attitude Adjustment	2.50	6.00
FF13	Million Dollar Dream	.75	2.00
FF14	KO Punch	1.25	3.00
FF15	Sister Abigail	2.00	5.00
FF16	F-5	2.00	5.00
FF17	Running Knee Smash	2.00	5.00
FF18	Camel Clutch	.75	2.00
FF19	Texas Cloverleaf	.75	2.00
FF20	World's Strongest Slam	.75	2.00
FF21	Razor's Edge	1.25	3.00
FF22	Banzai Drop	.75	2.00
FF23	Patriot Lock	.75	2.00
FF24	Spear	1.25	3.00
FF25	Perfectplex	.75	2.00
FF26	DDT	.75	2.00
FF27	Coup de Grace	1.50	4.00
FF28	Figure Eight	1.50	4.00
FF29	Skull-Crushing Finale	.75	2.00
FF30	Red Arrow	1.00	2.50

2015 Topps WWE Undisputed Famous Rivalries Dual Autographed Jumbo Relics

STATED PRINT RUN 5 SER.#'d SETS
UNPRICED DUE TO SCARCITY

FRARAR D.Ambrose/S.Rollins
FRARBB Nikki & Brie Bella
FRARCO J.Cena/R.Orton
FRARSH Big Show/M.Henry
FRARZM D.Ziggler/Miz

2015 Topps WWE Undisputed Famous Rivalries Dual Autographs

STATED PRINT RUN 25 SER.#'d SETS

FRACO	J.Cena/R.Orton	150.00	300.00
FRAHL	B.Hart/J.Lawler	75.00	150.00
FRAMR	S.Michaels/R.Ramon	100.00	200.00

2015 Topps WWE Undisputed Fistographs

STATED PRINT RUN 10 SER.#'d SETS

NNO	Big Show	100.00	200.00
NNO	Bray Wyatt	100.00	200.00
NNO	Bret Hit Man Hart	125.00	250.00
NNO	Bruno Sammartino	125.00	250.00
NNO	Daniel Bryan		
NNO	Dean Ambrose	150.00	300.00
NNO	Edge	125.00	250.00
NNO	Jack Swagger		
NNO	John Cena		
NNO	Kane	100.00	200.00
NNO	King Barrett		
NNO	Lita	150.00	300.00
NNO	Mark Henry	75.00	150.00
NNO	Randy Orton	125.00	250.00
NNO	Ric Flair		
NNO	Roman Reigns	250.00	500.00
NNO	Rowdy Roddy Piper		
NNO	Rusev	75.00	150.00
NNO	Shawn Michaels	300.00	450.00
NNO	Sheamus		
NNO	Trish Stratus	250.00	400.00

2015 Topps WWE Undisputed Four Corners Quadragraphs

STATED PRINT RUN 10 SER.#'d SETS

FCQBBSL	Lita/Trish/Bellas	300.00	600.00
FCQBBYS	Bryan/Young/Barrett/Slater	125.00	250.00
FCQDNZO	Dallas/Neville/Zayn/Owens	125.00	250.00
FCQHHLD	J.Hart/B.Hart/Lawler/DiBiase	150.00	300.00

2015 Topps WWE Undisputed NXT In Line Autographs

*BLACK/50: .6X TO 1.5X BASIC AUTOS
*PURPLE/25: .75X TO 2X BASIC AUTOS
*GOLD/1: UNPRICED DUE TO SCARCITY

NABD	Bull Dempsey	5.00	12.00
NABL	Becky Lynch	150.00	300.00
NABM	Murphy	5.00	12.00
NACC	Colin Cassady	6.00	15.00
NACH	Charlotte	125.00	250.00
NAEA	Enzo Amore	10.00	25.00
NAFB	Finn Balor	50.00	100.00
NAHI	Hideo Itami	8.00	20.00
NAKO	Kevin Owens	25.00	60.00
NASB	Sasha Banks	150.00	300.00
NASJ	Samoa Joe	10.00	25.00
NASZ	Sami Zayn	10.00	25.00
NATB	Tyler Breeze	8.00	20.00
NAWB	Blake	5.00	12.00
NABCO	Baron Corbin	6.00	15.00

2015 Topps WWE Undisputed NXT Prospects

COMPLETE SET (25) 100.00 200.00
*RED: .5X TO 1.2X BASIC CARDS
*BLACK/99: .6X TO 1.5X BASIC CARDS
*PURPLE/50: .75X TO 2X BASIC CARDS
*SILVER/25: 1.2X TO 3X BASIC CARDS
*GOLD/1: UNPRICED DUE TO SCARCITY
*PP BLACK/1: UNPRICED DUE TO SCARCITY
*PP CYAN/1: UNPRICED DUE TO SCARCITY
*PP MAGENTA/1: UNPRICED DUE TO SCARCITY
*PP YELLOW/1: UNPRICED DUE TO SCARCITY

NXT1	Angelo Dawkins	1.50	4.00
NXT2	Sasha Banks	12.00	30.00
NXT3	Finn Balor	4.00	10.00
NXT4	Sami Zayn	2.00	5.00
NXT5	Charlotte	10.00	25.00
NXT6	Blake	1.25	3.00
NXT7	Murphy	1.25	3.00
NXT8	Carmella	5.00	12.00
NXT9	Enzo Amore	1.25	3.00
NXT10	Baron Corbin	2.00	5.00
NXT11	Hideo Itami	1.25	3.00
NXT12	Tyler Breeze	1.25	3.00
NXT13	Solomon Crowe	1.25	3.00
NXT14	Becky Lynch	15.00	40.00
NXT15	Bayley	5.00	12.00
NXT16	Bull Dempsey	2.00	5.00
NXT17	Alexa Bliss	50.00	100.00
NXT18	Tye Dillinger	2.00	5.00
NXT19	Jason Jordan	1.25	3.00
NXT20	Colin Cassady	2.00	5.00
NXT21	Aiden English	1.50	4.00
NXT22	Simon Gotch	1.25	3.00
NXT23	Mojo Rawley	1.25	3.00
NXT24	Marcus Louis	2.00	5.00
NXT25	Samoa Joe	3.00	8.00

2016 Topps WWE Undisputed

COMPLETE SET (100) 25.00 60.00
UNOPENED BOX (10 PACKS)
UNOPENED PACK (5 CARDS)
*BRONZE/99: .5X TO 1.2X BASIC CARDS
*SILVER/50: .75X TO 2X BASIC CARDS
*BLUE/25: 1.2X TO 3X BASIC CARDS
*GOLD/10: 2X TO 5X BASIC CARDS
*RED/1: UNPRICED DUE TO SCARCITY
*P.P.BLACK/1: UNPRICED DUE TO SCARCITY
*P.P.CYAN/1: UNPRICED DUE TO SCARCITY
*P.P.MAGENTA/1: UNPRICED DUE TO SCARCITY
*P.P.YELLOW/1: UNPRICED DUE TO SCARCITY

1	Alberto Del Rio	1.00	2.50
2	Big E	.60	1.50
3	Big Show	1.25	3.00
4	Braun Strowman RC	.75	2.00
5	Bray Wyatt	2.50	6.00
6	Brock Lesnar	3.00	8.00
7	Bubba Ray Dudley	1.25	3.00
8	Cesaro	1.25	3.00
9	Chris Jericho	1.50	4.00
10	D-Von Dudley	1.00	2.50
11	Dean Ambrose	2.00	5.00
12	Dolph Ziggler	.75	2.00
13	Erick Rowan	.60	1.50
14	Goldust	1.00	2.50
15	Jerry The King Lawler	1.25	3.00
16	John Cena	3.00	8.00

17	Kane	1.00	2.50
18	Kevin Owens	1.50	4.00
19	King Barrett	.60	1.50
20	Kofi Kingston	.60	1.50
21	Luke Harper	.60	1.50
22	Mark Henry	.75	2.00
23	The Miz	1.00	2.50
24	Neville	1.50	4.00
25	Paul Heyman	.75	2.00
26	R-Truth	.60	1.50
27	Randy Orton	1.50	4.00
28	The Rock	3.00	8.00
29	Roman Reigns	2.00	5.00
30	Rusev	1.50	4.00
31	Ryback	.75	2.00
32	Seth Rollins	1.00	2.50
33	Sheamus	1.50	4.00
34	Sting	1.50	4.00
35	Triple H	2.50	6.00
36	Tyler Breeze	.60	1.50
37	Tyson Kidd	.60	1.50
38	Undertaker	2.50	6.00
39	Xavier Woods	.60	1.50
40	Zack Ryder	.60	1.50
41	The American Dream Dusty Rhodes	.60	1.50
42	Andre the Giant	2.00	5.00
43	Bam Bam Bigelow	.75	2.00
44	Batista	1.25	3.00
45	Big Boss Man	1.00	2.50
46	Big John Studd	1.00	2.50
47	Bob Backlund	.60	1.50
48	Bobby The Brain Heenan	1.00	2.50
49	Bret Hit Man Hart	1.50	4.00
50	Brian Pillman	.75	2.00
51	The British Bulldog	.75	2.00
52	Cowboy Bob Orton	1.00	2.50
53	Diamond Dallas Page	1.00	2.50
54	Doink the Clown	.60	1.50
55	Eddie Guerrero	1.50	4.00
56	Edge	1.50	4.00
57	General Adnan	.60	1.50
58	George The Animal Steele	.75	2.00
59	Hacksaw Jim Duggan	.60	1.50
60	High Chief Peter Maivia	.60	1.50
61	Honky Tonk Man	.60	1.50
62	Jake The Snake Roberts	1.25	3.00
63	Jim The Anvil Neidhart	.60	1.50
64	Jim Ross	1.00	2.50
65	J.J. Dillon	.60	1.50
66	Junkyard Dog	1.00	2.50
67	Kamala	.60	1.50
68	The King Harley Race	.60	1.50
69	Kevin Nash	1.50	4.00
70	Lex Luger	1.00	2.50
71	Macho Man Randy Savage	1.50	4.00
72	Mean Gene Okerlund	.75	2.00
73	Michael P.S. Hayes	.60	1.50
74	Million Dollar Man Ted DiBiase	.75	2.00
75	The Mouth of the South Jimmy Hart	.75	2.00
76	Mr. Perfect Curt Hennig	1.50	4.00
77	Mr. Wonderful Paul Orndorff	.60	1.50
78	Papa Shango	.75	2.00
79	Paul Bearer	1.00	2.50
80	Ravishing Rick Rude	1.00	2.50
81	Ric Flair	2.50	6.00
82	Ricky The Dragon Steamboat	.75	2.00
83	Rikishi	.75	2.00
84	Road Dogg	1.00	2.50
85	Rob Van Dam	1.25	3.00
86	Rocky Johnson	.75	2.00
87	Rowdy Roddy Piper	2.00	5.00
88	Scott Hall	1.50	4.00
89	Sgt. Slaughter	.75	2.00
90	Shawn Michaels	2.50	6.00
91	Superstar Billy Graham	.60	1.50
92	Stone Cold Steve Austin	3.00	8.00
93	Tatanka	.60	1.50
94	Tatsumi Fujinami RC	.60	1.50
95	Tito Santana	.75	2.00
96	Ultimate Warrior	1.50	4.00
97	Vader	1.25	3.00
98	Virgil	.60	1.50
99	X-Pac	1.00	2.50
100	Yokozuna	1.25	3.00

2016 Topps WWE Undisputed Autographed Diva Kiss and Relic Booklets

STATED PRINT RUN 5 SER. #'d SETS
UNPRICED DUE TO SCARCITY

ADRAF Alicia Fox
ADRBA Bayley
ADRBB Brie Bella
ADRLA Lana
ADRNB Nikki Bella

2016 Topps WWE Undisputed Autographed Relics

*SILVER/50: .6X TO 1.5X BASIC AUTOS
*BLUE/25: 1X TO 2.5X BASIC MEM
*GOLD/10: 1.2X TO 3X BASIC AUTOS
*RED/1: UNPRICED DUE TO SCARCITY
*P.P.BLACK/1: UNPRICED DUE TO SCARCITY
*P.P.CYAN/1: UNPRICED DUE TO SCARCITY
*P.P.MAGENTA/1: UNPRICED DUE TO SCARCITY
*P.P.YELLOW/1: UNPRICED DUE TO SCARCITY
STATED PRINT RUN 99 SER.#'d SETS

UARAC	Alicia Fox	6.00	15.00
UARAE	Aiden English	6.00	15.00
UARBB	Brie Bella	12.00	30.00
UARBC	Baron Corbin	6.00	15.00
UARBE	Big E	6.00	15.00
UARBL	Becky Lynch	20.00	50.00
UARBW	Bray Wyatt	10.00	25.00
UARCC	Colin Cassady	8.00	20.00
UARCH	Charlotte	15.00	40.00
UARDA	Dean Ambrose	12.00	30.00
UARDD	D-Von Dudley	6.00	15.00
UARDZ	Dolph Ziggler	6.00	15.00
UAREA	Enzo Amore	12.00	30.00
UARFB	Finn Balor	15.00	40.00
UARJU	Jey Uso	6.00	15.00
UARKA	Kalisto	6.00	15.00
UARKK	Kofi Kingston	6.00	15.00
UARKO	Kevin Owens	12.00	30.00
UARMR	Mojo Rawley	6.00	15.00
UARNE	Neville	8.00	20.00
UARRR	Roman Reigns	10.00	25.00
UARRY	Ryback	6.00	15.00
UARSB	Sasha Banks	25.00	60.00
UARSC	Sin Cara	8.00	20.00
UARSG	Simon Gotch	6.00	15.00
UARSH	Sheamus	6.00	15.00
UARSJ	Samoa Joe	6.00	15.00
UARSR	Seth Rollins	10.00	25.00
UARTB	Tyler Breeze	6.00	15.00
UARTM	The Miz	6.00	15.00
UARXW	Xavier Woods	6.00	15.00
UARZR	Zack Ryder	6.00	15.00
UARADR	Alberto Del Rio	6.00	15.00
UARAPC	Apollo Crews	6.00	15.00
UARBAY	Bayley	20.00	50.00
UARBRD	Bubba Ray Dudley	6.00	15.00
UARJIU	Jimmy Uso	8.00	20.00

2016 Topps WWE Undisputed Autographs

*BRONZE/99: .5X TO 1.2X BASIC AUTOS
*SILVER/50: .75X TO 2X BASIC AUTOS
*BLUE/25: 1.2X TO 3X BASIC AUTOS
*GOLD/10: 1.5X TO 4X BASIC AUTOS
*RED/1: UNPRICED DUE TO SCARCITY
*P.P.BLACK/1: UNPRICED DUE TO SCARCITY
*P.P.CYAN/1: UNPRICED DUE TO SCARCITY
*P.P.MAGENTA/1: UNPRICED DUE TO SCARCITY
*P.P.YELLOW/1: UNPRICED DUE TO SCARCITY
RANDOMLY INSERTED INTO PACKS

UAAF	Alicia Fox	5.00	12.00
UAAS	Asuka	25.00	60.00
UABA	Bayley	15.00	40.00
UABB	Brie Bella	8.00	20.00
UABE	Big E	6.00	15.00
UABH	Bret Hit Man Hart	12.00	30.00
UABL	Becky Lynch	30.00	75.00
UABS	Braun Strowman	6.00	15.00
UABT	Booker T	6.00	15.00
UACA	Carmella	10.00	25.00
UACC	Colin Cassady	6.00	15.00
UACE	Cesaro	6.00	15.00
UACH	Charlotte	25.00	60.00
UADA	Dean Ambrose	10.00	25.00
UADB	Daniel Bryan	10.00	25.00
UADD	D-Von Dudley	6.00	15.00
UAEA	Enzo Amore	10.00	25.00
UAER	Erick Rowan	5.00	12.00
UAFB	Finn Balor	10.00	25.00
UAGO	Goldust	10.00	25.00
UAHI	Hideo Itami	5.00	12.00
UAJC	John Cena	75.00	150.00
UAJN	Jim The Anvil Neidhart	6.00	15.00
UAKA	Kalisto	5.00	12.00
UAKK	Kofi Kingston	10.00	25.00
UALA	Lana	10.00	25.00
UALH	Luke Harper	6.00	15.00
UALI	Lita	25.00	60.00
UANA	Natalya	10.00	25.00
UANB	Nikki Bella	10.00	25.00
UANJ	Nia Jax	5.00	12.00
UARR	Roman Reigns	20.00	50.00
UASB	Sasha Banks	30.00	75.00
UASC	Sin Cara	6.00	15.00
UASJ	Samoa Joe	5.00	12.00
UASR	Seth Rollins	8.00	20.00
UAST	Sting	25.00	60.00
UATS	Trish Stratus	30.00	75.00
UAXW	Xavier Woods	5.00	12.00
UAAJS	AJ Styles	10.00	25.00
UABAC	Baron Corbin	6.00	15.00
UABRD	Bubba Ray Dudley	6.00	15.00
UABRW	Bray Wyatt	6.00	15.00
UANAO	Naomi	5.00	12.00
UASTR	Stevie Ray	5.00	12.00

2016 Topps WWE Undisputed Cut Signatures

STATED PRINT RUN 1 SER.#'d SET
UNPRICED DUE TO SCARCITY

UCSRS Macho Man Randy Savage
UCSCFB Classy Freddie Blassie
UCSMIE Miss Elizabeth

2016 Topps WWE Undisputed Divas Revolution

COMPLETE SET (30) 60.00 120.00
*BRONZE/99: .5X TO 1.2X BASIC CARDS
*SILVER/50: .75X TO 2X BASIC CARDS
*BLUE/25: 1.2X TO 3X BASIC CARDS
*GOLD/10: UNPRICED DUE TO SCARCITY
*RED/1: UNPRICED DUE TO SCARCITY
*P.P.BLACK/1 UNPRICED DUE TO SCARCITY
*P.P.CYAN/1 UNPRICED DUE TO SCARCITY
*P.P.MAGENTA/1 UNPRICED DUE TO SCARCITY
*P.P.YELLOW/1 UNPRICED DUE TO SCARCITY
RANDOMLY INSERTED INTO PACKS

DR1	Alundra Blayze	1.50	4.00
DR2	Eve	2.50	6.00
DR3	Lita	4.00	10.00
DR4	Miss Elizabeth	1.25	3.00
DR5	Sensational Sherri	2.00	5.00
DR6	Trish Stratus	6.00	15.00
DR7	Alicia Fox	2.00	5.00
DR8	Asuka	5.00	12.00
DR9	Bayley	3.00	8.00
DR10	Becky Lynch	4.00	10.00
DR11	Brie Bella	2.50	6.00
DR12	Cameron	1.25	3.00
DR13	Charlotte	4.00	10.00
DR14	Dasha Fuentes	1.25	3.00
DR15	Eden	1.50	4.00
DR16	Emma	2.50	6.00
DR17	Eva Marie	2.50	6.00
DR18	JoJo	1.25	3.00
DR19	Lana	5.00	12.00
DR20	Mandy Rose	3.00	8.00
DR21	Naomi	2.00	5.00
DR22	Natalya	2.00	5.00
DR23	Nikki Bella	4.00	10.00
DR24	Paige	4.00	10.00
DR25	Renee Young	3.00	8.00
DR26	Rosa Mendes	1.25	3.00
DR27	Sasha Banks	4.00	10.00
DR28	Maryse	2.50	6.00
DR29	Summer Rae	3.00	8.00
DR30	Tamina	1.50	4.00

2016 Topps WWE Undisputed Faction Triple Autograph Booklets

STATED PRINT RUN 10 SER. #'d SETS

FTAARR	Ambrose/Rollins/Reigns	125.00	250.00
FTABBF	The Bellas/Fox	100.00	200.00
FTAKBW	Kingston/Big E/Woods	75.00	150.00
FTANBT	Naomi/Banks/Tamina	125.00	250.00
FTASKV	Stardust/Konnor/Viktor	60.00	120.00

2016 Topps WWE Undisputed Family Ties Dual Autographs

STATED PRINT RUN 25 SER.#'d SETS

FTABB	Nikki & Brie Bella	120.00	200.00
FTAFC	Ric & Charlotte Flair	120.00	200.00

FTAGS Goldust/Stardust	60.00	120.00
FTANN J.Neidhart/Natalya	60.00	120.00
FTATR Booker T/S. Ray	30.00	75.00

2016 Topps WWE Undisputed NXT Prospects

COMPLETE SET (30) 30.00 80.00
*BRONZE/99: .5X TO 1.2X BASIC CARDS
*SILVER/50: .75X TO 2X BASIC CARDS
*BLUE/25: 1.2X TO 3X BASIC CARDS
*GOLD/10: UNPRICED DUE TO SCARCITY
*RED/1: UNPRICED DUE TO SCARCITY
*P.P.BLACK/1: UNPRICED DUE TO SCARCITY
*P.P.CYAN/1: UNPRICED DUE TO SCARCITY
*P.P.MAGENTA/1: UNPRICED DUE TO SCARCITY
*P.P.YELLOW/1: UNPRICED DUE TO SCARCITY
RANDOMLY INSERTED INTO PACKS

NXT1 Aiden English	1.25	3.00
NXT2 Alexa Bliss	6.00	15.00
NXT3 Angelo Dawkins	1.25	3.00
NXT4 Apollo Crews	1.25	3.00
NXT5 Asuka	5.00	12.00
NXT6 Austin Aries	1.50	4.00
NXT7 Baron Corbin	1.50	4.00
NXT8 Bayley	3.00	8.00
NXT9 Billie Kay	3.00	8.00
NXT10 Blake	1.25	3.00
NXT11 Carmella	3.00	8.00
NXT12 Chad Gable	1.50	4.00
NXT13 Colin Cassady	2.50	6.00
NXT14 Dana Brooke	3.00	8.00
NXT15 Dash Wilder	1.50	4.00
NXT16 Elias Samson	1.25	3.00
NXT17 Enzo Amore	2.50	6.00
NXT18 Finn Balor	4.00	10.00
NXT19 Hideo Itami	1.50	4.00
NXT20 Jason Jordan	1.50	4.00
NXT21 Mojo Rawley	1.25	3.00
NXT22 Murphy	1.25	3.00
NXT23 Nia Jax	2.00	5.00
NXT24 Peyton Royce	3.00	8.00
NXT25 Sami Zayn	2.00	5.00
NXT26 Samoa Joe	3.00	8.00
NXT27 Sawyer Fulton	1.50	4.00
NXT28 Scott Dawson	1.25	3.00
NXT29 Simon Gotch	2.00	5.00
NXT30 Tye Dillinger	1.50	4.00

2016 Topps WWE Undisputed Relics

STATED PRINT RUN 175 SER.#'d SETS

UARAC Alicia Fox	3.00	8.00
UARAE Aiden English	2.00	5.00
UARBB Brie Bella	4.00	10.00
UARBC Baron Corbin	2.50	6.00
UARBE Big E	2.00	5.00
UARBL Becky Lynch	6.00	15.00
UARBW Bray Wyatt	8.00	20.00
UARCC Colin Cassady	4.00	10.00
UARCH Charlotte	6.00	15.00
UARDA Dean Ambrose	6.00	15.00
UARDD D-Von Dudley	3.00	8.00
UARDZ Dolph Ziggler	2.50	6.00
UAREA Enzo Amore	4.00	10.00
UARFB Finn Balor	6.00	15.00
UARJU Jey Uso	2.00	5.00
UARKA Kalisto	5.00	12.00
UARKB King Barrett	2.00	5.00
UARKK Kofi Kingston	2.00	5.00
UARKO Kevin Owens	5.00	12.00
UARMR Mojo Rawley	2.00	5.00
UARNE Neville	5.00	12.00
UARRR Roman Reigns	6.00	15.00
UARRY Ryback	2.50	6.00
UARSB Sasha Banks	6.00	15.00
UARSC Sin Cara	2.50	6.00
UARSG Simon Gotch	3.00	8.00
UARSH Sheamus	5.00	12.00
UARSJ Samoa Joe	5.00	12.00
UARSR Seth Rollins	3.00	8.00
UARTB Tyler Breeze	2.00	5.00
UARTM The Miz	3.00	8.00
UARXW Xavier Woods	2.00	5.00
UARZR Zack Ryder	2.00	5.00
UARADR Alberto Del Rio	3.00	8.00
UARAPC Apollo Crews	2.00	5.00
UARBAY Bayley	5.00	12.00
UARBRD Bubba Ray Dudley	4.00	10.00
UARJIU Jimmy Uso	2.00	5.00

2016 Topps WWE Undisputed Tag Teams

COMPLETE SET (40) 50.00 100.00
*BRONZE/99: .5X TO 1.2X BASIC CARDS
*SILVER/50: .75X TO 2X BASIC CARDS
*BLUE/25: 1.2X TO 3X BASIC CARDS
*GOLD/10: UNPRICED DUE TO SCARCITY
*RED/1: UNPRICED DUE TO SCARCITY
*P.P.BLACK/1: UNPRICED DUE TO SCARCITY
*P.P.CYAN/1: UNPRICED DUE TO SCARCITY
*P.P.MAGENTA/1: UNPRICED DUE TO SCARCITY
*P.P.YELLOW/1: UNPRICED DUE TO SCARCITY
RANDOMLY INSERTED INTO PACKS

UTT1 The Allied Powers	1.50	4.00
UTT2 The APA	2.50	6.00
UTT3 The Ascension	1.00	2.50
UTT4 Blake and Murphy	1.00	2.50
UTT5 The Brain Busters	1.00	2.50
UTT6 Brothers of Destruction	4.00	10.00
UTT7 The Bushwhackers	1.00	2.50
UTT8 D-Generation X	3.00	8.00
UTT9 The Dudley Boyz	2.00	5.00
UTT10 Edge and Christian	2.50	6.00
UTT11 The Enforcers	1.00	2.50
UTT12 The Foreign Legion	1.25	3.00
UTT13 The Funks	1.00	2.50
UTT14 Gold and Stardust	1.50	4.00
UTT15 Harlem Heat	2.00	5.00
UTT16 The Hart Foundation	2.50	6.00
UTT17 The Hollywood Blonds	5.00	12.00
UTT18 The Hype Bros.	1.00	2.50
UTT19 J and J Security	1.00	2.50
UTT20 Jeri-Show	2.50	6.00
UTT21 The Insiders	2.50	6.00
UTT22 The Lucha Dragons	2.50	6.00
UTT23 The Mega Bucks	3.00	8.00
UTT24 Money Inc.	1.25	3.00
UTT25 The Nasty Boys	1.25	3.00
UTT26 The Natural Disasters	1.00	2.50
UTT27 The Outsiders	2.50	6.00
UTT28 The Prime Time Players	1.00	2.50
UTT29 Rated-RKO	2.50	6.00
UTT30 Rhythm and Blues	1.25	3.00
UTT31 ShoMiz	2.00	5.00
UTT32 Team Hell No	4.00	10.00
UTT33 Team Rhodes Scholars	1.00	2.50
UTT34 Dudes with Attitude	4.00	10.00
UTT35 Two Man Power Trip	5.00	12.00
UTT36 Unholy Alliance	4.00	10.00
UTT37 Miz/Mizdow	1.50	4.00
UTT38 The Usos	1.00	2.50
UTT39 The Vaudevillains	1.50	4.00
UTT40 The Revival	1.25	3.00

2017 Topps WWE Undisputed

COMPLETE SET (70) 20.00 50.00
UNOPENED BOX (10 PACKS)
UNOPENED PACK (5 CARDS)
*BRONZE/99: .5X TO 1.2X BASIC CARDS
*SILVER/50: .75X TO 2X BASIC CARDS
*GREEN/25: 1.2X TO 3X BASIC CARDS
*GOLD/10: 2X TO 5X BASIC CARDS
*RED/1: UNPRICED DUE TO SCARCITY
*P.P.BLACK/1: UNPRICED DUE TO SCARCITY
*P.P.CYAN/1: UNPRICED DUE TO SCARCITY
*P.P.MAGENTA/1: UNPRICED DUE TO SCARCITY
*P.P.YELLOW/1: UNPRICED DUE TO SCARCITY

1 John Cena	3.00	8.00
2 AJ Styles	3.00	8.00
3 Big Cass	.75	2.00
4 Big E	.75	2.00
5 The Brian Kendrick	.60	1.50
6 Bray Wyatt	1.50	4.00
7 Brock Lesnar	3.00	8.00
8 Cesaro	1.25	3.00
9 Chad Gable	.75	2.00
10 Chris Jericho	1.50	4.00
11 Daniel Bryan	2.50	6.00
12 Dean Ambrose	2.00	5.00
13 Dolph Ziggler	1.00	2.50
14 Finn Balor	2.50	6.00
15 Goldberg	2.50	6.00
16 James Ellsworth RC	.60	1.50
17 Jason Jordan	.75	2.00
18 Kane	.75	2.00
19 Karl Anderson	.60	1.50
20 Kevin Owens	1.50	4.00
21 Kofi Kingston	.75	2.00
22 Luke Gallows	1.00	2.50
23 Luke Harper	.60	1.50
24 Mick Foley	1.50	4.00
25 The Miz	1.25	3.00
26 Neville	1.00	2.50
27 Randy Orton	1.50	4.00
28 Rich Swann RC	.60	1.50
29 The Rock	3.00	8.00
30 Roman Reigns	2.00	5.00
31 Rusev	1.25	3.00
32 Sami Zayn	.75	2.00
33 Seth Rollins	2.00	5.00
34 Shane McMahon	1.00	2.50
35 Sheamus	1.25	3.00
36 TJ Perkins RC	.60	1.50
37 Triple H	1.50	4.00
38 Undertaker	2.50	6.00
39 Xavier Woods	.75	2.00
40 Zack Ryder	.60	1.50
41 Alexander Wolfe RC	.75	2.00
42 Andrade Cien Almas	.60	1.50
43 Austin Aries	1.25	3.00
44 Bobby Roode	1.50	4.00
45 Dash Wilder	.60	1.50
46 Eric Young	1.25	3.00
47 Hideo Itami	1.00	2.50
48 Johnny Gargano	.60	1.50
49 Nick Miller RC	.60	1.50
50 No Way Jose	.60	1.50
51 Oney Lorcan	.60	1.50
52 Roderick Strong RC	.75	2.00
53 Samoa Joe	2.00	5.00
54 Sawyer Fulton	.60	1.50
55 Scott Dawson	.60	1.50
56 Shane Thorne RC	.60	1.50
57 Shinsuke Nakamura	1.50	4.00
58 Tommaso Ciampa	.60	1.50
59 Tye Dillinger	.60	1.50
60 William Regal	.75	2.00
61 Andre the Giant	1.25	3.00
62 Bret Hit Man Hart	1.25	3.00
63 Macho Man Randy Savage	1.25	3.00
64 Million Dollar Man Ted DiBiase	.75	2.00
65 Ric Flair	1.50	4.00
66 Rowdy Roddy Piper	1.25	3.00
67 Shawn Michaels	1.50	4.00
68 Sting	2.00	5.00
69 Stone Cold Steve Austin	2.50	6.00
70 Ultimate Warrior	1.25	3.00

2017 Topps WWE Undisputed Autographed Relics

*SILVER/50: .5X TO 1.2X BASIC AUTOS
*GREEN/25: .6X TO 1.5X BASIC AUTOS
*GOLD/10: UNPRICED DUE TO SCARCITY
*RED/1: UNPRICED DUE TO SCARCITY
RANDOMLY INSERTED INTO PACKS

UARAE Aiden English	5.00	12.00
UARAB Alexa Bliss	60.00	120.00
UARAF Alicia Fox	6.00	15.00
UARAS Asuka	25.00	60.00
UARAA Austin Aries	5.00	12.00
UARBC Baron Corbin	6.00	15.00
UARBE Becky Lynch	25.00	60.00
UARBCA Big Cass	5.00	12.00
UARBIG Big E	6.00	15.00
UARBS Big Show	6.00	15.00
UARBD Bo Dallas	6.00	15.00
UARBR Bobby Roode	6.00	15.00
UARBRS Braun Strowman	15.00	40.00
UARBW Bray Wyatt	10.00	25.00
UARBB Brie Bella	12.00	30.00
UARCA Carmella	12.00	30.00
UARCU Curtis Axel	5.00	12.00
UARDY Darren Young	6.00	15.00
UARDZ Dolph Ziggler	6.00	15.00
UARFA Fandango	5.00	12.00
UARFB Finn Balor	12.00	30.00
UARGO Goldust	6.00	15.00
UARHS Heath Slater	5.00	12.00
UARJG Johnny Gargano	5.00	12.00
UARJO JoJo	6.00	15.00
UARKA Kalisto	8.00	20.00
UARLH Luke Harper	50.00	100.00
UARMR Mojo Rawley	5.00	12.00
UARNA Natalya	6.00	15.00
UARNE Neville	8.00	20.00
UARRO Randy Orton	15.00	40.00
UARRY Renee Young	8.00	20.00
UARRR Roman Reigns	15.00	40.00
UARSJ Samoa Joe	6.00	15.00

UARSB Sasha Banks	60.00	120.00
UARSR Seth Rollins	12.00	30.00
UARSH Sheamus	6.00	15.00
UARSG Simon Gotch	5.00	12.00
UARSU Summer Rae	8.00	20.00
UARTA Tamina	6.00	15.00
UARTC Tommaso Ciampa	8.00	20.00
UARVI Viktor	5.00	12.00
UARZR Zack Ryder	6.00	15.00

2017 Topps WWE Undisputed Autographs

*BRONZE/99: SAME VALUE AS BASIC AUTOS
*SILVER/50: .5X TO 1.2X BASIC AUTOS
*GREEN/25: .6X TO 1.5X BASIC AUTOS
*GOLD/10: UNPRICED DUE TO SCARCITY
*BLACK/5: UNPRICED DUE TO SCARCITY
*RED/1: UNPRICED DUE TO SCARCITY
*P.P.BLACK/1: UNPRICED DUE TO SCARCITY
*P.P.CYAN/1: UNPRICED DUE TO SCARCITY
*P.P.MAGENTA/1: UNPRICED DUE TO SCARCITY
*P.P.YELLOW/1: UNPRICED DUE TO SCARCITY
RANDOMLY INSERTED INTO PACKS

UAA Asuka	15.00	40.00
UAC Cesaro	6.00	15.00
UAE Edge	10.00	25.00
UAM Maryse	12.00	30.00
UAN Natalya	8.00	20.00
UAR Rhyno	6.00	15.00
UAS Sting	25.00	60.00
UAAA Austin Aries	6.00	15.00
UAAB Alexa Bliss	60.00	120.00
UAAF Alicia Fox	8.00	20.00
UAAS AJ Styles	20.00	50.00
UABA Bayley	15.00	40.00
UABC Big Cass	6.00	15.00
UABE Big E	5.00	12.00
UABH Bret Hit Man Hart	15.00	40.00
UABL Becky Lynch	25.00	60.00
UABR Bobby Roode	10.00	25.00
UABW Bray Wyatt	8.00	20.00
UACA Carmella	12.00	30.00
UACF Charlotte Flair	15.00	40.00
UACJ Chris Jericho	10.00	25.00
UADA Dean Ambrose	10.00	25.00
UADB Dana Brooke	10.00	25.00
UADD Diamond Dallas Page	12.00	30.00
UAEA Enzo Amore	8.00	20.00
UAEM Ember Moon	8.00	20.00
UAEY Eric Young	6.00	15.00
UAFB Finn Balor	15.00	40.00
UAHS Heath Slater	5.00	12.00
UAJG Johnny Gargano	6.00	15.00
UAKA Karl Anderson	6.00	15.00
UAKO Kevin Owens	8.00	20.00
UALG Luke Gallows	5.00	12.00
UALM Liv Morgan	12.00	30.00
UANA Naomi	8.00	20.00
UANB Nikki Bella	10.00	25.00
UARR Roman Reigns	25.00	60.00
UARS Roderick Strong	6.00	15.00
UARY Renee Young	8.00	20.00
UASB Sasha Banks	15.00	40.00
UASH Sheamus	5.00	12.00
UASN Shinsuke Nakamura	20.00	50.00
UASR Seth Rollins	10.00	25.00
UASZ Sami Zayn	6.00	15.00
UATC Tommaso Ciampa	6.00	15.00
UATM The Miz	5.00	12.00
UATP TJ Perkins	5.00	12.00
UATS Trish Stratus	25.00	60.00
UAXW Xavier Woods	5.00	12.00
UABAC Baron Corbin	8.00	20.00
UAEMM Emma	10.00	25.00
UAKOK Kofi Kingston	5.00	12.00

2017 Topps WWE Undisputed Autographs Bronze

UAG Goldberg	50.00	100.00
UAU Undertaker	150.00	300.00
UARO Randy Orton	15.00	40.00
UABRL Brock Lesnar	50.00	100.00

2017 Topps WWE Undisputed Dream Matches

COMPLETE SET (10)	10.00	25.00

*BRONZE/99: .5X TO 1.2X BASIC CARDS
*SILVER/50: .6X TO 1.5X BASIC CARDS
*GREEN/25: .75X TO 2X BASIC CARDS
*GOLD/10: UNPRICED DUE TO SCARCITY
*RED/1: UNPRICED DUE TO SCARCITY
*P.P.BLACK/1: UNPRICED DUE TO SCARCITY
*P.P.CYAN/1: UNPRICED DUE TO SCARCITY
*P.P.MAGENTA/1: UNPRICED DUE TO SCARCITY
*P.P.YELLOW/1: UNPRICED DUE TO SCARCITY
STATED ODDS 1:

D1 Sting/Undertaker	2.00	5.00
D2 Goldberg/Steve Austin	1.50	4.00
D3 Steve Austin/Brock Lesnar	1.50	4.00
D4 Shawn Michaels/The Rock	2.00	5.00
D5 Shawn Michaels/Eddie Guerrero	1.25	3.00
D6 John Cena/Steve Austin	1.50	4.00
D7 Edge/Bret Hit Man Hart	1.00	2.50
D8 Undertaker/Goldberg	1.50	4.00
D9 Batista/Brock Lesnar	1.25	3.00
D10 Nakamura/Daniel Bryan	1.00	2.50

2017 Topps WWE Undisputed Dual Autographs

STATED PRINT RUN 25 SER.#'d SETS

UDAAE Asuka/E.Moon	60.00	120.00
UDABA B.Roode/A.Aries	30.00	75.00
UDABG B.Lesnar/Goldberg	120.00	250.00
UDACR Charlotte & Ric Flair	75.00	150.00
UDAJT J.Gargano/T.Ciampa	50.00	100.00
UDAKC K.Owens/C.Jericho	60.00	120.00
UDASB S.Banks/Bayley	75.00	150.00
UDASR S.Rollins/R.Reigns	100.00	200.00

2017 Topps WWE Undisputed Quad Autographed Booklets

STATED PRINT RUN 5 SER.#'d SETS
UNPRICED DUE TO SCARCITY
UQACSBB Charlotte/Banks/Lynch/Bayley
UQAFAKL Balor/Styles/Anderson/Gallows
UQAGBJR Goldberg/Lesnar/Cena/Orton
UQASBER Nakamura/Roode/Young/Strong

2017 Topps WWE Undisputed Relics

*SILVER/50: .5X TO 1.2X BASIC MEM
*GREEN/25: .6X TO 1.5X BASIC MEM
*GOLD/10: UNPRICED DUE TO SCARCITY
*RED/1: UNPRICED DUE TO SCARCITY
RANDOMLY INSERTED INTO PACKS

URAA Austin Aries	3.00	8.00
URAB Alexa Bliss	8.00	20.00
URAE Aiden English	1.50	4.00
URAF Alicia Fox	2.50	6.00
URAS Asuka	5.00	12.00
URBB Brie Bella	4.00	10.00
URBD Bo Dallas	1.50	4.00
URBE Becky Lynch	5.00	12.00
URBL Brock Lesnar	8.00	20.00
URBR Bobby Roode	4.00	10.00
URBS Big Show	2.00	5.00
URBW Bray Wyatt	4.00	10.00
URCA Carmella	4.00	10.00
URCU Curtis Axel	1.50	4.00
URDY Darren Young	1.50	4.00
URFB Finn Balor	6.00	15.00
URGO Goldust	2.00	5.00
URJC John Cena	8.00	20.00
URJO JoJo	2.50	6.00
URLH Luke Harper	1.50	4.00
URMR Mojo Rawley	2.00	5.00
URNA Natalya	3.00	8.00
URNE Neville	2.50	6.00
URRO Randy Orton	4.00	10.00
URRY Renee Young	2.50	6.00
URSB Sasha Banks	5.00	12.00
URSG Simon Gotch	1.50	4.00
URSH Sheamus	3.00	8.00
URSJ Samoa Joe	5.00	12.00
URSR Seth Rollins	5.00	12.00
URSR Summer Rae	4.00	10.00
URTA Tamina	2.00	5.00
URVI Viktor	1.50	4.00
URXW Xavier Woods	2.00	5.00
URZR Zack Ryder	1.50	4.00
URBCA Big Cass	2.00	5.00
URBIG Big E	2.00	5.00

2017 Topps WWE Undisputed Cut Signature

STATED PRINT RUN 1 SER.#'d SET
UNPRICED DUE TO SCARCITY
UTCYO Yokozuna

2017 Topps WWE Undisputed Triple Autographs

STATED PRINT RUN 10 SER.#'d SETS

UTAAKL Styles/Anderson/Gallows	100.00	200.00
UTABAE Bayley/Asuka/Moon	150.00	300.00
UTACSB Flair/Banks/Lynch	250.00	400.00
UTADSR Ambrose/Rollins/Reigns	125.00	250.00
UTANCA N.Bella/Carmella/Bliss	200.00	350.00

2017 Topps WWE Undisputed Women's Division

*BRONZE/99: .75X TO 2X BASIC CARDS
*SILVER/50: 1X TO 2.5X BASIC CARDS
*GREEN/25: 1.5X TO 4X BASIC CARDS
*GOLD/10: UNPRICED DUE TO SCARCITY
*RED/1: UNPRICED DUE TO SCARCITY
*P.P.BLACK/1: UNPRICED DUE TO SCARCITY
*P.P.CYAN/1: UNPRICED DUE TO SCARCITY
*P.P.MAGENTA/1: UNPRICED DUE TO SCARCITY
*P.P.YELLOW/1: UNPRICED DUE TO SCARCITY
RANDOMLY INSERTED INTO PACKS

W1 Alexa Bliss	4.00	10.00
W2 Alicia Fox	1.25	3.00
W3 Bayley	2.50	6.00
W4 Becky Lynch	2.50	6.00
W5 Carmella	2.00	5.00
W6 Charlotte Flair	3.00	8.00
W7 Dana Brooke	1.50	4.00
W8 Eva Marie	2.00	5.00
W9 Lana	2.50	6.00
W10 Maryse	1.50	4.00
W11 Mickie James	1.25	3.00
W12 Naomi	1.50	4.00
W13 Natalya	1.50	4.00
W14 Nia Jax	1.25	3.00
W15 Nikki Bella	2.00	5.00
W16 Sasha Banks	2.50	6.00
W17 Asuka	2.50	6.00
W18 Ember Moon	2.00	5.00
W19 Liv Morgan	1.25	3.00

2018 Topps WWE Undisputed

COMPLETE SET (50)	20.00	50.00
UNOPENED BOX (10 PACKS)	200.00	250.00
UNOPENED PACK (5 CARDS)	20.00	25.00

*ORANGE/99: .6X TO 1.5X BASIC CARDS
*GREEN/50: .75X TO 2X BASIC CARDS
*BLUE/25: 1X TO 2.5X BASIC CARDS
*GOLD/10: 2X TO 5X BASIC CARDS
*PURPLE/5: UNPRICED DUE TO SCARCITY
*RED/1: UNPRICED DUE TO SCARCITY
*P.P.BLACK/1: UNPRICED DUE TO SCARCITY
*P.P.CYAN/1: UNPRICED DUE TO SCARCITY
*P.P.MAGENTA/1: UNPRICED DUE TO SCARCITY
*P.P.YELLOW/1: UNPRICED DUE TO SCARCITY

1 AJ Styles	2.50	6.00
2 Alexa Bliss	3.00	8.00
3 Asuka	2.00	5.00
4 Bayley	1.00	2.50
5 Becky Lynch	1.50	4.00
6 Big E	.75	2.00
7 Bobby Roode	1.00	2.50
8 Brie Bella	1.25	3.00
9 Braun Strowman	1.50	4.00
10 Bray Wyatt	1.50	4.00
11 Brock Lesnar	2.50	6.00
12 Carmella	1.25	3.00
13 Cesaro	1.25	3.00
14 Charlotte Flair	2.00	5.00
15 Chris Jericho	1.50	4.00
16 Daniel Bryan	1.50	4.00
17 Dean Ambrose	1.25	3.00
18 Finn Balor	1.50	4.00
19 Jason Jordan	.60	1.50
20 Jeff Hardy	1.25	3.00
21 John Cena	2.50	6.00
22 Kane	1.00	2.50
23 Kevin Owens	1.50	4.00
24 Kofi Kingston	.75	2.00
25 Kurt Angle	1.50	4.00
26 Woken Matt Hardy	1.50	4.00
27 Mickie James	1.25	3.00
28 Naomi	.75	2.00
29 Natalya	.75	2.00
30 Nia Jax	1.00	2.50
31 Nikki Bella	1.25	3.00
32 Paige	1.50	4.00
33 Randy Orton	1.50	4.00
34 Roman Reigns	1.50	4.00
35 Ruby Riott	1.00	2.50

36 Sami Zayn	.60	1.50
37 Samoa Joe	1.25	3.00
38 Sasha Banks	2.00	5.00
39 Seth Rollins	1.50	4.00
40 Sheamus	1.25	3.00
41 Shinsuke Nakamura	1.50	4.00
42 The Miz	1.25	3.00
43 Triple H	1.50	4.00
44 Undertaker	2.50	6.00
45 Xavier Woods	.75	2.00
46 Adam Cole RC	.75	2.00
47 Aleister Black	.75	2.00
48 Drew McIntyre	1.00	2.50
49 Ember Moon	1.25	3.00
50 Kairi Sane RC	1.50	4.00

2018 Topps WWE Undisputed 30 Years of Royal Rumble

COMPLETE SET (25) 12.00 30.00
*ORANGE/99: .5X TO 1.2X BASIC CARDS
*GREEN/50: .6X TO 1.5X BASIC CARDS
*BLUE/25: .75X TO 2X BASIC CARDS
*GOLD/10: 1.2X TO 3X BASIC CARDS
*PURPLE/5: UNPRICED DUE TO SCARCITY
*RED/1: UNPRICED DUE TO SCARCITY
*P.P.BLACK/1: UNPRICED DUE TO SCARCITY
*P.P.CYAN/1: UNPRICED DUE TO SCARCITY
*P.P.MAGENTA/1: UNPRICED DUE TO SCARCITY
*P.P.YELLOW/1: UNPRICED DUE TO SCARCITY
RANDOMLY INSERTED INTO PACKS

RR1 Hacksaw Jim Duggan	.60	1.50
RR2 Big John Studd	.60	1.50
RR3 Ric Flair	2.00	5.00
RR4 Yokozuna	.75	2.00
RR5 Bret Hit Man Hart	1.50	4.00
RR6 Lex Luger	.75	2.00
RR7 Shawn Michaels	2.00	5.00
RR8 Shawn Michaels	2.00	5.00
RR9 Stone Cold Steve Austin	3.00	8.00
RR10 Stone Cold Steve Austin	3.00	8.00
RR11 The Rock	3.00	8.00
RR12 Stone Cold Steve Austin	3.00	8.00
RR13 Triple H	1.50	4.00
RR14 Brock Lesnar	2.50	6.00
RR15 Batista	1.00	2.50
RR16 Undertaker	2.50	6.00
RR17 John Cena	2.50	6.00
RR18 Randy Orton	1.50	4.00
RR19 Edge	1.50	4.00
RR20 Sheamus	1.25	3.00
RR21 John Cena	2.50	6.00
RR22 Batista	1.00	2.50
RR23 Roman Reigns	1.50	4.00
RR24 Triple H	1.50	4.00
RR25 Randy Orton	1.50	4.00

2018 Topps WWE Undisputed 30 Years of Survivor Series

COMPLETE SET (25) 12.00 30.00
*ORANGE/99: .5X TO 1.2X BASIC CARDS
*GREEN/50: .6X TO 1.5X BASIC CARDS
*BLUE/25: .75X TO 2X BASIC CARDS
*GOLD/10: 1.2X TO 3X BASIC CARDS
*PURPLE/5: UNPRICED DUE TO SCARCITY
*RED/1: UNPRICED DUE TO SCARCITY
*P.P.BLACK/1: UNPRICED DUE TO SCARCITY
*P.P.CYAN/1: UNPRICED DUE TO SCARCITY
*P.P.MAGENTA/1: UNPRICED DUE TO SCARCITY
*P.P.YELLOW/1: UNPRICED DUE TO SCARCITY
RANDOMLY INSERTED INTO PACKS

SS1 Andre The Giant	1.25	3.00
SS2 Macho Man Randy Savage	2.00	5.00
SS3 Ultimate Warrior	2.50	6.00
SS4 Ultimate Warrior	2.50	6.00
SS5 Big Boss Man	.60	1.50
SS6 The Nasty Boys	.60	1.50
SS7 Lex Luger	.75	2.00
SS8 Million Dollar Man Ted DiBiase	.75	2.00
SS9 Shawn Michaels	2.00	5.00
SS10 Ken Shamrock	.75	2.00
SS11 The Rock	3.00	8.00
SS12 Chris Jericho	1.50	4.00
SS13 Randy Orton	1.50	4.00
SS14 Batista	1.00	2.50
SS15 John Cena	2.50	6.00
SS16 Randy Orton	1.50	4.00
SS17 Mickie James	1.25	3.00
SS18 Kofi Kingston	.75	2.00
SS19 Dolph Ziggler	.75	2.00
SS20 Dolph Ziggler	.75	2.00
SS21 Natalya	.75	2.00
SS22 John Cena	2.50	6.00
SS23 The Usos	1.00	2.50
SS24 AJ Styles	2.50	6.00
SS25 Kurt Angle	1.50	4.00

2018 Topps WWE Undisputed Autographed Kiss and Shirt Relic Booklets

STATED ODDS 1:1,500
STATED PRINT RUN 5 SER.#'d SETS
UNPRICED DUE TO SCARCITY

KSAF Alicia Fox
KSEM Ember Moon
KSNA Natalya
KSNB Nikki Bella
KSRY Renee Young

2018 Topps WWE Undisputed Autographed Relics

*SILVER/50: .5X TO 1.2X BASIC AUTOS
*BLUE/25: UNPRICED DUE TO SCARCITY
*GOLD/10: UNPRICED DUE TO SCARCITY
*PURPLE/5: UNPRICED DUE TO SCARCITY
*RED/1: UNPRICED DUE TO SCARCITY
*P.P.BLACK/1: UNPRICED DUE TO SCARCITY
*P.P.CYAN/1: UNPRICED DUE TO SCARCITY
*P.P.MAGENTA/1: UNPRICED DUE TO SCARCITY
*P.P.YELLOW/1: UNPRICED DUE TO SCARCITY
STATED ODDS 1:10
STATED PRINT RUN 99 SER.#'d SETS

URAA Andrade Cien Almas	8.00	20.00
URAB Alexa Bliss	60.00	120.00
URAE Aiden English	5.00	12.00
URAF Alicia Fox	15.00	40.00
URAK Akam	6.00	15.00
URAP Apollo Crews	5.00	12.00
URAW Alexander Wolfe	6.00	15.00
URAX Curtis Axel	5.00	12.00
URBK Becky Lynch	30.00	75.00
URCA Carmella	20.00	50.00
URCF Charlotte Flair	20.00	50.00
URCG Chad Gable	6.00	15.00
URDW Dash Wilder	6.00	15.00
UREY Eric Young	8.00	20.00
URFN Fandango	5.00	12.00
URGD Goldust	10.00	25.00
URHA Harper	6.00	15.00
URJJ JoJo	15.00	40.00
URJO Jason Jordan	5.00	12.00
URJU Jimmy Uso	6.00	15.00
URKA Karl Anderson	5.00	12.00
URLG Luke Gallows	6.00	15.00
URNA Naomi	10.00	25.00
URNC Nikki Cross	10.00	25.00
URNT Natalya	12.00	30.00
URNW No Way Jose	8.00	20.00
URRE Rezar	6.00	15.00
URRY Renee Young	15.00	40.00
URSB Sasha Banks	25.00	60.00
URSD Scott Dawson	6.00	15.00
URSR Seth Rollins	15.00	40.00
URTC Tommaso Ciampa	8.00	20.00
URZR Zack Ryder	6.00	15.00

2018 Topps WWE Undisputed Autographs

*ORANGE/99: .5X TO 1.2X BASIC AUTOS
*GREEN/50: .6X TO 1.5X BASIC AUTOS
*BLUE/25: UNPRICED DUE TO SCARCITY
*GOLD/10: UNPRICED DUE TO SCARCITY
*PURPLE/5: UNPRICED DUE TO SCARCITY
*RED/1: UNPRICED DUE TO SCARCITY
*P.P.BLACK/1: UNPRICED DUE TO SCARCITY
*P.P.CYAN/1: UNPRICED DUE TO SCARCITY
*P.P.MAGENTA/1: UNPRICED DUE TO SCARCITY
*P.P.YELLOW/1: UNPRICED DUE TO SCARCITY
RANDOMLY INSERTED INTO PACKS

UAAB Alexa Bliss	30.00	75.00
UAAC Adam Cole	12.00	30.00
UAAJ AJ Styles	20.00	50.00
UAAS Asuka	15.00	40.00
UABA Bayley	15.00	40.00
UABC Baron Corbin	6.00	15.00
UABE Big E	6.00	15.00
UABF Bobby Fish	8.00	20.00
UABL Becky Lynch	25.00	60.00
UABR Bobby Roode	10.00	25.00
UABW Bray Wyatt	10.00	25.00
UACA Carmella	12.00	30.00
UACE Cesaro	6.00	15.00
UACF Charlotte Flair	15.00	40.00
UACG Chad Gable	4.00	10.00
UADA Dean Ambrose	8.00	20.00
UADB Daniel Bryan	15.00	40.00
UADM Drew McIntyre	10.00	25.00
UADW Dash Wilder	5.00	12.00
UAEL Elias	15.00	40.00
UAEY Eric Young	5.00	12.00
UAFA Fandango	8.00	20.00
UAFB Finn Balor	15.00	40.00
UAHI Hideo Itami	6.00	15.00
UAJH Jeff Hardy	12.00	30.00
UAJJ Jason Jordan	6.00	15.00
UAJM Jinder Mahal	6.00	15.00
UAKA Karl Anderson	4.00	10.00
UAKK Kofi Kingston	4.00	10.00
UAKO Kevin Owens	12.00	30.00
UAKS Kairi Sane	25.00	60.00
UALA Lana	8.00	20.00
UAMH Matt Hardy	10.00	25.00
UAMK Maria Kanellis	8.00	20.00
UAMR Mojo Rawley	4.00	10.00
UANA Naomi	5.00	12.00
UANJ Nia Jax	10.00	25.00
UARS Roderick Strong	6.00	15.00
UARU Rusev	5.00	12.00
UASB Sasha Banks	20.00	50.00
UASD Scott Dawson	4.00	10.00
UASH Sheamus	6.00	15.00
UASJ Samoa Joe	10.00	25.00
UASN Shinsuke Nakamura	10.00	25.00
UASR Seth Rollins	12.00	30.00
UAST Sting	15.00	40.00
UASZ Sami Zayn	5.00	12.00
UATB Tyler Breeze	6.00	15.00
UATD Tye Dillinger	5.00	12.00
UATM The Miz	8.00	20.00
UAVD Velveteen Dream	15.00	40.00
UAXW Xavier Woods	5.00	12.00
UAZR Zack Ryder	4.00	10.00
UAABL Aleister Black	10.00	20.00
UABCA Big Cass	5.00	12.00
UABRS Braun Strowman	12.00	30.00
UAEMB Ember Moon	12.00	30.00
UAKOH Kassius Ohno	6.00	15.00
UAKUA Kurt Angle	12.00	30.00
UAKYO Kyle O'Reilly	6.00	15.00
UAMAR Maryse	10.00	25.00
UANAT Natalya	8.00	20.00
UARRI Ruby Riott	8.00	20.00
UASBE Shelton Benjamin	6.00	15.00

2018 Topps WWE Undisputed Classic Matches Dual Autographed Relics

*PURPLE/5: UNPRICED DUE TO SCARCITY
*RED/1: UNPRICED DUE TO SCARCITY
STATED ODDS 1:766
STATED PRINT RUN 10 SER.#'d SETS
UNPRICED DUE TO SCARCITY

ARBH HHH/D.Bryan
ARDS Sheamus/D.Bryan
ARRH HHH/S.Rollins
ARRU Undertaker/R.Reigns

2018 Topps WWE Undisputed Cut Signatures

STATED ODDS 1:19,120
STATED PRINT RUN 1 SER.#'d SET
UNPRICED DUE TO SCARCITY

CSCH Mr. Perfect Curt Hennig
CSEG Eddie Guerrero

2018 Topps WWE Undisputed Dual Autographs

*GOLD/10: UNPRICED DUE TO SCARCITY
*PURPLE/5: UNPRICED DUE TO SCARCITY
*RED/1: UNPRICED DUE TO SCARCITY
STATED ODDS 1:154
STATED PRINT RUN 25 SER.#'d SETS

DAAJ K.Angle/J.Jordan	25.00	60.00
DAAR D.Ambrose/S.Rollins	30.00	75.00
DABG S.Benjamin/C.Gable	15.00	40.00
DACS Sheamus/Cesaro	15.00	40.00
DAFB T.Breeze/Fandango	30.00	75.00
DAGA K.Anderson/L.Gallows	25.00	60.00
DAHH J.Hardy/M.Hardy	60.00	120.00
DARR M.Rawley/Z.Ryder	30.00	75.00

DATM	HHH/S.McMahon	150.00	300.00
DAWD	S.Dawson/D.Wilder	15.00	40.00

2018 Topps WWE Undisputed Quad Autographed Booklets

QAAUTH HHH/McMahon/Rollins/Orton
QATEAMA Benjamin/Jordan/Gable/Angle
QAWYATT Wyatt/Strowman/Harper/Rowan
QASANITY Cross/Wolfe/Dain/Young
QATHEMIZ Axel/Maryse/Miz/Dallas

2018 Topps WWE Undisputed Relics

*GREEN/50: .6X TO 1.2X BASIC MEM
*BLUE/25: .75X TO 2X BASIC MEM
*GOLD/10: 1.5X TO 4X BASIC MEM
*PURPLE/5: UNPRICED DUE TO SCARCITY
*RED/1: UNPRICED DUE TO SCARCITY
*P.P.BLACK/1: UNPRICED DUE TO SCARCITY
*P.P.CYAN/1: UNPRICED DUE TO SCARCITY
*P.P.MAGENTA/1: UNPRICED DUE TO SCARCITY
*P.P.YELLOW/1: UNPRICED DUE TO SCARCITY
STATED ODDS 1:10
STATED PRINT RUN 99 SER.#'d SETS

URAA	Andrade Cien Almas	5.00	12.00
URAB	Alexa Bliss	12.00	30.00
URAE	Aiden English	2.00	5.00
URAF	Alicia Fox	5.00	12.00
URAK	Akam	2.00	5.00
URAW	Alexander Wolfe	2.50	6.00
URAX	Curtis Axel	3.00	8.00
URBC	Baron Corbin	2.50	6.00
URBE	Big E	2.50	6.00
URBK	Becky Lynch	10.00	25.00
URBL	Brock Lesnar	6.00	15.00
URBR	Bobby Roode	2.50	6.00
URCA	Carmella	8.00	20.00
URCF	Charlotte Flair	6.00	15.00
URCG	Chad Gable	2.50	6.00
URDB	Daniel Bryan	5.00	12.00
URDW	Dash Wilder	3.00	8.00
UREM	Ember Moon	5.00	12.00
UREY	Eric Young	2.50	6.00
URGD	Goldust	3.00	8.00
URHA	Harper	2.00	5.00
URHI	Hideo Itami	2.00	5.00
URJC	John Cena	10.00	25.00
URJJ	JoJo	6.00	15.00
URJO	Jason Jordan	2.00	5.00
URJU	Jimmy Uso	3.00	8.00
URKA	Karl Anderson	3.00	8.00
URKK	Kofi Kingston	2.50	6.00
URKO	Kevin Owens	2.50	6.00
URLG	Luke Gallows	2.00	5.00
URNA	Naomi	2.50	6.00
URNC	Nikki Cross	6.00	15.00
URNT	Natalya	3.00	8.00
URNW	No Way Jose	2.00	5.00
URRE	Rezar	2.00	5.00
URRR	Roman Reigns	6.00	15.00
URRY	Renee Young	5.00	12.00
URSB	Sasha Banks	12.00	30.00
URSD	Scott Dawson	2.00	5.00
URSR	Seth Rollins	2.50	6.00
URTC	Tommaso Ciampa	6.00	15.00
URXW	Xavier Woods	2.50	6.00

2018 Topps WWE Undisputed Rivals Dual Autograph and Championship Booklets

STATED ODDS 1:1,500
STATED PRINT RUN 5 SER.#'d SETS
UNPRICED DUE TO SCARCITY

ACAC B.Corbin/D.Ambrose
ACBF Bayley/C.Flair
ACNB A.Bliss/Naomi
ACOJ C.Jericho/K.Owens
ACOW B.Wyatt/R.Orton

2018 Topps WWE Undisputed Triple Autographs

*PURPLE/5: UNPRICED DUE TO SCARCITY
*RED/1: UNPRICED DUE TO SCARCITY
STATED ODDS 1:475
STATED PRINT RUN 10 SER.#'d SETS

TACFO O'Reilly/Cole/Fish
TAKBW Kingston/Woods/Big E
TAMAD Miz/Axel/Dallas
TAOTC O'Neil/Crews/Tozawa
TASGA Anderson/Gallows/Styles
TAUUN J.Uso/J.Uso/Naomi
TAYWD Dain/Young/Wolfe

2018 Topps WWE Undisputed Triple Shirt Relics

*GOLD/10: UNPRICED DUE TO SCARCITY
*PURPLE/5: UNPRICED DUE TO SCARCITY
*RED/1: UNPRICED DUE TO SCARCITY
STATED ODDS 1:310
STATED PRINT RUN 25 SER.#'d SETS

TSBGA	Gallows/Balor/Anderson	20.00	50.00
TSDAY	Woods/Kingston/Big E	12.00	30.00
TSNUU	The Usos/Naomi	15.00	40.00
TSOZB	Zayn/Bryan/Owens	12.00	30.00
TSRRJ	Rollins/Reigns/Jordan	15.00	40.00

2019 Topps WWE Undisputed

COMPLETE SET (100) 25.00 60.00
UNOPENED BOX (10 PACKS)
UNOPENED PACK (5 CARDS)
*ORANGE/99: .6X TO 1.5X BASIC CARDS
*GREEN/50: .75X TO 2X BASIC CARDS
*BLUE/25: 1X TO 2.5X BASIC CARDS
*GOLD/10: UNPRICED DUE TO SCARCITY
*PURPLE/5: UNPRICED DUE TO SCARCITY
*RED/1: UNPRICED DUE TO SCARCITY
*P.P.BLACK/1: UNPRICED DUE TO SCARCITY
*P.P.CYAN/1: UNPRICED DUE TO SCARCITY
*P.P.MAGENTA/1: UNPRICED DUE TO SCARCITY
*P.P.YELLOW/1: UNPRICED DUE TO SCARCITY

1	Aiden English	.50	1.25
2	AJ Styles	2.50	6.00
3	Alexa Bliss	2.50	6.00
4	Alexander Wolfe	.50	1.25
5	Andrade	.60	1.50
6	Asuka	1.50	4.00
7	Baron Corbin	.75	2.00
8	Bayley	1.00	2.50
9	Becky Lynch	2.00	5.00
10	Big E	.50	1.25
11	Billie Kay	1.00	2.50
12	Bo Dallas	.60	1.50
13	Bobby Lashley	1.00	2.50
14	Bobby Roode	1.00	2.50
15	Braun Strowman	1.25	3.00
16	Bray Wyatt	1.25	3.00
17	Carmella	1.25	3.00
18	Cedric Alexander	.50	1.25
19	Cesaro	.60	1.50
20	Charlotte Flair	2.00	5.00
21	Curtis Axel	.60	1.50
22	Daniel Bryan	2.00	5.00
23	Dash Wilder	.50	1.25
24	Dolph Ziggler	1.00	2.50
25	Drake Maverick	.50	1.25
26	Drew Gulak	.50	1.25
27	Drew McIntyre	.60	1.50
28	Elias	1.00	2.50
29	Ember Moon	1.25	3.00
30	Eric Young	.60	1.50
31	Finn Balor	1.25	3.00
32	Harper	.60	1.50
33	Jeff Hardy	1.25	3.00
34	Jey Uso	.60	1.50
35	Jimmy Uso	.60	1.50
36	Jinder Mahal	1.00	2.50
37	John Cena	2.00	5.00
38	Karl Anderson	.75	2.00
39	Kevin Owens	1.25	3.00
40	Killian Dain	.50	1.25
41	Kofi Kingston	.75	2.00
42	Kurt Angle	1.00	2.50
43	Lacey Evans	1.00	2.50
44	Lio Rush	.60	1.50
45	Liv Morgan	1.50	4.00
46	Luke Gallows	.75	2.00
47	Mustafa Ali	.50	1.25
48	Naomi	.75	2.00
49	Natalya	1.00	2.50
50	Nia Jax	1.00	2.50
51	Paige	2.00	5.00
52	Peyton Royce	1.25	3.00
53	Randy Orton	1.25	3.00
54	Rey Mysterio	1.25	3.00
55	Roman Reigns	1.25	3.00
56	Ronda Rousey	2.50	6.00
57	Rowan	.50	1.25
58	Ruby Riott	1.00	2.50
59	Rusev	1.00	2.50
60	Sami Zayn	1.00	2.50
61	Samoa Joe	1.00	2.50
62	Sarah Logan	.60	1.50
63	Sasha Banks	2.00	5.00
64	Scott Dawson	.50	1.25
65	Seth Rollins	1.25	3.00
66	Sheamus	.75	2.00
67	Shelton Benjamin	.60	1.50
68	Shinsuke Nakamura	1.25	3.00
69	The Miz	1.00	2.50
70	The Rock	2.50	6.00
71	Titus O'Neil	.60	1.50
72	Triple H	1.25	3.00
73	Undertaker	2.50	6.00
74	Xavier Woods	.60	1.50
75	Zelina Vega	.75	2.00
76	Adam Cole	.60	1.50
77	Aleister Black	.60	1.50
78	Deonna Purrazzo RC	.50	1.25
79	EC3	.50	1.25
80	Johnny Gargano	.50	1.25
81	Kairi Sane	1.00	2.50
82	Keith Lee RC	.50	1.25
83	Nikki Cross	.75	2.00
84	Ricochet	1.25	3.00
85	Shayna Baszler	1.00	2.50
86	Tommaso Ciampa	.50	1.25
87	Goldberg	1.50	4.00
88	Shawn Michaels	1.25	3.00
89	Sting	1.25	3.00
90	Trish Stratus	2.50	6.00
RS1	Finn Balor	1.25	3.00
RS2	Jeff Hardy	1.25	3.00
RS3	Sasha Banks	2.00	5.00
RS4	Bayley	1.00	2.50
RS5	Seth Rollins	1.25	3.00
RS6	Shinsuke Nakamura	1.25	3.00
RS7	Aleister Black	.60	1.50
RS8	Ricochet	1.25	3.00
RS9	Sting	1.25	3.00
RS10	Ric Flair	1.50	4.00

2019 Topps WWE Undisputed Autographed Kiss and Shirt Relic Booklet

STATED PRINT RUN 5 SER.#'d SETS
UNPRICED DUE TO SCARCITY

AKSAF Alicia Fox

2019 Topps WWE Undisputed Autographed Relics

*GREEN/50: .5X TO 1.2X BASIC AUTOS
*BLUE/25: .6X TO 1.5X BASIC AUTOS
*GOLD/10: UNPRICED DUE TO SCARCITY
*PURPLE/5: UNPRICED DUE TO SCARCITY
*RED/1: UNPRICED DUE TO SCARCITY
STATED PRINT RUN 120 SER.#'d SETS

UAR4H	Shayna Baszler	10.00	25.00
UARAA	Andrade	12.00	30.00
UARAB	Alexa Bliss	60.00	120.00
UARAC	Adam Cole	10.00	25.00
UARAE	Aiden English	6.00	15.00
UARAK	Asuka	20.00	50.00
UARBD	Bo Dallas	6.00	15.00
UARBS	Braun Strowman	12.00	30.00
UARCA	Curtis Axel	6.00	15.00
UARCM	Carmella	15.00	40.00
UARCS	Cesaro	6.00	15.00
UARDW	Dash Wilder	6.00	15.00
UAREL	Elias	10.00	25.00
UARFB	Finn Balor	12.00	30.00
UARJH	Jeff Hardy	12.00	30.00
UARKD	Killian Dain	6.00	15.00
UARKK	Kofi Kingston	12.00	30.00
UARLG	Luke Gallows	6.00	15.00
UARLM	Liv Morgan	25.00	60.00
UARMG	Karl Anderson	6.00	15.00
UARNJ	Nia Jax	8.00	20.00
UARNM	Naomi	8.00	20.00
UARNN	Natalya	10.00	25.00
UARNW	No Way Jose	6.00	15.00
UARRB	Ruby Riott	12.00	30.00
UARRC	Ricochet	20.00	50.00
UARSB	Sasha Banks	20.00	50.00
UARSD	Scott Dawson	6.00	15.00
UARSM	Sheamus	6.00	15.00
UARSR	Seth Rollins	8.00	20.00
UARSZ	Sami Zayn	6.00	15.00
UARTC	Tommaso Ciampa	10.00	25.00

UARTM The Miz 10.00 25.00
UARVD Velveteen Dream 10.00 25.00
UARXW Xavier Woods 6.00 15.00
UARZR Zack Ryder 6.00 15.00

2019 Topps WWE Undisputed Autographed Relics Blue

UARCH Curt Hawkins 10.00 25.00

2019 Topps WWE Undisputed Autographed Relics Green

UARAF Alicia Fox 8.00 20.00

2019 Topps WWE Undisputed Autographed Tag Team Championship Medallion Booklets

STATED PRINT RUN 5 SER.#'d SETS
UNPRICED DUE TO SCARCITY

DACBT C.Axel/B.Dallas
DACND X.Woods/K.Kingston
DACTB Cesaro/Sheamus
DACUSO Jey and Jimmy Uso

2019 Topps WWE Undisputed Autographs

*GOLD/10: UNPRICED DUE TO SCARCITY
*PURPLE/5: UNPRICED DUE TO SCARCITY
*RED/1: UNPRICED DUE TO SCARCITY
*P.P.BLACK/1: UNPRICED DUE TO SCARCITY
*P.P.CYAN/1: UNPRICED DUE TO SCARCITY
*P.P.MAGENTA/1: UNPRICED DUE TO SCARCITY
*P.P.YELLOW/1: UNPRICED DUE TO SCARCITY
STATED PRINT RUN 199 SER.#'d SETS

AAA Andrade Almas 5.00 12.00
AAB Alexa Bliss 50.00 100.00
AAC Adam Cole 10.00 25.00
AAL Aleister Black 8.00 20.00
AAS AJ Styles 15.00 40.00
AAW Alexander Wolfe 5.00 12.00
ABC Baron Corbin 5.00 12.00
ABD Bo Dallas 5.00 12.00
ABE Big E 6.00 15.00
ABL Becky Lynch 25.00 60.00
ABR Bobby Roode 8.00 20.00
ABS Braun Strowman 10.00 25.00
ACA Cedric Alexander 5.00 12.00
ACE Cesaro 5.00 12.00
ACF Charlotte Flair 20.00 50.00
ACJ Cactus Jack 15.00 40.00
ACU Curtis Axel 5.00 12.00
ADK Dakota Kai 12.00 30.00
ADM Drew McIntyre 6.00 15.00
ADP Deonna Purrazzo 20.00 50.00
AEC EC3 5.00 12.00
AEY Eric Young 5.00 12.00
AFB Finn Balor 12.00 30.00
AJF Jeff Hardy 12.00 30.00
AJG Johnny Gargano 6.00 15.00
AJM Jinder Mahal 5.00 12.00
AKA Kurt Angle 10.00 25.00
AKD Killian Dain 5.00 12.00
AKK Kofi Kingston 10.00 25.00
AKL Keith Lee 6.00 15.00
AKR Kyle O'Reilly 5.00 12.00
AKS Kairi Sane 15.00 40.00
ALR Lio Rush 5.00 12.00
AMA Maryse 10.00 25.00
AME Carmella 10.00 25.00
AMR Mandy Rose 15.00 40.00
ANA Naomi 6.00 15.00
ANJ Nia Jax 8.00 20.00
ANN Natalya 5.00 12.00
APD Pete Dunne 6.00 15.00
ARI Ricochet 20.00 50.00
ARM Rey Mysterio 12.00 30.00
ARS Roderick Strong 5.00 12.00
ARU Rusev 5.00 12.00
ARY Renee Young 6.00 15.00
ASD Sonya Deville 12.00 30.00
ASH Sheamus 5.00 12.00
ASN Shinsuke Nakamura 10.00 25.00
AST Sting 15.00 40.00
ASU Asuka 15.00 40.00
ASZ Sami Zayn 5.00 12.00
ATC Tommaso Ciampa 8.00 20.00
ATM The Miz 10.00 25.00
ATN Titus O'Neil 5.00 12.00
AVD Velveteen Dream 10.00 25.00
AXW Xavier Woods 5.00 12.00
AZV Zelina Vega 12.00 30.00
ABAS Shayna Baszler 10.00 25.00
AE Elias 8.00 20.00

2019 Topps WWE Undisputed Cut Signatures

STATED PRINT RUN 1 SER.#'d SET
UNPRICED DUE TO SCARCITY

CSDR Dusty Rhodes
CSEG Eddie Guerrero
CSJN Jim "The Anvil" Neidhart

2019 Topps WWE Undisputed Dual Autographs

*GOLD/10: UNPRICED DUE TO SCARCITY
*PURPLE/5: UNPRICED DUE TO SCARCITY
*RED/1: UNPRICED DUE TO SCARCITY
STATED PRINT RUN 25 SER.#'d SETS

DTI B.Kay/P.Royce 125.00 250.00
DTR D.Wilder/S.Dawson 50.00 100.00
DUE R.Strong/K.O'Reilly 25.00 60.00
DWR Hanson/Rowe 100.00 200.00

2019 Topps WWE Undisputed Quad Autographs Booklets

STATED PRINT RUN 5 SER.#'d SETS
UNPRICED DUE TO SCARCITY

QHW Flair/Lynch/Banks/Bayley
QUE Strong/O'Reilly/Fish/Cole

2019 Topps WWE Undisputed Relics

*GREEN/50: .5X TO 1.2X BASIC MEM
*BLUE/25: .6X TO 1.5X BASIC MEM
*GOLD/10: UNPRICED DUE TO SCARCITY
*PURPLE/5: UNPRICED DUE TO SCARCITY
*RED/1: UNPRICED DUE TO SCARCITY
STATED PRINT RUN 99 SER.#'d SETS

UR4H Shayna Baszler 4.00 10.00
URAA Andrade 4.00 10.00
URAB Alexa Bliss 12.00 30.00
URAC Adam Cole 6.00 15.00
URAF Alicia Fox 4.00 10.00
URAK Asuka 5.00 12.00
URBD Bo Dallas 4.00 10.00
URBS Braun Strowman 5.00 12.00
URCA Curtis Axel 5.00 12.00
URCF Charlotte Flair 10.00 25.00
URCM Carmella 6.00 15.00
URCS Cesaro 3.00 8.00
URDW Dash Wilder 3.00 8.00
URDZ Dolph Ziggler 4.00 10.00
UREL Elias 3.00 8.00
UREM Ember Moon 5.00 12.00
URFB Finn Balor 5.00 12.00
URJC John Cena 6.00 15.00
URJH Jeff Hardy 5.00 12.00
URKD Killian Dain 5.00 12.00
URKK Kofi Kingston 4.00 10.00
URKO Kevin Owens 5.00 12.00
URLG Luke Gallows 4.00 10.00
URLM Liv Morgan 10.00 25.00
URMG Karl Anderson 4.00 10.00
URNJ Nia Jax 5.00 12.00
URNM Naomi 3.00 8.00
URNN Natalya 4.00 10.00
URNW No Way Jose 4.00 10.00
URRB Ruby Riott 4.00 10.00
URRC Ricochet 5.00 12.00
URRR Roman Reigns 6.00 15.00
URSB Sasha Banks 8.00 20.00
URSD Scott Dawson 3.00 8.00
URSM Sheamus 3.00 8.00
URSR Seth Rollins 5.00 12.00
URSZ Sami Zayn 3.00 8.00
URTC Tommaso Ciampa 5.00 12.00
URTM The Miz 3.00 8.00
URVD Velveteen Dream 4.00 10.00
URXW Xavier Woods 4.00 10.00
URZR Zack Ryder 5.00 12.00
URUCE Jey Uso 3.00 8.00
URUSO Jimmy Uso 3.00 8.00

2019 Topps WWE Undisputed Triple Autographs

*PURPLE/5: UNPRICED DUE TO SCARCITY
*RED/1: UNPRICED DUE TO SCARCITY
STATED PRINT RUN 10 SER.#'d SETS
UNPRICED DUE TO SCARCITY

TLP Kalisto/Metalik/Dorado
TND Big E/Woods/Kingston
TRD Rusev/Lana/English
TRS Logan/Riott/Morgan

2020 Topps WWE Undisputed

COMPLETE SET (90) 25.00 60.00
*ORANGE/99: .75X TO 2X BASIC CARDS
*GREEN/50: 1.2X TO 3X BASIC CARDS
*BLUE/25: UNPRICED DUE TO SCARCITY
*GOLD/10: UNPRICED DUE TO SCARCITY
*PURPLE/5: UNPRICED DUE TO SCARCITY
*RED/1: UNPRICED DUE TO SCARCITY
*P.P.BLACK/1: UNPRICED DUE TO SCARCITY
*P.P.CYAN/1: UNPRICED DUE TO SCARCITY
*P.P.MAGENTA/1: UNPRICED DUE TO SCARCITY
*P.P.YELLOW/1: UNPRICED DUE TO SCARCITY

1 Aleister Black 1.00 2.50
2 Andrade .75 2.00
3 Asuka 2.00 5.00
4 Becky Lynch 2.00 5.00
5 Bianca Belair 1.25 3.00
6 Bobby Lashley 1.00 2.50
7 Buddy Murphy .60 1.50
8 Charlotte Flair 2.00 5.00
9 Drew McIntyre 1.00 2.50
10 Edge 1.00 2.50
11 Erik .50 1.25
12 Humberto Carrillo .75 2.00
13 Ivar .50 1.25
14 Kairi Sane 1.00 2.50
15 Kevin Owens .60 1.50
16 Lana 1.25 3.00
17 Nia Jax .75 2.00
18 Randy Orton 1.25 3.00
19 Ricochet .75 2.00
20 Ruby Riott .75 2.00
21 R-Truth .50 1.25
22 Samoa Joe .75 2.00
23 Seth Rollins 1.00 2.50
24 Zelina Vega 1.00 2.50
25 AJ Styles 1.50 4.00
26 Alexa Bliss 3.00 8.00
27 Bayley 1.00 2.50
28 Big E .50 1.25
29 Braun Strowman 1.25 3.00
30 The Fiend Bray Wyatt 1.50 4.00
31 Carmella 1.25 3.00
32 Cesaro .50 1.25
33 Dana Brooke .75 2.00
34 Daniel Bryan 1.50 4.00
35 Dolph Ziggler .50 1.25
36 Elias .50 1.25
37 King Corbin .60 1.50
38 Kofi Kingston .75 2.00
39 Lacey Evans 1.25 3.00
40 Matt Riddle 1.00 2.50
41 Mustafa Ali .75 2.00
42 Naomi 1.00 2.50
43 Nikki Cross 1.00 2.50
44 Robert Roode .50 1.25
45 Roman Reigns 1.25 3.00
46 Sami Zayn .60 1.50
47 Sasha Banks 2.50 6.00
48 Sheamus .60 1.50
49 Shinsuke Nakamura 1.00 2.50
50 The Miz .75 2.00
51 Xavier Woods .50 1.25
52 Adam Cole 1.25 3.00
53 Bobby Fish .50 1.25
54 Candice LeRae 1.50 4.00
55 Dakota Kai 1.00 2.50
56 Damian Priest RC .50 1.25
57 Dominik Dijakovic .50 1.25
58 Finn Balor 1.25 3.00
59 Io Shirai .75 2.00
60 Johnny Gargano 1.00 2.50
61 Kay Lee Ray RC .75 2.00
62 Karrion Kross RC 1.00 2.50
63 Keith Lee .50 1.25
64 Kushida RC .60 1.50
65 Kyle OíReilly .60 1.50
66 Mia Yim 1.00 2.50
67 Pete Dunne .50 1.25
68 Rhea Ripley 2.00 5.00
69 Roderick Strong 1.00 2.50
70 Scarlett RC 2.00 5.00
71 Shayna Baszler 1.50 4.00
72 Tommaso Ciampa 1.00 2.50
73 Toni Storm 1.25 3.00
74 Velveteen Dream .60 1.50

75 Walter RC	1.00	2.50
76 John Cena	2.00	5.00
77 Ronda Rousey	2.50	6.00
78 Undertaker	2.00	5.00
79 Batista	.75	2.00
80 Booker T	1.00	2.50
81 Bret Hit Man Hart	1.25	3.00
82 Diesel	.75	2.00
83 Howard Finkel	.50	1.25
84 Hulk Hogan	1.50	4.00
85 Lita	1.25	3.00
86 Mr. T	1.00	2.50
87 Razor Ramon	.75	2.00
88 Rowdy Roddy Piper	1.25	3.00
89 Trish Stratus	2.50	6.00
90 Stone Cold Steve Austin	2.50	6.00

2020 Topps WWE Undisputed Autographed Dual Relics

*GREEN/50: .75X TO 2X BASIC AUTOS
*BLUE/25: UNPRICED DUE TO SCARCITY
*GOLD/10: UNPRICED DUE TO SCARCITY
*PURPLE/5: UNPRICED DUE TO SCARCITY
*RED/1: UNPRICED DUE TO SCARCITY
*P.P.BLACK/1: UNPRICED DUE TO SCARCITY
*P.P.CYAN/1: UNPRICED DUE TO SCARCITY
*P.P.MAGENTA/1: UNPRICED DUE TO SCARCITY
*P.P.YELLOW/1: UNPRICED DUE TO SCARCITY
STATED PRINT RUN 99 SER.#'d SETS

DRAAB Aleister Black	12.00	30.00
DRAAC Adam Cole	8.00	20.00
DRAAD Angelo Dawkins	8.00	20.00
DRAAJ AJ Styles	15.00	40.00
DRAAN Andrade/62	8.00	20.00
DRABB Bianca Belair	15.00	40.00
DRABF Bobby Fish	8.00	20.00
DRABO Bobby Lashley	8.00	20.00
DRABS Braun Strowman	10.00	25.00
DRACC Cesaro	6.00	15.00
DRACF Charlotte Flair	25.00	60.00
DRACS Cesaro	6.00	15.00
DRADZ Dolph Ziggler	6.00	15.00
DRAEK Erik	6.00	15.00
DRAFB Finn Balor	10.00	25.00
DRAJD Mia Yim	12.00	30.00
DRAJG Johnny Gargano	10.00	25.00
DRAKD Killian Dain	6.00	15.00
DRAKE Kevin Owens	8.00	20.00
DRAKK Kofi Kingston	8.00	20.00
DRAKO Kevin Owens	8.00	20.00
DRAKR Kyle OíReilly	6.00	15.00
DRALE Lacey Evans	15.00	40.00
DRALS Bobby Lashley	8.00	20.00
DRAMR Matt Riddle	12.00	30.00
DRAMZ The Miz	8.00	20.00
DRANJ Nia Jax	6.00	15.00
DRANT Natalya	10.00	25.00
DRAOT Otis	12.00	30.00
DRAPD The Demon Finn Balor	15.00	40.00
DRAPP Ricochet	10.00	25.00
DRARB Ruby Riott	15.00	40.00
DRARC Ricochet	10.00	25.00
DRARH Rhea Ripley	50.00	100.00
DRARS Roderick Strong	6.00	15.00
DRASH Shayna Baszler	15.00	40.00
DRASR Seth Rollins	8.00	20.00
DRATC Tommaso Ciampa	6.00	15.00
DRAVD Velveteen Dream/46		
DRAXW Xavier Woods	6.00	15.00

2020 Topps WWE Undisputed Autographed Match Books

STATED PRINT RUN 5 SER.#'d SETS
UNPRICED DUE TO SCARCITY

MBCAS AJ Styles/Samoa Joe
MBCDT D.Bryan/Miz
MBCJT J.Gargano/T.Ciampa

2020 Topps WWE Undisputed Autographed Oversized Boxloaders

STATED PRINT RUN 5 SER.#'d SETS
UNPRICED DUE TO SCARCITY

BLAC Adam Cole
BLAJ AJ Styles
BLBA Bayley
BLBW The Fiend Bray Wyatt
BLKK Kofi Kingston
BLMR Matt Riddle
BLSB Sasha Banks
BLSN Shinsuke Nakamura
BLTM The Miz
BL4HW Shayna Baszler

2020 Topps WWE Undisputed Autographs

*ORANGE/99: .5X TO 1.2X BASIC AUTOS
*GREEN/50: .6X TO 1.5X BASIC AUTOS
*BLUE/25: UNPRICED DUE TO SCARCITY
*GOLD/10: UNPRICED DUE TO SCARCITY
*PURPLE/5: UNPRICED DUE TO SCARCITY
*RED/1: UNPRICED DUE TO SCARCITY
*P.P.BLACK/1: UNPRICED DUE TO SCARCITY
*P.P.CYAN/1: UNPRICED DUE TO SCARCITY
*P.P.MAGENTA/1: UNPRICED DUE TO SCARCITY
*P.P.YELLOW/1: UNPRICED DUE TO SCARCITY
STATED PRINT RUN 199 SER.#'d SETS

AAB Alexa Bliss	50.00	100.00
AAC Adam Cole	10.00	25.00
AAJ AJ Styles	12.00	30.00
AAN Andrade	6.00	15.00
AAS Asuka	30.00	75.00
AAT Aleister Black	8.00	20.00
AAZ Zelina Vega	15.00	40.00
ABA Bayley EXCH	15.00	40.00
ABB Bianca Belair	12.00	30.00
ABD Daniel Bryan	10.00	25.00
ABE Big E	6.00	15.00
ABF Bobby Fish	8.00	20.00
ABM Buddy Murphy	6.00	15.00
ABS Braun Strowman EXCH	10.00	25.00
ABT Booker T	10.00	25.00
ABW The Fiend Bray Wyatt	50.00	100.00
ACF Charlotte Flair	20.00	50.00
ACL Candice LeRae	15.00	40.00
ACM Carmella EXCH	15.00	40.00
ACS Cesaro	5.00	15.00
ADB Dana Brooke	10.00	25.00
ADD Dominik Dijakovic	8.00	20.00
ADK Dakota Kai	20.00	50.00
ADM Drew McIntyre	12.00	30.00
ADP Damian Priest	8.00	20.00
ADZ Dolph Ziggler	8.00	20.00
AHC Humberto Carrillo	6.00	15.00
AIO Io Shirai	30.00	75.00
AIV Ivar	6.00	15.00
AJG Johnny Gargano	6.00	15.00
AKC King Corbin	8.00	20.00
AKK Kofi Kingston	6.00	15.00
AKO Kevin Owens	6.00	15.00
AKS Kairi Sane	20.00	50.00
AKU Kushida	8.00	20.00
ALE Lacey Evans	15.00	40.00
ALN Lana EXCH	10.00	25.00
ALT Lita	20.00	50.00
AMA Mustafa Ali	8.00	20.00
AMR Matt Riddle	12.00	30.00
AMY Mia Yim	10.00	25.00
ANC Nikki Cross	10.00	25.00
ARB Ruby Riott	12.00	30.00
ARC Ricochet	8.00	20.00
ARD Kyle OíReilly	6.00	15.00
ARR Roman Reigns EXCH	15.00	40.00
ART R-Truth	12.00	30.00
ASB Sasha Banks	30.00	75.00
ASG Shorty G EXCH	8.00	20.00
ASJ Samoa Joe	6.00	15.00
ASM Sheamus	8.00	20.00
ASN Shinsuke Nakamura	6.00	15.00
ASR Seth Rollins	10.00	25.00
ASZ Sami Zayn	6.00	15.00
ATC Tommaso Ciampa	8.00	20.00
ATM The Miz	8.00	20.00
AVD Velveteen Dream EXCH	6.00	15.00
AVR Erik	8.00	20.00
A4HW Shayna Baszler	12.00	30.00
ABOB Bobby Lashley	8.00	20.00
ALEE Keith Lee	10.00	25.00
ARIP Rhea Ripley	60.00	120.00
AROD Roderick Strong EXCH	8.00	20.00

2020 Topps WWE Undisputed Cut Signatures

CSBB Bam Bam Bigelow
CSBH Bobby The Brain Heenan
CSBM Big Boss Man
CSBS Bruno Sammartino
CSDR Dusty Rhodes
CSEG Eddie Guerrero
CSGO Mean Gene Okerlund
CSJN Jim The Anvil Neidhart
CSJS Big John Studd
CSJT Earthquake
CSMP Mr. Perfect
CSNV Nikolai Volkoff
CSPB Paul Bearer
CSRP Rowdy Roddy Piper
CSRR Ravishing Rick Rude
CSRS Macho Man Randy Savage
CSUM Umaga
CSUW Ultimate Warrior
CSVD Big Van Vader
CSYO Yokozuna
CSDBS Davey Boy Smith

2020 Topps WWE Undisputed Dual Relics

*GREEN/50: .75X TO 2X BASIC MEM
*BLUE/25: UNPRICED DUE TO SCARCITY
*GOLD/10: UNPRICED DUE TO SCARCITY
*PURPLE/5: UNPRICED DUE TO SCARCITY
*RED/1: UNPRICED DUE TO SCARCITY
*P.P.BLACK/1: UNPRICED DUE TO SCARCITY
*P.P.CYAN/1: UNPRICED DUE TO SCARCITY
*P.P.MAGENTA/1: UNPRICED DUE TO SCARCITY
*P.P.YELLOW/1: UNPRICED DUE TO SCARCITY
STATED PRINT RUN 99 SER.#'d SETS

DRAB Aleister Black	3.00	8.00
DRAC Adam Cole	2.50	6.00
DRAD Angelo Dawkins	2.50	6.00
DRAJ AJ Styles	4.00	10.00
DRAN Andrade	2.00	5.00
DRBB Bianca Belair	3.00	8.00
DRBF Bobby Fish	2.00	5.00
DRBO Bobby Lashley	2.50	6.00
DRBS Braun Strowman	3.00	8.00
DRCF Charlotte Flair	5.00	12.00
DRCM Carmella	8.00	20.00
DRCS Cesaro	2.50	6.00
DRDZ Dolph Ziggler	2.50	6.00
DREK Erik	2.00	5.00
DREL Elias	2.50	6.00
DRFB Finn Balor	6.00	15.00
DRJD Mia Yim	5.00	12.00
DRJG Johnny Gargano	4.00	10.00
DRKD Killian Dain	2.00	5.00
DRKE Kevin Owens	3.00	8.00
DRKK Kofi Kingston	3.00	8.00
DRKO Kevin Owens	3.00	8.00
DRKR Kyle OíReilly	2.50	6.00
DRKS Kairi Sane	12.00	30.00
DRLE Lacey Evans	6.00	15.00
DRMR Matt Riddle	4.00	10.00
DRMZ The Miz	2.50	6.00
DRNJ Nia Jax	2.50	6.00
DRNT Natalya	3.00	8.00
DROT Otis	2.00	5.00
DRPD The Demon Finn Balor	6.00	15.00
DRRB Ruby Riott	5.00	12.00
DRRC Ricochet	3.00	8.00
DRRO Randy Orton	3.00	8.00
DRRR Roman Reigns	4.00	10.00
DRRS Roderick Strong	2.00	5.00
DRSM Shawn Michaels	4.00	10.00
DRSR Seth Rollins	3.00	8.00
DRTC Tommaso Ciampa	2.50	6.00
DRVD Velveteen Dream	2.00	5.00
DRXW Xavier Woods	2.50	6.00
DRHHH Triple H	4.00	10.00

2020 Topps WWE Undisputed Framed Autograph

STATED PRINT RUN 150 SER.#'d SETS

AFF Bray Wyatt	50.00	100.00

2020 Topps WWE Undisputed Quad Autographs

STATED PRINT RUN 5 SER.#'d SETS
UNPRICED DUE TO SCARCITY

QHW Banks/Flair/Lynch/Bayley
QIP Walter/Barthel/Aichner/Wolfe
QUE Cole/Fish/O'Reilly/Strong

2020 Topps WWE Undisputed Schamberger Art

COMPLETE SET (10)	20.00	50.00
RANDOMLY INSERTED INTO PACKS		
RS1 Mustafa Ali	3.00	8.00

RS2	Asuka	5.00	12.00
RS3	Becky Lynch	5.00	12.00
RS4	Bianca Belair	3.00	8.00
RS5	Eddie Guerrero	4.00	10.00
RS6	Macho Man Randy Savage	6.00	15.00
RS7	The Miz	2.50	6.00
RS8	Toni Storm	6.00	15.00
RS9	Undertaker	4.00	10.00
RS10	Walter	2.00	5.00

2020 Topps WWE Undisputed Schamberger Art Autographs

STATED PRINT RUN 10 SER.#'d SETS
UNPRICED DUE TO SCARCITY

RSRSAS Schamberger/Ali
RSRSBB Schamberger/Asuka
RSRSBL Schamberger/Lynch
RSRSMA Schamberger/Belair
RSRSRG Schamberger/Guerrero
RSRSRS Schamberger/Savage
RSRSTM Schamberger/Miz
RSRSTS Schamberger/Storm
RSRSUT Schamberger/Undertaker
RSRSWT Schamberger/WALTER

2020 Topps WWE Undisputed Schamberger Art Superstar Autographs

STATED PRINT RUN 10 SER.#'d SETS
UNPRICED DUE TO SCARCITY

ARSAS Asuka
ARSBB Bianca Belair
ARSMA Mustafa Ali
ARSTM The Miz

2020 Topps WWE Undisputed Tag Team Autographs

*GOLD/10: UNPRICED DUE TO SCARCITY
*PURPLE/5: UNPRICED DUE TO SCARCITY
*RED/1: UNPRICED DUE TO SCARCITY
STATED PRINT RUN 25 SER.#'d SETS

DAKW	K.Sane/Asuka	125.00	250.00
DASP	A.Dawkins/M.Ford	30.00	75.00
DAVR	Erik/Ivar	20.00	50.00

2020 Topps WWE Undisputed Triple Autographs

*PURPLE/5: UNPRICED DUE TO SCARCITY
*RED/1: UNPRICED DUE TO SCARCITY
STATED PRINT RUN 10 SER.#'d SETS
UNPRICED DUE TO SCARCITY

TALP Dorado/Metalik/Kalisto
TAND Woods/Big E/Kingston

2021 Topps WWE Undisputed

COMPLETE SET (74) 20.00 50.00
*PURPLE/99: .75X TO 2X BASIC CARDS
*GREEN/50: 1.2X TO 3X BASIC CARDS
*BLACK/25: UNPRICED DUE TO SCARCITY
*BLUE/10: UNPRICED DUE TO SCARCITY
*RED/5: UNPRICED DUE TO SCARCITY
*GOLD/1: UNPRICED DUE TO SCARCITY
*P.P.BLACK/1: UNPRICED DUE TO SCARCITY
*P.P.CYAN/1: UNPRICED DUE TO SCARCITY
*P.P.MAGENTA/1: UNPRICED DUE TO SCARCITY
*P.P.YELLOW/1: UNPRICED DUE TO SCARCITY

1	AJ Styles	1.50	4.00
2	Alexa Bliss	3.00	8.00
3	Angel Garza	.60	1.50
4	Becky Lynch	2.00	5.00
5	Bobby Lashley	1.25	3.00
6	The Fiend Bray Wyatt	2.00	5.00
7	Charlotte Flair	2.50	6.00
8	Damian Priest	.75	2.00
9	Dana Brooke	.50	1.25
10	Drew McIntyre	1.25	3.00
11	Elias	.50	1.25
12	Eva Marie	1.25	3.00
13	John Morrison	1.00	2.50
14	Keith Lee	1.00	2.50
15	MACE	.50	1.25
16	Mandy Rose	2.50	6.00
17	Mustafa Ali	.60	1.50
18	MVP	.50	1.25
19	Nia Jax	1.00	2.50
20	Omos RC	1.00	2.50
21	Rhea Ripley	1.50	4.00
22	Riddle	1.25	3.00
23	R-Truth	.60	1.50
24	Shayna Baszler	1.00	2.50
25	Sheamus	.75	2.00
26	T-BAR	.60	1.50
27	Xavier Woods	.50	1.25
28	Angelo Dawkins	.60	1.50
29	Apollo Crews	.60	1.50
30	Bianca Belair	1.25	3.00
31	Big E	1.00	2.50
32	Carmella	1.25	3.00
33	Cesaro	.50	1.25
34	Chad Gable	.50	1.25
35	Commander Azeez RC	.60	1.50
36	Dominik Mysterio RC	.60	1.50
37	Jey Uso	.50	1.25
38	Jimmy Uso	.50	1.25
39	Kevin Owens	1.00	2.50
40	Baron Corbin	.50	1.25
41	Liv Morgan	2.00	5.00
42	Mia Yim	.60	1.50
43	Montez Ford	.50	1.25
44	Natalya	.75	2.00
45	Otis	.60	1.50
46	Sami Zayn	.75	2.00
47	Shinsuke Nakamura	1.25	3.00
48	Tamina	.60	1.50
49	Adam Cole	1.50	4.00
50	Candice LeRae	2.00	5.00
51	Dakota Kai	1.00	2.50
52	Danny Burch	.60	1.50
53	Ember Moon	.60	1.50
54	Finn Balor	1.25	3.00
55	Indi Hartwell RC	1.50	4.00
56	Io Shirai	1.00	2.50
57	Johnny Gargano	1.00	2.50
58	Karrion Kross	2.00	5.00
59	Kushida	.75	2.00
60	LA Knight RC	.60	1.50
61	Nash Carter RC	.50	1.25
62	Oney Lorcan	.50	1.25
63	Pete Dunne	1.00	2.50
64	Santos Escobar	.75	2.00
65	Tommaso Ciampa	1.25	3.00
66	Toni Storm	1.50	4.00
67	Wes Lee RC	.50	1.25
68	Lex Luger	.60	1.50
69	Ric Flair	2.00	5.00
70	The Godfather	.60	1.50
71	Undertaker	2.50	6.00
72	William Regal	.75	2.00
73	Yokozuna	.75	2.00
74	John Cena	2.50	6.00

2021 Topps WWE Undisputed Autographed Framed Boxloaders

*BLUE/25: UNPRICED DUE TO SCARCITY
*GOLD/10: UNPRICED DUE TO SCARCITY
*BLACK/5: UNPRICED DUE TO SCARCITY
*ORANGE/3: UNPRICED DUE TO SCARCITY
STATED PRINT RUN 150 SER.#'d SETS

FRA	Asuka	30.00	75.00
FRK	Kane	25.00	60.00
FRM	MVP	8.00	20.00
FRR	Riddle	15.00	40.00
FRAB	Alexa Bliss	100.00	200.00
FRCA	Cedric Alexander	10.00	25.00
FRIS	Io Shirai	20.00	50.00
FRJH	Jeff Hardy	30.00	75.00
FRJM	John Morrison	12.00	30.00
FRKU	Kushida		
FRLL	Lex Luger	15.00	40.00
FRMA	Mustafa Ali	8.00	20.00
FRRM	Rey Mysterio	25.00	60.00
FRRR	Robert Roode	8.00	20.00
FRSB	Shelton Benjamin	10.00	25.00
FRTC	Tommaso Ciampa	12.00	30.00
FRWR	William Regal	15.00	40.00

2021 Topps WWE Undisputed Autographed Mat Relics

*GREEN/50: .5X TO 1.2X BASIC AUTOS
*BLUE/25: UNPRICED DUE TO SCARCITY
*GOLD/10: UNPRICED DUE TO SCARCITY
*BLACK/5: UNPRICED DUE TO SCARCITY
STATED PRINT RUN 99 SER.#'d SETS

MB	Bayley	15.00	40.00
MC	Cesaro	8.00	20.00
ME	Edge	20.00	50.00
MG	Goldberg		
MM	MVP	6.00	15.00
MO	Otis	6.00	15.00
M$$	Sasha Banks	30.00	75.00
MAC	Adam Cole	15.00	40.00
MAD	Angelo Dawkins	5.00	12.00
MAG	Angel Garza	5.00	12.00
MAN	Angelo Dawkins	5.00	12.00
MAP	Apollo Crews	5.00	12.00
MAS	Asuka	15.00	40.00
MAT	Austin Theory	6.00	15.00
MBF	Bobby Fish	5.00	12.00
MBL	Becky Lynch	30.00	75.00
MBO	Bobby Lashley	10.00	25.00
MBW	The Fiend Bray Wyatt		
MCF	Charlotte Flair		
MDD	Dominik Dijakovic		
MDG	Drew Gulak	5.00	12.00
MDM	Drew McIntyre	10.00	25.00
MDO	Dominik Mysterio	12.00	30.00
MDR	Drew McIntyre	10.00	25.00
MES	Elias	6.00	15.00
MFB	Finn Balor	10.00	25.00
MGA	Angel Garza	5.00	12.00
MJC	John Cena	100.00	200.00
MJG	Johnny Gargano	5.00	12.00
MJM	John Morrison		
MJU	Jimmy Uso	5.00	12.00
MKC	King Corbin	5.00	12.00
MKK	Kofi Kingston	6.00	15.00
MKL	Keith Lee	10.00	25.00
MKO	Kevin Owens	8.00	20.00
MKR	Kyle O'Reilly	8.00	20.00
MMF	Montez Ford	5.00	12.00
MMO	Montez Ford	5.00	12.00
MMR	Matt Riddle	12.00	30.00
MPD	Pete Dunne	6.00	15.00
MRR	Rhea Ripley	25.00	60.00
MSB	Shayna Baszler	6.00	15.00
MSE	Seth Rollins	12.00	30.00
MSR	Seth Rollins	12.00	30.00
MTC	Tommaso Ciampa	8.00	20.00

2021 Topps WWE Undisputed Autographed Match-Up Dual Relics

*GOLD/10: UNPRICED DUE TO SCARCITY
*BLACK/5: UNPRICED DUE TO SCARCITY
STATED PRINT RUN 25 SER.#'d SETS

AMABN Natalya/Becky Lynch
AMABS Shayna Baszler/Becky Lynch
AMACD Drew Gulak/Cesaro
AMACT Charlotte Flair/Trish Stratus
AMADG Goldberg/Drew McIntyre
AMADO Drew Gulak/Oney Lorcan
AMADT Tegan Nox/Dakota Kai
AMAEK Elias/King Corbin
AMAFJ Johnny Gargano/Finn Balor
AMAFR Charlotte Flair/Rhea Ripley
AMAIC Io Shirai/Candice LeRae
AMAKD Keith Lee/Dominik Dijakovic
AMAKS Seth Rollins/Kevin Owens
AMALK Asuka/Bayley
AMALN Natalya/Liv Morgan
AMAMS Mandy Rose/Sonya Deville
AMARJ Ricochet/Johnny Gargano
AMARO Kevin Owens/Roman Reigns
AMART Rhea Ripley/Toni Storm
AMASA Sasha Banks/Asuka
AMASC Sasha Banks/Carmella
AMASM Mia Yim/Shayna Baszler

2021 Topps WWE Undisputed Autographed Oversized Boxloaders

STATED ODDS 1:93 BOXES
STATED PRINT RUN 5 SER.#'d SETS
UNPRICED DUE TO SCARCITY

OAC Carmella
OAR Ricochet
OAAG Angel Garza
OACF Charlotte Flair
OADZ Dolph Ziggler
OAJG Johnny Gargano
OAJU Jey Uso
OAKO Kevin Owens
OANJ Nia Jax
OAPD Pete Dunne
OASZ Sami Zayn

2021 Topps WWE Undisputed Autographs

*PURPLE/99: .5X TO 1.2X BASIC AUTOS
*GREEN/50: .6X TO 1.5X BASIC AUTOS

*BLUE/25: UNPRICED DUE TO SCARCITY
*GOLD/10: UNPRICED DUE TO SCARCITY
*BLACK/5: UNPRICED DUE TO SCARCITY
*RED/1: UNPRICED DUE TO SCARCITY
*P.P.BLACK/1: UNPRICED DUE TO SCARCITY
*P.P.CYAN/1: UNPRICED DUE TO SCARCITY
*P.P.MAGENTA/1: UNPRICED DUE TO SCARCITY
*P.P.YELLOW/1: UNPRICED DUE TO SCARCITY
STATED PRINT RUN 199 SER.#'d SETS

AC Carmella	12.00	30.00
AE Elias	6.00	15.00
AK Kushida	4.00	10.00
AM MACE	4.00	10.00
AO Omos	12.00	30.00
AR Riddle	10.00	25.00
AU Undertaker		
AAB Alexa Bliss	30.00	75.00
AAC Adam Cole	10.00	25.00
AAD Angelo Dawkins	6.00	15.00
AAG Angel Garza	3.00	8.00
AAS AJ Styles	10.00	25.00
ABB Bianca Belair EXCH	15.00	40.00
ABE Big E	4.00	10.00
ABL Becky Lynch	25.00	60.00
ABO Bobby Lashley EXCH	8.00	20.00
ACF Charlotte Flair EXCH	20.00	50.00
ACG Chad Gable	6.00	15.00
ACL Candice LeRae	10.00	25.00
ACS Cesaro	5.00	12.00
ADB Danny Burch	3.00	8.00
ADK Dakota Kai	10.00	25.00
ADM Drew McIntyre		
ADO Dominik Mysterio	6.00	15.00
ADZ Dolph Ziggler	5.00	12.00
AEM Ember Moon	6.00	15.00
AFB Finn Balor	8.00	20.00
AIH Indi Hartwell	10.00	25.00
AIS Io Shirai	12.00	30.00
AJC John Cena		
AJG Johnny Gargano	5.00	12.00
AJU Jey Uso	4.00	10.00
AKC King Corbin	5.00	12.00
AKK Karrion Kross	8.00	20.00
AKL Keith Lee	6.00	15.00
AKO Kevin Owens	8.00	20.00
ALL Lex Luger	12.00	30.00
AMA Mustafa Ali	4.00	10.00
AMF Montez Ford	4.00	10.00
AMR Mandy Rose	20.00	50.00
AMVP MVP	5.00	12.00
ANJ Nia Jax	4.00	10.00
AOD Otis	6.00	15.00
ARP Rhea Ripley	15.00	40.00
ARR Robert Roode	5.00	12.00
ART R-Truth	4.00	10.00
ASB Shayna Baszler	5.00	12.00
ASE Santos Escobar	5.00	12.00
ASH Sheamus	6.00	15.00
ASN Shinsuke Nakamura	8.00	20.00
ASZ Sami Zayn	6.00	15.00
ATB T-BAR	5.00	12.00
ATC Tommaso Ciampa	6.00	15.00
ATG The Godfather	8.00	20.00
ATS Toni Storm	12.00	30.00
AWR William Regal	10.00	25.00
AXW Xavier Woods	4.00	10.00

2021 Topps WWE Undisputed Cut Signatures

CSBB Bam Bam Bigelow
CSBH Bobby "The Brain" Heenan
CSCJS Chief Jay Strongbow

2021 Topps WWE Undisputed Dual Autographs

*BLUE/25: UNPRICED DUE TO SCARCITY
*GOLD/10: UNPRICED DUE TO SCARCITY
*BLACK/5: UNPRICED DUE TO SCARCITY
*RED/1: UNPRICED DUE TO SCARCITY
STATED PRINT RUN 50 SER.#'d SETS

DACS Cesaro/Shinsuka Nakamura	25.00	60.00
DADM Dana Brooke/Mandy Rose		
DADR Raquel Gonzalez/Dakota Kai	20.00	50.00
DAHB Shelton Benjamin/Cedric Alexander		
DAIM Marcel Barthel/Fabian Aichner	10.00	25.00
DAKS Scarlett/Karrion Kross	50.00	100.00
DALF Joaquin Wilde/Raul Mendoza	12.00	30.00
DALH Gran Metalik/Lince Dorado	12.00	30.00
DAMF Dominik and Rey Mysterio	30.00	75.00
DAND Kofi Kingston/Xavier Woods	10.00	25.00
DANS Nia Jax/Shayna Baszler	10.00	25.00
DAOD Oney Lorcan/Danny Burch	10.00	25.00
DAPC Candice LeRae/Johnny Gargano	50.00	100.00
DARB Mace/T-Bar	10.00	25.00
DAVR Ivar/Erik	10.00	25.00
DAZR Dolph Ziggler/Robert Roode	10.00	25.00
DAGYZ Zack Gibson/James Drake	10.00	25.00

2021 Topps WWE Undisputed Fistographs

STATED ODDS 1:19 BOXES
STATED PRINT RUN 25 SER.#'d SETS

FIO Omos	125.00	250.00
FIAS AJ Styles	200.00	400.00
FIBB Bianca Belair	200.00	400.00
FIBE Big E	100.00	200.00
FIDM Drew McIntyre	200.00	400.00
FIOD Otis	100.00	200.00
FIRR Rhea Ripley	250.00	500.00
FISB Sasha Banks	400.00	800.00
FISN Shinsuke Nakamura	200.00	400.00
FISR Seth Rollins	250.00	500.00

2021 Topps WWE Undisputed Grand Slam Champions Autographs

*PURPLE/99: .5X TO 1.2X BASIC AUTOS
*GREEN/50: .6X TO 1.5X BASIC AUTOS
*BLUE/25: UNPRICED DUE TO SCARCITY
*GOLD/10: UNPRICED DUE TO SCARCITY
*BLACK/5: UNPRICED DUE TO SCARCITY
*RED/1: UNPRICED DUE TO SCARCITY
*P.P.BLACK/1: UNPRICED DUE TO SCARCITY
*P.P.CYAN/1: UNPRICED DUE TO SCARCITY
*P.P.MAGENTA/1: UNPRICED DUE TO SCARCITY
*P.P.YELLOW/1: UNPRICED DUE TO SCARCITY
STATED PRINT RUN 199 SER.#'d SETS

GAA Asuka	15.00	40.00
GAE Edge	15.00	40.00
GAK Kane	20.00	50.00
GABT Booker T	12.00	30.00
GAJH Jeff Hardy	12.00	30.00
GAKK Kofi Kingston	6.00	15.00
GARM Rey Mysterio	15.00	40.00
GATM The Miz	10.00	25.00

2021 Topps WWE Undisputed Grand Slam Champions Autographs Purple

STATED PRINT RUN 99 SER.#'d SETS

GASB Sasha Banks	50.00	100.00
GASR Seth Rollins	12.00	30.00

2021 Topps WWE Undisputed Grand Slam Champions

COMPLETE SET (16)	20.00	50.00
RANDOMLY INSERTED INTO PACKS		
GS1 Asuka	3.00	8.00
GS2 Bayley	2.00	5.00
GS3 Booker T	1.50	4.00
GS4 Eddie Guerrero	4.00	10.00
GS5 Edge	3.00	8.00
GS6 Jeff Hardy	2.00	5.00
GS7 Kane	1.25	3.00
GS8 Kofi Kingston	2.00	5.00
GS9 Randy Orton	2.50	6.00
GS10 Rey Mysterio	2.00	5.00
GS11 Roman Reigns	4.00	10.00
GS12 Sasha Banks	4.00	10.00
GS13 Seth Rollins	2.00	5.00
GS14 Shawn Michaels	3.00	8.00
GS15 The Miz	1.25	3.00
GS16 Triple H	3.00	8.00

2021 Topps WWE Undisputed Mat Relics

*GREEN/50: .5X TO 1.2X BASIC MEM
*BLUE/25: UNPRICED DUE TO SCARCITY
*GOLD/10: UNPRICED DUE TO SCARCITY
*BLACK/5: UNPRICED DUE TO SCARCITY
*RED/1: UNPRICED DUE TO SCARCITY
*P.P.BLACK/1: UNPRICED DUE TO SCARCITY
*P.P.CYAN/1: UNPRICED DUE TO SCARCITY
*P.P.MAGENTA/1: UNPRICED DUE TO SCARCITY
*P.P.YELLOW/1: UNPRICED DUE TO SCARCITY
STATED PRINT RUN 99 SER.#'d SETS

MB Bayley	4.00	10.00
MC Cesaro	1.50	4.00
MG Goldberg	6.00	15.00
MM MVP	1.50	4.00
M$$ Sasha Banks	8.00	20.00
MAC Adam Cole	5.00	12.00
MAD Angelo Dawkins	2.00	5.00
MAG Angel Garza	2.00	5.00
MAP Apollo Crews	2.00	5.00
MBF Bobby Fish	2.00	5.00
MBL Becky Lynch	6.00	15.00
MCF Charlotte Flair	8.00	20.00
MDD Dominik Dijakovic	2.00	5.00
MDG Drew Gulak	2.00	5.00
MES Elias	1.50	4.00
MFB Finn Balor	4.00	10.00
MJG Johnny Gargano	3.00	8.00
MKC King Corbin	1.50	4.00
MKL Keith Lee	3.00	8.00
MKR Kyle O'Reilly	2.50	6.00
MMF Montez Ford	1.50	4.00
MMR Matt Riddle	4.00	10.00
MPD Pete Dunne	3.00	8.00
MRA Randy Orton	5.00	12.00
MRR Rhea Ripley	5.00	12.00
MSB Shayna Baszler	3.00	8.00
MSE Seth Rollins	4.00	10.00
MTC Tommaso Ciampa	4.00	10.00

2021 Topps WWE Undisputed Match-Up Dual Autographed Books

*GOLD/5: UNPRICED DUE TO SCARCITY
*RED/1: UNPRICED DUE TO SCARCITY
STATED PRINT RUN 10 SER.#'d SETS
UNPRICED DUE TO SCARCITY

MAC Charlotte Flair/Asuka
MAS AJ Styles/Shinsuke Nakamura
MBS Sasha Banks/Bayley
MCS Cesaro/Sheamus
MEJ Edge/Jeff Hardy
MJR Roman Reigns/John Cena
MSR Seth Rollins/Finn Balor
MTM Triple H/Mankind
MUK Kane/Undertaker

2021 Topps WWE Undisputed Match-Up Dual Relics

*GREEN/50: .5X TO 1.2X BASIC MEM
*BLUE/25: UNPRICED DUE TO SCARCITY
*RED/1: UNPRICED DUE TO SCARCITY
*GOLD/10: UNPRICED DUE TO SCARCITY
*P.P.BLACK/1: UNPRICED DUE TO SCARCITY
*P.P.CYAN/1: UNPRICED DUE TO SCARCITY
*P.P.MAGENTA/1: UNPRICED DUE TO SCARCITY
*P.P.YELLOW/1: UNPRICED DUE TO SCARCITY
STATED PRINT RUN 99 SER.#'d SETS

MABA Asuka/B.Lynch	6.00	15.00
MABJ B.Wyatt/J.Cena	8.00	20.00
MABL L.Evans/Bayley	4.00	10.00
MABS B.Lynch/S.Baszler	6.00	15.00
MACP A.Crews/MVP	2.00	5.00
MACS S.Baszler/C.Flair	8.00	20.00
MADG D.McIntyre/Goldberg	6.00	15.00
MADR R.Reigns/D.McIntyre	8.00	20.00
MAEK King Corbin/Elias	1.50	4.00
MAER R.Orton/Edge	6.00	15.00
MAFR C.Flair/R.Ripley	8.00	20.00
MAKS K.Owens/S.Rollins	4.00	10.00
MALK Bayley/Asuka	6.00	15.00
MAMO R.Orton/D.McIntyre	5.00	12.00
MAMS S.Deville/M.Rose	8.00	20.00
MARB B.Belair/R.Ripley	5.00	12.00
MARM D.Mysterio/S.Rollins	4.00	10.00
MARO K.Owens/R.Reigns	8.00	20.00
MASA S.Banks/Asuka	8.00	20.00
MASC S.Bannks/Carmella	8.00	20.00

2021 Topps WWE Undisputed Rob Schamberger Illustrations

COMPLETE SET (10)	12.00	30.00
RANDOMLY INSERTED INTO PACKS		
RS1 AJ Styles	2.00	5.00
RS2 Big E	1.25	3.00
RS3 Charlotte Flair	3.00	8.00
RS4 Johnny Gargano	1.25	3.00
RS5 Natalya	1.00	2.50
RS6 Rey Mysterio	1.50	4.00
RS7 Roman Reigns	3.00	8.00
RS8 Shotzi Blackheart	2.50	6.00
RS9 Stone Cold Steve Austin	3.00	8.00
RS10 The Fiend Bray Wyatt	2.50	6.00

2021 Topps WWE Undisputed Rob Schamberger Illustrations Artist Autographs

STATED PRINT RUN 10 SER.#'d SETS
UNPRICED DUE TO SCARCITY

AAAS Rob Schamberger
AABE Rob Schamberger
AABW Rob Schamberger
AACF Rob Schamberger
AAJG Rob Schamberger
AANT Rob Schamberger
AARM Rob Schamberger
AARR Rob Schamberger
AASA Rob Schamberger
AASB Rob Schamberger

2021 Topps WWE Undisputed Rob Schamberger Illustrations Superstar Autographs

STATED PRINT RUN 10 SER.#'d SETS
UNPRICED DUE TO SCARCITY

SAAS AJ Styles
SABE Big E
SABW The Fiend Bray Wyatt
SAJG Johnny Gargano
SANT Natalya
SARM Rey Mysterio
SASB Shotzi Blackheart

2017 Topps WWE Women's Division

UNOPENED BLASTER BOX (81 CARDS)
UNOPENED HANGER BOX (40 CARDS)
UNOPENED FAT PACK (18 CARDS)
*SILVER/50: 1.2X TO 3X BASIC CARDS
*BLUE/25: 2X TO 5X BASIC CARDS
*GOLD/10: UNPRICED DUE TO SCARCITY
*RED/1: UNPRICED DUE TO SCARCITY

R1 Aliyah	.40	1.00
R2 Asuka	1.00	2.50
R3 Billie Kay	.40	1.00
R4 Cathy Kelley	.30	.75
R5 Ember Moon	.75	2.00
R6 Kimberly Frankele RC	.30	.75
R7 Liv Morgan	.50	1.25
R8 Mandy Rose	.40	1.00
R9 Nikki Cross RC	.60	1.50
R10 Peyton Royce	.50	1.25
R11 Ruby Riot RC	.40	1.00
R12 Brie Bella	.75	2.00
R13 Alexa Bliss	1.50	4.00
R14 Alicia Fox	.50	1.25
R15 Bayley	1.00	2.50
R16 Charly Caruso RC	.30	.75
R17 Dana Brooke	.60	1.50
R18 Emma	.75	2.00
R19 JoJo	.50	1.25
R20 Maryse	.60	1.50
R21 Mickie James	.50	1.25
R22 Nia Jax	.50	1.25
R23 Sasha Banks	1.00	2.50
R24 Stephanie McMahon	.40	1.00
R25 Summer Rae	.75	2.00
R26 Lita	.60	1.50
R27 Becky Lynch	1.00	2.50
R28 Carmella	.75	2.00
R29 Charlotte Flair	1.25	3.00
R30 Dasha Fuentes	.40	1.00
R31 Lana	1.00	2.50
R32 Naomi	.60	1.50
R33 Natalya	.60	1.50
R34 Nikki Bella	.75	2.00
R35 Renee Young	.50	1.25
R36 Tamina	.40	1.00
R37 Alundra Blayze	.40	1.00
R38 Eve Torres	.50	1.25
R39 Miss Elizabeth	.50	1.25
R40 Sherri Martel	.40	1.00
R41 Terri Runnels	.30	.75
R42 Trish Stratus	1.25	3.00
R43 Wendi Richter	.40	1.00
R44 Beth Phoenix	.30	.75
R45 Ivory	.30	.75
R46 Judy Martin RC	.30	.75
R47 Kelly Kelly	.60	1.50
R48 Leilani Kai	.30	.75
R49 Princess Victoria RC	.30	.75
R50 Torrie Wilson	.75	2.00

2017 Topps WWE Women's Division Autographed Kiss and Mat Relics

STATED ODDS 1:1,054 BLASTER BOX EXCLUSIVE
STATED PRINT RUN 5 SER.#'d SETS
UNPRICED DUE TO SCARCITY

WARCA Carmella
WARNA Natalya

2017 Topps WWE Women's Division Autographed Mat Relics

STATED ODDS 1:68 BLASTER BOX
STATED ODDS 1:6,012 HANGER BOX
STATED ODDS 1:11,988 HANGER PACK
STATED PRINT RUN 10 SER.#'d SETS
UNPRICED DUE TO SCARCITY

MRAB Alexa Bliss
MRAF Alicia Fox
MRAS Asuka
MRBA Bayley
MRBL Becky Lynch
MRCA Carmella
MRCF Charlotte Flair
MRNJ Nia Jax
MRSR Summer Rae
MRSU Summer Rae
MRTA Tamina
MRASA Asuka
MRASU Asuka
MRBAY Bayley
MRBEC Becky Lynch
MRBLY Bayley
MRCAR Carmella
MRCHA Charlotte Flair
MRCHF Charlotte Flair
MRCRM Carmella
MREMM Emma
MRNAO Naomi
MRNAT Natalya
MRNIA Nia Jax
MRSUM Summer Rae
MRTAM Tamina
MRCHAR Charlotte Flair
MREMMA Emma

2017 Topps WWE Women's Division Autographs

*SILVER/50: .5X TO 1.2X BASIC AUTOS
*BLUE/25: .6X TO 1.5X BASIC AUTOS
*GOLD/10: UNPRICED DUE TO SCARCITY
*RED/1: UNPRICED DUE TO SCARCITY
STATED ODDS 1:13 BLASTER BOX
STATED ODDS 1:802 HANGER BOX
STATED ODDS 1:1,599 HANGER PACK
STATED PRINT RUN 99 OR FEWER SER.#'d SETS

R1 Aliyah/99	6.00	15.00
R2 Asuka/99	20.00	50.00
R3 Billie Kay/99	10.00	25.00
R4 Cathy Kelley/99	8.00	20.00
R5 Ember Moon/94	8.00	20.00
R7 Liv Morgan/99	25.00	60.00
R8 Mandy Rose/99	20.00	50.00
R10 Peyton Royce/99	10.00	25.00
R11 Ruby Riot/99	20.00	50.00
R12 Brie Bella/56	10.00	25.00
R13 Alexa Bliss/99	50.00	100.00
R14 Alicia Fox/61	10.00	25.00
R18 Emma/99	12.00	30.00
R19 JoJo/99	6.00	15.00
R22 Nia Jax/99	10.00	25.00
R23 Sasha Banks/68	25.00	60.00
R27 Becky Lynch/99	15.00	40.00
R28 Carmella/99	20.00	50.00
R29 Charlotte Flair/57	20.00	50.00
R30 Dasha Fuentes/99	6.00	15.00
R32 Naomi/99	8.00	20.00
R33 Natalya/78	8.00	20.00
R34 Nikki Bella/99	10.00	25.00
R36 Tamina/99	6.00	15.00
R37 Alundra Blayze/99	8.00	20.00
R41 Terri Runnels/99	10.00	25.00
R43 Wendi Richter/99	6.00	15.00
R44 Beth Phoenix/99	8.00	20.00
R45 Ivory/99	6.00	15.00
R46 Judy Martin/99	6.00	15.00
R47 Kelly Kelly/99	10.00	25.00
R48 Leilani Kai/99	6.00	15.00
R49 Princess Victoria/99	10.00	25.00
R50 Torrie Wilson/99	12.00	30.00

2017 Topps WWE Women's Division Autographs Blue

STATED ODDS 1:39 BLASTER BOX
STATED ODDS 1:3,280 HANGER BOX
STATED ODDS 1:6,539 HANGER PACK
STATED PRINT RUN 25 SER.#'d SETS

R25 Summer Rae	15.00	40.00

2017 Topps WWE Women's Division Autographs Silver

STATED ODDS 1:20 BLASTER BOX
STATED ODDS 1:1,569 HANGER BOX
STATED ODDS 1:3,128 HANGER PACK
STATED PRINT RUN 50 SER.#'d SETS

R15 Bayley	15.00	40.00
R20 Maryse	8.00	20.00
R38 Eve Torres	20.00	50.00
R42 Trish Stratus	25.00	60.00

2017 Topps WWE Women's Division Diva's Championship Medallions

*SILVER/50: .5X TO 1.2X BASIC MEM
*BLUE/25: .6X TO 1.5X BASIC MEM
*GOLD/10: UNPRICED DUE TO SCARCITY
*RED/1: UNPRICED DUE TO SCARCITY
STATED ODDS 1:15 BLASTER BOX
STATED ODDS 1:1,203 HANGER BOX
STATED ODDS 1:2,398 HANGER PACK
STATED PRINT RUN 99 SER.#'d SETS

DCM Maryse	5.00	12.00
DCN Natalya	5.00	12.00
DCAF Alicia Fox	4.00	10.00
DCBB Brie Bella	6.00	15.00
DCBP Beth Phoenix	2.50	6.00
DCCF Charlotte Flair	10.00	25.00
DCET Eve Torres	4.00	10.00
DCKK Kelly Kelly	5.00	12.00
DCMJ Mickie James	4.00	10.00
DCNB Nikki Bella	6.00	15.00

2017 Topps WWE Women's Division Finishers and Signature Moves

*SILVER/50: 1X TO 2.5X BASIC CARDS
*BLUE/25: 1.2X TO 3X BASIC CARDS
*GOLD/10: 2X TO 5X BASIC CARDS
*RED/1: UNPRICED DUE TO SCARCITY
STATED ODDS 5:1 HANGER BOX EXCLUSIVE

F1 Alexa Bliss	3.00	8.00
F2 Nikki Bella	1.50	4.00
F3 Bayley	2.00	5.00
F4 Natalya	1.25	3.00
F5 Brie Bella	1.50	4.00
F6 Sasha Banks	2.00	5.00
F7 Becky Lynch	2.00	5.00
F8 Beth Phoenix	.60	1.50
F9 Sasha Banks	2.00	5.00
F10 Charlotte Flair	2.50	6.00
F11 Eve Torres	1.00	2.50
F12 Mickie James	1.00	2.50
F13 Trish Stratus	2.50	6.00
F14 Naomi	1.25	3.00
F15 Alicia Fox	1.00	2.50
F16 Tamina	.75	2.00
F17 Dana Brooke	1.25	3.00
F18 Emma	1.50	4.00
F19 Carmella	1.50	4.00
F20 Summer Rae	1.50	4.00
F21 Nia Jax	1.00	2.50
F22 Stephanie McMahon	.75	2.00
F23 Kelly Kelly	1.25	3.00
F24 Charlotte Flair	2.50	6.00

2017 Topps WWE Women's Division Kiss

*GOLD/10: UNPRICED DUE TO SCARCITY
*RED/1: UNPRICED DUE TO SCARCITY
STATED ODDS 1:67 BLASTER BOX
STATED ODDS 1:1,503 HANGER BOX
STATED ODDS 1:2,997 HANGER PACK
STATED PRINT RUN 99 SER.#'d SETS

KAF Alicia Fox/99	15.00	40.00
KBK Billie Kay/99	25.00	60.00
KCA Carmella/99	25.00	60.00
KDB Dana Brooke/69	15.00	40.00
KNA Naomi/54	15.00	40.00

KPR Peyton Royce/99	20.00	50.00
KRY Renee Young/68	25.00	60.00

2017 Topps WWE Women's Division Kiss Autographs

*GOLD/10: UNPRICED DUE TO SCARCITY
*RED/1: UNPRICED DUE TO SCARCITY
STATED ODDS 1:211 BLASTER BOX
STATED ODDS 1:6,012 HANGER BOX
STATED ODDS 1:11,988 HANGER PACK
STATED PRINT RUN 25 SER.#'d SETS

KAF Alicia Fox		
KAS Asuka		
KBK Billie Kay	50.00	100.00
KCA Carmella	50.00	100.00
KDB Dana Brooke	30.00	75.00
KMR Mandy Rose	125.00	250.00
KPR Peyton Royce	125.00	250.00
KRY Renee Young	30.00	75.00

2017 Topps WWE Women's Division Mat Relics

*SILVER/50: .5X TO 1.2X BASIC MEM
*BLUE/25: .6X TO 1.5X BASIC MEM
*GOLD/10: UNPRICED DUE TO SCARCITY
*RED/1: UNPRICED DUE TO SCARCITY
STATED ODDS 1:10 BLASTER BOX
STATED ODDS 1:262 HANGER BOX
STATED ODDS 1:522 HANGER PACK
STATED PRINT RUN 199 SER.#'d SETS

MRAB Alexa Bliss	8.00	20.00
MRAF Alicia Fox	2.50	6.00
MRAL Alexa Bliss	8.00	20.00
MRAS Asuka	5.00	12.00
MRBA Bayley	5.00	12.00
MRBB Brie Bella	4.00	10.00
MRBL Becky Lynch	5.00	12.00
MRBR Brie Bella	4.00	10.00
MRCA Carmella	4.00	10.00
MRCF Charlotte Flair	6.00	15.00
MRDB Dana Brooke	3.00	8.00
MRLA Lana	5.00	12.00
MRNB Nikki Bella	4.00	10.00
MRNC Nikki Cross	3.00	8.00
MRNI Nikki Bella	4.00	10.00
MRNJ Nia Jax	2.50	6.00
MRSB Sasha Banks	5.00	12.00
MRSM Stephanie McMahon	2.00	5.00
MRSR Summer Rae	4.00	10.00
MRSU Summer Rae	4.00	10.00
MRTA Tamina	2.00	5.00
MRASA Asuka	5.00	12.00
MRASU Asuka	5.00	12.00
MRBAY Bayley	5.00	12.00
MRBEC Becky Lynch	5.00	12.00
MRBLY Bayley	5.00	12.00
MRBRI Brie Bella	4.00	10.00
MRCAR Carmella	4.00	10.00
MRCHA Charlotte Flair	6.00	15.00
MRCHF Charlotte Flair	6.00	15.00
MRCRM Carmella	4.00	10.00
MREMM Emma	4.00	10.00
MRLAA Lana	5.00	12.00
MRLAN Lana	5.00	12.00
MRNAO Naomi	3.00	8.00
MRNAT Natalya	3.00	8.00
MRNIA Nia Jax	2.50	6.00
MRNIK Nikki Cross	3.00	8.00
MRSAS Sasha Banks	5.00	12.00
MRSTE Stephanie McMahon	2.00	5.00
MRSUM Summer Rae	4.00	10.00
MRTAM Tamina	2.00	5.00
MRCHAR Charlotte Flair	6.00	15.00
MREMMA Emma	4.00	10.00

2017 Topps WWE Women's Division NXT Matches and Moments

*SILVER/50: 1.2X TO 3X BASIC CARDS
*BLUE/25: 2X TO 5X BASIC CARDS
*GOLD/10: UNPRICED DUE TO SCARCITY
*RED/1: UNPRICED DUE TO SCARCITY

NXT1 Emma	.75	2.00
NXT2 Billie Kay	.40	1.00
NXT3 Peyton Royce	.50	1.25
NXT4 Asuka	1.00	2.50
NXT5 Asuka	1.00	2.50
NXT6 Bayley	1.00	2.50
NXT7 Nia Jax	.50	1.25
NXT8 Bayley	1.50	4.00
NXT9 Bayley	1.00	2.50
NXT10 Carmella	1.00	2.50
NXT11 Bayley	1.00	2.50
NXT12 Bayley	1.00	2.50
NXT13 Asuka	1.00	2.50
NXT14 Asuka	1.00	2.50
NXT15 Nia Jax	.50	1.25
NXT16 Nia Jax	.50	1.25
NXT17 Asuka	1.00	2.50
NXT18 Bayley	1.00	2.50
NXT19 Mandy Rose	.40	1.00
NXT20 Ember Moon	.75	2.00
NXT21 Asuka	1.00	2.50
NXT22 Asuka	1.00	2.50
NXT23 Nikki Cross	.60	1.50
NXT24 Asuka	1.00	2.50
NXT25 Asuka	1.00	2.50
NXT26 Ember Moon	.75	2.00

2017 Topps WWE Women's Division Rivalries

*SILVER/50: 1.2X TO 3X BASIC CARDS
*BLUE/25: 2X TO 5X BASIC CARDS
*GOLD/10: UNPRICED DUE TO SCARCITY
*RED/1: UNPRICED DUE TO SCARCITY
STATED ODDS 3:1 HANGER PACK EXCLUSIVE

RV1 Charlotte Flair/Bayley	1.25	3.00
RV2 Charlotte Flair/Dana Brooke	1.25	3.00
RV3 Sasha Banks/Dana Brooke	1.00	2.50
RV4 Sasha Banks/Nia Jax	1.00	2.50
RV5 Bayley/Dana Brooke	1.00	2.50
RV6 Nikki Bella/Maryse	.75	2.00
RV7 Nikki Bella/Natalya	.75	2.00
RV8 Nikki Bella/Carmella	.75	2.00
RV9 Becky Lynch/Alexa Bliss	1.50	4.00
RV10 Becky Lynch/Mickie James	1.00	2.50
RV11 Alexa Bliss/Mickie James	1.50	4.00
RV12 Alexa Bliss/Naomi	1.50	4.00
RV13 Alexa Bliss/Bayley	1.50	4.00
RV14 Naomi/Charlotte Flair	1.25	3.00
RV15 Asuka/Ember Moon	1.00	2.50
RV16 Asuka/Peyton Royce	1.00	2.50
RV17 Asuka/Billie Kay	1.00	2.50
RV18 Asuka/Nikki Cross	1.00	2.50
RV19 Ruby Riot/Nikki Cross	.60	1.50
RV20 Wendi Richter/Leilani Kai	.40	1.00
RV21 Trish Stratus/Mickie James	1.25	3.00
RV22 Mickie James/Beth Phoenix	.50	1.25
RV23 Mickie James/Maryse	.60	1.50
RV24 Eve Torres/Maryse	.60	1.50
RV25 Eve Torres/Natalya	.60	1.50

2017 Topps WWE Women's Division Shirt Relics

*SILVER/50: .5X TO 1.2X BASIC MEM
*BLUE/25: .6X TO 1.5X BASIC MEM
*GOLD/10: UNPRICED DUE TO SCARCITY
*RED/1: UNPRICED DUE TO SCARCITY
STATED ODDS 1:12 BLASTER BOX
STATED ODDS 1:950 HANGER BOX
STATED ODDS 1:1,893 HANGER PACK
STATED PRINT RUN 199 SER.#'d SETS

SRAB Alexa Bliss	15.00	40.00
SRAF Alicia Fox	5.00	12.00
SRBA Bayley	10.00	25.00
SRBL Becky Lynch	10.00	25.00
SRCA Carmella	8.00	20.00
SRCF Charlotte Flair	12.00	30.00
SRJO JoJo	5.00	12.00
SRNA Naomi	6.00	15.00
SRNT Natalya	6.00	15.00
SRRY Renee Young	5.00	12.00
SRSB Sasha Banks	10.00	25.00
SRSR Summer Rae	8.00	20.00

2017 Topps WWE Women's Division Women's Championship Medallions

*SILVER/50: .5X TO 1.2X BASIC MEM
*BLUE/25: .6X TO 1.5X BASIC MEM
*GOLD/10: UNPRICED DUE TO SCARCITY
*RED/1: UNPRICED DUE TO SCARCITY
STATED ODDS 1:15 BLASTER BOX
STATED ODDS 1:1,203 HANGER BOX
STATED ODDS 1:2,398 HANGER PACK
STATED PRINT RUN 99 SER.#'d SETS

WCI Ivory	2.50	6.00
WCAB Alundra Blayze	3.00	8.00
WCBP Beth Phoenix	2.50	6.00
WCLK Leilani Kai	2.50	6.00
WCMJ Mickie James	4.00	10.00
WCSM Stephanie McMahon	3.00	8.00
WCSS Sensational Sherri	3.00	8.00
WCTS Trish Stratus	10.00	25.00
WCWR Wendi Richter	3.00	8.00

2017 Topps WWE Women's Division WWE Matches and Moments

*SILVER/50: 1.2X TO 3X BASIC CARDS
*BLUE/25: 2X TO 5X BASIC CARDS
*GOLD/10: UNPRICED DUE TO SCARCITY
*RED/1: UNPRICED DUE TO SCARCITY

WWE1 Sasha Banks	1.00	2.50
WWE2 Charlotte	1.25	3.00
WWE3 Nikki Bella	.75	2.00
WWE4 Bayley	1.00	2.50
WWE5 Becky Lynch	1.00	2.50
WWE6 Alexa Bliss	1.50	4.00
WWE7 Charlott Flair	1.25	3.00
WWE8 Alexa Bliss	1.50	4.00
WWE9 Charlotte Flair	1.25	3.00
WWE10 Sasha Banks	1.00	2.50
WWE11 Nikki Bella	.75	2.00
WWE12 Charlotte Flair	1.25	3.00
WWE13 Team Raw	1.25	3.00
WWE14 Sasha Banks	1.00	2.50
WWE15 Nikki Bella	.75	2.00
WWE16 Alexa Bliss	1.50	4.00
WWE17 Charlotte Flair	1.25	3.00
WWE18 Charlotte Flair	1.25	3.00
WWE19 Bayley	1.00	2.50
WWE20 Natalya	.75	2.00
WWE21 La Luchadora	.50	1.25
WWE22 Bayley	1.00	2.50
WWE23 Alexa Bliss	1.50	4.00
WWE24 Mickie James	1.50	4.00

2018 Topps WWE Women's Division

UNOPENED BOX (24 PACKS)
UNOPENED PACK (7 CARDS)
*SILVER/50: .6X TO 1.5X BASIC CARDS
*BLUE/25: 1.2X TO 3X BASIC CARDS
*GOLD/10: UNPRICED DUE TO SCARCITY
*RED/1: UNPRICED DUE TO SCARCITY

1 Alexa Bliss	2.00	5.00
2 Alicia Fox	.60	1.50
3 Asuka	1.25	3.00
4 Bayley	.60	1.50
5 Becky Lynch	1.00	2.50
6 Brie Bella	.75	2.00
7 Carmella	.75	2.00
8 Cathy Kelley	.75	2.00
9 Charlotte Flair	1.25	3.00
10 Charly Caruso	.60	1.50
11 Dana Brooke	.75	2.00
12 Dasha Fuentes	.60	1.50
13 JoJo	.40	1.00
14 Lana	1.00	2.50
15 Liv Morgan	.75	2.00
16 Mandy Rose	1.00	2.50
17 Maria Kanellis	1.00	2.50
18 Maryse	.75	2.00
19 Mickie James	.75	2.00
20 Naomi	.50	1.25
21 Natalya	.50	1.25
22 Nia Jax	.60	1.50
23 Nikki Bella	.75	2.00
24 Renee Young	.60	1.50
25 Ronda Rousey	2.00	5.00
26 Ruby Riott	.60	1.50
27 Sarah Logan RC	.40	1.00
28 Sasha Banks	1.25	3.00
29 Sonya Deville	.75	2.00
30 Stephanie McMahon	.75	2.00
31 Tamina	.40	1.00
32 Aliyah	.60	1.50
33 Bianca Belair RC	.50	1.25
34 Billie Kay	.75	2.00
35 Candice LeRae RC	.50	1.25
36 Dakota Kai RC	.50	1.25
37 Ember Moon	.75	2.00
38 Kairi Sane RC	1.00	2.50
39 Kayla Braxton RC	.40	1.00
40 Lacey Evans	.50	1.25
41 Nikki Cross	.60	1.50
42 Peyton Royce	1.00	2.50
43 Shayna Baszler	1.00	2.50
44 Taynara Conti RC	.40	1.00
45 Vanessa Borne	.40	1.00
46 Zelina Vega RC	.40	1.00

47	Alundra Blayze	.40	1.00
48	Lita	1.00	2.50
49	Trish Stratus	1.50	4.00
50	Wendi Richter	.40	1.00

2018 Topps WWE Women's Division Autographed Kiss and Shirt Relic Booklets

STATED PRINT RUN 5 SER.#'d SETS
UNPRICED DUE TO SCARCITY

ASKAB Alexa Bliss
ASKCF Charlotte Flair
ASKCR Carmella
ASKEM Ember Moon

2018 Topps WWE Women's Division Autographed Mat Relics

STATED ODDS 1:1,866
STATED PRINT RUN 10 SER.#'d SETS
UNPRICED DUE TO SCARCITY

AMRAK Asuka
AMRAS Asuka
AMRBB Brie Bella
AMRBL Becky Lynch
AMRBP Beth Phoenix
AMRBY Bayley
AMRCR Carmella
AMRDB Dana Brooke
AMREB Ember Moon
AMREM Ember Moon
AMRKR Kairi Sane
AMRKS Kairi Sane
AMRLA Lana
AMRLM Liv Morgan
AMRLT Lita
AMRMJ Mickie James
AMRMR Mandy Rose
AMRNA Naomi
AMRNB Nikki Bella
AMRNC Nikki Cross
AMRNJ Nia Jax
AMRNT Natalya
AMRNY Natalya
AMRPR Peyton Royce
AMRRR Ruby Riott
AMRSB Sasha Banks
AMRSD Sonya Deville
AMRSL Sarah Logan
AMRTM Tamina
AMRTS Trish Stratus

2018 Topps WWE Women's Division Autographed Shirt Relics

STATED ODDS 1:4,547
STATED PRINT RUN 10 SER.#'d SETS
UNPRICED DUE TO SCARCITY

ASRAB Alexa Bliss
ASRAF Alicia Fox
ASRBL Becky Lynch
ASRCF Charlotte Flair
ASRCM Carmella
ASREM Ember Moon
ASRJO JoJo
ASRNA Naomi
ASRNC Nikki Cross
ASRNT Natalya
ASRRY Renee Young
ASRSB Sasha Banks

2018 Topps WWE Women's Division Autographs

*GREEN/150: SAME VALUE AS BASIC AUTOS
*PURPLE/99: .5X TO 1.2X BASIC AUTOS
*BRONZE/75: .6X TO 1.5X BASIC AUTOS
*SILVER/50: .75X TO 2X BASIC AUTOS
*BLUE/25: 1X TO 2.5X BASIC AUTOS
*GOLD/10: UNPRICED DUE TO SCARCITY
*BLACK/5: UNPRICED DUE TO SCARCITY
*RED/1: UNPRICED DUE TO SCARCITY
*P.P.BLACK/1: UNPRICED DUE TO SCARCITY
*P.P.CYAN/1: UNPRICED DUE TO SCARCITY
*P.P.MAGENTA/1: UNPRICED DUE TO SCARCITY
*P.P.YELLOW/1: UNPRICED DUE TO SCARCITY
STATED ODDS 1:86
STATED PRINT RUN 199 SER.#'d SETS

1	Alexa Bliss	30.00	75.00
2	Alicia Fox	5.00	12.00
3	Asuka	12.00	30.00
4	Bayley	10.00	25.00
5	Becky Lynch	12.00	30.00
6	Brie Bella	10.00	25.00
7	Carmella	8.00	20.00
9	Charlotte Flair	15.00	40.00
11	Dana Brooke	6.00	15.00
12	Dasha Fuentes	5.00	12.00
14	Lana	6.00	15.00
15	Liv Morgan	15.00	40.00
16	Mandy Rose	12.00	30.00
19	Mickie James	10.00	25.00
20	Naomi	6.00	15.00
21	Natalya	8.00	20.00
22	Nia Jax	12.00	30.00
23	Nikki Bella	10.00	25.00
26	Ruby Riott	15.00	40.00
27	Sarah Logan	10.00	25.00
28	Sasha Banks	15.00	40.00
29	Sonya Deville	8.00	20.00
31	Tamina	5.00	12.00
32	Aliyah	6.00	15.00
33	Bianca Belair	15.00	40.00
34	Billie Kay	10.00	25.00
35	Candice LeRae	15.00	40.00
36	Dakota Kai	25.00	60.00
37	Ember Moon	10.00	25.00
38	Kairi Sane	15.00	40.00
40	Lacey Evans	12.00	30.00
42	Peyton Royce	15.00	40.00
43	Shayna Baszler	8.00	20.00
44	Taynara Conti	12.00	30.00
45	Vanessa Borne	8.00	20.00

2018 Topps WWE Women's Division Autographs Green

24	Renee Young	6.00	15.00

2018 Topps WWE Women's Division Commemorative Championship Relics

*PURPLE/99: SAME VALUE AS BASIC
*SILVER/50: .5X TO 1.2X BASIC MEM
*BLUE/25: .6X TO 1.5X BASIC MEM
*GOLD/10: UNPRICED DUE TO SCARCITY
*BLACK/5: UNPRICED DUE TO SCARCITY
*RED/1: UNPRICED DUE TO SCARCITY
STATED ODDS 1:183
STATED PRINT RUN 199 SER.#'d SETS

CCAB	Alundra Blayze	2.00	5.00
CCAL	Alexa Bliss	10.00	25.00
CCAS	Asuka	5.00	12.00
CCBL	Becky Lynch	8.00	20.00
CCBP	Beth Phoenix	2.50	6.00
CCBY	Bayley	2.50	6.00
CCCF	Charlotte Flair	6.00	15.00
CCCH	Charlotte Flair	6.00	15.00
CCET	Eve Torres	2.00	5.00
CCLT	Lita	4.00	10.00
CCMJ	Mickie James	5.00	12.00
CCMR	Maryse	2.00	5.00
CCNA	Naomi	2.50	6.00
CCNB	Nikki Bella	3.00	8.00
CCNT	Natalya	3.00	8.00
CCPG	Paige	10.00	25.00
CCSB	Sasha Banks	6.00	15.00
CCSS	Sensational Sherri	2.00	5.00
CCTS	Trish Stratus	4.00	10.00
CCWR	Wendi Richter	2.00	5.00

2018 Topps WWE Women's Division Kiss

*GOLD/10: UNPRICED DUE TO SCARCITY
*RED/1: UNPRICED DUE TO SCARCITY
STATED ODDS 1:1,797
STATED PRINT RUN 99 SER.#'d SETS

KCCF	Charlotte Flair	30.00	75.00
KCCR	Carmella	25.00	60.00
KCEM	Ember Moon	25.00	60.00
KCLM	Liv Morgan	20.00	50.00

2018 Topps WWE Women's Division Kiss Autographs

*GOLD/10: UNPRICED DUE TO SCARCITY
*RED/1: UNPRICED DUE TO SCARCITY
STATED ODDS 1:7,658
STATED PRINT RUN 25 SER.#'d SETS

AKCAB	Alexa Bliss	150.00	300.00
AKCCF	Charlotte Flair	200.00	400.00
AKCLM	Liv Morgan	60.00	120.00

2018 Topps WWE Women's Division Mat Relics

*GREEN/150: SAME AS BASIC MEM
*PURPLE/99: .5X TO 1.2X BASIC MEM
*BRONZE/75: .6X TO 1.5X BASIC MEM
*SILVER/50: .75X TO 2X BASIC MEM
*BLUE/25: 1X TO 2.5X BASIC MEM
*GOLD/10: UNPRICED DUE TO SCARCITY
*BLACK/5: UNPRICED DUE TO SCARCITY
*RED/1: UNPRICED DUE TO SCARCITY
STATED ODDS 1:123

AMRAK	Asuka	4.00	10.00
AMRAS	Asuka	4.00	10.00
AMRBB	Brie Bella	3.00	8.00
AMRBL	Becky Lynch	5.00	12.00
AMRBP	Beth Phoenix	3.00	8.00
AMRBY	Bayley	2.50	6.00
AMRCR	Carmella	4.00	10.00
AMRDB	Dana Brooke	2.50	6.00
AMREB	Ember Moon	5.00	12.00
AMREM	Ember Moon	5.00	12.00
AMRKR	Kairi Sane	5.00	12.00
AMRKS	Kairi Sane	5.00	12.00
AMRLA	Lana	5.00	12.00
AMRLM	Liv Morgan	4.00	10.00
AMRLT	Lita	3.00	8.00
AMRMJ	Mickie James	4.00	10.00
AMRMR	Mandy Rose	3.00	8.00
AMRNA	Naomi	2.00	5.00
AMRNB	Nikki Bella	5.00	12.00
AMRNC	Nikki Cross	2.00	5.00
AMRNJ	Nia Jax	2.00	5.00
AMRNT	Natalya	5.00	12.00
AMRNY	Natalya	5.00	12.00
AMRPR	Peyton Royce	3.00	8.00
AMRRR	Ruby Riott	4.00	10.00
AMRSB	Sasha Banks	6.00	15.00
AMRSD	Sonya Deville	3.00	8.00
AMRSL	Sarah Logan	3.00	8.00
AMRTM	Tamina	2.00	5.00
AMRTS	Trish Stratus	8.00	20.00

2018 Topps WWE Women's Division Matches and Moments

*SILVER/50: .6X TO 1.5X BASIC CARDS
*BLUE/25: 1.2X TO 3X BASIC CARDS
*GOLD/10: UNPRICED DUE TO SCARCITY
*RED/1: UNPRICED DUE TO SCARCITY

NXT1	Ember Moon	.75	2.00
NXT2	Asuka	1.25	3.00
NXT3	Asuka	1.25	3.00
NXT4	Ruby Riott	.60	1.50
NXT5	Asuka	1.25	3.00
NXT6	Asuka	1.25	3.00
NXT7	Asuka	1.25	3.00
NXT8	Sarah Logan	.40	1.00
NXT9	NXT Women's Triple Threat	1.25	3.00
NXT10	Asuka	1.25	3.00
NXT11	Bianca Belair	.50	1.25
NXT12	Vanessa Borne	.40	1.00
NXT13	Ember Moon	.75	2.00
NXT14	Asuka	1.25	3.00
NXT15	Shayna Baszler	1.00	2.50
NXT16	Dakota Kai	.50	1.25
NXT17	Bianca Belair	.50	1.25
NXT18	Candice LeRae	.50	1.25
NXT19	Lacey Evans	.50	1.25
NXT20	Kairi Sane	1.00	2.50
NXT21	Kairi Sane	1.00	2.50
NXT22	Shayna Baszler	1.00	2.50
NXT23	Dakota Kai	.50	1.25
NXT24	Candice LeRae	.50	1.25
NXT25	Shayna Baszler	1.00	2.50
NXT26	Kairi Sane	1.00	2.50
NXT27	Shayna Baszler	1.00	2.50
NXT28	Kairi Sane	1.00	2.50
NXT29	Asuka	1.25	3.00
NXT30	Kairi Sane	1.00	2.50
RAW1	Charlotte Flair	1.25	3.00
RAW2	Bayley	.60	1.50
RAW3	Sasha Banks	1.25	3.00
RAW4	Sasha Banks	1.25	3.00
RAW5	Bayley	.60	1.50
RAW6	Sasha Banks	1.25	3.00
RAW7	Nia Jax	.60	1.50
RAW8	Bayley & Sasha Banks	1.25	3.00
RAW9	Bayley	.60	1.50
RAW10	Alexa Bliss/Mickie James	2.00	5.00

SDL1	Becky Lynch	1.00	2.50
SDL2	Naomi	.50	1.25
SDL3	Naomi	.50	1.25
SDL4	Alexa Bliss	2.00	5.00
SDL5	Natalya	.50	1.25
SDL6	Mickie James	.75	2.00
SDL7	John Cena & Nikki Bella	1.50	4.00
SDL8	Naomi	.50	1.25
SDL9	Charlotte Flair	1.25	3.00
SDL10	Charlotte Flair	1.25	3.00

2018 Topps WWE Women's Division Mixed Match Challenge

COMPLETE SET (24) 8.00 20.00
*SILVER/50: .6X TO 1.5X BASIC CARDS
*BLUE/25: .75X TO 2X BASIC CARDS
*GOLD/10: UNPRICED DUE TO SCARCITY
*RED/1: UNPRICED DUE TO SCARCITY
RANDOMLY INSERTED INTO PACKS

MM1	Bliss/Strowman	1.50	4.00
MM2	Banks/Balor	1.00	2.50
MM3	Jax/Crews	.50	1.25
MM4	Miz/Asuka	1.00	2.50
MM5	Rose/Goldust	.75	2.00
MM6	Bayley/Elias	.75	2.00
MM7	Roode/Flair	1.00	2.50
MM8	Lana/Rusev	.75	2.00
MM9	Natalya/Nakamura	.75	2.00
MM10	Jimmy Uso/Naomi	.40	1.00
MM11	Zayn/Lynch	.75	2.00
MM12	Big E/Carmella	.60	1.50
MM13	The Boss Club	1.00	2.50
MM14	Team Awe-ska	1.00	2.50
MM15	Team Little Big	1.50	4.00
MM16	Glowish	.30	.75
MM17	Ravishing Rusev Day!	.50	1.25
MM18	The Robe Warriors	.50	1.25
MM19	Team Awe-ska	1.00	2.50
MM20	Team Little Big	.75	2.00
MM21	The Robe Warriors	1.00	2.50
MM22	Team Awe-ska	1.00	2.50
MM23	Roode & Lynch	.75	2.00
MM24	Team Awe-ska	1.00	2.50

2018 Topps WWE Women's Division Power Couples

*SILVER/50: .5X TO 1.2X BASIC CARDS
*BLUE/25: .6X TO 1.5X BASIC CARDS
*GOLD/10: UNPRICED DUE TO SCARCITY
*RED/1: UNPRICED DUE TO SCARCITY
RANDOMLY INSERTED INTO PACKS

PC1	Brie Bella/Daniel Bryan	1.50	4.00
PC2	Stephanie McMahon/Triple H	1.50	4.00
PC3	Maryse/The Miz	1.25	3.00
PC4	Renee Young/Dean Ambrose	1.25	3.00
PC5	Naomi/Jimmy Uso	.75	2.00
PC6	Lana/Rusev	1.50	4.00
PC7	Maria Kanellis/Mike Kanellis	1.50	4.00
PC8	Candice LeRae/Johnny Gargano	.75	2.00
PC9	Beth Phoenix/Edge	1.50	4.00
PC10	Alicia Fox/Noam Dar	1.00	2.50
PC11	Alicia Fox/Cedric Alexander	1.00	2.50
PC12	Lana/Dolph Ziggler	1.50	4.00
PC13	Eve Torres/Zack Ryder	1.25	3.00
PC14	Maria Kanellis/Dolph Ziggler	1.50	4.00
PC15	Stephanie McMahon/Kurt Angle	1.50	4.00
PC16	Trish Stratus/Chris Jericho	2.50	6.00
PC17	Trish Stratus/Jeff Hardy	2.50	6.00
PC18	Marlena/Goldust	1.25	3.00
PC19	Miss Elizabeth/Randy Savage	2.00	5.00
PC20	Queen Sherri/Randy Savage	2.00	5.00
PC21	Sherri/Shawn Michaels	2.00	5.00
PC22	Lita/Kane	1.50	4.00

2018 Topps WWE Women's Division Shirt Relics

*PURPLE/99: .5X TO 1.2X BASIC MEM
*SILVER/50: .6X TO 1.5X BASIC MEM
*BLUE/25: .75X TO 2X BASIC MEM
*GOLD/10: UNPRICED DUE TO SCARCITY
*BLACK/5: UNPRICED DUE TO SCARCITY
*RED/1: UNPRICED DUE TO SCARCITY
STATED ODDS 1:516

ASRAB	Alexa Bliss	15.00	40.00
ASRAF	Alicia Fox	5.00	12.00
ASRBL	Becky Lynch	8.00	20.00
ASRCF	Charlotte Flair	10.00	25.00
ASRCM	Carmella	6.00	15.00
ASREM	Ember Moon	6.00	15.00
ASRJO	JoJo	5.00	10.00
ASRNA	Naomi	5.00	12.00
ASRNC	Nikki Cross	4.00	10.00
ASRNT	Natalya	6.00	15.00
ASRRY	Renee Young	5.00	12.00
ASRSB	Sasha Banks	8.00	20.00

2018 Topps WWE Women's Division Women's Champion

COMPLETE SET (25) 10.00 25.00
RANDOMLY INSERTED INTO PACKS

WC1	Maryse	.75	2.00
WC2	Mickie James	.75	2.00
WC3	Eve Torres	.75	2.00
WC4	Alicia Fox	.60	1.50
WC5	Natalya	.50	1.25
WC6	Brie Bella	.75	2.00
WC7	Beth Phoenix	.75	2.00
WC8	Nikki Bella	.75	2.00
WC9	Paige	1.00	2.50
WC10	Charlotte Flair	1.25	3.00
WC11	Paige	1.00	2.50
WC12	Charlotte Flair	1.25	3.00
WC13	Sasha Banks	1.25	3.00
WC14	Bayley	.60	1.50
WC15	Asuka	1.25	3.00
WC16	Ember Moon	.75	2.00
WC17	Charlotte Flair	1.25	3.00
WC18	Sasha Banks	1.25	3.00
WC19	Bayley	.60	1.50
WC20	Alexa Bliss	2.00	5.00
WC21	Becky Lynch	1.00	2.50
WC22	Alexa Bliss	2.00	5.00
WC23	Naomi	.50	1.25
WC24	Natalya	.50	1.25
WC25	Charlotte Flair	1.25	3.00

2018 Topps WWE Women's Division Women's Royal Rumble

COMPLETE SET (24) 12.00 30.00
*SILVER/50: .5X TO 1.5X BASIC CARDS
*BLUE/25: 1.2X TO 3X BASIC CARDS
*GOLD/10: UNPRICED DUE TO SCARCITY
*RED/1: UNPRICED DUE TO SCARCITY
STATED ODDS 1:2

RR1	Sasha Banks	2.00	5.00
RR2	Becky Lynch	1.50	4.00
RR3	Sarah Logan	.60	1.50
RR4	Mandy Rose	1.50	4.00
RR5	Lita	1.50	4.00
RR6	Kairi Sane	1.50	4.00
RR7	Tamina	.60	1.50
RR8	Dana Brooke	1.25	3.00
RR9	Sonya Deville	1.25	3.00
RR10	Liv Morgan	1.25	3.00
RR11	Lana	1.50	4.00
RR12	Ruby Riott	1.00	2.50
RR13	Carmella	1.25	3.00
RR14	Natalya	.75	2.00
RR15	Naomi	.75	2.00
RR16	Nia Jax	1.00	2.50
RR17	Ember Moon	1.25	3.00
RR18	Beth Phoenix	1.25	3.00
RR19	Asuka	2.00	5.00
RR20	Mickie James	1.25	3.00
RR21	Nikki Bella	1.25	3.00
RR22	Brie Bella	1.25	3.00
RR23	Bayley	1.00	2.50
RR24	Trish Stratus	2.50	6.00

2019 Topps WWE Women's Division

COMPLETE SET (100) 8.00 20.00
*PURPLE/99: .6X TO 1.5X BASIC CARDS
*BRONZE/75: .75X TO 2X BASIC CARDS
*ORANGE/50: 1X TO 2.5X BASIC CARDS
*BLUE/25: 1.5X TO 4X BASIC CARDS
*GOLD/10: UNPRICED DUE TO SCARCITY
*RED/1: UNPRICED DUE TO SCARCITY
*P.P.BLACK/1: UNPRICED DUE TO SCARCITY
*P.P.CYAN/1: UNPRICED DUE TO SCARCITY
*P.P.MAGENTA/1: UNPRICED DUE TO SCARCITY
*P.P.YELLOW/1: UNPRICED DUE TO SCARCITY

1	Alexa Bliss	1.25	3.00
2	Alicia Fox	.50	1.25
3	Bayley	.50	1.25
4	Dana Brooke	.50	1.25
5	Ember Moon	.60	1.50
6	Lacey Evans	.50	1.25
7	Liv Morgan	.75	2.00
8	Mickie James	.60	1.50
9	Natalya	.50	1.25
10	Nia Jax	.50	1.25
11	Ronda Rousey	1.25	3.00
12	Ruby Riott	.50	1.25
13	Sarah Logan	.30	.75
14	Sasha Banks	1.00	2.50
15	Tamina	.25	.60
16	Renee Young	.40	1.00
17	Stephanie McMahon	.60	1.50
18	Maria Kanellis	.60	1.50
19	Asuka	.75	2.00
20	Becky Lynch	1.00	2.50
21	Billie Kay	.50	1.25
22	Carmella	.60	1.50
23	Mandy Rose	.60	1.50
24	Maryse	.30	.75
25	Naomi	.40	1.00
26	Nikki Cross	.40	1.00
27	Peyton Royce	.60	1.50
28	Sonya Deville	.50	1.25
29	Zelina Vega	.40	1.00
30	Paige	1.00	2.50
31	Aliyah	.25	.60
32	Bianca Belair	.25	.60
33	Candice LeRae	.50	1.25
34	Chelsea Green RC	.25	.60
35	Dakota Kai	.50	1.25
36	Deonna Purrazzo RC	.25	.60
37	Io Shirai RC	.25	.60
38	Jessamyn Duke	.30	.75
39	Jessi Kamea RC	.25	.60
40	Kacy Catanzaro RC	.60	1.50
41	Kairi Sane	.50	1.25
42	Lacey Lane RC	.25	.60
43	Marina Shafir RC	.25	.60
44	Mia Yim RC	.25	.60
45	MJ Jenkins RC	.25	.60
46	Shayna Baszler	.50	1.25
47	Taynara Conti	.30	.75
48	Vanessa Borne	.30	.75
49	Xia Li RC	.25	.60
50	Toni Storm RC	1.00	2.50
51	Nina Samuels RC	.30	.75
52	Alundra Blayze	.30	.75
53	Beth Phoenix	.40	1.00
54	Eve Torres	.30	.75
55	Marlena	.25	.60
56	Lita	.60	1.50
57	Sherri Martel	.40	1.00
58	Miss Elizabeth	.50	1.25
59	Trish Stratus	1.25	3.00
60	Wendi Richter	.25	.60
61	Asuka	.75	2.00
62	Ember Moon	.60	1.50
63	Asuka	.75	2.00
64	Asuka	.75	2.00
65	Alexa Bliss	1.25	3.00
66	Shayna Baszler	.50	1.25
67	Naomi	.40	1.00
68	Nia Jax	1.25	3.00
69	Ronda Rousey	1.25	3.00
70	Candice LeRae	.50	1.25
71	Carmella	.60	1.50
72	Asuka	.75	2.00
73	Shayna Baszler	.50	1.25
74	Kairi Sane	.50	1.25
75	Shayna Baszler	.50	1.25
76	Bayley	.50	1.25
77	Alexa Bliss	1.25	3.00
78	Carmella	.75	2.00
79	Alexa Bliss	1.25	3.00
80	Sasha Banks & Bayley	1.00	2.50
81	Kairi Sane	.50	1.25
82	Ronda Rousey	1.25	3.00
83	Asuka	.75	2.00
84	Ronda Rousey	1.25	3.00
85	Iiconics	.60	1.50
86	Io Shirai	.25	.60
87	Becky Lynch	1.00	2.50
88	Bianca Belair	.25	.60
89	Shayna Baszler	.50	1.25
90	Team RAW/Team SmackDown	.75	2.00
91	Nikki Cross	.40	1.00
92	Mia Yim	.25	.60
93	Io Shirai	.50	1.25
94	Natalya	.50	1.25
95	Ronda Rousey	1.25	3.00
96	Asuka	.75	2.00
97	Natalya	.50	1.25
98	Asuka	.75	2.00

99 Bayley/Sasha Banks/Ember Moon	.60	1.50
100 Bianca Belair	.25	.60

2019 Topps WWE Women's Division Autographed Mat Relics

*RED/1: UNPRICED DUE TO SCARCITY
STATED PRINT RUN 10 SER.#'d SETS
UNPRICED DUE TO SCARCITY

MRAAS Asuka
MRABL Becky Lynch
MRABY Bayley
MRACA Carmella
MRAIS Io Shirai
MRAKS Kairi Sane
MRANA Natalya
MRANM Naomi
MRAQA Shayna Baszler
MRASD Sonya Deville
MRATA Tamina

2019 Topps WWE Women's Division Autographed Shirt Relics

*RED/1: UNPRICED DUE TO SCARCITY
STATED PRINT RUN 10 SER.#'d SETS
UNPRICED DUE TO SCARCITY

SRAAB Alexa Bliss
SRACM Carmella
SRALE Lacey Evans
SRANM Naomi
SRANT Natalya
SRAQA Shayna Baszler
SRARY Renee Young
SRATM Tamina

2019 Topps WWE Women's Division Autographs

*GREEN/150: SAME VALUE AS BASIC
*PURPLE/99: .5X TO 1.2X BASIC AUTOS
*BRONZE/75: .5X TO 1.2X BASIC AUTOS
*ORANGE/50: .6X TO 1.5X BASIC AUTOS
*BLUE/25: UNPRICED DUE TO SCARCITY
*GOLD/10: UNPRICED DUE TO SCARCITY
*BLACK/5: UNPRICED DUE TO SCARCITY
*RED/1: UNPRICED DUE TO SCARCITY
*P.P.BLACK/1: UNPRICED DUE TO SCARCITY
*P.P.CYAN/1: UNPRICED DUE TO SCARCITY
*P.P.MAGENTA/1: UNPRICED DUE TO SCARCITY
*P.P.YELLOW/1: UNPRICED DUE TO SCARCITY
RANDOMLY INSERTED INTO PACKS

AAB Alexa Bliss	30.00	75.00
ABE Bayley	12.00	30.00
ABK Billie Kay	10.00	25.00
ABZ Shayna Baszler	8.00	20.00
ACG Chelsea Green	20.00	50.00
ACL Candice LeRae	10.00	25.00
ACM Carmella	12.00	30.00
ADB Dana Brooke	6.00	15.00
ADK Dakota Kai	10.00	25.00
ADP Deonna Purrazzo	6.00	15.00
AEM Ember Moon	8.00	20.00
AIS Io Shirai	30.00	75.00
AJD Jessamyn Duke	10.00	25.00
AJE Jessi Kamea	8.00	20.00
AKC Kacy Catanzaro	15.00	40.00
ALE Lacey Evans	10.00	25.00
AMR Mandy Rose	15.00	40.00
AMS Marina Shafir	8.00	20.00
AMY Mia Yim	12.00	30.00
ANC Nikki Cross	8.00	20.00
ANT Natalya	6.00	15.00
APR Peyton Royce	10.00	25.00
ARY Renee Young	6.00	15.00
ASD Sonya Deville	10.00	25.00
ATC Taynara Conti	6.00	15.00
ATM Tamina	6.00	15.00
AVB Vanessa Borne	6.00	15.00
AEST Bianca Belair	10.00	25.00

2019 Topps WWE Women's Division Championship Side Plate Commemorative Patches

*PURPLE/99: .5X TO 1.2X BASIC MEM
*ORANGE/50: .6X TO 1.5X BASIC MEM
*BLUE/25: .75X TO 2X BASIC MEM
*GOLD/10: UNPRICED DUE TO SCARCITY
*RED/1: UNPRICED DUE TO SCARCITY
STATED PRINT RUN 199 SER.#'d SETS

PCAB Alexa Bliss	15.00	40.00
PCAK Asuka	8.00	20.00
PCBL Becky Lynch	10.00	25.00
PCBY Bayley	8.00	20.00
PCCM Carmella	6.00	15.00
PCEM Ember Moon	5.00	12.00
PCKS Kairi Sane	12.00	30.00
PCNJ Nia Jax	5.00	12.00
PCNM Naomi	4.00	10.00
PCNT Natalya	4.00	10.00
PCQA Shayna Baszler	5.00	12.00
PCRR Ronda Rousey	12.00	30.00
PCSB Sasha Banks	8.00	20.00

2019 Topps WWE Women's Division Dual Autographs

*GOLD/10: UNPRICED DUE TO SCARCITY
*BLACK/5: UNPRICED DUE TO SCARCITY
*RED/1: UNPRICED DUE TO SCARCITY
RANDOMLY INSERTED INTO PACKS
STATED PRINT RUN 25 SER.#'d SETS

DABC A.Bliss/N.Cross	200.00	300.00
DADD B.Phoenix/Natalya	60.00	120.00
DAII B.Kay/P/Royce	125.00	250.00

2019 Topps WWE Women's Division Mat Relics

*GREEN/150: SAME VALUE AS BASIC
*PURPLE/99: .5X TO 1.2X BASIC MEM
*BRONZE/75: .6X TO 1.5X BASIC MEM
*ORANGE/50: .75X TO 2X BASIC MEM
*BLUE/25: 1.2X TO 3X BASIC MEM
*GOLD/10: UNPRICED DUE TO SCARCITY
*BLACK/5: UNPRICED DUE TO SCARCITY
*RED/1: UNPRICED DUE TO SCARCITY
RANDOMLY INSERTED INTO PACKS
STATED PRINT RUN 199 SER.#'d SETS

MRAB Alexa Bliss	10.00	25.00
MRAF Alicia Fox	3.00	8.00
MRAK Asuka	5.00	12.00
MRAS Asuka	4.00	10.00
MRBE Becky Lynch	10.00	25.00
MRBK Billie Kay	4.00	10.00
MRBL Becky Lynch	10.00	25.00
MRBP Beth Phoenix	3.00	8.00
MRBY Bayley	2.50	6.00
MRCA Carmella	3.00	8.00
MRCH Charlotte Flair	4.00	10.00
MRCM Carmella	3.00	8.00
MREM Ember Moon	4.00	10.00
MRIS Io Shirai	6.00	15.00
MRJJ JoJo	2.50	6.00
MRKS Kairi Sane	5.00	12.00
MRLI Liv Morgan	6.00	15.00
MRLM Liv Morgan	5.00	12.00
MRLT Lita	3.00	8.00
MRMD Alundra Blayze	2.50	6.00
MRMJ Mickie James	2.50	6.00
MRNA Natalya	2.50	6.00
MRNI Nia Jax	3.00	8.00
MRNJ Nia Jax	3.00	8.00
MRNM Naomi	2.50	6.00
MRNT Natalya	2.50	6.00
MRQA Shayna Baszler	2.50	6.00
MRRB Ruby Riott	3.00	8.00
MRRO Ronda Rousey	10.00	25.00
MRRR Ronda Rousey	10.00	25.00
MRRU Ruby Riott	3.00	8.00
MRRY Renee Young	3.00	8.00
MRSA Sarah Logan	2.50	6.00
MRSB Sasha Banks	6.00	15.00
MRSD Sonya Deville	5.00	12.00
MRSF Trish Stratus	4.00	10.00
MRSL Sarah Logan	2.50	6.00
MRTA Tamina	2.50	6.00
MRTM Tamina	2.50	6.00
MRTS Toni Storm	8.00	20.00

2019 Topps WWE Women's Division Mixed Match Challenge Season 2

COMPLETE SET (25)	8.00	20.00

*ORANGE/50: 1.2X TO 3X BASIC CARDS
*BLUE/25: 2X TO 5X BASIC CARDS
*GOLD/10: UNPRICED DUE TO SCARCITY
*RED/1: UNPRICED DUE TO SCARCITY
RANDOMLY INSERTED INTO PACKS

MMC1 Monster Eclipse	.60	1.50
MMC2 Country Dominance	.60	1.50
MMC3 B'N'B	.60	1.50
MMC4 Mahalicia	.50	1.25
MMC5 Team Pawz	.50	1.25
MMC6 Awe-ska	.75	2.00
MMC7 Day One Glow	.40	1.00
MMC8 Ravishing Rusev Day	.50	1.25
MMC9 Fabulous Truth	.60	1.50
MMC10 Monster Eclipse	.60	1.50
MMC11 Country Dominance	.60	1.50
MMC12 Awe-ska	.75	2.00
MMC13 B'N'B	.60	1.50
MMC14 Robert Roode/Team Pawz	.50	1.25
MMC15 Awe-ska	.75	2.00
MMC16 Monster Eclipse	.60	1.50
MMC17 Fabulous Truth	.60	1.50
MMC18 Curt Hawkins/Monster Eclipse	.60	1.50
MMC19 Mahalicia	.50	1.25
MMC20 B'N'B	.60	1.50
MMC21 Awe-ska	.75	2.00
MMC22 Apollo Crews/B'N'B	.50	1.25
MMC23 Mahalicia	.50	1.25
MMC24 Fabulous Truth	.60	1.50
MMC25 Fabulous Truth Win	.60	1.50

2019 Topps WWE Women's Division Shirt Relics

*PURPLE/99: .5X TO 1.2X BASIC CARDS
*ORANGE/50: .6X TO 1.5X BASIC CARDS
*BLUE/25: .75X TO 2X BASIC CARDS
*GOLD/10: UNPRICED DUE TO SCARCITY
*RED/1: UNPRICED DUE TO SCARCITY
STATED PRINT RUN 199 SER.#'d SETS

SRAB Alexa Bliss	12.00	30.00
SRAF Alicia Fox	5.00	12.00
SRAS Asuka	6.00	15.00
SRCM Carmella	5.00	12.00
SRJJ JoJo	4.00	10.00
SRLE Lacey Evans	5.00	12.00
SRNM Naomi	4.00	10.00
SRNT Natalya	4.00	10.00
SRQA Shayna Baszler	4.00	10.00
SRSB Sasha Banks		

2019 Topps WWE Women's Division Team Bestie

COMPLETE SET (20)	8.00	20.00

*ORANGE/50: 1.5X TO 4X BASIC CARDS
*BLUE/25: 2.5X TO 6X BASIC CARDS
*GOLD/10: UNPRICED DUE TO SCARCITY
*RED/1: UNPRICED DUE TO SCARCITY
RANDOMLY INSERTED INTO PACKS

TB1 Trish Stratus	.75	2.00
TB2 Trish Stratus	.75	2.00
TB3 Trish Stratus	.75	2.00
TB4 Trish Stratus	.75	2.00
TB5 Team Bestie	1.00	2.50
TB6 Trish Stratus	.75	2.00
TB7 Trish Stratus	.75	2.00
TB8 Trish Stratus	.75	2.00
TB9 Trish Stratus	1.25	3.00
TB10 Trish Stratus	.75	2.00
TB11 Lita	.60	1.50
TB12 Lita/The Rock	1.00	2.50
TB13 Lita	.60	1.50
TB14 Team Bestie	.75	2.00
TB15 Lita	.60	1.50
TB16 Lita	.60	1.50
TB17 Lita	.60	1.50
TB18 Lita	.60	1.50
TB19 Lita	.60	1.50
TB20 Lita	.60	1.50

2019 Topps WWE Women's Division Triple Autographs

STATED PRINT RUN 10 SER.#'d SETS
UNPRICED DUE TO SCARCITY

TA4H Shafir/Duke/Baszler

2019 Topps WWE Women's Division Women's Evolution

COMPLETE SET (10)	8.00	20.00

*ORANGE/50: 1.2X TO 1.5X BASIC CARDS
*BLUE/25: 2X TO 3X BASIC CARDS
*GOLD/10: UNPRICED DUE TO SCARCITY
*RED/1: UNPRICED DUE TO SCARCITY

WE1 Lita	1.50	4.00
WE2 Alundra Blayze	.75	2.00
WE3 Nia Jax/Tamina	.60	1.50
WE4 Carmella	1.50	4.00
WE5 Mandy Rose	1.50	4.00

WE6	Toni Storm	2.50	6.00
WE7	Sasha/Bayley/Natalya	2.50	6.00
WE8	Jessamyn Duke/Marina Shafir	.75	2.00
WE9	Becky Lynch	2.50	6.00
WE10	Women's Division	3.00	8.00

2019 Topps WWE Women's Division Women's Royal Rumble

COMPLETE SET (25) 12.00 30.00
*ORANGE/50: 2X TO 5X BASIC CARDS
*BLUE/25: 3X TO 8X BASIC CARDS
*GOLD/10: UNPRICED DUE TO SCARCITY
*RED/1: UNPRICED DUE TO SCARCITY
RANDOMLY INSERTED INTO PACKS

RR1	Lacey Evans	1.00	2.50
RR2	Natalya	1.00	2.50
RR3	Mandy Rose	1.25	3.00
RR4	Mickie James	1.25	3.00
RR5	Ember Moon	1.25	3.00
RR6	Billie Kay	1.00	2.50
RR7	Nikki Cross	.75	2.00
RR8	Peyton Royce	1.25	3.00
RR9	Tamina	.50	1.25
RR10	Kairi Sane	1.00	2.50
RR11	Naomi	.75	2.00
RR12	Candice LeRae	1.00	2.50
RR13	Alicia Fox	1.00	2.50
RR14	Kacy Catanzaro	1.25	3.00
RR15	Zelina Vega	.75	2.00
RR16	Ruby Riott	1.00	2.50
RR17	Io Shirai	.50	1.25
RR18	Sonya Deville	1.00	2.50
RR19	Alexa Bliss	2.50	6.00
RR20	Bayley	1.00	2.50
RR21	Becky Lynch	2.00	5.00
RR22	Nia Jax	1.00	2.50
RR23	Carmella	1.25	3.00
RR24	Maria Kanellis	1.25	3.00
RR25	Xia Li	.50	1.25

2020 Topps WWE Women's Division

COMPLETE SET (100) 15.00 40.00
*PURPLE/99: .6X TO 1.5X BASIC CARDS
*GREEN/75: .75X TO 2X BASIC CARDS
*ORANGE/50: 1X TO 2.5X BASIC CARDS
*BLUE/25: 1.5X TO 4X BASIC CARDS
*GOLD/10: UNPRICED DUE TO SCARCITY
*BLACK/5: UNPRICED DUE TO SCARCITY
*RED/1: UNPRICED DUE TO SCARCITY
*P.P.BLACK/1: UNPRICED DUE TO SCARCITY
*P.P.CYAN/1: UNPRICED DUE TO SCARCITY
*P.P.MAGENTA/1: UNPRICED DUE TO SCARCITY
*P.P.YELLOW/1: UNPRICED DUE TO SCARCITY

1	Becky Lynch	1.00	2.50
2	Toni Storm	.60	1.50
3	Nikki Cross	.50	1.25
4	Becky Lynch	1.00	2.50
5	Asuka	1.00	2.50
6	Shayna Baszler	.75	2.00
7	Ronda Rousey	1.25	3.00
8	Asuka	1.00	2.50
9	Lacey Evans	.60	1.50
10	Becky Lynch	1.00	2.50
11	Boss 'n' Hug Connection	1.25	3.00
12	Ronda Rousey	1.25	3.00
13	Mandy Rose	1.25	3.00
14	Shayna Baszler	.75	2.00
15	Asuka	1.00	2.50
16	Becky Lynch	1.00	2.50
17	Boss 'n' Hug Connection	1.25	3.00
18	IIconics	.50	1.25
19	Charlotte Flair	1.00	2.50
20	Shayna Baszler	.75	2.00
21	IIconics	.50	1.25
22	Becky Lynch	1.25	3.00
23	Lacey Evans	.60	1.50
24	Kairi Sane	.50	1.25
25	Shayna Baszler	.75	2.00
26	Charlotte Flair	1.00	2.50
27	Toni Storm	.60	1.50
28	Kabuki Warriors	.50	1.25
29	Bayley	.50	1.25
30	Becky Lynch	1.00	2.50
31	Charlotte Flair	1.00	2.50
32	Bayley	.50	1.25
33	Shayna Baszler	.75	2.00
34	Alexa Bliss	1.50	4.00
35	Kay Lee Ray	.40	1.00
36	Bayley	.50	1.25
37	Becky Lynch	1.00	2.50
38	Baron Corbin & Lacey Evans	.60	1.50
39	Nikki Cross	.50	1.25
40	Shayna Baszler	.75	2.00
41	Io Shirai	.75	2.00
42	Nikki Cross	1.50	4.00
43	Mia Yim	.50	1.25
44	Nikki Cross	.50	1.25
45	Seth Rollins & Becky Lynch	1.00	2.50
46	Io Shirai	.40	1.00
47	Bayley	.50	1.25
48	Seth Rollins & Becky Lynch	1.00	2.50
49	Natalya	.40	1.00
50	Bayley & Ember Moon	.50	1.25
51	IIconics	.50	1.25
52	Ember Moon	.50	1.25
53	Candice LeRae	.75	2.00
54	Natalya	1.00	2.50
55	Alexa Bliss & Nikki Cross	1.50	4.00
56	Charlotte Flair	1.25	3.00
57	Shayna Baszler	.75	2.00
58	Becky Lynch & Charlotte Flair	1.00	2.50
59	Alexa Bliss & Nikki Cross	1.50	4.00
60	Io Shirai	.40	1.00
61	Shayna Baszler	.75	2.00
62	Alexa Bliss & Nikki Cross	1.50	4.00
63	Becky Lynch	1.00	2.50
64	Bayley	.50	1.25
65	Charlotte Flair	1.25	3.00
66	Alexa Bliss & Nikki Cross	1.50	4.00
67	Sasha Banks	1.25	3.00
68	Charlotte Flair	1.00	2.50
69	Alexa Bliss & Nikki Cross	1.50	4.00
70	Charlotte Flair	1.50	4.00
71	Mia Yim	.50	1.25
72	Sasha Banks	1.25	3.00
73	Rhea Ripley	1.00	2.50
74	Kay Lee Ray	.40	1.00
75	Sasha Banks	1.25	3.00
76	Bayley	.50	1.25
77	Bayley & Sasha Banks	1.25	3.00
78	Fire & Desire	1.25	3.00
79	Becky Lynch & Charlotte Flair	1.00	2.50
80	Nikki Cross	1.50	4.00
81	Shayna Baszler	1.00	2.50
82	Alexa Bliss & Nikki Cross	1.50	4.00
83	Bayley	.50	1.25
84	Sasha Banks	1.25	3.00
85	Becky Lynch & Charlotte Flair	1.00	2.50
86	Candice LeRae	.75	2.00
87	Kabuki Warriors	1.00	2.50
88	Dakota Kai	.50	1.25
89	Shayna Baszler	.75	2.00
90	Charlotte Flair	1.00	2.50
91	Kabuki Warriors	1.00	2.50
92	Becky Lynch	1.00	2.50
93	Kabuki Warriors	1.00	2.50
94	Bayley	1.00	2.50
95	Tegan Nox	.60	1.50
96	Nikki Cross	.50	1.25
97	Rhea Ripley	1.00	2.50
98	Dakota Kai & Tegan Nox	.60	1.50
99	Kabuki Warriors	.60	1.50
100	Kabuki Warriors	1.00	2.50

2020 Topps WWE Women's Division Autographed Championship Plate Patches

*RED/1: UNPRICED DUE TO SCARCITY
STATED PRINT RUN 10 SER.#'d SETS
UNPRICED DUE TO SCARCITY

CPAB	Alexa Bliss
CPAS	Asuka
CPCM	Carmella
CPKS	Kairi Sane
CPNJ	Nia Jax
CPNM	Naomi
CPNT	Natalya
CPQU	Charlotte Flair
CPSB	Sasha Banks
CPSP	Shayna Baszler
CPALX	Alexa Bliss
CPBAY	Bayley
CPRIP	Rhea Ripley

2020 Topps WWE Women's Division Autographed Mat Relics

*RED/1: UNPRICED DUE TO SCARCITY
STATED PRINT RUN 10 SER.#'d SETS
UNPRICED DUE TO SCARCITY

MRABA	Bayley
MRABB	Bianca Belair
MRABP	Beth Phoenix
MRACG	Chelsea Green
MRACL	Candice LeRae
MRADB	Dana Brooke
MRADK	Dakota Kai
MRAKS	Kairi Sane
MRALE	Lacey Evans
MRALM	Liv Morgan
MRAMM	Mercedes Martinez
MRAMR	Mandy Rose
MRAMY	Mia Yim
MRANM	Naomi
MRAZI	Shotzi Blackheart
MRAZV	Zelina Vega

2020 Topps WWE Women's Division Autographs

*PINK/150: SAME PRICE AS BASIC
*PURPLE/99: .5X TO 1.2X BASIC AUTO
*GREEN/75: .6X TO 1.5X BASIC AUTO
*ORANGE/50: .75X TO 2X BASIC AUTO
*BLUE/25: UNPRICED DUE TO SCARCITY
*GOLD/10: UNPRICED DUE TO SCARCITY
*BLACK/5: UNPRICED DUE TO SCARCITY
*RED/1: UNPRICED DUE TO SCARCITY
*P.P.BLACK/1: UNPRICED DUE TO SCARCITY
*P.P.CYAN/1: UNPRICED DUE TO SCARCITY
*P.P.MAGENTA/1: UNPRICED DUE TO SCARCITY
*P.P.YELLOW/1: UNPRICED DUE TO SCARCITY
STATED ODDS

AAB	Alexa Bliss	60.00	120.00
AAL	Aliyah	12.00	30.00
AAS	Asuka	20.00	50.00
ABB	Bianca Belair	25.00	60.00
ABI	Billie Kay	10.00	25.00
ABL	Bayley	15.00	40.00
ACC	Charly Caruso	10.00	25.00
ACG	Chelsea Green	15.00	40.00
ACL	Candice LeRae	12.00	30.00
ACM	Carmella	15.00	40.00
ADK	Dakota Kai	20.00	50.00
AEM	Ember Moon	8.00	20.00
AIS	Io Shirai	30.00	75.00
AJD	Jessamyn Duke	8.00	20.00
AKB	Kayla Braxton	20.00	50.00
AKC	Kayden Carter	10.00	25.00
ALE	Lacey Evans	15.00	40.00
ALM	Liv Morgan	20.00	50.00
ALN	Lana	12.00	30.00
AMJ	Mickie James	12.00	30.00
AMR	Mandy Rose	15.00	40.00
AMS	Marina Shafir	6.00	15.00
AMY	Mia Yim	6.00	15.00
ANC	Nikki Cross	10.00	25.00
ANJ	Nia Jax	6.00	15.00
ANM	Naomi	8.00	20.00
ANT	Natalya	6.00	15.00
APR	Peyton Royce	15.00	40.00
ARB	Ruby Riott	12.00	30.00
ARR	Rhea Ripley	50.00	100.00
ASB	Sasha Banks	30.00	75.00
ASG	Santana Garrett	15.00	40.00
ASH	Shotzi Blackheart	75.00	150.00
ASP	Shayna Baszler	10.00	25.00
ATN	Tegan Nox	25.00	60.00
ATS	Toni Storm	50.00	100.00
AXL	Xia Li	20.00	50.00
AKLR	Kay Lee Ray	20.00	50.00

2020 Topps WWE Women's Division Breaking Barriers

COMPLETE SET (10) 8.00 20.00
*BLUE/25: UNPRICED DUE TO SCARCITY
*GOLD/10: UNPRICED DUE TO SCARCITY
*BLACK/5: UNPRICED DUE TO SCARCITY
*RED/1: UNPRICED DUE TO SCARCITY
STATED ODDS 1:

BB1	Chyna	1.25	3.00
BB2	Chyna	1.25	3.00
BB3	Chyna	1.25	3.00
BB4	Chyna	1.25	3.00
BB5	Alundra Blayze	.75	2.00
BB6	Chyna	1.25	3.00
BB7	Ronda Rousey	2.50	6.00
BB8	WWE Evolution	2.00	5.00
BB9	Nia Jax	.75	2.00
BB10	Main Event WrestleMania	2.00	5.00

2020 Topps WWE Women's Division Championship Plate Patches

*PURPLE/99: .5X TO 1.2X BASIC MEM
*GREEN/75: .6X TO 1.5X BASIC MEM
*ORANGE/50: .6X TO 1.5X BASIC MEM
*BLUE/25: UNPRICED DUE TO SCARCITY
*GOLD/10: UNPRICED DUE TO SCARCITY
*RED/1: UNPRICED DUE TO SCARCITY
STATED PRINT RUN 150 SER.#'d SETS

CPA Asuka	12.00	30.00
CPC Charlotte Flair	6.00	15.00
CPAB Alexa Bliss	15.00	40.00
CPAS Asuka	12.00	30.00
CPBL Becky Lynch	10.00	25.00
CPBS Sasha Banks	10.00	25.00
CPCF Charlotte Flair	6.00	15.00
CPCM Carmella	5.00	12.00
CPEM Ember Moon	4.00	10.00
CPHG Bayley	6.00	15.00
CPKS Kairi Sane	5.00	12.00
CPNJ Nia Jax	4.00	10.00
CPNM Naomi	3.00	8.00
CPNT Natalya	3.00	8.00
CPPG Paige		
CPQU Charlotte Flair	6.00	15.00
CPRH Rhea Ripley	15.00	40.00
CPRM Bayley	6.00	15.00
CPRR Ronda Rousey	12.00	30.00
CPSB Sasha Banks	10.00	25.00
CPSP Shayna Baszler	10.00	25.00
CPTS Toni Storm	15.00	40.00
CPALX Alexa Bliss	15.00	40.00
CPBAY Bayley	6.00	15.00
CPKLR Kay Lee Ray	8.00	20.00
CPMAN Becky Lynch	10.00	25.00
CPRIP Rhea Ripley	15.00	40.00

2020 Topps WWE Women's Division Cut Signatures

CSCY Chyna
CSMA Mae Young
CSME Miss Elizabeth

2020 Topps WWE Women's Division Dual Autographs

*GOLD/10: UNPRICED DUE TO SCARCITY
*BLACK/5: UNPRICED DUE TO SCARCITY
*RED/1: UNPRICED DUE TO SCARCITY
STATED ODDS

DAAN A.Bliss/N.Cross	100.00	200.00
DAHI V.Borne/Aliyah	50.00	100.00
DAKW K.Sane/Asuka	125.00	250.00

2020 Topps WWE Women's Division Four Horsewomen of MMA Autographed Book

QMMA Shafir/Rousey/Baszler/Duke	500.00	1000.00

2020 Topps WWE Women's Division Four Horsewomen of WWE Autographed Book

QWWE Bayley/Lynch/Flair/Banks	1000.00	1500.00

2020 Topps WWE Women's Division Mat Relics

*PURPLE/99: .5X TO 1.2X BASIC MEM
*ORANGE/50: .6X TO 1.5X BASIC MEM
*BLUE/25: UNPRICED DUE TO SCARCITY
*GOLD/10: UNPRICED DUE TO SCARCITY
*RED/1: UNPRICED DUE TO SCARCITY
STATED PRINT RUN 150 SER.#'d SETS

MRAB Alexa Bliss	12.00	30.00
MRAS Asuka	10.00	25.00
MRBA Bayley	5.00	12.00
MRBB Bianca Belair	3.00	8.00
MRBL Becky Lynch	8.00	20.00
MRBP Beth Phoenix	2.00	5.00
MRCF Charlotte Flair	6.00	15.00
MRCG Chelsea Green	4.00	10.00
MRCL Candice LeRae	6.00	15.00
MRDB Dana Brooke	2.50	6.00
MRDK Dakota Kai	8.00	20.00
MRET Asuka	10.00	25.00
MRIS Io Shirai	5.00	12.00
MRKS Kairi Sane	6.00	15.00
MRLE Lacey Evans	4.00	10.00
MRLM Liv Morgan	8.00	20.00
MRMH Mighty Molly	3.00	8.00
MRMM Mercedes Martinez	3.00	8.00
MRMR Mandy Rose	6.00	15.00
MRMY Mia Yim	3.00	8.00
MRNC Nikki Cross	4.00	10.00
MRNM Naomi	3.00	8.00
MRNT Natalya	2.50	6.00
MRQU Charlotte Flair	6.00	15.00
MRRR Rhea Ripley	6.00	15.00
MRSB Shayna Baszler	6.00	15.00
MRSD Sonya Deville	2.00	5.00
MRTM Becky Lynch	8.00	20.00
MRTN Tegan Nox	5.00	12.00
MRTO Toni Storm	10.00	25.00
MRTS Tamina	2.00	5.00
MRXL Xia Li	4.00	10.00
MRZI Shotzi Blackheart	12.00	30.00
MRZV Zelina Vega	3.00	8.00
MREST Bianca Belair	3.00	8.00

2020 Topps WWE Women's Division Roster

COMPLETE SET (60) 20.00 50.00
*BLUE/25: UNPRICED DUE TO SCARCITY
*GOLD/10: UNPRICED DUE TO SCARCITY
*BLACK/5: UNPRICED DUE TO SCARCITY
*RED/1: UNPRICED DUE TO SCARCITY
STATED ODDS 1:

RC1 Alexa Bliss	2.50	6.00
RC2 Alicia Taylor	.40	1.00
RC3 Aliyah	.75	2.00
RC4 Asuka	1.50	4.00
RC5 Bayley	.75	2.00
RC6 Becky Lynch	1.50	4.00
RC7 Beth Phoenix	.60	1.50
RC8 Bianca Belair	1.00	2.50
RC9 Billie Kay	.75	2.00
RC10 Candice LeRae	1.25	3.00
RC11 Carmella	1.00	2.50
RC12 Charlotte Flair	1.50	4.00
RC13 Charly Caruso	.40	1.00
RC14 Chelsea Green	2.00	5.00
RC15 Chyna	1.00	2.50
RC16 Dakota Kai	.75	2.00
RC17 Dana Brooke	.60	1.50
RC18 Ember Moon	.75	2.00
RC19 Io Shirai	.60	1.50
RC20 Jessamyn Duke	.60	1.50
RC21 Jessi Kamea	.40	1.00
RC22 Kairi Sane	.75	2.00
RC23 Kay Lee Ray	.60	1.50
RC24 Kayden Carter	.40	1.00
RC25 Kayla Braxton	.50	1.25
RC26 Lacey Evans	1.00	2.50
RC27 Lana	1.00	2.50
RC28 Liv Morgan	1.00	2.50
RC29 Lita	1.00	2.50
RC30 Mandy Rose	2.00	5.00
RC31 Marina Shafir	.60	1.50
RC32 Maryse	.75	2.00
RC33 Mia Yim	.75	2.00
RC34 Mickie James	.60	1.50
RC35 Naomi	.75	2.00
RC36 Natalya	.60	1.50
RC37 Nia Jax	.60	1.50
RC38 Nikki Cross	.75	2.00
RC39 Paige	1.00	2.50
RC40 Peyton Royce	.75	2.00
RC41 Piper Niven	.50	1.25
RC42 Renee Young	.50	1.25
RC43 Rhea Ripley	1.50	4.00
RC44 Ronda Rousey	2.00	5.00
RC45 Ruby Riott	.60	1.50
RC46 Santana Garrett	.40	1.00
RC47 Sarah Schreiber	.40	1.00
RC48 Sasha Banks	2.00	5.00
RC49 Shayna Baszler	1.25	3.00
RC50 Shotzi Blackheart	1.25	3.00
RC51 Sonya Deville	1.00	2.50
RC52 Stephanie McMahon	1.00	2.50
RC53 Tamina	.50	1.25
RC54 Tegan Nox	1.00	2.50
RC55 Toni Storm	1.00	2.50
RC56 Trish Stratus	2.00	5.00
RC57 Vanessa Borne	.75	2.00
RC58 Xia Li	.75	2.00
RC59 Zelina Vega	.75	2.00
RC60 Raquel Gonzalez	.60	1.50

2020 Topps WWE Women's Division Superstar Transformations

COMPLETE SET (15) 20.00 50.00
*BLUE/25: UNPRICED DUE TO SCARCITY
*GOLD/10: UNPRICED DUE TO SCARCITY
*BLACK/5: UNPRICED DUE TO SCARCITY
*RED/1: UNPRICED DUE TO SCARCITY
STATED ODDS 1:

ST1 Alexa Bliss	6.00	15.00
ST2 Asuka	3.00	8.00
ST3 Bayley	2.50	6.00
ST4 Becky Lynch	4.00	10.00
ST5 Carmella	2.00	5.00
ST6 Charlotte Flair	4.00	10.00
ST7 Io Shirai	2.50	6.00
ST8 Kairi Sane	3.00	8.00
ST9 Liv Morgan	2.50	6.00
ST10 Naomi	1.50	4.00
ST11 Paige	1.50	4.00
ST12 Peyton Royce	2.50	6.00
ST13 Ruby Riott	2.50	6.00
ST14 Sasha Banks	5.00	12.00
ST15 Sonya Deville	1.50	4.00

2020 Topps WWE Women's Division Triple Autographs

*GOLD/10: UNPRICED DUE TO SCARCITY
*BLACK/5: UNPRICED DUE TO SCARCITY
*RED/1: UNPRICED DUE TO SCARCITY
STATED PRINT RUN 25 SER.#'d SETS

TAUK Ray/Storm/Ripley	150.00	300.00
TABAD Naomi/Tamina/Banks	100.00	200.00

2021 Topps WWE Women's Division

COMPLETE SET (100) 10.00 25.00
*FOIL: .5X TO 1.2X BASIC CARDS
*PURPLE/99: .6X TO 1.5X BASIC CARDS
*ORANGE/75: .75X TO 2X BASIC CARDS
*GREEN/50: 1X TO 2.5X BASIC CARDS
*BLUE/25: 1.5X TO 4X BASIC CARDS
*GOLD/10: UNPRICED DUE TO SCARCITY
*BLACK/5: UNPRICED DUE TO SCARCITY
*RED/1: UNPRICED DUE TO SCARCITY
*P.P.BLACK/1: UNPRICED DUE TO SCARCITY
*P.P.CYAN/1: UNPRICED DUE TO SCARCITY
*P.P.MAGENTA/1: UNPRICED DUE TO SCARCITY
*P.P.YELLOW/1: UNPRICED DUE TO SCARCITY

1 Bianca Belair	.60	1.50
2 Io Shirai	.50	1.25
3 Alexa Bliss & Nikki Cross	1.50	4.00
4 Bayley	1.25	3.00
5 Sonya Deville	1.25	3.00
6 Tamina	.30	.75
7 Charlotte Flair	1.25	3.00
8 Mia Yim	.30	.75
9 Alexa Bliss & Nikki Cross	1.50	4.00
10 Charlotte Flair	1.25	3.00
11 Rhea Ripley	.75	2.00
12 Sonya Deville	1.25	3.00
13 Tamina & Lacey Evans	.60	1.50
14 Bayley	.60	1.50
15 Asuka	1.00	2.50
16 Becky Lynch	1.00	2.50
17 Nia Jax	1.00	2.50
18 Charlotte Flair	1.25	3.00
19 Bayley	.60	1.50
20 Nia Jax	.50	1.25
21 Sasha Banks	1.50	4.00
22 Nia Jax	.50	1.25
23 Golden Role Models	1.25	3.00
24 Io Shirai	.50	1.25
25 Charlotte Flair	1.25	3.00
26 Golden Role Models	1.25	3.00
27 Asuka	.50	1.25
28 Asuka	1.00	2.50
29 Golden Role Models	1.25	3.00
30 Sonya Deville	1.25	3.00
31 Asuka	1.00	2.50
32 Rhea Ripley	.75	2.00
33 Nikki Cross	.50	1.25
34 Sasha Banks	1.25	3.00
35 Rhea Ripley	.75	2.00
36 Tegan Nox	.60	1.50
37 Io Shirai	1.25	3.00
38 Nikki Cross	.60	1.50
39 Asuka	1.00	2.50
40 Golden Role Models	1.25	3.00
41 Golden Role Models	1.25	3.00
42 Aliyah	.50	1.25
43 Io Shirai	.50	1.25
44 Dakota Kai	.50	1.25

45 Golden Role Models	1.25	3.00
46 RAW Title Match Controversy	.60	1.50
47 Bayley	.60	1.50
48 Shotzi Blackheart	1.00	2.50
49 Nikki Cross	.50	1.25
50 Nia Jax & Shayna Baszler	.50	1.25
51 Mercedes Martinez	.40	1.00
52 Bayley	.60	1.50
53 The Fiend	1.50	4.00
54 Asuka	1.00	2.50
55 Dakota Kai	.50	1.25
56 Asuka	1.00	2.50
57 Rhea Ripley & Shotzi Blackheart	1.00	2.50
58 Asuka	1.00	2.50
59 Rhea Ripley & Shotzi Blackheart	1.00	2.50
60 Dakota Kai	.60	1.50
61 Sonya Deville	.60	1.50
62 Sasha Banks	1.25	3.00
63 Io Shirai	.50	1.25
64 Mandy Rose	1.25	3.00
65 Bayley	.60	1.50
66 Asuka	1.00	2.50
67 Shayna Baszler & Nia Jax	.50	1.25
68 Asuka	1.25	3.00
69 Dakota Kai & Raquel Gonzalez	.60	1.50
70 Shayna Baszler & Nia Jax	.50	1.25
71 Bayley	1.25	3.00
72 Rhea Ripley	.75	2.00
73 Alexa Bliss	1.50	4.00
74 Candice LeRae	1.00	2.50
75 Alexa Bliss	1.50	4.00
76 Sasha Banks	1.25	3.00
77 Candice LeRae & Johnny Gargano	1.00	2.50
78 Io Shirai	1.00	2.50
79 Ember Moon	.30	.75
80 Nia Jax & Shayna Baszler	.50	1.25
81 Ember Moon & Rhea Ripley	.75	2.00
82 Candice LeRae	1.00	2.50
83 Toni Storm	.75	2.00
84 Dakota Kai	.50	1.25
85 Sasha Banks	1.25	3.00
86 Sasha Banks	1.25	3.00
87 Rhea Ripley	.75	2.00
88 Io Shirai	.50	1.25
89 Nia Jax & Shayna Baszler	.50	1.25
90 Dakota Kai	.60	1.50
91 Toni Storm	.75	2.00
92 Sasha Banks	1.25	3.00
93 Carmella	.60	1.50
94 Candice LeRae	1.00	2.50
95 Carmella	.60	1.50
96 Toni Storm & Ember Moon	.75	2.00
97 Io Shirai	.75	2.00
98 Sasha Banks	1.25	3.00
99 Alexa Bliss	1.50	4.00
100 Toni Storm	.75	2.00

2021 Topps WWE Women's Division 5th Anniversary Women's Championship Tribute

*BLUE/25: 1.2X TO 3X BASIC CARDS
*GOLD/10: UNPRICED DUE TO SCARCITY
*BLACK/5: UNPRICED DUE TO SCARCITY
*RED/1: UNPRICED DUE TO SCARCITY
RANDOMLY INSERTED INTO PACKS

RC1 Sasha Banks def. Charlotte Flair	2.50	6.00
RC2 Charlotte Flair def. Sasha Banks	2.50	6.00
RC3 Sasha Banks def. Charlotte Flair	2.50	6.00
RC4 Bayley def. Charlotte Flair	1.25	3.00
RC5 Alexa Bliss def. Bayley	3.00	8.00
RC6 Alexa Bliss	3.00	8.00
RC7 Becky Lynch def. Sasha Banks	2.00	5.00
RC8 Becky Lynch def. Sasha Banks	2.00	5.00
RC9 Becky Lynch def. Asuka	2.00	5.00
RC10 Sasha Banks def. Asuka	2.50	6.00
SC1 Alexa Bliss def. Becky Lynch	3.00	8.00
SC2 Charlotte Flair def. Asuka	2.50	6.00
SC3 Charlotte Flair def. Becky Lynch and Carmella	2.50	6.00
SC4 Becky Lynch def. Charlotte Flair	2.00	5.00
SC5 Charlotte Flair def. Becky Lynch	2.50	6.00
SC6 Becky Lynch def. Charlotte Flair	2.00	5.00
SC7 Asuka def. Becky Lynch and Charlotte Flair	2.00	5.00
SC8 Asuka def. Becky Lynch	2.00	5.00
SC9 Bayley def. Charlotte Flair	1.25	3.00
SC10 Sasha Banks def. Bayley	2.50	6.00

2021 Topps WWE Women's Division 5th Anniversary Women's Championship Autographs

*ORANGE/75: .5X TO 1.2X BASIC AUTOS
*GREEN/50: .6X TO 1.5X BASIC AUTOS
*BLUE/25: .75X TO 2X BASIC AUTOS
*GOLD/10: UNPRICED DUE TO SCARCITY
*RED/1: UNPRICED DUE TO SCARCITY
STATED PRINT RUN 99 SER.#'d SETS
UNPRICED DUE TO SCARCITY

5AAB Alexa Bliss	75.00	150.00
5AAS Asuka	30.00	75.00
5ABL Becky Lynch	50.00	100.00
5ACF Charlotte Flair	50.00	100.00
5ACM Carmella	15.00	40.00
5ANJ Nia Jax	10.00	25.00
5ANM Naomi	10.00	25.00
5ANT Natalya	10.00	25.00
5ASB Sasha Banks	60.00	120.00

2021 Topps WWE Women's Division Autographed Mat Relics

STATED PRINT RUN 10 SER.#'d SETS
UNPRICED DUE TO SCARCITY

MC Carmella
MN Naomi
MT Tamina
MAB Alexa Bliss
MBB Bianca Belair
MBZ Shayna Baszler
MCF Charlotte Flair
MDB Dana Brooke
MDK Dakota Kai
MEM Ember Moon
MLM Liv Morgan
MMR Mandy Rose
MNC Nikki Cross
MNJ Nia Jax
MNT Natalya
MRP Rhea Ripley
MSB Shotzi Blackheart
MSD Sonya Deville
MTN Tegan Nox
MTS Toni Storm

2021 Topps WWE Women's Division Autographed Superstar Logo Patches

STATED PRINT RUN 10 SER.#'d SETS
UNPRICED DUE TO SCARCITY

ARAS Asuka
ARBB Bianca Belair
ARBZ Shayna Baszler
ARCF Charlotte Flair
ARCL Candice LeRae
ARCM Carmella
ARDB Dana Brooke
ARDK Dakota Kai
ARMR Mandy Rose
ARNJ Nia Jax
ARNT Natalya
ARRP Rhea Ripley
ARSD Sonya Deville
ARSZ Shotzi Blackheart

2021 Topps WWE Women's Division Autographs

*PURPLE/99: .5X TO 1.2X BASIC AUTOS
*ORANGE/75: .6X TO 1.5X BASIC AUTOS
*GREEN/50: .75X TO 2X BASIC AUTOS
*BLUE/25: 1X TO 2.5X BASIC AUTOS
*GOLD/10: UNPRICED DUE TO SCARCITY
*BLACK/5: UNPRICED DUE TO SCARCITY
*RED/1: UNPRICED DUE TO SCARCITY
*P.P.BLACK/1: UNPRICED DUE TO SCARCITY
*P.P.CYAN/1: UNPRICED DUE TO SCARCITY
*P.P.MAGENTA/1: UNPRICED DUE TO SCARCITY
*P.P.YELLOW/1: UNPRICED DUE TO SCARCITY
STATED PRINT RUN 199 SER.#'d SETS

AAA Alyse Ashton	12.00	30.00
AAB Alexa Bliss	75.00	150.00
AAL Aliyah	8.00	20.00
AAS Asuka	15.00	40.00
AAT Alicia Taylor	5.00	12.00
ABL Becky Lynch	30.00	75.00
ABP Beth Phoenix	8.00	20.00
ABZ Shayna Baszler	6.00	15.00
ACJ Cora Jade	75.00	150.00
ACL Candice LeRae	8.00	20.00
ACM Carmella	10.00	25.00
ADK Dakota Kai	10.00	25.00
AEM Ember Moon	6.00	15.00
AFM Franky Monet	12.00	30.00
AGD Gigi Dolin	75.00	150.00
AIH Indi Hartwell	15.00	40.00
AIS Io Shirai	12.00	30.00
AJK Jessi Kamea	6.00	15.00
AKB Kayla Braxton	6.00	15.00
AKC Kacy Catanzaro	12.00	30.00
AKD Kayden Carter	5.00	12.00
AKT Katrina Cortez	6.00	15.00
ALE Lacey Evans	10.00	25.00
ALM Liv Morgan	30.00	75.00
AMH Molly Holly	20.00	50.00
AMM McKenzie Mitchell	8.00	20.00
AMZ Maryse	10.00	25.00
ANC Nikki Cross	8.00	20.00
ANJ Nia Jax	5.00	12.00
ANT Natalya	6.00	15.00
APN Piper Niven	10.00	25.00
ARG Raquel Gonzalez	10.00	25.00
ARP Rhea Ripley	15.00	40.00
ASC Scarlett	30.00	75.00
ASD Sonya Deville	8.00	20.00
ASR Sarray	30.00	75.00
ASS Sarah Schreiber	10.00	25.00
AST Stephanie McMahon	125.00	250.00
ASZ Shotzi Blackheart	15.00	40.00
ATI Mei Ying	12.00	30.00
ATM Tamina	5.00	12.00
ATN Tegan Nox	12.00	30.00
ATS Toni Storm	15.00	40.00
AXL Xia Li	15.00	40.00
AZS Zoey Stark	6.00	15.00
AKLR Kay Lee Ray	6.00	15.00
ANEM Eva Marie	12.00	30.00

2021 Topps WWE Women's Division Autographs Purple

ACF Charlotte Flair	50.00	100.00
ANM Naomi	8.00	20.00

2021 Topps WWE Women's Division Best Roommates Ever Autograph Book

QBRE Kai/Duke/Baszler/Yim

2021 Topps WWE Women's Division Diamond Cuts

COMPLETE SET (14)
*BLUE/25: 2X TO 5X BASIC CARDS
*GOLD/10: UNPRICED DUE TO SCARCITY
*BLACK/5: UNPRICED DUE TO SCARCITY
*RED/1: UNPRICED DUE TO SCARCITY
RANDOMLY INSERTED INTO PACKS

DC1 Charlotte Flair	4.00	10.00
DC2 Lacey Evans	2.00	5.00
DC3 Mandy Rose	4.00	10.00
DC4 Jessi Kamea	1.50	4.00
DC5 Bianca Belair	2.00	5.00
DC6 Dana Brooke	.75	2.00
DC7 Carmella	2.00	5.00
DC8 Franky Monet	1.50	4.00
DC9 Liv Morgan	3.00	8.00
DC10 Natalya	1.25	3.00
DC11 Sasha Banks	4.00	10.00
DC12 Aliyah	1.50	4.00
DC13 Dakota Kai	1.50	4.00
DC14 Indi Hartwell	2.50	6.00

2021 Topps WWE Women's Division Dual Autographs

*GOLD/10: UNPRICED DUE TO SCARCITY
*RED/1: UNPRICED DUE TO SCARCITY
STATED PRINT RUN 25 SER.#'d SETS
UNPRICED DUE TO SCARCITY

DADR D.Kai/R.Gonzalez		
DAKK K.Carter/K/Catanzaro	50.00	100.00
DAMD M.Rose/D.Brooke	60.00	120.00
DANS S.Baszler/N.Jax	15.00	40.00
DANT Tamina/Natalya	25.00	60.00
DASE E.Moon/S.Blackheart	50.00	100.00

2021 Topps WWE Women's Division Legends of the Women's Division Autograph Book

QWDL Eve/Holly/Stratus/Phoenix

2021 Topps WWE Women's Division Mat Relics

*PINK/150: SAME VALUE AS BASIC
*PURPLE/99: .5X TO 1.2X BASIC MEM
*ORANGE/75: .6X TO 1.5X BASIC MEM
*GREEN/50: .75X TO 2X BASIC MEM
*BLUE/25: 1X TO 2.5X BASIC MEM
*GOLD/10: UNPRICED DUE TO SCARCITY
*BLACK/5: UNPRICED DUE TO SCARCITY
*RED/1: UNPRICED DUE TO SCARCITY
STATED PRINT RUN 250 SER.#'d SETS

M$ Sasha Banks	10.00	25.00
MA Asuka	6.00	15.00
MB Bayley	6.00	15.00
MC Carmella	3.00	8.00
MN Naomi	3.00	8.00
MT Tamina	2.50	6.00
MAB Alexa Bliss	15.00	40.00
MAK Asuka	6.00	15.00
MAL Alexa Bliss	15.00	40.00
MBB Bianca Belair	5.00	12.00
MBE Becky Lynch	12.00	30.00
MBL Bayley	6.00	15.00
MBY Bayley	6.00	15.00
MBZ Shayna Baszler	5.00	12.00
MCF Charlotte Flair	6.00	15.00
MCH Charlotte Flair	6.00	15.00
MDA Dakota Kai	5.00	12.00
MDB Dana Brooke	2.50	6.00
MDK Dakota Kai	5.00	12.00
MEM Ember Moon	2.50	6.00
MLA Lacey Evans	4.00	10.00
MLE Lacey Evans	4.00	10.00
MLM Liv Morgan	10.00	25.00
MLV Liv Morgan	10.00	25.00
MMR Mandy Rose	6.00	15.00
MNC Nikki Cross	2.50	6.00
MNJ Nia Jax	2.50	6.00
MNT Natalya	3.00	8.00
MRP Rhea Ripley	8.00	20.00
MSA Sasha Banks	10.00	25.00
MSB Shotzi Blackheart	8.00	20.00
MSD Sonya Deville	4.00	10.00
MTN Tegan Nox	3.00	8.00
MTS Toni Storm	5.00	12.00
MALE Alexa Bliss	15.00	40.00
MASU Asuka	6.00	15.00
MBIA Bianca Belair	5.00	12.00
MMRS Mandy Rose	6.00	15.00
MNIA Nia Jax	2.50	6.00
MRHE Rhea Ripley	8.00	20.00
MSAS Sasha Banks	10.00	25.00
MSHA Shayna Baszler	5.00	12.00

2021 Topps WWE Women's Division Roster

COMPLETE SET (55)	12.00	30.00

*BLUE/25: 1.2X TO 3X BASIC CARDS
*GOLD/10: UNPRICED DUE TO SCARCITY
*BLACK/5: UNPRICED DUE TO SCARCITY
*RED/1: UNPRICED DUE TO SCARCITY
RANDOMLY INSERTED INTO PACKS

R1 Alexa Bliss	2.50	6.00
R2 Asuka	1.50	4.00
R3 Becky Lynch	1.50	4.00
R4 Charlotte Flair	2.00	5.00
R5 Dana Brooke	.40	1.00
R6 Doudrop	.60	1.50
R7 Lacey Evans	1.00	2.50
R8 Mandy Rose	2.00	5.00
R9 Maryse	.60	1.50
R10 Naomi	.50	1.25
R11 Nia Jax	.75	2.00
R12 Nikki A.S.H.	.75	2.00
R13 Rhea Ripley	1.25	3.00
R14 Sarah Schreiber	.40	1.00
R15 Shayna Baszler	.75	2.00
R16 Alyse Ashton	.40	1.00
R17 Bayley	1.00	2.50
R18 Bianca Belair	1.00	2.50
R19 Carmella	1.00	2.50
R20 Kayla Braxton	.75	2.00
R21 Liv Morgan	1.50	4.00
R22 Natalya	.60	1.50
R23 Sasha Banks	2.00	5.00
R24 Sonya Deville	1.00	2.50
R25 Tamina	.50	1.25
R26 Alicia Taylor	.40	1.00
R27 Aliyah	.75	2.00
R28 Beth Phoenix	.75	2.00
R29 Candice LeRae	1.50	4.00
R30 Dakota Kai	.75	2.00
R31 Ember Moon	.50	1.25
R32 Franky Monet	.75	2.00
R33 Gigi Dolin	.40	1.00
R34 Indi Hartwell	1.25	3.00
R35 Io Shirai	.75	2.00
R36 Jessi Kamea	.75	2.00
R37 Kacy Catanzaro	.75	2.00
R38 Kavita Devi	.40	1.00
R39 Kayden Carter	.75	2.00
R40 Mei Ying	.60	1.50
R41 McKenzie Mitchell	.50	1.25
R42 Mercedes Martinez	.60	1.50
R43 Raquel Gonzalez	1.00	2.50
R44 Sarray	.50	1.25
R45 Scarlett	2.00	5.00
R46 Shotzi	1.50	4.00
R47 Nox	1.00	2.50
R48 Toni Storm	1.25	3.00
R49 Xia Li	.75	2.00
R50 Zoey Stark	.50	1.25
R51 Kay Lee Ray	1.00	2.50
R52 Stephanie McMahon	1.00	2.50
R53 Eva Marie	1.00	2.50
R54 Marlena	.60	1.50
R55 Molly Holly	.50	1.25

2021 Topps WWE Women's Division Sketches

NNO Carlos Cabaleiro

2021 Topps WWE Women's Division Superstar Logo Patches

*PINK/150: SAME PRICE AS BASIC
*PURPLE/99: .5X TO 1.2X BASIC MEM
*ORANGE/75: .6X TO 1.5X BASIC MEM
*GREEN/50: .75X TO 2X BASIC MEM
*BLUE/25: 1X TO 2.5X BASIC MEM
*GOLD/10: UNPRICED DUE TO SCARCITY
*BLACK/5: UNPRICED DUE TO SCARCITY
*RED/1: UNPRICED DUE TO SCARCITY
STATED PRINT RUN 199 SER.#'d SETS

SLPAB Alexa Bliss	15.00	40.00
SLPAS Asuka	10.00	25.00
SLPBA Bayley	8.00	20.00
SLPBB Bianca Belair	6.00	15.00
SLPBL Becky Lynch	15.00	40.00
SLPBP Beth Phoenix	4.00	10.00
SLPBZ Shayna Baszler	3.00	8.00
SLPCF Charlotte Flair	6.00	15.00
SLPCL Candice LeRae	4.00	10.00
SLPCM Carmella	4.00	10.00
SLPDB Dana Brooke	3.00	8.00
SLPDK Dakota Kai	5.00	12.00
SLPEM Ember Moon	5.00	12.00
SLPEV Eve	3.00	8.00
SLPLE Lacey Evans	3.00	8.00
SLPLM Liv Morgan	10.00	25.00
SLPMM Mercedes Martinez	4.00	10.00
SLPMR Mandy Rose	6.00	15.00
SLPNJ Nia Jax	3.00	8.00
SLPNM Naomi	5.00	12.00
SLPNT Natalya	4.00	10.00
SLPRP Rhea Ripley	6.00	15.00
SLPSB Sasha Banks	8.00	20.00
SLPSC Scarlett	10.00	25.00
SLPSD Sonya Deville	3.00	8.00
SLPSZ Shotzi	5.00	12.00
SLPTN Nox	8.00	20.00
SLPTR Trish Stratus	8.00	20.00

2019 Topps WWE Women's Revolution

COMPLETE SET (40)	25.00	60.00
SEMISTARS	1.00	2.50
UNLISTED STARS	1.25	3.00

RANDOMLY INSERTED INTO PACKS

DR1 Paige	2.00	5.00
DR2 Charlotte/Becky/Sasha	2.00	5.00
DR3 Charlotte Flair	2.00	5.00
DR4 Team PCB	2.00	5.00
DR5 Charlotte Flair	2.00	5.00
DR6 Nikki Bella	2.00	5.00
DR7 Charlotte Flair	2.00	5.00
DR8 Paige	2.00	5.00
DR9 Natalya	2.00	5.00
DR10 Charlotte Flair	2.00	5.00
DR11 Paige	2.00	5.00
DR12 Charlotte Flair	2.00	5.00
DR13 Paige	2.00	5.00
DR14 Charlotte Flair	2.00	5.00
DR15 Charlotte Flair	2.00	5.00
DR16 Nikki Bella	1.25	3.00
DR17 Charlotte Flair	2.00	5.00
DR18 Sasha Banks	2.00	5.00
DR19 Brie Bella	1.25	3.00
DR20 Team B.A.D./Sasha Banks	2.00	5.00
DR21 Lita	1.25	3.00
DR22 Charlotte Flair	2.00	5.00
DR23 Charlotte Flair	2.00	5.00
DR24 SD Women's Championship	2.50	6.00
DR25 Becky Lynch	2.00	5.00
DR26 Charlotte Flair	2.00	5.00
DR27 Sasha Banks & Charlotte Flair	2.00	5.00
DR28 Mickie James & Asuka	1.25	3.00
DR29 Alexa Bliss	2.50	6.00
DR30 Mickie James & Alexa Bliss	2.50	6.00
DR31 Bayley	1.00	2.50
DR32 Naomi	.75	2.00
DR33 Naomi & Charlotte	.75	2.00
DR34 Alexa Bliss	2.50	6.00
DR35 Carmella	1.25	3.00
DR36 Asuka	1.50	4.00
DR37 Charlotte Flair	2.00	5.00
DR38 Absolution	2.00	5.00
DR39 Riott Squad	1.50	4.00
DR40 Asuka	1.50	4.00

1985 Topps WWF

COMPLETE SET W/HOGAN (66)	200.00	400.00
COMPLETE SET W/O HOGAN (60)	100.00	200.00
UNOPENED BOX (36 PACKS)	1000.00	1500.00
UNOPENED PACK (9 CARDS+1 STICKER)	30.00	40.00
RACK PACK (26 CARDS+3 STICKERS)	150.00	200.00

RINGSIDE ACTION (22-56)
SUPERSTARS SPEAK (57-66)
*OPC: SAME VALUE AS TOPPS

1 Hulk Hogan RC	150.00	300.00
2 The Iron Sheik RC	1.00	2.50
3 Captain Lou Albano RC	.75	2.00
4 Junk Yard Dog RC	1.00	2.50
5 Paul Mr. Wonderful Orndorff RC	.60	1.50
6 Jimmy Superfly Snuka RC	.60	1.50
7 Rowdy Roddy Piper RC	8.00	20.00
8 Wendi Richter RC	.75	2.00
9 Greg The Hammer Valentine RC	1.00	2.50
10 Brutus Beefcake RC	1.00	2.50
11 Jesse The Body Ventura RC	3.00	8.00
12 Big John Studd RC	.60	1.50
13 Fabulous Moolah RC	1.25	3.00
14 Tito Santana RC	1.25	3.00
15 Hillbilly Jim RC	1.00	2.50
16 Hulk Hogan RC	75.00	150.00
17 Mr. Fuji RC	.75	2.00
18 Rotundo & Windham	.75	2.00
19 Moondog Spot RC	.50	1.25
20 Chief Jay Strongbow RC	.50	1.25
21 George The Animal Steele RC	1.25	3.00
22 Let Go of My Toe! RA	.50	1.25
23 Lock 'Em Up! RA	.50	1.25
24 Scalp 'Em! RA	.50	1.25
25 Going for the Midsection! RA	.75	2.00
26 Up in the Air! RA	.60	1.50
27 All Tied Up! RA	1.50	4.00
28 Here She Comes! RA	.50	1.25
29 Stretched to the Limit! RA	3.00	8.00
30 Over He Goes! RA	1.00	2.50
31 An Appetite for Mayhem! RA	.60	1.50
32 Putting on Pressure! RA	.50	1.25
33 Smashed on a Knee! RA	.75	2.00
34 A Fist Comes Flying! RA	.50	1.25
35 Lemme' Out of This! RA	.50	1.25
36 No Fair Chokin'! RA	.50	1.25
37 Attacked by an Animal! RA	.50	1.25
38 One Angry Man! RA	1.25	3.00
39 Someone's Going Down! RA	1.25	3.00
40 Strangle Hold! RA	2.00	5.00
41 Bending an Arm! RA	.50	1.25
42 Ready for a Pile Driver! RA	.75	2.00
43 Face to the Canvas! RA	.50	1.25
44 Paul Wants It All! RA	.75	2.00
45 Kick to the Face! RA	3.00	8.00
46 Ready for Action! RA	.50	1.25
47 Putting on the Squeeze! RA	.60	1.50
48 Giants in Action! RA	1.50	4.00
49 Camel Clutch! RA	.60	1.50
50 Pile Up! RA	2.00	5.00

51 Can't Get Away! RA	.60	1.50
52 Going for the Pin! RA	.50	1.25
53 Ready to Fly! RA	2.00	5.00
54 Crusher in a Crusher! RA	.50	1.25
55 Fury of the Animal! RA	.75	2.00
56 Wrong Kind of Music! RA	6.00	15.00
57 Who's your next challenger? SS	2.50	6.00
58 This dog has got a mean bite! SS	.75	2.00
59 I don't think I'll ask that... SS	1.25	3.00
60 You Hulkster fans lift... SS	8.00	20.00
61 This ain't my idea... SS	1.00	2.50
62 You mean Freddie Blassie is... SS	1.25	3.00
63 Mppgh Ecch Oong. SS	1.00	2.50
64 It's the rock n' wrestling... SS	.75	2.00
65 Arrrggghhhh! SS	.60	1.50
66 They took my reindeer! SS	.60	1.50

1985 Topps WWF Stickers

COMPLETE SET W/HOGAN (22)	50.00	100.00
COMPLETE SET W/O HOGAN (17)	12.00	30.00
1 Hulk Hogan	15.00	40.00
2 Captain Lou Albano	.75	2.00
3 Brutus Beefcake	1.25	3.00
4 Jesse Ventura	2.00	5.00
5 The Iron Sheik	1.50	4.00
6 Wendi Richter	1.25	3.00
7 Jimmy Snuka	.75	2.00
8 Ivan Putski	1.00	2.50
9 Hulk Hogan	4.00	10.00
10 Junk Yard Dog	1.25	3.00
11 Hulk Hogan	6.00	15.00
12 Captain Lou Albano	.75	2.00
13 Captain Lou Albano	.75	2.00
14 Freddie Blassie & The Iron Sheik	.75	2.00
15 Jimmy Snuka	.75	2.00
16 Hulk Hogan	10.00	25.00
17 Iron Sheik	1.50	4.00
18 Rene Goulet & S.D. Jones	1.25	3.00
19 Junk Yard Dog	.75	2.00
20 Wendi Richter	1.25	3.00
21 Andre the Giant	3.00	8.00
22 Hulk Hogan	8.00	20.00

1987 Topps WWF

COMPLETE SET (75)	60.00	120.00
UNOPENED BOX (36 PACKS)		
UNOPENED PACK (9 CARDS+1 STICKER)		
1 Bret "Hit Man" Hart RC	25.00	60.00
2 Andre the Giant RC	6.00	15.00
3 Hulk Hogan	5.00	12.00
4 Frankie	.75	2.00
5 Koko B. Ware RC	.75	2.00
6 Tito Santana	.60	1.50
7 Randy Savage & Elizabeth	10.00	25.00
8 Billy Jack Haynes RC	.40	1.00
9 Hercules & Bobby Heenan	.40	1.00
10 King Harley Race RC	.60	1.50
11 Kimchee & Kamala	.40	1.00
12 Bravo/Johnny V/Valentine	.50	1.25
13 Honky Tonk Man RC	1.00	2.50
14 Outback Jack RC	.40	1.00
15 King Kong Bundy	1.25	3.00
16 The Magnificent Muraco	.40	1.00
17 Mr. Fuji and Killer Khan	.75	2.00
18 The Natural Butch Reed RC	.60	1.50
19 Davey Boy Smith	.75	2.00
20 The Dynamite Kid RC	.40	1.00
21 Ricky The Dragon Steamboat	1.50	4.00
22 Two-Man Clothesline RA	.40	1.00
23 Ref Turned Wrestler RA	.75	2.00
24 Ready to Strike RA	.60	1.50
25 In the Outback RA	.40	1.00
26 The Hulkster Explodes RA	2.00	5.00
27 Double Whammy RA	.40	1.00
28 Spoiling for a Fight RA	.40	1.00
29 Flip Flop RA	.40	1.00
30 Islanders Attack RA	.40	1.00
31 King Harley Parades RA	.40	1.00
32 Backbreaker RA	.40	1.00
33 Double Dropkick RA	.40	1.00
34 The Loser Must Bow RA	.40	1.00
35 American-Made RA	2.50	6.00
36 A Challenge Answered RA	2.00	5.00
37 Champ in the Ring RA	4.00	10.00
38 Listening to Hulkamania RA	2.00	5.00
39 Heading for the Ring RA	.40	1.00
40 Out to Destroy RA	.40	1.00
41 Tama Takes a Beating RA	.40	1.00
42 Bundy in Mid-Air RA	.40	1.00
43 Karate Stance RA	.40	1.00
44 Her Eyes on Randy RA	2.50	6.00
45 The Olympian Returns RA	.40	1.00
46 Reed Is Riled RA	.40	1.00
47 Flying Bodypress RA	.40	1.00
48 Hooking the Leg RA	.40	1.00
49 A Belly Buster WMIII	.40	1.00
50 Revenge on Randy WMIII	.75	2.00
51 Fighting the Full Nelson WMIII	.40	1.00
52 Honky Tonk Goes Down WMIII	.40	1.00
53 Over the Top WMIII	.40	1.00
54 The Giant Is Slammed WMIII	1.25	3.00
55 Out of the Ring WMIII	.75	2.00
56 And Still Champion WMIII	1.50	4.00
57 Harts Hit Concrete WMIII	.40	1.00
58 The Challenge RA	1.25	3.00
59 Bearhug RA	.40	1.00
60 Fantastic Bodypress RA	.40	1.00
61 Aerial Maneuvers RA	.40	1.00
62 Ready to Sting! RA	.40	1.00
63 Showing Off RA	.40	1.00
64 Scare Tactics RA	.40	1.00
65 Taking a Bow RA	.60	1.50
66 Out to Eat a Turnbuckle RA	.40	1.00
67 Nice guys finish last! SS	.40	1.00
68 Here's how we keep... SS	.40	1.00
69 Urrggh. Nice! SS	.40	1.00
70 No Kamala...him not dinner! SS	.40	1.00
71 We are the original destroyers. SS	.40	1.00
72 I think the fans are mad at me. SS	.40	1.00
73 You ain't nothin'... SS	.40	1.00
74 I'm gonna take a big bit... SS	.40	1.00
75 Good! SS	.40	1.00

1987 Topps WWF Stickers

COMPLETE SET (22)	20.00	50.00
1 Bret Hit Man Hart	5.00	12.00
2 Hulk Hogan	8.00	20.00
3 Koko B. Ware	.40	1.00
4 Randy Savage & Elizabeth	10.00	25.00
5 Billy Jack Haynes	.40	1.00
6 Hercules & Bobby Heenan	.60	1.50
7 King Harley Race	.60	1.50
8 Kimchee & Kamala	.40	1.00
9 Bravo/Johnny V/Valentine	.60	1.50
10 Honky Tonk Man	.60	1.50
11 Outback Jack	.40	1.00
12 King Kong Bundy	.60	1.50
13 Magnificent Muraco	.40	1.00
14 Mr. Fuji & Killer Khan	.40	1.00
15 Ricky The Dragon Steamboat	.60	1.50
16 Danny Davis	.40	1.00
17 Andre the Giant	6.00	15.00
18 Ken Patera	.40	1.00
19 Smash Demolition	.40	1.00
20 Jim The Anvil Neidhart	.40	1.00
21 George The Animal Steele	.60	1.50
22 WWF Logo	.40	1.00

1985 Topps WWF 3-D Pro Wrestling Stars

COMPLETE SET (12)	500.00	1000.00
UNOPENED BOX (24 PACKS)		
UNOPENED PACK (1 CARD)		
1 Hulk Hogan	250.00	500.00
2 Wendi Richter	50.00	100.00
3 Jimmy Superfly Snuka	50.00	100.00
4 The Iron Sheik	60.00	120.00
5 Hillbilly Jim	30.00	75.00
6 Captain Lou Albano	50.00	100.00
7 Paul Orndorff	75.00	150.00
8 Jesse The Body Ventura	60.00	120.00
9 Brutus Beefcake	30.00	75.00
10 Andre the Giant	200.00	350.00
11 Rocky Johnson	30.00	75.00
12 Junk Yard Dog	60.00	120.00

2009 TRISTAR Hulk Hogan Joins TNA Commemoratives

COMPLETE SET (2)

H1 Hulk Hogan

H2 Hulk Hogan

2008 TRISTAR TNA Cross the Line

COMPLETE SET (100)	8.00	20.00
UNOPENED BOX (20 PACKS)		
UNOPENED PACK (6 CARDS)		
*GOLD/50: 2X TO 5X BASIC CARDS		
*RED/10: UNPRICED DUE TO SCARCITY		
*PURPLE/1: UNPRICED DUE TO SCARCITY		
1 A.J. Styles	.40	1.00
2 Motor City Machineguns	.15	.40
3 Brother Ray	.20	.50
4 LAX	.15	.40
5 Consequences Creed RC	.15	.40
6 Taylor Wilde RC	.60	1.50
7 Sheik Abdul Bashir RC	.20	.50
8 Main Event Mafia	.20	.50
9 Hector Guerrero & Willie Urbina	.12	.30
10 Lauren RC	.40	1.00
11 Kyra Angle RC	.40	1.00
12 Suicide	.12	.30
13 Rhaka Khan RC	.20	.50
14 Mick Foley	.60	1.50
15 Shane Sewell RC	.12	.30
16 Dutch Mantel	.12	.30
17 Beer Money Inc.	.15	.40
18 Prince Justice Brotherhood	.12	.30
19 Jeff Jarrett	.75	2.00
20 A.J. Styles	.40	1.00
21 Cowboy James Storm	.15	.40
22 Mike Tenay	.15	.40
23 Don West	.12	.30
24 Rudy Charles	.12	.30
25 Andrew Thomas	.12	.30
26 Jeremy Borash	.12	.30
27 Hermie Sadler	.12	.30
28 Kevin Nash	.60	1.50
29 Brother Devon	.20	.50
30 Beautiful People	.60	1.50
31 Roxxi RC	.40	1.00
32 Abyss	.40	1.00
33 Dixie Carter RC	.30	.75
34 Christian Cage	.30	.75
35 Booker T	.75	2.00
36 Shark Boy	.12	.30
37 Johnny Devine RC	.15	.40
38 Petey Williams RC	.12	.30
39 Homicide RC	.15	.40
40 Angelina Love RC	.60	1.50
41 Scott Steiner	.60	1.50
42 Alex Shelley RC	.15	.40
43 Jacqueline	.40	1.00
44 Curry Man	.12	.30
45 Kip James	.15	.40
46 Earl Hebner RC	.15	.40
47 Velvet Sky RC	.50	1.25
48 Kurt Angle	.75	2.00
49 Jim Cornette	.15	.40
50 Sting	.60	1.50
51 Traci Brooks	.50	1.25
52 Jay Lethal RC	.12	.30
53 Robert Roode RC	.12	.30
54 Petey Williams RC	.12	.30
55 Sonjay Dutt	.12	.30
56 Sharmell	.40	1.00
57 Chris Sabin	.12	.30
58 Matt Morgan	.15	.40
59 ODB RC	.40	1.00
60 Tomko	.12	.30
61 Kurt Angle	.75	2.00
62 Christian Cage	.30	.75
63 ODB RC	.40	1.00
64 Team 3D	.20	.50
65 A.J. Styles	.40	1.00
66 James Storm	.15	.40
67 Raisha Saeed RC	.30	.75
68 Sonjay Dutt	.12	.30
69 Kevin Nash	.60	1.50
70 Matt Morgan	.15	.40
71 BG James	.12	.30
72 Hernandez RC	.15	.40
73 A.J. Styles	.40	1.00
74 Kurt Angle	.75	2.00
75 Christian Cage	.30	.75
76 Jeff Jarrett	.75	2.00
77 Sting	.60	1.50
78 Christian Cage	.30	.75
79 Jeff Jarrett	.75	2.00
80 Kurt Angle Meets Samoa Joe	.75	2.00
81 Sharmell	.40	1.00
82 Sting	.60	1.50
83 Most Important Moment in TNA History	.12	.30
84 Christian†Cage vs. Abyss	.40	1.00
85 Samoa Joe vs. Daniels vs. Styles	.40	1.00
86 Kurt Angle	.75	2.00
87 Styles vs. Angle	.75	2.00
88 Eric Young RC	.12	.30
89 Rhino	.30	.75

90 Samoa Joe RC	.20	.50
91 SoCal Val RC	.60	1.50
92 Curry Man	.12	.30
93 Lance Rock RC	.15	.40
94 Jimmy Rave RC	.15	.40
95 Sting vs. Samoa Joe	.60	1.50
96 Kurt Angle vs. Jeff Jarrett	.75	2.00
97 Awesome Kong/TNA Knockouts	.30	.75
98 Beer Money vs. LAX	.15	.40
99 Steve McMichael	.30	.75
100 Checklist	.12	.30

2008 TRISTAR TNA Cross the Line Autographed Memorabilia Silver

*GOLD/50: .6X TO 1.2X BASIC AU MEM
*RED/25: .75X TO 1.5 BASIC AU MEM
*GREEN/5: UNPRICED DUE TO SCARCITY
*PURPLE/1: UNPRICED DUE TO SCARCITY
STATED PRINT RUN 99 SER.#'d SETS

MAA Abyss	15.00	30.00
MOA ODB	15.00	30.00
MSA Sting	25.00	50.00
MABA Sheik Abdul Bashir	10.00	20.00
MALA Angelina Love	20.00	40.00
MASA A.J. Styles	20.00	40.00
MCCA Christian Cage	15.00	30.00
MCHA Christy Hemme	20.00	40.00
MCMA Curry Man	10.00	20.00
MDCA Dixie Carter	15.00	30.00
MJBA Jeremy Borash	10.00	20.00
MKAA Kurt Angle	15.00	30.00
MKNA Kevin Nash	20.00	40.00
MRCA Rudy Charles	10.00	20.00
MRSA Raisha Saeed	10.00	20.00
MSEA Super Eric	10.00	20.00
MSJA Samoa Joe	20.00	40.00
MSVA SoCal Val	15.00	30.00
MTWA Taylor Wilde	15.00	30.00
MVSA Velvet Sky	20.00	40.00

2008 TRISTAR TNA Cross the Line Autographs Silver

*GOLD/50: .5X TO 1.2X BASIC AUTOS
*RED/25: .6X TO 1.5X BASIC AUTOS
*PURPLE/1: UNPRICED DUE TO SCARCITY
*P.P.BLACK/1: UNPRICED DUE TO SCARCITY
*P.P.CYAN/1: UNPRICED DUE TO SCARCITY
*P.P.MAGENTA/1: UNPRICED DUE TO SCARCITY
*P.P.YELLOW/1: UNPRICED DUE TO SCARCITY

CA Abyss	8.00	20.00
CJ Jacqueline	6.00	15.00
CL Lauren	6.00	15.00
CO ODB	6.00	15.00
CS Sting	20.00	50.00
CAB Sheik Abdul Bashir	6.00	15.00
CAJ A.J. Styles	10.00	25.00
CAK Awesome Kong	6.00	15.00
CAL Angelina Love	10.00	25.00
CAS Alex Shelley	6.00	15.00
CAT Andrew Thomas	6.00	15.00
CBD Brother Devon	8.00	20.00
CBR Brother Ray	8.00	20.00
CBT Booker T	8.00	20.00
CCC Christian Cage	8.00	20.00
CCH Christy Hemme	10.00	25.00
CCM Curry Man	8.00	20.00
CCS Chris Sabin	6.00	15.00
CDC Dixie Carter	8.00	20.00
CDW Don West	8.00	20.00
CEH Earl Hebner	6.00	15.00
CEY Eric Young	6.00	15.00
CH1 Hernandez	6.00	15.00
CH2 Homicide	6.00	15.00
CHG Hector Guerrero	6.00	15.00
CHS Hermie Sadler	6.00	15.00
CJB Jeremy Borash	6.00	15.00
CJC Jim Cornette	6.00	15.00
CJD Johnny Devine	6.00	15.00
CJJ Jeff Jarrett	8.00	20.00
CJL Jay Lethal	6.00	15.00
CJR Jimmy Rave	6.00	15.00
CJS James Storm	6.00	15.00
CKA Kurt Angle	12.00	30.00
CKJ Kip James	6.00	15.00
CKN Kevin Nash	12.00	30.00
CLR Lance Rock	6.00	15.00
CMF Mick Foley	12.00	30.00
CMM Matt Morgan	8.00	20.00
CMT Mike Tenay	6.00	15.00
CPW Petey Williams	6.00	15.00
CR2 Roxxi	8.00	20.00
CRC Rudy Charles		
CRR Robert Roode	6.00	15.00
CRS Raisha Saeed	8.00	20.00
CRS Rhino	6.00	15.00
CS2 Sharmell	6.00	15.00
CS3 Suicide	8.00	20.00
CSB Shark Boy	6.00	15.00
CSD Sonjay Dutt	6.00	15.00
CSE Super Eric	6.00	15.00
CSJ Slick Johnson	6.00	15.00
CSJ Samoa Joe	12.00	30.00
CSM Steve McMichael	8.00	20.00
CSS Scott Steiner	12.00	30.00
CSV SoCal Val	8.00	20.00
CTB Traci Brooks	8.00	20.00
CTW Taylor Wilde	8.00	20.00
CVS Velvet Sky	10.00	25.00
CWU Willie Urbina	8.00	20.00
CCC2 Consequences Creed	6.00	15.00
CKA2 Karen Angle	8.00	20.00
CSS2 Shane Sewell	6.00	15.00

2008 TRISTAR TNA Cross the Line Dual Autographs Silver

*GOLD/50: .5X TO 1.2X BASIC AUTOS
*RED/25: .6X TO 1.5X BASIC AUTOS
*BLUE/5: UNPRICED DUE TO SCARCITY
*PURPLE/1: UNPRICED DUE TO SCARCITY
*P.P.BLACK/1: UNPRICED DUE TO SCARCITY
*P.P.CYAN/1: UNPRICED DUE TO SCARCITY
*P.P.MAGENTA/1: UNPRICED DUE TO SCARCITY
*P.P.YELLOW/1: UNPRICED DUE TO SCARCITY
RANDOMLY INSERTED INTO PACKS

C2BS Booker T/Sharmell	15.00	30.00
C2CB J.Cornette/T.Brooks	12.50	25.00
C2CR C.Cage/Rhino	12.50	25.00
C2HH Hernandez/Homicide	7.50	15.00
C2JK S.Joe/K.Nash	15.00	30.00
C2KS A.Kong/R.Saeed	12.50	25.00
C2KW A.Kong/T.Wilde	20.00	40.00
C2LS A.Love/V.Sky	20.00	40.00
C2RD BroRay/BroDevon	15.00	30.00
C2SA Sting/K.Angle	20.00	40.00
C2SA A.J. Styles/K.Angle	15.00	30.00
C2SR J.Storm/R.Roode	15.00	30.00
C2SS A.Shelley/C.Sabin	15.00	30.00
C2SW S.Steiner/P.Williams	12.50	25.00
C2WC P.Williams/C.Creed	7.50	15.00

2008 TRISTAR TNA Cross the Line Dual Memorabilia Silver

*GOLD/50: .5X TO 1.2X BASIC MEM
*RED/25: .6X TO 1.5X BASIC MEM
*GREEN/5: UNPRICED DUE TO SCARCITY
*PURPLE/1: UNPRICED DUE TO SCARCITY
STATED PRINT RUN 99 SER.#'d SETS

MS2 Sting	20.00	50.00
MAS2 Kurt Angle/A.J. Styles	8.00	20.00
MDL2 Sonjay Dutt/Jay Lethal	6.00	15.00
MLV2 Jay Lethal	5.00	12.00
SoCal Val		

2008 TRISTAR TNA Cross the Line High Impact Championship Inserts

STATED ODDS 1:CASE
NO PRICING DUE TO SCARCITY

NNO Velvet Sky Auto Baseball EXCH
NNO Booker T Auto Baseball EXCH
NNO A.J. Styles Auto Baseball EXCH
NNO TNA Wrestler Auto Photo EXCH

2008 TRISTAR TNA Cross the Line Memorabilia Silver

*GOLD/50: .5X TO 1.2X BASIC MEM
*RED/25: .6X TO 1.5X BASIC MEM
*GREEN/5: UNPRICED DUE TO SCARCITY
*PURPLE/1: UNPRICED DUE TO SCARCITY
STATED PRINT RUN 99 SER.#'d SETS

MA Abyss	8.00	20.00
MS Sting	10.00	25.00
MAB Sheik Abdul Bashir	6.00	15.00
MAS A.J. Styles	8.00	20.00
MBP The Beautiful People	10.00	25.00
MCC Christian Cage	8.00	20.00
MCM Curry Man	6.00	15.00
MDC Dixie Carter	8.00	20.00
MKA Kurt Angle	10.00	25.00
MKN Kevin Nash	8.00	20.00
MSE Super Eric	6.00	15.00
MTW Taylor Wilde	8.00	20.00

2008 TRISTAR TNA Cross the Line Quad Autographs Silver

*GOLD/50: .6X TO 1.2X BASIC AUTOS
*RED/25: .75X TO 1.5X BASIC AUTOS
*BLUE/5: UNPRICED DUE TO SCARCITY
*PURPLE/1: UNPRICED DUE TO SCARCITY
*P.P.BLACK/1: UNPRICED DUE TO SCARCITY
*P.P.CYAN/1: UNPRICED DUE TO SCARCITY
*P.P.MAGENTA/1: UNPRICED DUE TO SCARCITY
*P.P.YELLOW/1: UNPRICED DUE TO SCARCITY
RANDOMLY INSERTED INTO PACKS

1 Love/Sky/Brooks/Hemme	60.00	120.00
2 Sting/Nash/Jarrett/Steiner	125.00	200.00
3 Hebner/Johnson/Thomas/Charles	25.00	50.00
4 Tenay/West/Guerrero/Urbina	25.00	50.00
5 Storm/Roode/Homic/Hrndz	25.00	50.00
6 Love/Sky/Kong/Jacqueline	30.00	60.00
7 Bashir/Dutt/Curry/Guer	25.00	50.00

2008 TRISTAR TNA Cross the Line Triple Autographs Silver

*GOLD/50: .6X TO 1.2X BASIC AUTOS
*RED/25: .75X TO 1.5X BASIC AUTOS
*BLUE/5: UNPRICED DUE TO SCARCITY
*PURPLE/1: UNPRICED DUE TO SCARCITY
*P.P.BLACK/1: UNPRICED DUE TO SCARCITY
*P.P.CYAN/1: UNPRICED DUE TO SCARCITY
*P.P.MAGENTA/1: UNPRICED DUE TO SCARCITY
*P.P.YELLOW/1: UNPRICED DUE TO SCARCITY
RANDOMLY INSERTED INTO PACKS

C3B Tenay/West/Borash	20.00	40.00
C3BP Love/Sky/James	40.00	80.00
C3RR Hemme/Rock/Rave	25.00	50.00
C3BSS Booker/Sting/Samoa	40.00	80.00
C3LVD Lethal/SoCal/Dutt	25.00	50.00
C3PJB Shark/Curry/SuperEric	20.00	40.00

2010 TRISTAR TNA Icons

COMPLETE SET (100)	10.00	25.00
UNOPENED BOX (20 PACKS)		
UNOPENED PACK (6 CARDS)		

*GOLD/25: 2.5X TO 6X BASIC CARDS
*RED/5: UNPRICED DUE TO SCARCITY
*PURPLE/1: UNPRICED DUE TO SCARCITY

1 Hulk Hogan	1.00	2.50
2 Ric Flair	.75	2.00
3 Sting	.60	1.50
4 Jeff Hardy	.60	1.50
5 Mick Foley	.75	2.00
6 Kevin Nash	.60	1.50
7 Rob Van Dam	.40	1.00
8 Jeff Jarrett	.40	1.00
9 Kurt Angle	.60	1.50
10 Eric Bischoff	.15	.40
11 Earl Hebner	.15	.40
12 Mr. Anderson	.25	.60
13 Team 3D	.25	.60
14 AJ Styles	.40	1.00
15 Tara	.60	1.50
16 Tommy Dreamer	.15	.40
17 Ric Flair	.75	2.00
18 Sting	.60	1.50
19 Jeff Hardy	.60	1.50
20 Jeff Jarrett	.40	1.00
21 Kevin Nash	.60	1.50
22 Kurt Angle	.60	1.50
23 Mick Foley	.75	2.00
24 Rob Van Dam	.40	1.00
25 Ric Flair	.75	2.00
26 Sting	.60	1.50
27 Jeff Hardy	.60	1.50
28 Mick Foley	.75	2.00
29 Kevin Nash	.60	1.50
30 Rob Van Dam	.40	1.00
31 Team 3D	.25	.60
32 Kurt Angle	.60	1.50
33 Eric Bischoff	.15	.40
34 Dixie Carter	.40	1.00
35 Desmond Wolfe RC	.15	.40
36 Jay Lethal	.15	.40
37 Matt Morgan	.15	.40
38 Abyss	.25	.60
39 AJ Styles	.40	1.00
40 Hulk Hogan	1.00	2.50
41 Velvet Sky	.75	2.00
42 Angelina Love	.60	1.50

43 Taylor Wilde	.40	1.00
44 Sarita	.40	1.00
45 Daffney	.60	1.50
46 Madison Rayne	.60	1.50
47 Lacey Von Erich RC	.75	2.00
48 Christy Hemme	.60	1.50
49 SoCal Val	.60	1.50
50 Chelsea	.60	1.50
51 Miss Tessmacher RC	.75	2.00
52 Rosie Lottalove RC	.40	1.00
53 Motor City Machineguns	.20	.50
54 Rob Terry	.15	.40
55 Kazarian	.15	.40
56 D'Angelo Dinero	.15	.40
57 Douglas Williams	.15	.40
58 Desmond Wolfe	.15	.40
59 Eric Young	.15	.40
60 Generation Me	.15	.40
61 Beer Money Inc.	.25	.60
62 Abyss	.25	.60
63 Matt Morgan	.15	.40
64 Samoa Joe	.25	.60
65 Hernandez	.15	.40
66 Ink Inc.	.15	.40
67 Jay Lethal	.15	.40
68 Magnus	.15	.40
69 Lacey Von Erich RC	.75	2.00
70 Hulk Hogan	.75	2.00
71 Ric Flair	.60	1.50
72 Sting	.50	1.25
73 Jeff Hardy	.50	1.25
74 Mick Foley	.60	1.50
75 Kevin Nash	.50	1.25
76 Rob Van Dam	.30	.75
77 Jeff Jarrett	.30	.75
78 Kurt Angle	.50	1.25
79 Mr. Anderson	.20	.50
80 Tommy Dreamer	.15	.40
81 Hulk Hogan	.75	2.00
82 Ric Flair	.60	1.50
83 Sting	.50	1.25
84 Jeff Hardy	.50	1.25
85 Mick Foley	.60	1.50
86 Kevin Nash	.50	1.25
87 Rob Van Dam	.30	.75
88 Jeff Jarrett	.30	.75
89 Kurt Angle	.50	1.25
90 Mick Foley	.60	1.50
91 Mick Foley	.60	1.50
92 Mick Foley	.60	1.50
93 Mick Foley	.60	1.50
94 Mick Foley	.60	1.50
95 Sting	.50	1.25
96 Kevin Nash	.50	1.25
97 Rob Van Dam	.30	.75
98 Mr. Anderson	.20	.50
99 Jeff Jarrett	.30	.75
100 Kurt Angle	.50	1.25

2010 TRISTAR TNA Icons Dual Memorabilia Silver

STATED PRINT RUN 199 SER.#'d SETS

M8 Rob Van Dam
Jeff Hardy
M9 Ric Flair
AJ Styles

2010 TRISTAR TNA Icons Hogangraphs Green

OVERALL AUTO ODDS TWO PER BOX

H1 Hulk Hogan	75.00	150.00
H2 Hulk Hogan	75.00	150.00
H3 Hulk Hogan	75.00	150.00
H4 Hulk Hogan	75.00	150.00
H5 Hulk Hogan	75.00	150.00

2010 TRISTAR TNA Icons Hulk Hogan Die-Cut Letter Memorabilia Silver

*GOLD/50: .5X TO 1.2X BASIC MEM
*RED/25: .6X TO 1.5 BASIC MEM
*PURPLE/1: UNPRICED DUE TO SCARCITY
STATED ODDS OVERALL MEM 1:BOX
STATED PRINT RUN 199 SER.#'d SETS

HH1 Hulk Hogan Bandana H	12.00	30.00
HH2 Hulk Hogan Bandana O	12.00	30.00
HH3 Hulk Hogan Bandana G	12.00	30.00
HH4 Hulk Hogan Bandana A	12.00	30.00
HH5 Hulk Hogan Bandana N	12.00	30.00

2010 TRISTAR TNA Icons Hulk Hogan Dual Autographs Gold

*GREEN/50: UNPRICED DUE TO SCARCITY
*RED/5: UNPRICED DUE TO SCARCITY
*PURPLE/1: UNPRICED DUE TO SCARCITY
STATED PRINT RUN 99 SER.#'d SETS

H21 Hulk Hogan/Abyss
H22 Hulk Hogan/AJ Styles
H23 Hulk Hogan/Jeff Hardy
H24 Hulk Hogan/Jeff Jarrett
H25 Hulk Hogan/Kevin Nash
H26 Hulk Hogan/Kurt Angle
H27 Hulk Hogan/Lacey Von Erich
H28 Hulk Hogan/Mick Foley
H29 Hulk Hogan/Ric Flair
H210 Hulk Hogan/Rob Van Dam
H211 Hulk Hogan/Sting
H212 Hulk Hogan/Tara
H213 Hulk Hogan/Velvet Sky

2010 TRISTAR TNA Icons Hulk Hogan Quad Autographs Gold

*GREEN/50: UNPRICED DUE TO SCARCITY
*RED/5: UNPRICED DUE TO SCARCITY
*PURPLE/1: UNPRICED DUE TO SCARCITY
STATED PRINT RUN 99 SER. #'d SETS

H41 Hogan/Sky/Rayne/Von Erich
H42 Hogan/Magnus/Williams/Terry
H43 Hogan/Flair/Abyss/Styles
H44 Hogan/Flair/Sting/Foley

2010 TRISTAR TNA Icons Iconigraphs Gold

*GREEN/25: .5X TO 1.2X BASIC AUTOS
*RED/5: UNPRICED DUE TO SCARCITY
*PURPLE/1: UNPRICED DUE TO SCARCITY
STATED ODDS OVERALL 2:BOX
STATED PRINT RUN 50 SER.#'d SETS

I1 Ric Flair		
I2 Sting		
I3 Jeff Hardy	25.00	50.00
I4 Mick Foley	12.00	30.00
I5 Kevin Nash	10.00	20.00
I6 Rob Van Dam	20.00	40.00
I7 Jeff Jarrett	10.00	20.00
I8 Kurt Angle	12.00	25.00
I9 Earl Hebner	12.00	25.00
I10 Mr. Anderson	12.00	25.00
I11 AJ Styles	10.00	20.00
I12 Syxx-Pac	12.00	25.00
I13 Tara	12.00	25.00
I14 Tommy Dreamer	10.00	20.00
I15 Sting/Icon		
I16 Jeff Hardy/Twist of Fate		
I17 Mick Foley/Bang Bang		
I18 Kevin Nash (inscribed)		
I19 Rob Van Dam/Mr. Monday Night		
I20 Rob Van Dam/Whole F'n Show		
I21 Rob Van Dam/420		
I22 Jeff Jarrett/TNA Founder		
I23 Jeff Jarrett/Guitar Show		
I24 Jeff Jarrett/Slapnutz		
I25 Jeff Jarrett/The Chosen One		
I26 Jeff Jarrett/Music City USA		
I27 Kurt Angle/Olympic Champ		
I28 Kurt Angle/It's Real		
I29 Earl Hebner/Montreal Screw Job		
I30 Mr. Anderson/Mic Check		
I31 Mr. Anderson/Go Pack Go		
I32 AJ Styles/Grand Slam Winner		
I33 AJ Styles/Phenomenal		
I34 AJ Styles/TNA Original		
I35 Tommy Dreamer/Extreme Original		

2010 TRISTAR TNA Icons Memorabilia Silver

*GOLD: .5X TO 1.2X BASIC MEM
*RED: .6X TO 1.5X BASIC MEM
*PURPLE/1: UNPRICED DUE TO SCARCITY
STATED ODDS OVERALL 1:BOX
STATED PRINT RUN 199 SER.#'d SETS

M1 Ric Flair		
M2 Rob Van Dam	4.00	10.00
M3 Jeff Hardy	6.00	15.00
M4 Sting		
M5 Mick Foley	8.00	20.00
M6 Kevin Nash	6.00	15.00
M7 Tommy Dreamer	4.00	10.00

2010 TRISTAR TNA Icons Memorabilia Gold

*GOLD: .5X TO 1.2X BASIC MEM
STATED PRINT RUN 50 SER.#'d SETS

M1 Ric Flair		
M2 Rob Van Dam	5.00	12.00
M3 Jeff Hardy	8.00	20.00
M4 Sting	10.00	25.00
M5 Mick Foley	10.00	25.00
M6 Kevin Nash	8.00	20.00
M7 Tommy Dreamer	5.00	12.00

2010 TRISTAR TNA Icons The Next Generation Autographs Gold

*GREEN/25: .5X TO 1.2X BASIC AUTOS
*RED/5: UNPRICED DUE TO SCARCITY
*PURPLE/1: UNPRICED DUE TO SCARCITY
STATED ODDS OVERALL 2:BOX
STATED PRINT RUN 50 SER.#'d SETS

NEXT1 Alex Shelley	6.00	15.00
NEXT2 Chris Sabin	4.00	10.00
NEXT3 Rob Terry	4.00	10.00
NEXT4 Kazarian	4.00	10.00
NEXT5 D'Angelo Dinero	4.00	10.00
NEXT6 Douglas Williams	4.00	10.00
NEXT7 Desmond Wolfe	4.00	10.00
NEXT8 Eric Young	4.00	10.00
NEXT9 Abyss	6.00	15.00
NEXT10 Matt Morgan	4.00	10.00
NEXT11 Samoa Joe	6.00	15.00
NEXT12 Hernandez	4.00	10.00
NEXT13 Jay Lethal	4.00	10.00
NEXT14 Magnus	4.00	10.00

2010 TRISTAR TNA Icons Quad Memorabilia Silver

COMPLETE SET (1)
HH8 Hogan/Flair/Sting/Foley

2010 TRISTAR TNA Icons Six Autographs Gold

*GREEN/50: UNPRICED DUE TO SCARCITY
*RED/5: UNPRICED DUE TO SCARCITY
*PURPLE/1: UNPRICED DUE TO SCARCITY
STATED PRINT RUN 99 SER.#'d SETS

A61 Hogan/Foley/Sting/Nash/Flair/Jarr
A62 RVD/Moore/Hardy/Foley/Anderson/Angle
A63 Devon/Young/Ray/Storm/Nash/Roode
A64 Sky/Love/Rayne/Wilde/Von Erich/Sarita

2010 TRISTAR TNA Icons Sugar and Spice Autographs Gold

*GREEN/25: .5X TO 1.2X BASIC AUTOS
*RED/5: UNPRICED DUE TO SCARCITY
*PURPLE/1: UNPRICED DUE TO SCARCITY
STATED ODDS OVERALL 2:BOX
STATED PRINT RUN 50 SER.#'d SETS

SS1 Velvet Sky	10.00	25.00
SS2 Angelina Love	8.00	20.00
SS3 Taylor Wilde	8.00	20.00
SS4 Sarita	8.00	20.00
SS5 Daffney	10.00	25.00
SS6 Madison Rayne	8.00	20.00
SS7 Lacey Von Erich	12.00	30.00
SS8 Christy Hemme	8.00	20.00
SS9 SoCal Val	8.00	20.00
SS10 Chelsea	10.00	25.00
SS11 Miss Tessmacher	12.00	30.00
SS12 Rosie Lottalove	10.00	25.00

2010 TRISTAR TNA Icons Triple Memorabilia Silver

STATED PRINT RUN 199 SER.#'d SETS

HH6 Hulk Hogan/Bandana
HH7 Hulk Hogan/Bandana/Shirt/Mat
M10 Sky/Rayne/Von Erich

2008 TRISTAR TNA Impact

COMPLETE SET (69)	8.00	20.00
UNOPENED BOX (18 PACKS)	30.00	50.00
UNOPENED PACK (8 CARDS)		

*GOLD/50: 2X TO 5X BASIC CARDS
*RUBY/10: UNPRICED DUE TO SCARCITY
*P.P.BLACK/1: UNPRICED DUE TO SCARCITY
*P.P.CYAN/1: UNPRICED DUE TO SCARCITY
*P.P.MAGENTA/1: UNPRICED DUE TO SCARCITY
*P.P.YELLOW/1: UNPRICED DUE TO SCARCITY

1 Kurt Angle	.75	2.00

2 Christian Cage	.30	.75
3 Samoa Joe RC	.20	.50
4 A.J. Styles	.40	1.00
5 Tomko	.12	.30
6 Booker T	.75	2.00
7 Jay Lethal RC	.12	.30
8 Jeff Jarrett	.75	2.00
9 Rhino	.30	.75
10 Curry Man	.12	.30
11 Sting	.60	1.50
12 Scott Steiner	.60	1.50
13 Robert Roode RC	.12	.30
14 Eric Young RC	.12	.30
15 Homicide RC	.15	.40
16 Hernandez RC	.15	.40
17 Petey Williams RC	.12	.30
18 Shark Boy	.12	.30
19 Consequences Creed RC	.15	.40
20 Alex Shelley RC	.15	.40
21 Jimmy Rave RC	.15	.40
22 Rellik RC	.15	.40
23 Brother Devon	.20	.50
24 Brother Ray	.20	.50
25 Kip James	.15	.40
26 Abyss	.40	1.00
27 Lance Hoyt RC	.15	.40
28 BG James	.12	.30
29 Chris Sabin	.12	.30
30 Kaz	.12	.30
31 Johnny Devine RC	.15	.40
32 Super Eric RC	.12	.30
33 Black Reign RC	.15	.40
34 James Storm	.15	.40
35 Sonjay Dutt	.12	.30
36 A.Styles/Tomko	.40	1.00
37 Team 3D	.20	.50
38 LAX	.40	1.00
39 Rock n' Rave Infection	.75	2.00
40 Motor Sity Machineguns	.15	.40
41 Karen Angle RC	.50	1.25
42 ODB RC	.40	1.00
43 Awesome Kong RC	.30	.75
44 Traci Brooks	.50	1.25
45 Christy Hemme	.75	2.00
46 Sharmell	.40	1.00
47 Gail Kim	.40	1.00
48 Angelina Love RC	.60	1.50
49 Raisha Saeed RC	.30	.75
50 SoCal Val RC	.60	1.50
51 Velvet Sky RC	.50	1.25
52 Hermie Sadler	.40	1.00
53 Jacqueline	.40	1.00
54 Roxxi Laveaux RC	.40	1.00
55 Salinas RC	.40	1.00
56 Vince Russo	.12	.30
57 James Mitchell	.15	.40
58 Matt Morgan	.15	.40
59 Jim Cornette	.15	.40
60 Earl Hebner RC	.15	.40
61 Andrew Thomas	.12	.30
62 Rudy Charles	.12	.30
63 Mark Johnson RC	.12	.30
64 Mike Tenay	.15	.40
65 Don West	.12	.30
66 Jeremy Borash	.12	.30
67 Terry Taylor	.12	.30
68 Dixie Carter RC	.30	.75
69 Kevin Nash	.60	1.50

2008 TRISTAR TNA Impact Autographs Silver

*GOLD/50: .5X TO 1.2X BASIC AUTOS
*RED/25: .6X TO 1.5X BASIC AUTOS
*BLUE/5: UNPRICED DUE TO SCARCITY
*PURPLE/1: UNPRICED DUE TO SCARCITY

AA Abyss	6.00	15.00
AJ Jacqueline	4.00	10.00
AK Kaz	4.00	10.00
AO ODB	4.00	10.00
AR Rellik	4.00	10.00
AS Sting SP	40.00	80.00
AT Tomko	6.00	15.00
AAJ A.J. Styles	15.00	40.00
AAK Awesome Kong	5.00	12.00
AAL Angelina Love	6.00	15.00
AAS Alex Shelley	5.00	12.00
ABD Brother Devon	6.00	15.00
ABG BG James	5.00	12.00
ABR Black Reign	4.00	10.00
ABR Brother Ray	6.00	15.00
ABT Booker T SP	15.00	40.00
ACC Christian Cage SP	6.00	15.00
ACH Christy Hemme	10.00	25.00
ACM Curry Man	4.00	10.00
ACS Chris Sabin	5.00	12.00
ADC Dixie Carter SP	15.00	40.00
ADW Don West	4.00	10.00
AEY Eric Young	4.00	10.00
AGK Gail Kim	20.00	40.00
AH1 Hernandez	4.00	10.00
AH2 Homicide	4.00	10.00
AJB Jeremy Borash	4.00	10.00
AJC Jim Cornette	5.00	12.00
AJD Johnny Devine	4.00	10.00
AJJ Jeff Jarrett	6.00	15.00
AJL Jay Lethal	4.00	10.00
AJM James Mitchell	4.00	10.00
AJR Jimmy Rave	5.00	12.00
AJS James Storm	4.00	10.00
AKA Kurt Angle SP	30.00	60.00
AKJ Kip James	5.00	12.00
AKN Kevin Nash	12.00	30.00
ALH Lance Hoyt	4.00	10.00
AMM Matt Morgan	5.00	12.00
AMT Mike Tenay	4.00	10.00
APB Payton Banks	5.00	12.00
APW Petey Williams	4.00	10.00
AR2 Rhino	5.00	12.00
ARL Roxxi Laveaux	5.00	12.00
ARR Robert Roode	5.00	12.00
ARS Raisha Saeed	4.00	10.00
AS2 Sharmell	4.00	10.00
AS3 Salinas	5.00	12.00
ASB Shark Boy	4.00	10.00
ASD Sonjay Dutt	4.00	10.00
ASE Super Eric	4.00	10.00
ASJ Samoa Joe SP	15.00	40.00
ASS Scott Steiner	12.00	30.00
ASV SoCal Val	5.00	12.00
ATB Traci Brooks	5.00	12.00
AVS Velvet Sky	10.00	25.00
ACC2 Consequences Creed	4.00	10.00
AKA2 Karen Angle SP	20.00	40.00

2008 TRISTAR TNA Impact Dual Autographs Gold

COMPLETE SET (10)
*RED/25: .5X TO 1.2X BASIC AUTOS
*BLUE/5: UNPRICED DUE TO SCARCITY
*PURPLE/1: UNPRICED DUE TO SCARCITY
STATED PRINT RUN 50 SER.#'d SETS

A2AA Ku.Angle/Ka.Angle	50.00	100.00
A2BS Booker T/Sharmell	25.00	50.00
A2DR Brothers Devon & Ray	25.00	50.00
A2HH Homicide/Hernandez	20.00	40.00
A2LS A.Love/V.Sky	40.00	80.00
A2LV J.Lethal/S.Val	20.00	40.00
A2RB R.Roode/P.Banks	25.00	50.00
A2SJ J.Storm/Jacqueline	20.00	40.00
A2SS A.Shelley/C.Sabin	30.00	60.00
A2TW M.Tenay/D.West	15.00	30.00

2008 TRISTAR TNA Impact Memorabilia Black

*RAINBOW FOIL/10-50
*GOLD/25: .5X TO 1.2X BASIC MEM
*RED/1: UNPRICED DUE TO SCARCITY
STATED PRINT RUN 250 SER.#'d SETS

AAO ODB	6.00	15.00
AAS Sting	10.00	25.00
AAT Tomko	5.00	12.00
AAAL Angelina Love	10.00	25.00
AAAS A.J. Styles	6.00	15.00
AACC Christian Cage	5.00	12.00
AACH Christy Hemme	8.00	20.00
AAGK Gail Kim	8.00	20.00
AAJL Jay Lethal	6.00	15.00
AAKA Kurt Angle	8.00	20.00
AAKN Kevin Nash	8.00	20.00
AASD Sonjay Dutt	5.00	12.00
AASJ Samoa Joe	5.00	12.00
AASS Scott Steiner	8.00	20.00
AASV SoCal Val	8.00	20.00
AATB Traci Brooks	8.00	20.00
AAVS Velvet Sky	10.00	25.00
AAKA2 Karen Angle	10.00	25.00

2008 TRISTAR TNA Impact Mike's Magical Moments

COMPELETE SET (5)	1.00	2.50

*GOLD/50: 2X TO 5X BASIC CARDS
*RED/10: UNPRICED DUE TO SCARCITY
*PURPLE/1: UNPRICED DUE TO SCARCITY
*P.P.BLACK/1: UNPRICED DUE TO SCARCITY
*P.P.CYAN/1: UNPRICED DUE TO SCARCITY
*P.P.MAGENTA/1: UNPRICED DUE TO SCARCITY
*P.P.YELLOW/1: UNPRICED DUE TO SCARCITY

M1 First Night	.12	.30
M2 Kurt Angle/Samoa Joe	.75	2.00
M3 Big Name Newcomers/Arrivals	.12	.30
M4 X Division	.12	.30
M5 Sporting Superstars	.12	.30

2008 TRISTAR TNA Impact Muscles Ink

COMPLETE SET (10)	3.00	8.00

*GOLD/50: 2X TO 5X BASIC CARDS
*RED/10: UNPRICED DUE TO SCARCITY
*PURPLE/1: UNPRICED DUE TO SCARCITY
*P.P.BLACK/1: UNPRICED DUE TO SCARCITY
*P.P.CYAN/1: UNPRICED DUE TO SCARCITY
*P.P.MAGENTA/1: UNPRICED DUE TO SCARCITY
*P.P.YELLOW/1: UNPRICED DUE TO SCARCITY

MI1 Scott Steiner	.60	1.50
MI2 Robert Roode	.12	.30
MI3 Petey Williams	.12	.30
MI4 Traci Brooks	.50	1.25
MI5 Brother Devon	.20	.50
MI6 Booker T	.75	2.00
MI7 Christy Hemme	.75	2.00
MI8 Kevin Nash	.60	1.50
MI9 Tomko	.12	.30
MI10 Kurt Angle	.75	2.00

2008 TRISTAR TNA Impact Then and Now

COMPLETE SET (4)	1.50	4.00

*GOLD/50: 2X TO 5X BASIC CARDS
*RED/10: UNPRICED DUE TO SCARCITY
*PURPLE/1: UNPRICED DUE TO SCARCITY
*P.P.BLACK/1: UNPRICED DUE TO SCARCITY
*P.P.CYAN/1: UNPRICED DUE TO SCARCITY
*P.P.MAGENTA/1: UNPRICED DUE TO SCARCITY
*P.P.YELLOW/1: UNPRICED DUE TO SCARCITY

TN1 Jeff Jarrett	.75	2.00
TN2 Robert Roode	.12	.30
TN3 Kevin Nash	.60	1.50
TN4 Scott Steiner	.60	1.50

2008 TRISTAR TNA Impact Thoughts by Big Sexy Kevin Nash

COMPLETE SET (5)	2.00	5.00

*GOLD/50: 2X TO 5X BASIC CARDS
*RED/10: UNPRICED DUE TO SCARCITY
*PURPLE/1: UNPRICED DUE TO SCARCITY
*P.P.BLACK/1: UNPRICED DUE TO SCARCITY
*P.P.CYAN/1: UNPRICED DUE TO SCARCITY
*P.P.MAGENTA/1: UNPRICED DUE TO SCARCITY
*P.P.YELLOW/1: UNPRICED DUE TO SCARCITY

BS1 TNA's X-Division	.60	1.50
BS2 Samoa Joe	.60	1.50
BS3 Sting	.60	1.50
BS4 Scott Steiner	.60	1.50
BS5 Trading Cards	.60	1.50

2008 TRISTAR TNA Impact Triple Autographs Red

STATED PRINT RUN 25 SER.#'d SETS

A3AAS Angle/Angle/Styles	75.00	150.00
A3RHH Rave/Hoyt/Hemme	25.00	50.00

2008 TRISTAR TNA Impact We Are TNA

COMPLETE SET (7)	2.50	6.00

*GOLD/50: 2X TO 5X BASIC CARDS
*RED/10: UNPRICED DUE TO SCARCITY
*PURPLE/1: UNPRICED DUE TO SCARCITY
*P.P.BLACK/1: UNPRICED DUE TO SCARCITY
*P.P.CYAN/1: UNPRICED DUE TO SCARCITY
*P.P.MAGENTA/1: UNPRICED DUE TO SCARCITY
*P.P.YELLOW/1: UNPRICED DUE TO SCARCITY

T1 6-Sided Ring	.40	1.00
T2 X-Division	.20	.50
T3 History	.75	2.00
T4 TNA World Championship	.75	2.00
T5 TNA X-Division Championship	.40	1.00

T6 TNA World Tag Team Champ.	.40	1.00
T7 TNA Womens Championship	.40	1.00

2009 TRISTAR TNA Impact

COMPLETE SET (100)	12.50	25.00
UNOPENED BOX (20 PACKS)		
UNOPENED PACK (6 CARDS)		

*WHITE: SAME VALUE
*SILVER/20: 4X TO 10X BASIC CARDS
*GOLD/5: UNPRICED DUE TO SCARCITY
*PURPLE/1: UNPRICED DUE TO SCARCITY

1 Sting	.60	1.50
2 Mick Foley	.60	1.50
3 Daniels	.12	.30
4 Angelina Love	.60	1.50
5 Bobby Lashley	.30	.75
6 James Storm	.15	.40
7 Jeff Jarrett	.60	1.50
8 Taz	.12	.30
9 Brother Ray	.20	.50
10 Tara	.50	1.25
11 Samoa Joe	.20	.50
12 Kevin Nash	.75	2.00
13 Suicide	.12	.30
14 Velvet Sky	.60	1.50
15 Scott Steiner	.60	1.50
16 Daffney RC	.30	.75
17 Amazing Red RC	.12	.30
18 Matt Morgan	.15	.40
19 Hernandez	.15	.40
20 ODB	.20	.50
21 AJ Styles	.30	.75
22 Jay Lethal	.12	.30
23 Awesome Kong	.20	.50
24 Robert Roode	.15	.40
25 Kurt Angle	.75	2.00
26 Brutus Magnus RC	.12	.30
27 SoCal Val	.50	1.25
28 Mike Tenay	.12	.30
29 Jenna Morasca RC	.50	1.25
30 Booker T	.12	.30
31 Alex Shelley	.15	.40
32 Kiyoshi RC	.12	.30
33 Sojournor Bolt RC	.20	.50
34 Abyss	.30	.75
35 Christy Hemme	.75	2.00
36 Doug Williams RC	.12	.30
37 Consequences Creed	.12	.30
38 Taylor Wilde	.50	1.25
39 Jesse Neal RC	.12	.30
40 Brother Devon	.20	.50
41 Lauren Brooke	.30	.75
42 Shark Boy	.12	.30
43 Homicide	.15	.40
44 Sharmell	.20	.50
45 Jim Cornette	.12	.30
46 Cody Deaner RC	.12	.30
47 Eric Young	.12	.30
48 Raisha Saeed	.20	.50
49 Rhino	.20	.50
50 Sarita RC	.30	.75
51 Don West	.12	.30
52 Traci Brooks	.50	1.25
53 Sheik Abdul Bashir	.12	.30
54 Dr. Stevie	.15	.40
55 Madison Rayne RC	.50	1.25
56 Chris Sabin	.12	.30
57 Kip James	.15	.40
58 Dixie Carter	.30	.75
59 Jeremy Borash	.12	.30
60 Rob Terry RC	.12	.30
61 Hermie Sadler	.12	.30
62 Rocco & Sally Boy	.12	.30
63 Ayako Hamada RC	.30	.75
64 The Beautiful People	.60	1.50
65 Beer Money, Inc.	.15	.40
66 Danny Bonaduce	.30	.75
67 Curtis Granderson	.20	.50
68 THE ICON: STING	.60	1.50
69 THE ICON: STING	.60	1.50
70 THE ICON: STING	.60	1.50
71 THE ICON: STING	.60	1.50
72 THE ICON: STING	.60	1.50
73 Mick Foley	.60	1.50
74 Kurt Angle	.75	2.00
75 Booker T	.12	.30
76 AJ Styles	.30	.75
77 Suicide	.12	.30
78 Daniels	.12	.30
79 Team 3D	.20	.50
80 Sting/Kurt Angle	.75	2.00
81 Angelina Love	.60	1.50
82 Awesome Kong	.20	.50
83 Kurt Angle	.75	2.00
84 Jenna Morasca RC	.50	1.25
85 Daniels	.12	.30
86 Madison Rayne RC	.50	1.25
87 Mike Tenay	.12	.30
88 Alex Shelley	.15	.40
89 Sheik Abdul Bashir	.12	.30
90 Jeff Jarrett	.60	1.50
91 Consequences Creed	.12	.30
92 Lauren Brooke	.30	.75
93 Mick Foley	.60	1.50
94 James Storm	.15	.40
95 Jenna Morasca RC	.50	1.25
96 Kip James	.15	.40
97 Mike Tenay	.12	.30
98 Daniels	.12	.30
99 Tweet n' Tweak Connection	.20	.50
NNO Checklist	.12	.30

2009 TRISTAR TNA Impact Autographs Silver

SEMISTARS (IA1-IA84)
UNLISTED STARS (IA1-IA84)
*GOLD/60: .5X TO 1.2X BASIC AUTOS
*BLUE/25: .6X TO 1.5X BASIC AUTOS
*GREEN/10: UNPRICED DUE TO SCARCITY
*PURPLE/1: UNPRICED DUE TO SCARCITY

IA1 Abyss	5.00	12.00
IA2 AJ Styles	6.00	15.00
IA3 Alex Shelley	4.00	10.00
IA4 Amazing Red	4.00	10.00
IA5 Angelina Love	8.00	20.00
IA6 Awesome Kong	5.00	12.00
IA7 Bobby Lashley		
IA8 Booker T		
IA9 Brother Devon	4.00	10.00
IA10 Brother Ray	4.00	10.00
IA11 Brutus Magnus	4.00	10.00
IA12 Chris Sabin	5.00	12.00
IA13 Christy Hemme		
IA14 Cody Deaner	4.00	10.00
IA15 Consequences Creed	4.00	10.00
IA16 Curtis Granderson		
IA17 Daffney	8.00	20.00
IA18 Daniels	5.00	12.00
IA19 Danny Bonaduce	6.00	15.00
IA20 Dixie Carter	5.00	12.00
IA21 Doug Williams	4.00	10.00
IA22 Dr. Stevie	5.00	12.00
IA23 Eric Young	4.00	10.00
IA24 Hernandez		
IA25 Homicide	4.00	10.00
IA26 Hermie Sadler	4.00	10.00
IA27 James Storm	5.00	12.00
IA28 Jay Lethal	4.00	10.00
IA29 Jeff Jarrett	6.00	15.00
IA30 Jenna Morasca	6.00	15.00
IA31 Jesse Neal	4.00	10.00
IA32 Jeremy Borash	4.00	10.00
IA33 Jim Cornette		
IA34 Kevin Nash		
IA35 Kip James	4.00	10.00
IA36 Kiyoshi	4.00	10.00
IA37 Kurt Angle		
IA38 Lauren Brooke	5.00	12.00
IA39 Madison Rayne	6.00	15.00
IA40 Matt Morgan		
IA41 Mick Foley		
IA42 ODB	4.00	10.00
IA43 Raisha Saeed	5.00	12.00
IA44 Rhino		
IA45 Rob Terry	5.00	12.00
IA46 Robert Roode	5.00	12.00
IA47 Samoa Joe	5.00	12.00
IA48 Sarita	6.00	15.00
IA49 Scott Steiner		
IA50 Shark Boy	5.00	12.00
IA51 Sharmell		
IA52 Sheik Abdul Bashir		10.00
IA53 SoCal Val	6.00	15.00
IA54 Sojournor Bolt		
IA55 Sting		
IA56 Suicide	4.00	10.00
IA57 Tara	8.00	20.00
IA58 Taylor Wilde	8.00	20.00
IA59 Traci Brooks	6.00	15.00
IA60 Velvet Sky	8.00	20.00
IA61 Jeff Jarrett / Mick Foley		
IA62 Angelina Love / Velvet Sky	12.00	30.00
IA63 Chris Sabin / Alex Shelley		
IA64 Daffney / The Governor	12.00	30.00
IA65 Bobby Lashley / Kurt Angle		
IA66 Kevin Nash / Jenna Morasca		
IA67 Abyss / Lauren		
IA68 Mick Foley / Sting		
IA69 Consequences Creed / Jay Lethal		
IA70 Jesse Neal / Rhino		
IA71 Mike Tenay / Don West		
IA72 ODB / Cody Deaner		
IA73 Brother Devon / Brother Ray		
IA74 Sting / Kurt Angle		
IA75 Kevin Nash / Samoa Joe		
IA76 Scott Steiner / Booker T		
IA77 Angelina Love / Velvet Sky / Madison Rayne		
IA78 Sting / Kurt Angle / Mick Foley		
IA79 Tara / Christy Hemme / Traci Brooks		
IA80 Brutus Magnus / Rob Terry / Doug Williams		
IA81 Brother Devon / Brother Ray / James Storm / Robert Roode		
IA82 Kurt Angle / Kevin Nash / Booker T / Scott Steiner		
IA83 Angelina Love / Velvet Sky / Tara / Christy Hemme		
IA84 Chris Sabin / Alex Shelley / Jay Lethal / Consequences Creed		

2009 TRISTAR TNA Impact High Impact Championship Inserts

NNO Phone Call EXCH
NNO 2 Tickets and Backstage Pass EXCH
NNO 2 Tickets EXCH
NNO Autographed Baseball EXCH
NNO Autographed Photo EXCH

2009 TRISTAR TNA Impact Knockout Autographed Dual Kiss Gold

*BLUE/10: UNPRICED DUE TO SCARCITY
*PURPLE/1: UNPRICED DUE TO SCARCITY
STATED PRINT RUN 25 SER.#'d SETS

2K1 A.Love/V.Sky		
2K2 C.Hemme/T.Brooks		
2K3 J.Morasca/Sharmell	15.00	30.00
2K4 SoCal Val/L.Brooke	25.00	50.00

2009 TRISTAR TNA Impact Knockout Kiss Gold

*BLUE/25: .6X TO 1.5X BASIC KISS
*GREEN/10: UNPRICED DUE TO SCARCITY
*PURPLE/1: UNPRICED DUE TO SCARCITY
STATED PRINT RUN 99 SER.#'d SETS

K1 Angelina Love	15.00	40.00
K2 Awesome Kong	8.00	20.00
K3 Christy Hemme	15.00	40.00
K4 Jenna Morasca	10.00	25.00

K5 ODB	8.00	20.00
K6 Sharmell	8.00	20.00
K7 Tara	15.00	40.00
K8 Taylor Wilde	12.00	30.00
K9 Traci Brooks	12.00	30.00
K10 Velvet Sky	15.00	40.00

2009 TRISTAR TNA Impact Sting Autographed Face Paint Silver

STATED PRINT RUN 10 SER. #'d SETS
NOT PRICED DUE TO SCARCITY

S1 Sting Black
S2 Sting White

2009 TRISTAR TNA Impact Sting Event-Worn Face Paint Silver

*PURPLE/1: UNPRICED DUE TO SCARCITY
STATED PRINT RUN 5 SER. #'d SETS
UNPRICED DUE TO SCARCITY

S1 Sting Black
S2 Sting White

2009 TRISTAR TNA Impact Sting Face Paint Gold

*GREEN/10: UNPRICED DUE TO SCARCITY
*PURPLE/1: UNPRICED DUE TO SCARCITY
STATED PRINT RUN 60 SER.#'d SETS

S1 Sting Black	25.00	60.00
S2 Sting White	25.00	60.00

2013 TRISTAR TNA Impact Glory

COMPLETE SET (109)	20.00	50.00
COMPLETE SET W/O SP (100)	8.00	20.00

UNOPENED BOX (20 PACKS)
UNOPENED PACK (6 CARDS)
*RED/40: 2X TO 5X BASIC CARDS
*RED SP/40: .5X TO 1.2X BASIC CARDS
*BLUE/10: UNPRICED DUE TO SCARCITY
*BLUE SP/10: UNPRICED DUE TO SCARCITY
*RAINBOW/1: UNPRICED DUE TO SCARCITY
*RAINBOW SP/1: UNPRICED DUE TO SCARCITY
STATED ODDS SP 1:1 HOBBY BOX

1 Jeff Hardy	.60	1.50
2 Hulk Hogan	.75	2.00
3 Kurt Angle	.25	.60
4 Sting	.60	1.50
5 Rampage Jackson	.25	.60
6 Tito Ortiz	.25	.60
7 Mickie James	.75	2.00
8 Chris Sabin	.15	.40
9 Bully Ray	.15	.40
10 Bobby Roode	.15	.40
11 AJ Styles	.25	.60
12 Gail Kim	.40	1.00
13 Velvet Sky	.60	1.50
14 Chavo Guerrero Jr.	.15	.40
15 James Storm	.15	.40
16 ODB	.15	.40
17 Christopher Daniels	.15	.40
18 Sting	.60	1.50
19 Joseph Park	.25	.60
20 Jessie Godderz	.15	.40
21 Mr. Anderson	.25	.60
22 Garett Bischoff	.25	.60
23 Samoa Joe	.15	.40
24 Austin Aries	.25	.60
25 Hernandez	.15	.40
26 Jeremy Borash	.15	.40
27 Manik RC	.15	.40
28 Velvet Sky	.60	1.50
29 Jeff Hardy	.60	1.50
30 Christy Hemme	.50	1.25
31 Robbie E	.15	.40
32 Dixie Carter	.25	.60
33 Christopher Daniels	.15	.40
34 Taryn Terrell	.40	1.00
35 Eric Young	.15	.40
36 Miss Tessmacher	.40	1.00
37 Magnus	.15	.40
38 AJ Styles	.25	.60
39 Hulk Hogan	.75	2.00
40 Sting	.60	1.50
41 Gail Kim	.40	1.00
42 Wes Brisco RC	.15	.40
43 Rob Terry	.15	.40
44 Chavo Guerrero Jr.	.15	.40
45 Gunner	.15	.40
46 Velvet Sky	.60	1.50
47 Knux	.15	.40
48 Jeff Hardy	.60	1.50
49 Chris Sabin	.15	.40
50 Kazarian	.15	.40
51 King Mo	.15	.40
52 Austin Aries	.25	.60
53 Jay Bradley RC	.15	.40
54 Kenny King RC	.15	.40
55 Taz	.15	.40
56 Hernandez	.15	.40
57 Eric Young	.15	.40
58 Hulk Hogan	.75	2.00
59 Velvet Sky	.60	1.50
60 Sting	.60	1.50
61 AJ Styles	.25	.60
62 Rockstar Spud RC	.15	.40
63 Bully Ray	.15	.40
64 Dixie Carter	.25	.60
65 Velvet Sky	.60	1.50
66 Rampage Jackson	.25	.60
67 Jeff Hardy	.60	1.50
68 Christopher Daniels	.15	.40
69 Abyss	.25	.60
70 Chris Sabin	.15	.40
71 Mike Tenay	.15	.40
72 Mickie James	.75	2.00
73 AJ Styles	.25	.60
74 ODB	.15	.40
75 Magnus	.15	.40
76 Hector Guerrero	.15	.40
77 Hulk Hogan	.75	2.00
78 Brooke Hogan	.40	1.00
79 Austin Aries	.25	.60
80 Jessie Godderz	.15	.40
81 Jessie Godderz	.15	.40
82 Jessie Godderz	.15	.40
83 Garett Bischoff	.25	.60
84 Chavo Guerrero Jr.	.15	.40
85 Sam Shaw RC	.15	.40
86 Bobby Roode	.15	.40
87 Dixie Carter	.25	.60
88 Jeff Hardy	.60	1.50
89 Hulk Hogan	.75	2.00
90 Jeff Hardy Original Art	.50	1.25
91 Jeff Hardy Original Art	.50	1.25
92 Jeff Hardy Original Art	.50	1.25
93 Jeff Hardy Original Art	.50	1.25
94 Jeff Hardy Original Art	.50	1.25
95 Jeff Hardy Original Art	.50	1.25
96 Jeff Hardy Original Art	.50	1.25
97 Jeff Hardy Original Art	.50	1.25
98 Jeff Hardy Original Art	.50	1.25
99 Jeff Hardy Original Art	.50	1.25
100 Aces and Eights SP	3.00	8.00
101 Jeff Hardy SP	3.00	8.00
102 Rampage Jackson SP	1.25	3.00
103 Velvet Sky SP	3.00	8.00
104 AJ Styles SP	1.25	3.00
105 Gail Kim SP	2.00	5.00
106 Sting SP	3.00	8.00
107 Jeff Hardy SP	3.00	8.00
108 Dixie Carter SP	1.25	3.00
109 Hulk Hogan SP	4.00	10.00

2013 TRISTAR TNA Impact Glory Autographed Mat Relics Gold

*BLUE/10: UNPRICED DUE TO SCARCITY
*RED/5: UNPRICED DUE TO SCARCITY
*RAINBOW/1: UNPRICED DUE TO SCARCITY
STATED PRINT RUN 50 SER.#'d SETS

MAS AJ Styles	12.00	30.00
MBH Brooke Hogan	20.00	50.00
MBR Bully Ray	8.00	20.00
MBR Bobby Roode	8.00	20.00
MCG Chavo Guerrero Jr.	8.00	20.00
MCH Christy Hemme	12.00	30.00
MCS Chris Sabin	8.00	20.00
MD Devon	8.00	20.00
MHH Hulk Hogan	50.00	100.00
MJG Jessie Godderz	8.00	20.00
MJH Jeff Hardy	20.00	50.00
MKA Kurt Angle	15.00	40.00
MMA Mr. Anderson	8.00	20.00
MMJ Mickie James	20.00	50.00
MRJ Rampage Jackson	12.00	30.00
MS Sting	30.00	60.00
MT Tara	8.00	20.00
MTT Taryn Terrell	12.00	30.00

2013 TRISTAR TNA Impact Glory Autographed Memorabilia Red

M1 Hulk Hogan		
M2 Jeff Hardy		
M3 Sting	40.00	80.00
M4 Austin Aries		
M5 Rampage Jackson	15.00	40.00
M6 Tito Ortiz		

2013 TRISTAR TNA Impact Glory Dual Autographs Gold

*RED/50: .5X TO 1.2X BASIC AUTOS
*BLUE/10: UNPRICED DUE TO SCARCITY
*GREEN/5: UNPRICED DUE TO SCARCITY
*RAINBOW/1: UNPRICED DUE TO SCARCITY
*P.P.BLACK/1: UNPRICED DUE TO SCARCITY
*P.P.CYAN/1: UNPRICED DUE TO SCARCITY
*P.P.MAGENTA/1: UNPRICED DUE TO SCARCITY
*P.P.YELLOW/1: UNPRICED DUE TO SCARCITY
STATED PRINT RUN 99 SER.#'d SETS

4 J.Park/Abyss	8.00	20.00
7 M.James/G.Kim	10.00	25.00
8 C.Daniels/Kazarian	4.00	10.00
10 E.Young/ODB	4.00	10.00
12 G.Kim/V.Sky	8.00	20.00
14 B.Roode/J.Storm	5.00	12.00
16 J.Storm/Gunner	5.00	12.00
20 A.Styles/S.Joe	8.00	20.00
21 C.Hemme/S.Val	8.00	20.00

2013 TRISTAR TNA Impact Glory Dual Memorabilia Gold

*RED/50: .5X TO 1.2X BASIC MEM
*BLUE/10: UNPRICED DUE TO SCARCITY
*GREEN/5: UNPRICED DUE TO SCARCITY
*RAINBOW/1: UNPRICED DUE TO SCARCITY
STATED PRINT RUN 99 SER.#'d SETS

M8 B.Ray/M.Tessmacher	5.00	12.00
M9 T.Ortiz/R.Jackson	5.00	12.00

2013 TRISTAR TNA Impact Glory Dual Memorabilia Red

*RED/50: .5X TO 1.2X BASIC MEM

M8 B.Ray/M.Tessmacher	6.00	15.00
M9 T.Ortiz/R.Jackson	6.00	15.00

2013 TRISTAR TNA Impact Glory Jeff Hardy Autographed Face Paint Green

H1 Jeff Hardy
H2 Jeff Hardy

2013 TRISTAR TNA Impact Glory Memorabilia Red

STATED PRINT RUN 50 SER.#'d SETS

M10 Tito Ortiz	5.00	12.00
M11 Rampage Jackson	5.00	12.00
M12 Bully Ray	5.00	12.00
M13 Mickie James	15.00	40.00
M14 Sting	12.00	30.00

2013 TRISTAR TNA Impact Glory On-Card Autographs Gold

*RED/50: .5X TO 1.2X BASIC AUTOS
*BLUE/10: UNPRICED DUE TO SCARCITY
*GREEN/5: UNPRICED DUE TO SCARCITY
*RAINBOW/1: UNPRICED DUE TO SCARCITY
STATED PRINT RUN 199 SER.#'d SETS

GAS AJ Styles	8.00	20.00
GBR Bobby Roode	6.00	15.00
GCH Christy Hemme	6.00	15.00
GGK Gail Kim	8.00	20.00
GJG Jessie Godderz	5.00	12.00
GJS James Storm	5.00	12.00
GKA Kurt Angle	12.00	30.00
GMJ Mickie James	8.00	20.00
GT Tara	6.00	15.00
GVS Velvet Sky	10.00	25.00

2013 TRISTAR TNA Impact Glory Quad Memorabilia Gold

*RED/50: X TO X BASIC MEM
*BLUE/10: UNPRICED DUE TO SCARCITY
*GREEN/5: UNPRICED DUE TO SCARCITY
*RAINBOW/1: UNPRICED DUE TO SCARCITY
STATED PRINT RUN 99 SER.#'d SETS

M7 Kim/James/Tessmacher/Sky

2013 TRISTAR TNA Impact Glory Sticker Autographs Gold

*RED/50: .5X TO 1.2X BASIC AUTOS

*BLUE/10: UNPRICED DUE TO SCARCITY
*GREEN/5: UNPRICED DUE TO SCARCITY
*RAINBOW/1: UNPRICED DUE TO SCARCITY
*P.P.BLACK/1: UNPRICED DUE TO SCARCITY
*P.P.CYAN/1: UNPRICED DUE TO SCARCITY
*P.P.MAGENTA/1: UNPRICED DUE TO SCARCITY
*P.P.YELLOW/1: UNPRICED DUE TO SCARCITY
STATED PRINT RUN 99 SER.#'d SETS

G5 Chris Sabin	4.00	10.00
G11 Manik	4.00	10.00
G15 Knux	4.00	10.00
G26 Wes Brisco	4.00	10.00
G27 Jay Bradley	4.00	10.00
G31 Brooke Hogan	15.00	40.00
G32 Garett Bischoff	4.00	10.00
G33 Magnus	4.00	10.00
G37 Devon	4.00	10.00

2013 TRISTAR TNA Impact Glory Triple Autographs Red

*BLUE/10: UNPRICED DUE TO SCARCITY
*GREEN/5: UNPRICED DUE TO SCARCITY
*RAINBOW/1: UNPRICED DUE TO SCARCITY
STATED PRINT RUN 50 SER.#'d SETS

1 Bobby Roode Christopher Daniels Kazarian	8.00	20.00
3 Brisco/G.Bischoff/Knux	8.00	20.00
5 James/ODB/Tessmacher	12.00	30.00

2013 TRISTAR TNA Impact Live

COMPLETE SET (109)	25.00	50.00
COMPLETE SET W/O SP (99)	8.00	20.00

UNOPENED BOX (20 PACKS)
UNOPENED PACK (6 CARDS)
*GOLD/50: 2X TO 5X BASIC CARDS
*GOLD SP/50: .6X TO 1.5X BASIC CARDS
*RED/10: UNPRICED DUE TO SCARCITY
*RED SP/10: UNPRICED DUE TO SCARCITY
*RAINBOW/1: UNPRICED DUE TO SCARCITY
*RAINBOW/1: UNPRICED DUE TO SCARCITY
STATED SP ODDS 1:BOX

1 Hulk Hogan	.75	2.00
2 Brooke Hogan	.40	1.00
3 Hulk Hogan/Brooke Hogan	.75	2.00
4 Sting	.60	1.50
5 Jeff Hardy	.60	1.50
6 Austin Aries	.25	.60
7 Gail Kim	.40	1.00
8 AJ Styles	.25	.60
9 Bobby Roode	.15	.40
10 Bully Ray	.15	.40
11 Kurt Angle	.25	.60
12 Garett Bischoff	.25	.60
13 Hernandez	.15	.40
14 King Mo	.15	.40
15 Jessie Godderz	.15	.40
16 Tara	.50	1.25
17 James Storm	.15	.40
18 Kazarian	.15	.40
19 Christopher Daniels	.15	.40
20 Matt Morgan	.15	.40
21 Rob Van Dam	.25	.60
22 Douglas Williams	.15	.40
23 SoCal Val	.40	1.00
24 Sting	.60	1.50
25 Christy Hemme	.50	1.25
26 Jesse Sorensen	.15	.40
27 Taz	.15	.40
28 Earl Hebner	.15	.40
29 Magnus	.15	.40
30 AJ Styles	.25	.60
31 Kenny King RC	.15	.40
32 Taryn Terrell	.40	1.00
33 Devon	.15	.40
34 Velvet Sky	.60	1.50
35 Jeff Hardy	.60	1.50
36 Joseph Park	.25	.60
37 Eric Young	.15	.40
38 Tara	.50	1.25
39 Chris Sabin	.15	.40
40 Sting	.60	1.50
41 Bully Ray	.15	.40
42 Robbie E	.15	.40
43 Rob Terry	.15	.40
44 James Storm	.15	.40
45 Crimson	.15	.40
46 DOC	.15	.40
47 Jessie Godderz	.15	.40
48 Samoa Joe	.15	.40
49 Rob Van Dam	.25	.60
50 Hulk Hogan	.75	2.00
51 Jeff Hardy	.60	1.50
52 Christy Hemme	.50	1.25
53 Jessie Godderz	.15	.40
54 Madison Rayne	.40	1.00
55 TNA Referees	.15	.40
56 Zema Ion RC	.15	.40
57 Christopher Daniels	.15	.40
58 Mr. Anderson	.25	.60
59 Garett Bischoff	.25	.60
60 AJ Styles	.25	.60
61 Mike Tenay	.15	.40
62 Aces and Eights	.15	.40
63 Matt Morgan	.15	.40
64 James Storm	.15	.40
65 Hernandez	.15	.40
66 Kurt Angle	.25	.60
67 Douglas Williams	.15	.40
68 Jeff Hardy	.60	1.50
69 ODB	.15	.40
70 Abyss	.25	.60
71 Bully Ray	.15	.40
72 Jeremy Borash	.15	.40
73 Gunner	.15	.40
74 Christopher Daniels	.15	.40
75 AJ Styles	.25	.60
76 Gut Check	.15	.40
77 Alex Silva	.15	.40
78 Christian York RC	.15	.40
79 Sam Shaw RC	.15	.40
80 Joey Ryan RC	.15	.40
81 Taeler Hendrix RC	.25	.60
82 Wes Brisco RC	.15	.40
83 Al Snow	.25	.60
84 D'Lo Brown	.15	.40
85 Chavo Guerrero Jr.	.15	.40
86 Hector Guerrero	.15	.40
87 World Tag Team Champions: Hernandez and Chavo Guerrero Jr.	.15	.40
88 The Guerrero Legacy	.15	.40
89 Gail Kim	.40	1.00
90 Mr. Anderson	.25	.60
91 Miss Tessmacher	.40	1.00
92 Robbie E	.15	.40
93 Tara	.50	1.25
94 Mickie James	.75	2.00
95 Chavo Guerrero Jr.	.15	.40
96 Destination X	.15	.40
97 Slammiversary	.15	.40
98 Bound For Glory	.15	.40
99 Sting's Hall of Fame Induction	.60	1.50
100 Hulk Hogan SP	4.00	10.00
101 Sting SP	3.00	8.00
102 Bully Ray SP	.75	2.00
103 Samoa Joe SP	.75	2.00
104 Kurt Angle SP	1.25	3.00
105 Hulk Hogan SP	4.00	10.00
106 Sting SP	3.00	8.00
107 Kurt Angle SP	1.25	3.00
108 Miss Tessmacher SP	2.00	5.00
109 Jeff Hardy SP	3.00	8.00
CL Checklist	.15	.40

2013 TRISTAR TNA Impact Live Autographed Memorabilia Gold

M17 Gail Kim

2013 TRISTAR TNA Impact Live Autographed Memorabilia Rainbow

STATED PRINT RUN 1 SER.#'d SET
UNPRICED DUE TO SCARCITY

M15 Hulk Hogan
M16 Jeff Hardy
M17 Gail Kim
M18 Sting

2013 TRISTAR TNA Impact Live Autographs Gold

*GREEN/50: .5X TO 1.2X BASIC AUTOS
*BLUE/25: .6X TO 1.5X BASIC AUTOS
*RED/5: UNPRICED DUE TO SCARCITY
*RAINBOW/1: UNPRICED DUE TO SCARCITY
STATED PRINT RUN 99 SER. #'d SETS

L16 Gail Kim	8.00	20.00
L17 James Storm	5.00	12.00
L20 Mr. Anderson	6.00	15.00
L23 Taryn Terrell	12.00	30.00
L24 Doug Williams	3.00	8.00
L25 Matt Morgan	5.00	12.00
L26 Christy Hemme	10.00	25.00
L27 Abyss	3.00	8.00
L29 Samoa Joe	3.00	8.00
L32 Bully Ray	5.00	12.00
L33 Robbie E	3.00	8.00
L34 Winter	4.00	10.00
L35 Jesse Sorensen	3.00	8.00
L36 Kazarian	4.00	10.00
L37 Garett Bischoff	3.00	8.00
L38 Kenny King	6.00	15.00
L39 Christian York	8.00	20.00
L40 Hector Guerrero	3.00	8.00
L41 ODB	5.00	12.00
L42 Bobby Roode	3.00	8.00
L43 Chris Sabin	4.00	10.00
L44 SoCal Val	5.00	12.00
L45 Rosita	5.00	12.00
L46 Hernandez	3.00	8.00
L47 Kid Kash	3.00	8.00
L48 Austin Aries	8.00	20.00

2013 TRISTAR TNA Impact Live Dual Autographs Gold

*GREEN/50: .5X TO 1.2X BASIC AUTOS
*BLUE/25: .6X TO 1.5X BASIC AUTOS
*RED/5: UNPRICED DUE TO SCARCITY
*RAINBOW/1: UNPRICED DUE TO SCARCITY
STATED PRINT RUN 99 SER.#'d SETS

2 Chavo & Hector Guerrero		
3 K.Angle/W.Brisco		
4 E.Young/ODB		
5 C.Daniels/Kazarian	4.00	10.00
6 Tara/J.Godderz	6.00	15.00
7 C.Hemme/J.Borash	6.00	15.00
8 M.Morgan/J.Ryan	6.00	15.00
9 Sarita/Rosita	5.00	12.00
10 C.Guerrero/Hernandez		
11 G.Kim/M.James	12.00	30.00
12 J.Storm/B.Roode		
13 B.Roode/J.Hardy		
14 B.Hogan/B.Ray		
15 A.Aries/M.Morgan		
16 M.Tessmacher/Tara	8.00	20.00
17 W.Brisco/G.Bischoff	5.00	12.00
18 S.Shaw/C.York		
19 M.James/Tara		
20 C.Daniels/C.Sabin	4.00	10.00
21 C.Sabin/J.Sorensen	4.00	10.00
22 K.Angle/M.Anderson		
23 B.Roode/A.Aries		
24 M.Anderson/Devon		
25 Sting/J.Hardy		

2013 TRISTAR TNA Impact Live Dual Memorabilia Silver

*GOLD/50: .5X TO 1.2X BASIC MEM
*BLUE/25: .6X TO 1.5X BASIC MEM
*RED/5: UNPRICED DUE TO SCARCITY
*RAINBOW/1: UNPRICED DUE TO SCARCITY
STATED ODDS OVERALL 1:BOX

M11 Tara Jessie Godderz	4.00	10.00
M12 C.Guerrero Jr./Hernandez	4.00	10.00

2013 TRISTAR TNA Impact Live Eight Autographs Gold

*GREEN/50: X TO X BASIC AUTOS
*BLUE/25: UNPRICED DUE TO SCARCITY
*RED/5: UNPRICED DUE TO SCARCITY
*RAINBOW/1: UNPRICED DUE TO SCARCTIY
STATED PRINT RUN 99 SER.#'d SETS

3 Brooke Hogan
Tara
Velvet Sky
Madison Rayne
Gail Kim
Mickie James
Christy Hemme
Ms. Tessmacher

2013 TRISTAR TNA Impact Live Jeff Hardy Die-Cut Letter Memorabilia Gold

*BLUE/25: .5X TO 1.2X BASIC MEM
*RED/5: .75X TO 2X BASIC MEM
*RAINBOW/1: UNPRICED DUE TO SCARCITY
STATED PRINT RUN 50 SER.#'d SETS

M1 Jeff Hardy H	15.00	40.00
M2 Jeff Hardy A	15.00	40.00
M3 Jeff Hardy R	15.00	40.00
M4 Jeff Hardy D	15.00	40.00
M5 Jeff Hardy Y	15.00	40.00

2013 TRISTAR TNA Impact Live Memorabilia Silver

*GOLD/50: .5X TO 1.2X BASIC MEM
*BLUE/25: .6X TO 1.5X BASIC MEM
*RED/5: UNPRICED DUE TO SCARCITY
*RAINBOW/1: UNPRICED DUE TO SCARCITY
STATED ODDS OVERALL 1:BOX

M6 Hulk Hogan	10.00	25.00
M7 Sting	8.00	20.00
M8 Kurt Angle	6.00	15.00
M9 Austin Aries	4.00	10.00
M10 Chavo Guerrero Jr.	4.00	10.00

2013 TRISTAR TNA Impact Live Quad Autographs Gold

*GREEN/50: X TO X BASIC AUTOS
*BLUE/25: UNPRICED DUE TO SCARCITY
*RED/5: UNPRICED DUE TO SCARCITY
*RAINBOW/1: UNPRICED DUE TO SCARCITY
STATED PRINT RUN 99 SER.#'d SETS

1 Gail Kim
Mickie James
Tara
Velvet Sky
2 Angle/Brisco/G.Bischoff/Samoa Joe

2013 TRISTAR TNA Impact Live Quad Memorabilia Silver

*GOLD/50: .5X TO 1.2X BASIC MEM
*BLUE/25: .6X TO 1.5X BASIC MEM
*RED/5: UNPRICED DUE TO SCARCITY
*RAINBOW/1: UNPRICED DUE TO SCARCITY
STATED ODDS OVERALL 1:BOX

M13 Hulk Hogan
Sting
Jeff Hardy
Kurt Angle
M14 Kim/James/Tessmacher/Sky 12.00 30.00

2013 TRISTAR TNA Impact Live Six Autographs Gold

2 Kim/Tara/James
Sky/Tessmacher/Rayne

2013 TRISTAR TNA Impact Live Ten Autographs Gold

2 Styles/Morgan/Sabin/Daniels/Roode
Young/Hernandez/Kazarian/Storm/Robbie

2013 TRISTAR TNA Impact Live Triple Autographs Gold

2 Jeff Hardy
Austin Aries
Bobby Roode
4 Angle/Anderson/Hardy

2013 TRISTAR TNA Impact Live Twelve Autographs Gold

2 Brooke/Tara/Hemme/Sarita
Kim/Sky/Tessmacher/Terrell
James/Rayne/ODB/Val

2012 TRISTAR TNA Impact Reflexxions

COMPLETE SET (100)	10.00	25.00
UNOPENED BOX (20 PACKS)		
UNOPENED PACK (6 CARDS)		

*SILVER/40: 2.5X TO 6X BASIC CARDS
*GOLD/10: UNPRICED DUE TO SCARCITY
*PURPLE/1: UNPRICED DUE TO SCARCITY
SUBSET CARDS SAME PRICE AS BASE CARDS
EXCHANGE DEADLINE 6/1/2013

1 Hulk Hogan	1.00	2.50
2 Ric Flair	.75	2.00
3 Sting	.60	1.50
4 Bobby Roode	.15	.40
5 James Storm	.15	.40
6 Jeff Hardy	.60	1.50
7 AJ Styles	.25	.60
8 Dixie Carter	.40	1.00
9 Jeff Jarrett	.25	.60
10 Rob Van Dam	.25	.60
11 Velvet Sky	.75	2.00
12 Bully Ray	.15	.40
13 Angelina Love	.60	1.50
14 Kurt Angle	.25	.60
15 Crimson	.15	.40
16 Christy Hemme	.60	1.50
17 Gail Kim	.40	1.00
18 Austin Aries RC	.25	.60
19 Mickie James	1.00	2.50
20 Samoa Joe	.15	.40
21 Eric Bischoff	.15	.40
22 Garrett Bischoff	.25	.60
23 Mr. Anderson	.25	.60
24 Alex Shelley	.15	.40
25 Mark Haskins RC	.15	.40
26 Rob Terry	.15	.40
27 Karen Jarrett	.25	.60
28 Douglas Williams	.15	.40
29 Rosita	.25	.60
30 Kazarian	.15	.40
31 Scott Steiner	.25	.60
32 Zema Ion RC	.15	.40
33 Anarquia	.15	.40
34 Gunner	.15	.40
35 Kid Kash	.25	.60
36 D'Angelo Dinero	.15	.40
37 Magnus	.15	.40
38 Tara	.60	1.50
39 Abyss	.25	.60
40 Matt Morgan	.15	.40
41 ODB	.15	.40
42 Chris Sabin	.15	.40
43 Jesse Sorensen RC	.15	.40
44 Mike Tenay	.15	.40
45 Madison Rayne	.40	1.00
46 Devon	.15	.40
47 Sarita	.25	.60
48 Eric Young	.15	.40
49 Traci Brooks	.40	1.00
50 Anthony Nese	.15	.40
51 Taz	.15	.40
52 Hernandez	.15	.40
53 Brooke Tessmacher	.40	1.00
54 Christopher Daniels	.15	.40
55 Jesse Neal	.15	.40
56 Robbie E	.15	.40
57 SoCal Val	.40	1.00
58 Brian Kendrick	.15	.40
59 Jeremy Borash	.15	.40
60 Shannon Moore	.15	.40
61 Winter	.60	1.50
62 Ric Flair US	.75	2.00
63 Sting US	.60	1.50
64 Christy Hemme US	.60	1.50
65 Jeff Jarrett US	.25	.60
66 Velvet Sky US	.75	2.00
67 Mr. Anderson US	.25	.60
68 Gail Kim US	.40	1.00
69 Scott Steiner US	.25	.60
70 Traci Brooks US	.40	1.00
71 Jeff Hardy US	.60	1.50
72 Dixie Carter US	.40	1.00
73 Sting FT	.60	1.50
74 Ric Flair FT	.75	2.00
75 Velvet Sky FT	.75	2.00
76 Jeff Jarrett FT	.25	.60
77 Scott Steiner FT	.25	.60
78 Jeff Hardy FT	.60	1.50
79 Mr. Anderson FT	.25	.60
80 Velvet Sky BMV	.75	2.00
81 Christy Hemme BMV	.60	1.50
82 Gail Kim BMV	.40	1.00
83 Karen Jarrett BMV	.25	.60
84 Traci Brooks BMV	.40	1.00
85 Madison Rayne BMV	.40	1.00
86 Brooke Tessmacher BMV	.40	1.00
87 Hulk Hogan SW	1.00	2.50
88 Sting SW	.60	1.50
89 Kurt Angle SW	.25	.60
90 Crimson SW	.15	.40
91 Jeff Hardy LH	.60	1.50
92 Sting LH	.60	1.50
93 Christy Hemme LH	.60	1.50
94 Ric Flair LH	.75	2.00
95 Mr. Anderson LH	.25	.60
96 Velvet Sky LH	.75	2.00
97 Scott Steiner LH	.25	.60
98 Gail Kim LH	.40	1.00
99 Jeff Jarrett LH	.25	.60
CL Checklist	.15	.40
NNO Jeff Hardy Art Redemption EXCH		

2012 TRISTAR TNA Impact Reflexxions Autographed Mat Relics Gold

*BLUE/25: X TO X BASIC AU RELICS
*RED/5: UNPRICED DUE TO SCARCITY
*PURPLE/1: UNPRICED DUE TO SCARCITY
STATED PRINT RUN 50 SER.#'d SETS

M3 Kurt Angle		
M4 Velvet Sky	25.00	50.00
M5 AJ Styles		
M6 Bobby Roode		
M7 Tara		
M8 Mr. Anderson		
M9 James Storm	15.00	30.00
M10 Angelina Love	20.00	40.00
M11 Jeff Jarrett		
M12 Gail Kim	20.00	40.00
M13 Rob Van Dam		

2012 TRISTAR TNA Impact Reflexxions Autographed Memorabilia Blue

*RED/5: UNPRICED DUE TO SCARCITY
*PURPLE/1: UNPRICED DUE TO SCARCITY
STATED PRINT RUN 25 SER.#'d SETS

M14 Hulk Hogan		
M15 Ric Flair	75.00	125.00
M16 Sting	50.00	100.00
M17 Rob Van Dam	20.00	40.00
M18 Kurt Angle	25.00	50.00
M19 Mickie James	75.00	125.00
M20 Jeff Hardy	40.00	80.00
M21 Mr. Anderson	15.00	30.00
M22 Garett Bischoff	15.00	30.00
M23 Velvet Sky	40.00	80.00

2012 TRISTAR TNA Impact Reflexxions Autographs Silver

*GOLD/50: .5X TO 1.2X BASIC AUTOS
*RED/25: X TO X BASIC AUTOS
*GREEN/5: UNPRICED DUE TO SCARCITY
*PURPLE/1: UNPRICED DUE TO SCARCITY
STATED PRINT RUN 99 SER.#'d SETS

16 Christy Hemme	10.00	25.00
20 Samoa Joe	4.00	10.00
22 Garrett Bischoff	4.00	10.00
26 Rob Terry	4.00	10.00
29 Rosita	6.00	15.00
30 Kazarian	4.00	10.00
33 Anarquia	4.00	10.00
34 Gunner	4.00	10.00
35 Kid Kash	6.00	15.00
36 D'Angelo Dinero	4.00	10.00
37 Magnus	4.00	10.00
39 Abyss	5.00	12.00
41 ODB	4.00	10.00
43 Jesse Sorensen	5.00	12.00
45 Madison Rayne	6.00	15.00
47 Sarita	5.00	12.00
48 Eric Young	4.00	10.00
49 Traci Brooks	5.00	12.00
52 Hernandez	4.00	10.00
53 Brooke Tessmacher	8.00	20.00
55 Jesse Neal	4.00	10.00
56 Robbie E	4.00	10.00
57 SoCal Val	5.00	12.00
61 Winter	8.00	20.00

2012 TRISTAR TNA Impact Reflexxions Blue Foil Inserts

COMPLETE SET (50)	60.00	120.00

*RED/10: UNPRICED DUE TO SCARCITY
*PURPLE/1: UNPRICED DUE TO SCARCITY
STATED PRINT RUN 40 SER.#'d SETS

R1 Hulk Hogan	4.00	10.00
R2 Hulk Hogan	4.00	10.00
R3 Hulk Hogan	4.00	10.00
R4 Hulk Hogan	4.00	10.00
R5 Hulk Hogan	4.00	10.00
R6 Ric Flair	3.00	8.00
R7 Ric Flair	3.00	8.00
R8 Sting	2.50	6.00
R9 Sting	2.50	6.00
R10 Kurt Angle	1.00	2.50
R11 Kurt Angle	1.00	2.50

R12 Jeff Jarrett	1.00	2.50
R13 Rob Van Dam	1.00	2.50
R14 Velvet Sky	3.00	8.00
R15 AJ Styles	1.00	2.50
R16 Eric Bischoff	.60	1.50
R17 Scott Steiner	1.00	2.50
R18 Angelina Love	2.50	6.00
R19 Mr. Anderson	1.00	2.50
R20 Bobby Roode	.60	1.50
R21 James Storm	.60	1.50
R22 Abyss	1.00	2.50
R23 Gail Kim	1.50	4.00
R24 Samoa Joe	.60	1.50
R25 Crimson	.60	1.50
R26 Dixie Carter	1.50	4.00
R27 Tara	2.50	6.00
R28 Hernandez	.60	1.50
R29 Christopher Daniels	.60	1.50
R30 Devon	.60	1.50
R31 Mickie James	4.00	10.00
R32 Matt Morgan	.60	1.50
R33 Bully Ray	.60	1.50
R34 Garett Bischoff	1.00	2.50
R35 Brooke Tessmacher	1.50	4.00
R36 Karen Jarrett	1.00	2.50
R37 The Immortal Battles	4.00	10.00
R38 The Immortal Battles	4.00	10.00
R39 The Immortal Battles	4.00	10.00
R40 Jeff Hardy	2.50	6.00
R41 Jeff Hardy Original Art	5.00	12.00
R42 Jeff Hardy Original Art	5.00	12.00
R43 Jeff Hardy Original Art	5.00	12.00
R44 Jeff Hardy Original Art	5.00	12.00
R45 Jeff Hardy Original Art	5.00	12.00
R46 Jeff Hardy Original Art	5.00	12.00
R47 Jeff Hardy Original Art	5.00	12.00
R48 Jeff Hardy Original Art	5.00	12.00
R49 Jeff Hardy Original Art	5.00	12.00
R50 Jeff Hardy Original Art	5.00	12.00

2012 TRISTAR TNA Impact Reflexxions Dual Autographs Silver

*GOLD/50: .5X TO 1.25X BASIC AUTOS
*RED/25: .6X TO 1.5X BASIC AUTOS
*GREEN/5: UNPRICED DUE TO SCARCITY
*PURPLE/1: UNPRICED DUE TO SCARCITY
STATED PRINT RUN 99 SER.#'d SETS

7 Tara/Tessmacher	8.00	20.00
8 Crimson/Morgan	6.00	15.00
9 Kim/Sky	15.00	30.00
10 K.Jarrett/Brooks	10.00	25.00
12 Hernandez/Anarquia	5.00	12.00
14 Robbie E/Robbie T	5.00	12.00
15 Sarita/Rosita	8.00	20.00
17 Aries/Kash	8.00	20.00
19 Hemme/SoCal Val	8.00	20.00
20 Tenay/Borash	5.00	12.00
29 Aries/Kendrick	6.00	15.00
30 Sky/Love	8.00	20.00

2012 TRISTAR TNA Impact Reflexxions Dual Memorabilia Silver

*GOLD/50: .5X TO 1.2X BASIC MEM
*BLUE/25: .6X TO 1.5X BASIC MEM
*RED/5: UNPRICED DUE TO SCARCITY
*PURPLE/1: UNPRICED DUE TO SCARCITY
STATED PRINT RUN 199 SER.#'d SETS

M26 J.Jarrett/K.Jarrett	4.00	10.00
M27 Roode/Storm	4.00	10.00
M29 Jarrett/Brooks	5.00	12.00

2012 TRISTAR TNA Impact Reflexxions Quad Memorabilia Silver

*GOLD/50: X TO X BASIC MEM
*BLUE/25: X TO X BASIC MEM
*RED/5: UNPRICED DUE TO SCARCITY
*PURPLE/1: UNPRICED DUE TO SCARCITY
STATED PRINT RUN 199 SER.#'d SETS

M36 Styles/Abyss/Mrgn/Dnls	8.00	20.00

2012 TRISTAR TNA Impact Reflexxions Quad Memorabilia Gold

*GOLD: .5X TO 1.2X BASIC MEM
STATED PRINT RUN 50 SER.#'d SETS

M34 James/Tara/Sky/Love	15.00	40.00
M36 Styles/Abyss/Mrgn/Dnls	10.00	25.00

2012 TRISTAR TNA Impact Reflexxions Quad Memorabilia Red

STATED PRINT RUN 5 SER.#'d SETS
UNPRICED DUE TO SCARCITY

M34 James/Tara/Sky/Love
M35 Hulk/Flair/Sting/Angle
M36 Styles/Abyss/Mrgn/Dnls

2012 TRISTAR TNA Impact Reflexxions Six Autographs Red

*GREEN/5: UNPRICED DUE TO SCARCITY
*PURPLE/1: UNPRICED DUE TO SCARCITY
STATED PRINT RUN 25 SER.#'d SETS

1 Sky/Tara/Tess/Love/Wint/Rayn
3 Rood/Strm/Styl/VDam/Hard/Angle

2012 TRISTAR TNA Impact Reflexxions Triple Autographs Red

*GREEN/5: UNPRICED DUE TO SCARCITY
*PURPLE/1: UNPRICED DUE TO SCARCITY
STATED PRINT RUN 25 SER.#'d SETS

2 Angle/Jarrett/Jarrett	20.00	40.00
3 Roode/Styles/Hardy	40.00	80.00
4 Kim/James/Sky	40.00	80.00
5 Hemme/Kim/Brooks	30.00	60.00

2012 TRISTAR TNA Impact Reflexxions Triple Memorabilia Silver

*GOLD/50: .5X TO 1.2X BASIC MEM
*BLUE/25: X TO X BASIC MEM
*RED/5: UNPRICED DUE TO SCARCITY
*PURPLE/1: UNPRICED DUE TO SCARCITY
STATED PRINT RUN 199 SER.#'d SETS

M32 Sting/Steiner/Jarrett	8.00	20.00
M33 RVD/Anderson/Styles	6.00	15.00

2012 TRISTAR TNA Impact Reflexxions Triple Memorabilia Blue

*BLUE: .6X TO 1.5X BASIC MEM
STATED PRINT RUN 25 SER.#'d SETS

M31 Hogan/Flair/Sting		
M32 Sting/Steiner/Jarrett	12.00	30.00
M33 RVD/Anderson/Styles	10.00	25.00

2012 TRISTAR TNA Impact Reflexxions Triple Memorabilia Purple

STATED PRINT RUN 1 SER.#'d SET
UNPRICED DUE TO SCARCITY

M31 Hogan/Flair/Sting
M32 Sting/Steiner/Jarrett
M33 RVD/Anderson/Styles

2012 TRISTAR TNA Impact TENacious

COMPLETE SET (120)		
COMPLETE SET W/O SP (100)	8.00	20.00
UNOPENED BOX (20 PACKS)		
UNOPENED PACK (6 CARDS)		

*SILVER/30: 2.5X TO 6X BASIC CARDS
*GOLD/RED/10: UNPRICED DUE TO SCARCITY
*PURPLE/1: UNPRICED DUE TO SCARCITY

1 Jeff Jarrett	.25	.60
2 AJ Styles	.25	.60
3 James Storm	.15	.40
4 Jeremy Borash	.15	.40
5 Mike Tenay	.15	.40
6 Hulk Hogan	1.00	2.50
7 Brooke Hogan	.60	1.50
8 Sting	.60	1.50
9 Gail Kim	.40	1.00
10 Jeff Jarrett	.25	.60
11 Jeff Hardy	.60	1.50
12 Kurt Angle	.25	.60
13 Chris Sabin	.15	.40
14 Austin Aries RC	.25	.60
15 Bully Ray	.15	.40
16 Hector Guerrero RC	.15	.40
17 Kazarian	.15	.40
18 Eric Bischoff	.15	.40
19 Hernandez	.15	.40
20 Jeff Jarrett	.25	.60
21 Mickie James	1.00	2.50
22 Christopher Daniels	.15	.40
23 Mr. Anderson	.25	.60
24 ODB	.15	.40
25 Devon	.15	.40
26 Matt Morgan	.15	.40
27 Ric Flair	.75	2.00
28 AJ Styles	.25	.60
29 Rob Terry	.15	.40
30 Jeff Jarrett	.25	.60
31 Rob Van Dam	.25	.60
32 Jeff Hardy	.60	1.50
33 Kid Kash	.25	.60
34 Robbie E	.15	.40
35 Madison Rayne	.40	1.00
36 Bobby Roode	.15	.40
37 Bobby Roode	.15	.40
38 Bobby Roode	.15	.40
39 Bobby Roode	.15	.40
40 Jeff Jarrett	.25	.60
41 Jeremy Borash	.15	.40
42 Jeremy Borash	.15	.40
43 Jeremy Borash	.15	.40
44 Joseph Park	.25	.60
45 Alex Silva RC	.15	.40
46 Gunner	.15	.40
47 Mr. Anderson	.25	.60
48 Rosita	.25	.60
49 Samoa Joe	.15	.40
50 Jeff Jarrett	.25	.60
51 Sarita	.25	.60
52 Eric Young	.15	.40
53 Kurt Angle	.25	.60
54 Miss Tessmacher	.40	1.00
55 Sting	.60	1.50
56 Tara	.60	1.50
57 Garett Bischoff RC	.25	.60
58 Taz	.15	.40
59 SoCal Val	.40	1.00
60 Jeff Jarrett	.25	.60
61 Velvet Sky	.75	2.00
62 Angelina Love	.60	1.50
63 Jeff Hardy	.60	1.50
64 Zema Ion RC	.15	.40
65 Winter	.60	1.50
66 James Storm	.15	.40
67 Jessie Godderz RC	.15	.40
68 Matt Morgan	.15	.40
69 ODB	.15	.40
70 Jeff Jarrett	.25	.60
71 Christopher Daniels	.15	.40
72 Gail Kim	.40	1.00
73 Velvet Sky	.75	2.00
74 Doug Williams	.15	.40
75 Abyss	.25	.60
76 Crimson	.15	.40
77 Karen Jarrett	.25	.60
78 Eric Young	.15	.40
79 Magnus	.15	.40
80 Jeff Jarrett	.25	.60
81 D'Angelo Dinero	.15	.40
82 Jesse Sorensen RC	.15	.40
83 Jeff Hardy	.60	1.50
84 Christy Hemme	.60	1.50
85 Christopher Daniels	.15	.40
86 Hulk Hogan	1.00	2.50
87 Tara	.60	1.50
88 ODB	.15	.40
89 Magnus	.15	.40
90 AJ Styles	.25	.60
91 Miss Tessmacher	.40	1.00
92 Joe vs. Daniels vs. Styles	.15	.40
93 MSG Hulk Hogan Press Conference	1.00	2.50
94 IMPACT Wrestling Live on 1/4/2010	1.00	2.50
95 Beer Money vs. MCMG Best of 5	.15	.40
96 RVD Defeats Hardy and Styles	.25	.60
97 Sting Defeats Jarrett	.60	1.50
98 Samoa Joe vs. Kurt Angle	.25	.60
99 Gail Kim Wins 1st Knockouts Title	.40	1.00
100 Jeff Hardy/100	8.00	20.00
101 Team 3D/100	2.50	6.00
102 Kurt Angle/100	3.00	8.00
103 Hulk Hogan/100	4.00	10.00
104 Ric Flair/100	4.00	10.00
105 Jeff Hardy ART/100	8.00	20.00
106 Jeff Hardy ART/100	8.00	20.00
107 Jeff Hardy ART/100	8.00	20.00
108 Jeff Hardy ART/100	8.00	20.00
109 Jeff Hardy ART/100	8.00	20.00
110 Hulk Hogan/100	4.00	10.00
111 Hulk Hogan/100	4.00	10.00
112 Hulk Hogan/100	4.00	10.00
113 Hulk Hogan/100	4.00	10.00
114 Hulk Hogan/100	4.00	10.00
115 Sting/100	3.00	8.00
116 Sting/100	3.00	8.00
117 Sting/100	3.00	8.00
118 Sting/100	3.00	8.00

119 Sting/100	3.00	8.00
CL Checklist	.15	.40

2012 TRISTAR TNA Impact TENacious Autographed Memorabilia Silver

COMPLETE SET (5)
*GOLD/80: .5X TO 1.2X BASIC AU MEM
*BLUE/50: .6X TO 1.5X BASIC AU MEM
*RED/10: UNPRICED DUE TO SCARCITY
*PURPLE/1: UNPRICED DUE TO SCARCITY
STATED PRINT RUN 100 SER.#'d SETS

T2 Jeff Hardy	12.00	30.00
T3 Bobby Roode	5.00	12.00
T4 Sting	25.00	60.00
T5 Mickie James	15.00	40.00
T6 Rob Van Dam	10.00	25.00

2012 TRISTAR TNA Impact TENacious Autographed Memorabilia Blue

T2 Jeff Hardy	20.00	50.00
T3 Bobby Roode	8.00	20.00
T4 Sting	50.00	100.00
T5 Mickie James	30.00	60.00
T6 Rob Van Dam	15.00	40.00

2012 TRISTAR TNA Impact TENacious Autographs Gold

*RED/10: UNPRICED DUE TO SCARCITY
*PURPLE/1: UNPRICED DUE TO SCARCITY
STATED PRINT RUN 100 SER.#'d SETS

TEN1 Jeff Jarrett	6.00	15.00
TEN2 AJ Styles	5.00	12.00
TEN3 James Storm	4.00	10.00
TEN4 Gail Kim		
TEN8 Sting		
TEN9 Bobby Roode	4.00	10.00
TEN10 Jeff Hardy	25.00	50.00
TEN11 Kurt Angle	10.00	25.00
TEN12 Eric Bischoff		
TEN13 Mickie James	12.00	30.00
TEN14 Mr. Anderson	5.00	12.00
TEN15 Ric Flair		
TEN16 Rob Van Dam	10.00	25.00
TEN17 Austin Aries	10.00	25.00
TEN18 Brooke Tessmacher	10.00	25.00
TEN19 Samoa Joe	4.00	10.00
TEN20 Tara	8.00	20.00
TEN21 Bully Ray	5.00	12.00
TEN22 Devon	4.00	10.00
TEN23 Velvet Sky	8.00	20.00
TEN24 Garett Bischoff	4.00	10.00
TEN25 Abyss	4.00	10.00
TEN26 Christy Hemme	10.00	25.00
TEN27 Jeremy Borash	4.00	10.00
TEN28 ODB	4.00	10.00
TEN29 Magnus	4.00	10.00
TEN30 Crimson	4.00	10.00
TEN31 Doug Williams	4.00	10.00
TEN32 Robbie E	4.00	10.00
TEN33 Alex Shelley	4.00	10.00
TEN34 Rosita	5.00	12.00
TEN35 Gunner	5.00	12.00
TEN36 Kazarian	4.00	10.00
TEN37 Angelina Love	8.00	20.00
TEN38 Matt Morgan	4.00	10.00
TEN39 Chris Sabin	4.00	10.00
TEN40 Gail Kim	10.00	25.00
TEN41 Hernandez	5.00	12.00
TEN42 Madison Rayne	8.00	20.00
TEN43 Anarquia	4.00	10.00
TEN44 Winter	6.00	15.00
TEN45 Eric Young	4.00	10.00
TEN46 Sarita	5.00	12.00
TEN47 Shannon Moore	4.00	10.00
TEN48 Christopher Daniels	4.00	10.00
TEN49 Mike Tenay	4.00	10.00
TEN50 SoCal Val	5.00	12.00

2012 TRISTAR TNA Impact TENacious Celebrity Cut Signatures Gold

STATED PRINT RUN 5 SER.#'d SETS
UNPRICED DUE TO SCARCITY

1 Ace Young
2 Adam Pac-Man Jones
3 AJ Pierzynski
4 Brandon Jacobs
5 Brian Urlacher
6 Brooke Hogan
7 Chris Rock
8 Curtis Granderson
9 David Eckstein
10 Dennis Rodman
11 Johnny Damon
12 Juan Pablo Montoya
13 Ken Shamrock
14 Rowdy Roddy Piper
15 Steve McMichael
16 Tito Ortiz
17 Toby Keith
18 Tom Arnold

2012 TRISTAR TNA Impact TENacious Dual Autographs Gold

*RED/10: UNPRICED DUE TO SCARCITY
*PURPLE/1: UNPRICED DUE TO SCARCITY
STATED PRINT RUN 100 SER. #'d SETS

TEN21 B.Roode/J.Storm	8.00	20.00
TEN22 Eric & Garett Bischoff		
TEN23 J.Hardy/K.Angle		
TEN24 V.Sky/G.Kim	12.00	30.00
TEN25 K.Angle/AJ Styles		
TEN26 Sting/J.Hardy		
TEN28 ODB/E.Young	5.00	12.00
TEN210 B.Roode/E.Young	5.00	12.00
TEN211 A.Shelley/C.Sabin	5.00	12.00
TEN212 K.Angle/Samoa Joe	10.00	25.00
TEN213 Sting/B.Roode		
TEN214 Sting/J.Jarrett		
TEN215 B.Ray/Devon		
TEN216 Jeff & Karen Jarrett		
TEN217 Kazarian/T.Brooks	8.00	20.00
TEN218 K.Angle/Sting		
TEN219 Hernandez/Anarquia	5.00	12.00
TEN220 Kazarian/C.Daniels	5.00	12.00

2012 TRISTAR TNA Impact TENacious Dual Memorabilia Silver

*GOLD/80: .5X TO 1.2X BASIC MEM
*BLUE/50: .6X TO 1.5X BASIC MEM
*RED/10: UNPRICED DUE TO SCARCITY
*PURPLE/1: UNPRICED DUE TO SCARCITY
STATED PRINT RUN 100 SER.#'d SETS

T10 Eric & Garett Bischoff	3.00	8.00
T11 Devon/B.Ray	3.00	8.00
T12 B.Roode/J.Storm	3.00	8.00
T13 J.Hardy/Mr.Anderson	6.00	15.00
T14 K.Angle/AJ Styles	3.00	8.00

2012 TRISTAR TNA Impact TENacious Quad Autographs Gold

*RED/10: UNPRICED DUE TO SCARCITY
*PURPLE/1: UNPRICED DUE TO SCARCITY

TEN41 Jarrett/Styles/Storm/Borash		
TEN43 Storm/Roode/Sabin/Shelley	10.00	25.00

2012 TRISTAR TNA Impact TENacious Six Autographs Gold

*RED/10: UNPRICED DUE TO SCARCITY
*PURPLE/1: UNPRICED DUE TO SCARCITY
STATED ODDS

TEN61 Styles/Samoa Joe/Daniels
Aries/Sabin/Kash
TEN62 Young/Styles/Terry
Abyss/Williams/Devon
TEN63 Angle/Sting/Styles
Roode/RVD/Hardy
TEN64 Kim/Love/Tara
Rayne/James/Sky

2012 TRISTAR TNA Impact TENacious Triple Autographs Gold

*RED/10: UNPRICED DUE TO SCARCITY
*PURPLE/1: UNPRICED DUE TO SCARCITY
STATED ODDS

TEN31 Styles/Samoa Joe/Daniels
TEN32 Kurt & Karen Angle/Jarrett

2012 TRISTAR TNA Impact TENacious Triple Memorabilia Blue

T15 Jarrett/Storm/Styles	6.00	15.00
T17 Kim/Sky/James	10.00	25.00

2009 TRISTAR TNA Knockouts

COMPLETE SET W/SP (108)	20.00	50.00
COMPLETE SET W/O SP (90)	12.00	30.00
UNOPENED BOX (18 PACKS)		
UNOPENED PACK (4 CARDS)		

*SILVER: 4X TO 10X BASIC CARDS
*GOLD/10: UNPRICED DUE TO SCARCITY
*PURPLE/1: UNPRICED DUE TO SCARCITY
*P.P.BLACK/1: UNPRICED DUE TO SCARCITY
*P.P.CYAN/1: UNPRICED DUE TO SCARCITY
*P.P.MAGENTA/1: UNPRICED DUE TO SCARCITY
*P.P.YELLOW/1: UNPRICED DUE TO SCARCITY
INSTANT WIN CARD RANDOMLY INSERTED
90-107 ARE REVEALED PACKS EXCLUSIVE

1 Angelina Love	.50	1.25
2 Awesome Kong	.15	.40
3 Christy Hemme	.60	1.50
4 The Governor	.25	.60
5 Jacqueline	.20	.50
6 Jenna Morasca	.40	1.00
7 Lauren	.25	.60
8 Madison Rayne KO RC	.40	1.00
9 ODB	.15	.40
10 Raisha Saeed	.15	.40
11 Rhaka Khan	.20	.50
12 Roxxi	.20	.50
13 Sharmell	.15	.40
14 SoCal Val	.40	1.00
15 Sojournor Bolt KO RC	.15	.40
16 Taylor Wilde	.40	1.00
17 Traci Brooks	.40	1.00
18 Velvet Sky	.50	1.25
19 Cute Kip	.12	.30
20 The Beautiful People	.50	1.25
21 Angelina Love	.50	1.25
22 Christy Hemme	.60	1.50
23 Lauren	.25	.60
24 ODB	.15	.40
25 Roxxi	.20	.50
26 Sharmell	.15	.40
27 SoCal Val	.40	1.00
28 Taylor Wilde	.40	1.00
29 Traci Brooks	.40	1.00
30 Velvet Sky	.50	1.25
31 Angelina Love	.50	1.25
32 Awesome Kong	.15	.40
33 Dixie Carter	.25	.60
34 Jacqueline	.20	.50
35 Lauren	.25	.60
36 ODB	.15	.40
37 Raisha Saeed	.15	.40
38 Traci Brooks	.40	1.00
39 Christy Hemme	.60	1.50
40 Rhaka Khan	.20	.50
41 Roxxi	.20	.50
42 Sharmell	.15	.40
43 SoCal Val	.40	1.00
44 Sojournor Bolt TT	.15	.40
45 Taylor Wilde	.40	1.00
46 Velvet Sky	.50	1.25
47 Jacqueline	.20	.50
48 Sojournor Bolt FF	.15	.40
49 ODB	.15	.40
50 Traci Brooks	.40	1.00
51 Angelina Love	.50	1.25
52 Awesome Kong	.15	.40
53 Christy Hemme	.60	1.50
54 Jacqueline	.20	.50
55 Lauren	.25	.60
56 ODB	.15	.40
57 Sharmell	.15	.40
58 SoCal Val	.40	1.00
59 Sojournor Bolt OUT	.15	.40
60 Taylor Wilde	.40	1.00
61 Traci Brooks	.40	1.00
62 Velvet Sky	.50	1.25
63 Angelina Love	.50	1.25
64 Awesome Kong	.15	.40
65 Christy Hemme	.60	1.50
66 Dixie Carter	.25	.60
67 Roxxi	.20	.50
68 Sharmell	.15	.40
69 ODB	.15	.40
70 Taylor Wilde	.40	1.00
71 Traci Brooks	.40	1.00
72 Velvet Sky	.50	1.25
73 Angelina Love / AJ Styles	.50	1.25
74 Awesome Kong / Samoa Joe	.15	.40
75 Christy Hemme / Robert Roode	.60	1.50
76 Dixie Carter / Mick Foley	.50	1.25
77 Jacqueline / James Storm	.20	.50
78 Jenna Morasca / Brother Ray	.40	1.00
79 Lauren / Chris Sabin	.25	.60
80 ODB / Rhino	.15	.40
81 Raisha Saeed / Alex Shelley	.15	.40
82 Rhaka Khan / Kurt Angle	.60	1.50

83 Roxxi / Jim Cornette	.20	.50
84 Sharmell / Mike Tenay	.15	.40
85 SoCal Val / Consequences Creed	.40	1.00
86 Sojournor Bolt/Don West MC	.15	.40
87 Taylor Wilde / Jay Lethal	.40	1.00
88 Traci Brooks / Sting	.50	1.25
89 Velvet Sky / Brother Devon	.50	1.25
90 Traci Brooks	1.25	3.00
91 Angelina Love	1.50	4.00
92 SoCal Val	1.25	3.00
93 Christy Hemme	2.00	5.00
94 Velvet Sky	1.50	4.00
95 Lauren	.75	2.00
96 ODB	.50	1.25
97 Traci Brooks	1.25	3.00
98 SoCal Val	1.25	3.00
99 Christy Hemme	2.00	5.00
100 Angelina Love	1.50	4.00
101 Roxxi	.60	1.50
102 Jenna Morasca	1.25	3.00
103 Velvet Sky	1.50	4.00
104 SoCal Val	1.25	3.00
105 Christy Hemme	2.00	5.00
106 Angelina Love/Velvet Sky	1.50	4.00
107 Traci Brooks/SoCal Val	1.25	3.00
CL Checklist	.20	.50
NNO Instant Winner		

2009 TRISTAR TNA Knockouts Autographed Dual Kiss Gold

*TURQUOISE/10: UNPRICED DUE TO SCARCITY
*PURPLE/1: UNPRICED DUE TO SCARCITY
STATED PRINT RUN 25 SER.#'d SETS

2K1 A.Love/V.Sky
2K2 C.Hemme/T.Brooks
2K3 Jenna/Sharmell
2K4 S.Val/Lauren

2009 TRISTAR TNA Knockouts Autographed Kiss

STATED PRINT RUN 10 SER.#'d SETS

K1 Angelina Love
K2 Awesome Kong
K3 Jacqueline
K4 Jenna
K5 Lauren
K6 Madison Rayne
K7 ODB
K8 Roxxi
K9 Sharmell
K10 Sojournor Bolt
K11 Taylor Wilde
K12 Velvet Sky
K13 Christy Hemme
K14 SoCal Val
K15 Traci Brooks

2009 TRISTAR TNA Knockouts Knockout Kiss

*TURQUOISE/25: .5X TO 1.25X BASIC KISS
*GREEN/5: UNPRICED DUE TO SCARCITY
*PURPLE/1: UNPRICED DUE TO SCARCITY
*P.P.BLACK/1: UNPRICED DUE TO SCARCITY
*P.P.CYAN/1: UNPRICED DUE TO SCARCITY
*P.P.MAGENTA/1: UNPRICED DUE TO SCARCITY
*P.P.YELLOW/1: UNPRICED DUE TO SCARCITY
STATED PRINT RUN 75 SER.#'d SETS
K12-K15 ARE REVEALED PACKS EXCLUSIVE

K1 Angelina Love	30.00	60.00
K2 Awesome Kong	12.00	30.00
K3 Jacqueline	8.00	20.00
K4 Jenna	25.00	50.00
K5 Lauren	15.00	40.00
K6 Madison Rayne	25.00	50.00
K7 ODB	12.00	30.00
K8 Roxxi	10.00	25.00
K9 Sharmell	10.00	25.00
K10 Sojournor Bolt	8.00	20.00
K11 Taylor Wilde	25.00	50.00
K12 Velvet Sky	30.00	60.00
K13 Christy Hemme	25.00	50.00
K14 SoCal Val	15.00	40.00
K15 Traci Brooks	12.00	30.00

2009 TRISTAR TNA Knockouts Signature Curves

*GOLD/75: .5X TO 1.2X BASIC AUTOS
*TURQUOISE/25: UNPRICED DUE TO SCARCITY
*PINK/10: UNPRICED DUE TO SCARCITY
*GREEN/5: UNPRICED DUE TO SCARCITY
*PURPLE/1: UNPRICED DUE TO SCARCITY
*P.P.BLACK/1: UNPRICED DUE TO SCARCITY
*P.P.CYAN/1: UNPRICED DUE TO SCARCITY
*P.P.MAGENTA/1: UNPRICED DUE TO SCARCITY
*P.P.YELLOW/1: UNPRICED DUE TO SCARCITY
STATED ODDS 1:9

KA1 Angelina Love	10.00	25.00
KA2 Awesome Kong	6.00	15.00
KA3 Christy Hemme	10.00	25.00
KA4 Dixie Carter	6.00	15.00
KA5 Jacqueline	6.00	15.00
KA6 Jenna	8.00	20.00
KA7 Madison Rayne	10.00	25.00
KA8 Raisha Saeed	6.00	15.00
KA9 Roxxi	6.00	15.00
KA10 Sharmell	6.00	15.00
KA11 SoCal Val	8.00	20.00
KA12 Sojournor Bolt	8.00	20.00
KA13 Taylor Wilde	8.00	20.00
KA14 Traci Brooks	8.00	20.00
KA15 Velvet Sky	10.00	25.00
KA24 Lauren	10.00	25.00
KA25 ODB	8.00	20.00

2009 TRISTAR TNA Knockouts Six-Person Signature Curves Gold

*TURQUOISE/25: X TO X BASIC AUTOS
*GREEN/5: UNPRICED DUE TO SCARCITY
*PURPLE/1: UNPRICED DUE TO SCARCITY
*P.P.BLACK/1: UNPRICED DUE TO SCARCITY
*P.P.CYAN/1: UNPRICED DUE TO SCARCITY
*P.P.MAGENTA/1: UNPRICED DUE TO SCARCITY
*P.P.YELLOW/1: UNPRICED DUE TO SCARCITY
STATED ODDS

KA27 Sharmell/Booker T/Nash Angle/Sting/Steiner

2009 TRISTAR TNA Knockouts Top Drawer Memorabilia Gold

*TURQUOISE/75: .5X TO 1.2X BASIC MEM
*PINK/10: UNPRICED DUE TO SCARCITY
*PURPLE/1: UNPRICED DUE TO SCARCITY
STATED PRINT RUN 175 SER.#'d SETS

TD1 Angelina Love	10.00	25.00
TD2 Christy Hemme	10.00	25.00
TD3 Jenna Morasca	6.00	15.00
TD4 Lauren	10.00	25.00
TD5 Madison Rayne	10.00	25.00
TD6 Roxxi	6.00	15.00
TD7 SoCal Val	8.00	20.00
TD8 Sojournor Bolt	6.00	15.00
TD9 Taylor Wilde	10.00	25.00
TD10 Traci Brooks	6.00	15.00
TD11 Velvet Sky	10.00	25.00

2010 TRISTAR TNA New Era

COMPLETE SET (101)	30.00	75.00
UNOPENED BOX (20 PACKS)		
UNOPENED PACK (6 CARDS)		
COMPLETE SET W/O SP (90)	10.00	25.00

*SILVER: 2.5X TO 6X BASIC CARDS
*GOLD/10: UNPRICED DUE TO SCARCITY
*PURPLE/1: UNPRICED DUE TO SCARCITY
OBAK STATED ODDS 2:HOBBY BOX
OBAK ANNOUNCED PRINT RUN 600

1 Hulk Hogan	1.00	2.50
2 Hulk Hogan	1.00	2.50
3 Hulk Hogan	1.00	2.50
4 Hulk Hogan	1.00	2.50
5 Hulk Hogan	1.00	2.50
6 Hulk Hogan	1.00	2.50
7 Hulk Hogan	1.00	2.50
8 Ric Flair	.75	2.00
9 Jeff Hardy	.60	1.50
10 Scott Hall	.15	.40
11 Syxx-Pac	.25	.60
12 Eric Bischoff	.15	.40
13 Shannon Moore	.15	.40
14 Orlando Jordan	.15	.40
15 Bubba the Love Sponge RC	.25	.60
16 Mr. Anderson	.25	.60
17 The Nasty Boys	.15	.40
18 Generation Me	.15	.40
19 The Pope D'Angelo Dinero	.15	.40
20 Desmond Wolfe RC	.15	.40
21 Brian Kendrick	.25	.60
22 Jimmy Hart	.25	.60
23 Sting	.60	1.50
24 Kurt Angle	.60	1.50
25 Mick Foley	.75	2.00
26 Kevin Nash	.60	1.50
27 Jeff Jarrett	.40	1.00
28 James Storm	.25	.60
29 Alex Shelley	.25	.60
30 AJ Styles	.40	1.00
31 Team 3D	.25	.60
32 British Invasion	.15	.40
33 Taz & Mike Tenay	.15	.40
34 Motor City Machineguns	.25	.60
35 Matt Morgan	.15	.40
36 Amazing Red	.15	.40
37 Robert Roode	.15	.40
38 Suicide	.15	.40
39 Abyss	.25	.60
40 Lethal Consequences	.15	.40
41 Eric Young	.15	.40
42 Beer Money, Inc.	.25	.60
43 Samoa Joe	.25	.60
44 Daniels	.15	.40
45 Taylor Wilde	.40	1.00
46 Homicide	.20	.50
47 Daffney	.60	1.50
48 Hernandez	.15	.40
49 The Beautiful People	.75	2.00
50 Rob Terry	.15	.40
51 Lacey Von Erich RC	.75	2.00
52 Tara	.60	1.50
53 Hamada	.40	1.00
54 Sarita	.40	1.00
55 ODB	.25	.60
56 Jesse Neal	.15	.40
57 Velvet Sky	.75	2.00
58 Magnus	.15	.40
59 Angelina Love	.60	1.50
60 Doug Williams	.15	.40
61 Madison Rayne	.60	1.50
62 Rhino	.25	.60
63 Kazarian	.15	.40
64 Chris Sabin	.15	.40
65 Dr. Stevie	.15	.40
66 Christy Hemme	.60	1.50
67 Jeremy Borash	.15	.40
68 Dixie Carter	.40	1.00
69 Bob Carter RC	.15	.40
70 Rob Van Dam	.40	1.00
71 Destination X	.15	.40
72 Lockdown	.15	.40
73 Hulk Hogan/Eric Bischoff	.75	2.00
74 Ric Flair/AJ Styles	.60	1.50
75 Scott Hall/Syxx-Pac	.20	.50
76 Hulk Hogan/Abyss	.75	2.00
77 Matt Morgan/Hernandez	.15	.40
78 Ric Flair	.60	1.50
79 Ric Flair	.60	1.50
80 Ric Flair	.60	1.50
81 TNA iMPACT! Moves	.75	2.00
82 Hogan's Wrestling Return	.75	2.00
83 H.Hogan/R.Flair	.75	2.00
84 The Main Event	.75	2.00
85 Why, Sting, Why?	.50	1.25
86 Van Dam Arrives in TNA	.30	.75
87 The Band: Off Key	.20	.50
88 Kurt Angle	.50	1.25
89 Jeff Hardy Returns	.50	1.25
90 What A Night!	.75	2.00
91 Hulk Hogan OBAK SP	4.00	10.00
92 Ric Flair OBAK SP	3.00	8.00
93 Sting OBAK SP	2.50	6.00
94 Kevin Nash OBAK SP	2.50	6.00
95 Jeff Jarrett OBAK SP	1.50	4.00
96 Kurt Angle OBAK SP	2.50	6.00
97 Mick Foley OBAK SP	3.00	8.00
98 AJ Styles OBAK SP	1.50	4.00
99 Beautiful People OBAK SP	3.00	8.00
100 Hogan/Flair OBAK SP	4.00	10.00
CL Checklist	.15	.40

2010 TRISTAR TNA New Era Autographed Hulk Hogan Bonus Red

*PURPLE/1: UNPRICED DUE TO SCARCITY
STATED PRINT RUN 9 SER.#'d SETS
UNPRICED DUE TO SCARCITY

H1 Hulk Hogan holding rope
H2 Hulk Hogan black shirt in ring
H3 Hulk Hogan ripping shirt
H4 Hulk Hogan no shirt white bkgrnd

H5 Hulk Hogan w/boa		
H6 Hulk Hogan black shirt white bkgrnd		

2010 TRISTAR TNA New Era Autographed Memorabilia Silver

STATED PRINT RUN 199 SER.#'d SETS

M13 Hulk Hogan		
M14 Ric Flair		
M15 Mick Foley		
M16 Sting		
M17 AJ Styles		
M18 Velvet Sky	15.00	40.00

2010 TRISTAR TNA New Era Autographs Silver

*GOLD/50: .5X TO 1.2X BASIC AUTOS
*GREEN/15-25: X TO X BASIC AUTOS
*RED/5: UNPRICED DUE TO SCARCITY
*PURPLE/1: UNPRICED DUE TO SCARCITY

A1 Hulk Hogan		
A2 Sting		
A3 Mick Foley	10.00	25.00
A4 Kurt Angle	8.00	20.00
A5 Sean Morley	6.00	15.00
A6 Mr. Anderson	8.00	20.00
A7 Orlando Jordan	8.00	20.00
A8 D'Angelo Dinero	8.00	20.00
A9 Tara	6.00	15.00
A10 Desmond Wolfe	4.00	10.00
A11 Taz	4.00	10.00
A12 Kevin Nash	8.00	20.00
A13 Brian Kendrick	6.00	15.00
A14 AJ Styles	8.00	20.00
A15 Jeff Jarrett	5.00	12.00
A16 Sarita	6.00	15.00
A17 Amazing Red	4.00	10.00
A18 Lacey Von Erich	12.00	30.00
A19 Abyss	4.00	10.00
A20 Rob Van Dam	12.00	30.00
A21 Hernandez	4.00	10.00
A22 Taylor Wilde	6.00	15.00
A23 Samoa Joe	8.00	20.00
A24 Awesome Kong	5.00	12.00
A25 Dr. Stevie	5.00	12.00
A26 Brutus Magnus	4.00	10.00
A27 Velvet Sky	10.00	25.00
A28 Jeremy Borash	4.00	10.00
A29 Madison Rayne	8.00	20.00
A30 Doug Williams	4.00	10.00
A31 Christy Hemme	10.00	25.00
A32 Suicide	4.00	10.00
A33 Hamada	8.00	20.00
A34 Robert Roode	4.00	10.00
A35 Brian Knobs	4.00	10.00
A36 Dixie Carter	5.00	12.00
A37 Daniels	4.00	10.00
A38 Bubba the Love Sponge	10.00	25.00
A39 ODB	5.00	12.00
A40 Homicide	4.00	10.00
A41 Matt Morgan	4.00	10.00
A42 Daffney	10.00	25.00
A43 Jesse Neal	4.00	10.00
A44 James Storm	4.00	10.00
A45 SoCal Val	6.00	15.00
A46 Jeff Hardy	20.00	40.00
A47 Traci Brooks	6.00	15.00
A48 Jerry Sags	4.00	10.00
A49 Angelina Love	8.00	20.00
A50 Alex Shelley	4.00	10.00
A51 Syxx-Pac	6.00	15.00
A52 Shannon Moore	6.00	15.00
A53 Jay Lethal	4.00	10.00
A54 Rob Terry	4.00	10.00
A55 Ric Flair		

2010 TRISTAR TNA New Era Dual Autographs Silver

*GOLD/50: X TO X BASIC AUTOS
*GREEN/25: X TO X BASIC AUTOS
*RED/5: UNPRICED DUE TO SCARCITY
*PURPLE/1: UNPRICED DUE TO SCARCITY
RANDOMLY INSERTED INTO RETAIL PACKS

1 H.Hogan/Sting
2 M.Foley/Abyss
3 H.Hogan/D.Carter
4 K.Angle/J.Jarrett
5 K.Nash/E.Young
6 H.Hogan/M.Foley
7 K.Angle/Mr.Anderson
8 Taz/M.Tenay
9 H.Hogan/K.Nash
10 A.Love/Lacey Von Erich
11 D.Dinero/O.Jordan
12 B.Knobs/J.Sags
13 A.Kong/Hamada
14 K.Angle/D.Wolfe
15 M.Morgan/Hernandez
16 V.Sky/M.Rayne
17 H.Hogan/K.Angle
18 A.Shelley/C.Sabin
19 J.Storm/R.Roode
20 R.Flair/AJ Styles
21 Sting/R.Flair
22 H.Hogan/R.Flair

2010 TRISTAR TNA New Era Dual Autographs Gold

STATED PRINT RUN 50 SER.#'d SETS

1 H.Hogan/Sting
2 M.Foley/Abyss
3 H.Hogan/D.Carter
4 K.Angle/J.Jarrett
5 K.Nash/E.Young
6 H.Hogan/M.Foley
7 K.Angle/Mr.Anderson
8 Taz/M.Tenay
9 H.Hogan/K.Nash
10 Angelina Love/L.Von Erich
11 D.Dinero/O.Jordan
12 B.Knobs/J.Sags
13 A.Kong/Hamada
14 K.Angle/D.Wolfe
15 M.Morgan/Hernandez
16 V.Sky/M.Rayne
17 H.Hogan/K.Angle
18 A.Shelley/C.Sabin
19 J.Storm/R.Roode
20 R.Flair/AJ Styles
21 Sting/R.Flair
22 H.Hogan/R.Flair

2010 TRISTAR TNA New Era Dual Autographs Green

*GREEN: X TO X BASIC AUTOS
STATED PRINT RUN 25 SER.#'d SETS

1 H.Hogan/Sting		
2 M.Foley/Abyss	20.00	40.00
3 H.Hogan/D.Carter		
4 K.Angle/J.Jarrett	25.00	50.00
5 K.Nash/E.Young	15.00	30.00
6 H.Hogan/M.Foley		
7 K.Angle/Mr.Anderson	20.00	40.00
8 Taz/M.Tenay	10.00	20.00
9 H.Hogan/K.Nash		
10 Angelina Love/L.Von Erich	20.00	40.00
11 D.Dinero/O.Jordan	20.00	40.00
12 B.Knobs/J.Sags	15.00	30.00
13 A.Kong/Hamada	15.00	30.00
14 K.Angle/D.Wolfe	20.00	40.00
15 M.Morgan/Hernandez	15.00	30.00
16 V.Sky/M.Rayne	20.00	40.00
17 H.Hogan/K.Angle		
18 A.Shelley/C.Sabin	10.00	20.00
19 J.Storm/R.Roode	15.00	30.00
20 R.Flair/AJ Styles		
21 Sting/R.Flair		
22 H.Hogan/R.Flair		

2010 TRISTAR TNA New Era Dual Memorabilia Silver

STATED ODDS

M10 J.Storm/R.Roode	4.00	10.00

2010 TRISTAR TNA New Era Memorabilia Silver

*GOLD/50: .5X TO 1.2X BASIC MEM
*RED/25: .6X TO 1.5X BASIC MEM
*PURPLE/1: UNPRICED DUE TO SCARCITY
OVERALL MEM ODDS ONE PER HOBBY BOX
STATED PRINT RUN 99-199

M1 Hulk Hogan		
M2 Ric Flair		
M3 Mick Foley	5.00	12.00
M4 Sting	6.00	15.00
M5 Kurt Angle	5.00	12.00
M6 Rob Van Dam	4.00	10.00
M7 Mr. Anderson	4.00	10.00
M8 Syxx-Pac	4.00	10.00

2010 TRISTAR TNA New Era Quad Autographs Silver

*GOLD/50: X TO X BASIC AUTOS
*GREEN/25: X TO X BASIC AUTOS
*RED/5: UNPRICED DUE TO SCARCITY
*PURPLE/1: UNPRICED DUE TO SCARCITY
RANDOMLY INSERTED INTO RETAIL PACKS

1 Hogan/Jarrett/Angle/Foley
2 Sky/Rayne/Von Erich/Love
3 Hogan/Flair/Sting/Nash
4 Wilde/Sarita/Hamada/A.Kong
5 Hogan/Abyss/Flair/Styles

2010 TRISTAR TNA New Era Triple Autographs Silver

*GOLD/50: X TO X BASIC AUTOS
*GREEN/25: X TO X BASIC AUTOS
*RED/5: UNPRICED DUE TO SCARCITY
*PURPLE/1: UNPRICED DUE TO SCARCITY
RANDOMLY INSERTED INTO RETAIL PACKS

1 Hogan/Nash/6-Pac
2 Sky/Rayne/Von Erich
3 Terry/Magnus/Williams
4 Tara/Hemme/Brooks

2010 TRISTAR TNA New Era Triple Autographs Green

*GREEN: X TO X BASIC AUTOS
STATED PRINT RUN 25 SER.#'d SETS

1 Hogan/Nash/6-Pac		
2 Sky/Rayne/Von Erich	30.00	60.00
3 Terry/Magnus/Williams	15.00	30.00
4 Tara/Hemme/Brooks	20.00	40.00

2010 TRISTAR TNA New Era Triple Autographs Red

STATED PRINT RUN 5 SER.#'d SETS
UNPRICED DUE TO SCARCITY

1 Hogan/Nash/6-Pac
2 Sky/Rayne/Von Erich
3 Terry/Magnus/Williams
4 Tara/Hemme/Brooks

2010 TRISTAR TNA Obak National Convention

COMPLETE SET (3)	4.00	10.00
TNA1 Rob Van Dam	2.00	5.00
TNA2 Mick Foley	2.50	6.00
TNA3 Kurt Angle	2.00	5.00

2011 TRISTAR TNA Signature Impact

COMPLETE SET (100)	20.00	40.00
COMPLETE SET W/O SP (90)	10.00	25.00
UNOPENED BOX (20 PACKS)		
UNOPENED PACK (6 CARDS)		

*SILVER/50: 2.5X TO 6X BASIC CARDS
*SILVER SP/50: .75X TO 2X BASIC CARDS
*GOLD/5: UNPRICED DUE TO SCARCITY
*PURPLE/1: UNPRICED DUE TO SCARCITY

1 Hulk Hogan	1.00	2.50
2 Ric Flair	.75	2.00
3 Sting	.60	1.50
4 Jeff Jarrett	.25	.60
5 Scott Steiner	.25	.60
6 Jeff Hardy	.60	1.50
7 Matt Hardy	.40	1.00
8 Velvet Sky	.75	2.00
9 Abyss	.25	.60
10 Kurt Angle	.25	.60
11 Sting	.60	1.50
12 Ric Flair	.75	2.00
13 Matt Hardy/Jeff Hardy	.60	1.50
14 AJ Styles	.25	.60
15 Velvet Sky	.75	2.00
16 Scott Steiner	.25	.60
17 Mr. Anderson	.25	.60
18 Anarquia RC	.15	.40
19 Devon	.15	.40
20 Dixie Carter	.40	1.00
21 Crimson	.15	.40
22 Angelina Love	.60	1.50
23 Eric Bischoff	.15	.40
24 AJ Styles	.25	.60
25 Daniels	.15	.40
26 Gunner RC	.15	.40
27 Murphy RC	.15	.40
28 Tara	.60	1.50

29 Ric Flair	.75	2.00
30 Hulk Hogan	1.00	2.50
31 Mickie James	1.00	2.50
32 Sting	.60	1.50
33 Abyss	.25	.60
34 Mr. Anderson	.25	.60
35 James Storm	.15	.40
36 Karen Jarrett	.25	.60
37 Bully Ray	.15	.40
38 Douglas Williams	.15	.40
39 Mickie James	1.00	2.50
40 Mr. Anderson	.25	.60
41 Alex Shelley	.15	.40
42 Chris Sabin	.15	.40
43 Matt Morgan	.15	.40
44 Rob Van Dam	.25	.60
45 Hulk Hogan	1.00	2.50
46 Samoa Joe	.15	.40
47 Taz	.15	.40
48 RVD	.25	.60
49 Madison Rayne	.40	1.00
50 Orlando Jordan	.15	.40
51 Mike Tenay	.15	.40
52 Taz	.15	.40
53 Jeremy Borash	.15	.40
54 Christy Hemme	.60	1.50
55 Eric Young	.15	.40
56 Ms. Tessmacher	.40	1.00
57 Rob Terry	.15	.40
58 Amazing Red	.15	.40
59 Hernandez	.15	.40
60 Magnus	.15	.40
61 K.Angle/J.Jarrett	.25	.60
62 Lockdown 2011	.15	.40
63 Karen Jarrett's TNA Return	.25	.60
64 Karen on Angle & Jarrett	.25	.60
65 The Jarrett/Angle Bunch	.15	.40
66 Robbie E	.15	.40
67 Robert Roode	.15	.40
68 Shannon Moore	.15	.40
69 Jesse Neal	.15	.40
70 Cookie	.15	.40
71 D'Angelo Dinero	.15	.40
72 Rosita RC	.25	.60
73 Generation Me	.15	.40
74 Samoa Joe	.15	.40
75 Mexican America	.15	.40
76 Sarita	.25	.60
77 Suicide	.15	.40
78 Brian Kendrick	.15	.40
79 Winter	.60	1.50
80 Kazarian	.15	.40
81 Immortal	.15	.40
82 Fortune	.15	.40
83 Bully Ray	.15	.40
84 Christy Hemme	.60	1.50
85 Kurt Angle	.25	.60
86 Beer Money	.15	.40
87 Eric Bischoff	.15	.40
88 Scott Steiner	.25	.60
89 Samoa Joe	.15	.40
90 Hogan/Flair/Sting	3.00	8.00
91 Hulk Hogan SP	3.00	8.00
92 Hulk Hogan SP	3.00	8.00
93 Hulk Hogan SP	3.00	8.00
94 Ric Flair SP	3.00	8.00
95 Ric Flair SP	3.00	8.00
96 Ric Flair SP	3.00	8.00
97 Sting SP	3.00	8.00
98 Sting SP	3.00	8.00
99 Sting SP	3.00	8.00
CL Checklist	.15	.40

2011 TRISTAR TNA Signature Impact Autographs Silver

*GOLD/25: .6X TO 1.25X BASIC AUTOS
*RED/5: UNPRICED DUE TO SCARCITY
*PURPLE/1: UNPRICED DUE TO SCARCITY
STATED PRINT RUN 99 SER.#'d SETS

S8 Jeff Hardy	25.00	50.00
S9 Matt Hardy	15.00	30.00
S10 Rob Van Dam	15.00	30.00
S11 Mickie James	30.00	60.00
S12 Scott Steiner		
S13 Anarquia	15.00	30.00
S14 Jeff Jarrett	12.00	25.00
S15 Kazarian	6.00	15.00
S16 Winter	12.00	25.00
S17 Kurt Angle	20.00	40.00
S18 Karen Jarrett	6.00	15.00
S19 Abyss	6.00	15.00
S20 Matt Morgan	6.00	15.00
S21 Kendrick	6.00	15.00
S22 Mr. Anderson	10.00	20.00
S23 Velvet Sky	20.00	40.00
S24 Robert Roode	10.00	20.00
S25 Ms. Tessmacher	12.00	25.00
S26 Sarita	6.00	15.00
S27 Jesse Neal	6.00	15.00
S28 Amazing Red	6.00	15.00
S29 D'Angelo Dinero	6.00	15.00
S30 Magnus	6.00	15.00
S31 Angelina Love	10.00	20.00
S32 Orlando Jordan	6.00	15.00
S33 Mick Foley	10.00	20.00
S34 Crimson	6.00	15.00
S35 Daniels	6.00	15.00
S36 Madison Rayne	10.00	20.00
S37 Murphy		
S38 Tara	10.00	20.00
S39 James Storm	6.00	15.00
S40 Jeremy Buck	6.00	15.00
S41 Rosita	12.00	25.00
S42 Rob Terry	6.00	15.00
S43 SoCal Val	10.00	20.00
S44 Jay Lethal	6.00	15.00
S45 Mike Tenay	6.00	15.00
S46 Jeremy Borash	6.00	15.00
S47 Samoa Joe	6.00	15.00
S48 Eric Young	6.00	15.00
S49 AJ Styles	10.00	20.00
S50 Christy Hemme	10.00	20.00
S51 Shannon Moore	6.00	15.00
S52 Max Buck	6.00	15.00
S53 Chyna	10.00	25.00
S54 Eric Bischoff		

2011 TRISTAR TNA Signature Impact Dual Autographs Silver

*GOLD/25: .6X TO 1.25X BASIC AUTOS
*RED/5: UNPRICED DUE TO SCARCITY
*PURPLE/1: UNPRICED DUE TO SCARCITY
STATED PRINT RUN 99 SER.#'d SETS

1 H.Hogan/R.Flair		
2 Jeff & Matt Hardy		
3 Jeff & Karen Jarrett		
4 Sting/RVD		
5 H.Hogan/Sting		
6 M.Hardy/RVD		
7 H.Hogan/M.Hardy		
8 Sarita/Rosita	10.00	20.00
9 Hernandez/Anarquia		
10 AJ Styles/Daniels	10.00	20.00
11 RVD/H.Hogan		
12 M.James/Tara	20.00	40.00
13 Tara/M.Rayne	10.00	20.00
14 Gunner/Murphy	6.00	15.00
15 Magnus/D.Williams	6.00	15.00
16 Max & Jeremy Buck	6.00	15.00
17 S.Steiner/H.Hogan		
18 Crimson/Abyss	6.00	15.00
19 K.Angle/J.Jarrett		
20 S.Moore/J.Neal		
21 M.Foley/RVD		
22 C.Hemme/S.Val	10.00	20.00
23 Hernandez/M.Morgan	6.00	15.00
24 Robbie E/Cookie	6.00	15.00
25 Winter/A.Love	10.00	20.00
26 A.Love/V.Sky	15.00	30.00
27 Chyna/K.Angle		

2011 TRISTAR TNA Signature Impact Dual Memorabilia Silver

STATED PRINT RUN 199 SER.#'d SETS

M11 Jeff & Matt Hardy

2011 TRISTAR TNA Signature Impact Eight Autographs Silver

*GOLD/25: UNPRICED DUE TO SCARCITY
*RED/5: UNPRICED DUE TO SCARCITY
*PURPLE/1: UNPRICED DUE TO SCARCITY
STATED PRINT RUN 99 SER.#'d SETS

1 Hogan/Flair/Sting/Steiner
Angle/J.Hardy/RVD/M.Hardy
2 Hogan/Tara/Flair/James
Sting/Sky/J.Hardy/Love
3 James/Tara/Love/Sky
Rayne/Winter/Rosita/Sarita

2011 TRISTAR TNA Signature Impact Five Autographs Silver

*GOLD/25: X TO X BASIC AUTOS
*RED/5: UNPRICED DUE TO SCARCITY
*PURPLE/1: UNPRICED DUE TO SCARCITY
STATED PRINT RUN 99 SER.#'d SETS

1 Hogan/Steiner/Sting/Jarrett/Flair		
2 Love/Sky/Tara/James/Rayne	30.00	60.00
3 Jeff & Matt Hardy/RVD/Foley/Angle		

2011 TRISTAR TNA Signature Impact Memorabilia Silver

*GOLD/50: .6X TO 1.25X BASIC MEM
*BLUE/25: .75X TO 1.5X BASIC MEM
*RED/5: UNPRICED DUE TO SCARCITY
*PURPLE/1: UNPRICED DUE TO SCARCITY
STATED PRINT RUN 199 SER.#'d SETS

M6 Hulk Hogan		
M7 Sting	12.00	25.00
M8 Chyna	12.00	25.00
M9 Jeff Hardy		
M10 Rob Van Dam	10.00	20.00

2011 TRISTAR TNA Signature Impact Quad Autographs Silver

*GOLD/25: .6X TO 1.25X BASIC AUTOS
*RED/5: UNPRICED DUE TO SCARCITY
*PURPLE/1: UNPRICED DUE TO SCARCITY
STATED PRINT RUN 99 SER.#'d SETS

1 Flair/Hardy/Abyss/Styles		
2 Hogan/Flair/The Hardys		
3 Hernandez/Anarquia/Sarita/Rosita	15.00	30.00
4 Angle/Chyna/Karen & Jeff Jarrett		

2011 TRISTAR TNA Signature Impact Quad Memorabilia Silver

M14 Sky/Love/Winter/James	15.00	40.00
M15 Hernandez/Anarquia Sarita/Rosita	8.00	20.00

2011 TRISTAR TNA Signature Impact Ric Flair Die-Cut Letter Memorabilia Silver

COMPLETE SET (5)

M1 Ric Flair F
M2 Ric Flair L
M3 Ric Flair A
M4 Ric Flair I
M5 Ric Flair R

2011 TRISTAR TNA Signature Impact Seven Autographs Silver

*GOLD/25: UNPRICED DUE TO SCARCITY
*RED/5: UNPRICED DUE TO SCARCITY
*PURPLE/1: UNPRICED DUE TO SCARCITY
STATED PRINT RUN 99 SER.#'d SETS
UNPRICED DUE TO SCARCITY

1 Sting/RVD/Anderson/Hogan
Flair/Jeff & Matt Hardy
2 Hogan/James/Flair
Love/RVD/Sky/J.Hardy

2011 TRISTAR TNA Signature Impact Six Autographs Silver

*GOLD/25: UNPRICED DUE TO SCARCITY
*RED/5: UNPRICED DUE TO SCARCITY
*PURPLE/1: UNPRICED DUE TO SCARCITY
STATED PRINT RUN 99 SER.#'d SETS
UNPRICED DUE TO SCARCITY

1 Hogan/Flair/Sting
Angle/Jarrett/Steiner
2 Tara/James/Sky
Love/Rayne/Hemme

2011 TRISTAR TNA Signature Impact Triple Autographs Silver

*GOLD/25: UNPRICED DUE TO SCARCITY
*RED/5: UNPRICED DUE TO SCARCITY
*PURPLE/1: UNPRICED DUE TO SCARCITY
STATED PRINT RUN 99 SER.#'d SETS
UNPRICED DUE TO SCARCITY

1 Jeff & Karen Jarrett/Angle
2 Sky/Winter/Love
3 Sting/RVD/Anderson
4 Hogan/Flair/Sting
5 Jeff & Matt Hardy/RVD

2011 TRISTAR TNA Signature Impact Triple Memorabilia Silver

M12 Hogan/Flair/Sting		
M13 Jeff & Karen Jarrett/Angle	8.00	20.00

2010 TRISTAR TNA Xtreme

COMPLETE SET W/SP (111)	60.00	120.00
COMPLETE SET W/O SP (101)	10.00	25.00
UNOPENED BOX (20 PACKS)		
UNOPENED PACK (6 CARDS)		

*SILVER/40: 3X TO 8X BASIC CARDS
*GOLD/10: UNPRICED DUE TO SCARCITY
*PURPLE/1: UNPRICED DUE TO SCARCITY
SP STATED ODDS 1:BOX

1 Hulk Hogan	1.00	2.50
2 Eric Bischoff	.15	.40
3 Jeff Jarrett	.40	1.00
4 Samoa Joe	.25	.60
5 Robbie E RC	.15	.40
6 Sting	.60	1.50
7 Ric Flair	.75	2.00
8 AJ Styles	.40	1.00
9 Matt Morgan	.15	.40
10 Cowboy James Storm	.25	.60
11 Robert Roode	.15	.40
12 Kazarian	.15	.40
13 Tommy Dreamer	.15	.40
14 Mick Foley	.75	2.00
15 Brother Devon	.25	.60
16 Stevie Richards	.15	.40
17 Rhino	.25	.60
18 Brian Kendrick	.25	.60
19 Raven	.25	.60
20 Taz	.15	.40
21 Sabu	.15	.40
22 Al Snow	.40	1.00
23 Hardcore Justice	.15	.40
24 RVD/Sabu	.40	1.00
25 Raven/Tommy Dreamer	.25	.60
26 So.Philly Street Fight	.15	.40
27 Rhino/Al Snow/Brother Runt	.40	1.00
28 Stevie Richards/PJ Polaco	.15	.40
29 Too Cold Scorpio/CW Anderson	.15	.40
30 The FBI/Kash/Diamond/Swinger	.15	.40
31 Jason Hervey	.15	.40
32 Rob Van Dam	.40	1.00
33 Jeff Hardy	.60	1.50
34 Kurt Angle	.60	1.50
35 D'Angelo Dinero	.15	.40
36 Brother Ray	.25	.60
37 Mr. Anderson	.25	.60
38 TNA Tag Team Champ	.15	.40
39 Falls Count Anywhere	.25	.60
40 Jarrett/Joe/Sting/Nash	.60	1.50
41 Tommy Dreamer/AJ Styles	.40	1.00
42 Jeff Hardy/Kurt Angle	.60	1.50
43 London Brawling	.15	.40
44 Generation Me	.15	.40
45 Rob Terry	.15	.40
46 Douglas Williams	.15	.40
47 Motorcity Machine Guns	.25	.60
48 Amazing Red	.15	.40
49 Magnus	.15	.40
50 Hernandez	.15	.40
51 Jeremy Borash	.15	.40
52 Orlando Jordan	.15	.40
53 TNA Tag Team Champ	.15	.40
54 Classic Knockouts	.25	.60
55 RVD Overcomes the Odds	.40	1.00
56 Lethal Lockdown	.15	.40
57 Cookie RC	.25	.60
58 Mickie James	.75	2.00
59 Angelina Love	.60	1.50
60 Velvet Sky	.75	2.00
61 Lacey Von Erich RC	.75	2.00
62 Madison Rayne	.60	1.50
63 Taylor Wilde	.40	1.00
64 Hamada	.40	1.00
65 Daffney	.60	1.50
66 Sarita	.40	1.00
67 SoCal Val	.60	1.50
68 Tara	.60	1.50
69 Miss Tessmacher RC	.75	2.00
70 Ink Inc.	.15	.40
71 Abyss SS	.25	.60
72 AJ Styles SS	.40	1.00
73 Hulk Hogan SS	1.00	2.50
74 Kurt Angle SS	.60	1.50
75 Jeff Jarrett SS	.40	1.00
76 Jeff Hardy SS	.60	1.50
77 Dixie Carter SS	.40	1.00
78 Rob Van Dam SS	.40	1.00
79 Lacey Von Erich SS	.75	2.00
80 Jay Lethal SS	.15	.40
81 Tommy Dreamer SS	.15	.40
82 Mick Foley SS	.75	2.00
83 Sting PC	.60	1.50
84 Madison Rayne PC	.60	1.50
85 D'Angelo Dinero PC	.15	.40
86 Christy Hemme PC	.60	1.50
87 Jeff Hardy PC	.60	1.50
88 Angelina Love PC	.60	1.50
89 Mickie James PC	.75	2.00
90 Dixie Carter PC	.40	1.00
91 Kurt Angle PC	.60	1.50
92 Mike Tenay PC	.15	.40
93 Mickie James	.75	2.00
94 Rob Van Dam UX	.40	1.00
95 Sting UX	.60	1.50
96 Jeff Hardy UX	.60	1.50
97 Abyss UX	.25	.60
98 Tommy Dreamer UX	.15	.40
99 AJ Styles UX	.40	1.00
100 Hulk Hogan UX	1.00	2.50
101 Jeff Hardy Original Art SP	6.00	15.00
102 Jeff Hardy Original Art SP	6.00	15.00
103 Jeff Hardy Original Art SP	6.00	15.00
104 Jeff Hardy Original Art SP	6.00	15.00
105 Jeff Hardy Original Art SP	6.00	15.00
106 Jeff Hardy Original Art SP	6.00	15.00
107 Jeff Hardy Original Art SP	6.00	15.00
108 Jeff Hardy Original Art SP	6.00	15.00
109 Jeff Hardy Original Art SP	6.00	15.00
110 Jeff Hardy Original Art SP	6.00	15.00
CL Checklist	.15	.40

2010 TRISTAR TNA Xtreme Autographed Memorabilia Gold

*GREEN/25: UNPRICED DUE TO SCARCITY
*RED/5: UNPRICED DUE TO SCARCITY
*PURPLE/1: UNPRICED DUE TO SCARCITY
STATED PRINT RUN 99 SER.#'d SETS
UNPRICED DUE TO SCARCITY

XA1 Hulk Hogan
XA2 Mickie James
XA3 Rob Van Dam
XA4 Jeff Hardy
XA5 Sting
XA6 AJ Styles

2010 TRISTAR TNA Xtreme Autographs Gold

COMMON AUTO	5.00	12.00

*GREEN/25: .6X TO 1.5X BASIC AUTOS
*RED/5: UNPRICED DUE TO SCARCITY
*PURPLE/1: UNPRICED DUE TO SCARCITY
STATED PRINT RUN 99 SER.#'d SETS

X1 Rob Van Dam		
X2 Rhino	6.00	15.00
X3 Mick Foley		
X4 Tommy Dreamer	6.00	15.00
X5 Sabu	6.00	15.00
X6 Raven		
X7 Stevie Richards	6.00	15.00
X8 Al Snow	8.00	20.00
X9 Kid Kash	5.00	12.00
X10 New Jack	5.00	12.00
X11 P.J. Polaco	5.00	12.00
X12 Tracy Smothers	5.00	12.00
X13 Axl Rotten	5.00	12.00
X14 Too Cold Scorpio	5.00	12.00
X15 Bill Alfonso	5.00	12.00
X16 Tony Luke	5.00	12.00
X17 Blue Tillie	5.00	12.00
X18 Swinger	5.00	12.00
X19 Brother Runt	5.00	12.00
X20 Stephen DeAngelis	5.00	12.00
X21 Simon Diamond	5.00	12.00
X22 Nova	5.00	12.00
X23 Guido Maritato	5.00	12.00
X24 Big Sal	5.00	12.00
X25 Mustafa	5.00	12.00
X26 C.W. Anderson	5.00	12.00
X27 Joel Gertner		
X28 John Rechner		
X29 Taz	5.00	12.00
X30 Brian Kendrick	6.00	15.00
X31 Tara	8.00	20.00
X32 Jason Hervey	6.00	15.00
X33 Mickie James	15.00	30.00
X34 Jeremy Borash	5.00	12.00
X35 Samoa Joe	8.00	20.00
X36 Alex Shelley	5.00	12.00
X37 Shannon Moore	8.00	20.00
X38 Jay Lethal	5.00	12.00
X39 Jeff Hardy		
X40 Chris Sabin	5.00	12.00
X41 Kazarian	5.00	12.00
X42 Mr. Anderson	6.00	15.00
X43 Sting		
X44 Abyss	6.00	15.00
X45 AJ Styles	8.00	20.00
X46 Angelina Love	10.00	25.00
X47 Madison Rayne	10.00	25.00
X48 Velvet Sky	10.00	25.00
X49 Lacey Von Erich	10.00	25.00
X50 Christy Hemme	10.00	25.00
X51 Kevin Nash	10.00	25.00
X52 Kurt Angle	10.00	25.00
X53 Ric Flair		
X54 Hulk Hogan		
X55 Hulk Hogan		
X56 Hulk Hogan		

2010 TRISTAR TNA Xtreme Autographs Green

*GREEN: .6X TO 1.5X BASIC AUTOS
STATED PRINT RUN 25 SER.#'d SETS

X1 Rob Van Dam		
X2 Rhino	10.00	25.00
X3 Mick Foley		
X4 Tommy Dreamer	10.00	25.00
X5 Sabu	10.00	25.00
X6 Raven		
X7 Stevie Richards	10.00	25.00
X8 Al Snow	12.00	30.00
X9 Kid Kash	8.00	20.00
X10 New Jack	8.00	20.00
X11 P.J. Polaco	8.00	20.00
X12 Tracy Smothers	8.00	20.00
X13 Axl Rotten	8.00	20.00
X14 Too Cold Scorpio	8.00	20.00
X15 Bill Alfonso	8.00	20.00
X16 Tony Luke	8.00	20.00
X17 Blue Tillie	8.00	20.00
X18 Swinger	8.00	20.00
X19 Brother Runt	8.00	20.00
X20 Stephen DeAngelis	8.00	20.00
X21 Simon Diamond	8.00	20.00
X22 Nova	8.00	20.00
X23 Guido Maritato	8.00	20.00
X24 Big Sal	8.00	20.00
X25 Mustafa	8.00	20.00
X26 C.W. Anderson	8.00	20.00
X27 Joel Gertner		
X28 John Rechner		
X29 Taz	8.00	20.00
X30 Brian Kendrick	10.00	25.00
X31 Tara	15.00	30.00
X32 Jason Hervey	10.00	25.00
X33 Mickie James	25.00	50.00
X34 Jeremy Borash	8.00	20.00
X35 Samoa Joe	12.00	30.00
X36 Alex Shelley	8.00	20.00
X37 Shannon Moore	12.00	30.00
X38 Jay Lethal	8.00	20.00
X39 Jeff Hardy		
X40 Chris Sabin	8.00	20.00
X41 Kazarian	8.00	20.00
X42 Mr. Anderson	10.00	25.00
X43 Sting		
X44 Abyss	10.00	25.00
X45 AJ Styles	12.00	30.00
X46 Angelina Love	20.00	40.00
X47 Madison Rayne	20.00	40.00
X48 Velvet Sky	20.00	40.00
X49 Lacey Von Erich	20.00	40.00
X50 Christy Hemme	20.00	40.00
X51 Kevin Nash	20.00	40.00
X52 Kurt Angle	20.00	40.00
X53 Ric Flair		
X54 Hulk Hogan		
X55 Hulk Hogan		
X56 Hulk Hogan		

2010 TRISTAR TNA Xtreme Dual Autographed Memorabilia Gold

STATED PRINT RUN 50 SER.#'d SETS

XA7 RVD/Sabu		
XA8 A.Love/V.Sky	35.00	70.00
XA9 J.Hardy/RVD		

2010 TRISTAR TNA Xtreme Dual Autographs Gold

1 R.Flair/M.Foley		
2 Sting/K.Nash		
3 RVD/Sabu		
4 A.Love/V.Sky	12.00	30.00
5 A.Shelley/C.Sabin	8.00	20.00
6 Max & Jeremy Buck	8.00	20.00
7 J.Neal/S.Moore	12.00	25.00
8 Robbie E/Cookie	12.00	30.00
9 Tommy & Trisa Dreamer	12.00	30.00
10 N.Jack/Mustafa		
11 J.Finegan/M.Kehner		
12 Scorpio/C.Anderson		
13 M.Tenay/Taz		
14 Raven/T.Dreamer		
15 H.Hogan/R.Flair		

2010 TRISTAR TNA Xtreme Dual Memorabilia

*GOLD/50: .5X TO 1.2X BASIC MEM
*GREEN/25: .6X TO 1.5X BASIC MEM
*RED/5: UNPRICED DUE TO SCARCITY
*PURPLE/1: UNPRICED DUE TO SCARCITY
STATED PRINT RUN 199 SER.#'d SETS

X12 Robbie E/Cookie	8.00	20.00
X13 Jeremy & Max Buck	6.00	15.00

2010 TRISTAR TNA Xtreme Dual Memorabilia Gold

*GOLD: .5X TO 1.2X BASIC MEM
STATED PRINT RUN 50 SER.#'d SETS

X12 Robbie E/Cookie	10.00	25.00
X13 Jeremy & Max Buck	8.00	20.00

2010 TRISTAR TNA Xtreme Lovely Locks Hair Autographs Turquoise

*PINK/1: UNPRICED DUE TO SCARCITY
STATED PRINT RUN 3 SER.#'d SETS
UNPRICED DUE TO SCARCITY

LL1 Velvet Sky
LL2 Angelina Love
LL3 SoCal Val
LL4 Christy Hemme

2010 TRISTAR TNA Xtreme Memorabilia

*GOLD/50: .5X TO 1.2X BASIC MEM
*GREEN/10: UNPRICED DUE TO SCARCITY
*RED/5: UNPRICED DUE TO SCARCITY
*PURPLE/1: UNPRICED DUE TO SCARCITY
OVERALL MEMORABILIA ODDS ONE PER HOBBY BOX
STATED PRINT RUN 199 SER.#'d SETS

X1 Hulk Hogan		
X2 Rob Van Dam		
X3 Jeff Hardy		
X4 Mr. Anderson	6.00	15.00
X5 Kurt Angle	6.00	15.00
X6 Mickie James		
X7 AJ Styles		
X8 D'Angelo Dinero		
X9 Sabu	6.00	15.00
X10 Al Snow	6.00	15.00
X11 Brother Runt	6.00	15.00

2010 TRISTAR TNA Xtreme Obak

COMPLETE SET (8)	15.00	40.00
STATED PRINT RUN 310 SER.#'d SETS		
X1 Hulk Hogan	8.00	20.00
X2 Jeff Hardy	5.00	12.00
X3 Rob Van Dam	3.00	8.00
X4 Mickie James	6.00	15.00
X5 AJ Styles	3.00	8.00
X6 Tommy Dreamer	1.25	3.00
X7 Jeff Jarrett	3.00	8.00
X8 Sting	5.00	12.00

2010 TRISTAR TNA Xtreme Quad Autographs

*GOLD/99: UNPRICED DUE TO SCARCITY
*GREEN/25: UNPRICED DUE TO SCARCITY
*RED/5: UNPRICED DUE TO SCARCITY
*PURPLE/1: UNPRICED DUE TO SCARCITY
UNPRICED DUE TO SCARCITY

1 Hogan/Flair/Jarrett/Hardy
2 Angle/Sting/Nash/Foley
3 Sky/Love/Rayne/Tara
4 Tommy & Trisa Dreamer/Kimberly/Brianna

2010 TRISTAR TNA Xtreme Quad Memorabilia Gold

*GREEN/10: UNPRICED DUE TO SCARCITY
*RED/5: UNPRICED DUE TO SCARCITY
*PURPLE/1: UNPRICED DUE TO SCARCITY
STATED PRINT RUN 50 SER.#'d SETS

X14 Hogan/Sting/RVD/Hardy		
X15 Sky/Love/Von Erich/Rayne		
X16 Hogan/Flair/Foley/Sting		
X17 Tara/James/Sky/Love		
X18 Snow/B.Runt/Scorpio/Tillie	15.00	30.00
X19 Dreamer/RVD/Sabu/Snow	15.00	30.00

2010 TRISTAR TNA Xtreme Six Autographs

*GOLD/99: UNPRICED DUE TO SCARCITY
*GREEN/25: UNPRICED DUE TO SCARCITY
*RED/5: UNPRICED DUE TO SCARCITY
*PURPLE/1: UNPRICED DUE TO SCARCITY
UNPRICED DUE TO SCARCITY

1 Flair/Styles/Storm
Roode/Kazarian/Morgan
2 Hogan/Flair/Hardy
Jarrett/Angle/Sting
3 Dreamer/Foley/Richards
Rhino/Raven/Sabu
4 Smothers/Luke/Maritato
Kash/Diamond/Swinger

2010 TRISTAR TNA Xtreme Six Autographs Gold

STATED PRINT RUN 99 SER. #'d SETS

1 Flair/Styles/Storm
Roode/Kazarian/Morgan
2 Hogan/Flair/Hardy
Jarrett/Angle/Sting
3 Dreamer/Foley/Richards
Rhino/Raven/Sabu
4 Smothers/Luke/Maritato
Kash/Diamond/Swinger

2010 TRISTAR TNA Xtreme Sting Die-Cut Letter Memorabilia Green

STATED PRINT RUN 10 SER.#'d SETS

S1 Sting S	20.00	40.00
S2 Sting T	20.00	40.00
S3 Sting I	20.00	40.00
S4 Sting N	20.00	40.00
S5 Sting G	20.00	40.00

2010 TRISTAR TNA Xtreme Sting Face Paint Red

STATED PRINT RUN 5 SER.#'d SETS
UNPRICED DUE TO SCARCITY

S3 Sting
S4 Sting

2010 TRISTAR TNA Xtreme Triple Autographs Gold

STATED PRINT RUN 99 SER.#'d SETS

1 Hogan/Jarrett/Flair
2 Foley/Angle/Anderson
3 Raven/Dreamer/Foley
4 Richards/Nova/Polaco
5 Rhino/Runt/Snow
6 Ray/Devon/Gertner
7 Sabu/VanDam/Alfonso

2010 TRISTAR TNA Xtreme Velvet Sky Die-Cut Letter Memorabilia Gold

STATED PRINT RUN 50 SER.#'d SETS

VS1 Velvet Sky S	25.00	50.00
VS2 Velvet Sky K	25.00	50.00
VS3 Velvet Sky Y	25.00	50.00

1993 Unbeatables Mid-South Wrestling

COMPLETE SET (25)
STATED PRINT RUN 1,000 SETS

1 Big Mike Norman
2 Ricky Morton
3 The Sheik
4 Ben Jordan
5 Chris Champion
6 Reno Riggins
7 The Mongolian Mauler
8 Billy Montana
9 Gary Valiant
10 The Scorpion
11 The Medic
12 Jeff Daniels with Dominique
13 PG-13
14 Mephisto and Dante
15 Wild Boys
16 The Hickersons
17 Rhodes and Lawler
18 Woodrow Foundation
19 Madd Maxx
20 Little Farmer John
21 Cowabunga
22 Willie the Wrestling Clown
23 Chris Keirn
24 Freddie Morton
25 The Fireball

2006 Unilever WWE

NNO Batista	5.00	12.00
NNO Booker T	3.00	8.00
NNO Carlito	5.00	12.00
NNO Hulk Hogan	8.00	20.00
NNO The Hurricane	1.25	3.00
NNO John Cena	8.00	20.00
NNO Kurt Angle	8.00	20.00
NNO Rey Mysterio	5.00	12.00
NNO Stone Cold Steve Austin	8.00	20.00
NNO The Undertaker	6.00	15.00

2008 Unilever WWE

COMPLETE SET (10)

NNO Batista
NNO Bobby Lashley
NNO Carlito
NNO CM Punk
NNO Edge
NNO Jeff Hardy
NNO John Cena
NNO Rob Van Dam
NNO Shawn Michaels
NNO Triple H

1998 Up Front Sports WCW/nWo American Pop 3-D

COMPLETE SET (3)

NNO Goldberg
NNO Randy Savage
NNO Sting

1998 Up Front Sports WCW/nWo Pop-Up Real Action

COMPLETE SET (10)

1 Bret Hart
2 Sting
3 DDP
4 Goldberg
5 Hollywood Hogan
6 Kevin Nash
7 Lex Luger
8 Macho Man Randy Savage
9 Scott Steiner
10 Scott Hall

2021 Upper Deck AEW

COMPLETE SET W/SP (100)	100.00	200.00
COMPLETE SET W/O SP (60)	30.00	75.00
COMMON TT (61-70)	.60	1.50
COMMON CREW (71-80)	.60	1.50
COMMON MAG (81-100)	1.25	3.00

*GOLD: .5X TO 1.2X BASIC CARDS
*GOLD TT: .5X TO 1.2X BASIC CARDS
*GOLD CREW: .5X TO 1.2X BASIC CARDS
*GOLD MAG: .5X TO 1.2X BASIC CARDS
*PYRO: .75X TO 2X BASIC CARDS
*PYRO TT: .75X TO 2X BASIC CARDS
*PYRO CREW: .75X TO 2X BASIC CARDS
*PYRO MAG: .75X TO 2X BASIC CARDS
*DYNAMITE: 1.2X TO 3X BASIC CARDS
*DYNA.TT: 1.2X TO 3X BASIC CARDS

*DYNA.CREW: 1.2X TO 3X BASIC CARDS
*DYNA.MAG: 1.2X TO 3X BASIC CARDS
*FINISHER: 1.5X TO 4X BASIC CARDS
*FINISH.TT: 1.5X TO 4X BASIC CARDS
*FINISH.CREW: 1.5X TO 4X BASIC CARDS
*FINISH.MAG: 1.5X TO 4X BASIC CARDS
*YELLOW: X TO X BASIC CARDS
*EXCLUSIVES/100: 8X TO 20X BASIC CARDS
*HIGH GLOSS/10: UNPRICED DUE TO SCARCITY
*BLACK/1: UNPRICED DUE TO SCARCITY

1 Cody Rhodes 1.00 2.50
2 Kris Statlander RC .50 1.25
3 Shawn Spears .50 1.25
4 Dustin Rhodes .60 1.50
5 Lance Archer .75 2.00
6 Penelope Ford RC .50 1.25
7 Hangman Adam Page RC 2.00 5.00
8 Scorpio Sky RC .30 .75
9 Miro .60 1.50
10 QT Marshall RC .40 1.00
11 Dr. Britt Baker RC 1.50 4.00
12 Joey Janela RC .30 .75
13 Jon Moxley .75 2.00
14 Isiah Kassidy RC .40 1.00
15 Sammy Guevara RC .75 2.00
16 Kenny Omega RC 2.00 5.00
17 The Blade RC .50 1.25
18 John Silver RC .30 .75
19 Jake Hager .50 1.25
20 Nick Jackson RC 1.25 3.00
21 PAC .60 1.50
22 Abadon RC .30 .75
23 Jungle Boy RC 1.25 3.00
24 Marq Quen RC .40 1.00
25 Riho RC 1.25 3.00
26 Ricky Starks RC .75 2.00
27 Frankie Kazarian .40 1.00
28 Anna Jay RC 1.50 4.00
29 Matt Jackson RC 1.25 3.00
30 Ortiz RC .50 1.25
31 Cash Wheeler .50 1.25
32 Stu Grayson RC .30 .75
33 Darby Allin RC 2.00 5.00
34 Chuck Taylor RC .40 1.00
35 Trent? .75 2.00
36 Alex Reynolds RC .30 .75
37 Matt Hardy .60 1.50
38 The Butcher RC .50 1.25
39 Tay Conti 1.25 3.00
40 Orange Cassidy RC .75 2.00
41 Big Swole RC .50 1.25
42 Penta el Zero M RC .75 2.00
43 Kip Sabian RC .60 1.50
44 Christopher Daniels .50 1.25
45 Brian Cage RC .40 1.00
46 Luchasaurus RC 1.00 2.50
47 Colt Cabana RC .40 1.00
48 The Bunny RC .75 2.00
49 Wardlow RC .60 1.50
50 Nyla Rose RC .60 1.50
51 MJF RC 2.00 5.00
52 Santana RC .50 1.25
53 Brandi Rhodes 1.50 4.00
54 Chris Jericho 1.25 3.00
55 Hikaru Shida RC 1.00 2.50
56 Powerhouse Hobbs RC .60 1.50
57 Dax Harwood .50 1.25
58 Rey Fenix RC .75 2.00
59 Evil Uno RC .60 1.50
60 Mr. Brodie Lee .75 2.00
61 Trent?/Chuck Taylor SP 1.25 3.00
62 The Butcher/The Blade SP .75 2.00
63 Dax Harwood/Cash Wheeler SP .75 2.00
64 Santana/Ortiz SP .75 2.00
65 Jungle Boy/Luchasaurus SP 2.00 5.00
66 Rey Fenix/Penta el Zero M SP 1.25 3.00
67 Evil Uno/Stu Grayson SP 1.00 2.50
68 Marq Quen/Isiah Kassidy SP .60 1.50
69 Frankie Kazarian/Scorpio Sky SP .60 1.50
70 Matt Jackson/Nick Jackson SP 2.00 5.00
71 Arn Anderson SP 1.00 2.50
72 Billy Gunn SP .75 2.00
73 Jake Roberts SP 1.00 2.50
74 Jim Ross SP 1.50 4.00
75 Justin Roberts SP .60 1.50
76 Paul Turner SP RC .60 1.50
77 Sting SP 2.50 6.00
78 Taz SP .75 2.00
79 Tony Schiavone SP .75 2.00
80 Tully Blanchard SP 1.00 2.50
81 Sting SP 4.00 10.00
82 Brian Cage SP 1.25 3.00
83 Dr. Britt Baker SP 5.00 12.00
84 Chris Jericho SP 4.00 10.00
85 Cody Rhodes SP 3.00 8.00
86 Colt Cabana SP 1.25 3.00
87 Darby Allin SP 6.00 15.00
88 Hikaru Shida SP 3.00 8.00
89 Jon Moxley SP 2.50 6.00
90 Kenny Omega SP 6.00 15.00
91 Lance Archer SP 2.50 6.00
92 Matt Hardy SP 2.00 5.00
93 Matt Jackson SP 4.00 10.00
94 MJF SP 6.00 15.00
95 Mr. Brodie Lee SP 2.50 6.00
96 Nick Jackson SP 4.00 10.00
97 Nyla Rose SP 2.00 5.00
98 Orange Cassidy SP 2.50 6.00
99 Rey Fenix SP 2.50 6.00
100 Sammy Guevara SP 2.50 6.00

2021 Upper Deck AEW Autographs

*PYRO/25: UNPRICED DUE TO SCARCITY
*DYNAMITE/5: UNPRICED DUE TO SCARCITY
*GOLD/1: UNPRICED DUE TO SCARCITY
*P.P.BLACK/1: UNPRICED DUE TO SCARCITY
*P.P.CYAN/1: UNPRICED DUE TO SCARCITY
*P.P.MAGENTA/1: UNPRICED DUE TO SCARCITY
*P.P.YELLOW/1: UNPRICED DUE TO SCARCITY
GROUP A ODDS 1:7,581
GROUP B ODDS 1:1,832
GROUP C ODDS 1:913
GROUP D ODDS 1:464
GROUP E ODDS 1:341
STATED ODDS 1:146 HOBBY/EPACK
STATED ODDS 1:113 BLASTER/FAT PACKS
STATED TT ODDS 1:2,048 HOBBY
STATED TT ODDS 1:1,700 EPACK/BLAST/FAT
STATED CREW ODDS 1:1,024 HOBBY/EPACK
STATED CREW ODDS 1:800 BLASTER/FAT
STATED MAG ODDS 1:768 HOBBY/EPACK
STATED MAG ODDS 1:600 BLASTER/FAT

1 Cody Rhodes B 125.00 250.00
2 Kris Statlander E 100.00 200.00
3 Shawn Spears D 25.00 60.00
4 Dustin Rhodes D 30.00 75.00
5 Lance Archer C 50.00 100.00
6 Penelope Ford E 125.00 300.00
7 Hangman Adam Page D 200.00 400.00
8 Scorpio Sky D 75.00 150.00
9 Miro D 30.00 75.00
10 QT Marshall E 20.00 50.00
11 Dr. Britt Baker C 500.00 1000.00
12 Joey Janela D 15.00 40.00
13 Jon Moxley B
14 Isiah Kassidy C
15 Sammy Guevara C
16 Kenny Omega B 200.00 400.00
17 The Blade C
18 John Silver D 25.00 60.00
19 Jake Hager E 20.00 50.00
20 Nick Jackson A 75.00 150.00
21 PAC E 60.00 120.00
22 Abadon E 30.00 75.00
23 Jungle Boy D 200.00 400.00
24 Marq Quen D 8.00 20.00
25 Riho E 100.00 200.00
26 Ricky Starks D 25.00 60.00
27 Frankie Kazarian C 15.00 40.00
28 Anna Jay E 100.00 200.00
29 Matt Jackson A 100.00 200.00
30 Ortiz D 30.00 75.00
31 Cash Wheeler D 20.00 50.00
32 Stu Grayson D
33 Darby Allin B 500.00 1000.00
34 Chuck Taylor D 25.00 60.00
35 Trent? D 50.00 100.00
36 Alex Reynolds E 25.00 60.00
37 Matt Hardy B 25.00 60.00
38 The Butcher C 75.00 150.00
39 Tay Conti E 125.00 250.00
40 Orange Cassidy B 200.00 400.00
41 Big Swole E 50.00 100.00
42 Penta el Zero M C
43 Kip Sabian E 25.00 60.00
44 Christopher Daniels E 20.00 50.00
45 Brian Cage C
46 Luchasaurus C 125.00 250.00
47 Colt Cabana C 50.00 100.00
48 The Bunny E 75.00 150.00
49 Wardlow E 150.00 300.00
50 Nyla Rose C 60.00 120.00
51 MJF B 300.00 600.00
52 Santana D 50.00 100.00
53 Brandi Rhodes E 60.00 120.00
54 Chris Jericho B 175.00 350.00
55 Hikaru Shida B
56 Powerhouse Hobbs D
57 Dax Harwood D 25.00 60.00
58 Rey Fenix A 30.00 75.00
59 Evil Uno D 50.00 100.00
61 Chuck Taylor/Trent? B 60.00 120.00
62 The Butcher/The Blade B 100.00 200.00
63 Dax Harwood/Cash Wheeler B 75.00 150.00
64 Santana/Ortiz B
65 Jungle Boy/Luchasaurus B 300.00 600.00
66 Rey Fenix/Penta el Zero M B
67 Evil Uno/Stu Grayson B 75.00 150.00
68 Marq Quen/Isiah Kassidy B
69 Frankie Kazarian/Scorpio Sky B 60.00 120.00
70 Matt Jackson/Nick Jackson A
71 Arn Anderson B 30.00 75.00
72 Billy Gunn A 60.00 120.00
73 Jake Roberts B 25.00 60.00
74 Jim Ross B 60.00 120.00
75 Justin Roberts B 30.00 75.00
76 Paul Turner B 15.00 40.00
77 Sting A 250.00 500.00
78 Taz B
79 Tony Schiavone B 75.00 150.00
80 Tully Blanchard B 75.00 150.00
81 Sting B
82 Brian Cage C 50.00 100.00
83 Dr. Britt Baker C 500.00 1000.00
84 Chris Jericho A 150.00 300.00
85 Cody Rhodes A 150.00 300.00
86 Colt Cabana C 50.00 100.00
87 Darby Allin C 500.00 1000.00
88 Hikaru Shida C 200.00 400.00
89 Jon Moxley B 100.00 200.00
90 Kenny Omega C 250.00 500.00
91 Lance Archer C 50.00 100.00
92 Matt Hardy C 30.00 75.00
93 Matt Jackson B
94 MJF C 250.00 500.00
96 Nick Jackson B 60.00 120.00
97 Nyla Rose C 60.00 120.00
98 Orange Cassidy C 150.00 300.00
99 Rey Fenix B 50.00 100.00
100 Sammy Guevara C 125.00 250.00

2021 Upper Deck AEW Canvas

COMPLETE SET W/O SP (30) 125.00 250.00
STATED ODDS 1:5
STATED SP ODDS 1:40

C1 Matt Hardy 3.00 8.00
C2 Brian Cage 3.00 8.00
C3 Dustin Rhodes 5.00 12.00
C4 Jungle Boy 8.00 20.00
C5 Brandi Rhodes 5.00 12.00
C6 Darby Allin 12.00 30.00
C7 Dr. Britt Baker 15.00 40.00
C8 Austin Gunn 2.50 6.00
C9 Tay Conti 8.00 20.00
C10 PAC 2.50 6.00
C11 Best Friends 4.00 10.00
C12 Colt Cabana 2.50 6.00
C13 Taz 4.00 10.00
C14 Nyla Rose 2.50 6.00
C15 The Butcher/The Blade 2.50 6.00
C16 Santana/Ortiz 3.00 8.00
C17 Lance Archer 5.00 12.00
C18 Sting 10.00 25.00
C19 Ricky Starks 4.00 10.00
C20 Luchasaurus 6.00 15.00
C21 Scorpio Sky 2.50 6.00
C22 Anna Jay 8.00 20.00
C23 Dax Harwood/Cash Wheeler 4.00 10.00

C24 Jim Ross	5.00	12.00
C25 Big Swole	2.50	6.00
C26 Joey Janela	2.50	6.00
C27 Rey Fenix/Penta el Zero M	6.00	15.00
C28 Tony Schiavone	3.00	8.00
C29 Sammy Guevara	5.00	12.00
C30 Hikaru Shida	10.00	25.00
C31 Cody Rhodes SP	15.00	40.00
C32 Nick Jackson SP	15.00	40.00
C33 Matt Jackson SP	15.00	40.00
C34 Mr. Brodie Lee SP	20.00	50.00
C35 Chris Jericho SP	15.00	40.00
C36 Hangman Adam Page SP	25.00	60.00
C37 Orange Cassidy SP	15.00	40.00
C38 MJF SP	20.00	50.00
C39 Kenny Omega SP	30.00	75.00
C40 Jon Moxley SP	15.00	40.00

2021 Upper Deck AEW The Dotted Line Autographs

STATED ODDS 1:1,536 HOBBY/EPACK
STATED ODDS 1:3,072 BLASTER
STATED ODDS 1:6,144 FAT PACKS

DLCJ Chris Jericho	250.00	400.00
DLCR Cody Rhodes		
DLDA Darby Allin		
DLHS Hikaru Shida		
DLJM Jon Moxley		
DLKO Kenny Omega	1500.00	3000.00
DLMF MJF		
DLMH Matt Hardy		
DLMJ Matt Jackson		
DLNJ Nick Jackson		
DLOC Orange Cassidy		

2021 Upper Deck AEW Main Features

COMPLETE SET (40) 30.00 75.00
*SILVER: .5X TO 1.2X BASIC CARDS
*GREEN/199: 1.5X TO 4X BASIC CARDS
*GOLD: .6X TO 1.5X BASIC CARDS
*RED/50: 2X TO 5X BASIC CARDS
*PURPLE/25: 2.5X TO 6X BASIC CARDS
*BLACK/1: UNPRICED DUE TO SCARCITY
STATED ODDS 1:1

MF1 Cody Rhodes	1.25	3.00
MF2 Darby Allin	2.50	6.00
MF3 Lance Archer	1.00	2.50
MF4 Chris Jericho	1.50	4.00
MF5 Riho	1.50	4.00
MF6 Santana	.60	1.50
MF7 Orange Cassidy	1.00	2.50
MF8 Hikaru Shida	1.25	3.00
MF9 Dax Harwood	.60	1.50
MF10 Kenny Omega	2.50	6.00
MF11 Big Swole	.60	1.50
MF12 Dustin Rhodes	.75	2.00
MF13 Shawn Spears	.60	1.50
MF14 PAC	.75	2.00
MF15 Brandi Rhodes	2.00	5.00
MF16 Cash Wheeler	.60	1.50
MF17 Frankie Kazarian	.50	1.25
MF18 Tay Conti	1.50	4.00
MF19 Nick Jackson	1.50	4.00
MF20 Penta el Zero M	1.00	2.50
MF21 Nyla Rose	.75	2.00
MF22 Brian Cage	.50	1.25
MF23 Sting	1.50	4.00
MF24 Ortiz	.60	1.50
MF25 Hangman Adam Page	2.50	6.00
MF26 Luchasaurus	1.25	3.00
MF27 Scorpio Sky	.40	1.00
MF28 MJF	2.50	6.00
MF29 Jungle Boy	1.50	4.00
MF30 The Blade	.60	1.50
MF31 Matt Jackson	1.50	4.00
MF32 Matt Hardy	.75	2.00
MF33 Colt Cabana	.50	1.25
MF34 Rey Fenix	1.00	2.50
MF35 Dr. Britt Baker	2.00	5.00
MF36 Anna Jay	2.00	5.00
MF37 Ricky Starks	1.00	2.50
MF38 Sammy Guevara	1.00	2.50
MF39 Jake Hager	.60	1.50
MF40 Jon Moxley	1.00	2.50

2021 Upper Deck AEW Memorabilia

*GOLD/199: .75X TO 2X BASIC MEM
*RED/50: 1.5X TO 4X BASIC MEM
STATED ODDS 1:

1 Cody Rhodes	20.00	50.00
2 Kris Statlander	20.00	50.00
3 Shawn Spears	5.00	12.00
4 Dustin Rhodes	6.00	15.00
5 Lance Archer	6.00	15.00
6 Penelope Ford		
7 Hangman Adam Page	30.00	75.00
8 Scorpio Sky	12.00	30.00
9 Miro	8.00	20.00
10 QT Marshall	4.00	10.00
11 Dr. Britt Baker	20.00	50.00
12 Joey Janela	4.00	10.00
13 Jon Moxley		
14 Isiah Kassidy	6.00	15.00
15 Sammy Guevara	10.00	25.00
16 Kenny Omega	30.00	75.00
17 The Blade	4.00	10.00
18 John Silver	5.00	12.00
19 Jake Hager	5.00	12.00
20 Nick Jackson		
21 PAC	5.00	12.00
22 Abadon		
23 Jungle Boy	15.00	40.00
24 Marq Quen	4.00	10.00
26 Ricky Starks	8.00	20.00
27 Frankie Kazarian	6.00	15.00
28 Anna Jay	8.00	20.00
29 Matt Jackson		
30 Ortiz		
31 Cash Wheeler	6.00	15.00
32 Stu Grayson	8.00	20.00
33 Darby Allin	25.00	60.00
34 Chuck Taylor	4.00	10.00
35 Trent?		
36 Alex Reynolds		
37 Matt Hardy	5.00	12.00
38 The Butcher	4.00	10.00
39 Tay Conti	15.00	40.00
40 Orange Cassidy	15.00	40.00
41 Big Swole	6.00	15.00
42 Penta el Zero M	8.00	20.00
43 Kip Sabian	4.00	10.00
44 Christopher Daniels		
45 Brian Cage	6.00	15.00
46 Luchasaurus	12.00	30.00
47 Colt Cabana	6.00	15.00
48 The Bunny	20.00	50.00
49 Wardlow	8.00	20.00
50 Nyla Rose	5.00	12.00
51 MJF	15.00	40.00
52 Santana	5.00	12.00
53 Brandi Rhodes	10.00	25.00
54 Chris Jericho		
55 Hikaru Shida	20.00	50.00
56 Powerhouse Hobbs		
57 Dax Harwood	8.00	20.00
58 Rey Fenix		
59 Evil Uno		
61 Chuck Taylor/Trent?		
62 The Butcher/The Blade		
63 Dax Harwood/Cash Wheeler		
64 Santana/Ortiz		
65 Jungle Boy/Luchasaurus		
66 Rey Fenix/Penta el Zero M		
67 Evil Uno/Stu Grayson		
68 Marq Quen/Isiah Kassidy		
69 Frankie Kazarian/Scorpio Sky		
70 Matt Jackson/Nick Jackson		
71 Arn Anderson	8.00	20.00
72 Billy Gunn		
73 Jake Roberts		
74 Jim Ross		
78 Taz		
80 Tully Blanchard	5.00	12.00

2021 Upper Deck AEW Memorabilia Gold

*RED/50: .75X TO 2X BASIC MEM
STATED PRINT RUN 199 OR FEWER

2021 Upper Deck AEW NYCC Promo Sheet

PV1 Cody Rhodes	20.00	50.00
PV2 Miro		
PV3 Dr. Britt Baker		
PV4 Kenny Omega		
NNO Cover Card		
PV5 Chris Jericho		
PV6 Hikaru Shida		
PV7 Sting		
PV8 Jon Moxley		

2021 Upper Deck AEW NYCC Promos

NNO Cover Card	1.50	4.00
PV1 Cody Rhodes	2.00	5.00
PV2 Miro	2.00	5.00
PV3 Dr. Britt Baker	12.00	30.00
PV4 Kenny Omega	8.00	20.00
PV5 Chris Jericho	3.00	8.00
PV6 Hikaru Shida	5.00	12.00
PV7 Sting	6.00	15.00
PV8 Jon Moxley	4.00	10.00

2021 Upper Deck AEW Preview

0 CM Punk	20.00	50.00
PP1 Adam Cole	12.00	30.00
PP2 Bryan Danielson	15.00	40.00
PP3 Keith Lee		

2021 Upper Deck AEW Preview Autograph

0 CM Punk

2021 Upper Deck AEW Rhodes to Success

COMPLETE SET (10) 15.00 40.00
*SILVER: .5X TO 1.2X BASIC CARDS
*GOLD: .6X TO 1.5X BASIC CARDS
*RED/50: 1.5X TO 4X BASIC CARDS
*BLACK/1: UNPRICED DUE TO SCARCITY
STATED ODDS 1:10 HOBBY/EPACK/BLASTER
STATED ODDS 1:5 FAT PACKS

RS1 Cody Rhodes	2.00	5.00
RS2 Cody Rhodes	2.00	5.00
RS3 Cody Rhodes	2.00	5.00
RS4 Cody Rhodes	2.00	5.00
RS5 Cody Rhodes	2.00	5.00
RS6 Cody Rhodes	2.00	5.00
RS7 Cody Rhodes	2.00	5.00
RS8 Cody Rhodes	2.00	5.00
RS9 Cody Rhodes	2.00	5.00
RS10 Cody Rhodes	2.00	5.00

2021 Upper Deck AEW Top Rope

COMPLETE SET (10) 12.00 30.00
*SILVER: .5X TO 1.2X BASIC CARDS
*GOLD: .6X TO 1.5X BASIC CARDS
*RED/50: 2X TO 5X BASIC CARDS
*BLACK/1: UNPRICED DUE TO SCARCITY
STATED ODDS 1:10 HOBBY/EPACK/BLASTER
STATED ODDS 1:5 FAT PACKS

TR1 PAC	1.00	2.50
TR2 Darby Allin	3.00	8.00
TR3 Nick Jackson	2.00	5.00
TR4 Riho	2.00	5.00
TR5 Kenny Omega	3.00	8.00
TR6 Joey Janela	.50	1.25
TR7 Rey Fenix	1.25	3.00
TR8 Hangman Adam Page	3.00	8.00
TR9 Marq Quen	.60	1.50
TR10 Sammy Guevara	1.25	3.00

2021 Upper Deck AEW Wednesday in Action

COMPLETE SET (33) 250.00 500.00
STATED ODDS 1:64

WIA1 Orange Cassidy	8.00	20.00
WIA2 Luchasaurus	10.00	25.00
WIA3 Chris Jericho	12.00	30.00
WIA4 Anna Jay	15.00	40.00
WIA5 Dax Harwood	5.00	12.00
WIA6 Matt Hardy	6.00	15.00
WIA7 Brian Cage	4.00	10.00
WIA8 Santana	5.00	12.00
WIA9 Jon Moxley	8.00	20.00
WIA10 Hikaru Shida	10.00	25.00
WIA11 Matt Jackson	12.00	30.00
WIA12 Nick Jackson	12.00	30.00
WIA13 Dustin Rhodes	6.00	15.00
WIA14 Ricky Starks	8.00	20.00

WIA15 Dr. Britt Baker	15.00	40.00
WIA16 MJF	20.00	50.00
WIA17 Lance Archer	8.00	20.00
WIA18 Kenny Omega	20.00	50.00
WIA19 Penta el Zero M	8.00	20.00
WIA20 Sammy Guevara	8.00	20.00
WIA21 Ortiz	5.00	12.00
WIA22 Tay Conti	12.00	30.00
WIA23 Cody Rhodes	10.00	25.00
WIA24 Joey Janela	3.00	8.00
WIA25 Scorpio Sky	3.00	8.00
WIA26 Rey Fenix	8.00	20.00
WIA27 Sting	12.00	30.00
WIA28 Brandi Rhodes	15.00	40.00
WIA29 Cash Wheeler	5.00	12.00
WIA30 Christopher Daniels	5.00	12.00
WIA31 Jungle Boy	12.00	30.00
WIA32 Nyla Rose	6.00	15.00
WIA33 Hangman Adam Page	20.00	50.00

2022 Upper Deck AEW

COMPLETE SET (100)
UNOPENED BOX (16 PACKS)
UNOPENED PACK (8 CARDS)
*GOLD: .75X TO 2X BASIC CARDS
*PYRO: 1.2X TO 3X BASIC CARDS
*GREEN PYRO/399: 1.5X TO 4X BASIC CARDS
*DYNAMITE/299: 2X TO 5X BASIC CARDS
*PURPLE PYRO/199: 2.5X TO 6X BASIC CARDS
*EXCLUSIVE/100: 4X TO 10X BASIC CARDS
*HIGH GLOSS/10: UNPRICED DUE TO SCARCITY
*BLACK/1: UNPRICED DUE TO SCARCITY

1 Chris Jericho	1.25	3.00
2 Colt Cabana	.40	1.00
3 MJF	1.50	4.00
4 Brian Pillman Jr. RC	1.25	3.00
5 The Bunny	.75	2.00
6 Powerhouse Hobbs	.60	1.50
7 Max Caster	.40	1.00
8 Ethan Page	.75	2.00
9 Christian Cage	.50	1.25
10 Luchasaurus	.60	1.50
11 Trent?	.40	1.00
12 Nyla Rose	.60	1.50
13 Sammy Guevara	1.00	2.50
14 Daniel Garcia RC	1.00	2.50
15 CM Punk	1.50	4.00
16 QT Marshall	.40	1.00
17 Ricky Starks	.60	1.50
18 Jake Hager	.50	1.25
19 The Blade	.30	.75
20 Jungle Boy	1.00	2.50
21 Penelope Ford	1.50	4.00
22 Santana	.60	1.50
23 Paul Wight	.60	1.50
24 Evil Uno	.60	1.50
25 John Silver	.30	.75
26 Scorpio Sky	.60	1.50
27 Adam Cole	1.00	2.50
28 Billy Gunn	.40	1.00
29 Ruby Soho	.60	1.50
30 Stu Grayson	.60	1.50
31 Red Velvet	.50	1.25
32 Jay Lethal	.50	1.25
33 Tay Conti	1.25	3.00
34 Lance Archer	.75	2.00
35 Kris Statlander	.60	1.50
36 Angelico RC	.40	1.00
37 The Butcher	.30	.75
38 Serena Deeb	.30	.75
39 Pac	.60	1.50
40 Jon Moxley	.75	2.00
41 Matt Hardy	.60	1.50
42 Dax Harwood	.50	1.25
43 Matt Sydal	.30	.75
44 Cash Wheeler	.50	1.25
45 Miro	.60	1.50
46 Dustin Rhodes	.60	1.50
47 Eddie Kingston	1.00	2.50
48 Rey Fenix	.75	2.00
49 Anthony Bowens	.40	1.00
50 Frankie Kazarian	.40	1.00
51 Malakai Black	.75	2.00
52 Orange Cassidy	1.00	2.50
53 Dante Martin RC	.60	1.50
54 Riho	.60	1.50
55 Matt Jackson	.75	2.00
56 Nick Jackson	.75	2.00
57 Bryan Danielson	1.25	3.00
58 Hangman Adam Page	1.50	4.00
59 Darby Allin	1.50	4.00
60 Jamie Hayter RC	2.00	5.00
61 Kenny Omega	1.50	4.00
62 Andrade El Idolo	.40	1.00
63 Thunder Rosa	.75	2.00
64 Dr. Britt Baker	1.25	3.00
65 Chuck Taylor	.30	.75
66 Wardlow	.75	2.00
67 Keith Lee	.75	2.00
68 Diamante	.30	.75
69 Kyle O'Reilly	.30	.75
70 Ortiz	.60	1.50
71 Shawn Spears	.50	1.25
72 Alex Reynolds	.30	.75
73 Jade Cargill	1.50	4.00
74 Penta el Zero M	.75	2.00
75 Lee Johnson	.30	.75
76 Sting	1.25	3.00
77 Anna Jay	1.25	3.00
78 Hikaru Shida	.75	2.00
79 Griff Garrison	.30	.75
80 Hook RC	2.50	6.00
81 Dax Harwood/Cash Wheeler	.50	1.25
82 Rey Fenix/Penta El Zero M	.75	2.00
83 Griff Garrison/Brian Pillman Jr.	.50	1.25
84 Anthony Bowens/Max Caster	.40	1.00
85 Jeff Parker/Matt Lee	.40	1.00
86 Santana/Ortiz	.60	1.50
87 Jungle Boy/Luchasaurus	1.00	2.50
88 Marq Quen/Isiah Kassidy	.40	1.00
89 The Butcher/The Blade	.30	.75
90 Matt Jackson/Nick Jackson	.75	2.00
91 Jim Ross	.75	2.00
92 Tony Schiavone	.40	1.00
93 Vickie Guerrero	.30	.75
94 Bryce Remsburg RC	.40	1.00
95 Arn Anderson	.50	1.25
96 Justin Roberts	.30	.75
97 Tully Blanchard	.40	1.00
98 Rick Knox RC	.40	1.00
99 Mark Henry	.40	1.00
100 Taz	.40	1.00

2022 Upper Deck AEW Autographs

*PYRO/25: UNPRICED DUE TO SCARCITY
*DYNAMITE/5: UNPRICED DUE TO SCARCITY
*GOLD/1: UNPRICED DUE TO SCARCITY
*P.P.BLACK/1: UNPRICED DUE TO SCARCITY
*P.P.CYAN/1: UNPRICED DUE TO SCARCITY
*P.P.MAGENTA/1: UNPRICED DUE TO SCARCITY
*P.P.YELLOW/1: UNPRICED DUE TO SCARCITY
STATED OVERALL ODDS 1:144 HOBBY/EPACK
STATED OVERALL ODDS 1:187 BLASTER
TAG TEAM OVERALL ODDS 1:3,072 HOBBY/EPACK
TAG TEAM OVERALL ODDS 1:6,000 BLASTER
CREW OVERALL ODDS 1:768 HOBBY/EPACK
CREW OVERALL ODDS 1:1,000 BLASTER
GROUP A ODDS 1:14,037
GROUP B ODDS 1:2,562
GROUP C ODDS 1:154

1 Chris Jericho A		
2 Colt Cabana C	6.00	15.00
3 MJF C	200.00	500.00
4 Brian Pillman Jr. B	10.00	25.00
5 The Bunny C	25.00	60.00
6 Powerhouse Hobbs B		
7 Max Caster C	40.00	100.00
8 Ethan Page C	40.00	100.00
9 Christian Cage C	15.00	40.00
10 Luchasaurus C	20.00	50.00
11 Trent? C	10.00	25.00
12 Nyla Rose C	12.00	30.00
13 Sammy Guevara C	25.00	60.00
14 Daniel Garcia C	15.00	40.00
15 CM Punk A		
16 QT Marshall C	10.00	25.00
17 Ricky Starks B		
18 Jake Hager C	10.00	25.00
19 The Blade C	6.00	15.00
20 Jungle Boy C	30.00	75.00
21 Penelope Ford C	40.00	100.00
22 Santana C	10.00	25.00
23 Paul Wight B	10.00	25.00
24 Evil Uno C	15.00	40.00
25 John Silver C	8.00	20.00
26 Scorpio Sky C	10.00	25.00
27 Adam Cole C		
28 Billy Gunn C	20.00	50.00
29 Ruby Soho B		
30 Stu Grayson C	10.00	25.00
31 Red Velvet B		
32 Jay Lethal C	15.00	40.00
33 Tay Conti C	40.00	100.00
34 Lance Archer C	10.00	25.00
35 Kris Statlander C	60.00	150.00
36 Angelico C	12.00	30.00
37 The Butcher C	6.00	15.00
38 Serena Deeb C	15.00	40.00
39 PAC C	15.00	40.00
40 Jon Moxley A		
41 Matt Hardy B		
42 Dax Harwood C		
43 Matt Sydal C		
44 Cash Wheeler B		
45 Miro C	15.00	40.00
46 Dustin Rhodes B	15.00	40.00
47 Eddie Kingston C	50.00	125.00
48 Rey Fenix C	25.00	60.00
49 Anthony Bowens C	25.00	60.00
50 Frankie Kazarian B		
51 Malakai Black C	25.00	60.00
52 Orange Cassidy C		
53 Dante Martin C	50.00	125.00
54 Riho C	30.00	75.00
55 Matt Jackson B	15.00	40.00
56 Nick Jackson B		
57 Bryan Danielson C	20.00	50.00
58 Hangman Adam Page C	60.00	150.00
59 Darby Allin C	60.00	150.00
60 Jamie Hayter C	125.00	300.00
61 Kenny Omega A		
62 Andrade El Idolo C	20.00	50.00
63 Thunder Rosa B	40.00	100.00
64 Dr. Britt Baker C	125.00	300.00
65 Chuck Taylor C	10.00	25.00
66 Wardlow C	25.00	60.00
67 Keith Lee A	25.00	60.00
68 Diamante C	10.00	25.00
69 Kyle O'Reilly C	12.00	30.00
70 Ortiz C	10.00	25.00
71 Shawn Spears C	10.00	25.00
72 Alex Reynolds C	6.00	15.00
73 Jade Cargill C	100.00	250.00
74 Penta el Zero M C	30.00	75.00
75 Lee Johnson C	15.00	40.00
76 Sting C	60.00	150.00
77 Anna Jay C	50.00	125.00
78 Hikaru Shida B	75.00	200.00
79 Griff Garrison C	10.00	25.00
80 Hook C	150.00	400.00
81 Dax Harwood/Cash Wheeler	75.00	200.00
82 Rey Fenix/Penta El Zero M		
83 Griff Garrison/Brian Pillman Jr.	25.00	60.00
84 Anthony Bowens/Max Caster	60.00	150.00
85 Jeff Parker/Matt Lee	40.00	100.00
86 Santana/Ortiz		
87 Jungle Boy/Luchasaurus		
88 Marq Quen/Isiah Kassidy		
89 The Butcher/The Blade	30.00	75.00
90 Matt Jackson/Nick Jackson		
91 Jim Ross	12.00	30.00
92 Tony Schiavone	12.00	30.00
93 Vickie Guerrero	12.00	30.00
94 Bryce Remsburg	10.00	25.00
95 Arn Anderson	15.00	40.00
96 Justin Roberts	12.00	30.00
97 Tully Blanchard	20.00	50.00
98 Rick Knox	15.00	40.00
99 Mark Henry		
100 Taz	10.00	25.00

2022 Upper Deck AEW Breakouts

COMMON SP (BO26-BO35)	20.00	50.00

STATED ODDS 1:73 HOBBY/EPACK/BLASTER
SP ODDS 1:512 HOBBY/EPACK/BLASTER

BO1 Christian Cage	6.00	15.00
BO2 Thunder Rosa	15.00	40.00

B03 Matt Hardy	6.00	15.00
B04 Jade Cargill	40.00	100.00
B05 Cash Wheeler	25.00	60.00
B06 Adam Cole	20.00	50.00
B07 Dustin Rhodes	10.00	25.00
B08 Kris Statlander	15.00	40.00
B09 Malakai Black	12.00	30.00
B010 Paul Wight	4.00	15.00
B011 Jungle Boy	12.00	30.00
B012 Sting	20.00	50.00
B013 Rey Fenix	12.00	30.00
B014 Darby Allin	30.00	75.00
B015 Max Caster	8.00	20.00
B016 Luchasaurus	8.00	20.00
B017 Tay Conti	12.00	30.00
B018 Penta el Zero M	15.00	40.00
B019 Bryan Danielson	15.00	40.00
B020 Lance Archer	8.00	20.00
B021 Dr. Britt Baker	25.00	60.00
B022 Dax Harwood	6.00	15.00
B023 Wardlow	12.00	30.00
B024 Powerhouse Hobbs	10.00	25.00
B025 Ricky Starks	8.00	20.00
B026 Orange Cassidy SP	20.00	50.00
B027 Chris Jericho SP	30.00	75.00
B028 Keith Lee SP	30.00	75.00
B029 Kenny Omega SP	60.00	150.00
B030 Jon Moxley SP	30.00	75.00
B031 Hangman Adam Page SP		100.00
B032 Miro SP	20.00	50.00
B033 CM Punk SP	40.00	100.00
B034 Matt Jackson SP	20.00	50.00
B035 Nick Jackson SP	20.00	50.00

2022 Upper Deck AEW Canvas

STATED ODDS 1:4 HOBBY/EPACK/BLASTER/FAT
SP ODDS 1:40 HOBBY/EPACK/BLASTER/FAT

C1 Brian Pillman Jr.	1.00	2.50
C2 Penta el Zero M	1.50	4.00
C3 Tay Conti	2.50	6.00
C4 Ruby Soho	1.25	3.00
C5 Dax Harwood	1.00	2.50
C6 Dustin Rhodes	1.25	3.00
C7 Rey Fenix	1.50	4.00
C8 Jungle Boy	2.00	5.00
C9 Luchasaurus	1.25	3.00
C10 Ricky Starks	1.25	3.00
C11 Dr. Britt Baker	2.50	6.00
C12 Thunder Rosa	1.50	4.00
C13 Sammy Guevara	2.00	5.00
C14 Mark Henry	.75	2.00
C15 Isiah Kassidy/Marq Quen	.75	2.00
C16 Jamie Hayter	3.00	8.00
C17 Anthony Bowens/Max Caster	.75	2.00
C18 Dante Martin	.60	1.50
C19 Lance Archer	1.50	4.00
C20 Bryan Danielson	2.50	6.00
C21 Matt Hardy	1.25	3.00
C22 Powerhouse Hobbs	1.25	3.00
C23 MJF	3.00	8.00
C24 Santana/Ortiz	1.25	3.00
C25 Paul Wight	1.25	3.00
C26 Jade Cargill	3.00	8.00
C27 Christian Cage	1.00	2.50
C28 CM Punk	3.00	8.00
C29 Hikaru Shida	1.50	4.00
C30 Cash Wheeler	1.00	2.50
C31 Hangman Adam Page SP	8.00	20.00
C32 Matt Jackson SP	4.00	10.00
C33 Orange Cassidy SP	5.00	12.00
C34 Kenny Omega SP	8.00	20.00
C35 Chris Jericho SP	6.00	15.00
C36 Miro SP	3.00	8.00
C37 Sting SP	6.00	15.00
C38 Nick Jackson SP	4.00	10.00
C39 Keith Lee SP	4.00	10.00
C40 Darby Allin SP	8.00	20.00

2022 Upper Deck AEW Debut Dates

COMPLETE SET (10)	10.00	25.00

*SILVER: .5X TO 1.2X BASIC CARDS
*GOLD: .6X TO 1.5X BASIC CARDS
*RED/50: .75X TO 2X BASIC CARDS
*GOLD SPECTRUM/1: UNPRICED DUE TO SCARCITY
STATED ODDS 1:10 HOBBY/EPACK/BLASTER
STATED ODDS 1:5 FAT PACKS

DD1 Thunder Rosa	1.50	4.00
DD2 Paul Wight	1.25	3.00
DD3 Ruby Soho	1.25	3.00
DD4 Christian Cage	1.00	2.50
DD5 Andrade El Idolo	.75	2.00
DD6 Malakai Black	1.50	4.00
DD7 Adam Cole	2.00	5.00
DD8 CM Punk	3.00	8.00
DD9 Bryan Danielson	2.50	6.00
DD10 Mark Henry	.75	2.00

2022 Upper Deck AEW Jumbo Mat Relic Signatures

STATED PRINT RUN 10 SER.#'d SETS
UNPRICED DUE TO SCARCITY

JMS2 Rey Fenix
JMS3 Chris Jericho
JMS5 Nick Jackson
JMS6 Kenny Omega
JMS7 Christian Cage
JMS8 Lance Archer
JMS9 Tay Conti
JMS10 Powerhouse Hobbs
JMS11 Darby Allin
JMS12 Miro
JMS14 Matt Jackson
JMS15 Orange Cassidy
JMS16 Matt Hardy
JMS17 Jungle Boy
JMS18 Brian Cage
JMS19 MJF

2022 Upper Deck AEW Main Features

*SILVER: .5X TO 1.2X BASIC CARDS
*GOLD: .6X TO 1.5X BASIC CARDS
*GREEN/199: .75X TO 2X BASIC CARDS
*RED/50: 1.2X TO 3X BASIC CARDS
*PURPLE/25: UNPRICED DUE TO SCARCITY
*GOLD SPECTRUM/1: UNPRICED DUE TO SCARCITY
STATED ODDS 1:1 HOBBY/EPACK/BLASTER
STATED ODDS 2:1 FAT PACKS

MF1 Kenny Omega	4.00	10.00
MF2 Thunder Rosa	2.00	5.00
MF3 Cash Wheeler	1.25	3.00
MF4 Darby Allin	4.00	10.00
MF5 Adam Cole	2.50	6.00
MF6 Dr. Britt Baker	3.00	8.00
MF7 Max Caster	1.00	2.50
MF8 Luchasaurus	1.50	4.00
MF9 MJF	4.00	10.00
MF10 Orange Cassidy	2.50	6.00
MF11 Sting	3.00	8.00
MF12 Christian Cage	1.25	3.00
MF13 Hangman Adam Page	4.00	10.00
MF14 Penta el Zero M	2.00	5.00
MF15 Ruby Soho	1.50	4.00
MF16 Tay Conti	3.00	8.00
MF17 PAC	1.50	4.00
MF18 Matt Jackson	2.00	5.00
MF19 Bryan Danielson	3.00	8.00
MF20 Chris Jericho	3.00	8.00
MF21 Powerhouse Hobbs	1.50	4.00
MF22 Jungle Boy	2.50	6.00
MF23 Lance Archer	2.00	5.00
MF24 Nyla Rose	1.50	4.00
MF25 Anthony Bowens	1.00	2.50
MF26 Keith Lee	2.00	5.00
MF27 Paul Wight	1.50	4.00
MF28 Rey Fenix	2.00	5.00
MF29 Dax Harwood	1.25	3.00
MF30 Dustin Rhodes	1.50	4.00
MF31 Nick Jackson	2.00	5.00
MF32 Mark Henry	1.00	2.50
MF33 Ricky Starks	1.50	4.00
MF34 Miro	1.50	4.00
MF35 Hikaru Shida	2.00	5.00
MF36 Brian Cage	1.00	2.50
MF37 Red Velvet	1.25	3.00
MF38 Sammy Guevara	2.50	6.00
MF39 CM Punk	4.00	10.00
MF40 Jon Moxley	2.00	5.00

2022 Upper Deck AEW Mat Relics

*GOLD: .5X TO 1.2X BASIC MEM
*RED/50: .6X TO 1.5X BASIC MEM
STATED ODDS 1:23 BLASTER

1 Chris Jericho	6.00	15.00
2 Colt Cabana	2.00	5.00
3 MJF	8.00	20.00
4 Brian Pillman Jr.	2.50	6.00
5 The Bunny	4.00	10.00
6 Powerhouse Hobbs	3.00	8.00
7 Max Caster	2.00	5.00
8 Ethan Page	4.00	10.00
9 Christian Cage	2.50	6.00
10 Luchasaurus	3.00	8.00
11 Trent?	2.00	5.00
12 Nyla Rose	3.00	8.00
13 Sammy Guevara	5.00	12.00
14 Daniel Garcia	2.00	5.00
15 CM Punk	8.00	20.00
16 QT Marshall	2.00	5.00
17 Ricky Starks	3.00	8.00
18 Jake Hager	2.50	6.00
19 The Blade	1.50	4.00
20 Jungle Boy	5.00	12.00
21 Penelope Ford	8.00	20.00
22 Santana	3.00	8.00
23 Paul Wight	3.00	8.00
24 Evil Uno	3.00	8.00
25 John Silver	1.50	4.00
26 Scorpio Sky	3.00	8.00
27 Adam Cole	5.00	12.00
28 Billy Gunn	2.00	5.00
29 Ruby Soho	3.00	8.00
30 Stu Grayson	3.00	8.00
31 Red Velvet	2.50	6.00
32 Jay Lethal	2.50	6.00
33 Tay Conti	6.00	15.00
34 Lance Archer	4.00	10.00
35 Kris Statlander	3.00	8.00
36 Angelico	1.50	4.00
37 The Butcher	1.50	4.00
38 Serena Deeb	1.50	4.00
39 PAC	3.00	8.00
40 Jon Moxley	4.00	10.00
41 Matt Hardy	3.00	8.00
42 Dax Harwood	2.50	6.00
43 Matt Sydal	1.50	4.00
44 Cash Wheeler	2.50	6.00
45 Miro	3.00	8.00
46 Dustin Rhodes	3.00	8.00
47 Eddie Kingston	5.00	12.00
48 Rey Fenix	4.00	10.00
49 Anthony Bowens	2.00	5.00
50 Frankie Kazarian	2.00	5.00
51 Malakai Black	4.00	10.00
52 Orange Cassidy	5.00	12.00
53 Dante Martin	1.50	4.00
54 Riho	3.00	8.00
55 Matt Jackson	4.00	10.00
56 Nick Jackson	4.00	10.00
57 Bryan Danielson	6.00	15.00
58 Hangman Adam Page	8.00	20.00
59 Darby Allin	8.00	20.00
60 Jamie Hayter	8.00	20.00
61 Kenny Omega	8.00	20.00
62 Andrade El Idolo	2.00	5.00
63 Thunder Rosa	4.00	10.00
64 Dr. Britt Baker	6.00	15.00
65 Chuck Taylor	1.50	4.00
66 Wardlow	4.00	10.00
67 Keith Lee	4.00	10.00
68 Diamante	1.50	4.00
69 Kyle O'Reilly	1.50	4.00
70 Ortiz	3.00	8.00
71 Shawn Spears	2.50	6.00
72 Alex Reynolds	1.50	4.00
73 Jade Cargill	8.00	20.00
74 Penta el Zero M	4.00	10.00
75 Lee Johnson	1.50	4.00
76 Sting	6.00	15.00
77 Anna Jay	6.00	15.00
78 Hikaru Shida	4.00	10.00
79 Griff Garrison	1.50	4.00
80 Hook	6.00	15.00
81 Dax Harwood/Cash Wheeler	2.50	6.00
82 Rey Fenix/Penta El Zero M	4.00	10.00
83 Griff Garrison/Brian Pillman Jr.	2.50	6.00
84 Anthony Bowens/Max Caster	2.00	5.00
85 Jeff Parker/Matt Lee	2.00	5.00

86 Santana/Ortiz	3.00	8.00
87 Jungle Boy/Luchasaurus	5.00	12.00
88 Marq Quen/Isiah Kassidy	2.00	5.00
89 The Butcher/The Blade	1.50	4.00
90 Matt Jackson/Nick Jackson	4.00	10.00
91 Jim Ross	4.00	10.00
92 Tony Schiavone	2.00	5.00
93 Vickie Guerrero	1.50	4.00
94 Bryce Remsburg	1.50	4.00
95 Arn Anderson	2.50	6.00
96 Justin Roberts	1.50	4.00
97 Tully Blanchard	2.00	5.00
98 Rick Knox	1.50	4.00
99 Mark Henry	2.00	5.00
100 Taz	2.00	5.00

2022 Upper Deck AEW Match Dated Moments Grand Slam

COMPLETE SET (6)

GS1 Toni Storm	2.00	5.00
GS2 The Wizard Chris Jericho	2.50	6.00
GS3 Jon Moxley	2.00	5.00
GS4 The Great Muta	1.25	3.00
GS5 Hook and Action Bronson S	12.00	30.00
GS6 The Acclaimed G	30.00	75.00

2022 Upper Deck AEW Match Dated Moments Top Ranked Achievements

COMPLETE SET (6)
*SILVER: UNPRICED DUE TO SCARCITY
*GOLD: UNPRICED DUE TO SCARCITY

TR1 MJF
TR2 Jon Moxley
TR3 Bryan Danielson
TR4 Dr. Britt Baker DMD
TR5 Jade Cargill
TR6 Kenny Omega

2022 Upper Deck AEW Outside the Ring

COMPLETE SET (10) 6.00 15.00
*SILVER: .5X TO 1.2X BASIC CARDS
*GOLD: .6X TO 1.5X BASIC CARDS
*RED/50: .75X TO 2X BASIC CARDS
*GOLD SPECTRUM/1: UNPRICED DUE TO SCARCITY
STATED ODDS 1:10 HOBBY/EPACK/BLASTER
STATED ODDS 1:5 FAT PACKS

OTR1 Santana	1.25	3.00
OTR2 Ortiz	1.25	3.00
OTR3 Varsity Blonds	1.00	2.50
OTR4 Best Friends	.75	2.00
OTR5 Tony Schiavone	.75	2.00
OTR6 Hikaru Shida	1.50	4.00
OTR7 Shawn Spears	1.00	2.50
OTR8 Sammy Guevara	2.00	5.00
OTR9 Powerhouse Hobbs	1.25	3.00
OTR10 Mark Henry	.75	2.00

2022 Upper Deck AEW Shirt Relics

*RED/50: .75X TO 2X BASIC MEM
RANDOMLY INSERTED INTO PACKS

1 Chris Jericho	6.00	15.00
2 Colt Cabana	2.00	5.00
3 MJF	8.00	20.00
4 Brian Pillman Jr.	2.50	6.00
5 The Bunny	4.00	10.00
6 Powerhouse Hobbs	3.00	8.00
7 Max Caster	2.00	5.00
8 Ethan Page	4.00	10.00
9 Christian Cage	2.50	6.00
10 Luchasaurus	3.00	8.00
11 Trent?	2.00	5.00
12 Nyla Rose	3.00	8.00
13 Sammy Guevara	5.00	12.00
14 Daniel Garcia	2.00	5.00
15 CM Punk	8.00	20.00
16 QT Marshall	2.00	5.00
17 Ricky Starks	3.00	8.00
18 Jake Hager	2.50	6.00
19 The Blade	1.50	4.00
20 Jungle Boy	5.00	12.00
21 Penelope Ford	8.00	20.00
22 Santana	3.00	8.00
23 Paul Wight	3.00	8.00
24 Evil Uno	3.00	8.00
25 John Silver	1.50	4.00
26 Scorpio Sky	3.00	8.00
27 Adam Cole	5.00	12.00
28 Billy Gunn	2.00	5.00
29 Ruby Soho	3.00	8.00
30 Stu Grayson	3.00	8.00
31 Red Velvet	2.50	6.00
32 Jay Lethal	2.50	6.00
33 Tay Conti	6.00	15.00
34 Lance Archer	4.00	10.00
35 Kris Statlander	3.00	8.00
36 Angelico	1.50	4.00
37 The Butcher	1.50	4.00
38 Serena Deeb	1.50	4.00
39 PAC	3.00	8.00
40 Jon Moxley	4.00	10.00
41 Matt Hardy	3.00	8.00
42 Dax Harwood	2.50	6.00
43 Matt Sydal	1.50	4.00
44 Cash Wheeler	2.50	6.00
45 Miro	3.00	8.00
46 Dustin Rhodes	3.00	8.00
47 Eddie Kingston	5.00	12.00
48 Rey Fenix	4.00	10.00
49 Anthony Bowens	2.00	5.00
50 Frankie Kazarian	2.00	5.00
51 Malakai Black	4.00	10.00
52 Orange Cassidy	5.00	12.00
53 Dante Martin	1.50	4.00
54 Riho	3.00	8.00
55 Matt Jackson	4.00	10.00
56 Nick Jackson	4.00	10.00
57 Bryan Danielson	6.00	15.00
58 Hangman Adam Page	8.00	20.00
59 Darby Allin	8.00	20.00
60 Jamie Hayter	8.00	20.00
61 Kenny Omega	8.00	20.00
62 Andrade El Idolo	2.00	5.00
63 Thunder Rosa	4.00	10.00
64 Dr. Britt Baker	6.00	15.00
65 Chuck Taylor	1.50	4.00
66 Wardlow	4.00	10.00
67 Keith Lee	4.00	10.00
68 Diamante	1.50	4.00
69 Kyle O'Reilly	1.50	4.00
70 Ortiz	3.00	8.00
71 Shawn Spears	2.50	6.00
72 Alex Reynolds	1.50	4.00
73 Jade Cargill	8.00	20.00
74 Penta el Zero M	4.00	10.00
75 Lee Johnson	1.50	4.00
76 Sting	6.00	15.00
77 Anna Jay	6.00	15.00
78 Hikaru Shida	4.00	10.00
79 Griff Garrison	1.50	4.00
80 Hook	6.00	15.00
81 Dax Harwood/Cash Wheeler	2.50	6.00
82 Rey Fenix/Penta El Zero M	4.00	10.00
83 Griff Garrison/Brian Pillman Jr.	2.50	6.00
84 Anthony Bowens/Max Caster	2.00	5.00
85 Jeff Parker/Matt Lee	2.00	5.00
86 Santana/Ortiz	3.00	8.00
87 Jungle Boy/Luchasaurus	5.00	12.00
88 Marq Quen/Isiah Kassidy	2.00	5.00
89 The Butcher/The Blade	1.50	4.00
90 Matt Jackson/Nick Jackson	4.00	10.00
91 Jim Ross	4.00	10.00
92 Tony Schiavone	2.00	5.00
93 Vickie Guerrero	1.50	4.00
94 Bryce Remsburg	1.50	4.00
95 Arn Anderson	2.50	6.00
96 Justin Roberts	1.50	4.00
97 Tully Blanchard	2.00	5.00
98 Rick Knox	1.50	4.00
99 Mark Henry	2.00	5.00
100 Taz	2.00	5.00

2022 Upper Deck AEW Match Dated Moments

COMPLETE SET (30)

1 Hangman Adam Page	3.00	8.00
2 Jade Cargill	4.00	10.00
3 Sting/Darby Allin/Sammy Guevara	3.00	8.00
4 Dr. Britt Baker DMD	5.00	12.00
5 CM Punk S	10.00	25.00
6 Willam Regal G	25.00	60.00
7 Wardlow	2.00	5.00
8 Thunder Rosa	8.00	20.00
9 The Hardys	2.00	5.00
10 CM Punk	3.00	8.00
11 Adam Cole & Britt Baker S	6.00	15.00
12 Jericho Appreciation Society G	30.00	75.00
13 FTR	4.00	10.00
14 Jericho/Guevara/Suzuki	3.00	8.00
15 PAC	2.00	5.00
16 Jon Moxley	2.50	6.00
17 Orange Cassidy/Will Ospreay S	6.00	15.00
18 Allin/Sting/Takagi G	15.00	40.00
19 CM Punk		8.00
20 Toni Storm	2.50	6.00
21 Lionheart Chris Jericho	2.50	6.00
22 The Joker (MJF)	4.00	10.00
23 The Elite S	10.00	25.00
24 MJF G	40.00	100.00

25 Death Triangle
26 Saraya
27 Danhausen
28 Jamie Hayter
29 MJF S
30 Jungle Boy G

2021 Upper Deck AEW Happy Holidays Promo

UDHC2021 Tis the Season
(Kenny Omega/Britt Baker/Jade Cargill/CM Punk)

2022 Upper Deck AEW New Arrivals

COMPLETE SET (15)
*SILVER: .6X TO 1.5X BASIC CARDS

1 Athena	3.00	8.00
2 Stokely Hathaway	2.00	5.00
3 Claudio Castagnoli	4.00	10.00
4 Madison Rayne	3.00	8.00
5 Trustbusters	2.50	6.00
6 W. Morrissey	2.00	5.00
7 Saraya	5.00	12.00
8 Rush	2.00	5.00
9 Renee Paquette	2.00	5.00
10 Willow Nightingale	3.00	8.00
11 Jeff Jarrett	2.00	5.00
12 Bandido	3.00	8.00

13 Konosuke Takeshita
14 AR Fox
15 Action Andretti

2021 Upper Deck AEW Spectrum

UNOPENED BOX (7 CARDS)
*DARK/99: .6X TO 1.5X BASIC CARDS
*RED/50: .75X TO 2X BASIC CARDS
*GREEN/25: UNPRICED DUE TO SCARCITY
*BEACH/10: UNPRICED DUE TO SCARCITY
*GOLD/1: UNPRICED DUE TO SCARCITY

1 Kenny Omega RC	6.00	15.00
2 Hikaru Shida RC	2.50	6.00
3 Joey Janela RC	1.50	4.00
4 Tay Conti	1.50	4.00
5 Isiah Kassidy RC	1.25	3.00
6 Jake Hager	.60	1.50
7 Rey Fenix RC	1.25	3.00
8 Anthony Bowens RC	1.50	4.00
9 Sonny Kiss RC	.75	2.00
10 Hangman Adam Page RC	4.00	10.00
11 MJF RC	10.00	25.00
12 Tony Schiavone	.50	1.25
13 Ricky Starks RC	1.25	3.00
14 Serpentico RC	.75	2.00
15 Christopher Daniels	.60	1.50
16 Wardlow RC	2.00	5.00
17 CM Punk	2.00	5.00
18 Trent?	.50	1.25
19 Penta el Zero M RC	1.50	4.00
20 Frankie Kazarian	.50	1.25
21 Chuck Taylor RC	.75	2.00
22 Darby Allin RC	3.00	8.00
23 Evil Uno RC	1.25	3.00
24 Paul Wight	.75	2.00
25 Leva Bates RC	.75	2.00

26 Powerhouse Hobbs RC	1.25	3.00
27 Aubrey Edwards RC	2.00	5.00
28 The Butcher RC	.75	2.00
29 Nyla Rose RC	1.50	4.00
30 Yuka Sakazaki RC	.75	2.00
31 Excalibur RC	.75	2.00
32 Cody Rhodes	1.25	3.00
33 Billy Gunn	.50	1.25
34 Marq Quen RC	.75	2.00
35 Ortiz RC	.75	2.00
36 Marko Stunt RC	.75	2.00
37 Malakai Black	1.00	2.50
38 Sting	1.50	4.00
39 Sammy Guevara RC	2.00	5.00
40 Miro	.75	2.00
41 The Bunny	1.00	2.50
42 Penelope Ford RC	3.00	8.00
43 Kip Sabian RC	1.00	2.50
44 The Blade RC	.75	2.00
45 Cash Wheeler	.60	1.50
46 Santana RC	.75	2.00
47 John Silver RC	.75	2.00
48 Matt Jackson RC	1.50	4.00
49 Colt Cabana RC	.75	2.00
50 Riho RC	1.25	3.00
51 Eddie Kingston RC	2.00	5.00
52 Ryo Mizunami RC	.75	2.00
53 Stu Grayson RC	.75	2.00
54 Matt Sydal	.40	1.00
55 Jon Moxley	1.00	2.50
56 Luchasaurus RC	2.50	6.00
57 Nick Jackson RC	1.50	4.00
58 Jade Cargill RC	5.00	12.00
59 Adam Cole	1.25	3.00
60 Griff Garrison RC	.75	2.00
61 Pres10 Vance RC	.75	2.00
62 Red Velvet RC	.75	2.00
63 Bryan Danielson	1.50	4.00
64 Orange Cassidy RC	2.00	5.00
65 Serena Deeb	.40	1.00
66 Dax Harwood	.60	1.50
67 Jim Ross	1.00	2.50
68 Leyla Hirsch RC	1.25	3.00
69 Brandi Rhodes	2.00	5.00
70 Diamante RC	.75	2.00
71 Austin Gunn RC	.75	2.00
72 Shawn Spears	.60	1.50
73 Luther RC	.75	2.00
74 Scorpio Sky RC	1.25	3.00
75 Chris Jericho	1.50	4.00
76 Jungle Boy RC	3.00	8.00
77 Brian Cage RC	.75	2.00
78 Max Caster RC	1.25	3.00
79 Thunder Rosa RC	5.00	12.00
80 Ethan Page RC	1.50	4.00
81 Dustin Rhodes	.75	2.00
82 Lee Johnson RC	.75	2.00
83 Dr. Britt Baker RC	2.50	6.00
84 Lance Archer	1.00	2.50
85 Kris Statlander RC	1.25	3.00
86 Matt Hardy	.75	2.00
87 Christian Cage	.60	1.50
88 Taz	.50	1.25
89 Alex Reynolds RC	.75	2.00
90 Pac	.75	2.00

2021 Upper Deck AEW Spectrum Autographed Diamond Battle Royale Relics

STATED PRINT RUN 12 SER.#'d SETS
UNPRICED DUE TO SCARCITY

DBR1 MJF
DBR2 Hangman Adam Page
DBR3 Sammy Guevara
DBR4 John Silver
DBR5 Alex Reynolds
DBR6 Isiah Kassidy
DBR7 Marq Quen
DBR8 Matt Hardy
DBR9 Scorpio Sky
DBR10 Shawn Spears
DBR11 Orange Cassidy
DBR12 Kip Sabian
DBR13 Miro
DBR14 Wardlow
DBR15 Jungle Boy

2021 Upper Deck AEW Spectrum Autographed Memorabilia

*DARK/10: UNPRICED DUE TO SCARCITY
*GOLD/1: UNPRICED DUE TO SCARCITY
STATED PRINT RUN 20 SER.#'d SETS

1 Kenny Omega
2 Hikaru Shida
3 Joey Janela
4 Tay Conti
5 Isiah Kassidy
6 Jake Hager
7 Rey Fenix
8 Anthony Bowens
9 Sonny Kiss
10 Hangman Adam Page
11 MJF
12 Tony Schiavone
13 Ricky Starks
14 Serpentico
15 Christopher Daniels
16 Wardlow
17 CM Punk
18 Trent?
19 Penta el Zero M
20 Frankie Kazarian
21 Chuck Taylor
22 Darby Allin
23 Evil Uno
24 Paul Wight
25 Leva Bates
26 Powerhouse Hobbs
27 Aubrey Edwards
28 The Butcher
29 Nyla Rose
31 Excalibur
32 Cody Rhodes
33 Billy Gunn
34 Marq Quen
35 Ortiz
36 Marko Stunt
37 Malakai Black
38 Sting
39 Sammy Guevara
40 Miro
41 The Bunny
42 Penelope Ford
43 Kip Sabian
44 The Blade
45 Cash Wheeler
46 Santana
47 John Silver
48 Matt Jackson
49 Colt Cabana
50 Riho
51 Eddie Kingston
53 Stu Grayson
55 Jon Moxley
56 Luchasaurus
57 Nick Jackson
58 Jade Cargill
60 Griff Garrison
61 Pres10 Vance
62 Red Velvet
64 Orange Cassidy
65 Serena Deeb
66 Dax Harwood
67 Jim Ross
68 Leyla Hirsch
69 Brandi Rhodes
70 Diamante
71 Austin Gunn
72 Shawn Spears
73 Luther
74 Scorpio Sky
75 Chris Jericho
76 Jungle Boy
77 Brian Cage
78 Max Caster
79 Thunder Rosa
80 Ethan Page
81 Dustin Rhodes
82 Lee Johnson
83 Dr. Britt Baker
84 Lance Archer
85 Kris Statlander
86 Matt Hardy
87 Christian Cage
88 Taz
89 Alex Reynolds
90 Pac

2021 Upper Deck AEW Spectrum Autographed On the Mat Relics

STATED PRINT RUN 25 SER.#'d SETS

OTM1 Tay Conti		
OTM2 Ethan Page	60.00	150.00
OTM3 Penelope Ford	75.00	200.00
OTM4 Chuck Taylor		
OTM5 The Bunny	40.00	100.00
OTM6 Kris Statlander	60.00	150.00
OTM7 Austin Gunn		
OTM8 Diamante		
OTM9 Red Velvet	15.00	40.00
OTM10 Jake Hager		
OTM11 Dr. Britt Baker	125.00	300.00
OTM12 Jungle Boy	30.00	75.00
OTM13 Marko Stunt		
OTM14 Anthony Bowens	30.00	75.00
OTM15 Pres10 Vance	20.00	50.00
OTM16 Trent?		
OTM17 Lee Johnson		
OTM18 Jade Cargill	60.00	150.00
OTM19 Angelico		
OTM20 Ricky Starks	30.00	75.00
OTM21 Christopher Daniels	12.00	30.00
OTM22 Powerhouse Hobbs	15.00	40.00
OTM23 Max Caster	50.00	125.00
OTM24 Riho	25.00	60.00

2021 Upper Deck AEW Spectrum Autographed Ring Generals Relics

STATED PRINT RUN 16 SER.#'d SETS
UNPRICED DUE TO SCARCITY

RL1 Rey Fenix
RL2 Cody Rhodes
RL3 Darby Allin
RL4 Pac
RL5 Thunder Rosa
RL6 Nick Jackson
RL7 Billy Gunn
RL8 Frankie Kazarian
RL9 Serena Deeb
RL10 Brian Cage
RL11 Powerhouse Hobbs
RL12 Jon Moxley
RL13 Sting
RL14 Hikaru Shida
RL15 Ortiz
RL16 Orange Cassidy
RL17 Matt Jackson
RL18 Paul Wight
RL19 MJF
RL20 Kenny Omega
RL21 Dr. Britt Baker
RL22 Miro
RL23 Santana
RL24 Chris Jericho

2021 Upper Deck AEW Spectrum Autographed Table for 2 Relics

STATED PRINT RUN 12 SER.#'d SETS
UNPRICED DUE TO SCARCITY

T21 Pac/A.Page
T22 J.Moxley/E.Kingston
T23 C.Rhodes/D.Rhodes
T24 B.Baker/T.Schiavone
T25 H.Shida/Abadon
T26 D.Allin/R.Starks
T27 M.Hardy/S.Guevara
T28 R.Velvet/J.Cargill
T29 N.Rose/Riho
T210 Sting/L.Archer
T211 C.Cage/K.Omega

T212 O.Cassidy/Miro
T213 MJF/C.Jericho

2021 Upper Deck AEW Spectrum Autographed Table for 4 Relics

STATED PRINT RUN 12 SER.#'d SETS
UNPRICED DUE TO SCARCITY

T41 Sting/Allin/Cage/Starks
T42 Wheeler/Harwood/Santana/Ortiz
T43 Miro/Sabian/Cassidy/Taylor
T44 Fenix/el Zero/Jacksons
T45 Butcher/Blade/Luchasaurus/Jungle Boy
T46 Pillman Jr./Garrison/Bowens/Caster
T47 Kassidy/Quen/Reynolds/Silver
T48 Page/Sky/Uno/Grayson

2021 Upper Deck AEW Spectrum Autographs

*DARK/25: UNPRICED DUE TO SCARCITY
*BEACH/5: UNPRICED DUE TO SCARCITY
*GOLD/1: UNPRICED DUE TO SCARCITY
*P.P.BLACK/1: UNPRICED DUE TO SCARCITY
*P.P.CYAN/1: UNPRICED DUE TO SCARCITY
*P.P.MAGENTA/1: UNPRICED DUE TO SCARCITY
*P.P.YELLOW/1: UNPRICED DUE TO SCARCITY
GROUP A ODDS 1:44
GROUP B ODDS 1:16
GROUP C ODDS 1:6
GROUP D ODDS 1:3
STATED ODDS 1:7 HOBBY/EPACK

1 Kenny Omega B	75.00	200.00
2 Hikaru Shida A	40.00	100.00
3 Joey Janela D	8.00	20.00
4 Tay Conti C	30.00	75.00
5 Isiah Kassidy D	8.00	20.00
6 Jake Hager B	10.00	25.00
7 Rey Fenix B	20.00	50.00
8 Anthony Bowens D	20.00	50.00
9 Sonny Kiss D	10.00	25.00
10 Hangman Adam Page A	50.00	125.00
11 MJF A	200.00	500.00
12 Tony Schiavone D	15.00	40.00
13 Ricky Starks D	30.00	75.00
14 Serpentico D	10.00	25.00
15 Christopher Daniels D	12.00	30.00
16 Wardlow D	30.00	75.00
17 CM Punk A	125.00	300.00
18 Trent? C	10.00	25.00
19 Penta el Zero M C	30.00	75.00
20 Frankie Kazarian C	12.00	30.00
21 Chuck Taylor D	12.00	30.00
22 Darby Allin B	60.00	150.00
23 Evil Uno D	12.00	30.00
24 Paul Wight B	12.00	30.00
25 Leva Bates D	10.00	25.00
26 Powerhouse Hobbs C	20.00	50.00
27 Aubrey Edwards D	30.00	75.00
28 The Butcher C	8.00	20.00
29 Nyla Rose C	12.00	30.00
30 Yuka Sakazaki B	12.00	30.00
31 Excalibur D	12.00	30.00
32 Cody Rhodes A	100.00	250.00
33 Billy Gunn C	12.00	30.00
34 Marq Quen D	8.00	20.00
35 Ortiz C	10.00	25.00
36 Marko Stunt D	8.00	20.00
37 Malakai Black C	30.00	75.00
38 Sting B	60.00	150.00
39 Sammy Guevara B	25.00	60.00
40 Miro B	10.00	25.00
41 The Bunny D	30.00	75.00
42 Penelope Ford D	40.00	100.00
43 Kip Sabian D	12.00	30.00
44 The Blade D	8.00	20.00
45 Cash Wheeler D	15.00	40.00
46 Santana C	12.00	30.00
47 John Silver D	10.00	25.00
48 Matt Jackson B	20.00	50.00
49 Colt Cabana D	12.00	30.00
50 Riho D	30.00	75.00
51 Eddie Kingston C	30.00	75.00
53 Stu Grayson C	12.00	30.00
54 Matt Sydal C	8.00	20.00
55 Jon Moxley A	50.00	125.00
56 Luchasaurus D	30.00	75.00
57 Nick Jackson B	20.00	50.00
58 Jade Cargill D	75.00	200.00
59 Adam Cole A	40.00	100.00
60 Griff Garrison D	12.00	30.00
61 Pres10 Vance D	12.00	30.00
62 Red Velvet D	15.00	40.00
63 Bryan Danielson A	40.00	100.00
64 Orange Cassidy B	40.00	100.00
65 Serena Deeb D	12.00	30.00
66 Dax Harwood D	15.00	40.00
67 Jim Ross C	15.00	40.00
68 Leyla Hirsch D	10.00	25.00
69 Brandi Rhodes C	20.00	50.00
70 Diamante D	12.00	30.00
71 Austin Gunn D	12.00	30.00
72 Shawn Spears D	8.00	20.00
73 Luther D	15.00	40.00
74 Scorpio Sky C	8.00	20.00
75 Chris Jericho B	60.00	150.00
76 Jungle Boy D	25.00	60.00
77 Brian Cage C	12.00	30.00
78 Max Caster D	25.00	60.00
79 Thunder Rosa C	60.00	150.00
80 Ethan Page D	30.00	75.00
81 Dustin Rhodes C	12.00	30.00
82 Lee Johnson D	10.00	25.00
83 Dr. Britt Baker C	75.00	200.00
84 Lance Archer C	10.00	25.00
85 Kris Statlander D	50.00	125.00
86 Matt Hardy B	15.00	40.00
87 Christian Cage C	15.00	40.00
88 Taz C	10.00	25.00
89 Alex Reynolds C	12.00	30.00
90 Pac C	15.00	40.00

2021 Upper Deck AEW Spectrum Banner Year Relics

RANDOMLY INSERTED INTO PACKS

BY1 Chris Jericho	15.00	40.00
May 25th, 2020		
BY2 Chris Jericho	15.00	40.00
September 5th, 2020		
BY3 Chris Jericho	15.00	40.00
October 7th, 2020		
BY4 Chris Jericho	15.00	40.00
November 7th, 202		
BY5 Chris Jericho	15.00	40.00
March 7th, 2021		
BY6 Chris Jericho	15.00	40.00
April 14th, 2021		
BY7 Chris Jericho	15.00	40.00
May 5th, 2021		
BY8 Chris Jericho	15.00	40.00
May 30th, 2021		

2021 Upper Deck AEW Spectrum Chair Shots

STATED ODDS 1:8 HOBBY/EPACK

CS1 Shawn Spears	3.00	8.00
CS2 Lance Archer	5.00	12.00
CS3 Dustin Rhodes	4.00	10.00
CS4 Dr. Britt Baker	10.00	25.00
CS5 Matt Hardy	4.00	10.00
CS6 Santana	3.00	8.00
CS7 Miro	4.00	10.00
CS8 Jon Moxley	5.00	12.00
CS9 The Blade	3.00	8.00
CS10 Penta el Zero M	5.00	12.00
CS11 Thunder Rosa	8.00	20.00
CS12 Sammy Guevara	5.00	12.00
CS13 Darby Allin	12.00	30.00
CS14 The Butcher	3.00	8.00
CS15 Joey Janela	2.00	5.00
CS16 Eddie Kingston	6.00	15.00
CS17 Ethan Page	5.00	12.00
CS18 Chris Jericho	8.00	20.00
CS19 Ortiz	3.00	8.00
CS20 Kenny Omega	12.00	30.00

2021 Upper Deck AEW Spectrum Diamond Battle Royale Relics

STATED PRINT RUN 25 SER.#'d SETS

DBR1 MJF	75.00	200.00
DBR2 Hangman Adam Page	75.00	200.00
DBR3 Sammy Guevara	30.00	75.00
DBR4 John Silver	25.00	60.00
DBR5 Alex Reynolds	20.00	50.00
DBR6 Isiah Kassidy	20.00	50.00
DBR7 Marq Quen	20.00	50.00
DBR8 Matt Hardy	25.00	60.00
DBR9 Scorpio Sky	25.00	60.00
DBR10 Shawn Spears	20.00	50.00
DBR11 Orange Cassidy	40.00	100.00
DBR12 Kip Sabian	30.00	75.00
DBR13 Miro	25.00	60.00
DBR14 Wardlow	60.00	150.00
DBR15 Jungle Boy	60.00	150.00

2021 Upper Deck AEW Spectrum Full Gear

STATED ODDS 1:4 HOBBY/EPACK

FG1 Jon Moxley	8.00	20.00
FG2 Dr. Britt Baker	20.00	50.00
FG3 Orange Cassidy	6.00	15.00
FG4 Darby Allin	12.00	30.00
FG5 MJF	15.00	40.00
FG6 Hangman Adam Page	12.00	30.00
FG7 Riho	10.00	25.00
FG8 Nyla Rose	6.00	15.00
FG9 Cash Wheeler	6.00	15.00
FG10 Dax Harwood	6.00	15.00
FG11 Serena Deeb	5.00	12.00
FG12 Matt Jackson	12.00	30.00
FG13 Nick Jackson	12.00	30.00
FG14 Eddie Kingston	15.00	40.00
FG15 John Silver	5.00	12.00
FG16 Hikaru Shida	12.00	30.00
FG17 Chris Jericho	10.00	25.00
FG18 Cody Rhodes	12.00	30.00
FG19 Matt Hardy	5.00	12.00
FG20 Kenny Omega	30.00	75.00

2021 Upper Deck AEW Spectrum Memorabilia

*DARK/25: UNPRICED DUE TO SCARCITY
*GOLD/1: UNPRICED DUE TO SCARCITY
STATED ODDS 1:1 HOBBY/EPACK

1 Kenny Omega	8.00	20.00
2 Hikaru Shida	4.00	10.00
3 Joey Janela	1.25	3.00
4 Tay Conti	5.00	12.00
5 Isiah Kassidy	1.50	4.00
6 Jake Hager	2.00	5.00
7 Rey Fenix	3.00	8.00
8 Anthony Bowens	1.25	3.00
9 Sonny Kiss	1.25	3.00
10 Hangman Adam Page	8.00	20.00
11 MJF	8.00	20.00
12 Tony Schiavone	1.50	4.00
13 Ricky Starks	3.00	8.00
14 Serpentico	1.25	3.00
15 Christopher Daniels	2.00	5.00
16 Wardlow	2.50	6.00
17 CM Punk	6.00	15.00
18 Trent?	1.50	4.00
19 Penta el Zero M	3.00	8.00
20 Frankie Kazarian	1.50	4.00
21 Chuck Taylor	1.50	4.00
22 Darby Allin	8.00	20.00
23 Evil Uno	2.50	6.00
24 Paul Wight	2.50	6.00
25 Leva Bates	1.25	3.00
26 Powerhouse Hobbs	2.50	6.00
27 Aubrey Edwards	3.00	8.00
28 The Butcher	2.00	5.00
29 Nyla Rose	2.50	6.00
31 Excalibur	1.25	3.00
32 Cody Rhodes	4.00	10.00
33 Billy Gunn	1.50	4.00
34 Marq Quen	1.50	4.00
35 Ortiz	2.00	5.00
36 Marko Stunt	1.25	3.00
37 Malakai Black	3.00	8.00
38 Sting	5.00	12.00
39 Sammy Guevara	3.00	8.00
40 Miro	2.50	6.00
41 The Bunny	3.00	8.00
42 Penelope Ford	2.00	5.00
43 Kip Sabian	2.50	6.00
44 The Blade	2.00	5.00
45 Cash Wheeler	2.00	5.00
46 Santana	2.00	5.00
47 John Silver	1.25	3.00
48 Matt Jackson	5.00	12.00

49 Colt Cabana	1.50	4.00
50 Riho	5.00	12.00
51 Eddie Kingston	4.00	10.00
53 Stu Grayson	1.25	3.00
55 Jon Moxley	3.00	8.00
56 Luchasaurus	4.00	10.00
57 Nick Jackson	5.00	12.00
58 Jade Cargill	6.00	15.00
60 Griff Garrison	1.25	3.00
61 Pres10 Vance	1.25	3.00
62 Red Velvet	1.25	3.00
64 Orange Cassidy	3.00	8.00
65 Serena Deeb	1.25	3.00
66 Dax Harwood	2.00	5.00
67 Jim Ross	3.00	8.00
68 Leyla Hirsch	1.50	4.00
69 Brandi Rhodes	6.00	15.00
70 Diamante	1.25	3.00
71 Austin Gunn	1.50	4.00
72 Shawn Spears	2.00	5.00
73 Luther	1.25	3.00
74 Scorpio Sky	1.25	3.00
75 Chris Jericho	5.00	12.00
76 Jungle Boy	5.00	12.00
77 Brian Cage	1.50	4.00
78 Max Caster	1.50	4.00
79 Thunder Rosa	5.00	12.00
80 Ethan Page	3.00	8.00
81 Dustin Rhodes	2.50	6.00
82 Lee Johnson	1.25	3.00
83 Dr. Britt Baker	6.00	15.00
84 Lance Archer	3.00	8.00
85 Kris Statlander	2.00	5.00
86 Matt Hardy	2.50	6.00
87 Christian Cage	2.00	5.00
88 Taz	1.50	4.00
89 Alex Reynolds	1.25	3.00
90 Pac	2.50	6.00

2021 Upper Deck AEW Spectrum On the Mat Relics

RANDOMLY INSERTED INTO PACKS

OTM1 Tay Conti	10.00	25.00
OTM2 Ethan Page	6.00	15.00
OTM3 Penelope Ford	4.00	10.00
OTM4 Chuck Taylor	3.00	8.00
OTM5 The Bunny	6.00	15.00
OTM6 Kris Statlander	4.00	10.00
OTM/ Austin Gunn	3.00	8.00
OTM8 Diamante	2.50	6.00
OTM9 Red Velvet	2.50	6.00
OTM10 Jake Hager	4.00	10.00
OTM11 Dr. Britt Baker	12.00	30.00
OTM12 Jungle Boy	10.00	25.00
OTM13 Marko Stunt	2.50	6.00
OTM14 Anthony Bowens	2.50	6.00
OTM15 Pres10 Vance	2.50	6.00
OTM16 Trent?	3.00	8.00
OTM17 Lee Johnson	2.50	6.00
OTM18 Jade Cargill	12.00	30.00
OTM19 Angelico	2.50	6.00
OTM20 Ricky Starks	6.00	15.00
OTM21 Christopher Daniels	4.00	10.00
OTM22 Powerhouse Hobbs	5.00	12.00
OTM23 Max Caster	3.00	8.00
OTM24 Riho	10.00	25.00

2021 Upper Deck AEW Spectrum Ring Generals Relics

STATED PRINT RUN 50 SER.#'d SETS

RL1 Rey Fenix	15.00	40.00
RL2 Cody Rhodes	40.00	100.00
RL3 Darby Allin	30.00	75.00
RL4 Pac	20.00	50.00
RL5 Thunder Rosa	30.00	75.00
RL6 Nick Jackson	25.00	60.00
RL7 Billy Gunn	10.00	25.00
RL8 Frankie Kazarian	12.00	30.00
RL9 Serena Deeb	10.00	25.00
RL10 Brian Cage	15.00	40.00
RL11 Powerhouse Hobbs	15.00	40.00
RL12 Jon Moxley	15.00	40.00
RL13 Sting	40.00	100.00
RL14 Hikaru Shida	25.00	60.00
RL15 Ortiz	10.00	25.00
RL16 Orange Cassidy		50.00
RL17 Matt Jackson	20.00	50.00
RL18 Paul Wight	10.00	25.00
RL19 MJF	75.00	200.00
RL20 Kenny Omega	40.00	100.00
RL21 Dr. Britt Baker	40.00	100.00
RL22 Miro	12.00	30.00
RL23 Santana	12.00	30.00
RL24 Chris Jericho	30.00	75.00

2021 Upper Deck AEW Spectrum Table for 2 Relics

STATED ODDS 1:9 HOBBY/EPACK

T21 Pac/A.Page	15.00	40.00
T22 J.Moxley/E.Kingston	15.00	40.00
T23 C.Rhodes/D.Rhodes	30.00	75.00
T24 B.Baker/T.Schiavone	20.00	50.00
T25 H.Shida/Abadon	15.00	40.00
T26 D.Allin/R.Starks	20.00	50.00
T27 M.Hardy/S.Guevara	15.00	40.00
T28 R.Velvet/J.Cargill	30.00	75.00
T29 N.Rose/Riho	15.00	40.00
T210 Sting/L.Archer	25.00	60.00
T211 C.Cage/K.Omega	30.00	75.00
T212 O.Cassidy/Miro	15.00	40.00
T213 MJF/C.Jericho	20.00	50.00

2021 Upper Deck AEW Spectrum Table for 4 Relics

*GOLD/12: UNPRICED DUE TO SCARCITY
STATED ODDS 1:36 HOBBY/EPACK

T41 Sting/Allin/Cage/Starks	50.00	125.00
T42 Wheeler/Harwood/Santana/Ortiz	20.00	50.00
T43 Miro/Sabian/Cassidy/Taylor	12.00	30.00
T44 Fenix/el Zero/Jacksons	15.00	40.00
T45 Butcher/Blade/Luchasaurus/Jungle Boy12.0030.00		
T46 Pillman Jr./Garrison/Bowens/Caster12.00		30.00
T47 Kassidy/Quen/Reynolds/Silver	12.00	30.00
T48 Page/Sky/Uno/Grayson	20.00	50.00

2022 Upper Deck AEW Spectrum Revolution Fan Fest Promo Sheet

FF1 Tay Conti/FF2 "Hangman" Adam Page/FF3 MJF/FF4 CM Punk
NNO Cover Card/Bryan Danielson/Jade Cargill/Jungle Boy/Dr. Britt Baker DMD

2022 Upper Deck AEW Spectrum Revolution Fan Fest Promos

FF1 Tay Conti
FF2 Hangman Adam Page
FF3 MJF
FF4 CM Punk
FF5 Bryan Danielson
FF6 Jade Cargill
FF7 Jungle Boy
FF8 Dr. Britt Baker DMD
NNO Cover Card

2000 Waldenbooks WWF Limited Edition

COMPLETE SET (2)	8.00	20.00
1 Have a Nice Day!	3.00	8.00
2 The Rock Says	6.00	15.00

1993 WCW Magazine Collector's Special 3

10 Steve Austin	75.00	150.00
11 Johnny B. Badd		
12 Cactus Jack		
13 Shane Douglas		
14 Van Hammer		
15 Missy Hyatt	2.50	6.00
16 Jushin Liger		
17 Madusa		
18 Brian Pillman		
19 Dustin Rhodes		
20 Rick Rude	3.00	8.00
21 Ron Simmons		
22 Ricky Steamboat		
23 Sting		
24 Big Van Vader		
25 Erik Watts	3.00	8.00
26 Barry Windham	2.50	6.00
27 Tom Zenk		

1988 Wonderama NWA

COMPLETE SET (343)	300.00	600.00
1 Ric Flair RC	75.00	150.00
2 Tommy Angel RC	.40	1.00
3 Dusty Rhodes/Tully Blanchard	2.50	6.00
4 Baby Doll RC	1.25	3.00
5 Eddie Gilbert RC	2.00	5.00
6 Rocky King RC	.75	2.00
7 Lex Luger/Arn Anderson	1.50	4.00
8 Mike Rotunda vs. Ivan Koloff	.60	1.50
9 Barry Windham/Sting	5.00	12.00
10 Ron Simmons RC	.20	3.00
11 Mighty Wilbur RC	.40	1.00
12 Skandor Akbar RC	.60	1.50
13 Precious RC	1.50	4.00
14 Shaska Whatley vs. Jimmy Valiant	.40	1.00
15 Curtis Thompson RC	.75	2.00
16 Kendall Windham RC	2.00	5.00
17 Sting RC	20.00	50.00
18 Paul Ellering RC	1.25	3.00
19 Johnny Ace RC	.75	2.00
20 Kat Leroux w/Linda Dallas	.75	2.00
21 Michael Hayes RC	1.00	2.50
22 Terry Taylor RC	.40	1.00
23 Barry Windham RC	2.50	6.00
24 Johnny Weaver vs. J.J. Dillon	.40	1.00
25 Tully Blanchard RC	1.00	2.50
26 Dick Murdoch RC	.75	2.00
27 Stan Lane RC	.75	2.00
28 Barbarian w/Paul Jones	.40	1.00
29 Linda Dallas w/Misty Blue	.75	2.00
30 Road Warriors	15.00	40.00
31 Stan Lane vs. Sean Royal	.50	1.25
32 Ricky Santana RC	.40	1.00
33 Jimmy Valiant RC	1.25	3.00
34 Larry Zbyszko vs. Kendall Windham	.75	2.00
35 Lex Luger RC	2.00	5.00
36 Shaska Whatley RC	.40	1.00
37 Warlord RC	.40	1.00
38 Bobby Eaton RC	2.00	5.00
39 Dusty Rhodes RC	2.50	6.00
40 Paul Jones RC	.40	1.00
41 Eddie Gilbert/Sting	2.00	5.00
42 Butch Miller RC	.40	1.00
43 Barry Windham/Arn Anderson	3.00	8.00
44 Michael Hayes RC	1.00	2.50
45 Larry Stephens RC	.40	1.00
46 Black Bart RC	.40	1.00
47 Gladiator #2 RC	.40	.30
48 Ric Flair/Sting	3.00	8.00
49 Ivan Koloff RC	1.25	3.00
50 Jamie West RC	.40	1.00
51 Larry Zbyszko RC	.75	2.00
52 Sean Royal vs. Bobby Eaton	.40	1.00
53 Arn Anderson vs. Lex Luger	2.00	5.00
54 Baby Doll RC	.60	1.50
55 Tim Horner vs. Shaska Whatley	.40	1.00
56 Jimmy Garvin vs. Tully Blanchard	1.00	2.50
57 Kendall Windham vs. Gladiator	.40	1.00
58 Terry Taylor vs. Eddie Gilbert	.75	2.00
59 Dick Murdoch RC	.50	1.25
60 Stan Lane vs. Sean Royal	.40	.30
61 Magnum T.A. RC	.75	.75
62 Ricky Santana RC	.40	.30
63 Luke Williams RC	.40	.30
64 Robert Gibson RC	1.50	4.00
65 Ron Garvin RC	.40	1.00
66 Ivan Koloff RC	.50	.50
67 Larry Zbyszko vs. Kendall Windham	.50	.50
68a Butch Miller RC	1.25	3.00
68b Ric Flair logo	6.00	15.00
69 Ricky Morton RC	1.50	4.00
70 Tommy Angel RC	.40	1.00
71 Stan Lane vs. Sean Royal	.40	.30
72 Kendall Windham RC	.40	.30
73 Baby Doll RC	.50	.50
74a Black Bart RC		
74b Barry Windham logo	1.00	2.50
75 Road Warrior Hawk RC	1.50	4.00
76 Mike Rotunda	.60	1.50
77 Ron Simmons/Arn Anderson	1.00	2.50
78 J.J. Dillon RC	.40	1.00
79 Shaska Whatley vs. Jimmy Valiant	.60	1.50
80 Kat Leroux RC	.50	1.25
81 Kendall Windham vs. Larry Zbyszko	.50	1.25
82 Road Warrior Animal RC	2.00	5.00
83 D.Murdoch/Steve Williams	.50	1.25
84 Tully Blanchard RC	2.50	6.00
85 Barbarian RC	.75	2.00
86 Robert Gibson RC	1.25	3.00
87 Ricky Santana RC	.40	1.00
88 Jimmy Valiant RC	.60	1.50

89 Nikita Koloff/Ric Flair	4.00	10.00
90 Kat Leroux vs. Misty Blue	.50	1.25
91 Kevin Sullivan RC	6.00	15.00
92 Luke Williams RC	.40	1.00
93 Lex Luger/Arn Anderson	1.00	2.50
94 Big Bubba Rogers RC	1.25	3.00
95 Bobby Eaton RC	.60	1.50
96 Paul Jones RC	.40	1.00
97 Butch Miller RC	.40	.30
98 Jimmy Garvin w/Precious	1.25	3.00
99a Warlord vs. Sting	2.00	5.00
99b Dusty Rhodes logo	3.00	8.00
100 Ivan Koloff RC	.50	1.25
101 Larry Zbyszko RC	.50	.50
102 Sting RC	20.00	50.00
103 Larry Zbyszko/Baby Doll	.60	1.50
104 Eddie Gilbert/Sting	1.00	2.50
105 Dusty Rhodes RC	2.00	5.00
106 Mighty Wilbur RC	.40	1.00
107 Michael Hayes/Ric Flair	.60	1.50
108 Brad Armstorng w/Tom Horner	.40	.30
109 Terry Taylor RC	.40	.30
110 Dick Murdoch RC	.50	.50
111 Tully Blanchard RC	.75	2.00
112 Ricky Santana vs. Warlord	.40	1.00
113 Jimmy Valiant RC	1.25	3.00
114 Kevin Sullivan RC	.60	1.50
115 Paul Jones RC	.40	1.00
116 Lex Luger/Sting	8.00	20.00
117 Ivan Koloff RC	.50	1.25
118 Larry Zbyszko/Barry Windham	.50	.50
119 Italian Stallion RC	.40	.30
120 Dusty Rhodes RC	2.00	5.00
121 Tim Horner vs. Chris Champion	.40	1.00
122 Eddie Gilbert/Sting	1.50	4.00
123 Mighty Wilbur vs. Ivan Koloff	.50	1.25
124 Barry Windham RC	.50	.50
125 Dick Murdoch RC	.50	1.25
126 Lex Luger RC	3.00	8.00
127 Dusty Rhodes/Nikita Koloff	1.00	2.50
128 Barbarian/Warlord/Ivan Koloff	.50	1.25
129 Paul Jones RC	.40	.30
130 Arn Anderson/Barry Windham	.75	2.00
131 Ivan Koloff RC	.75	2.00
132 Baby Doll/Dusty Rhodes	1.50	4.00
133 Eddie Gilbert w/Terry Taylor	.60	1.50
134 Rocky King w/Kendall Windham	.40	1.00
135 Jimmy Garvin vs. Tully Blanchard	.75	2.00
136a Ricky Morton vs. Ric Flair	1.50	4.00
136b Lex Luger logo	1.50	4.00
137 Tim Horner vs. Gladiator	.40	1.00
138 Kendall Windham RC	.40	.30
139 Magnum T.A. RC	.75	.75
140 Terry Taylor RC	.40	.30
141 Dick Murdoch/Steve Williams	.60	.60
142 Barbarian RC	.40	.30
143 Mad Dog Debbie RC	.40	.30
144 Dr. Death Steve Williams RC	.50	.50
145 Italian Stallion RC	.40	.30
146 Jimmy Valiant RC	3.00	8.00
147 Kevin Sullivan vs. Jimmy Garvin	.40	1.00
148 Ron Garvin RC	.40	.30
149 Ricky Morton RC	1.00	2.50
150 Luke Williams RC	.40	1.00
151 Paul Jones RC	.40	.30
152 Butch Miller RC	.40	.30
153 Warlord/Sting	1.50	4.00
154 Ricky Morton/Ric Flair	1.25	3.00
155 Black Bart RC	.40	1.00
156 Gladiators 1 & 2	.40	1.00
157 Ivan Koloff RC	.50	1.25
158 Larry Zbyszko w/Baby Doll	.60	1.50
159 Road Warrior Hawk RC	1.50	4.00
160 Bobby Eaton vs. Chris Champion	.40	1.00
161 Paul Jones RC	.40	1.00
162 Ric Flair RC	10.00	25.00
163 Luke Williams RC	.40	.30
164 Dick Murdoch/Steve Williams	.50	.50
165 J.J. Dillon RC	.40	.30
166 Linda Dallas vs. Misty Blue	.50	.50
167 Mike Rotunda	.40	1.00
168 Tommy Angel RC	.40	.30
169 Baby Doll RC	.50	.50
170 Animal/I.Koloff	.60	.60
171 Mike Rotunda w/Kevin Sullivan	.40	.30
172 Ron Garvin RC	.40	.30
173 Ron Simmons RC	.50	.50
174 Robert Gibson RC	.40	.30
175 Four Horsemen logo	4.00	10.00
176 Pee Wee Anderson RC	.40	1.00
177 Tony Schiavone RC	1.50	4.00
178 Tiger Conway RC	.40	1.00
179 Nikita Koloff RC	.75	2.00
180 Chris Champion RC	.40	1.00
181 Kendall Windham RC	.40	.30
182 Paul Ellering vs. Paul Jones	.40	.30
183 Lex Luger RC	1.50	4.00
184 Johnny Ace RC	.40	1.00
185 Cougar Jay RC	.40	1.00
186 Missy Hyatt w/Magnum T.A.	.75	.75
187 Precious RC	1.00	2.50
188 Kat Leroux vs. Misty Blue	.50	1.25
189 Denny Brown w/Nelson Royal	.40	.30
190 Johnny Weaver RC	.40	.30
191 Sting/Eddie Gilbert	6.00	15.00
192 Dick Murdoch RC	.50	1.25
193 Ole Anderson RC	.40	.30
194 Sting RC	20.00	50.00
195 Barbarian RC	.40	1.00
196 Road Warrior Animal RC	2.00	5.00
197 Michael Hayes/Ric Flair	.60	1.50
198 Paul Jones RC	.40	.30
199 Ricky Santana RC	.40	.30
200 Ron Garvin RC	.40	.30
201 Jimmy Valiant RC	.40	.30
202 Tully Blanchard RC	.50	.50
203 Shaska Whatley RC	.40	.30
204 Rock 'N Roll Express	5.00	12.00
205 Brad Armstrong RC	.40	1.00
206 Misty Blue RC	.50	.50
207 Road Warriors	5.00	12.00
208 Larry Zbyszko RC	.50	1.25
209 Bobby Eaton RC	.40	.30
210 Paul Jones w/Warlord	.40	.30
211 Butch Miller RC	.40	.30
212 Lex Luger RC	.75	2.00
213 Larry Stephens RC	.40	1.00
214 Warlord/Sting	1.25	3.00
215 Dr. Death Steve Williams RC	.50	1.25
216 Tommy Young RC	.40	.30
217 Nikita Koloff RC	.40	.30
218 George South RC	.40	.30
219 Dusty Rhodes/Ric Flair	3.00	8.00
220 Black Bart RC	.40	1.00
221 Ivan Koloff RC	.50	.50
222 Barry Windham RC	.50	.50
223 Larry Zbyszko RC	.50	.50
224 Sean Royal RC	.40	.30
225 Kevin Sullivan vs. Jimmy Garvin	.40	.30
226 Eddie Gilbert RC	1.00	2.50
227 Ric Flair/Robert Gibson	2.50	6.00
228 Eddie Gilbert RC	1.00	2.50
229 Rocky King vs. Nelson Royal	.40	.30
230 Mike Rotunda	.40	1.00
231 Arn Anderson RC	.50	.50
232 Ron Simmons RC	1.25	3.00
233 Mighty Wilbur RC	.40	.30
234 Tony Schiavone RC	1.50	4.00
235 Skandor Akbar RC	.40	.30
236 Jimmy Garvin vs. Tully Blanchard	.50	.50
237 Jive Tones	.40	.30
238 Tim Horner RC	.40	.30
239 Arn Anderson RC	1.25	3.00
240 Ivan Koloff w/Paul Jones	.50	1.25
241 Paul Jones RC	.40	.30
242 Magnum T.A./Arn Anderson	.75	.75
243 Kevin Sullivan w/Mike Rotunda	.40	.30
244 Ricky Santana RC	.40	.30
245 Baby Doll RC	.50	.50
246 Eddie Gilbert/Ron Garvin	.50	.50
247 Dr. Death Steve Williams RC	.50	.50
248 Mike Rotunda vs. Jimmy Garvin	.40	.30
249 Mighty Wilbur RC	.40	.30
250 Kevin Sullivan vs. Jimmy Garvin	.40	.30
251 Dick Murdoch RC	.50	.50
252 Ron Garvin/Ric Flair	.60	1.50
253 Trent Knight RC	.40	.30
254 Curtis Thompson RC	.40	.30
255 Mighty Wilbur RC	.40	.30
256 Luke Williams RC	.40	.30
257 Ricky Morton/Ric Flair	.60	1.50
258 Missy Hyatt RC	2.00	5.00
259 Road Warrior Animal RC	1.50	4.00
260 Nelson Royal RC	.40	1.00
261 Magnum T.A. RC	.75	.75
262 Road Warriors	2.00	5.00
263 Johnny Weaver RC	.40	1.00
264 Precious RC	.50	1.25
265 Robert Gibson RC	.40	.30
266 Dick Murdoch RC	.50	.50
267 Arn Anderson RC	.50	.50
268 Ole Anderson RC	.50	.50
269 Barbarian RC	.40	.30
270 Ric Flair/Ron Garvin	2.00	5.00
271 Linda Dallas vs. Venus	.50	.50
272 Gene Ligon RC	.40	1.00
273 Ricky Santana RC	.40	.30
274 Lex Luger/Nikita Koloff	.40	1.00
275 Misty Blue vs. Linda Dallas	.50	.50
276 J.J. Dillon RC	.40	.30
277 David Isley RC	.40	.30
278 Teddy Long RC	.40	1.00
279 Road Warriors	2.00	5.00
280 Kevin Sullivan RC	.40	1.00
281 Road Warrior Animal RC	1.25	3.00
282 Luke Williams RC	.40	.30
283 Big Bubba Rogers RC	1.25	3.00
284 Jimmy Garvin RC	.40	.30
285 Denny Brown RC	.40	.30
286 Bobby Eaton RC	.40	.30
287 Robert Gibson RC	.40	.30
288 Paul Jones RC	.40	.30
289 Butch Miller RC	.40	.30
290 Warlord vs. Road Warrior Animal	.60	1.50
291 Tommy Young RC	.40	.30
292 Nikita Koloff RC	.40	.30
293 Black Bart RC	.40	.30
294 Gladiator #1 RC	.40	.30
295 Ivan Koloff RC	.50	.50
296 Ricky Nelson RC	.40	.30
297 Dr. Death Steve Williams RC	.50	.50
298 Rick Steiner RC	.40	1.00
299 Larry Zbyszko RC	.60	.60
300 Sean Royal RC	.40	.30
301 Road Warriors	.60	.60
302 Baby Doll RC	.50	.50
303 J.J. Dillon/Lex Luger	.50	1.25
304 Tim Horner RC	.40	.30
305 Paul Ellering RC	.40	.30
306 Lex Luger/Gladiator	.40	1.00
307 J.J. Dillon RC	.40	.30
308 Midnight Express	.40	.30
309 Sheepherders w/Johnny Ace	.40	.30
310 Jimmy Garvin w/Precious	.40	.30
311 Kat Leroux RC	.50	.50
312 Jimmy Garvin RC	.40	.30
313 Road Warriors.	.60	.60
314 Ricky Morton RC	.40	.30
315 Barbarian RC	.40	.30
316 Linda Dallas RC	.50	.50
317 Sting/Eddie Gilbert	2.50	6.00
318 Italian Stallion RC	.40	.30
319 Ricky Santana RC	.40	.30
320 Jimmy Valiant RC	.40	.30
321 Shaska Whatley RC	.40	.30
322 Michael Hayes RC	.40	.30
323 Misty Blue RC	.50	.50
324 Magnum T.A. RC	.75	.75
325 Venus RC	.40	1.00
326 Luke Williams RC	.40	.30
327 Road Warrior Animal RC	1.25	3.00
328 Dr. Death Steve Williams RC	.50	.50
329 Bobby Eaton RC	.40	.30
330 Paul Jones RC	.40	.30
331 Butch Miller RC	.40	.30
332 Tully Blanchard RC	1.25	3.00
333 Warlord vs. Road Warrior Hawk	.75	.75
334 Ivan Koloff w/Paul Jones	.50	.50
335 Jamie West RC	.40	.30
336 Larry Zbyszko/Dusty Rhodes	.75	.75
337 Lex Luger RC	.40	1.00
338 Sean Royal RC	.40	.30
339 Four Horsemen	30.00	75.00
340 Jimmy Garvin RC	.40	.30
341 Road Warriors/Paul Ellering	.60	.60
342 Comrade Orga RC	.40	.30
343 Magnum T.A. RC	.75	.75
NNO Checklist 1	.75	2.00
NNO Checklist 2	.75	2.00
NNO Checklist 3	.75	2.00
NNO Checklist 4	.75	2.00

2019-20 WWE Bray Wyatt Collector's Boxes

Box 1 Firefly Funhouse/500*	125.00	250.00
Box 2 Wyatt Gym/1000*	30.00	75.00
Box 3 The Holidays with Ramblin' Rabbit	30.00	75.00
Box 4 Mercy the Buzzard		

Action Figures & Figurines

2017 Bleacher Creatures WWE

NNO AJ Styles	12.50	25.00
NNO Bayley	12.50	25.00
NNO Braun Strowman		
NNO Finn Balor	7.50	15.00
NNO Jeff Hardy		
NNO Kevin Owens	12.50	25.00
NNO Seth Rollins	10.00	20.00
NNO Shinsuke Nakamura		
NNO Stone Cold Steve Austin		

2013-18 Bleacher Creatures WWE Shop Exclusives

NNO Hulk Hogan
NNO John Cena
NNO Roman Reigns
NNO Ultimate Warrior

2013 Bleacher Creatures WWE Series 1

NNO CM Punk
NNO Daniel Bryan
NNO John Cena
NNO Kane
NNO Ryback
NNO Sheamus

2013 Bleacher Creatures WWE Series 2

NNO CM Punk
NNO John Cena
NNO Randy Orton

2014 Bleacher Creatures WWE WrestleMania 30

NNO New Orleans Bear

2010 Burger King WWEKids.com Plush 6-Inch

NNO John Cena
NNO Triple H
NNO Undertaker

2021 Creative Ventures Brawler Ballz

NNO Lucha Bros.
NNO Road Warriors
NNO Rowdy Roddy Piper

2016 Figures Toy Co. Ring of Honor Series 1

NNO Jay Briscoe
NNO Jay Lethal
NNO Kevin Steen
NNO Mark Briscoe

2016 Figures Toy Co. Ring of Honor Series 1 2-Packs

NNO Jay & Mark Briscoe
NNO Kevin Steen & Jay Lethal

2016 Figures Toy Co. Ring of Honor Series 1 4-Pack

NNO Kevin Steen/Jay Briscoe/Mark Briscoe/Jay Lethal

2017 Figures Toy Co. Ring of Honor Series 2

NNO Adam Cole
NNO Bobby Fish
NNO Delirious
NNO Kyle O'Reilly

2018 Figures Toy Co. Ring of Honor Series 3

NNO Hanson
NNO Nigel McGuinness
NNO Raymond Rowe
NNO Roderick Strong

2019 Figures Toy Co. Ring of Honor Series 4

NNO ACH
NNO Dalton Castle
NNO Matt Taven
NNO Moose

2008 FOCO Bobbleheads WWE

NNO CM Punk
NNO Hornswoggle
NNO Jeff Hardy
NNO John Cena
NNO Mr. Kennedy
NNO Rey Mysterio
NNO Shawn Michaels
NNO Stone Cold Steve Austin
NNO Triple H
NNO Undertaker

2021 FOCO Bobbleheads WWE

NNO AJ Styles
NNO Andre the Giant
NNO Asuka
NNO Daniel Bryan (Moment)
NNO Edge
NNO Edge vs. Jeff Hardy (Moment)
NNO Hulk Hogan (red and yellow pose)
NNO Hulk Hogan nWo
NNO Kane (Brothers of Destruction)
NNO Kevin Nash nWo
NNO Mankind & Undertaker (HIAC)
NNO Rey Mysterio
NNO Ric Flair
NNO Roman Reigns
NNO Ronda Rousey
NNO Sasha Banks
NNO Scott Hall nWo
NNO Stone Cold Steve Austin
NNO The Fiend Bray Wyatt
NNO Triple H
NNO Ultimate Warrior (Moment)
NNO Undertaker
NNO Undertaker (Brothers of Destruction)

2015 Funko Mystery Minis WWE Series 1

COMPLETE SET (15)	55.00	110.00
UNOPENED CASE (12 BOXES)		
UNOPENED BOX (1 MINI)		
NNO Andre the Giant	3.00	6.00
NNO Brie Bella	3.00	6.00
NNO Daniel Bryan	3.00	6.00
NNO George The Animal Steele	6.00	12.00
NNO Hacksaw Jim Duggan WM	10.00	20.00
NNO Hulk Hogan	12.50	25.00
NNO Iron Sheik	6.00	12.00
NNO John Cena	3.00	6.00
NNO Nikki Bella	4.00	8.00
NNO Randy Savage WM	12.50	25.00
NNO Ric Flair	12.50	25.00
NNO Rock	7.50	15.00
NNO Rowdy Roddy Piper WM	15.00	30.00
NNO Ultimate Warrior	6.00	12.00
NNO Undertaker	4.00	8.00

2016 Funko Mystery Minis WWE Series 2

COMPLETE SET (15)	50.00	100.00
UNOPENED CASE (12 BOXES)		
UNOPENED BOX (1 MINI)		
NNO Bret Hitman Hart	3.00	6.00
NNO Brock Lesnar	4.00	8.00
NNO Dusty Rhodes	3.00	6.00
NNO Goldust	3.00	6.00
NNO Jake The Snake Roberts TAR	20.00	40.00
NNO John Cena	4.00	8.00
NNO Kevin Nash	3.00	6.00
NNO Million Dollar Man Ted Dibiase	3.00	6.00
NNO Randy Orton	3.00	6.00
NNO Razor Ramon TAR	15.00	30.00
NNO Roman Reigns	3.00	6.00
NNO Seth Rollins	3.00	6.00
NNO Sgt. Slaughter TAR	10.00	20.00
NNO Sting	3.00	6.00
NNO Stone Cold Steve Austin	6.00	12.00

2017 Funko Pint Size Heroes WWE

COMPLETE SET (19)	75.00	150.00
NNO Andre the Giant	10.00	20.00
NNO Big E	4.00	8.00
NNO Bray Wyatt	4.00	8.00
NNO Brock Lesnar	3.00	6.00
NNO Enzo Amore	5.00	10.00
NNO Finn Balor TRU	10.00	20.00
NNO John Cena	3.00	6.00
NNO Kevin Owens	4.00	8.00
NNO Kofi Kingston	5.00	10.00
NNO Macho Man Randy Savage	15.00	30.00
NNO Nikki Bella	4.00	8.00
NNO Ric Flair TRU	7.50	15.00
NNO Roman Reigns	4.00	8.00
NNO Sasha Banks	4.00	8.00
NNO Seth Rollins	3.00	6.00
NNO Stone Cold Steve Austin TRU	10.00	20.00
NNO Ultimate Warrior	7.50	15.00
NNO Undertaker	4.00	8.00
NNO Xavier Woods	3.00	6.00

2020-22 Funko Pop Vinyl Art Series

44 The Rock WM

2011-22 Funko Pop Vinyl Freddy Funko

COMMON FUNKO POP	12.50	25.00
34A Hulk Hogan/500* FD	600.00	1200.00
34B Hulk Hogan Injured /500* FD	600.00	1200.00
52 Sting/500* FD	600.00	1200.00

2022 Funko Pop Vinyl Magazine Covers

17 Hulk Hogan
(2023 Target Exclusive)
18 Mr. T
(2023 Target Exclusive)

2015-19 Funko Pop Vinyl Pocket Pop Keychains WWE

NNO Hulk Hogan	7.50	15.00
NNO John Cena V	7.50	15.00
NNO John Cena WM DVD	6.00	12.00
NNO Macho Man WM DVD	6.00	12.00
NNO The Rock WM DVD	6.00	12.00
NNO Sting WM DVD	5.00	10.00
NNO Ultimate Warrior WM DVD	7.50	15.00
NNO Undertaker WM DVD	10.00	20.00

2018-19 Funko Pop Vinyl Pro Wrestling

1 Kenny Omega	7.50	15.00
2 The American Nightmare Cody	7.50	15.00

2018-19 Funko Pop Vinyl Pro Wrestling Multi-Packs

NNO Young Bucks	7.50	15.00
NNO Young Bucks Purple/Gold HT	10.00	20.00

2011-23 Funko Pop Vinyl Rides

284 Eddie Guerrero w/Low Rider GS	30.00	75.00

2011-23 Funko Pop Vinyl WWE

1A John Cena	30.00	60.00
1B J.Cena Black Pants WWE.com	200.00	400.00

1C J.Cena Green-Orange	25.00	50.00
1D J.Cena Green Hat WWE.com	600.00	1200.00
2A CM Punk V	125.00	250.00
2B CM Punk Pink Trunks HT	250.00	500.00
3 The Rock V	30.00	75.00
4 Sheamus V	30.00	75.00
5A Stone Cold Steve Austin V	40.00	80.00
5B SC Steve Austin 2K16 PRE	60.00	125.00
5C SC Steve Austin 2K16 GS	25.00	50.00
5D SC Steve Austin 2K16 EB	25.00	50.00
6A Rey Mysterio V	150.00	300.00
6B R.Mysterio Bright Blue 7-11	250.00	500.00
6C Rey Mysterio Dark SDCC	500.00	1000.00
7A Daniel Bryan V	60.00	125.00
7B Daniel Bryan Red Trunks HT/UT	60.00	125.00
7C Daniel Bryan Patterned WWE.com	300.00	600.00
8 Undertaker	30.00	75.00
9 Triple H V	50.00	100.00
10A Macho Man Randy Savage V	30.00	60.00
10B Savage Pink WWE.com	250.00	500.00
10C Macho Man Randy Savage Purple FYE	50.00	100.00
11A Hulk Hogan	30.00	75.00
11B Hogan Hulk Rules WWE.com	600.00	1200.00
11C Hollywood Hogan WWE 2K15	200.00	400.00
12 AJ Lee WWE.com	300.00	600.00
13 Brock Lesnar WM	50.00	100.00
14 Brie Bella	12.50	25.00
15 Nikki Bella	15.00	30.00
16 Paige V	75.00	150.00
17 Ric Flair TAR	25.00	50.00
18 Roddy Piper TAR	30.00	75.00
19A Sting	60.00	125.00
19B Wolfpac Sting GS	75.00	150.00
20 Ultimate Warrior	40.00	80.00
21 Andre the Giant	25.00	50.00
23 Roman Reigns	20.00	40.00
24A Seth Rollins V	30.00	75.00
24B Seth Rollins White Attire FYE	30.00	60.00
25 Bret Hart	50.00	100.00
26 Eva Marie	7.50	15.00
27 Kevin Owens V	30.00	60.00
28 Bray Wyatt V	25.00	50.00
29 Big E	12.50	25.00
30 Xavier Woods	7.50	15.00
31 Kofi Kingston	10.00	20.00
32 Shawn Michaels WG	20.00	40.00
33 Kane WG	40.00	80.00
34A Finn Balor	15.00	30.00
34B Finn Balor Demon Mask CH	30.00	60.00
35 Mick Foley	50.00	100.00
36 Goldberg	20.00	40.00
37 AJ Styles	25.00	50.00
38 The Demon Finn Balor FYE	15.00	30.00
39 Bayley TRU	25.00	50.00
40A Chris Jericho Red	20.00	40.00
40B Chris Jericho Blue FYE	20.00	40.00
41A Million Dollar Man Black	20.00	40.00
41B Million Dollar Man White CH	30.00	60.00
42 Sasha Banks	50.00	100.00
43A Iron Sheik White	15.00	30.00
43B Iron Sheik Red CH	20.00	40.00
44A Zack Ryder NYCC	30.00	75.00
44B Zack Ryder FCE	20.00	40.00
44C Zack Ryder Green Tights/500* FHQ	400.00	800.00
45 Shinsuke Nakamura TRU	20.00	40.00
46A The Rock	15.00	30.00
46B The Rock Black Jacket CH	25.00	50.00
46C The Rock Gold NYCC	25.00	50.00
46D The Rock Gold TAR	15.00	30.00
47A Razor Ramon	15.00	30.00
47B Razor Ramon nWo Trunks CH	50.00	100.00
47C Razor Ramon Purple GS	10.00	20.00
48 Braun Strowman	20.00	40.00
49 Alexa Bliss	30.00	75.00
50 Shawn Michaels	25.00	50.00
51A Jake The Snake Robers Green	20.00	40.00
51B Jake The Snake Roberts Blue CH	30.00	75.00
52A Triple H	12.50	25.00
52B Triple H Masked CH	50.00	100.00
53A Mr. McMahon	12.50	25.00
53B Mr. McMahon Pink Jacket CH	50.00	100.00
54 Sgt. Slaughter	20.00	40.00
55 Kurt Angle	30.00	75.00
56A Asuka SDCC	40.00	80.00
56B Asuka SCE	10.00	20.00
56C Asuka w/Mask WM	20.00	40.00
56D Asuka w/Mask TAR	20.00	40.00
57 Ric Flair Classic 2K19	40.00	80.00
58 Ronda Rousey	12.50	25.00
59 John Cena Clear AMZ	30.00	60.00
60 Randy Orton	30.00	60.00
61 Batista	12.50	25.00
62A Charlotte Flair	7.50	15.00
62B Charlotte Flair Blue Robe FL	15.00	30.00
63 Ric Flair Red Robe	30.00	60.00
64 Andre the Giant 6" WM	12.50	25.00
65 Becky Lynch	7.50	15.00
66A Trish Stratus	7.50	15.00
66B Trish Stratus DC Web Exclusive	25.00	50.00
67 Elias	7.50	15.00
68 Bret Hit Man Hart Pink	30.00	75.00
69A Undertaker Hooded	12.50	25.00
69B Undertaker Hooded Purple Translucent AMZ	12.50	25.00
70 Becky Lynch The Man AMZ	15.00	30.00
71 Hulk Hogan Python Power WM	12.50	25.00
72 The Miz	10.00	20.00
73 Mean Gene Okerlund	7.50	15.00
74A Diesel	10.00	20.00
74B Kevin Nash CH	50.00	100.00
75A Naomi	7.50	15.00
75B Naomi GITD CH	20.00	40.00
76 John Cena Thuganomics	10.00	20.00
77 The Fiend Bray Wyatt AMZ	20.00	40.00
78 The Rock w/Microphone	12.50	25.00
79 Macho Man Randy Savage DC GS	12.50	25.00
80 Mr. T	7.50	15.00
81 Undertaker ABA AMZ	10.00	20.00
82 Ric Flair '92 Royal Rumble GS	15.00	30.00
83 Macho Man Randy Savage Checkered Glasses GS	7.50	15.00
84 Stone Cold Steve Austin w/Belt	10.00	20.00
85 Chyna	7.50	15.00
86 Edge	7.50	15.00
87 Drew McIntyre	7.50	15.00
88 Otis MITB	7.50	15.00
89 Stone Cold Steve Austin 2 Belts 711	15.00	30.00
90 Eddie Guerrero w/Pop Pin GS	12.50	25.00
91 The Rock Bring It Shirt EE	10.00	20.00
92 Xavier Woods Up Up Down Down MET TAR	10.00	20.00
93A Rey Mysterio	10.00	20.00
93B Rey Mysterio GITD AMZ	15.00	30.00
94 Angelo Dawkins	7.50	15.00
95 Montez Ford	7.50	15.00
96 Asuka	7.50	15.00
97 Jerry Lawler	7.50	15.00
98 Roman Reigns MET AMZ	20.00	40.00
99 Triple H DX GS	12.50	25.00
100 The Fiend Bray Wyatt Santa WM	25.00	50.00
101 Shawn Michaels DX GS	20.00	40.00
102 Becky Lynch w/Two Belts TAR	10.00	20.00
103 Mankind GS	25.00	50.00
104 Alexa Bliss w/Lilly WM	12.50	25.00
105 Cactus Jack GS	10.00	20.00
106 Undertaker Coffin GS	15.00	30.00
107A Alexa Bliss White Dress	10.00	20.00
107B Alexa Bliss Black Dress CH	25.00	50.00
108A Bianca Belair Purple	7.50	15.00
108B Bianca Belair Red		
109 Dude Love	7.50	15.00
110 Brock Lesnar Cowboy	15.00	30.00
111 Roman Reigns HOTT WM	30.00	60.00
112 Macho Man Randy Savage EE	10.00	20.00
113 Paul Heyman GS	12.50	25.00
114 Dusty Rhodes	10.00	20.00
115 Riddle	15.00	30.00
116 Randy Orton	10.00	20.00
117 Rob Van Dam GS	12.50	25.00
118 Finn Balor AMZ	7.50	15.00
119 Bam Bam Bigelow GITD WM	20.00	40.00
120A Rocky Maivia	10.00	20.00
120B Rocky Maivia MET FS	25.00	50.00
121 Ricky The Dragon Steamboat	10.00	20.00
122 Rhea Ripley	15.00	30.00
123 American Nightmare Cody Rhodes WM		
124A Ted DiBiase GS		
124B Ted DiBiase DC GS CH		

1991 Galoob WCW Superstars 14-Inch

NNO Lex Luger	50.00	100.00
NNO Ric Flair	60.00	120.00
NNO Sid Vicious	50.00	100.00
NNO Sting	100.00	200.00

1991 Galoob WCW Superstars 14-Inch (loose)

NNO Lex Luger	20.00	40.00
NNO Ric Flair	30.00	75.00
NNO Sid Vicious	30.00	75.00
NNO Sting	30.00	60.00

1991 Galoob WCW Superstars Accessories

NNO 12-Figure Collector's Case	30.00	75.00
NNO Championship Belt	75.00	150.00
NNO Slam Action Wrestling Arena	125.00	250.00

1991 Galoob WCW Superstars Series 1

NNO Arn Anderson	30.00	60.00
NNO Barry Windham	25.00	50.00
NNO Brian Pillman	30.00	60.00
NNO Butch Reed	20.00	40.00
NNO Lex Luger	15.00	30.00
NNO Ric Flair	50.00	90.00
NNO Rick Steiner	20.00	40.00
NNO Ron Simmons	20.00	40.00
NNO Scott Steiner	20.00	40.00
NNO Sid Vicious	30.00	60.00
NNO Sting/Blue Tights	30.00	60.00
NNO Sting/Orange Tights	150.00	300.00
NNO Tom Zenk	20.00	40.00

1991 Galoob WCW Superstars Series 1 (loose)

NNO Arn Anderson	7.50	15.00
NNO Barry Windham	7.50	15.00
NNO Brian Pillman	7.50	15.00
NNO Butch Reed	10.00	20.00
NNO Lex Luger	7.50	15.00
NNO Ric Flair	10.00	20.00
NNO Rick Steiner	7.50	15.00
NNO Ron Simmons	7.50	15.00
NNO Scott Steiner	7.50	15.00
NNO Sid Vicious	10.00	20.00
NNO Sting/Blue Tights	12.50	25.00
NNO Sting/Orange Tights	25.00	50.00
NNO Tom Zenk	6.00	12.00

1991 Galoob WCW Superstars Series 2

NNO Arn Anderson/Red Trunks	125.00	250.00
NNO Barry Windham/Blue Trunks	125.00	250.00
NNO Brian Pillman/Lt Blue Trunks	100.00	200.00
NNO Lex Luger/Green Trunks	125.00	250.00
NNO Ric Flair/Red Trunks	150.00	300.00
NNO Rick Steiner/Green Tights	100.00	200.00
NNO Ron Simmons/Blue Tights	25.00	50.00
NNO Scott Steiner/Red & Blue Tights	125.00	250.00
NNO Sid Vicious/Pink Tights	100.00	200.00
NNO Sting/Black Tights	150.00	300.00

1991 Galoob WCW Superstars Series 2 (loose)

NNO Arn Anderson/Red Trunks	15.00	30.00
NNO Barry Windham/Blue Trunks	12.50	25.00
NNO Brian Pillman/Lt Blue Trunks	25.00	50.00
NNO Lex Luger/Green Trunks	20.00	40.00
NNO Ric Flair/Red Trunks	15.00	30.00
NNO Rick Steiner/Green Tights	15.00	30.00
NNO Ron Simmons/Blue Tights	20.00	40.00
NNO Scott Steiner/Red & Blue Tights	25.00	50.00
NNO Sid Vicious/Pink Tights	20.00	40.00
NNO Sting/Black Tights	20.00	40.00

1991 Galoob WCW Superstars UK

NNO Big Josh	500.00	1000.00
NNO Dustin Rhodes	100.00	200.00
NNO El Gigante	150.00	300.00
NNO Jimmy Garvin	150.00	300.00
NNO Lex Luger/Robe		
NNO Michael Hayes	200.00	350.00
NNO Sting/Robe	250.00	400.00

1991 Galoob WCW Superstars UK (loose)

NNO Big Josh	150.00	300.00
NNO Dustin Rhodes	75.00	150.00
NNO El Gigante	30.00	75.00
NNO Jimmy Garvin	20.00	40.00
NNO Lex Luger/Robe	75.00	150.00
NNO Michael Hayes	20.00	40.00
NNO Sting/Robe	60.00	120.00

1991 Galoob WCW Tag Team Superstars UK

NNO Lex Luger/Sting
NNO Michael Haynes/Jimmy Garvin
NNO Ric Flair/Arn Anderson
NNO Rick & Scott Steiner

1990 Galoob WCW Tag Team Superstars US

NNO	Lex Luger/Sting	75.00	150.00
NNO	Ric Flair/Arn Anderson	75.00	150.00
NNO	Rick & Scott Steiner	60.00	120.00
NNO	Ron Simmons/Butch Reed	100.00	200.00

1990 Hasbro WWF Series 1

NNO	Akeem	200.00	350.00
NNO	Andre the Giant	150.00	300.00
NNO	Ax	125.00	250.00
NNO	Big Boss Man	75.00	150.00
NNO	Brutus The Barber Beefcake	60.00	120.00
NNO	Hulk Hogan	150.00	300.00
NNO	Jake The Snake Roberts	100.00	200.00
NNO	Macho Man Randy Savage	300.00	600.00
NNO	Million Dollar Man Ted DiBiase	125.00	250.00
NNO	Ravishing Rick Rude	125.00	250.00
NNO	Smash	60.00	120.00
NNO	Ultimate Warrior	200.00	350.00

1990 Hasbro WWF Series 1 (loose)

NNO	Akeem	10.00	20.00
NNO	Andre the Giant	25.00	50.00
NNO	Ax	12.50	25.00
NNO	Big Boss Man	10.00	20.00
NNO	Brutus The Barber Beefcake	12.50	25.00
NNO	Hulk Hogan	15.00	30.00
NNO	Jake The Snake Roberts	12.50	25.00
NNO	Macho Man Randy Savage	20.00	40.00
NNO	Million Dollar Man Ted DiBiase	10.00	20.00
NNO	Ravishing Rick Rude	7.50	15.00
NNO	Smash	7.50	15.00
NNO	Ultimate Warrior	10.00	20.00

1991 Hasbro WWF Series 2

NNO	Dusty Rhodes	600.00	1000.00
NNO	Hacksaw Jim Duggan	75.00	150.00
NNO	Honky Tonk Man	60.00	120.00
NNO	Hulk Hogan	75.00	150.00
NNO	Macho King	150.00	300.00
NNO	Million Dollar Man	75.00	150.00
NNO	Rowdy Roddy Piper	75.00	150.00
NNO	Superfly Jim Snuka	60.00	120.00
NNO	Ultimate Warrior	125.00	250.00

1991 Hasbro WWF Series 2 (loose)

NNO	Dusty Rhodes	50.00	100.00
NNO	Hacksaw Jim Duggan	10.00	20.00
NNO	Honky Tonk Man	15.00	30.00
NNO	Hulk Hogan	12.50	25.00
NNO	Macho King	25.00	50.00
NNO	Million Dollar Man	7.50	15.00
NNO	Rowdy Roddy Piper	7.50	15.00
NNO	Superfly Jim Snuka	7.50	15.00
NNO	Ultimate Warrior	15.00	30.00

1991 Hasbro WWF Series 2 Tag Teams

NNO	The Bushwhackers	60.00	120.00
NNO	Demolition	150.00	300.00
NNO	The Rockers	60.00	120.00

1991 Hasbro WWF Series 2 Tag Teams (loose)

NNO	Butch	12.50	25.00
NNO	Crush	10.00	20.00
NNO	Luke	12.50	25.00
NNO	Marty Jannetty	10.00	20.00
NNO	Shawn Michaels	10.00	20.00
NNO	Smash	10.00	20.00

1992 Hasbro WWF Series 3

NNO	Big Boss Man	60.00	120.00
NNO	Brutus Beefcake/Zebra Tights	200.00	400.00
NNO	Earthquake	75.00	150.00
NNO	Greg The Hammer Valentine	50.00	100.00
NNO	Hulk Hogan	100.00	200.00
NNO	Koko B. Ware	75.00	150.00
NNO	Macho Man Randy Savage	90.00	175.00
NNO	Mr. Perfect	60.00	120.00
NNO	Sgt. Slaughter	60.00	120.00
NNO	Texas Tornado	60.00	120.00
NNO	Typhoon	50.00	100.00
NNO	Ultimate Warrior	125.00	250.00

1992 Hasbro WWF Series 3 (loose)

NNO	Big Boss Man	10.00	20.00
NNO	Brutus The Barber Beefcake	30.00	60.00
NNO	Earthquake	12.50	25.00
NNO	Greg The Hammer Valentine	10.00	20.00
NNO	Hulk Hogan	15.00	30.00
NNO	Koko B. Ware	15.00	30.00
NNO	Macho Man Randy Savage	10.00	20.00
NNO	Mr. Perfect	15.00	30.00
NNO	Sgt. Slaughter	15.00	30.00
NNO	Texas Tornado	12.50	25.00
NNO	Typhoon	10.00	20.00
NNO	Ultimate Warrior	25.00	50.00

1992 Hasbro WWF Series 3 Tag Teams

NNO	Legion of Doom	125.00	250.00
NNO	Nasty Boys	125.00	250.00

1992 Hasbro WWF Series 3 Tag Teams (loose)

NNO	Animal	20.00	40.00
NNO	Hawk	20.00	40.00
NNO	Knobbs	10.00	20.00
NNO	Sags	10.00	20.00

1992 Hasbro WWF Series 4

NNO	Bret Hart	200.00	350.00
NNO	British Bulldog	75.00	150.00
NNO	Ricky The Dragon Steamboat	50.00	100.00
NNO	Undertaker	75.00	150.00

1992 Hasbro WWF Series 4 (loose)

NNO	Bret Hart	20.00	40.00
NNO	British Bulldog	12.50	25.00
NNO	Ricky The Dragon Steamboat	12.50	25.00
NNO	Undertaker	20.00	40.00

1993 Hasbro WWF Series 5

NNO	Hulk Hogan	75.00	150.00
NNO	IRS	50.00	100.00
NNO	Jim Neidhart	60.00	120.00
NNO	Macho Man	100.00	200.00
NNO	Mountie	50.00	100.00
NNO	Rick Martel	50.00	100.00
NNO	Sid Justice	60.00	120.00
NNO	Skinner	50.00	100.00
NNO	Virgil	30.00	75.00
NNO	Warlord	60.00	120.00

1993 Hasbro WWF Series 5 (loose)

NNO	Hulk Hogan	12.50	25.00
NNO	IRS	10.00	20.00
NNO	Jim Neidhart	10.00	20.00
NNO	Macho Man	20.00	40.00
NNO	Mountie	20.00	40.00
NNO	Rick Martel	12.50	25.00
NNO	Sid Justice	12.50	25.00
NNO	Skinner	12.50	25.00
NNO	Virgil	10.00	20.00
NNO	Warlord	15.00	30.00

1993 Hasbro WWF Series 6

NNO	Berzerker	75.00	150.00
NNO	El Matador	30.00	75.00
NNO	Papa Shango	75.00	150.00
NNO	Repo Man	60.00	120.00
NNO	Ric Flair	125.00	250.00
NNO	Tatanka	50.00	100.00

1993 Hasbro WWF Series 6 (loose)

NNO	Berzerker	20.00	40.00
NNO	El Matador	12.50	25.00
NNO	Papa Shango	15.00	30.00
NNO	Repo Man	12.50	25.00
NNO	Ric Flair	15.00	30.00
NNO	Tatanka	10.00	20.00

1993 Hasbro WWF Series 7

NNO	Crush	75.00	150.00
NNO	Kamala/Star on Belly	100.00	200.00
NNO	Kamala/Crescent Moon Belly	4000.00	8000.00
NNO	Nailz	125.00	250.00
NNO	Owen Hart	150.00	300.00
NNO	Razor Ramon	75.00	150.00
NNO	Shawn Michaels	75.00	150.00

1993 Hasbro WWF Series 7 (loose)

NNO	Crush	15.00	30.00
NNO	Kamala/Star on Belly	20.00	40.00
NNO	Kamala/Crescent Moon Belly	750.00	1500.00
NNO	Nailz	25.00	50.00
NNO	Owen Hart	25.00	50.00
NNO	Razor Ramon	25.00	50.00
NNO	Shawn Michaels	25.00	50.00

1993 Hasbro WWF Series 8

NNO	Bam Bam Bigelow	125.00	250.00
NNO	Bret Hart	200.00	400.00
NNO	Lex Luger	75.00	150.00
NNO	Mr. Perfect	100.00	200.00
NNO	Undertaker	250.00	500.00
NNO	Yokozuna	100.00	200.00

1993 Hasbro WWF Series 8 (loose)

NNO	Bam Bam Bigelow	25.00	50.00
NNO	Bret Hart	30.00	75.00
NNO	Lex Luger	15.00	30.00
NNO	Mr. Perfect	15.00	30.00
NNO	Undertaker	60.00	120.00
NNO	Yokozuna	30.00	75.00

1993 Hasbro WWF Series 9

NNO	Doink the Clown	100.00	200.00
NNO	Hacksaw Jim Duggan	100.00	200.00
NNO	Million Dollar Man	75.00	150.00
NNO	Rick Steiner	60.00	120.00
NNO	Scott Steiner	50.00	100.00
NNO	Tatanka	60.00	120.00

1993 Hasbro WWF Series 9 (loose)

NNO	Doink the Clown	25.00	50.00
NNO	Hacksaw Jim Duggan	30.00	75.00
NNO	Million Dollar Man	20.00	40.00
NNO	Rick Steiner	20.00	40.00
NNO	Scott Steiner	15.00	30.00

1993 Hasbro WWF Series 10

NNO	Butch	50.00	100.00
NNO	Fatu	50.00	100.00
NNO	Giant Gonzalez	60.00	120.00
NNO	Luke	50.00	100.00
NNO	Marty Jannetty	30.00	75.00
NNO	Razor Ramon/Purple Shorts	125.00	250.00
NNO	Razor Ramon/Red Shorts	150.00	300.00
NNO	Samu	30.00	75.00
NNO	Shawn Michaels/Black Tights	200.00	400.00
NNO	Shawn Michaels/White Tights	150.00	300.00

1993 Hasbro WWF Series 10 (loose)

NNO	Butch	15.00	30.00
NNO	Fatu	10.00	20.00
NNO	Giant Gonzalez	12.50	25.00
NNO	Luke	15.00	30.00
NNO	Marty Jannetty	15.00	30.00
NNO	Razor Ramon/Purple Shorts	50.00	100.00
NNO	Razor Ramon/Red Shorts	15.00	30.00
NNO	Samu	10.00	20.00
NNO	Shawn Michaels/Black Tights	50.00	100.00
NNO	Shawn Michaels/White Tights	10.00	20.00

1994 Hasbro WWF Series 11

NNO	1-2-3 Kid	500.00	1000.00
NNO	Adam Bomb	125.00	250.00
NNO	Bart Gunn	150.00	300.00
NNO	Billy Gunn	150.00	300.00
NNO	Crush	300.00	600.00
NNO	Ludvig Borga	150.00	300.00
NNO	Yokozuna	300.00	600.00

1994 Hasbro WWF Series 11 (loose)

NNO	1-2-3 Kid	200.00	400.00
NNO	Adam Bomb	100.00	200.00
NNO	Bart Gunn	100.00	200.00
NNO	Billy Gunn	125.00	250.00
NNO	Crush	125.00	250.00
NNO	Ludvig Borga	75.00	150.00
NNO	Yokozuna	75.00	150.00

1992 Hasbro WWF Accessories and Playsets

NNO	King of the Ring (yellow)		
NNO	Official Wrestling Ring (blue)		
NNO	Official Wrestling Ring (sound effects)		

1993 Hasbro WWF Magazine Series

NNO	Bret Hart	600.00	1200.00
NNO	Hulk Hogan	600.00	1200.00
NNO	Undertaker	1500.00	2500.00

1993 Hasbro WWF Magazine Series (loose)

NNO	Bret Hart	50.00	100.00
NNO	Hulk Hogan	400.00	800.00
NNO	Undertaker	1000.00	1500.00

1992 Hasbro WWF Mini Wrestlers

NNO	Brutus Beefcake/Butch		

Luke/Greg Valentine 30.00 75.00
NNO Mr. Perfect/Jim Duggan
Roddy Piper/Texas Tornado 30.00 75.00
NNO Typhoon/Earthquake/Animal/Hawk25.00 60.00

1992 Hasbro WWF Mini Wrestlers Playset

NNO Royal Rumble Wrestling Ring
(w/Hogan/Slaughter/Roberts/DiBiase/Boss Man/Savage

1992 Hasbro WWF Mini Wrestlers Playset Figures (loose)

NNO Big Boss Man 10.00 20.00
NNO Hulk Hogan 20.00 40.00
NNO Jake The Snake Roberts 15.00 30.00
NNO Macho Man Randy Savage 20.00 40.00
NNO Million Dollar Man Ted DiBiase 10.00 20.00
NNO Sgt. Slaughter 20.00 40.00

2019 HeroClix WWE Series 1 Mixed Match Challenge

107 Charlotte Flair
108 Sasha Banks
109 Finn Balor
110 AJ Styles
111 WWE Ring

2019 HeroClix WWE Series 1 Mixed Match Challenge Maps

M001 WWE Backstage Area
M001 WWE Arena

2019 HeroClix WWE Series 1 Rock 'N Sock Starter Set

101 The Rock
102 Mankind
103 Stone Cold Steve Austin
104 Triple H
105 Ric Flair
106 Shawn Michaels

2019 HeroClix WWE Series 1 Rock 'N Sock Starter Set Maps

M001 WWE Training Center
M002 WWE War Games

1998 The Idea Factory WCW Beanbag Brawlers Series 1

NNO Bret "Hit Man" Hart/21,000*
NNO Diamond Dallas Page/28,000*
NNO Goldberg/35,000*
NNO Hollywood Hogan/21,000*
NNO Kevin Nash/28,000*
NNO Sting/35,000*

1999 The Idea Factory WCW Beanbag Brawlers Series 2

NNO Booker T/
NNO Buff Bagwell/
NNO Goldberg/
NNO Jeff Jarrett/
NNO Scott Steiner/
NNO Sting/
NNO Vampiro/

2017 Jada Toys WWE Metalfigs 2.5-Inch

M228 John Cena
M229 Brock Lesnar
M230 Triple H
M231 Finn Balor
M232 Paige
M243 Sasha Banks

2017 Jada Toys WWE Metalfigs 4-Inch

M200 Finn Balor
M202 Paige
M203 Brock Lesnar
M205 John Cena
M206 Sami Zayn
M207 Sasha Banks
M210 Seth Rollins
M211 The Rock
M212 Charlotte Flair
M213 Kevin Owens
M218 AJ Styles
M220 The Rock
M242 John Cena
M275 Finn Balor

2017 Jada Toys WWE Metalfigs 6-Inch

M209 Triple H

2017 Jada Toys WWE Nano Metalfigs

W1 John Cena
W2 Triple H
W3 The Rock
W4 Roman Reigns
W5 Charlotte Flair
W6 Bayley
W7 Sami Zayn
W8 Chris Jericho
W9 Dean Ambrose
W10 Macho Man Randy Savage
W11 Sting
W12 Undertaker
W13 AJ Styles
W14 Kevin Owens
W15 Seth Rollins
W16 Finn Balor
W17 Sasha Banks
W18 Brock Lesnar
W19 Becky Lynch
W20 Kalisto
W21 Bray Wyatt
W22 Nikki Bella
W23 Ultimate Warrior
W24 Rowdy Roddy Piper

2017 Jada Toys WWE Nano Metalfigs 20-Pack

NNO Cena/Triple H/Rock/Reigns/Charlotte
Bayley/Zayn/Jericho/Ambrose/Savage
Sting/Undertaker/Styles/Owens/Rollins
Balor/Banks/Lesnar/Kalisto/Wyatt
(2017 Toys R Us Exclusive)

2007-08 Jakks Pacific ECW Wrestling Series 1

NNO CM Punk 20.00 40.00
NNO Kevin Thorn 25.00 50.00
NNO Rob Van Dam 15.00 30.00
NNO Sandman 25.00 50.00
NNO Tommy Dreamer 25.00 50.00

2007-08 Jakks Pacific ECW Wrestling Series 2

NNO Ariel 15.00 30.00
NNO Balls Mahoney 12.50 25.00
NNO Elijah Burke 25.00 50.00
NNO Joey Styles 20.00 40.00
NNO Kelly Kelly 25.00 50.00
NNO Mike Knox 15.00 30.00

2007-08 Jakks Pacific ECW Wrestling Series 3

NNO Layla 12.50 25.00
NNO Marcus Cor Von
NNO Matt Striker 7.50 15.00
NNO Nunzio 6.00 12.00
NNO Snitsky
NNO Stevie Richards
NNO Tazz

2007-08 Jakks Pacific ECW Wrestling Series 4

NNO Boogeyman
NNO CM Punk 7.50 15.00
NNO Elijah Burke 15.00 30.00
NNO John Morrison 10.00 20.00
NNO Matt Striker
NNO Tommy Dreamer

2007-08 Jakks Pacific ECW Wrestling Series 5

NNO Christian 12.50 25.00
NNO Evan Bourne
NNO Fit Finlay 12.50 25.00
NNO Jack Swagger
NNO Mark Henry
NNO Tyson Kidd 6.00 12.00

2010 Jakks Pacific TNA Wrestling Cross the Line Series 1

NNO James Storm/Bobby Roode 30.00 75.00
NNO Samoa Joe/Mick Foley 30.00 60.00
NNO Scott Steiner/Kevin Nash 25.00 50.00

2010 Jakks Pacific TNA Wrestling Cross the Line Series 2

NNO AJ Styles/Jeff Jarrett
NNO Alex Shelley/Chris Sabin 30.00 75.00
NNO Brother Ray/Brother Devon

2010 Jakks Pacific TNA Wrestling Cross the Line Series 3

NNO AJ Styles/Jeff Hardy
NNO Kurt Angle/Mr. Anderson 20.00 40.00
NNO Stevie Richards/Daffney 12.50 25.00

2010 Jakks Pacific TNA Wrestling Cross the Line Series 4

NNO Eric Young/Kevin Nash 15.00 30.00
NNO Hulk Hogan/Abyss 30.00 75.00
NNO Sting/Rob Van Dam 20.00 40.00

2010 Jakks Pacific TNA Wrestling Deluxe Impact Series 1

NNO AJ Styles/No Stubble
NNO AJ Styles/Stubble
NNO Jeff Jarrett/Dk Blonde Hair 10.00 20.00
NNO Jeff Jarrett/Lt Blonde Hair
NNO Kurt Angle 10.00 20.00
NNO Samoa Joe 15.00 30.00
NNO Sting
NNO Suicide

2010 Jakks Pacific TNA Wrestling Deluxe Impact Series 1 Slammin' Celebration Exclusives

NNO AJ Styles
NNO Jeff Jarrett
NNO Kurt Angle
NNO Samoa Joe
NNO Sting
NNO Suicide

2010 Jakks Pacific TNA Wrestling Deluxe Impact Series 2

NNO AJ Styles
NNO Amazing Red
NNO Eric Young
NNO Hernandez 25.00 50.00
NNO Hulk Hogan 40.00 80.00
NNO Mick Foley

2010 Jakks Pacific TNA Wrestling Deluxe Impact Series 3

NNO Jay Lethal 15.00 30.00
NNO Kevin Nash 12.50 25.00
NNO Matt Morgan 20.00 40.00
NNO Shark Boy 15.00 30.00
NNO Sting
NNO Velvet Sky 20.00 40.00

2010 Jakks Pacific TNA Wrestling Deluxe Impact Series 4

NNO Abyss 50.00 100.00
NNO D'Angelo Dinero
NNO Desmond Wolfe 25.00 50.00
NNO Hulk Hogan 30.00 60.00
NNO Jeff Hardy
NNO Rob Van Dam

2010 Jakks Pacific TNA Wrestling Deluxe Impact Series 5

NNO Angelina Love 20.00 40.00
NNO Jeff Hardy
NNO Mr. Anderson
NNO Raven LOTR
NNO Rob Terry 10.00 20.00
NNO Samoa Joe 20.00 40.00

2011 Jakks Pacific TNA Wrestling Deluxe Impact Series 6

NNO Doug Williams
NNO Kazarian 12.50 25.00
NNO Kurt Angle 15.00 30.00
NNO Madison Rayne 20.00 40.00
NNO Sting 15.00 30.00
NNO Terry Taylor LOTR 17.50 35.00

2012 Jakks Pacific TNA Wrestling Deluxe Impact Series 7

NNO Bobby Roode 10.00 20.00
NNO James Storm
NNO James Storm/Belt 30.00 75.00
NNO Jeff Hardy 30.00 60.00
NNO Mr. Anderson 10.00 20.00
NNO Velvet Sky 12.50 25.00

2012 Jakks Pacific TNA Wrestling Deluxe Impact Series 8

NNO AJ Styles
NNO Hulk Hogan 30.00 60.00
NNO Matt Morgan 7.50 15.00
NNO Rob Van Dam
NNO Rob Van Dam/Belt
NNO Sting

2013 Jakks Pacific TNA Wrestling Deluxe Impact Series 9

NNO Austin Aries
NNO Christopher Daniels
NNO Gail Kim
NNO Jeff Hardy
NNO Jeff Hardy/Belt
NNO Magnus

2013 Jakks Pacific TNA Wrestling Deluxe Impact Series 10

NNO Crimson
NNO Kurt Angle
NNO Miss Tessmacher
NNO Rob Terry
NNO Rob Van Dam

2013 Jakks Pacific TNA Wrestling Deluxe Impact Series 11

NNO AJ Styles
NNO Austin Aries
NNO Jeff Hardy
NNO Velvet Sky

2014 Jakks Pacific TNA Wrestling Deluxe Impact Series 12

NNO Bully Ray 12.50 25.00
NNO Chris Sabin 20.00 40.00
NNO Hernandez 12.50 25.00
NNO Magnus

2014 Jakks Pacific TNA Wrestling Deluxe Impact Series 13

NNO Angelina Love 12.50 25.00
NNO Mr. Anderson 7.50 15.00

2010 Jakks Pacific TNA Wrestling Genesis

NNO AJ Styles
NNO AJ Styles/Belt
NNO Jeff Jarrett
NNO Jeff Jarrett/Belt
NNO Kurt Angle
NNO Kurt Angle/Belt
NNO Samoa Joe
NNO Samoa Joe/Belt
NNO Sting
NNO Sting/Belt
NNO Suicide
NNO Suicide/Belt

2010 Jakks Pacific TNA Wrestling Genesis 3-Packs

NNO AJ Styles/Kurt Angle/Suicide
NNO Jeff Jarrett/Samoa Joe/Sting

2010 Jakks Pacific TNA Wrestling Genesis 4-Packs

NNO AJ Styles/Kurt Angle/
Sting/Suicide
NNO Jeff Jarrett/Kurt Angle/
Samoa Joe/Sting

2010 Jakks Pacific TNA Wrestling Impact Series 1

NNO Abyss 15.00 30.00
NNO Jay Lethal 10.00 20.00
NNO Kevin Nash 7.50 15.00
NNO Kurt Angle 7.50 15.00
NNO Sting 12.50 25.00
NNO Suicide 20.00 40.00

2010 Jakks Pacific TNA Wrestling Legends of the Ring

NNO Hulk Hogan
NNO Jeff Jarrett
NNO Kevin Nash
NNO Kurt Angle
NNO Sting
NNO Sting USA Gear RSC

2010 Jakks Pacific TNA Wrestling Micro Impact Series 1

NNO Abyss/Shark Boy/Suicide
NNO AJ Styles/Jeff Jarrett/Mick Foley
NNO C. Daniels/Creed/Jay Lethal
NNO Kevin Nash/Kurt Angle/Sting

2010 Jakks Pacific TNA Wrestling Micro Impact Series 1 10-Pack

NNO Sting/Shark Boy/Jeff Jarrett/Suicide/Abyss
Jay Lethal/AJ Styles/Mick Foley/Kurt Angle/Kevin Nash

2010 Jakks Pacific TNA Wrestling Micro Impact Series 2

NNO Abyss/Hulk Hogan/Jeff Hardy
NNO Eric Young/Lethal/Nash
NNO James Storm/Morgan/Roode 15.00 30.00
NNO Jeff Jarrett/RVD/Sting

1998 Jakks Pacific WWF 2 Tuff Series 1

NNO Chyna/HHH 12.50 25.00
NNO D.O.A. 7.50 15.00
NNO Goldust/Marlena 10.00 20.00
NNO Truth Commission 7.50 15.00

1998 Jakks Pacific WWF 2 Tuff Series 2

NNO B. Christopher/J. Lawler 7.50 15.00
NNO Kama Mustafa/D'Lo Brown 10.00 20.00
NNO Kurrgan/Jackal 7.50 15.00
NNO Road Dogg/B.A. Billy Gunn 12.50 25.00

1999 Jakks Pacific WWF 2 Tuff Series 3

NNO Kane/Corporate Mankind 10.00 20.00
NNO LOD 2000 15.00 30.00
NNO Steve Austin/Undertaker 12.50 25.00
NNO The Rock/Owen Hart 15.00 30.00

1999 Jakks Pacific WWF 2 Tuff Series 4

NNO Big Boss Man vs. Steve Austin 12.50 25.00
NNO The Rock vs. Mankind 10.00 20.00
NNO Undertaker vs. Kane 12.50 25.00
NNO Val Venis vs. B.A. Billy Gunn 7.50 15.00

1999 Jakks Pacific WWF 2 Tuff Series 5

NNO Billy Gunn vs. Road Dogg 10.00 20.00
NNO Debra McMichaels vs. Double J 7.50 15.00
NNO Stone Cold Steve Austin vs. The Rock12.5025.00
NNO Viscera vs. Undertaker 10.00 20.00

2003 Jakks Pacific WWE Adrenaline Series 1

NNO Big Show/Brock Lesnar 25.00 50.00
NNO Shawn Michaels/RVD 15.00 30.00
NNO Tommy Dreamer
Jeff Hardy

2003 Jakks Pacific WWE Adrenaline Series 2

NNO Johnny Stamboli 15.00 30.00
Chavo Guerrero
NNO Rey Mysterio/Matt Hardy 20.00 40.00
NNO Test/Stacy Keibler 20.00 40.00

2003 Jakks Pacific WWE Adrenaline Series 3

NNO Kurt Angle/Brock Lesnar 20.00 40.00
NNO Shawn Michaels/Y2J
NNO Steve Austin/Eric Bischoff 20.00 40.00

2003 Jakks Pacific WWE Adrenaline Series 4

NNO Billy Gunn/Torrie Wilson 12.50 25.00
NNO Chris Benoit/Rhyno 17.50 35.00
NNO Undertaker/John Cena 25.00 50.00

2003 Jakks Pacific WWE Adrenaline Series 5

NNO Eddie Guerrero 25.00 50.00
John Cena
NNO Rey Mysterio 15.00 30.00
Billy Kidman
NNO Shelton Benjamin 10.00 20.00
Charlie Haas

2003 Jakks Pacific WWE Adrenaline Series 6

NNO Eddie and Chavo Guerrero 15.00 30.00
NNO Faarooq/Bradshaw 10.00 20.00
NNO The Hurricane/Rosey 10.00 20.00

2004 Jakks Pacific WWE Adrenaline Series 7

NNO Batista/Randy Orton 17.50 35.00
NNO Chris Jericho/Christian
NNO Scott Steiner/Test 12.50 25.00

2004 Jakks Pacific WWE Adrenaline Series 8

NNO Bubba Ray/D-Von Dudley 10.00 20.00
NNO Rene Dupree 12.50 25.00
Rob Conway
NNO Steven Richards/Victoria 15.00 30.00

2004 Jakks Pacific WWE Adrenaline Series 9

NNO Charlie Haas/Rico 12.50 25.00
NNO Eddie Guerrero 20.00 40.00
John Bradshaw Layfield
NNO Matt Hardy/Lita 20.00 40.00

2004 Jakks Pacific WWE Adrenaline Series 10

NNO Christian/Trish Stratus 20.00 40.00
NNO Doug and Danny Basham 12.50 25.00
NNO Triple H/Randy Orton 20.00 40.00

2005 Jakks Pacific WWE Adrenaline Series 11

NNO Billy Kidman/Paul London 12.50 25.00
NNO Heidenreich/Paul Heyman 12.50 25.00
NNO John Cena/Funaki 20.00 40.00

2005 Jakks Pacific WWE Adrenaline Series 12

NNO Batista/Triple H 15.00 30.00
NNO JBL/Orlando Jordan 12.50 25.00
NNO RVD/Rey Mysterio 15.00 30.00

2005 Jakks Pacific WWE Adrenaline Series 13

NNO Luther Reigns/Kurt Angle 12.50 25.00
NNO Rey Mysterio/Teddy Long 15.00 30.00
NNO Rob Conway 12.50 25.00
Sylvain Grenier

2005 Jakks Pacific WWE Adrenaline Series 14

NNO Eddie Guerrero/Booker T 15.00 30.00
NNO M. Hassan/Daivari 20.00 40.00
NNO William Regal/Tajiri 12.50 25.00

2005 Jakks Pacific WWE Adrenaline Series 15

NNO John Cena/JBL 15.00 30.00
NNO Kane/Edge 20.00 40.00
NNO Rey Mysterio 25.00 50.00
Eddie Guerrero

2005 Jakks Pacific WWE Adrenaline Series 16

NNO Batista/JBL 15.00 30.00
NNO Chris Jericho/John Cena 20.00 40.00
NNO Johnny Nitro 12.50 25.00
Joey Mercury

2006 Jakks Pacific WWE Adrenaline Series 17

NNO John Cena/Kurt Angle 12.50 25.00
NNO Matt Hardy/Edge 12.50 25.00
NNO Super Crazy/Psicosis 15.00 30.00

2006 Jakks Pacific WWE Adrenaline Series 18

NNO Bobby Lashley 17.50 35.00
Orlando Jordan
NNO Lance Cade 15.00 30.00
Trevor Murdoch
NNO Johnny Nitro
Road Warrior Animal

2006 Jakks Pacific WWE Adrenaline Series 19

NNO John Cena/Edge 15.00 30.00
NNO Johnny Nitro 10.00 20.00
Joey Mercury
NNO Rey Mysterio/Mark Henry 20.00 40.00

2006 Jakks Pacific WWE Adrenaline Series 20

NNO Triple H/John Cena		
NNO Trish Stratus/HBK	15.00	30.00
NNO William Regal	12.50	25.00
Paul Burchill		

2006 Jakks Pacific WWE Adrenaline Series 21

NNO Booker T/Boogeyman	12.50	25.00
NNO Gymini	12.50	25.00
NNO Mikey vs. Big Show	15.00	30.00

2006 Jakks Pacific WWE Adrenaline Series 22

NNO Johnny/Mitch	10.00	20.00
NNO Psicosis/Super Crazy	15.00	30.00
NNO Umaga/Armando Estrada	15.00	30.00

2007 Jakks Pacific WWE Adrenaline Series 23

NNO Booker T vs. Batista	12.50	25.00
NNO Elijah Burke	15.00	30.00
Sylvester Terkay		
NNO Jeff Hardy vs. Johnny Nitro	20.00	40.00

2007 Jakks Pacific WWE Adrenaline Series 24

NNO Brian Kendrick/Paul London	12.50	25.00
NNO HHH/Shawn Michaels	17.50	35.00
NNO Undertaker/Kane	15.00	30.00

2007 Jakks Pacific WWE Adrenaline Series 25

NNO Charlie Haas/Shelton Benjamin	12.50	25.00
NNO John Cena vs. The Great Khali	20.00	40.00
NNO MVP vs. Kane	15.00	30.00

2007 Jakks Pacific WWE Adrenaline Series 26

NNO Cryme Tyme	12.50	25.00
NNO The Highlanders	12.50	25.00
NNO King Booker/Queen Sharmell	15.00	30.00

2007 Jakks Pacific WWE Adrenaline Series 27

NNO Deuce/Domino	15.00	30.00
NNO Jeff and Matt Hardy	17.50	35.00
NNO Lance Cade/Trevor Murdoch	12.50	25.00

2007 Jakks Pacific WWE Adrenaline Series 28

NNO CM Punk/Elijah Burke	15.00	30.00
NNO Mr. Kennedy/Edge	12.50	25.00
NNO Umage/Vince McMahon	12.50	25.00

2008 Jakks Pacific WWE Adrenaline Series 29

NNO Cody & Dusty Rhodes	12.50	25.00
NNO Miz/Layla	12.50	25.00
NNO MVP/Matt Hardy	15.00	30.00

2008 Jakks Pacific WWE Adrenaline Series 30

NNO Balls Mahoney/Kelly Kelly	20.00	40.00
NNO HHH/Umaga	15.00	30.00
NNO Rey Mysterio/Finlay		

2008 Jakks Pacific WWE Adrenaline Series 31

NNO Big Daddy V/Matt Striker	12.50	25.00
NNO Chuck Palumbo	15.00	30.00
Michelle McCool		
NNO The Highlanders	12.50	25.00

2008 Jakks Pacific WWE Adrenaline Series 32

NNO Jesse/Festus	10.00	20.00
NNO John Morrison/The Miz	15.00	30.00
NNO Santino Marella/Maria	15.00	30.00

2008 Jakks Pacific WWE Adrenaline Series 33

NNO Chavo Guerrero/Kane	15.00	30.00
NNO Katie Lea/Paul Burchill	15.00	30.00
NNO Vickie Guerrero/Edge	20.00	40.00

2008 Jakks Pacific WWE Adrenaline Series 34

NNO Hornswoggle/Finlay	30.00	60.00
NNO Randy Orton/JBL		
NNO Tommy Dreamer	20.00	40.00
Joey Styles		

2009 Jakks Pacific WWE Adrenaline Series 35

NNO Cody Rhodes/Ted DiBiase Jr.		
NNO Curt Hawkins/Zach Ryder	15.00	30.00
NNO Evan Bourne/Rey Mysterio		

2009 Jakks Pacific WWE Adrenaline Series 36

NNO Brian Kendrick/Ezekiel Jackson	15.00	30.00
NNO Mark Henry/Tony Atlas	15.00	30.00
NNO Shad Gaspard/JTG	20.00	40.00

2009 Jakks Pacific WWE Adrenaline Series 37

NNO Jeff Hardy/The Undertaker	20.00	40.00
NNO Million Dollar Man/DiBiase Jr.		
NNO Triple H/Randy Orton	12.50	25.00

2009 Jakks Pacific WWE Adrenaline Series 38

NNO Edge vs. Big Show		
NNO Finlay/Hornswoggle	25.00	50.00
NNO Jack Swagger vs. Christian		

2009 Jakks Pacific WWE Adrenaline Series 39

NNO Undertaker/HBK	12.50	25.00
NNO Triple H/Stephanie		
NNO Natalya/Tyson Kidd		

2000 Jakks Pacific WWF Back Talkin' Crushers Exclusive

NNO Stone Cold Steve Austin TF	10.00	20.00

1999 Jakks Pacific WWF Back Talkin' Crushers Series 1

NNO Big Show	6.00	12.00
NNO The Rock	7.50	15.00
NNO Steve Austin	10.00	20.00
NNO Undertaker	7.50	15.00

2000 Jakks Pacific WWF Back Talkin' Crushers Series 2

NNO Mankind	7.50	15.00
NNO Road Dogg	6.00	12.00
NNO The Rock	10.00	20.00

2000 Jakks Pacific WWF Back Talkin' Crushers Series 3

NNO Chris Jericho	10.00	20.00
NNO Steve Austin	10.00	20.00
NNO Triple H	7.50	15.00

2001 Jakks Pacific WWF Back Talkin' Slammers Series 1

NNO The Rock	12.50	25.00
NNO Stone Cold Steve Austin	12.50	25.00
NNO Triple H	10.00	20.00

2001 Jakks Pacific WWF Back Talkin' Slammers Series 2

NNO Chris Jericho	10.00	20.00
NNO Kurt Angle	12.50	25.00
NNO Undertaker		

2001 Jakks Pacific WWF Back Talkin' Slammers Series 3

NNO Chris Jericho	10.00	20.00
NNO Kurt Angle	12.50	25.00
NNO Stone Cold Steve Austin	10.00	20.00
NNO The Rock	10.00	20.00
NNO Triple H	7.50	15.00
NNO Undertaker		

2002 Jakks Pacific WWF Back Talkin' Slammers Series 4

NNO Chris Jericho		
NNO Kurt Angle		
NNO Triple H		

2000 Jakks Pacific WWF Backlash Series 1

NNO Al Snow	12.50	25.00
NNO Kane	6.00	12.00
NNO Shawn Michaels	15.00	30.00
NNO Stone Cold Steve Austin	10.00	20.00
NNO The Rock	12.50	25.00
NNO Triple H	10.00	20.00
NNO Undertaker	10.00	20.00
NNO X-Pac	7.50	15.00

2000 Jakks Pacific WWF Backlash Series 2

NNO Big Boss Man		
NNO Edge		
NNO Hardcore Holly		
NNO Road Dogg		
NNO The Rock		
NNO Stone Cold Steve Austin		
NNO Triple H	7.50	15.00
NNO X-Pac	6.00	12.00

2000 Jakks Pacific WWF Backlash Series 3

NNO Billy Gunn	7.50	15.00
NNO Edge	10.00	20.00
NNO Kane	7.50	15.00
NNO The Rock		
NNO Stone Cold Steve Austin		
NNO Test		
NNO Triple H		
NNO Undertaker		

2000 Jakks Pacific WWF Backlash Series 4

NNO Big Boss Man	6.00	12.00
NNO Billy Gunn	7.50	15.00
NNO Edge	10.00	20.00
NNO Kane	10.00	20.00
NNO The Rock		
NNO Stone Cold Steve Austin	12.50	25.00
NNO Triple H		
NNO Undertaker	15.00	30.00

2000 Jakks Pacific WWF Backlash Series 5

NNO Al Snow		
NNO Hardcore Holly	6.00	12.00
NNO Rock		
NNO Stone Cold Steve Austin	12.50	25.00
NNO Test		
NNO Undertaker	15.00	30.00
NNO Val Venis		
NNO X-Pac		

2005 Jakks Pacific WWE Backlash Series 7

NNO Batista	12.50	25.00
NNO Chris Benoit	12.50	25.00
NNO Kurt Angle	10.00	20.00
NNO Undertaker	15.00	30.00

2005 Jakks Pacific WWE Backlash Series 8

NNO Batista	12.50	25.00
NNO Edge	10.00	20.00
NNO Kurt Angle	12.50	25.00
NNO Triple H	10.00	20.00

2005 Jakks Pacific WWE Backlash Series 9

NNO Carlito	12.50	25.00
NNO Kurt Angle	20.00	40.00
NNO Randy Orton	7.50	15.00
NNO Rob Van Dam	12.50	25.00
NNO Shawn Michaels		
NNO Undertaker		

2005 Jakks Pacific WWE Backlash Series 10

NNO Batista	12.50	25.00
NNO Chris Benoit	7.50	15.00
NNO John Cena	12.50	25.00
NNO Rob Van Dam	7.50	15.00
NNO Shawn Michaels	15.00	30.00
NNO Triple H	10.00	20.00

2007 Jakks Pacific WWE Backlash Series 11

NNO Bobby Lashley	12.50	25.00
NNO Edge	15.00	30.00
NNO Finlay	15.00	30.00
NNO Jeff Hardy	15.00	30.00
NNO Rey Mysterio	20.00	40.00
NNO Undertaker	20.00	40.00

2008 Jakks Pacific WWE Backlash Series 12

NNO	Kane		
NNO	Matt Hardy		
NNO	Miz		
NNO	Mr. Kennedy		
NNO	Randy Orton		
NNO	Triple H		

2009 Jakks Pacific WWE Backlash Series 13

NNO	Batista		
NNO	Chavo Guerrero		
NNO	Chris Jericho		
NNO	Elijah Burke		
NNO	John Cena		
NNO	Nunzio		

2009 Jakks Pacific WWE Backlash Series 14

NNO	Chavo Guerrero		
NNO	Cody Rhodes		
NNO	Matt Hardy	10.00	20.00
NNO	Stone Cold Steve Austin		
NNO	Triple H		

2009 Jakks Pacific WWE Backlash Series 15

NNO	Chris Jericho	15.00	30.00
NNO	CM Punk		
NNO	John Cena	10.00	20.00
NNO	Rey Mysterio	20.00	40.00
NNO	Shawn Michaels	12.50	25.00
NNO	Triple H	15.00	30.00

2008 Jakks Pacific WWE Best of Classic Superstars

NNO	Andre the Giant	20.00	40.00
NNO	Bret Hit Man Hart	20.00	40.00
NNO	Eddie Guerrero	12.50	25.00
NNO	Rowdy Roddy Piper		
NNO	Shawn Michaels	12.50	25.00

2009 Jakks Pacific WWE Best of Deluxe Aggression

NNO	Chris Jericho		
NNO	John Cena		
NNO	Randy Orton		
NNO	Rey Mysterio		
NNO	Triple H		
NNO	Undertaker		

2006 Jakks Pacific WWE Best of Deluxe Aggression

NNO	Batista	7.50	15.00
NNO	John Cena	15.00	30.00
NNO	Kane	10.00	20.00
NNO	Rey Mysterio	10.00	20.00
NNO	Triple H	7.50	15.00
NNO	Undertaker	20.00	40.00

2008 Jakks Pacific WWE Best of Deluxe Aggression

NNO	Chris Jericho	15.00	30.00
NNO	CM Punk		
NNO	John Cena	10.00	20.00
NNO	Rey Mysterio	17.50	35.00
NNO	Shawn Michaels	12.50	25.00
NNO	Undertaker	20.00	40.00

2005 Jakks Pacific WWE Best of ECW

NNO	Bubba Ray Dudley	15.00	30.00
NNO	D-Von Dudley	12.50	25.00
NNO	Rey Mysterio	12.50	25.00
NNO	Rhyno	7.50	15.00
NNO	Rob Van Dam	15.00	30.00
NNO	Stevie Richards	7.50	15.00

2005 Jakks Pacific WWE Best of WCW

NNO	Billy Kidman	10.00	20.00
NNO	Chris Benoit	15.00	30.00
NNO	Chris Jericho	12.50	25.00
NNO	Eddie Guerrero	10.00	20.00
NNO	Rey Mysterio	15.00	30.00
NNO	Ric Flair	20.00	40.00

1998 Jakks Pacific WWF Bone Crunchin' Buddies

NNO	Animal		
NNO	Dude Love		
NNO	Hawk		
NNO	Shawn Michaels		

1999 Jakks Pacific WWF Bone Crunchin' Buddies

NNO	Kane		
NNO	The Rock		
NNO	Steve Austin/Ring Gear	20.00	40.00
NNO	Steve Austin/Street Clothes		
NNO	Triple H	20.00	40.00
NNO	Undertaker		

2001 Jakks Pacific WWF Bone Crunchin' Buddies

NNO	Animal		
NNO	Hawk		
NNO	The Rock		
NNO	Stone Cold Steve Austin		
NNO	Undertaker		

1999 Jakks Pacific WWF Break Down In Your House

NNO	D'Lo Brown	7.50	15.00
NNO	Droz	6.00	12.00
NNO	Goldust	6.00	12.00
NNO	Mankind	12.50	25.00
NNO	Steve Austin	10.00	20.00
NNO	X-Pac	6.00	12.00

1999 Jakks Pacific WWF Break Down In Your House Multi-Packs

NNO	Steve Austin/D'Lo Brown/Droz BJ		
NNO	Steve Austin/Droz/Goldust/X-Pac SC		
NNO	X-Pac/Mankind/Goldust BJ		

2003 Jakks Pacific WWE Bring the Noise

NNO	Matt Hardy	10.00	20.00
NNO	Shawn Michaels	7.50	15.00
NNO	The Rock	20.00	40.00
NNO	Tommy Dreamer	12.50	25.00
NNO	Triple H	12.50	25.00
NNO	Undertaker		

2008 Jakks Pacific WWE Build N' Brawl Playset

NNO	Wrestling Ring (w/HHH & Orton TRU		

2008 Jakks Pacific WWE Build N' Brawl Series 1

NNO	Batista		
NNO	Bobby Lashley		
NNO	Edge		
NNO	John Cena		
NNO	Triple H		
NNO	Undertaker		

2008 Jakks Pacific WWE Build N' Brawl Series 2

NNO	Batista		
NNO	Kane		
NNO	Mr. Kennedy		
NNO	Randy Orton		
NNO	Rey Mysterio		
NNO	Shawn Michaels		

2008 Jakks Pacific WWE Build N' Brawl Series 3

NNO	Boogeyman		
NNO	CM Punk		
NNO	Jeff Hardy		
NNO	Matt Hardy		
NNO	MVP		
NNO	Umaga		

2008 Jakks Pacific WWE Build N' Brawl Series 4

NNO	Chris Jericho		
NNO	Deuce		
NNO	Domino		
NNO	The Miz		
NNO	John Morrison		
NNO	Stone Cold Steve Austin		

2008 Jakks Pacific WWE Build N' Brawl Series 5

NNO	Chavo Guerrero		
NNO	Elijah Burke		
NNO	Finlay		
NNO	JBL		
NNO	Razor Ramon		
NNO	William Regal		

2008 Jakks Pacific WWE Build N' Brawl Series 6

NNO	Curt Hawkins		
NNO	Kofi Kingston		
NNO	Rey Mysterio		
NNO	Santino Marella		
NNO	Sgt. Slaughter		
NNO	Zack Ryder		

2008 Jakks Pacific WWE Build N' Brawl Series 7

NNO	Bret Hart		
NNO	John Cena		
NNO	Mark Henry		
NNO	Matt Hardy		
NNO	Rey Mysterio		
NNO	Undertaker		

2008 Jakks Pacific WWE Build N' Brawl Series 8

NNO	Batista		
NNO	Big Show		
NNO	Rey Mysterio		
NNO	The Rock		
NNO	Roddy Piper		
NNO	Shawn Michaels		

2008 Jakks Pacific WWE Build N' Brawl Series 9

NNO	John Cena		
NNO	Rey Mysterio		
NNO	Undertaker		

2008 Jakks Pacific WWE Build N' Brawl WrestleMania

NNO	John Cena		
NNO	Rey Mysterio	12.50	25.00
NNO	Triple H	10.00	20.00

1999 Jakks Pacific WWF Camo Carnage

NNO	B.A. Billy Gunn	6.00	12.00
NNO	Billy Gunn SI	7.50	15.00
NNO	Billy Gunn w/Gun	7.50	15.00
NNO	Chyna	6.00	12.00
NNO	Chyna SI	7.50	15.00
NNO	Chyna w/Gun	7.50	15.00
NNO	HHH	6.00	12.00
NNO	HHH SI	7.50	15.00
NNO	HHH w/Gun	7.50	15.00
NNO	Road Dogg	5.00	10.00
NNO	Road Dogg SI	6.00	12.00
NNO	Road Dogg w/Gun	6.00	12.00
NNO	Stone Cold Steve Austin	7.50	15.00
NNO	Steve Austin SI	10.00	20.00
NNO	Steve Austin w/Gun	10.00	20.00
NNO	X-Pac	5.00	10.00
NNO	X-Pac SI	6.00	12.00
NNO	X-Pac w/Gun	6.00	12.00

2004 Jakks Pacific WWE Classic Superstars Series 1

NNO	Andre the Giant	20.00	40.00
NNO	Bret Hart	30.00	75.00
NNO	Hunter Hearst Helmsley	10.00	20.00
NNO	Shawn Michaels	25.00	50.00
NNO	Ultimate Warrior	15.00	30.00
NNO	Undertaker	15.00	30.00

2004 Jakks Pacific WWE Classic Superstars Series 2

NNO	Big John Studd Chair & Microphone	12.50	25.00
NNO	Big John Studd Ring Bell & Stretcher	20.00	40.00
NNO	Dude Love Tye-Dye Wrist Bands	15.00	30.00
NNO	Dude Love Yellow Wrist Bands	12.50	25.00
NNO	George The Animal Steele Painted Body Hair	15.00	30.00
NNO	George The Animal Steele Synthetic Body Hair	25.00	50.00
NNO	Mankind	20.00	40.00
NNO	Ric Flair	20.00	40.00
NNO	Sgt. Slaughter/Jacket Off		
NNO	Sgt. Slaughter/Jacket On	15.00	30.00

2004 Jakks Pacific WWE Classic Superstars Series 3

NNO Bret Hit Man Hart	15.00	30.00
NNO Jake The Snake Roberts	15.00	30.00
NNO Million Dollar Man Ted DiBiase	25.00	50.00
NNO Superfly Jimmy Snuka	15.00	30.00
NNO Undertaker	12.50	25.00
NNO Ultimate Warrior		
NNO Hollywood Hogan Small World Title	15.00	30.00
NNO Hulk Hogan/'80s WWF Title	30.00	75.00
NNO Hulk Hogan/'90s WWF Title	20.00	40.00
NNO Jerry The King Lawler	15.00	30.00
NNO Vader	25.00	50.00

2004 Jakks Pacific WWE Classic Superstars Series 4

NNO Hacksaw Jim Duggan	20.00	40.00
NNO Hillbilly Jim	15.00	30.00
NNO Junkyard Dog	12.50	25.00
NNO Rowdy Roddy Piper	15.00	30.00
NNO Tito Santana	12.50	25.00
NNO Yokozuna Smooth Belt Strap		
NNO Yokozuna Textured Belt Strap	20.00	40.00

2004 Jakks Pacific WWE Classic Superstars Series 5

NNO Brutus The Barber Beefcake	15.00	30.00
NNO Iron Sheik	15.00	30.00
NNO King Kong Bundy	20.00	40.00
NNO Mr. Wonderful Paul Orndorff	15.00	30.00
NNO Nikolai Volkoff	20.00	40.00
NNO Terry Funk	25.00	50.00

2005 Jakks Pacific WWE Classic Superstars Series 6

NNO Andre the Giant	15.00	30.00
NNO Bobby The Brain Heenan	12.50	25.00
NNO Doink	15.00	30.00
NNO Earthquake Painted Chest Hair	10.00	20.00
NNO Earthquake Synthetic Chest Hair	12.50	25.00
NNO Koko B. Ware	25.00	50.00
NNO One Man Gang	20.00	40.00
NNO Road Warrior Animal	20.00	40.00
NNO Road Warrior Hawk	15.00	30.00
NNO Shawn Michaels	12.50	25.00

2005 Jakks Pacific WWE Classic Superstars Series 7

NNO Andre the Giant	15.00	30.00
NNO British Bulldog	12.50	25.00
NNO Don Muraco	15.00	30.00
NNO Eddie Guerrero	10.00	20.00
NNO Gorilla Monsoon	12.50	25.00
NNO Jimmy Hart	15.00	30.00
NNO King Harley Race	20.00	40.00
NNO Superstar Billy Graham	12.50	25.00
NNO The Ultimate Warrior	15.00	30.00

2005 Jakks Pacific WWE Classic Superstars Series 8

NNO Bruiser Brody	25.00	50.00
NNO Chief Jay Strongbow	15.00	30.00
NNO Classy Freddie Blassie	10.00	20.00
NNO Cowboy Bob Orton Ace on Boots	20.00	40.00
NNO Cowboy Bob Orton Plain Boots	15.00	30.00
NNO Hollywood Hogan Large World Title	20.00	40.00

2006 Jakks Pacific WWE Classic Superstars Series 9

NNO Akeem	12.50	25.00
NNO Bam Bam Bigelow	25.00	50.00
NNO The Godfather	15.00	30.00
NNO Kamala	15.00	30.00
NNO Papa Shango	20.00	40.00
NNO Paul Bearer/Bow Tie	15.00	30.00
NNO Paul Bearer/Windsor Tie	15.00	30.00
NNO Ric Flair/Smooth Wrists	15.00	30.00
NNO Ric Flair/Taped Wrists	10.00	20.00
NNO Road Warrior Animal	10.00	20.00
NNO Road Warrior Hawk	10.00	20.00

2006 Jakks Pacific WWE Classic Superstars Series 10

NNO Bruno Sammartino	12.50	25.00
NNO Dusty Rhodes	20.00	40.00
NNO Gorilla Monsoon	25.00	50.00
NNO Greg The Hammer Valentine	20.00	40.00
NNO Harley Race	15.00	30.00
NNO Mr. Perfect	15.00	30.00
NNO Rocky Maivia	20.00	40.00
NNO Sabu	20.00	40.00

2006 Jakks Pacific WWE Classic Superstars Series 11

NNO 123 Kid	20.00	40.00
NNO Barry Windham	10.00	20.00
NNO Diesel	15.00	30.00
NNO Fabulous Moolah	10.00	20.00
NNO Hulk Hogan Black Weightlifting Belt	12.50	25.00
NNO Hulk Hogan Yellow Weightlifting Belt	20.00	40.00
NNO Irwin R. Schyster	15.00	30.00
NNO Ken Shamrock	12.50	25.00
NNO Rick Steiner	15.00	30.00

2006 Jakks Pacific WWE Classic Superstars Series 12

NNO Arn Anderson	12.50	25.00
NNO Brooklyn Brawler	15.00	30.00
NNO Captain Lou Albano	15.00	30.00
NNO Dean Malenko	12.50	25.00
NNO Handsome Jimmy Valiant	20.00	40.00
NNO Hollywood Hulk Hogan	30.00	60.00
NNO Killer Kowalski	12.50	25.00
NNO Nasty Boy Brian Knobbs	12.50	25.00
NNO Nasty Boy Jerry Sags	12.50	25.00
NNO Ultimate Warrior Facing Back	15.00	30.00
NNO Ultimate Warrior Facing Forward	15.00	30.00

2006 Jakks Pacific WWE Classic Superstars Series 13

NNO Al Snow	15.00	30.00
NNO Bad News Brown	10.00	20.00
NNO Bret Hit Man Hart	15.00	30.00
NNO Brother Love	25.00	50.00
NNO Droz	10.00	20.00
NNO Dusty Rhodes	15.00	30.00
NNO Ernie Ladd	15.00	30.00
NNO Luna Vachon	20.00	40.00
NNO The Mountie	25.00	50.00
NNO Mr. Perfect	15.00	30.00
NNO Ravishing Rick Rude	20.00	40.00
NNO Undertaker/LJN Style	25.00	50.00

2007 Jakks Pacific WWE Classic Superstars Series 14

NNO Abdullah the Butcher	30.00	60.00
NNO Bob Backlund	20.00	40.00
NNO Demolition Ax	20.00	40.00
NNO Demolition Smash	20.00	40.00
NNO Diamond Dallas Page	20.00	40.00
NNO Honky Tonk Man	17.50	35.00
NNO Mean Gene Okerlund	30.00	60.00
NNO Rick The Model Martel	25.00	50.00
NNO Sensational Sherri	15.00	30.00
NNO Steve Austin/LJN Black Card	15.00	30.00
NNO Steve Austin/LJN Blue Card		
NNO The Ultimate Warrior	15.00	30.00

2007 Jakks Pacific WWE Classic Superstars Series 15

NNO The Genius	20.00	40.00
NNO Johnny Rodz	12.50	25.00
NNO Lex Luger	15.00	30.00
NNO Outlaw Ron Bass	12.50	25.00
NNO Razor Ramon	20.00	40.00
NNO The Rock/LJN Style	12.50	25.00
NNO Shawn Michaels w/Entrance Gear	15.00	30.00
NNO Shawn Michaels w/o Entrance Gear	15.00	30.00
NNO Tank Abbott w/Chair+Barbell	15.00	30.00
NNO Tank Abbott w/Chair	20.00	40.00
NNO Tully Blanchard	15.00	30.00
NNO Zeus w/Chain+Pipe	40.00	80.00
NNO Zeus w/Chain	20.00	40.00

2007 Jakks Pacific WWE Classic Superstars Series 16

NNO Barbarian	20.00	40.00
NNO Giant Gonzalez/Painted Fur	25.00	50.00
NNO Giant Gonzalez Synthetic Fur/500*	60.00	120.00
NNO Shawn Michaels/LJN Style	12.50	25.00
NNO Sycho Sid w/Knee Pads & {WWF Belt by Feet	15.00	30.00
NNO Sycho Sid w/Knee Pads & {WWF Belt by Waist	20.00	40.00
NNO Sycho Sid w/o Knee Pads & {WWF Belt by Feet	20.00	40.00
NNO Sycho Sid w/o Knee Pads & {WWF Belt by Waist	12.50	25.00
NNO Vince McMahon	20.00	40.00
NNO Warlord	20.00	40.00
NNO The Ultimate Warrior	25.00	50.00
NNO X-Pac/Belt by Feet	12.50	25.00
NNO X-Pac/Belt by Waist		

2007 Jakks Pacific WWE Classic Superstars Series 17

NNO Eddie Guerrero	17.50	35.00
NNO Ivan Putski	15.00	30.00
NNO Ken Patera	25.00	50.00
NNO Repo Man	17.50	35.00
NNO The Rock	20.00	40.00
NNO Rocky Johnson	15.00	30.00
NNO Shane McMahon Centered Jersey Logo	15.00	30.00
NNO Shane McMahon Off-Centered Jersey Logo		
NNO Triple H/LJN Style	15.00	30.00
NNO Typhoon	17.50	35.00

2007 Jakks Pacific WWE Classic Superstars Series 18

NNO Honky Tonk Man	15.00	30.00
NNO Jim Ross	30.00	75.00
NNO Kane	25.00	50.00
NNO King Mabel	30.00	75.00
NNO Mae Young	30.00	60.00
NNO Ric Flair/LJN Style	15.00	30.00
NNO Rikishi	15.00	30.00
NNO Stone Cold Steve Austin	15.00	30.00
NNO Sunny	20.00	40.00
NNO Val Venis Cruiserweight Torso		
NNO Val Venis Heavyweight Torso	20.00	40.00

2008 Jakks Pacific WWE Classic Superstars Series 19

NNO Adam Bomb	30.00	75.00
NNO Cactus Jack	12.50	25.00
NNO Eddie Guerrero	15.00	30.00
NNO Evil Doink	20.00	40.00
NNO Howard Finkel	20.00	40.00
NNO Kevin Sullivan	15.00	30.00
NNO Mankind/LJN Style	17.50	35.00
NNO Nikita Koloff	30.00	60.00
NNO The Rock	15.00	30.00
NNO Tatanka	15.00	30.00

2008 Jakks Pacific WWE Classic Superstars Series 20

NNO Dynamite Kid	20.00	40.00
NNO John Cena/LJN Style	12.50	25.00
NNO Rey Mysterio	17.50	35.00
NNO Ric Flair	25.00	50.00
NNO The Rock	15.00	30.00
NNO Ron Simmons	15.00	30.00
NNO Tony Atlas	20.00	40.00

2008 Jakks Pacific WWE Classic Superstars Series 21

NNO Brian Pillman	12.50	25.00
NNO Buff Bagwell	30.00	60.00
NNO Chris Jericho	15.00	30.00
NNO Jeff Hardy	20.00	40.00
NNO Jesse The Body Ventura	15.00	30.00
NNO Rey Mysterio/LJN Style	20.00	40.00
NNO Tazz	12.50	25.00

2008 Jakks Pacific WWE Classic Superstars Series 22

NNO Andy Kaufman	50.00	100.00
NNO Bob Spark Plugg Holly	15.00	30.00
NNO Chainsaw Charlie	15.00	30.00
NNO Earthquake	17.50	35.00
NNO Eddie Guerrero/LJN Style	15.00	30.00
NNO Matt Hardy	20.00	40.00
NNO Mr. McMahon	15.00	30.00
NNO Stone Cold Steve Austin	25.00	50.00

2009 Jakks Pacific WWE Classic Superstars Series 23

NNO The Berzerker	25.00	50.00
NNO Big Boss Man	30.00	60.00
NNO Billy Kidman	15.00	30.00
NNO Lance Storm	25.00	50.00
NNO Road Warrior Animal	15.00	30.00
NNO Road Warrior Hawk	15.00	30.00
NNO Rob Van Dam	17.50	35.00
NNO Spike Dudley	25.00	50.00
NNO Trish Stratus/LJN Style	25.00	50.00

2009 Jakks Pacific WWE Classic Superstars Series 24

NNO B. Brian Blair	20.00	40.00
NNO Davey Boy Smith	15.00	30.00
NNO Dynamite Kid	15.00	30.00
NNO Hunter-Hearst-Helmsley	15.00	30.00
NNO Jim Brunzell	15.00	30.00
NNO Rey Mysterio	20.00	40.00
NNO Rob Van Dam/LJN Style	15.00	30.00
NNO Stephanie McMahon	15.00	30.00
NNO Trish Stratus	30.00	60.00

2009 Jakks Pacific WWE Classic Superstars Series 25

NNO Bastion Booger	30.00	75.00
NNO Big Boss Man	15.00	30.00
NNO Big Show	15.00	30.00
NNO Goldberg	50.00	100.00
NNO Haku	50.00	100.00
NNO Jack Brisco	30.00	60.00
NNO Jeff Hardy/LJN Style	20.00	40.00
NNO Jerry Brisco	30.00	75.00
NNO Jesse The Body Ventura	40.00	80.00

2009 Jakks Pacific WWE Classic Superstars Series 26

NNO Bret Hit Man Hart	15.00	30.00
NNO Dangerous Danny Davis	20.00	40.00
NNO Dr. Death Steve Williams	30.00	60.00
NNO Giant Machine/Andre	20.00	40.00
NNO The Iron Sheik	20.00	40.00
NNO Junkyard Dog	12.50	25.00
NNO Matt Hardy/LJN Style	12.50	25.00
NNO Meng	15.00	30.00
NNO Mr. Fuji	20.00	40.00
NNO The Sheik	25.00	50.00
NNO The Shockmaster	25.00	50.00

2009 Jakks Pacific WWE Classic Superstars Series 27

NNO The Barbarian	15.00	30.00
NNO Bill Goldberg	50.00	100.00
NNO Evil Doink	15.00	30.00
NNO The Giant		
NNO Kona Crush	50.00	100.00
NNO Sgt. Slaughter	15.00	30.00
NNO Steve Blackman	25.00	50.00
NNO The Warlord	15.00	30.00

2009 Jakks Pacific WWE Classic Superstars Series 28

NNO Bret Hit Man Hart	20.00	40.00
NNO Rey Mysterio/LJN Style	30.00	60.00
NNO Rowdy Roddy Piper	20.00	40.00
NNO Shawn Michaels	12.50	25.00
NNO Triple H	12.50	25.00
NNO The Undertaker	25.00	50.00

2004 Jakks Pacific WWE Classic Superstars 2-Packs Series 1

NNO Hart Foundation	75.00	150.00
Black Knee Pads on Bret UK		
NNO Hart Foundation	30.00	75.00
Pink Knee Pads		
NNO Road Warriors		
NNO Rockers	30.00	75.00

2005 Jakks Pacific WWE Classic Superstars 2-Packs Series 2

NNO Jake Roberts/Steve Austin	30.00	75.00
NNO Mankind/Undertaker	30.00	60.00
NNO Roddy Piper/Jimmy Snuka	30.00	60.00

2005 Jakks Pacific WWE Classic Superstars 2-Packs Series 3

NNO Bushwhackers	25.00	50.00
NNO Steve Austin/Roddy Piper	25.00	50.00
NNO Wild Samoans	20.00	40.00

2006 Jakks Pacific WWE Classic Superstars 2-Packs Series 4

NNO Hulk Hogan/Freddie Blassie	25.00	50.00
NNO Sgt. Slaughter/Col. Mustafa	20.00	40.00
NNO Undertaker/Paul Bearer	25.00	50.00

2006 Jakks Pacific WWE Classic Superstars 2-Packs Series 5

NNO Demolition	40.00	80.00
NNO Hulk Hogan/Ultimate Warrior	60.00	120.00
NNO Hulk Hogan/Ultimate Warrior Head Variant		
NNO Ted DiBiase/Virgil	20.00	40.00

2007 Jakks Pacific WWE Classic Superstars 2-Packs Series 6

NNO Hollywood Blondes	30.00	60.00
NNO Midnight Express	50.00	75.00
NNO Strike Force	30.00	60.00

2007 Jakks Pacific WWE Classic Superstars 2-Packs Series 7

NNO Arn Anderson/Tully Blanchard	25.00	50.00
NNO Lex Luger/Dean Malenko	25.00	50.00
NNO Ric Flair/Barry Windham	25.00	50.00

2008 Jakks Pacific WWE Classic Superstars 2-Packs Series 8

NNO Giant Gonzales	30.00	75.00
Harvey Wippleman		
NNO Jerry Lawler vs.	50.00	100.00
(Andy Kaufman		
NNO Killer Bees	40.00	80.00

2008 Jakks Pacific WWE Classic Superstars 2-Packs Series 9

NNO British Bulldogs	75.00	150.00
NNO Ivan & Nikita Koloff	30.00	75.00
NNO Rock 'n Roll Express	60.00	120.00

2009 Jakks Pacific WWE Classic Superstars 2-Packs Series 10

NNO Tony Atlas/Rocky Johnson		
NNO Too Cool		
NNO Yokozuna vs. Bret Hart	30.00	60.00

2009 Jakks Pacific WWE Classic Superstars 2-Packs Series 11

NNO Jake Roberts vs. Rick Martel		
NNO Jake Roberts vs. Rick Martel/Blindfolds		
NNO Rob Van Dam vs. Tazz	25.00	50.00
NNO Rowdy Roddy Piper vs. Mr. Fuji	40.00	80.00

2009 Jakks Pacific WWE Classic Superstars 2-Packs Series 12

NNO Cowboy Bob Orton/Randy Orton	30.00	60.00
NNO Jim Neidhart/Natalya	30.00	75.00
NNO Million Dollar Man/DiBiase Jr.	20.00	40.00

2009 Jakks Pacific WWE Classic Superstars 2-Packs Series 13

NNO Steve Austin vs. Rock	30.00	60.00
NNO Triple H/X-Pac	20.00	40.00
NNO Bobby Heenan/Abe Schwartz	30.00	60.00

2004 Jakks Pacific WWE Classic Superstars 3-Packs Series 1

NNO Jake Roberts/Andre Single Strap	150.00	300.00
John Studd		
NNO Jake Roberts/Andre Double Strap	30.00	75.00
John Studd		

2005 Jakks Pacific WWE Classic Superstars 3-Packs Series 2

NNO Bret Hart/Rock/HBK	30.00	75.00

2005 Jakks Pacific WWE Classic Superstars 3-Packs Series 3

NNO 3 Faces of Undertaker	60.00	120.00
NNO Jim Neidhart/Tito Santana	20.00	40.00
Marty Janetty		

2005 Jakks Pacific WWE Classic Superstars 3-Packs Series 4

NNO King Kong Bundy	45.00	90.00
Volkoff & Sheik		
NNO Hart Foundation w/J. Hart	30.00	75.00

2006 Jakks Pacific WWE Classic Superstars 3-Packs Series 5

NNO Fabulous Freebirds	30.00	60.00
NNO Fabulous Freebirds		
Taped Wrists		
NNO Mega-Maniacs	25.00	50.00
w/Jimmy Hart		

2006 Jakks Pacific WWE Classic Superstars 3-Packs Series 6

NNO Captain Lou Albano	20.00	40.00
Wild Samoans		
NNO Rowdy Roddy Piper/Cowboy Bob Orton/Mr. Wonderful	25.00	50.00

2006 Jakks Pacific WWE Classic Superstars 3-Packs Series 7

NNO Terry Funk/Cactus Jack/Sabu	25.00	50.00
NNO Undertaker/Kane/Paul Bearer	25.00	50.00

2007 Jakks Pacific WWE Classic Superstars 3-Packs Series 8

NNO Jake Roberts/British	40.00	80.00
(Bulldog/Koko B. Ware		
NNO Ric Flair/Perfect/Heenan	25.00	50.00

2008 Jakks Pacific WWE Classic Superstars 3-Packs Series 9

NNO Rhythm & Blues	30.00	75.00
(w/Jimmy Hart		
NNO Rocky Johnson/Peter		
Maivia/The Rock	40.00	80.00

2009 WWE Classic Superstars 3-Packs Series 10

NNO Brainbusters w/Bobby Heenan	25.00	50.00
NNO Demolition/Ax/	75.00	150.00
Smash/Crush		

2009 Jakks Pacific WWE Classic Superstars 3-Packs Series 11

NNO LOD 2000 w/Sunny	75.00	150.00
NNO Nasty Boys w/Jimmy Hart	30.00	60.00

2009 Jakks Pacific WWE Classic Superstars 3-Packs Series 12

NNO Powers of Pain w/Mr. Fuji		
NNO Tito Santana/HBK w/Sherri		

1999 Jakks Pacific WWF Deadly Games

NNO Droz	6.00	12.00
NNO HHH	6.00	12.00
NNO Stone Cold Steve Austin	7.50	15.00

2005 Jakks Pacific WWE Deluxe Aggression Series 1

NNO Batista	20.00	40.00
NNO Kurt Angle	12.50	25.00
NNO John Cena	30.00	60.00
NNO Randy Orton	15.00	30.00
NNO Rey Mysterio	20.00	40.00
NNO Triple H	15.00	30.00

2006 Jakks Pacific WWE Deluxe Aggression Series 2

NNO Booker T	10.00	20.00
NNO Carlito Cool	10.00	20.00
NNO Edge	10.00	20.00
NNO Kane	15.00	30.00
NNO Rey Mysterio	15.00	30.00
NNO Undertaker	25.00	50.00

2006 Jakks Pacific WWE Deluxe Aggression Series 3

NNO Batista	12.50	25.00
NNO Chris Benoit	15.00	30.00
NNO John Cena		
NNO Kurt Angle	12.50	25.00
NNO Lashley	7.50	15.00
NNO Shawn Michaels		

2006 Jakks Pacific WWE Deluxe Aggression Series 4

NNO Boogeyman	12.50	25.00
NNO Chris Masters	10.00	20.00
NNO JBL	7.50	15.00
NNO Mr. Kennedy		
NNO Randy Orton	10.00	20.00
NNO Rob Conway	7.50	15.00
NNO Shelton Benjamin		

2006 Jakks Pacific WWE Deluxe Aggression Series 5

NNO	Batista	10.00	20.00
NNO	Big Show	15.00	30.00
NNO	John Cena	20.00	40.00
NNO	Matt Hardy	10.00	20.00
NNO	Rob Van Dam	10.00	20.00
NNO	Triple H		

2007 Jakks Pacific WWE Deluxe Aggression Series 6

NNO Booker T
NNO Edge
NNO Finlay
NNO John Cena
NNO Kenny
NNO Rob Van Dam

2007 Jakks Pacific WWE Deluxe Aggression Series 7

NNO Carlito
NNO Chris Benoit
NNO Mr. Kennedy
NNO Jeff Hardy
NNO Sabu
NNO Rey Mysterio

2007 Jakks Pacific WWE Deluxe Aggression Series 8

NNO Bobby Lashley
NNO CM Punk
NNO Sandman
NNO Gregory Helms
NNO Undertaker
NNO Johnny Nitro

2007 Jakks Pacific WWE Deluxe Aggression Series 8 (loose)

NNO Bobby Lashley
NNO CM Punk
NNO Sandman
NNO Gregory Helms
NNO Undertaker
NNO Johnny Nitro

2007 Jakks Pacific WWE Deluxe Aggression Series 9

NNO Mr. McMahon
NNO Kenny Dykstra
NNO Kevin Thorn
NNO John Cena
NNO Jimmy Wang Yang
NNO Tommy Dreamer

2007 Jakks Pacific WWE Deluxe Aggression Series 10

NNO Batista
NNO Daivari
NNO JBL
NNO Matt Hardy
NNO Randy Orton
NNO Shawn Michaels

2007 Jakks Pacific WWE Deluxe Aggression Series 11

NNO Chavo Guerrero
NNO Elijah Burke
NNO John Cena
NNO MVP
NNO Snitsky
NNO William Regal

2007 Jakks Pacific WWE Deluxe Aggression Series 12

NNO Batista
NNO Boogeyman
NNO CM Punk
NNO Paul London
NNO Shawn Michaels
NNO Umaga

2008 Jakks Pacific WWE Deluxe Aggression Series 13

NNO	Cody Rhodes	12.50	25.00
NNO	John Cena	12.50	25.00
NNO	Miz	10.00	20.00
NNO	Rey Mysterio	12.50	25.00
NNO	Stone Cold Steve Austin	15.00	30.00
NNO	Triple H	17.50	35.00

2008 Jakks Pacific WWE Deluxe Aggression Series 14

NNO	John Morrison	20.00	40.00
NNO	Armando Estrada	10.00	20.00
NNO	Brian Kendrick	10.00	20.00
NNO	MVP	10.00	20.00
NNO	Randy Orton	12.50	25.00
NNO	Undertaker	20.00	40.00

2008 Jakks Pacific WWE Deluxe Aggression Series 15

NNO	Chris Jericho		
NNO	Finlay		
NNO	Matt Striker	15.00	30.00
NNO	Mr. Kennedy		
NNO	Tazz		
NNO	Undertaker		

2008 Jakks Pacific WWE Deluxe Aggression Series 16

NNO	Batista		
NNO	Edge	15.00	30.00
NNO	JBL	10.00	20.00
NNO	Nunzio		
NNO	Randy Orton		
NNO	Shelton Benjamin		

2008 Jakks Pacific WWE Deluxe Aggression Series 17

NNO	Curt Hawkins		
NNO	DH Smith	12.50	25.00
NNO	Kofi Kingston	15.00	30.00
NNO	Paul Burchill	10.00	20.00
NNO	Santino Marella	10.00	20.00
NNO	Zack Ryder		

2008 Jakks Pacific WWE Deluxe Aggression Series 18

NNO	Chris Jericho	15.00	30.00
NNO	Festus	10.00	20.00
NNO	Hardcore Holly	10.00	20.00
NNO	Jesse	10.00	20.00
NNO	John Morrison	10.00	20.00
NNO	The Miz		

2009 Jakks Pacific WWE Deluxe Aggression Series 19

NNO	Chris Jericho		
NNO	John Cena	15.00	30.00
NNO	JTG	10.00	20.00
NNO	Matt Hardy	15.00	30.00
NNO	Shad	10.00	20.00
NNO	Ted DiBiase	12.50	25.00

2009 Jakks Pacific WWE Deluxe Aggression Series 20

NNO	Big Show	10.00	20.00
NNO	Evan Bourne		
NNO	Shawn Michaels		
NNO	Stone Cold Steve Austin		
NNO	R-Truth	10.00	20.00
NNO	Rey Mysterio	17.50	35.00

2009 Jakks Pacific WWE Deluxe Aggression Series 21

NNO	Edge	12.50	25.00
NNO	Goldust		
NNO	Jeff Hardy	25.00	50.00
NNO	John Cena	12.50	25.00
NNO	Rey Mysterio	20.00	40.00
NNO	Vladimir Kozlov	10.00	20.00

2009 Jakks Pacific WWE Deluxe Aggression Series 22

NNO	Batista		
NNO	Christian	25.00	50.00
NNO	CM Punk	30.00	60.00
NNO	Jack Swagger	12.50	25.00
NNO	Randy Orton		
NNO	Triple H		

2009 Jakks Pacific WWE Deluxe Aggression Series 23

NNO	Batista		
NNO	Big Show	10.00	20.00
NNO	John Cena	10.00	20.00
NNO	Randy Orton		
NNO	Rey Mysterio		
NNO	Triple H	15.00	30.00

2009 Jakks Pacific WWE Deluxe Aggression Series 24

NNO	Kofi Kingston		
NNO	Matt Hardy		
NNO	MVP		
NNO	Rey Mysterio	15.00	30.00

2007 Jakks Pacific WWE Deluxe Aggression 2-Packs

NNO Edge/Batista
NNO Undertaker/Kane
NNO Shawn Michaels/Triple H

2006 Jakks Pacific WWE Deluxe Aggression 3-Packs Series 1

NNO	Triple H/John Cena/Edge	15.00	30.00
NNO	Rey Mysterio/Randy Orton/Kurt Angle	25.00	50.00

2007 Jakks Pacific WWE Deluxe Aggression 3-Packs Series 2

NNO DX & The Big Show
NNO Rey Mysterio
Lashley/Batista

2007 Jakks Pacific WWE Deluxe Aggression 3-Packs Series 3

NNO Lashley/Sabu/RVD
NNO Randy Orton/Edge/Jeff Hardy

2008 Jakks Pacific WWE Deluxe Aggression 3-Packs Series 4

NNO	Shawn Michaels/John Cena/Edge		
NNO	Mr. Kennedy/Undertaker/Fit Finlay	20.00	40.00

2008 Jakks Pacific WWE Deluxe Aggression 3-Packs Series 5

NNO	Umaga/Triple H/Randy Orton	25.00	50.00
NNO	Rey Mysterio/Undertaker/Fit Finlay	25.00	50.00

2009 Jakks Pacific WWE Deluxe Aggression 3-Packs Series 6

NNO Chris Jericho/Kane/Shawn Michaels
NNO CM Punk/Edge/Chavo Guerrero

2006 Jakks Pacific WWE Deluxe Classic Superstars Series 1

NNO	Hulk Hogan	25.00	50.00
NNO	Ric Flair	25.00	50.00
NNO	Rowdy Roddy Piper (black tape)	15.00	30.00
NNO	Rowdy Roddy Piper (gold tape)		
NNO	Stone Cold Steve Austin	15.00	30.00
NNO	The Rock	20.00	40.00

2007 Jakks Pacific WWE Deluxe Classic Superstars Series 2

NNO Bret Hart
NNO British Bulldog
NNO Kevin Nash
NNO Mr. Perfect
NNO Shawn Michaels

2007 Jakks Pacific WWE Deluxe Classic Superstars Series 3

NNO Jake The Snake Roberts
NNO Lex Luger
NNO Ravishing Rick Rude
NNO Scott Hall
NNO Undertaker

2007 Jakks Pacific WWE Deluxe Classic Superstars Series 4

NNO Brutus Beefcake
NNO Honky Tonk Man
NNO Iron Sheik
NNO Million Dollar Man Ted DiBiase
NNO Shawn Michaels

2008 Jakks Pacific WWE Deluxe Classic Superstars Series 5

NNO	Buff Bagwell	12.50	25.00
NNO	Diamond Dallas Page		
NNO	Jim The Anvil Neidhart	20.00	40.00
NNO	Jimmy Superfly Snuka	12.50	25.00

2008 Jakks Pacific WWE Deluxe Classic Superstars Series 6

NNO	Eddie Guerrero	25.00	50.00
NNO	Hillbilly Jim	20.00	40.00
NNO	Kane	30.00	60.00
NNO	Sgt. Slaughter	17.50	35.00
NNO	Triple H	12.50	25.00

2009 Jakks Pacific WWE Deluxe Classic Superstars Series 7

NNO Bret Hart 20.00 40.00
NNO Shawn Michaels 15.00 30.00
NNO The Rock 15.00 30.00
NNO Tito Santana 12.50 25.00
NNO Undertaker 20.00 40.00

2009 Jakks Pacific WWE Deluxe Classic Superstars Series 8

NNO Big John Studd 30.00 40.00
NNO British Bulldog 12.50 25.00
NNO Chainsaw Charlie 10.00 20.00
NNO Dynamite Kid 20.00 40.00
NNO Stone Cold Steve Austin 25.00 50.00

2000 Jakks Pacific WWF Double Slam Series 1

NNO Edge/Christian 17.50 35.00
NNO Kane/X-Pac 10.00 20.00
NNO Stone Cold Steve Austin 15.00 30.00
Shane McMahon
NNO Vince McMahon/Undertaker 10.00 20.00

2000 Jakks Pacific WWF Double Slam Series 2

NNO Big Show 12.50 25.00
Stone Cold Steve Austin
NNO HHH/X-Pac
NNO The Rock/Billy Gunn 10.00 20.00
NNO Undertaker/Kane

2000 Jakks Pacific WWF Double Slam Series 3

NNO Big Show/Test 7.50 15.00
NNO Billy Gunn/Hardcore Holly 7.50 15.00
NNO Debra/Stone Cold Steve Austin 15.00 30.00
NNO Mankind/Undertaker 15.00 30.00

2000 Jakks Pacific WWF Double Slam Series 4

NNO Chyna/Chris Jericho 17.50 35.00
NNO Matt Hardy/Jeff Hardy 17.50 35.00
NNO Triple H/Billy Gunn 10.00 20.00

2000 Jakks Pacific WWF Double Slam Series 5

NNO Bradshaw/Faarooq 10.00 20.00
NNO Edge/Christian 12.50 25.00
NNO Triple H/The Rock

1998 Jakks Pacific WWF DTA Tour Series 1

NNO 8-Ball 6.00 12.00
NNO Chainz 7.50 15.00
NNO Dude Love 7.50 15.00
NNO Faarooq 6.00 12.00
NNO HHH 6.00 12.00
NNO Kane 12.50 25.00
NNO Shawn Michaels 10.00 20.00
NNO Vader 6.00 12.00

1999 Jakks Pacific WWF DTA Tour Series 2

NNO Double J Jeff Jarrett 6.00 12.00
NNO Al Snow 6.00 12.00
NNO Blue Blazer 15.00 30.00
NNO Edge 7.50 15.00
NNO Steve Blackman 6.00 12.00
NNO Undertaker 10.00 20.00

1999 Jakks Pacific WWF DTA Tour Series 3

NNO Christian 5.00 10.00
NNO Godfather 5.00 10.00
NNO HHH 7.50 15.00
NNO Ken Shamrock 7.50 15.00
NNO Stone Cold Steve Austin 12.50 25.00
NNO X-Pac 6.00 12.00

2004 Jakks Pacific WWE Exclusives

NNO Legion of Doom 150.00 300.00
(Ringside Collectibles Exclusive)
NNO Roddy Piper/100* TFM 1000.00 2000.00
NNO Roddy Piper/1800* RSF 150.00 300.00
NNO Roddy Piper/3000* TFM 75.00 150.00
NNO Ultimate Warrior/100* NYC TF1500.00 3000.00

2005 Jakks Pacific WWE Exclusives

NNO Hillbilly Jim/5000* 30.00 75.00
RTWM21 TOUR
NNO Hulk Hogan vs. Shawn Michaels/3000* RSC 75.00 150.00
NNO Mankind vs. Terry Funk KM 25.00 50.00
NNO Sgt. Slaughter/100* TFM 500.00 1000.00
NNO Sgt. Slaughter/3000* TFM 30.00 60.00
NNO Superstar B. Graham/3000* TRU CAN
NNO Superstar B.Graham
Blue Jeans/14000* TRU
NNO Superstar B. Graham
Green Gear/7000* TRU
NNO Superstar B. Graham
Pink Suit/7000 TRU
NNO Superstar B. Graham
Red Suit/400* TRU Orland
NNO Terry Funk/100* NYC TF

2006 Jakks Pacific WWE Exclusives

NNO Bobby Heenan Weasel/100* NYC TF 300.00 500.00
NNO Bret Hart vs. Shawn Michaels RSF125.00 250.00
NNO British Bulldog & William Regal 50.00 100.00
Best of British ARGO UK
NNO Diesel & Shawn Michaels 60.00 120.00
2 Dudes with Attitudes RSC
NNO Dusty Rhodes/3000* OL 50.00 100.00
NNO Hulk Hogan/Blue Trunks & 30.00 75.00
{White Boots WM CAN
NNO Hulk Hogan/Blue Trunks & 25.00 60.00
{White Boots WM US
NNO Hulk Hogan/Tye Dye &
{Knee Brace WM US
NNO Hulk Hogan/Tye Dye & 30.00 75.00
{No Knee Brace WM US
NNO Hulk Hogan/Tye Dye WM CAN
NNO Hulk Hogan 2-in-1 MANIA TIX 75.00 150.00
NNO Hulk Hogan vs. 60.00 120.00
{Andre the Giant ARGO/BL
NNO Hulk Hogan/100* TFM 1500.00 3000.00
NNO Hulk Hogan/3000* TFM 60.00 120.00
NNO Jimmy Hart/100* NYC TF 600.00 1200.00
NNO Steve Austin WWE SZ 30.00 75.00
NNO Tazz/Towel Around Waist RSC
NNO Tazz/Towel in Package RSC 60.00 120.00

2007 Jakks Pacific WWE Exclusives

NNO Bret Hart vs. Jeff Hardy OL 100.00 200.00
NNO Razor Ramon vs. HBK RSC 60.00 120.00
NNO Roddy Piper Deluxe 100* NYC TF 1000.00 2000.00
NNO Scott Hall & Kevin Nash 75.00 150.00
The Outsiders RSC
NNO Steve Austin vs. Bret Hart RSF 150.00 300.00
NNO Ultimate Warrior Classic
Superstars Marble Finish/20*
NNO Ultimate Warrior Classic Superstars 2000.00 3500.00
One Warrior Nation/20*
NNO Ultimate Warrior Classic
Superstars Warrior America/5*
NNO Ultimate Warrior Classic
Superstars WCW 1998/20*
NNO Ultimate Warrior Ring Giant 1800.00 3000.00
Warrior America/25*
NNO Ultimate Warrior Unmatched Fury 4000.00 6000.00
Warrior America Gear/15*

2008 Jakks Pacific WWE Exclusives

NNO Cactus Jack/3000* TFM 50.00 100.00
NNO D-Generation X RSC 75.00 150.00
NNO Eddie Guerrero vs. Rey Mysterio 400.00 750.00
{Halloween Havoc RSC
NNO Eddie Guerrero/100* NYC TF 1000.00 2000.00
NNO Hardy Boys RSC
NNO Hardy Boys WWE SZ
NNO Hart Foundation PROFIG
NNO Ric Flair/3000* WWE 24/7 30.00 75.00
NNO Stephanie & Triple H RSC 60.00 120.00
NNO Undertaker vs. Kane RSC 300.00 600.00
NNO Undertaker GITD/100* TFM 1000.00 2000.00
NNO Undertaker/3000* TFM 75.00 150.00

2009 Jakks Pacific WWE Exclusives

NNO Edge/3000* TFM 125.00 250.00
NNO Goldust Shattered RSC 125.00 250.00
NNO Kane vs. Vader OL 30.00 60.00
NNO Rey Mysterio/100* TFM 300.00 600.00
NNO Shawn Michaels/ 125.00 250.00
Multi-Belts PROFIG
NNO Shawn Michaels vs. 75.00 150.00
{Steve Austin WWE SZ
NNO Shawn Michaels vs. 100.00 200.00
{Undertaker RSC
NNO Sunny/100* TFM 300.00 500.00
NNO Sunny/3000* TFM 30.00 75.00
NNO Undertaker vs. 100.00 200.00
{Triple H WWE SZ

2005 Jakks Pacific WWE Face Flippin' Fighters

NNO Batista 12.50 25.00
NNO Chris Benoit 10.00 20.00
NNO Eddie Guerrero 12.50 25.00
NNO John Cena 20.00 40.00
NNO Randy Orton 12.50 25.00
NNO Undertaker 20.00 40.00

2001 Jakks Pacific WWF Famous Scenes Series 1

NNO Jeff Hardy/Matt Hardy 15.00 30.00
NNO Mick Foley/Undertaker 20.00 50.00
NNO The Rock/Triple H 12.50 25.00

2001 Jakks Pacific WWF Famous Scenes Series 2

NNO Chris Benoit/Chris Jericho 12.50 25.00
NNO HHH/Cactus Jack 20.00 40.00
NNO Kurt Angle/Rikishi 15.00 30.00

2001 Jakks Pacific WWF Famous Scenes Series 3

NNO Bubba Ray Dudley/D-Von Dudley15.00 30.00
NNO Stone Cold Steve Austin
Vince McMahon

2001 Jakks Pacific WWF Famous Scenes Series 4

NNO Lita/Test 15.00 30.00
NNO The Rock/Billy Gunn
NNO Stone Cold Steve Austin 12.50 25.00
Undertaker

1998 Jakks Pacific WWF Fantasy Warfare

NNO Stone Cold Steve Austin vs. Andre the Giant 12.50 25.00
NNO Undertaker vs. Mankind 15.00 30.00

2002 Jakks Pacific WWF Fatal 4-Way Series 1

NNO Bubba Ray Dudley 6.00 12.00
NNO Edge 10.00 20.00
NNO Jeff Hardy 15.00 30.00
NNO Lita 12.50 25.00

2002 Jakks Pacific WWF Fatal 4-Way Series 2

NNO Chris Jericho 20.00 40.00
NNO Christian 7.50 15.00
NNO Stone Cold Steve Austin 12.50 25.00
NNO Undertaker 20.00 40.00

2002 Jakks Pacific WWF Fatal 4-Way Series 3

NNO Bubba Ray Dudley 6.00 12.00
NNO Chris Jericho 10.00 20.00
NNO Christian 10.00 20.00
NNO Jeff Hardy 12.50 25.00

1999 Jakks Pacific WWF Federation Fighters

NNO Kane
(two sleeves)
NNO Stone Cold Steve Austin 15.00 30.00
NNO Steve Austin/Jumpsuit 20.00 40.00

1999 Jakks Pacific WWF Federation Fighters Series 2

NNO Big Show 15.00 30.00
NNO Rock 25.00 50.00
NNO Stone Cold Steve Austin 15.00 30.00
NNO Undertaker 20.00 40.00

2001 Jakks Pacific WWF-WWE Final Count Series 1

NNO Billy Gunn vs. Edge
Downward Spiral
NNO Billy Gunn vs. Edge
Famous-er
NNO Lita vs. Matt Hardy
Litacanrana
NNO Lita vs. Matt Hardy
Twist of Fate
NNO Undertaker vs. Steve Austin

The Last Ride
NNO Undertaker vs. Steve Austin
Stone Cold Stunner

2002 Jakks Pacific WWF-WWE Final Count Series 2

NNO Kane vs. Steve Austin
NNO Kurt Angle vs. Triple H 12.50 25.00
NNO The Rock vs. Chris Jericho 20.00 40.00

2002 Jakks Pacific WWF-WWE Final Count Series 3

NNO Billy Gunn/Jeff Hardy 12.50 25.00
NNO Chris Jericho/Steve Austin
NNO Rikishi/Bubba Ray Dudley

2002 Jakks Pacific WWF-WWE Final Count Series 4

NNO Albert/Scotty Too Hotty
NNO The Rock/Kurt Angle 15.00 30.00
NNO Test/Christian

2002 Jakks Pacific WWF-WWE Final Count Series 5

NNO Bradshaw/Undertaker
NNO Jeff Hardy/Trish Stratus 12.50 25.00
NNO Rob Van Dam 25.00 50.00
Eddie Guerrero

2002 Jakks Pacific WWF-WWE Final Count Series 6

NNO Billy vs. Chuck 10.00 20.00
Famous-er
NNO Billy vs. Chuck 10.00 20.00
Jungle Kick
NNO C.Jericho vs. C.Benoit 15.00 30.00
Crippler Crossface
NNO C.Jericho vs. C.Benoit 15.00 30.00
Walls of Jericho
NNO Hulk Hogan vs. HHH 12.50 25.00
Pedigree
NNO Hulk Hogan vs. HHH 12.50 25.00
Running Leg Drop

2002 Jakks Pacific WWF-WWE Final Count Series 7

NNO Batista
NNO Billy Kidman
NNO Hurricane

2001 Jakks Pacific WWF Finishing Moves Series 1

NNO Chris Jericho/Kurt Angle
NNO The Hardy Boyz
NNO Triple H/The Rock

2001 Jakks Pacific WWF Finishing Moves Series 2

NNO Chris Jericho/The Rock
NNO Kane/Undertaker
NNO Rikishi/Triple H

2001 Jakks Pacific WWF Finishing Moves Series 3

NNO Chris Benoit/Chris Jericho
NNO Eddie Guerrero/Billy Gunn
NNO The Hardy Boyz

2001 Jakks Pacific WWF Finishing Moves Series 4

NNO Kane/Edge
NNO Lita/Buh Buh Dudley
NNO The Rock/Stone Cold Steve Austin

2002 Jakks Pacific WWE Flex 'Ems Series 1

NNO Chris Jericho 7.50 15.00
NNO Edge 7.50 15.00
NNO Hulk Hogan 10.00 20.00
NNO Kurt Angle 7.50 15.00
NNO The Rock 10.00 20.00
NNO Triple H 7.50 15.00

2002 Jakks Pacific WWE Flex 'Ems Series 2

NNO Batista 10.00 20.00
NNO Booker T 7.50 15.00
NNO Brock Lesnar 6.00 12.00
NNO Chris Benoit 6.00 12.00
NNO Hurricane 7.50 15.00
NNO Rob Van Dam 7.50 15.00

2002 Jakks Pacific WWE Flex 'Ems Series 3

NNO Batista 7.50 15.00
NNO Chris Benoit 7.50 15.00
NNO Chris Jericho 7.50 15.00
NNO Hurricane 7.50 15.00
NNO Rob Van Dam 7.50 15.00
NNO The Rock 10.00 20.00

2003 Jakks Pacific WWE Flex 'Ems Series 4

NNO Booker T
NNO Kane
NNO Kurt Angle
NNO Rey Mysterio
NNO Triple H
NNO Undertaker

2003 Jakks Pacific WWE Flex 'Ems Series 5

NNO Booker T
NNO Brock Lesnar
NNO Chris Benoit
NNO Chris Jericho
NNO Rey Mysterio
NNO Rob Van Dam

2003 Jakks Pacific WWE Flex 'Ems Series 8

NNO Chris Jericho
NNO Eddie Guerrero
NNO Kurt Angle
NNO Matt Hardy
NNO Randy Orton
NNO Rey Mysterio

2003 Jakks Pacific WWE Flex 'Ems Series 9

NNO Batista
NNO Chris Benoit
NNO Eddie Guerrero
NNO Randy Orton
NNO Rey Mysterio
NNO Rob Van Dam

2003 Jakks Pacific WWE Flex 'Ems Series 10

NNO Batista
NNO Booker T
NNO Chris Benoit
NNO Chris Jericho
NNO Eddie Guerrero
NNO Rey Mysterio

2003 Jakks Pacific WWE Flex 'Ems Series 11

NNO Batista
NNO Kurt Angle
NNO Randy Orton
NNO Rey Mysterio
NNO Triple H
NNO Undertaker

2003 Jakks Pacific WWE Flex 'Ems Series 12

NNO Kane
NNO Rey Mysterio
NNO Shawn Michaels
NNO Triple H

2003 Jakks Pacific WWE Flex 'Ems Series 13

NNO Batista
NNO Chris Benoit
NNO Randy Orton
NNO Rob Van Dam

2003 Jakks Pacific WWE Flex 'Ems Series 14

NNO Rey Mysterio
NNO Shawn Michaels
NNO Triple H
NNO Undertaker

1998 Jakks Pacific WWF Fully Loaded Series 1

NNO Al Snow 6.00 12.00
NNO B.A. Billy Gunn 7.50 15.00
NNO HHH 6.00 12.00
NNO Kane 7.50 15.00
NNO Road Dogg 5.00 10.00
NNO The Rock 10.00 20.00

1999 Jakks Pacific WWF Fully Loaded Series 2

NNO Road Dogg Jesse James 6.00 12.00
NNO The Rock 10.00 20.00
NNO Shane McMahon 12.50 25.00
NNO Stone Cold Steve Austin 10.00 20.00
NNO Test
NNO X-Pac 7.50 15.00

2003 Jakks Pacific WWE Grudge Brawlers

NNO Christian
NNO Chris Jericho
NNO Kurt Angle
NNO Jeff Hardy 30.00 60.00
NNO Triple H
NNO Undertaker

1997 Jakks Pacific WWF Grudge Match

NNO Bret Hitman Hart vs.
Stone Cold Steve Austin 10.00 20.00
NNO Goldust vs. Savio Vega 6.00 12.00
NNO Shawn Michaels vs. Owen Hart 7.50 15.00
NNO Sycho Sid vs. Vader 10.00 20.00
NNO The Undertaker vs. Mankind 15.00 30.00
NNO Yokozuna vs. Ahmed Johnson 6.00 12.00

1998 Jakks Pacific WWF Grudge Match Series 1

NNO HHH vs. Owen Hart 7.50 15.00
NNO Ken Shamrock vs. Dan Severn 7.50 15.00
NNO Luna vs. Sable 20.00 40.00
NNO Marvelous Marc Mero vs. Lethal Weapon Steve Blackman
NNO Stone Cold Steve
Austin vs. Shawn Michaels 10.00 20.00
NNO Undertaker vs. Kane 10.00 20.00

1998 Jakks Pacific WWF Grudge Match Series 2

NNO HHH vs. Shawn Michaels 7.50 15.00
NNO Road Dogg Jesse James vs. Al Snow
NNO Stone Cold Steve Austin vs.
Vince McMahon 12.50 25.00

1998 Jakks Pacific WWF Grudge Match Series 3

NNO Stone Cold Steve Austin vs. The Rock7.50 15.00
NNO X-Pac vs. Double J Jeff Jarrett 10.00 20.00

2005 Jakks Pacific WWE Havoc Unleashed Series 1

NNO Booker T 10.00 20.00
NNO Chris Benoit 7.50 15.00
NNO Edge 7.50 15.00
NNO Kurt Angle 12.50 25.00
NNO Scotty 2 Hotty 10.00 20.00
NNO Triple H 10.00 20.00

2006 Jakks Pacific WWE Havoc Unleashed Series 2

NNO Batista 10.00 20.00
NNO JBL 7.50 15.00
NNO RVD 12.50 25.00
NNO Shawn Michaels 12.50 25.00

2007 Jakks Pacific WWE Havoc Unleashed Series 3

NNO Bobby Lashley
NNO Edge
NNO HHH
NNO John Cena
NNO Kane
NNO Matt Hardy

2009 Jakks Pacific WWE Havoc Unleashed Series 4

NNO Batista 10.00 20.00
NNO HHH 6.00 12.00
NNO JBL 7.50 15.00
NNO Matt Hardy 7.50 15.00
NNO Undertaker 10.00 20.00

1997 Jakks Pacific WWF Heroes of Wrestling

NNO Sycho Sid 10.00 20.00
NNO Undertaker 12.50 25.00

2000 Jakks Pacific WWF House of Pain

NNO HHH	7.50	15.00
NNO Rock	12.50	25.00
NNO Stone Cold Steve Austin	12.50	25.00
NNO Tori	7.50	15.00
NNO Undertaker	12.50	25.00
NNO X-Pac	6.00	12.00

2000 Jakks Pacific WWF House of Pain (loose)

NNO HHH
NNO The Rock
NNO Stone Cold Steve Austin
NNO Tori
NNO Undertaker
NNO X-Pac

1998 Jakks Pacific WWF Jakk'd Up

NNO Sable
NNO Stone Cold Steve Austin
NNO Kane
NNO Undertaker

1998 Jakks Pacific WWF Jakk'd Up (loose)

NNO Sable
NNO Stone Cold Steve Austin
NNO Kane
NNO Undertaker

1997 Jakks Pacific WWF Boxed Sets

NNO Championship Title Series
Undertaker/Rocky/Bulldog/Owen
NNO King of the Iron Rungs
Hart/Austin/Ref/Johnson
NNO Nation of Domination
Mason/Faarooq/Vega/Crush
NNO RAW Is War 1
Sunny/Bret Hart/Sid/Vince
NNO Survivor Series 1996
Bearer/Mankind/Undertaker/Executioner
NNO Triple Threat
Johnson/Mero/Yokozuna

1998 Jakks Pacific WWF Boxed Sets

NNO Bad to the Bonz Steve Austin TRU
NNO Badd Blood
Bearer/Undertaker/Kane/Austin WM CAN
NNO DX
HHH/Chyna/Billy/Road Dogg MEI
NNO Go Mental
HHH/Dude Love/Austin/Undertaker SAM
NNO Legends of the Past and Present
Andre/Undertaker/Austin WM
NNO Mankind Grapple KM
NNO No Holds Barred
Kane/Austin/Cactus Jack KB
NNO Off the Mat
Austin/Rock/Billy Gunn/Road Dogg TRU
NNO RAW Is War 2
Austin/Undertaker/Rock/Mankind)
NNO Rock Bottom KM
NNO Shotgun Saturday Night
Austin/Kane/HBK/The Rock
NNO Slammers
Mankind/HBK/Undertaker/Austin
NNO Stone Cold Steve Austin Breakaway Table KM
NNO Stone Cold Steve Austin Grapple KM
NNO Stone Cold Steve Austin Special Collection HILLS
NNO Survivor Series
Undertaker/Kane/Austin/Rock
NNO Undertaker Special Collection HILLS
NNO WrestleMania XV Fully Loaded
Undertaker/Austin/Road Dogg/Billy Gunn
NNO WrestleMania XV Judgment Day
Undertaker/Austin/Vince

1999 Jakks Pacific WWF Boxed Sets

NNO Buried Alive	30.00	75.00
HHH/Vince/Undertaker/Austin		
NNO Championship Title Series	20.00	40.00
Austin/X-Pac/Kane/The Rock TRU		
NNO Hardcore Champions	20.00	40.00
Big Boss Man/Mankind/Al Snow/Hardcore Holly		
NNO Mick Foley's Triple Threat	25.00	50.00
Mankind/Dude Love/Cactus Jack KB		
NNO No Chance	20.00	40.00
Vince/Austin/Paul Wight		
NNO Over the Edge	15.00	30.00
Austin/Rock/HHH/Kane		
NNO Perfect 10		
Austin/Rock/Kane/Undertaker/Mankind/Big Show X-Pac/HHH/Road Dogg/Billy Gunn TRU		
NNO SummerSlam '99 Camo Carnage	17.50	35.00
HHH/Billy Gunn/Ausin		
NNO SummerSlam Expect No Mercy		
Austin/Rock/Vince/Undertaker		
NNO SummerSlam '99 Last Man Standing	20.00	40.00
Austin/Rock/Vince/Shane		
NNO Survivor Series Mayhem	17.50	35.00
HHH/Rock/Austin		
NNO WWF Attitude	20.00	40.00
HBK/Animal/Austin/Hawk KM		

2001 Jakks Pacific WWF Boxed Sets

NNO 2 Extreme	30.00	75.00
Lita & The Hardys		
NNO Back in the Ring/Undertaker	25.00	50.00
Stone Cold Steve Austin/Mick Foley KM		
NNO Brothers of Destruction		
Austin/Undertaker/Kane TRU		
NNO Cold Day in Dudleyville	30.00	60.00
Rock/D-Von/Buh Buh Ray TRU		
NNO Get in the Groove	50.00	100.00
(Scottie/Rikishi/Sexay MEI		
NNO Insurrextion		
HHH/Austin/Bubba/Edge/Kane Rock/Test/Jeff Hardy/Y2J/Regal UK		
NNO KOTR Lead Me to My Throne		
D-Von/Edge/Austin/Angle/Hardys		
NNO Picture Perfect	20.00	40.00
Edge/Christian KM		
NNO Renegades		
Raven/Austin/Shane McMahon KM		
NNO Team Extreme	20.00	40.00
Matt & Jeff Hardy/Lita		
NNO Triple Threat	12.50	25.00
Y2J/Rock/HHH		

2002 Jakks Pacific WWE Boxed Sets

NNO nWo Federation Poison	25.00	50.00
Nash/X-Pac/Hall		
NNO RAW Draft		
Bubba Ray/Undertaker/Flair/Austin		
NNO Rock Solid	20.00	40.00
Rock/Scorpion King		
NNO SmackDown Draft		
Y2J/Hogan/Vince/Rock		

2004 Jakks Pacific WWE Employee Gift Exclusives

NNO Ric Flair/25*
NNO Rowdy Roddy Piper/20*
NNO Sgt. Slaughter/20*

2002 Jakks Pacific WWF-WWE King of the Ring Series 1

NNO D-Von Dudley	7.50	15.00
NNO Edge	20.00	40.00
NNO Jeff Hardy	12.50	25.00
NNO Kurt Angle	10.00	20.00
NNO Matt Hardy	7.50	15.00
NNO Stone Cold Steve Austin		

2002 Jakks Pacific WWF-WWE King of the Ring Series 2

NNO Brock Lesnar	15.00	30.00
NNO Chris Jericho	12.50	25.00
NNO Hardcore Holly	12.50	25.00
NNO Rob Van Dam	15.00	30.00
NNO Test	10.00	20.00
NNO X-Pac	10.00	20.00

1998 Jakks Pacific WWF Legends

NNO Andre the Giant	20.00	40.00
NNO Captain Lou Albano	7.50	15.00
NNO Classy Freddie Blassie	7.50	15.00
NNO Jimmy Superfly Snuka	10.00	20.00

1999 Jakks Pacific WWF Live Wire Series 1

NNO Chyna	10.00	20.00
NNO Ken Shamrock	7.50	15.00
NNO Mankind	10.00	20.00
NNO Stone Cold Steve Austin	12.50	25.00
NNO Undertaker	15.00	30.00
NNO Vader	7.50	15.00

1999 Jakks Pacific WWF Live Wire Series 2

NNO Mark Henry	7.50	15.00
NNO Marvelous Marc Mero	6.00	12.00
NNO Rock	10.00	20.00
NNO Shawn Michaels	7.50	15.00
NNO Val Venis	6.00	12.00
NNO X-Pac	7.50	15.00

2003 Jakks Pacific WWE Main Event

NNO Hulk Hogan	12.50	25.00
NNO Shawn Michaels		
NNO Spike Dudley	15.00	30.00
NNO Stacy Keibler	10.00	20.00
NNO Tazz		
NNO Torrie Wilson	10.00	20.00
NNO Triple H		

1997 Jakks Pacific WWF Managers Series 1

NNO Bob Backlund/Sultan	12.50	25.00
NNO Clarence Mason/Crush	10.00	20.00
NNO Paul Bearer/Mankind	12.50	25.00
NNO Sable/Marc Mero	10.00	20.00

2002 Jakks Pacific WWE Match Champs

NNO Booker T	10.00	20.00
NNO Jeff Hardy	10.00	20.00
NNO Ric Flair	7.50	15.00
NNO Rob Van Dam	7.50	15.00
NNO The Rock	10.00	20.00
NNO Triple H	7.50	15.00

2002 Jakks Pacific WWF Match Enders

NNO Billy Gunn/Famous-er		
NNO Edge/Downward Spiral		
NNO Lita/Litacanrana		
NNO Matt Hardy/Twist of Fate		
NNO Triple H/Pedigree		
NNO Undertaker/Last Ride	12.50	25.00

2007 Jakks Pacific WWE Maximum Aggression Series 1

NNO Bobby Lashley
NNO Carlito
NNO CM Punk
NNO Rey Mysterio
NNO Triple H

2008 Jakks Pacific WWE Maximum Aggression Series 2

NNO Carlito	20.00	40.00
NNO Chris Jericho		
NNO Elijah Burke	25.00	50.00
NNO Undertaker	20.00	40.00

2008 Jakks Pacific WWE Maximum Aggression Series 3

NNO Edge	20.00	40.00
NNO John Cena	15.00	30.00
NNO John Morrison		
NNO Randy Orton	15.00	30.00

2008 Jakks Pacific WWE Maximum Aggression Series 4

NNO Matt Hardy
NNO Kane
NNO Mr. Kennedy
NNO Shelton Benjamin

2009 Jakks Pacific WWE Maximum Aggression Series 5

NNO CM Punk	15.00	30.00
NNO John Cena	20.00	40.00
NNO Matt Hardy		
NNO Triple H	15.00	30.00

2009 Jakks Pacific WWE Maximum Aggression Series 6

NNO Rey Mysterio	25.00	50.00
NNO Shawn Michaels		
NNO Triple H	15.00	30.00
NNO Undertaker	20.00	40.00

1999 Jakks Pacific WWF Maximum Sweat Series 1

NNO Hunter Hearst-Helmsley	6.00	12.00
NNO Kane/Mask Off	10.00	20.00
NNO Kane/Mask On	12.50	25.00
NNO Rock The People's Champion	15.00	30.00
NNO Shawn Michaels	12.50	25.00

NNO Stone Cold Steve Austin 10.00 20.00
NNO Undertaker 15.00 30.00

1999 Jakks Pacific WWF Maximum Sweat Series 2

NNO B.A. Billy Gunn 10.00 20.00
NNO Edge 7.50 15.00
NNO Ken Shamrock 7.50 15.00
NNO Road Dogg 10.00 20.00
NNO Stone Cold Steve Austin 12.50 25.00
NNO Undertaker 10.00 20.00

1999 Jakks Pacific WWF Maximum Sweat Series 3

NNO Big Show 10.00 20.00
NNO Gangrel/Blue Shirt
NNO Gangrel/Lt. Blue Shirt 12.50 25.00
NNO Mankind 7.50 15.00
NNO The Rock 10.00 20.00
NNO Stone Cold Steve Austin 10.00 20.00

1999 Jakks Pacific WWF Maximum Sweat Series 4

NNO Billy Gunn 7.50 15.00
NNO Droz 7.50 15.00
NNO Kane 7.50 15.00
NNO Road Dogg 7.50 15.00
NNO Stone Cold Steve Austin 10.00 20.00
NNO Undertaker

1999 Jakks Pacific WWF Maximum Sweat Special Series

NNO B.A. Billy Gunn
NNO Edge
NNO Ken Shamrock
NNO Road Dogg

2008 Jakks Pacific WWE Micro Aggression 10-Packs

NNO Batista/Jeff Hardy/HBK/Kennedy/Cena Mysterio/Undertaker/Carlito/HHH/Kane
NNO John Cena/Kennedy/HBK/CM Punk/Batista Kane/HHH/Carlito/Undertaker/Mysterio
NNO John Cena/Matt Hardy/Orton/MVP/Primo Kane/HHH/Carlito/Undertaker/Mysterio

2006 Jakks Pacific WWE Micro Aggression Playset

NNO Crash and Bash Playset 30.00 75.00
Chris Benoit/Triple H/Kane/Rey Mysterio

2007 Jakks Pacific WWE Micro Aggression Playset

NNO Crash and Bash Arena
w/John Cena/HBK/Lashley/Edge

2008 Jakks Pacific WWE Micro Aggression Playsets

NNO Crash and Bash Cell 60.00 120.00
w/Cena/Undertaker/HBK/CM Punk
NNO Crash and Bash El. Chamber 30.00 75.00
w/Cena/Rey Mysterio/Umaga/Kane

2006 Jakks Pacific WWE Micro Aggression Series 1

NNO Kane/Undertaker/Chris Benoit 15.00 30.00
NNO Rey Mysterio/John Cena
Rob Van Dam 12.50 25.00
NNO Triple H/Shawn Michaels/John Cena12.50 25.00

2007 Jakks Pacific WWE Micro Aggression Series 2

NNO Edge/Cena/RVD
NNO Rey Mysterio/Batista/Hogan
NNO Triple H/HBK/Orton

2007 Jakks Pacific WWE Micro Aggression Series 3

NNO Jeff Hardy/Cena/Carlito
NNO Jimmy Wang Yang/Undertaker/Kennedy
NNO Shawn Michaels/CM Punk/Tommy Dreamer

2007 Jakks Pacific WWE Micro Aggression Series 4

NNO Batista/Finlay/Rey Mysterio
NNO CM Punk/Lashley/Hardcore Holly
NNO Edge/Cena/Orton

2008 Jakks Pacific WWE Micro Aggression Series 5

NNO CM Punk/Lashley/T.Dreamer
NNO Jeff Hardy/Cena/HBK
NNO Undertaker/Kennedy/Batista

2008 Jakks Pacific WWE Micro Aggression Series 6

NNO Carlito/King Booker/HHH
NNO Chris Masters/MVP/Edge
NNO Hardcore Holly/Burke/Boogeyman

2008 Jakks Pacific WWE Micro Aggression Series 7

NNO John Cena/Umaga/Kennedy
NNO John Morrison/CM Punk/Tommy Dreamer
NNO Matt Hardy/Batista/Rey Mysterio

2008 Jakks Pacific WWE Micro Aggression Series 8

NNO Edge/Kane/Finlay
NNO Miz/Boogeyman/Burke
NNO Triple H/Jeff Hardy/Lashley

2008 Jakks Pacific WWE Micro Aggression Series 9

NNO CM Punk/Finlay/Morrison
NNO Rey Mysterio/MVP/Undertaker
NNO Shawn Michaels/Cena/Kennedy

2008 Jakks Pacific WWE Micro Aggression Series 10

NNO Chris Jericho/John Cena/JBL
NNO CM Punk/Elijah Burke/Domino
NNO Great Khali/Undertaker/Deuce

2008 Jakks Pacific WWE Micro Aggression Series 11

NNO Chavo/Big Daddy V/Benjamin
NNO Edge/Ric Flair/Kane
NNO Triple H/Cody Rhodes/Umaga

2008 Jakks Pacific WWE Micro Aggression Series 12

NNO Carlito/Santino/Orton
NNO Matt Hardy/Ryder/Hawkins
NNO Tommy Dreamer/Kofi/Miz

2009 Jakks Pacific WWE Micro Aggression Series 13

NNO Kane/Mysterio/Cena 10.00 20.00
NNO MVP/Undertaker/Jeff Hardy
NNO Shawn Michaels/CM Punk/Y2J 12.50 25.00

2009 Jakks Pacific WWE Micro Aggression Series 14

NNO Carlito/Ryder/Hawkins 7.50 15.00
NNO Cody Rhodes/DiBiase/JBL 7.50 15.00
NNO Finlay/Dreamer/Matt Hardy

2009 Jakks Pacific WWE Micro Aggression Series 15

NNO Cody Rhodes/Mysterio/Cena 10.00 20.00
NNO Edge/Jeff Hardy/HHH 7.50 15.00
NNO MVP/Matt Hardy/Morrison

Jakks Pacific WWE Micro Aggression Series 16

NNO John Cena/Mysterio/Undertaker 12.50 25.00
NNO Randy Orton/Rhodes/DiBiase
NNO Triple H/MVP/Edge 10.00 20.00

2009 Jakks Pacific WWE Micro Aggression Series 17

NNO Finlay/Dreamer/Morrison
NNO John Cena/Mysterio/Kane 12.50 25.00
NNO Undertaker/Hawkins/Ryder

2001 Jakks Pacific WWF No Way Out Series 1

NNO Chris Jericho 10.00 20.00
NNO Grandmaster Sexay 7.50 15.00
NNO Kurt Angle
NNO The Rock 15.00 30.00
NNO Scotty 2 Hotty 7.50 15.00
NNO Stone Cold Steve Austin 12.50 25.00

2001 Jakks Pacific WWF No Way Out Series 2

NNO Chris Benoit 15.00 30.00
NNO Chris Jericho 15.00 30.00
NNO Christian 10.00 20.00
NNO Kurt Angle 12.50 25.00
NNO Lita 10.00 20.00
NNO Matt Hardy 12.50 25.00
NNO Raven 10.00 20.00
NNO Undertaker 15.00 30.00

2002 Jakks Pacific WWE nWo

NNO Hulk Hogan/Tights 15.00 30.00
NNO Hulk Hogan/T-Shirt 12.50 25.00
NNO Kevin Nash/Tights 12.50 25.00
NNO Kevin Nash/T-Shirt 10.00 20.00
NNO Scott Hall/Tights 12.50 25.00
NNO Scott Hall/T-Shirt 10.00 20.00

2002 Jakks Pacific WWE nWo 2-Packs

NNO Hulk Hogan vs. The Rock 12.50 25.00
NNO Kane vs. Kevin Nash 20.00 40.00
NNO Steve Austin vs. Scott Hall 20.00 40.00

2002 Jakks Pacific WWE nWo Playset

NNO Metal Match 30.00 60.00

2002 Jakks Pacific WWE Off the Ropes Series 1

NNO Booker T 7.50 15.00
NNO Brock Lesnar 10.00 20.00
NNO Edge 7.50 15.00
NNO Hollywood Hulk Hogan 15.00 30.00
NNO Triple H 10.00 20.00
NNO Trish Stratus 20.00 40.00

2003 Jakks Pacific WWE Off the Ropes Series 2

NNO Chris Benoit 12.50 25.00
NNO Hurricane 15.00 30.00
NNO Kurt Angle 10.00 20.00
NNO Matt Hardy
NNO Rikishi

2003 Jakks Pacific WWE Off the Ropes Series 2 (loose)

NNO Brock Lesnar 12.50 25.00
NNO Chris Jericho 10.00 20.00
NNO Christian 10.00 20.00
NNO Rey Mysterio 15.00 30.00

2003 Jakks Pacific WWE Off the Ropes Series 4

NNO Jamie Noble 7.50 15.00
NNO Rob Van Dam 10.00 20.00
NNO Scott Steiner 4.00 15.00
NNO Undertaker

2003 Jakks Pacific WWE Off the Ropes Series 5

NNO Billy Gunn 10.00 20.00
NNO Brock Lesnar 12.50 25.00
NNO Eddie Guerrero 10.00 20.00
NNO Ric Flair 7.50 15.00
NNO Stone Cold Steve Austin 12.50 25.00
NNO Triple H 10.00 20.00

2003 Jakks Pacific WWE Off the Ropes Series 6

NNO Al Snow 12.50 25.00
NNO A-Train 10.00 20.00
NNO Big Show 7.50 15.00
NNO Spike Dudley 10.00 20.00
NNO Tajiri 12.50 25.00

2004 Jakks Pacific WWE Off the Ropes Series 7

NNO Brock Lesnar 10.00 20.00
NNO Chris Benoit 10.00 20.00
NNO Lance Storm 7.50 15.00
NNO Matt Hardy 12.50 25.00
NNO Rob Van Dam 12.50 25.00
NNO Triple H 10.00 20.00

2004 Jakks Pacific WWE Off the Ropes Series 8

NNO JBL 10.00 20.00
NNO Maven 10.00 20.00
NNO Rob Van Dam 10.00 20.00
NNO The Rock 15.00 30.00
NNO Stacy Keibler 20.00 40.00
NNO Steven Richards 7.50 15.00

2005 Jakks Pacific WWE Off the Ropes Series 9

NNO Chris Benoit	12.50	25.00
NNO Rey Mysterio	10.00	20.00
NNO Triple H	10.00	20.00

2006 Jakks Pacific WWE Off the Ropes Series 10

NNO Batista	7.50	15.00
NNO Chris Masters	7.50	15.00
NNO John Cena	10.00	20.00
NNO Kurt Angle	10.00	20.00
NNO Shawn Michaels	12.50	25.00

2007 Jakks Pacific WWE Off the Ropes Series 11

NNO Boogeyman		
NNO JBL		
NNO John Cena		
NNO Randy Orton		
NNO Ric Flair		
NNO Shawn Michaels		

2007 Jakks Pacific WWE Off the Ropes Series 12

NNO Batista		
NNO Elijah Burke		
NNO The Great Khali		
NNO Jeff Hardy		
NNO Mr. Kennedy		
NNO Tommy Dreamer		

2009 Jakks Pacific WWE Off the Ropes Series 13

NNO Big Show	10.00	20.00
NNO Chris Jericho	15.00	30.00
NNO Festus	7.50	15.00
NNO Hornswoggle		
NNO JBL	7.50	15.00
NNO Kofi Kingston	7.50	15.00

2003 Jakks Pacific WWE Pay Per View Series 1

NNO Booker T	12.50	25.00
NNO Goldberg	20.00	40.00
NNO Ric Flair	10.00	20.00
NNO Scott Steiner	30.00	75.00
NNO Stone Cold Steve Austin		
NNO Triple H		

2003 Jakks Pacific WWE Pay Per View Series 2

NNO Eddie Guerrero		
NNO Goldberg		
NNO Kurt Angle		
NNO Stone Cold Steve Austin		
NNO Triple H		
NNO Undertaker		

2003 Jakks Pacific WWE Pay Per View Series 3

NNO Eric Bischoff		
NNO Goldberg		
NNO John Cena		
NNO Kane		
NNO Kurt Angle		
NNO Randy Orton		

2004 Jakks Pacific WWE Pay Per View Series 4

NNO Chris Benoit	10.00	20.00
NNO Chris Jericho	15.00	30.00
NNO Edge	10.00	20.00
NNO Hurricane	12.50	25.00
NNO Randy Orton	15.00	30.00
NNO Shelton Benjamin	12.50	25.00

2004 Jakks Pacific WWE Pay Per View Series 6

NNO Chris Jericho	10.00	20.00
NNO Edge	15.00	30.00
NNO JBL	10.00	20.00
NNO John Cena	12.50	25.00
NNO Kane	7.50	15.00
NNO Torrie Wilson	20.00	40.00

2004 Jakks Pacific WWE Pay Per View Series 7

NNO Eddie Guerrero	10.00	20.00
NNO Edge	7.50	15.00
NNO JBL	6.00	12.00
NNO Randy Orton	12.50	25.00
NNO Trish Stratus	15.00	30.00
NNO Undertaker	12.50	25.00

2005 Jakks Pacific WWE Pay Per View Series 8

NNO Batista	12.50	25.00
NNO Eugene	10.00	20.00
NNO Kane	15.00	30.00
NNO Maven	7.50	15.00
NNO Shawn Michaels/Ref Gear	15.00	30.00
NNO Triple H	7.50	15.00

2005 Jakks Pacific WWE Pay Per View Series 9

NNO Bubba Ray Dudley	12.50	25.00
NNO D-Von Dudley	10.00	20.00
NNO Eric Bischoff		
NNO JBL	7.50	15.00
NNO Kurt Angle/Referee Gear		
NNO Paul Heyman	10.00	20.00
NNO Rey Mysterio	15.00	30.00
NNO Rob Van Dam	10.00	20.00
NNO Stone Cold Steve Austin		
NNO Tajiri	12.50	25.00
NNO Tazz	7.50	15.00
NNO Tommy Dreamer	15.00	30.00

2006 Jakks Pacific WWE Pay Per View Series 10

NNO Animal	7.50	15.00
NNO Batista	7.50	15.00
NNO JBL/Vest		
NNO Orlando Jordan	12.50	25.00
NNO Rey Mysterio	12.50	25.00
NNO Undertaker	15.00	30.00

2006 Jakks Pacific WWE Pay Per View Series 11

NNO Batista	15.00	30.00
NNO Daivari/Ref Gear		
NNO John Cena		
NNO Kurt Angle	7.50	15.00
NNO Randy Orton	10.00	20.00
NNO Undertaker		

2006 Jakks Pacific WWE Pay Per View Series 12

NNO Gregory Helms	10.00	20.00
NNO Kurt Angle	12.50	25.00
NNO Matt Hardy	12.50	25.00
NNO Randy Orton	15.00	30.00
NNO Rey Mysterio	15.00	30.00
NNO Undertaker	12.50	25.00

2006 Jakks Pacific WWE Pay Per View Series 13

NNO Carlito		
NNO Edge	15.00	30.00
NNO John Cena	20.00	40.00
NNO Ric Flair	12.50	25.00
NNO Rob Van Dam	10.00	20.00
NNO Shawn Michaels		

2007 Jakks Pacific WWE Pay Per View Series 14

NNO Carlito		
NNO Eric Bischoff/Ref Gear		
NNO Jeff Hardy		
NNO John Cena		
NNO King Booker		
NNO Umaga		

2007 Jakks Pacific WWE Pay Per View Series 15

NNO Batista		
NNO Brian Kendrick		
NNO Finlay		
NNO John Cena		
NNO Johnny Nitro		
NNO Kane		

2007 Jakks Pacific WWE Pay Per View Series 16

NNO Bobby Lashley		
NNO Deuce		
NNO Edge		
NNO John Cena		
NNO Mark Henry		
NNO Matt Hardy		

2008 Jakks Pacific WWE Pay Per View Series 17

NNO Batista		
NNO CM Punk		
NNO Randy Orton		
NNO Rey Mysterio		
NNO Triple H		
NNO Umaga		

2008 Jakks Pacific WWE Pay Per View Series 18

NNO Chavo Guerrero		
NNO Edge		
NNO JBL		
NNO John Cena		
NNO Triple H		
NNO Undertaker		

2008 Jakks Pacific WWE Pay Per View Series 19

NNO Batista		
NNO Big Show		
NNO JBL		
NNO Triple H		
NNO Umaga		
NNO Undertaker		

2008 Jakks Pacific WWE Pay Per View Series 20

NNO Batista		
NNO Jeff Hardy		
NNO Matt Hardy		
NNO Rey Mysterio		
NNO Triple H		
NNO Undertaker		

2008 Jakks Pacific WWE Pay Per View Series 21

NNO Edge		
NNO Jack Swagger		
NNO Randy Orton		
NNO Shane McMahon		
NNO Shawn Michaels		
NNO Triple H		

2001 Jakks Pacific WWF Playsets

NNO Attitude Ring	25.00	50.00
NNO Hardcore Action Ring w/Ref/Jim Ross	20.00	40.00
NNO Hardcore Action Ring w/Ref/Jim Ross/Mick Foley	20.00	40.00

2016-17 Jakks Pacific WWE Plush Hangers

NNO AJ Styles		
NNO Brock Lesnar		
NNO Dean Ambrose		
NNO Finn Balor		
NNO John Cena		
NNO Roman Reigns		
NNO Seth Rollins		
NNO Undertaker		

2000 Jakks Pacific WWF Prop Boxes

NNO Back Alley Street Fight	12.50	25.00
NNO Break Room Brawl		
NNO House of Pain	20.00	40.00

2004 Jakks Pacific WWE Pump 'N Flex Series 1

NNO Chris Benoit	7.50	15.00
NNO Eddie Guerrero	15.00	30.00
NNO John Cena	20.00	40.00
NNO Kane	12.50	25.00
NNO Kurt Angle	10.00	20.00
NNO Triple H	10.00	20.00

2004 Jakks Pacific WWE Pump 'N Flex Series 2

NNO Batista		
NNO Booker T	12.50	25.00
NNO John Cena	12.50	25.00
NNO Randy Orton	7.50	15.00
NNO Rene Dupree		

2003 Jakks Pacific WWE RAW 10th Anniversary

NNO Goldust	10.00	20.00
NNO Jeff Hardy	15.00	30.00
NNO Jerry Lawler	12.50	25.00
NNO Kurt Angle	10.00	20.00

NNO The Rock	15.00	30.00
NNO RVD	12.50	25.00
NNO Shane McMahon	15.00	30.00
NNO Shawn Michaels	12.50	25.00
NNO Steve Austin	20.00	40.00
NNO Triple H	10.00	20.00
NNO Trish Stratus	15.00	30.00
NNO Undertaker	17.50	35.00

2002 Jakks Pacific WWE RAW Draft

1 Undertaker/27,500*	12.50	25.00
2A Kevin Nash/8,750*	12.50	25.00
2B Scott Hall/8,750*	12.50	25.00
2C X-Pac/10,000*	7.50	15.00
3 Kane/25,000*	12.50	25.00
4 Rob Van Dam/21,250*	10.00	20.00
5 Booker T/20,000*	12.50	25.00
6 Big Show/18,750*	10.00	20.00
7 Bubba Ray/18,750*	12.50	25.00
8 Brock Lesnar		
9 William Regal/16,250*	10.00	20.00
10 Lita/16,250*	15.00	30.00
11 Bradshaw/13,750*	7.50	15.00
12 Steven Richards/12,500*		
13 Matt Hardy/11,250*	10.00	20.00
14 Raven/8,750*	12.50	25.00
15 Jeff Hardy/7,500*	20.00	40.00
16 Mr. Perfect		
17 Spike Dudley/5,000*		
18 D'Lo Brown		
19 Shawn Stasiak		
20 Terri		

1999 Jakks Pacific WWF RAW Is War

NNO Mankind	7.50	15.00
NNO The Rock	15.00	30.00
NNO Stone Cold Steve Austin	7.50	15.00
NNO Undertaker	10.00	20.00

2003 Jakks Pacific WWE RAW Uncovered

NNO Jeff Hardy	20.00	40.00
NNO Kane	50.00	100.00
NNO Kurt Angle	15.00	30.00
NNO Matt Hardy	15.00	30.00
NNO Rey Mysterio	20.00	40.00
NNO Rob Van Dam	12.50	25.00

2002 Jakks Pacific WWF Real Reaction R-3 Tech Series 1

NNO Chris Benoit	12.50	25.00
NNO Chris Jericho	10.00	20.00
NNO Kane	15.00	30.00
NNO Matt Hardy	10.00	20.00
NNO The Rock	10.00	20.00
NNO Stone Cold Steve Austin	12.50	25.00

2002 Jakks Pacific WWF Real Reaction R-3 Tech Series 2

NNO Big Show	12.50	25.00
NNO Edge	10.00	20.00
NNO Jeff Hardy	15.00	30.00
NNO Rock	10.00	20.00
NNO Stone Cold Steve Austin	10.00	20.00
NNO Undertaker	15.00	30.00

2002 Jakks Pacific WWF Real Reaction R-3 Tech Series 3

NNO Big Show	12.50	25.00
NNO Jeff Hardy	15.00	30.00
NNO Kane		
NNO Matt Hardy	7.50	15.00
NNO Stone Cold Steve Austin		
NNO Undertaker	10.00	20.00

2002 Jakks Pacific WWF Real Reaction R-3 Tech Series 4

NNO Billy Gunn	7.50	15.00
NNO Chuck Palumbo	7.50	15.00
NNO Kurt Angle	7.50	15.00
NNO Rikishi	7.50	15.00
NNO Test	6.00	12.00
NNO Triple H	12.50	25.00

2002 Jakks Pacific WWF Real Reaction R-3 Tech Series 5

NNO Booker T	7.50	15.00
NNO Chris Benoit	7.50	15.00
NNO Jeff Hardy	10.00	20.00
NNO Kevin Nash	7.50	15.00
NNO Rob Van Dam	6.00	12.00
NNO Undertaker	12.50	25.00

2000 Jakks Pacific WWF Rebellion Series 1

NNO Chris Benoit	10.00	20.00
NNO Chris Jericho	12.50	25.00
NNO Jeff Hardy	7.50	15.00
NNO The Rock	12.50	25.00
NNO Undertaker	15.00	30.00
NNO X-Pac	7.50	15.00

2001 Jakks Pacific WWF Rebellion Series 2

NNO Chris Benoit	10.00	20.00
NNO Chris Jericho	7.50	15.00
NNO Crash Holly	10.00	20.00
NNO Kurt Angle	10.00	20.00
NNO The Rock	15.00	30.00

2001 Jakks Pacific WWF Rebellion Series 3

NNO D-Von Dudley	7.50	15.00
NNO Jeff Hardy	12.50	25.00
NNO Kurt Angle	10.00	20.00
NNO Stone Cold Steve Austin	20.00	40.00
NNO The Rock	12.50	25.00
NNO Triple H	7.50	15.00
NNO Undertaker	12.50	25.00

2001 Jakks Pacific WWF Rebellion Series 4

NNO Billy Gunn	7.50	15.00
NNO Chris Benoit	10.00	20.00
NNO Edge	10.00	20.00
NNO HHH	10.00	20.00
NNO Lita	10.00	20.00
NNO X-Pac	7.50	15.00

2002 Jakks Pacific WWE Relentless

NNO Booker T		
NNO Edge	10.00	20.00
NNO Rob Van Dam	15.00	30.00
NNO Triple H		

2005 Jakks Pacific WWE Ring Giants Classic Series 1

NNO Rowdy Roddy Piper	30.00	60.00
NNO Ted DiBiase	25.00	50.00
NNO Ultimate Warrior	30.00	75.00

2005 Jakks Pacific WWE Ring Giants Series 1

NNO Chris Benoit	20.00	40.00
NNO Eddie Guerrero	15.00	30.00
NNO John Cena	15.00	30.00
NNO Triple H	15.00	30.00

2005 Jakks Pacific WWE Ring Giants Series 2

NNO Batista	12.50	25.00
NNO Booker T	15.00	30.00
NNO Kurt Angle	20.00	40.00
NNO Randy Orton	15.00	30.00

2005 Jakks Pacific WWE Ring Giants Series 3

NNO Carlito/Hair	20.00	40.00
NNO Carlito/No Hair		
NNO Kane	12.50	25.00
NNO Rey Mysterio Red White Blue Pants	30.00	75.00
NNO Shawn Michaels	20.00	40.00

2005 Jakks Pacific WWE Ring Giants Series 4

NNO Batista	15.00	30.00
NNO John Cena	20.00	40.00
NNO Rey Mysterio	15.00	30.00
NNO Undertaker	20.00	40.00

2006 Jakks Pacific WWE Ring Giants Series 5

NNO Batista		
NNO John Cena		
NNO Kurt Angle		
NNO Rey Mysterio		

2006 Jakks Pacific WWE Ring Giants Series 6

NNO Bobby Lashley		
NNO Boogeyman		
NNO Kurt Angle		
NNO Rey Mysterio		

2006 Jakks Pacific WWE Ring Giants Series 7

NNO Batista		
NNO Hulk Hogan		
NNO John Cena		
NNO Rob Van Dam		

2007 Jakks Pacific WWE Ring Giants Series 8

NNO Edge		
NNO John Cena		
NNO Rey Mysterio		
NNO Shawn Michaels		

2007 Jakks Pacific WWE Ring Giants Series 9

NNO Carlito		
NNO Shawn Michaels		
NNO Triple H		
NNO Undertaker		

2007 Jakks Pacific WWE Ring Giants Series 10

NNO Batista		
NNO Jeff Hardy		
NNO Mr. Kennedy		
NNO Randy Orton		

2007 Jakks Pacific WWE Ring Giants Series 11

NNO Boogeyman		
NNO Edge		
NNO Fit Finlay		
NNO Matt Hardy		

2007 Jakks Pacific WWE Ring Giants Series 12

NNO Jeff Hardy		
NNO John Cena		
NNO Rey Mysterio		
NNO Triple H		

2007 Jakks Pacific WWE Ring Giants Series 13

NNO Boogeyman		
NNO Finlay		
NNO Matt Hardy		
NNO Randy Orton		

1997 Jakks Pacific WWF Ring Masters

NNO Bret Hit Man Hart	10.00	20.00
NNO Goldust	6.00	12.00
NNO Shawn Michaels	10.00	20.00
NNO Sycho Sid	6.00	12.00
NNO Undertaker	7.50	15.00
NNO Yokozuna		

2002 Jakks Pacific WWE Ringleader Collection

NNO Chris Jericho	10.00	20.00
NNO Hollywood Hulk Hogan	17.50	35.00
NNO The Rock	10.00	20.00
NNO Triple H	15.00	30.00
NNO Undertaker	15.00	30.00

2002 Jakks Pacific WWE Ringside Rebels Series 1

NNO The Rock	20.00	40.00
NNO Stone Cold Steve Austin		
NNO Undertaker	25.00	50.00

2002 Jakks Pacific WWE Ringside Rebels Series 2

NNO Chris Jericho	15.00	30.00
NNO The Rock	15.00	30.00
NNO Triple H	12.50	25.00

2002 Jakks Pacific WWE Ringside Rebels Series 3

NNO Booker T	10.00	20.00
NNO Rob Van Dam	15.00	30.00
NNO Triple H	12.50	25.00

2002 Jakks Pacific WWE Ringside Rebels Series 4

NNO Hulk Hogan	20.00	40.00
NNO Jeff Hardy	15.00	30.00

2002 Jakks Pacific WWE Ringside Rivals Fatal Showdown

NNO Chris Jericho vs. Triple H
NNO Jeff Hardy vs. Eddie Guerrero
NNO Undertaker vs. Hollywood Hogan

2002 Jakks Pacific WWE Ringside Rivals Head to Head

NNO Edge vs. Kurt Angle
NNO Rob Van Dam vs. Booker T
NNO Test vs. Tajiri

2002 Jakks Pacific WWE Ringside Rivals New Series

NNO Billy Gunn vs. Chuck Palumbo
NNO Matt Hardy vs. Jeff Hardy
NNO The Rock vs. Brock Lesnar

2002 Jakks Pacific WWE Ringside Rivals Raging Tempers

NNO Rob Van Dam vs. Test
NNO The Rock vs. Booker T
NNO Vince McMahon vs. Ric Flair

2001 Jakks Pacific WWF Ringside Rivals Series 1

NNO Bradshaw vs. Test	10.00	20.00
NNO Father (Vince) vs. Son (Shane)	12.50	25.00
NNO The Rock vs. Stone Cold Steve Austin	15.00	30.00

2001 Jakks Pacific WWF Ringside Rivals Series 2

NNO Edge vs. Christian	25.00	50.00
NNO Kurt Angle vs. Undertaker	15.00	30.00
NNO Matt Hardy vs. Bubba Ray Dudley	12.50	25.00
NNO The Rock vs. Chris Jericho	25.00	50.00
NNO Triple H vs. Stone Cold Steve Austin	20.00	40.00
NNO William Regal vs. Mick Foley	20.00	40.00

2002 Jakks Pacific WWF Ringside Rivals Series 3

NNO D-Von vs. Spike
NNO Edge vs. William Regal
NNO Triple H vs. Kurt Angle

1998 Jakks Pacific WWF Ringside Collection Series 1

NNO Referee	5.00	10.00
NNO Sable	7.50	15.00
NNO Sunny	10.00	20.00
NNO Vince McMahon	6.00	12.00

1998 Jakks Pacific WWF Ringside Collection Series 2

NNO Honky Tonk Man	6.00	12.00
NNO Jim Cornette	15.00	30.00
NNO Jim Ross	12.50	25.00
NNO Referee	5.00	10.00
NNO Sgt. Slaughter	7.50	15.00
NNO Vince McMahon	7.50	15.00

1997 Jakks Pacific WWF Ripped and Ruthless Series 1

NNO Goldust	5.00	10.00
NNO Mankind	7.50	15.00
NNO Stone Cold Steve Austin	10.00	20.00
NNO Undertaker	12.50	25.00

1998 Jakks Pacific WWF Ripped and Ruthless Series 2

NNO Kane	15.00	30.00
NNO Sable	12.50	25.00
NNO Shawn Michaels	10.00	20.00
NNO Triple H	10.00	20.00

1998 Jakks Pacific WWF Ripped and Ruthless 2-Pack

NNO Undertaker/Stone Cold Steve Austin

1999 Jakks Pacific WWF Road Rage

NNO Al Snow	7.50	15.00
NNO Gangrel	7.50	15.00
NNO Godfather	10.00	20.00
NNO Hardcore Holly	6.00	12.00
NNO The Rock	12.50	25.00
NNO Test	6.00	12.00

2002 Jakks Pacific WWF Road to WrestleMania

NNO Bubba Ray Dudley
NNO Chris Benoit
NNO Chris Jericho
NNO D-Von Dudley
NNO Jeff Hardy
NNO Undertaker

2006 Jakks Pacific WWE Road to WrestleMania 22 Gear and Figure Sets

NNO Kane/Glove & Elbow Pad
NNO Rey Mysterio/Mask
NNO Triple H/Crown

2006 Jakks Pacific WWE Road to WrestleMania 22 Series 1

NNO Chris Benoit
NNO Eddie Guerrero
NNO John Cena
NNO Kurt Angle
NNO Rey Mysterio
NNO Shawn Michaels
NNO Shawn Michaels
Hulk Hogan Costume

2006 Jakks Pacific WWE Road to WrestleMania 22 2-Packs Series 1

NNO Batista/JBL
NNO Edge/Matt Hardy
NNO Undertaker/Randy Orton

2006 Jakks Pacific WWE Road to WrestleMania 22 Series 2

NNO Batista
NNO Carlito
NNO Chris Masters
NNO John Cena
NNO Kurt Angle
NNO Shawn Michaels

2006 Jakks Pacific WWE Road to WrestleMania 22 2-Packs Series 2

NNO Kane/Big Show
NNO Rey Mysterio/Matt Hardy
NNO Rob Conway/Tyson Tomko

2006 Jakks Pacific WWE Road to WrestleMania 22 Series 3

NNO Bobby Lashley
NNO Finlay
NNO Matt Hardy
NNO Ric Flair
NNO RVD
NNO Shelton Benjamin

2006 Jakks Pacific WWE Road to WrestleMania 22 2-Packs Series 3

NNO John Cena/Edge
NNO Kurt Angle/Rey Mysterio
NNO Undertaker/Mark Henry

2007 Jakks Pacific WWE Road to WrestleMania 23 Series 1

NNO Batista
NNO King Booker
NNO Rey Mysterio
NNO Ric Flair
NNO Shawn Michaels
NNO Triple H

2007 Jakks Pacific WWE Road to WrestleMania 23 2-Packs Series 1

NNO John Cena/Edge
NNO Randy Orton/Hulk Hogan
NNO Sabu/Big Show

2007 Jakks Pacific WWE Road to WrestleMania 23 Series 2

NNO Batista
NNO Chris Benoit
NNO CM Punk
NNO Ron Simmons
NNO Triple H

2007 Jakks Pacific WWE Road to WrestleMania 23 2-Packs Series 2

NNO Bobby Lashley/John Cena
NNO Matt Hardy/Jeff Hardy
NNO Undertaker/Mr. Kennedy

2007 Jakks Pacific WWE Road to WrestleMania 23 Series 3

NNO CM Punk
NNO Elijah Burke
NNO Jeff Hardy
NNO Matt Hardy
NNO Mr. Kennedy
NNO MVP

2007 Jakks Pacific WWE Road to WrestleMania 23 2-Packs Series 3

NNO Batista/Undertaker
NNO Bobby Lashley/Umaga
NNO John Cena/Shawn Michaels

2008 Jakks Pacific WWE Road to WrestleMania 24 Series 1

NNO Batista
NNO Carlito
NNO CM Punk/Blue Trunks
NNO Kane
NNO Mr. Kennedy
NNO Umaga

2008 Jakks Pacific WWE Road to WrestleMania 24 Series 1 2-Packs

NNO Randy Orton/John Cena		
NNO Rey Mysterio/Chavo Guerrero	15.00	30.00
NNO Triple H/Mr. McMahon		

2008 Jakks Pacific WWE Road to WrestleMania 24 Series 2

NNO Batista
NNO CM Punk/Red Trunks
NNO Kane
NNO Triple H
NNO Umaga
NNO Undertaker

2008 Jakks Pacific WWE Road to WrestleMania 24 Series 2 2-Packs

NNO Finlay & Mysterio
NNO Mr. Kennedy & Jeff Hardy
NNO Shawn Michaels & Randy Orton

2008 Jakks Pacific WWE Road to WrestleMania 24 Series 3

NNO Chris Jericho
NNO CM Punk/Black Trunks
NNO Finlay
NNO John Cena
NNO Kane
NNO Randy Orton

2008 Jakks Pacific WWE Road to WrestleMania 24 Series 3 2-Packs

NNO Batista & Umaga
NNO Edge & Undertaker
NNO Ric Flair & Shawn Michaels

2008 Jakks Pacific WWE Road to WrestleMania 24 Best of WrestleMania

NNO Batista
NNO John Cena
NNO Kane
NNO Rey Mysterio
NNO Shawn Michaels
NNO Triple H

2008 Jakks Pacific WWE Road to WrestleMania 24 Mask and Figure Sets

NNO Rey Mysterio
Black and Green Pants
NNO Rey Mysterio/Blue Pants
NNO Rey Mysterio/Silver Pants

2002 Jakks Pacific WWE Rollin' Rebels

NNO Hulk Hogan	30.00	75.00
NNO Undertaker	30.00	60.00

2002 Jakks Pacific WWE Royal Rumble

NNO Chris Jericho	7.50	15.00
NNO Referee Earl Hebner	6.00	12.00
NNO Ric Flair	10.00	20.00
NNO Tazz	6.00	12.00
NNO Triple H	7.50	15.00
NNO William Regal	6.00	12.00

2006 Jakks Pacific WWE Royal Rumble

NNO Carlito		
NNO Randy Orton		
NNO Rey Mysterio		
NNO Rob Van Dam	12.50	25.00
NNO Shawn Michaels		
NNO Triple H		

2007 Jakks Pacific WWE Royal Rumble

NNO Batista		
NNO Bobby Lashley		
NNO John Cena		
NNO Mr. Kennedy		
NNO Shawn Michaels		
NNO Undertaker		

2008 Jakks Pacific WWE Royal Rumble

NNO Chris Jericho		
NNO Edge		
NNO JBL		
NNO John Cena		
NNO Randy Orton		
NNO Ric Flair		

2009 Jakks Pacific WWE Royal Rumble

NNO Kane		
NNO Mark Henry		
NNO Ted DiBiase		
NNO Vladimir Kozlov		
NNO Cody Rhodes		
NNO Great Khali		

2008 Jakks Pacific WWE Royal Rumble Playset

NNO Deluxe Ring {w/Cena/Y2J/Mysterio/Edge		

2000 Jakks Pacific WWF Rulers of the Ring Series 1

NNO Al Snow	6.00	12.00
NNO Buh Buh Ray	7.50	15.00
NNO D-Von	7.50	15.00
NNO Edge	6.00	12.00
NNO Ivory	10.00	20.00
NNO Tazz	10.00	20.00

2000 Jakks Pacific WWF Rulers of the Ring Series 2

NNO Big Boss Man	7.50	15.00
NNO Brian Christopher	7.50	15.00
NNO Crash Holly	6.00	12.00
NNO Rikishi	7.50	15.00
NNO Scotty 2 Hotty	6.00	12.00
NNO Steve Blackman	10.00	20.00

2001 Jakks Pacific WWF Rulers of the Ring Series 3

NNO Eddie Guerrero	12.50	25.00
NNO Perry Saturn	10.00	20.00
NNO Prince Albert	10.00	20.00
NNO Raven	12.50	25.00
NNO Stephanie McMahon-Helmsley	10.00	20.00
NNO Steven Richards	7.50	15.00

2001 Jakks Pacific WWF Rulers of the Ring Series 4

NNO Bob Holly	10.00	20.00
NNO Christian	7.50	15.00
NNO Justin Credible	10.00	20.00
NNO Molly Holly	10.00	20.00
NNO Shane McMahon	15.00	30.00

2003 Jakks Pacific WWE Ruthless Aggression Best of 2003

NNO A-Train		
NNO Chavo Guerrero		
NNO Eric Bischoff		
NNO Goldust		
NNO Rey Mysterio		
NNO Rico		
NNO Scott Steiner		

2006 Jakks Pacific WWE Ruthless Aggression Best of 2006

NNO Boogeyman		
NNO Carlito		
NNO Chris Masters		
NNO Edge		
NNO John Cena		
NNO Kurt Angle		
NNO Rey Mysterio		
NNO Rob Van Dam		
NNO Shawn Michaels		

2007 Jakks Pacific WWE Ruthless Aggression Best of 2007

NNO Great Khali	15.00	30.00
NNO John Cena	10.00	20.00
NNO Rey Mysterio	12.50	25.00
NNO Shawn Michaels	10.00	20.00
NNO Umaga		
NNO Undertaker		

2008 Jakks Pacific WWE Ruthless Aggression Best of 2008

NNO Batista		
NNO John Cena	10.00	20.00
NNO Ric Flair	12.50	25.00
NNO Triple H	10.00	20.00
NNO Umaga	10.00	20.00
NNO Undertaker		

2009 Jakks Pacific WWE Ruthless Aggression Best of 2009

NNO Batista		
NNO Hornswoggle		
NNO John Cena		
NNO Randy Orton		
NNO Rey Mysterio	15.00	30.00
NNO Triple H		

2002 Jakks Pacific WWE Ruthless Aggression Series 1

NNO Brock Lesnar	15.00	30.00
NNO Chavo Guerrero	7.50	15.00
NNO Eric Bischoff	20.00	40.00
NNO John Cena	15.00	30.00
NNO Randy Orton	10.00	20.00
NNO Rey Mysterio		

2003 Jakks Pacific WWE Ruthless Aggression Series 2

NNO Batista	6.00	12.00
NNO Billy Kidman	7.50	15.00
NNO Jamie Noble	6.00	12.00
NNO Rico	6.00	12.00
NNO Scott Steiner	7.50	15.00
NNO Tommy Dreamer	15.00	30.00

2003 Jakks Pacific WWE Ruthless Aggression Series 3

NNO A-Train		
NNO Goldust	10.00	20.00
NNO John Cena	15.00	30.00
NNO Rey Mysterio	12.50	25.00
NNO Rob Van Dam	12.50	25.00
NNO Scott Steiner	25.00	50.00

2003 Jakks Pacific WWE Ruthless Aggression Series 3.5

NNO Chavo Guerrero		
NNO Eric Bischoff	12.50	25.00
NNO Goldust		
NNO Rey Mysterio		
NNO Rico		
NNO Scott Steiner		

2003 Jakks Pacific WWE Ruthless Aggression Series 4

NNO Bill Goldberg	25.00	50.00
NNO Chris Benoit	15.00	30.00
NNO Eddie Guerrero	10.00	20.00
NNO The Hurricane	15.00	30.00
NNO The Rock	25.00	50.00
NNO Undertaker	12.50	25.00

2003 Jakks Pacific WWE Ruthless Aggression Series 5

NNO Billy Kidman	7.50	15.00
NNO John Cena	15.00	30.00
NNO Kane	15.00	30.00
NNO Kevin Nash	7.50	15.00
NNO Shawn Michaels	12.50	25.00
NNO Tajiri	7.50	15.00

2003 Jakks Pacific WWE Ruthless Aggression Series 6

NNO Bill Goldberg	30.00	60.00
NNO Kurt Angle	7.50	15.00
NNO Maven	6.00	12.00
NNO Rey Mysterio	12.50	25.00
NNO Rob Van Dam	6.00	12.00
NNO Triple H	20.00	40.00

2003 Jakks Pacific WWE Ruthless Aggression Series 7

NNO Brock Lesnar	15.00	30.00
NNO Chris Benoit	25.00	50.00
NNO Chris Jericho	12.50	25.00
NNO Kane/Unmasked	10.00	20.00
NNO Matt Hardy	10.00	20.00
NNO Randy Orton	10.00	20.00

2003 Jakks Pacific WWE Ruthless Aggression Series 7.5

NNO Bill Goldberg		
NNO Chris Jericho		
NNO Goldust		
NNO Rey Mysterio	6.00	12.00
NNO Rob Van Dam		
NNO Stone Cold Steve Austin		

2004 Jakks Pacific WWE Ruthless Aggression Series 8

NNO Bill Goldberg	30.00	75.00
NNO Christian (long sleeves)	12.50	25.00
NNO Christian (short sleeves)		
NNO Kurt Angle	6.00	12.00
NNO Test		
NNO The Rock	15.00	30.00
NNO Ultimo Dragon	20.00	40.00

2004 Jakks Pacific WWE Ruthless Aggression Series 8.5

NNO A-Train		
NNO Big Show	6.00	12.00
NNO Eddie Guerrero	7.50	15.00
NNO John Cena	6.00	12.00
NNO Rey Mysterio		
NNO Undertaker		

2004 Jakks Pacific WWE Ruthless Aggression Series 9

NNO Booker T SE	15.00	30.00
NNO Jamie Noble	7.50	15.00
NNO Kane	10.00	20.00
NNO Matt Hardy	12.50	25.00
NNO Matt Morgan	10.00	20.00
NNO Rob Van Dam	10.00	20.00
NNO Stone Cold Steve Austin	12.50	25.00

2004 Jakks Pacific WWE Ruthless Aggression Series 10

NNO Chris Benoit	10.00	20.00
NNO Chris Jericho	7.50	15.00
NNO Edge	15.00	30.00
NNO Kurt Angle	10.00	20.00
NNO Rey Mysterio	12.50	25.00
NNO Ultimo Dragon	12.50	25.00

2004 Jakks Pacific WWE Ruthless Aggression Series 10.5

NNO Charlie Haas		
NNO Jamie Noble	7.50	15.00
NNO John Bradshaw Layfield		
NNO Matt Hardy	10.00	20.00
NNO Shelton Benjamin		
NNO Tajiri		

2004 Jakks Pacific WWE Ruthless Aggression Series 11

NNO Batista	7.50	15.00
NNO Booker T	12.50	25.00
NNO Eugene	7.50	15.00
NNO John Cena	7.50	15.00
NNO Rene Dupree	6.00	12.00
NNO Undertaker	10.00	20.00

2004 Jakks Pacific WWE Ruthless Aggression Series 11.5

NNO Charlie Haas		
NNO John Cena		
NNO Randy Orton	10.00	20.00
NNO Rene Dupree		
NNO Rob Conway		
NNO Shelton Benjamin		

2004 Jakks Pacific WWE Ruthless Aggression Series 12

NNO	Booker T	7.50	15.00
NNO	Chris Jericho	7.50	15.00
NNO	Eric Bischoff	10.00	20.00
NNO	Kurt Angle	12.50	25.00
NNO	Randy Orton	7.50	15.00
NNO	Rey Mysterio	12.50	25.00

2004 Jakks Pacific WWE Ruthless Aggression Series 12.5

NNO Chris Benoit
NNO Edge
NNO Eric Bischoff
NNO Randy Orton
NNO Shelton Benjamin
NNO Triple H

2005 Jakks Pacific WWE Ruthless Aggression Series 13

NNO	Chavo Guerrero	7.50	15.00
NNO	Kurt Angle	10.00	20.00
NNO	Rosey	12.50	25.00
NNO	Shelton Benjamin	10.00	20.00
NNO	Tyson Tomko	7.50	15.00
NNO	William Regal	10.00	20.00

2005 Jakks Pacific WWE Ruthless Aggression Series 14

NNO	John Cena	15.00	30.00
NNO	Ric Flair	10.00	20.00
NNO	Shelton Benjamin	7.50	15.00
NNO	Triple H	10.00	20.00
NNO	Trish Stratus	12.50	25.00
NNO	Undertaker	7.50	15.00

2005 Jakks Pacific WWE Ruthless Aggression Series 15

NNO	Big Show	17.50	35.00
NNO	Carlito	7.50	15.00
NNO	Christian	12.50	25.00
NNO	Gene Snitsky	15.00	30.00
NNO	Johnathan Coachman	7.50	15.00
NNO	Mark Jindrak	7.50	15.00

2005 Jakks Pacific WWE Ruthless Aggression Series 15.5

NNO Chris Masters
NNO Eric Bischoff
NNO Heidenreich
NNO Scotty 2 Hotty
NNO Shannon Moore
NNO Simon Dean

2005 Jakks Pacific WWE Ruthless Aggression Series 16

NNO	Batista	10.00	20.00
NNO	Kurt Angle	12.50	25.00
NNO	Rey Mysterio	12.50	25.00
NNO	Stone Cold Steve Austin	10.00	20.00
NNO	Triple H	10.00	20.00
NNO	Undertaker	12.50	25.00

2005 Jakks Pacific WWE Ruthless Aggression Series 16.5

NNO	Chris Jericho		
NNO	John Cena		
NNO	Rob Van Dam		
NNO	Shawn Michaels		
NNO	Undertaker		
NNO	Viscera	15.00	30.00

2005 Jakks Pacific WWE Ruthless Aggression Series 17

NNO	Hardcore Holly	10.00	20.00
NNO	Nunzio	7.50	15.00
NNO	Orlando Jordan	7.50	15.00
NNO	Paul London	7.50	15.00
NNO	Steven Richards	10.00	20.00
NNO	Tajiri	6.00	12.00

2005 Jakks Pacific WWE Ruthless Aggression Series 17.5

NNO	Batista	10.00	20.00
NNO	The Hurricane	20.00	40.00
NNO	John Cena	7.50	15.00
NNO	Rey Mysterio	10.00	20.00
NNO	Shawn Michaels		
NNO	Undertaker		

2006 Jakks Pacific WWE Ruthless Aggression Series 18

NNO	Batista		
NNO	Carlito	20.00	40.00
NNO	Eddie Guerrero	10.00	20.00
NNO	Heidenreich	12.50	25.00
NNO	John Cena	20.00	40.00
NNO	Shawn Michaels		

2006 Jakks Pacific WWE Ruthless Aggression Series 18.5

NNO Batista
NNO Chris Benoit
NNO Edge
NNO John Cena
NNO Matt Hardy
NNO Randy Orton

2006 Jakks Pacific WWE Ruthless Aggression Series 19

NNO	Chris Benoit		
NNO	Ken Kennedy		
NNO	Kurt Angle	15.00	30.00
NNO	Randy Orton	7.50	15.00
NNO	Rey Mysterio		
NNO	Rob Conway		

2006 Jakks Pacific WWE Ruthless Aggression Series 20

NNO	Boogeyman	10.00	20.00
NNO	Booker T		
NNO	Chris Masters	7.50	15.00
NNO	Kid Kash		
NNO	Ric Flair	15.00	30.00

2006 Jakks Pacific WWE Ruthless Aggression Series 20.5

NNO Batista
NNO Ken Kennedy
NNO Randy Orton
NNO Rey Mysterio
NNO Undertaker

2006 Jakks Pacific WWE Ruthless Aggression Series 21

NNO Carlito
NNO Chavo Guerrero
NNO Edge
NNO John Cena
NNO Rob Van Dam
NNO Triple H

2006 Jakks Pacific WWE Ruthless Aggression Series 22

NNO	Kurt Angle	15.00	30.00
NNO	Matt Striker	12.50	25.00
NNO	Nicky	6.00	12.00
NNO	Rey Mysterio		
NNO	Torrie Wilson	12.50	25.00
NNO	Victoria		20.00

2006 Jakks Pacific WWE Ruthless Aggression Series 22.5

NNO Big Show
NNO Edge
NNO Lita
NNO Psicosis
NNO Rey Mysterio
NNO Shawn Michaels
NNO Undertaker

2006 Jakks Pacific WWE Ruthless Aggression Series 23

NNO	John Cena		
NNO	Paul London		
NNO	Rey Mysterio	15.00	30.00
NNO	Shelton Benjamin		
NNO	Tatanka		
NNO	Triple H		

2006 Jakks Pacific WWE Ruthless Aggression Series 23.5

NNO Carlito
NNO Chris Masters
NNO Edge
NNO John Cena
NNO Rob Van Dam
NNO Shawn Michaels

2006 Jakks Pacific WWE Ruthless Aggression Series 24

NNO	Big Show		
NNO	Booker T		
NNO	Kane		
NNO	Kenny	10.00	20.00
NNO	Sabu	15.00	30.00
NNO	The Great Khali	20.00	40.00

2006 Jakks Pacific WWE Ruthless Aggression Series 24.5

NNO	Batista		
NNO	John Cena		
NNO	Paul Heyman	15.00	30.00
NNO	Tommy Dreamer		
NNO	Triple H		
NNO	Undertaker		

2006 Jakks Pacific WWE Ruthless Aggression Series 25

NNO	Batista		
NNO	Brian Kendrick		
NNO	Carlito		
NNO	Rey Mysterio	6.00	12.00
NNO	Shawn Michaels		
NNO	Test		

2007 Jakks Pacific WWE Ruthless Aggression Series 26

NNO	Candice Michelle	12.50	25.00
NNO	Chris Benoit	15.00	30.00
NNO	Finlay	10.00	20.00
NNO	Hardcore Holly	7.50	15.00
NNO	John Cena	7.50	15.00
NNO	William Regal	15.00	30.00

2007 Jakks Pacific WWE Ruthless Aggression Series 27

NNO	Batista	6.00	12.00
NNO	Bobby Lashley	15.00	30.00
NNO	Chris Masters	7.50	15.00
NNO	John Cena	6.00	12.00
NNO	Mr. Kennedy	7.50	15.00
NNO	Rey Mysterio	6.00	12.00

2007 Jakks Pacific WWE Ruthless Aggression Series 28

NNO	Kenny Dykstra		
NNO	Miz	10.00	20.00
NNO	Mr. McMahon		
NNO	Rey Mysterio	12.50	25.00
NNO	Super Crazy	10.00	20.00
NNO	Torrie Wilson	20.00	40.00
NNO	Victoria	15.00	30.00

2007 Jakks Pacific WWE Ruthless Aggression Series 29

NNO	Batista	7.50	15.00
NNO	Candice Michelle	12.50	25.00
NNO	Edge	12.50	25.00
NNO	Ken Kennedy	10.00	20.00
NNO	Matt Hardy	12.50	25.00
NNO	Melina	15.00	30.00
NNO	Shawn Michaels	12.50	25.00

2007 Jakks Pacific WWE Ruthless Aggression Series 30

NNO	Boogeyman	12.50	25.00
NNO	John Cena	7.50	15.00
NNO	Mark Henry	10.00	20.00
NNO	MVP	10.00	20.00
NNO	Sandman	12.50	25.00
NNO	Triple H	10.00	20.00

2007 Jakks Pacific WWE Ruthless Aggression Series 31

NNO	Batista	6.00	12.00
NNO	Jillian Hall	12.50	25.00
NNO	John Cena	7.50	15.00
NNO	John Morrison	10.00	20.00
NNO	Kelly Kelly	12.50	25.00
NNO	Kevin Thorn	10.00	20.00
NNO	Ric Flair	12.50	25.00

2007 Jakks Pacific WWE Ruthless Aggression Series 31.5

NNO	Batista	10.00	20.00
NNO	Boogeyman	10.00	20.00
NNO	CM Punk	12.50	25.00
NNO	John Morrison	10.00	20.00
NNO	Matt Hardy	10.00	20.00
NNO	Randy Orton	12.50	25.00

2007 Jakks Pacific WWE Ruthless Aggression Series 32

NNO	Carlito	12.50	25.00

NNO	John Morrison	12.50	25.00
NNO	Randy Orton	10.00	20.00
NNO	Triple H	10.00	20.00
NNO	Umaga	10.00	20.00
NNO	Undertaker	12.50	25.00

2008 Jakks Pacific WWE Ruthless Aggression Series 33

NNO	Candice Michelle	15.00	30.00
NNO	CM Punk	15.00	30.00
NNO	John Cena	7.50	15.00
NNO	Melina	20.00	40.00
NNO	Randy Orton	7.50	15.00
NNO	Rey Mysterio	15.00	30.00
NNO	Triple H	12.50	25.00

2008 Jakks Pacific WWE Ruthless Aggression Series 34

NNO	Chris Jericho	10.00	20.00
NNO	Funaki	7.50	15.00
NNO	Great Khali		
NNO	Lilian Garcia	12.50	25.00
NNO	Mickie James	15.00	30.00
NNO	Nunzio		
NNO	Shelton Benjamin		

2008 Jakks Pacific WWE Ruthless Aggression Series 34.5

NNO	Batista		
NNO	Cody Rhodes		
NNO	Jamie Noble		
NNO	The Miz		
NNO	Ric Flair	10.00	20.00
NNO	Great Khali		

2008 Jakks Pacific WWE Ruthless Aggression Series 35

NNO	Beth Phoenix	6.00	12.00
NNO	Edge	7.50	15.00
NNO	Hornswoggle	15.00	30.00
NNO	Joey Styles	6.00	12.00
NNO	Rey Mysterio		
NNO	Santino		
NNO	Victoria	15.00	30.00

2008 Jakks Pacific WWE Ruthless Aggression Series 35.5

NNO	Carlito	10.00	20.00
NNO	Edge	7.50	15.00
NNO	Elijah Burke	10.00	20.00
NNO	Matt Hardy	10.00	20.00
NNO	Ken Kennedy		
NNO	Triple H	15.00	30.00

2008 Jakks Pacific WWE Ruthless Aggression Series 36

NNO	Big Show	12.50	25.00
NNO	Charlie Haas	10.00	20.00
NNO	David Hart Smith	15.00	30.00
NNO	Kofi Kingston	15.00	30.00
NNO	Maryse	12.50	25.00
NNO	Mickie James	15.00	30.00
NNO	Umaga	12.50	25.00

2008 Jakks Pacific WWE Ruthless Aggression Series 37

NNO	Cherry	17.50	35.00
NNO	Colin Delaney	15.00	30.00
NNO	Festus	7.50	15.00
NNO	Katie Lee Burchill	20.00	40.00
NNO	MVP		
NNO	Paul Burchill		
NNO	Santino Marella	12.50	25.00

2008 Jakks Pacific WWE Ruthless Aggression Series 38

NNO	Batista	10.00	20.00
NNO	The Brian Kendrick	15.00	30.00
NNO	Hornswoggle	12.50	25.00
NNO	Jesse		
NNO	John Cena	10.00	20.00
NNO	Rey Mysterio	15.00	30.00

2008 Jakks Pacific WWE Ruthless Aggression Series 38.5

NNO	Big Show		
NNO	Chris Jericho		
NNO	Festus	10.00	20.00
NNO	Jesse		
NNO	Kane		
NNO	Kofi Kingston	12.50	25.00

2009 Jakks Pacific WWE Ruthless Aggression Series 39

NNO	Evan Bourne	10.00	20.00
NNO	Jeff Hardy	15.00	30.00
NNO	Mark Henry		
NNO	Rey Mysterio	15.00	30.00
NNO	Ted DiBiase	15.00	30.00
NNO	Vladimir Kozlov	10.00	20.00

2009 Jakks Pacific WWE Ruthless Aggression Series 40

NNO	Chris Jericho	20.00	40.00
NNO	Edge	17.50	35.00
NNO	Matt Hardy	12.50	25.00
NNO	Randy Orton	12.50	25.00
NNO	R-Truth		
NNO	Undertaker	12.50	25.00

2009 Jakks Pacific WWE Ruthless Aggression Series 40.5

NNO	Cody Rhodes	10.00	20.00
NNO	Matt Hardy	10.00	20.00
NNO	Ted DiBiase		
NNO	Triple H	12.50	25.00
NNO	Undertaker	20.00	40.00
NNO	Vladimir Kozlov	10.00	20.00

2009 Jakks Pacific WWE Ruthless Aggression Series 41

NNO	The Brian Kendrick	20.00	40.00
NNO	CM Punk	20.00	40.00
NNO	Goldust	15.00	30.00
NNO	Hornswoggle	25.00	50.00
NNO	John Cena	25.00	50.00
NNO	Rey Mysterio	20.00	40.00

2009 Jakks Pacific WWE Ruthless Aggression Series 42

NNO	Christian	20.00	40.00
NNO	CM Punk	20.00	40.00
NNO	The Great Khali		
NNO	Jack Swagger		
NNO	Shawn Michaels	25.00	50.00
NNO	Triple H	10.00	20.00

2009 Jakks Pacific WWE Ruthless Aggression Series 43

NNO	Batista	15.00	30.00
NNO	John Cena	20.00	40.00
NNO	Randy Orton	20.00	40.00
NNO	Rey Mysterio	25.00	50.00
NNO	Triple H		
NNO	Undertaker		

2009 Jakks Pacific WWE Ruthless Aggression Series 44

NNO	Edge	15.00	30.00
NNO	John Cena	12.50	25.00
NNO	Kane	15.00	30.00
NNO	Matt Hardy		
NNO	MVP		
NNO	Rey Mysterio		

1998 Jakks Pacific WWF Shotgun Saturday Night Series 1

NNO	Animal	7.50	15.00
NNO	Hawk	7.50	15.00
NNO	Henry Godwinn	6.00	12.00
NNO	Phineas Godwinn	6.00	12.00
NNO	Rocky Maivia	12.50	25.00
NNO	Savio Vega	10.00	20.00
NNO	Steve Austin	12.50	25.00
NNO	Undertaker	7.50	15.00
NNO	Stone Cold Steve Austin/Kane Shawn Michaels/Rocky Maivia		

1998 Jakks Pacific WWF Shotgun Saturday Night Series 2

NNO	B.A. Billy Gunn	7.50	15.00
NNO	Jeff Jarrett	6.00	12.00
NNO	Jesse James	7.50	15.00
NNO	Kane	10.00	20.00
NNO	Sable	7.50	15.00
NNO	Shawn Michaels	7.50	15.00

1999 Jakks Pacific WWF Shotgun Saturday Night Series 3

NNO	Droz	5.00	10.00
NNO	Edge	7.50	15.00
NNO	Kurgann	6.00	12.00
NNO	Road Dogg Jesse James	6.00	12.00
NNO	Stone Cold Steve Austin	10.00	20.00
NNO	Triple H	7.50	15.00

1999 Jakks Pacific WWF Shotgun Saturday Night Series 4

NNO	Al Snow	6.00	12.00
NNO	Gangrel	6.00	12.00
NNO	Godfather	6.00	12.00
NNO	Hardcore Holly	5.00	10.00
NNO	Rock	7.50	15.00
NNO	Test		

2001 Jakks Pacific WWF Signature Jams Series 1

NNO	Billy Gunn	7.50	15.00
NNO	Chris Jericho	12.50	25.00
NNO	Jeff Hardy	15.00	30.00
NNO	Kurt Angle	7.50	15.00
NNO	The Rock	12.50	25.00
NNO	Triple H	7.50	15.00

2001 Jakks Pacific WWF Signature Jams Series 2

NNO	Chris Benoit		
NNO	D-Von Dudley	7.50	15.00
NNO	Kane		
NNO	Matt Hardy	12.50	25.00
NNO	Stone Cold Steve Austin		
NNO	Undertaker		

2002 Jakks Pacific WWF Signature Jams Series 3

NNO	Kane		
NNO	Matt Hardy		
NNO	Stone Cold Steve Austin		
NNO	Undertaker		

2002 Jakks Pacific WWF Signature Jams Slam Grooves

NNO	Billy Gunn		
NNO	Jeff Hardy		
NNO	Stone Cold Steve Austin		
NNO	Undertaker		

1997 Jakks Pacific WWF Signature Series 1

NNO	Goldust	7.50	15.00
NNO	HHH	6.00	12.00
NNO	Mankind	10.00	20.00
NNO	Road Warrior Animal	7.50	15.00
NNO	Road Warrior Hawk	7.50	15.00
NNO	Steve Austin	7.50	15.00

1998 Jakks Pacific WWF Signature Series 2

NNO	B.A. Billy Gunn	5.00	10.00
NNO	Dude Love	10.00	20.00
NNO	Kane	10.00	20.00
NNO	Road Dogg	5.00	10.00
NNO	Shawn Michaels	7.50	15.00
NNO	Undertaker	7.50	15.00

1998 Jakks Pacific WWF Signature Series 3

NNO	Edge	6.00	12.00
NNO	HHH	7.50	15.00
NNO	Jacqueline	10.00	20.00
NNO	The Rock	10.00	20.00
NNO	Stone Cold Steve Austin	7.50	15.00
NNO	Undertaker	12.50	25.00

1999 Jakks Pacific WWF Signature Series 4

NNO	Big Show	10.00	20.00
NNO	Edge	7.50	15.00
NNO	Ken Shamrock	7.50	15.00
NNO	Rock	10.00	20.00
NNO	Stone Cold Steve Austin	7.50	15.00
NNO	X-Pac	6.00	12.00

1999 Jakks Pacific WWF Signature Series 5

NNO	Al Snow	7.50	15.00
NNO	Big Bossman	6.00	12.00
NNO	Billy Gunn	6.00	12.00
NNO	Kane	10.00	20.00
NNO	Road Dogg	6.00	12.00
NNO	Stone Cold Steve Austin	10.00	20.00

1999 Jakks Pacific WWF Signature Series 6

NNO Hardcore Holly	5.00	10.00
NNO HHH	7.50	15.00
NNO Mankind	7.50	15.00
NNO Stone Cold Steve Austin	10.00	20.00
NNO Undertaker	7.50	15.00
NNO Vince McMahon	7.50	15.00

1998 Jakks Pacific WWF Slammers Series 1

NNO Bret Hart	7.50	15.00
NNO Faarooq	6.00	12.00
NNO Goldust	6.00	12.00
NNO Mankind	6.00	12.00
NNO Steve Austin	7.50	15.00
NNO Undertaker	7.50	15.00

1998 Jakks Pacific WWF Slammers Series 2

NNO Brian Pillman	6.00	12.00
NNO Dude Love	7.50	15.00
NNO Kane	7.50	15.00
NNO Patriot	6.00	12.00
NNO Shawn Michaels	7.50	15.00
NNO Taka	6.00	12.00

2002 Jakks Pacific WWE SmackDown Draft

1 The Rock/26,250*	10.00	20.00
2 Kurt Angle/25,000*	12.50	25.00
3 Chris Benoit/23,750*	10.00	20.00
4 Hollywood Hogan/22,500*	15.00	30.00
6 Edge/18,750*	10.00	20.00
7 Rikishi/17,500*		
8 D-Von Dudley/16,250*	12.50	25.00
9 Mark Henry		
10 Maven/15,000*		
11 Billy Kidman		
12 Tajiri/13,750*	15.00	30.00
13 Chris Jericho/11,250*	15.00	30.00
14 Ivory/11,250*	15.00	30.00
15 Albert/8,750*	20.00	40.00
16 The Hurricane/7,500*	25.00	50.00
17 Al Snow/6,250*	12.50	25.00
18 Lance Storm/5,000*	25.00	50.00
19 DDP/3,750*	30.00	75.00
20 Torrie Wilson		
5A Billy/11,250*	15.00	30.00
5B Chuck/11,250*	15.00	30.00

2002 Jakks Pacific WWF Snappin' Bashers

NNO Chris Benoit	12.50	25.00
NNO Chris Jericho		
NNO Jeff Hardy	15.00	30.00
NNO The Rock		
NNO Stone Cold Steve Austin	7.50	15.00
NNO Undertaker		

1997 Jakks Pacific WWF Special Edition Series 1

NNO Ahmed Johnson	6.00	12.00
NNO British Bulldog	6.00	12.00
NNO Rocky Maivia	10.00	20.00
NNO Sunny	7.50	15.00
NNO Undertaker	7.50	15.00
NNO Vader	12.50	25.00
NNO Yokozuna/18000*	15.00	30.00

1998 Jakks Pacific WWF Special Edition Series 2

NNO Faarooq	6.00	12.00
NNO Goldust	6.00	12.00
NNO HHH	7.50	15.00
NNO Sable	10.00	20.00
NNO Savio Vega	6.00	12.00
NNO Stone Cold Steve Austin	7.50	15.00

1998 Jakks Pacific WWF Special Edition Series 3

NNO Animal	10.00	20.00
NNO Dan Severn	12.50	25.00
NNO Hawk	10.00	20.00
NNO Hunter Hearst-Helmsley	7.50	15.00
NNO Marvelous Marc Mero	7.50	15.00
NNO Shamrock	6.00	12.00

1999 Jakks Pacific WWF Special Edition Series 4

NNO B.A. Billy Gunn	7.50	15.00
NNO Chyna	10.00	20.00
NNO Mankind	12.50	25.00
NNO Road Dogg	7.50	15.00
NNO Stone Cold Steve Austin	10.00	20.00
NNO Undertaker		

1999 Jakks Pacific WWF Special Edition Series 5

NNO Al Snow	6.00	12.00
NNO Edge	7.50	15.00
NNO Mark Henry		
NNO Shamrock		
NNO Val Venis	6.00	12.00
NNO X-Pac		

1999 Jakks Pacific WWF Special Edition Series 6

NNO Double J	7.50	15.00
NNO Hardcore Holly	6.00	12.00
NNO HHH	7.50	15.00
NNO Stone Cold Steve Austin	10.00	20.00
NNO Test		
NNO The Rock	10.00	20.00

1997 Jakks Pacific WWF S.T.O.M.P. Series 1

NNO Ahmed Johnson	7.50	15.00
NNO Brian Pillman	5.00	10.00
NNO Crush	6.00	12.00
NNO Ken Shamrock	7.50	15.00
NNO Stone Cold Steve Austin	10.00	20.00
NNO Undertaker	7.50	15.00

1998 Jakks Pacific WWF S.T.O.M.P. Series 2

NNO Chyna	10.00	20.00
NNO Headbanger Mosh	7.50	15.00
NNO Headbanger Thrash	7.50	15.00
NNO Owen Hart	10.00	20.00
NNO Rocky Maivia	12.50	25.00
NNO Stone Cold Steve Austin	10.00	20.00

1998 Jakks Pacific WWF S.T.O.M.P. Series 3

NNO Animal	7.50	15.00
NNO Hawk	7.50	15.00
NNO Kane	7.50	15.00
NNO Marc Mero	15.00	30.00
NNO Sable	10.00	20.00
NNO Undertaker	10.00	20.00

2000 Jakks Pacific WWF S.T.O.M.P. Series 4

NNO B.A. Billy Gunn		
NNO Chyna		
NNO Road Dogg Jesse James		
NNO Stone Cold Steve Austin		
NNO Triple H		
NNO X-Pac		

1997 Jakks Pacific WWF Stretchin'

NNO Bret Hit Man Hart	12.50	25.00
NNO Shawn Michaels		
NNO Sycho Sid	10.00	20.00
NNO Undertaker	12.50	25.00

2001 Jakks Pacific WWF Stunt Action Superstars Series 1

NNO Jeff Hardy	12.50	25.00
NNO Kurt Angle	10.00	20.00
NNO Rikishi	7.50	15.00
NNO Stephanie McMahon	15.00	30.00
NNO Triple H	10.00	20.00
NNO X-Pac	7.50	15.00

2005 Jakks Pacific WWE SummerSlam Limited Edition

NNO Chris Benoit		
NNO Chris Jericho		
NNO Kane		
NNO Matt Hardy		
NNO Stone Cold Steve Austin		
NNO Test		
NNO The Rock		
NNO X-Pac		

1999 Jakks Pacific WWF Sunday Night Heat

NNO B.A. Billy Gunn	7.50	15.00
NNO Road Dogg		
NNO The Rock		
NNO Sable	7.50	15.00
NNO Stone Cold Steve Austin		
NNO Undertaker		

2016-17 Jakks Pacific WWE Superstar Buddies

NNO AJ Styles		
NNO John Cena		
NNO The Rock		

1997 Jakks Pacific WWF Superstars Best of 1997

NNO Bret Hart		
NNO British Bulldog	7.50	15.00
NNO Owen Hart	10.00	20.00

1997 Jakks Pacific WWF Superstars Best of 1997 Tag Teams

NNO Godwinns	12.50	25.00
NNO Headbangers	15.00	30.00
NNO Legion of Doom		
NNO New Blackjacks	10.00	20.00

1998 Jakks Pacific WWF Superstars Best of 1998 Series 1

NNO 8-Ball	6.00	12.00
NNO Blackjack Bradshaw	10.00	20.00
NNO Brian Christopher	6.00	12.00
NNO Chyna	12.50	25.00
NNO Shawn Michaels	10.00	20.00
NNO Skull	6.00	12.00
NNO Stone Cold Steve Austin	12.50	25.00
NNO Vader	6.00	12.00

1998 Jakks Pacific WWF Superstars Best of 1998 Series 2

NNO Dan Severn	5.00	10.00
NNO Dude Love	6.00	12.00
NNO HHH	7.50	15.00
NNO Jeff Jarrett	6.00	12.00
NNO Ken Shamrock	6.00	12.00
NNO Mark Henry	6.00	12.00
NNO Stone Cold Steve Austin	10.00	20.00
NNO Undertaker	7.50	15.00

1998 Jakks Pacific WWF Superstars Best of 1998 Tag Teams

NNO Headbangers		
NNO LOD 2000		
NNO New Age Outlaws		

1996 Jakks Pacific WWF Superstars Series 1

NNO Bret Hart	20.00	40.00
NNO Diesel	15.00	30.00
NNO Goldust	15.00	30.00
NNO Razor Ramon	20.00	40.00
NNO Shawn Michaels	12.50	25.00
NNO Undertaker	15.00	30.00

1996 Jakks Pacific WWF Superstars Series 2

NNO Bret Hart	12.50	25.00
NNO Owen Hart	20.00	40.00
NNO Shawn Michaels	15.00	30.00
NNO Ultimate Warrior	20.00	40.00
NNO Undertaker GITD	25.00	50.00
NNO Vader	10.00	20.00

1997 Jakks Pacific WWF Superstars Series 3

NNO Ahmed Johnson	10.00	20.00
NNO Bret Hart	12.50	25.00
NNO British Bulldog	7.50	15.00
NNO Mankind	10.00	20.00
NNO Shawn Michaels	10.00	20.00
NNO Sycho Sid	7.50	15.00

1997 Jakks Pacific WWF Superstars Series 4

NNO Faarooq	5.00	10.00
NNO Hunter Hearst Helmsley	6.00	12.00
NNO Jerry Lawler	7.50	15.00
NNO Justin Hawk Bradshaw	12.50	25.00
NNO Stone Cold Steve Austin	7.50	15.00
NNO Vader	7.50	15.00

1997 Jakks Pacific WWF Superstars Series 5

NNO Flash Funk	10.00	20.00
NNO Ken Shamrock	6.00	12.00

NNO Rocky Maivia	12.50	20.00
NNO Savio Vega	7.50	15.00
NNO Stone Cold Steve Austin	12.50	25.00
NNO Sycho Sid	6.00	12.00

1998 Jakks Pacific WWF Superstars Series 6

NNO Jeff Jarrett	10.00	20.00
NNO Marc Mero	6.00	12.00
NNO Mark Henry	7.50	15.00
NNO Owen Hart	12.50	25.00
NNO Steve Blackman	12.50	25.00
NNO Triple H	7.50	15.00

1998 Jakks Pacific WWF Superstars Series 7

NNO Dr. Death Steve Williams	12.50	25.00
NNO Edge	7.50	15.00
NNO Steve Austin	7.50	15.00
NNO Undertaker	7.50	15.00
NNO Val Venis	7.50	15.00
NNO X-Pac	6.00	12.00

1999 Jakks Pacific WWF Superstars Series 8

NNO Big Boss Man	6.00	12.00
NNO Kane	7.50	15.00
NNO Ken Shamrock		
NNO The Rock	7.50	15.00
NNO Shane McMahon	7.50	15.00
NNO Shawn Michaels	7.50	15.00

1999 Jakks Pacific WWF Superstars Series 9

NNO Bob Holly	6.00	12.00
NNO Christian	6.00	12.00
NNO Gangrel	10.00	20.00
NNO Paul Wight	7.50	15.00
NNO Undertaker	7.50	15.00
NNO Vince McMahon	7.50	15.00

2006 Jakks Pacific WWE Superstars Series 1

NNO Hulk Hogan
NNO The Rock
NNO Ric Flair
NNO Roddy Piper
Black Wrist Tape
NNO Roddy Piper
White Wrist Tape
NNO Stone Cold Steve Austin

2007 Jakks Pacific WWE Superstars Series 2

NNO Bret Hit Man Hart
NNO British Bulldog
NNO Kevin Nash
NNO Mr. Perfect
NNO Shawn Michaels

2007 Jakks Pacific WWE Superstars Series 3

NNO Jake The Snake Roberts
NNO Lex Luger
NNO Ravishing Rick Rude
NNO Scott Hall
NNO Undertaker

2008 Jakks Pacific WWE Superstars Series 4

NNO Brutus The Barber Beefcake
NNO Honky Tonk Man
NNO Iron Sheik
NNO Million Dollar Man
NNO Shawn Michaels

2008 Jakks Pacific WWE Superstars Series 5

NNO Buff Bagwell
NNO Diamond Dallas Page
NNO Jim The Anvil Neidhart
NNO Superfly Jimmy Snuka

2009 Jakks Pacific WWE Superstars Series 6

NNO Eddie Guerrero
NNO Hillbilly Jim
NNO Hunter Hearst Helmsley
NNO Kane
NNO Sgt. Slaughter

2009 Jakks Pacific WWE Superstars Series 7

NNO Bret Hit Man Hart
NNO Shawn Michaels
NNO El Matador
NNO The Rock
NNO Undertaker

2009 Jakks Pacific WWE Superstars Series 8

NNO Big John Studd
NNO Chainsaw Charlie
NNO Davey Boy Smith
NNO Dynamite Kid
NNO Stone Cold Steve Austin

2003 Jakks Pacific WWE Superstars Uncovered

NNO Hulk Hogan	20.00	40.00
NNO Kurt Angle	12.50	25.00
NNO Rob Van Dam	12.50	25.00
NNO The Rock	30.00	60.00
NNO Triple H	10.00	20.00
NNO Undertaker	15.00	30.00

2004 Jakks Pacific WWE Talkin' Pounders

NNO The Hurricane
NNO John Cena
NNO Randy Orton
NNO Rey Mysterio

1997 Jakks Pacific WWF Talking Undertaker 14-Inch

NNO Undertaker	25.00	50.00

1997 Jakks Pacific WWF Thumb Wrestlers

NNO Bulldog vs. Shamrock	10.00	20.00
NNO HHH vs. Mankind	10.00	20.00
NNO Steve Austin vs. Owen Hart	12.50	25.00
NNO Undertaker vs. HBK	15.00	30.00

1999 Jakks Pacific WWF Titan Tron Live Series 1

NNO Kane	7.50	15.00
NNO Mankind	7.50	15.00
NNO Road Dogg	6.00	12.00
NNO Rock	10.00	20.00
NNO Stone Cold Steve Austin	15.00	30.00
NNO Undertaker	15.00	30.00

2000 Jakks Pacific WWF Titan Tron Live Series 2

NNO Big Show	6.00	12.00
NNO Kane	17.50	35.00
NNO Ken Shamrock	7.50	15.00
NNO The Rock	12.50	25.00
NNO Stone Cold Steve Austin	7.50	15.00
NNO X-Pac	6.00	12.00

2000 Jakks Pacific WWF Titan Tron Live Series 3

NNO Big Boss Man	7.50	15.00
NNO Chris Jericho	7.50	15.00
NNO Chyna	12.50	25.00
NNO The Rock	7.50	15.00
NNO Stone Cold Steve Austin	10.00	20.00
NNO Test	6.00	12.00

2000 Jakks Pacific WWF Titan Tron Live Series 4

NNO Big Show		
NNO Cactus Jack	10.00	20.00
NNO Road Dogg		
NNO The Rock		
NNO Triple H		
NNO X-Pac		

2000 Jakks Pacific WWF Titan Tron Live Series 5

NNO Chris Jericho	6.00	15.00
NNO Kurt Angle	6.00	15.00
NNO The Rock	10.00	20.00
NNO Stone Cold Steve Austin	10.00	20.00
NNO Test	6.00	12.00
NNO Undertaker	10.00	20.00

2000 Jakks Pacific WWF Titan Tron Live Series 6

NNO Big Show
NNO Edge
NNO Jeff Hardy
NNO Rock
NNO Tazz
NNO Triple H

2000 Jakks Pacific WWF Titan Tron Live Series 7

NNO Chris Jericho
NNO Kane
NNO Kurt Angle
NNO Stephanie McMahon
NNO Triple H
NNO Undertaker

2000 Jakks Pacific WWF Titan Tron Live Series 8

NNO Bubba Ray Dudley
NNO Jeff Hardy
NNO Matt Hardy
NNO Rikishi
NNO Road Dogg
NNO The Rock

2001 Jakks Pacific WWF Titan Tron Live Series 9

NNO Chyna
NNO Kurt Angle
NNO Mick Foley
NNO Rikishi
NNO The Rock
NNO Triple H

2001 Jakks Pacific WWF Titan Tron Live Series 10

NNO Billy Gunn	7.50	15.00
NNO Kane	7.50	15.00
NNO Matt Hardy	7.50	15.00
NNO Rikishi	7.50	15.00
NNO Stone Cold Steve Austin	10.00	20.00
NNO Triple H	10.00	20.00

2001 Jakks Pacific WWF Titan Tron Live Series 11

NNO Jeff Hardy	7.50	15.00
NNO Kurt Angle	7.50	15.00
NNO Rikishi	7.50	15.00
NNO Stephanie McMahon	10.00	20.00
NNO Stone Cold Steve Austin	10.00	20.00
NNO Triple H	10.00	20.00

2001 Jakks Pacific WWF Titan Tron Live Series 12

NNO Big Show	6.00	12.00
NNO Chris Jericho	7.50	15.00
NNO Kurt Angle	6.00	12.00
NNO Rock	10.00	20.00
NNO Stone Cold Steve Austin	10.00	20.00
NNO Undertaker	12.50	25.00

2001 Jakks Pacific WWF Titan Tron Live Series 13

NNO Chris Jericho	6.00	12.00
NNO Lita	7.50	15.00
NNO Rock	10.00	20.00
NNO Stone Cold Steve Austin	12.50	25.00
NNO Triple H	7.50	15.00
NNO Undertaker	12.50	25.00

2000 Jakks Pacific WWF ToyFare Exclusives

NNO Big Show	12.50	25.00
NNO Debra	15.00	30.00
NNO The Rock	20.00	40.00

2002 Jakks Pacific WWE Trash Talkin' Champions

NNO Chris Jericho	20.00	40.00
NNO Kurt Angle	10.00	20.00

2005 Jakks Pacific WWE Treacherous Trios Series 1

NNO Kurt Angle/Eddie Guerrero/Big Show		
NNO Triple H/Ric Flair/Batista	12.50	25.00
NNO Undertaker/JBL/Heidenreich	15.00	30.00

2005 Jakks Pacific WWE Treacherous Trios Series 2

NNO Mark Jindrak/Booker T/Kurt Angle15.00 30.00
NNO Orlando Jordan/Danny Basham
Doug Basham 12.50 25.00
NNO Trish Stratus/Tyson Tomko/Christian15.00 30.00

2005 Jakks Pacific WWE Treacherous Trios Series 3

NNO Edge/Lita/Matt Hardy 30.00 60.00
NNO Randy Orton/Undertaker 25.00 50.00
Cowboy Bob Orton Jr.
NNO Rey Mysterio/Chris Benoit/Batista25.00 50.00

2006 Jakks Pacific WWE Treacherous Trios Series 4

NNO Chris Benoit/Booker T/Randy Orton
NNO Melina/Johnny Nitro/Joey Mercury
NNO Kurt Angle/Daivari/Mark Henry

2007 Jakks Pacific WWE Treacherous Trios Series 5

NNO Randy Orton/Edge/Carlito
NNO Rey Mysterio/Booker T/Chavo
NNO Shawn Michaels/HHH/
Coachman

2007 Jakks Pacific WWE Treacherous Trios Series 6

NNO Batista/Long/Undertaker
NNO Brian Kendrick/Yang/London
NNO Umaga/Cena/Armando Estrada

2008 Jakks Pacific WWE Treacherous Trios Series 7

NNO Elijah Burke/CM Punk/ 25.00 50.00
Tommy Dreamer
NNO Great Khali/Batista/Undertaker
NNO Randy Orton/John Cena/
Jonathan Coachman

2008 Jakks Pacific WWE Treacherous Trios Series 8

NNO Curt Hawkins/Edge/Zack Ryder
NNO Deuce/Cherry/Domino 30.00 75.00
NNO Triple H/John Cena/Orton 15.00 30.00

2009 Jakks Pacific WWE Treacherous Trios Series 9

NNO Finlay/JBL/Hornswoggle
NNO JTG/John Cena/Shad 20.00 40.00
NNO Miz/Matt Hardy/Morrison 25.00 50.00

2009 Jakks Pacific WWE Treacherous Trios Series 10

NNO Big Show/Undertaker/Khali
NNO Chris Jericho/Cena/CM Punk
NNO Matt Hardy/Edge/Jeff Hardy

2002 Jakks Pacific WWE Unchained Fury Series 1

NNO Booker T 10.00 20.00
NNO Hurricane Helms 12.50 25.00
NNO Lance Storm 10.00 20.00
NNO Ric Flair 12.50 25.00

2002 Jakks Pacific WWE Unchained Fury Series 1 2-Packs

NNO Booker T/Steve Austin 20.00 40.00
NNO Ric Flair/Vince McMahon 25.00 50.00
NNO Rob Van Dam/Chris Jericho

2002 Jakks Pacific WWE Unchained Fury Series 2

NNO Booker T 10.00 20.00
NNO Kevin Nash 15.00 30.00
NNO Kurt Angle 10.00 20.00
NNO Rhyno 12.50 25.00
NNO Rob Van Dam 15.00 30.00
NNO Tajiri 10.00 20.00

2002 Jakks Pacific WWE Unchained Fury Series 2 2-Packs

NNO Christian/DDP 12.50 25.00
NNO Chuck Palumbo/Billy Gunn 15.00 30.00
NNO Kurt Angle/Edge 15.00 30.00

2003 Jakks Pacific WWE Unlimited Series 1

NNO Chris Jericho 12.50 25.00
NNO Edge 12.50 25.00
NNO Hulk Hogan 15.00 30.00
NNO Kurt Angle 10.00 20.00
NNO Rob Van Dam 7.50 15.00
NNO The Rock 12.50 25.00

2003 Jakks Pacific WWE Unlimited Series 2

NNO Batista 15.00 30.00
NNO Billy Kidman 10.00 20.00
NNO Booker T 12.50 25.00
NNO Brock Lesnar 15.00 30.00
NNO Eddie Guerrero 12.50 25.00
NNO Triple H 10.00 20.00

2003 Jakks Pacific WWE Unlimited Series 3

NNO Booker T 12.50 25.00
NNO Brock Lesnar 20.00 40.00
NNO Chris Benoit 10.00 20.00
NNO Chris Jericho 10.00 20.00
NNO Hulk Hogan 15.00 30.00
NNO The Rock 15.00 30.00

2003 Jakks Pacific WWE Unlimited Series 4

NNO Chris Benoit
NNO Kurt Angle
NNO Rob Van Dam 10.00 20.00
NNO The Rock 15.00 30.00
NNO Triple H 12.50 25.00

2006 Jakks Pacific WWE Unmatched Fury Series 1

NNO Batista
NNO Hulk Hogan
NNO John Cena
NNO Rey Mysterio

2007 Jakks Pacific WWE Unmatched Fury Series 2

NNO Rob Van Dam 20.00 40.00
NNO Shawn Michaels 30.00 60.00
NNO Triple H 12.50 25.00
NNO Undertaker 20.00 40.00
NNO Undertaker GITD 300.00 500.00
100* NYC TF

2007 Jakks Pacific WWE Unmatched Fury Series 3

NNO Carlito 15.00 30.00
NNO Jeff Hardy 20.00 40.00
NNO John Cena 15.00 30.00
NNO Sabu 15.00 30.00

2007 Jakks Pacific WWE Unmatched Fury Series 4

NNO Ken Kennedy 12.50 25.00
NNO Mr.Perfect 20.00 40.00
NNO Ric Flair 15.00 30.00
NNO Umaga 12.50 25.00

2007 Jakks Pacific WWE Unmatched Fury Series 5

NNO Bobby Lashley 25.00 50.00
NNO Mick Foley 15.00 30.00
NNO The Rock 20.00 40.00
NNO Undertaker

2007 Jakks Pacific WWE Unmatched Fury Series 6

NNO Eddie Guerrero 15.00 30.00
NNO Kane 12.50 25.00
NNO Randy Orton 25.00 50.00
NNO Rowdy Roddy Piper 30.00 60.00

2008 Jakks Pacific WWE Unmatched Fury Series 7

NNO British Bulldog
NNO Edge
NNO Ravishing Rick Rude
NNO Undertaker

2008 Jakks Pacific WWE Unmatched Fury Series 8

NNO Boogeyman
NNO Iron Sheik
NNO Matt Hardy
NNO Shawn Michaels

2008 Jakks Pacific WWE Unmatched Fury Series 9

NNO Bret Hitman Hart 30.00 60.00
NNO Finlay 12.50 25.00
NNO Hornswoggle 20.00 50.00
NNO Hornswoggle LE 200.00 350.00
(Green/Gold/500*
NNO Undertaker

2008 Jakks Pacific WWE Unmatched Fury Series 10

NNO Great Khali
NNO Junk Yard Dog
NNO MVP
NNO Ultimate Warrior

2008 Jakks Pacific WWE Unmatched Fury Series 11

NNO Chris Jericho
NNO CM Punk
NNO Honkytonk Man
NNO Million Dollar Man

2008 Jakks Pacific WWE Unmatched Fury Series 12

NNO Big Show
NNO JBL
NNO Razor Ramon
NNO Undertaker

2009 Jakks Pacific WWE Unmatched Fury Series 14

NNO Bret Hitman Hart 30.00 60.00
NNO Hornswoggle 20.00 40.00
NNO John Cena 15.00 30.00
NNO Rey Mysterio 20.00 40.00

2009 Jakks Pacific WWE Unmatched Fury Series 15

NNO CM Punk 60.00 120.00
NNO Eddie Guerrero 25.00 50.00
NNO Rowdy Roddy Piper 30.00 60.00
NNO Stone Cold Steve Austin 20.00 40.00

2003 Jakks Pacific WWE Unrelenting

NNO Booker T 7.50 15.00
NNO Chris Jericho 10.00 20.00
NNO Edge
NNO Jeff Hardy
NNO Rob Van Dam
NNO Triple H

2008 Jakks Pacific WWE Vinyl Aggression Exclusive

NNO Bret Hart RSC 20.00 40.00

2009 Jakks Pacific WWE Vinyl Aggression Exclusive

NNO Jesse Ventura/100* NYC TF

2008 Jakks Pacific WWE Vinyl Aggression Series 1

NNO Carlito
NNO ECW Stylized
NNO Hornswoggle
NNO John Cena
NNO Mankind
NNO Umaga
NNO Undertaker

2008 Jakks Pacific WWE Vinyl Aggression Series 2

NNO Batista
NNO Chris Jericho
NNO CM Punk
NNO DX Stylized
NNO Finlay
NNO Honkytonk Man
NNO Mr. Kennedy
NNO MVP
NNO Rey Mysterio
NNO Rock
NNO Shawn Michaels
NNO Tommy Dreamer
NNO Triple H Stylized

2008 Jakks Pacific WWE Vinyl Aggression Series 3

NNO Batista
NNO Chris Jericho
NNO Shawn Michaels

NNO Rock
NNO Tommy Dreamer
NNO Triple H

2008 Jakks Pacific WWE Vinyl Aggression Series 4

NNO Edge
NNO Jimmy Wang Yang
NNO Miz
NNO Randy Orton
NNO Santino
NNO Ted DiBiase

2008 Jakks Pacific WWE Vinyl Aggression Series 5

NNO Big Show
NNO DX Stylized
NNO Jake Roberts
NNO Kane
NNO Kofi Kingston
NNO Matt Hardy

2008 Jakks Pacific WWE Vinyl Aggression Series 6

NNO Festus
NNO Jesse
NNO John Morrison
NNO JTG
NNO Rowdy Roddy Piper
NNO Shad

2008 Jakks Pacific WWE Vinyl Aggression Series 7

NNO Beth Phoenix
NNO Boogeyman
NNO Great Khali
NNO Kane/Classic Mask
NNO Ricky Ortiz
NNO Triple H

1999 Jakks Pacific WWF White's Exclusives

NNO Sable
NNO Undertaker

1998 Jakks Pacific WWF WrestleMania XIV

NNO Headbanger Mosh	6.00	12.00
NNO Headbanger Thrasher	6.00	12.00
NNO HHH	10.00	20.00
NNO Rocky Maivia	7.50	15.00
NNO Shawn Michaels	10.00	20.00
NNO Stone Cold Steve Austin	7.50	15.00

2001 Jakks Pacific WWF WrestleMania X-7

NNO Chris Jericho	7.50	15.00
NNO Chyna	10.00	20.00
NNO Eddie Guerrero	7.50	15.00
NNO Edge	7.50	15.00
NNO Kane	10.00	20.00
NNO Stone Cold Steve Austin	12.50	25.00

2002 Jakks Pacific WWE WrestleMania X-8

NNO Billy Gunn	7.50	15.00
NNO Chuck Palumbo	7.50	15.00
NNO Diamond Dallas Page	7.50	15.00
NNO HHH	15.00	30.00
NNO Maven	7.50	15.00
NNO Rob Van Dam	12.50	25.00

2002 Jakks Pacific WWE WrestleMania X-8 2-Packs

NNO Booker T/Edge	15.00	30.00
NNO Kurt Angle/Kane	12.50	25.00
NNO The Rock vs. Hollywood Hogan	30.00	60.00
NNO Undertaker vs. Ric Flair	30.00	75.00

2004 Jakks Pacific WWE WrestleMania 19 Winners

NNO Chris Benoit
NNO Chris Jericho
NNO Kane
NNO Kurt Angle
NNO The Rock

2004 Jakks Pacific WWE WrestleMania 19 Winners 2-Packs

NNO D-Von and Bubba Ray Dudley
NNO La Resistance
Conway/Dupree
NNO Team Angle
Benjamin/Haas

2004 Jakks Pacific WWE WrestleMania 20 Series 1

NNO Edge
NNO Hardcore Holly
NNO Rob Van Dam
NNO Shane McMahon
NNO Stone Cold Steve Austin
NNO Triple H

2004 Jakks Pacific WWE WrestleMania 20 Series 3

NNO Booker T
NNO Chris Benoit
NNO Chris Jericho
NNO Kane
NNO Kurt Angle
NNO The Rock

2004 Jakks Pacific WWE WrestleMania 20 Series 3 2-Packs

NNO Bubba Ray & D-Von
NNO Rob Conway & Rene Dupree
NNO Shelton Benjamin & Charlie Haas

2004 Jakks Pacific WWE WrestleMania 20 Mask and Figure Sets Series 1

NNO Hurricane
NNO Kane
NNO Mankind
NNO Rey Mysterio

2004 Jakks Pacific WWE WrestleMania 20 Mask and Figure Sets Series 2

NNO Rey Mysterio
NNO Rosey
NNO Ultimo Dragon

2004 Jakks Pacific WWE WrestleMania 20 Playset

NNO Stage Entrance and Stunt Ring

2004 Jakks Pacific WWE WrestleMania 20 Times Square Limited Edition

NNO Ric Flair/600*
NNO Triple H/600*

2004 Jakks Pacific WWE WrestleMania 20 Series 2

NNO Chavo Guerrero
NNO Chris Benoit
NNO Christian
NNO Eddie Guerrero
NNO John Cena
NNO Undertaker

2004 Jakks Pacific WWE WrestleMania 20 Series 2 2-Packs

NNO Booker T/Rob Van Dam
NNO Ric Flair/Randy Orton
NNO Rikishi/Scotty 2 Hotty

2004 Jakks Pacific WWE WrestleMania 20 Series 1 2-Packs

NNO Brock Lesnar/Kurt Angle
NNO Edge/Christian
NNO Steve Austin/HBK

2005 Jakks Pacific WWE WrestleMania 21 Series 1

NNO Eddie Guerrero	12.50	25.00
NNO Rey Mysterio		
NNO Triple H		
NNO Victoria		

2005 Jakks Pacific WWE WrestleMania 21 Series 1 2-Packs

NNO Chris Jericho vs. Shawn Michaels
NNO John Cena vs. Big Show
NNO Kane vs. Kurt Angle

2005 Jakks Pacific WWE WrestleMania 21 Series 2

NNO Batista		
NNO Booker T		
NNO Charlie Haas		
NNO Chris Benoit		
NNO Eddie Guerrero	12.50	25.00
NNO Lita		

2005 Jakks Pacific WWE WrestleMania 21 Series 2 2-Packs

NNO Maven/Eugene
NNO Rey Mysterio/Rene Dupree
NNO Rob Conway/William Regal

2005 Jakks Pacific WWE WrestleMania 21 Series 3

NNO Booker T
NNO Carlito
NNO Edge
NNO Randy Orton
NNO Stone Cold Steve Austin
NNO Undertaker

2005 Jakks Pacific WWE WrestleMania 21 Series 3 2-Packs

NNO John Cena/John Bradshaw Layfield
NNO Kurt Angle/Shawn Michaels
NNO Triple H/Batista

2005 Jakks Pacific WWE WrestleMania 21 Gear and Figure Sets Series 1

NNO Edge	10.00	20.00
NNO Hurricane		
NNO JBL		
NNO Kurt Angle		
NNO Rey Mysterio	12.50	25.00
NNO Undertaker		

2005 Jakks Pacific WWE WrestleMania 21 Gear and Figure Sets Series 2

NNO John Cena		
NNO Rey Mysterio	12.50	25.00
NNO Undertaker	10.00	20.00

2005 Jakks Pacific WWE WrestleMania 21 Gear and Figure Sets Series 3

NNO Edge	10.00	20.00
NNO JBL		
NNO Kurt Angle		

2005 Jakks Pacific WWE WrestleMania 21 Gear and Figure Sets Series 4

NNO Hurricane		
NNO John Cena		
NNO Rey Mysterio	12.50	25.00

2005 Jakks Pacific WWE WrestleMania 21 Gear and Figure Sets 2-Packs

NNO Rey Mysterio/Rey Mysterio
NNO Rosey/Hurricane

2002 Jakks Pacific WWE Wrestling's Most Wanted

NNO Rock n' Roll Rivals
Edge/Y2J
NNO Ultimate Hardcore Match
RVD/Hardcore Holly
NNO Iron Man Match
HHH/Chris Benoit

2020-21 Jazwares AEW Exclusives

NNO Britt Baker Lights Out	25.00	50.00
NNO Chris Jericho Bubbly	30.00	75.00
NNO Cody & Dustin Rhodes Blood Brothers	30.00	75.00
NNO Darby Allin Coffin Drop	30.00	60.00
NNO Jurassic Express	50.00	100.00
NNO Jurassic Express (Package Variant)	75.00	150.00
NNO Kenny Omega & Jon Moxley Death Match	40.00	80.00

2022 Jazwares AEW Exclusives

NNO Brodie Lee & Negative 1 (Ringside Collectibles Exclusive)	20.00	40.00
NNO CM Punk First Dance (Ringside Collectibles Exclusive)	30.00	60.00

NNO Jim Ross (announcer) 25.00 50.00
(Ringside Collectibles Exclusive)
NNO King of Harts Owen Hart 30.00 75.00
(Ringside Collectibles Exclusive)
NNO Tony Schiavone (announcer) 20.00 40.00
(Ringside Collectibles Exclusive)

2023 Jazwares AEW Exclusives

NNO Excalibur
(Ringside Collectibles Exclusive)
NNO Thunder Rosa Blood & Guts
(Ringside Collectibles Exclusive)

2021 Jazwares AEW Unmatched Series 1

NNO Britt Baker DMD 30.00 75.00
NNO Britt Baker DMD/3,000* R 60.00 125.00
NNO Cody (LJN style) 25.00 50.00
NNO Darby Allin 30.00 75.00
NNO Darby Allin/5,000* CH 75.00 150.00
NNO Dustin Rhodes 25.00 50.00
NNO Kenny Omega 30.00 60.00
NNO Miro 30.00 75.00

2021 Jazwares AEW Unmatched Series 2

NNO MJF 15.00 30.00
NNO MJF/3,000* R 60.00 125.00
NNO Ortiz 10.00 20.00
NNO Santana 10.00 20.00
NNO Sting 20.00 40.00
NNO Sting/5,000* CH 75.00 150.00
NNO Tay Conti 15.00 30.00
NNO Wardlow 20.00 40.00

2022 Jazwares AEW Unmatched Series 3

NNO Anna Jay 15.00 30.00
NNO Anna Jay/3,000 R 50.00 100.00
NNO Evil Uno 12.50 25.00
NNO John Silver 15.00 30.00
NNO Mr. Brodie Lee 20.00 40.00
NNO Mr. Brodie Lee/5,000* CH 60.00 125.00
NNO Stu Grayson 12.50 25.00

2022 Jazwares AEW Unmatched Series 4

NNO CM Punk 15.00 30.00
NNO CM Punk/5,000* CH 75.00 150.00
NNO Cody Rhodes 15.00 30.00
NNO Cody Rhodes/3,000* R 75.00 150.00
NNO Corazon de Leon Chris Jericho 12.50 25.00
NNO Hangman Adam Page 12.50 25.00
NNO Jade Cargill 15.00 30.00
NNO MJF 12.50 25.00

2022 Jazwares AEW Unmatched Series 5

NNO Bryan Danielson 25.00 50.00
NNO Bryan Danielson/5,000* CH
NNO Darby Allin (LJN) 30.00 60.00
NNO Kenny Omega 15.00 30.00
NNO Red Velvet 20.00 40.00
NNO Sammy Guevara 15.00 30.00
NNO Shawn Spears 15.00 30.00
NNO Shawn Spears/3,000* R 100.00 200.00

2023 Jazwares AEW Unmatched Series 6

NNO Brodie Lee
NNO Malakai Black
NNO Ortiz
NNO Owen Hart
NNO Ruby Soho
NNO Santana

2020-21 Jazwares AEW Unrivaled Collection Playsets

NNO Action Ring 30.00 75.00
NNO Action Ring w/Cody UK 75.00 150.00
NNO Authentic Scale Ring
(w/Aubrey Edwards) 75.00 150.00
NNO Authentic Scale Ring
(w/Kenny Omega) 100.00 200.00

2020 Jazwares AEW Unrivaled Collection Series 1

NNO Brandi Rhodes 50.00 100.00
NNO Chris Jericho 20.00 40.00
NNO Chris Jericho/1000* CH 300.00 600.00
NNO Cody Rhodes 20.00 40.00
NNO Cody Rhodes/500* R 1500.00 3000.00
NNO Kenny Omega 30.00 75.00
NNO Matt Jackson 20.00 40.00
NNO Nick Jackson 25.00 50.00

2020 Jazwares AEW Unrivaled Collection Series 2

NNO Dustin Rhodes 10.00 20.00
NNO Hangman Adam Page 12.50 25.00
NNO Jon Moxley 20.00 40.00
NNO Jon Moxley/500* R 150.00 300.00
NNO MJF 25.00 50.00
NNO MJF/1,000* CH 200.00 400.00
NNO Pentagon Jr. 30.00 60.00
NNO Rey Fenix 15.00 30.00

2021 Jazwares AEW Unrivaled Collection Series 3

NNO Darby Allin 30.00 60.00
NNO Darby Allin/500* R 300.00 600.00
NNO Matt Jackson 20.00 40.00
NNO Nick Jackson 20.00 40.00
NNO Orange Cassidy 25.00 50.00
NNO Pac 25.00 50.00
NNO Riho 20.00 40.00
NNO Riho/1,000* CH 100.00 200.00

2021 Jazwares AEW Unrivaled Collection Series 4

NNO Cody 25.00 50.00
NNO Cody/1,000* CH 200.00 400.00
NNO Kenny Omega 30.00 60.00
NNO Matt Hardy 25.00 50.00
NNO Matt Hardy/500* R 200.00 400.00
NNO Ortiz 20.00 40.00
NNO Sammy Guevara 30.00 75.00
NNO Santana 30.00 60.00

2021 Jazwares AEW Unrivaled Collection Series 5

NNO Hangman Adam Page 25.00 50.00
NNO Hangman Adam Page w
chaps/3,000* R 125.00 250.00
NNO Jon Moxley 30.00 75.00
NNO Jon Moxley Paradigm Shift
5,000* CH 100.00 200.00
NNO Jungle Boy/black tights 30.00 60.00
NNO Kazarian 25.00 50.00
NNO Luchasaurus/black tights 30.00 75.00
NNO Scorpio Sky 25.00 50.00

2021 Jazwares AEW Unrivaled Collection Series 6

NNO Chris Jericho 25.00 50.00
NNO Chris Jericho/5,000* CH 75.00 150.00
NNO Hikaru Shida 20.00 40.00
NNO Jake Hager 25.00 50.00
NNO Jake Hager/3,000* R 200.00 400.00
NNO MJF 20.00 40.00
NNO Pentagon Jr. 30.00 75.00
NNO Rey Fenix 20.00 40.00

2021 Jazwares AEW Unrivaled Collection Series 7

NNO Cash Wheeler 15.00 30.00
NNO Dax Harwood 15.00 30.00
NNO Lance Archer 10.00 20.00
NNO Lance Archer w
silver tights/3,000* R 50.00 100.00
NNO Matt Jackson 20.00 40.00
NNO Nick Jackson 20.00 40.00
NNO Nyla Rose 10.00 20.00
NNO Nyla Rose w/orange scarf/5,000* CH40.00 80.00

2021 Jazwares AEW Unrivaled Collection Series 8

NNO Chris Jericho 15.00 30.00
NNO Chris Jericho/3,000* R 50.00 100.00
NNO Chuck Taylor 10.00 20.00
NNO Jon Moxley 15.00 30.00
NNO Jon Moxley/5,000* CH 60.00 125.00
NNO Kris Statlander 20.00 40.00
NNO Orange Cassidy 15.00 30.00
NNO Trent? 12.50 25.00

2022 Jazwares AEW Unrivaled Collection Series 9

NNO Brian Cage
NNO Christian Cage
NNO Eddie Kingston
NNO Powerhouse Hobbs
NNO Ricky Starks
NNO Ricky Starks/3,000* R
NNO Thunder Rosa
NNO Thunder Rosa/5,000* CH

2022 Jazwares AEW Unrivaled Collection Series 10

NNO Britt Baker
NNO Britt Baker/5,000* CH
NNO El Idolo
NNO Jake Hager
NNO Miro
NNO Taz
NNO Taz/3,000* R
NNO Wardlow

2023 Jazwares AEW Unrivaled Collection Series 11

NNO Adam Cole
NNO Chris Jericho
NNO Darby Allin
NNO Jungle Boy
NNO Kip Sabian
NNO Penelope Ford

2022 Jazwares AEW Unrivaled Playsets

NNO Authentic Scale Ring (w/Sting)

2022 Jazwares AEW Unrivaled Supreme Collection Series 1

NNO Britt Baker 30.00 60.00
NNO Cody Rhodes 30.00 60.00

2022 Jazwares AEW Unrivaled Supreme Collection Series 2

NNO Kenny Omega 60.00 125.00
NNO Malakai Black 75.00 150.00

1990 JusToys WCW Bend-Ems

NNO Arn Anderson 20.00 40.00
NNO Barry Windham 20.00 40.00
NNO Brian Pillman 15.00 30.00
NNO Butch Reed 15.00 30.00
NNO Lex Luger 15.00 30.00
NNO Ric Flair 30.00 60.00
NNO Rick Steiner 12.50 25.00
NNO Ron Simmons 15.00 30.00
NNO Scott Steiner 20.00 40.00
NNO Sid Vicious 15.00 30.00
NNO Sting 25.00 50.00
NNO Tom Zenk 30.00 75.00

1990 JusToys WCW Bend-Ems Challenge 2-Pack

NNO The Steiner Brothers

2001 JusToys WWF Bend-Ems Gear

NNO Chris Jericho
NNO Jeff Hardy 20.00 40.00
NNO Kane 25.00 50.00
NNO Matt Hardy 20.00 40.00
NNO Road Dogg 15.00 30.00
NNO Rock (black & white) 12.50 25.00
NNO Rock (blue & yellow) 15.00 30.00
NNO Steve Austin 12.50 25.00
NNO Triple H 20.00 40.00

1998 JusToys WWF Bend-Ems Playsets

NNO Super Slam Wrestling Ring (w/Austin & Michaels)
NNO Super Slam Wrestling Ring
(w/Paul Bearer) 30.00 60.00

1994 JusToys WWF Bend-Ems Series I

NNO Bret Hitman Hart 12.50 25.00
NNO Diesel 7.50 15.00
NNO Doink 7.50 15.00
NNO Lex Luger 10.00 20.00
NNO Razor Ramon 10.00 20.00

1995 JusToys WWF Bend-Ems Series II

NNO 1-2-3 Kid 6.00 12.00
NNO British Bulldog 7.50 15.00
NNO Mabel 6.00 12.00
NNO Undertaker 7.50 15.00

1996 JusToys WWF Bend-Ems Series III

NNO Ahmed Johnson 5.00 10.00

NNO Goldust	6.00	12.00
NNO Shawn Michaels	7.50	15.00
NNO Yokozuna	6.00	12.00

1996 JusToys WWF Bend-Ems Series IV

NNO Sunny	7.50	15.00
NNO Sycho Sid	6.00	12.00
NNO Vader	6.00	12.00
NNO Wildman Marc Mero	5.00	10.00

1997 JusToys WWF Bend-Ems Series V

NNO Faarooq	6.00	12.00
NNO Mankind	10.00	20.00
NNO Rocky Maivia	12.50	25.00
NNO Stone Cold Steve Austin	6.00	12.00

1997 JusToys WWF Bend-Ems Series VI

NNO Animal	6.00	12.00
NNO Hawk	6.00	12.00
NNO Hunter Hearts Helmsley	5.00	10.00
NNO Undertaker	10.00	20.00

1997 JusToys WWF Bend-Ems Series VII

NNO Crush	7.50	15.00
NNO Ken Shamrock	7.50	15.00
NNO Owen Hart	12.50	25.00
NNO The Patriot	10.00	20.00

1998 JusToys WWF Bend-Ems Series IX

NNO Brian Christopher	6.00	12.00
NNO Cactus Jack	7.50	15.00
NNO Sable	10.00	20.00
NNO X-Pac	6.00	12.00

1998 JusToys WWF Bend-Ems Series VIII

NNO Chyna	7.50	15.00
NNO Jeff Jarrett	6.00	12.00
NNO Kane	7.50	15.00
NNO Taka	5.00	10.00

1998 JusToys WWF Bend-Ems Series X

NNO B.A. Billy Gunn	6.00	12.00
NNO Edge	7.50	15.00
NNO Road Dogg	6.00	12.00
NNO Steve Blackman	5.00	10.00

1999 JusToys WWF Bend-Ems Series XI

NNO Al Snow	6.00	12.00
NNO Godfather	7.50	15.00
NNO Mr. McMahon	7.50	15.00
NNO Val Venis	5.00	10.00

1999 JusToys WWF Bend-Ems Series XII

NNO Big Boss Man	5.00	10.00
NNO Mankind	7.50	15.00
NNO Paul Wight	5.00	10.00
NNO Steve Austin	10.00	20.00
NNO Undertaker	7.50	15.00

1999 JusToys WWF Bend-Ems Series XIII

NNO Droz	5.00	10.00
NNO D'Lo Brown	5.00	10.00
NNO Hardcore Holly	5.00	10.00
NNO Shane McMahon	6.00	12.00
NNO Steve Austin	7.50	15.00

2000 JusToys WWF Bend-Ems Series XIV

NNO Chris Jericho	6.00	12.00
NNO Jeff Hardy	6.00	12.00
NNO Matt Hardy	5.00	10.00
NNO The Rock	7.50	15.00

2001 JusToys WWF Bend-Ems Series XV

NNO Tazz		
NNO Grandmaster Sexay		
NNO Rikishi		
NNO The Rock/Repack		
NNO Scotty 2 Hotty		

1994 Kelian AAA Wrestling Figures

NNO Blue Panther		
NNO Cien Caras	30.00	60.00
NNO Fuerza Guerrera		
NNO Heavy Metal	50.00	100.00
NNO Hijo Del Santo	60.00	120.00
NNO Konnan		
NNO La Parka	60.00	120.00
NNO Mascara Sagrada		
NNO Octagon		
NNO Perro Aguayo	40.00	80.00
NNO Psicosis		
NNO Rey Misterio		

1994 Kelian AAA Wrestling Figures (loose)

NNO Blue Panther		
NNO Cien Caras	20.00	40.00
NNO Fuerza Guerrera		
NNO Heavy Metal		
NNO Hijo Del Santo		
NNO Konnan		
NNO La Parka		
NNO Mascara Sagrada		
NNO Octagon	12.50	25.00
NNO Perro Aguayo		
NNO Psicosis	30.00	75.00
NNO Rey Misterio	25.00	60.00

2019 Kidrobot Collectible Vinyl Mini Series WWE

NNO AJ Styles	6.00	12.00
NNO Alexa Bliss	7.50	15.00
NNO Andre the Giant	4.00	8.00
NNO Charlotte Flair	6.00	12.00
NNO John Cena	7.50	15.00
NNO Ric Flair	6.00	12.00
NNO Roman Reigns	5.00	10.00
NNO Ronda Rousey	5.00	10.00
NNO Sasha Banks	7.50	15.00
NNO Shawn Michaels	5.00	10.00
NNO The Rock	7.50	15.00
NNO Triple H Mystery CH		
NNO Ultimate Warrior	20.00	40.00
NNO Undertaker	7.50	15.00

1985 LJN WWF Wrestling Superstars 16-Inch

NNO Hulk Hogan	225.00	450.00
NNO Rowdy Roddy Piper	175.00	350.00

1985 LJN WWF Wrestling Superstars 16-Inch (loose)

NNO Hulk Hogan	60.00	120.00
NNO Rowdy Roddy Piper	75.00	150.00

1985 LJN WWF Wrestling Superstars Bendies

NNO Andre the Giant	50.00	100.00
NNO Big John Studd	30.00	75.00
NNO Bobby Heenan	50.00	100.00
NNO Brutus Beefcake	20.00	40.00
NNO Captain Lou Albano	50.00	100.00
NNO Corporal Kirchner	20.00	40.00
NNO George Steele	30.00	75.00
NNO Hillbilly Jim	30.00	75.00
NNO Hulk Hogan/Blue Knee Pads	25.00	50.00
NNO Hulk Hogan/Red Knee Pads	25.00	50.00
NNO Iron Sheik	25.00	60.00
NNO Jesse Ventura	30.00	60.00
NNO Junk Yard Dog	30.00	75.00
NNO King Kong Bundy	20.00	40.00
NNO Mr. Wonderful	25.00	60.00
NNO Nikolai Volkoff	25.00	60.00
NNO Randy Macho Man Savage	75.00	150.00
NNO Ricky The Dragon Steamboat	30.00	75.00
NNO Rowdy Roddy Piper	50.00	100.00

1985 LJN WWF Wrestling Superstars Bendies (loose)

NNO Andre the Giant	10.00	20.00
NNO Big John Studd	10.00	20.00
NNO Bobby Heenan	10.00	20.00
NNO Brutus Beefcake	7.50	15.00
NNO Captain Lou Albano	12.50	25.00
NNO Corporal Kirchner	6.00	12.00
NNO George Steele	7.50	15.00
NNO Hillbilly Jim	6.00	12.00
NNO Hulk Hogan/Blue Knee Pads	10.00	20.00
NNO Hulk Hogan/Red Knee Pads	10.00	20.00
NNO Iron Sheik	6.00	12.00
NNO Jesse Ventura	7.50	15.00
NNO Junk Yard Dog	7.50	15.00
NNO King Kong Bundy	5.00	10.00
NNO Mr. Wonderful	7.50	15.00
NNO Nikolai Volkoff	6.00	12.00
NNO Randy Macho Man Savage	20.00	40.00
NNO Ricky The Dragon Steamboat	15.00	30.00
NNO Rowdy Roddy Piper	15.00	30.00

1985 LJN WWF Wrestling Superstars Bendies Playset

NNO Cage Match Challenge w Hogan Blue Knee Pads	150.00	300.00

1985 LJN WWF Wrestling Superstars Bendies Playset (loose)

NNO Cage Match Challenge	50.00	100.00

1985 LJN WWF Wrestling Superstars Bendies Tag Teams

NNO Hulk Hogan/Junk Yard Dog		
NNO Iron Sheik/Nikolai Volkoff	25.00	50.00
NNO George Steele/Captain Lou Albano	25.00	50.00
NNO King Kong Bundy/Big John Studd	50.00	100.00
NNO Randy Savage/Jesse Ventura	50.00	100.00
NNO Ricky Steamboat/Corporal Kirchner	60.00	120.00

1989 LJN WWF Wrestling Superstars Black Card Re-Release

NNO Adrian Adonis		
NNO Bam Bam Bigelow	50.00	100.00
NNO Big John Studd		
NNO Bret Hitman Hart		
NNO Brutus The Barber Beefcake		
NNO Demolition Ax		
NNO Elizabeth/Gold Skirt		
NNO Elizabeth/Purple Skirt		
NNO Hacksaw Jim Duggan	350.00	500.00
NNO Honky Tonk Man	450.00	900.00
NNO Hulk Hogan/Red Shirt		
NNO Hulk Hogan/White Shirt	1000.00	2000.00
NNO Jake The Snake Roberts	150.00	300.00
NNO Randy Macho Man Savage		
NNO Ted DiBiase		

1984 LJN WWF Wrestling Superstars Series 1

NNO Andre the Giant/Long Hair	250.00	500.00
NNO Big John Studd	125.00	250.00
NNO Hillbilly Jim	150.00	300.00
NNO Hulk Hogan	350.00	700.00
NNO Iron Sheik	200.00	400.00
NNO Jimmy Snuka	125.00	250.00
NNO Junk Yard Dog/Red Chain	125.00	250.00
NNO Junk Yard Dog/Silver Chain	150.00	300.00
NNO Nikolai Volkoff	125.00	250.00
NNO Rowdy Roddy Piper/Brown Boots		
NNO Rowdy Roddy Piiper/Red Boots	125.00	250.00

1984 LJN WWF Wrestling Superstars Series 1 (loose)

NNO Andre the Giant/Long Hair	25.00	50.00
NNO Big John Studd	15.00	40.00
NNO Hillbilly Jim	15.00	40.00
NNO Hulk Hogan	30.00	60.00
NNO Iron Sheik	15.00	30.00
NNO Jimmy Snuka	15.00	40.00
NNO Junk Yard Dog/Red Chain	25.00	50.00
NNO Junk Yard Dog/Silver Chain	15.00	30.00
NNO Nikolai Volkoff	15.00	30.00
NNO Rowdy Roddy Piper/Brown Boots		
NNO Rowdy Roddy Piper/Red Boots	30.00	60.00

1985 LJN WWF Wrestling Superstars Series 2

NNO Andre the Giant/Short Hair	300.00	600.00
NNO Brutus Beefcake	200.00	400.00
NNO George Steele	100.00	200.00
NNO Greg Valentine/Dk. Blonde Hair		
NNO Greg Valentine/Lt. Blonde Hair	100.00	200.00
NNO King Kong Bundy	100.00	200.00
NNO Mr. Wonderful	150.00	300.00

1985 LJN WWF Wrestling Superstars Series 2 (loose)

NNO Andre the Giant/Short Hair	50.00	100.00
NNO Brutus Beefcake	15.00	30.00
NNO George Steele	15.00	30.00
NNO Greg Valentine/Dk Blond Hair	12.50	25.00
NNO Greg Valentine/Lt. Blonde Hair	10.00	20.00
NNO King Kong Bundy	20.00	40.00
NNO Mr. Wonderful	15.00	30.00

1986 LJN WWF Wrestling Superstars Series 3

NNO Bobby Heenan/No Scrolls
NNO Bobby Heenan/Scrolls 75.00 150.00
NNO Bruno Sammartino 60.00 120.00
NNO Captain Lou Albano/Red Lapel 50.00 100.00
NNO Captain Lou Albano/White Lapel 75.00 150.00
NNO Classy Freddie Blassie 60.00 120.00
NNO Corporal Kirchner/Beard
NNO Corporal Kirchner/No Stubble 60.00 120.00
NNO Corporal Kirchner/Stubble
NNO Don Muraco 100.00 200.00
NNO Jesse Ventura 125.00 250.00
NNO Jimmy Hart/Hearts on Megaphone 60.00 120.00
NNO Jimmy Hart/No Hearts on Megaphone 60.00 120.00
NNO Randy Savage 300.00 500.00
NNO Ricky Steamboat 100.00 200.00
NNO SD Jones/Hawaiian Shirt 75.00 150.00
NNO SD Jones/Red Shirt 60.00 120.00
NNO Terry Funk 125.00 250.00
NNO Tito Santana 100.00 200.00

1986 LJN WWF Wrestling Superstars Series 3 (loose)

NNO Bobby Heenan/No Scrolls 30.00 60.00
NNO Bobby Heenan/Scrolls 20.00 50.00
NNO Bruno Sammartino 20.00 40.00
NNO Captain Lou Albano/Red Lapel 12.50 25.00
NNO Captain Lou Albano/White Lapel 15.00 30.00
NNO Classy Freddie Blassie 30.00 60.00
NNO Corporal Kirchner/Beard
NNO Corporal Kirchner/No Stubble 15.00 30.00
NNO Corporal Kirchner/Stubble 15.00 30.00
NNO Don Muraco 20.00 40.00
NNO Jesse Ventura 20.00 40.00
NNO Jimmy Hart/Hearts on Megaphone 20.00 40.00
NNO Jimmy Hart/No Hearts on Megaphone 10.00 20.00
NNO Randy Savage 30.00 60.00
NNO Ricky Steamboat 15.00 30.00
NNO SD Jones/Hawaiian Shirt 20.00 40.00
NNO SD Jones/Red Shirt 12.50 25.00
NNO Terry Funk 30.00 75.00
NNO Tito Santana 20.00 40.00

1987 LJN WWF Wrestling Superstars Series 4

NNO Adrian Adonis 75.00 150.00
NNO Billy Jack Haynes 200.00 350.00
NNO Bret Hart/Pink Tights 300.00 600.00
NNO Bret Hart/Purple Tights
NNO Brian Blair/Non-Tan 75.00 150.00
NNO Brian Blair/Tan 125.00 250.00
NNO Cowboy Bob Orton 100.00 200.00
NNO Elizabeth/Gold Skirt 125.00 250.00
NNO Elizabeth/Purple Skirt 1200.00 1800.00
NNO Hercules Hernandez 100.00 200.00
NNO Jake the Snake Roberts 200.00 400.00
NNO Jim Brunzell/Non-Tan 125.00 250.00
NNO Jim Brunzell/Tan 150.00 300.00
NNO Jim Neidhart/Pink Tights 300.00 600.00
NNO Jim Neidhart/Purple Tights
NNO Kamala 150.00 300.00
NNO King Harley Race 300.00 500.00
NNO Koko B. Ware 200.00 350.00
NNO Mean Gene Okerlund 100.00 200.00
NNO Mr. Fuji 125.00 250.00
NNO Outback Jack 100.00 200.00
NNO Ted Arcidi 150.00 300.00

1987 LJN WWF Wrestling Superstars Series 4 (loose)

NNO Adrian Adonis 25.00 50.00
NNO Billy Jack Haynes 50.00 100.00
NNO Bret Hart/Pink Tights 50.00 100.00
NNO Bret Hart/Purple Tights
NNO Brian Blair/Non-Tan 20.00 40.00
NNO Brian Blair/Tan
NNO Cowboy Bob Orton 30.00 60.00
NNO Elizabeth/Gold Skirt 50.00 100.00
NNO Elizabeth/Purple Skirt 200.00 350.00
NNO Hercules Hernandez 20.00 40.00
NNO Jake the Snake Roberts 50.00 100.00
NNO Jim Brunzell/Non-Tan 15.00 30.00
NNO Jim Brunzell/Tan
NNO Jim Neidhart/Pink Tights 30.00 75.00
NNO Jim Neidhart/Purple Tights
NNO Kamala 30.00 60.00
NNO King Harley Race 60.00 120.00
NNO Koko B. Ware 30.00 75.00
NNO Mean Gene Okerlund 20.00 40.00
NNO Mr. Fuji 30.00 60.00
NNO Outback Jack 30.00 75.00
NNO Ted Arcidi 20.00 40.00

1988 LJN WWF Wrestling Superstars Series 5

NNO Ax 300.00 600.00
NNO Bam Bam Bigelow 200.00 400.00
NNO Hacksaw Jim Duggan 300.00 450.00
NNO Honky Tonk Man 300.00 500.00
NNO Hulk Hogan/Red Shirt
NNO Hulk Hogan/White Shirt
NNO Johnny V 90.00 175.00
NNO Ken Patera 150.00 300.00
NNO One Man Gang 200.00 400.00
NNO Referee/Blue Shirt 200.00 400.00
NNO Referee/White Shirt 400.00 750.00
NNO Rick Martel 300.00 600.00
NNO Slick 150.00 300.00
NNO Ted Dibiase 300.00 500.00
NNO Tito Santana/White Trunks 200.00 350.00
NNO Vince McMahon 150.00 300.00

1988 LJN WWF Wrestling Superstars Series 5 (loose)

NNO Ax 50.00 100.00
NNO Bam Bam Bigelow 50.00 100.00
NNO Hacksaw Jim Duggan 100.00 200.00
NNO Honky Tonk Man 50.00 100.00
NNO Hulk Hogan/Red Shirt 125.00 250.00
NNO Hulk Hogan/White Shirt 125.00 250.00
NNO Johnny V 20.00 40.00
NNO Ken Patera 30.00 60.00
NNO One Man Gang 30.00 75.00
NNO Referee/Blue Shirt 50.00 100.00
NNO Referee/White Shirt 60.00 120.00
NNO Rick Martel 30.00 60.00
NNO Slick 30.00 75.00
NNO Ted Dibiase 60.00 120.00
NNO Tito Santana 25.00 50.00
NNO Vince McMahon 60.00 120.00

1989 LJN WWF Wrestling Superstars Series 6

NNO Andre the Giant 2000.00 4000.00
NNO Big Boss Man 1250.00 2500.00
NNO Haku 500.00 1000.00
NNO Rick Rude 500.00 1000.00
NNO Ultimate Warrior 3000.00 6000.00
NNO Warlord 1500.00 3000.00

1984 LJN WWF Wrestling Superstars Accessories

NNO Hulkamania Barbell Workout Set
NNO Hulkamania Deluxe Workout Set 300.00 600.00

1986 LJN WWF Wrestling Superstars Stretch Wrestlers

NNO George The Animal Steele 125.00 250.00
NNO Hulk Hogan 300.00 600.00
NNO Junkyard Dog 125.00 250.00
NNO King Kong Bundy 125.00 250.00
NNO Macho Man Randy Savage 250.00 400.00
NNO Mr. Wonderful Paul Orndorff 75.00 150.00
NNO Ricky The Dragon Steamboat 150.00 300.00
NNO Rowdy Roddy Piper 250.00 500.00

1985 LJN WWF Wrestling Superstars Tag Teams

NNO British Bulldogs 400.00 800.00
NNO Greg Valentine & Brutus Beefcake 200.00 400.00
NNO Hart Foundation 1000.00 1500.00
NNO Hillbilly Jim & Hulk Hogan 250.00 500.00
NNO Iron Sheik & Nikolai Volkoff 150.00 300.00
NNO Killer Bees 200.00 400.00
NNO Strike Force 300.00 500.00

1986 LJN WWF Wrestling Superstars Thumb Wrestlers

NNO Hillbilly Jim/Big John Studd 75.00 150.00
NNO Hillbilly Jim/Macho Man Randy Savage 15.00 30.00
NNO Hillbilly Jim/Nikolai Volkoff 12.50 25.00
NNO Hillbilly Jim/Rowdy Roddy Piper 30.00 60.00
NNO Hillbilly Jim/The Iron Sheik 30.00 75.00
NNO Hulk Hogan/Big John Studd 25.00 50.00
NNO Hulk Hogan/Jake The Snake Roberts 30.00 75.00
NNO Hulk Hogan/King Kong Bundy 20.00 40.00
NNO Hulk Hogan/Macho Man Randy Savage 25.00 50.00
NNO Hulk Hogan/Nikolai Volkoff 30.00 75.00
NNO Hulk Hogan/Rowdy Roddy Piper 60.00 120.00
NNO Hulk Hogan/The Iron Sheik 20.00 40.00
NNO Junkyard Dog/Big John Studd 15.00 30.00
NNO Junkyard Dog/Nikolai Volkoff 30.00 75.00
NNO Junkyard Dog/Rowdy Roddy Piper 100.00 200.00
NNO Junkyard Dog/The Iron Sheik 15.00 30.00
NNO Mr. Wonderful Paul Orndorff/Big John Studd 30.00 75.00
NNO Mr. Wonderful Paul Orndorff/King Kong Bundy 15.00 30.00
NNO Mr. Wonderful Paul Orndorff/Rowdy Roddy Piper 50.00 100.00
NNO Ricky The Dragon Steamboat Jake The Snake Roberts 30.00 75.00
NNO Ricky The Dragon Steamboat Macho Man Randy Savage 25.00 50.00
NNO Ricky The Dragon Steamboat Nikolai Volkoff 12.50 25.00
NNO Ricky The Dragon Steamboat Rowdy Roddy Piper 15.00 30.00

1986 LJN WWF Wrestling Superstars Thumb Wrestlers (loose)

NNO Big John Studd 5.00 10.00
NNO Hillbilly Jim 5.00 10.00
NNO Hulk Hogan 7.50 15.00
NNO Iron Sheik 3.00 8.00
NNO Jake The Snake Roberts 5.00 10.00
NNO Junkyard Dog 3.00 8.00
NNO King Kong Bundy 6.00 12.00
NNO Macho Man Randy Savage 7.50 15.00
NNO Mr. Wonderful Paul Orndorff 3.00 8.00
NNO Nikolai Volkoff 3.00 8.00
NNO Ricky The Dragon Steamboat 5.00 10.00
NNO Rowdy Roddy Piper 6.00 12.00

2018 The Loyal Subjects Action Vinyls WWE

NNO AJ Styles
NNO Brock Lesnar 10.00 20.00
NNO Demon King Finn Balor 12.50 25.00
NNO Demon King Finn Balor Black and White
NNO Finn Balor/Blue Trunks 30.00 75.00
NNO John Cena 7.50 15.00
NNO Macho Man Randy Savage/Gold/2*
NNO Macho Man Randy Savage 12.50 25.00
NNO Macho Man Randy Savage American Flag 30.00 75.00
NNO Referee
NNO Referee/GITD
NNO Roman Reigns 10.00 20.00
NNO Sasha Banks CH 40.00 80.00
NNO Shinsuke Nakamura 7.50 15.00
NNO Shinsuke Nakamura/Black Pants 15.00 30.00
NNO Sting 15.00 30.00
NNO Undertaker 12.50 25.00
NNO RAW Ring/Bottom Left 10.00 20.00
NNO RAW Ring/Bottom Right 10.00 20.00
NNO RAW Ring/Top Left 10.00 20.00
NNO RAW Ring/Top Right 10.00 20.00

2018 The Loyal Subjects Action Vinyls WWE SDCC Exclusives

NNO AJ Styles vs. Shinsuke Nakamura 20.00 40.00
NNO Brock Lesnar vs. Roman Reigns 12.50 25.00
NNO John Cena vs. Undertaker 30.00 75.00

2020 Major Wrestling Figure Podcast Ringside Collectibles Exclusives

NNO Zack Ryder/Curt Hawkins/500
NNO Zack Ryder/Curt Hawkins (NY Mets colors)/250

2015 Mattel Create A WWE Superstar Series 1

NNO Bray Wyatt 10.00 20.00
NNO Hulk Hogan 20.00 40.00
NNO John Cena 12.50 25.00
NNO The Rock 15.00 30.00

2015 Mattel Create A WWE Superstar Series 1 Sets

NNO Gladiator Set 10.00 20.00
NNO Lucha Set 10.00 20.00
NNO Rocker Set 10.00 20.00

2015 Mattel Create A WWE Superstar Series 2

NNO Kane 12.50 25.00
NNO Randy Orton 10.00 20.00
NNO Sheamus 10.00 20.00
NNO Stone Cold Steve Austin

2015 Mattel Create A WWE Superstar Series 2 Sets

NNO Samurai Set
NNO Special Ops Set 20.00 40.00
NNO Zombie Set 15.00 30.00

2015 Mattel Create A WWE Superstar Series 3

NNO Goldust 25.00 50.00
NNO John Cena 15.00 30.00
NNO Rusev
NNO Triple H
NNO Ultimate Warrior 12.50 25.00

2015 Mattel Create A WWE Superstar Series 3 Sets

NNO Enforcer Set 10.00 20.00
NNO Hip Hop Set 10.00 20.00
NNO Vigilante Set 15.00 30.00

2015 Mattel Create A WWE Superstar Series Playset

NNO Ring Builder 30.00 75.00

2019 Mattel Masters of the WWE Universe

NNO Finn Balor 20.00 40.00
NNO Sting 30.00 60.00
NNO Triple H 20.00 40.00
NNO Ultimate Warrior 15.00 30.00

2019 Mattel Masters of the WWE Universe Playsets

NNO Grayskull Mania (w/John Cena & Terror Claws Triple H) 25.00 50.00
NNO Grayskull Ring 20.00 40.00

2020 Mattel Masters of the WWE Universe Wave 2

NNO Macho Man 20.00 40.00
NNO John Cena 15.00 30.00
NNO Roman Reigns 20.00 40.00
NNO Rey Mysterio 25.00 50.00

2020 Mattel Masters of the WWE Universe Wave 3

NNO Braun Strowman 25.00 50.00
NNO The New Day 30.00 75.00
NNO The Rock 30.00 75.00
NNO Undertaker 50.00 100.00

2020 Mattel Masters of the WWE Universe Wave 4

NNO The Fiend Bray Wyatt 30.00 60.00
NNO Jake "The Snake" Roberts 25.00 50.00
NNO Mr. T 45.00 90.00
NNO Seth Rollins 25.00 50.00

2020 Mattel Masters of the WWE Universe Wave 5

NNO Becky Lynch 15.00 30.00
NNO Macho Man Randy Savage 20.00 40.00
NNO Ricky "The Dragon" Steamboat 15.00 30.00
NNO Rowdy Roddy Piper 15.00 30.00

2020 Mattel Masters of the WWE Universe Wave 6

NNO Goldberg 12.50 25.00
NNO Kane 12.50 25.00
NNO Stephanie McMahon 10.00 20.00
NNO Ultimate Warrior 12.50 25.00

2021 Mattel Masters of the WWE Universe Wave 7

NNO Bret "Hit Man" Hart 20.00 40.00
NNO Andre the Giant 30.00 75.00
NNO Junkyard Dog 20.00 40.00
NNO Sgt. Slaughter 20.00 40.00

2021 Mattel Masters of the WWE Universe Wave 8

NNO Chyna 20.00 40.00
NNO Rey Mysterio 20.00 40.00
NNO Stone Cold Steve Austin 15.00 30.00

2016 Mattel WWE 3-Count Crushers

NNO John Cena
NNO The Rock
NNO Roman Reigns
NNO Seth Rollins

2010 Mattel WWE Battle Packs Series 1

NNO Santino/Beth Phoenix 15.00 30.00
NNO Shawn Michaels vs. Chris Jericho 20.00 40.00
NNO Ted DiBiase/Cody Rhodes 30.00 75.00

2010 Mattel WWE Battle Packs Series 2

NNO Carlito/Primo 12.50 25.00
NNO Finlay/Hornswoggle 20.00 40.00
NNO John Morrison/The Miz 15.00 30.00

2010 Mattel WWE Battle Packs Series 3

NNO Edge/Big Show
NNO Rey Mysterio/Evan Bourne 25.00 50.00
NNO Shad/JTG 30.00 60.00

2010 Mattel WWE Battle Packs Series 4

NNO Chavo vs. Hornswoggle 7.50 15.00
NNO Christian/Tommy Dreamer 40.00 80.00
NNO Hart Dynasty 20.00 40.00

2010 Mattel WWE Battle Packs Series 5

NNO Carlito/Primo 20.00 40.00
NNO D-Generation X 25.00 50.00
NNO Ricky Steamboat vs. Y2J 15.00 30.00

2010 Mattel WWE Battle Packs Series 6

NNO Mark Henry & MVP
NNO Undertaker vs. Batista
NNO Vladimir Kozlov & Ezekiel Jackson7.50 15.00

2010 Mattel WWE Battle Packs Series 7

NNO CM Punk & Luke Gallows 20.00 40.00
NNO Dolph Ziggler vs. John Morrison
NNO The Miz & Big Show

2011 Mattel WWE Battle Packs Series 8

NNO John Cena vs. Randy Orton
NNO Matt Hardy/Great Khali
NNO Ted DiBiase/Cody Rhodes

2011 Mattel WWE Battle Packs Series 9

NNO Christian/Heath Slater 7.50 15.00
NNO Hart Dynasty 15.00 30.00
NNO Sheamus/Triple H 12.50 25.00

2011 Mattel WWE Battle Packs Series 10

NNO Darren Young/Justin Gabriel 15.00 30.00
NNO David Otunga/ Michael Tarver 15.00 30.00
NNO Randy Orton vs. Edge 40.00 80.00

2011 Mattel WWE Battle Packs Series 11

NNO Drew McIntyre/ Cody Rhodes 75.00 150.00
NNO Jimmy Uso/Jey Uso 25.00 50.00
NNO Undertaker/Kane 30.00 75.00

2011 Mattel WWE Battle Packs Series 13

NNO John Cena vs. R-Truth 15.00 30.00
NNO The Miz vs. Alex Riley 20.00 40.00
NNO Rey Mysterio vs. Cody Rhodes 30.00 60.00

2012 Mattel WWE Battle Packs Series 14

NNO Heath Slater/Justin Gabriel 12.50 25.00
NNO Macho Man Randy Savage vs. CM Punk 25.00 50.00
NNO Randy Orton vs. Mason Ryan 12.50 25.00

2012 Mattel WWE Battle Packs Series 15

NNO Brie Bella/Nikki Bella 30.00 60.00
NNO Sin Cara vs. Daniel Bryan 25.00 50.00
NNO The Rock vs. John Cena 12.50 25.00

2012 Mattel WWE Battle Packs Series 16

NNO Alberto Del Rio vs. Big Show
NNO David Otunga/ Michael McGillicutty 12.50 25.00
NNO Randy Orton vs. Christian 15.00 30.00

2012 Mattel WWE Battle Packs Series 17

NNO John Cena vs. CM Punk 15.00 30.00
NNO Mark Henry vs. Trent Barreta 15.00 30.00
NNO Rey Mysterio vs. The Miz 25.00 50.00

2012 Mattel WWE Battle Packs Series 18

NNO CM Punk vs. Triple H 20.00 40.00
NNO Randy Orton vs. Wade Barrett
NNO Zack Ryder vs. Dolph Ziggler 15.00 30.00

2012 Mattel WWE Battle Packs Series 19

NNO Daniel Bryan vs. Big Show 15.00 30.00
NNO Epico/Primo 25.00 50.00
NNO John Cena vs. Kane

2013 Mattel WWE Battle Packs Series 20

NNO Brock Lesnar vs. Triple H 15.00 30.00
NNO Brodus Clay vs. Curt Hawkins 10.00 20.00
NNO Kofi Kingston/R-Truth 15.00 30.00

2013 Mattel WWE Battle Packs Series 21

NNO Darren Young/Titus O'Neil 12.50 25.00
NNO Kane vs. Daniel Bryan 20.00 40.00
NNO Sheamus vs. Randy Orton 15.00 30.00

2013 Mattel WWE Battle Packs Series 22

NNO Dolph Ziggler/ Vickie Guerrero 12.50 25.00
NNO Ryback vs. Jinder Mahal 12.50 25.00
NNO Sin Cara/Rey Mysterio 7.50 15.00

2013 Mattel WWE Battle Packs Series 23

NNO CM Punk vs. Mr. McMahon 20.00 40.00
NNO Rey Mysterio vs. Kofi Kingston 15.00 30.00
NNO Sin Cara vs. Cody Rhodes 15.00 30.00

2013 Mattel WWE Battle Packs Series 24

NNO Naomi/Cameron 20.00 40.00
NNO The Rock vs. John Cena 17.50 35.00
NNO Seth Rollins/Roman Reigns 15.00 30.00

2013 Mattel WWE Battle Packs Series 25

NNO Brock Lesnar/Paul Heyman 15.00 30.00
NNO CM Punk vs. Undertaker 25.00 50.00
NNO Mark Henry vs. Ryback 20.00 40.00

2014 Mattel WWE Battle Packs Series 26

NNO Nikki Bella/Brie Bella 20.00 40.00
NNO Seth Rollins/Dean Ambrose 15.00 30.00
NNO Triple H vs. Curtis Axel 12.50 25.00

2014 Mattel WWE Battle Packs Series 27

NNO Big Show/Mark Henry 12.50 25.00
NNO Brodus Clay/Tensai 10.00 20.00
NNO Daniel Bryan/Randy Orton 12.50 25.00

2014 Mattel WWE Battle Packs Series 28

NNO Big E/AJ Lee 20.00 40.00
NNO Jimmy Uso/Jey Uso 10.00 20.00
NNO Luke Harper/Erick Rowan 15.00 30.00

2014 Mattel WWE Battle Packs Series 29

NNO CM Punk vs. Ryback 25.00 50.00
NNO Goldust/Cody Rhodes 20.00 40.00
NNO Los Matadores 12.50 25.00

2014 Mattel WWE Battle Packs Series 30

NNO Brock Lesnar vs. Undertaker 15.00 30.00
NNO Jake Roberts/Dean Ambrose 15.00 30.00
NNO Xavier Woods/R-Truth 12.50 25.00

2014 Mattel WWE Battle Packs Series 31

NNO John Cena/Ultimate Warrior 12.50 25.00

NNO	Luke Harper/Erick Rowan	12.50	30.00
NNO	Sin Cara/Alberto Del Rio	10.00	20.00

2015 Mattel WWE Battle Packs Series 32

NNO	Daniel Bryan/Triple H	15.00	30.00
NNO	Jimmy Uso/Jey Uso	20.00	40.00
NNO	Road Dogg/Billy Gunn	15.00	30.00

2015 Mattel WWE Battle Packs Series 33

NNO	Andre the Giant/Big Show	25.00	50.00
NNO	Rey Mysterio/RVD	15.00	30.00
NNO	Shawn Michaels/Undertaker	7.50	15.00

2015 Mattel WWE Battle Packs Series 34

NNO	Animal/Hawk	30.00	75.00
NNO	Hornswoggle/El Torito	30.00	60.00
NNO	Lana/Rusev	15.00	30.00

2015 Mattel WWE Battle Packs Series 35

NNO	Kane/Roman Reigns	12.50	25.00
NNO	Ryback/Curtis Axel	15.00	30.00
NNO	Zeb Colter/Jack Swagger	12.50	25.00

2015 Mattel WWE Battle Packs Series 36

NNO	Big E/Kofi Kingston	15.00	30.00
NNO	Dean Ambrose/Seth Rollins	10.00	20.00
NNO	Kevin Nash/Scott Hall	15.00	30.00

2015 Mattel WWE Battle Packs Series 37

NNO	Jamie Noble/Joey Mercury	12.50	25.00
NNO	Jey Uso/Jimmy Uso	12.50	25.00
NNO	Konnor/Viktor	10.00	20.00

2015 Mattel WWE Battle Packs Series 38

NNO	Adam Rose/Bunny	10.00	20.00
NNO	Bray Wyatt/Undertaker	15.00	30.00
NNO	Nikki Bella/Brie Bella	20.00	40.00

2016 Mattel WWE Battle Packs Series 39

NNO	Darren Young/Titus O'Neill	10.00	20.00
NNO	John Cena/Kevin Owens	7.50	15.00
NNO	Tyson Kidd/Cesaro	7.50	15.00

2016 Mattel WWE Battle Packs Series 40

NNO	Bushwhackers	10.00	20.00
NNO	Enzo Amore/Big Cass	15.00	30.00
NNO	Steve Austin/Mr. McMahon	15.00	30.00

2016 Mattel WWE Battle Packs Series 41

NNO	Bubba Ray/Devon Dudley	15.00	30.00
NNO	Charlotte/Ric Flair	12.50	25.00
NNO	Simon Gotch/Aiden English		

2016 Mattel WWE Battle Packs Series 42

NNO	Edge/Christian	10.00	20.00
NNO	Sin Cara/Kalisto	15.00	30.00
NNO	Triple H/Stephanie	12.50	25.00

2016 Mattel WWE Battle Packs Series 43A

NNO	Big E/Kofi Kingston	15.00	30.00
NNO	Nikki Bella/Brie Bella	20.00	40.00
NNO	Undertaker/Kane	12.50	25.00

2016 Mattel WWE Battle Packs Series 43B

NNO	Dean Ambrose/Brock Lesnar	12.50	25.00
NNO	Finn Balor/Samoa Joe	20.00	40.00
NNO	John Cena/Seth Rollins	10.00	20.00
NNO	Roman Reigns/Sheamus	12.50	25.00

2016 Mattel WWE Battle Packs Series 44

NNO	American Alpha	10.00	20.00
NNO	Sami Zayn/Kevin Owens	12.50	25.00
NNO	The Usos	15.00	30.00

2017 Mattel WWE Battle Packs Series 45

NNO	AJ Styles/Roman Reigns	15.00	30.00
NNO	Enzo Amore/Big Cass	20.00	40.00
NNO	Scott Dawson/Dash Wilder	15.00	30.00
NNO	Triple H/Road Dogg	15.00	30.00

2017 Mattel WWE Battle Packs Series 46

NNO	Dean Ambrose/Shane McMahon	15.00	30.00
NNO	Karl Anderson/Luke Gallows	25.00	50.00
NNO	The Miz & Maryse	15.00	30.00
NNO	The New Day (Kingston/Woods)	15.00	30.00

2017 Mattel WWE Battle Packs Series 47

NNO	Bray Wyatt/Luke Harper	12.50	25.00
NNO	The Hart Foundation	12.50	25.00
NNO	Roman Reigns vs. Rusev	12.50	25.00
NNO	Sasha Banks vs. Charlotte Flair	15.00	30.00

2017 Mattel WWE Battle Packs Series 48

NNO	American Alpha	12.50	25.00
NNO	Hype Bros.	10.00	20.00
NNO	Shawn Michaels/Diesel	12.50	25.00

2017 Mattel WWE Battle Packs Series 49

NNO	Daniel Bryan/The Miz	12.50	25.00
NNO	Sheamus/Cesaro	12.50	25.00
NNO	Stephanie McMahon/Mick Foley	10.00	20.00

2017 Mattel WWE Battle Packs Series 50

NNO	Konnor/Viktor	10.00	20.00
NNO	Luke Gallows/Karl Anderson	20.00	40.00
NNO	Randy Orton/Bray Wyatt	12.50	25.00

2017 Mattel WWE Battle Packs Series 51

NNO	Big E/Xavier Woods	12.50	25.00
NNO	The Miz/Maryse	10.00	20.00
NNO	Scott Dawson/Dash Wilder	15.00	30.00

2018 Mattel WWE Battle Packs Series 52

NNO	Jey Uso/Jimmy Uso	30.00	60.00
NNO	Roman Reigns/Brock Lesnar	12.50	25.00
NNO	Sheamus/Cesaro	15.00	30.00

2018 Mattel WWE Battle Packs Series 53

NNO	Carmella/James Ellsworth	12.50	25.00
NNO	Matt Hardy/Jeff Hardy	25.00	50.00
NNO	S. Nakamura/D. Ziggler	12.50	25.00

2018 Mattel WWE Battle Packs Series 54

NNO	B. Strowman/R. Reigns	15.00	30.00
NNO	Bray Wyatt/Finn Balor	12.50	25.00
NNO	Nia Jax/Alexa Bliss	25.00	50.00
NNO	Tyler Breeze/Fandango	10.00	20.00

2018 Mattel WWE Battle Packs Series 55

NNO	Big Show/Big Cass	17.50	35.00
NNO	Charlotte Flair/Becky Lynch	20.00	40.00
NNO	Seth Rollins/Dean Ambrose	15.00	30.00

2018 Mattel WWE Battle Packs Series 56

NNO	Miztourage		
NNO	Roman Reigns vs. John Cena		
NNO	Kurt Angle/Jason Jordan		

2019 Mattel WWE Battle Packs Series 57

NNO	Braun Strowman vs. Kane		
NNO	Sunil &Samir Singh		
NNO	Finn Balor vs. Shinsuke Nakamura		

2019 Mattel WWE Battle Packs Series 58

NNO	Kevin Owens/Sami Zayn		
NNO	S. Benjamin/C. Gable		
NNO	Triple H/HBK		

2019 Mattel WWE Battle Packs Series 59

NNO	The Hardy Boyz		
NNO	Jinder Mahal vs. AJ Styles		
NNO	The Shield (Ambrose/Rollins)		

2019 Mattel WWE Battle Packs Series 60

NNO	The Bar (Cesaro/Sheamus)		
NNO	Goldberg vs. Stone Cold Steve Austin		
NNO	Sasha Banks vs. Alexa Bliss		

2019 Mattel WWE Battle Packs Series 61

NNO	AJ Styles/Daniel Bryan		
NNO	The IIconics (Billie Kay/Peyton Royce)		
NNO	Jimmy and Jey Uso		

2019 Mattel WWE Battle Packs Series 62

NNO	Akam & Rezar		
NNO	Andrade/Zelina Vega		
NNO	Rey Mysterio/Shinsuke Nakamura		

2019 Mattel WWE Battle Packs Series 63

NNO	Bobby Lashley vs. Finn Balor		
NNO	The New Day (Big E/Xavier Woods)		
NNO	Seth Rollins vs. Brock Lesnar		

2020 Mattel WWE Battle Packs Series 64

NNO	Daniel Bryan vs. AJ Styles	15.00	30.00
NNO	Lita & Trish Stratus	30.00	75.00
NNO	The Usos	60.00	120.00

2020 Mattel WWE Battle Packs Series 65

NNO	Ali & Kevin Owens	20.00	40.00
NNO	The Hardy Boyz	25.00	50.00
NNO	Ricochet & Velveteen	20.00	40.00

2020 Mattel WWE Battle Packs Series 66

NNO	Seth Rollins & Becky Lynch	25.00	50.00
NNO	Roman Reigns & Undertaker	30.00	60.00
NNO	Shane McMahon & Drew McIntyre	15.00	30.00

2016 Mattel WWE Battle Packs SummerSlam Heritage

NNO	John Cena/Brock Lesnar	12.50	25.00
NNO	Roman Reigns/Dean Ambrose	10.00	20.00

2017 Mattel WWE Battle Packs SummerSlam Heritage

NNO	Brock Lesnar/Randy Orton	15.00	30.00
NNO	Ultimate Warrior/Honkytonk Man	15.00	30.00

2016 Mattel WWE Battle Packs Then Now Forever

NNO	Dean Ambrose/Brian Pillman	10.00	20.00
NNO	John Cena/Steve Austin	15.00	30.00
NNO	Ultimate Warrior/Sting	12.50	25.00

2010 Mattel WWE Battle Packs WrestleMania 26

NNO	John Cena/Batista		
NNO	The Miz/Big Show	20.00	40.00
NNO	R-Truth/John Morrison		

2014 Mattel WWE Battle Packs WrestleMania 30 Heritage

NNO	Batista vs. Brock Lesnar	15.00	30.00
NNO	Sheamus vs. Ultimate Warrior	12.50	25.00

2015 Mattel WWE Battle Packs WrestleMania 31 Heritage

NNO	Daniel Bryan vs. Rey Mysterio	20.00	40.00
NNO	Triple H vs. Roman Reigns	20.00	40.00

2016 Mattel WWE Battle Packs WrestleMania 32 Heritage

NNO	Bret Hart & Steve Austin	15.00	30.00
NNO	Ric Flair & The Rock	12.50	25.00

2016 Mattel WWE Battle Packs WrestleMania 33 Heritage

NNO	Andre the Giant/ Ted DiBiase	10.00	20.00
NNO	The Rock/John Cena	12.50	25.00

2018 Mattel WWE Battle Packs WrestleMania 34 Heritage

NNO	Sting/Triple H	10.00	20.00
NNO	John Cena/Nikki Bella	15.00	30.00
NNO	Roman Reigns/Undertaker	12.50	25.00

2018 Mattel WWE Battle Packs WrestleMania 35 Heritage

NNO	AJ Styles vs. Shinsuke Nakamura	15.00	30.00
NNO	Jeff Hardy vs. Edge	15.00	30.00
NNO	The Miz vs. Seth Rollins	12.50	25.00

2020 Mattel WWE Beast Mode

NNO	AJ Styles	7.50	15.00
NNO	Becky Lynch	7.50	15.00
NNO	Braun Strowman	5.00	10.00
NNO	Daniel Bryan	6.00	12.00
NNO	Finn Balor	7.50	15.00
NNO	The Rock	5.00	10.00
NNO	Roman Reigns	10.00	20.00
NNO	Triple H	7.50	15.00

2021 Mattel WWE Beast Mode

NNO Becky Lynch
NNO Big E
NNO Bray Wyatt
NNO Kofi Kingston
NNO Seth Rollins
NNO The Rock
NNO Undertaker
NNO Xavier Woods

2022 Mattel WWE Bend 'N Bash Series 1

NNO	John Cena	15.00	30.00
NNO	Rey Mysterio	15.00	30.00
NNO	The Rock	20.00	40.00
NNO	Roman Reigns	15.00	30.00

2022 Mattel WWE Bend 'N Bash Series 2

NNO	Bobby Lashley	12.50	25.00
NNO	Drew McIntyre	12.50	25.00
NNO	Kofi Kingston		
NNO	Undertaker	12.50	25.00

2010 Mattel WWE Best of 2010

NNO	Batista	12.50	25.00
NNO	Evan Bourne	7.50	15.00
NNO	Hornswoggle	20.00	40.00
NNO	John Cena	10.00	20.00
NNO	Mark Henry	7.50	15.00
NNO	Rey Mysterio	12.50	25.00

2011 Mattel WWE Best of 2011

NNO	Big Show	12.50	25.00
NNO	John Cena	6.00	12.00
NNO	Kofi Kingston		
NNO	Randy Orton	7.50	15.00
NNO	Rey Mysterio	25.00	50.00
NNO	Santino Marella	7.50	15.00

2012 Mattel WWE Best of 2012

NNO	Alberto Del Rio		
NNO	Brodus Clay		
NNO	Daniel Bryan	15.00	30.00
NNO	Great Khali	40.00	80.00
NNO	Rey Mysterio	12.50	25.00
NNO	Sin Cara	25.00	50.00

2013 Mattel WWE Best of 2013

NNO Brock Lesnar
NNO Great Khali
NNO Kaitlyn
NNO Rey Mysterio
NNO Tensai
NNO Undertaker

2014 Mattel WWE Best of 2014

NNO	Cesaro	7.50	15.00
NNO	El Torito	12.50	25.00
NNO	John Cena	10.00	20.00
NNO	Roman Reigns	20.00	40.00
NNO	Sin Cara	25.00	50.00
NNO	Undertaker	10.00	20.00

2012 Mattel WWE Best of PPV Series 1

NNO	Christian		
NNO	John Cena		
NNO	Mark Henry		
NNO	Rey Mysterio	30.00	75.00

2012 Mattel WWE Best of PPV Series 2

NNO John Cena
NNO The Rock
NNO Sheamus
NNO Triple H

2013 Mattel WWE Best of PPV Series 3

NNO Alberto Del Rio
NNO John Cena
NNO Mark Henry
NNO Rey Mysterio

2013 Mattel WWE Best of PPV Series 4

NNO	Alberto Del Rio	7.50	15.00
NNO	Sheamus	7.50	15.00
NNO	The Rock	12.50	25.00
NNO	Undertaker	10.00	20.00

2014 Mattel WWE Best of PPV Series 5

NNO Damien Sandow
NNO Daniel Bryan
NNO Dolph Ziggler
NNO Kofi Kingston

2016 Mattel WWE Best of PPV

NNO	Chris Jericho	10.00	20.00
NNO	Neville		
NNO	Rusev		
NNO	Undertaker		

2023 Mattel WWE Best of Ultimate Edition Series 1

NNO Bret "Hit Man" Hart
NNO Triple H

2015 Mattel WWE Big Reveal 12-Inch

NNO Rey Mysterio
NNO Triple H
NNO Ultimate Warrior
NNO Undertaker

2012 Mattel WWE Brawlin' Buddies

NNO John Cena
NNO Randy Orton
NNO Rey Mysterio
NNO Sheamus

2013 Mattel WWE Brawlin' Buddies

NNO John Cena
NNO Kofi Kingston
NNO Rey Mysterio
NNO Zack Ryder

2012 Mattel WWE Brawlin' Buddies 2-Pack

NNO Rey Mysterio/John Cena
(Toys R Us Exclusive)

2013 Mattel WWE Brawlin' Buddies Championship Buddies

NNO Brodus Clay
NNO John Cena
NNO The Rock
NNO Sheamus

2014 Mattel WWE Dollar Store Series 1

NNO CM Punk
NNO John Cena
NNO Kane
NNO Randy Orton
NNO Rey Mysterio
NNO Sheamus

2014 Mattel WWE Dollar Store Series 2

NNO Alberto Del Rio
NNO Big Show
NNO Brodus Clay
NNO Daniel Bryan
NNO John Cena
NNO Undertaker

2017 Mattel WWE Dollar Store

NNO Brock Lesnar
NNO John Cena
NNO Roman Reigns
NNO Undertaker

2019 Mattel WWE Dollar Store

NNO AJ Styles
NNO Finn Balor
NNO John Cena
NNO The Rock
NNO Roman Reigns

2019 Mattel WWE Dollar Store 5-Pack

NNO Cena/Rock/Styles/Balor/Reigns

2020 Mattel WWE Elite Collection 2-Packs

NNO	Bret "Hit Man" Hart & Goldberg	30.00	75.00
NNO	Brood Hardy Boyz (Ringside Exclusive)	50.00	100.00
NNO	Chyna & Triple H	30.00	75.00
NNO	Mr. T & "Rowdy" Roddy Piper	60.00	120.00

2021 Mattel WWE Elite Collection 2-Packs

NNO	The Rock & Mankind (Rock 'N' Sock Connection)	50.00	100.00
NNO	Jeff Hardy vs. Triple H	25.00	50.00

2010 Mattel WWE Elite Collection Best of 2010

NNO	John Cena	20.00	40.00
NNO	Kane	50.00	100.00
NNO	Randy Orton	50.00	90.00
NNO	Rey Mysterio	60.00	120.00
NNO	Triple H	25.00	50.00
NNO	Undertaker	30.00	60.00

2011 Mattel WWE Elite Collection Best of 2011

NNO	John Cena	25.00	50.00
NNO	John Morrison	60.00	120.00
NNO	Randy Orton	20.00	40.00
NNO	Rey Mysterio	30.00	75.00
NNO	Sheamus		

2018 Mattel WWE Elite Collection Best of Attitude Era

NNO	Chris Jericho	10.00	20.00
NNO	The Rock	20.00	40.00
NNO	Stone Cold Steve Austin	20.00	40.00
NNO	Triple H	12.50	25.00

2012 Mattel WWE Elite Collection Best of PPV Series 1

NNO Bret Hart
NNO Daniel Bryan
NNO John Cena
NNO Triple H

2012 Mattel WWE Elite Collection Best of PPV Series 2

NNO Big Show
NNO CM Punk
NNO The Miz
NNO Shawn Michaels
NNO Undertaker EXCL

2013 Mattel WWE Elite Collection Best of PPV Series 3

NNO	Christian	60.00	120.00
NNO	John Cena	25.00	50.00
NNO	Sheamus	15.00	30.00
NNO	Sin Cara	30.00	75.00

2013 Mattel WWE Elite Collection Best of PPV Series 4

NNO	Brock Lesnar	15.00	30.00
NNO	CM Punk	30.00	60.00
NNO	Daniel Bryan	15.00	30.00
NNO	John Cena	12.50	25.00

2014 Mattel WWE Elite Collection Best of PPV Series 5

NNO	Alberto Del Rio	20.00	40.00
NNO	CM Punk	30.00	60.00
NNO	Curtis Axel	25.00	50.00
NNO	Paul Bearer	15.00	30.00
NNO	Randy Orton	17.50	35.00

2014 Mattel WWE Elite Collection Best of PPV Series 6

NNO	Bray Wyatt	12.50	25.00
NNO	Daniel Bryan	20.00	40.00
NNO	John Cena	12.50	25.00
NNO	Undertaker	20.00	40.00

2017 Mattel WWE Elite Collection Booty-O's 3-Pack

NNO	The New Day	25.00	50.00

2011 Mattel WWE Elite Collection Defining Moments Series 1

NNO	Macho Man Randy Savage	50.00	100.00
NNO	Shawn Michaels	75.00	150.00

2011 Mattel WWE Elite Collection Defining Moments Series 2

NNO	The Rock	100.00	200.00
NNO	Ultimate Warrior	60.00	120.00

2011 Mattel WWE Elite Collection Defining Moments Series 3

NNO	Ricky Steamboat	40.00	80.00
NNO	Triple H	125.00	250.00

2011 Mattel WWE Elite Collection Defining Moments Series 4

NNO	Stone Cold Steve Austin	40.00	80.00
NNO	Undertaker	100.00	200.00

2011 Mattel WWE Elite Collection Defining Moments Series 5

NNO	Bret Hart	100.00	200.00
NNO	John Cena	30.00	60.00

2014 Mattel WWE Elite Collection Defining Moments Series 6

NNO	Hulk Hogan	30.00	75.00
NNO	Ric Flair	40.00	80.00

2015 Mattel WWE Elite Collection Defining Moments Series 7

NNO	Hulk Hogan		
NNO	Razor Ramon		
NNO	Sting		
NNO	Undertaker		

2016 Mattel WWE Elite Collection Defining Moments Series 8

NNO	John Cena		
NNO	Ric Flair/Retirement		
NNO	Stone Cold Steve Austin		
NNO	Sting/Surfer Gear		
NNO	Ultimate Warrior		

2017 Mattel WWE Elite Collection Defining Moments Series 9

NNO	Chris Jericho	15.00	30.00
NNO	Macho Man Randy Savage	20.00	40.00
NNO	Shinsuke Nakamura	20.00	40.00

2018 Mattel WWE Elite Collection Entrance Greats

NNO	Bobby Roode	20.00	40.00
NNO	Elias		
NNO	Finn Balor		
NNO	Goldberg	25.00	50.00
NNO	Jeff Hardy	30.00	60.00
NNO	Kurt Angle		

2010 Mattel WWE Elite Collection Entrance Greats Series 1

NNO	Rey Mysterio	50.00	100.00
NNO	Shawn Michaels	25.00	50.00
NNO	Triple H	20.00	40.00

2010 Mattel WWE Elite Collection Entrance Greats Series 2

NNO	Chris Jericho	30.00	60.00
NNO	Million Dollar Man	20.00	40.00
NNO	Rowdy Roddy Piper	25.00	50.00

2010 Mattel WWE Elite Collection Entrance Greats Series 3

NNO	The Rock	30.00	75.00
NNO	Undertaker	50.00	100.00

2018 Mattel WWE Elite Collection Epic Moments

NNO	Festival of Friendship Chris Jericho/Kevin Owens	30.00	75.00
NNO	Milk-O-Mania Kurt Angle/Stone Cold Steve Austin/Stephanie McMahon	25.00	50.00
NNO	Shield Reunion Seth Rollins/Roman Reigns/Dean Ambrose	50.00	100.00
NNO	Team Xtreme Matt & Jeff Hardy	30.00	60.00
NNO	Undisputed Era Adam Cole/Bobby Fish/Kyle O'Reilly	60.00	120.00

2010 Mattel WWE Elite Collection Exclusives

NNO	Rey Mysterio Flash RSC	150.00	300.00

2011 Mattel WWE Elite Collection Exclusives

NNO	Bret Hart P&B Attack RSC	150.00	300.00
NNO	CM Punk Straight Edge RSC	200.00	350.00
NNO	Macho King RSC	150.00	300.00
NNO	Undertaker SDCC	75.00	150.00
NNO	Vince McMahon MA	60.00	120.00

2012 Mattel WWE Elite Collection Exclusives

NNO	Macho Man nWo RSC	75.00	150.00
NNO	Steve Austin Rattlesnake RSC		
NNO	Triple H COO MA	20.00	40.00

2013 Mattel WWE Elite Collection Exclusives

NNO	Brock Lesnar Pain RSC	30.00	75.00
NNO	Cactus Jack Bang RSC	30.00	60.00
NNO	Undertaker 21-0 TRU		

2014 Mattel WWE Elite Collection Exclusives

NNO	CM Punk ECW (Flashback RSC	60.00	120.00
NNO	Edge Rated R RSC	100.00	200.00
NNO	Kane Hardcore RSC	125.00	250.00
NNO	Kane Unmasked RSC		
NNO	The Rock IC Champ RSC	25.00	50.00
NNO	Mankind AMZ	25.00	50.00
NNO	Rocky Maivia TAR	30.00	75.00
NNO	Brock Lesnar 21-1 TRU	25.00	50.00

2015 Mattel WWE Elite Collection Exclusives

NNO	Hulk Hogan American RSC	60.00	120.00
NNO	John Cena TRU	50.00	100.00
NNO	Scott Hall nWo RSC	50.00	100.00
NNO	Seth Rollins TRU	30.00	60.00
NNO	Shawn Michaels DX SE WG	30.00	60.00
NNO	Shawn Michaels SS RSC	50.00	100.00
NNO	Triple H DX SE WG	30.00	60.00
NNO	Virgil Convention Sign	30.00	60.00

2016 Mattel WWE Elite Collection Exclusives

NNO	Chris Jericho WM XIX RSC	25.00	50.00
NNO	Finn Balor Balor Club RSC	30.00	75.00
NNO	Kevin Nash nWo RSC	75.00	150.00
NNO	Nation of Domination KM OL	60.00	120.00
NNO	Sting nWo Wolfpac RSC	60.00	120.00
NNO	Brock Lesnar/ WWE 2K17 GS	25.00	50.00
NNO	Shockmaster SDCC	60.00	120.00

2017 Mattel WWE Elite Collection Exclusives

NNO	AJ Styles WRMS	25.00	50.00
NNO	Andre the Giant AMZ	30.00	75.00
NNO	Becky Lynch WG	20.00	40.00
NNO	Bret Hit Man Hart KOTR RSC	60.00	120.00
NNO	Chris Jericho List GS	30.00	75.00
NNO	Hardy Boyz WWE SZ		
NNO	Isaac Yankem DDS TRU	60.00	120.00
NNO	Macho Man Wolfpack RSC	75.00	150.00
NNO	Maryse WG	20.00	40.00
NNO	Samoa Joe GS	20.00	40.00
NNO	Sasha Banks Title WG	25.00	50.00
NNO	Shano Mac RSC	30.00	75.00

2018 Mattel WWE Elite Collection Exclusives

NNO	AJ Styles TRU	25.00	50.00
NNO	The Brian Kendrick RSC	20.00	40.00
NNO	Hardy Boyz Brood RSC	50.00	100.00
NNO	Kurt Angle Shield RSC	15.00	30.00
NNO	Matt Hardy ECW RSC	25.00	50.00
NNO	Pete Dunne	30.00	75.00
NNO	The Shark SDCC	20.00	40.00

2019 Mattel WWE Elite Collection Exclusives

NNO	Alexa Bliss WG	25.00	50.00
NNO	Alexander Wolfe TAR	20.00	40.00
NNO	Andrade Cien Almas (NXT TakeOver) RSC	30.00	60.00
NNO	Bob Backlund WM	20.00	40.00
NNO	Gorilla Monsoon WM	60.00	120.00
NNO	Kassius Ohno TAR	75.00	150.00
NNO	Liv Morgan TAR	60.00	120.00
NNO	Macho Man Randy Savage (Slim Jim) SDCC	75.00	150.00
NNO	Paige TAR	50.00	100.00
NNO	Pat Patterson WM	20.00	40.00
NNO	Red Rooster TAR	50.00	100.00
NNO	Rock (SmackDown Live) WM	20.00	40.00
NNO	Sensational Sherri WG	20.00	40.00
NNO	Sonya Deville TAR	30.00	60.00
NNO	Tyler Bate (UK Champion)	25.00	50.00
NNO	Undertaker as Kane (Deadman's Revenge) RSC	30.00	60.00

2020 Mattel WWE Elite Collection Exclusives

NNO	Finn Balor/AJ Styles	30.00	75.00
NNO	Rey Mysterio/Samoa Joe (WrestleMania Moment)	60.00	120.00

2021 Mattel WWE Elite Collection Exclusives

NNO	Bray Wyatt Firefly Funhouse RSC	30.00	75.00
NNO	Cactus Jack ECW RSC	25.00	50.00
NNO	John Cena nWo RSC	30.00	60.00
NNO	Ultimate Warrior WrestleMania 12 RSC	20.00	40.00
NNO	Undertaker Tag Champ RSC		
NNO	Walter RSC	25.00	50.00

2022 Mattel WWE Elite Collection Exclusives

NNO	Cameron Grimes (To the Moon) (Ringside Collectibles Exclusive)	25.00	50.00
NNO	Mega Powers (Hogan & Savage) 2-Pack (Ringside Collectibles Exclusive)	50.00	100.00
NNO	Tommaso Ciampa (Blackheart) (Ringside Collectibles Exclusive)	40.00	80.00
NNO	Wolfpac Hulk Hogan (Ringside Collectibles Exclusive)	30.00	75.00

2018 Mattel WWE Elite Collection Fan Central

NNO	Carmella	25.00	50.00

2019 Mattel WWE Elite Collection Fan Central

NNO	Akira Tozawa	20.00	40.00
NNO	Big Show	25.00	50.00
NNO	Bobby The Brain Heenan	20.00	40.00
NNO	Daniel Bryan	15.00	30.00
NNO	Mark Henry	25.00	50.00
NNO	Mojo Rawley	15.00	30.00
NNO	Triple H	15.00	30.00

2018 Mattel WWE Elite Collection Flashback Series 1

NNO	Mean Gene Okerlund	30.00	75.00
NNO	Syxx	25.00	50.00
NNO	Ultimate Warrior	25.00	50.00
NNO	Yokozuna	20.00	40.00

2018 Mattel WWE Elite Collection Flashback Series 2

NNO	Alundra Blayze	15.00	30.00
NNO	Razor Ramon	15.00	30.00
NNO	Shawn Michaels	20.00	40.00

2019 Mattel WWE Elite Collection Ghostbusters

NNO	John Cena	12.50	25.00
NNO	The Rock	15.00	30.00
NNO	Shawn Michaels	12.50	25.00
NNO	Stone Cold Steve Austin	12.50	25.00
NNO	Undertaker	15.00	30.00

2022 Mattel WWE Elite Collection Greatest Hits Series 1

NNO	Bam Bam Bigelow	20.00	40.00
NNO	Jake The Snake Roberts	25.00	50.00
NNO	Rey Mysterio	20.00	40.00
NNO	Rikishi	30.00	75.00
NNO	The Rock	20.00	40.00
NNO	Undertaker	20.00	40.00

2018 Mattel WWE Elite Collection Hall of Champions Series 3

NNO	Billy Gunn	15.00	30.00
NNO	Paul Bearer	25.00	50.00
NNO	Road Dogg	15.00	30.00
NNO	Ultimate Warrior	25.00	50.00

2016 Mattel WWE Elite Collection Hall of Fame 2-Packs

NNO	Papa Shango/Ultimate Warrior	25.00	50.00
NNO	Wild Samoans	20.00	40.00

2017 Mattel WWE Elite Collection Hall of Fame 4-Pack

NNO	Eddie Guerrero/Kevin Nash/ Scott Hall/Larry Zybysko	25.00	50.00

2015 Mattel WWE Elite Collection Hall of Fame Four Horsemen 4-Pack

NNO	Ric Flair/Arn Anderson/Barry Windham/Tully Blanchard	30.00	75.00

2015 Mattel WWE Elite Collection Hall of Fame Series 1

NNO	Sgt. Slaughter	20.00	40.00
NNO	Stone Cold Steve Austin	25.00	50.00
NNO	Trish Stratus	25.00	50.00
NNO	Ultimate Warrior	20.00	40.00

2015 Mattel WWE Elite Collection Hall of Fame Series 2

NNO	Eddie Guerrero	15.00	30.00
NNO	Hulk Hogan	25.00	50.00
NNO	Tito Santana	10.00	20.00
NNO	Yokozuna	20.00	40.00

2016 Mattel WWE Elite Collection Hall of Fame Series 3

NNO	Jimmy Hart	20.00	40.00
NNO	Macho Man Randy Savage	25.00	50.00
NNO	Million Dollar Man Ted DiBiase	17.50	35.00

2016 Mattel WWE Elite Collection Hall of Fame Series 4

NNO	Edge	25.00	50.00
NNO	Jerry Lawler	15.00	30.00
NNO	King Booker	20.00	40.00
NNO	Sting	20.00	40.00

2017 Mattel WWE Elite Collection Hall of Fame Series 5

NNO	Diesel	17.50	35.00
NNO	George The Animal Steele		
NNO	Jake Roberts	12.50	25.00
NNO	Roddy Piper	12.50	25.00

2010 Mattel WWE Elite Collection Legends Hall of Fame Series

NNO	Am. Dream Dusty Rhodes	25.00	50.00
NNO	Jimmy Superfly Snuka	25.00	50.00
NNO	Ricky Steamboat	30.00	75.00
NNO	Sgt. Slaughter		
NNO	Stone Cold Steve Austin	50.00	100.00
NNO	Terry Funk	25.00	50.00

2010 Mattel WWE Elite Collection Legends Series 1

NNO	Am. Dream Dusty Rhodes	30.00	75.00
NNO	Ricky Steamboat	30.00	75.00
NNO	Road Warrior Animal	50.00	100.00
NNO	Road Warrior Hawk	50.00	100.00
NNO	Sgt. Slaughter	25.00	50.00
NNO	Stone Cold Steve Austin	40.00	80.00

2010 Mattel WWE Elite Collection Legends Series 1 2-Packs

NNO	Bushwhackers	30.00	75.00
NNO	Iron Sheik/Nikolai Volkoff	50.00	100.00
NNO	Rowdy Roddy Piper Cowboy Bob Orton	50.00	100.00

2010 Mattel WWE Elite Collection Legends Series 2

NNO	Iron Sheik	30.00	60.00
NNO	Jake The Snake Roberts	30.00	60.00
NNO	Jimmy Superfly Snuka	50.00	100.00
NNO	Kamala	20.00	40.00
NNO	Ravishing Rick Rude	30.00	75.00
NNO	Terry Funk	20.00	40.00

2010 Mattel WWE Elite Collection Legends Series 2 2-Packs

NNO	Kerry and Kevin Von Erich		
NNO	Marty Jannetty/HBK		

2010 Mattel WWE Elite Collection Legends Series 3

NNO	Brian Pillman	60.00	120.00
NNO	British Bulldog	30.00	75.00
NNO	Hacksaw Jim Duggan	50.00	100.00
NNO	Mr. Perfect	30.00	75.00
NNO	The Rock	25.00	50.00
NNO	Vader/Black Mask	75.00	150.00
NNO	Vader/Red Mask	50.00	100.00

2011 Mattel WWE Elite Collection Legends Series 4

NNO	Ax	60.00	120.00
NNO	George The Animal Steele	30.00	60.00
NNO	Hillbilly Jim	30.00	75.00
NNO	Paul Orndorff	75.00	150.00
NNO	Smash	60.00	120.00
NNO	Ultimate Warrior	30.00	60.00

2011 Mattel WWE Elite Collection Legends Series 5

NNO	Akeem	100.00	200.00
NNO	Bam Bam Bigelow	30.00	60.00
NNO	Macho Man Randy Savage	30.00	75.00
NNO	Rick Martel	100.00	200.00

2011 Mattel WWE Elite Collection Legends Series 6

NNO	Eddie Guerrero	75.00	150.00
NNO	Kerry Von Erich	100.00	200.00
NNO	Kevin Von Erich	125.00	250.00
NNO	Texas Tornado	75.00	150.00
NNO	Ultimate Warrior	30.00	75.00

2015 Mattel WWE Elite Collection Network Spotlight

NNO	The Ringmaster Steve Austin	15.00	30.00
NNO	Big Boss Man	20.00	40.00
NNO	Hunter Hearst Helmsley	15.00	30.00

2016 Mattel WWE Elite Collection Network Spotlight

NNO	Bayley	17.50	35.00
NNO	Roman Reigns	20.00	40.00
NNO	Shawn Michaels	25.00	50.00

2017 Mattel WWE Elite Collection Network Spotlight

NNO	Dean Ambrose	17.50	35.00
NNO	Finn Balor	20.00	40.00
NNO	TJ Perkins	25.00	50.00
NNO	Undertaker	25.00	50.00
NNO	Vince McMahon	15.00	30.00

2019 Mattel WWE Elite Collection Network Spotlight

NNO	Asuka	20.00	40.00
NNO	Diesel	17.50	35.00
NNO	Jinder Mahal	15.00	30.00
NNO	Rey Mysterio	25.00	50.00

2020 Mattel WWE Elite Collection Network Spotlight

NNO	Kurt Angle	25.00	50.00
NNO	Matt Hardy	20.00	40.00
NNO	Ricochet	20.00	40.00
NNO	Wendi Richter	12.50	25.00

2017 Mattel WWE Elite Collection NXT Series 1

NNO	Austin Aries	20.00	40.00
NNO	No Way Jose	30.00	60.00
NNO	Seth Rollins	20.00	40.00

2017 Mattel WWE Elite Collection NXT Series 2

NNO	Asuka	25.00	50.00
NNO	Dash Wilder	17.50	35.00
NNO	Scott Dawson	17.50	35.00
NNO	Shinsuke Nakamura	15.00	30.00

2018 Mattel WWE Elite Collection NXT Series 3

NNO	Alexander Rusev	15.00	30.00
NNO	Bobby Roode	20.00	40.00
NNO	Ember Moon	20.00	40.00
NNO	Roman Reigns	20.00	40.00

2021 Mattel WWE Elite Collection Royal Rumble 2021

NNO	Stone Cold Steve Austin	20.00	40.00
NNO	Titus O'Neil	15.00	30.00
NNO	Ultimate Warrior	30.00	60.00
NNO	Umaga	20.00	40.00

2022 Mattel WWE Elite Collection Royal Rumble 2023

NNO	Brie Bella	15.00	30.00
NNO	Damian Priest	15.00	30.00
NNO	Rey Mysterio (red pants)	20.00	40.00
NNO	Vader	25.00	50.00

2010 Mattel WWE Elite Collection Series 1

NNO	CM Punk	75.00	150.00
NNO	Edge	30.00	75.00
NNO	MVP		
NNO	Rey Mysterio	75.00	150.00
NNO	Undertaker	50.00	100.00

2010 Mattel WWE Elite Collection Series 2

NNO	Batista		
NNO	Matt Hardy		
NNO	R-Truth	30.00	75.00
NNO	Randy Orton	60.00	120.00
NNO	Ted Dibiase	40.00	80.00
NNO	Triple H	30.00	75.00
NNO	Triple H (bottle pack)		

2010 Mattel WWE Elite Collection Series 3

NNO	Christian	60.00	120.00
NNO	Cody Rhodes	30.00	60.00
NNO	John Cena	40.00	80.00
NNO	The Miz	25.00	50.00
NNO	Santino Marella		
NNO	Shawn Michaels	60.00	120.00

2010 Mattel WWE Elite Collection Series 4

NNO	Big Show	25.00	50.00
NNO	Chris Jericho/Blue Gear	40.00	80.00
NNO	Chris Jericho/Purple Gear	50.00	100.00
NNO	Finlay		
NNO	John Morrison/ Bright Red Robe		
NNO	John Morrison/ Dk Red Robe	125.00	250.00
NNO	Kane	60.00	120.00
NNO	Kofi Kingston		

2010 Mattel WWE Elite Collection Series 5

NNO	Chavo Guerrero	25.00	50.00
NNO	Dolph Ziggler	20.00	40.00
NNO	Jack Swagger/No Singlet	20.00	40.00
NNO	Jack Swagger/Singlet	30.00	60.00
NNO	Mark Henry	20.00	40.00
NNO	Rey Mysterio	75.00	150.00
NNO	Vladimir Kozlov/ Jacket Sleeves		
NNO	Vladimir Kozlov/ No Jacket Sleeves		

2010 Mattel WWE Elite Collection Series 6

NNO	Batista	50.00	100.00
NNO	CM Punk	60.00	120.00
NNO	Goldust	30.00	75.00
NNO	JTG	45.00	90.00
NNO	Matt Hardy	50.00	100.00
NNO	Shad	45.00	90.00

2011 Mattel WWE Elite Collection Series 7

NNO	David Hart Smith	25.00	50.00
NNO	Hornswoggle	60.00	120.00
NNO	John Cena	30.00	75.00
NNO	Shawn Michaels	75.00	150.00
NNO	Triple H	30.00	75.00
NNO	Tyson Kidd	25.00	50.00

2011 Mattel WWE Elite Collection Series 8

NNO	Drew McIntyre	30.00	60.00
NNO	Edge	30.00	75.00
NNO	Evan Bourne	50.00	100.00

NNO	Sheamus	25.00	50.00
NNO	Undertaker	30.00	60.00
NNO	William Regal	40.00	80.00

2011 Mattel WWE Elite Collection Series 9

NNO	Kofi Kingston		
NNO	Luke Gallows	25.00	50.00
NNO	The Miz	30.00	75.00
NNO	MVP	60.00	120.00
NNO	Randy Orton	25.00	50.00
NNO	Zack Ryder	25.00	50.00

2011 Mattel WWE Elite Collection Series 10

NNO	Big Show	30.00	75.00
NNO	John Morrison	50.00	100.00
NNO	Kane	50.00	100.00
NNO	R-Truth	25.00	50.00
NNO	Ted Dibiase	30.00	60.00
NNO	Yoshi Tatsu	30.00	75.00

2011 Mattel WWE Elite Collection Series 11

NNO	Christian	30.00	60.00
NNO	CM Punk	50.00	100.00
NNO	John Cena		
NNO	The Miz	40.00	80.00
NNO	Rey Mysterio	60.00	120.00
NNO	Wade Barrett	40.00	80.00

2011 Mattel WWE Elite Collection Series 12

NNO	Alberto Del Rio	15.00	30.00
NNO	Daniel Bryan	20.00	40.00
NNO	Justin Gabriel	30.00	60.00
NNO	Kane FB	50.00	100.00
NNO	Papa Shango FB	25.00	50.00
NNO	Randy Orton	20.00	40.00

2012 Mattel WWE Elite Collection Series 13

NNO	Big Show	25.00	50.00
NNO	Cody Rhodes	45.00	90.00
NNO	Dolph Ziggler	20.00	40.00
NNO	Edge FB	30.00	75.00
NNO	Rey Mysterio	75.00	150.00
NNO	Sheamus	20.00	40.00

2012 Mattel WWE Elite Collection Series 14

NNO	Alberto Del Rio	20.00	40.00
NNO	Big Boss Man FB	30.00	75.00
NNO	John Cena	30.00	75.00
NNO	King Booker FB	25.00	50.00
NNO	The Rock	20.00	40.00
NNO	Undertaker	30.00	60.00

2012 Mattel WWE Elite Collection Series 15

NNO	Evan Bourne	30.00	75.00
NNO	Mark Henry	25.00	50.00
NNO	R-Truth	30.00	75.00
NNO	Rey Mysterio		
NNO	Sin Cara	30.00	60.00
NNO	Yokozuna FB	20.00	40.00

2012 Mattel WWE Elite Collection Series 16

NNO	CM Punk	50.00	100.00
NNO	Diesel FB	30.00	60.00
NNO	Ezekiel Jackson	30.00	75.00
NNO	Heath Slater	20.00	40.00
NNO	Kevin Nash FB	60.00	120.00
NNO	Randy Orton	15.00	30.00
NNO	The Rock	30.00	60.00

2012 Mattel WWE Elite Collection Series 17

NNO	John Cena	20.00	40.00
NNO	Kelly Kelly	30.00	60.00
NNO	Kofi Kingston	20.00	40.00
NNO	Mankind FB	30.00	75.00
NNO	Sheamus	15.00	30.00
NNO	Zack Ryder	30.00	60.00

2012 Mattel WWE Elite Collection Series 18

NNO	Brodus Clay	10.00	20.00
NNO	Jerry Lawler FB	15.00	30.00
NNO	Rey Mysterio	50.00	100.00
NNO	Sin Cara	75.00	150.00
NNO	Undertaker FB	30.00	75.00
NNO	Wade Barrett	15.00	30.00

2013 Mattel WWE Elite Collection Series 19

NNO	Brock Lesnar	20.00	40.00
NNO	Daniel Bryan	20.00	40.00
NNO	Dolph Ziggler	15.00	30.00
NNO	Kane	30.00	60.00
NNO	Miss Elizabeth FB	20.00	40.00
NNO	Shawn Michaels	20.00	40.00

2013 Mattel WWE Elite Collection Series 20

NNO	Chris Jericho	20.00	40.00
NNO	Christian FB	30.00	60.00
NNO	CM Punk	50.00	100.00
NNO	Cody Rhodes	20.00	40.00
NNO	John Cena	25.00	50.00
NNO	Santino Morella	30.00	75.00

2013 Mattel WWE Elite Collection Series 21

NNO	AJ Lee	25.00	50.00
NNO	Alberto Del Rio	15.00	30.00
NNO	Honky Tonk Man FB	25.00	50.00
NNO	Randy Orton	17.50	35.00
NNO	Rey Mysterio	60.00	120.00
NNO	Ryback	15.00	30.00

2013 Mattel WWE Elite Collection Series 22

NNO	Big Show	25.00	50.00
NNO	Damien Sandow	12.50	25.00
NNO	The Giant FB	50.00	100.00
NNO	Kane	20.00	40.00
NNO	The Rock	30.00	60.00
NNO	Tensai	15.00	30.00

2013 Mattel WWE Elite Collection Series 23

NNO	Antonio Cesaro	15.00	30.00
NNO	JBL FB	25.00	50.00
NNO	John Cena	20.00	40.00
NNO	Macho Man Randy Savage	25.00	50.00
NNO	Triple H FB	15.00	30.00
NNO	Undertaker FB	20.00	40.00

2013 Mattel WWE Elite Collection Series 24

NNO	Dolph Ziggler	20.00	40.00
NNO	The Miz	12.50	25.00
NNO	Rey Mysterio	30.00	75.00
NNO	Ryback	15.00	30.00
NNO	Trish Stratus FB	30.00	75.00
NNO	Wade Barrett	15.00	30.00

2013 Mattel WWE Elite Collection Series 25

NNO	Brodus Clay	12.50	25.00
NNO	Bruno Sammartino FB	30.00	60.00
NNO	Dean Ambrose	20.00	40.00
NNO	Seth Rollins	20.00	40.00
NNO	Sheamus	15.00	30.00
NNO	Sin Cara	25.00	50.00

2014 Mattel WWE Elite Collection Series 26

NNO	Big E Langston	12.50	25.00
NNO	Jack Swagger	25.00	50.00
NNO	Mark Henry	20.00	40.00
NNO	Road Dogg FB	25.00	50.00
NNO	Roman Reigns	20.00	40.00
NNO	Ultimate Warrior FB	15.00	30.00

2014 Mattel WWE Elite Collection Series 27

NNO	Billy Gunn FB	25.00	50.00
NNO	Fandango	12.50	25.00
NNO	Kofi Kingston	12.50	25.00
NNO	Rikishi FB/Gear on Side	25.00	50.00
NNO	Rikishi FB/Wearing Gear	20.00	40.00
NNO	Rob Van Dam	30.00	75.00
NNO	Undertaker	20.00	40.00

2014 Mattel WWE Elite Collection Series 28

NNO	Big Show	20.00	40.00
NNO	Bray Wyatt	20.00	40.00
NNO	Daniel Bryan	20.00	40.00
NNO	Demolition Crush FB	20.00	50.00
NNO	John Cena	20.00	40.00
NNO	Triple H	15.00	30.00

2014 Mattel WWE Elite Collection Series 29

NNO	Andre the Giant FB	30.00	60.00
NNO	CM Punk	30.00	75.00
NNO	Damien Sandow	15.00	30.00
NNO	Erick Rowan	20.00	40.00
NNO	Goldust	15.00	30.00
NNO	Luke Harper	20.00	40.00

2014 Mattel WWE Elite Collection Series 30

NNO	Batista	20.00	40.00
NNO	Brock Lesnar	15.00	30.00
NNO	Lex Luger FB	20.00	40.00
NNO	Road Warrior Animal FB	60.00	120.00
NNO	Road Warrior Hawk FB	60.00	120.00
NNO	Ryback	15.00	30.00

2014 Mattel WWE Elite Collection Series 31

NNO	Dean Ambrose	25.00	50.00
NNO	Jey Uso	15.00	30.00
NNO	Jimmy Uso	15.00	30.00
NNO	Kane	30.00	75.00
NNO	The Rock FB	25.00	50.00
NNO	Vader FB	50.00	100.00

2014 Mattel WWE Elite Collection Series 32

NNO	Big E Langston	12.50	25.00
NNO	Cody Rhodes	25.00	50.00
NNO	Daniel Bryan	17.50	35.00
NNO	Mark Henry	20.00	40.00
NNO	Rey Mysterio FB	50.00	100.00
NNO	Sin Cara	40.00	80.00

2015 Mattel WWE Elite Collection Series 33

NNO	Batista	25.00	50.00
NNO	Cesaro	12.50	25.00
NNO	Junkyard Dog FB	15.00	30.00
NNO	Roman Reigns	15.00	30.00
NNO	Seth Rollins	12.50	25.00
NNO	X-Pac FB	20.00	40.00

2015 Mattel WWE Elite Collection Series 34

NNO	Bad News Barrett	12.50	25.00
NNO	Doink the Clown FB	20.00	40.00
NNO	Hulk Hogan	25.00	50.00
NNO	John Cena	20.00	40.00
NNO	Paige	25.00	50.00
NNO	Rusev	12.50	25.00

2015 Mattel WWE Elite Collection Series 35

NNO	Diego	10.00	20.00
NNO	Earthquake FB	17.50	35.00
NNO	Fernando	15.00	30.00
NNO	Luke Harper	20.00	40.00
NNO	Randy Orton	15.00	30.00
NNO	Triple H	12.50	25.00

2015 Mattel WWE Elite Collection Series 36

NNO	Bo Dallas	12.50	25.00
NNO	Bray Wyatt	12.50	25.00
NNO	Dean Ambrose	15.00	30.00
NNO	DDP FB	25.00	50.00
NNO	Goldust	17.50	35.00
NNO	Stardust	20.00	40.00

2015 Mattel WWE Elite Collection Series 37

NNO	Brock Lesnar	15.00	30.00
NNO	Dean Malenko FB	17.50	35.00
NNO	John Cena	15.00	30.00
NNO	The Miz	12.50	25.00
NNO	Seth Rollins	25.00	50.00
NNO	Stephanie McMahon	12.50	25.00

2015 Mattel WWE Elite Collection Series 38

NNO	Adam Rose	10.00	20.00
NNO	Bradshaw FB	15.00	30.00
NNO	Daniel Bryan	30.00	60.00
NNO	Faarooq FB	15.00	30.00
NNO	Macho Man Randy Savage FB	15.00	30.00
NNO	Roman Reigns	20.00	40.00

2015 Mattel WWE Elite Collection Series 39

NNO	British Bulldog FB	15.00	30.00
NNO	Damien Mizdow	10.00	20.00
NNO	Dolph Ziggler	25.00	50.00
NNO	Godfather FB	15.00	30.00
NNO	Sting	20.00	40.00
NNO	Sycho Sid FB	12.50	25.00

2016 Mattel WWE Elite Collection Series 40

NNO	Irwin R. Schyster FB	10.00	20.00
NNO	John Cena	25.00	50.00
NNO	Ravishing Rick Rude FB	15.00	30.00
NNO	Sami Zayn	10.00	20.00
NNO	Tyson Kidd	12.50	25.00
NNO	Umaga FB	12.50	25.00

2016 Mattel WWE Elite Collection Series 41

NNO	123 Kid FB	15.00	30.00
NNO	Dean Ambrose	15.00	30.00
NNO	Finn Balor	15.00	30.00
NNO	Lita FB	12.50	25.00
NNO	Ryback	15.00	30.00
NNO	Terry Funk FB	20.00	40.00

2016 Mattel WWE Elite Collection Series 42

NNO	Kalisto	20.00	40.00
NNO	Nasty Boy Brian Knobbs FB	12.50	25.00
NNO	Nasty Boy Jerry Sags FB	12.50	25.00
NNO	Neville	10.00	20.00
NNO	Triple H	12.50	25.00
NNO	Xavier Woods	10.00	20.00

2016 Mattel WWE Elite Collection Series 43

NNO	Alberto Del Rio	7.50	15.00
NNO	Bret Hart FB	25.00	50.00
NNO	Jim Neidhart FB	12.50	25.00
NNO	Kevin Owens	10.00	20.00
NNO	Kofi Kingston	10.00	20.00
NNO	Samoa Joe	10.00	20.00

2016 Mattel WWE Elite Collection Series 44

NNO	Big E	10.00	20.00
NNO	Braun Strowman	20.00	40.00
NNO	Randy Savage FB	15.00	30.00
NNO	Sasha Banks	15.00	30.00
NNO	Sin Cara	30.00	75.00
NNO	Tugboat FB	10.00	20.00

2016 Mattel WWE Elite Collection Series 45

NNO	Bubba Ray Dudley	25.00	50.00
NNO	D-Von Dudley	25.00	50.00
NNO	Lord Steven Regal FB	12.50	25.00
NNO	Narcissist Lex Luger FB	10.00	20.00
NNO	Roman Reigns	15.00	30.00
NNO	Seth Rollins	20.00	40.00

2016 Mattel WWE Elite Collection Series 46

NNO	Booker T FB	15.00	30.00
NNO	Finn Balor	12.50	25.00
NNO	John Cena	12.50	25.00
NNO	Rusev	10.00	20.00
NNO	Sheamus	10.00	20.00
NNO	Stevie Ray FB	12.50	25.00

2016 Mattel WWE Elite Collection Series 47A

NNO	AJ Styles	15.00	30.00
NNO	Asuka	20.00	40.00
NNO	Big Boss Man FB	12.50	25.00
NNO	Cesaro	15.00	30.00
NNO	Kevin Owens	10.00	20.00
NNO	Tatanka FB	12.50	25.00

2016 Mattel WWE Elite Collection Series 47B

NNO	Brian Pillman FB		
NNO	Demon Kane		
NNO	Goldust FB		
NNO	Konnor		
NNO	The Rock FB		
NNO	Viktor		

2017 Mattel WWE Elite Collection Series 48

NNO	Boogeyman FB	25.00	50.00
NNO	Cactus Jack FB	25.00	50.00
NNO	Dean Ambrose	20.00	40.00
NNO	Dolph Ziggler	20.00	40.00
NNO	Erick Rowan	15.00	30.00
NNO	Kalisto	25.00	50.00

2017 Mattel WWE Elite Collection Series 49

NNO	Apollo Crews	15.00	30.00
NNO	Becky Lynch	12.50	25.00
NNO	Big Cass	10.00	20.00
NNO	Brutus Beefcake FB	10.00	20.00
NNO	Enzo Amore	10.00	20.00
NNO	Randy Orton FB	20.00	40.00

2017 Mattel WWE Elite Collection Series 50

NNO	Baron Corbin	7.50	15.00
NNO	John Cena	12.50	25.00
NNO	Rhyno	10.00	20.00
NNO	Shane McMahon	15.00	30.00
NNO	Stephanie McMahon	15.00	30.00
NNO	Warlord FB	12.50	25.00

2017 Mattel WWE Elite Collection Series 51

NNO	AJ Styles	12.50	25.00
NNO	Berzerker FB	7.50	15.00
NNO	Mankind FB	12.50	25.00
NNO	Roman Reigns	12.50	25.00
NNO	Sami Zayn	7.50	15.00
NNO	Scott Hall FB	12.50	25.00

2017 Mattel WWE Elite Collection Series 52

NNO	Braun Strowman	20.00	40.00
NNO	D'Lo Brown FB	12.50	25.00
NNO	Ken Shamrock FB	12.50	25.00
NNO	Kofi Kingston	10.00	20.00
NNO	Seth Rollins	12.50	25.00
NNO	Xavier Woods	7.50	15.00

2017 Mattel WWE Elite Collection Series 53

NNO	Alexa Bliss	15.00	30.00
NNO	Big E	10.00	20.00
NNO	Chris Jericho	10.00	20.00
NNO	Heath Slater	12.50	25.00
NNO	Kevin Owens	10.00	20.00
NNO	The Miz	10.00	20.00

2017 Mattel WWE Elite Collection Series 54

NNO	Bray Wyatt	15.00	30.00
NNO	Charlotte Flair	15.00	30.00
NNO	Jey Uso	12.50	25.00
NNO	Jimmy Uso	12.50	25.00
NNO	John Cena	15.00	30.00
NNO	Rich Swann	15.00	30.00

2017 Mattel WWE Elite Collection Series 55

NNO	Big Cass	10.00	20.00
NNO	Brock Lesnar	25.00	50.00
NNO	Enzo Amore	30.00	60.00
NNO	James Ellsworth	15.00	30.00
NNO	Neville FB	25.00	50.00
NNO	Undertaker	25.00	50.00

2017 Mattel WWE Elite Collection Series 56

NNO	AJ Styles	15.00	30.00
NNO	Jack Gallagher	10.00	20.00
NNO	Karl Anderson	15.00	30.00
NNO	Luke Gallows	15.00	30.00
NNO	Roman Reigns	20.00	40.00
NNO	Samoa Joe	10.00	20.00

2017 Mattel WWE Elite Collection Series 57

NNO	Baron Corbin	10.00	20.00
NNO	Jeff Hardy	30.00	75.00
NNO	Scotty 2 Hotty	12.50	25.00
NNO	Seth Rollins	15.00	30.00
NNO	Shinsuke Nakamura	15.00	30.00
NNO	Tye Dillinger	15.00	30.00

2017 Mattel WWE Elite Collection Series 58

NNO	Braun Strowman	15.00	30.00
NNO	Cesaro	12.50	25.00
NNO	Dean Ambrose	12.50	25.00
NNO	Matt Hardy	25.00	50.00
NNO	Mickie James	17.50	35.00
NNO	Sheamus	12.50	25.00

2017 Mattel WWE Elite Collection Series 59

NNO	Chad Gable	15.00	30.00
NNO	Finn Balor	15.00	30.00
NNO	Jason Jordan	15.00	30.00
NNO	Kurt Angle	12.50	25.00
NNO	The Miz	12.50	25.00
NNO	Zack Ryder	10.00	20.00

2017 Mattel WWE Elite Collection Series 60

NNO	Andre/Giant Machine	20.00	40.00
NNO	Elias	20.00	40.00
NNO	John Cena	15.00	30.00
NNO	Kofi Kingston	12.50	25.00
NNO	Triple H	20.00	40.00
NNO	Xavier Woods	12.50	25.00

2018 Mattel WWE Elite Collection Series 61

NNO	AJ Styles	15.00	30.00
NNO	Big E	12.50	25.00
NNO	Fandango	12.50	25.00
NNO	Kevin Owens	12.50	25.00
NNO	Shane McMahon	15.00	30.00
NNO	Tyler Breeze	12.50	25.00

2018 Mattel WWE Elite Collection Series 62

NNO	Roman Reigns	17.50	35.00
NNO	Braun Strowman	20.00	40.00
NNO	Dude Love	15.00	30.00
NNO	Akam	12.50	25.00
NNO	Rezar	12.50	25.00
NNO	Sting/Surfer Gear	17.50	35.00

2018 Mattel WWE Elite Collection Series 63

NNO	Dean Ambrose	12.50	25.00
NNO	Dusty Rhodes	17.50	35.00
NNO	Kane	12.50	25.00
NNO	Sami Zayn	12.50	25.00
NNO	Shelton Benjamin	20.00	40.00
NNO	Shelton Benjamin Gold Tights CH		
NNO	Shinsuke Nakamura	12.50	25.00

2018 Mattel WWE Elite Collection Series 64

NNO	Curt Hawkins	25.00	50.00
NNO	Curt Hawkins Black Gear CH		
NNO	Jey Uso	15.00	30.00
NNO	Jimmy Uso	15.00	30.00
NNO	John Cena	20.00	40.00
NNO	Samoa Joe	20.00	40.00
NNO	Seth Rollins	25.00	50.00

2018 Mattel WWE Elite Collection Series 65

NNO	Aiden English		
NNO	Aiden English Black Scarf CH		
NNO	Eric Young	17.50	35.00
NNO	Nia Jax	15.00	30.00
NNO	Roman Reigns	15.00	30.00
NNO	Ronda Rousey	20.00	40.00
NNO	Rusev		

2018 Mattel WWE Elite Collection Series 66

NNO	AJ Styles	20.00	40.00
NNO	Erick Rowan	15.00	30.00
NNO	Kevin Owens	10.00	20.00
NNO	Kevin Owens (KO Mania) (CHASE)		
NNO	Kurt Angle	15.00	30.00
NNO	Luke Harper	15.00	30.00
NNO	Nikki Cross	25.00	50.00

2019 Mattel WWE Elite Collection Series 67

NNO	Cedric Alexander FP	12.50	25.00
NNO	Jeff Hardy	12.50	25.00
NNO	Jeff Hardy USA Face Paint CH		

NNO Randy Orton 10.00 20.00
NNO Rey Mysterio 15.00 30.00
NNO Shayna Baszler FP 15.00 30.00
NNO Velveteen Dream FP 12.50 25.00

2019 Mattel WWE Elite Collection Series 68

NNO Braun Strowman 12.50 25.00
NNO Brie Bella 12.50 25.00
NNO Daniel Bryan 12.50 25.00
NNO King Mabel FP 10.00 20.00
NNO King Mabel FP Lightning CH
NNO Roman Reigns 12.50 25.00
NNO Undertaker 20.00 40.00

2019 Mattel WWE Elite Collection Series 69

NNO Bobby Lashley 10.00 20.00
NNO Miz 10.00 20.00
NNO Mustafa Ali 12.50 25.00
NNO Mustafa Ali (orange pants) (CHASE)
NNO Rey Mysterio 12.50 25.00
NNO Ricochet 15.00 30.00
NNO Tommaso Ciampa 12.50 25.00

2019 Mattel WWE Elite Collection Series 70

NNO Demon Finn Balor 15.00 30.00
NNO Dolph Ziggler 12.50 25.00
NNO Dolph Ziggler Pink CH 25.00 50.00
NNO EC3 10.00 20.00
NNO Johnny Gargano 15.00 30.00
NNO Seth Rollins/Shield Fatigues 15.00 30.00
NNO Vince McMahon 15.00 30.00

2019 Mattel WWE Elite Collection Series 71

NNO Adam Cole
NNO Big Show
NNO Drew McIntyre
NNO Jeff Hardy
NNO John Cena
NNO Nikki Bella
NNO Nikki Bella Red Gear CH

2019 Mattel WWE Elite Collection Series 72

NNO Batista
NNO Becky Lynch
NNO Buddy Murphy
NNO Buddy Murphy Black Shorts CH
NNO Rey Mysterio
NNO Roderick Strong
NNO Velveteen Dream

2019 Mattel WWE Elite Collection Series 73

NNO Aleister Black
NNO Daniel Bryan
NNO Elias
NNO Gran Metalik
NNO Gran Metalik Black Shirt CH
NNO Kairi Sane
NNO Triple H

2019 Mattel WWE Elite Collection Series 74

NNO AJ Styles
NNO Andrade
NNO Finn Balor
NNO Goldberg
NNO Lince Dorado
NNO Lince Dorado Gold CH
NNO Natalya

2020 Mattel WWE Elite Collection Series 75

NNO Hurricane 20.00 40.00
NNO Hurricane White Boots CH 30.00 60.00
NNO Jeff Hardy 15.00 30.00
NNO Kalisto 30.00 60.00
NNO Mandy Rose 20.00 40.00
NNO Pete Dunne 20.00 40.00
NNO Seth Rollins 20.00 40.00

2020 Mattel WWE Elite Collection Series 76

NNO Braun Strowman 20.00 40.00
NNO Christian Black Shirt CH 20.00 40.00
NNO Christian White Shirt 20.00 40.00
NNO John Cena 25.00 50.00
NNO Lacey Evans 20.00 40.00
NNO Tucker 15.00 30.00

2020 Mattel WWE Elite Collection Series 77

NNO AJ Styles 20.00 40.00
NNO Classy Freddie Blassie RSC 30.00 60.00
NNO The Fiend Bray Wyatt 25.00 50.00
NNO Miss Elizabeth 20.00 40.00
NNO Ravishing Rick Rude Ult. Warrior Tights 20.00 40.00
NNO Ravishing Rick Rude Yellow Tights CH 30.00 60.00
NNO Ronda Rousey 15.00 30.00
NNO Viscera 20.00 40.00

2020 Mattel WWE Elite Collection Series 78

NNO Drake Maverick 15.00 30.00
NNO Kofi Kingston 20.00 40.00
NNO Matt Riddle 25.00 50.00
NNO Naomi 15.00 30.00
NNO Naomi Glow CH 20.00 40.00
NNO Randy Orton 25.00 50.00
NNO R-Truth 15.00 30.00
NNO Superstar Billy Graham TAR 20.00 40.00

2020 Mattel WWE Elite Collection Series 79

NNO Big E 15.00 30.00
NNO Bobby Fish 20.00 40.00
NNO Bobby Fish Black Gear CH 25.00 50.00
NNO Daniel Bryan 15.00 30.00
NNO Io Shirai 20.00 40.00
NNO Roman Reigns 15.00 30.00
NNO Xavier Woods 15.00 30.00

2020 Mattel WWE Elite Collection Series 80

NNO Bayley 25.00 50.00
NNO Erik 15.00 30.00
NNO Ivar 15.00 30.00
NNO Kevin Owens 20.00 40.00
NNO Kyle O'Reilly 20.00 40.00
NNO Kyle O'Reilly Black Gear CH 25.00 50.00
NNO Ricochet 15.00 30.00
NNO Rocky Johnson TAR 20.00 40.00

2020 Mattel WWE Elite Collection Series 81

NNO Angelo Dawkins 15.00 30.00
NNO Bianca Belair 30.00 60.00
NNO Mae Young WM 25.00 50.00
NNO Montez Ford 15.00 30.00
NNO The Rock 20.00 40.00
NNO Shinsuke Nakamura 20.00 40.00
NNO S.Nakamura Black CH 25.00 50.00
NNO Stunning Steve Austin 25.00 50.00

2021 Mattel WWE Elite Collection Series 82

NNO Alexa Bliss 20.00 40.00
NNO Finn Balor 15.00 30.00
NNO Jerry The King Lawler 15.00 30.00
NNO John Morrison 15.00 30.00
NNO Keith Lee 15.00 30.00
NNO Keith Lee White Gear CH 20.00 40.00
NNO Rob Gronkowski 40.00 80.00

2021 Mattel WWE Elite Collection Series 83

NNO Drew McIntyre 15.00 30.00
NNO Dusty Rhodes 15.00 30.00
NNO Edge 20.00 40.00
NNO Edge Black Gear CH 20.00 40.00
NNO King Baron Corbin 15.00 30.00
NNO Michael PS Hayes TAR 20.00 40.00
NNO Sasha Banks 20.00 40.00

2021 Mattel WWE Elite Collection Series 84

NNO Angel Garza 15.00 30.00
NNO Jeff Hardy 15.00 30.00
NNO Jeff Hardy CH 20.00 40.00
NNO Murphy 15.00 30.00
NNO Rhea Ripley 15.00 30.00
NNO Roman Reigns 25.00 50.00
NNO Sheamus 15.00 30.00

2021 Mattel WWE Elite Collection Series 85

NNO Aleister Black 15.00 30.00
NNO Aleister Black CH 30.00 60.00
NNO Becky Lynch 15.00 30.00
NNO Bray Wyatt 20.00 40.00
NNO Karrion Kross 25.00 50.00
NNO Liv Morgan 20.00 40.00
NNO Undertaker 25.00 50.00

2021 Mattel WWE Elite Collection Series 86

NNO Carmella 20.00 40.00
NNO The Fiend Bray Wyatt 25.00 50.00
NNO The Miz 20.00 40.00
NNO Seth Rollins 20.00 40.00
NNO Sid Justice 20.00 40.00
NNO Triple H Purple 15.00 30.00
NNO Triple H Red CH 20.00 40.00

2021 Mattel WWE Elite Collection Series 87

NNO Apollo Crews (blue trunks) 15.00 30.00
NNO Apollo Crews (white trunks) 20.00 40.00
(CHASE)
NNO Asuka 15.00 30.00
NNO Braun Strowman 15.00 30.00
NNO Candice LeRae 15.00 30.00
NNO Otis 12.50 25.00
NNO Santos Escobar 12.50 25.00

2021 Mattel WWE Elite Collection Series 88

NNO Kushida 12.50 25.00
NNO Matt Riddle 25.00 50.00
NNO MVP 20.00 40.00
NNO Rey Mysterio 20.00 40.00
NNO Trish Stratus 15.00 30.00
NNO Trish Stratus (Canadian gear) 25.00 50.00
(CHASE)

2021 Mattel WWE Elite Collection Series 89

NNO Bobby Lashley 15.00 30.00
NNO Damian Priest 20.00 40.00
NNO Dominik Mysterio 30.00 60.00
NNO Drew McIntyre 15.00 30.00
NNO Nia Jax 12.50 25.00
NNO Nia Jax (purple gear) 15.00 30.00
(CHASE)
NNO Sgt. Slaughter 20.00 40.00

2021 Mattel WWE Elite Collection Series 90

NNO Big Bossman 15.00 30.00
NNO Big Bossman (black gear) 25.00 50.00
(CHASE)
NNO Bronson Reed 12.50 25.00
NNO Jey Uso 17.50 35.00
NNO Mustafa Ali 15.00 30.00
NNO Randy Orton 15.00 30.00

2022 Mattel WWE Elite Collection Series 91

NNO Austin Theory 20.00 40.00
NNO Bianca Belair 12.50 25.00
NNO Hulk Hogan 15.00 30.00
NNO Kevin Owens 15.00 30.00
NNO Rob Van Dam 12.50 25.00
NNO Rob Van Dam
(CHASE)
NNO Sami Zayn 20.00 40.00

2022 Mattel WWE Elite Collection Series 92

NNO Adam Cole 10.00 20.00
NNO Adam Cole (camo trunks) 20.00 40.00
(CHASE)
NNO Burnt Fiend 15.00 30.00
NNO Charlotte Flair 12.50 25.00
NNO Rey Mysterio 12.50 25.00
NNO Ric Flair 12.50 25.00
NNO Scarlett 15.00 30.00

2022 Mattel WWE Elite Collection Series 93

NNO Cesaro 12.50 25.00
NNO Karrion Kross 12.50 25.00
NNO Raquel Gonzalez 12.50 25.00
NNO Ricky Steamboat (white gear) 12.50 25.00
NNO Ricky Steamboat (yellow year) 20.00 40.00
(CHASE)

NNO	Seth Rollins	15.00	30.00
NNO	T-Bar	12.50	25.00

2022 Mattel WWE Elite Collection Series 94

NNO	Bret Hart (black tights) (CHASE)	25.00	50.00
NNO	Bret Hart (pink tights)	12.50	25.00
NNO	British Bulldog	20.00	40.00
NNO	Edge	15.00	30.00
NNO	Mace	12.50	25.00
NNO	Nash Carter	15.00	30.00
NNO	Stephanie McMahon	15.00	30.00
NNO	Wes Lee	12.50	25.00

2022 Mattel WWE Elite Collection Series 95

NNO	Big E	12.50	25.00
NNO	Bobby Lashley	15.00	30.00
NNO	Eddie Guerrero (black gear) (CHASE)	25.00	50.00
NNO	Eddie Guerrero (green gear)	15.00	30.00
NNO	Jimmy Uso	30.00	60.00
NNO	John Cena	20.00	40.00
NNO	Shotzi	20.00	40.00

2022 Mattel WWE Elite Collection Series 96

NNO	Brock Lesnar	15.00	30.00
NNO	Doudrop (blue gear)	12.50	25.00
NNO	Doudrop (metallic green) (CHASE)	20.00	40.00
NNO	Hulk Hogan	12.50	25.00
NNO	Ilja Dragunov	12.50	25.00
NNO	Kofi Kingston	15.00	30.00
NNO	Shinsuke Nakamura	12.50	25.00

2022 Mattel WWE Elite Collection Series 97

NNO	Alexa Bliss	20.00	40.00
NNO	Chainsaw Charlie	15.00	30.00
NNO	Omos	12.50	25.00
NNO	Ronda Rousey	10.00	20.00
NNO	Sheamus	12.50	25.00
NNO	Xavier Woods (red He-Man gear) (CHASE)	20.00	40.00
NNO	Xavier Woods (white gear)	12.50	25.00

2022 Mattel WWE Elite Collection Series 98

NNO	Big E	12.50	25.00
NNO	Demon Finn Balor	20.00	40.00
NNO	Faarooq	25.00	50.00
NNO	Mandy Rose	20.00	40.00
NNO	Randy Orton	12.50	25.00
NNO	Rick Boogs (grey tights)	15.00	30.00
NNO	Rick Boogs (red tights) (CHASE)	20.00	40.00

2023 Mattel WWE Elite Collection Series 99

NNO	Boogeyman		
NNO	Boogeyman (red head) (CHASE)		
NNO	Brock Lesnar		
NNO	Happy Corbin		
NNO	Matt Riddle		
NNO	Queen Zelina		
NNO	Seth Rollins		

2023 Mattel WWE Elite Collection Series 100

NNO	Andre the Giant		
NNO	Becky Lynch		
NNO	John Cena		
NNO	Rey Mysterio		
NNO	The Rock		
NNO	Stunning Steve Austin		

2023 Mattel WWE Elite Collection Series 101

NNO	Cody Rhodes		
NNO	Johnny Knoxville		
NNO	Kevin Owens as Stone Cold		
NNO	Mr. America		
NNO	Ricochet		
NNO	Sonya Deville		

2018 Mattel WWE Elite Collection SummerSlam 2018

NNO	Dean Ambrose	20.00	40.00
NNO	Edge	12.50	25.00
NNO	Matt Hardy	10.00	20.00
NNO	Seth Rollins	15.00	30.00

2022 Mattel WWE Elite Collection SummerSlam 2022

NNO	Randy Orton	20.00	40.00
NNO	Rey Mysterio	20.00	40.00
NNO	Sensational Sherri	15.00	30.00
NNO	Shawn Michaels	15.00	30.00

2019 Mattel WWE Elite Collection Survivor Series

NNO	Alicia Fox		
NNO	Don Muraco		
NNO	Jeff Hardy		
NNO	Shinsuke Nakamura		

2021 Mattel WWE Elite Collection Survivor Series 2021

NNO	Bayley	20.00	40.00
NNO	Bret "Hit Man" Hart	25.00	50.00
NNO	Hulk Hogan	25.00	50.00
NNO	Keith Lee	20.00	40.00

2022 Mattel WWE Elite Collection Survivor Series 2022

NNO	AJ Styles	20.00	40.00
NNO	Becky Lynch	15.00	30.00
NNO	Drew McIntyre	15.00	30.00
NNO	Ultimate Warrior	20.00	40.00

2017 Mattel WWE Elite Collection Then Now Forever 3-Packs

NNO	Lex Luger/Randy Savage/Sting	30.00	60.00
NNO	The Shield - Seth Rollins/Dean Ambrose/Roman Reigns	75.00	150.00

2016 Mattel WWE Elite Collection Then Now Forever Series 1

NNO	Bam Bam Bigelow FB	25.00	50.00
NNO	Rusev	15.00	30.00
NNO	The Rock FB	20.00	40.00
NNO	Tyler Breeze	15.00	30.00

2017 Mattel WWE Elite Collection Then Now Forever Series 2

NNO	Earthquake FB	15.00	30.00
NNO	Macho Man Randy Savage FB	17.50	35.00
NNO	Sami Zayn	7.50	15.00
NNO	Typhoon FB	15.00	30.00

2017 Mattel WWE Elite Collection Then Now Forever Series 3

NNO	Chad Gable	12.50	25.00
NNO	Jason Jordan	10.00	20.00
NNO	Miss Elizabeth	15.00	30.00
NNO	Seth Rollins	12.50	25.00

2020 Mattel WWE Elite Collection Top Picks 2020

NNO	Braun Strowman	20.00	40.00
NNO	Ricochet	20.00	40.00
NNO	Roman Reigns	20.00	40.00
NNO	Seth Rollins	20.00	40.00

2021 Mattel WWE Elite Collection Top Picks 2021

NNO	Drew McIntyre	15.00	30.00
NNO	The Fiend Bray Wyatt	20.00	40.00
NNO	Kofi Kingston	12.50	25.00
NNO	Roman Reigns	12.50	25.00

2021 Mattel WWE Elite Collection Top Picks 2022

NNO	Drew McIntyre	15.00	30.00
NNO	John Cena	17.50	35.00
NNO	Rey Mysterio	25.00	50.00
NNO	Roman Reigns	15.00	30.00

2021 Mattel WWE Elite Collection Top Picks 2023

NNO	Rey Mysterio		
NNO	The Rock		
NNO	Undertaker		

2022 Mattel WWE Elite Collection Top Picks 2023 Wave 2

NNO	Rey Mysterio	15.00	30.00
NNO	Roman Reigns	15.00	30.00
NNO	Seth Rollins	12.50	25.00

2018 Mattel WWE Elite Collection Top Talent 2018

NNO	AJ Styles	20.00	40.00
NNO	Braun Strowman	15.00	30.00
NNO	Finn Balor	15.00	30.00
NNO	Seth Rollins	15.00	30.00

2019 Mattel WWE Elite Collection Top Talent 2019

NNO	AJ Styles	15.00	30.00
NNO	Braun Strowman	12.50	25.00
NNO	Finn Balor	12.50	25.00
NNO	Seth Rollins	10.00	20.00

2021 Mattel WWE Elite Collection Top Talent 2022

NNO	Goldberg	8.00	20.00
NNO	Jeff Hardy	12.00	30.00
NNO	Roman Reigns	12.00	30.00

2022 Mattel WWE Elite Collection Top Talent 2023

NNO	Drew McIntyre		
NNO	John Cena		
NNO	Randy Orton		
NNO	Rey Mysterio (gray)		

2017 Mattel WWE Elite Collection Women's Division

NNO	Alexa Bliss	20.00	40.00
NNO	Becky Lynch	20.00	40.00
NNO	Maryse	15.00	30.00
NNO	Sasha Banks	17.50	35.00

2010 Mattel WWE Elite Collection WrestleMania 26

NNO	Jack Swagger	25.00	50.00
NNO	Rey Mysterio	30.00	60.00
NNO	Triple H		
NNO	Undertaker	30.00	60.00

2011 Mattel WWE Elite Collection WrestleMania 27

NNO	Kofi Kingston	17.50	35.00
NNO	The Miz	20.00	40.00
NNO	The Rock	30.00	75.00
NNO	Stone Cold Steve Austin	30.00	60.00
NNO	Undertaker	30.00	75.00

2014 Mattel WWE Elite Collection WrestleMania 30 Heritage

NNO	Bret Hart	25.00	50.00
NNO	Shawn Michaels	30.00	60.00

2015 Mattel WWE Elite Collection WrestleMania 31 Heritage

NNO	Kane	30.00	75.00
NNO	Undertaker	25.00	50.00

2016 Mattel WWE Elite Collection WrestleMania 32 Heritage

NNO	Brock Lesnar	20.00	40.00
NNO	Undertaker	20.00	40.00

2017 Mattel WWE Elite Collection WrestleMania 33 Heritage

NNO	Shawn Michaels	25.00	50.00
NNO	Triple H	15.00	30.00

2018 Mattel WWE Elite Collection WrestleMania 34 Heritage

NNO	Brutus Beefcake FB	7.50	15.00
NNO	John Cena	12.50	25.00
NNO	Kevin Owens	10.00	20.00
NNO	Randy Orton	20.00	40.00

2018 Mattel WWE Elite Collection WrestleMania 35 Heritage

NNO	Sasha Banks	15.00	30.00
NNO	Scott Hall	15.00	30.00
NNO	Triple H	12.50	25.00
NNO	Undertaker	17.50	35.00

2020 Mattel WWE Elite Collection WrestleMania 36 Heritage

NNO	Booker T	20.00	40.00
NNO	Kofi Kingston	15.00	30.00

NNO Mick Foley 20.00 40.00
NNO Woken Matt Hardy 12.50 25.00

2021 Mattel WWE Elite Collection WrestleMania 37 Heritage

NNO Chyna 12.50 25.00
NNO Edge 20.00 40.00
NNO Goldberg 15.00 30.00
NNO Shawn Michaels 30.00 60.00

2021 Mattel WWE Elite Collection WrestleMania 37 Heritage (loose)

NNO Paul Ellering w/Rocco (Build-A-Figure)

2021 Mattel WWE Elite Collection WrestleMania 38 Heritage

NNO AJ Styles 15.00 30.00
NNO Bret "Hit Man" Hart 15.00 30.00
NNO Shawn Michaels 12.50 25.00
NNO Stone Cold Steve Austin 15.00 30.00

2021 Mattel WWE Elite Collection WrestleMania 38 Heritage (loose)

NNO Vince McMahon (Build-A-Figure)

2022 Mattel WWE Elite Collection WrestleMania 39

NNO Dusty Rhodes 20.00 40.00
NNO Hollywood Hulk Hogan 25.00 50.00
NNO Macho King Randy Savage 25.00 50.00
NNO The Rock 30.00 60.00

2011 Mattel WWE Elite Collection WWE All-Stars 2-Packs

NNO Jake The Snake Roberts vs. Randy Orton 60.00 120.00
NNO Macho Man Randy Savage vs. John Morrison 50.00 100.00
NNO Stone Cold Steve Austin vs. CM Punk 125.00 250.00

2012 Mattel WWE Fan Central

NNO Big Show
NNO John Cena
NNO Kane
NNO Kofi Kingston

2014 Mattel WWE Fan Central

NNO Daniel Bryan 30.00 60.00
NNO The Rock

2014-15 Mattel WWE Fan Central

NNO Dean Ambrose 12.50 25.00
NNO John Cena 10.00 20.00
NNO Randy Orton 10.00 20.00

2015 Mattel WWE Fan Central

NNO Bad News Barrett
NNO Daniel Bryan
NNO Ultimate Warrior

2016 Mattel WWE Fan Central

NNO Finn Balor 10.00 20.00
NNO John Cena 7.50 15.00
NNO Ryback 7.50 15.00
NNO Triple H 6.00 12.00

2018 Mattel WWE Fan Central

NNO Finn Balor 12.50 25.00
NNO Kevin Nash 15.00 30.00
NNO Randy Orton 10.00 20.00
NNO Rusev 7.50 15.00

2018 Mattel WWE Flashback Series 1

NNO Cowboy Bob Orton 7.50 15.00
NNO The Million Dollar Man 7.50 15.00
NNO Ravishing Rick Rude 7.50 15.00
NNO Sgt. Slaughter 10.00 20.00

2018 Mattel WWE Flashback Series 2

NNO Booker T 12.50 25.00
NNO Lex Luger 10.00 20.00
NNO Ric Flair 12.50 25.00
NNO Sting 15.00 30.00

2010-11 Mattel WWE Flex Force

NNO R-Truth
NNO Shawn Michaels (flip kickin')
NNO Shawn Michaels (hook throwin')
NNO Sheamus
NNO Triple H
NNO Undertaker (fist poundin' w/belt) (Toys R Us Exclusive)
NNO Undertaker (fist poundin')
NNO Undertaker (fist poundin') (card variant)
NNO Batista
NNO Big Show
NNO Big Show (card variant)
NNO Chris Jericho
NNO CM Punk (back flippin')
NNO CM Punk (hook throwin' w/belt) (Toys R Us Exclusive)
NNO CM Punk (hook throwin')
NNO CM Punk (super jumpin')
NNO Edge
NNO Evan Bourne (back flippin')
NNO Evan Bourne (flip kickin')
NNO Jack Swagger
NNO John Cena (body slammin')
NNO John Cena (fist poundin' w/belt) (Toys R Us Exclusive)
NNO John Cena (fist poundin')
NNO John Cena (hook throwin')
NNO John Cena (hook throwin') (card variant)
NNO John Morrison (flip kickin')
NNO John Morrison (super jumpin')
NNO Kane
NNO Kofi Kingston
NNO Matt Hardy
NNO Matt Hardy (w/belt) (Toys R Us Exclusive)
NNO Miz (back flippin')
NNO Miz (hook throwin')
NNO Randy Orton (fist poundin')
NNO Randy Orton (flip kickin')
NNO Randy Orton (hook throwin')
NNO Rey Mysterio (fist poundin')
NNO Rey Mysterio (flip kickin' green)
NNO Rey Mysterio (flip kickin' red)
NNO Rey Mysterio (flip kickin' yellow w/belt) (Toys R Us Exclusive)
NNO Rey Mysterio (flip kickin' yellow)
NNO Rey Mysterio (super jumpin')

2011-12 Mattel WWE Flex Force

NNO Alberto Del Rio
NNO Big Show
NNO Christian
NNO Evan Bourne
NNO John Cena (body slammin')
NNO John Cena (hook throwin')
NNO Kofi Kingston
NNO Randy Orton (flip kickin')
NNO Randy Orton (scissor kickin')
NNO Rey Mysterio (super jumpin')
NNO Rey Mysterio (swing kickin')
NNO The Rock
NNO Sheamus
NNO Sin Cara
NNO Wade Barrett

2010 Mattel WWE Flex Force Big Talkin'

NNO CM Punk
NNO MVP
NNO Randy Orton
NNO Triple H

2011 Mattel WWE Flex Force Champions Series 1

NNO John Cena vs. Sheamus
NNO The Miz vs. R-Truth
NNO Randy Orton vs. Rey Mysterio

2012 Mattel WWE Flex Force Champions Series 2

NNO Alberto Del Rio vs. Rey Mysterio
NNO John Cena vs. Undertaker
NNO Randy Orton vs. Kane
NNO Sheamus vs. Kofi Kingston

2010 Mattel WWE Flex Force Deluxe

NNO CM Punk
NNO John Cena
NNO Matt Hardy
NNO Rey Mysterio
NNO Undertaker

2010 Mattel WWE Flex Force DVD Heroes

NNO CM Punk
NNO John Cena
NNO John Morrison
NNO Rey Mysterio

2011-12 Mattel WWE Flex Force Lightning

NNO Big Show
NNO Evan Bourne
NNO John Cena (fist poundin')
NNO John Cena (hook throwin')
NNO Kane
NNO Kofi Kingston
NNO The Miz
NNO Randy Orton
NNO Rey Mysterio (blue)
NNO Rey Mysterio (red)
NNO Sheamus
NNO Sin Cara

2010 Mattel WWE Flex Force Playsets

NNO Breakdown Brawl Ring
NNO Breakdown Brawl Ring (w/Big Show) (Walmart Exclusive)
NNO Colossal Crashdown Arena
NNO Launchin' Entrance Ring

2011 Mattel WWE Flex Force Playsets

NNO High Flyin' Fury
NNO Money in the Bank Ring

2012 Mattel WWE Flex Force Playsets

NNO Tornado Takedown Ring

2010 Mattel WWE Flex Force Smash Scenes

NNO CM Punk
NNO John Cena (body slammin')
NNO John Cena (fist poundin')
NNO Matt Hardy
NNO Randy Orton
NNO Rey Mysterio

2018 Mattel WWE Flextremes

NNO Finn Balor
NNO John Cena
NNO The Rock
NNO Roman Reigns

2018 Mattel WWE Flextremes 4-Pack

NNO Cena/Rock/Balor/Reigns 15.00 30.00

2011 Mattel WWE Heritage Series

NNO CM Punk
NNO John Cena
NNO Kane
NNO Melina
NNO Randy Orton
NNO Triple H

2011-12 Mattel WWE Legends Mattyshop Exclusives

NNO Andre the Giant 125.00 250.00
NNO Arn Anderson 100.00 200.00
NNO Diamond Dallas Page 60.00 120.00
NNO King Kong Bundy 125.00 250.00
NNO The Rockers (Jannetty/Michaels) 200.00 350.00
NNO Tully Blanchard 100.00 200.00

2017 Mattel WWE Make-A-Wish Foundation

NNO John Cena 15.00 30.00

2015 Mattel WWE Mighty Minis Series 1

NNO Bret Hart (blue)
NNO Bret Hart (pink)
NNO Daniel Bryan 2.50 5.00
NNO Dolph Ziggler 2.00 4.00
NNO John Cena 3.00 6.00
NNO Roman Reigns 2.00 4.00
NNO Rusev 2.50 5.00
NNO Seth Rollins 2.00 4.00
NNO Ted DiBiase 2.00 4.00
NNO Undertaker 3.00 6.00

2015 Mattel WWE Mighty Minis Series 2

NNO Brock Lesnar		
NNO Dean Ambrose		
NNO Goldust		
NNO John Cena		
NNO Kane	2.00	4.00
NNO The Rock	4.00	8.00
NNO Stone Cold Steve Austin		
NNO Triple H		
NNO Ultimate Warrior (orange)		
NNO Ultimate Warrior (white)		

2016 Mattel WWE Mighty Minis SDCC Exclusive

NNO Dean Ambrose	5.00	10.00

2017 Mattel WWE Monsters

NNO Asuka as The Phantom	7.50	15.00
NNO Braun Strowman as Frankenstein	12.50	25.00
NNO Chris Jericho as The Mummy	7.50	15.00
NNO Jake Roberts as The Creature	12.50	25.00
NNO Roman Reigns as The Werewolf	10.00	20.00
NNO Undertaker as The Vampire	12.50	25.00

2018 Mattel WWE M.U.S.C.L.E. SDCC Exclusives

NNO Andre the Giant		
NNO Hacksaw Jim Duggan		
NNO Iron Sheik		
NNO Jake The Snake Roberts		
NNO Junkyard Dog		
NNO Macho Man Randy Savage		
NNO Mean Gene Okerlund		
NNO Million Dollar Man		
NNO Ric Flair		
NNO Rowdy Roddy Piper		
NNO Sgt. Slaughter		
NNO Ultimate Warrior		

2018 Mattel WWE M.U.S.C.L.E. SDCC Exclusives 3-Pack

NNO WWE Figurines	3.00	6.00

2016 Mattel WWE Mutants

NNO Bray Wyatt	6.00	12.00
NNO Brock Lesnar	20.00	40.00
NNO Finn Balor	12.50	25.00
NNO John Cena	7.50	15.00
NNO Stardust	6.00	12.00
NNO Sting	7.50	15.00

2017 Mattel WWE Network Spotlight

NNO Big Cass	6.00	12.00
NNO Brock Lesnar	7.50	15.00
NNO Enzo Amore	12.50	25.00
NNO Sting Surfer Gear FB	10.00	20.00

2017 Mattel WWE NXT Series 1

NNO Andrade Cien Almas	15.00	30.00
NNO Hideo Itami	7.50	15.00
NNO Kevin Owens	6.00	12.00
NNO Sami Zayn	6.00	12.00
NNO Samoa Joe	7.50	15.00
NNO Tye Dillinger	6.00	12.00

2017 Mattel WWE NXT Series 2

NNO Akam	12.50	25.00
NNO Bobby Roode	10.00	20.00
NNO Eva Marie	20.00	40.00
NNO Johnny Gargano		
NNO Rezar	12.50	25.00
NNO Tommaso Ciampa		

2017 Mattel WWE NXT Series 3

NNO Johnny Gargano	15.00	30.00
NNO Tommaso Ciampa	15.00	30.00

2018 Mattel WWE NXT Series 4

NNO Billie Kay		
NNO Paige		
NNO Roderick Strong		
NNO Triple H		
NNO Xavier Woods		

2012 Mattel WWE Power Slammers

NNO Brodus Clay	10.00	20.00
NNO John Cena		
NNO Kofi Kingston		
NNO Rey Mysterio	12.50	25.00
NNO Sheamus		
NNO The Miz		
NNO Zack Ryder		

2010 Mattel WWE PPV Series 1

NNO Batista		
NNO Edge		
NNO John Cena		
NNO Randy Orton		
NNO Steve Austin		
NNO Undertaker		

2010 Mattel WWE PPV Series 2

NNO John Cena		
NNO John Morrison		
NNO Kofi Kingston		
NNO The Miz		
NNO Rey Mysterio		
NNO Undertaker		

2010 Mattel WWE PPV Series 3

NNO Beth Phoenix		
NNO Chris Jericho		
NNO CM Punk		
NNO Cody Rhodes		
NNO Edge		
NNO Triple H		

2010 Mattel WWE PPV Series 4

NNO Batista		
NNO Chris Jericho		
NNO Drew McIntyre		
NNO John Cena		
NNO Rey Mysterio		
NNO Undertaker		

2010 Mattel WWE PPV Series 5

NNO Big Show		
NNO CM Punk		
NNO Jack Swagger		
NNO John Cena		
NNO Rey Mysterio		
NNO R-Truth		

2010 Mattel WWE PPV Series 6

NNO Christian		
NNO John Cena		
NNO Randy Orton		
NNO Rey Mysterio		
NNO Sheamus		
NNO Undertaker		

2011 Mattel WWE PPV Series 7

NNO CM Punk		
NNO John Cena		
NNO Kane		
NNO Melina		
NNO Randy Orton		
NNO Triple H		

2011 Mattel WWE PPV Series 8

NNO Edge		
NNO John Cena	20.00	40.00
NNO John Morrison		
NNO Rey Mysterio		
NNO Sheamus		
NNO Wade Barrett		

2011 Mattel WWE PPV Series 9

NNO Edge	15.00	30.00
NNO Great Khali	20.00	40.00
NNO John Cena		
NNO Randy Orton		
NNO Rey Mysterio		
NNO Triple H		

2011 Mattel WWE PPV Series 10

NNO Alberto Del Rio		
NNO Christian		
NNO John Cena		
NNO Rey Mysterio		
NNO R-Truth		
NNO Sheamus		

2011 Mattel WWE PPV Series 11

NNO Big Show		
NNO Chris Masters		
NNO Evan Bourne		
NNO John Cena		
NNO The Rock		
NNO Sheamus		

2016 Mattel WWE Retro Series 1

NNO Brock Lesnar	15.00	30.00
NNO John Cena	20.00	40.00
NNO Kevin Owens	20.00	40.00
NNO Roman Reigns	75.00	150.00
NNO Ultimate Warrior	15.00	30.00
NNO Undertaker	25.00	50.00

2017 Mattel WWE Retro Series 2

NNO Kane	20.00	40.00
NNO Mankind	20.00	40.00
NNO The Rock	12.50	25.00
NNO Sting	15.00	30.00
NNO Stone Cold Steve Austin	15.00	30.00
NNO Triple H	15.00	30.00

2017 Mattel WWE Retro Series 3

NNO AJ Styles	6.00	12.00
NNO Dean Ambrose	7.50	15.00
NNO Goldberg	6.00	12.00
NNO Seth Rollins	10.00	20.00

2017 Mattel WWE Retro Series 4

NNO Finn Balor	15.00	30.00
NNO Kevin Owens	10.00	20.00
NNO Ric Flair	30.00	60.00
NNO Sami Zayn	7.50	15.00

2017 Mattel WWE Retro Series 5

NNO Big E	7.50	15.00
NNO Kofi Kingston	10.00	20.00
NNO Macho Man Randy Savage	12.50	25.00
NNO Macho Man/Arms Down	12.50	25.00
NNO Xavier Woods	6.00	12.00

2018 Mattel WWE Retro Series 6

NNO Bray Wyatt	7.50	15.00
NNO Daniel Bryan	10.00	20.00
NNO Shinsuke Nakamura	7.50	15.00
NNO Sting/Wolfpac	12.50	25.00

2018 Mattel WWE Retro Series 7

NNO Chris Jericho	7.50	15.00
NNO Kurt Angle	7.50	15.00
NNO Shawn Michaels	10.00	20.00
NNO Sheamus	7.50	15.00

2019 Mattel WWE Retro Series 8

NNO Braun Strowman	7.50	15.00
NNO Iron Sheik	7.50	15.00
NNO Jeff Hardy	7.50	15.00
NNO Zack Ryder	7.50	15.00

2019 Mattel WWE Retro Series 9

NNO Goldust	7.50	15.00
NNO Macho Man Randy Savage	12.50	25.00
NNO Randy Orton	7.50	15.00
NNO Samoa Joe	12.50	25.00

2019 Mattel WWE Retro Series 10

NNO Diesel	10.00	20.00
NNO Elias	7.50	15.00
NNO Junkyard Dog	15.00	30.00
NNO Matt Hardy	6.00	12.00

2018 Mattel WWE Retro Series Playset

NNO Collectible Retro Ring		

2018-19 Mattel WWE Retrofest

NNO Hacksaw Jim Duggan	10.00	20.00
NNO Honky Tonk Man	10.00	20.00
NNO Macho Man Randy Savage	12.50	25.00
NNO Mr. Perfect	15.00	30.00
NNO Ric Flair	10.00	20.00
NNO Shawn Michaels	12.50	25.00

2010 Mattel WWE Series 1

NNO Batista		
NNO Batista w/Title Belt/1000		
NNO Big Show		
NNO Big Show w/Title Belt/1000		
NNO Evan Bourne		
NNO Evan Bourne w/Title Belt/1000		
NNO John Cena		
NNO John Cena w/Title Belt/1000		
NNO Kofi Kingston		
NNO Kofi Kingston w/Title Belt/1000		
NNO Triple H		
NNO Triple H w/Title Belt/1000		

2010 Mattel WWE Series 2

NNO CM Punk		

NNO CM Punk w/Title Belt/1000		
NNO Jack Swagger		
NNO Jack Swagger w/Title Belt/1000		
NNO Kane		
NNO Kane w/Title Belt/1000		
NNO Mark Henry	10.00	20.00
NNO Mark Henry w/Title Belt/1000		
NNO Rey Mysterio/Dk Blue		
NNO Rey Mysterio/Dk Blue w/Title Belt/1000		
NNO Rey Mysterio/Lt Blue	25.00	50.00
NNO Rey Mysterio/Lt Blue w/Title Belt/1000		
NNO Vladimir Kozlov		
NNO Vladimir Kozlov w/Title Belt/1000		

2010 Mattel WWE Series 3

NNO Chris Jericho	10.00	20.00
NNO Chris Jericho w/Title Belt/1000		
NNO Chris Jericho Alt Head		
NNO Chris Jericho Alt Head w/Title Belt/1000		
NNO Great Khali		
NNO Great Khali w/Title Belt/1000		
NNO Mickie James	12.50	25.00
NNO Mickie James w/Title Belt/1000		
NNO Randy Orton		
NNO Randy Orton w/Title Belt/1000		
NNO Shelton Benjamin		
NNO Shelton Benjamin w/Title Belt/1000		
NNO Undertaker		
NNO Undertaker w/Title Belt/1000		

2010 Mattel WWE Series 4

NNO Dolph Ziggler	12.50	25.00
NNO Dolph Ziggler w/Title Belt/1000		
NNO Goldust	12.50	25.00
NNO Goldust w/Title Belt/1000		
NNO Matt Hardy	12.50	25.00
NNO Matt Hardy w/Title Belt/1000		
NNO MVP	15.00	30.00
NNO MVP w/Title Belt/1000		
NNO Shawn Michaels	17.50	35.00
NNO Shawn Michaels w/Title Belt/1000		
NNO William Regal	10.00	20.00
NNO William Regal w/Title Belt/1000		

2010 Mattel WWE Series 5

NNO Batista	12.50	25.00
NNO Hurricane	12.50	25.00
NNO Hurricane w/Title Belt/1000		
NNO John Cena	10.00	20.00
NNO Melina	20.00	40.00
NNO Melina w/Title Belt/1000		
NNO Mike Knox	25.00	50.00
NNO Mike Knox w/Title Belt/1000		
NNO R-Truth		
NNO R-Truth w/Title Belt/1000		

2010 Mattel WWE Series 6

NNO Big Show	10.00	20.00
NNO Drew McIntyre	15.00	30.00
NNO Edge		
NNO Kelly Kelly	20.00	40.00
NNO The Miz		
NNO Ted DiBiase	12.50	25.00

2010 Mattel WWE Series 7

NNO Kofi Kingston		
NNO Michelle McCool	25.00	50.00
NNO Rey Mysterio	25.00	50.00
NNO Sheamus		
NNO Undertaker		
NNO Yoshi Tatsu	12.50	25.00
NNO Yoshi Tatsu w/Title Belt/1000		
NNO Sheamus w/Title Belt/1000		
NNO Michelle McCool w/Title Belt/1000		

2011 Mattel WWE Series 8

NNO Chris Masters	15.00	30.00
NNO Christian	10.00	20.00
NNO Finlay	12.50	25.00
NNO Kane	12.50	25.00
NNO Kofi Kingston	15.00	30.00
NNO Maryse	30.00	60.00

2011 Mattel WWE Series 9

NNO Evan Bourne	7.50	15.00
NNO Jack Swagger	6.00	12.00
NNO JTG	10.00	20.00
NNO Mark Henry		
NNO Natalya	20.00	40.00
NNO Rey Mysterio		

2011 Mattel WWE Series 10

NNO Dolph Ziggler	10.00	20.00
NNO John Cena	12.50	25.00
NNO Kofi Kingston	10.00	20.00
NNO Triple H		
NNO Wade Barrett	7.50	15.00
NNO Zack Ryder	10.00	20.00

2011 Mattel WWE Series 11

NNO Big Show	12.50	25.00
NNO Daniel Bryan	7.50	15.00
NNO Eve	12.50	25.00
NNO Sheamus	6.00	12.00
NNO Skip Sheffield	12.50	25.00

2011 Mattel WWE Series 12

NNO Alberto Del Rio	7.50	15.00
NNO Evan Bourne	7.50	15.00
NNO John Morrison		
NNO Randy Orton	7.50	15.00
NNO Rey Mysterio		
NNO Wade Barrett	7.50	15.00

2012 Mattel WWE Series 13

1 Rey Mysterio		
2 Vickie Guerrero	15.00	30.00
3 John Morrison		
4 R-Truth	15.00	30.00
5 Ezekiel Jackson		
6 Undertaker		

2012 Mattel WWE Series 14

7 Bret Hit Man Hart		
8 Shawn Michaels		
9 Goldust		
10 Rey Mysterio		
11 John Morrison		
12 Alberto Del Rio		

2012 Mattel WWE Series 15

13 Layla	30.00	75.00
14 Kofi Kingston	15.00	30.00
15 John Cena	7.50	15.00
16 Wade Barrett	20.00	40.00
17 Brodus Clay		
18 Kane		

2012 Mattel WWE Series 16

19 Ultimate Warrior	15.00	30.00
20 John Cena	10.00	20.00
21 Eddie Guerrero	17.50	35.00
22 Triple H		
23 Undertaker		
24 Jack Swagger	7.50	15.00

2012 Mattel WWE Series 17

25 Rey Mysterio	15.00	30.00
26 Dolph Ziggler	10.00	20.00
27 Zack Ryder	10.00	20.00
28 The Miz	7.50	15.00
29 Alex Riley	7.50	15.00
30 Mark Henry	10.00	20.00

2012 Mattel WWE Series 18

31 Kelly Kelly	12.50	25.00
32 Sin Cara		
33 Hunico	15.00	30.00
34 CM Punk	10.00	20.00
35 John Cena	7.50	15.00
36 Cody Rhodes		

2012 Mattel WWE Series 19

37 Hornswoggle		
38 Evan Bourne	10.00	20.00
39 Kofi Kingston	7.50	15.00
40 Justin Gabriel	6.00	12.00
41 Jinder Mahal	7.50	15.00
42 Randy Orton	7.50	15.00

2012 Mattel WWE Series 20

43 Natalya		
44 Rey Mysterio		
45 Yoshi Tatsu	7.50	15.00
46 John Cena	7.50	15.00
47 Sheamus	10.00	20.00
48 Wade Barrett		

2012 Mattel WWE Series 21

49 Beth Phoenix	25.00	50.00
50 R-Truth		
51 The Miz		
52 Mason Ryan		
53 Jack Swagger		
54 Big Show		

2012 Mattel WWE Series 22

55 Booker T	12.50	25.00
56 Mark Henry		
57 Chris Jericho	6.00	12.00
58 Christian	10.00	20.00
59 John Cena	7.50	15.00
60 Zack Ryder	7.50	15.00

2012 Mattel WWE Series 23

61 Rey Mysterio	15.00	30.00
62 Alicia Fox	15.00	30.00
63 Hunico	10.00	20.00
64 Santino Marella	7.50	15.00
65 Triple H		
66 Kane		

2013 Mattel WWE Series 24

1 John Cena		
2 CM Punk		
3 Zack Ryder	15.00	30.00
4 Drew McIntyre	15.00	30.00
5 Sheamus		
6 AJ	20.00	40.00

2013 Mattel WWE Series 25

7 Big Show		
8 Brock Lesnar		
9 Randy Orton		
10 The Miz	12.50	25.00
11 Eve	20.00	40.00
12 David Otunga	10.00	20.00

2013 Mattel WWE Series 26

13 Macho Man Randy Savage	12.50	25.00
14 Shawn Michaels	12.50	25.00
15 Undertaker	10.00	20.00
16 Kane	25.00	50.00
17 Mark Henry		
18 Daniel Bryan	10.00	20.00

2013 Mattel WWE Series 27

19 Cody Rhodes		
20 Kofi Kingston		
21 Wade Barrett		
22 Ryback	12.50	25.00
23 Brodus Clay		
24 Antonio Cesaro	10.00	20.00

2013 Mattel WWE Series 28

25 Rey Mysterio		
26 R-Truth	10.00	20.00
27 Heath Slater	10.00	20.00
28 Sin Cara	20.00	50.00
29 Tensai	7.50	15.00
30 Damien Sandow	7.50	15.00

2013 Mattel WWE Series 29

31 Ultimate Warrior		
32 Eddie Guerrero	15.00	30.00
33 Stone Cold Steve Austin		
34 Big Show		
35 John Cena	7.50	15.00
36 CM Punk		

2013 Mattel WWE Series 30

37 The Miz		
38 Hornswoggle	30.00	60.00
39 Santino Marella		
40 Sheamus	10.00	20.00
41 Daniel Bryan	10.00	20.00
42 AJ Lee	20.00	40.00

2013 Mattel WWE Series 31

43 Kane		
44 R-Truth	10.00	20.00
45 Zack Ryder		
46 Rosa Mendes	10.00	20.00
47 Wade Barrett	7.50	15.00
48 Alberto Del Rio	7.50	15.00

2013 Mattel WWE Series 32

49 Chris Jericho	10.00	20.00
50 The Rock	12.50	25.00
51 Randy Orton	12.50	25.00
52 John Cena	7.50	15.00
53 Ryback		
54 Antonio Cesaro	7.50	15.00

2013 Mattel WWE Series 33

55 Big Show		

56 Dolph Ziggler	10.00	20.00
57 Great Khali		
58 CM Punk	12.50	25.00
59 Tamina Snuka	10.00	20.00
60 Dean Ambrose		

2013 Mattel WWE Series 34

61 John Cena	7.50	15.00
62 The Miz		
63 Rey Mysterio		
64 Sin Cara	20.00	40.00
65 Ricardo Rodriguez	12.50	25.00
66 Brodus Clay	7.50	15.00

2014 Mattel WWE Series 35

1 Kane		
2 Damien Sandow	7.50	15.00
3 Daniel Bryan	17.50	35.00
4 Triple H		
5 Cody Rhodes	7.50	15.00
6 Jinder Mahal	10.00	20.00

2014 Mattel WWE Series 36

7 CM Punk	15.00	30.00
8 Big E Langston	7.50	15.00
9 Christian		
10 Jack Swagger		
11 Fandango		
12 Kaitlyn	12.50	25.00

2014 Mattel WWE Series 37

13 Mr. Perfect		
14 Batista		
15 Roman Reigns		
16 Ryback		
17 Zeb Colter		
18 Randy Orton		

2014 Mattel WWE Series 38

19 Chris Jericho		
20 Dolph Ziggler	7.50	15.00
21 Vickie Guerrero	10.00	20.00
22 Sheamus		
23 The Miz		
24 Kofi Kingston	7.50	15.00

2014 Mattel WWE Series 39

25 Bray Wyatt	7.50	15.00
26 Rob Van Dam	12.50	25.00
27 Justin Gabriel	10.00	20.00
28 John Cena		
29 Christian		
30 Heath Slater	10.00	20.00

2014 Mattel WWE Series 40

31 CM Punk	17.50	35.00
32 Alberto Del Rio	7.50	15.00
33 Rey Mysterio		
34 The Great Khali		
35 Zack Ryder	7.50	15.00
36 Edge	12.50	25.00

2014 Mattel WWE Series 41

37 Daniel Bryan	10.00	20.00
38 Santino Marella		
39 Cesaro		
40 Drew McIntyre		
41 Bray Wyatt		
42 Fandango		

2014 Mattel WWE Series 42

43 Natalya	12.50	25.00
44 Batista		
45 El Torito	10.00	20.00
46 Big Show		
47 Roman Reigns	10.00	20.00
48 Sin Cara		

2014 Mattel WWE Series 43

49 Mark Henry		
50 Eva Marie	10.00	20.00
51 Rob Van Dam	17.50	35.00
52 John Cena	7.50	15.00
54 Dolph Ziggler	7.50	15.00
55 Rey Mysterio		

2014 Mattel WWE Series 44

53 Kane	20.00	40.00
56 Big E		
57 Randy Orton		
58 Seth Rollins	10.00	20.00
59 Titus O'Neil		
60 Goldust	10.00	20.00

2015 Mattel WWE Series 45

1 Triple H	6.00	12.00
2 Chris Jericho	10.00	20.00
3 Mankind	10.00	20.00
4 The Miz	7.50	15.00
5 Ricky The Dragon Steamboat	10.00	20.00
6 Daniel Bryan	15.00	30.00

2015 Mattel WWE Series 46

8 Big Show	12.50	25.00
9 Kofi Kingston	10.00	20.00
10 Bad News Barrett	7.50	15.00
11 Jerry The King Lawler	20.00	40.00
12 Batista	17.50	35.00

2015 Mattel WWE Series 47

13 Alicia Fox	7.50	15.00
14 Rusev	6.00	12.00
15 Brock Lesnar	10.00	20.00
16 Kane	20.00	40.00
17 Christian	10.00	20.00
18 Cesaro	10.00	20.00

2015 Mattel WWE Series 48

19 Ric Flair	10.00	20.00
20 Hulk Hogan	12.50	25.00
21 Brie Bella	10.00	20.00
22 John Cena	7.50	15.00
23 Booker T	15.00	30.00
24 Randy Orton		

2015 Mattel WWE Series 49

25 Ryback		
26 Bray Wyatt	7.50	15.00
27 Roman Reigns	10.00	20.00
28 Bret Hart	12.50	25.00
29 Bo Dallas	7.50	15.00
30A Emma FP	12.50	25.00
30B Emma FP/Legs Variant		

2015 Mattel WWE Series 50

31 Daniel Bryan	10.00	20.00
32 Adam Rose	6.00	12.00
33 Seth Rollins	7.50	15.00
34 Goldust	10.00	20.00
35 Summer Rae FP	15.00	30.00
36 Sami Zayn FP	6.00	12.00

2015 Mattel WWE Series 51

37 Dolph Ziggler	7.50	15.00
38 Dean Ambrose	10.00	20.00
39 Stardust	25.00	50.00
40 Stephanie McMahon	10.00	20.00
41 Stone Cold Steve Austin FB	12.50	25.00
42 Heath Slater	7.50	15.00

2015 Mattel WWE Series 52

43 John Cena		
44 Chris Jericho	6.00	12.00
45 The Miz	7.50	15.00
46 Nikki Bella	7.50	15.00
47 Mark Henry		
48 Adrian Neville FP	10.00	20.00

2015 Mattel WWE Series 53

49 Brock Lesnar	7.50	15.00
50 The Rock	10.00	20.00
51 Triple H	7.50	15.00
52 Damien Mizdow	6.00	12.00
53 AJ Lee	30.00	75.00
54 Tyler Breeze FP	6.00	12.00

2015 Mattel WWE Series 54

55 Roman Reigns	10.00	20.00
56 The Rock	10.00	20.00
57 Rusev	6.00	12.00
58 Big Show	12.50	25.00
59 Dolph Ziggler	7.50	15.00
60 Tyson Kidd	6.00	12.00

2015 Mattel WWE Series 55

60 Sting FB	10.00	20.00
61 John Cena	7.50	15.00
62 El Torito	20.00	40.00
63 Kane	7.50	15.00
64 Randy Orton	10.00	20.00
65 Bray Wyatt	10.00	20.00
66 Undertaker	12.50	25.00
67 Charlotte FP	15.00	30.00

2015 Mattel WWE Series 56

NNO Dean Ambrose	7.50	15.00
NNO Dean Ambrose/WWE Title		
NNO Hideo Itami FP	6.00	12.00
NNO John Cena	10.00	20.00
NNO John Cena/WWE Title	15.00	30.00
NNO Naomi	7.50	15.00
NNO Naomi/WWE Title	12.50	25.00
NNO Ultimate Warrior FB	12.50	25.00
NNO Ultimate Warrior FB/WWE Title		
NNO Xavier Woods	6.00	12.00
NNO Xavier Woods/WWE Title		

2015 Mattel WWE Series 57

NNO Big Show		
NNO Big Show/WWE Title	15.00	30.00
NNO Daniel Bryan	7.50	15.00
NNO Daniel Bryan/WWE Title	12.50	25.00
NNO Erick Rowan	6.00	12.00
NNO Erick Rowan/WWE Title	10.00	20.00
NNO Finn Balor FP	10.00	20.00
NNO Paige	12.50	25.00
NNO Paige/WWE Title	20.00	40.00
NNO Ryback	6.00	12.00
NNO Ryback/WWE Title		

2015 Mattel WWE Series 58

NNO Bad News Barrett	7.50	15.00
NNO Bad News Barrett/WWE Title		
NNO Bayley	10.00	20.00
NNO Bayley/WWE Title		
NNO Edge FB	7.50	15.00
NNO Edge FB/WWE Title		
NNO Fandango	6.00	12.00
NNO Fandango/WWE Title		
NNO Kevin Owens	7.50	15.00
NNO Kevin Owens/WWE Title		
NNO Lana	7.50	15.00
NNO Lana/WWE Title	15.00	30.00
NNO Paul Orndorff FB	7.50	15.00
NNO Paul Orndorff FB/WWE Title		
NNO Stardust	10.00	20.00
NNO Stardust/WWE Title		
NNO Undertaker	12.50	25.00
NNO Undertaker/WWE Title	20.00	40.00

2016 Mattel WWE Series 59

NNO Bray Wyatt	7.50	15.00
NNO Bray Wyatt/WWE Title		
NNO Eva Marie	10.00	20.00
NNO Eva Marie/WWE Title	12.50	25.00
NNO Honky Tonk Man FB	6.00	12.00
NNO Honky Tonk Man FB/WWE Title		
NNO Iron Sheik FB	10.00	20.00
NNO Iron Sheik FB/WWE Title		
NNO R-Truth	12.50	25.00
NNO R-Truth/WWE Title		
NNO Sasha Banks FP	10.00	20.00
NNO Sasha Banks FP/WWE Title		
NNO Sheamus	6.00	12.00
NNO Sheamus/WWE Title	7.50	15.00
NNO Triple H	6.00	12.00
NNO Triple H/WWE Title		

2016 Mattel WWE Series 60

NNO Brock Lesnar	7.50	15.00
NNO Brock Lesnar/WWE Title		
NNO John Cena	10.00	20.00
NNO John Cena/WWE Title		
NNO Kalisto FP	12.50	25.00
NNO Kalisto FP/WWE Title		
NNO Kofi Kingston	7.50	15.00
NNO Kofi Kingston/WWE Title		
NNO Luke Harper	6.00	12.00
NNO Luke Harper/WWE Title		
NNO Randy Orton	7.50	15.00
NNO Randy Orton/WWE Title		
NNO Renee Young	7.50	15.00
NNO Renee Young/WWE Title	10.00	20.00
NNO Seth Rollins	7.50	15.00
NNO Seth Rollins/WWE Title		

2016 Mattel WWE Series 61

NNO Big E	7.50	15.00
NNO Dean Ambrose	6.00	12.00
NNO Dolph Ziggler	7.50	15.00
NNO Finn Balor	10.00	20.00
NNO John Cena	7.50	15.00
NNO Natalya	10.00	20.00
NNO Neville	6.00	12.00
NNO Sami Zayn	6.00	12.00
NNO Zack Ryder	7.50	15.00

2016 Mattel WWE Series 62

NNO	Becky Lynch FP	20.00	40.00
NNO	The Miz	7.50	15.00
NNO	Roman Reigns	10.00	20.00
NNO	Sin Cara	20.00	40.00
NNO	Sting FB	15.00	30.00

2016 Mattel WWE Series 63

NNO	Alberto Del Rio	10.00	20.00
NNO	Baron Corbin FP	7.50	15.00
NNO	Paul Heyman	12.50	25.00
NNO	Rusev	10.00	20.00
NNO	Ryback	10.00	20.00
NNO	Seth Rollins	7.50	15.00
NNO	Sid Justice FB	10.00	20.00
NNO	Undertaker	12.50	25.00

2016 Mattel WWE Series 64

NNO	Apollo Crews FP	10.00	20.00
NNO	Braun Strowman	15.00	30.00
NNO	Brock Lesnar	12.50	25.00
NNO	Dolph Ziggler	7.50	15.00
NNO	John Cena	7.50	15.00
NNO	Lana	10.00	20.00
NNO	Xavier Woods	6.00	12.00

2016 Mattel WWE Series 65

NNO	Emma	10.00	20.00
NNO	Kane	10.00	20.00
NNO	Kevin Owens	7.50	15.00
NNO	The Rock	12.50	25.00
NNO	Roman Reigns	7.50	15.00
NNO	Samoa Joe	7.50	15.00
NNO	Sheamus	7.50	15.00

2016 Mattel WWE Series 66

NNO	Alberto Del Rio	7.50	15.00
NNO	Big Show		
NNO	Daniel Bryan	12.50	25.00
NNO	Dean Ambrose	7.50	15.00
NNO	Paige	15.00	30.00
NNO	Roman Reigns	12.50	25.00
NNO	Tyler Breeze	6.00	12.00

2016 Mattel WWE Series 67

NNO	Cesaro	6.00	12.00
NNO	Cesaro/Slammy		
NNO	Goldust	10.00	20.00
NNO	Goldust/Slammy	12.50	25.00
NNO	JBL	7.50	15.00
NNO	JBL/Slammy		
NNO	John Cena	7.50	15.00
NNO	John Cena/Slammy	12.50	25.00
NNO	Luke Harper	7.50	15.00
NNO	Luke Harper/Slammy	7.50	15.00
NNO	Naomi	10.00	20.00
NNO	Naomi/Slammy	7.50	15.00
NNO	Randy Orton	7.50	15.00
NNO	Randy Orton/Slammy	12.50	25.00
NNO	Xavier Woods	7.50	15.00
NNO	Xavier Woods/Slammy		

2016 Mattel WWE Series 68A

NNO	Bo Dallas	7.50	15.00
NNO	Bo Dallas/Slammy	7.50	15.00
NNO	Dana Brooke	12.50	25.00
NNO	Dana Brooke/Slammy	7.50	15.00
NNO	DDP FB	10.00	20.00
NNO	Diamond Dallas Page/Slammy	7.50	15.00
NNO	Finn Balor	7.50	15.00
NNO	Finn Balor/Slammy	7.50	15.00
NNO	Kalisto	15.00	30.00
NNO	Kalisto/Slammy	12.50	25.00
NNO	Neville	6.00	12.00
NNO	Neville/Slammy	6.00	12.00

2016 Mattel WWE Series 68B

NNO	AJ Styles	6.00	12.00
NNO	AJ Styles/Slammy	6.00	12.00
NNO	Alexa Bliss FP	20.00	40.00
NNO	Alexa Bliss FP/Slammy	12.50	25.00
NNO	Chris Jericho	7.50	15.00
NNO	Chris Jericho/Slammy	7.50	15.00
NNO	The Rock	10.00	20.00
NNO	The Rock/Slammy	15.00	30.00
NNO	Seth Rollins	7.50	15.00
NNO	Seth Rollins/Slammy	7.50	15.00
NNO	Sting FB	7.50	15.00
NNO	Sting FB/Slammy		

2016 Mattel WWE Series 69

NNO	Bray Wyatt	7.50	15.00
NNO	Bray Wyatt/Slammy	10.00	20.00
NNO	John Cena	6.00	12.00
NNO	John Cena/Slammy	7.50	15.00
NNO	Sami Zayn	6.00	12.00
NNO	Sami Zayn/Slammy	6.00	12.00
NNO	Sgt. Slaughter FB	6.00	12.00
NNO	Sgt. Slaughter FB/Slammy	10.00	20.00
NNO	Tamina	7.50	15.00
NNO	Tamina/Slammy	7.50	15.00
NNO	Triple H	7.50	15.00
NNO	Triple H/Slammy	7.50	15.00

2017 Mattel WWE Series 70

NNO	Apollo Crews	7.50	15.00
NNO	Brie Bella	10.00	20.00
NNO	Carmella FP	12.50	25.00
NNO	Ric Flair	7.50	15.00
NNO	The Rock FB	12.50	25.00
NNO	Roman Reigns	10.00	20.00
NNO	Samoa Joe	12.50	25.00
NNO	Ultimate Warrior	15.00	30.00

2017 Mattel WWE Series 71

NNO	Austin Aries FP	6.00	12.00
NNO	Baron Corbin	6.00	12.00
NNO	Charlotte Flair	10.00	20.00
NNO	Finn Balor	12.50	25.00
NNO	John Cena	7.50	15.00
NNO	Seth Rollins	7.50	15.00
NNO	Undertaker	20.00	40.00

2017 Mattel WWE Series 72

NNO	Dean Ambrose	10.00	20.00
NNO	Dolph Ziggler	7.50	15.00
NNO	Nia Jax FP	7.50	15.00
NNO	Sheamus	10.00	20.00
NNO	Shinsuke Nakamura	7.50	15.00
NNO	Zack Ryder	10.00	20.00

2017 Mattel WWE Series 73

NNO	AJ Styles	10.00	20.00
NNO	Big E	10.00	20.00
NNO	Cesaro	7.50	15.00
NNO	Kevin Owens	10.00	20.00
NNO	Seth Rollins	7.50	15.00
NNO	Triple H	6.00	12.00

2017 Mattel WWE Series 74

NNO	Bayley	10.00	20.00
NNO	John Cena	7.50	15.00
NNO	Kane	20.00	40.00
NNO	Neville	7.50	15.00
NNO	Roman Reigns	7.50	15.00
NNO	Samoa Joe	10.00	20.00

2017 Mattel WWE Series 75

NNO	Braun Strowman	12.50	25.00
NNO	Brock Lesnar	10.00	20.00
NNO	Chris Jericho	6.00	12.00
NNO	Finn Balor	6.00	12.00
NNO	Lana	7.50	15.00
NNO	Randy Orton	15.00	30.00

2017 Mattel WWE Series 76

NNO	AJ Styles	6.00	12.00
NNO	Dolph Ziggler	7.50	15.00
NNO	John Cena	7.50	15.00
NNO	Macho King Randy Savage FB	10.00	20.00
NNO	The Rock FB	12.50	25.00
NNO	Sami Zayn	6.00	12.00

2017 Mattel WWE Series 77

NNO	Corey Graves	6.00	12.00
NNO	Dean Ambrose	6.00	12.00
NNO	Finn Balor	10.00	20.00
NNO	Roman Reigns	10.00	20.00
NNO	Seth Rollins	12.50	25.00

2017 Mattel WWE Series 78

NNO	AJ Styles	10.00	20.00
NNO	AJ Styles/Case	7.50	15.00
NNO	Braun Strowman	20.00	40.00
NNO	Braun Strowman/Case		
NNO	Kevin Owens	7.50	15.00
NNO	Kevin Owens/Case		
NNO	Natalya	10.00	20.00
NNO	Natalya/Case	7.50	15.00
NNO	The Rock FB	12.50	25.00
NNO	The Rock FB/Case	12.50	25.00
NNO	Shane McMahon	10.00	20.00
NNO	Shane McMahon/Case	10.00	20.00

2017 Mattel WWE Series 79

NNO	Baron Corbin	7.50	15.00
NNO	Baron Corbin/Case	7.50	15.00
NNO	Neville	7.50	15.00
NNO	Neville/Case		
NNO	Nia Jax	7.50	15.00
NNO	Nia Jax/Case	7.50	15.00
NNO	Samoa Joe	7.50	15.00
NNO	Samoa Joe/Case	10.00	20.00
NNO	Stone Cold Steve Austin	10.00	20.00
NNO	Steve Austin/Case	15.00	30.00
NNO	TJ Perkins	10.00	20.00
NNO	TJ Perkins/Case		

2017 Mattel WWE Series 80

NNO	Brock Lesnar	7.50	15.00
NNO	Chris Jericho	7.50	15.00
NNO	Chris Jericho/Case	7.50	15.00
NNO	Rich Swann	6.00	12.00
NNO	Rich Swann/Case	6.00	12.00
NNO	Roman Reigns	7.50	15.00
NNO	Roman Reigns/Case	10.00	20.00
NNO	Sasha Banks	10.00	20.00
NNO	Sasha Banks/Case	12.50	25.00

2017 Mattel WWE Series 81

NNO	Dana Brooke	7.50	15.00
NNO	Dana Brooke/Case	7.50	15.00
NNO	Kofi Kingston	7.50	15.00
NNO	Kofi Kingston/Case	7.50	15.00
NNO	Rhyno	10.00	20.00
NNO	Rhyno/Case	10.00	20.00
NNO	Sami Zayn	7.50	15.00
NNO	Sami Zayn/Case	7.50	15.00
NNO	Seth Rollins	7.50	15.00
NNO	Seth Rollins/Case	7.50	15.00

2017 Mattel WWE Series 82

NNO	AJ Styles	10.00	20.00
NNO	AJ Styles/Case	10.00	20.00
NNO	Becky Lynch	15.00	30.00
NNO	Becky Lynch/Case	10.00	20.00
NNO	John Cena	6.00	12.00
NNO	John Cena/Case	6.00	12.00
NNO	Luke Harper	7.50	15.00
NNO	Luke Harper/Case	7.50	15.00
NNO	Shinsuke Nakamura	7.50	15.00
NNO	Shinsuke Nakaura/Case		

2017 Mattel WWE Series 83

NNO	Alicia Fox	7.50	15.00
NNO	Alicia Fox/Case	7.50	15.00
NNO	Kurt Angle	7.50	15.00
NNO	Kurt Angle/Case	7.50	15.00
NNO	Randy Orton	12.50	25.00
NNO	Randy Orton/Case	10.00	20.00
NNO	Triple H	7.50	15.00
NNO	Triple H/Case	7.50	15.00
NNO	Tye Dillinger	6.00	12.00
NNO	Tye Dillinger/Case	7.50	15.00

2017 Mattel WWE Series 84

NNO	Dean Ambrose	7.50	15.00
NNO	Dean Ambrose/Case	7.50	15.00
NNO	Finn Balor	7.50	15.00
NNO	Finn Balor/Case	10.00	20.00
NNO	Kevin Owens	10.00	20.00
NNO	Kevin Owens/Case		
NNO	Naomi	7.50	15.00
NNO	Naomi/Case		
NNO	Rusev	7.50	15.00
NNO	Rusev/Case		

2017 Mattel WWE Series 85

NNO	AJ Styles	10.00	20.00
NNO	AJ Styles/Case	10.00	20.00
NNO	Alexa Bliss	10.00	30.00
NNO	Alexa Bliss/Case		
NNO	Bobby Roode	12.50	25.00
NNO	Bobby Roode/Case		
NNO	John Cena	7.50	15.00
NNO	John Cena/Case	7.50	15.00
NNO	Seth Rollins	10.00	20.00
NNO	Seth Rollins/Case	10.00	20.00

2018 Mattel WWE Series 86

NNO	Akira Tozawa	6.00	12.00
NNO	Charlotte Flair	7.50	15.00
NNO	Dolph Ziggler	12.50	25.00
NNO	The Rock	15.00	30.00
NNO	Roman Reigns	12.50	25.00

2018 Mattel WWE Series 87

NNO	AJ Styles	10.00	20.00
NNO	Bayley	7.50	15.00
NNO	Dean Ambrose	10.00	20.00
NNO	Jason Jordan	6.00	12.00
NNO	The Miz	7.50	15.00

2018 Mattel WWE Series 88

NNO	Baron Corbin	7.50	15.00
NNO	Chad Gable	6.00	12.00
NNO	Elias	7.50	15.00
NNO	John Cena	7.50	15.00
NNO	Sasha Banks	10.00	20.00

2018 Mattel WWE Series 89

NNO	Carmella	10.00	20.00
NNO	Cesaro	6.00	12.00
NNO	Kalisto	12.50	25.00
NNO	Kurt Angle	7.50	15.00
NNO	Sheamus	10.00	20.00

2018 Mattel WWE Series 90

NNO	Aiden English	6.00	12.00
NNO	Kane	12.50	25.00
NNO	The Miz	7.50	15.00
NNO	Roman Reigns	7.50	15.00
NNO	Roman Reigns/Shield Shirt	10.00	20.00
NNO	Ronda Rousey	15.00	30.00

2018 Mattel WWE Series 91

NNO	Alexa Bliss	10.00	20.00
NNO	Dean Ambrose	7.50	15.00
NNO	Dean Ambrose/Shield Shirt		
NNO	Drew Gulak	10.00	20.00
NNO	Finn Balor	7.50	15.00
NNO	Shinsuke Nakamura	7.50	15.00

2018 Mattel WWE Series 92

NNO	Jeff Hardy	10.00	20.00
NNO	John Cena	7.50	15.00
NNO	Mandy Rose	15.00	30.00
NNO	Samoa Joe	12.50	25.00
NNO	Seth Rollins	6.00	12.00
NNO	Seth Rollins/Shield Shirt		

2019 Mattel WWE Series 93

NNO	Bayley	7.50	15.00
NNO	Jinder Mahal	6.00	12.00
NNO	Macho Man Randy Savage	7.50	15.00
NNO	Macho Man/White Lightning CH	12.50	25.00
NNO	Triple H	6.00	12.00
NNO	Undertaker	7.50	15.00

2019 Mattel WWE Series 94

NNO	Big E	6.00	12.00
NNO	Kofi Kingston	10.00	20.00
NNO	Matt Hardy	6.00	12.00
NNO	Matt Hardy Mower of Lawn CH	12.50	25.00
NNO	Randy Orton		
NNO	Xavier Woods	6.00	12.00

2019 Mattel WWE Series 95

NNO	AJ Styles		
NNO	Bray Wyatt	7.50	15.00
NNO	Kurt Angle	7.50	15.00
NNO	Rusev	6.00	12.00
NNO	Sonya Deville	6.00	12.00
NNO	Sonya Deville Black Attire CH	10.00	20.00

2019 Mattel WWE Series 96

NNO	Bobby Roode		
NNO	Daniel Bryan	7.50	15.00
NNO	Kevin Owens	6.00	12.00
NNO	Sami Zayn	6.00	12.00
NNO	Sami Zayn Arabic CH		
NNO	Sasha Banks	10.00	20.00

2019 Mattel WWE Series 97

NNO	AJ Styles	7.50	15.00
NNO	Bret Hitman Hart	7.50	15.00
NNO	Jeff Hardy	7.50	15.00
NNO	Miz White Trunks	6.00	12.00
NNO	Miz Black Trunks CH	10.00	20.00
NNO	Razor Ramon	7.50	15.00

2019 Mattel WWE Series 98

NNO	Finn Balor	10.00	20.00
NNO	Elias	6.00	12.00
NNO	Ruby Riott	10.00	20.00
NNO	Tony Nese White Tights FP	7.50	15.00
NNO	Tony Nese Gray Tights FP CH	12.50	25.00
NNO	Ultimate Warrior	7.50	15.00

2019 Mattel WWE Series 99

NNO	Ariya Daivari White Tights CH	6.00	12.00
NNO	Ariya Daivari Black Tights CH	7.50	15.00
NNO	Becky Lynch	10.00	20.00
NNO	Drew McIntyre	10.00	20.00
NNO	Rey Mysterio	7.50	15.00
NNO	Shinsuke Nakamura	10.00	20.00

2019 Mattel WWE Series 100

NNO	John Cena	10.00	20.00
NNO	The Rock	10.00	20.00
NNO	Stone Cold Steve Austin	12.50	25.00
NNO	Shawn Michaels	10.00	20.00
NNO	Shawn Michaels Red & White CH	20.00	40.00
NNO	Undertaker	12.50	25.00

2019 Mattel WWE Series 101

NNO	AJ Styles		
NNO	Bobby Lashley		
NNO	Ali		
NNO	Ali Green Tights CH		
NNO	Ronda Rousey		
NNO	Sarah Logan		

2019 Mattel WWE Series 102

NNO	Constable Baron Corbin		
NNO	Drake Maverick		
NNO	Drake Maverick (black gear) (CHASE)		
NNO	Jeff Hardy		
NNO	The Miz		
NNO	Seth Rollins		

2019 Mattel WWE Series 103

NNO	AJ Styles		
NNO	Becky Lynch		
NNO	Becky Lynch Orange Shirt CH		
NNO	Brock Lesnar		
NNO	Kofi Kingston		
NNO	Matt Riddle		

2019 Mattel WWE Series 104

NNO	Alexa Bliss		
NNO	Daniel Bryan		
NNO	Keith Lee		
NNO	Keith Lee Black Tights CH		
NNO	Randy Orton		
NNO	Rey Mysterio		

2019 Mattel WWE Series 105

NNO	John Cena		
NNO	Lars Sullivan		
NNO	Paige GM		
NNO	Roman Reigns		
NNO	Ronda Rousey		
NNO	Ronda Rousey (CHASE)		

2020 Mattel WWE Series 106

NNO	Carmella	15.00	30.00
NNO	Carmella Orange/Purple CH	15.00	30.00
NNO	Finn Balor	7.50	15.00
NNO	Johnny Gargano	10.00	20.00
NNO	R-Truth	10.00	20.00
NNO	Triple H	7.50	15.00

2020 Mattel WWE Series 107

NNO	Bianca Belair	10.00	20.00
NNO	Braun Strowman	12.50	25.00
NNO	EC3	12.50	25.00
NNO	The Rock	15.00	30.00
NNO	Shinsuke Nakamura Black Gear	7.50	15.00
NNO	Shinsuke Nakamura Blue Gear CH	12.50	25.00

2020 Mattel WWE Series 108

NNO	AJ Styles Red/Gray	15.00	30.00
NNO	AJ Styles White/Gold CH	25.00	50.00
NNO	Aleister Black	12.50	25.00
NNO	Angelo Dawkins		
NNO	Montez Ford	7.50	15.00
NNO	Roman Reigns	15.00	30.00

2020 Mattel WWE Series 109

NNO	Becky Lynch	10.00	20.00
NNO	Lana Blue Gear CH	12.50	25.00
NNO	Lana Red Gear	7.50	15.00
NNO	Ricochet	10.00	20.00
NNO	Seth Rollins	7.50	15.00
NNO	Undertaker	12.50	25.00

2020 Mattel WWE Series 110

NNO	Finn Balor	7.50	15.00
NNO	John Cena	10.00	20.00
NNO	Kofi Kingston	7.50	15.00
NNO	Liv Morgan	15.00	30.00
NNO	Mike Kanellis Barbed Wire Tights	7.50	15.00
NNO	Mike Kanellis Name on Tights CH	12.50	25.00

2020 Mattel WWE Series 111

NNO	Bray Wyatt	12.50	25.00
NNO	Erick Rowan	7.50	15.00
NNO	Jeff Hardy	10.00	20.00
NNO	Kevin Owens	12.50	25.00
NNO	Nikki Cross	10.00	20.00
NNO	Nikki Cross Gray Pants CH	12.50	25.00

2020 Mattel WWE Series 112

NNO	Adam Cole	10.00	20.00
NNO	Bobby Lashley	10.00	20.00
NNO	Bobby Lashley Red CH	12.50	25.00
NNO	Braun Strowman	12.50	25.00
NNO	Sasha Banks	20.00	40.00
NNO	Seth Rollins	10.00	20.00

2020 Mattel WWE Series 113

NNO	Buddy Murphy	15.00	30.00
NNO	Drew McIntyre	15.00	30.00
NNO	Edge	12.50	25.00
NNO	Edge Silver Boots CH	15.00	30.00
NNO	John Cena	12.50	25.00
NNO	Mia Yim	15.00	30.00

2020 Mattel WWE Series 114

NNO	The Fiend Bray Wyatt	20.00	40.00
NNO	Kofi Kingston	7.50	15.00
NNO	Rhea Ripley	15.00	30.00
NNO	Ricochet	10.00	20.00
NNO	Ricochet (yellow gear) (CHASE)	12.50	25.00
NNO	Shorty G	7.50	15.00

2021 Mattel WWE Series 115

NNO	Becky Lynch	12.50	25.00
NNO	Big E	6.00	12.00
NNO	Braun Strowman	10.00	20.00
NNO	Humberto Carrillo	7.50	15.00
NNO	Humberto Carrillo Blue/White CH	12.50	25.00
NNO	Tegan Nox	10.00	20.00

2021 Mattel WWE Series 116

NNO	Dakota Kai	15.00	30.00
NNO	Kevin Owens	12.50	25.00
NNO	Roderick Strong	10.00	20.00
NNO	Roderick Strong Black Gear CH	12.50	25.00
NNO	Seth Rollins	12.50	25.00
NNO	Sheamus	7.50	15.00

2021 Mattel WWE Series 117

NNO	Otis	10.00	20.00
NNO	Roman Reigns	10.00	20.00
NNO	Toni Storm	20.00	40.00
NNO	Toni Storm Red Gear CH	25.00	50.00
NNO	Tucker		
NNO	Undertaker	15.00	30.00

2021 Mattel WWE Series 118

NNO	Austin Theory	7.50	15.00
NNO	Austin Theory Red Tights CH	10.00	20.00
NNO	Erik	10.00	20.00
NNO	Finn Balor	7.50	15.00
NNO	Ivar	7.50	15.00
NNO	Jeff Hardy	7.50	15.00

2021 Mattel WWE Series 119

NNO	Dominik Dijakovic	7.50	15.00
NNO	John Cena	12.50	25.00
NNO	Lacey Evans Red CH	12.50	25.00
NNO	Lacey Evans Yellow	6.00	12.00
NNO	Randy Orton	12.50	25.00
NNO	Triple H	7.50	15.00

2021 Mattel WWE Series 120

NNO	Edge	10.00	20.00
NNO	Karrion Kross	10.00	20.00
NNO	Pete Dunne	12.50	25.00
NNO	Scarlett (trunks and top)) (CHASE)	15.00	30.00
NNO	Scarlett (body suit)	12.50	25.00
NNO	Shawn Michaels	7.50	15.00

2021 Mattel WWE Series 121

NNO	Apollo Crews (black trunks) (CHASE)	12.50	25.00

NNO	Apollo Crews (gray trunks)	7.50	15.00
NNO	Bayley	6.00	12.00
NNO	Kane	12.50	25.00
NNO	Rey Mysterio	10.00	20.00
NNO	Roman Reigns	7.50	15.00

2021 Mattel WWE Series 122

NNO	Charlotte Flair	10.00	20.00
NNO	Drew McIntyre	7.50	15.00
NNO	Chelsea Green (black gear) (CHASE)	15.00	30.00
NNO	Chelsea Green (purple gear)	12.50	25.00
NNO	Damian Priest	7.50	15.00

2021 Mattel WWE Series 123

NNO	Bobby Lashley	12.50	25.00
NNO	Braun Strowman	7.50	15.00
NNO	Dexter Lumis	10.00	20.00
NNO	Jake Atlas	7.50	15.00
NNO	Jake Atlas (white gear) (CHASE)	12.50	25.00
NNO	Otis	6.00	12.00

2021 Mattel WWE Series 124

NNO	Angel Garza	7.50	15.00
NNO	Angel Garza (green gear) (CHASE)	12.50	25.00
NNO	Io Shirai	10.00	20.00
NNO	Kyle O'Reilly	10.00	20.00
NNO	Rey Mysterio	10.00	20.00
NNO	Seth Rollins	7.50	15.00

2021 Mattel WWE Series 125

NNO	Elias	6.00	12.00
NNO	Ember Moon	12.50	25.00
NNO	Isaiah Swerve Scott	10.00	20.00
NNO	Isaiah Swerve Scott (red shorts) (CHASE)	15.00	30.00
NNO	Jeff Hardy	12.50	25.00
NNO	The Rock	12.50	25.00

2021 Mattel WWE Series 126

NNO	Bobby Fish	15.00	30.00
NNO	Drew McIntyre		
NNO	Macho Man Randy Savage	12.50	25.00
NNO	Mandy Rose	15.00	30.00
NNO	Mandy Rose (pink gear) (CHASE)	20.00	40.00
NNO	Seth Rollins	10.00	20.00

2021 Mattel WWE Series 127

NNO	Joaquin Wilde	10.00	20.00
NNO	Joaquin Wilde (no face paint) (CHASE)	15.00	30.00
NNO	Keith Lee	12.50	25.00
NNO	Rey Mysterio		
NNO	Santos Escobar	7.50	15.00
NNO	Shayna Baszler	12.50	25.00

2021 Mattel WWE Series 128

NNO	Big E	10.00	20.00
NNO	Edge	7.50	15.00
NNO	MVP	7.50	15.00
NNO	Raul Mendoza	10.00	20.00
NNO	Raul Mendoza (w/face paint) (CHASE)	12.50	25.00
NNO	Sasha Banks	15.00	30.00

2022 Mattel WWE Series 129

NNO	Carmella	10.00	20.00
NNO	Dominik Mysterio	30.00	60.00
NNO	The Miz	10.00	20.00
NNO	Noam Dar	12.50	25.00
NNO	Roman Reigns	12.50	25.00

2022 Mattel WWE Series 130

NNO	AJ Styles	15.00	30.00
NNO	Gran Metalik	10.00	20.00
NNO	John Cena	7.50	15.00
NNO	Johnny Gargano (black & red gear) (CHASE)	12.50	25.00
NNO	Johnny Gargano (The Way)	10.00	20.00
NNO	Omos	10.00	20.00

2022 Mattel WWE Series 131

NNO	Bianca Belair	10.00	20.00
NNO	Candice LeRae (purple gear) (CHASE)	20.00	40.00
NNO	Candice LeRae (The Way)	7.50	15.00
NNO	Happy Corbin	6.00	12.00
NNO	Lince Dorado	12.50	25.00
NNO	Randy Orton	6.00	12.00

2022 Mattel WWE Series 132

NNO	Bobby Lashley	7.50	15.00
NNO	Kushida	15.00	30.00
NNO	Matt Riddle	15.00	30.00
NNO	Rey Mysterio	7.50	15.00
NNO	Tamina (blue highlights)	10.00	20.00
NNO	Tamina (green highlights) (CHASE)	12.50	25.00

2022 Mattel WWE Series 133

NNO	Cedric Alexander (black & gold gear)	7.50	15.00
NNO	Cedric Alexander (red & yellow gear) (CHASE)	12.50	25.00
NNO	Finn Balor	10.00	20.00
NNO	Natalya	12.50	25.00
NNO	Roman Reigns	10.00	20.00
NNO	Stone Cold Steve Austin	10.00	20.00

2022 Mattel WWE Series 134

NNO	Becky Lynch	10.00	20.00
NNO	Indi Hartwell	15.00	30.00
NNO	Sami Zayn	12.50	25.00
NNO	Seth Rollins	10.00	20.00
NNO	Shelton Benjamin (black & white) (CHASE)	15.00	30.00
NNO	Shelton Benjamin (gold standard)	10.00	20.00

2022 Mattel WWE Series 135

NNO	Brock Lesnar	12.50	25.00
NNO	Bron Breakker	25.00	50.00
NNO	Damian Priest	12.50	25.00
NNO	Nikki A.S.H.	10.00	20.00
NNO	Reggie (orange pants)	7.50	15.00
NNO	Reggie (white pants) (CHASE)		

2022 Mattel WWE Series 136

NNO	Cody Rhodes	20.00	40.00
NNO	Dolph Ziggler (pink tights)	10.00	20.00
NNO	Dolph Ziggler (blue tights) (CHASE)	10.00	20.00
NNO	Goldberg	12.50	25.00
NNO	Robert Roode	7.50	15.00
NNO	Xia Li	30.00	75.00

2023 Mattel WWE Series 137

NNO	Aliyah		
NNO	Austin Theory		
NNO	Commander Azeez		
NNO	Roman Reigns		
NNO	Seth Rollins		
NNO	Seth Rollins (CHASE)		

2020 Mattel WWE Showdown 2-Packs Series 1

NNO	Roman Reigns vs. Finn Balor	15.00	30.00
NNO	Sasha Banks vs. Alexa Bliss	25.00	50.00
NNO	Undertaker vs. Jeff Hardy	20.00	40.00

2020 Mattel WWE Showdown 2-Packs Series 2

NNO	Bobby Lashley vs. King Booker	20.00	40.00
NNO	Randy Orton vs. John Cena	25.00	50.00
NNO	The Rock vs. Triple H	20.00	40.00

2020 Mattel WWE Showdown 2-Packs Series 3

NNO	The Fiend Bray Wyatt vs. Daniel Bryan		
NNO	The Giant vs. Ric Flair		
NNO	Kane vs. Edge		

2021 Mattel WWE Showdown 2-Packs Series 4

NNO	Drew McIntyre vs. Seth Rollins	15.00	30.00
NNO	John Morrison vs. Kofi Kingston	15.00	30.00
NNO	Riddle vs. AJ Styles	20.00	40.00

2021 Mattel WWE Showdown 2-Packs Series 5

NNO	Mankind vs. Stone Cold Steve Austin	15.00	30.00
NNO	British Bulldog vs. Big Boss Man	17.50	35.00
NNO	Chyna vs. Trish Stratus	15.00	30.00

2021 Mattel WWE Showdown 2-Packs Series 6

NNO	Angelo Dawkins & Montez Ford	20.00	40.00
NNO	Shawn Michaels & John Cena	17.50	35.00
NNO	The Usos	30.00	75.00

2021 Mattel WWE Showdown 2-Packs Series 7

NNO	Cesaro vs. Roman Reigns	20.00	40.00
NNO	Kane vs. "Stone Cold" Steve Austin	15.00	30.00
NNO	Rhea Ripley vs. Charlotte Flair	12.50	25.00

2021 Mattel WWE Showdown 2-Packs Series 8

NNO	Bret "Hit Man" Hart vs. Undertaker	25.00	50.00
NNO	Goldberg vs. Drew McIntyre	15.00	30.00
NNO	Street Profits	15.00	30.00

2022 Mattel WWE Showdown 2-Packs Series 9

NNO	Bayley vs. Sasha Banks	20.00	40.00
NNO	The Rock vs. John Cena	25.00	50.00
NNO	Sheamus vs. Ricochet	15.00	30.00

2022 Mattel WWE Showdown 2-Packs Series 10

NNO	The Miz vs. Bobby Lashley	15.00	30.00
NNO	Omos & AJ Styles	12.50	25.00

2022 Mattel WWE Showdown 2-Packs Series 11

NNO	Becky Lynch vs. Bianca Belair	30.00	60.00
NNO	Roman Reigns vs. John Cena	15.00	30.00
NNO	The Usos	30.00	60.00

2023 Mattel WWE Showdown 2-Packs Series 12

NNO	Bobby Lashley vs. Big E		
NNO	Charlotte Flair vs. Alexa Bliss		
NNO	Riddle & Randy Orton RKBro		

2010 Mattel WWE Signature Series

NNO	Chris Jericho		
NNO	Dave Batista	12.50	25.00
NNO	John Cena	10.00	20.00
NNO	Shawn Michaels		

2011 Mattel WWE Signature Series

NNO	Edge		
NNO	Edge/Black		
NNO	John Cena	7.50	15.00
NNO	Randy Orton	10.00	20.00
NNO	Rey Mysterio	7.50	15.00
NNO	Triple H		
NNO	Undertaker		

2012 Mattel WWE Signature Series

NNO	Big Show		
NNO	CM Punk		
NNO	John Cena/Dk Shorts		
NNO	John Cena/ Green Wristbands		
NNO	John Cena/Lt Shorts		
NNO	Kane		
NNO	Randy Orton		
NNO	Rey Mysterio/Gray		
NNO	Rey Mysterio Red and White		
NNO	Rey Mysterio/Red		
NNO	Sheamus		
NNO	Sin Cara		
NNO	The Miz		
NNO	The Rock		

2015 Mattel WWE Signature Series

NNO	Bray Wyatt	7.50	15.00
NNO	Daniel Bryan	15.00	30.00
NNO	Dave Batista	7.50	15.00
NNO	Dean Ambrose	7.50	15.00
NNO	Hulk Hogan	15.00	30.00
NNO	John Cena	7.50	15.00

2013 Mattel WWE Slam City Series 1

NNO	Alberto Del Rio		
NNO	Big Show	15.00	30.00
NNO	Brock Lesnar		
NNO	John Cena	7.50	15.00
NNO	Kane	20.00	40.00
NNO	Rey Mysterio	15.00	30.00

2018 Mattel WWE Sound Slammers Playset

NNO	Destruction Zone	50.00	100.00

2018 Mattel WWE Sound Slammers Series 1

NNO	Dean Ambrose	12.50	25.00

NNO John Cena 20.00 40.00
NNO Kevin Owens 12.50 25.00
NNO Roman Reigns 12.50 25.00
NNO Seth Rollins 12.50 25.00

2018 Mattel WWE Sound Slammers Series 2

NNO AJ Styles 10.00 20.00
NNO Bobby Roode 10.00 20.00
NNO Finn Balor 20.00 40.00
NNO Kurt Angle 10.00 20.00
NNO The Miz 10.00 20.00

2018 Mattel WWE SummerSlam Heritage

NNO John Cena 6.00 12.00
NNO Kurt Angle 6.00 12.00
NNO Ric Flair 7.50 15.00
NNO Roman Reigns 7.50 15.00
NNO Shane McMahon 7.50 15.00
NNO Shinsuke Nakamura 12.50 25.00

2014 Mattel WWE SummerSlam Heritage

NNO CM Punk 15.00 30.00
NNO Million Dollar Man Ted DiBiase 12.50 25.00
NNO Rey Mysterio
NNO Shawn Michaels 12.50 25.00
NNO Triple H 10.00 20.00
NNO Undertaker 12.50 25.00

2016 Mattel WWE SummerSlam Heritage

NNO British Bulldog FB 6.00 12.00
NNO Dave Batista FB 6.00 12.00
NNO Jim Duggan FB 7.50 15.00
NNO Undertaker FB 12.50 25.00

2017 Mattel WWE SummerSlam Heritage

NNO Dusty Rhodes FB 7.50 15.00
NNO Nikki Bella 12.50 25.00
NNO The Rock FB 10.00 20.00
NNO Seth Rollins 7.50 15.00

2013 Mattel WWE Super Strikers

NNO Alberto Del Rio
NNO Big Show 7.50 15.00
NNO Brock Lesnar
NNO CM Punk 10.00 20.00
NNO Daniel Bryan 12.50 25.00
NNO Dolph Ziggler
NNO John Cena
NNO Kofi Kingston 7.50 15.00
NNO The Miz
NNO Randy Orton 10.00 20.00
NNO The Rock
NNO Roman Reigns 15.00 30.00
NNO Ryback
NNO Sheamus 10.00 20.00
NNO Undertaker 12.50 25.00

2012 Mattel WWE Superstar Entrances Series 1

NNO CM Punk 20.00 40.00
NNO Dolph Ziggler
NNO John Cena 12.50 25.00
NNO The Miz 7.50 15.00
NNO R-Truth 7.50 15.00
NNO Randy Orton 12.50 25.00
NNO Triple H 10.00 20.00

2013 Mattel WWE Superstar Entrances Series 2

NNO Daniel Bryan 15.00 30.00
NNO John Cena 10.00 20.00
NNO Ryback
NNO Santino Marella
NNO The Rock 10.00 20.00
NNO Zack Ryder

2014 Mattel WWE Superstar Entrances Series 3

NNO Brock Lesnar 10.00 20.00
NNO CM Punk 20.00 40.00
NNO Cody Rhodes 15.00 30.00
NNO John Cena 10.00 20.00
NNO Macho Man Randy Savage 15.00 30.00
NNO Sheamus 10.00 20.00
NNO The Rock 10.00 20.00

2014 Mattel WWE Superstar Entrances Series 4

NNO AJ Lee 30.00 60.00
NNO Daniel Bryan 15.00 30.00
NNO Dolph Ziggler
NNO John Cena 10.00 20.00
NNO Rob Van Dam 15.00 30.00
NNO The Rock 7.50 15.00

2015 Mattel WWE Superstar Entrances Series 5

NNO Daniel Bryan 15.00 30.00
NNO John Cena 10.00 20.00
NNO Randy Orton 10.00 20.00
NNO Rowdy Roddy Piper 15.00 30.00
NNO Triple H 7.50 15.00

2015 Mattel WWE Superstar Entrances Series 6

NNO Bo Dallas 7.50 15.00
NNO Hulk Hogan 20.00 40.00
NNO John Cena 10.00 20.00
NNO Kofi Kingston 7.50 15.00
NNO Wade Barrett 6.00 12.00

2011 Mattel WWE Superstar Matchups Series 4

NNO Rey Mysterio/
Blue and White
NNO Rey Mysterio/Black and Blue
NNO Sin Cara

2017 Mattel WWE Superstars Dolls 12-Inch

NNO Alicia Fox
NNO Asuka
NNO Bayley
NNO Becky Lynch 15.00 30.00
NNO Carmella
NNO Charlotte Flair 12.50 25.00
NNO Eva Marie 10.00 20.00
NNO Lana
NNO Natalya

2017 Mattel WWE Superstars Dolls 12-Inch Fashions

NNO Alexa Bliss
NNO Bayley
NNO Becky Lynch
NNO Brie Bella 12.50 25.00
NNO Natalya 12.50 25.00
NNO Nikki Bella 15.00 30.00
NNO Sasha Banks 12.50 25.00

2017 Mattel WWE Superstars Dolls 12-Inch Multi-Packs

NNO Charlotte Flair/Sasha Banks SDCC
NNO Natalya/Becky Lynch/Sasha Banks/Bellas

2017 Mattel WWE Superstars Dolls Action Figures Playset

NNO Ultimate Entrance Playset (w/Nikki Bella)

2017 Mattel WWE Superstars Dolls Action Figures Series 1

NNO Brie Bella
NNO Charlotte Flair
NNO Nikki Bella

2017 Mattel WWE Superstars Dolls Action Figures Series 2

NNO Alexa Bliss
NNO Brie Bella
NNO Natalya
NNO Nikki Bella

2017 Mattel WWE Superstars Dolls Action Figures Ultimate Fan Packs

NNO Bayley
NNO Charlotte Flair
NNO Sasha Banks

2017 Mattel WWE Surf's Up 2 WaveMania Action Figure DVD Combo

NNO Batista
NNO Big Show
NNO Bray Wyatt
NNO Daniel Bryan
NNO Dean Ambrose (black shirt)
NNO Dean Ambrose (white shirt)
NNO Dolph Ziggler
NNO El Torito
NNO Goldust
NNO John Cena (black shorts)
NNO John Cena (blue shorts)
NNO John Cena (green shorts)
NNO John Cena (tan shorts/blue armband)
NNO John Cena (tan shorts/red armband)
NNO Justin Gabriel
NNO Kane
NNO Mankind
NNO Miz
NNO Randy Orton
NNO Rey Mysterio
NNO Ric Flair
NNO Ricky "The Dragon" Steamboat
NNO Roman Reigns
NNO Rusev
NNO Ryback
NNO Santino Marella
NNO Seth Rollins
NNO Titus O'Neill
NNO Triple H

2013 Mattel WWE Survivor Series 2013

NNO CM Punk
NNO Ryback

2019 Mattel WWE Tag Team Buddies Plush Dolls 14"

NNO Bayley
NNO Becky Lynch
NNO Sasha Banks

2016 Mattel WWE Teenage Mutant Ninja Turtles Ninja Superstars Series 1

NNO Donatello as Undertaker 15.00 30.00
NNO Leonardo as John Cena 10.00 20.00
NNO Michelangelo as Macho Man Randy Savage 12.50 25.00
NNO Raphael as Sting 12.50 25.00

2017 Mattel WWE Teenage Mutant Ninja Turtles Ninja Superstars Series 2

NNO Donatello as Ultimate Warrior 12.50 25.00
NNO Leonardo as Finn Balor 10.00 20.00
NNO Michelangelo as Rowdy Roddy Piper7.50 15.00
NNO Raphael as The Rock 15.00 30.00

2016 Mattel WWE Then Now Forever Series 1

NNO Chris Jericho 6.00 12.00
NNO Seth Rollins 10.00 20.00
NNO Sin Cara 40.00 80.00
NNO Undertaker 15.00 30.00

2017 Mattel WWE Then Now Forever Series 2

NNO Neville 6.00 12.00
NNO Sheamus 10.00 20.00
NNO Stone Cold Steve Austin FB 10.00 20.00
NNO Ultimate Warrior FB 12.50 25.00

2017 Mattel WWE Then Now Forever Series 3

NNO Bray Wyatt 7.50 15.00
NNO Kevin Owens 6.00 12.00
NNO Seth Rollins 10.00 20.00
NNO Triple H 12.50 25.00
NNO X-Pac 12.50 25.00

2013 Mattel WWE TLC 2013

NNO Alberto Del Rio
NNO Kofi Kingston
NNO Mark Henry
NNO Sheamus

2020 Mattel WWE Top Picks 2020

NNO John Cena 15.00 30.00
NNO Kofi Kingston 15.00 30.00
NNO The Rock 20.00 40.00
NNO Roman Reigns 12.50 25.00

2021 Mattel WWE Top Picks 2021

NNO Braun Strowman
NNO John Cena
NNO The Rock
NNO Roman Reigns

2021 Mattel WWE Top Picks 2022

NNO	Drew McIntyre	6.00	12.00
NNO	The Fiend Bray Wyatt	6.00	12.00
NNO	John Cena	12.50	25.00
NNO	The Rock	12.00	30.00

2022 Mattel WWE Top Picks 2023

NNO Bray Wyatt
NNO Roman Reigns
NNO Undertaker

2022 Mattel WWE Top Picks 2023 Wave 2

NNO John Cena
NNO Randy Orton
NNO Rey Mysterio

2023 Mattel WWE Top Picks 2023 Wave 3

NNO AJ Styles
NNO Brock Lesnar
NNO The Rock

2018 Mattel WWE Top Talent 2018

NNO	AJ Styles	15.00	20.00
NNO	John Cena	7.50	15.00
NNO	Roman Reigns	7.50	15.00
NNO	Seth Rollins	6.00	12.00

2019 Mattel WWE Top Talent 2019

NNO	AJ Styles		
NNO	Jeff Hardy	7.50	15.00
NNO	John Cena	12.50	25.00
NNO	Seth Rollins	7.50	15.00

2020 Mattel WWE Top Talent 2020

NNO	AJ Styles		
NNO	Braun Strowman	15.00	30.00
NNO	Finn Balor		
NNO	John Cena	12.50	25.00

2021 Mattel WWE Top Talent 2022

NNO John Cena
NNO The Rock
NNO Roman Reigns

2022 Mattel WWE Top Talent 2023

NNO Brock Lesnar
NNO Rock
NNO Seth Rollins

2017 Mattel WWE Tough Talkers Series 1

NNO	Bray Wyatt	15.00	30.00
NNO	Dean Ambrose	12.50	25.00
NNO	John Cena	15.00	30.00
NNO	Kevin Owens	10.00	20.00
NNO	Roman Reigns	12.50	25.00
NNO	Seth Rollins	12.50	25.00

2017 Mattel WWE Tough Talkers Series 2

NNO	Big E	7.50	15.00
NNO	Brock Lesnar	12.50	25.00
NNO	Dean Ambrose	12.50	25.00
NNO	John Cena	20.00	40.00
NNO	Kofi Kingston	10.00	20.00
NNO	Xavier Woods	10.00	20.00

2017 Mattel WWE Tough Talkers 2-Packs Series 1

NNO	The Rock/Stone Cold Steve Austin	25.00	50.00
NNO	Undertaker/Brock Lesnar	25.00	50.00

2017 Mattel WWE Tough Talkers 2-Packs Series 2

NNO	AJ Styles/Seth Rollins	20.00	40.00
NNO	Triple H/Roman Reigns	17.50	35.00

2017 Mattel WWE Tough Talkers Hall of Fame Series

NNO	Macho Man Randy Savage	12.50	25.00
NNO	Ric Flair	12.50	25.00
NNO	Rowdy Roddy Piper	12.50	25.00

2017 Mattel WWE Tough Talkers Total Tag Team

NNO	AJ Styles	15.00	30.00
NNO	Randy Orton	12.50	25.00
NNO	Sting	12.50	25.00
NNO	Xavier Woods	10.00	20.00

2017 Mattel WWE Tough Talkers Total Tag Team 2-Packs

NNO	Big E/Kofi Kingston	17.50	35.00
NNO	Kevin Owens & Chris Jericho	15.00	30.00

2012 Mattel WWE Tribute to the Troops

NNO	Big Show/Brown Hat		
NNO	Big Show/Green Hat		
NNO	John Cena	12.50	25.00
NNO	Randy Orton/Brown Vest	10.00	20.00
NNO	Randy Orton/Green Vest	10.00	20.00
NNO	Rey Mysterio	20.00	40.00

2010 Mattel WWE Triple Threat 3-Packs

NNO Evan Bourne/Swagger/Kozlov
NNO John Cena/Batista/Y2J
NNO Kane/John Cena/Big Show
NNO Kane/Triple H/Great Khali
NNO Sheamus/John Cena/Triple H

2018 Mattel WWE True Moves 12-Inch

NNO	AJ Styles	12.50	25.00
NNO	Kane	10.00	20.00
NNO	Randy Orton	10.00	20.00
NNO	Kevin Owens	12.50	25.00
NNO	Kurt Angle	10.00	20.00
NNO	Kalisto	15.00	30.00
NNO	Seth Rollins	12.50	25.00

2019 Mattel WWE Ultimate Edition Series 1

NNO	Ultimate Warrior	20.00	40.00
NNO	Ronda Rousey	25.00	50.00

2019 Mattel WWE Ultimate Edition Series 2

NNO	Bret "Hitman" Hart	25.00	50.00
NNO	Shinsuke Nakamura	20.00	40.00

2019 Mattel WWE Ultimate Edition Series 3

NNO Finn Balor
NNO Triple H

2020 Mattel WWE Ultimate Edition Series 4

NNO	Brock Lesnar	30.00	60.00
NNO	Shawn Michaels	60.00	120.00

2020 Mattel WWE Ultimate Edition Series 5

NNO	Becky Lynch	30.00	60.00
NNO	John Cena	40.00	80.00

2020 Mattel WWE Ultimate Edition Series 6

NNO	Charlotte Flair	30.00	60.00
NNO	The Rock	60.00	120.00

(Amazon Exclusive)

2020 Mattel WWE Ultimate Edition Series 7

NNO	The Fiend Bray Wyatt	30.00	75.00
NNO	Hollywood Hulk Hogan	50.00	100.00

2021 Mattel WWE Ultimate Edition Series 8

NNO	Edge	25.00	50.00
NNO	Macho Man Randy Savage	25.00	50.00

2021 Mattel WWE Ultimate Edition Series 9

NNO	Stone Cold Steve Austin	30.00	60.00
NNO	Ric Flair	30.00	75.00

2021 Mattel WWE Ultimate Edition Series 10

NNO	John Cena	20.00	40.00
NNO	The Rock	25.00	50.00

2021 Mattel WWE Ultimate Edition Series 11

NNO	Kane	30.00	60.00
NNO	Undertaker	30.00	60.00

2022 Mattel WWE Ultimate Edition Series 12

NNO	Alexa Bliss	20.00	40.00
NNO	The Fiend Bray Wyatt	25.00	50.00

2022 Mattel WWE Ultimate Edition Series 13

NNO	Hulk Hogan	25.00	50.00
NNO	Mr. T	20.00	40.00

2022 Mattel WWE Ultimate Edition Series 14

NNO	Jeff Hardy	20.00	40.00
NNO	Roman Reigns	20.00	40.00

2022 Mattel WWE Ultimate Edition Series 15

NNO	Brock Lesnar	30.00	60.00
NNO	Ultimate Warrior	25.00	50.00

2023 Mattel WWE Ultimate Edition Series 16

NNO AJ Styles
NNO Razor Ramon

2017 Mattel WWE Undertaker 5-Pack

NNO	1990/1994/1998/2014/2016	30.00	75.00

2019 Mattel WWE Wrekkin' Playsets

NNO	Entrance Stage Playset	40.00	80.00
NNO	Performance Center Playset	30.00	75.00
NNO	Slam Mobile (w/Braun Strowman)	20.00	40.00

2019 Mattel WWE Wrekkin' Series 1

NNO	AJ Styles	10.00	20.00
NNO	John Cena	12.50	25.00
NNO	Seth Rollins	10.00	20.00
NNO	Undertaker	15.00	30.00

2019 Mattel WWE Wrekkin' Series 2

NNO Miz
NNO Woken Matt Hardy

2019 Mattel WWE Wrekkin' Series 3

NNO Daniel Bryan
NNO Rey Mysterio

2020 Mattel WWE Wrekkin' Playsets

NNO	Collision Cage	60.00	120.00
NNO	Slambulance	50.00	100.00
NNO	Slamcycle (w/Drew McIntyre)	30.00	60.00
NNO	Slamcycle (w/Undertaker)	30.00	60.00

2020 Mattel WWE Wrekkin' Series 4

NNO	Elias	20.00	40.00
NNO	Roman Reigns	25.00	50.00

2010 Mattel WWE WrestleMania 26

NNO	Chris Jericho		
NNO	Christian	15.00	30.00
NNO	Drew McIntyre	12.50	25.00
NNO	Kane		
NNO	Matt Hardy		
NNO	Shawn Michaels		
NNO	Shelton Benjamin		

2011 Mattel WWE WrestleMania 27

NNO	Alberto Del Rio	6.00	12.00
NNO	Christian	20.00	40.00
NNO	John Cena	12.50	25.00
NNO	John Morrison	10.00	20.00
NNO	Randy Orton	10.00	20.00
NNO	Triple H	12.50	25.00

2021 Mattel WWE WrestleMania 37 Celebration

NNO	Andre the Giant	20.00	40.00
NNO	Macho Man Randy Savage	20.00	40.00

2014 Mattel WWE WrestleMania 30 Heritage

NNO	Brock Lesnar		
NNO	John Cena	12.50	25.00
NNO	The Rock	12.50	25.00
NNO	Undertaker	10.00	20.00

2015 Mattel WWE WrestleMania 31 Heritage

NNO	Hulk Hogan	15.00	30.00
NNO	John Cena		
NNO	The Rock	12.50	25.00
NNO	Shawn Michaels	10.00	20.00

2016 Mattel WWE WrestleMania 32 Heritage

NNO	Cesaro	6.00	12.00

NNO Eddie Guerrero 10.00 20.00
NNO Razor Ramon 17.50 35.00
NNO Roman Reigns 7.50 15.00

2017 Mattel WWE WrestleMania 33 Heritage

NNO Chris Jericho 12.50 25.00
NNO Roman Reigns 15.00 30.00
NNO Stone Cold Steve Austin 10.00 20.00
NNO Undertaker 15.00 30.00

2018 Mattel WWE WrestleMania 34 Heritage

NNO AJ Styles 7.50 15.00
NNO Bayley 7.50 15.00
NNO Big Show 20.00 40.00
NNO Dean Ambrose 7.50 15.00
NNO Mojo Rawley 6.00 12.00
NNO Seth Rollins 7.50 15.00

2018 Mattel WWE WrestleMania 35 Heritage

NNO Charlotte Flair 12.50 25.00
NNO Elias 7.50 15.00
NNO John Cena
NNO Kevin Nash 10.00 20.00
NNO Matt Hardy 7.50 15.00
NNO Trish Stratus 12.50 25.00

2020 Mattel WWE WrestleMania 36 Heritage

NNO Batista 20.00 40.00
NNO Becky Lynch 12.50 25.00
NNO The Rock 15.00 30.00
NNO Seth Rollins 10.00 20.00
NNO Shane McMahon 15.00 30.00
NNO Stephanie McMahon 12.50 25.00

2021 Mattel WWE WrestleMania 37 Heritage

NNO Andrade 6.00 12.00
NNO Drew McIntyre 12.50 25.00
NNO The Fiend Bray Wyatt 12.50 25.00
NNO Ricochet 6.00 12.00

2021 Mattel WWE WrestleMania 38 Heritage

NNO Bianca Belair 15.00 30.00
NNO Hulk Hogan 12.50 25.00
NNO Seth Rollins 10.00 20.00
NNO Sheamus 10.00 20.00

2022 Mattel WWE WrestleMania 39 Heritage

NNO Andre the Giant 25.00 50.00
NNO Bianca Belair 15.00 30.00
NNO Kane 12.50 25.00
NNO Undertaker 12.50 25.00

2016 Mattel WWE Zombies Series 1

NNO Bray Wyatt 7.50 15.00
NNO Dean Ambrose 15.00 30.00
NNO John Cena 15.00 30.00
NNO Paige 7.50 15.00
NNO The Rock 12.50 25.00
NNO Roman Reigns 12.50 25.00
NNO Triple H 7.50 15.00
NNO Undertaker 12.50 25.00

2017 Mattel WWE Zombies Series 2

NNO Stone Cold Steve Austin 12.50 25.00
NNO AJ Styles 7.50 15.00
NNO Brock Lesnar 7.50 15.00
NNO Kevin Owens 6.00 12.00
NNO Sasha Banks 12.50 25.00
NNO Seth Rollins 7.50 15.00

2018 Mattel WWE Zombies Series 3

NNO Charlotte Flair 10.00 20.00
NNO Finn Balor 12.50 25.00
NNO Jeff Hardy 10.00 20.00
NNO Kane 20.00 40.00
NNO Matt Hardy 10.00 20.00
NNO Shinsuke Nakamura 10.00 20.00

1990 Multi Toys WWF Power Grip Squirts

NNO Big Boss Man
NNO Hulk Hogan
NNO Jake The Snake Roberts
NNO Macho King Randy Savage
NNO Million Dollar Man Ted Dibiase
NNO Ultimate Warrior

1990 Multi Toys WWF Power Grip Squirts Tag Teams

NNO Bushwhackers
NNO Legion of Doom
NNO The Rockers

1990 Multi Toys WWF Squirt Heads

NNO Big Boss Man
NNO Hulk Hogan
NNO Jake The Snake Roberts
NNO Macho King Randy Savage
NNO Million Dollar Man Ted Dibiase
NNO Ultimate Warrior

2017 Ooshies WWE Series 1

NNO Asuka R
NNO Booker T Black Trunks R
NNO Booker T R
NNO Bray Wyatt C
NNO Brie Bella R
NNO Brock Lesnar C
NNO Cesaro C
NNO Charlotte Flair R
NNO Dean Ambrose C
NNO Dolph Ziggler C
NNO Finn Balor (hologram) LE
NNO Finn Balor R
NNO Jey Uso R
NNO Jimmy Uso R
NNO John Cena C
NNO John Cena Never Give Up R
NNO Junkyard Dog R
NNO Kalisto (golden) LE
NNO Kalisto R
NNO Kane R
NNO Kevin Owens C
NNO Kofi Kingston Green Tights R
NNO Kofi Kingston R
NNO Macho Man Randy Savage (glow-in-the-dark) R
NNO Macho Man Randy Savage C
NNO The Miz C
NNO Nikki Bella R
NNO Randy Orton (glow-in-the-dark) R
NNO Randy Orton C
NNO The Rock (glow-in-the-dark) R
NNO The Rock C
NNO Roman Reigns C
NNO Seth Rollins C
NNO Sheamus C
NNO Sting R
NNO Sting Wolfpack LE
NNO Stone Cold Steve Austin C
NNO Ultimate Warrior (glow-in-the-dark) R
NNO Ultimate Warrior C
NNO Undertaker R

1991 Original San Francisco Toymakers CMLL Luchadores

NNO Atlantis 25.00 50.00
NNO Lizmark 30.00 75.00
NNO Pierroth
NNO Rayo de Jalisco
NNO Ultimo Dragon 50.00 100.00
NNO Vampiro Canadiense 60.00 120.00

1999-00 Original San Francisco Toymakers ECW Wrestling Accessories

NNO Hardcore Grapple Gear
NNO Wrestling Ring Gift Set (w/Rob Van Dam & Sabu) (Toys R Us Exclusive)

1999-00 Original San Francisco Toymakers ECW Wrestling Series 1

NNO Chris Candido 25.00 50.00
NNO Justin Credible 15.00 30.00
NNO Rob Van Dam 30.00 60.00
NNO Sabu 20.00 40.00
NNO Shane Douglas 15.00 30.00
NNO Taz 25.00 50.00

1999-00 Original San Francisco Toymakers ECW Wrestling Series 2

NNO Buh Buh Ray Dudley 20.00 40.00
NNO D-Von Dudley 20.00 40.00
NNO Lance Storm 15.00 30.00
NNO New Jack 30.00 75.00
NNO Tommy Dreamer 15.00 30.00

1999-00 Original San Francisco Toymakers ECW Wrestling Series 3

NNO Justin Credible
NNO New Jack
NNO Taz

1999-00 Original San Francisco Toymakers ECW Wrestling Series 4

NNO Axl Rotten 20.00 40.00
NNO Balls Mahoney 20.00 40.00
NNO Jerry Lynn 30.00 75.00
NNO Raven 25.00 50.00
NNO Rhino 30.00 60.00
NNO Rob Van Dam 30.00 60.00
NNO Taz 20.00 40.00
NNO Yoshihiro Tajiri 30.00 60.00

1999-00 Original San Francisco Toymakers ECW Wrestling Series 5

NNO Justin Credible 15.00 30.00
NNO Little Guido
NNO Mike Awesome 60.00 120.00
NNO Nova 25.00 50.00
NNO Sabu 30.00 60.00
NNO Sandman 30.00 75.00
NNO Steve Corino
NNO Super Crazy

1999-00 Original San Francisco Toymakers ECW Wrestling Series 6

NNO Balls Mahoney 25.00 50.00
NNO Chris Candido 30.00 60.00
NNO Lance Storm 20.00 40.00
NNO New Jack 30.00 75.00
NNO Raven 30.00 75.00
NNO Rhino 50.00 100.00
NNO Rob Van Dam 30.00 60.00
NNO Tommy Dreamer 20.00 40.00

1998 Original San Francisco Toymakers WCW

NNO Bret Hart 10.00 20.00
NNO Chris Benoit 12.50 25.00
NNO Diamond Dallas Page 20.00 40.00
NNO Goldberg 15.00 30.00
NNO Raven 7.50 15.00
NNO Rey Mysterio 12.50 25.00
NNO Ric Flair 10.00 20.00
NNO Sting 10.00 20.00

1998 Original San Francisco Toymakers WCW 12-Inch

NNO Bill Goldberg 20.00 40.00
NNO Hollywood Hulk Hogan 15.00 30.00
NNO Macho Man Randy Savage 20.00 40.00
NNO Sting/Black & White 15.00 30.00
NNO Sting/Red & Black 12.50 25.00

1998 Original San Francisco Toymakers WCW 4.5-Inch

NNO Goldberg 7.50 15.00
NNO Ric Flair 7.50 15.00
NNO Rick Steiner 6.00 12.00
NNO Sting 7.50 15.00

1997-98 Original San Francisco Toymakers WCW Boxed Sets

NNO Clash of the Champions 25.00 50.00
Lex Luger/Scott Hall
NNO Fall Brawl 10.00 20.00
Sting/Giant
NNO Fearsome Foursome 20.00 40.00
Goldberg/Flair/DDP/Chris Benoit
NNO Halloween Havoc 20.00 40.00
Giant/Savage
NNO Live on Forever 30.00 75.00
Hogan/Bagwell/Giant/Scott Steiner
NNO No Retreat No Surrender 25.00 50.00
Nash/Sting/Savage/Luger
NNO Starrcade 20.00 40.00
Hogan/Sting
NNO We Are the Champions 25.00 50.00
Goldberg/Giant/Hall/Hart
NNO World War 3 12.50 25.00
Page/Nash

1997 Original San Francisco Toymakers WCW Fly Buddies

NNO Giant 10.00 20.00
NNO Hollywood Hulk Hogan 15.00 30.00
NNO Sting 10.00 20.00

1998 Original San Francisco Toymakers WCW nWo 4.5-Inch

NNO Giant	5.00	10.00
NNO Hollywood Hogan	6.00	12.00
NNO Kevin Nash	5.00	10.00
NNO Lex Luger	3.00	8.00
NNO Macho Man Randy Savage	5.00	10.00
NNO Scott Hall	5.00	10.00
NNO Scott Steiner	3.00	8.00

1998 Original San Francisco Toymakers WCW nWo Series

NNO Curt Henning UER	6.00	12.00
NNO The Giant	6.00	12.00
NNO Hollywood Hogan	7.50	15.00
NNO Kevin Nash	6.00	12.00
NNO Lex Luger	5.00	10.00
NNO Macho Man Randy Savage	7.50	15.00
NNO Marcus Bagwell	3.00	8.00
NNO Scott Hall	6.00	12.00
NNO Scott Steiner	5.00	10.00
NNO Sting	6.00	12.00

1995 Original San Francisco Toymakers WCW Playsets

NNO Wrestling Ring & Cage	25.00	50.00

1998 Original San Francisco Toymakers WCW Playsets

NNO Battle Royal Wrestling Ring & Cage
Hogan/Nash/Savage/Sting/Rick Steiner/Luger
NNO Thunder Wrestling Ring & Cage 30.00 60.00
Nash/Giant/Luger/Sting
NNO Wrestling Ring & Cage w
Action Sounds 20.00 40.00
NNO Wrestling Ring & Cage w/Giant/Luger30.0075.00
NNO Wrestling Ring & Cage w/Sting KMART
NNO Wrestling Ring & Cage 20.00 40.00
Hogan/Rick Steiner/Savage/Sting

1995 Original San Francisco Toymakers WCW Series 1

1 Brian Knobbs	12.50	25.00
2 Hulk Hogan	30.00	75.00
3 Jerry Sags	10.00	20.00
4 Jimmy Hart ERR/Dk. Skin	150.00	300.00
5 Jimmy Hart/Lt. Skin	12.50	25.00
6 Johnny B. Badd	20.00	40.00
7 Kevin Sullivan	12.50	25.00
8 Ric Flair/Blue Tights	15.00	30.00
9 Ric Flair/Purple Tights	15.00	30.00
10 Sting	25.00	50.00
11 Vader	20.00	40.00

1995 Original San Francisco Toymakers WCW Series 1 (loose)

NNO Brian Knobbs
NNO Hulk Hogan
NNO Jerry Sags
NNO Jimmy Hart
NNO Johnny B. Badd
NNO Kevin Sullivan
NNO Ric Flair/Blue Tights
NNO Ric Flair/Purple Tights
NNO Sting
NNO Vader

1996 Original San Francisco Toymakers WCW Series 2

NNO Hulk Hogan	20.00	40.00
NNO Jimmy Hart	12.50	25.00
NNO Johnny B. Badd	15.00	30.00
NNO Kevin Sullivan	10.00	20.00
NNO Macho Man Randy Savage	50.00	100.00
NNO Ric Flair/Green Tights	15.00	30.00
NNO Ric Flair/Purple Tights	15.00	30.00
NNO Sting	20.00	40.00
NNO Vader	25.00	50.00

1996 Original San Francisco Toymakers WCW Series 3

NNO Alex Wright	12.50	25.00
NNO Big Bubba Rogers	10.00	20.00
NNO Booker T	7.50	15.00
NNO Craig Pittman	7.50	15.00
NNO Giant	12.50	25.00
NNO Hulk Hogan	15.00	30.00
NNO Macho Man Randy Savage	15.00	30.00
NNO Ric Flair	12.50	25.00
NNO Stevie Ray	10.00	20.00
NNO Sting	15.00	30.00

1998 Original San Francisco Toymakers WCW Special Edition

NNO Sting/Diamond Dallas Page		
NNO Diamond Dallas Page		
NNO nWo Wolfpack Sting		
NNO Sting/nWo Wolfpack Sting		
NNO Sting	15.00	30.00

1995 Original San Francisco Toymakers WCW Tag Teams Series 1

NNO Harlem Heat	25.00	50.00
NNO Hulk Hogan/Sting	60.00	120.00
NNO Nasty Boys/Black	15.00	30.00
NNO Nasty Boys/Green	75.00	150.00

1995 Original San Francisco Toymakers WCW Tag Teams Series 1 (loose)

NNO Booker T
NNO Brian Knobbs/Black
NNO Brian Knobbs/Green
NNO Hulk Hogan
NNO Jerry Sags/Black
NNO Jerry Sags/Green
NNO Stevie Ray
NNO Sting

1996 Original San Francisco Toymakers WCW Tag Teams Series 2

NNO Harlem Heat	30.00	60.00
NNO Hulk Hogan/Sting	75.00	150.00
NNO Nasty Boys	25.00	50.00

1996 Original San Francisco Toymakers WCW Tag Teams Series 3

NNO Blue Bloods	25.00	50.00
NNO Harlem Heat	20.00	40.00
NNO Hollywood Hogan/Macho Man	20.00	40.00

1997 Original San Francisco Toymakers WCW Vibrating Action Figures

NNO Chris Benoit	7.50	15.00
NNO Giant	7.50	15.00
NNO Hollywood Hulk Hogan	12.50	25.00
NNO Lex Luger	6.00	12.00
NNO Scott Hall	7.50	15.00
NNO Sting	10.00	20.00
NNO Taskmaster Kevin Sullivan	6.00	12.00

1999 Planet Toys WWF Head Crushers

NNO Mankind
NNO The Rock
NNO Stone Cold Steve Austin

2010 Playmates Lucha Libre Masked Warriors

NNO Charly Malice
NNO Lizmark Jr.
NNO Marco Corleone
NNO Super Nova
NNO Sydistiko
NNO Tinieblas Jr.

2010 Playmates Lucha Libre Masked Warriors Accessories

NNO Hexalateral Wrestling Ring

2010 Playmates Lucha Libre Masked Warriors Combo Packs

NNO Super Nova
NNO Tinieblas Jr.

2010 Playmates Lucha Libre Masked Warriors Masks

NNO Super Nova
NNO Tinieblas Jr.

2016 Playmates WWE Nitro Machines

NNO Dean Ambrose	3.00	8.00
NNO John Cena	6.00	12.00
NNO The Rock	7.50	15.00
NNO Undertaker	7.50	15.00

2016 Playmates WWE Nitro Machines (loose)

NNO Brock Lesnar	7.50	15.00
NNO John Cena	7.50	15.00
NNO The Rock	10.00	20.00
NNO Undertaker	7.50	15.00

2021 Pro Wrestling Tees Micro Brawlers AEW Wave 1

NNO Brodie Lee	20.00	40.00
NNO Chris Jericho	25.00	50.00
NNO Darby Allin	20.00	40.00
NNO Dr. Britt Baker, DMD	30.00	60.00
NNO Hikaru Shida	25.00	50.00
NNO Jon Moxley	25.00	50.00
NNO Orange Cassidy	30.00	75.00

2021-22 Pro Wrestling Tees Micro Brawlers AEW Crate Exclusive

NNO Sting	30.00	75.00
NNO Nyla Rose	15.00	30.00

2021-22 Pro Wrestling Tees Micro Brawlers AEW Limited Edition

NNO Christian Cage	25.00	50.00
NNO Sting (retro blue and orange)		
NNO Sting (retro black and green chase)		

2017 Pro Wrestling Tees Micro Brawlers Crate Exclusives

NNO Big Van Vader	20.00	40.00
NNO CM Punk	30.00	75.00
NNO Colt Cabana	15.00	30.00
NNO Joey Ryan	12.50	25.00
NNO Kenny Omega	20.00	40.00
NNO Matt Jackson		
NNO Nick Jackson		
NNO Penta El Zero M	30.00	60.00
NNO Taz	75.00	150.00
NNO :Villain" Marty Scurll	15.00	30.00

2018 Pro Wrestling Tees Micro Brawlers Crate Exclusives

NNO American Nightmare Cody	15.00	30.00
NNO Andre the Giant	25.00	50.00
NNO Bad Boy Tama Tonga	12.50	25.00
NNO Candice LeRae	10.00	20.00
NNO Eddie Guerrero	20.00	40.00
NNO Hangman Adam Page	25.00	50.00
NNO Kazuchika Okada	20.00	40.00
NNO Papa Shango	15.00	30.00
NNO Road Warrior Animal	30.00	60.00
NNO Road Warrior Hawk	25.00	50.00
NNO Tetsuya Naito	20.00	40.00
NNO ZSJ Zack Sabre Jr.	10.00	20.00

2019 Pro Wrestling Tees Micro Brawlers Crate Exclusives

NNO Bruiser Brody	20.00	40.00
NNO Brutus "The Barber" Beefcake	10.00	20.00
NNO Demolition Ax	15.00	30.00
NNO Demolition Smash	20.00	40.00
NNO Jeff Cobb	7.50	15.00
NNO Jim Ross	12.50	25.00
NNO Kota Ibushi	12.50	25.00
NNO Macho Man Randy Savage	30.00	60.00
NNO MJF	12.50	25.00
NNO Raven	20.00	40.00
NNO Rey Fenix	15.00	30.00
NNO Warrior	25.00	50.00

2020 Pro Wrestling Tees Micro Brawlers Crate Exclusives

NNO The Boogeyman	10.00	20.00
NNO Bret "The Hitman" Hart	20.00	40.00
NNO Brian Meyers		
NNO Chris Hero	7.50	15.00
NNO El Generico	12.50	25.00
NNO Hacksaw Jim Duggan	10.00	20.00
NNO Honky Tonk Man	10.00	20.00
NNO Kamala	10.00	20.00
NNO Koko B. Ware	15.00	30.00
NNO Matt Cardona	15.00	30.00
NNO Tatanka	7.50	15.00
NNO Tommy Dreamer	15.00	30.00

2021 Pro Wrestling Tees Micro Brawlers Crate Exclusives

NNO Jake "The Snake" Roberts (blue and yellow tights)	15.00	30.00
NNO Jake "The Snake" Roberts (black and yellow tights chase)		
NNO Owen Hart	12.50	25.00

(blue tights)
NNO Owen Hart
(red tights chase)
NNO Kevin Nash (Super Shredder) 15.00 30.00
(black tights)
NNO Kevin Nash (Super Shredder) 15.00 30.00
(purple tights chase)
NNO Tanga Loa 15.00 30.00
(camo tights)
NNO Tanga Loa 30.00 75.00
(black camo tights chase)
NNO Iron Sheik
(red and black boots)
NNO Iron Sheik
(yellow boots chase)
NNO Bully Ray 15.00 30.00
(black and white attire)
NNO Bully Ray 25.00 50.00
(black and red attire chase)
NNO Flyin' Brian Pillman 10.00 20.00
(tiger print tights)
NNO Flyin' Brian Pillman 30.00 60.00
(blue tights chase)
NNO Lex Luger 12.50 25.00
(red white and blue tights)
NNO Lex Luger 30.00 75.00
(red white and blue tights chase)
NNO Adam Bomb 12.50 25.00
(red and yellow tights)
NNO Adam Bomb 50.00 100.00
(orange and yellow tights chase)
NNO Shane Helms 15.00 30.00
(brown hair)
NNO Shane Helms 50.00 100.00
(green hair chase)
NNO Virgil 10.00 20.00
NNO Virgil 30.00 60.00
(chase)
NNO Glacier 15.00 30.00
(blue and white)
NNO Glacier 30.00 75.00
(light blue and white chase)

2020-21 Pro Wrestling Tees Micro Brawlers Limited Edition

NNO Big Van Vader
NNO Brian Knobs/350* 20.00 40.00
NNO Dragon Lee 20.00 40.00
(Online Exclusive)
NNO Dynamite Kid 25.00 50.00
NNO Francine/300* 50.00 100.00
NNO Frank the Clown/300* 20.00 40.00
NNO Iron Sheik/150* 75.00 150.00
NNO Jerry Sags/350* 20.00 40.00
NNO Jonathan Gresham 15.00 30.00
NNO Josh Mathews
NNO Kevin Nash/350* 30.00 75.00
NNO Kurt Angle/150* 100.00 200.00
NNO Loose Cannon Brian Pillman 20.00 40.00
(Online Exclusive)
NNO Luna Vachon 25.00 50.00
NNO Macho Man (black & white) 20.00 40.00
(Online Exclusive)
NNO Macho Man (classic orange) 15.00 30.00
(Online Exclusive)
NNO Macho Man (classic pink) 12.50 25.00
(Online Exclusive)
NNO Macho Man (lime green) 10.00 20.00
(Online Exclusive)
NNO Macho Man (Mega Powers) 20.00 40.00
(Online Exclusive)
NNO Macho Man (USA Edition) 25.00 50.00
(Online Exclusive)
NNO New Jack 20.00 40.00
(Online Exclusive)
NNO Owen Hart (Japanese Tour) 20.00 40.00
(Online Exclusive)
NNO Owen Hart/150* 100.00 200.00
NNO Psychosis 20.00 40.00
(Online Exclusive)
NNO Rob Van Dam (green tights) 125.00 250.00
(Online Exclusive chase)
NNO Rob Van Dam 30.00 60.00
(Online Exclusive)
NNO Sabu 20.00 40.00
(Online Exclusive)
NNO Sandman 20.00 40.00
(Online Exclusive)
NNO Sommarhausen 30.00 60.00
(Online Exclusive)
NNO Terry Funk

2022 Pro Wrestling Tees Micro Brawlers Limited Edition

NNO Andre the Giant
NNO British Bulldog

2021 Pro Wrestling Tees Micro Brawlers MLW Exclusives

NNO Alexander Hammerstone 30.00 60.00
NNO LA Park 60.00 120.00
NNO Richard Holliday 30.00 60.00

2020-21 Pro Wrestling Tees Micro Brawlers ROH Exclusives

NNO Angelina Love 20.00 40.00
NNO Danhausen 30.00 75.00
NNO Jonathan Gresham
NNO Session Moth Martina 10.00 20.00
NNO Shane Taylor 15.00 30.00

2021 Pro Wrestling Tees Micro Brawlers Staff Edition Exclusives

NNO Barracuda Mailbox Bomber/150*75.00 150.00
NNO Marvelous Matt Knicks/150* 20.00 40.00

2022 Pro Wrestling Tees Micro Brawlers Talk 'N Shop-a-Mania

NNO Sex Ferguson
NNO Chico El Luchador
NNO Chad 2 Badd

2018 Pro Wrestling Tees Micro Brawlers Wave 1

NNO British Bulldog
NNO Brooklyn Brawler
NNO Burnard the Business Bear 30.00 60.00
NNO Cheeseburger
NNO Chris Hero 7.50 15.00
NNO Cody 12.50 25.00
NNO Dalton Castle
NNO Jay Lethal
NNO Jay White 20.00 40.00
NNO Kenny Omega 25.00 50.00
NNO Ricky The Dragon Steamboat
NNO Rosemary
NNO Rowdy Roddy Piper 300.00 500.00
NNO Sami Callihan
NNO Swoggle
NNO Tenille Dashwood
NNO Vickie Guerrero 15.00 30.00
NNO Villain Marty Scurll 17.50 35.00

2018 Pro Wrestling Tees Micro Brawlers Wave 1 Limited Edition Tag Team 2-Packs

NNO The Briscoes
NNO The Young Bucks

2019 Pro Wrestling Tees Micro Brawlers Wave 2

NNO Brandi Rhodes
NNO Bushi
NNO Christopher Daniels
NNO Evil 10.00 20.00
NNO Flip Gordon
NNO Frankie Kazarian 17.50 35.00
NNO Hiromu Takahashi 20.00 40.00
NNO Joey Ryan 15.00 30.00
NNO Sanada 20.00 40.00
NNO Scorpio Sky
NNO Tetsuya Naito 15.00 30.00

2019 Pro Wrestling Tees Micro Brawlers Wave 3

NNO Blue Meanie
NNO Brian Cage
NNO Colt Cabana 12.50 25.00
NNO Fat Ass Masa 50.00 100.00
NNO Hiroshi Tanahashi/250* 25.00 50.00
NNO Hot Mess Chelsea Green 30.00 60.00
NNO Johnny Gimmick Name 25.00 50.00
NNO King Kong Bundy
NNO Mandy Leon 30.00 75.00
NNO Villain Marty Scurll

2019 Pro Wrestling Tees Micro Brawlers Wave 4

NNO Bandido 15.00 30.00
NNO Big Poppa Pump Scott Steiner 30.00 75.00
NNO Bone Soldier Taiji Ishimora
NNO Flamboyant Juice Robinson 25.00 50.00
NNO Penta El Zero M
NNO Rush 7.50 15.00
NNO Tomohiro Ishii

2019 Pro Wrestling Tees Micro Brawlers Wave 4 Limited Edition Multi-Packs

NNO The Kingdom 3-Pack 30.00 75.00
NNO The Road Warriors 2-Pack

2020 Pro Wrestling Tees Micro Brawlers Wave 5

NNO Crown Jewel Chase Owens
NNO Dustin Rhodes
NNO Kazuchika Okada 20.00 40.00
NNO Terry Funk 25.00 50.00
NNO The Enforcer Arn Anderson
NNO Underboss Bad Luck Fale 20.00 40.00

2020 Pro Wrestling Tees Micro Brawlers Wave 6

NNO Brody King 20.00 40.00
NNO Ian Riccaboni 15.00 30.00
NNO PCO
NNO Rhino 25.00 50.00
NNO Taya Valkyrie
NNO Undeniable Tessa B 20.00 40.00

1985 Remco AWA Wrestling Accessories and Playsets

NNO Battle Royal Playset (w/7 figures)400.00 600.00
NNO Battle Royal Playset 2 (w/7 figures)500.00800.00
NNO Championship Belt Figure Holder200.00 400.00
NNO Regular Ring Playset 125.00 200.00
NNO Steel Cage Match 300.00 600.00

1986 Remco AWA Wrestling Mini-Mashers

NNO Animal
NNO Barbarian
NNO Boris Zhukov
NNO Curt Henning
NNO Hawk
NNO Larry Zbyszko
NNO Marty Jannetty
NNO Nick Bockwinkel
NNO Ric Flair
NNO Scott Hall
NNO Shawn Michaels
NNO Stan Hansen

1986 Remco AWA Wrestling Mini-Mashers Green

NNO Animal
NNO Barbarian
NNO Boris Zhukov
NNO Curt Henning
NNO Hawk
NNO Larry Zbyszko
NNO Marty Jannetty
NNO Nick Bockwinkel
NNO Ric Flair
NNO Scott Hall
NNO Shawn Michaels
NNO Stan Hansen

1986 Remco AWA Wrestling Mini-Mashers Packs

NNO 4-Pack 25.00 50.00
NNO 8-Pack 50.00 100.00
NNO 12-Pack 60.00 120.00

1986 Remco AWA Wrestling Mini-Mashers Purple

NNO Animal
NNO Barbarian
NNO Boris Zhukov
NNO Curt Henning
NNO Hawk
NNO Larry Zbyszko
NNO Marty Jannetty
NNO Nick Bockwinkel
NNO Ric Flair
NNO Scott Hall
NNO Shawn Michaels
NNO Stan Hansen

1986 Remco AWA Wrestling Mini-Mashers Red

NNO Animal
NNO Barbarian
NNO Boris Zhukov
NNO Curt Henning
NNO Hawk
NNO Larry Zbyszko
NNO Marty Jannetty
NNO Nick Bockwinkel
NNO Ric Flair
NNO Scott Hall
NNO Shawn Michaels
NNO Stan Hansen

1985 Remco AWA Wrestling Series 1

NNO Fabulous Ones	100.00	200.00
Steve Keirn/Stan Lane		
NNO High Flyers	100.00	200.00
Greg Gagne/Jim Brunzell		
NNO Ric Flair/Larry Zbyszko	125.00	250.00
NNO Rick Martel/Baron von Raschke w/AWA Ring	125.00	250.00
NNO Rick Martel/Baron von Raschke w/AWA Sticker	75.00	150.00
NNO Road Warriors	200.00	400.00
Animal/Hawk No Belts		
NNO Road Warriors	150.00	300.00
Animal/Hawk w/Belts		

1985 Remco AWA Wrestling Series 1 (loose)

NNO Animal	6.00	12.00
NNO Baron Von Raschke	7.50	15.00
NNO Greg Gagne	7.50	15.00
NNO Hawk	6.00	12.00
NNO Jim Brunzell	6.00	12.00
NNO Larry Zbyszko	6.00	12.00
NNO Ric Flair	15.00	30.00
NNO Rick Martel	12.50	25.00
NNO Stan Lane	6.00	15.00
NNO Steve Keirn	6.00	12.00

1985 Remco AWA Wrestling Series 2

NNO Fabulous Freebirds	100.00	200.00
Buddy Roberts/Terry Gordy/Michael Hayes		
NNO Gagne's Raiders	125.00	250.00
Greg Gagne/Curt Henning		
NNO Jimmy Garvin/Precious/Steve Regal	75.00	150.00
NNO Long Riders	100.00	200.00
Wild Bill Irwin/Scott Hog Irwin		
NNO Road Warriors	150.00	300.00
Animal/Hawk/Paul Ellering		

1985 Remco AWA Wrestling Series 2 (loose)

NNO Animal	10.00	20.00
NNO Buddy Roberts	12.50	25.00
NNO Curt Henning	10.00	20.00
NNO Greg Gagne	6.00	12.00
NNO Hawk	10.00	20.00
NNO Jimmy Garvin	10.00	20.00
NNO Michael Hayes	12.50	25.00
NNO Paul Ellering	12.50	25.00
NNO Precious	10.00	20.00
NNO Scott Hog Irwin	7.50	15.00
NNO Steve Regal	6.00	12.00
NNO Terry Gordy	12.50	25.00
NNO Wild Bill Irwin	7.50	15.00

1985 Remco AWA Wrestling Series 2 Fight to the Finish 2-Pack

NNO Steve Regal vs. Curt Hennig (w/VHS Tape)	50.00	100.00

1985 Remco AWA Wrestling Series 3

NNO Nick Bockwinkel vs. Larry Zbyszko	150.00	300.00
NNO Scott Hall vs. Gorgeous Jimmy Garvin	150.00	300.00
NNO Stan Hansen vs. Jerry Blackwell	100.00	200.00
NNO Carlos Colon vs. Abdullah the Butcher	150.00	300.00

1985 Remco AWA Wrestling Series 3 (loose)

NNO Abdullah the Butcher	20.00	40.00
NNO Carlos Colon	7.50	15.00
NNO Gorgeous Jimmy Garvin	5.00	10.00
NNO Jerry Blackwell	10.00	20.00
NNO Larry Zbyszko	15.00	30.00
NNO Nick Bockwinkel	20.00	40.00
NNO Referee Curley Brown	12.50	25.00
NNO Referee Nasty Ned	15.00	30.00
NNO Scott Hall	30.00	75.00
NNO Stan Hansen	20.00	40.00

1986 Remco AWA Wrestling Series 4

NNO Boris Zhukov	300.00	600.00
NNO Buddy Rose	250.00	500.00
NNO Doug Somers	200.00	400.00
NNO Marty Jannetty	400.00	800.00
NNO Nick Bockwinkel		
NNO Nord the Barbarian	250.00	500.00
NNO Paul Ellering		
NNO Referee Dick Woehrle	200.00	350.00
NNO Ric Flair	500.00	1000.00
NNO Shawn Michaels	750.00	1500.00
NNO Sheik Adnan Al-Kaissie	200.00	400.00

1986 Remco AWA Wrestling Series 4 (loose)

NNO Boris Zhukov	125.00	250.00
NNO Buddy Rose	125.00	250.00
NNO Doug Somers	100.00	200.00
NNO Marty Jannetty	150.00	300.00
NNO Nord the Barbarian	150.00	300.00
NNO Referee Dick Woehrle	60.00	120.00
NNO Shawn Michaels	250.00	400.00
NNO Sheik Adnan Al-Kaissie	250.00	500.00

1985 Remco AWA Wrestling Thumbsters

NNO Greg Gagne vs. Hawk	30.00	75.00
NNO Ric Flair vs. Larry Zbyszko	50.00	100.00
NNO Rick Martel vs. Animal	30.00	75.00

1985 Remco AWA Wrestling Thumbsters (loose)

NNO Animal	7.50	15.00
NNO Greg Gagne	5.00	10.00
NNO Hawk	7.50	15.00
NNO Larry Zbyszko	5.00	10.00
NNO Ric Flair	10.00	20.00
NNO Rick Martel	7.50	15.00

1998 Ringside Supplies WWF Squirt Heads Cellophane Package

NNO The Rock
NNO Stone Cold Steve Austin
NNO Undertaker

1998 Ringside Supplies WWF Squirt Heads Mesh Package

NNO The Rock
NNO Stone Cold Steve Austin
NNO Undertaker

2017 S.H. Figuarts WWE

NNO Kane	30.00	75.00
NNO The Rock	30.00	60.00
NNO Stone Cold Steve Austin	20.00	40.00
NNO Triple H	12.50	25.00
NNO Undertaker	30.00	75.00
NNO Vince McMahon		

1990 Spectra Star WWF Rad Rollers Collection

NNO Hulk Hogan/Jake The Snake Roberts/Macho King Randy Savage
Big Boss Man/Million Dollar Man Ted DiBiase/Ultimate Warrior

1990 Spectra Star WWF Rad Rollers Collection (loose)

NNO Big Boss Man
NNO Hulk Hogan
NNO Jake The Snake Roberts
NNO Macho King Randy Savage
NNO Million Dollar Man Ted DiBiase
NNO Ultimate Warrior

1990 Spectra Star WWF Superstars Radical Flying Discs

NNO Ultimate Warrior (green)
NNO Ultimate Warrior (pink)

1991 Spectra Star WWF Superstars Radical Flying Discs

NNO Hulk Hogan

2019 Super 7 ReAction Wrestling Figures

NNO Andre the Giant (singlet)
NNO Andre the Giant (w/vest)

2021 Super 7 Ultimate Wrestling Figures

NNO Brian Meyers
NNO Doc Gallows
NNO Karl Anderson
NNO Matt Cardona

2017 TeenyMates WWE Collector Sets

NNO WWE Hall of Fame Inductees
NNO WWE Superstars (w/Andre the Giant GITD)

2016 TeenyMates WWE Series 1

NNO Big Show C
NNO Bray Wyatt C
NNO Bret Hart C
NNO Brie Bella C
NNO Brock Lesnar C
NNO Daniel Bryan C
NNO Dean Ambrose C
NNO Dolph Ziggler C
NNO Goldust C
NNO Jey Uso C
NNO Jimmy Uso C
NNO John Cena (crystal clear) R
NNO John Cena C
NNO Kane C
NNO Kofi Kingston C
NNO Macho Man Randy Savage (orange) C
NNO Macho Man Randy Savage (glow-in-the-dark) R (Collector Tin Exclusive)
NNO Macho Man Randy Savage (purple) R
NNO Nikki Bella C
NNO Randy Orton C
NNO The Rock C
NNO The Rock (metallic gold) UR
NNO Roman Reigns C
NNO Seth Rollins C
NNO Sheamus C
NNO Sin Cara C
NNO Stardust C
NNO Sting C
NNO Stone Cold Steve Austin C
NNO Triple H C
NNO Ultimate Warrior C
NNO Undertaker (glow-in-the-dark) R
NNO Undertaker C

2017 TeenyMates WWE Series 2

NNO AJ Styles C
NNO Andre the Giant C
NNO Andre the Giant (glow-in-the-dark) R (Collector's Set Exclusive)
NNO Becky Lynch C
NNO Big E C
NNO Bray Wyatt C
NNO Brock Lesnar C
NNO Chris Jericho C
NNO Dean Ambrose C
NNO Finn Balor C
NNO Finn Balor (glow-in-the-dark) R
NNO Jake the Snake Roberts C
NNO John Cena (ice blue) R
NNO John Cena C
NNO Kane C
NNO Kevin Owens C
NNO Kofi Kingston C
NNO Macho Man Randy Savage C
NNO Mankind C
NNO Ric Flair (blue robe) UR
NNO Ric Flair (pink robe) C
NNO The Rock C
NNO Roman Reigns C
NNO Rowdy Roddy Piper C
NNO Sasha Banks C
NNO Seth Rollins C
NNO Sgt. Slaughter R

NNO Shawn Michaels C		
NNO Sting C		
NNO Triple H C		
NNO Ultimate Warrior C		
NNO Ultimate Warrior (metallic gold) UR		
NNO Xavier Woods C		

2019 Tomy WWE Blitz Brawlers

NNO AJ Styles		
NNO John Cena		

1990 Tonka WWF Wrestling Buddies

NNO Big Boss Man	100.00	200.00
NNO Hulk Hogan	250.00	500.00
NNO Jake "The Snake" Roberts	325.00	650.00
NNO Macho King Randy Savage	150.00	300.00
NNO Million Dollar Man Ted DiBiase	400.00	800.00
NNO Ultimate Warrior	250.00	500.00

1990 Tonka WWF Wrestling Buddies (loose)

NNO Animal (Legion of Doom)		
NNO Big Boss Man		
NNO Hawk (Legion of Doom)		
NNO Hulk Hogan		
NNO Jake "The Snake" Roberts		
NNO Macho King Randy Savage		
NNO Million Dollar Man Ted DiBiase		
NNO Ultimate Warrior		

1990 Tonka WWF Wrestling Buddies Tag Team

NNO Legion of Doom		

2005 Toy Biz Best of TNA Series 1

NNO AJ Styles		
NNO Elix Skipper		
NNO Jeff Hardy		
NNO Ron Killings		

2006 Toy Biz Best of TNA Series 2

NNO AJ Styles		
NNO Chris Sabin		
NNO Jeff Hardy		
NNO Monty Brown		
NNO Raven		
NNO Ron Killings		

2005 Toy Biz TNA Wrestling 2-Packs Series 1

NNO BG James/Konnan	15.00	30.00
NNO Elix Skipper/C. Daniels	12.50	25.00
NNO James Storm/Chris Harris	30.00	75.00

2006 Toy Biz TNA Wrestling 2-Packs Series 2

NNO AJ Styles vs. Samoa Joe	20.00	40.00
NNO Jeff Hardy vs. Abyss	50.00	100.00
NNO Jeff Jarrett vs. Monty Brown	20.00	40.00

2006 Toy Biz TNA Wrestling 2-Packs Series 3

NNO BG James/Kip James	20.00	40.00
NNO Raven vs. Sabu	30.00	75.00
NNO Sting vs. Jeff Jarrett	25.00	50.00

2007 Toy Biz TNA Wrestling 2-Packs Series 4

NNO Christian Cage/Rhyno	20.00	40.00
NNO Christopher Daniels Homicide	15.00	30.00
NNO Kevin Nash/Chris Sabin	20.00	40.00

2007 TNA Wrestling Bashin' Brawlers Series 1

NNO Samoa Joe	12.50	25.00
NNO Sting	15.00	30.00

2007 TNA Wrestling Bashin' Brawlers Series 2

NNO Christian Cage	10.00	20.00
NNO Kevin Nash	10.00	20.00

2007 Toy Biz TNA Wrestling Collector's Edition 12-Inch Series 1

NNO AJ Styles	30.00	60.00
NNO Sting	30.00	75.00

2007 Toy Biz TNA Wrestling Collector's Edition 12-Inch Series 2

NNO Christopher Daniels	15.00	30.00
NNO Kurt Angle	25.00	50.00

2006 Toy Biz TNA Wrestling Masked Fury

NNO Abyss	20.00	40.00
NNO Shark Boy	20.00	40.00
NNO Sting	25.00	50.00

2005 Toy Biz TNA Wrestling Playsets

NNO 6-Sided Wrestling Ring w/AJ Styles	75.00	150.00

2006 Toy Biz TNA Wrestling Playsets

NNO Lockdown Six Sides of Steel w/Christian Cage		
NNO Champion X Ring w/AJ Styles		
NNO Championship Belt w/AJ Styles & Jeff Jarrett Blue Package		
NNO Championship Belt w/AJ Styles & Jeff Jarrett Red Package		

2007 Toy Biz TNA Wrestling Playsets

NNO Ultimate X Ring w/Christopher Daniels	50.00	100.00

2005 Toy Biz TNA Wrestling Series 1

NNO Abyss	15.00	30.00
NNO AJ Styles	20.00	40.00
NNO Jeff Jarrett	12.50	25.00
NNO Raven	12.50	25.00

2005 Toy Biz TNA Wrestling Series 2

NNO Christopher Daniels	12.50	25.00
NNO Jeff Hardy	20.00	40.00
NNO Ron The Truth Killings	15.00	30.00
NNO Shark Boy	12.50	25.00

2005 Toy Biz TNA Wrestling Series 3

NNO AJ Styles	15.00	30.00
NNO Alpha Male Monty Brown	20.00	40.00
NNO Chris Sabin	20.00	40.00
NNO Raven/Straight Jacket	12.50	25.00

2006 Toy Biz TNA Wrestling Series 4

NNO Kevin Nash		
NNO Petey Williams	12.50	25.00
NNO Rhino	20.00	40.00
NNO Wildcat Chris Harris Mustache	7.50	15.00
NNO Wildcat Chris Harris No Mustache		

2006 Toy Biz TNA Wrestling Series 5

NNO James Cowboy Storm	10.00	20.00
NNO Kip James	10.00	20.00
NNO Kip James/Black Trunks		
NNO Lance Hoyt	15.00	30.00
NNO Lance Hoyt/White Pants		
NNO Samoa Joe	12.50	25.00
NNO Samoa Joe Blue and Black Trunks		
NNO Sting	15.00	30.00

2007 Toy Biz TNA Wrestling Series 6

NNO Alex Shelley	10.00	20.00
NNO Alex Shelley Green on Shorts		
NNO Christian Cage	12.50	25.00
NNO Jay Lethal	12.50	25.00
NNO Jay Lethal/Green Gear		
NNO Sonjay Dutt	7.50	15.00
NNO Sonjay Dutt/Green Gear		

2007 Toy Biz TNA Wrestling Series 7

NNO Brother Devon	10.00	20.00
NNO Matt Bentley	10.00	20.00
NNO Robert Roode	12.50	25.00
NNO Robert Roode/Team Canada		
NNO Scott Steiner	15.00	30.00
NNO Scott Steiner/Black Pants		

2007 Toy Biz TNA Wrestling Series 8

NNO Chase Stevens	15.00	30.00
NNO Chase Stevens Headband and Jacket		
NNO Eric Young	12.50	25.00
NNO Eric Young/Team Canada	20.00	40.00
NNO James Mitchell CH	20.00	40.00
NNO Kurt Angle	10.00	20.00
NNO Senshi	20.00	40.00
NNO Senshi/Black Pants	25.00	50.00

2000 Toy Biz WCW Bash at the Beach

NNO Bret Hitman Hart		
NNO Diamond Dallas Page		
NNO Goldberg	10.00	20.00
NNO Lex Luger	6.00	12.00
NNO Sting		

1998 Toy Biz WCW Bashin' Brawlers

NNO Big Poppa Pump Scott Steiner		
NNO Diamond Dallas Page	30.00	75.00
NNO Goldberg	60.00	120.00
NNO Hollywood Hogan	75.00	150.00
NNO Kevin Nash		
NNO Macho Man Randy Savage	50.00	100.00
NNO Sting	60.00	120.00
NNO Sting (Wolfpac)		

2000 Toy Biz WCW Battle Arms

NNO Sting	12.50	25.00
NNO Goldberg	15.00	30.00
NNO Bret Hitman Hart	12.50	25.00

1999 Toy Biz WCW Bend 'N Flex

NNO Booker T	7.50	15.00
NNO Bret Hart	6.00	12.00
NNO Diamond Dallas Page	6.00	12.00
NNO Goldberg	10.00	20.00
NNO Kevin Nash	12.50	25.00
NNO Scott Hall	7.50	15.00
NNO Scott Steiner	6.00	12.00
NNO Sting	7.50	15.00

1999 Toy Biz WCW Bend 'N Flex 6-Pack

NNO Sting/Goldberg/DDP Hall/Steiner/Nash	25.00	50.00

1999 Toy Biz WCW Boxed Sets

NNO Heavyweight Champions Hogan/Goldberg/Sting	30.00	75.00
NNO IV Horsemen Flair/Benoit/Malenko/Mongo	15.00	30.00
NNO Red & Black Attack Hogan/Bischoff/Nash	30.00	60.00

1999 Toy Biz WCW Brawlin' Bikers

NNO DDP		
NNO Goldberg	7.50	15.00
NNO Hulk Hogan	20.00	40.00
NNO Sting	10.00	20.00

2001 Toy Biz WCW Bruisers

NNO Bam Bam Bigelow	7.50	15.00
NNO DDP	12.50	25.00
NNO Disco Inferno	10.00	20.00
NNO Goldberg	20.00	40.00
NNO Kevin Nash	10.00	20.00
NNO Kidman	10.00	20.00
NNO Randy Macho Man Savage	12.50	25.00
NNO Raven	7.50	15.00
NNO Rey Mysterio Jr.	15.00	30.00
NNO Stevie Ray	10.00	20.00
NNO Sting	15.00	30.00
NNO Wrath	7.50	15.00

1999 Toy Biz WCW Collector's Edition 8-Inch Figures

NNO Hollywood Hogan TAR		
NNO Kevin Nash TAR		
NNO Sting KB		

2000 Toy Biz WCW Grip 'N Flip Series 2

NNO Kevin Nash vs. Konnan	10.00	20.00

NNO Scott Steiner vs. Rick Steiner 7.50 15.00
NNO Sting vs. Buff Bagwell 7.50 15.00

2000 Toy Biz WCW Gross-Out Wrestlers

NNO Goldberg 30.00 75.00
NNO Sid Vicious 25.00 50.00
NNO Sting 50.00 100.00

1999 Toy Biz WCW Head Ringers

NNO Bret Hart
NNO Buff Bagwell
NNO Diamond Dallas Page
NNO Goldberg
NNO Hulk Hogan
NNO Kevin Nash
NNO Konnan
NNO Sting

1999 Toy Biz WCW Head Ringers (loose)

NNO Bret Hart
NNO Buff Bagwell
NNO Diamond Dallas Page
NNO Goldberg
NNO Hulk Hogan
NNO Kevin Nash
NNO Konnan
NNO Sting

2000 Toy Biz WCW Main Event 2-Packs

NNO Goldberg/Sid Vicious
NNO Hulk Hogan/Ric Flair 40.00 80.00
NNO Sting/The Total Package 30.00 60.00

2000 Toy Biz WCW Nitro Active Wrestlers

NNO Buff Bagwell/Black Pants
NNO Buff Bagwell/Red Pants
NNO Goldberg
NNO Jeff Jarrett
NNO Kevin Nash

1999 Toy Biz WCW Playset

NNO Electronic Monday Nitro Arena 125.00 250.00

2000 Toy Biz WCW Power Slam

NNO Buff Bagwell 7.50 15.00
NNO Dennis Rodman/Blue Hair 10.00 20.00
NNO Dennis Rodman/Green Hair
NNO Dennis Rodman/Orange Hair 15.00 30.00
NNO Goldberg 25.00 50.00
NNO Hak 15.00 30.00
NNO Hollywood Hogan 12.50 25.00
NNO Hulk Hogan 12.50 25.00
NNO Kanyon 6.00 12.00
NNO Kevin Nash 10.00 20.00
NNO Rowdy Roddy Piper 10.00 20.00
NNO Sid Vicious 7.50 15.00
NNO Sting 7.50 15.00

1999 Toy Biz WCW Ring Announcers

NNO Mean Gene 30.00 60.00
(w/Nash & Goldberg
NNO Michael Buffer 15.00 30.00
(w/Scott Steiner & DDP

2001 Toy Biz WCW Ring Fighters

NNO Booker T/Dk Tights 12.50 25.00
NNO Booker T/White Tights 10.00 20.00
NNO Bret Hart 7.50 15.00
NNO Chris Benoit/Red Tights 7.50 15.00
NNO Chris Benoit/Blue Tights 10.00 20.00
NNO Goldberg 10.00 20.00
NNO Scott Steiner/Black Tights
NNO Scott Steiner/White Tights 10.00 20.00
NNO Sting 12.50 25.00

1999 Toy Biz WCW Ring Masters

NNO Bret Hart 10.00 20.00
NNO Chris Jericho 10.00 20.00
NNO Goldberg 15.00 30.00
NNO Hulk Hogan 12.50 25.00
NNO Lex Luger 7.50 15.00
NNO Rick Steiner 10.00 20.00

2000 Toy Biz WCW Road Rebels

NNO Goldberg
NNO Hulk Hogan
NNO Sting

1999 Toy Biz WCW Road Wild Wrestlers

NNO Goldberg 25.00 50.00
NNO Hollywood Hogan 30.00 60.00
NNO Kevin Nash 15.00 30.00
NNO Sting 20.00 40.00

1999 Toy Biz WCW Rumble 'N Roar

NNO Goldberg 25.00 50.00
NNO Sting 30.00 60.00

1999 Toy Biz WCW Slam 'N Crunch

NNO Buff Bagwell 10.00 20.00
NNO Goldberg 15.00 30.00
NNO Kevin Nash 10.00 20.00
NNO Konnan 15.00 30.00
NNO Saturn
NNO Sting 12.50 25.00

2001 Toy Biz WCW Slam Force

NNO Bret Hart 20.00 40.00
NNO Goldberg
NNO Hollywood Hogan
NNO Kevin Nash 12.50 25.00
NNO Lex Luger

1999 Toy Biz WCW Smash 'N Slam

NNO DDP/No Vest 12.50 25.00
NNO DDP/Vest 6.00 12.00
NNO Giant w/Luchadore 10.00 20.00
NNO Goldberg KB
NNO Goldberg w/Blue 10.00 20.00
(Masked Lucha
NNO Goldberg w/Red 15.00 30.00
Masked Lucha
NNO Hollywood Hogan/ 10.00 20.00
No Tank Top
NNO Hollywood Hogan/ 12.50 25.00
Tank Top
NNO Kevin Nash w/Referee/ 7.50 15.00
No Red Pants
NNO Kevin Nash w/Referee/ 7.50 15.00
Red Pants
NNO Lex Luger/No Shirt 6.00 12.00
NNO Lex Luger/Shirt 12.50 25.00
NNO Macho Man/Black and Red 15.00 30.00
NNO Macho Man/Black and White 10.00 20.00
NNO Scott Hall/Black and Red 12.50 25.00
NNO Scott Hall/Black and White 12.50 25.00
NNO Sting/Black and Red 10.00 20.00
NNO Sting/Black and White 15.00 30.00

1999 Toy Biz WCW Smash 'N Slam 2-Packs

NNO The Giant/Kevin Nash
NNO Macho Man/Miss Elizabeth
NNO Sting/Hulk Hogan 15.00 30.00

2001 Toy Biz WCW Target Exclusives

NNO Hollywood Hogan 20.00 40.00
NNO Kevin Nash 12.50 25.00

2000 Toy Biz WCW Thunder Slam

NNO Bagwell/Jarrett/Vampiro
NNO Goldberg/Bam Bam Bigelow 10.00 20.00
NNO Scott Hall/KevinNash 20.00 40.00
NNO Sting/Bret Hart 10.00 20.00

2001 Toy Biz WCW TNT

NNO Goldberg 17.50 35.00
NNO Jeff Jarrett 12.50 25.00
NNO Scott Steiner 15.00 30.00
NNO Vampiro 12.50 25.00

2000 Toy Biz WCW Tuff Talkin' Wrestlers

NNO Scott Steiner 15.00 30.00
NNO Buff Bagwell 15.00 30.00
NNO Macho Man Randy Savage 25.00 50.00
NNO Konnan 12.50 25.00

2000 Toy Biz WCW Tuff Talkin' Wrestlers 2-Packs

NNO Goldberg/Kevin Nash 30.00 75.00
NNO Sting/Diamond Dallas Page 30.00 60.00

2000 Toy Biz WCW Unleashed

NNO Franchise (Shane Douglas) 15.00 30.00
NNO Kidman 15.00 30.00
NNO Mike Awesome 10.00 20.00
NNO Vampiro 12.50 25.00

2000 Toy Biz WCW Whiplashers

NNO Kidman vs. Rey Mysterio
NNO Scott Steiner vs. Buff Bagwell
NNO Sting vs. Goldberg

2000 Toy Biz WCW Window Crashers

NNO Goldberg
NNO Hulk Hogan
NNO Kevin Nash
NNO Sting

1991 Toymax WCW Finger Fighters

NNO Lex Luger & Sid Vicious
NNO Sting & Ric Flair

1991 Toymax WCW Wrestling Champs

NNO Lex Luger
NNO Ric Flair
NNO Rick Steiner
NNO Sid Vicious
NNO Sting

2014 Wicked Cool Toys WWE Bobblestars

NNO CM Punk
NNO Daniel Bryan
NNO John Cena
NNO Rey Mysterio
NNO Road Warrior Animal
NNO Road Warrior Hawk
NNO Undertaker

2019 Wicked Cool Toys WWE Micro Maniax Battle Game On!

NNO Wrestling Ring

2019 Wicked Cool Toys WWE Micro Maniax Series 1

NNO Alexa Bliss
NNO Braun Strowman
NNO Daniel Bryan
NNO Finn Balor
NNO John Cena
NNO Macho Man Randy Savage
NNO Roman Reigns
NNO Ronda Rousey

1985 Winston Toys WWF Hulk Hogan Rock 'n' Wrestling Figurine Erasers

NNO Hulk Hogan 75.00 150.00
NNO Iron Sheik 100.00 200.00
NNO Jimmy "Superfly" Snuka 30.00 75.00
NNO Junkyard Dog
NNO Rowdy Roddy Piper
NNO Wendi Richter

1985 Winston Toys WWF Hulk Hogan Rock 'n' Wrestling Figurine Erasers (loose)

NNO Hulk Hogan
NNO Iron Sheik
NNO Jimmy "Superfly" Snuka
NNO Junkyard Dog
NNO Rowdy Roddy Piper
NNO Wendi Richter

2019 Zag Toys Domez WWE

NNO Andre the Giant
NNO Jake The Snake Roberts
NNO Macho Man Randy Savage
NNO Ric Flair
NNO Rowdy Roddy Piper
NNO Sting
NNO Stone Cold Steve Austin
NNO Undertaker
NNO Undertaker Clear CH